JEE MAIN & ADVANCED TEST SERIES

50+ Tests

CHEMISTRY

Author
Sailajananda Raychaudhuri
M.Sc. Chemistry

ARIHANT PRAKASHAN (SERIES), MEERUT

ARIHANT PRAKASHAN (SERIES), MEERUT

ADMINISTRATIVE & PRODUCTION OFFICES

Regd. Office
'Ramchhaya' 4577/15, Agarwal Road, Darya Ganj, New Delhi -110002
Tele: 011- 47630600, 43518550

Head Office
Kalindi, TP Nagar, Meerut (UP) - 250002, Tel: 0121-7156203, 7156204

SALES & SUPPORT OFFICES

Agra, Ahmedabad, Bengaluru, Bareilly, Chennai, Delhi, Guwahati, Hyderabad, Jaipur, Jhansi, Kolkata, Lucknow, Nagpur & Pune.

ISBN 978-93-27194-15-9

PRICE ₹ 375.00

PO No. : TXT-59-T050999-12-22

Published By Arihant Publications (India) Ltd.

For further information about the books published by Arihant, log on to www.arihantbooks.com or e-mail at info@arihantbooks.com

Follow us on    

Contents

SYLLABUS

JEE MAIN

Section A : PHYSICAL CHEMISTRY

UNIT I Some Basic Concepts in Chemistry

Matter and its nature, Dalton's atomic theory; Concept of atom, molecule, element and compound; Physical quantities and their measurements in Chemistry, precision and accuracy, significant figures, S.I. Units, dimensional analysis; Laws of chemical combination; Atomic and molecular masses, mole concept, molar mass, percentage composition, empirical and molecular formulae; Chemical equations and stoichiometry.

UNIT II States of Matter

Classification of matter into solid, liquid and gaseous states.

Gaseous State Measurable properties of gases; Gas laws - Boyle's law, Charle's law, Graham's law of diffusion, Avogadro's law, Dalton's law of partial pressure; Concept of Absolute scale of temperature; Ideal gas equation, Kinetic theory of gases (only postulates); Concept of average, root mean square and most probable velocities; Real gases, deviation from Ideal behaviour, compressibility factor, van der Waals' equation, liquefaction of gases, critical constants.

Liquid State Properties of liquids - vapour pressure, viscosity and surface tension and effect of temperature on them (qualitative treatment only).

Solid State Classification of solids: molecular, ionic, covalent and metallic solids, amorphous and crystalline solids (elementary idea); Bragg's Law and its applications, Unit cell and lattices, packing in solids (fcc, bcc and hcp lattices), voids, calculations involving unit cell parameters, imperfection in solids; electrical, magnetic and dielectric properties.

UNIT III Atomic Structure

Discovery of sub-atomic particles (electron, proton and neutron); Thomson and Rutherford atomic models and their limitations; Nature of electromagnetic radiation, photoelectric effect; spectrum of hydrogen atom, Bohr model of hydrogen atom - its postulates, derivation of the relations for energy of the electron and radii of the different orbits, limitations of Bohr's model; dual nature of matter, de-Broglie's relationship, Heisenberg uncertainty principle.

Elementary ideas of quantum mechanics, quantum mechanical model of atom, its important features, ψ and ψ_2, concept of atomic orbitals as one electron wave functions; Variation of ψ and ψ_2 with *r* for 1*s* and 2*s*-orbitals; various quantum numbers (principal, angular momentum and magnetic quantum numbers) and their significance; shapes of *s*, *p* and *d* - orbitals, electron spin and spin quantum number; rules for filling electrons in orbitals – Aufbau principle, Pauli's exclusion principle and Hund's rule, electronic configuration of elements, extra stability of half-filled and completely filled orbitals.

UNIT IV Chemical Bonding and Molecular Structure

Kossel Lewis approach to chemical bond formation, concept of ionic and covalent bonds.

Ionic Bonding Formation of ionic bonds, factors affecting the formation of ionic bonds; calculation of lattice enthalpy.

Covalent Bonding Concept of electronegativity, Fajan's rule, dipole moment; Valence Shell Electron Pair Repulsion (VSEPR) theory and shapes of simple molecules.

Quantum mechanical approach to covalent bonding Valence bond theory - Its important features, concept of hybridization involving *s*, *p* and *d*-orbitals; Resonance.

Molecular Orbital Theory Its important features, LCAOs, types of molecular orbitals (bonding, antibonding), sigma and pi-bonds, molecular orbital electronic configurations of homonuclear diatomic molecules, concept of bond order, bond length and bond energy.

Elementary idea of metallic bonding. Hydrogen bonding and its applications.

UNIT V Chemical Thermodynamics

Fundamentals of thermodynamics System and surroundings, extensive and intensive properties, state functions, types of processes.

First law of thermodynamics Concept of work, heat internal energy and enthalpy, heat capacity, molar heat capacity, Hess's law of constant heat summation; Enthalpies of bond dissociation, combustion, formation, atomization, sublimation, phase transition, hydration, ionization and solution.

Second law of thermodynamics Spontaneity of processes; ΔS of the universe and ΔG of the system as criteria for spontaneity, ΔG° (Standard Gibb's energy change) and equilibrium constant.

UNIT VI Solutions

Different methods for expressing concentration of solution - molality, molarity, mole fraction, percentage (by volume and mass both), vapour pressure of solutions and Raoult's Law - Ideal and non-ideal solutions, vapour pressure - composition plots for ideal and non-ideal solutions.

Colligative properties of dilute solutions - relative lowering of vapour pressure, depression of freezing point, elevation of boiling point and osmotic pressure; Determination of molecular mass using colligative properties; Abnormal value of molar mass, van't Hoff factor and its significance.

UNIT VII Equilibrium

Meaning of equilibrium, concept of dynamic equilibrium.

Equilibria involving physical processes Solid -liquid, liquid - gas and solid - gas equilibria, Henry's law, general characteristics of equilibrium involving physical processes.

Equilibria involving chemical processes Law of chemical equilibrium, equilibrium constants (K and K) and their significance, significance of ΔG and ΔG° in chemical equilibria, factors affecting equilibrium concentration, pressure, temperature, effect of catalyst; Le -Chatelier's principle.

Ionic equilibrium Weak and strong electrolytes, ionization of electrolytes, various concepts of acids and bases (Arrhenius, Bronsted - Lowry and Lewis) and their ionization, acid-base equilibria (including multistage ionization) and ionization constants, ionization of water, pH scale, common ion effect, hydrolysis of salts and pH of their solutions, solubility of sparingly soluble salts and solubility products, buffer solutions.

UNIT VIII Redox Reactions and Electrochemistry

Electronic concepts of oxidation and reduction, redox reactions, oxidation number, rules for assigning oxidation number, balancing of redox reactions.

Eectrolytic and metallic conduction, conductance in electrolytic solutions, specific and molar conductivities and their variation with concentration: Kohlrausch's law and its applications.

Electrochemical cells - Electrolytic and Galvanic cells, different types of electrodes, electrode potentials including standard electrode potential, half - cell and cell reactions, emf of a Galvanic cell and its measurement; Nernst equation and its applications; Relationship between cell potential and Gibbs' energy change; Dry cell and lead accumulator; Fuel cells; Corrosion and its prevention.

UNIT IX Chemical Kinetics

Rate of a chemical reaction, factors affecting the rate of reactions concentration, temperature, pressure and catalyst; elementary and complex reactions, order and molecularity of reactions, rate law, rate constant and its units, differential and integral forms of zero and first order reactions, their characteristics and half - lives, effect of temperature on rate of reactions - Arrhenius theory, activation energy and its calculation, collision theory of bimolecular gaseous reactions (no derivation).

UNIT X Surface Chemistry

Adsorption - Physisorption and chemisorption and their characteristics, factors affecting adsorption of gases on solids- Freundlich and Langmuir adsorption isotherms, adsorption from solutions.

Catalysis Homogeneous and heterogeneous, activity and selectivity of solid catalysts, enzyme catalysis and its mechanism.

Colloidal state distinction among true solutions, colloids and suspensions, classification of colloids - lyophilic, lyophobic; multimolecular, macromolecular and associated colloids (micelles), preparation and properties of colloids Tyndall effect, Brownian movement, electrophoresis, dialysis, coagulation and flocculation; Emulsions and their characteristics.

Section B : INORGANIC CHEMISTRY

UNIT XI Classification of Elements and Periodicity in Properties

Periodic Law and Present Form of the Periodic Table, *s, p, d* and *f*-Block Elements, Periodic Trends in Properties of Elements-atomic and Ionic Radii, Ionization Enthalpy, Electron Gain Enthalpy, Valence, Oxidation States and Chemical Reactivity.

UNIT XII General Principles and Processes of Isolation of Metals

Modes of occurrence of elements in nature, minerals, ores; steps involved in the extraction of metals - concentration, reduction (chemical and electrolytic methods) and refining with special reference to the extraction of Al, Cu, Zn and Fe; Thermodynamic and electrochemical principles involved in the extraction of metals.

UNIT XIII Hydrogen

Position of hydrogen in periodic table, isotopes, preparation, properties and uses of hydrogen; physical and chemical properties of water and
heavy water; Structure, preparation, reactions and uses of hydrogen peroxide; Classification of hydrides ionic, covalent and interstitial; Hydrogen as a fuel.

UNIT XIV *s* - Block Elements (Alkali and Alkaline Earth Metals)

Group 1 and 2 Elements

General introduction, electronic configuration and general trends in physical and chemical properties of elements, anomalous properties of the first element of each group, diagonal relationships.

Preparation and properties of some important compounds - sodium carbonate, sodium chloride, sodium hydroxide and sodium hydrogen carbonate; Industrial uses of lime, limestone, Plaster of Paris and cement; Biological significance of Na, K, Mg and Ca.

UNIT XV *p* - Block Elements

Group 13 to Group 18 Elements

General Introduction Electronic configuration and general trends in physical and chemical properties of elements across the periods and down the groups; unique behaviour of the first element in each group.Group wise study of the *p* – block elements

Group 13 Preparation, properties and uses of boron and aluminium; structure, properties and uses of borax, boric acid, diborane, boron trifluoride, aluminium chloride and alums.

Group 14 Tendency for catenation; Structure, properties and uses of allotropes and oxides of carbon, silicon tetrachloride, silicates, zeolites and silicones.

Group 15 Properties and uses of nitrogen and phosphorus; Allotrophic forms of phosphorus; Preparation, properties, structure and uses of ammonia nitric acid, phosphine and phosphorus halides,(PCl_3, PCl_5); Structures of oxides and oxoacids of nitrogen and phosphorus.

Group 16 Preparation, properties, structures and uses of dioxygen and ozone; Allotropic forms of sulphur; Preparation, properties, structures and uses of sulphur dioxide, sulphuric acid (including its industrial preparation); Structures of oxoacids of sulphur.

Group 17 Preparation, properties and uses of chlorine and hydrochloric acid; Trends in the acidic nature of hydrogen halides; Structures of Interhalogen compounds and oxides and oxoacids of halogens.

Group 18 Occurrence and uses of noble gases; Structures of fluorides and oxides of xenon.

UNIT XVI *d*–and *f*–Block Elements

Transition Elements General introduction, electronic configuration, occurrence and characteristics, general trends in properties of the first row transition elements - physical properties, ionization enthalpy, oxidation states, atomic radii, colour, catalytic behaviour, magnetic properties, complex formation, interstitial compounds, alloy formation; Preparation, properties and uses of $K_2Cr_2O_7$ and $KMnO_4$.

Inner Transition Elements

Lanthanoids - Electronic configuration, oxidation states, chemical reactivity and lanthanoid contraction.

Actinoids - Electronic configuration and oxidation states.

UNIT XVII Coordination Compounds

Introduction to coordination compounds, Werner's theory; ligands, coordination number, denticity, chelation; IUPAC nomenclature of mononuclear coordination compounds, isomerism; Bonding Valence bond approach and basic ideas of Crystal field theory, colour and magnetic properties; importance of coordination compounds (in qualitative analysis, extraction of metals and in biological systems).

UNIT XVIII Environmental Chemistry

Environmental pollution Atmospheric, water and soil.

Atmospheric pollution - Tropospheric and stratospheric.

Tropospheric pollutants Gaseous pollutants Oxides of carbon, nitrogen and sulphur, hydrocarbons; their sources, harmful effects and prevention; Green house effect and Global warming; Acid rain;

Particulate pollutants Smoke, dust, smog, fumes, mist; their sources, harmful effects and prevention.

Stratospheric pollution Formation and breakdown of ozone, depletion of ozone layer - its mechanism and effects.

Water pollution Major pollutants such as, pathogens, organic wastes and chemical pollutants their harmful effects and prevention.

Soil pollution Major pollutants such as: Pesticides (insecticides, herbicides and fungicides), their harmful effects and prevention.

Strategies to control environmental pollution.

Section C : ORGANIC CHEMISTRY

UNIT XIX Purification & Characterisation of Organic Compounds

Purification Crystallisation, sublimation, distillation, differential extraction and chromatography principles and their applications.

Qualitative analysis Detection of nitrogen, sulphur, phosphorus and halogens.

Quantitative analysis (basic principles only) Estimation of carbon, hydrogen, nitrogen, halogens, sulphur, phosphorus.

Calculations of empirical formulae and molecular formulae; Numerical problems in organic quantitative analysis.

UNIT XX Some Basic Principles of Organic Chemistry

Tetravalency of carbon; Shapes of simple molecules hybridization (*s* and *p*); Classification of organic compounds based on functional groups: —C=C—,—C≡C— and those containing halogens, oxygen, nitrogen and sulphur, Homologous series; Isomerism - structural and stereoisomerism.

Nomenclature (Trivial and IUPAC)

Covalent bond fission Homolytic and heterolytic free radicals, carbocations and carbanions; stability of carbocations and free radicals, electrophiles and nucleophiles.

Electronic displacement in a covaient bond Inductive effect, electromeric effect, resonance and hyperconjugation.

Common types of organic reactions Substitution, addition, elimination and rearrangement.

UNIT XXI Hydrocarbons

Classification, isomerism, IUPAC nomenclature, general methods of preparation, properties and reactions.

Alkanes Conformations: Sawhorse and Newman projections (of ethane); Mechanism of halogenation of alkanes.

Alkenes Geometrical isomerism; Mechanism of electrophilic addition: addition of hydrogen, halogens, water, hydrogen halides (Markownikoff's and peroxide effect); Ozonolysis, oxidation, and polymerization.

Alkenes acidic character; addition of hydrogen, halogens, water and hydrogen halides; polymerization.

Aromatic hydrocarbons Nomenclature, benzene structure and aromaticity; Mechanism of electrophilic substitution: halogenation, nitration, Friedel – Craft's alkylation and acylation, directive influence of functional group in mono-substituted benzene.

UNIT XXII Organic Compounds Containing Halogens

General methods of preparation, properties and reactions; Nature of C—*X* bond; Mechanisms of substitution reactions.

Uses/environmental effects of chloroform, iodoform, freons and DDT.

UNIT XXIII Organic Compounds Containing Oxygen

General methods of preparation, properties, reactions and uses. Alcohols, Phenols and Ethers

Alcohols Identification of primary, secondary and tertiary alcohols; mechanism of dehydration.

Phenols Acidic nature, electrophilic substitution reactions: halogenation, nitration and sulphonation, Reimer - Tiemann reaction.

Ethers: Structure

Aldehyde and Ketones Nature of carbonyl group; Nucleophilic addition to >C=O group, relative reactivities of aldehydes and ketones; Important reactions such as - Nucleophilic addition reactions (addition of HCN, NH_3 and its derivatives), Grignard reagent; oxidation; reduction (Wolff Kishner and Clemmensen); acidity of α - hydrogen, aldol condensation, Cannizzaro reaction, Haloform reaction; Chemical tests to distinguish between aldehydes and Ketones.

Carboxylic Acids Acidic strength & factors affecting it.

UNIT XXIV Organic Compounds Containing Nitrogen

General methods of preparation, properties, reactions and uses.

Amines Nomenclature, classification, structure basic character and identification of primary, secondary and tertiary amines and their basic character.

Diazonium Salts Importance in synthetic organic chemistry.

UNIT XXV Polymers

General introduction and classification of polymers, general methods of polymerization-addition and condensation, copolymerization; Natural and synthetic rubber and vulcanization; some important polymers with emphasis on their monomers and uses - polythene, nylon, polyester and bakelite.

UNIT XXVI Biomolecules

General introduction and importance of biomolecules.
Carbohydrates Classification aldoses and ketoses; monosaccharides (glucose and fructose), constituent monosaccharides of oligosacchorides (sucrose, lactose, maltose) and polysaccharides (starch, cellulose, glycogen).

Proteins Elementary Idea of α-amino acids, peptide bond,. polypeptides; proteins: primary, secondary, tertiary and quaternary structure (qualitative idea only), denaturation of proteins, enzymes. Vitamins Classification and functions.

Nucleic Acids Chemical constitution of DNA and RNA. Biological functions of Nucleic acids.

UNIT XXVII Chemistry in Everyday Life

Chemicals in medicines Analgesics, tranquilizers, antiseptics, disinfectants, antimicrobials, antifertility drugs, antibiotics, antacids, antihistamins - their meaning and common examples.

Chemicals in food Preservatives, artificial sweetening agents - common examples.

Cleansing agents Soaps and detergents, cleansing action.

Unit XXVIII Principles Related to Practical Chemistry

- Detection of extra elements (N, S, halogens) in organic compounds; Detection of the following functional groups: hydroxyl (alcoholic and phenolic), carbonyl (aldehyde and ketone), carboxyl and amino groups in organic compounds.

Chemistry involved in the preparation of the following

- Inorganic compounds Mohr's salt, potash alum.
- Organic compounds Acetanilide, *p*-nitroacetan ilide, aniline yellow, iodoform.
- Chemistry involved in the titrimetric excercises - Acids bases and the use of indicators, oxali acid vs $KMnO_4$, Mohr's salt vs $KMnO_4$.
- Chemical principles involved in the qualitative salt analysis
- Cations — Pb^{2+}, Cu^{2+}, Al^{3+}, Fe^{3+}, Zn^{2+}, Ni^{2+}, Ca^{2+}, Ba^{2+}, Mg^{2+} NH^{4+}. Anions – CO_3^{2-}, S^{2-}, SO_4^{2-}, NO_2, NO_3, Cl^-, Br^-, I^- (Insoluble salts excluded).
- Chemical principles involved in the following experiments

1. Enthalpy of solution of $CuSO_4$
2. Enthalpy of neutralization of strong acid and strong base.
3. Preparation of lyophilic and lyophobic sols.
4. Kinetic study of reaction of iodide ion with hydrogen peroxide at room temperature.

JEE ADVANCED

General Topics
Concept of atoms and molecules; Dalton's atomic theory; Mole concept; Chemical formulae; Balanced chemical equations; Calculations (based on mole concept and stoichiometry) involving common oxidation-reduction, neutralisation, and displacement reactions; Concentration in terms of mole fraction, molarity, molality and normality.

States of Matter: Gases and Liquids
Gas laws and ideal gas equation, absolute scale of temperature; Deviation from ideality, van der Waals equation; Kinetic theory of gases, average, root mean square and most probable velocities and their relation with temperature; Law of partial pressures; Diffusion of gases. Intermolecular interactions: types, distance dependence, and their effect on properties; Liquids: vapour pressure, surface tension, viscosity.

Atomic Structure
Bohr model, spectrum of hydrogen atom; Wave-particle duality, de Broglie hypothesis; Uncertainty principle; Qualitative quantum mechanical picture of hydrogen atom: Energies, quantum numbers, wave function and probability density (plots only), shapes of *s*, *p* and *d*-orbitals; Aufbau principle; Pauli's exclusion principle and Hund's rule.

Chemical Bonding and Molecular Structure
Orbital overlap and covalent bond; Hybridisation involving *s*, *p* and *d*-orbitals only; Molecular orbital energy diagrams for homonuclear diatomic species (up to Ne_2); Hydrogen bond; Polarity in molecules, dipole moment; VSEPR model and shapes of molecules (linear, angular, triangular, square planar, pyramidal, square pyramidal, trigonal bipyramidal, tetrahedral and octahedral).

Chemical Thermodynamics
Intensive and extensive properties, state functions, First law of thermodynamics; Internal energy, work (pressure-volume only) and heat; Enthalpy, heat capacity, standard state, Hess's law; Enthalpy of reaction, fusion and vapourization, and lattice enthalpy; Second law of thermodynamics; Entropy; Gibbs energy; Criteria of equilibrium and spontaneity.

Chemical and Ionic Equilibrium
Law of mass action; Significance of ΔG and $\Delta G^{\ominus}$ in chemical equilibrium; Equilibrium constant (K_p and K_c) and reaction quotient, Le-Chatelier's principle (effect of concentration, temperature and pressure); Solubility product and its applications, common ion effect, pH and buffer solutions; Acids and bases (Bronsted and Lewis concepts); Hydrolysis of salts.

Electrochemistry
Electrochemical cells and cell reactions; Standard electrode potentials; Electrochemical work, Nernst equation; Electrochemical series, emf of galvanic cells; Faraday's laws of electrolysis; Electrolytic conductance, specific, equivalent and molar conductivity, Kohlrausch's law; Batteries: Primary and Secondary, fuel cells; Corrosion.

Chemical Kinetics
Rates of chemical reactions; Order and molecularity of reactions; Rate law, rate constant, half-life; Differential and integrated rate expressions for zero and first order reactions; Temperature dependence of rate constant (Arrhenius equation and activation energy); Catalysis: Homogeneous and heterogeneous, activity and selectivity of solid catalysts, enzyme catalysis and its mechanism.

Solid State
Classification of solids, crystalline state, seven crystal systems (cell parameters *a*, *b*, *c*, α, β, γ), close packed structure of solids (cubic and hexagonal), packing in fcc, bcc and hcp lattices; Nearest neighbours, ionic radii and radius ratio, point defects.

Solutions
Henry's law; Raoult's law; Ideal solutions; Colligative properties: lowering of vapour pressure, elevation of boiling point, depression of freezing point, and osmotic pressure; van't Hoff factor.

Surface Chemistry
Elementary concepts of adsorption: Physisorption and Chemisorption, Freundlich adsorption isotherm; Colloids: types, methods of preparation and general properties; Elementary ideas of emulsions, surfactants and micelles (only definitions and examples).

Classification of Elements and Periodicity in Properties

Modern periodic law and the present form of periodic table; electronic configuration of elements; periodic trends in atomic radius, ionic radius, ionization enthalpy, electron gain enthalpy, valence, oxidation states, electronegativity, and chemical reactivity.

Hydrogen

Position of hydrogen in periodic table, occurrence, isotopes, preparation, properties and uses of hydrogen; hydrides – ionic, covalent and interstitial; physical and chemical properties of water, heavy water; hydrogen peroxide-preparation, reactions, use and structure; hydrogen as a fuel.

s-Block Elements

Alkali and alkaline earth metals-reactivity towards air, water, dihydrogen, halogens, acids; their reducing nature including solutions in liquid ammonia; uses of these elements; general characteristics of their oxides, hydroxides, halides, salts of oxoacids; anomalous behaviour of lithium and beryllium; preparation, properties, and uses of compounds of sodium (sodium carbonate, sodium chloride, sodium hydroxide, sodium hydrogen carbonate) and calcium (calcium oxide, calcium hydroxide, calcium carbonate, calcium sulphate).

p-Block Elements

Oxidation state and trends in chemical reactivity of elements of groups 13-17; anomalous properties of boron, carbon, nitrogen, oxygen, and fluorine with respect to other elements in their respective groups.

Group 13: Reactivity towards acids, alkalis, and halogens; preparation, properties, and uses of borax, orthoboric acid, diborane, boron trifluoride, aluminium chloride, and alums; uses of boron and aluminium.

Group 14: Reactivity towards water and halogen; allotropes of carbon and uses of carbon; preparation, properties, and uses of carbon monoxide, carbon dioxide, silicon dioxide, silicones, silicates, zeolites.

Group 15: Reactivity towards hydrogen, oxygen, and halogen; allotropes of phosphorous; preparation, properties, and uses of dinitrogen, ammonia, nitric acid, phosphine, phosphorus trichloride, phosphorus pentachloride; oxides of nitrogen and oxoacids of phosphorus.

Group 16: Reactivity towards hydrogen, oxygen, and halogen; simple oxides; allotropes of sulphur; preparation/manufacture, properties, and uses of dioxygen, ozone, sulphur dioxide, sulphuric acid; oxoacids of sulphur.

Group 17: Reactivity towards hydrogen, oxygen, and metals; preparation/manufacture, properties, and uses of chlorine, hydrogen chloride and interhalogen compounds; oxoacids of halogens, bleaching powder.

Group 18: Chemical properties and uses; compounds of xenon with fluorine and oxygen.

d-Block Elements

Oxidation states and their stability; standard electrode potentials; interstitial compounds; alloys; catalytic properties; applications; preparation, structure, and reactions of oxoanions of chromium and manganese.

f-Block Elements

Lanthanoid and actinoid contractions; oxidation states; general characteristics.

Coordination Compounds

Werner's theory; Nomenclature, cis-trans and ionization isomerism, hybridization and geometries (linear, tetrahedral, square planar and octahedral) of mononuclear coordination compounds; Bonding [VBT and CFT (octahedral and tetrahedral fields)]; Magnetic properties (spin-only) and colour of 3*d*-series coordination compounds; Ligands and spectrochemical series; Stability; Importance and applications; Metal carbonyls.

Isolation of Metals

Metal ores and their concentration; extraction of crude metal from concentrated ores: thermodynamic (iron, copper, zinc) and electrochemical (aluminium) principles of metallurgy; cyanide process (silver and gold); refining.

Principles of Qualitative Analysis

Groups I to V (only Ag^+, Hg^{2+}, Cu^{2+}, Pb^{2+}, Fe^{3+}, Cr^{3+}, Al^{3+}, Ca^{2+}, Ba^{2+}, Zn^{2+}, Mn^{2+} and Mg^{2+}); Nitrate, halides (excluding fluoride), carbonate and bicarbonate, sulphate and sulphide.

Environmental Chemistry

Atmospheric pollution; water pollution; soil pollution; industrial waste; strategies to control environmental pollution; green chemistry.

Basic Principles of Organic Chemistry

Hybridisation of carbon; σ and π-bonds; Shapes of simple organic molecules; aromaticity; Structural and geometrical isomerism; Stereoisomers and stereochemical relationship (enantiomers, diastereomers, meso) of compounds containing only up to two asymmetric centres (*R*,*S* and *E*,*Z* configurations excluded); Determination of empirical and molecular formulae of simple compounds by combustion method only; IUPAC nomenclature of organic molecules (hydrocarbons, including simple cyclic hydrocarbons and their mono-functional and bi-functional derivatives only); Hydrogen bonding effects; Inductive, Resonance and Hyperconjugative effects; Acidity and basicity of organic compounds; Reactive intermediates produced during homolytic and heterolytic bond cleavage; Formation, structure and stability of carbocations, carbanions and free radicals.

Alkanes

Homologous series; Physical properties (melting points, boiling points and density) and effect of branching on them; Conformations of ethane and butane (Newman projections only); Preparation from alkyl halides and aliphatic carboxylic acids; Reactions: combustion, halogenation (including allylic and benzylic halogenation) and oxidation.

Alkenes and Alkynes

Physical properties (boiling points, density and dipole moments); Preparation by elimination reactions; Acid catalysed hydration (excluding the stereochemistry of addition and elimination); Metal acetylides; Reactions of alkenes with $KMnO_4$ and ozone; Reduction of alkenes and alkynes; Electrophilic addition reactions of alkenes with X_2, HX, HOX, (X=halogen); Effect of peroxide on addition reactions; cyclic polymerization reaction of alkynes.

Benzene

Structure; Electrophilic substitution reactions: halogenation, nitration, sulphonation, Friedel- Crafts alkylation and acylation; Effect of directing groups (monosubstituted benzene) in these reactions.

Phenols

Physical properties; Preparation, Electrophilic substitution reactions of phenol (halogenation, nitration, sulphonation); Reimer-Tiemann reaction, Kolbe reaction; Esterification; Etherification; Aspirin synthesis; Oxidation and reduction reactions of phenol.

Alkyl Halides

Rearrangement reactions of alkyl carbocation; Grignard reactions; Nucleophilic substitution reactions and their stereochemical aspects.

Alcohols

Physical properties; Reactions: esterification, dehydration (formation of alkenes and ethers); Reactions with: sodium, phosphorus halides, $ZnCl_2$/concentrated HCl, thionyl chloride; Conversion of alcohols into aldehydes, ketones and carboxylic acids.

Ethers

Preparation by Williamson's synthesis; C—O bond cleavage reactions.

Aldehydes and Ketones

Preparation of: aldehydes and ketones from acid chlorides and nitriles; aldehydes from esters; benzaldehyde from toluene and benzene; Reactions: oxidation, reduction, oxime and hydrazone formation; Aldol condensation, Cannizzaro reaction; Haloform reaction; Nucleophilic addition reaction with $RMgX$, $NaHSO_3$, HCN, alcohol, amine.

Carboxylic Acids

Physical properties; Preparation: from nitriles, Grignard reagents, hydrolysis of esters and amides; Preparation of benzoic acid from alkylbenzenes; Reactions: reduction, halogenation, formation of esters, acid chlorides and amides.

Amines

Preparation from nitro compounds, nitriles and amides; Reactions: Hoffmann bromamide degradation, Gabriel phthalimide synthesis; Reaction with nitrous acid, Azo coupling reaction of diazonium salts of aromatic amines; Sandmeyer and related reactions of diazonium salts; Carbylamine reaction, Hinsberg test, Alkylation and acylation reactions.

Haloarenes

Reactions: Fittig, Wurtz-Fittig; Nucleophilic aromatic substitution in haloarenes and substituted haloarenes (excluding benzyne mechanism and cine substitution).

Biomolecules

Carbohydrates: Classification; Mono- and di-saccharides (glucose and sucrose); Oxidation; Reduction; Glycoside formation and hydrolysis of disaccharides (sucrose, maltose, lactose); Anomers.

Proteins: Amino acids; Peptide linkage; Structure of peptides (primary and secondary); Types of proteins (fibrous and globular).

Nucleic acids: Chemical composition and structure of DNA and RNA.

Polymers

Types of polymerization (addition, condensation); Homo and copolymers; Natural rubber; Cellulose; Nylon; Teflon; Bakelite; PVC; Bio-degradable polymers; Applications of polymers.

Chemistry in Everyday Life

Drug-target interaction; Therapeutic action, and examples (excluding structures), of antacids, antihistamines, tranquilizers, analgesics, antimicrobials, and antifertility drugs; Artificial sweeteners (names only); Soaps, detergents, and cleansing action.

Practical Organic Chemistry

Detection of elements (N, S, halogens); Detection and identification of the following functional groups: hydroxyl (alcoholic and phenolic), carbonyl (aldehyde and ketone), carboxyl, amino and nitro.

JEE MAIN & ADVANCED

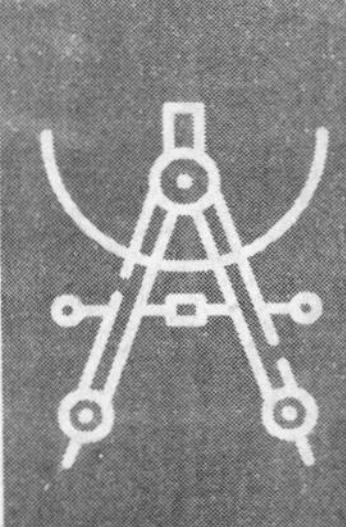

The Qualifier

One Test for each Unit of JEE Chemistry

To ensure good score in JEE, You must be sure of the good understanding to each unit of JEE Syllabus. You must complete these tests with atleast 75% score, then only move to the next section.

QUALIFIER 01

Some Basic Concepts of Chemistry

Section A Objective Type Questions

1. The number of significant digit in the number 134000 is ....

(a) 3 (b) 4
(c) 5 (d) 6

2. Which among the following statement(s) (I to IV) is/are correct about the laws of chemical combination?

I. Oxygen combines with two isotopes of hydrogen (^1_1H and ^2_1H) to form two samples of H_2O. These combinations follow the law of constant proportion.
II. Formation of H_2O and H_2O_2 follow the law of multiple proportions.
III. An analysis shows,
$H = 11.11\%$ in H_2O; $H = 5.88\%$ in H_2S; $S = 50\%$ in SO_2
The above data illustrate the law of reciprocal proportion.
IV. Law of multiple proportion cannot explain the formation of higher homologues of alkanes.

Choose the correct option.

(a) Only I (b) I, II and III
(c) II and III (d) II, III and IV

3. If Avogadro's number (N_A) is changed from 6.022×10^{23} mol^{-1} to 6.022×10^{21} mol^{-1}, this would change

(a) the definition of mass in units of gram or kilogram
(b) the mass of one mole of carbon-12
(c) the ratio of chemical species to each other in a balanced equation
(d) the ratio of number of atoms of elements to each other in a compound

4. A sample of impure sulphide ore contains 42.34% Zn. Percentage of pure ZnS in the sample is ......
[Atomic wt. of Zn = 65.38, S = 32.06]

(a) 67.10 (b) 45.38
(c) 60.15 (d) 63.10

5. If 30 mL of a gaseous hydrocarbon requires 90 mL of O_2 for complete combustion and 60 mL of CO_2 is formed in an eudiometer, the molecular formula of the hydrocarbon will be

(a) C_2H_2 (b) CH_4
(c) C_2H_4 (d) C_2H_6

6. Which of the following solution represents 1 M NaCl solution?

(a) 1 L solution containing 150 g NaCl.
(b) 250 mL solution containing 58.5 g NaCl.
(c) A solution containing 5.85 mg NaCl/mL solution.
(d) 5 L solution containing 292.5 g NaCl.

7. Orthoboric acid [H_3BO_3 or $B(OH)_3$] is an oxoacid of boron (atomic mass = 11 g mol^{-1}). 62 mg of H_3BO_3 is present in its 250 mL aqueous solution. Molarity and normality of the solution will be

(a) 4×10^{-3} M, 4×10^{-3} N
(b) 4×10^{-3} M, 1.34×10^{-3} N
(c) 1.34×10^{-3} M, 1.34×10^{-3} N
(d) 4×10^{-3} M, 12×10^{-3} N

8. Final concentration of solute after 250 mL of 5M antifreeze solution and 500 mL of 4 M antifreeze solution are combined and diluted to 2 L with water will be

(a) 3.24 M (b) 4.26 M
(c) 1.62 M (d) 2.13 M

9. Match the items given in Column I with those given in Column II. Choose the correct matching code from the codes given below.

Column I	Column II
A. 0.98% H_2SO_4 (w/w) [$d = 1.8$ g/mL]	1. 3 M, 4 N
B. 9.8% H_3PO_4 (w/w) [$d = 1.4$ g/mL, $\alpha\% = 100$]	2. 1.4 M, 4.2 N
C. $1.8 \times 10^{-3} \times N_A$ molecules of NH_3 in 0.5 L water	3. 0.18 M, 0.36 N
D. 250 mL 4N HCl + 250 mL 2 M H_2SO_4	4. 0.0036 M, 0.0036 N

Codes

	A	B	C	D		A	B	C	D
(a)	3	2	1	4	(b)	1	2	4	3
(c)	3	2	4	1	(d)	2	1	3	4

10. The volume of water needs to be added to 10 mL of HNO_3 (density : 1.40 g/mL) containing 70 per cent of mass of the acid to prepare 1.0 M solution would be

(a) 155.6 mL (b) 130.6 mL
(c) 135.6 mL (d) 145.6 mL

11. 1.8 g of Mg is burnt in a closed vessel which contains 0.8 g of oxygen. Which of the following statement is not correct? [Atomic weight of Mg = 24.3 g mol^{-1}]

(a) 0.05 mole of MgO is formed.
(b) 0.8 g of Mg remains unreacted.
(c) Oxygen is the limiting reactant.
(d) The extent of reaction at the completion of reaction is 0.025 mol.

12. 254 g of I_2 and 12.046×10^{23} molecules of Cl_2 are made to react completely to give a mixture of ICl and ICl_3. The moles of each compound formed respectively is [Atomic weights of I = 127, Cl = 35.5]

	ICl	ICl_3
(a)	0.1 mol	0.1 mol
(b)	1 mol	1 mol
(c)	0.5 mol	0.1 mol
(d)	0.5 mol	1 mol

13. When solutions containing 2 g of Na_2SO_4 and 3 g of $BaCl_2$ are mixed, what mass of $BaSO_4$ is produced?
[Molar mass (g mol^{-1}) : Na_2SO_4 = 142, $BaCl_2$ = 208.2 and $BaSO_4$ = 233.4]

(a) 3.29 g (b) 14.39 g (c) 4.12 g (d) 21.11 g

14. H_3PO_4 is a tribasic acid and it on reaction with NaOH, forms an acidic salt, NaH_2PO_4. What volume of 1 M NaOH solution should be added to 12 g of NaH_2PO_4 to convert it completely into Na_3PO_4?
[Atomic wt. of Na = 23, H = 1, P = 31, O = 16]

(a) 100 mL (b) 150 mL
(c) 200 mL (d) 250 mL

15. 25 mL of a solution of $Ba(OH)_2$ of density 1.2 g/mL gets neutralised completely by 35 mL of 0.1 M HCl solution. The molality of barium hydroxide [$Ba(OH)_2$] solution was [Atomic wt. of Ba = 137]

(a) 1.11 m (b) 0.140 m
(c) 0.119 m (d) 2.19 m

16. Volume of ammonia gas required at STP which on passing into 30 mL of 1 N H_2SO_4 solution will reduce the strength of acidic solution to 0.2 N is

(a) 1.514 L (b) 0.537 L
(c) 2.141 L (d) 0.0254 L

17. 0.4 g of a polybasic acid, AH_n requires 0.5 g of NaOH for complete neutralisation. If all hydrogen atoms of AH_n are acidic, the value of n and atomic weight of A will be respectively. [Molecular weight of AH_n = 96]

(a) 1, 95 (b) 2, 94
(c) 3, 93 (d) 4, 92

18. 0.70 g of a sample of $(NH_4)_2SO_4$ was boiled with 100 mL of 0.2 N NaOH solution till all the $NH_3(g)$ evolved and get dissolved in solution itself. The remaining solution was diluted to 250 mL. 25 mL of this solution was neutralised using 10 mL of 0.1 N H_2SO_4 solution. The percentage purity of the sample is

(a) 94.3 (b) 50.8
(c) 47.4 (d) 79.8

19. Given below are two statements, one is labelled as Assertion (A) and the other is labelled as Reason (R).
Assertion (A) Na_2CO_3 solution cannot be titrated with HCl solution completely with phenolphthalein indicator.
Reason (R) Phenolphthalein is a weak indicator.
In the light of the above statements, choose the correct answer from the options given below.

(a) Both A and R are true and R is the correct explanation of A.
(b) Both A and R are true but R is not the correct explanation of A.
(c) A is true but R is false.
(d) A is false but R is true.

20. 3 moles of ethane is mixed with 60 g of it and after sometimes 2.4×10^{24} molecules of the gas is removed. The left over gas is combusted with excess of oxygen [$N_A = 6.023 \times 10^{23}$ mol^{-1}, density of water = 1 g/mL].
Based on the above experiment, three statements can be made which need justification in accordance to the experiment.

I. 2 moles of C_2H_6 was left for combustion.
II. Volume of CO_2 produced at STP after combustion is 44.8 L.
III. Volume of water produced is 54 mL.

Which of the above statement(s) is (are) correct?

(a) Only I (b) II and III
(c) I, II and III (d) I and III

Section B *Numerical Value Questions*

21. The proper number of significant digits in (1.0042 – 0.0034) (1.23) are ....

22. Disilane (Si_2H_x), on compositional analysis results that it contains 90.9% Si by mass. The value of x is ....

23. When the Baeyer process is used for recovering aluminium from siliceous ore, some aluminium is always lost because of the formation of an unworkable mud having the following average formula : $3Na_2O \cdot 3Al_2O_3 \cdot 5SiO_2 \cdot 5H_2O$. A certain ore contained 13% (by weight) kaolin ($Al_2O_3 \cdot 2SiO_2 \cdot 2H_2O$; molar mass = 258 g mol^{-1}) and 87% gibbsite ($Al_2O_3 \cdot 3H_2$; molar mass = 156 g mol^{-1}). The percentage of the total aluminium in this ore that is recoverable in the Baeyer process is .... [Atomic mass of aluminium = 27 g mol^{-1}]

24. A sample of polystyrene prepared by heating styrene ($C_6H_5—CH=CH_2$) with tribromobenzoyl peroxide in absence of air has the formula, $Br_3C_6H_3(C_8H_8)_n$ which contains 10.46% of bromine by mass. The value of n is .... [Atomic mass of bromine $=80$ g mol^{-1}]

25. The volume (in L) of 0.5 M $BaCl_2$ that contains 3 moles of chloride ions is ....

26. A litre of milk weighs 1.032 kg. The butterfat it contains to the extent of 4% by volume has a density of 865 kg/m^3. The density (in kg/m^3) of the fat-free "skimmed" milk will be ....

27. The molarity of H^+ ions produced by bubbling excess H_2S into 1 L of 0.1 M $CuCl_2$ solution will be .... M.
The equation is, $Cu^{2+} + H_2S(g) \longrightarrow CuS(s) + 2H^+$
Assume no change in volume of the liquid.

28. The empirical formula of a commercial ion-exchange resin is $C_8H_7SO_3Na$. The resin can be used to soften hard water according to the reaction,

$$Ca^{2+} + 2C_8H_7SO_3Na \longrightarrow (C_8H_7SO_3)_2Ca\downarrow + 2Na^+$$

The maximum uptake of Ca^{2+} by the resin is found to be $x \times 10^{-3}$ mol/g resin. The value of x is ....

29. x% BaO is present in a 10 g mixture of BaO and CaO which requires 100 mL of 2.5 M HCl to react with it completely. The value of x is ....
[Molar mass (g/mol) : BaO = 153, CaO = 56]

30. After mixing 40 mL of 1.6 M HCl and 60 mL of 2 M NaOH, the molar concentrations of Na^+, Cl^- and OH^- in the resultant solution of volume 100 mL are found to be a M, b M and c M respectively. The value of $(a+b+c)$ is ......

Answers

Section A

1 (a)	2 (d)	3 (b)	4 (d)	5 (c)
6 (d)	7 (a)	8 (c)	9 (c)	10 (d)
11 (b)	12 (b)	13 (a)	14 (c)	15 (c)
16 (b)	17 (c)	18 (a)	19 (c)	20 (b)

Section B

21 (3)	22 (6)	23 (90.07)	24 (19)	25 (3)
26 (1038.96)	27 (0.20)	28 (2.43)	29 (47.27)	30 (2.40)

See detailed solutions on page no. 197

QUALIFIER 02

States of Matter

Section A Objective Type Questions

1. A 10 cm column of air is trapped by a 8 cm long column of Hg in a capillary tube of uniform bore. When the tube is held horizontally in a room at 0.94 atm pressure.

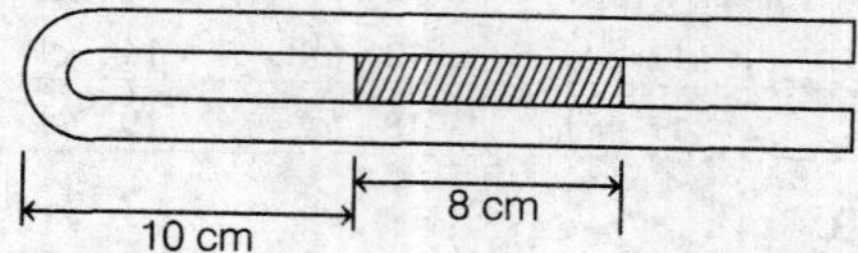

What will be the length of air column when the tube is held vertically with the open end up?

(a) 8.99 cm (b) 9.15 cm
(c) 10.99 cm (d) 7.56 cm

2. The graphs depicted below explain the behaviour of four gases –*A*, *B*, *C* and *D* with adopted restrictions as given

Gas	Constant parameters
A	Mole and pressure
B	Mole and temperature
C	Mole and volume
D	Mole and temperature

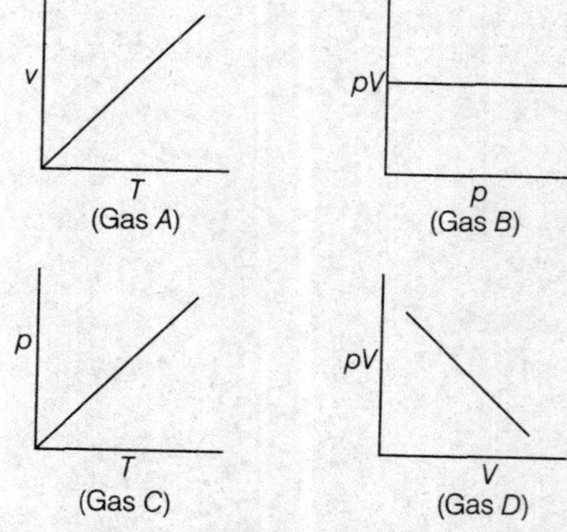

Which of these gases exhibit(s) behaviour that deviate(s) most significantly from that expected for an ideal gas?

(a) Only *A*
(b) *A* and *C*
(c) *B*, *C* and *D*
(d) Only *D*

3. The following *V-T* graph is constructed for a given amount of an ideal gas.

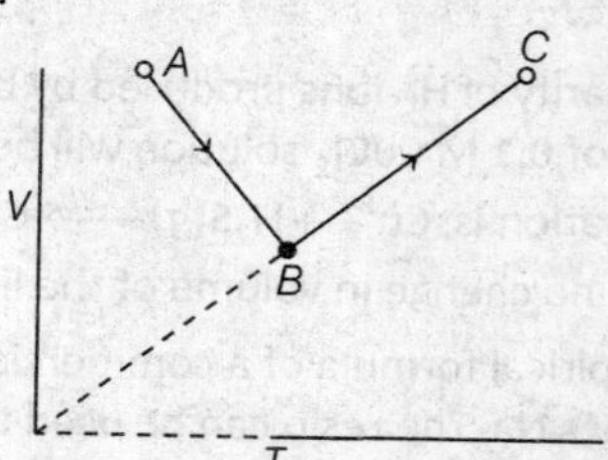

Which of the following statements correctly illustrate experimental verifications regarding the behaviour of the gas as depicted in the above plot?

I. Along $A \rightarrow B$, pressure will increase.
II. Along $B \rightarrow C$, pressure remains constant.
III. Pressure of the gas at *C* is greater than that at *A*.
IV. Along *BC*, the gas obeys Charles' law.

(a) I, II and III
(b) III and IV
(c) I, II and IV
(d) I, II, III and IV

4. If equal weights of oxygen and nitrogen are placed in separate containers of equal volume at the same temperature, which of the following statements is true?

(a) Both containers have the same number of molecules.
(b) The pressure in the nitrogen flask is greater than that in the oxygen flask.
(c) More molecules are present in the oxygen flask.
(d) Molecules in the oxygen flask are moving faster on the average than the molecules in the oxygen flask.

5. A mixture of two gases, *P* and *Q* in the mole ratio 2 : 3 is kept in a 2 L vessel. A second 3 L vessel has the same two gases in the mole ratio 3 : 5. Both of the gas mixture are kept at same pressure and temperature. They are allowed to intermix at constant temperature and pressure, so that final volume becomes 5 L. What is the mean molar mass of the final mixture?

[Molar mass for *P* is M_P and *Q* is M_Q]

(a) $\dfrac{77M_P + 123M_Q}{200}$ (b) $\dfrac{123M_P + 77M_Q}{200}$

(c) $\dfrac{77M_P + 123M_Q}{250}$ (d) $\dfrac{123M_P + 77M_Q}{250}$

6. A bulb with chlorine gas at ambient pressure contains 3.55 g at t°C. When the bulb is placed in a second thermostat at a temperature 30°C higher and stopcock of the bulb temporarily opened (and closed again) to restore the initial pressure. The bulb is now found to contain 3.2 g of chlorine. The value of t°C will be

(a) 2.81 (b) 8.21
(c) 8.12 (d) 2.23

7. The absolute viscosity of water at 298 K is 1.002×10^{-3} Pa-s. Time taken by equal volumes of water and chloroform to flow through a capillary tube are 39.7 s and 15 s respectively. Calculate the specific viscosity of chloroform at 298 K.

[Given, density of water $= 1 \times 10^3$ kg m^{-3}, density of chloroform $= 1.49 \times 10^3$ kg m^{-3}]

(a) 1.35 (b) 0.84 (c) 0.56 (d) 2.50

8. A large cylinder of helium filled at 100 bar had a small thin orifice through which helium escaped into an evacuated space at the rate of 6.4 mmol/h. How long would it take for 10 mmol of CO to leak through similar orifice, if the CO were confined at the same pressure?

(a) 5.21 h (b) 2.13 h (c) 4.13 h (d) 10.15 h

9. Air is essentially a mixture of nitrogen and oxygen in the ratio of 4 : 1 by volume. Assume that gases are ideal. Ignore the presence in air of small amounts of other gases and vapours. Partial pressure of nitrogen in air on a certain day when the barometric pressure is 740 mm Hg at a certain place will be

(a) 148 torr (b) 592 torr (c) 370 torr (d) 300.5 torr

10. At what temperature, would the average translational kinetic energy of gaseous hydrogen molecules equal to the energy required to dissociate the molecules into atoms (104 kcal/mol)?

(a) 2.59×10^3 K (b) 1.52×10^4 K
(c) 3.49×10^3 K (d) 3.49×10^4 K

11. Given below are two statements, one is labelled as Assertion (A) and the other is labelled as Reason (R).

Assertion (A) As velocity increases, distribution of molecules also increases and becomes maximum at most probable velocity, after which distribution of molecules decreases at a constant temperature.

Reason (R) Most probable velocity of an ideal gas is given by,

$$u_{mp} = \sqrt{\frac{2RT}{M}}$$

In the light of the above statements, choose the correct answer from the options given below.

(a) Both (A) and (R) are true and (R) is the correct explanation of (A).
(b) Both (A) and (R) are true but (R) is not the correct explanation of (A).
(c) (A) is true but (R) is false.
(d) (A) is false but (R) is true.

12. The density of oxygen at 273 K and 1 atm pressure is 1.4290 g dm^{-3}. Root mean square velocity of the gas at 273 K is

(a) 4.61 ms^{-1} (b) 183.42 ms^{-1} (c) 670.15 ms^{-1} (d) 461.15 ms^{-1}

13. When two molecules are present at a distance of r pm (where, $r \leq 600$ pm), they may exert different types of intermolecular forces of attraction which vary inversely with r as,

I. Dipole-dipole force (f_1) between stationary polar molecules, $f_1 \propto \frac{1}{r^x}$

II. Dipole-dipole force (f_2) between rotating polar molecules, $f_2 \propto \frac{1}{r^y}$

III. Dipole-induce dipole force (f_3) between polar and non-polar molecules, $f_3 \propto \frac{1}{r^a}$

IV. London force or dispersion force (f_4) between non-polar molecules, $f_4 \propto \frac{1}{r^b}$

Now, the value of $\frac{|a+b|}{|x+y|}$ is

(a) 1.34 (b) 2.60 (c) 0.84 (d) 0.68

14. What is the compressibility factor of water vapour at 20°C and 1.5 atm pressure, if molar volume of water vapour is 33.18 dm^3 ?

(a) 1.429 (b) 2.071 (c) 1.986 (d) 0.896

15. n moles of helium gas is placed in a vessel of volume V litre at temperature, T K. If V_i is the ideal volume of helium, the diameter of the molecule is

(a) $\left[\frac{3V_i}{2\pi n N_A}\right]^{1/3}$ (b) $\left[\frac{3(V-V_i)}{2\pi n N_A}\right]^{1/3}$

(c) $\left[\frac{6(V-V_i)}{\pi n N_A}\right]^{1/3}$ (d) $\left[\frac{6V_i}{\pi n N_A}\right]^{1/3}$

16. Oxygen gas follows van der Waals' equation of state. For 1 mole of O_2 when $b = 0$ and $T = 300$ K, the pV vs $\frac{1}{V}$ plot is shown below,

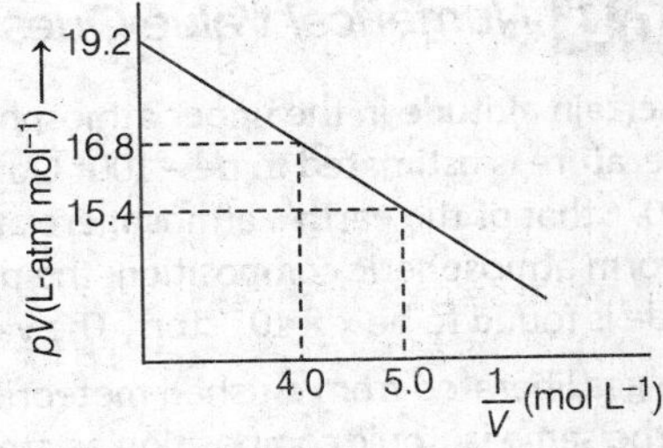

The value of van der Waals' constant, a (atm L^2 mol^{-2}) of O_2 will be

(a) 1.5 (b) 1.4 (c) 0.8 (d) 2.2

17. The van der Waals' constants a and b of a real gas are 3.6 atm L^2 mol^{-2} and 0.05 L mol^{-1} respectively. If 200 g of the gas of molar mass 40 g mol^{-1} is taken in a 10 L vessel at 300 K, match Column I with Column II. For this purpose, the matching order are given below.

	Column I		Column II
A.	Pressure correction (atm)	1.	0.25
B.	Free space for the molecules to move through (L)	2.	0.0125
C.	Actual volume of the gas molecules per mole of the gas (L)	3.	0.90
D.	Effective volume occupied by total gas molecules (L)	4.	9.75

Codes

	A	B	C	D		A	B	C	D
(a)	4	3	1	2	(b)	3	4	1	2
(c)	1	2	3	4	(d)	3	4	2	1

18. If, $\frac{p}{p_C} = \alpha$ (reduced pressure), $\frac{V}{V_C} = \beta$ (reduced volume) and $\frac{T}{T_C} = \gamma$ (reduced temperature), then van der Waals' equation for 1 mole of a real gas can be expressed in terms of critical states (c) as

(a) $\left(\alpha + \frac{3}{\beta^2}\right)(3\beta - 1) = 8\gamma$ (b) $\left(\alpha + \frac{3}{\beta^2}\right)(\beta - 1) = \gamma$

(c) $\left(\alpha - \frac{3}{\beta^2}\right)(3\beta + 1) = 8\gamma$ (d) $\left(\alpha - \frac{3}{\beta^2}\right)(3\beta - 1) = 8\gamma$

19. How much water vapour is contained in a cubic room 4 m along an edge if the relative humidity is 50% at 27°C? The vapour pressure of water at 27°C is 26.8 torr.

(a) 1026.5 g (b) 412.6 g (c) 111.2 g (d) 825.7 g

20. At 100°C and 1 atm pressure, for water, $\Delta_{vap}H° = 40.6$ kJ mol^{-1}. If water vapour behaves ideally, the value of $\frac{dT}{dp}$ for water at the boiling point is

(a) 28.5 K atm^{-1} (b) 0.0351 K atm^{-1}
(c) 0.076 K atm^{-1} (d) 13.08 K atm^{-1}

Section B Numerical Value Questions

21. At a certain altitude in the upper atmosphere, the temperature is estimated to be $-100°$ C and the density is just 10^{-9} that of the earth's atmosphere at STP. Assuming a uniform atmospheric composition, the pressure at this altitude is found to be $x \times 10^{-7}$ torr. The value of x is ....

22. Argon gas liberated from crushed meteorites does not have the same isotopic composition as atmospheric argon. The gas density of a particular sample of meteoritic Ar was found to be 1.481 g/L at 27°C and 740 torr. The average atomic weight (in g/mol) of this sample of argon is ....

23. The pressure in a vessel that contained pure oxygen dropped from 2000 torr to 1500 torr in 55 min as the oxygen leaked through a small hole into a vacuum. When the same vessel was filled with another gas, the pressure dropped from 2000 torr to 1500 torr in 85 min. Molar mass (in g/mol) of the second gas is ....

24. A certain gas effuses out of two different vessels I and II. I has a circular orifice, while II has a square orifice of length equal to the radius of the orifice of vessel. The ratio of rate of effusion of the gas from vessel I to that from vessel II is ....

25. When 0.75 mol solid 'A_4' and 1 mol gaseous O_2 are heated in a sealed vessel (bomb), completely using up the reactants and producing one compound, it is found that when the temperature is reduced to the initial temperature, the contents of the vessel exhibit a pressure equal to half the original pressure.
The molecular formula of the compound formed is reported as A_xO_y. The value of $\left(\frac{x}{y}\right)$ is ....

26. The value of $\frac{u_{rms}}{u_{av}}$ of a given gas molecule at a given temperature is ....

27. The molecular diameter of a CO molecule is 3.19×10^{-8} cm. At 27°C and a pressure of 250 mm Hg, the mean free path travelled by CO is $x \times 10^{-8}$ cm. The value of x will be ....

28. The van der Waals' constants are $a = 0.245$ atm L^2 mol^{-2} and $b = 26.7$ cm^3 mol^{-1} for hydrogen. Boyle temperature of H_2 in Kelvin will be ....

29. Compressibility factor for CO_2, if 2 moles of it occupies 0.4 L at 300 K and 40 atm is ....

30. A liquid of density 850 kg/m^3 have a surface tension of 0.055 N/m. Rise (in mm) in a glass capillary of 1.40 mm inside diameter will be .... mm.

Answers

Section A

1 (a)	2 (d)	3 (d)	4 (b)	5 (a)
6 (d)	7 (c)	8 (c)	9 (b)	10 (d)
11 (b)	12 (d)	13 (a)	14 (b)	15 (b)
16 (b)	17 (d)	18 (a)	19 (d)	20 (a)

Section B

21 (4.81)	22 (37.49)	23 (76.43)	24 (3.14)	25 (0.75)
26 (1.08)	27 (2.75)	28 (111.90)	29 (0.32)	30 (18.86)

See detailed solutions on page no. 199

QUALIFIER **03**

Atomic Structure

Section A *Objective Type Questions*

1. In an experiment to measure the quantum efficiency of photosynthesis in green plants, it was found that 8 quanta of red light at 6850 Å were needed to evolve 1 molecule of O_2. The average energy storage in the photosynthesis process is 112 kcal/mol O_2 evolved. Energy conversion efficiency of the photosynthesis process is

(a) 85% (b) 61.8% (c) 33.5% (d) 100%

2. If λ_0 is threshold wavelength for photoelectronic emission, λ is the wavelength of light falling on the surface of metal, and m is the mass of electron, then de-Broglie wavelength of the emitted electron is

(a) $\left[\dfrac{h(\lambda\lambda_0)}{2mc(\lambda_0-\lambda)}\right]^{1/2}$ (b) $\left[\dfrac{h(\lambda_0-\lambda)}{2\,mc\,\lambda\lambda_0}\right]^{1/2}$

(c) $\left[\dfrac{h(\lambda-\lambda_0)}{2mc\,\lambda\,\lambda_0}\right]^{1/2}$ (d) $\left[\dfrac{(h\lambda\lambda_0)}{2mc}\right]^{1/2}$

3. The angular momentum of electron in Li^{2+} ion is found to be $\dfrac{7h}{11}$, where, h is Planck's constant. The distance of the electron from the nucleus is

(a) 1.69 Å (b) 0.68 Å
(c) 2.82 Å (d) 8.19 Å

4. The distance of closest approach of an α-particle fired towards a nucleus with momentum p is r. What will be the distance of closest approach when the momentum of the α-particle is $2p$?

(a) $2r$ (b) $4r$
(c) $\dfrac{r}{2}$ (d) $\dfrac{r}{4}$

5. 'Hartree' or 'Ha' is the atomic unit of energy and 1 Ha is equal to

(a) – 13.6 eV atom^{-1} (b) – 27.2 eV atom^{-1}
(c) + 13.6 eV atom^{-1} (d) + 27.2 eV mol^{-1}

6. How fast should an electron have to move in order to eject an electron of neon, which has first ionisation energy equal to 2080 kJ mol^{-1}?

(a) 2.754×10^{6} ms^{-1}
(b) 3.021×10^{7} ms^{-1}
(c) 1.265×10^{8} ms^{-1}
(d) 4.012×10^{5} ms^{-1}

7. Given below are two statements.

Statement I An ideal black body emits and absorbs radiation of all frequencies.

Statement II Frequency of black body radiation is directly proportional to the temperature of the black body.

In the light of the above statements, choose the most appropriate answer from the options given below.

(a) Both statement I and statement II are correct.
(b) Both statement I and statement II are incorrect.
(c) Statement I is correct but statement II is incorrect.
(d) Statement I is incorrect but statement II is correct.

8. During transition, an electron present in hydrogen atom travels a distance of 0.7935 nm. During de-excitation of the electron, maximum number of spectral lines formed will be

(a) 5 (b) 6 (c) 8 (d) 10

9. The de-Broglie wavelength made by the electron present in the third orbit of He^{+} ion is

(a) 3.32 Å (b) 1.66 Å (c) 1.11 Å (d) 4.98 Å

10. Frequency of a matter wave is equal to

(a) $\dfrac{KE}{2h}$ (b) $\dfrac{2(KE)}{h}$
(c) $\dfrac{KE}{h}$ (d) $\left[\dfrac{2(KE)}{h}\right]^{1/2}$

11. In hydrogen atom, the electronic motion can be shown as,

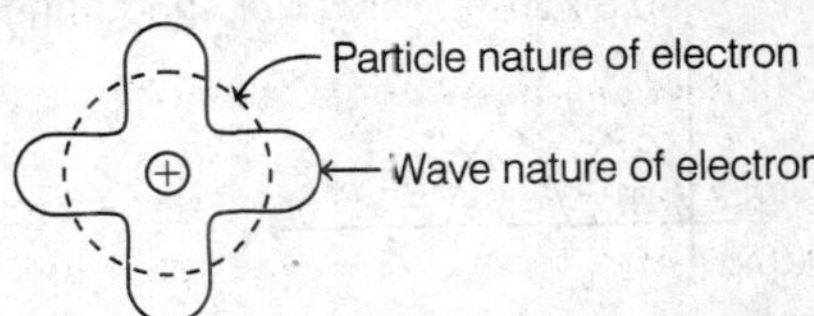

The number of revolutions made by the electron in the given orbit is

(a) 6.5×10^{15} s^{-1} (b) 2×10^{14} s^{-1}
(c) 2×10^{13} s^{-1} (d) 1.0×10^{14} s^{-1}

12. An automobile of mass 500 kg is moving with a speed of 50 ± 0.001 km/h. Which of the following will be the correct one regarding the uncertainty in position of the car and its interpretation?

(a) 3.798×10^{-34} m and negligible
(b) 3.798×10^{-34} m and not negligible
(c) 1.512×10^{-2} m and not negligible
(d) 4.151×10^{-40} m and negligible

13. For x-axis, wave function (ψ) can be written as,

$$\psi = A \sin\left(\frac{2\pi x}{\lambda}\right)$$

Thus, Schrodinger wave equation along x-axis can be written as

(a) $\frac{d^2\psi}{dx^2} - \frac{4\pi^2\psi}{\lambda^2} = 0$ (b) $\frac{d^2\psi}{dx^2} + \frac{2\pi\psi}{\lambda} = 0$

(c) $\frac{d^2\psi}{dx^2} + \frac{4\pi^2\psi}{\lambda^2} = 0$ (d) None of these

14. Given the wave function of an orbital of hydrogen atom as,

$$\Psi_{1,0} = \left[\frac{1}{\sqrt{\pi a_0^{3/2}}}\right] e^{-r/a_0}$$

The most probable distance of the electron present in the given orbital from the nucleus is

(a) $a_0 \times e^{-2r}$ (b) a_0

(c) $\frac{3}{2}a_0$ (d) $2a_0$

15. Match radial distribution curves given in Column I with the presentations of the respective curves given in Column II. Select the answer from the codes given below.

Column I	Column II [r = distance from the nucleus]
A. 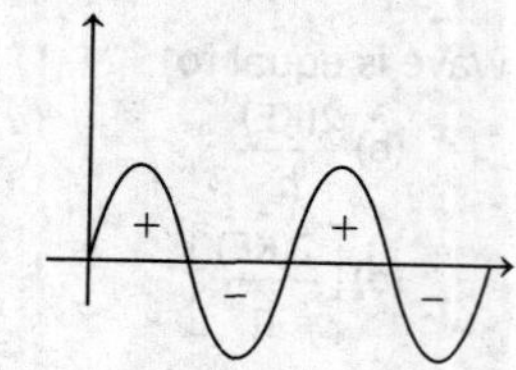	1. $R^2(r)$ vs r
B. 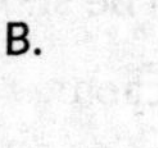	2. $R(r)$ vs r
C. 	3. ψ^2 vs r for 2s

Codes

	A	B	C		A	B	C
(a)	1	2	3	(b)	2	3	1
(c)	2	1	3	(d)	3	2	1

16. The r-dependent wave function of hydrogen atom is given by the expression,

$$\psi = (\text{constant})\left(3 - \frac{2\gamma}{a_0} + \frac{2\gamma^2}{9a_0^2}\right) e^{-\gamma/3a_0}$$

Using this expression, answer the following. One of the nodes lies at the distance r from the nucleus, where r is about

(a) $1.5\, a_0$ (b) $2.5 a_0$ (c) $5.5 a_0$ (d) $7.1\, a_0$

17. The nucleus of an atom is located at $x = y = z = 0$. If the probability of finding a s-electron in a tiny volume around $x = a, y = z = 0$ is 1.0×10^{-5}, what is the probability of finding the electron in the same sized volume around $x = z = 0, y = a$?

(a) 2.0×10^{-5} (b) 5.0×10^{-6}

(c) 1.0×10^{-5} (d) 1.0×10^{-2}

18. Which is a possible set of quantum numbers for a valence unpaired electron in ground state atom of phosphorus (atomic no. $Z = 15$)?

(a) $n = 2, l = 1, m = 0, s = +\frac{1}{2}$ (b) $n = 3, l = 2, m = 0, s = +\frac{1}{2}$

(c) $n = 3, l = 0, m = 0, s = +\frac{1}{2}$ (d) $n = 3, l = 1, m = +1, s = +\frac{1}{2}$

19. $1s^2 2s^2 2p^6 3s^2 3p^6 4s^2 3d^{10} 4p^6 5s^2 4d^{10}$ could be the ground state electronic configuration of

(a) Cd (b) Sb^{3+}

(c) Sn^{2+} (d) All of these

20. Quantum numbers of some electrons are given as

I. $n = 4, s = -\frac{1}{2}$ II. $n = 3, l = 0$ III. $n = 2, l = 1$

IV. $n = 2, m = 0$

How many electrons in an atom may have these quantum numbers ?

	I	II	III	IV		I	II	III	IV
(a)	16	2	6	6	(b)	32	18	8	8
(c)	16	6	8	6	(d)	16	2	6	4

Section B *Numerical Value Questions*

21. The wavelength of a beam of light is 24 μm. The energy (in J) of one of its photon with a multiple of value, 10^{-21} will be ....

22. To stop the ejection of photoelectrons produced by electromagnetic radiation incident on a certain metal, a negative or opposing potential of 300 V is required. If the photoelectric threshold wavelength of the metal is 1500 Å, frequency of incident radiation will be $x \times 10^{16}$ Hz. The value of x is ....

23. A photon of wavelength $a \times 10^{-7}$ m causes the transition of an electron of an atom from its ground state to its excited state of energy difference 4.4×10^{-19} J. The value of *a* will be ....

24. A corona is an aura of plasma that surrounds the Sun and other stars. High temperature ($>10^6$ K) of the plasma state of corona indicates strong ionisation of elements within it. Its spectroscopic measurement, coronagraph, indicates the presence of an emission spectral line of S^{15+} ion. From this observation, the most probable temperature of the corona state is found to be $x \times 10^6$ K. The value of *x* is ....

25. He^+ ions are in an excited state from where maximum 6 types of photons can be emitted. If *E* is the separation energy of He^+ from the excited state. The energy, *E* is required to ionise hydrogen atom is .... times.

26. At $T' \times 10^3$ K temperature, the transitional kinetic energy of atomic hydrogen is found to be equal to that for $e_1 \rightarrow e_3$ transition. The value of T' will be ....

27. An electron diffraction experiment was performed with a beam of electrons accelerated by a potential difference 20 kV. The wavelength of the electron beam was found to be $Y \times 10^{-12}$ m. The value of Y is ....

28. The diameter of an atomic nucleus is 1.34×10^{-15}m. The uncertainty in momentum of an electron if it like to exist inside the nucleus will be $x \times 10^{-20}$ kg ms^{-1}. The value of *x* is ....

29. In a compound of titanium ($Z = 22$), Ti is present in +2 oxidation state. The spin-only magnetic moment (in BM) of the compound is ....

30. Total orbital angular momentum (in Js) contributed by one orbital each of $3s, 3p$ and $3d$ in an atom is $x \times 10^{-34}$ Js. *x* is ....

Answers

Section A

1 (c)	2 (a)	3 (c)	4 (d)	5 (b)
6 (a)	7 (c)	8 (b)	9 (d)	10 (b)
11 (d)	12 (a)	13 (c)	14 (b)	15 (c)
16 (d)	17 (c)	18 (d)	19 (d)	20 (d)

Section B

21 (8.28)	22 (7.44)	23 (4.52)	24 (26.95)	25 (4)
26 (93.72)	27 (8.68)	28 (4)	29 (2.83)	30 (4)

See detailed solutions on page no. 202

QUALIFIER **04**

Chemical Bonding and Molecular Structure

Section A *Objective Type Questions*

1. If IE_1 of Na and EA_1 of Cl are 495.8 kJ mol^{-1} and 349.4 kJ mol^{-1} respectively. The correct statement regarding formation of sodium chloride crystal will be (lattice energy of NaCl = 776 kJ mol^{-1})

(a) Total energy released per mole of NaCl formed is 628.6 kJ
(b) The ionic bond formed in NaCl is unstable
(c) Total energy absorbed per mole of NaCl formed is 1125.4 kJ
(d) Net energy released in the process is 629.6 kJ

2. Which of the following order is correct regarding covalent bond nature of the molecules?

(a) $LiCl > BeCl_2 > BCl_3 > CCl_4$
(b) $CCl_4 > BCl_3 > BeCl_2 > LiCl$
(c) $LiCl > BeCl_2 > CCl_4 > BCl_3$
(d) $CCl_4 > BeCl_2 > BCl_3 > LiCl$

3. PCl_aF_{5-a} shows non-polar behaviour, when value(s) of '*a*' can be

(a) 2, 1 and 4 (b) 0, 3 and 5
(c) 0, 4 and 1 (d) 0

4. Which of the following species have the same number of lone pair(s) of electrons with their central atom?

I. XeF_5^- II. BrF_5 III. XeF_2 IV. H_3S^+ V. XeO_6^{4-}

Choose the correct option.

(a) IV and V (b) I and III
(c) I and II (d) II and IV

5. Select the correct statement(s) from the following.

I. $(CH_3)_3N$ is pyramidal but $(SiH_3)_3N$ is planar.
II. N in $(CH_3)_3N$ and N in $(SiH_3)_3N$ are sp^3 and sp^2 -hybridised respectively.
III. $(SiH_3)_3N$ is a stronger Lewis base compared to $(CH_3)_3N$
IV. $p\pi$ - $d\pi$ bond is absent in $(SiH_3)_3N$.

Choose the correct option.

(a) I, II, III and IV
(b) I, II and III
(c) I and II
(d) I, II and IV

6. AsF_5 molecule is trigonal bipyramidal. The hybrid atomic orbitals used by As-atom for bonding are

s p_x p_y p_z $d_{x^2-y^2}$ d_{xy} d_{z^2}
I II III IV V VI VII

(a) I, II, III, IV and V
(b) I, II, III, IV and VI
(c) I, II, III, IV and VII
(d) I, II, III, V and VI

7. In which of the following reactions, hybridisation state of the underlined atom of the reactant get(s) changed?

(a) $\underline{Sb}F_5 + HF \longrightarrow H[SbF_6]$
(b) $\underline{P}Cl_5 \longrightarrow PCl_3 + Cl_2$
(c) $\underline{B}Cl_3 + F^- \longrightarrow [BCl_3F]^-$
(d) All of the above

8. Among the following species, isostructural pairs are

CO_2 CH_4 SF_4 $SiCl_4$ XeF_2 BF_3
a *b* *c* *d* *e* *f*

(a) [*a*, *b*] and [*c*, *d*] (b) [*a*, *d*] and [*c*, *e*]
(c) [*a*, *c*] and [*d*, *f*] (d) [*a*, *e*] and [*b*, *d*]

9. Which of the following options contains a pair of species which are isostructural but not isolobal?

(a) PH_4^+, XeO_3 (b) CO_2, XeF_2
(c) BF_3, BF_4^- (d) XeF_4, SF_4

10. Statement I SiF_6^{2-} is known but $SiCl_6^{2-}$ is not.

Statement II Size of fluorine atom is smaller and its lone pair of electrons interacts with vacant *d*-orbitals of silicon strongly.

(a) Both statement I and statement II are correct.
(b) Statement I is incorrect but statement II is corrrect.
(c) Both statement I and statement II are incorrect.
(d) Statement I is correct but statement II is incorrect.

11. Choose one molecule or ion from each of the following sets having the smallest bond angle.

I. NH_3, PH_3 and AsH_3
II. O_3^+ and O_3
III. NO_2^- and O_3
IV. $SOCl_2$ and SOF_2 angle ($L \times Sx$)

Choose the correct option.

	I	II	III	IV
(a)	(NH_3)	(O_3^+)	(O_3)	$(SOCl_2)$
(b)	(AsH_3)	(O_3)	(NO_2^-)	(SOF_2)
(c)	(PH_3)	(O_3^+)	(NO_2^-)	
(d)	(AsH_3)	(O_3^+)	(O_3)	(SOF_2)

12. Which of the following statement(s) is not correct for NO_2, NO_2^+ and NO_2^-?

(a) NO_2 is paramagnetic.
(b) NO_2^+ is linear and NO_2 is bent with bond angle slightly lower than 120°.
(c) NO_2^+ ion has the shortest and strongest bonds.
(d) NO_2^- ion has the longest and weakest bonds.

13. Consider the aromatic molecule anthracene, $C_{14}H_{10}$.

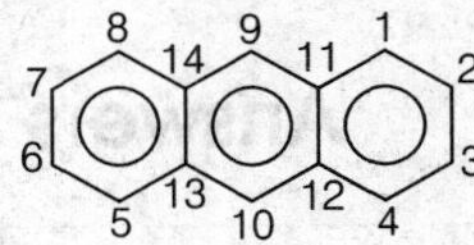

Approximate calculations of the π-bond order for carbon-carbon bonds yields the following results :

Bond	π-bond order
1-2	0.738
1-11	0.535
2-3	0.568
9-11	0.606
11-12	0.485

Which carbon-carbon bond would be the shortest and which the longest respectively?

(a) 1-2, 2-3 (b) 1-11, 9-11
(c) 1-2, 11-12 (d) 1-2, 9-11

14. If two atoms bonded along their *z*-axis, the various *d*-orbitals can combine to form σ, π or δ (delta) type molecular orbitals. Which of the following combination of atomic orbitals (*d*) will lead to form a δ-bond?

(a) + ⟶

(b) + ⟶

(c)
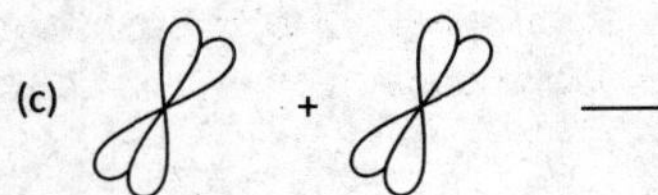

(d) None of the above

15. The electronic configuration of B_2 molecule is different from the electronic configuration of F_2 molecule, which is due to mixing of

(a) σ_{1s} and σ_{2s}-orbitals
(b) σ_{2s} and σ_{2p}-orbitals
(c) $\overset{*}{\sigma}_{2s}$ and σ_{2p}-orbitals
(d) $\overset{*}{\sigma}_{2s}$ and σ_{2p}-orbitals

16. During ionisation of N_2 to N_2^+ and O_2 to O_2^+, which of the following statements seems to be incorrect?

(a) In N_2^+, N—N bond weakens
(b) In O_2^+, O—O bond order increases
(c) In O_2^+, paramagnetic character decreases
(d) N_2^+ becomes diamagnetic

17. Which of the following sets of molecules show paramagnetic behaviour?

(a) B_2, O_2, N_2 (b) B_2, O_2, NO
(c) B_2, F_2, O_2 (d) B_2, O_2, Li_2

18. The MO (molecular orbital) electronic configuration of a molecule, X_2 can be represented as follows

$\overset{*}{\sigma}$ — 2s

E ↑ 2s σ 1 2s 2s

$\overset{*}{\sigma}$ 1 1s

1s ⥮ σ ⥮ 1s ⥮ 1s

From the MO diagram, select the correct statement(s) from the following

I. It is excited electronic configuration of X_2.
II. It is more stable than ground state X_2 molecule.
III. Bond order of X_2 in excited state is 1.
IV. It is more likely to dissociate into two X-atoms in ground state than in excited state.

Choose the correct option.

(a) Only III
(b) I and II
(c) I, III and IV
(d) I, II, III and IV

19. Which of the following octet structural formulae for azide ion (N_3^-) is incorrect?

(a) $[:\ddot{N}{=}N{=}\ddot{N}:]^-$ (b) $[:\ddot{N}{-}N{\equiv}N:]^-$

(c) $[:N{\equiv}N{-}\ddot{N}:]^-$ (d) $\left[\begin{matrix}:N{=}N: \\ \diagdown\ \diagup \\ :N:\end{matrix}\right]^-$

20. In the following compound, select the points or atomic sites of the molecule which can give molecular association through intermolecular hydrogen bonding predominantly.

(Structure: benzene ring bearing H—O— (site 1), —C(=O)—O—H with carbonyl O (site 3) and O—H (site 4), CH$_3$, and O—H (site 2))

(a) 1, 2, 3 (b) 1, 3, 4 (c) 1, 2, 4 (d) 1, 4

Section B Numerical Value Questions

21. The experimental value of the dipole moment of HCl is 1.03 D. The H—Cl bond length is 1.275 Å. The percentage of ionic character in HCl is x%. The value of x is ....

22. A diatomic molecule has a dipole moment 1.2 D. If its bond distance is 1.0 Å, fraction of an electronic charge e, exists on each atom will be ....

23. Dipole moment of H_2O is 1.85 debye. If the bond angle, $\angle HOH = 105°$ and bond length, O—H = 0.94 Å, the dipole moment (in D) of O—H bond in H_2O molecule is .... [$\cos 52.5° = 0.609$]

24. In Pauling scale, electronegativity values are given as,

$$\chi_F = 4.0, \chi_H = 2.1$$

% of covalent character of HF bond in HF molecule is ....

25. AX_4 forms square planar type structure. Distance between A and X-atoms is 2.2 Å. The distance (in Å) between two X-atoms in *trans*-position is ....

26. Total number of $d\pi$-$p\pi$ bond(s) present in XeO_4 molecule is ....

27. Number of nodal planes present in the σ^*_{2s}, π_{2p_x} and $\pi^*_{2p_y}$, MOs are x, y and z respectively.

The value of $(x + y + z)$ is ....

28. Bond order of CO^+ is 'a' and that of P—O bonds in PO_4^{3-} is 'b' where they have been calculated from their molecular orbital electronic configuration and resonance model respectively. The value of $(a + b)$ will be ....

29. The number of type(s) of chemical bond present in blue vitriol molecule is ....

30. Among the given compounds, the number of compounds in which intramolecular hydrogen bonding is ....

$KHCl_2$, KHF_2, 2-nitrophenol, 4-nitrophenol, benzoic acid, ice and water

Answers

Section A

1 (d)	2 (b)	3 (b)	4 (d)	5 (c)
6 (c)	7 (d)	8 (d)	9 (b)	10 (a)
11 (b)	12 (b)	13 (c)	14 (c)	15 (b)
16 (d)	17 (b)	18 (d)	19 (d)	20 (d)

Section B

21 (16.83)	22 (0.25)	23 (1.52)	24 (56.97)	25 (4.40)
26 (4)	27 (4)	28 (4.75)	29 (4)	30 (2)

See detailed solutions on page no. 205

QUALIFIER **05**

Chemical Thermodynamics

Section A Objective Type Questions

1. The value of ΔU for a certain change is – 1455 J. During the change, the system absorbs 812 J of heat. How much work, expressed in joules, was involved?

(a) – 2267 J (b) – 1325 J (c) – 3021 J (d) – 2856 J

2. Calculate the increase in internal energy of 1 kg of water at 100°C when it is converted into steam at the same temperature and at 1 atm (100 kPa). The density of water and steam are 1000 kgm^{-3} and 0.6 kgm^{-3} respectively. The latent heat of vaporisation of water $= 2.25 \times 10^6$ J kg^{-1}.

(a) 2.99×10^6 J (b) 3.26×10^6 J
(c) 3.02×10^6 J (d) 2.08×10^6 J

3. Two separate experiments were carried out involving adiabatic reversible expansion, taking monoatomic gas in one case and a diatomic gas in the second case. In each case, the initial temperature was T_I and expansion was from volume V_1 to volume V_2. The final temperatures attained were T_M for monoatomic gas and T_D for diatomic gas. Then

(a) $T_M = T_D < T_1$ (b) $T_M < T_D < T_1$
(c) $T_D > T_M > T_1$ (d) $T_D < T_M < T_1$

4. One mole of a monoatomic ideal gas expands adiabatically at initial temperature T against a constant external pressure of 1 atm from one litre to three litres. The final temperature of the gas is

(a) T (b) $T / 3^{(5R/2)}$
(c) $T - \dfrac{2}{(1.5 \times 0.082)}$ (d) $T + \dfrac{2}{(1.5 \times 0.082)}$

5. A steam boiler made up of steel weighs 900 kg. The boiler contains 400 kg of water. Assuming 70% of the heat is delivered to boiler and water, how much heat is required to raise the temperature of the whole from 10°C to 100°C? Heat capacity of steel is 0.11 kcal kg^{-1} K^{-1} and heat capacity of water is 1 kcal kg^{-1} K^{-1}.

(a) 65321 kcal (b) 64157 kcal
(c) 6869 kcal (d) 66549 kcal

6. A mole of an ideal gas for which $C_V = \dfrac{3}{2}R$ is heated reversibly at a constant pressure of 1 atm from 25°C to 100°C. The change in enthalpy of the process will be

(a) 3.725 cal mol^{-1} (b) 25.7 cal mol^{-1}
(c) 250 cal mol^{-1} (d) 372.56 cal mol^{-1}

7. The enthalpy change for a reaction does not depend upon the

(a) physical states of reactants and products
(b) use of different reactants for same product
(c) nature of intermediate reaction steps
(d) difference in initial and final temperature of involved substances

8. Given below are two statements, one is labelled as Assertion (A) and the other is labelled as Reason (R).

Assertion (A) Combustion of all organic compounds is an exothermic reaction.

Reason (R) The enthalpies of all elements in their standard state are zero.

In the light of the above statements, choose the correct answer from the options given below.

(a) Both A and R are true and R is the correct explanation of the A.
(b) Both A and R are true but R is not the correct explanation of the A.
(c) A is true but R is false.
(d) A is false but R is true.

9. What will be the enthalpy change for the combustion of cyclopropane at 298 K?

The enthalpies of formation of $CO_2(g)$, $H_2O(l)$ and propene (g) are –393.5, –285.8 and 20.42 kJ mol^{-1} respectively. The enthalpy of isomerisation of cyclopropane to propene is – 33.0 kJ mol^{-1}.

(a) 844.63 kJ mol^{-1}
(b) – 844.63 kJ mol^{-1}
(c) – 2091.32 kJ mol^{-1}
(d) 1893.44 kJ mol^{-1}

10. ΔH_f° of atom B is 134.5 kcal/mol, ΔH_f° of atoms F is 118.86 kcal/mol and ΔH_f° of $BF_3(g)$ is – 271.75 kcal/mol. Average B—F bond energy would be

(a) 97.7 kcal/mol
(b) 116.6 kcal/mol
(c) 135.4 kcal/mol
(d) 254.3 kcal/mol

11. If a bond dissociation energies of XY, X_2 and Y_2 (all diatomic molecules) are in the ratio of 1 : 1 : 0.5 and ΔH_f for the formation of XY is –200 kJ/mol. The bond dissociation energy of X_2 will be

(a) 100 kJ/mol (b) 200 kJ/mol
(c) 800 kJ/mol (d) 40 kJ/mol

12. $H_2(g) + \frac{1}{2}O_2(g) \longrightarrow H_2O(l)$;

BE(H—H) $= x_1$; BE(O═O) $= x_2$; BE (O—H) $= x_3$

Latent heat of vaporisation of water liquid into water vapour $= x_4$, then ΔH_f (heat of formation of liquid water) is

(a) $x_1 + \frac{x_2}{2} - x_3 + x_4$

(b) $2x_3 - x_1 - \frac{x_2}{2} - x_4$

(c) $x_1 + \frac{x_2}{2} - 2x_3 - x_4$

(d) $x_1 + \frac{x_2}{2} - 2x_3 + x_4$

13. Which of the following statement is not correct?

(a) Final temperature in reversible adiabatic expansion is greater than that in irreversible adiabatic expansion.

(b) When heat is supplied to an ideal gas in isothermal process, kinetic energy of gas remains constant.

(c) When an ideal gas is subjected to adiabatic expansion, it gets cooled.

(d) Entropy increases when an ideal gas expands isothermally.

14. Oxygen gas weighing 64 g is expanded from 1 atm to 0.25 atm at 30°C. Calculate entropy change, assuming the gas to be ideal.

(a) 23.1 JK^{-1} (b) 25.0 JK^{-1}

(c) 26.1 JK^{-1} (d) 22.4 JK^{-1}

15. Match Column I with Column II and choose the correct options using codes.

	Column I		Column II
A.	Entropy of vaporisation	1.	Decreases
B.	K (equilibrium constant) for spontaneous process	2.	is always +ve
C.	Crystalline solid state	3.	Lowest entropy
D.	ΔE in adiabatic expansion of ideal gas	4.	$\frac{\Delta H_{vap}}{T_b}$

Codes

	A	B	C	D		A	B	C	D
(a)	2,4	2	3	1	(b)	3	1,2	4	2
(c)	2	4	1	3	(d)	3,4	2	1	2

16. 100 J of heat was transferred reversibly to a block of gold at 25°C, from a thermal reservoir at 25.01°C and then exactly 100 J of heat was absorbed reversibly from the block of gold by a thermal reservoir at 24.99°C. Thus, entropy change of the system is

(a) 0.335 JK^{-1} (b) $-$ 0.33 JK^{-1}

(c) 0.670 JK^{-1} (d) 0.00 JK^{-1}

17. What is the maximum amount of useful work that could possibly be obtained at 25°C and 1 atm from the combustion of 48.0 g of methane, to give CO_2 and H_2O?

$\Delta_f G^\circ[CO_2(g)] = -394.4$ kg mol^{-1}, $\Delta_f G^\circ[H_2O(g)] = -228.6$ kJ mol^{-1}, $\Delta_f G^\circ[CH_4(g)] = -50.79$ kJ mol^{-1}.

(a) 2.40×10^3 kJ (b) -3.1×10^4 kJ

(c) 4.01×10^3 kJ (d) -5.2×10^3 kJ

18. In an irreversible process taking place at constant T and p in which only pressure volume work is being done, the change in Gibbs free energy (ΔG) and change in entropy (ΔS), satisfy the criteria

(a) $(\Delta S)_{V,E} < 0, (\Delta G)_{T,p} < 0$ (b) $(\Delta S)_{V,E} > 0, (\Delta G)_{T,p} < 0$

(c) $(\Delta S)_{V,E} = 0, (\Delta G)_{T,p} = 0$ (d) $(\Delta S)_{V,E} = 0, (\Delta G)_{T,p} > 0$

19. Using the data given below, pick the correct statement about the reaction :

$$TiO_2(s) + 2Cl_2(g) \longrightarrow TiCl_4(l) + O_2(g)$$

[Given that $\Delta_f H^\circ$ for $TiO_2(s)$, $TiCl_4(l)$, $Cl_2(g)$ and $O_2(g)$ are $-$ 944.7, $-$ 804.22, 0.0, 0.0 kJ mol^{-1} respectively. Also ΔS° for $TiO_2(s)$, $TiCl_4(l)$, $Cl_2(g)$ and $O_2(g)$ are 50.3, 252.3, 233.0, 205.1 J mol^{-1} K^{-1}, respectively.]

(a) The reaction is exothermic at standard conditions

(b) The standard entropy is favourable for the reaction in forward direction

(c) The reaction is not spontaneous at standard condition at 25°C

(d) Reaction becomes spontaneous at higher temperature

20. An ideal gas can be expanded from an initial state to a certain volume through two different processes.

(i) $pV^2 = K$ and (ii) $p = KV^2$,

where, K is a positive constant. Then, choose the correct option from the following.

(a) Final temperature in (i) will be greater than in (ii)

(b) Final temperature in (ii) will be greater than in (i)

(c) Work done by the gas in both the processes would be equal

(d) Total heat given to the gas in (i) is greater than in (ii)

Section B *Numerical Value Questions*

21. Assume an ideal gas obeys $\frac{p}{V}$ = constant. This gas confined in piston fitted cylinder having initial volume and pressure 2 L and 1 atm is allowed to expand to occupy finally 6 L. The work done (in L atm) by the system will be ....

22. One mole of an ideal gas at 300 K is heated at constant volume (V_1) until its temperature is doubled, then it is expanded isothermally till it reaches the original pressure. Finally, the gas is cooled at the constant pressure till system reached to the half of original volume $\left(\frac{V_1}{2}\right)$. The total work done ($W$) in calories will be ....

[Use : ln 2 = 0.70, R = 2 cal K^{-1} mol^{-1}]

23. The maximum possible temperature (in K) of a Bunsen burner flame is .... Assume that the gas is pure methane and that it is premixed with sufficient air to permit complete combustion. Given that

$CH_4(g) + 2O_2(g) \longrightarrow 2H_2O(l) + CO_2(g);$

$\Delta_r H^\circ_{298K} = -890.36 \text{ kJ mol}^{-1}$

$H_2O(l) \longrightarrow H_2O(g); \Delta_r H^\circ_{298K} = 44.02 \text{ kJmol}^{-1}$

C_p of $CO_2(g) = 37.11 \text{ JK}^{-1} \text{ mol}^{-1}$

C_p of $H_2O(g) = 33.58 \text{ JK}^{-1}\text{mol}^{-1}$

24. One mole of a gas at 300 K is compressed isothermally and reversibly from an initial volume of 10 dm^3 to a final volume of 0.2 $dm^3 \text{ mol}^{-1}$. Work done on system if the equation of state of the gas is $(V_m - b)\, p = RT$ with $b = 0.03 \text{ dm}^3$ is found to be $x \times 10^3 \text{ J mol}^{-1}$. The value of x is .... [Given, $\ln 58.65 = 4.07$]

25. Consider 2 moles of an ideal diatomic gas at 300 K and 0.507 MPa to be expanded adiabatically to a final pressure of 0.203 MPa against a constant pressure of 0.101 MPa. The final temperature (in K) is ....

26. 3000 J of heat is given to a gas at constant pressure of $2 \times 10^5 \text{ N/m}^2$. If the volume increases by 10 L during the process. The change in the internal energy of the gas will be .... J.

27. Bond enthalpy (in kJ mol^{-1}) of S—S bond from the following data :

$C_2H_5—S—C_2H_5; \Delta H_f^\circ = -147.2 \text{ kJ mol}^{-1}$

$C_2H_5—S—S—C_2H_5; \Delta H_f^\circ = -201.9 \text{ kJ mol}^{-1}$

$S(g); \Delta H_f^\circ = -222.8 \text{ kJ mol}^{-1}$ will be ....

28. In the combustion of solid naphthalene ($C_{10}H_8$) at 298 K and atmospheric pressure, 5175 kJ/mol of heat are evolved. Using this result together with the data below the resonance energy (in kJ/mol) of naphthalene will be ....

Heat of sublimation of naphthalene = 72 kJ/mol

ΔH_f° of H_2O and CO_2 are − 286 and − 393.5 kJ/mol respectively.

Bond energy of H_2 = 436 kJ/mol, enthalpy of atomisation of C is 715.5 kJ/mol BE : C—C = 345.5 kJ/mol, C=C = 617 kJ/mol and C—H = 415 kJ/mol

29. The heat of vaporisation of mercury is 60.7 kJ mol^{-1}. For Hg (l), $S^\circ = 76.1 \text{ J mol}^{-1} \text{ K}^{-1}$ and for Hg(g), $S^\circ = 175 \text{ J mol}^{-1} \text{ K}^{-1}$. The normal boiling point of liquid mercury (in K) is ......

30. In an ice calorimeter, a chemical reaction is allowed to occur in thermal contact with an ice-water mixture at 0°C. Any heat liberated by the reaction is used to melt some ice, the volume change of the ice-water mixture indicates the amount of melting.

When solutions containing 1.00 m mol each of $AgNO_3$ and NaCl were mixed in such a calorimeter, both solutions have been precooled to 0°C, 0.20 g of ice melted. Assuming complete reaction in this experiment, ΔH (in kcal mol^{-1}) for the reaction will be ......

$Ag^+ + Cl^- \longrightarrow AgCl$?

Answers

Section A

1 *(a)*	2 *(d)*	3 *(b)*	4 *(c)*	5 *(b)*
6 *(c)*	7 *(c)*	8 *(b)*	9 *(c)*	10 *(d)*
11 *(c)*	12 *(c)*	13 *(a)*	14 *(a)*	15 *(a)*
16 *(d)*	17 *(a)*	18 *(b)*	19 *(c)*	20 *(b)*

Section B

21 *(–8)*	22 *(60)*	23 *(7992.64)*	24 *(10.15)*	25 *(270)*
26 *(1000)*	27 *(277.50)*	28 *(253)*	29 *(613.75)*	30 *(–16)*

See detailed solutions on page no. 210

QUALIFIER 06

Solutions

Section A Objective Type Questions

1. A beaker containing 0.01 mole of $C_{12}H_{22}O_{11}$ in 100 g of $H_2O(l)$ and an another beaker containing 0.02 mole of $C_{12}H_{22}O_{11}$ in 100 g of $H_2O(l)$ are placed in a chamber and allowed to equilibriate. Thus, mole fraction of $C_{12}H_{22}O_{11}$ in two solutions are respectively.

(a) 0.00172, 0.00269 (b) 0.00269, 0.00269
(c) 0.00269, 0.00172 (d) 0.00172, 0.00172

2. A 5.2 molal aqueous solution of CH_3OH is taken. What is the mole fraction of methyl alcohol in the solution ?

(a) 0.05 (b) 0.1
(c) 0.086 (d) 0.19

3. 25 mL of a solution of $Ba(OH)_2$ on titration with a 0.1 molar solution of hydrochloric acid gave a litre value of 35 mL. The molarity of $Ba(OH)_2$ solution was

(a) 14 (b) 0.28 (c) 0.35 (d) 0.07

4. The volumes of 4 N HCl and 10 N HCl required to make 1 L 6 N HCl are

	4 N HCl	10 N HCl
(a)	0.75 L	0.25 L
(b)	0.25 L	0.75 L
(c)	0.80 L	0.20 L
(d)	0.67 L	0.33 L

5. The density (in g mL^{-1}) of a 3.60 M sulphuric acid solution that is 29% H_2SO_4 (Molar mass = 98 g mol^{-1}) by mass will be

(a) 1.64 (b) 1.88
(c) 1.22 (d) 1.45

6. At 40°C, the vapour pressure (in torr) of $CH_3OH(A)$ and $C_2H_5OH(B)$ solution is represented by $p = 120\chi_A + 138$, where, χ_A is mole fraction of CH_3OH.

The values of $\lim\limits_{\chi_A \to 0} \frac{p_B^\circ}{\chi_B}$ and $\lim\limits_{\chi_B \to 0} \frac{p_A^\circ}{\chi_A}$ are respectively.

(a) 138, 258 (b) 258, 138
(c) 120, 138 (d) 138, 125

7. A solution has 1:4 mole ratio of pentane to hexane. The vapour pressure of pure hydrocarbon at 20°C are 440 mm Hg for pentane and 120 mm Hg for hexane. The mole fraction of pentane in vapour phase would be

(a) 0.786 (b) 0.549
(c) 0.478 (d) 0.200

8. At 300 K, solubility of a gas in a liquid was measured at different partial pressures,

Mole fraction of gas (χ)	0.010	0.015	0.020
Partial pressure of gas (p) (kPa)	82	122	166

From this experiment, which of the following is correct for the gas in accordance with Henry's law ?

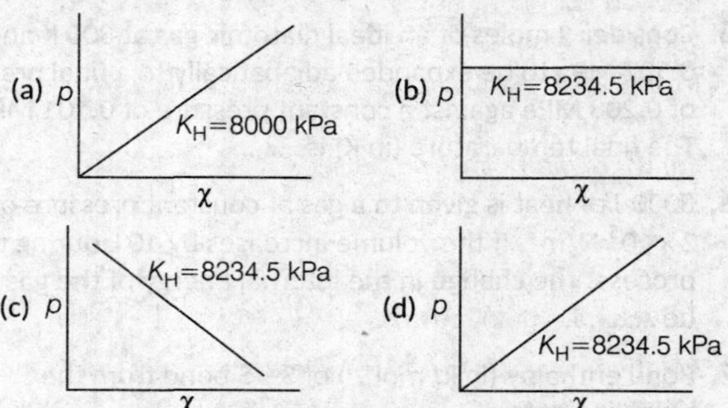

9. Based on the given diagram, which of the following statements regarding the solution of two miscible volatile liquids A and B are correct?

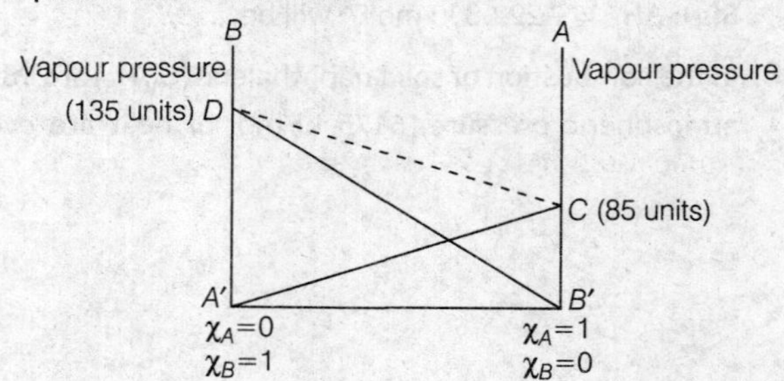

I. Plots $A'C$ and $B'D$ show Raoult's law is obeyed for the solution in which A is solute and B is solvent and as well as for that in which B is solute and A is solvent.

II. Plot CD shows that Dalton's law of partial pressure is observed for the binary solution of components A and B.

III. In pure state, vapour pressures of volatile A and B differ by 50 units.

IV. Vapour pressure of a mixture containing 40% mole of B is about 105 units.

Choose the correct option using the codes given below.

(a) All expect IV (b) All expect I
(c) Both I and III (d) All of these

10. Total vapour pressure of a solution is observed to be 200 torr by mixing 1 mole of A ($p_A^\circ = 150$ torr) and 2 moles of B ($p_B^\circ = 240$ torr). Which of the following statements correctly states nature of the solution?

(a) There is positive deviation from Raoult's law.
(b) It is an ideal solution.
(c) The solution shows negative deviation from Raoult's law.
(d) Without knowing molar masses of A and B, the deviation from Raoult's law given by the solution cannot be measured.

11. Given below are two statements, one is labelled as Assertion (A) and the other is labelled as Reason (R).

Assertion (A) 0.01 M aqueous solution of urea and 0.01 M aqueous solution of NaCl have same lowering of vapour pressure.

Reason (R) When non-volatile solute is dissolved in water, vapour pressure of solution always decreases.

In the light of the above statements, choose the correct answer from the options given below.

(a) Both A and R are true and R is the correct explanation of A.
(b) Both A and R are true but R is not the correct explanation of A.
(c) A is true but R is false.
(d) A is false but R is true.

12. Relative lowering of vapour pressure of non-volatile solute, χ in water is 0.15. If ΔT_b = elevation in boiling point assuming a dilute solution and, $\Delta T_b'$ = elevation in boiling point of a solution of moderate concentration then, $(\Delta T_b - \Delta T_b')$ will be [$K_b(H_2O) = 0.52 \text{ K m}^{-1}$]

(a) zero (b) – 0.87 K
(c) – 0.08 K (d) – 0.76 K

13. Based on the following graph, molar mass of the solute x (non-dissociable/ non-associable) is

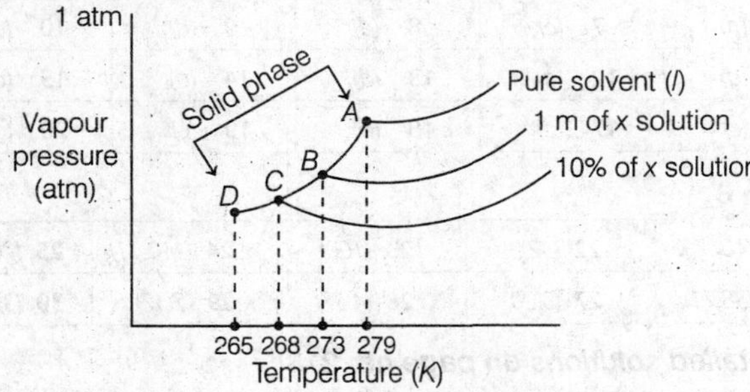

(a) 134 g mol^{-1} (b) 54.5 g mol^{-1}
(c) 76.8 g mol^{-1} (d) 60.6 g mol^{-1}

14. The latent heat of vaporisation of pure liquid (volatile) is 11217 cal mol^{-1} and its boiling point is 111°C. The value of K_b of the liquid in g mol^{-1} K will be (molar mass of the liquid = 92 g mol^{-1})

(a) 0.52 (b) 0.24
(c) 0.012 (d) 2.40

15. The diagram given below depicts boiling point as a function of composition of the mixture $CCl_4(l)$ and $SiCl_4(l)$. Which of the following statements about the diagram is (are) true?

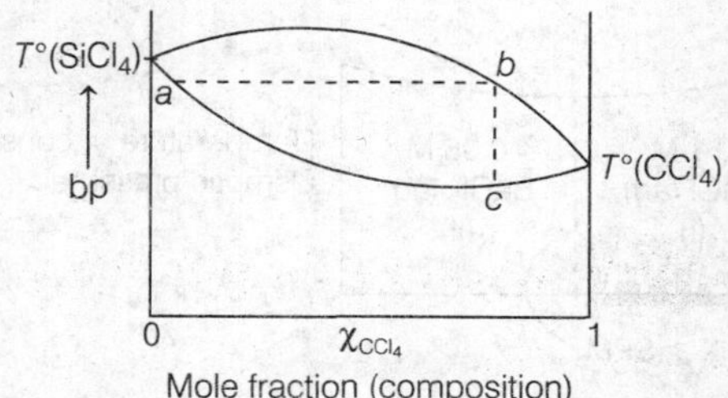

I. The point 'a' represents the composition of solution and point 'b' that of vapour in equilibrium.
II. The proportion of CCl_4 in the solution is smaller than that in the vapour in equilibrium.
III. bc represents the condensation of the vapour.
IV. The point 'c' represents the composition of the solution and point 'b' that of the vapour in equilibrium.

Choose the correct option.

(a) Only statement I is correct.
(b) Statements II and III are correct.
(c) Statements I, II and III are correct.
(d) Statements III and IV are correct.

16. One molal aqueous sucrose solution boils at 100.52°C and water boils at 100°C. 5% aqueous solution (by mass of water) of non-electrolyte AB_2 boils at 100.26°C and 9% aqueous solution (by mass of water) of non-electrolyte A_2B boils at 100.52°C.

Match the molar masses given in Column II with the species in Column I and select the answer from the codes given below.

	Column I		Column II
A.	AB_2	1.	10
B.	A_2B	2.	40
C.	A	3.	90
D.	B	4.	100

Codes

	A	B	C	D		A	B	C	D
(a)	1	4	3	2	(b)	2	3	1	4
(c)	4	3	2	1	(d)	1	2	4	3

17. The freezing point of a 0.08 molal aqueous solution of $NaHSO_4$ is –0.372°C. The dissociation constant for the following reaction is

$$HSO_4^- \rightleftharpoons H^+ + SO_4^{2-}$$

[K_f (H_2O) = 1.86 K kg mol^{-1}]

(a) 0.2 (b) 0.02
(c) 0.01 (d) 0.04

18. Study the following figure, regarding the study of osmotic pressure of two solutions (I and II) separated by a semipermeable membrane (SPM) and choose the correct option.

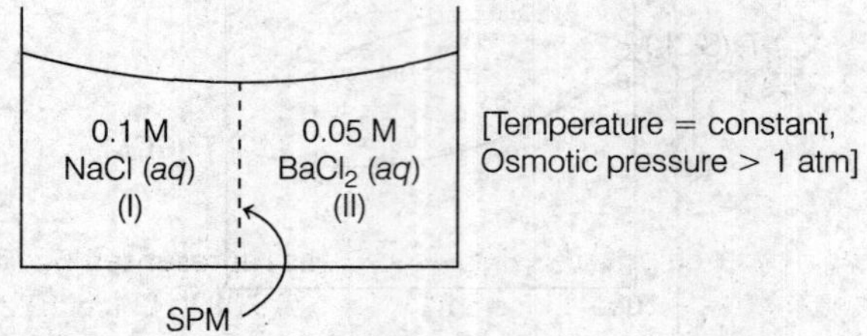

(a) There will be no movement of any solution across the SPM.
(b) Flow of solvent molecules from II to I
(c) Flow of NaCl molecule from I to II
(d) $\pi_{II} > \pi_I$ at constant temperature assuming complete dissociation of NaCl and $BaCl_2$ where, π is osmotic pressure

19. Insulin, $(C_6H_{10}O_5)_n$ dissolved in a medium shows osmotic pressure π-atm of concentration C gcm^{-3} and 300 K temperature. The slope of the plot π *vs* C is 4.1×10^{-3}. Molar mass (in g mol^{-1}) of insulin will be
(a) 3×10^3 (b) 3×10^6 (c) 6×10^6 (d) 6×10^3

20. For a dilute aqueous solution, density is 1 g cm^{-3} and the osmotic pressure of this solution at a height of 0.14 m will be (g = 10 ms^{-2})
(a) 0.0138 atm (b) 1.4×10^3 Pa
(c) Both (a) and (b) (d) None of these

Section B *Numerical Value Questions*

21. 109% labelled oleum has x mole of H_2SO_4 and y mole of SO_3. The value of $\left(\frac{x+y}{x-y}\right)$ in oleum is ....

22. The freezing point of 0.08 m $NaHSO_4$ is $-0.345°$ C. The percentage of HSO_4^{2-} that transfer a proton to water to form SO_4^{2-} ion will be ....
[K_f of $H_2O = 1.86$ kg mol^{-1}]

23. A dry air is passed through the solution containing 10 g of solute and 90 g water and then, it passes through pure water. There is a decrease in weight of solution by 2.5 g and in weight of pure water by 0.05 g. Molecular weight of the solute is ....

24. The mass (in g) of urea (NH_2CONH_2) that has to be dissolved in 100 g water in order to decrease the vapour pressure of water by 25% is ....

25. Vapour pressure of nitrobenzene (molar mass = 123 g mol^{-1}) is 3.6 K Nm^{-2} and that of water (molar mass = 18 g mol^{-1}) is 97.7 K Nm^{-2}. They form immiscible mixture at the given temperature percentage of nitrobenzene in the vapour phase will be ....

26. On cooling a solution containing 50 g of ethylene glycol in 200 g water to – 9.3°C, x g of ice gets separated out. The value of x is .... [K_f (H_2O) = 1.86 K kg mol^{-1}]

27. 25 mL of an aqueous solution of KCl was found to require 20 mL of 1 M $AgNO_3$ solution when titrated using K_2CrO_4 as indicator. Thus, the depression in freezing point of KCl solution with 100% ionistation will be (in degree) ....
[K_f (H_2O) = 2° mol^{-1} kg, molarity = molality]

28. At 0°C and 1 atm pressure of O_2, solubility of $O_2(g)$ in water is 48.9 mL O_2 per litre. Molarity of O_2 in a saturated aqueous solution when the O_2 is under the normal partial pressure of 0.2095 atm is found to be $x\times10^{-4}$ M. The value of x is ....

29. Osmotic pressure of a solution obtained by mixing 100 mL of 3.4% solution (w/V) of urea and 100 mL of 1.6% solution (w/V) of cane sugar at 20°C will be (in atm) ....
[Temperature = Constant, Osmotic pressure > 1 atm] ....

30. Osmotic pressure of a decinormal solution of $BaCl_2$ at 27°C showing 70% degree of ionisation is (in atm) ....

Answers

Section A

1 (b)	2 (c)	3 (d)	4 (d)	5 (c)
6 (a)	7 (c)	8 (d)	9 (d)	10 (c)
11 (d)	12 (d)	13 (d)	14 (d)	15 (c)
16 (c)	17 (a)	18 (b)	19 (c)	20 (c)

Section B

21 (10)	22 (32)	23 (100)	24 (111.11)	25 (20.12)
26 (38.71)	27 (3.20)	28 (4.57)	29 (7.37)	30 (3)

See detailed solutions on page no. 213

QUALIFIER **07**

Equilibrium

Section A Objective Type Questions

1. A sample $Na_2CO_3 \cdot H_2O$ weighing 0.62 g is added to 100 mL of 0.1 N $(NH_4)_2SO_4$ solution. What will be the nature of resulting solution?

(a) Acidic
(b) Neutral
(c) Basic
(d) None of the above

2. The rate of the elementary gaseous phase reaction, $2NO + O_2 \rightleftharpoons 2NO_2$ at 380°C is given by rate $= 2.6\times 10^3 [NO_2]^2[O_2]$.

The rate of the reverse reaction at 380°C is given by rate $= 4.1 [NO_2]^2$

Hence, equilibrium constant for the formation of NO_2 by chemical equation, $NO + \frac{1}{2} O_2 \rightleftharpoons NO_2$ is

(a) 6.34×10^2
(b) 1.577×10^{-3}
(c) 25.18
(d) 3.97×10^{-2}

3. During the experiment, 0.2 mol of H_2 and 0.2 mol of I_2 were placed into a 1L vessel where the reaction,

$$H_2(g) + I_2(g) \rightleftharpoons 2HI(g)$$

came to equilibrium. For this reaction, $K_C = 49.5$ at the temperature of the experiment. What were the equilibrium concentrations of H_2, I_2 and HI?

(a) 0.044 M, 0.044 M, 0.312 M
(b) 0.013 M, 0.013 M, 0.342 M
(c) 0.023 M, 0.023 M, 0.128 M
(d) 0.015 M, 0.015 M, 0.285 M

4. In a system, $A(s) \rightleftharpoons 2B(g) + 3C(g)$; if the concentration of C at equilibrium is increased by a factor of 2, it will cause the equilibrium concentration of B to change to

(a) two times of its original value
(b) one half of its original value
(c) $2\sqrt{2}$ times of its original value
(d) $\frac{1}{2\sqrt{2}}$ times of its original value

5. The first equilibrium expression (K_C) as represented by the first chemical equation is 5.81×10^{-7} at 700 K. Calculate the value of the equilibrium expression for the second equation at the same temperature.

$$2SO_3(g) \rightleftharpoons 2SO_2(g) + O_2(g)$$
$$SO_3(g) \rightleftharpoons SO_2(g) + \frac{1}{2} O_2(g)$$

(a) 7.62×10^{-4}
(b) 6.32×10^{-4}
(c) 5.90×10^{-5}
(d) 4.28×10^{-5}

6. At 27°C, $K_p = 1.5 \times 10^{18}$ for the reaction, $3NO(g) \rightleftharpoons N_2O(g) + NO_2(g)$. If 0.03 mole of NO were placed in a 1L vessel and equilibrium were established, what would be the equilibrium concentration of NO? $[R = 0.082 \text{ L atm mol}^{-1}\text{K}^{-1}]$

(a) 0
(b) 4×10^{-8} M
(c) 1.2×10^{-7} M
(d) 1.4×10^{-8} M

7. Match the items given in Column I with that of Column II.

	Column I	Column II
A.	$Q = K$	1. Reaction is nearer to completion
B.	$Q > K$	2. Reaction proceed in forward direction
C.	$Q < K$	3. Reaction proceed in backward direction
D.	$K >>> 1$	4. Reaction at equilibrium

	A	B	C	D
(a)	1	2	3	4
(b)	4	3	1	2
(c)	4	3	2	1
(d)	4	1	3	2

8. Equilibrium constant, K_C for the reaction $N_2(g) + 3H_2(g) \rightleftharpoons 2NH_3(g)$ at 500 K is 0.061. At a particular time, the analysis shows that the composition of the reaction mixture is 3.00 mol $L^{-1}N_2$, 2.00 mol $L^{-1}H_2$ and 0.500 mol $L^{-1}NH_3$. Is the reaction at equilibrium. If not, in which direction does the reaction tends to proceed to reach equilibrium?

(a) Yes, it will remain at equilibrium
(b) No, the reaction tends to move toward products side
(c) No, the reaction tends to move towards reactants side
(d) None of the above

9. The exothermic formation of ClF_3 is represented by the equation :

$$Cl_2(g) + 3F_2(g) \rightleftharpoons 2ClF_3(g); \Delta H = -329 \text{ kJ}$$

Which of the following will increase the quantity of ClF_3 in an equilibrium mixture of Cl_2, F_2 and ClF_3?

(a) Increasing the temperature
(b) Removing of Cl_2
(c) Increasing the volume of the container
(d) Adding F_2

10. The anions of sodium hydrogen sulphate, HSO_4^- react with the phosphate ion, PO_4^{3-}. Identify the two conjugate acid-base pairs.

$$HSO_4^-(aq) + PO_4^{3-}(aq) \longrightarrow SO_4^{2-}(aq) + HPO_4^{2-}(aq)$$

(a) HSO_4^-, PO_4^{3-} and HPO_4^{2-}, SO_4^{2-}
(b) HSO_4^-, SO_4^{2-} and HPO_4^{2-}, PO_4^{3-}
(c) HSO_4^-, HPO_4^{2-} and HPO_4^{2-}, SO_4^{2-}
(d) HSO_4^-, HPO_4^{2-} and PO_4^{3-}, SO_4^{2-}

11. Ascorbic acid (vitamin C) is a diprotic acid, $H_2C_6H_6O_6$. $[H^+]$, pH and $[C_6H_6O_6^{2-}]$ in a 0.10 M solution of ascorbic acid will be respectively.
[Given : $K_{a_1} = 6.8 \times 10^{-5}$ and $K_{a_2} = 2.7 \times 10^{-12}$ for ascorbic acid]

(a) 3.6×10^{-5} M, 2.58, 2.7×10^{-12} M
(b) 2.6×10^{-3} M, 5.18, 1.5×10^{-10} M
(c) 2.6×10^{-3} M, 2.58, 2.7×10^{-12} M
(d) 1.5×10^{-4} M, 3.67, 1.7×10^{-14} M

12. What is the pH of the mixture obtained by mixing 50 mL of 0.05 M NH_4OH and 50 mL of 0.05 M CH_3COOH ?
[$K_a = 1.8 \times 10^{-5}$ and $K_b = 1.8 \times 10^{-5}$]

(a) 2 (b) 7 (c) 5 (d) 6

13. 0.1 mole of CH_3NH_2 ($K_b = 6 \times 10^{-4}$) is added to 0.08 mole of HCl and the solution is diluted to 1L. The hydrogen ion concentration in the solution is

(a) 5×10^{-5} M (b) 8×10^{-2} M
(c) 1.6×10^{-11} M (d) 6.7×10^{-11} M

14. The degree of ionisation of 1.0 M weak acid, HA is 0.5%. If 2 mL of 1.0 M HA solution is diluted to 32 mL, the degree of ionisation of the acid and H_3O^+ ion concentration in the resulting solution will be respectively

(a) 0.02 and 3.125×10^{-4} M
(b) 0.02 and 1.25×10^{-3} M
(c) 1.25×10^{-3} and 0.02 M
(d) 0.02 and 8.0×10^{-12} M

15. For the reaction: $2HI(g) \rightleftharpoons H_2(g) + I_2(g)$, the degree of dissociation (α) of HI (g) is related to equilibrium constant K_p by the expression

(a) $\frac{1 + 2\sqrt{K_p}}{2}$ (b) $\sqrt{\frac{1 + 2K_p}{2}}$ (c) $\sqrt{\frac{2K_p}{1 + 2K_p}}$ (d) $\frac{2\sqrt{K_p}}{1 + 2\sqrt{K_p}}$

16. Ammonia under a pressure of 15 atm at 27°C is heated to 347°C in a closed vessel in the presence of catalyst. Under the conditions, NH_3 is partially decomposed according to the equation: $2NH_3 \rightleftharpoons N_2 + 3H_2$. The vessel is such that the volume remains effectively constant, whereas pressure increases at 50 atm. Calculate the percentage of NH_3 actually decomposed.

(a) 62% (b) 63.5%
(c) 65.3% (d) 66.6%

17. Given below are two statements, one is labelled as Assertion (A) and the other is labelled as Reason (R).

Assertion (A) According to the principle of common ion effect, the solubility of HgI_2 is expected to be less in aqueous solution of KI than in water. But HgI_2 dissolves in an aqueous solution of KI to form a clear solution.

Reason (R) Iodide ion (I^-) is highly polarisable.

In the light of the above statements, choose the correct answer from the options given below.

(a) Both A and R are true and R is the correct explanation of A.
(b) Both A and R are true but R is not the correct explanation of A.
(c) A is true but R is false.
(d) A is false but R is true.

18. HX is a weak acid ($K_a = 10^{-5}$). It forms a salt NaX (0.1 M) on reaction with caustic soda. The degree of hydrolysis of NaX is

(a) 0.01% (b) 0.0001%
(c) 0.1% (d) 0.5%

19. Given below are two statements, one is labelled as Assertion (A) and the other is labelled as Reason (R).

Assertion (A) On mixing equal volumes 1 M HCl and 2 M $CH_3COO^-Na^+$, acidic buffer solution is formed.

Reason (R) Resultant mixture contains CH_3COOH and $CH_3COO^-Na^+$ which are parts of acidic buffer.

In the light of the above statements, choose the correct answer from the options given below.

(a) Both A and R are true and R is the correct explanation of A.
(b) Both A and R are true but R is not the correct explanation of A.
(c) A is true but R is false.
(d) A is false but R is true.

20. Solubility product constant (K_{sp}) of salts of types MX, MX_2 and M_3X at temperature T are 4.0×10^{-8}, 3.2×10^{-14} and 2.7×10^{-15} respectively. Solubilities (mol dm^{-3}) of the salts at temperature T are in the order

(a) $MX > MX_2 > M_3X$
(b) $M_3X > MX_2 > MX$
(c) $MX_2 > M_3X > MX$
(d) $MX > M_3X > MX_2$

Section B *Numerical Value Questions*

21. For the reaction : $E + F \rightleftharpoons G + H$

If one starts with 6.0 moles of E and 7.0 moles of F in a 1.0 L vessel. When equilibrium is attained, 4.5 moles of G is formed. The value of the equilibrium constant for the reaction is ....

22. At 90°C, the following equilibrium is established

$$H_2(g) + S(s) \rightleftharpoons H_2S(g) : K = 6.8 \times 10^{-2}$$

If 0.20 mole of hydrogen and 1.0 mole of sulphur are heated to 90°C in a 1.0 L vessel, the partial pressure (in atm) of H_2S at equilibrium will be ....

23. A theoretically computed equilibrium constant for the polymerisation of formaldehyde, HCHO to glucose, $C_6H_{12}O_6$, in aqueous solution is 6×10^{22}.

$$6\ HCHO \longrightarrow C_6H_{12}O_6$$

If a 1.0 M solution of glucose were to reach dissociation equilibrium with respect to the above equation, the value of log [HCHO] in the solution will be ....

[log (0.167) = -0.777]

24. The equilibrium concentration ratio of C to A, [Given, $10^{(-0.334)} = 0.463$], if 2.0 moles each of A and B were allowed to come to equilibrium at 300 K as in $A + B \rightleftharpoons C + D$ will be .... $\Delta G° = 460$ cal mol^{-1} and $R = 1.99$ cal mol^{-1}K^{-1}

25. The basic ionisation constant for hydrazine, N_2H_4 is 9.6×10^{-7}. The per cent hydrolysis of 0.100 M N_2H_5Cl, a salt containing the acid ion conjugate to hydrazine base will be ....

26. The pH of a 1L solution prepared by addition of 0.01 mole of $HC_2H_3O_2$ and 0.02 mole of $NaC_2H_3O_2$ is ....

[Given, pK_a of $HC_2H_3O_2$ = 4.74]

27. The amount of volume in mL of 0.10 M sodium formate solution should be added to 50 mL of 0.05 M formic acid to produce a buffer solution of pH 4.1, pK_a for formic acid is 3.80 is ....

28. A solution of saturated CaF_2 is found to contain 4.1×10^{-4} M fluoride ion. The K_{sp} of CaF_2 is found to be $x \times 10^{-11}$. The value of x is .... Neglect hydrolysis.

29. The maximum pH of a solution 0.10 M of Mg^{2+} from which $Mg(OH)_2$ will not precipitate is ....

[Given, K_{sp} of $Mg(OH)_2 = 1.2 \times 10^{-11}$]

30. Sulphide ion in alkaline solution reacts with solid sulphur to form polysulphide ions having formulas S_2^{2-}, S_3^{2-}, S_4^{2-} and so on. The equilibrium constant for the formation of S_2^{2-} is 12 and for the formation of S_3^{2-} is 130, both from S and S^{2-}. The equilibrium constant for the formation of S_3^{2-} from S_2^{2-} and S is ....

Answers

Section A

1 (b)	2 (c)	3 (a)	4 (d)	5 (a)
6 (c)	7 (c)	8 (b)	9 (d)	10 (b)
11 (c)	12 (b)	13 (d)	14 (b)	15 (d)
16 (a)	17 (b)	18 (a)	19 (a)	20 (d)

Section B

21 (5.40)	22 (0.41)	23 (–3.79)	24 (0.68)	25 (0.03)
26 (5.04)	27 (50)	28 (3.44)	29 (9.04)	30 (11)

See detailed solutions on page no. 216

QUALIFIER 08

Redox Reactions

Section A Objective Type Questions

1. Consider the following reaction,

$$I^- + ClO_3^- + H_2SO_4 \longrightarrow Cl^- + HSO_4^- + I_2$$

The incorrect statement related to the balanced equation is

(a) iodide is oxidised
(b) H_2O is one of the product
(c) stoichiometric coefficient of HSO_4^- is 6
(d) sulphur is reduced.

2. When a solution of potassium chromate is treated with an excess of dilute nitric acid, then

(a) Cr^{3+} and $Cr_2O_7^{2-}$ are formed
(b) $Cr_2O_7^{2-}$ and H_2O are formed.
(c) $Cr_2O_7^{2-}$ is reduced to +3 oxidation state of Cr.
(d) $Cr_2O_7^{2-}$ is oxidised to +7 oxidation state of Cr.

3. The values of *x*, *y* and *z* in the following reaction are respectively,

$$xMnO_4^- + yC_2O_4^{2-} + 2H^+ \longrightarrow xMn^{2+} + 2yCO_2 + \frac{z}{2}H_2O$$

(a) 5, 2, 6 (b) 8, 2, 6
(c) 2, 5, 16 (d) 2, 5, 8

4. 2 moles of $FeSO_4$ in acidic medium are oxidised by '*a*' mole of $KMnO_4$, whereas 2 moles of FeC_2O_4 in acidic medium are oxidised by '*b*' moles of $KMnO_4$.

The ratio of '*a*' and '*b*' is

(a) $\frac{2}{3}$ (b) $\frac{3}{5}$ (c) $\frac{5}{2}$ (d) $\frac{1}{3}$

5. Given below are two statements.

Statement I Equal volume of 1 M each of $KMnO_4$ and $K_2Cr_2O_7$ are reduced separately by Fe^{2+} ion in acidic medium.

Statement II Fe^{2+} ion will be oxidised by $K_2Cr_2O_7$.

In the light of the above statements, choose the correct answer from the options given below.

(a) Both Statement I and Statement II are correct.
(b) Statement I is incorrect but Statement II is correct.
(c) Both Statement I and Statement II are incorrect.
(d) Statement I is correct but Statement II is incorrect.

6. $H_2C_2O_4$ and $NaHC_2O_4$ behave as acids as well as reducing agents. Which of the following statement(s) is (are) correct regarding $H_2C_2O_4$ and $NaHC_2O_4$?

I. Equivalent weights of $H_2C_2O_4$ and $NaHC_2O_4$ are equal to their molecular weights when acting as reducing agents.
II. Equivalent weights of $H_2C_2O_4$ and $NaHC_2O_4$ are equal to half of their molecular weights when acting as reducing agents.
III. 100 mL of 1 M solution of each is neutralised by equal volumes of 1M $Ca(OH)_2$.
IV. 100 mL of 1M solution of each is oxidised by equal volumes of 1 M $KMnO_4$ in presence of H_2SO_4.

Choose the correct option.

(a) I, III and IV
(b) II, III and IV
(c) I and III
(d) II and IV

7. Equivalent mass of $KMnO_4$ (molar mass = M) in the reaction is

$$2KMnO_4 \xrightarrow{\Delta} K_2MnO_4 + MnO_2 + O_2$$

(a) M (b) $\frac{M}{3}$
(c) $\frac{M}{4}$ (d) $\frac{M}{12}$

8. Three moles of a mixture of iron (II) sulphate and iron (III) sulphate required 100 mL of 2M $KMnO_4$ solution in acidic medium for complete oxidation.

Thus, mole fraction of iron (II) sulphate in the mixture is

(a) $\frac{1}{3}$ (b) $\frac{2}{3}$
(c) $\frac{2}{5}$ (d) $\frac{3}{5}$

9. What will be the molar concentration of I_3^- if 24.55 mL of 0.102 M $Na_2S_2O_3$ is needed to complete the reaction with 10 mL of the I_3^- solution?

(a) 0.125 M (b) 0.138 M
(c) 2.50 M (d) 0.02 M

10. What will be the % of oxalate ion in given sample of oxalate salt of which 0.45 g is present in 100 mL of solution which required 90 mL of N/20 $KMnO_4$ for complete oxidation ?

(a) 66%
(b) 44%
(c) 55%
(d) 19.8%

Section B *Numerical Value Questions*

11. When manganous salt is fused with KNO_3 and solid NaOH, then the value of *n*-factor of this salt is ....

12. Oxidation number of chromium in the following compounds are given as

$$K_2\overset{+x}{\underline{Cr}}O_4,\ \overset{+y}{\underline{Cr}}O_5,\ K_3[\overset{+a}{\underline{Cr}}O_8],\ \overset{+b}{\underline{Cr}}O_2Cl_2$$

The value of $\frac{(a+b)}{(x+y)}$ is ....

13. For the balanced chemical reaction,

$$aCrI_3 + bCl_2 + cNaOH \longrightarrow pNa_2CrO_4 + 2NaIO_4 + rNaCl + sH_2O$$

The value of $\left[\frac{(a+r)}{b}\right]$ will be

14. The weight of sodium bromate (= 151 g mol^{-1}) necessary to prepare 85.5 mL of 0.672 N solution, will be .... g, when the half-cell reaction is

$$2BrO_3^- + 12H^+ + 10e^- \longrightarrow Br_2 + 6H_2O$$

15. Gram equivalent mass of phosphorus (P = 31) in the following reaction will be ....

$$P + NaOH \longrightarrow PH_3 + NaH_2PO_2 + H_2O$$

Answers

Section A

1 (d)	2 (b)	3 (c)	4 (d)	5 (a)
6 (d)	7 (d)	8 (a)	9 (a)	10 (b)

Section B

11 (4)	12 (0.92)	13 (2.07)	14 (1.73)	15 (41.34)

See detailed solutions on page no. 219

QUALIFIER 09

Electrochemistry

Section A Objective Type Questions

1. Considering the Latimer diagram for the following,

$$MnO_4^- \xrightarrow{E_1^\circ = xV} MnO_2 \xrightarrow{E_2^\circ = 1.23V} Mn^{2+}$$
$$E_3^\circ = 1.51V \text{ (from } MnO_4^- \text{ to } Mn^{2+})$$

Calculate the value of x.

(a) 2.41 (b) 3.69
(c) 1.69 (d) 5.15

2. At what pressure of hydrogen gas at 298 K, the potential of hydrogen-electrode in pure water will be zero?

(a) 10^{-11} atm (b) 10^{-14} atm
(c) 10^{-8} atm (d) 10^{-7} atm

3. The emf of a voltaic cell with the cell reaction at 25°C,

$$H_2 + Hg_2^{2+} \rightleftharpoons 2Hg + 2H^+$$

is 0.65 V. When 5.6 L of H_2 at STP is consumed in the cell, the maximum electrical work done by the cell will be

(a) -6.27×10^4 J
(b) -6.27×10^5 J
(c) -3.13×10^4 J
(d) -1.25×10^4 J

4. EMF of the given cell,

Pt|H_2 (0.1 bar) |BOH (0.1 M) || HA (0.1 M) | H_2 (1 bar)/Pt
$[K_b = 1\times 10^{-5}][K_a = 1\times 10^{-7}]$

is

(a) 0.125 V (b) – 0.385 V
(c) 0.385 V (d) – 0.125 V

5. Standard reduction potential values of some half-cell reactions are given as

I. $MnO_4^- + 8H^+ + 5e^- \longrightarrow Mn^{2+} + 4H_2O; E^\circ = +1.51$ V
II. $Cr_2O_7^{2-} + 14H^+ + 6e^- \longrightarrow 2Cr^{3+} + 7H_2O; E^\circ = +1.38$ V
III. $Fe^{3+} + e^- \longrightarrow Fe^{2+}; E^\circ = +0.77$ V
IV. $Cl_2 + 2e^- \longrightarrow 2Cl^-; E^\circ = +1.41$

Select the incorrect comparison.

(a) Oxidising power : $Cl_2 > MnO_4^-$
(b) Oxidising power : $Cl_2 < Cr_2O_7^{2-}$
(c) Reducing power : $Fe^{3+} > MnO_4^-$
(d) Reducing power : $Cr_2O_7^{2-} > MnO_4^-$

6. Given below are two statements.

Statement I $E^\circ_{X^+/X}, E^\circ_{Y^+/Y}$ and $E^\circ_{Z^+/Z}$ are –2.71V, + 0.34 V and + 0.80 V respectively. The reducing power of the elements follows the order : $Y > Z > X$.

Statement II Lower the standard reduction potential, higher is the reducing power.

In the light of the above statements, choose the most appropriate answer from the options given below.

(a) Both Statement I and Statement II are correct.
(b) Statement I is incorrect but Statement II is correct.
(c) Both Statement I and Statement II are incorrect.
(d) Statement I is correct but Statement I is incorrect.

7. Calculate $E_{Cu^{2+}/Cu}$ at pH = 14. Given,

$K_{sp}[Cu(OH)_2] = 1\times 10^{-19}$, $E^\circ_{Cu^{2+}/Cu} = 0.34$ V

(a) – 0.11 V (b) – 0.22 V (c) + 0.11 V (d) + 0.22 V

8. From the following half-cell reactions,

$$MCl + e^- \longrightarrow M + Cl^-, E^\circ = 0.22 \text{ V}$$
$$M^+ + e^- \longrightarrow M, E^\circ = 0.812 \text{ V}$$

the solubility product of the sparingly soluble salt, MCl will be

(a) 2×10^{-5} M^2 (b) 1.5×10^{-10} M^2
(c) 4×10^{-20} M^2 (d) 1×10^{-10} M^2

9. In the measurement of molar conductivity, aqueous $AgNO_3$ is gradually added into aqueous KCl. Which of the following plots of molar conductivity (Λ_m) vs volume of $AgNO_3$ solution (V) correctly represent the experiment?

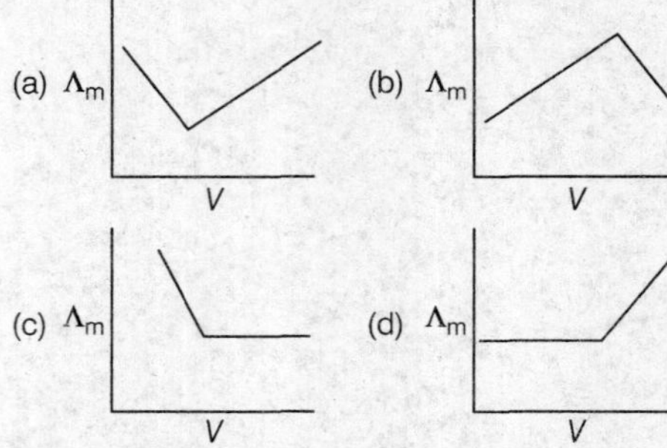

10. Three faraday of charge is passed through three aqueous solutions of $AgNO_3$, $GeCl_2$ and $Au(NO_3)_3$ connected in series. The molar ratio of Ag : Ge : Au get deposited at the cathode (inert) will be

(a) 1 : 2 : 3 (b) $\frac{2}{1}:\frac{3}{2}:\frac{4}{3}$ (c) 3 : 2 : 1 (d) 6 : 3 : 2

11. How many coulombs of electricity is required to coat a plate of 80 cm^2 area and 5×10^{-4} cm thick layer of Ag (molecular mass = 108 g mol^{-1}, $d = 10.5$ g cm^{-3}) from electrolysis of aqueous $AgNO_3$, if current efficiency is 90%?

(a) 375 C (b) 417 C (c) 543 C (d) 118 C

12. A 100 mL solution of 1M $CuSO_4$ is electrolysed with 0.8 ampere of current until its concentration becomes 0.4 M. If no change in volume takes place, during electrolysis, how long was the electrolysis continued?

(a) 5.45 h (b) 6.25 h (c) 4.02 h (d) 2 h

13. Calculate the number of coulombs delivered by a Daniell cell,initially containing 1 L each of 1M copper (II) ion and 1 M Zn (II) ion, which is operated until the potential drops to 1V. [$E^\circ_{Cu^{2+}, Cu} = 0.34$ V, $E^\circ_{Zn^{2+}, Zn} = -0.76$ V]

(a) 96500 C (b) 48250 C
(c) 193000 C (d) 289500 C

14. Which of the following statements is correct regarding a fuel cell?

(a) It is pollution free cell (b) It consumes H_2 at cathode
(c) It consumes O_2 at anode (d) It is about 90% efficient

15. Match the items of Column I and Column II.

Column I	Column II
A. Leclanche cell	1. Cell reaction $2H_2 + O_2 \longrightarrow 2H_2O$
B. Ni-Cd cell	2. Does not involve any ion in solution and is used in hearing aids.
C. Fuel cell	3. Rechargeable
D. Mercury cell	4. Reaction at anode $Zn \longrightarrow Zn^{2+} + 2e^-$
	5. Converts combustion energy into electrical energy.

Codes

	A	B	C	D		A	B	C	D
(a)	4	3	2	1, 5	(b)	1	3	2	4
(c)	4	1, 5	3	2	(d)	4	3	1, 5	2

Section B *Numerical Value Questions*

16. Exactly 0.2000 mole of electrons is passed through two electrolytic cells connected in series.

One contains Ag^+ ion and the other Zn^{2+} ion. Assuming that in each cell, reduction of metal ion into metal takes place, x g of Ag and y g of Zn get deposited.The value of $(x + y)$ in gram is ....

[Ag = 107.9, Zn = 65.38]

17. The emf of a Ag/AgCl electrode measured with respect to a saturated calomel electrode is −0.014 V. The value (in volt) of the standard reduction potential for the Ag/AgCl electrode will be ....
[Given : $Hg_2Cl_2 + 2e^- \rightarrow 2Hg + 2Cl^-$ (Satd. KCl); $E^\circ = 0.244$ V]

18. The amount of charge (in coulomb) present on one FeF_6^{3-} ion is $x \times 10^{-19}$ C. The value of x is ....

19. The mass of Hg_2Cl_2 (Molar mass = 472 g mol^{-1}) in gram that can be prepared by the reduction of Hg(II) ion in presence of chloride ion by the passage of 5A current for 3h is ....

20. The standard redox potentials for the following reactions are −1.20 V and 1.52 V respectively.

$$Mn^{2+} + 2e^- \longrightarrow Mn$$
$$Mn^{3+} + e^- \longrightarrow Mn^{2+}$$

The redox potential for the reaction in V is ....

$$Mn^{3+} + 3e^- \longrightarrow Mn$$

Answers

Section A

1 (c)	2 (b)	3 (a)	4 (c)	5 (a)
6 (b)	7 (b)	8 (d)	9 (d)	10 (d)
11 (b)	12 (c)	13 (c)	14 (a)	15 (d)

Section B

16 (28.12)	17 (0.23)	18 (4.8)	19 (132.06)	20 (−0.29)

See detailed solutions on page no. 220

QUALIFIER 10

Chemical Kinetics

Section A Objective Type Questions

1. For the given reaction, $4NH_3 + 5O_2 \longrightarrow 4NO + 6H_2O$

Which of the following relationship is correct?

(a) $\frac{d[O_2]}{dt} = 0.8\frac{d[NH_3]}{dt}$ (b) $\frac{d[H_2O]}{dt} = -1.5\frac{d[NH_3]}{dt}$

(c) $\frac{d[NO]}{dt} = -1.25\frac{d[O_2]}{dt}$ (d) $\frac{d[NH_3]}{dt} = -1.25\frac{d[O_2]}{dt}$

2. The reactant, *A* decomposes as

$$A(g) \begin{cases} \xrightarrow{k_1} 2B(g);\ k_1 = 4\times10^{-4}\,s^{-1} \\ \xrightarrow{k_2} C(g);\ k_2 = 1\times10^{-4}\,s^{-1} \end{cases}$$

If initial concentration of *A* is 4 M, the rate of appearance (in Ms^{-1}) of *B* will be

(a) 1.6×10^{-3} (b) 6.4×10^{-3}

(c) 3.2×10^{-3} (d) None of these

3. For the reaction,

$$2N_2O_5(g) \longrightarrow 4NO_2(g) + O_2(g);\ -\frac{\Delta[N_2O_5]}{\Delta t} = k_1[N_2O_5];$$

$$\frac{\Delta[NO_2]}{\Delta t} = k_2[N_2O_5];\ \frac{\Delta[O_2]}{\Delta t} = k_3[N_2O_5]$$

Thus,

(a) $k_1 = k_2 = k_3$ (b) $2k_1 = k_2 = 4k_3$

(c) $2k_1 = 4k_2 = k_3$ (d) None of these

4. Reaction between NO and H_2 takes place through a multi-step mechanism as,

I. $2NO(g) \underset{k_{-1}}{\overset{k_1}{\rightleftharpoons}} N_2O_2(g)$ [Fast]

II. $N_2O_2(g) + H_2(g) \xrightarrow{k_2} N_2O(g) + H_2O(g)$ [Slow]

III. $N_2O(g) + H_2(g) \xrightarrow{k_3} N_2(g) + H_2O(g)$ [Fast]

Now, select the correct expression of the rate of overall reaction

(a) Rate $= \frac{k_1k_2}{k_{-1}}[NO]^2[H_2]$ (b) Rate $= \frac{k_1k_2}{k_{-1}}[NO][H_2]^2$

(c) Rate $= k_1k_2[NO]^2[H_2]$ (d) Rate $= \frac{k_2}{k_1}[NO]^2[H_2]$

5. Select the correct statement(s) from the following:

I. The order of a reaction can be a fractional number.

II. The order of a reaction is an experimentally determined quantity.

III. The order of a reaction is always equal to the sum of the stoichiometric coefficients of reactants in the balanced chemical equation for a reaction.

IV. The order of a reaction is the sum of the powers of molar concentration of the reactants present in the expression of rate law.

Choose the correct option.

(a) I, II, III (b) I, II, IV (c) II, III (d) II, III, IV

6. Given below are two statements.

Statement I Order of a reaction is related to molecularity of a reaction.

Statement II Molecularity of a reaction cannot be fractional.

Justify both of the statements with a choice as given.

In the light of the above statements, choose the most appropriate answer from the options given below.

(a) Both statement I and statement II are correct.

(b) Statement I is incorrect but statement II is correct.

(c) Both statement I and statement II are incorrect.

(d) Statement I is correct but statement II is incorrect.

7. If *k* is the rate constant of a first order reaction, the expression of the fraction of reactant gets disappeared in time, *t* is

(a) $1 + e^{kt}$ (b) e^{-kt} (c) $\ln(kt)$ (d) $1 - e^{-kt}$

8. A certain reaction, $A + B \rightarrow$ Products, is the first order with respect to each reactant, with $k = 5\times10^{-3}\ M^{-1}s^{-1}$. Calculate the concentration of *A* remaining after 100 s, if initial concentration of *A* was 0.1 M and that of *B* was 6M. [Given antilog $(-2.30) = 5\times10^{-3}$ M]

(a) 4×10^{-2}M (b) 4×10^{-9}M

(c) 5×10^{-3}M (d) 1×10^{-5}M

9. *A first order sequential reaction,* $A \xrightarrow{k_1} B \xrightarrow{k_2} C$ is carried out with $k_1 = 10^{-1}s^{-1}$ and $k_2 = 10^{-2}s^{-1}$ with initial concentration of $A = 10$ M. The maximum concentration of *B* at any time is

(a) $\frac{10\times0.1}{(10)^{1/5}}$ M (b) $(10)^{1/2}$ M

(c) $(10)^{8/9}$ M (d) $10\times\frac{1}{(10)^{1/8}}$ M

10. In the reaction,

$$(CH_3)_3COOC(CH_3)_3\,(g) \xrightarrow{\Delta} 2CH_3COCH_3(g) + C_2H_6(g)$$

is carried out at constant volume with pressure, p_0 of $(CH_3)_3COOC(CH_3)_3$ and the decomposition follows first order reaction.

Select the expression from the following which holds good for this reaction.

[p = total pressure of the mixture at a time, t]

(a) $kt = \ln\left(\frac{3p_0 + p}{2p_0}\right)$ (b) $-kt = \ln\left(\frac{3p_0 - p}{2p_0}\right)$

(c) $-kt = \ln\left(\frac{2p_0 + 3p}{2p_0}\right)$ (d) $kt = \ln\left(\frac{2p_0 - 3p}{2p_0}\right)$

11. For a reaction, $A \rightarrow$ product, the following is the plot of $\log(t_{50})$ *vs* $\log a_0$, where a_0 is the initial concentration of A. Which of the following is the correct expression of the rate law of the reaction?

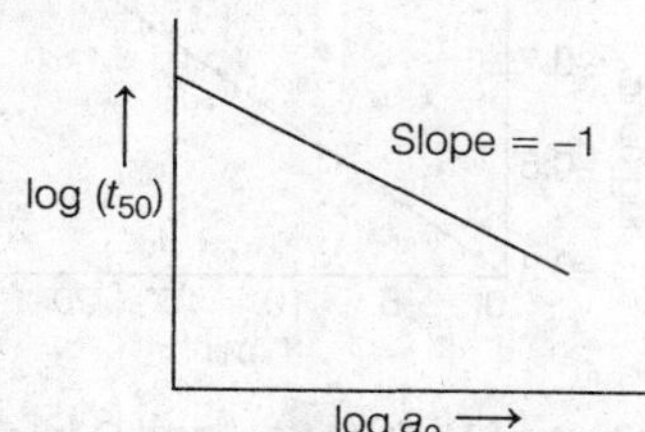

(a) $-\frac{d[A]}{dt} = k$ (b) $-\frac{d[A]}{dt} = k[A]$

(c) $-\frac{d[A]}{dt} = k[A]^2$ (d) $-\frac{d[A]}{dt} = k[A]^3$

12. In a zero order reaction, variation of $(a_o - a)$ with time (t) is represented as,

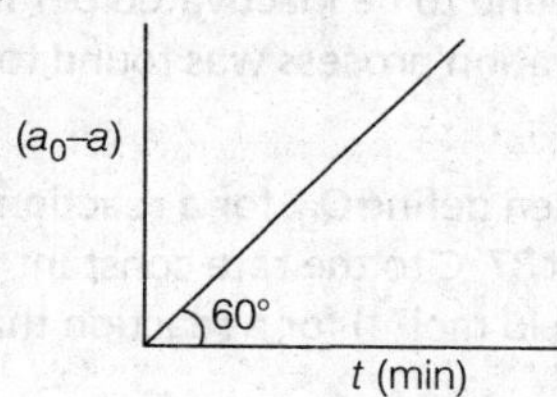

where, $(a_o - a)$ = decrease in molar concentration of the reactant in time, t minute.

Half-life of the reaction for $a_0 = 17.32$ M will be

(a) 5 min (b) 10 min

(c) 8.66 min (d) 15 min

13. Under the same reaction condition of $A \longrightarrow B$, initial concentration of 1.386 mol/L of a substance becomes half in 40s and 20s through first order and zero order kinetics respectively. Ratio (k_1 / k_0) of the rate constants for the first order (k_1) and zero order (k_0) of the reaction is

(a) 0.5 L/mol (b) 1 mol/L

(c) 1.5 mol/L (d) 2 mol/L

14. For a first order reaction, the correct order of its half-life (t_{50}), average life (t_{av}), time for 75% completion (t_{75}) and time for 99.9% completion $(t_{99.9})$ is

(a) $t_{50} > t_{av} > t_{75} > t_{99.9}$

(b) $t_{50} < t_{76} < t_{99.9} < t_{av}$

(c) $t_{av} < t_{50} < t_{99.9} > t_{15}$

(d) $t_{50} < t_{av} < t_{75} < t_{99.9}$

15. The reaction, $2NO\,(g) + H_2(g) \longrightarrow N_2O(g) + H_2O(g)$ follows the rate law, $\frac{dp_{(N_2O)}}{dt} = k(p_{NO})^2 p_{H_2}$

If the reaction is started with, $p_{NO} = 1500$ mm of Hg and $p_{H_2} = 8$ mm of Hg, the reaction may be considered to follow :

(a) zero order kinetics (b) first order kinetics

(c) second order kinetics (d) third order kinetics

16. Match the graphical presentation in Column I with the order of reactions in Column II and select the answer from the code given.

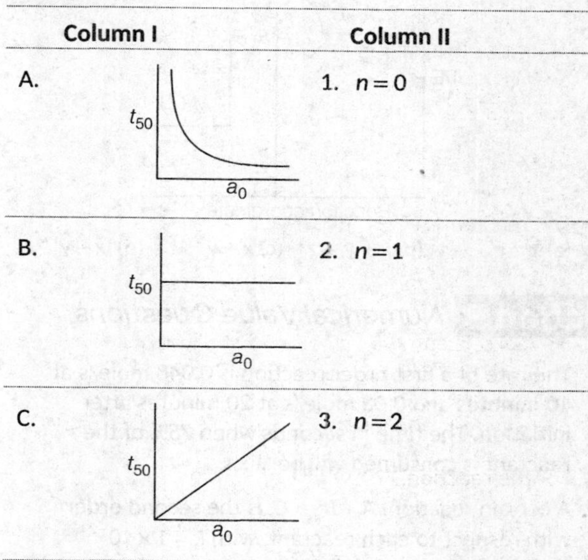

Column I	Column II
A. (graph of t_{50} vs a_0)	1. $n = 0$
B. (graph of t_{50} vs a_0)	2. $n = 1$
C. (graph of t_{50} vs a_0)	3. $n = 2$

[t_{50} = half-life, a_0 = initial concentration]

Codes

	A	B	C
(a)	1	2	3
(b)	2	3	1
(c)	2	1	3
(d)	3	1	2

17. The increase in the rate of a reaction with increase in temperature is mainly due to

(a) the increase in collision frequency.

(b) the decrease in activation energy.

(c) the increase in number of molecules having threshold energy.

(d) the increase in pre-exponential factor.

18. A reaction takes place in three steps, the rate constants are k_1, k_2 and k_3. The overall rate constant is expressed as, $k = \frac{k_1 k_3}{k_2}$.

If activation energy of three steps with rate constants k_1, k_2 and k_3 are 40, 30, and 20 kJ mol^{-1} respectively. The overall activation energy of the reaction will be [Arrhenius constant, A remains constant throughout the reaction.]

(a) 10 kJ mol^{-1} (b) 15 kJ mol^{-1}

(c) 30 kJ mol^{-1} (d) 60 kJ mol^{-1}

19. What fraction of number of moleules will cross over the energy barrier at 200 K for 3.684 kJ mol^{-1} activation energy if $R = 8\ J\ mol^{-1}\ K^{-1}$?

$$\left[\text{Given}: e^{(-2.303)} = \frac{1}{10}\right]$$

(a) 5% (b) 10%
(c) 15% (d) 20%

20. According to the following diagram, the activation energy of the reaction, $M + N \rightarrow A + B$ will be

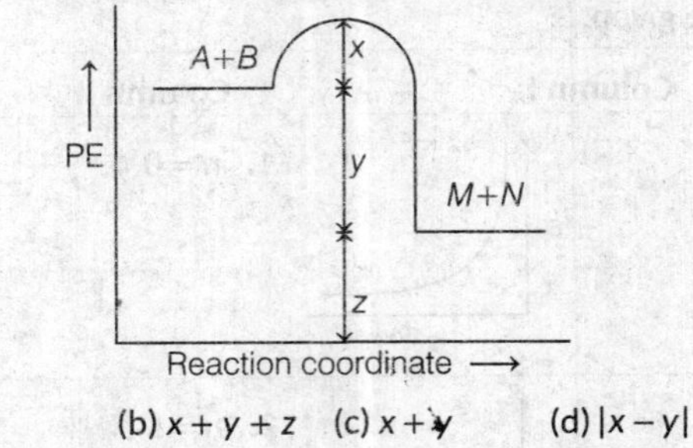

(a) x (b) $x + y + z$ (c) $x + y$ (d) $|x - y|$

Section B *Numerical Value Questions*

21. The rate of a first order reaction is 0.048 mole/s at 10 minutes and 0.03 mole/s at 20 minutes after initiation. The time in seconds when 75% of the reactant is consumed will be ....

22. A certain reaction, $A + B \rightarrow C$, is the second order with respect to each reactant, with $k = 1 \times 10^{-2}$ M^{-1}/s. The concentration (in M) of A remaining after 100s, if the initial concentration of each reactant was 0.1M will be ....

23. In an enzymatic solution of the fermentation of sugar, it is observed that on doubling the time the fractional reduction of the reactant concentration also doubles. In an experiment, initially 0.12 M the concentration of the sugar is reduced to 0.06 M in 10 h and to 0.03 M in 20h. Rate constant of the reaction is $x \times 10^{-5} s^{-1}$. The value of x is ....

24. The hydrolysis of methyl acetate in alkaline solution,

$$CH_3COOCH_3 + OH^- \longrightarrow CH_3COO^- + CH_3OH$$

followed rate $= [CH_3COOCH_3][OH^-]$, with $k = 0.137\ L\ mol^{-1}s^{-1}$ at 25°C. A reaction mixture was prepared to have initial concentrations of methyl acetate and OH^- of 0.05M each. Initial rate of the reaction is found to be $a \times 10^{-4}\ Ms^{-1}$. The value of '$a$' will be ....

25. The following data were obtained at a certain temperature for decomposition of ammonia in contact with tungsten :

p (mm Hg)	50	100	200
Relative $t_{1/2}$	3.64	1.82	0.91

The order of reaction is ....

26. Using the data sheet and its plot, rate constant (in min^{-1}) of the concerned reaction will be ....

t min	conc. M	log conc.
0.00	0.500	−0.301
5.00	0.389	−0.410
10.00	0.303	−0.519
15.00	0.236	−0.627
20.00	0.184	−0.735
25.00	0.143	−0.845

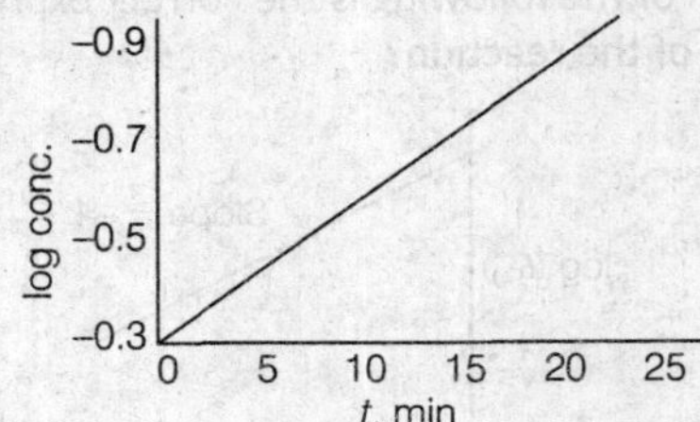

27. The decomposition of N_2O into N_2 and O in presence of gaseous argon follows the second order kinetics with, $k = (5 \times 10^{11} L\ mol^{-1}s^{-1}) \times e^{-29000\ k/T}$

The activation energy (in kJ mol^{-1}) of the reaction will be ....

28. A viral preparation was inactivated in a chemical bath. The inactivation process was found to be first order in virus concentration and at the beginning of the experiment 2% of the virus was found to be inactivated per minute. Evaluation of k for the inactivation process was found to be $x \times 10^{-9} s^{-1}$. The value of x is ....

29. Biochemists often define Q_{10} for a reaction as the ratio of the rate constant at 37°C to the rate constant at 27°C. The energy of activation (in kJ mol^{-1}) for a reaction that has a Q_{10} of 2.5 will be ....

30. For the overall reaction between P and Q to give R and S, two mechanisms are suggested

(i) $P + Q \rightarrow PQ^* \rightarrow R + S;\ k_1 = 3 \times 10^{-5} M^{-1}s^{-1}$

(ii) $P \rightarrow P^* \rightarrow X;\ k_2 = 5 \times 10^{-4} s^{-1}$

(iii) $X + Q \rightarrow R + S;\ k_3 = 1 \times 10^{10} M^{-1}s^{-1}$

The concentration (in mol L^{-1}) of P and/or Q with the inherent rates be equal is ....

Answers

Section A

1 (b)	2 (c)	3 (d)	4 (a)	5 (b)
6 (b)	7 (d)	8 (c)	9 (c)	10 (b)
11 (c)	12 (a)	13 (a)	14 (d)	15 (b)
16 (d)	17 (c)	18 (c)	19 (b)	20 (c)

Section B

21 (1770)	22 (0.09)	23 (1.92)	24 (3.42)	25 (2)
26 (0.05)	27 (241)	28 (3.34)	29 (71)	30 (16.67)

See detailed solutions on page no. 222

QUALIFIER 11

Surface Chemistry

Section A Objective Type Questions

1. Some important properties related to adsorption are as follows:

I. Reversible

II. Formation of unimolecular layer

III. Low heat of adsorption

IV. Occurs at low temperature and decreases with increase in temperature

Which of the above properties are true for physisorption?

(a) I, II and III (b) I, III and IV
(c) II, III and IV (d) I and II

2. During adsorption, the system has

(a) $\Delta H > 0$ (b) $\Delta G > 0$
(c) $\Delta S < 0$ (d) Both (a) and (b)

3. If x is the amount of adsorbate and m is the amount of adsorbent, which of the following relation is not related to adsorption process?

(a) $\frac{x}{m} = p \times T$ (b) $\frac{x}{m} = f(p)$ at constant T

(c) $\frac{x}{m} = f(T)$ at constant p (d) $p = f(T)$ at constant $\frac{x}{m}$

4. On adding $AgNO_3$ solution in KI solution, a negatively charged colloidal sol is obtained when they are in a mixture of

(a) 100 mL 0.2 M $AgNO_3$ + 100 mL 0.1 M KI
(b) 100 mL 0.1 M $AgNO_3$ + 100 mL 0.2 M KI
(c) 100 mL 0.15 M $AgNO_3$ + 100 mL 0.25 M KI
(d) Both (b) and (c)

5. If a freshly prepared precipitate of SnO_2 is peptised by a small amount of NaOH, these colloidal particles may be represented as,

(a) $[SnO_2]SnO_3^{2-} \cdot 2Na^+$
(b) $[SnO_2]Sn^{4+} \cdot 2O^{2-}$
(c) $[SnO_2]Na^+ \cdot OH^-$
(d) $[SnO_2]Sn^{4+} \cdot 4OH^-$

6. Which of the following is the adsorption isobar for chemisorption?

(a) 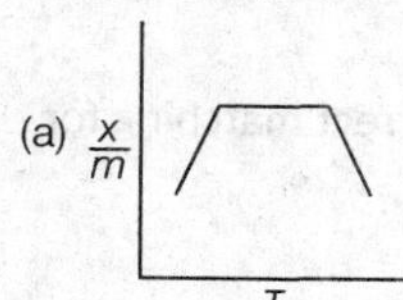

(b) 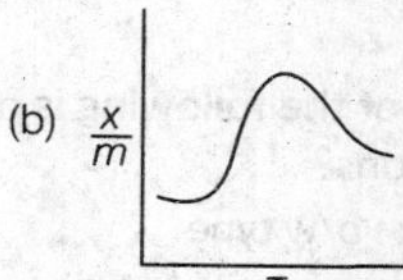

(c) 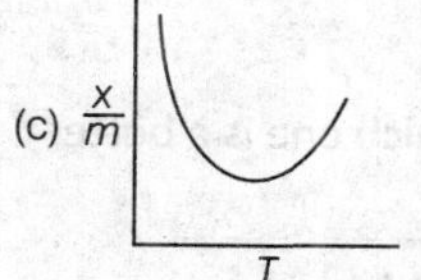

(d) 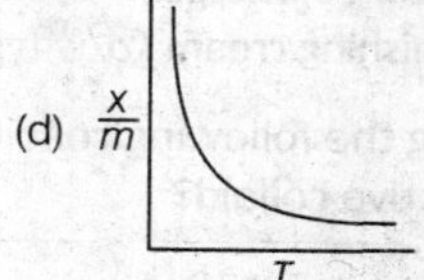

7. According to Freundlich adsorption, $\frac{x}{m} = k(p)^{1/n}$

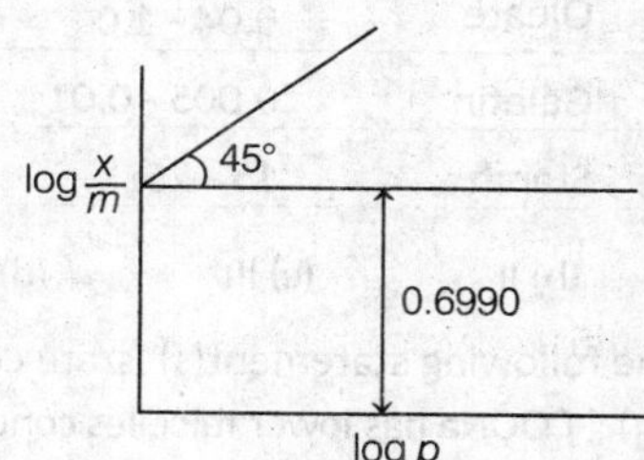

What is the value of n and k?

(a) 1, 5 (b) 2, 1
(c) 1, 2 (d) 5, 1

8. 1 g of a charcoal adsorbs 100 mL 0.5 M CH_3COOH to form a monolayer and thereby molarity of CH_3COOH reduces to 0.49 M. Surface area of charcoal is 3.015×10^2 m^2/g. The surface area of charcoal adsorbed by each molecule of CH_3COOH is found to be $x \times 10^{-19}$ m^2. The value of x is ....

(a) 4.02 (b) 2.7
(c) 5 (d) 3

9. Which one of the following electrolytes will be most effective in coagulation of arsenous sulphide (Ar_2S_3) sol?

(a) KCl (b) NaCl
(c) $MgCl_2$ (d) $AlCl_3$

10. The coagulation values in milli-moles per litre of electrolytes used for the coagulation of As_2S_3 sol are,

I. (NaCl) = 52 ; II. (KCl) = 51 ; III. ($BaCl_2$) = 0.69 ;
IV. ($MgSO_4$) = 0.22

The correct order of their flocculation power is

(a) I > II > III = IV (b) IV > III > II > I
(c) I > II > III > IV (d) I = II > III < IV

11. 0.0025 g of starch is required to prevent coagulation of 10 mL of gold sol, when 1 mL of 10% NaCl solution is present. Here, gold number of starch is

(a) 5.5 (b) 2.5
(c) 1.2 (d) 2.2

12. Which of the following is not a correct matching for emulsions?

(a) Milk : *o/w* type
(b) Cold cream : *w/o* type
(c) Butter : *o/w* type
(d) Vanishing cream : *o/w* type

13. Among the following colloids, which one is a better protective colloid?

	Colloids	Gold number
I.	Gum Arabic	0.15 - 0.25
II.	Oleate	0.04 - 1.0
III.	Gelatin	0.005 - 0.01
IV.	Starch	15 - 25

(a) I (b) II (c) III (d) IV

14. Which of the following statement(s) is/are correct?

(a) $CH_3(CH_2)_{14}$ COONa has lower micelles concentration (CMC) than $CH_3(CH_2)_{10}$ COONa.
(b) Peptisation works on the principle of relative adsorption of common ions of electrolyte.
(c) Above kraft temperature, with increase in temperature, CMC decreases.
(d) All of the above

15. Which of the following type of catalysis can be explained by the adsorption theory?

(a) Acid base catalysis (b) Enzyme catalysis
(c) Homogeneous catalysis (d) Heterogeneous catalysis

Section B *Numerical Value Questions*

16. Positively charged colloidal sol is formed by hydrolysis of $AlCl_3$. The number of total ions present in fixed layer and diffused layer of a double layer for one $AlCl_3$ molecule is ....

17. 50 mL of 1 M oxalic acid (molar mass = 126 g mol^{-1}) is shaken with 0.5 g of wood charcoal, concentration of the acid solution is decreased to 0.5 M. The amount (in gram) of oxalic acid adsorbed per gram of carbon will be ....

18. The coagulation of 100 mL of gold sol is prevented by addition of 0.7561 g of a lyophilic sol, X to it before addition of 1 mL of 10% NaCl solution. The gold number of X is ....

19. Coagulation value NaCl is 52 mmol/L and that of $AlCl_3$ is 0.093 mmol/L. So, flocculation power of $AlCl_3$ is $x \times 10^2$ times more than NaCl. The value of x is ....

20. 100 mL of colloidal solution is completely coagulated by addition of 4.75 mL of 1 M KCl solution. Flocculation value of KCl will be........ .

Answers

Section A

1 (b)	2 (c)	3 (a)	4 (d)	5 (a)
6 (b)	7 (a)	8 (c)	9 (d)	10 (b)
11 (b)	12 (c)	13 (c)	14 (d)	15 (d)

Section B

16 (4)	17 (6.30)	18 (75.61)	19 (5.59)	20 (47.5)

See detailed solutions on page no. 225

QUALIFIER 12

Classification of Elements and Periodicity in Properties

Section A Objective Type Questions

1. Match the atomic number in Column I with its IUPAC nomenclature in Column II and then select the correct choice with proper codes.

	Column I		Column II
A.	105	1.	Bue
B.	110	2.	Uun
C.	219	3.	Uns
D.	107	4.	Unp

Codes

	A	B	C	D		A	B	C	D
(a)	3	2	1	4	(b)	4	2	1	3
(c)	1	2	3	4	(d)	2	1	4	3

2. In the 6th period of the periodic table, the order of orbitals in which electrons being filled are

(a) *5s, 5p, 5d* (b) *6s, 6p, 6d, 6f*
(c) *6s, 5f, 6d, 6p* (d) *6s, 4f, 5d, 6p*

3. The correct order of ionic radii is

(a) $S^{2-} > Br^{-} > Cl^{-} > O^{2-} > Mg^{2+} > Na^{+}$
(b) $S^{2-} > O^{2-} > Br^{-} > Cl^{-} > Na^{+} > Mg^{2+}$
(c) $Br^{-} > S^{2-} > Cl^{-} > O^{2-} > Na^{+} > Mg^{2+}$
(d) $S^{2-} = O^{2-} > Br^{-} = Cl^{-} > Na^{+} > Mg^{2+}$

4. If the ionic radii of K^{+} and F^{-} are about 1.34Å each, then the expected values of atomic radii of K and F should be respectively

(a) 1.34Å and 1.34Å (b) 2.31Å and 0.64Å
(c) 0.64Å and 2.31Å (d) 2.31Å and 1.34Å

5. Which of the following is arranged in order of increasing radius of the hydrated ions?

(a) $K^{+} < Na^{+} < Li^{+}$ (b) $Na^{+} < K^{+} < Li^{+}$
(c) $K^{+} < Li^{+} < Na^{+}$ (d) $Li^{+} < Na^{+} < K^{+}$

6. Which of the following statements is incorrect?

(a) The second ionisation energy of sulphur is greater than that of chlorine.
(b) The third ionisation energy of phosphorus is greater than that of aluminium.
(c) The first ionisation energy of aluminium is nearly the same as that of gallium.
(d) The second ionisation energy of boron is greater than that of carbon.

7. The correct order of IE_1 values of Na, Mg, Al and Si will be

(a) Na<Mg>Al<Si (b) Na>Mg>Al>Si
(c) Na<Mg<Al>Si (d) Na<Mg<Al<Si

8. An element has successive ionisation energy values (in eV $atom^{-1}$) as : 7.1, 14.3, 34.5, 46.8 and 162.2. The element is likely to be

(a) Na (b) Ca
(c) Si (d) F

9. Which of the following configurations is expected to have maximum difference in second and third ionisation energy?

(a) $(1s)^2(2s)^2(2p)^2$ (b) $(1s)^2(2s)^2(2p)^6(3s)^1$
(c) $(1s)^2(2s)^2(2p)^6(3s)^2$ (d) $(1s)^2(2s)^2(2p)^1$

10. Given below are two statements.

Statement I IE_1 of Mg is larger than that of Na but the reverse is true for IE_2.

Statement II Mg has larger atomic number than Na.

In the light of the above statements, choose the most appropriate answer from the options given below.

(a) Both Statement I and Statement II are correct.
(b) Statement I is incorrect but Statement II is correct.
(c) Both Statement I and Statement II are incorrect.
(d) Statement I is correct but Statement II is incorrect.

11. The correct order of the second ionisation energy of C, N, O and F is

(a) C > N > O > F (b) O > N > F > C
(c) O > F > N > C (d) F > O > N > C

12. Which of the following elements has zero electron affinity?

(a) Fluorine (b) Nitrogen
(c) Oxygen (d) Neon

13. The correct order of negative electron gain enthalpy of group 16 elements will be

(a) O > S > Se > Te (b) O < S < Te < Se
(c) S > Se > Te > O (d) S > O > Se > Te

14. Which of the following conversions show minimum energy release?

(a) $C \rightarrow C^-$ (b) $N \rightarrow N^-$
(c) $O \rightarrow O^-$ (d) $F \rightarrow F^-$

15. Choose the incorrect statement from the following :

(a) $|IE|$ of $A^- = |EA|$ of A
(b) $O \longrightarrow O^-$ process is exothermic
(c) $O^- \longrightarrow O^{2-}$ process is exothermic
(d) $N^- \longrightarrow N$ process is endothermic

16. Aqueous solutions of two compounds, X—O—H and Y—O—H have been prepared in two flasks. If the electronegativity values of $X = 3$, $Y = 1.72$, $O = 3.5$ and $H = 2.1$, Then the solutions are respectively

(a) acidic, basic (b) basic, acidic
(c) acidic, acidic (d) basic, basic

17. The correct statement about electronegativity (EN) and electron affinity (EA) of an element is as

(a) both represent the same quantity.
(b) EA is a characteristic of single atom, while EN is the characteristic of bonded atom.
(c) EA is always lesser than EN of an element.
(d) EA and EN, both are accompanied by exchange of energy.

18. The correct order of acidity is

(a) $Cl_2O_7 > SO_3 > P_2O_5 > N_2O_5 > MgO > Na_2O$
(b) $Cl_2O_7 > P_2O_5 > N_2O_5 > MgO > SO_3 > Na_2O$
(c) $SO_3 > N_2O_5 > Cl_2O_7 > P_2O_5 > MgO > Na_2O$
(d) $Cl_2O_7 > SO_3 > N_2O_5 > P_2O_5 > MgO > Na_2O$

19. Beryllium shows a diagonal relationship with

(a) magnesium (b) aluminium
(c) boron (d) sodium

20. Which of the following statements regarding halogens is not true?

(a) Ionisation energy decreases with increase in atomic number
(b) Electronegativity decreases with increase in atomic number
(c) Electron affinity decreases with increase in atomic number
(d) Enthalpy of fusion increases with increase in atomic number

Section B *Numerical Value Questions*

21. Out of 18 groups of the periodic table, the number of elements present in all three physical states, *viz.*, solid, liquid and gas at 298 K and 1 bar pressure is/are ....

22. The more stable oxidation states (in compounds) of Al, Tl, C, F are $|a|$, $|b|$, $|c|$ and $|d|$ respectively. The value of $\left(\frac{|c|+|d|}{|a|+|b|}\right)$ is ....

23. Effective nuclear charge for the last electron in fluorine atom is ....

24. The dipole moment of HBr molecule if the bond length is 1.2476 is ....

25. The amount of energy releasd when one million of atoms of iodine in the vapour state are converted to I^- ions is 4.9×10^{-13} J. From this observation, we can express electron affinity of iodine as $x \times 10^4$ J/mol. The value of x is ....

26. In Pauling scale, electronegativity of Ge = 2.01. Electronegativity of Ge (germanium) in Mulliken's scale will be ....

27. $\Delta\chi$ (difference in electronegativity value in Pauling scale) of a heteronuclear covalent bond is 2.5. The bond is found to be x% ionic in nature. The value of x is ....

28. X—X and C—C bond length values are 1Å and 1.54Å respectively. Electronegativity values (in Pauling scale) of X and C are 3 and 2 respectively. The C—X bond length (in Å) is likely to be ....

29. Given, $E_{C-C} = 348$ kJ mol^{-1} ; $E_{C-H} = 412$ kJ mol^{-1}

$E_{H-H} = 436$ kJ mol^{-1}; $\chi_H = 2.1$

In Pauling scale, electronegativity (χ, chi) of carbon will be

30. If the Allred-Rochow scale of electronegativity is expressed as

$\chi = a + b \times \frac{Z_{eff}}{r^2_{cov}(\text{in Å})}$, the value of $(a + b)$ is ....

Answers

Section A

1 (b)	2 (d)	3 (c)	4 (b)	5 (a)
6 (a)	7 (a)	8 (c)	9 (c)	10 (c)
11 (c)	12 (d)	13 (c)	14 (b)	15 (c)
16 (a)	17 (b)	18 (d)	19 (b)	20 (c)

Section B

21 (1)	22 (1.25)	23 (5)	24 (6)	25 (30)
26 (5.63)	27 (61.87)	28 (1.18)	29 (3)	30 (1.10)

See detailed solutions on page no. 226

QUALIFIER 13

General Principles and Processes of Isolation of Metals

Section A Objective Type Questions

1. Which of the following is the least carbon content form of iron?

(a) Cast iron (b) Wrought iron
(c) Steel (d) None of these

2. Type metal is an alloy containing metals which consist of

(a) Pb, Sb and Sn (b) Al, Sb and Pb
(c) Pb, Cu and Sn (d) Pb, Sb and Si

3. I. ACl_2 (excess) $+ BCl_2 \longrightarrow ACl_4 + B\downarrow$

II. $BO \xrightarrow[>400°C]{\Delta} B + \frac{1}{2}O_2$

Ore of B would be

(a) siderite (b) cinnabar (c) malachite (d) horn silver

4. An ore contains PbS, ZnS and FeS_2. During separation of these sulphide ores by froth floatation, NaCN is added first followed by addition of $CuSO_4$. Here, roles of NaCN and $CuSO_4$ are respectively

(a) stabilising agent and wetting agent
(b) wetting agent and stabilising agent
(c) depressant and activator
(d) activator and depressant

5. Select the incorrect statement(s) regarding the roasting of zinc blende ore.

I. Both zinc oxide and zinc sulphate are formed during the process.
II. Impurities like arsenic and antimony cannot be removed.
III. Roasting is done to remove organic impurities.
IV. Chemical composition of the ore does not change.

Choose the correct option.

(a) I, II, and III (b) II, III and IV
(c) III and IV (d) I, II, III and IV

6. A sulphide ore is usually roasted to its oxide before reduction because

(a) $\Delta_f H°(CO_2, g) >, \Delta_f H°(CS_2, l)$
(b) a metal sulphide is more stable than its oxide
(c) no reducing agent is found suitable for reducing a metal sulphide ore
(d) a sulphide cannot be reduced at all

7. Auto or self-reduction is most important step in the copper metallurgy. In auto-reduction Cu_2O is reduced by Cu_2S. Which of the following statements is correct regarding auto-reduction?

(a) Auto-reduction occurs in blast furnace.
(b) Auto-reduction occurs in Bessemer converter in the supply of air.
(c) Auto-reduction occurs in blast furnace in absence of air.
(d) Auto-reduction occurs in Bessemer converter, when supply of air is cut off.

8. Match Column I (metallurgical step) with Column II (metal extracted/refined) and select answer from the codes given :

	Column I		Column II
A.	Extraction by reduction of ore with carbon	1.	Ag
B.	Extraction through formation of a soluble complex	2.	Zn
C.	An ingredient of anode mud obtained in electrorefining of copper	3.	Fe
D.	Metal involved in Parkes process	4.	Au

Codes

	A	B	C	D
(a)	2, 3	1, 4	1, 4	1, 2, 4
(b)	1, 2	1, 4	1, 4	2, 3
(c)	2	1	4	3, 1
(d)	3	1, 2	1	1

9. Near the mouth of blast furnace, iron oxides are reduced to sponge iron by

(a) CO (b) CO_2
(c) $CaCO_3$ (d) C

10. Liquation method could have been employed to purify

(a) Zn (b) Sn
(c) Hg (d) Both (b) and (c)

11. In sulphatising of zinc blende, the product(s) obtained is (are)

(a) $ZnO + SO_2$ (b) $ZnO + ZnSO_4 + SO_2$
(c) $ZnCl_2$ (d) $Zn + SO_2$

12. During electro-reduction of pure alumina into aluminium by Hall-Heroult method, the concentration of which substance in the electrolyte is decreased?

(a) Al_2O_3 (b) $AlF_3.3NaF$ (c) CaF_2 (d) AlF_3

13. Silicon is purified by zone refining. In this process, the melt formed contains

(a) same concentration of Si as it was in its solid state (crude form).
(b) lesser concentration of Si as it was in its solid state (crude form).
(c) slightly higher Si% as it was in its solid form (crude).
(d) minimum 99% of Si.

14. Given below are two statements.

Statement I Extraction of gold which occurs in native form can be done by forming an amalgam.

Statement II Due to the presence of completely filled 4*f* and 5*d*-orbitals, mercury has lower melting point.

In the light of the above statements, choose the most appropriate answer from the options given below.

(a) Both Statement I and Statement II are correct
(b) Statement I is incorrect but Statement II is correct
(c) Both Statement I and Statement II are incorrect
(d) Statement I is correct but Statement II is incorrect

15. In the Hoope's process for purification of aluminium, crude or impure Al, pure Al and electrolyte used form three layers which are separated

(a) by a perforated steel sheet.
(b) by carbon sheet which acts as anode.
(c) by density difference between them.
(d) by keeping them in different containers.

16. A sudden change in slope is seen when free energy change (ΔG) for formation of oxide is plotted graphically (Ellingham diagram) against temperature is due to

(a) free energy increases with temperature.
(b) change of state from solid metal to liquid metal.
(c) cutting across the line with $\Delta G = 0$.
(d) decomposition oxide at that temperature.

17. The Ellingham diagram of a certain metal *M* is represented in the figure. The points P_1 and P_2 correspond respectively to

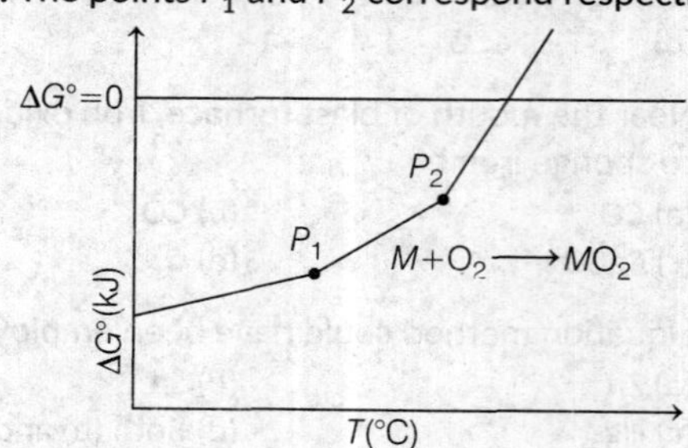

(a) oxidation and reduction of *M*.
(b) beginning and end of the reduction process.
(c) minimum and maximum value of ΔG.
(d) melting and boiling point of *M*.

18. Which of the following condition favours the reduction of a metal oxide to metal?

(a) $\Delta H = +ve, T\Delta S = +ve$; at low temperature
(b) $\Delta H = +ve, T\Delta S = -ve$; at any temperature
(c) $\Delta H = -ve, T\Delta S = -ve$; at high temperature
(d) $\Delta H = -ve, T\Delta S = +ve$; at any temperature

19. For which of the following reactions, slope of the straight line will be negative in Ellingham diagram (plot of $\Delta G°$ vs *T*)?

(a) $Mg + \frac{1}{2}O_2 \longrightarrow MgO$
(b) $2Ag + \frac{1}{2}O_2 \longrightarrow Ag_2O$
(c) $C + \frac{1}{2}O_2 \longrightarrow CO$
(d) $CO + \frac{1}{2}O_2 \longrightarrow CO_2$

20. Which of the following curves of Ellingham diagram indicates that the metal (*M*) is obtained in its vapour state by carbon reduction of the metal oxide (*MO*)?

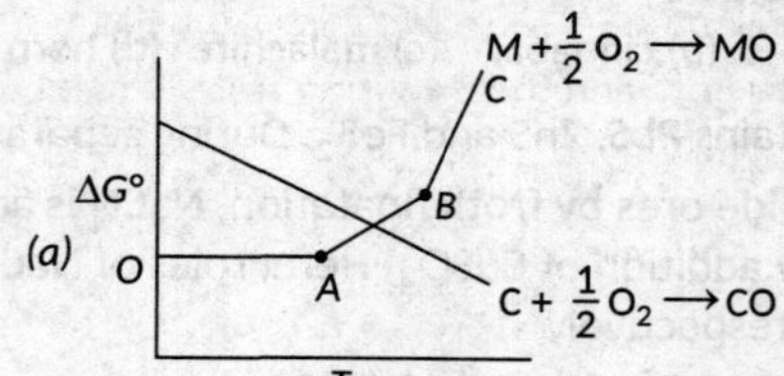

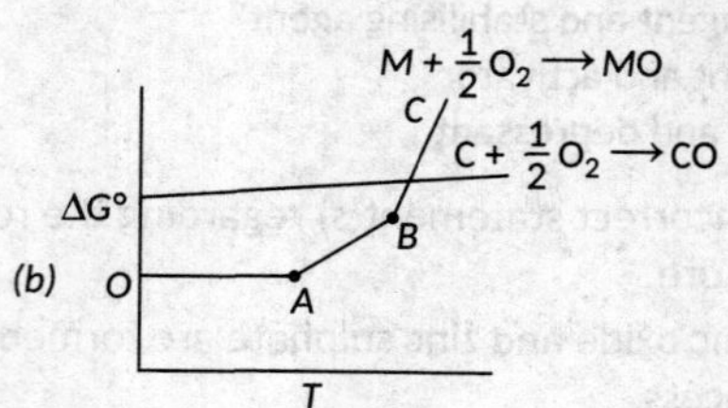

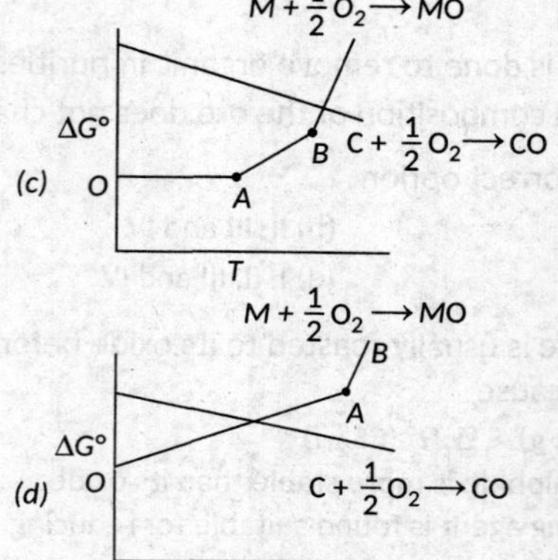

Section B *Numerical Value Questions*

21. A sample of the alloy duralumin contains 4.2% copper (Cu = 63.5) by mass. The percent of the alloy consists of the compound $CuAl_2$ will be .... (molar mass = 117.5 g mol^{-1})

22. The molecular formula of beryl is represented as, $Be_m\ Al_2Si_n\ O_{18}$. The value of *mn* is ....

23. The number of substance among the following which contain metal in its elemental form is/are ....
(Copper matte, argentite, pig iron, alumina, blister copper).

24. Considering average composition of Portland cement, we find the ratio of the following ranges from *a* (min.) to *b*(max.),

$$\frac{\%CaO}{\%SiO_2 + \%Al_2O_3 + \%Fe_2O_3} = a \text{ to } b$$

The value of (*b*/*a*) is ....

25. Among HgO, ZnO, CaO, PbO, Al_2O_3, SnO_2, WO_3, Cr_2O_3, Fe_2O_3– the number of oxides which can be reduced by carbon is ....

26. Consider the following reaction,

$$\text{Galena} \xrightarrow{\text{Roasting}} \text{Metal oxide + Gas}$$

The difference between the oxidation state of sulphur in product and reaction is ....

27. When a mixture of 0.25 mole of Li_2CO_3 and 0.5 mol of Na_2CO_3 is heated, *x* L of CO_2 gas is produced at STP. The value of *x* is ....

28. The number of metals among the following can be purified by vapour phase refining are ....
Zr, Zn, Cd, Ti, Fe, Hf, Pt, Pb, Cu, Ni, Mn

29. (i) $Ni + xCO \xrightarrow{330K} Ni(CO)_x \xrightarrow{470K} Ni + xCO$
(ii) $Zr + yI_2 \xrightarrow{523K} ZrI_{2y} \xrightarrow{1700K} Zr + yI_2$
The value, $(x + y)$ is ....

30. The minimum emf that to be maintained in Hall-Heroult process in volt is ....
$[\Delta_f G°(Al_2O_3) = -1520 \text{ kJ mol}^{-1}, \Delta_f G° (CO_2) = -394 \text{ kJ mol}^{-1}]$

Answers

Section A

1 (b)	2 (a)	3 (b)	4 (c)	5 (b)
6 (a)	7 (d)	8 (a)	9 (a)	10 (d)
11 (b)	12 (a)	13 (b)	14 (a)	15 (c)
16 (b)	17 (d)	18 (d)	19 (c)	20 (c)

Section B

21 (7.77)	22 (18)	23 (2)	24 (1.10)	25 (4)
26 (+2)	27 (5.6)	28 (3)	29 (6)	30 (–1.60)

See detailed solutions on page no. 228

QUALIFIER 14

Hydrogen

Section A Objective Type Questions

1. Which of the following is (are) the order of properties (as given) of diatomic molecules formed by three isotopes of hydrogen, P ($^1_1$H), D ($^2_1$H) and T ($^3_1$H)?

I. $T_2 > D_2 > P_2$ (boiling point)
II. $D_2 > P_2$ (bond dissociation enthalpy)
III. $D_2 = P_2$ (bond length)
IV. $P_2 > D_2$ (order of reactivity with Cl_2)

Choose the correct option.

(a) I, II, III and IV (b) Only IV
(c) I, II and III (d) II and IV

2. In context of commercial production of dihydrogen, which of the following statements is (are) true?

(a) Electrolysis of warm water in presence of a significant amount of $Ba(OH)_2$ by nickel electrodes yields very pure H_2 gas.
(b) In 'water-gas shift' reaction, H_2 gas can also be manufactured by using *syn* gas.
(c) Bosch reaction is also known as reverse water-gas shift reaction
(d) All of the above

3. Which statement is not correct for *ortho* and *para* hydrogen?

(a) With increase in temperature, the maximum amount of the *para* form becomes nearly 100%.
(b) They differ in nuclear spin.
(c) *ortho* form is more stable than *para* form at room temperature.
(d) They are the allotropes of hydrogen.

4. Match Column I with Column II and select answer from the codes given below.

	Column I (Compound)		Column II (Properties)
A.	Permutit	1.	Antichlor
B.	H_2O_2	2.	β^--emitter
C.	Tritium	3.	Water softener
D.	H_2O	4.	Amphoteric

Codes

	A	B	C	D		A	B	C	D
(a)	3	1	4	2	(b)	3	4	1	2
(c)	3	1	2	4	(d)	1	3	2	4

5. Which of the following process produce very pure hydrogen?

(a) By the reaction of methane with steam
(b) By electrolysis of water
(c) By reaction of salt hydrides with water.
(d) By mixing hydrocarbons of high molecular weight.

6. When H_2O_2 is added to a cold acidified solution of potassium dichromate followed by shaking with an ether in a separatory funnel, we observe

(a) a blue colour in ether layer due to formation of a Cr(III)-salt.
(b) a blue colour in ether layer due to formation of CrO_5.
(c) an orange colour in aqueous layer due to formation $CrO_2(OH)_2$.
(d) a green colour in aqueous layer due to formation of a Cr (IV) salt.

7. H_2O_2 acts as a reducing agent in which of the given below reactions?

I. $H_2O_2 + 2e^- \longrightarrow 2OH^-$
II. $H_2O_2 - 2e^- \longrightarrow O_2 + 2H^+$
III. $H_2O_2 + 2H^+ + 2e^- \longrightarrow 2H_2O$
IV. $H_2O_2 + 2OH^- - 2e^- \longrightarrow O_2 + 2H_2O$

(a) I and III (b) III and IV
(c) II and IV (d) II and III

8. In which of the following reactions, H_2O_2 acts as a reducing agent?

(a) $Na_2AsO_3 + H_2O_2 \longrightarrow Na_3AsO_4 + H_2O$
(b) $Fe^{2+} + H_2O_2 \longrightarrow Fe^{3+} + OH^-$
(c) $PbS + H_2O_2 \longrightarrow PbSO_4 + H_2O$
(d) $[Fe(CN)_6]^{3-} + OH^- + H_2O_2 \longrightarrow [Fe(CN)_6]^{4+} + H_2O + O_2$

9. Given below are two statements.

Statement I H_2O_2 undergoes disproportionation even on warming.

Statement II On thermal decomposition H_2O_2 produces H_2O and O_2 molecules.

In the light of the above statements, choose the most appropriate answer from the options given below.

(a) Both Statement I and Statement II are correct
(b) Statement I is incorrect but Statement II is correct
(c) Both Statement I and Statement II are incorrect
(d) Statement I is correct but Statement II is incorrect.

10. Among the following statements regarding heavy water, which one is incorrect?

(a) It reacts with CaC_2 to produce C_2D_2 and $Ca(OD)_2$.

(b) It reacts with Al_4C_3 to produce CD_4 and $Al(OD)_3$.

(c) It reacts with SO_3 to produce deuterated sulphuric acid (D_2SO_4).

(d) It reacts with $(CH_3)_3$ CMgCl to produce $(CH_3)_3CDCl$ and $Mg(OD)_2$.

Section B *Numerical Value Questions*

11. Normality of "0.9 volume" H_2O_2 solution is ....

12. Consider the following statements.

(a) $[Fe(CN)_6]^{4-}$ reacts with hydrogen peroxide in acidic medium to form $[Fe(CN)_6]^{3-}$ and water.

(b) In the preparation of sodium peroxoborate, H_2O_2 is treated with sodium metaborate.

(c) 2-ethylanthraquinol is used in the preparation of H_2O_2.

(d) On the decomposition of H_2O_2, oxygen gas is produced.

The number of correct statements is ....

13. If soluble hydroxide precipitates of Be and Al become soluble in excess of NaOH solution as,

$$Be(OH)_2(s) \xrightarrow[\text{(Excess)}]{OH^-} [Be(OH)_x]^{y-}(aq)$$

$$Al(OH)_3(s) \xrightarrow[\text{(Excess)}]{OH^-} [Al(OH)_a]^{b-}$$

The value of $\left(\frac{x+y}{a+b}\right)$ is ....

14. Degree of hardness (in ppm) of a 1 L water sample containing 12 mg of $MgSO_4$ is .... [density of water = 1 kg/L]

15. Permutit is a water softener. It is sodium aluminosilicate or sodium zeolite. If it is written as $Na_x[Al_ySi_zO_{x'} \cdot xH_2O]$. The value of $\left(\frac{x+y+z}{x'}\right)$ will be ....

Answers

Section A

1 (a)	2 (d)	3 (a)	4 (c)	5 (b)
6 (b)	7 (c)	8 (d)	9 (a)	10 (d)

Section B

11 (0.16)	12 (4)	13 (1.20)	14 (10)	15 (0.75)

See detailed solutions on page no. 230

QUALIFIER 15

s-Block Elements (Alkali and Alkaline Earth Metals)

Section A Objective Type Questions

1. Identify the correct matching of pairs from the following.

(a) CH_4 : Electron-precise covalent hydride
NH_3 : Metallic hydride

(b) BeH_2 : Electron-deficient covalent hydride
LiH : Ionic hydride

(c) NH_3 : Electron-rich covalent hydride
$LaH_{2.87}$: Ionic hydride

(d) CaH_2 : Ionic hydride
B_2H_6 : Electron-deficient covalent hydride

2. The correct order of thermal stability of group 1 metal hydrides is

(a) $LiH > NaH > KH > RbH > CsH$
(b) $LiH < NaH < KH < RbH < CsH$
(c) $KH > NaH > LiH > CsH > RbH$
(d) $NaH > LiH > KH > RbH > CsH$

3. Which of the following statements regarding alkali metals is/are not true?

I. The strength of alkali metal hydroxides decreases down the group.
II. The conductivity of alkali metal ions in water increases down the group.
III. Melting points of halides of a given alkali metal follow the order, $MF < MCl < MBr < MI$.
IV. Melting points of LiX (X can be F, Cl, Br and I) are greater than those of the corresponding halides of Na.

Choose the correct option.

(a) I, II, III and IV
(b) I, II and III
(c) I, III and IV
(d) II and IV

4. Lithium is the strongest reducing agent among all alkali metals ($E^\circ_{Li^+/Li} = -3.04V$) which is due to (in comparison to other alkali metals)

(a) highest positive value of $\Delta_{sub}H^\circ$ for Li.
(b) highest positive value of $\Delta_i H^\circ$ for Li.
(c) highest negative value of $\Delta_{hyd}H^\circ$ for Li^+.
(d) All of the above

5. K_2CO_3 cannot be prepared by Solvay process because

(a) $KHCO_3$ is fairly soluble in water at 298 K.
(b) K_2CO_3 is fairly soluble in water at 298 K.
(c) K_2CO_3 decomposes in water.
(d) $KHCO_3$ is hygroscopic in nature.

6. Given below are two statements.

Statement I We cannot store NaOH solution in a vessel made of Zn or Al.

Statement II A protective layer of ZnO or Al_2O_3 will be formed when Zn or Al reacts with NaOH solution.

In the light of the above statements, choose the most appropriate answer from the options given below.

(a) Both Statement I and Statement II are correct.
(b) Statement I is correct but Statement II is incorrect.
(c) Statement I is incorrect but Statement II is correct.
(d) Both Statement I and Statement II are incorrect.

7. A hard water sample containing $MgCl_2$ is passed through calgon. Mg^{2+} ions get removed by calgon due to formation of a precipitate of composition.

(a) $Mg[Na_4(PO_3)_6]$
(b) $Mg[Mg_2(PO_3)_6]$
(c) $Na_2[Mg_2(PO_3)_6]$
(d) $Mg[Na_2Mg(PO_3)_6]$

8. Which of the following statements is correct?

(a) Alkaline earth metals are harder and denser than alkali metals.
(b) Alkali metals are less electropositive than alkaline earth metals.
(c) IE_1 of Na is higher than that of Mg.
(d) None of the above

9. On heating separately : $LiNO_3$, $NaNO_3$ and $Mg(NO_3)_2$ produce a common substance (X) which is

(a) N_2, a diamagnetic gas
(b) O_2, a diamagnetic gas
(c) NO_2, a paramagnetic gas
(d) O_2, a paramagnetic gas

10. Among these group 2 metal hydrides,

CaH_2, BaH_2, MgH_2 and BeH_2

their order of ionic nature will be

(a) $CaH_2 > BaH_2 > MgH_2 > BeH_2$
(b) $BaH_2 > CaH_2 > MgH_2 > BeH_2$
(c) $BeH_2 > MgH_2 > CaH_2 > BaH_2$
(d) $MgH_2 > BeH_2 > CaH_2 > BaH_2$

11. Solubility of group 2 metal sulphates decreases down the group in contrary to their ionic character which increases down the group because

(a) they become more ionic down the group.

(b) lattice enthalpy (numerical value) increases down the group, so that it cannot overcome their respective enthalpy of solution (numerical value).

(c) numerical value of hydration enthalpy decreases significantly from Be^{2+} to Ba^{2+}.

(d) Both (b) and (c)

12. Which of the following statements is incorrect regarding beryllium and aluminium?

(a) Charge/radius ratio of Al^{3+} is higher than that of Be^{2+}.

(b) In excess of alkali, both of their hydroxides become soluble.

(c) $BeCl_2$ and $AlCl_3$ are dimeric in vapour phase.

(d) With excess of F^- ions, Be^{2+} and Al^{3+} can form complexes, which are $[BeF_4]^{2-}$ and $[AlF_6]^{3-}$ respectively.

13. Calcium imide on hydrolysis liberates a gas (*P*) which on reaction with bleaching powder liberates another gas (*Q*). (*Q*) on burning with Mg produces a white solid (*R*) which on boiling with water gives off the gas (*P*). (*P*), (*Q*) and (*R*) are respectively

(a) NH_3, NO_2 and $Mg(NO_3)_2$

(b) N_2, NH_3 and MgO

(c) NH_3, N_2 and Mg_3N_2

(d) NH_3, N_2, Mg(NH)

Section B *Numerical Value Questions*

14. *s*-block metals readily form liquid ammonia solution which is blue coloured, paramagnetic, strongly reducing and good conductor of electricity. Let us take, sodium and calcium for this purpose. They get dissolved in *aq*.NH_3 as,

(i) $Na(s) + (x + y)NH_3(l) \rightarrow \underbrace{[Na(NH_3)_x]^+ + [e(NH_3)_y]^-}_{\text{Ammoniated ions and electrons}}$

(ii) $Ca(s) + (a + b)NH_3 \longrightarrow \underbrace{[Ca(NH_3)_a]^{2+} + 2[e(NH_3)]^-}_{\text{Ammoniated ions and electrons}}$

The value of $(x + a)$ is ....

15. Among *s*-block metals (excluding Fr and Ra), *x* number and *y* number of metal(s) impart(s) crimson red colour to the flame and do(es) not impart colour to the flame in the flame test respectively. The value of (*xy*) is ....

16. When gypsum is heated at 120°C and above 120°C, *x* and *y* number molecules of H_2O get lost respectively form one gypsum molecule. The value of $(x \div y)$ is ....

17. A typical 70 kg adult body contains *x* g of Na, *y* g of K, *a* g of Mg and *b* g of Ca compared with only 5 g of Fe and 0.06 g Cu. The value of $\left(\frac{a+b}{x+y}\right)$ is ....

Answers

Section A

1 (d)	2 (a)	3 (c)	4 (d)	5 (a)
6 (b)	7 (c)	8 (a)	9 (d)	10 (b)
11 (d)	12 (a)	13 (c)		

Section B

14 (10)	15 (4)	16 (0.75)	17 (4.71)	

See detailed solutions on page no. 231

QUALIFIER 16

p-Block Elements

Section A Objective Type Questions

1. Aluminium and gallium have nearly the same atomic radii, which is due to
(a) greater shielding by s-electrons of Ga-atoms
(b) poor shielding by s-electrons of Al-atoms
(c) poor shielding by d-electrons of Ga-atoms
(d) poor shielding by d-electrons of Al-atoms

2. Consider the following reactions.

I. $Al + N_2 \xrightarrow{\Delta} P \xrightarrow[\Delta]{H_2O} Q + R$

II. $Al + R \xrightarrow{\Delta} P + S$ (gas, burns in air)

In the above reactions, P, Q, R and S are respectively
(a) $Al(NH_2)_3$, AlN, NH_3 and O_2 (b) AlN, AlH_3, N_2 and H_2
(c) AlN, $Al(OH)_3$, NH_3 and H_2 (d) Al_2N_3, Al_2O_3, NH_4OH and O_2

3. Match the following columns.

	Column I		Column II
A.	$2B + N_2 \rightarrow 2BN$	1.	Al, Ga and In only (M)
B.	$2M + 3I_2 \rightarrow 2MI_3]$	2.	At very high temperature
C.	$MI + I_2 \rightarrow M^+[I_3]^-$	3.	Tl only (M)
D.	$4M + 3O_2 \rightarrow 2M_2O_3$	4.	Ga only superficially oxidised (M)

Codes

	A	B	C	D		A	B	C	D
(a)	1	2	3	4	(b)	3	4	1	2
(c)	2	1	3	4	(d)	2	3	1	4

4. Anhydrous dimeric aluminium chloride (Al_2Cl_6) is a covalent compound but it is fairly soluble in water due to the formation of
(a) Al^{3+} and Cl^- ions
(b) $[Al(H_2O)_6]^{3+}$ and Cl^- ions
(c) $[Al(H_2O)_4Cl_2]^+$ and $[Al(H_2O)_2Cl_4]^-$ ions
(d) None of the above

5. Given below are two statements.
Statement I All B—H bonds in diborane are similar.
Statement II In diborane, the two H—B—H angles are nearly 97° and 120°.
In the light of the above statements, choose the most appropriate answer from the options given below.
(a) Both statement I and Statement II are correct.
(b) Statement I is incorrect but Statement II is correct.
(c) Both statement I and Statement II are incorrect.
(d) Statement I is correct but statement II is incorrect.

6. During the preparation of a silicon polymer, its chain length can be controlled by addition of
(a) $(CH_3)_3SiCl$ (b) $(CH_3)_2SiCl_2$
(c) CH_3SiCl_3 (d) $(CH_3)_4Si$

7. Given below are two statements.
Statement I PbF_4 is a good fluorinating agent.
Statement II PbF_2 is more stable than PbF_4 because effective nuclear charge on s-orbital electrons is higher due to poor shielding of d-orbitals.
In the light of the above statements, choose the most appropriate answer from the options given below.
(a) Both statement I and Statement II are correct.
(b) Statement I is incorrect but Statement II is correct.
(c) Both statement I and Statement II are incorrect.
(d) Statement I is correct but statement II is incorrect.

8. Silanol, $(CH_3)_3SiOH$ is more acidic than tertiary butyl alcohol, $(CH_3)_3COH$. It is because
(a) silicon is more electronegative than carbon.
(b) $d\pi(Si)$-$p\pi(O)$ bond is present in $(CH_3)_3SiOH$.
(c) $p\pi(C)$-$p\pi(O)$ bond is present in $(CH_3)_3COH$.
(d) CH_3 group shows $-I$ effect in $(CH_3)_3SiOH$.

9. The correct order of boiling points of group 15 hydrides of formula, $:MH_3$ is
(a) $NH_3 > BiH_3 > SbH_3 > AsH_3 > PH_3$
(b) $NH_3 > PH_3 > AsH_3 > SbH_3 > BiH_3$
(c) $BiH_3 > SbH_3 > AsH_3 > PH_3 > NH_3$
(d) $BiH_3 > SbH_3 > NH_3 > AsH_3 > PH_3$

10. Which of the following composition of the chlorides in solid state has (have) been represented correctly?
(a) Ga_2Cl_4 as $[Ga]^+[GaCl_4]^-$
(b) PCl_5 as $[PCl_4]^+[PCl_6]^-$
(c) ICl_3 as $[ICl_2]^+[ICl_4]^-$
(d) All of the above

11. Which of the following statements is not correct?
(a) Pure HNO_3 is a light yellow liquid
(b) H_2SO_4 with water forms an azeotropic mixture containing 98.3% of acid
(c) Conc. HNO_3 when mixed with conc. H_2SO_4 produces nitronium ion
(d) Covalent nitrates are less stable than ionic nitrates.

12. White phosphorus when separately reacts with thionyl chloride and sulphuryl chloride, we get respectively
(a) PCl_5 and PCl_3 (b) PCl_3 and PCl_5
(c) SO_2 and SO_2 (d) Both (b) and (c)

13. Which of the following acids does not include S—S linkage?
(a) Dithionous acid (b) Dithionic acid
(c) Polythionic acid (d) Pyrosulphuric acid

14. Identify *A*, *B* and *C* in the following reactions,
I. $A(aq) + H_2SO_4(\text{dil.}) \longrightarrow B(g) + H_2O(l)$
II. $B(g) + K_2Cr_2O_7 + H_2SO_4(\text{dil.}) \longrightarrow$ Green coloured solution of compound, $C(aq)$
(a) $A = H_2S, B = SO_2, C = CrO_3$
(b) $A = SO_3^{2-}$-salt, $B = SO_2$, $C = Cr_2(SO_4)_3$
(c) $A = SO_3^{2-}$-salt, $B = SO_3$, $C = Cr_2O_3$
(d) $A = SO_4^{2-}$-salt, $B = H_2$, $C = Cr_2(SO_4)_3$

15. Which of the following order is not in accordance with the property mentioned?
(a) $F_2 > Cl_2 > Br_2 > I_2$ (oxidising power)
(b) $Cl(OH) > OCl(OH) > O_2Cl(OH) > O_3Cl(OH)$ (oxidising power)
(c) $F_2 > Cl_2 > Br_2 > I_2$ (bond dissociation enthalpy)
(d) $HI > HBr > HCl > HF$ (acid strength)

16. For which of the following reactions, $\Delta G° > 0$?
(a) $2KCl + I_2 \longrightarrow 2KI + Cl_2$ (b) $2NaI + Br_2 \longrightarrow 2NaBr + I_2$
(c) $2KClO_3 + I_2 \longrightarrow KIO_3 + Cl_2$ (d) Both (a) and (c)

17. In the following reactions,
$F_2 \xrightarrow[\text{Cold, dilute}]{\text{NaOH}} A + B + H_2O$; $Cl_2 \xrightarrow[\text{Dry}]{\text{Ca(OH)}_2} C + D + H_2O$
Identify *A*, *B*, *C* and *D* from the options given as

	A	B	C	D		A	B	C	D
(a)	NaF	O_3	$CaOCl_2$	$CaCl_2$	(b)	NaF	O_2	$Ca(OCl)_2$	Cl_2O
(c)	NaF	OF_2	$Ca(OCl)_2$	$CaCl_2$	(d)	NaF	OF_2	Cl_2O_3	$CaCl_2$

18. In the reaction (Ph = Phenyl group, C_6H_5),
$[Ph_4As][Cl] + Cl_2 \xrightarrow{195K} [Ph_4As][Cl_3]$
(a) Cl_2 acts as a Lewis acid (b) Cl_2 acts as a Lewis base
(c) Cl_2 acts as a reducing agent (d) Cl_2 acts as an oxidising agent

19. In which of the following oxides, $d\pi$-$p\pi$ bond(s) is(are) present?
(a) Cl_2O_3 (b) XeO_3
(c) Both (a) and (b) (d) None of these

20. Which of the following statements is incorrect regarding xenon and xenon fluorides?
(a) The processes, $Xe(g) \longrightarrow Xe^+(g) + e^-$ and $O_2(g) \longrightarrow O_2^+(g) + e^-$, involved more or less equal ionisation energy.
(b) Shape of $XeOF_2$ molecule is trigonal planar.
(c) XeF_2 possesses a trigonal bipyramidal geometry where Xe and F-atoms are placed linearly and the three lone pairs are occupying equatorial positions.
(d) XeF_4 is regarded as pseudo-octahedral with fluorine occupying the corners of a square plane.

Section B Numerical Value Questions

21. The number of bases from which TlOH is stronger are ......
$Tl(OH)_3$, $Ga(OH)_3$, $In(OH)_3$, $B(OH)_3$, KOH, NH_4OH

22. Borax structure contains,
$BO_4 = x$ number of unit(s), $BO_3 = y$ number of unit(s)
Number of sp^2 boron atom(s) $= a$
Number of sp^3 boron atom(s) $= b$
The value of $(ab)^{xy}$ is ....

23. The number of disubstituted borazine molecules are possible without changing the basic ring structure are ....

24. Equivalent weight (in g) of boric acid and water is ....
(B = 11, O = 16, H = 1)

25. One fullerene unit (C_{60}) contains '*p*' number of pentagons and '*h*' number of hexagons. The value of $\frac{p}{h}$ is ....

26. Number of P—O—P bonds in P_4O_6 and P_4O_{10} are *x* and *y* respectively. If number of S—O—S bonds in S_3O_8 is *z*, the value of $\left(\frac{y+z}{x}\right)$ is ....

27. Among the following, the number of compounds that react with PCl_5 to give $POCl_3$ is ....
[O_2, CO_2, H_2O, SO_2, H_2SO_4, P_4O_{10}, C_2H_5OH, CH_3COOH]

28. Let the molecular formulae of sulphuric acid crystal is, $H_2SO_4.nH_2O$ is −190°C and chlorine water crystal at 0°C is $Cl_2.mH_2O$.
The value of (*mn*) is ....

29. In the general formula of monomeric interhalogen compounds in AB_n, the sum of the possible values of *n* will be ....

30. When Xe and F_2 react in presence of catalyst and at elevated conditions of pressure and temperature, we get xenon fluorides, XeF_n (n = 2, 4 and 6) for the molar ratio of Xe and F_2, 1 : *x* we get XeF_2 1 : *y* we get XeF_4 and 1 : *z* we get XeF_6
The value of $(x + y + z)$ is ....

Answers

Section A

1 (c)	2 (c)	3 (c)	4 (b)	5 (b)
6 (a)	7 (a)	8 (b)	9 (d)	10 (d)
11 (a)	12 (d)	13 (d)	14 (b)	15 (c)
16 (a)	17 (c)	18 (a)	19 (c)	20 (b)

Section B

21 (5)	22 (256)	23 (4)	24 (62)	25 (0.60)
26 (1.50)	27 (6)	28 (16)	29 (16)	30 (25.50)

See detailed solutions on page no. 232

QUALIFIER 17

d-and f-Block Elements

Section A Objective Type Questions

1. Anhydrous Co^{2+} compounds and hydrated Co^{2+} compounds absorb red and blue/green radiations respectively. The colour of these compounds will be respectively
(a) red and blue/green (b) blue/green and red
(c) red and red (d) blue/green and blue/green

2. Cu^+ ion is unstable in aqueous solution, because
(a) Cu^+ ion has $3d^{10}$ configuration
(b) Cu^+ ion undergoes disproportionation in aqueous solution with a value, $E° = 0.18$ V
(c) Cu^+ ion has pseudo inert configuration
(d) Both (a) and (b)

3. Consider the following statements for transition elements.
I. Transition elements show variable oxidation states because energy difference between $(n-1)d$ and ns sub-shells is small.
II. All transition elements exhibit a minimum oxidation state of (+2) except in case of Cr, Cu, Ag, Au and Hg, which show minimum oxidation state of (+1).
III. V^{2+} and Mn^{2+} salts are very weak reducing agents.
IV. Atomic radii of 3*d*-series first decreases till the middle, becomes almost constant, then decreases and finally reaches to a higher value.
The correct statements are
(a) I, II and III (b) II, III and IV
(c) I, III and IV (d) I, II, III and IV

4. Match the properties in Column I with the metals given in Column II.

	Column I		Column II
A.	An element which can show +8 oxidation state	1.	Mn
B.	An element of first row transition series able to show +7 oxidation state	2.	Cr
C.	Highest melting transition metal	3.	Os
D.	Radioactive lanthanoid	4.	W
		5.	Pm

Codes

	A	B	C	D		A	B	C	D
(a)	3	2	2	4	(b)	3	1	2	5
(c)	4	1	2	4	(d)	3	1	4	5

5. In +8 oxidation state of osmium (Os) its known compounds is/are
(a) OsF_8 (b) OsO_4 (c) $OsCl_8$ (d) All of these

6. Which transition elements do not show variable oxidation states?
(a) Sc and Y (b) Y and La
(c) Y and Ac (d) Sc, Y, La and Ac

7. The intense orange colour of $K_2Cr_2O_7$ is due to
(a) $M \rightarrow L$ charge transfer transition
(b) $L \rightarrow M$ charge transfer transition
(c) *d*-*d* transition
(d) σ-σ transition

8. Given below are two statements.
Statement I To a solution of potassium chromate, when H_2SO_4 is added, it changes its colour from yellow to orange.
Statement II The colour change is due to the change in oxidation state of chromium of potassium chromate.
In the light of the above statements, choose the most appropriate answer from the options given below.
(a) Both Statement I and Statement II are correct.
(b) Both Statement I and Statement II are incorrect.
(c) Statement I is correct but Statement II is incorrect.
(d) Statement II is correct but Statement I is incorrect.

9. For a paramagnetic substance, the ratio :
$$\frac{\text{Mass of a substance in a magnetic field}}{\text{Actual mass of the substance}}$$
(a) is greater than 1.0 (b) is less than 1.0
(c) is equal to 1.0 (d) cannot be predicted

10. Which of the following statement is incorrect?
(a) Across a period, from Sc to Cu the densities increase with increasing atomic number.
(b) Transition metals have high enthalpies of atomization and in 3*d*-series increase regularly from Sc to Cu.
(c) On going down a group, from 3*d* to 6*d*-series, the stability of higher oxidation state increases with increasing atomic number.
(d) The melting point of transition elements rise to a maximum from Sc to Cr and then decreases from Fe to Zn.

11. The conversion of chromate ion, CrO_4^{2-} to dichromate, $Cr_2O_7^{2-}$ in the acidic medium is an example of
(a) redox reaction (b) neutralisation reaction
(c) condensation reaction (d) rearrangement reaction

12. Potassium permanganate acts as an oxidising agent in both of the conditions, alkaline and acidic. Here, MnO_4^- changes into X and Y, which are respectively
(a) MnO_2 and MnO_4^{2-}
(b) MnO_4^{2-} and Mn^{2+}
(c) MnO_2 and Mn^{3+}
(d) MnO^{2+} and Mn^+

13. When MnO_2 is fused with KOH in presence of air, a coloured compound is formed which is
(a) $KMnO_4$, purple
(b) Mn_3O_4, black
(c) Mn_2O_3, brown
(d) K_2MnO_4, dark green

14. Which of the following elements has the largest atomic radius?
(a) $_{61}Nd$ (b) $_{62}Sm$
(c) $_{63}Eu$ (d) $_{64}Gd$

15. Which of the following statements regarding basicity of lanthanoid (III) ions (Ln^{3+}) is correct?
(a) Basicity decreases with increase in ionic radius
(b) Basicity decreases with decrease in ionic radius
(c) More basic oxo-salt decomposes more readily than the less basic oxo-salt
(d) More basic ions hydrolyse faster

16. Which of the following pair of ions have the same colour?
(a) $_{58}Ce^{3+}$, $_{63}Eu^{3+}$ (b) $_{59}Pr^{3+}$, $_{64}Gd^{3+}$
(c) $_{62}Sm^{3+}$, $_{66}Dy^{3+}$ (d) $_{71}Lu^{3+}$, $_{69}Tm^{3+}$

17. Basicity of lanthanoid, hydroxides, $Ln(OH)_3$ can be compared as
(a) $Sr(OH)_2 > Fe(OH)_3 > Ln(OH)_3$
(b) $Ln(OH)_3 > Fe(OH)_3 > Sr(OH)_2$
(c) $Ln(OH)_3 > Sr(OH)_2 > Fe(OH)_3$
(d) $Sr(OH)_2 > Ln(OH)_3 > Fe(OH)_3$

18. Which of the following statements is not correct?
(a) $La(OH)_3$ is less basic than $Lu(OH)_3$
(b) La does not belong to lanthanoids
(c) In the series of lanthanoids (Ln), ionic radius of Ln^{3+} decreases with increase in atomic number
(d) Atomic radii of Zr and Hf are same because of lanthanoid contraction

19. Which of the following tripositive lanthanoid ion(s), (Ln^{3+}) is(are) most likely to react with $CrCl_2$?
(a) Sm^{3+} (b) Eu^{3+}
(c) Yb^{3+} (d) All of these

20. Actinoids have higher tendency to form complex as compared to lanthanoids because
(a) they have higher charge density
(b) poor shielding 5*f* electrons compared to 4*f* electrons
(c) they show variable oxidation states
(d) they have higher atomic masses

Section B *Numerical Value Questions*

21. In acidic medium, equivalent weight of $KMnO_4$ (K = 39, Mn = 55, O = 16) as an oxidant is ....

22. In a dichromate ion, '*a*' number of Cr—O bonds are present which are of two types, type I and type II. Number of type-I and type-II bonds are '*b*' and '*c*' respectively where, $b < c$. The value of $\left(\frac{a}{bc}\right)$ is ....

23. $K_2Cr_2O_7$ on fusion with KOH and H_2O_2 produces a reddish brown compound, $K_3[CrO_a]$ in which oxidation state of Cr is $+b$. The value of $\frac{a}{b}$ is ....

24. Consider the following list of reagents, acidified $K_2Cr_2O_7$, alkaline $KMnO_4$, $CuSO_4$, H_2O_2, Cl_2, O_3, $FeCl_3$, HNO_3 and $Na_2S_2O_3$. The total number of reagents that can oxidise aqueous iodide to iodine is........

25. Solid potassium dichromate (K = 39, Cr = 52, O = 16) on thermal decomposition liberates oxygen gas. In this intramolecular redox reaction, equivalent weight of potassium dichromate is.......

26. How many of the following pairs have nearly same radii? (Zr, Hf); (Cr, Mn); (Nb^{3+}, Ta^{3+}); (Zr^{4+}, Hf^{4+}); (Nb, Ta); (Mn, Fe)

27. The spin only magnetic moment (in BM) of dipositive gadolinium ion is ....

28. From the given set of ions, *x* number of ions show reducing property and *y* number of ions show oxidising property in aqueous solution. The value of $\left(\frac{x}{y}\right)$ is ....
Cr^{2+}, Ce^{4+}, Pr^{4+}, Sm^{2+}, Eu^{2+}, Tb^{4+}, Dy^{4+}, Tm^{2+}, Yb^{2+}

29. Among the actinoids, if number of transuranic elements $= x$, and number of radioactive elements $= y$, then the value of $\frac{x}{y}$ is $a \times 10^{-2}$. The value of *a* is ....

30. Two common oxidation states of lanthanoids and actinoids are $+x$ and $+y$. The value of $\frac{x}{y}$ is (when $x < y$) ....

Answers

Section A

1 (b)	2 (d)	3 (d)	4 (d)	5 (b)
6 (d)	7 (b)	8 (c)	9 (a)	10 (b)
11 (c)	12 (b)	13 (d)	14 (c)	15 (b)
16 (c)	17 (d)	18 (a)	19 (d)	20 (a)

Section B

21 (31.60)	22 (0.67)	23 (1.6)	24 (7)	25 (14.7)
26 (6)	27 (8.94)	28 (1.25)	29 (78.57)	30 (0.75)

See detailed solutions on page no. 235

QUALIFIER 18

Coordination Compounds

Section A Objective Type Questions

1. An octahedral complex of molecular formula $[Co(en)_2(NCS)_2Br]$ reacts with ethylene diamine but fails to respond to $AgNO_3$ test. Hence, the complex is
(a) *trans-bis*(ethylenediamine)dithiocyanato(N) cobalt (III) bromide.
(b) *trans*-bromido*bis*(ethylenediamine)thiocyanato (N)cobalt(III) thiocyanate.
(c) *cis*-bromido*bis*(ethylenediamine)thiocyanato(N)cobalt(III) thiocyanate.
(d) *cis-bis*(ethylenediamine)dithiocyanato(N)cobalt(III) bromide.

2. Regarding the complex $[Pt(Gly)_2Cl_2]$ which of the following statements is false? (Gly $= H_2NCH_2COO^-$)
(a) For this complex, a total six isomers are possible.
(b) It can exhibit geometrical isomerism.
(c) It can have optical isomers.
(d) It can exhibit linkage isomerism.

3. The IUPAC name of $K_2[Cr(CN)_2O_2(O)_2(NH_3)]$ is
(a) potassium amminedicyanidodioxoperoxochromate (VI)
(b) potassium amminecyanidoperoxodioxochromium (VI)
(c) potassium amminecyanidoperoxodioxochromium (IV)
(d) potassium amminecyanidoperoxodioxochromate (IV)

4. Combination of NH_3, Cl^-, K^+ and one Pt(IV) results in the formation of complexes of coordination number 6 and 4 (which have different molecular formula). Out of which *y* number of complex(es) exists(s) as geometrical isomers. Find *y*.
(a) 2 (b) 4 (c) 6 (d) 5

5. The platinum complex of NH_3 and Cl ligands is an anti-tumor agent. The correct isomeric formula of the complex and its precursor are
(a) *cis*-$Pt(NH_3)_2Cl_2$ and $PtCl_4^{2-}$
(b) *trans*-$Pt(NH_3)_2Cl_2$ and $PtCl_4^{2-}$
(c) *cis*-$Pt(NH_3)_2Cl_2$ and $Pt(NH_3)_4^{2+}$
(d) *trans*-$Pt(NH_3)_2Cl_2$ and $Pt(NH_3)_4^{2+}$

6. Which of the following pairs of complexes are isomeric with each other but their aqueous solutions exhibit different molar conductivities?
(a) $[PtCl_2(NH_3)_4]Br_2$ and $[PtBr_2(NH_3)_4]Cl_2$
(b) $[CoCl_2(NH_3)_4]NO_2$ and $[CoCl(NO_2)(NH_3)_4]Cl$
(c) $[Co(NO_2)(NH_3)_5]Cl_2$ and $[Co(ONO)(NH_3)_5]Cl_2$
(d) $[CoBr(NH_3)_5]SO_4$ and $[Co(SO_4)(NH_3)_5]Br$

7. Match Column I and Column II and choose the correct option from the codes given below :

	Column I		Column II
A.	$[Ni(CN)_4]^{2-}$	1.	Ti^{4+}
B.	Chlorophyll	2.	sp^3, paramagnetic
C.	*Ziegler-Natta* catalyst	3.	Non-planar
D.	$[NiCl_4]^{2-}$	4.	Mg^{2+}
		5.	Planar
		6.	dsp^2; diamagnetic

Codes

	A	B	C	D		A	B	C	D
(a)	6	4	1	2,3	(b)	2	4	1	2,3
(c)	2	4	1	6,5	(d)	6	4	1	2,5

8. Which of the following is incorrect distribution of electron in *d*-orbitals of metal in corresponding complex?

(a) $[NiCl_4]^{2-}$
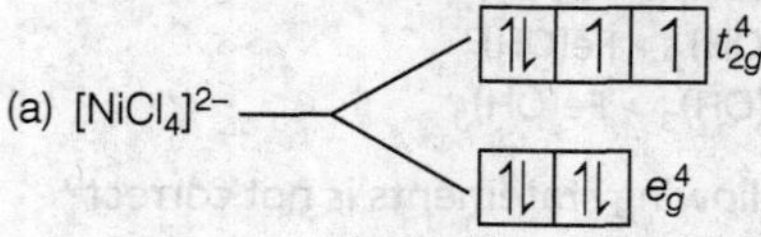

(b) $[Ni(NH_3)_6]^{2+}$
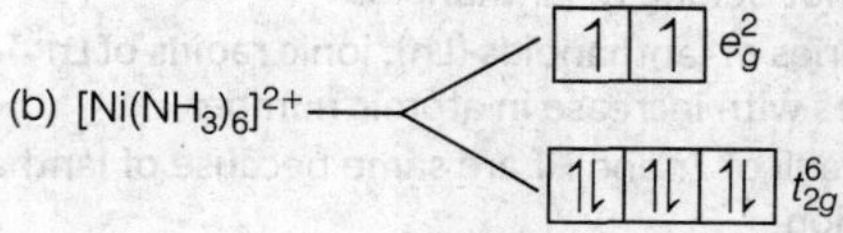

(c) $[Co(H_2O)_6]^{3+}$
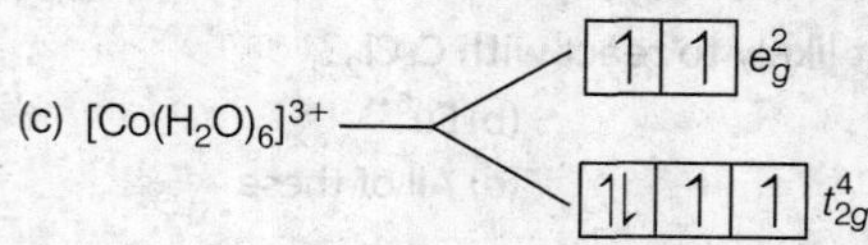

(d) $[Co(SCN)_4]^{2-}$
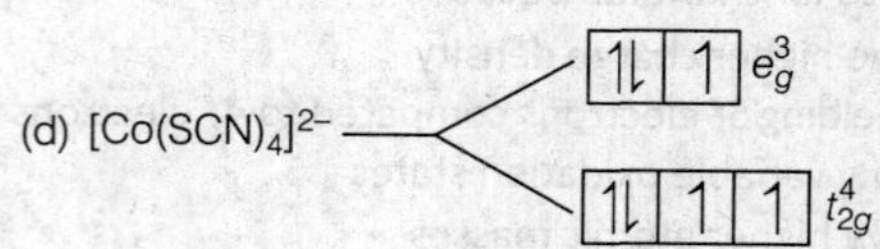

9. Which statement is incorrect regarding crystal field theory?
(a) There is no interaction between metal orbitals and ligand orbitals.
(b) In most transition metal complexes, either six or four ligands surround the metal because they give spherically symmetrical field.
(c) Generally the crystal field splitting energy (Δ) for different ligands is in the order, N-donors < O-donors < C-donors.
(d) Only CO among different ligands can form back bonding (π-bond from metal to ligand).

10. The Δ_t of (I) $[CoCl_4]^{2-}$, (II) $[CoBr_4]^{2-}$ and (III) $[Co(NCS)_4]^{2-}$ follows the order
(a) III > I > II (b) I > II > III (c) II > I > III (d) III > II > I

11. The magnetic moment of an octahedral Co^{+2} complex is 4.0 BM. The electronic configuration of the complex is
(a) $t_{2g}^5 e_g^2$ (b) $t_{2g}^6 e_g^1$ (c) $t_{2g}^3 e_g^4$ (d) $t_{2g}^4 e_g^3$

12. A $[M(H_2O)_6]^{2+}$ complex typically absorbs at around 600 nm. It is allowed to react with ammonia to form a new complex $[M(NH_3)_6]^{2+}$ that should have absorption at
(a) 800 nm (b) 580 nm (c) 620 nm (d) 320 nm

13. The light pink colour of $[Co(H_2O)_6]^{2+}$ and the deep blue colour of $[CoCl_4]^{2-}$ are due to
(a) *MLCT* transition in the first and *d-d* transition in the second
(b) *LMCT* transitions in both
(c) *d-d* transitions in both
(d) *d-d* transition in the first and *MLCT* transition in the second

14. The correct order of wavelength of absorption (λ_{max}) of the Cr-complexes is (en = ethylenediamine)
(a) $[CrF_6]^{3-} > [Cr(H_2O)_6]^{3+} > [Cr(en)_3]^{3+} > [Cr(CN)_6]^{3-}$
(b) $[Cr(H_2O)_6]^{3+} > [CrF_6]^{3-} > [Cr(en)_3]^{3+} > [Cr(CN)_6]^{3-}$
(c) $[Cr(CN)_6]^{3-} > [Cr(en)_3]^{3+} > Cr(H_2O)_6]^{3+} > [CrF_6]^{3-}$
(d) $[Cr(en)_3]^{3+} > [Cr(CN)_6]^{3-} > Cr(H_2O)_6]^{3+} > [CrF_6]^{3-}$

15. The red colour of oxy-haemoglobin is mainly due to the
(a) *d-d* transition
(b) metal to ligand charge transfer transition
(c) ligand to metal charge transfer transition
(d) inter-ligand $\pi \rightarrow \pi^*$ transition

16. Given below are two statements.
Statement I $[NiCl_4]^{2-}$ and $[Ni(CN)_4]^{2-}$ have different primary valencies of nickel but same secondary valency.
Statement II Both $[NiCl_4]^{2-}$ and $[Ni(CN)_4]^{2-}$ complexes absorb same wavelength radiation.
In the light of the above statements, choose the most appropriate answer from the options given below.
(a) Both statement I and Statement II are correct.
(b) Statement I is incorrect but Statement II is correct.
(c) Both statement I and Statement II are incorrect.
(d) Statement I is correct but statement II is incorrect.

17. Which one of the following configurations will show Jahn-Teller distortion in an octahedral field?
(a) High spin d^2
(b) High spin d^4
(c) High spin d^5
(d) Low spin d^6

18. In which of the following metal carbonyls the M—C bond is strongest?
(a) $[Cr(CO)_6]$
(b) $[Cr(CO)_5(CH_3NH_2)]$
(c) $[Cr(CO)_4(CH_3NH_2)_2]$
(d) $[Cr(CO)_3(CH_3NH_2)_3]$

19. Which of the following statement is incorrect?
(a) The stability constant of $[Co(NH_3)_6]^{3+}$ is larger than $[Co(NH_3)_6]^{2+}$.
(b) The cyano complexes are far more stable than those formed by halide ions.
(c) The stability of halide complexes follows the order $I^- < Br^- < Cl^-$.
(d) The stability constant of $[Cu(CN)_4]^{3-}$ is less than that of $[Cd(CN)_4]^{2-}$ ion.

20. Successive values of $\log K_f$ (30° C) for the Ni^{2+}—NH_3 system in water decreases. This is due to
(a) decrease in the probability for the attack of NH_3 on Ni—H_2O bonds.
(b) decrease in the enthalpy of substitution of H_2O by NH_3.
(c) decrease in the entropy by the substitution of H_2O by NH_3.
(d) increase in the electrostatic repulsion between ligands (their peripheral electrons).

Section B *Numerical Value Questions*

21. The value of *x* in the formula $Mo(CO)_x$ is ....

22. In *bis*(dimethylglyoximato)nickel(II), the number of Ni—N, Ni—O and intramolecular hydrogen bonds(s) are *x*, *y* and *z* respectively. The value of $(z-y)^x$ is ....

23. The optical absorption spectrum of $[Ti(H_2O)_6]^{3+}$ has an absorption maximum at 20300 cm^{-1}. The magnitude of the crystal field stabilisation energy in cm^{-1} is ....

24. For the $[Cr(H_2O_6]^{2+}$ ion, the mean pairing energy, *P* is found to be 23,500 cm^{-1}. The magnitude of Δ is 13,900 cm^{-1}. The crystal field stabilisation energy (in cm^{-1}) for the complex in configurations corresponding to low spin state will be ....

25. The enthalpy of hydration of Cr^{2+} is –460 kcal/mol. In the absence of crystal field stabilisation energy, the value of ΔH would be – 435 kcal/mol. The value of Δ_o for $[Cr(H_2O)_6]^{2+}$ is $x \times 10^4 cm^{-1}$, where x = ...

26. The enthalpy of hydration of Cr^{2+} is – 460 kcal mol^{-1}. In the absence of CFSE, the value for ΔH is – 424 kcal mol^{-1}. The value of Δ_o (in cm^{-1}) for $[Cr(H_2O)_6]^{2+}$ will be ....

27. $[Ti(NCS)_6]^{3-}$ ion exhibits a single absorption band at 544 nm. If the crystal field splitting energy is 21979×10^x kJ mol^{-1}, then the value of x is ....

28. The concentration of $[Cu(H_2O)_4]^{2+}$ (represented by $[Cu^{2+}]$) in 1.0 L of a solution made by dissolving 0.10 mol Cu^{2+} in 1.00 M aqueous ammonia found to be $x \times 10^{-13}$ M. The value of x is .... ($K_s = 1 \times 10^{12}$).

29. In dilute nitric acid solution, Fe^{3+} forms a dark red complex with thiocyanate ions (SCN^-) according to following reaction,

$$[Fe(H_2O)_6]^{3+} + SCN^- \rightleftharpoons H_2O + [Fe(H_2O)_5NCS]^{2+}$$

In one experiment, 1.0 mL of 0.20 M $[Fe(H_2O)_6]^{3+}$ was mixed with 1.0 mL of a 10^{-3} M KSCN solution and 8 mL dilute nitric acid was added. Final concentration of $[Fe(H_2O)_5(SCN)]^{2+}$ was found to be 7.3×10^{-5} M. The value of formation constant of the complex is ....

30. The overall formation constant of $[Co(NH_3)_6]^{2+}$ ion in aqueous solution is 10^5 and the standard potentials for the reduction of Co^{3+} (*aq.*) and $[Co(NH_3)_6]^{3+}$(*aq.*) are as follows:

$$Co^{3+}(aq) + e^- \rightleftharpoons Co^{2+}(aq);\ E^\circ = +1.9\ V$$

$$[Co(NH_3)_6]^{3+}(aq) + e^- \rightleftharpoons [Co(NH_3)_6]^{2+}(aq);\ E^\circ = +0.1\ V$$

The overall formation constant of the $[Co(NH_3)_6]^{3+}$ ion is 10^x where the value of 'x' is ....

Answers

Section A

1 (c)	2 (d)	3 (a)	4 (c)	5 (a)
6 (d)	7 (a)	8 (d)	9 (a)	10 (a)
11 (a)	12 (b)	13 (c)	14 (a)	15 (a)
16 (c)	17 (b)	18 (d)	19 (d)	20 (a)

Section B

21 (6)	22 (16)	23 (8120)	24 (1260)	25 (1.46)
26 (21000)	27 (–2)	28 (7.72)	29 (0.39)	30 (35)

See detailed solutions on page no. 237

QUALIFIER 19

Environmental Chemistry

Section A Objective Type Questions

1. Carbon monoxide emitted by automobiles prevents transport of oxygen in the body due to

(a) combining with oxygen to form carbon dioxide

(b) destruction of haemoglobin

(c) preventing reaction between oxygen and haemoglobin

(d) formation of stable compound with haemoglobin

2. Which of the following statements about Polar Stratospheric Clouds (PSCs) is wrong?

(a) Type I clouds are formed at about $-77°C$ and contain solid $HNO_3 \cdot 3H_2O$.

(b) Type II clouds are formed at about $-85°C$ and contain some ice.

(c) A tight whirlpool of wind called Polar Vortex is formed which surrounds Antarctica.

(d) PSCs do not show reactivity with chlorine nitrate and HCl.

3. In Antarctica, ozone depletion is due to the formation of

(a) chlorine nitrate

(b) peroxyacetyl nitrate

(c) SO_2

(d) SO_3

4. Choose the correct statement from the following.

(a) CO which is major pollutant resulting from the combustion of fuels in automobiles plays a major role in photochemical smog.

(b) Classical smog has an oxidising character, while the photochemical smog is reducing in character.

(c) Photochemical smog occurs in day time, whereas the classical smog occurs in early morning hours.

(d) During formation of smog the level of ozone in the atmosphere goes down.

5. Which of the following statements regarding photochemical smog is not true?

(a) It has high concentration of oxidising agents.

(b) It has low concentration of oxidising agents.

(c) It can be controlled by controlling the release of NO_2, hydrocarbons, ozone etc.

(d) Plantation of some plants like pinus helps in controlling photochemical smog.

6. Given below are two statements.

Statement I Freons, chlorofluorocarbons are inert. Chemically, they do not react with ozone in stratosphere.

Statement II Freons and chlorofluorocarbons liberate chlorine radical by action of ultraviolet light.

In the light of the above statements, choose the most appropriate answer from the options given below.

(a) Both statement I and Statement II are correct.

(b) Statement I is incorrect but Statement II is correct.

(c) Both statement I and Statement II are incorrect.

(d) Statement I is correct but statement II is incorrect.

7. Match the pollutants given in Column I with their effects in Column II.

	Column I		Column II
A.	Unsaturated hydrocarbons	1.	BOD level of water increases
B.	Methane in air	2.	Acid rain
C.	Synthetic detergents in water	3.	Global warming
D.	Nitrogen oxides in air	4.	Photochemical smog

Codes

	A	B	C	D		A	B	C	D
(a)	4	3	1	2	(b)	4	1	3	2
(c)	1	4	2	3	(d)	4	3	2	1

8. Sevin, an insecticide is obtained when methyl isocyanate reacts with

(a) α-naphthol

(b) β-naphthol

(c) catechol

(d) resorcinol

9. Which of the following practices will not come under green chemistry?

(a) Making use of soap made of vegetable oils instead of using synthetic detergents if possible.

(b) Using H_2O_2 for bleaching purpose instead of using chlorine based bleaching agents.

(c) Using bicycle for travelling small distances instead of using petrol/diesel based vehicles.

(d) Using plastic cans for storing substances.

10. The gas 'X' is non-toxic and non-flammable but dissociated by UV- radiations in stratosphere. The gas 'X' produces which of the following intermediates initially

(a) $\dot{C}H_3 + \dot{C}F_2Cl$ (b) $\dot{C}l + \dot{C}F_2Cl$

(c) $Cl\dot{O} + \dot{C}H_3$ (d) $Cl\dot{O} + \dot{C}F_2Cl$

Section B *Numerical Value Questions*

11. The number of gases cause global warming are ....

CO_2, N_2O, CH_4, O_3, N_2, CFCs, O_2, H_2

12. In case of thunderstorm, the types of nitrogeneous oxide formed during formation of nitric acid is ....

13. Average ozone concentration in Jakarta, Indonesia have been reported to be 0.015 mg m^{-3} and those in Tokyo, Japan are 20 ppmV. The approximate ratio of these two values, when expressed in the same unit is ....

14. 100 mL of a sample of water required 1.96 mg of potassium dichromate in the presence of 50% H_2SO_4 for the oxidation of dissolved organic matter in it. The chemical oxygen demand (COD) of sample of water (in ppm) will be ....

15. COD value of a water sample is 40 ppm. The amount of acidified $K_2Cr_2O_7$ (in gram) required to oxidise the organic matter present in 500 mL of that water sample will be ....

Answers

Section A

1 *(d)*	2 *(d)*	3 *(a)*	4 *(d)*	5 *(b)*
6 *(a)*	7 *(a)*	8 *(a)*	9 *(d)*	10 *(b)*

Section B

11 *(4)*	12 *(4)*	13 *(0.35)*	14 *(3.20)*	15 *(0.12)*

See detailed solutions on page no. 240

QUALIFIER 20

Purification and Characterisation of Organic Compounds

Section A Objective Type Questions

1. Match the following columns.

	Column I		Column II
A.	H_2O : Sugar	1.	Sublimation
B.	H_2O : Aniline	2.	Steam distillation
C.	H_2O : Toluene	3.	Differential extraction
		4.	Recrystallisation

Codes

	A	B	C		A	B	C		A	B	C		A	B	C
(a)	3	2	1	(b)	4	2	3	(c)	2	1	3	(d)	4	2	1

2. Two solids which are soluble in the same liquid to different extents may be separated by

(a) crystallisation (b) sublimation
(c) evaporation (d) fractional crystallisation

3. Given below are two statements.

Statement I Simple distillation can help in separating a mixture of propan-1-ol (boiling point 97°C) and propanone (boiling point 56°C).

Statement II Liquids with a difference of more than 20°C in their boiling points can be separated by simple distillation.

In the light of the above statements, choose the most appropriate answer from the options given below.

(a) Both Statement I and Statement II are correct.
(b) Both Statement I and Statement II are incorrect.
(c) Statement I is correct but Statement II is incorrect.
(d) Statement II is correct but Statement I is incorrect.

4. Which of the following statements is true regarding the fractional distillation of a mixture of two liquids?

(a) The distillate collected is the liquid of lower boiling point.
(b) The distillate collected is the liquid of higher boiling point.
(c) The liquid left behind in flask have lower boiling point.
(d) The compositions of distillate and the liquid left behind in the flask do not depend upon the length the fractionating coloumn.

5. The fragrance of flowers is due to the presence of some steam volatile organic compounds called essential oils. These are generally insoluble in water at room temperature but are miscible with water vapour in vapour phase. A suitable method for the extraction of these oils from the flowers is

(a) distillation
(b) crystallisation
(c) distillation under reduced pressure
(d) steam distillation

6. In chromatography technique, the purification of compound is independent of

(a) mobility or flow of solvent system
(b) solubility of the compound
(c) length of the column or TLC plate
(d) physical state of the pure compound

7. Chromatography is a valuable method for the separation, isolation, purification and identification of the constituents of a mixture and it is based on general principles of

(a) phase rule (b) phase distribution
(c) interphase separation (d) phase contact

8. The presence of halogen in an organic compound is detected by

(a) iodoform test (b) silver nitrate test
(c) Beilstein's test (d) Millon's test

9. In Kjeldahl's method, $CuSO_4$ acts as

(a) oxidising agent (b) reducing agent
(c) hydrolysing agent (d) catalytic agent

10. Sodium fusion extract of an organic compound gives a blood red colouration with few drops of $FeCl_3$ solution. This indicates the presence of

(a) nitrogen (b) sulphur
(c) both nitrogen and sulphur (d) both sulphur and chlorine

11. For which of the following compounds Lassaigne's test will fail?

(a) NH_2CONH_2 (b) $NH_2CONH\ NH_2 \cdot HCl$
(c) $NH_2NH_2 \cdot HCl$ (d) $C_6H_5NH_2NH_2 \cdot 2HCl$

12. Sodium extract is heated with concentrated HNO_3 before testing for halogens because

(a) Ag_2S and AgCN are soluble in acidic medium.
(b) silver halides are totally insoluble in nitric acid.
(c) S^{2-} and CN^-, if present, are decomposed by conc. HNO_3 and hence, do not interfere in the test.
(d) Ag reacts faster with halides in acidic medium.

13. In Kjeldahl's method, 295 mg of an organic compound containing nitrogen was digested and the evolved ammonia was absorbed in 20 mL of 0.1 M HCl solution. The excess of the acid required 15 mL of 0.1 M NaOH solution for complete neutralisation. The percentage of nitrogen in the compound is

(a) 29.5 (b) 59.0 (c) 47.4 (d) 23.7

14. In Carius method of estimation of halogens, 250 mg of an organic compound gave 141 mg of AgBr. The percentage of bromine in the compound is (Atomic mass : Ag = 108; Br = 80)

(a) 36 (b) 48 (c) 60 (d) 24

15. 1.4 g of an organic compound was digested according to Kjeldahl's method and the ammonia evolved was absorbed in 60 mL of $\frac{M}{10}$ H_2SO_4 solution. The excess sulphuric acid required 20 mL of $\frac{M}{10}$ NaOH solution for neutralisation. The percentage of nitrogen in the compound is

(a) 3 (b) 5 (c) 10 (d) 24

16. The ammonia evolved from the treatment of 0.30 g of an organic compound for the estimation of nitrogen was passed in 100 mL of 0.1 M sulphuric acid. The excess of acid required 20 mL of 0.5 M sodium hydroxide solution for complete neutralisation. The organic compound is

(a) acetamide (b) thiourea (c) urea (d) benzamide

17. $\frac{5}{19}$ g of an organic compound gave 22.4 cm^3 of moist nitrogen measured at 280 K and 732.7 mm pressure. The percentage of nitrogen in the substance is approximately (Aqueous tension at 280 K = 12.7 mm)

(a) 9.8 (b) 19.6 (c) 4.9 (d) 9.0

18. An organic compound having molecular mass 60 is found to contain C = 20%, H = 6.67% and N = 46.67%, while the rest is oxygen. On heating, it gives NH_3 along with a solid residue. The solid residue gives violet colour with alkaline copper sulphate solution. The compound is

(a) CH_3NCO (b) CH_3CONH_2
(c) $(NH_2)_2CO$ (d) $CH_3CH_2CONH_2$

19. Insulin contains 3.4% sulphur. The minimum weight of insulin is

(a) 350 (b) 470 (c) 560 (d) 940

20. The silver salt of a monobasic acid on ignition gave 60% of Ag. The molecular weight of the acid is (in g)

(a) 37 (b) 33 (c) 73 (d) 77

Section B *Numerical Value Questions*

21. 0.50 g of an organic compound was Kjeldahlised and the NH_3 evolved was absorbed in a certain volume of 1N H_2SO_4. The residual acid required 60 cm^3 of *N*/2 NaOH. If the percentage of N is 56. The volume of 1N H_2SO_4 taken (in mL) is ....

22. If 0.2 g of an organic compound containing carbon, hydrogen and oxygen on combustion yielded 0.147 g carbon dioxide and 0.12 g water. The percentage content of oxygen in the substance will be ....

23. 0.25 g of an organic compound gave 31.1 mL of N_2 by Duma's method. The % of N in this compound is ....

24. A dibasic organic acid gave the following results : C = 34.62%, H = 3.84%, 0.1075 g of this acid consumes 20 mL of 0.1 N NaOH for complete neutralisation. If the molecular formula of the acid is $C_aH_bO_c$, then the value of bc/a will be ....

25. 0.257 g of an organic substance was heated with conc. H_2SO_4 and then distilled with excess of strong alkali. The ammonia gas evolved was absorbed in 50 mL of $\frac{N}{10}$ HCl which required 23.2 mL of $\frac{N}{10}$ NaOH for neutralisation at the end of the process. The percentage of nitrogen in the compound is ....

26. 0.395 g of an organic compound by Carius method for the estimation of sulphur gave 0.582 g of $BaSO_4$. The percentage of sulphur in the compound is ....

27. In a Liebig's method, an organic compound weighing 0.198 g produced 0.524 g CO_2 and 0.132 g H_2O. The percentage of carbon and hydrogen in the given compound are *x* and *y* respectively. Then, the value of $\frac{x}{y}$ is ....

28. In Victor Meyer's method, 0.2 g of an organic substance displaced 15 mL of air at STP. The molecular mass of the compound is ....

29. 10 mL of a gaseous hydrocarbon was mixed with 100 mL of oxygen and exploded in an eudiometer tube. The volume of the residual gases was 95 mL of which 20 mL was absorbed by caustic soda and the remaining by pyrogallol. If the molecular formula of the gas is $C_x H_y$, then the value of $(x + y)$ is ....

30. 0.24 g of an organic compound gave 0.22 g of CO_2 on complete combustion. If it contains 1.66% hydrogen, then the percentage of O will be ....

Answers

Section A

1 (b)	2 (d)	3 (a)	4 (a)	5 (d)
6 (d)	7 (c)	8 (c)	9 (d)	10 (c)
11 (c)	12 (c)	13 (d)	14 (d)	15 (c)
16 (c)	17 (a)	18 (c)	19 (d)	20 (c)

Section B

21 (50)	22 (73.29)	23 (15.55)	24 (5.33)	25 (14.59)
26 (20.24)	27 (9.75)	28 (298.65)	29 (4)	30 (73.34)

See detailed solutions on page no. 241

QUALIFIER 21

Some Basic Principles of Organic Chemistry

Section A Objective Type Questions

1. The correct order of decreasing H— C—H angle in the following molecules is

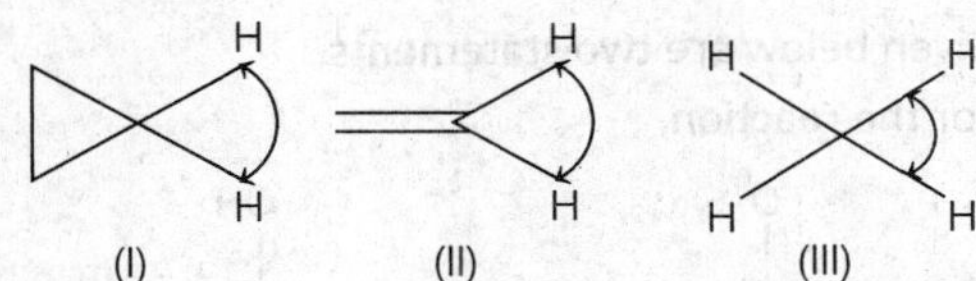

(a) I > II > III (b) II > I > III (c) III > II > I (d) I > III > II

2. A ketone can show all types of structural isomerism *viz.*, chain isomerism, position isomerism, functional isomerism, tautomerism and metamerism. For this feature, the number of carbon atoms present in ketone will be

(a) three (b) four (c) five (d) six

3. Tautomerism is not exhibited by

(a) Me_3COC, Me_3COC—C—H, Me_3COC (b) (c) (d)

4. The correct sequence of relationship between the compounds of the following pairs I to IV is

(I) COOH, H—NH$_2$, Me ; Me, H—NH$_2$, COOH

(II) Et, H—Br, Br—H, Me ; Me, H—Br, Br—H, Et

(III) Ph, HO—H, H$_2$N—H, Me ; Me, H—NH$_2$, HO—H, Ph

(IV) Et, H—Cl, H—Br, Me ; Me, Cl—H, Br—H, Et

Choose the correct option.

(a) identical, enantiomers, diastereomers and structural isomers respectively

(b) enantiomers, identical, structural isomers and diastereomers respectively

(c) enantiomers, identical, diastereomers and structural isomers respectively

(d) identical, identical, diastereomers and structural isomers respectively

5. The absolute configuration of C-2 and C-3 in the following compound is

HO, H, O, H_3C, OH, Br, H

(a) 2*R*, 3*S* (b) 2*S*, 3*R* (c) 2*S*, 3*S* (d) 2*R*, 3*R*

6. Which one of the following is *sec*-butyl phenyl vinyl methane?

(a) Ph, Me, Me, Me (b) Ph, Me, Me (c) Ph, Me, Me (d) Me, Ph, Me

7. The IUPAC name for the compound given below is

OH, Ph

(a) (2*R*, 3*Z*)-7-phenylhept-3-en-2-ol

(b) (2*S*, 3*Z*)-7-phenylhept-3-en-2-ol

(c) (2*R*, 3*E*)-7-phenylhept-3-en-2-ol

(d) (2*S*, 3*E*)-7-phenylhept-3-en-2-ol

8. What is the IUPAC nomenclature of the following molecule?

Et, I, COOH, Me, H, Me, Br, COMe

(a) (2*S*, 3*E*, 5*Z*) -4-bromo-5-iodo-2, 6-dimethyl-3-methoxycarbonyloctanoic acid
(b) (2*S*, 3*Z*, 5*Z*) -4-bromo-5-iodo-2, 6-dimethyl-3-methoxy oct-3, 5-dienoic acid
(c) (2*R*, 3*E*, 5*Z*)-4-bromo-5-iodo-2, 6-dimethyl-3-methoxycarbonyloctanoic acid
(d) (2*R*, 3*E*, 5*Z*)-4-bromo-5-iodo-2, 6-dimethyl-3-methoxycarbonyloctanoic acid

9. The homolytic breaking of C_a—C_b bond is easiest in

(a) C_aH_3—C_bH_3 (b) $CH_3C_aH_2C_bH_2CH_3$
(c) $Me_2C_aHC_bHMe_2$ (d) $Me_3C_aC_bMe_3$

10. The order of ease of the following leaving groups would be

A. CH_3COO^- B. MeO^-
C. $CH_3SO_3^-$ D. $CF_3SO_3^-$

(a) *A* > *B* > *C* > *D* (b) *D* > *C* > *A* > *B*
(c) *B* > *A* > *C* > *D* (d) *C* > *D* > *A* > *B*

11. Which one will be the most powerful nucleophile in water?

(a) F^- (b) Cl^-
(c) Br^- (d) I^-

12. The stability of $Me_2C{=}CH_2$ is more than that of $MeCH_2CH{=}CH_2$ due to

(a) inductive effect of —Me group
(b) resonance effect of the —Me group
(c) hyperconjugative effect of the —Me group
(d) resonance as well as inductive effect of the —Me group

13. Which of the following carbocations would have greatest stability ?

(a) 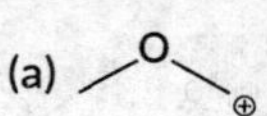 (b) 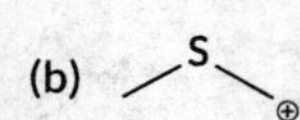 (c) 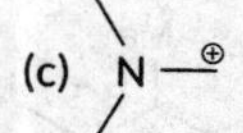 (d) $^{\oplus}$—F

14. The correct order of the pK_a values for the conjugate acids of heterocyclic compounds given below is

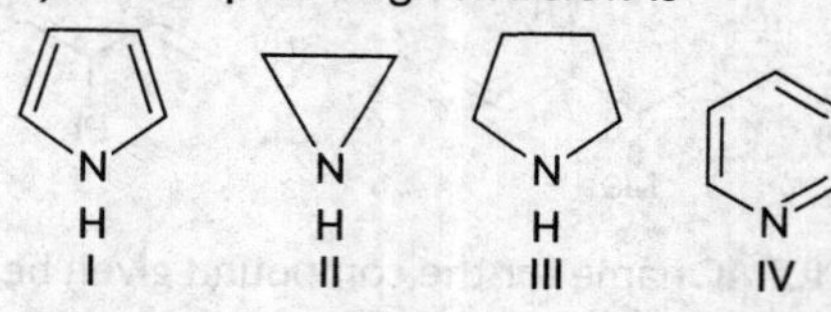

(a) II > III > I > IV (b) IV > II > III > I
(c) III > II > IV > I (d) III > IV > II > I

15. The decreasing order of the acidity of the marked H-atom of the following molecules is

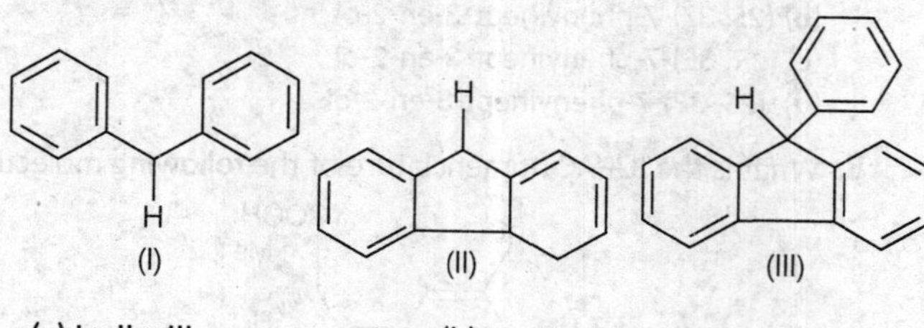

(a) I > II > III (b) III > I > II
(c) III > II > I (d) II > I > III

16. Consider the following compounds and

(I) (II) (III) (IV)

Choose the correct decreasing order the stability.

(a) IV > III > II > I (b) III > II > I > IV
(c) III > II > IV > I (d) III > I > II > IV

17. Given below are two statements.

For the reaction,

$$C_6H_5O^{\ominus} + H_2O \rightleftharpoons C_6H_5OH + \overset{\ominus}{O}H;\ K_1$$

$$C_2H_5O^{\ominus} + H_2O \rightleftharpoons C_2H_5OH + \overset{\ominus}{O}H;\ K_2$$

Statement I The value of K_2 is less than K_1.
Statement II Phenoxide is a weaker base than ethoxide.

In the light of the above statements, choose the most appropriate answer from the options given below.

(a) Both Statement I and Statement II are correct.
(b) Both Statement I and Statement II are incorrect.
(c) Statement I is correct but Statement II is incorrect.
(d) Statement II is correct but Statement I is incorrect.

18. In S_N2 substitution reaction given below,

$$R\text{—}Br + Cl^- \xrightarrow{DMF} R\text{—}Cl + Br^-$$

Which one of the following has the highest relative rate?

(a) Ethyl bromide
(b) 2-methyl propyl bromide
(c) Propyl bromide
(d) 2,3-dimethyl propyl bromide

19. Which one will not undergo substitution reaction ?

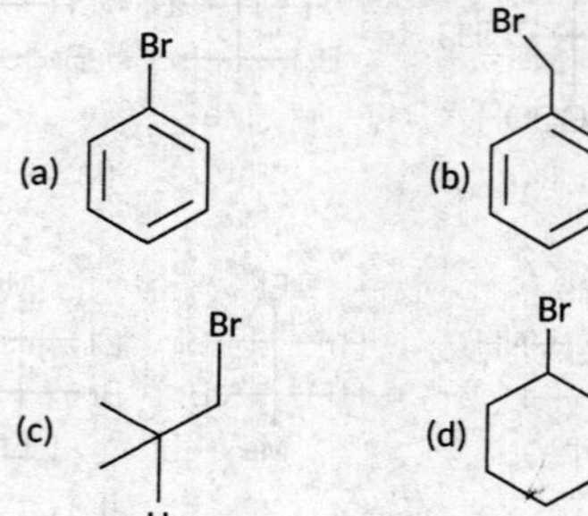

20. Which of the following are not correctly related with an S_N1 reaction?

I. Rearrangement is possible.
II. Rate is affected by solvent polarity.
III. The strength of the nucleophile is important in determining rate.
IV. Reactivity series is : $3° > 2° > 1°$.
V. Process with complete inversion of configuration.

(a) III and V (b) Only V
(c) II, III and V (d) Only III

Section B *Numerical Value Questions*

21. From the following structure, the value of degree of unsaturation is ....

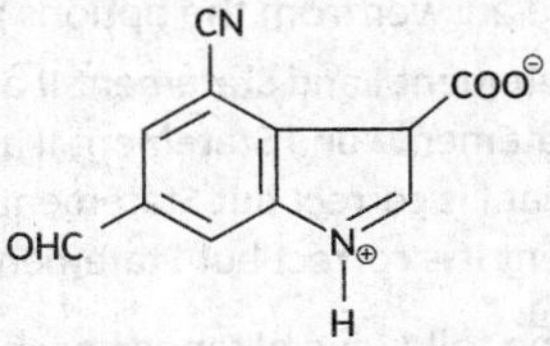

(Structure: pyridinium ring (N⊕–H) fused benzene ring bearing CN, $COO^{\ominus}$ and OHC substituents)

22. An optically active compound enriched with *R*-enantiomer (60% enantiomeric excess) exhibited $[\alpha]_D = +90°$. If the $[\alpha]_D$ value of the sample is $-135°$, the ratio of *S* and *R* enantiomers would be ....

23. The $[\alpha]_D$ of a 90% optically pure 2-acylpropanoic acid is $+135°$. On treatment with a base at room temperature for one hour, $[\alpha]_D$ changed to $+120°$. The optical purity is reduced to 40% after 3 hours. If so, the percent optical purity of the solution after 1 hour will be ....

24. A 0.1 M solution of an enantiometrically pure chiral compound (A) has an observed rotation of 0.40° in 1 dm tube. If the solution of A is diluted will an equal volume of the solution, the observed rotation will be θ. The value of θ is ....

25. Number of stereocentre(s) of the given compound is ....

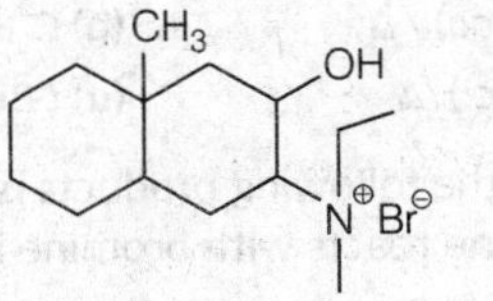

(Structure: decalin system with angular CH_3, OH, ethyl group and quaternary $N^{\oplus}Br^{\ominus}$)

26. The number of *meso*-form(s) of the following compound is ....

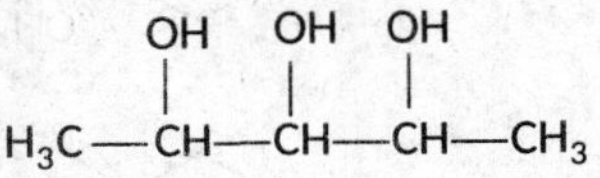

$H_3C—CH(OH)—CH(OH)—CH(OH)—CH_3$

27. The number of possible structural isomers of the molecular formula $C_4H_{11}N$ will be ....

28. The number of compounds which are more acidic than ethyne is ....

$CH_2{=}CH_2, NH_3, H_2O, CH_3—CH_3, HF,$
$CH_3CH_2—OH, CH_3—CH_2—CH_2—SH,$
(cyclopentadiene), (benzene)

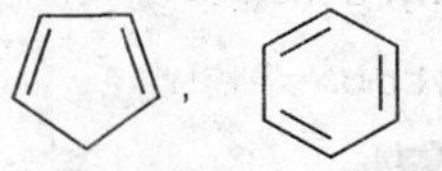

29. Among the following the number of cations that is(are) more stable than $CH_3—\overset{\oplus}{C}H—CH_3$ are ....

(I) $CH_3—\overset{\oplus}{C}H_2$ (II) 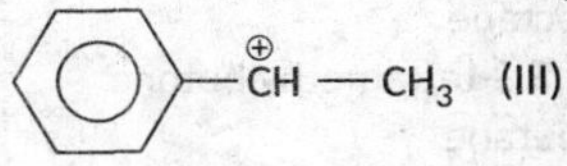 $C_6H_5—\overset{\oplus}{C}H—CH_3$ (III) 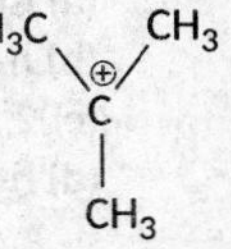 $(CH_3)_3\overset{\oplus}{C}$

(IV) $(CF_3)_3\overset{\oplus}{C}$ (V) $CF_3—\overset{\oplus}{C}H_2$

(VI) $CH_2{=}CH—\overset{\oplus}{C}H—CH_3$ (VII) $CF_3—\overset{\oplus}{C}H—CH_3$

(VIII) $CH_3—\overset{\oplus}{C}H—OCH_3$ (IX) $CH_3—\overset{\oplus}{C}H—C(=O)—OCH_3$

30. The number of conditions that affect the mechanism of nucleophilic substitution in a significant fashion is ....

I. concentration of the nucleophile
II. solvent polarity
III. reactivity of nucleophile
IV. structure of alkyl halide

Answers

Section A

1 (b)	2 (c)	3 (c)	4 (c)	5 (d)
6 (c)	7 (d)	8 (a)	9 (d)	10 (b)
11 (d)	12 (c)	13 (c)	14 (c)	15 (c)
16 (c)	17 (d)	18 (a)	19 (a)	20 (a)

Section B

21 (10)	22 (19)	23 (80)	24 (0.20)	25 (4)
26 (2)	27 (8)	28 (5)	29 (4)	30 (4)

See detailed solutions on page no. 244

QUALIFIER 22

Hydrocarbons

Section A *Objective Type Questions*

1. The highest boiling point is expected for
(a) *iso*-octane
(b) *n*-octane
(c) 2,2,3,3-tetramethylbutane
(d) *n*-butane

2. Which of the following statement is correct ?
(a) The electrolysis of concentrated solution of sodium, ethanoate by Pt-electrodes produces ethene.
(b) If the relative rates of abstraction of 2° and 1° hydrogen atoms are 3.8 and 1.0 respectively, then the percentage ratio of products 1-chloro-,2-chloro and 3-chloro-, obtained by photochlorination of *n*-hexane would be 16.48 : 41.76 : 41.76.
(c) The C—H bond in cyclopropane is longer than propane.
(d) The boat conformation of cyclohexane is more stable than chair conformation.

3. Which of the following conformations of cyclohexane is optically active?
(a) Boat (b) Twist boat
(c) Chair (d) Half chair

4. The following two representations,

CH_3; H; $C(CH_3)_3$; H; H; H — I and II are

(a) same configuration
(b) same molecule
(c) Both (a) and (b)
(d) None of the above

5. The correct order of acidity of the following hydrocarbons is

(I) (II)

(III) $HC \equiv CH$ (IV) $CH_3 - C \equiv CH$

(a) I > II > III > IV (b) III > IV > II > I
(c) I > III > IV > II (d) IV > III > I > II

6. Given below are two statements.
Statement I Addition of Br_2 to 1-butene in the presence of CCl_4 gives two optical isomers.
Statement II The product contains one asymmetric carbon.
In the light of the above statements, choose the most appropriate answer from the options given below.
(a) Both Statement I and Statement II are correct.
(b) Both Statement I and Statement II are incorrect.
(c) Statement I is correct but Statement II is incorrect.
(d) Statement II is correct but Statement I is incorrect.

7. Which of the following alkenes has maximum heat of hydrogenation value?

(a) 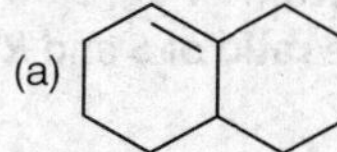 (b) 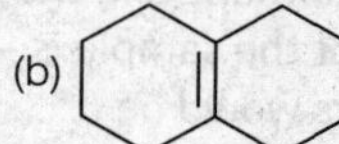

(c) 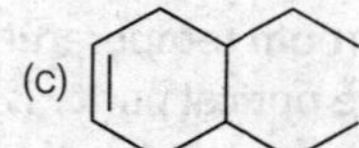 (d) 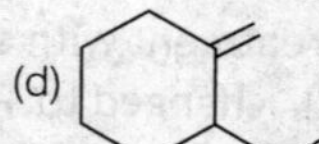

8. Which of the following reagents/ conditions would you employ to obtain the best yield of the product in the following reaction?

$$CH_3CH_2 - \underset{Br}{\overset{CH_3}{C}} - CH_3 \longrightarrow CH_3CH_2 - \overset{CH_3}{C} = CH_2$$

(a) NaOH (*aq*) /Δ (b) C_2H_5ONa / C_2H_5OH /Δ
(c) KOH (alc.) /Δ (d) *t*-BuOK/*t*-BuOH /Δ

9. Which of the following products is not possible when cyclohexene reacts with bromine in presence of brine?

(a) 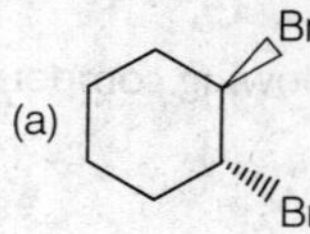

(b) 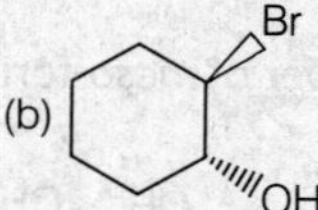

(c) 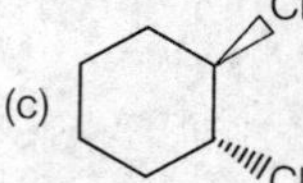

(d)
Br
Cl

10. The major product of the following reaction will be

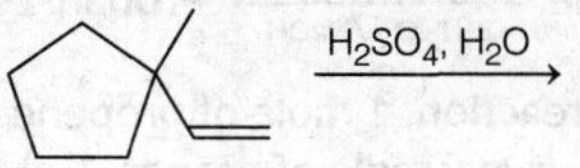

$\xrightarrow{H_2SO_4,\ H_2O}$

(a) 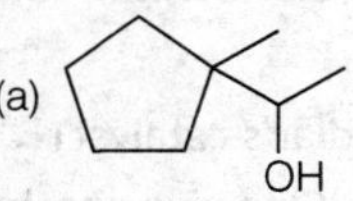 OH (b) 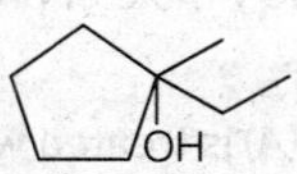 OH

(c) 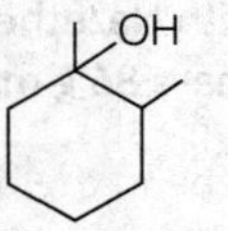 OH (d) 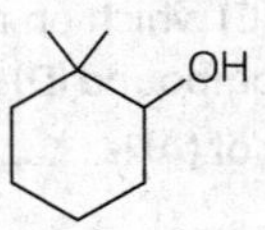 OH

11. Reaction of one molecule of 1,3-butadiene with one molecule of HBr at 40°C gives predominantly

(a) 3-bromobutene as kinetically controlled product.
(b) 1-bromo-2-butene as thermodynamically controlled product.
(c) 3-bromobutene as thermodynamically controlled product.
(d) 1-bromo-2-butene as kinetically controlled product.

12. $CH_3—C\equiv CH \xrightarrow[\text{(ii) } CH_3CH_2Br]{\text{(i) } NaNH_2} P \xrightarrow[\text{(ii) } NH_4Cl]{\text{(i) Li, } C_2H_5NH_2,\ -78°C} Q$ (major)

The major product *Q* in the given reaction is

(a) 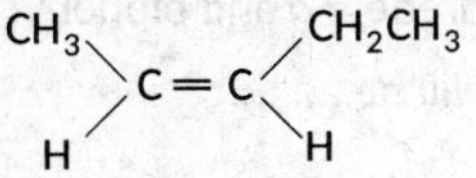 $CH_3(H)C=C(CH_2CH_3)(H)$ — CH_3 and CH_2CH_3 on the same side

(b) $CH_3(H)C=C(H)(CH_2CH_3)$ — CH_3 and CH_2CH_3 on opposite sides

(c) $CH_3(H)C=C(CH_3)(H)$ — CH_3 and CH_3 on the same side

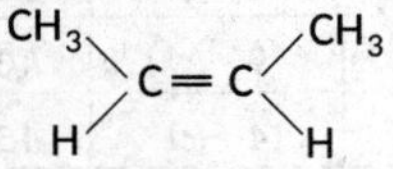

(d) 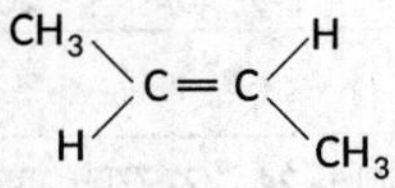 $CH_3(H)C=C(H)(CH_3)$ — CH_3 and CH_3 on opposite sides

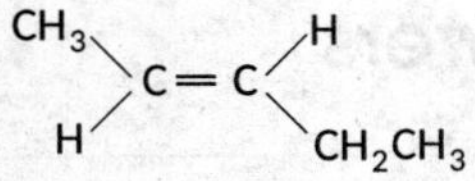

13. Ozonolysis of the following compound gives

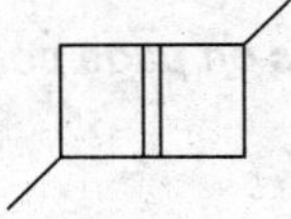

(a) 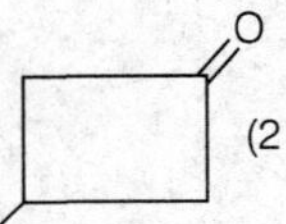 (2 mol) (b) 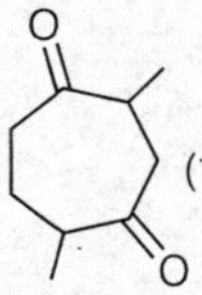 (1 mol)

(c) 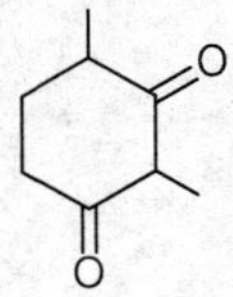 (1 mol) (d) 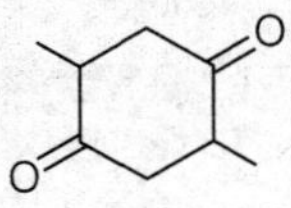 (1 mol)

14. The product formed (*A*) in the following reaction is

$\xrightarrow[NH_3(l)]{Na} A$

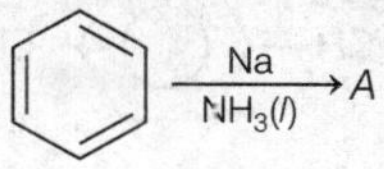

(a) 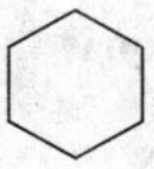 (b) 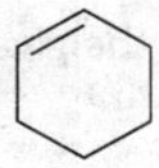 (c) 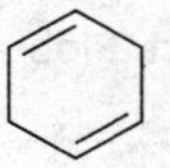 (d)

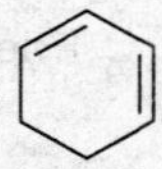

15. The number of structural and stereoisomers of a bromo compound, C_5H_9Br formed by the addition of HBr to 2-pentyne, respectively are

(a) 1 and 2 (b) 2 and 4
(c) 4 and 2 (d) 2 and 1

16. Which of the following has the highest melting point ?

(a) *o*-xylene (b) *m*-xylene
(c) Toluene (d) *p*-xylene

17. $C_6H_5—C\equiv C—CH_2CH_3 \xrightarrow[H_3O^+]{HgSO_4} A$ (Major) ;

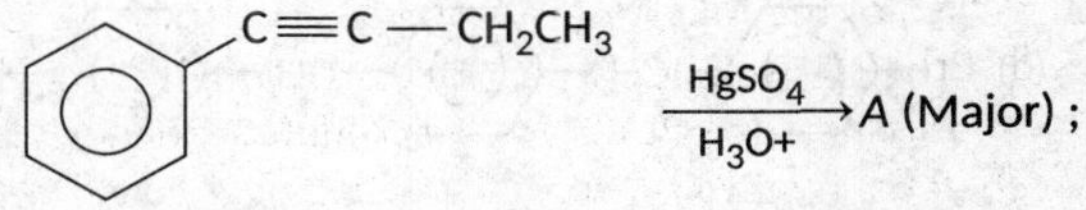

The major product (*A*) in the above reaction is

(a) 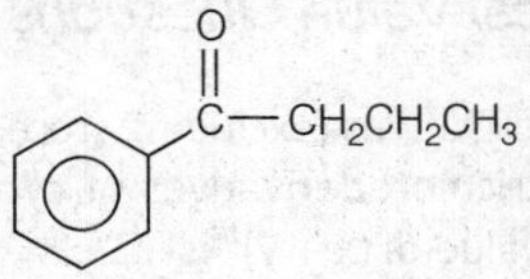 $C_6H_5—CO—CH_2CH_2CH_3$ (b) $C_6H_5—CH_2—CO—C_2H_5$

(c) $C_6H_5—C(OH)=CH—C_2H_5$ (d) 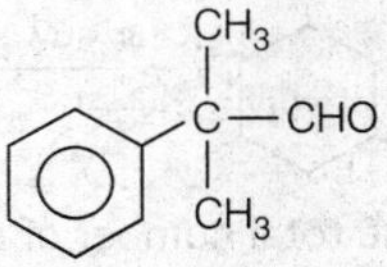 $C_6H_5—C(CH_3)_2—CHO$

18. In which of the following, polysubstitution may takes place?

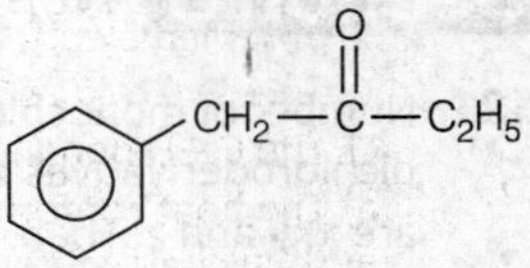

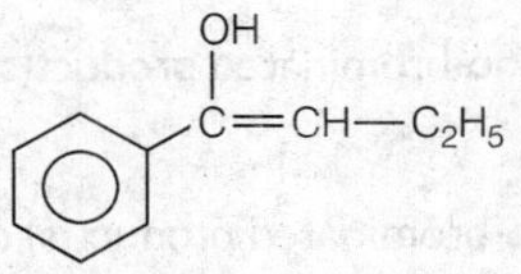

(a) $PhH + CH_3COCl \xrightarrow{\text{Anhyd. } AlCl_3} Ph—CO—CH_3$

(b) $PhH + CH_3Cl \xrightarrow{\text{Anhyd. } AlCl_3} Ph—CH_3$

(c) $PhH + HNO_3 \xrightarrow{H_2SO_4} Ph—NO_2$

(d) $PhH + H_2SO_4 \xrightarrow{90°C} Ph—SO_3H$

19. Product(s) of the following reaction is(are)

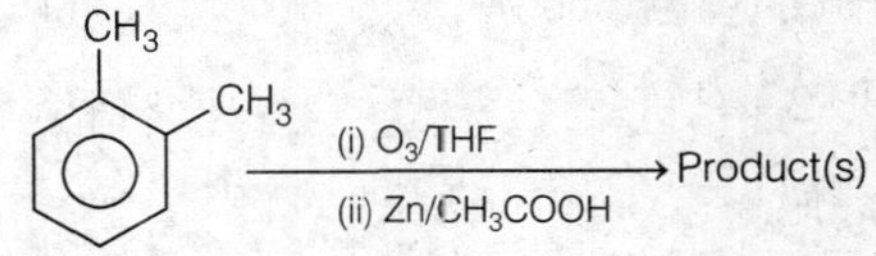

(*o*-xylene) $\xrightarrow[\text{(ii) Zn}/CH_3COOH]{\text{(i) } O_3/THF}$ Product(s)

(a) 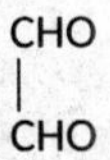 CHO–CHO

(b) 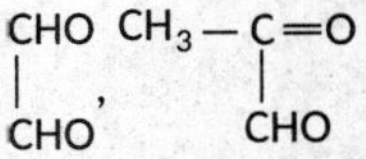 CHO–CHO, $CH_3—C(=O)—CHO$

(c) CHO–CHO, $CH_3—C(=O)—C(=O)—CH_3$

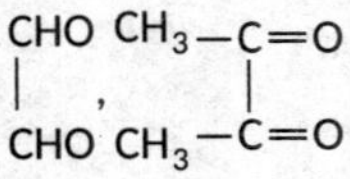

(d) 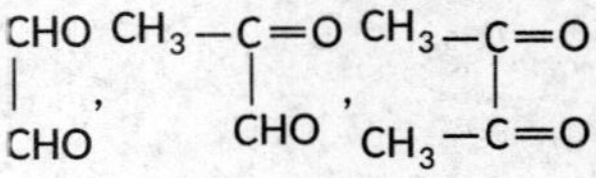 CHO–CHO, $CH_3—C(=O)—CHO$, $CH_3—C(=O)—C(=O)—CH_3$

20. C_6H_6 + Cl—CH_2—C_6H_4—CH_2—Cl $\xrightarrow{AlCl_3(anhyd.)}$ A $\xrightarrow[\Delta]{NBS}$ B
(Excess)

The product, B obtained in the given reaction is

(a) C_6H_5—CH_2—C_6H_4—CH_2—C_6H_5

(b) C_6H_5—CH(Br)—C_6H_4—CH(Br)—C_6H_5

(c) C_6H_5—C_6H_4—CH(Br)—C_6H_5

(d) Br—C_6H_4—CH_2—C_6H_4—CH_2—C_6H_4—Br

Section B *Numerical Value Questions*

21. Number of monochloroderivatives (excluding stereoisomers), dichloroderivatives and trichloroderivatives of cyclopentane are x, y and z. Then, the value of $(x+y)^z$ is ....

22. 1,3,5-trimethylcyclohexane $\xrightarrow{Br_2/UV}$ mono-brominated product(s).

The total number of mono-brominated product(s) obtained in the reaction is ....

23. Mass percentage of primary hydrogen atom(s) in *iso*-pentane is x%. The value of x is ....

24. 2-methylbutane $\xrightarrow[Cl_2/UV]{\text{Mono-chlorination}}$ 2-chloro-2-methylbutane (a%) + Other products

The value of a in the reaction is ....

25. Propene $\xrightarrow[2.\ H_2O_2/NaOH]{1.\ B_2H_6/THF}$ Propan-1-ol

In this reaction, 1 mole of propene reacts with x mole of B_2H_6 to give y mole of propan-1-ol. Now, the value of $(x+y)$ is ....

26. An alkyne (A) is treated with Lindlar's catalyst H_2 to give a compound (B). (B) reacts with HCl to give another compound (C) which on reaction with Na/ether produces compound (D) of molar mass 86 g mol^{-1}. Molar mass of (A) is .... g mol^{-1}.

27. A hydrocarbon of molecular formula C_4H_6 gives x numbers of structural isomers. The value of x is ....

28. Magnesium carbide $\xrightarrow{D_2O}$ A (deuterocarbon)
$\xrightarrow{H_2O}$ B (hydrocarbon)

The value of [molar mass of $A \times$ molar mass of B] is $x \times 10^3$g mol^{-1}. Here, the value of x is ....

29. The ratio of number of σ-bonds to number of π-bonds in toluene is ....

30. If, number of fused benzene rings in naphthalene $= x$, anthracene $= y$, phenanthrene $= a$ and biphenyl $= b$, then the value of $\frac{(a+b)}{(x+y)}$ will be ....

Answers

Section A

1 (b)	2 (b)	3 (b)	4 (b)	5 (c)
6 (a)	7 (d)	8 (d)	9 (c)	10 (c)
11 (b)	12 (b)	13 (d)	14 (c)	15 (b)
16 (d)	17 (a)	18 (b)	19 (d)	20 (b)

Section B

21 (256)	22 (3)	23 (12.50)	24 (27.77)	25 (1.16)
26 (40)	27 (8)	28 (1.76)	29 (5)	30 (0.60)

See detailed solutions on page no. 248

QUALIFIER 23

Organic Compounds Containing Halogens

Section A Objective Type Questions

1. In the following reaction, the ratio of *A* : *B* : *C* is
(* indicates labelled carbon)

$\xrightarrow[CCl_4/Heat]{NBS/AIBN}$ *A* + *B* + *C*

(a) 1 : 1 : 1 (b) 1 : 2 : 1 (c) 2 : 1 : 1 (d) 3 : 2 : 1

2. The major product *P* of the following reaction is

$\xrightarrow[Dark]{Br_2} P$

(a) (b) (c) (d)

3. Given below are two statements, one is labelled as Assertion (A) and the other is labelled as Reason (R).

Assertion (A) Bromobenzene upon reaction with Br_2/Fe gives 1, 4-dibromobenzene as the major product.

Reason (R) In bromobenzene, the inductive effect of the bromo group is more dominant than the mesomeric effect in directing the incoming electrophile.

In the light of the above statements, choose the correct answer from the options given below.

(a) Both Assertion and Reason are correct statements and Reason is the correct explanation of the Assertion.
(b) Both Assertion and Reason are correct statements but Reason is not the correct explanation of the Assertion.
(c) Assertion is correct but Reason is incorrect.
(d) Assertion is incorrect but Reason is correct.

4. The major product formed in the reaction of butadiene with bromine is

(a) $BrCH_2CH(Br)CH{=}CH_2$ (b) $CH_2{=}CH{-}CH_2CH_2Br$
(c) $CH_2{=}C(Br){-}C(Br){=}CH_2$ (d) $BrCH_2CH{=}CHCH_2Br$

5. The major product obtained in the reaction below is

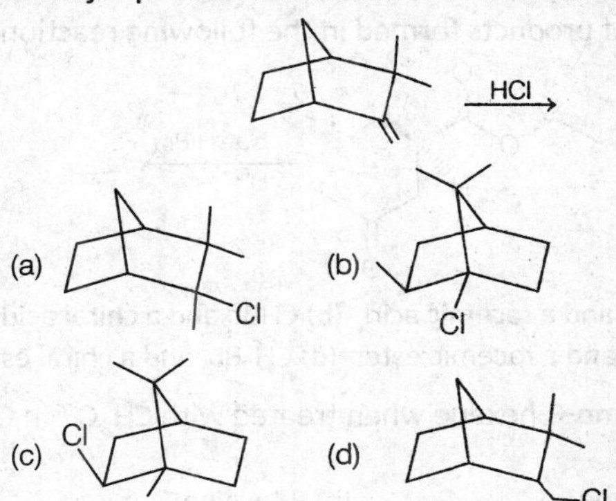

6. Molecular orbital interactions involved in the first step of the following reaction is

+ Br—Br ⟶

(a) $\pi_{C=C} \longrightarrow \sigma^*_{Br-Br}$ (b) $n_{Br} \longrightarrow \sigma^*_{C-C}$
(c) $\pi_{C=C} \longrightarrow \sigma_{Br-Br}$ (d) $n_{Br} \longrightarrow \pi_{C=C}$

7. Arrange the following compounds in the increasing order of their densities.

(i) (ii) (iii) (iv)

Choose the correct order.

(a) (i) < (ii) < (iii) < (iv) (b) (i) < (iii) < (iv) < (ii)
(c) (iv) < (iii) < (ii) < (i) (d) (ii) < (iv) < (iii) < (i)

8. The order of increasing dipole moment of the compound is

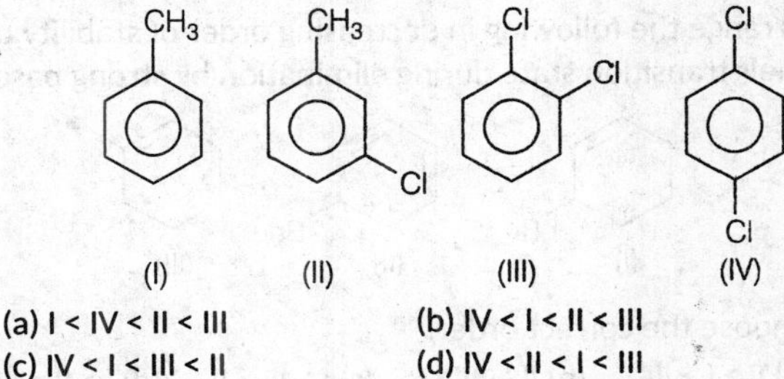

(a) I < IV < II < III (b) IV < I < II < III
(c) IV < I < III < II (d) IV < II < I < III

9. The major product formed in the following reaction is

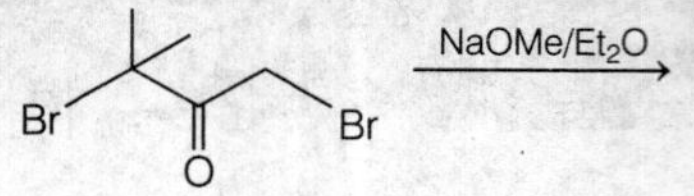

(Structure: dibromo ketone with Br and Br) $\xrightarrow{NaOMe/Et_2O}$

(a) 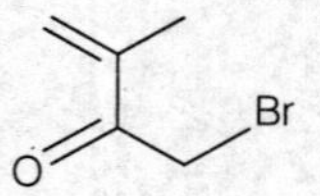 (structure with Br, ketone) (b)  (cyclopropanone structure)

(c) 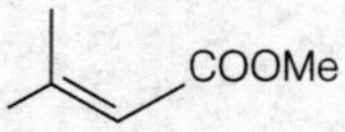 COOMe (d) 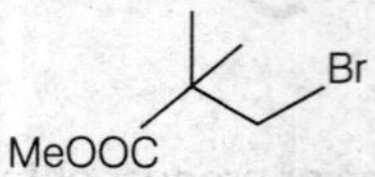 MeOOC, Br

10. The set of products formed in the following reaction is

(Structure) $\xrightarrow[2.\ H^{\oplus}]{1.\ NaOH/Br_2}$

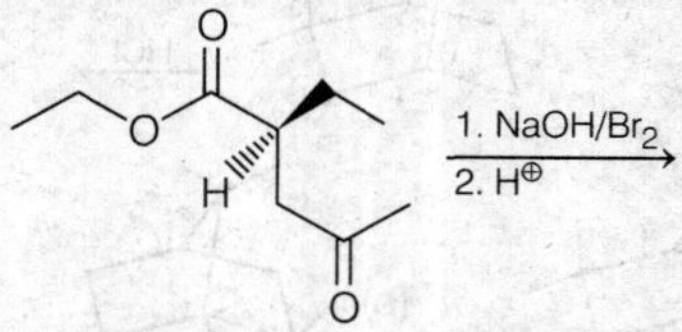

(a) $CHBr_3$ and a racemic acid (b) $CHBr_3$ and a chiral acid
(c) $CHBr_3$ and a racemic ester (d) CH_2Br_2 and a chiral ester

11. (*E*)-3-bromo-3-hexene when treated with CH_3O^- in CH_3OH gives

(a) 3-hexyne (b) 2-hexyne
(c) 2, 3-hexadiene (d) 2,4-hexadiene

12. Iodine from iodoethane can be substituted by cyanide group in a number of ways. Which of the following is true statement ?

(a) With AgCN, EtNC, while with KCN, EtCN is formed as major product.
(b) With AgCN, EtCN and with KCN, EtNC is formed.
(c) With either KCN or AgCN, EtNC is formed as major product.
(d) With either KCN or AgCN, EtCN is formed as major product.

13. The most probable product in the following reaction is

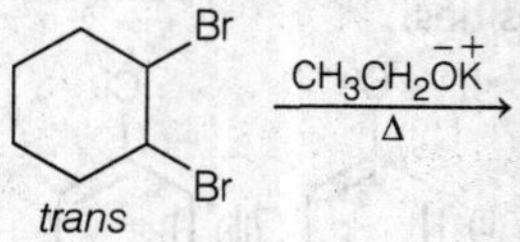

(trans-1,2-dibromocyclohexane, Br, Br, *trans*) $\xrightarrow[\Delta]{CH_3CH_2\overset{-}{O}\overset{+}{K}}$

(a) 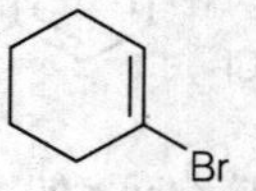 (1-bromocyclohexene, Br) (b) 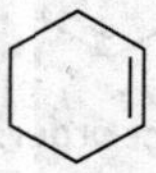 (cyclohexene)
(c) 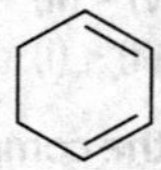 (cyclohexadiene) (d) 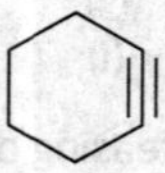 (cyclohexene)

14. Arrange the following in decreasing order of stability of their transition state during elimination by strong base

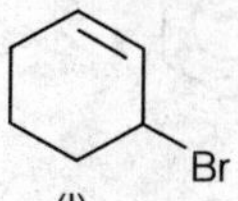

(I) 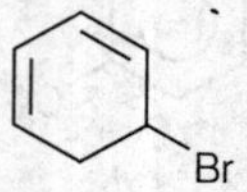 (II) 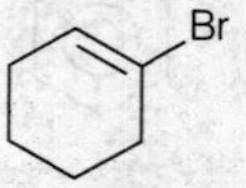 (III) (bromocyclohexene isomers, Br)

Choose the correct order.

(a) II > I > III (b) II > III > I (c) I > III > II (d) I > II > III

15. Match the Column I with Column II and choose the correct options using codes.

	Column I		Column II
A.	S_N1 reaction	1.	*Vic*-dibromides
B.	Bromination of alkenes	2.	*Gem*-dihalides
C.	Alkylidene halides	3.	Racemisation
D.	Elimination of HX from alkyl halide	4.	Saytzeff's rule

Codes

	A	B	C	D		A	B	C	D
(a)	3	1	2	4	(b)	1	3	2	4
(c)	3	2	1	4	(d)	2	4	3	1

16. Which one of the following ketones does not react with isopropyl magnesium bromide to give a tertiary alcohol?

(a) $H_3C-\overset{O}{\overset{\|}{C}}-CH_3$ (b) $H_3C-\underset{CH_3}{\overset{H_3C}{\overset{|}{\underset{|}{C}}}}-\overset{O}{\overset{\|}{C}}-\underset{CH_3}{\overset{CH_3}{\overset{|}{\underset{|}{C}}}}-CH_3$

(c) $H_5C_6-\overset{O}{\overset{\|}{C}}-CH_3$ (d) $H_3C-CH_2-\overset{O}{\overset{\|}{C}}-CH_3$

17. Which of these pairs are correctly matched ?

I. $RMgX/CH_2O \longrightarrow$ Primary alcohol
II. $RMgX/RCHO \longrightarrow$ Secondary alcohol
III. $RMgX/RCOR \longrightarrow$ Tertiary alcohol
IV. $R-C\equiv H/R-MgX \longrightarrow$ Primary alcohol

(a) Only (IV) (b) (I) and (II)
(c) (I), (II), and (III) (d) (I), (II), (III) and (IV)

18. From which of the following compound Grignard reagent cannot be prepared directly using ether and magnesium?

(a)  HO~~~Br (b) 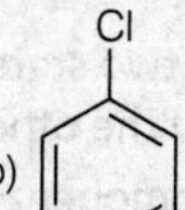 (chlorobenzene, Cl)
(c) 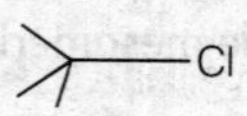 (tert-butyl chloride, Cl) (d) 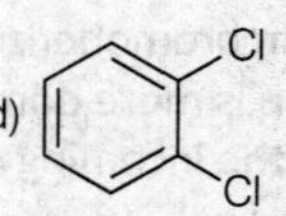 (dichlorobenzene, Cl, Cl)

19. The correct statement(s) regarding the mechanism of the following reaction is(are)

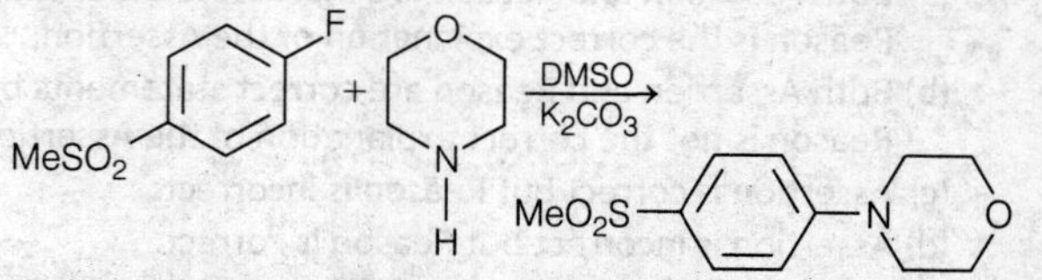

($MeSO_2$-C$_6$H$_4$-F) + (morpholine, N–H) $\xrightarrow[K_2CO_3]{DMSO}$ MeO_2S-C$_6$H$_4$-N(morpholine)

(a) Aromatic *ipso* substitution reaction
(b) Aromatic nucleophilic substitution
(c) Aromatic electrophilic substitution
(d) Both (a) and (b)

20. Ullmann reaction is fastest with

(a) C_6H_5 —Cl (b) H_3C—⟨benzene⟩—Cl

(c) ⟨benzene⟩—Cl with NO_2 (d) NO_2—⟨benzene⟩—Cl

Section B *Numerical Value Questions*

21.

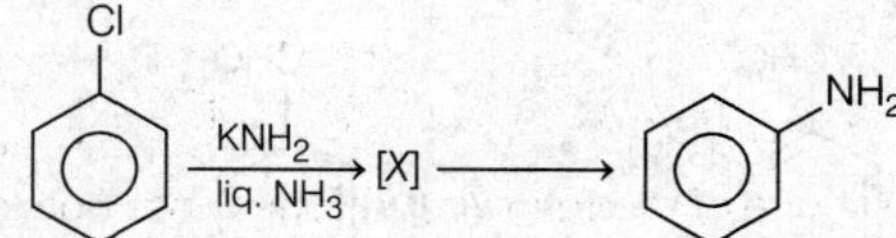

Total number of conjugated π-electrons in [X] is ....

22. A 10.0 g mixture of *n*-butane and 2-butene was treated with bromine in CCl_4 and it was consumed 8.0 g of bromine (Atomic weight = 80). Another 10.0 g of the same mixture was hydrogenated to get *n*-butane only.

The weight of 2-butene in the original mixture and the gain in the weight of the mixture after hydrogenation, are '*a*' g and '*b*' respectively. The value of $(a+b)$ is ....

23. 12.0 g of acetophenone on reaction with 76.2 g of iodine in presence of *aq*. NaOH gave solid *A* in 75% yield. Approximate amount of *A* obtained (in gram) in the reaction is [I = 127] ....

24. The number of substrate from the following that will show rearrangement during S_N1 reaction is ....

Br, Cl, I, Cl, Cl Br,

Br, Cl, Cl, Cl, Br

25. The number of substrates those can give both S_N1 and S_N2 reactions is ....

C_6H_5—CH_2—Br, H_3C—$C(CH_3)_2$—Cl, $(CH_3)_2CH$—Br, H_3C(Ph)C(Br)—, H_3C—Ö—CH_2—Cl, Br (bicyclic), OTs (with Ö), CH_3—CH_2—Cl, Cl (cyclopentadiene), Br (cyclohexane), Cl (cyclopentylmethyl)

26. Consider the following reaction,

$$\text{PhCH}_2\text{CH(Br)CH}_3 \xrightarrow{\text{KOH, EtOH}} (B) + (C)$$

In an experiment, 1.99 g of bromine *A* on reaction with ethanolic potassium hydroxide gave 1.062 g of a mixture of the olefins *B* and *C*. If the ratio of olefins *B* : *C* formed is 2 : 1, then % yield of *A* is ....

27. $$\text{Cl—C(=O)—OC}_2\text{H}_5 \xrightarrow[(2)\ H_3O^+]{(1)\ 'x'\ \text{RMgBr}} 3°\text{-alcohol}$$

The value of *x* is ....

28. HO—(chain with SH)—C(=O)—OC_2H_5

$\xrightarrow[\text{(ii) } H_2O]{\text{(i) 'a' mole of } CH_3\text{—MgBr}}$ HO—(chain with SH)—C(OH) + (Q) [gas] '*b*' mol

The value of $(a+b)$ is ....

29. 1.5 mole of BrMg—$CH_2CH_2CH_2$—MgBr reacts with excess of ethanol to give *x* L of propane gas at STP.

The value of '*x*' is ....

30. Total number of π-electrons present in *X* and *Y* is ....

$$\text{(bicyclic amine)} \xrightarrow{CH_3I} \xrightarrow{Ag_2O(aq)} X \xrightarrow[\text{excess}]{CH_3I} \xrightarrow[\Delta]{Ag_2O(aq)} Y$$

Answers

Section A

1 (c)	2 (d)	3 (c)	4 (d)	5 (a)
6 (a)	7 (a)	8 (b)	9 (c)	10 (b)
11 (c)	12 (a)	13 (c)	14 (a)	15 (a)
16 (b)	17 (c)	18 (a)	19 (d)	20 (d)

Section B

21 (6)	22 (2.97)	23 (29.55)	24 (6)	25 (6)
26 (60)	27 (3)	28 (6)	29 (33.6)	30 (6)

See detailed solutions on page no. 252

QUALIFIER 24

Organic Compounds Containing Oxygen

Section A Objective Type Questions

1. Arrange the following in decreasing order of their reactivity toward S_N2 reaction.

I. Me_3CO^- II. MeO^-

III. $MeCH_2O^-$ IV. Me_2CHO^-

V. 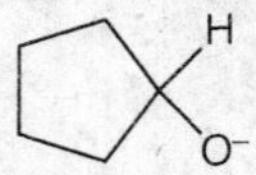 (cyclopentyl with H and O^-)

Choose the correct option.

(a) II > III > V > IV > I

(b) V > III > II > I > IV

(c) I > V > II > III > IV

(d) III > V > I > II > III

2. Identify the correct product of following reaction,

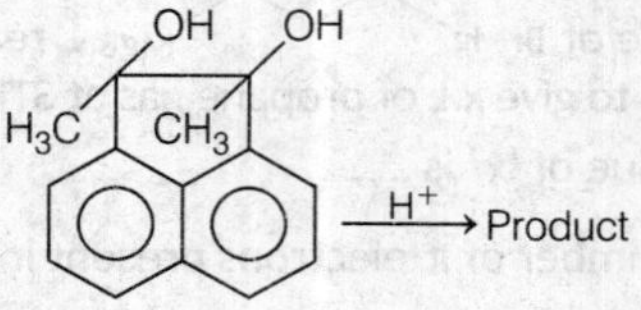

$\xrightarrow{H^+}$ Product

(a) 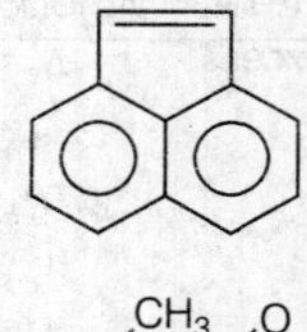 (b) 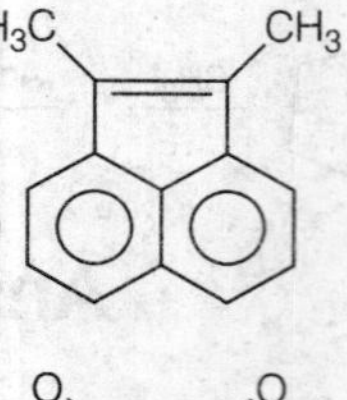 (c) 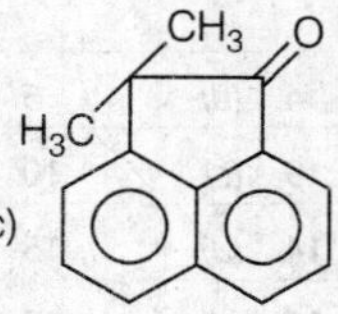 (d)

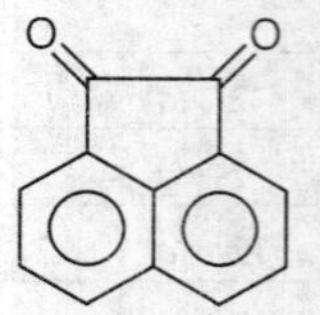

3. The major product of the reaction is

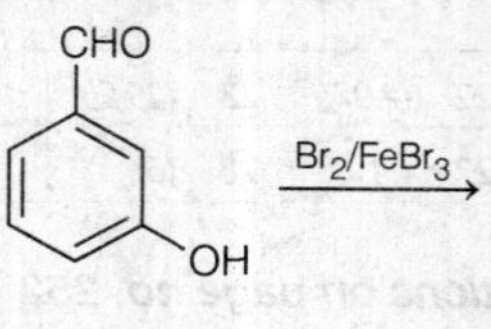

$\xrightarrow{Br_2/FeBr_3}$

(a) 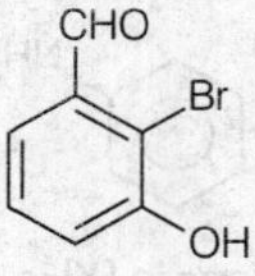 (b) 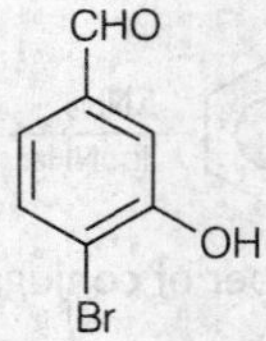 (c) 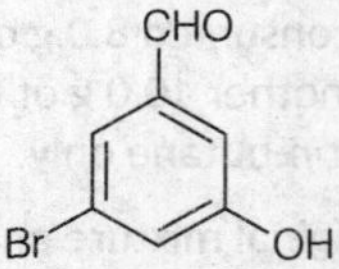 (d)

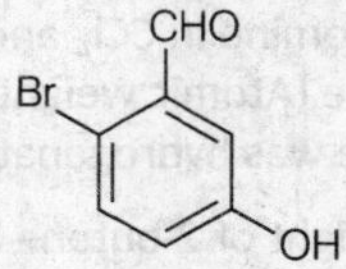

4. In the following reaction, the major products *E* and *F* respectively are

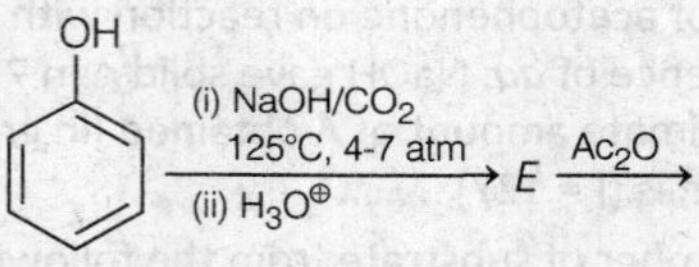

$\xrightarrow[\text{(ii) } H_3O^{\oplus}]{\text{(i) NaOH/}CO_2\text{, 125°C, 4-7 atm}} E \xrightarrow{Ac_2O} F$

(a) (E) (F)

(b) (E) (F)

(c) (E) (F)

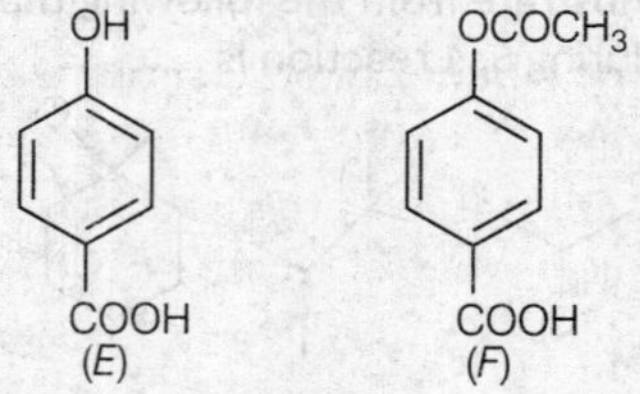

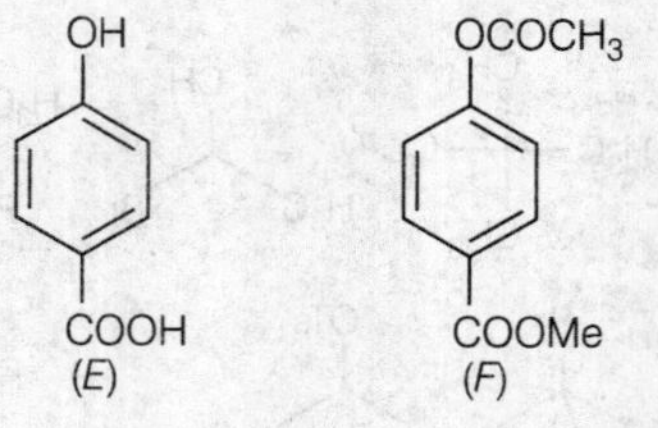

(d) 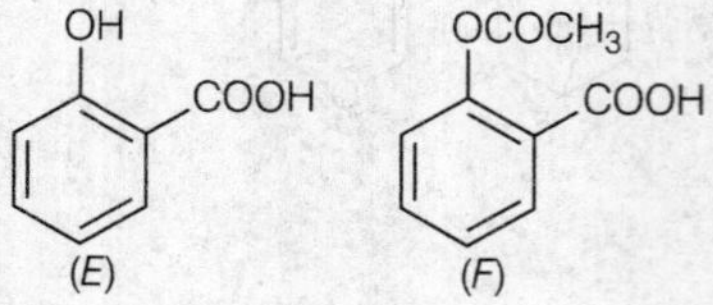 (E) (F)

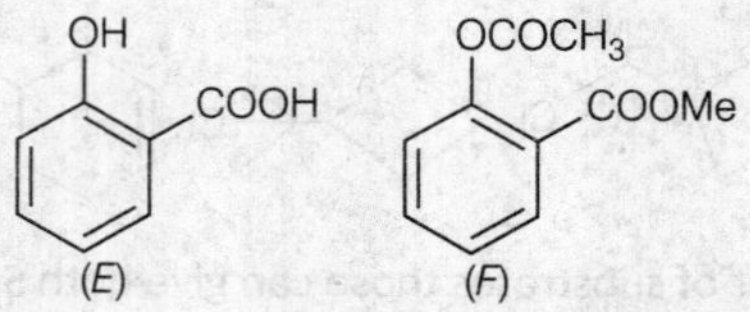

5. An unknown compound (*A*), $C_9H_{12}O$ have four isomeric structures as given. All the compounds react with sodium to give odourless and colourless gas. The three out of the four compounds can be oxidised by hot $KMnO_4/H^+$ to produce benzoic acid and do not respond to iodoform test. Only one isomer out of these four, fulfills all the conditions. The isomer is

(a) 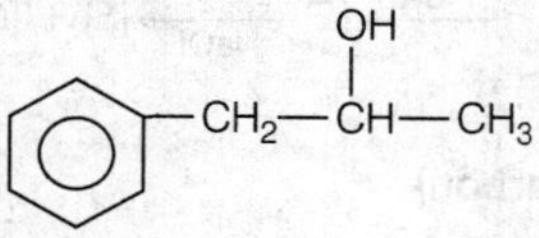 $C_6H_5-CH_2-CH(OH)-CH_3$ (b) $C_6H_5-C(CH_3)(OH)-CH_3$

(c) $C_6H_5-CH(OH)-CH_2-CH_3$ (d) 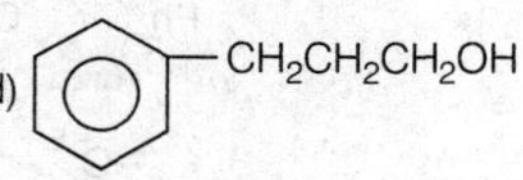 $C_6H_5-CH_2CH_2CH_2OH$

6. Hydroboration of 1-methylcyclopentene using B_2D_6/THF, followed by the treatment with alkaline hydrogen peroxide gives

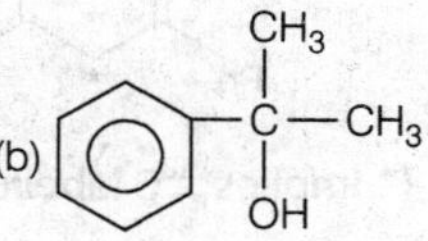

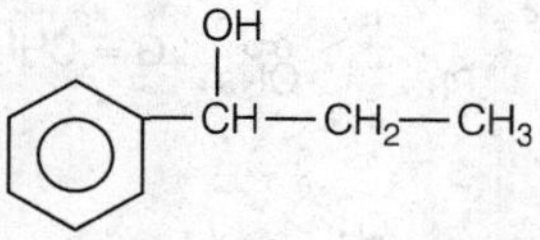

(a) 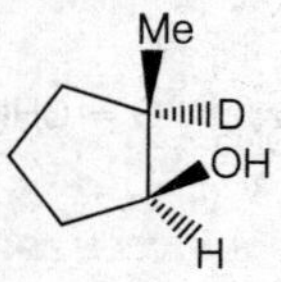 Me, D, OH, H (b) Me, D, OH, H

(c) Me, OH, D, H (d) Me, OH, H, H

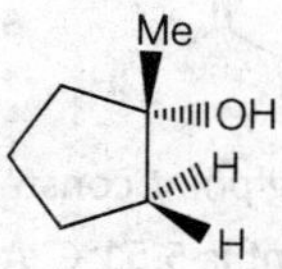

7. An organic diketone *A* having molecular formula $C_{14}H_{10}O_2$ when undergo reaction with hydroxyl ion (OH^-) converted into benzylic acid *B* after acidification. The molecular structure of *A* and *B* respectively are

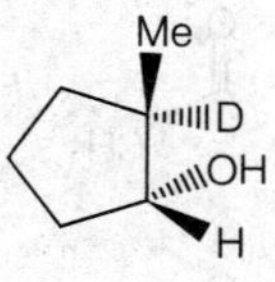

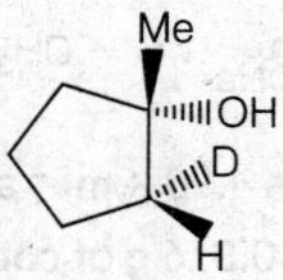

(a) 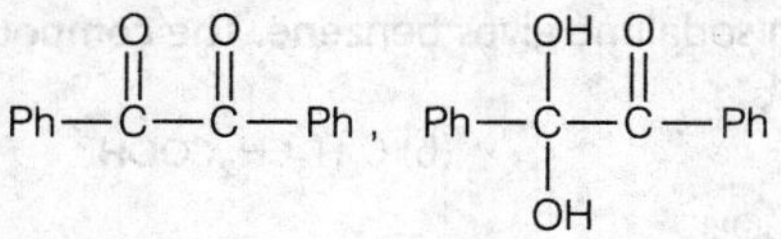 $Ph-CO-CO-Ph$, $Ph-C(OH)(OH)-CO-Ph$

(b) $Ph-CO-CO-Ph$, $Ph-C(OH)(Ph)-CO-OH$

(c) $Ph-C(OH)(Ph)-CO-CO-C_5H_5$ (cyclopentadienyl), $C_5H_5-C(OH)(H)-CO-C_6H_5$

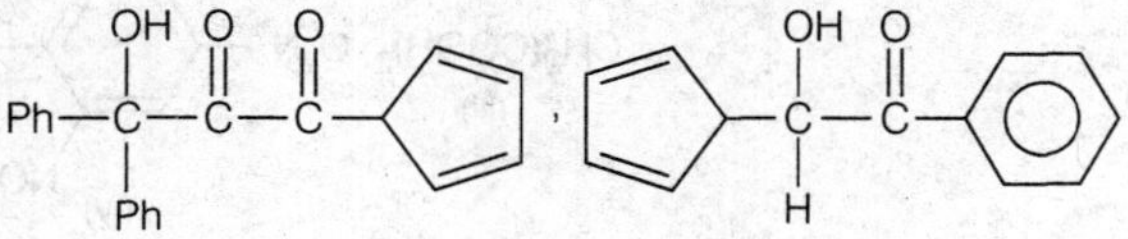

(d) 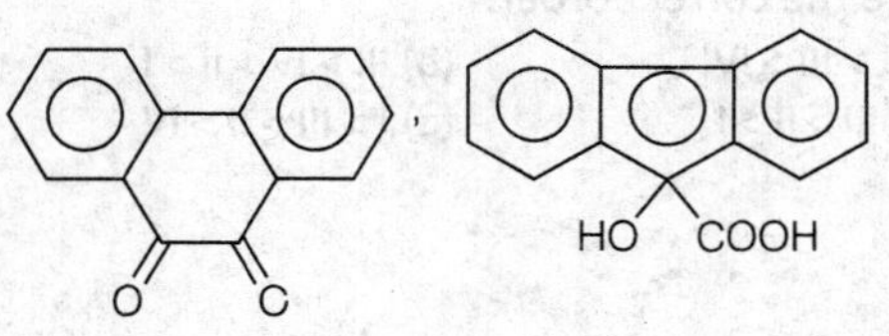 Phenanthrene-9,10-dione (O, O), 9-hydroxyfluorene-9-carboxylic acid (HO, COOH)

8. Which of the following will undergo oxidation reaction with MnO_2?

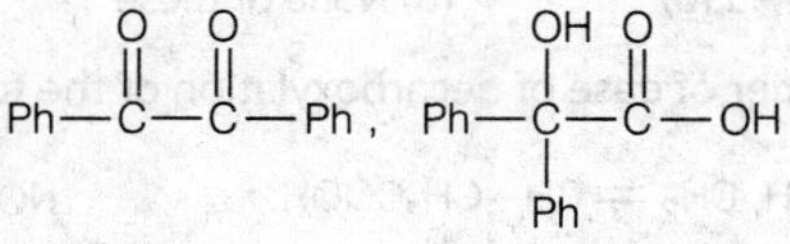

(a) Hex-3-en-1-ol (b) Cyclohex-3-en-1-ol

(c) Hex-2-en-1-ol (d) All of these

9. An organic compound *A* having molecular formula $C_9H_{10}O$, an orange red precipitate with 2, 4-DNP reagent and yellow precipitate on heating with I_2/NaOH. It neither reduces Tollen's reagent or Fehling solution nor it decolourises bromine water solution. On drastic oxidation with CrO_3, it produces a carboxylic acid having molecular formula $C_7H_6O_2$. Identify the correct structure of compound *A*.

(a) 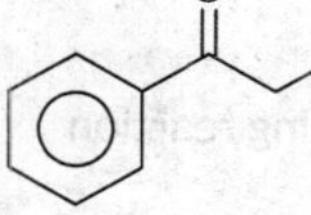 $C_6H_5-CO-CH_2CH_3$ (b) $C_6H_5-CH_2CH_2-CHO$

(c) $C_6H_5-CH_2-CO-CH_3$ (d) 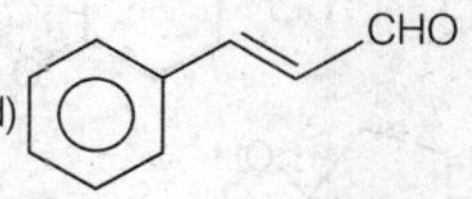 $C_6H_5-CH=CH-CHO$

10. What will be the correct structural formula of product (*C*) for the following reaction?

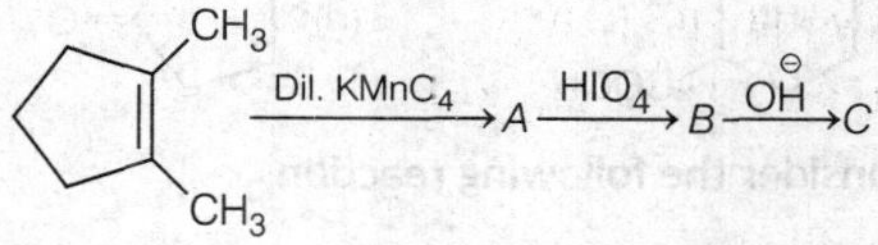

1,2-Dimethylcyclopentene (CH$_3$, CH$_3$) $\xrightarrow{\text{Dil. KMnO}_4} A \xrightarrow{HIO_4} B \xrightarrow{\overset{\ominus}{OH}} C$

(a) 3-methylcyclohex-2-en-1-one (O, CH$_3$) (b) 2-methylcyclopent-1-ene-1-carbaldehyde (CHO, CH$_3$)

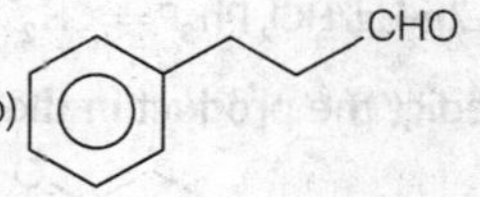

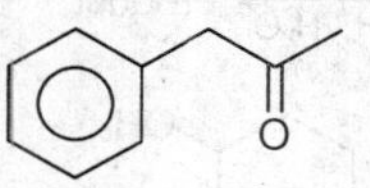

(c) cyclohexene-1-carbaldehyde (CHO) (d) 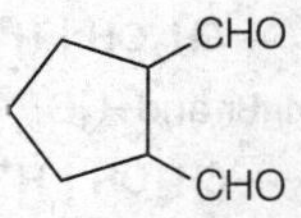 cyclopentane with two CHO

11. The product *R* in the following reaction is

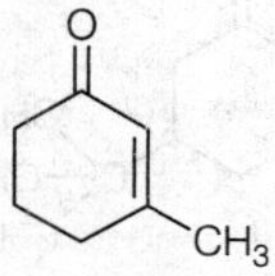

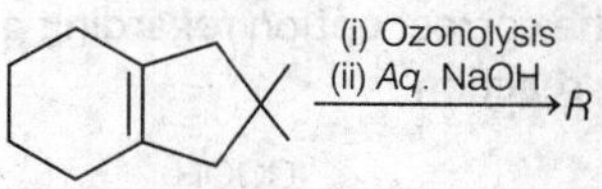

Bicyclic alkene with gem-dimethyl alkylidene $\xrightarrow[\text{(ii) Aq. NaOH}]{\text{(i) Ozonolysis}} R$

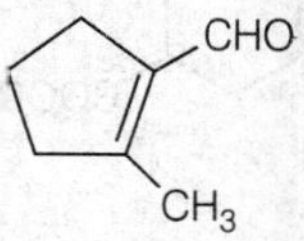

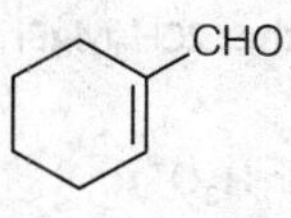

(a) 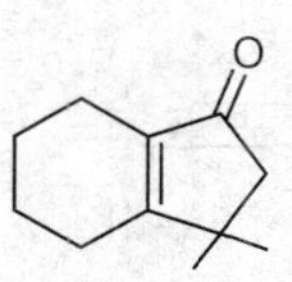 (b) 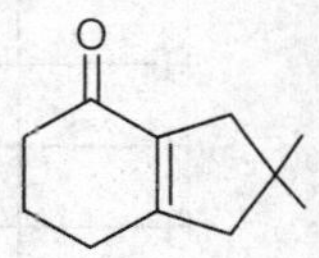 (c) 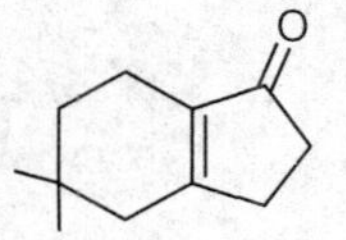 (d)

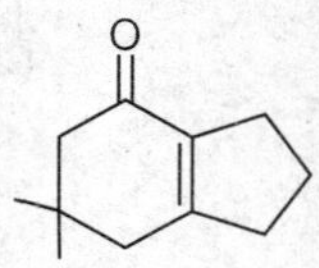

12. On the basis of following reaction, choose the correct option for *A* and *B* respectively.

(Cyclopentyl methyl ketone $\xrightarrow{A}$ ethylcyclopentane; cyclopentyl methyl ketone $\xrightarrow{B}$ cyclopentyl–C($=CH_2$)CH_3)

(a) $Ph_3P = CH_2$, Zn-Hg/HCl
(b) $Ph_3P = CH_2$, $LiAlH_4$
(c) $NaBH_4$, Zn-Hg/HCl
(d) Zn-Hg/HCl, $Ph_3P = CH_2$

13. Predict the product in the following reaction

(Cyclohexane-1,2-dione $\xrightarrow[\text{(ii) } H^+/H_2O]{\text{(i) } OH^{\ominus}}$ Product)

(a) 1-hydroxycyclopentanecarboxylic acid (OH, COOH) (b) cyclohexenol (OH)
(c) 2-hydroxycyclohexanecarboxylic acid (OH, COOH) (d) cyclopentanone

14. Consider the following reaction,

(3-(COOCH$_3$)cyclohexanone $\xrightarrow{\text{'X'}}$ 3-(C(CH$_3$)$_2$OH)cyclohexanone)

The reagent *X* in the reaction is
(a) $HOCH_2—CH_2OH$ | H^+, $LiAlH_4$ | ether $2CH_3MgBr$, H_3O^+
(b) $2CH_3MgBr$ and H_3O^+
(c) $HOCH_2 — CH_2OH$ | H^+, $2CH_3MgBr$, H_3O^+
(d) $HOCH_2—CH_2OH$ | H^+, H_2 | Pt, CH_3OH, H^+

15. Choose the correct option regarding product(s) of following reaction.

(Fischer projection: COOH; H—NH$_2$; H—OH; H—OH; CH$_3$ $\xrightarrow{HIO_4}$)

(a) CHO—COOH + CH_3CHO + HCOOH
(b) 4HCOOH + CH_3CHO
(c) 3HCOOH + CH_3CHO
(d) 2HCOOH + CHO—COOH + CH_3CHO

16. In the following reaction sequence, the correct structures of *E*, *F* and *G* are

(Ph–CO–C*H$_2$–COOH $\xrightarrow{\text{Heat}}$ [*E*] $\xrightarrow[\text{NaOH}]{I_2}$ [*F*] + [*G*])

(* implies ^{13}C labelled carbon)

(a) *E* = Ph–C*(=O)–CH$_3$; *F* = Ph–C*(=O)–$\overset{\ominus\oplus}{O}$Na ; *G* = CHI_3
(b) *E* = Ph–C(=O)–C*H$_3$; *F* = Ph–C(=O)–$\overset{\ominus\oplus}{O}$Na ; *G* = CHI_3
(c) *E* = Ph–C(=O)–C*H$_3$; *F* = Ph–C(=O)–$\overset{\ominus\oplus}{O}$Na ; *G* = C*HI$_3$
(d) *E* = Ph–C(=O)–C*H$_3$; *F* = Ph–C(=O)–$\overset{\ominus\oplus}{O}$Na ; *G* = C*H$_3$I

17. The freezing point constant of C_6H_6 is 4.90 K m^{-1} and its melting point is 5.51°C. A solution of 0.816 g of compound *A* when dissolved in 7.5 g of benzene, freezes at 1.59°C. The compound *A* has C = 70.58%, H = 5.88% and the rest is oxygen. Compound *A* on heating with sodalime gives another compound *B* which on oxidation and subsequent acidification gives an acid *C* of equivalent weight 122. *C* on heating with sodalime gives benzene. The compound *A* is

(a) C_6H_4(CH$_3$)(COOH) (b) $C_6H_5CH_2COOH$
(c) Both (a) and (b) (d) None of these

18. Give the order of ease of decarboxylation of the following acids.

CH_3COOH (I); $CH_2 = CH—CH_2COOH$ (II);
$CH_2(COOH)_2$ (III); O_2N–C$_6$H$_2$(NO$_2$)$_2$–COOH (IV) (2,4,6-trinitrobenzoic acid)

Choose the correct order.
(a) I > II > III > IV (b) III > IV > II > I
(c) IV > III > II > I (d) I > III > II > IV

19. An ester (*A*) with molecular formula $C_9H_{10}O_2$ was treated with excess of CH_3MgBr and the complex so formed was treated with H_2SO_4 to give an olefin (*B*). Ozonolysis of (*B*) gave a ketone with molecular formula C_8H_8O which shows positive iodoform test. The structure of (*A*) is

(a) $C_6H_5COOC_2H_5$ (b) $C_6H_5COOC_6H_5$
(c) $C_6H_5COOCH_3$ (d) *p*-$H_3CO—C_6H_4COCH_3$

20. Given below are two statements, one is labelled as Assertion (A) and the other is labelled as Reason (R).

Assertion (A) Acetyl chloride is more reactive than ethyl acetate for hydrolysis reaction.

Reason (R) Ethyl acetate is more stable than acetyl chloride due to resonance and electronegativity of oxygen and chlorine respectively.

In the light of the above statements, choose the correct answer from the options given below.

(a) Both Assertion and Reason are true and Reason is the correct explanation of Assertion.
(b) Both Assertion and Reason are true but Reason is not the correct explanation of Assertion.
(c) Assertion is true but Reason is false.
(d) Assertion is false but Reason is true.

Section B *Numerical Value Questions*

21. The number of organic products which are possible for the given stereoselective and regioselective reaction is ....

1-methylcyclopentene (CH₃) $\xrightarrow[\text{(ii) } \overset{\ominus}{O}H/H_2O_2]{\text{(i) } BH_3,\ THF}$

22. 0.436 g of acetyl derivative of a polyhydric alcohol (molecular mass = 92) requires 0.336 of KOH for hydrolysis. The number of hydroxyl groups in the alcohol is ....

23. $R—CH_2—OH \xrightarrow{?} R—CH_2—Cl$. The number of reagents that can be used for above conversion from following is ....

$HCl/ZnCl_2$, PCl_3, PCl_5, $POCl_3$, $SOCl_2$, NaCl, TsCl

24. Moles of HI reacts with glycerol to give 3-iodopropene are ....

25. Consider the pairs of ether A to F shown below. To the right of each pairs, there is a description of reaction conditions to be applied to each. One compound of the pair will react more rapidly than the other. The number of reactions in which first ether more rapidly cleaved than second is ....

	Ether pairs	Conditions
A.	C_6H_5—O—$CH(CH_3)_2$ and 3,5-$(H_3C)_2C_6H_3$—O—CH_3	Treated with HBr in $CH_3—CN$, 40°C
B.	1,1-$(H_3C)_2$-cyclohexyl—O—$C(CH_3)_3$ and 1,1-$(H_5C_2)_2$-cyclohexyl—O—CH_3	Treated with H_2SO_4 in CH_3CN, 40°C
C.	C_6H_5—O—CH(vinyl)(ethyl) and C_6H_5—O—(bicyclic)	Treated with H_2SO_4 in CH_3CN, 40°C
D.	CH_3O—(tetrahydropyran)—OH and HO—(tetrahydropyran)—OCH_3	Treated with 5% aqueous H_2SO_4, 25°C
E.	$CH_2=CH—CH_2—O—CH(CH_3)_2$ and $CH_3—CH=CH—O—CH(CH_3)_2$	Treated with 5% aqueous H_2SO_4, 25°C
F.	C_6H_5—$CH_2—O—C_2H_5$ and C_6H_5—$(CH_2)_3—O—CH_3$	Treated with $H^{\oplus}/H_2O$

26. .... number of compound(s) from the following that is/are enol tautomers of butan-2-one.

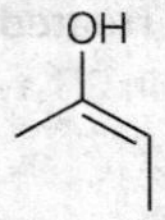

(A) 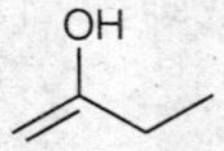 (B) 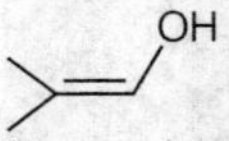 (C) 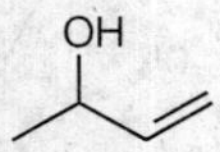 (D)

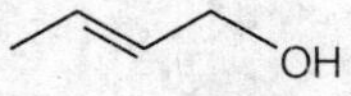

(E) 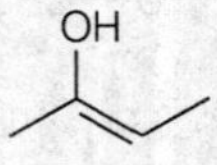 (F) 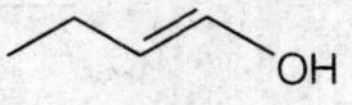 (G)

27. 0.535 g mixture of ethanol and acetaldehyde when heated with Fehling solution give 1.2 g of a red precipitate. The percentage of acetaldehyde, present in the mixture is ....

28. $CO_2 + H_2 \xleftarrow[\text{High pressure}]{160^\circ} (X) \xrightarrow{P_2O_5/\Delta} CO + H_2O$, then number of oxygen atom in (X) is ....

29. $(X) \xrightarrow{\Delta}$ Carboxylic acid $+ CO_2\uparrow$;

$(Y) \xrightarrow{\Delta}$ Acid anhydride $+ H_2O$;
(5-membered)

$(Z) \xrightarrow{\Delta}$ Cyclopentanone $+ H_2O + CO_2\uparrow$

Then the numbers of carbon atoms in *X*, *Y* and *Z* are *x*, *y* and *z* respectively.

The value of $(x + y + z)$ is ....

30. CH_3COCl is used to detect number of amino groups in the organic compounds. When a compound of molecular mass 180 is acetylated, it gives a compound of molecular mass 390. The number of amino groups in the compound is ......

Answers

Section A

1 *(a)*	2 *(c)*	3 *(b)*	4 *(d)*	5 *(a)*
6 *(b)*	7 *(b)*	8 *(c)*	9 *(c)*	10 *(a)*
11 *(d)*	12 *(d)*	13 *(a)*	14 *(c)*	15 *(a)*
16 *(c)*	17 *(c)*	18 *(c)*	19 *(a)*	20 *(a)*

Section B

21 *(2)*	22 *(3)*	23 *(4)*	24 *(3)*	25 *(5)*
26 *(3)*	27 *(69)*	28 *(2)*	29 *(13)*	30 *(5)*

See detailed solutions on page no. 256

QUALIFIER 25

Organic Compounds Containing Nitrogen

Section A *Objective Type Questions*

1. Examine the following two structures for the anilinium ion and choose the correct statement from the ones given below.

Structure (I): $\overset{+}{N}H_3$ attached to benzene ring; Structure (II): NH_3 double bonded (=) to ring carbon with + charge on ring; (I) ⟷ (II)

(a) Structure II is not an acceptable canonical structure because carbonium ions are less stable then ammonium ions.

(b) Structure II is not an acceptable canonical structure because it is non-aromatic.

(c) Structure II is not an acceptable canonical structure because the nitrogen has 10 valence electrons.

(d) Structure II is an acceptable canonical structure.

2. Product (*B*) in the given reaction is

$$\begin{matrix} CH_2-COOH \\ | \\ CH_2-COOH \end{matrix} \xrightarrow{Urea/\Delta} [A] \xrightarrow{KOBr} [B]$$

(a) $CH_2(COOH)-CH_2(NH_2)$ (COOH / NH_2)

(b) $CH_2(COO^{\ominus})-CH_2(NH_2)$ ($COO^{\ominus}$ / NH_2)

(c) Succinic anhydride (cyclic, ring O with two C=O)

(d) Succinimide (cyclic, ring NH with two C=O)

3. For preparing 2° amine, the most appropriate method is

(a) $NH_3 + 2\underset{1°}{RBr} \longrightarrow$

(b) $2\underset{1°}{RBr} + NaCN \longrightarrow \xrightarrow{Pt/H_2}$

(c) $RNH_2 \xrightarrow{RCHO} \xrightarrow{Pt/H_2}$

(d) $2\underset{1°}{R—Br} + C_6H_4\langle {}^{CO}_{CO} \rangle NH \xrightarrow{H_3O^+}$

4. The correct order of basic strength of the following compounds is

I. $C_6H_5-NHCOCH_3$ II. $C_6H_5-\overset{O}{\overset{\|}{C}}-NHCH_3$

III. $C_6H_5-\overset{O}{\overset{\|}{C}}-CH_2NH_2$ IV. $H_2N-C_6H_4-COCH_3$

(a) I > II > III > IV (b) IV > II > III > I

(c) III > IV > II > I (d) III > II > IV > I

5. RNH_2 reacts with $C_6H_5SO_2Cl$ in *aq*. KOH to give a clear solution. On acidification, a precipitate is obtained which is due to the formation of

(a) $R-\overset{H}{\underset{H}{N^+}}-SO_2C_6H_5OH^-$ (b) $R—N^-SO_2C_6H_5K^+$

(c) $C_6H_5SO_2NH_2$ (d) $R—NH—SO_2—C_6H_5$

6. Consider the following reaction sequence,

I. Toluene ($C_6H_5CH_3$) $\xrightarrow[\Delta]{Conc.\ H_2SO_4}$ *o*-isomer + *p*-isomer

II. *o*-isomer $\xrightarrow{PCl_5} \xrightarrow{NH_3} \xrightarrow[35°C]{aq.\ KMnO_4} \xrightarrow[35°C]{\Delta} A$

The structure of compound *A* is

(a) Benzene ring with COOH and ortho SO_2NH_2

(b) Benzene ring with CO and SO_2 bridged by NH (cyclic)

(c) Benzene ring with CH_3 and para SO_2NH_2

(d) Benzene ring with CH_3 and para $SO_2—\overset{Cl}{\underset{\ominus}{N}}\overset{\oplus}{Na}$

7. Nitration of aniline also gives *m*-nitroaniline in strong acidic medium because

(a) in electrophilic, substitution reaction amino group is *meta*-directive.
(b) inspite of substitutents, nitro group always goes to *meta*-position.
(c) in acidic (strong) medium aniline is present as anilinium ion.
(d) None of the above

8. Given below are two statements, one is labelled as Assertion (A) and the other is labelled as Reason (R).

Assertion (A) Nitration of aniline can be conveniently done by protecting the amino group by acetylation.

Reason (R) Acetylation increases the electron-density in the benzene ring.

In the light of the above statements, choose the correct answer from the options given below.

(a) Both A and R are true and R is the correct explanation of A.
(b) Both A and R are true but R is not the correct explanation of A.
(c) A is true but R is false.
(d) A is false but R is true.

9. The major product formed on nitration of N, N-dimethyl aniline with conc. H_2SO_4 and HNO_3 mixture is

(a) 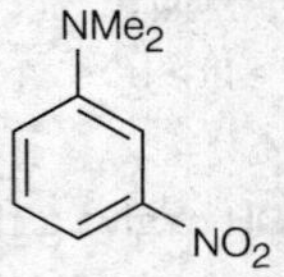 NMe_2, NO_2 (b) 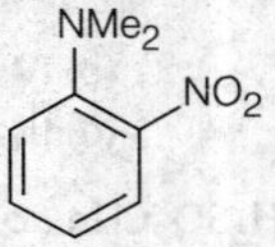 NMe_2, NO_2 (c) 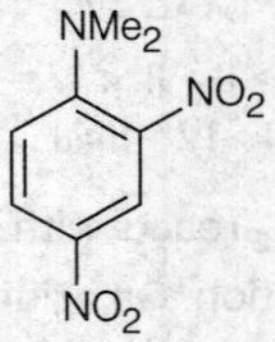 NMe_2, NO_2, NO_2 (d) 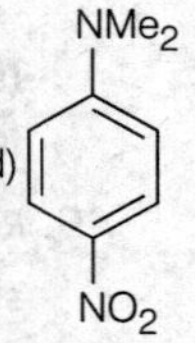 NMe_2, NO_2

10. Predict the product of the reaction.

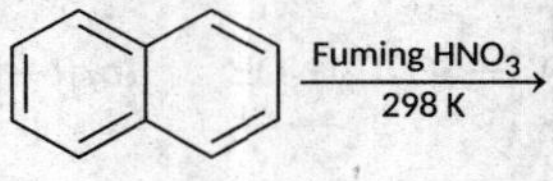

Fuming HNO_3, 298 K

(a) 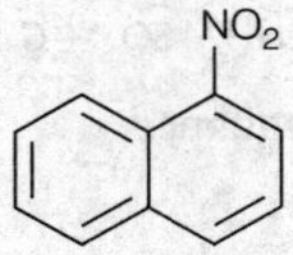 NO_2 (b) 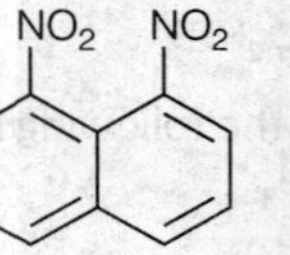 NO_2 NO_2 (c) 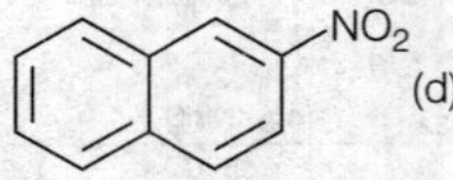 NO_2 (d) 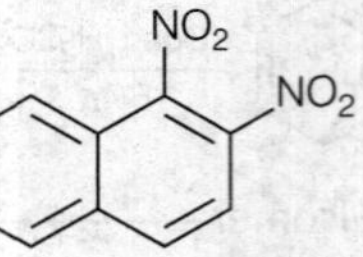 NO_2, NO_2

11. The best method to synthesize *m*-dibromobenzene can be achieved by which of the following reaction sequence?

(a) Benzene $\xrightarrow{Br_2/FeBr_3/Heat}$

(b) Aniline $\xrightarrow{Br_2, H_2O}$ [ ] $\xrightarrow[\text{(ii) CuBr}]{\text{(i) HONO}}$

(c) Nitrobenzene $\xrightarrow[H_2SO_4, \Delta]{\text{Fuming } HNO_3}$ [ ] $\xrightarrow[C_2H_5OH, \text{ Heat}]{Fe/HCl}$ [ ] $\xrightarrow[\text{(ii) CuBr}]{\text{(i) HONO}}$

(d) Bromobenzene $\xrightarrow[H_2SO_4]{HNO_3}$ [ ] $\xrightarrow[C_2H_5OH, \text{ Heat}]{Fe/HCl}$ [ ] $\xrightarrow[\text{(ii) CuBr}]{\text{(i) HONO}}$

12. Product (*P*) of the given reaction is

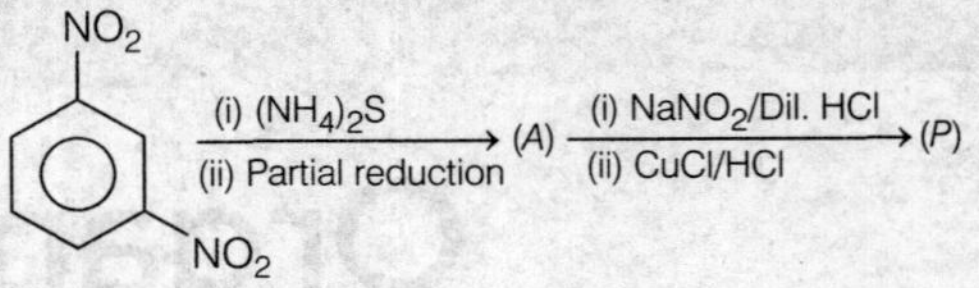

NO_2, NO_2 $\xrightarrow[\text{(ii) Partial reduction}]{\text{(i) } (NH_4)_2S}$ (*A*) $\xrightarrow[\text{(ii) CuCl/HCl}]{\text{(i) NaNO}_2\text{/Dil. HCl}}$ (*P*)

(a) Cl, Cl (b) 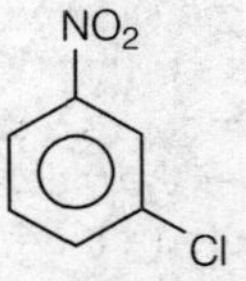 NO_2, Cl
(c) 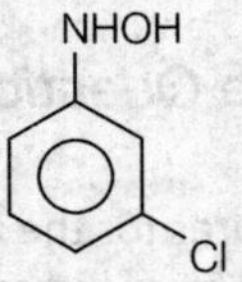 NHOH, Cl (d) 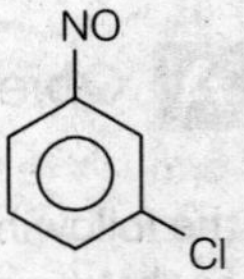 NO, Cl

13. 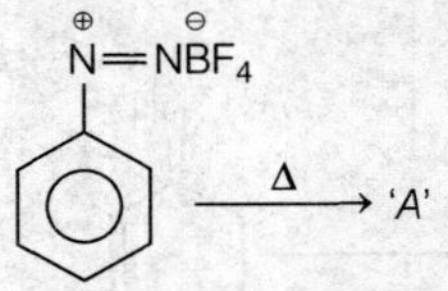 $\overset{\oplus}{N}{=}N\overset{\ominus}{B}F_4$ $\xrightarrow{\Delta}$ '*A*'

In the above reaction, product *A* is

(a) fluorobenzene (b) benzene
(c) 1, 4-difluorobenzene (d) 1, 3-difluorobenzene

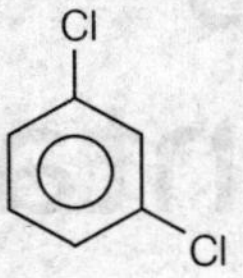

14. The major product formed in the reaction given below is

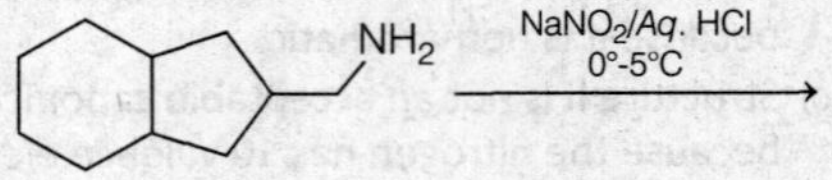

NH_2 $\xrightarrow[0°\text{-}5°C]{NaNO_2/Aq.\ HCl}$

(a) NO_2 (b) OH
(c) NO_2 (d) 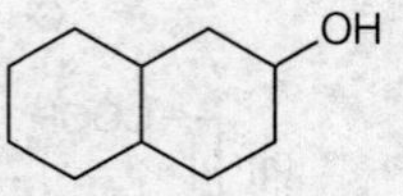 OH

15. Under the following sequence of reactions, *A* gives

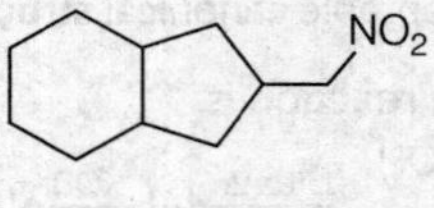

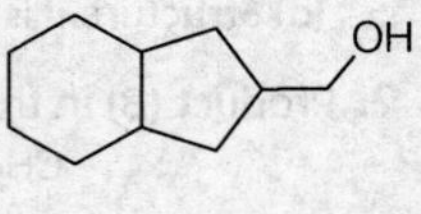

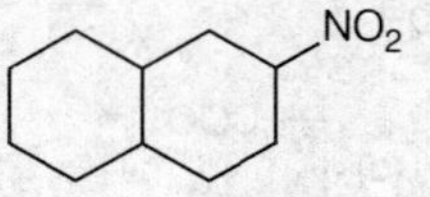

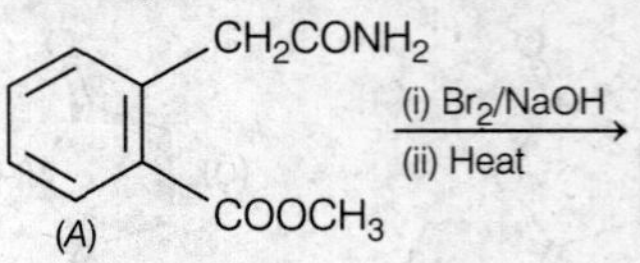

CH_2CONH_2, $COOCH_3$ (*A*) $\xrightarrow[\text{(ii) Heat}]{\text{(i) } Br_2/NaOH}$

(a) O, O, O (b) 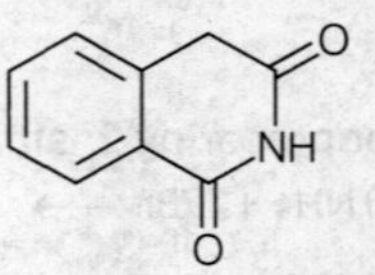 O, NH, O
(c) 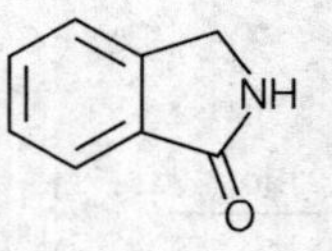 NH, O (d) 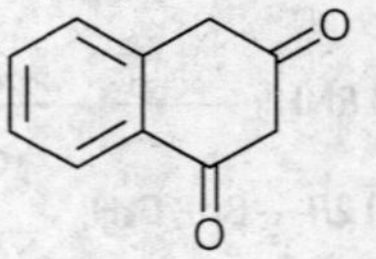 O, O

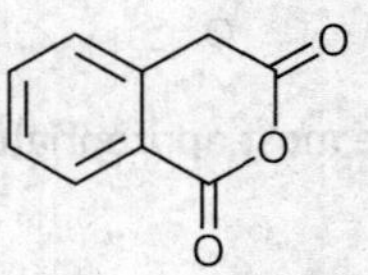

16. The correct statement about the following reaction is

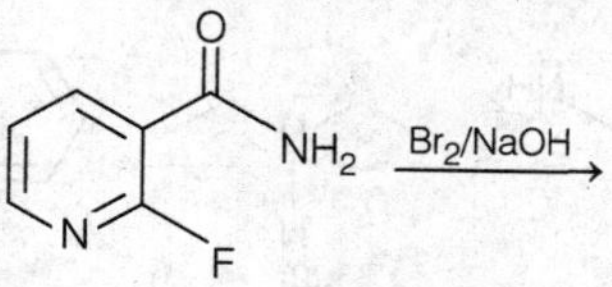

$\xrightarrow{Br_2/NaOH}$

(a) The product is 2-fluoropyridine-3- amine and the reaction involves the nitrene intermediate

(b) The product is 2-fluoropyridine-3- amine and the reaction involves the radical intermediate

(c) The product is 2-hydroxynicotinamide and the reaction involves the benzyne like intermediate

(d) The product is 2-fluoropyridine-3-amine and the reaction involves the addition-elimination mechanism

17. The compound which on reaction with aniline will not form an acetanilide is

(a) 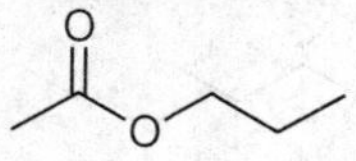 (b) 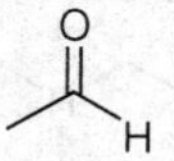 (c) 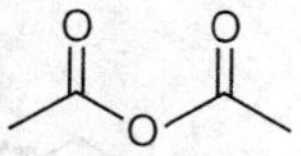 (d)

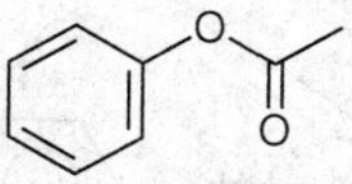

18. In the reaction shown below, identify the correct combination of the intermediate *P* and the product *Q*.

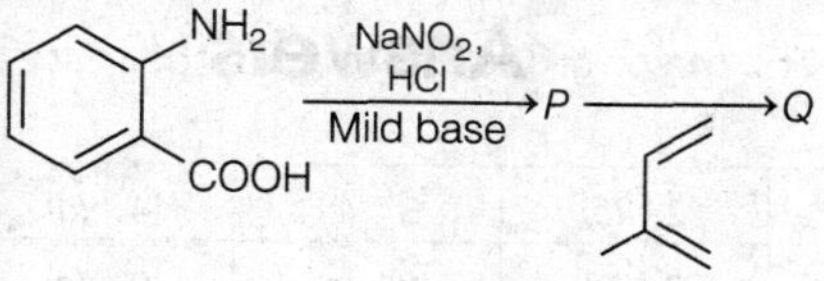

$\xrightarrow[\text{Mild base}]{NaNO_2, HCl} P \longrightarrow Q$

(a) COOH (*P*) ; COOH (*Q*)

(b) 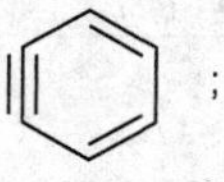 (*P*) ; 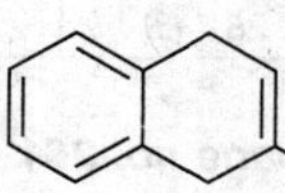 (*Q*)

(c) 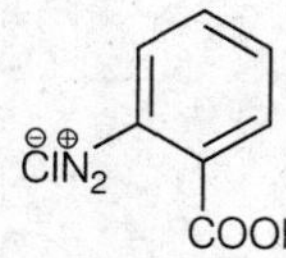 $\overset{\ominus\oplus}{ClN_2}$ COOH (*P*) ; COOH (*Q*)

(d) 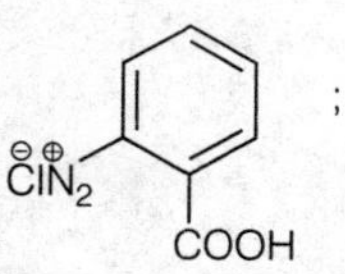 $\overset{\ominus\oplus}{ClN_2}$ COOH (*P*) ; HO O (*Q*)

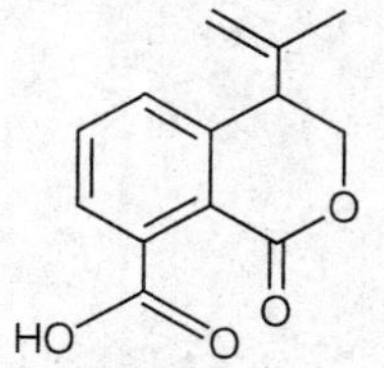

19. Observe the following reaction,

(*R'*)-1-phenylethylamine + (*R*+*S*)-2-Chloropropanoic acid $\xrightarrow{(1)}$ [(*R'R*)+(*R'S*)] $\xrightarrow[\text{(2)}]{\text{Separation by recrystallisation}}$ (*R'R*) $\xrightarrow[(3)]{\text{Hydrolysis}}$ (*R'*)+(*R*) ; (*R'S*) $\xrightarrow[(3)]{\text{Hydrolysis}}$ (*R'*)+(*S*)

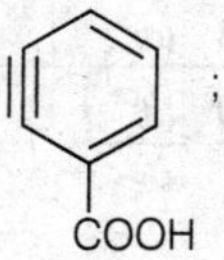

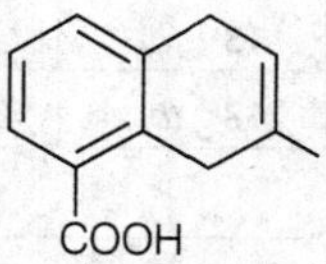

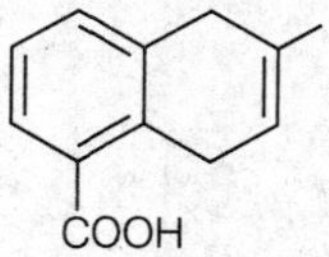

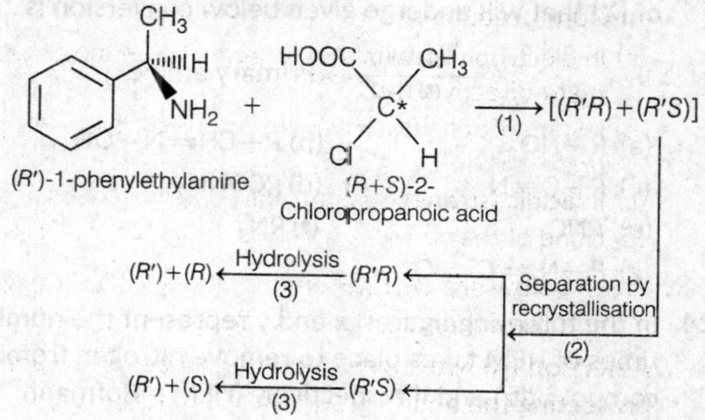

Which statement is not correct about the above reaction?

(a) The product mixture of step-1 is optically active

(b) The product (*R'R*) and (*R'S*) have identical structural formula

(c) (*R'R*) is non-superimposable on (*R'S*)

(d) (*R'R*) and (*R'S*) have same solubility in water

20. Product (*P*) of the given reaction is

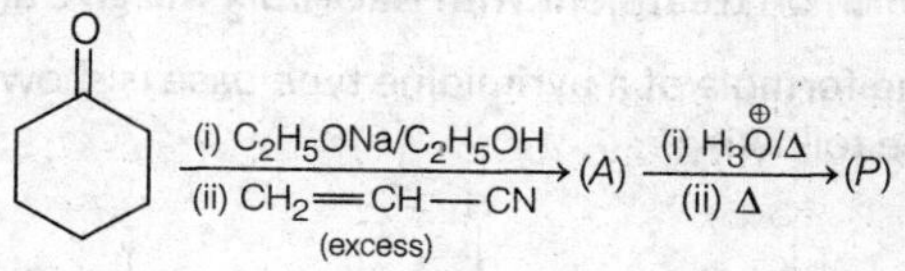

$\xrightarrow[\text{(ii) } CH_2{=}CH{-}CN \text{ (excess)}]{\text{(i) } C_2H_5ONa/C_2H_5OH} (A) \xrightarrow[\text{(ii) } \Delta]{\text{(i) } H_3\overset{\oplus}{O}/\Delta} (P)$

(a) $HOOC-CH_2-CH_2-$ ... $-CH_2-CH_2-COOH$

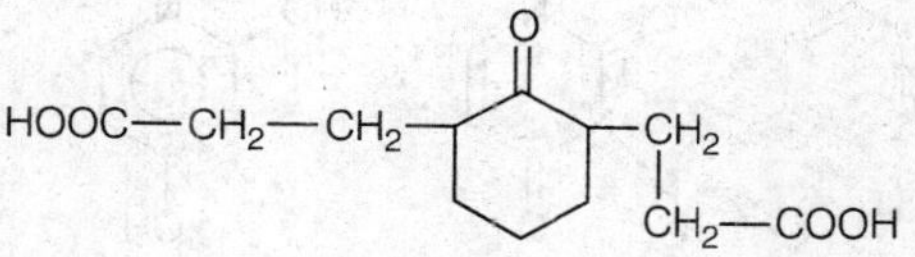

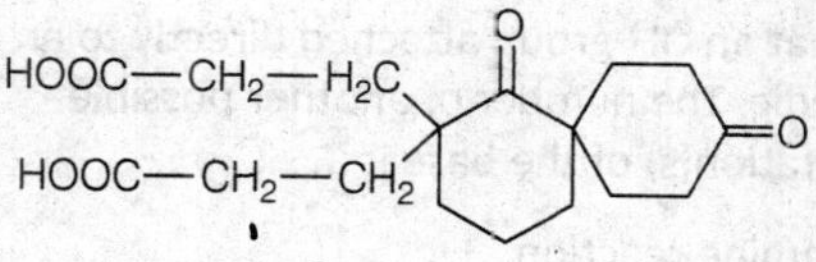

(b) $HOOC-CH_2-H_2C$, $HOOC-CH_2-CH_2$ ... =O

(c) O= ... =O

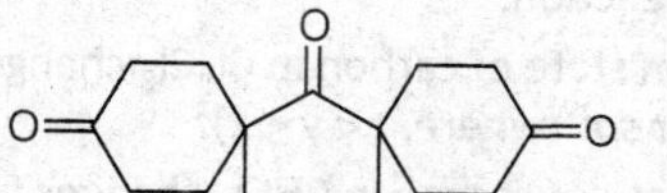

(d) 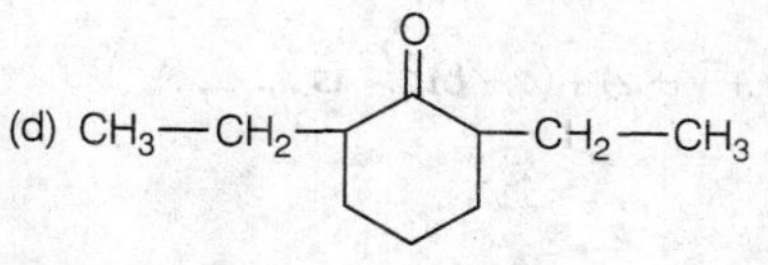 CH_3-CH_2- ... $-CH_2-CH_3$

Section B Numerical Value Questions

21. The number of possible structural isomers for the molecular formula $C_2H_8N_2$ is ....

22. The number of reagents used for this conversion is ....

$R-\overset{\oplus}{N}\equiv\overset{\ominus}{C} \longrightarrow R-NH-CH_3$

I. H_2 / Ni / Δ II. metal/acid

III. $LiAlH_4$ IV. Na/EtOH

V. P_2O_5 / Δ VI. $CHCl_3$ / Alc. KOH / Δ

23. In the given reaction, the total number of different types(s) of [X] that will undergo given below conversion is ....

$$X \xrightarrow[\text{(ii) } H_2O]{\text{(i) } LiAlH_4} \text{Primary amine}$$

(a) $R—NO_2$ (b) $R—CH{=}N—OH$
(c) $R—C{\equiv}N$ (d) $RCONH_2$
(e) RNC (f) RN_3
(g) $R—N{=}C{=}O$

24. In the following figures, x and y represent the number of times of HEM takes place to remove nitrogen from the compounds I and II respectively (HEM = Hofmann Exhaustive Methylation), $x + y$ is ....

I. II.

25. .... number of amide isomer(s) exist(s) for $C_5H_{11}ON$ which on treatment with $NaOH/Br_2$ will give amines,

26. The formula of a pyrimidine type base is shown as one of the following,

Noting that an OH-group attached directly to an aromatic ring is acidic. The number of another possible representation(s) of the base is ....

27. In carbylamine reaction,

(a) hybridisation state of carbon in $CHCl_3$ changes from sp^x to sp^y or sp^z (where, $z < y < x$).

(b) oxidation state of carbon in $CHCl_3$ changes from $|a|$ to $|b|$.

The value of $[(x + y + z) + (a - b)]^{1/2}$ is ....

28. Out of the following amines, ... give carbylamine reaction

(1) ; (2) ; (3) ; (4) ; (5) ; (6)

29. 0.1 mole of aniline reacts with x g of bromine in water to give a white precipitate. The value of x is .... (Br = 80).

30. Out of the following .... number of amines(s) amines that can participate in Hofmann's mustard oil reaction.

Answers

Section A

1 (c)	2 (b)	3 (c)	4 (d)	5 (b)
6 (b)	7 (c)	8 (c)	9 (a)	10 (a)
11 (c)	12 (b)	13 (a)	14 (d)	15 (c)
16 (a)	17 (b)	18 (b)	19 (d)	20 (c)

Section B

21 (5)	22 (4)	23 (5)	24 (5)	25 (5)
26 (4)	27 (2.45)	28 (3)	29 (48)	30 (4)

See detailed solutions on page no. 261

QUALIFIER 26

Polymers

Section A Objective Type Questions

1. Free radical polymerisation requires a free radical initiator. The most commonly used free radical initiator is

(a) Ph—CO—O—O—COPh, benzoylperoxide
(b) $(CH_3)_3C—O—O—C(CH_3)_3$, *tert*-butylperoxide
(c) $C_6H_5—N\rightarrow O$ ($=N—C_6H_5$), azoxybenzene
(d) CH_2N_2, diazomethane

2. Which monomer will give cross-linked polymer?

(a) COOH—C_6H_4—COOH
(b) $NH_2—CH_2—COOH$
(c) HOH_2CHN—(triazine ring)—$NH—CH_2OH$, with $NH—CH_2OH$ on the third ring carbon
(d) $CH_2OH—CH_2OH$

3. Which of the following is not correctly matched?

(a) Neoprene : $\left[CH_2—\underset{}{\overset{Cl}{\overset{|}{C}}}=CH—CH_2 \right]_n$

(b) Nylon-6,6 : $\left[NH—(CH_2)—NH—CO—(CH_2)_4\overset{O}{\overset{\|}{C}} \right]_n$

(c) Terylene : $\left[O—CH_2CH_2—O—\underset{O}{\underset{\|}{C}}—C_6H_4—\underset{O}{\underset{\|}{C}} \right]_n$

(d) PMMA : $\left[CH_2—\overset{CH_3}{\overset{|}{\underset{COOCH_3}{\underset{|}{C}}}} \right]_n$

4. Which of the following monomers can undergo radical, cationic as well as anionic polymerisation with equal ease?

(a) $CH_3—\underset{CH_3}{\underset{|}{C}}=CH_2$
(b) $CH_2=CH_2$
(c) $C_6H_5—CH=CH_2$
(d) $CH_3—CH=CH_2$

5. Match the Column I and Column II and choose the correct answer by using codes as given:

	Column I		Column II
A.	Nylon-6	1.	Polyvinyl chloride
B.	PVC	2.	Polyacrylonitrile
C.	Acrilan	3.	Polycaprolactam
D.	Natural rubber	4.	*cis*-polyisoprene

Codes

	A	B	C	D
(a)	3	1	2	4
(b)	1	2	4	3
(c)	4	1	2	3
(d)	1	4	3	2

6. Arrange the following in increasing order of their intermolecular forces.

Nylon-6,6 (I), Buna-S (II), Polythene (III)

Choose the correct order.

(a) II < I < III
(b) III < II < I
(c) I < II < III
(d) II < III < I

7. In the reaction sequence,

$$\text{Cyclohexanone oxime (C=NOH)} \xrightarrow{H_2SO_4} [X] \xrightarrow{540K} \text{Nylon-6}$$

The intermediate [X] is

(a) cyclohexanone
(b) caprolactam
(c) $HO(CH_2)_6NH_2$
(d) hexamethylene diisocyanate

8. Consider the following reactions,

(a) Caprolactam $\xrightarrow{\text{Hydrolysis}}$ A (b) A + Glycine $\longrightarrow$ B (Polymer)

Here, B is

I. condensation polymer II. addition polymer
III. polyamide polymer IV. polyester polymer
V. boidegradable polymer

Choose the correct option.

(a) I, III and V (b) II and IV (c) II, III and IV (d) II, IV and V

9. Which of the following pairs of monomers form biodegradable polymers?

I. 3-hydroxybutanoic acid + 3-hydroxypentanoic acid
II. Glycine + Amino caproic acid
III. Ethylene glycol + Phthalic acid
IV. Caprolactam

Choose the correct option.

(a) I and II (b) II and III (c) I, II and III (d) III and IV

10. Which of the following polymers is biodegradable?

(a) $\left[CH_2—\underset{Cl}{\underset{|}{C}}=CH—CH_2 \right]_n$

(b) $\left(CH_2—CH=CH—CH_2—CH_2—CH \right)_n$

(c) $\left[O—\underset{CH_3}{\underset{|}{CH}}—CH_2—\underset{O}{\underset{||}{C}}—O—\underset{CH_2CH_3}{\underset{|}{CH}}—CH_2—\underset{O}{\underset{||}{C}} \right]_n$

(d) $\left[\overset{H}{\overset{|}{N}}—(CH_2)_6—\overset{H}{\overset{|}{N}}—\overset{O}{\overset{||}{C}}—(CH_2)_4—\overset{O}{\overset{||}{C}} \right]_n$

Section B Numerical Value Questions

11. .... of the following are chain growth (addition) polymers.
[PVC, PAN, nylon-6, neoprene, PMMA, polystyrene, dacron, novolac.]

12. The number of polymers that contain isoprene as one of the monomers is ....
[Neoprene, *Gutta-percha*, Buna-N, Buna-S, SBR, Natural rubber, Thiokol, Glyptal, LDP.]

13. A regular copolymer of ethylene and vinyl chloride contains alternate monomers of each type. Weight per cent of ethylene in this copolymer is ....

14. The number average molecular mass and mass average molecular mass of a polymer are respectively 30,000 and 40,000. The polydispersity index of the polymer is ....

15. A compound 'X' reacts with formaldehyde to form a resin intermediate 'Y'. Polymerisation of this resin gives melamine polymer.

If x and y are number of carbon atoms, number of nitrogen atoms respectively in compound 'X' and z is the number of double bonds in compound 'X' and 'Y'.

The value of $(z-x)^y$ is ....

Answers

Section A

1 *(a)*	2 *(c)*	3 *(b)*	4 *(c)*	5 *(a)*
6 *(d)*	7 *(b)*	8 *(a)*	9 *(a)*	10 *(c)*

Section B

11 *(5)*	12 *(2)*	13 *(30.94)*	14 *(1.33)*	15 *(729)*

See detailed solutions on page no. 265

QUALIFIER 27

Biomolecules

Section A Objective Type Questions

1. The term invert sugar refers to an equimolar mixture of

(a) D-glucose and D-galactose

(b) D-glucose and D-fructose

(c) D-glucose and D-mannose

(d) D-glucose and D-ribose

2. Cellulose upon acetylation with excess acetic anhydride/ H_2SO_4 (catalytic) gives cellulose triacetate whose structure is

(a)

(b)

(c)

(d)

3. Compound A, $C_5H_{10}O_5$ gives a tetraacetate with Ac_2O and oxidation of 'A' with Br_2 / H_2O gives an acid, $C_5H_{10}O_6$. Reduction of 'A' with HI gives *iso*-pentane. What is the possible structure of A?

(a) COOH
HO—C—CH_2OH
CHOH
CH_2OH

(b) CHO
HO—C—CH_2OH
CHOH
CH_2OH

(c) CHO
HO—C—H
$(CHOH)_2$
CH_2OH

(d) CH_2OH
HO—C=O
HO—C—CH_2OH
CHOH
CH_2OH

4. Given below are two statements, one is labelled as Assertion (A) and the other is labelled as Reason (R).

Assertion (A) β-glycosidic linkage is present in maltose.

Reason (R) Maltose is composed of two glucose units in which C-1 of one glucose unit is linked to C-4 of another glucose unit.

(a) Both A and R are true and R is the correct explanation of A.

(b) Both A and R are true but R is not the correct explanation of A.

(c) A is true but R is false.

(d) A is false but R is true.

5. The correct epimeric pair of the following is

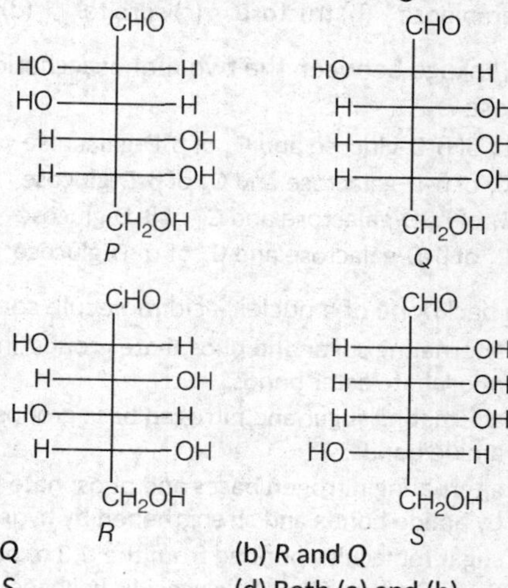

(a) P and Q

(b) R and Q

(c) Q and S

(d) Both (a) and (b)

6. The major products *A* and *B* in the following reaction sequences are

$$A \xleftarrow[\text{(iii) } H_2O_2,\ Fe_2(SO_4)_3]{\text{(i) } Br_2/H_2O \quad \text{(ii) } Ca(OH)_2} \begin{array}{c} CHO \\ H-\!\!\!\!-OH \\ H-\!\!\!\!-OH \\ H-\!\!\!\!-OH \\ CH_2OH \end{array} \xrightarrow[\text{(ii) } H_2,\ Pd/BaSO_4 \quad \text{(iii) } H^+/H_2O]{\text{(i) KCN, HCN}} B$$

(a) *A* = D-threose, *B* = D-glucose
(b) *A* = D-erythrose, *B* = D-glucose + D-mannose
(c) *A* = D-threose, *B* = D-glucose + D-mannose
(d) *A* = D-tartaric acid, *B* = D-glucose

7. A disaccharide that will not give Benedict's test and will not form osazone is
(a) maltose (b) lactose (c) cellobiose (d) sucrose

8. The major product of the following reaction is

(Pyranose ring with CH_2OH (OH), HO, HO, OH, OH) $\xrightarrow[\text{(ii) HCl, } H_2O]{\text{(i) } Me_2SO_4,\ NaOH}$

(a) Pyranose ring with OMe (C-6), MeO, MeO, OMe, OMe
(b) Pyranose ring with OH (C-6), MeO, MeO, OMe, OMe
(c) Pyranose ring with OMe (C-6), MeO, MeO, OMe, OH
(d) Pyranose ring with OH (C-6), HO, HO, OH, OMe

9. Which of the following gives violet colour with conc. HCl?
(a) Fructose (b) Glucose (c) Maltose (d) Starch

10. Consider the following sequence of the reactions

$$\text{Glucose} \xrightarrow[\text{(Excess)}]{PhNH-NH_2} (A) \xrightarrow[\text{Heat}]{H_3O^{\oplus}} (B) \xrightarrow{\text{Zn/ AcOH}} (C)$$

The product (*C*) is expected to be
(a) arabinose (b) fructose (c) sorbitol (d) mannose

11. The linkage between the two monosaccharide units in lactose is
(a) C_1 of β-D-glucose and C_4 of β-D-galactose
(b) C_1 of β-D-galactose and C_4 of β-D-glucose
(c) C_1 of α-D-galactose and C_4 of β-D-glucose
(d) C_1 of β-D-galactose and C_4 of α-D-glucose

12. The backbone of a nucleic acid molecule consists of
(a) alternating sugar and phosphate groups linked by phosphate ester bonds.
(b) alternating sugar and nitrogen base groups linked by amide bonds.
(c) alternating nitrogen bases and phosphate groups linked by amide bonds and strengthened by hydrogen bonds.
(d) sugar molecules bonded from the C-3 of one molecule to the C-5 of the other by glycosidic linkages.

13. Among the following, the correct statement(s) is/are
(a) guanine is purine nucleobase.
(b) glycine and proline are achiral and chiral amino acids respectively.
(c) DNA contains glycosidic bonds and pentose sugars.
(d) All of the above

14. If one strand of DNA has the sequence ATCGTATG, the sequence in the complementary strand would be
(a) TAGCTTAC (b) TCACATAC
(c) TAGCATAC (d) TACGATAC

15. Following amino acid has been found in protein prothrombin, but remained undetected due to formation of another common acid (*A*)

$$H_3\overset{\oplus}{N}-CH(COO^{\ominus})-CH_2-CH(COO^{\ominus})_2 \longrightarrow (A)$$

Identify '*A*'

(a) $H_3\overset{\oplus}{N}-CH(COO^{\ominus})-CH_2-CH_2-COO^{\ominus}$
(b) $H_3\overset{\oplus}{N}-CH(COO^{\ominus})-CH(COO^{\ominus})_2$
(c) $H_2N-CH(COO^{\ominus})-CH_2COOH$
(d) $H_2N-CH(COOH)-CH(COO^{\ominus})_2$

16. The secondary structure of a protein refers to
(a) α-helical backbone.
(b) hydrophobic interaction.
(c) sequence of α-amino acids.
(d) fixed configuration of the polypeptide back bone.

17. Which one of the following statements is true for protein synthesis (translation)?
(a) Amino acids are directly recognized by *m*-RNA.
(b) The third base of the codon is less specific.
(c) Only one codon codes for an amino acid.
(d) Every *t*-RNA molecules has more than one amino acid attachments.

18. Product (*B*) of the given reaction is

$$C_6H_5-CH(COOC_2H_5)_2 \xrightarrow{Br_2/CCl_4} (A) \xrightarrow{C_6H_4(CO)_2\overset{-}{N}\overset{+}{K}} (B)$$

(a) NH_2-CH_2-COOH
(b) $NH_2-CH_2-CH_2-COOH$
(c) $C_6H_5-CH(NH_2)-COOH$
(d) All of the above

19. Consider the following statements concerning proteins.

I. All natural amino acids which are constituents of proteins, are α-amino acids.

II. α-amino acids are all optically active and have *L*-configuration.

III. α-amino acids are connected by ester linkages.

IV. An especially favourable conformation for the peptide linkages in protein is the α-helix arrangement.

Of these statements,

(a) I and II are correct. (b) II and III are correct.
(c) I and IV are correct. (d) I, II, III and IV are correct.

20. Match the isoelectric points with the amino acids

Amino acids		Isoelectric points
A. H_2NCH_2COOH	1.	9.5
B. $HOOCCH_2CH_2CH(NH_2)COOH$	2.	6.0
C. $H_2N(CH_2)_4CH(NH_2)COOH$	3.	3.1

Codes

	A	B	C		A	B	C
(a)	2	3	1	(b)	3	1	2
(c)	1	2	3	(d)	2	1	3

Section B *Numerical Value Questions*

21. Specific rotations of freshly prepared aqueous solutions of (I) and (II) are +112° and +18.7°, respectively. On standing, the optical rotation of aqueous solution of (I) slowly decrease to give a final value of +52.7° due to equilibrium with (II). Under this state of equilibrium, the ratio (II) : (I) is ....

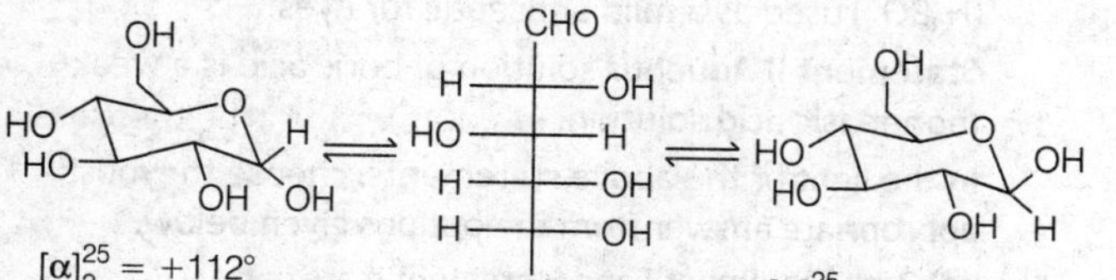

(I) $[\alpha]_2^{25} = +112°$ ⇌ CHO / H—OH / HO—H / H—OH / H—OH / CH_2OH ⇌ (II) $[\alpha]_2^{25} = +18.7°$

22. Periodic acid splits D-glucose and D-fructose into formic acid and formaldehyde. Sum of the ratio of formic acid and formaldehyde from glucose and fructose is ....

23. Glucose molecule reacts with X number of molecules of phenylhydrazine to yield osazone. The value of X is ....

24. The optical rotation of the α-form of a pyranose is +150.7°; that of the β-form is +52.8°. In solution, an equilibrium mixture of the anomers has an optical rotation of +80.2°. The percentage of the α-form at equilibrium is ....

25. A compound of molecular weight 180 is acetylated to give a compound of molecular weight 390. The number of amino groups in the intial compound is ....

26. Moles of HIO_4 is required to breakdown one mole of the given molecule here are ....

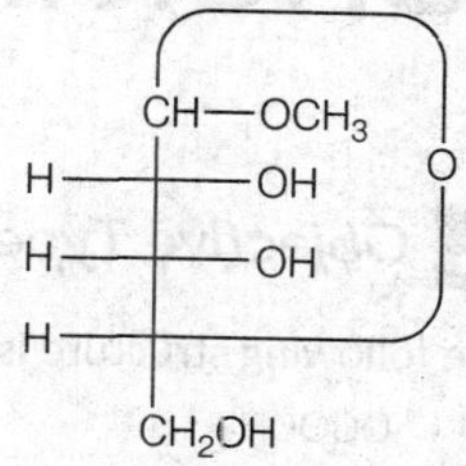

CH—OCH_3 / H—OH / H—OH / H— (ring O) / CH_2OH

27. The pK_a values for three ionisable groups *X*, *Y* and *Z* of glutamic acid are 4.3, 9.7 and 2.2 respectively.

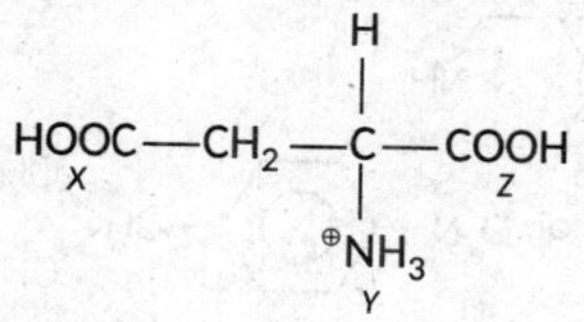

$\underset{X}{HOOC}—CH_2—\overset{H}{C}(\underset{Y}{{}^{\oplus}NH_3})—\underset{Z}{COOH}$

The isoelectric point for the amino acid is ....

28. .... number of tetrapeptides can be possible from three different amino acids.

29. A decapeptide (molecular weight 796) on complete hydrolysis gives glycine (molecular weight 75), alanine and phenylalanine. Glycine contributes 47.0% to the total weight of the hydrolysed products. The number of glycine units present in the decapeptide is ......

30. The net charge on the given amino acid at pH = 14 is ....

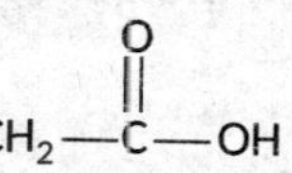

$H_2N—CH(COOH)—CH_2—C(=O)—OH$

Answers

Section A

1 (b)	2 (a)	3 (c)	4 (d)	5 (d)
6 (b)	7 (d)	8 (c)	9 (b)	10 (b)
11 (b)	12 (a)	13 (d)	14 (c)	15 (a)
16 (a)	17 (b)	18 (c)	19 (c)	20 (a)

Section B

21 (1.74)	22 (7.00)	23 (3.00)	24 (27.99)	25 (4.88)
26 (1.00)	27 (3.25)	28 (81.00)	29 (5.00)	30 (−2.00)

See detailed solutions on page no. 266

QUALIFIER 28

Chemistry in Everyday Life

Section A Objective Type Questions

1. Which of the following structure is not correct?

(a) Aspirin, [benzene ring with $OCOCH_3$ and $COOH$]

(b) Piperazine, HN[ring]NH

(c) Chloramphenicol, O_2N–[benzene]–CH(OH)–CH(CH_2OH)($NHCOCHI_2$)

(d) Paracetamol, C_2H_5O–[benzene]–$NHCOCH_3$

2. Which of the following is not true for reserpine?

(a) It is an alkaloid.
(b) It is also known as serpasil.
(c) It is obtained from the plant Raowolfia serpentina.
(d) It is not a tranquilizer.

3. The following compounds are the examples of which category of drugs?

[Structure (I): benzene ring–C(=O)–$NHNHCH(CH_3)_2$] (I)

[Structure (I): benzene ring–CH_2CH_2–$NHNH_2$] (I)

(a) Narcotic analgesics (b) Antidepressant drugs
(c) Antibiotics (d) Antiseptics

4. A narrow spectrum antibiotic like penicillin-G is active against

(a) gram-positive or gram negative bacteria.
(b) gram-negative bacteria only.
(c) single organism or one disease.
(d) gram-positive only.

5. Among the given compounds, which are not an antacid?

I. Phenelzine II. Cimetidine
III. Equanil IV. Ranitidine

(a) I and II (b) II and III
(c) I and III (d) II and IV

6. Match the classes of medicines in Column I with their functions/definitions in Column II and select answer from the codes given.

	Column I		Column II
A.	Pathogen	1.	Kills the microorganisms of the body.
B.	Bacteriostatic	2.	Kills or prevents the growth of microorganism.
C.	Bactericidal	3.	Prevents the normal growth of microorganism.
D.	Disinfectant	4.	Causes disease

Codes

	A	B	C	D		A	B	C	D
(a)	2	1	3	4	(b)	4	3	1	2
(c)	1	2	3	4	(d)	2	1	4	3

7. Given below are two statements.

Statement I Dilute aqueous solution of boric acid is (H_3BO_3) used as a mild antiseptic for eyes.

Statement II Aqueous solution of boric acid is a weak monobasic acid solution.

In the light of the above statements, choose the most appropriate answer from the options given below.

(a) Both Statement I and Statement II are correct.
(b) Both Statement I and Statement II are incorrect.
(c) Statement I is correct and Statement II is incorrect.
(d) Statement II is incorrect and Statement I is correct.

8. Which of the following detergent can be used as germicide also?

(a) A cationic detergent (b) An anionic detergent
(c) A non-ionic detergent (d) None of these

9. Which of the following is/are biodegradable detergent ?

(a) $CH_3(CH_2)_{11}$–[benzene]–$\overset{-}{SO_3}\overset{+}{Na}$

(b) $CH_3(CH_2)_{11}$—O—$\overset{-}{SO_3}\overset{+}{Na}$

(c) Both (a) and (b)

(d) None of the above

10. Which of the following distillation technique is best for separating glycerol from spent-lye used in the soap industry?

(a) Steam distillation
(b) Simple distillation
(c) Distillation under reduced pressure
(d) Fractional distillation

Section B *Numerical Value Questions*

11. Consider the following statements.

I. Drugs that bind the receptor site and inhibit its natural function are called agonists.
II. Majority of receptors are embedded in cell membranes.
III. Drugs usually interact with biomolecules such as carbohydrates, lipids, proteins and nucleic acids.
IV. Aspirin inhibits the synthesis of chemicals known as prostaglandins which stimulate inflammation in the tissue and cause pain.

The number of correct statements is ....

12. Among the given drugs, the total number of antibiotic(s) is/are ....

Salvarsan, Chloramphenicol, Prontosil, Azo dye, Chlordiazepoxide, Terfenadine, Sulphanilamide.

13. Consider the following reaction.

Glyceryl ester of stearic acid + x Sodium hydroxide $\longrightarrow$ y Sodium stearate + Glycerol

The value of $x + y$ is ....

14. If sweetness of sucrose is x, sweetness of

Alitame $= xy$ Saccharin $= xz$ Sucralose $= xw$

The value of $w(y+z)$ is $p \times 10^6$ when $x = 1$.

The value of p is ....

15. The value of $(a+b)$ in the following chemical formula of sodium laurylsulphate and cetyltrimethyl ammonium bromide is ....

$CH_3(CH_2)_aCH_2OSO_3\overset{-}{O}\overset{+}{Na}$ and $CH_3(CH_2)_b-\overset{+}{N}(CH_3)_3\overset{-}{Br}$

Answers

Section A

1 *(d)*	2 *(d)*	3 *(b)*	4 *(a)*	5 *(c)*
6 *(b)*	7 *(a)*	8 *(a)*	9 *(c)*	10 *(c)*

Section B

11 *(3)*	12 *(5)*	13 *(6)*	14 *(1.53)*	15 *(25)*

See detailed solutions on page no. 270

QUALIFIER 29

Principles Related to Practical Chemistry

Section A Objective Type Questions

1. Detection of the chlorine is not possible without preparing sodium extract in

(a) 2,4-dinitro-substituted ring: O_2N–(benzene ring with two NO_2)–Cl

(b) $CHCl_3$

(c) C_6H_5–CH_2Cl

(d) $CH_2{=}CHCH_2Cl$

2. Compound C_7H_8O (*A*) gives colour with neutral $FeCl_3$ and can be nitrated to form three types of nitro compound. *A* can be

(a) o-cresol (OH, CH_3 ortho)

(b) m-cresol (OH, CH_3 meta)

(c) p-cresol (OH, CH_3 para)

(d) $C_6H_5CH_2OH$

3. In the preparation of acetanilide ($C_6H_5NHCOCH_3$) in laboratory, 5 mL aniline, 5 mL acetic anhydride, 5 mL glacial acetic acid and 0.05 g zinc dust are taken in a 100 mL round bottom flask. The role of Zn in this reaction is

(a) as a seeding agent. (b) as a reducing agent.
(c) as a complexing agent. (d) as a colourant.

4. Dilute HCl precipitated only group I cations and not other cations. This is because of the fact that

(a) solubility product of first group chlorides are less than the chlorides of other metals.
(b) solubility product of group I chlorides is maximum among all metal chlorides.
(c) all metal chlorides are soluble whereas group I metal chlorides are insoluble.
(d) all metal chlorides are insoluble only group I metal chlorides are soluble.

5. Aqueous solution of *A* can dissolve AgBr forming a soluble complex *B*. *A* also reacts with aqueous $AgNO_3$ solution giving a white ppt., *C* changing to black ppt. *D*. *A*, *B*, *C* and *D* are

	A	B	C	D
(a)	$Na_2S_2O_3$	$Na_3[Ag(S_2O_3)_2]$	$Ag_2S_2O_3$	Ag_2S
(b)	$Na_2S_2O_3$	$Ag_2S_2O_3$	Ag_2S	$Na_3[Ag(S_2O_3)_2]$
(c)	NH_3	$[Ag(NH_3)_2]Br$	$Ag(OH)$	Ag_2O
(d)	NH_3	$Na[Ag(OH)_2]$	Ag_2O	$[Ag(NH_3)_2]Br$

6. A mixture contains Cu^{2+}, Al^{3+} and Ni^{2+}. Following steps have been adopted but written in disorder

I. Filter, boil off H_2S gas and add NH_4Cl, heat and add NH_4OH
II. Filter, add NH_4OH and pass H_2S gas
III. Pass H_2S gas into acidified solution of the mixture

Choose the correct order of the steps.

(a) I, II and III
(b) III, I and II
(c) III, II and I
(d) I, III and II

7. Which of the compounds is/are soluble in NaOH?

(a) $Al(OH)_3$ (b) $Cr(OH)_3$
(c) Both (a) and (b) (d) $Fe(OH)_3$

8. In mixture analysis, the filtrate of group II is treated with H_2S which gives ppt. of metal sulphide. This precipitate is insoluble in dil. HCl but soluble in *aqua-regia*. The solution on treatment with sodium bicarbonate followed by bromine water gives green solution. The above observations show the presence of

(a) Zn^{2+} (b) Mn^{2+}
(c) Co^{2+} (d) Ni^{2+}

9. $CoCl_2$ forms coloured complex with
(a) sodium bicarbonate in presence of Br_2 water
(b) NH_4SCN
(c) KNO_2 in presence of CH_3COOH
(d) All of the above

10. Sulphide of group IV is soluble in dil. HCl. The acidic solution gives white ppt. with NH_4OH. The white precipitate when boil with conc. HNO_3 in presence of PbO_2 gives pink colour solution. The group IV sulphide and pink colour solution are respectively
(a) MnS and NH_4MnO_2
(b) MnS and $HMnO_4$
(c) ZnS and $Zn(NO_3)_2$
(d) CoS and ammonium cobalt nitrate

11. Turnbull's blue and Prussian's blue respectively are
I. $Fe^{II}[Fe^{II}(CN)_6]$ II. $Fe^{III}[Fe^{III}(CN)_6]$
III. $Fe_3^{II}[Fe^{III}(CN)_6]_2$ IV. $Fe_4^{III}[Fe^{II}(CN)_6]_3$
(a) I, II (b) I, III (c) III, IV (d) IV, III

12. Match the following and choose the correct option.

	Ion + Reagent		Colour
A.	$Fe^{3+} + [Fe(CN)_6]^{4-}$	1.	Cherry red
B.	$Fe^{3+} + CNS^-$	2.	Pink
C.	Ni^{2+} + DMG	3.	Blood red
D.	$Mn^{2+} + PbO_2 + H^+$	4.	Blue

Codes

	A	B	C	D		A	B	C	D
(a)	1	4	2	3	(b)	4	3	1	2
(c)	3	4	2	1	(d)	3	1	4	3

13. $(NH_4)_2CO_3$ is added to precipitate out the carbonates of group V cations. Na_2CO_3 is not added because
(a) $CaCO_3$ is soluble in Na_2CO_3
(b) Na_2CO_3 increases the solubility of group V cations
(c) $MgCO_3$ will be precipitated out in group V
(d) None of the above

14. Which of the following statements is (are) correct regarding the experiment, the determination of rate of reaction of I^- ions with H_2O_2 at room temperature?
I. Equivalent concentration of $Na_2S_2O_3$ should be kept slightly less than that of KI or H_2O_2.
II. Time of appearance of blue colour produced by the reaction of I_2 and starch is measured by varying concentration of either I^- or H_2O_2.
III. Since, the time taken for appearance of blue colour is noted, the reaction is said to be a 'clock reaction'.
(a) Only I (b) II and III
(c) I and II (d) I, II and III

15. SO_2 and CO_2 both turn lime water (*A*) milky, SO_2 also turns $K_2Cr_2O_7/H^+$ (*B*) green, while O_2 is soluble in pyrogallol (*C*) turning it black. These gases are to be detected in order by using these reagents in a mixture. The order is
(a) (*A*), (*B*) and (*C*) (b) (*B*), (*C*) and (*A*)
(c) (*B*), (*A*) and (*C*) (d) (*A*), (*C*) and (*B*)

16. A translucent white waxy solid *A* on heating in an inert atmosphere is converted to its allotropic form *B*. Allotrope *A* on reaction with very dilute aqueous KOH liberates a highly poisonous gas *C* having rotten fish smell, while excess of chlorine *A* forms *D* which hydrolyses to its another compound *E*. Identify compound *A*.
(a) White phosphorus (b) Red phosphorus
(c) Phosphine (d) Phosphorus pentachloride

17. A gaseous mixture containing *X*, *Y* and *Z* gases, when passed into acidified $K_2Cr_2O_7$ solution, gas *X* was absorbed and the solution was turned green. The remaining gas mixture was then pass through lime water, which turns milky by absorbed gas *Y*. Then residual gas when passed through alkaline pyrogallol solution, it turned black. The gases *X*, *Y* and *Z* are respectively.
(a) SO_2, CO_2, O_2 (b) O_2, CO_2, SO_2
(c) SO_2, O_2, H_2S (d) H_2S, SO_2, O_2

18. Given below are two statements, one is labelled as Assertion (A) and the other is labelled as Reason (R).
Assertion (A) NO_2^- is decomposed by urea in the mixture of NO_3^- and NO_2^-.
Reason (R) NO_2^- interfere in the ring test.
In the light of the above statements, choose the correct answer from the options given below.
(a) Both A and R are true and R is the correct explanation of A.
(b) Both A and R are true but R is not the correct explanation of A.
(c) A is true but R is false.
(d) A is false but R is true.

19. In determination of enthalpy of dissolution of hydrated copper sulphate ($CuSO_4 \cdot 5H_2O$) in laboratory, *w* g of $CuSO_4 \cdot 5H_2O$ is taken in calorimeter (polythene bottle) containing 200 g of water at t_1°C. After complete dissolution of $CuSO_4 \cdot 5H_2O$, temperature of the solution is noted to be t_2°C ($t_2 > t_1$). The expression of enthalpy of dissolution of the salt will be
[Molar mass of $CuSO_4 \cdot 5H_2O = 249.5$ g mol^{-1}; water equivalent of polythene bottle = *w* g]
(a) $\frac{(w+200)\times(t_2-t_1)}{W\times 249.5}$ J/mol
(b) $\frac{(w+200)\times(t_2-t_1)}{w\times 249.5}$ J/mol
(c) $\frac{(w+200)\times 4.2\times(t_2-t_1)\times 249.5}{w}$ J/mol
(d) $\frac{(w+200)\times 4.2\times(t_2-t_1)\times 249.5}{w}$ J/mol

20. Which of the following experiments lead to the formation of a lyophobic sol?

(a) Starch powder + Distilled water $\xrightarrow{\text{Stirring}}$

(b) 5% NaCl solution + Distilled water + Colourless part of an egg $\xrightarrow{\text{Stirring}}$

(c) 2% $FeCl_3$ solution + distilled water $\xrightarrow{\text{Boiling}}$

(d) None of the above

Section B Numerical Value Questions

21. In the following synthesis

$$CH_3CH_2\underset{\displaystyle CH_3}{\underset{|}{C}H}CH_2OH \xrightarrow[\Delta]{\text{Conc. } H_2SO_4} \text{Major product} \xrightarrow[\text{(ii) } H_2O_2 \cdot OH^-]{\text{(i) } BH_3 \cdot THF} A$$

The number of reagents that will be used to identify *A* is ....

$NaOH/I_2$, Conc. $HCl/ZnCl_2$, $K_2Cr_2O_7/H^+$, MnO_4^-/H^+ CAN, Cu/300°c, Fehling's solution, Tollen's reagent.

22. The number of isomeric carbonyl compound(s) $C_5H_{10}O$ which reduce Tollen's reagent is ....

23. .... number of the following compounds will liberate CO_2 with $NaHCO_3$.

(I) (squaric acid: cyclobutene ring with two OH and two C=O) , (II) (phenol, OH on benzene) , (III) (2,4,6-trinitrophenol: OH with O_2N, NO_2, NO_2)

CH_3OH (IV) · CH_3CH_2OH (V)

24. Benzene diazonium chloride undergoes coupling reaction with alkaline β-naphthol, forming azo coloured dye. The number of π-bonds involved on conjugation with each other is ....

25. Out of the compounds given below the number of compound(s) that will give white ppt. with $AgNO_3$ solution is ....

Cl-cycloheptatriene (Cl on cycloheptatriene ring), chlorobenzene (Cl on benzene), CH_3Cl, benzyl chloride (CH_2—Cl on benzene), $CH_2{=}CH{-}Cl$, 3-chlorocyclopropene (Cl on cyclopropene), $CH_3{-}CH{=}CH{-}CH_2{-}Cl$

26. A mixture of oxalic acid and Mohr's salt is titrated against $KMnO_4$ (excess). The total change in the oxidation state of the reducing agents is ....

27. Among PbS, CuS, HgS, MnS, CoS, Bi_2S_3 and SnS_3, the number of compounds which are black in colour is ....

28. $FeCl_3$ gives blood red colour of formula, $[Fe(CNS)(H_2O)_5]^{2+}$ with KCNS. If *P* is the coordination no. of Fe, *Q* is the no. of unpaired electrons, *R* is the no. of paired electrons in *d*-orbital and *S* is the oxidation state of Fe. Then, the value of $(P+Q)+R^2-S$ is ......

29. Brown coloured ring formed in the nitrate test has formula $[Fe(H_2O)_5NO]SO_4$. Unpaired electrons in Fe is ......

30. Among $Cr(OH)_3$, $Al(OH)_3$, $Zn(OH)_2$, $Fe(OH)_3$, the number of compound(s) that can dissolve in NaOH is ....

Answers

Section A

1 (b)	2 (b)	3 (b)	4 (a)	5 (a)
6 (b)	7 (c)	8 (c)	9 (d)	10 (b)
11 (c)	12 (b)	13 (c)	14 (d)	15 (c)
16 (a)	17 (a)	18 (d)	19 (c)	20 (c)

Section B

21 (6)	22 (4)	23 (1)	24 (2)	25 (4)
26 (3)	27 (5)	28 (8)	29 (3)	30 (2)

See detailed solutions on page no. 271

JEE MAIN & ADVANCED

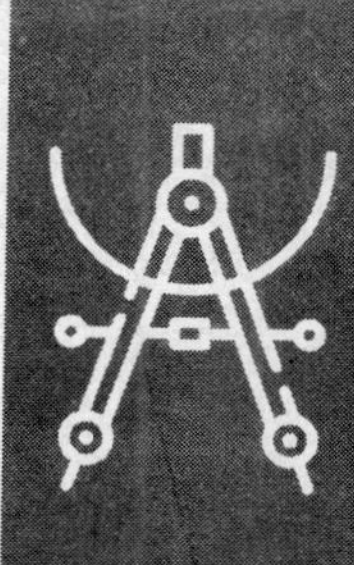

Part Tests

Based on Complete Class 11th & 12th Syllabus

This section will check your overall understanding of complete syllabus of class 11 & 12, respectively.

Part Test 01

(Based on Complete Class 11 Syllabus)

JEE MAIN

Chemistry

Instructions

- This question paper contains of 30 Questions of Chemistry, divided into two sections : **Section A** Objective Type Questions and **Section B** Numerical Value Questions.
- Section A contains 20 Objective questions and all Questions are cumpulsory (Marking Scheme : Correct + 4, Incorrect – 1).
- Section B contains 10 Numerical value questions out of which only 5 questions are to be attempted (Marking Scheme : Correct + 4, Incorrect 0)

Section A *Objective Type Questions*

1. In which of the following arrangements, the order is not according to the property indicated against it?

(a) $Al^{3+} < Mg^{2+} < Na^{+} < F^{-}$ (increasing ionic size)

(b) B < C < N < O (increasing first ionisation enthalpy)

(c) I < Br < F < Cl (increasing electron gain enthalpy with negative sign)

(d) Li < Na < K < Rb (increasing metallic radius)

2. The hydration energy of alkali metals decreases from Li to Cs. The order of their electrical conductance will be

(a) $Li^{+} > Na^{+} > K^{+} > Rb^{+} > Cs^{+}$

(b) $Li^{+} < Na^{+} < K^{+} < Rb^{+} < Cs^{+}$

(c) $Li^{+} > K^{+} > Na^{+} > Cs^{+} > Rb^{+}$

(d) $Li^{+} < Na^{+} < K^{+} > Rb^{+} > Cs^{+}$

3. 100 mL of pure phosphine is decomposed to produce vapours of phosphorus (P_4) and H_2. The change in volume during reaction at constant temperature is

(a) 75 mL (b) 50 mL

(c) 25 mL (d) 150 mL

4. For the reaction, $CO(g) + \frac{1}{2}O_2(g) \longrightarrow CO_2(g)$, ΔH and ΔS are -283 kJ and $-97\ JK^{-1}$. It was intended to carry out this reaction at 1000 K, 1500 K and 3500 K. At which of these temperature would this reaction be thermodynamically spontaneous?

(a) 1500 K and 3500 K

(b) 1000 K and 1500 K

(c) 1000 K, 1500 K and 3500 K

(d) 1500 K, 3000 K and 3500 K

5. The numbers of spherical nodal planes present in 4*s*, 4*p* and 4*d* subshells are respectively

(a) 3,2,1 (b) 1, 2, 3

(c) 0, 1, 2 (d) 2, 1, 3

6. 200 g sample of hard water is passed through a cation exchanger in which H^{+} ions are exchanged by Ca^{2+} ions. The water coming out of cation exchanger needed 75 mL of 0.1 N NaOH for complete neutralisation. The hardness of water due to Ca^{2+} ion is

(a) 250 ppm (b) 500 ppm

(c) 750 ppm (d) 1000 ppm

7. Which of the following is a chiral molecule?

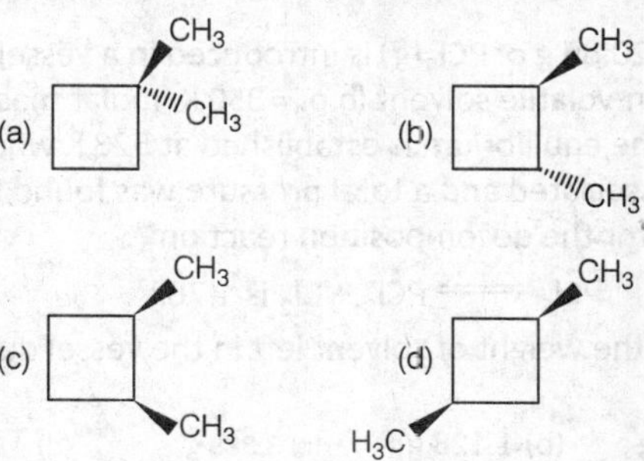

8. Consider three hypothetical ionic compounds *AB*, A_2B and A_2B_3 where in all the compounds *B* is in (–2) oxidation state and *A* has a variable oxidation state. What is the correct order of lattice energy of these compounds?

(a) $A_2B > AB > A_2B_3$

(b) $A_2B_3 > AB > A_2B$

(c) $AB > A_2B > A_2B_3$

(d) $A_2B_3 > A_2B > AB$

9. Match the orbital overlap figures shown in List-I with the description given in List-II and select the correct answer using the code given below the lists.

List-I	List-II
A.	1. p-$d\pi$ antibonding
B.	2. d-$d\sigma$ bonding
C.	3. p-$d\pi$ bonding
D.	4. d-$d\sigma$ antibonding

Codes

	A	B	C	D		A	B	C	D
(a)	2	1	3	4	(b)	4	3	1	2
(c)	2	3	1	4	(d)	4	1	3	2

10. A real gas obeys the equation of state $p(V - nb) = nRT$ where b is van der Waals' constant and R is the gas constant. If the pressure and temperature are such that the molar volume of the gas is 10 b, what is the value of compressibility factor?

(a) 10/9 (b) 8/9 (c) 12/11 (d) 10/11

11. In a system $A(s) \rightleftharpoons 2B(g) + 3C(g)$. If the concentration of C at equilibrium is increased by a factor of 2, it will cause the equilibrium concentration of B to change to

(a) two times of its original value

(b) one-half of its original value

(c) $2\sqrt{2}$ times of its original value

(d) $\frac{1}{2\sqrt{2}}$ times of its original value

12. Suppose 20.85 g of $PCl_5(g)$ is introduced in a vessel washed with a non-volatile solvent (b.p. = 350 K, molar mass 154 g mol^{-1}). The equilibrium is established at 523 K when $PCl_5(g)$ is 52% dissociated and a total pressure was found to be 5.5 bar. If K_p for the decomposition reaction

$$PCl_5 \rightleftharpoons PCl_3 + Cl_2 \text{ is } 1.78,$$

calculate the weight of solvent left in the vessel during washing.

(a) 2.188 g (b) 1.128 g (c) 3.388 g (d) 4.212 g

13. Metallic tin in the presence of HCl is oxidised by $K_2Cr_2O_7$ to stannic chloride. What volume of decinormal dichromate solution will be reduced by 1 g of tin?

(Atomic weight of Sn = 118.7 u)

(a) 336.9 mL (b) 235.6 mL (c) 465.23 mL (d) 398.56 mL

14. Of the two solvents, H_2O and D_2O, sodium chloride dissolves

(a) equally in both (b) more in D_2O

(c) more in H_2O (d) only in H_2O

15. Given below are two statements.

Statement I Alkali metals dissolve in liquid ammonia to give blue solution.

Statement II Alkali metals in liquid ammonia give solvated species of the type $[M(NH_3)_n]^+$ (M = alkali metals).

In the light of the above statements, choose the most appropriate answer from the options given below.

(a) Both Statement I and Statement II are correct.

(b) Both Statement I and Statement II are incorrect.

(c) Statement I is correct but Statement II is incorrect.

(d) Statement I is incorrect but Statement II is correct.

16. The gas evolved on heating CaF_2 and SiO_2 with concentrated H_2SO_4, on hydrolysis gives a white gelatinous precipitate. The precipitate is

(a) hydrofluorosilicic acid (b) silica gel

(c) silicic acid (d) calciumfluorosilicate

17. Match the List-I and List-II and pick the correct matching from the codes given below.

List-I	List-II
A. Peroxy acetyl nitrate	1. Waste incineration
B. Polycyclic aromatic	2. Global warming
C. Dioxins	3. Photochemical smog
D. IR active molecules	4. Carcinogens

Codes

	A	B	C	D		A	B	C	D
(a)	3	4	1	2	(b)	2	4	3	1
(c)	3	1	2	4	(d)	4	3	1	2

18. What product would you expect from addition of deuterium chloride to 2 cyclohexyl-4-methyl 2-pentene?

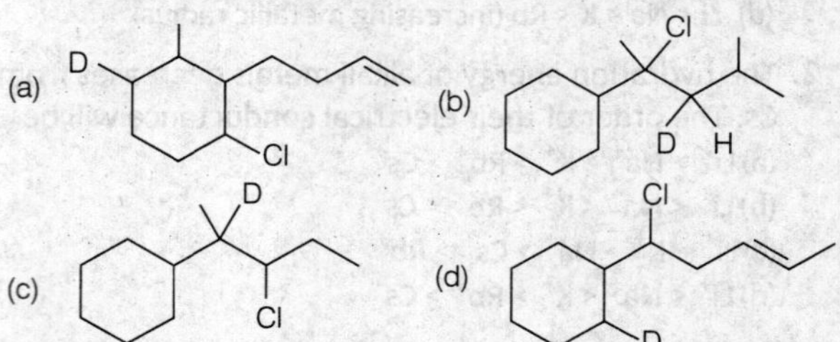

19. Predict the major product in the following reaction.

Ph–C_6H_4–CH=CH–C_6H_5 $\xrightarrow{HBr}$

(a) Br on ring; –CH=CH–

(b) Br– ; –CH=CH–

(c) –CH–CH_2– with Br on CH

(d) –CH_2–CH– with Br on CH

20. $KMnO_4$ is a good oxidising agent in acidic/basic/neutral medium. Match the reducing agent in List-I with its number of moles in List-II which can be oxidised by 1 mole of $KMnO_4$ in acidic medium.

List-I	List-II
A. Iron (III) oxalate	1. 2.0 mol
B. Iron (II) sulphate (IV)	2. 0.0 mol
C. Iron (II) oxalate	3. 0.83 mol
D. Iron (III) sulphate (VI)	4. 1.67 mol
E. Iron (III) sulphate (IV)	5. 2.50 mol

Codes

	A	B	C	D	E		A	B	C	D	E
(a)	3	4	4	2	3	(b)	3	4	2	1	2
(c)	1	2	3	4	5	(d)	5	4	3	2	1

Section B *Numerical Value Questions*

21. One mole of $N_2O(g)$ is kept in a closed container along with gold catalyst at 450 K under one atmosphere. It is heated to 900 K when it dissociates to $N_2(g)$ and $O_2(g)$ giving an equilibrium pressure of 2.4 atm. The degree of dissociation of N_2O in percentage will be ....

22. In how many of the following pairs, first intermediate is more stable than the second one?

(i) $CH_3—\overset{(+)}{C}H=CH, CH_3—\overset{(+)}{C}H=CH_3$

(ii)

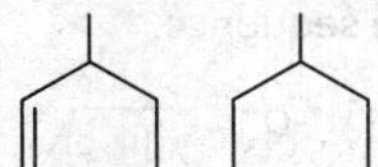

(iii) $CH_3—O—\overset{(+)}{C}H_2, CH_3—\overset{(+)}{C}(CH_3)_2$

(iv) 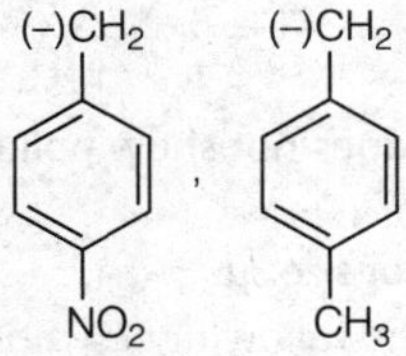 (–)CH_2 / NO_2 , (–)CH_2 / CH_3

(v) 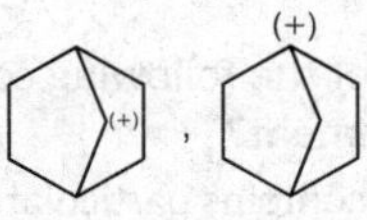 (+) , (+)

(vi) 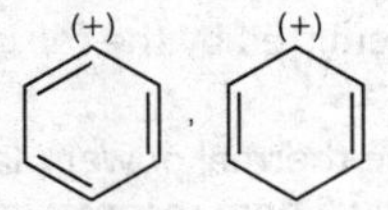 (+) . (+)

(vii) 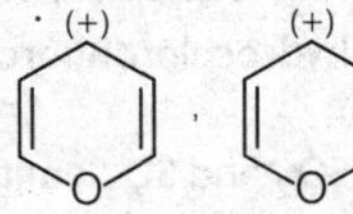 (+) , (+)

(viii) $\overset{(-)}{C}Cl_3, \overset{(-)}{C}F_3$

(ix) $CH_2=CH—\dot{C}H_2, CH_3—\dot{C}H—CH_3$

(x) $\uparrow\downarrow CCl_2, \uparrow\downarrow CF_2$ (both are singlet)

23. Number of $\angle FMF = 90°$ bonds (M = central atom) in SF_6, SF_4, IF_5 and XeF_4 are a, b, c and d respectively. The value of $(b+c+d) \div (a)$ is ....

24. The reaction of powdered aluminium and iron (III) oxide,

$$2Al + Fe_2O_3 \longrightarrow Al_2O_3 + 2Fe$$

produces so much heat that the iron forms is molten. Because of this, railroads use the reaction to provide molten steel to weld steel rails together when laying track. Suppose that in one batch of reactants, 4.20 moles of Al are mixed with 1.75 moles of Fe_2O_3, then calculate the number of grams of iron that can be formed from this mixture of reactants.

25. In the spectrum of hydrogen, there is a line with a wavelength of 410.3 nm. Use the Rydberg equation to calculate the value of *n* for the higher energy Bohr orbit involved in the emission of this light. Assume the value of *n* for the lower energy orbit equals 2.

26. Calculate the lattice enthalpy (in kJ mol^{-1}) of $CaCl_2$. Given that the enthalpy of

(i) sublimation of Ca is 121 kJ mol^{-1}

(ii) dissociation of Cl_2 to Cl is 242.8 kJ mol^{-1}

(iii) ionisation of Ca to Ca^{2+} is 2422 kJ mol^{-1}

(iv) electron gain enthalpy for Cl to Cl^- is – 355 kJ mol^{-1}

(v) formation of $CaCl_2$ is – 795 kJ mol^{-1}

27. Methanol, a potential replacement for gasoline as an auto-motive fuel, can be made from H_2 and CO by the reaction. $CO(g) + 2H_2(g) \rightleftharpoons CH_3OH(g)$

At 500 K, this reaction has $K_p = 6.25 \times 10^{-3}$

ΔG°_{500} for this reaction is .... $\times 10^4$ J.

28. The K_{sp} of Ag_2CrO_4 is 1.1×10^{-12} at 298 K. The solubility in (mol L^{-1}) of Ag_2CrO_4 in a 0.1 M $AgNO_3$ solution is .... $\times 10^{-10}$ mol L^{-1}.

29. How many chiral carbons are there in the following compound?

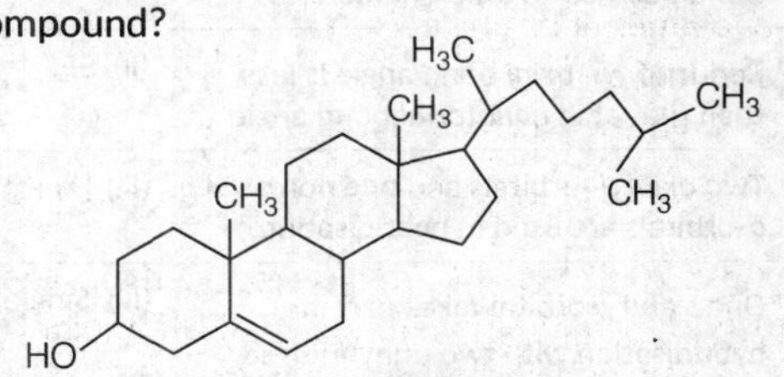

H_3C, CH_3, CH_3, CH_3, CH_3, HO

30. The total number of alkenes possible by dehydrobromination of 3-bromo-3-cyclopentylhexane using alcoholic KOH is ....

Answers

Section A

1 *(b)*	2 *(b)*	3 *(a)*	4 *(b)*	5 *(a)*
6 *(c)*	7 *(b)*	8 *(b)*	9 *(c)*	10 *(a)*
11 *(d)*	12 *(c)*	13 *(a)*	14 *(c)*	15 *(a)*
16 *(c)*	17 *(a)*	18 *(b)*	19 *(c)*	20 *(a)*

Section B

21 *(40)*	22 *(7)*	23 *(0.33)*	24 *(195.46)*	25 *(6)*
26 *(– 2870.80)*	27 *(2.11)*	28 *(1.10)*	29 *(8)*	30 *(5)*

See detailed solutions on page no. 275

Part Test 02

(Based on Complete Class 11 Syllabus)

JEE ADVANCED

Chemistry

SECTION 1

- This section contains **FOUR (04)** questions.
- Each question has **FOUR** options (a), (b), (c) and (d). **ONLY ONE** of these four options is the correct answer.
- For each question, choose the option corresponding to the correct answer.
- Answer to each question will be evaluated according to the following marking scheme:

Full Marks : +3 If ONLY the correct option is chosen;
Zero Marks : 0 If none of the options is chosen (i.e., the question is unanswered);
Negative Marks : −1 In all other cases.

1. Match List-I with List-II and choose the correct option.

	List-I (Statement)	List-II (Example)
A.	Bond pair has > 75% *p*-character.	(i) HF
B.	Reduction in *axial* bond angle is less than that of in *equatorial* bond angle.	(ii) SF_4
C.	Two *axial d* -orbitals and one non axial *d*-orbitals are used in hybridisation.	(iii) $[XeF_5]^-$
D.	One *s* and *p*-orbital takes part in hybridisation with two unhybridised *p*-orbitals having one electron and another empty respectively.	(iv) Singlet (carbene)

Codes

(a) A-(ii), B-(i), C-(iv), D-(iii)
(b) A-(i), B-(ii), C-(iii), D-(iv)
(c) A-(iii), B-(iv), C-(i), D-(ii)
(d) A-(iii), B-(ii), C-(i), D-(iv)

2. Consider the following reaction.

$$H_3C-C\equiv C-H \xrightarrow[\text{(ii)TsO}-\text{cyclohexyl}]{\text{(i)NaNH}_2} A \xrightarrow{Na/NH_3(l)} B \xrightarrow{mCPBA} C$$

Find out C from the given reaction sequence.

(a) H_3C–CH(–O–)CH–cyclohexyl (epoxide, both H on same side)
(b) H_3C–CH(–O–)CH–cyclohexyl (epoxide, H on opposite sides)
(c) $H_3C-C(=O)-$cyclohexyl
(d) $H_3C-CH_2-C(=O)-$cyclohexyl

3. Which of the following condition does not show pollute air environment?

(a) Air contains particulate matter of size 3μ.
(b) The rain falling has pH of 4.5.
(c) The hydrochlorofluorocarbons emitted by the refrigeration plant.
(d) The SO_2 and SO_3 emitted by the thermal power plant have concentration of 7 ppm and 2 ppm respectively in the air.

4. Calculate the $[H^+]$ in a solution containing 0.1 M HCOOH and 0.1 M HOCN. [K_a for HCOOH and HOCN are 1.8×10^{-4} and 3.3×10^{-4} respectively].

(a) 28.01×10^{-3} M
(b) 30.21×10^{-3} M
(c) 22.59×10^{-3} M
(d) 26.25×10^{-3} M

SECTION 2

- This section contains **FOUR (04)** question stems.
- There are **TWO (02)** questions corresponding to each question stem.
- The answer to each question is a **NUMERICAL VALUE.**
- For each question, enter the correct numerical value corresponding to the answer in the designated place using the mouse and the on-screen virtual numeric keypad.
- If the numerical value has more than two decimal places, **truncate/round-off** the value to **TWO** decimal places.
- Answer to each question will be evaluated according to the following marking scheme:

Full Marks : +2 If ONLY the correct numerical value is entered at the designated place;
Zero marks : 0 In all other cases.

Question Stem for Question Nos. 5 and 6

A mixture contains CH_3OH, CH_3CH_2OH and H_2O and mole fractions are shown below.

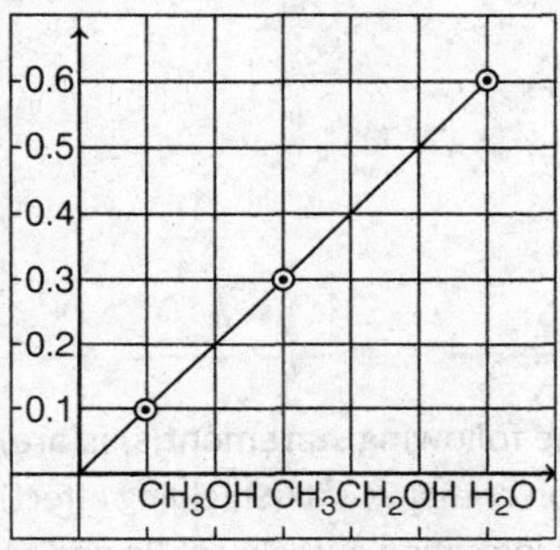

5. Molality of CH_3OH in the above case is ....

6. Mass percentage of CH_3CH_2OH is ....

Question Stem Nos. 7 and 8

A balloon of radius 3.0 m is to be inflated by H_2 at a pressure of 1.0 bar and 298 K, when density of air is 1.22 kg m^{-3} at sea level.

7. The amount of H_2 needed is .... kmol.

8. What mass (in kg) can the balloon lift at the sea level?

Question Stem Nos. 9 and 10

One litre of saturated CaC_2O_4 solution required 200 mL of 1×10^{-4} M $KMnO_4$ in acidic medium.

9. K_{sp} of CaC_2O_4 will be .... $\times 10^{-9}$ M^2.

10. If same solution is titrated in presence of 1×10^{-3} M $CaCl_2$ solution, 1×10^{-4} M $KMnO_4$ required is .... mL.

Question Stem Nos. 11 and 12

Based on the following figure

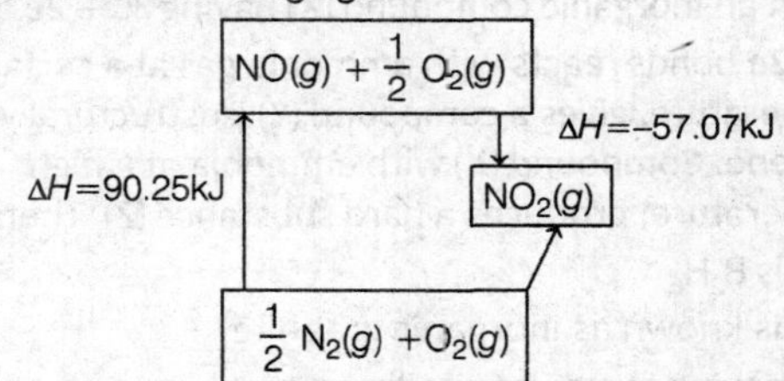

11. $\Delta_f H°(NO_2)$ is .... kJ mol^{-1}.

12. $\Delta_C H°$ (enthalpy of combustion) of NO(*g*) is .... kJ mol^{-1}.

SECTION 3

- This section contains **SIX (06)** questions.
- Each question has **FOUR** options (a), (b), (c) and (d). **ONE OR MORE THAN ONE** of these four option(s) is (are) correct answer(s).
- For each question, choose the option(s) corresponding to (all) the correct answer(s).
- Answer to each question will be evaluated according to the following marking scheme:

Full Marks : +4 If only (all) the correct option(s) is(are) chosen;
Partial Marks : +3 If all the four options are correct but ONLY three options are chosen;
Partial Marks : +2 If three or more options are correct but ONLY two options are chosen, both of which are correct;
Partial Marks : +1 If two or more options are correct but ONLY one option is chosen and it is a correct option;
Zero Marks : 0 If unanswered;
Negative Marks : −2 In all other cases.

- For example, in a question, if (a), (b) and (d) are the ONLY three options corresponding to correct answers, then
choosing ONLY (a), (b) and (d) will get +4 marks;
choosing ONLY (a) and (b) will get +2 marks;
choosing ONLY (a) and (d) will get +2 marks;
choosing ONLY (b) and (d) will get +2 marks;
choosing ONLY (a) will get +1 mark;
choosing ONLY (b) will get +1 mark;
choosing ONLY (d) will get +1 mark;
choosing no option(s) (i.e., the question is unanswered) will get 0 marks and
choosing any other option(s) will get –2 marks.

13. When an inorganic compound (*X*) having $3C-2e$ as well as $2C-2e$ bonds reacts with ammonia gas at a certain temperature, gives a compound (*Y*) isostructural with benzene. Compound (*X*) with ammonia at a high temperature, produces a hard substance (*Z*). Then

(a) (*X*) is B_2H_6
(b) (*Z*) is known as inorganic graphite
(c) (*Z*) having structure similar to graphite
(d) (*Z*) having structure similar to (*X*)

14. When zeolite, which is hydrated sodium aluminium silicate, is treated with hard water, the sodium ions are exchanged with

(a) H^+ ions
(b) Ca^{2+} ions
(c) SO_4^{2-}
(d) Mg^{2+} ions

15. $H_2C_2O_4$ and $NaHC_2O$ behave as acids as well as reducing agents. Which of the following is (are) the correct statement(s) ?

(a) Equivalent weights of $H_2C_2O_4$ and $NaHC_2O_4$ are equal to their molecular weights when acting as reducing agents.
(b) Equivalent weight of $H_2C_2O_4$ and $NaHC_2O_4$ are equal to half of their molecular weights when acting as reducing agents.
(c) 100 mL of 1 M solution of each is neutralised by equal volumes of 1 M $Ca(OH)_2$
(d) 100 mL of 1 M solution of each is oxidised by equal volume of 1 M $KMnO_4$

16. Which of the following statement(s) is(are) true?

(a) Ionisation enthalpy $\propto$ 1/(Shielding effect)
(b) The first ionisation enthalpy of Be and Mg are more than ionisation enthalpy of B and Al, respectively
(c) Atomic and ionic radii of niobium and tantalum are almost the same.
(d) Metallic and covalent radii of potassium are 2.3 Å and 2.03 Å respectively.

17. Benzoic acid may be prepared by the oxidation of

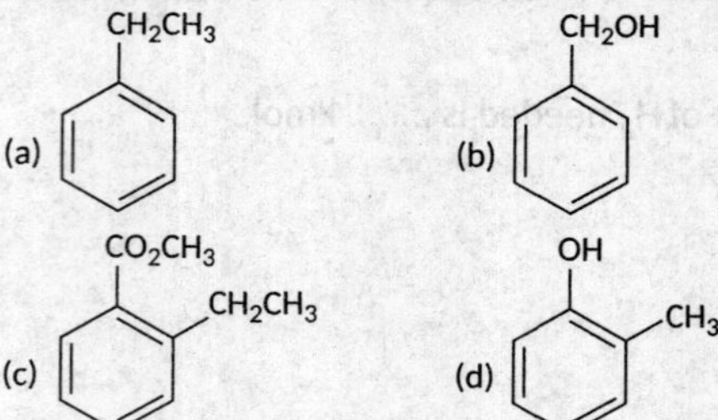

18. Which of the following represent(s) the resonating structure of the given compound?

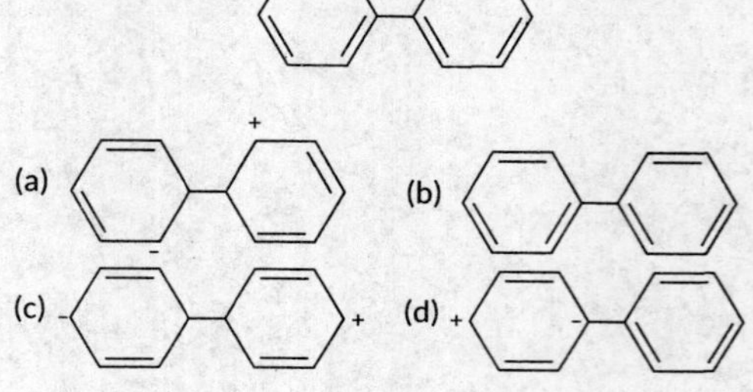

SECTION 4

- This section contains **THREE (03)** questions.
- The answer to each question is a **NON-NEGATIVE INTEGER.**
- For each question, enter the correct integer corresponding to the answer using the mouse and the on-screen virtual numeric keypad in the place designated to enter the answer.
- Answer to each question will be evaluated according to the following marking scheme:
Full Marks : +4 If ONLY the correct integer is entered;
Zero Marks : 0 In all other cases.

19. The ratio of $\frac{pM_m}{RT}$ for a real gas obeying van der Waals' equation is $\frac{x}{24}$ at a temperature, where $\left(\frac{\partial p}{\partial V_m}\right)=0$. The value of x is ....

20. For the following graph, it is given that

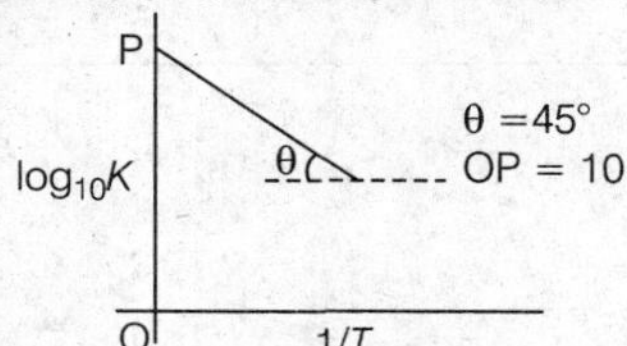

If the value of $\Delta H°$ is Q cal/mol, then the value of $10Q$ is .... [$R = 2$ cal mol^{-1} K^{-1}].

21. A 3 g sample containing Fe_3O_4, Fe_2O_3 along with an inert impurity is treated with excess KI solution in presence of dil. H_2SO_4 The entire iron is converted into Fe^{2+} alongwith liberation of iodine. The resulting solution is diluted to 100 mL, 20 mL of the diluted solution requires 11 mL of 0.5 M $Na_2S_2O_3$ for complete reduction of iodine present. 50 mL of the diluted solution after complete extraction of iodine requires 12.8 mL of 0.25 M $KMnO_4$ acidified with dil H_2SO_4, the percentage of Fe_3O_4 in the original sample is [Fe = 56] ....

SECTION 5

- This section contains **TWO (02) paragraphs.** Based on each paragraph, there are **TWO (02)** questions.
- Each question has **FOUR** options (A), (B), (C) and (D). **ONLY ONE** of these four options is the correct answer.
- For each question, choose the option corresponding to the correct answer.
- Answer to each question will be evaluated according to the following marking scheme:
Full Marks : +3 If ONLY the correct integer is entered;
Zero Marks : 0 If none of the options is chosen (i.e. question is unanswered);
Negative Marks : –1 In all other cases.

Paragraph-I

Ionisation potential is the minimum amount of energy needed to remove the outermost electron from the gaseous isolated atom. Its unit is eV atom^{-1} or kJ mol^{-1}.

Successive ionisation energy is the amount of energy needed to remove electron successively from a gaseous ion, it may be termed as IE_1, IE_3...... . The difference in the values of IE_3, IE_2 .... helps to determine electronic configuration of the elements.

Element	IE_1	IE_2	IE_3 (kcal mol^{-1})
P	497	947	1500
Q	98	735	1100
R	176	347	1850
S	296	530	2050

22. Which of the element (X) can make MX type compound (where X is the halogen and M is alkali metal) ?
(a) P (b) Q
(c) R (d) S

23. The order of ionic mobility in aqueous solution of the following ions will be
(a) $R^{2+}(aq) > S^{2+}(aq)$ (b) $S^{2+}(aq) > R^{2+}(aq)$
(c) $S^{2+}(aq) = R^{2+}(aq)$ (d) Cannot be correlated

Paragraph-II

Alkenes on catalytic hydrogenation give alkanes. The reactions are exothermic. The heat of hydrogenation is a measure of stability of alkenes.

Lesser the heat of hydrogenation more is the stablity of the alkene.

24. The relative rate of catalytic hydrogenation of the following alkenes is

I II III IV

(a) II > III > IV > I
(b) I > IV > III > II
(c) II > IV > I > III
(d) III > IV > I > II

25. In the reaction,

CH_3, Br (cyclohexane) $\xrightarrow{\text{Alc. KOH}}$ X (Major)
$\xrightarrow{Et_3N}$ Y (Major)

which of the following statements is correct?

(a) The heat of hydrogenation of *X* is more than *Y*
(b) The heat of hydrogenation of *Y* is more than *X*
(c) Both *X* and *Y* has the same heat of hydrogenation
(d) Both *X* and *Y* have same reactivity towards catalytic hydrogenation

Answers

1 *(a)*	2 *(b)*	3 *(c)*	4 *(c)*	5 *(4.06)*	6 *(49.64)*	7 *(4.56)*	8 *(128.90)*	9 *(2.50)*	10 *(10.00)*
11 *(33.18)*	12 *(–57.07)*	13 *(a,b,c)*	14 *(b, d)*	15 *(b, c, d)*	16 *(a, b, c, d)*	17 *(a, b)*	18 *(a, b, c, d)*	19 *(9)*	20 *(46)*
21 *(35)*	22 *(b)*	23 *(a)*	24 *(a)*	25 *(b)*					

See detailed solutions on page no. 277

Part Test 03

(Based on Complete Class 12 Syllabus)

JEE MAIN

Chemistry

Instructions

- This question paper contains of 30 Questions of Chemistry, divided into two sections : **Section A** Objective Type Questions and **Section B** Numerical Value Questions.
- Section A contains 20 Objective questions and all Questions are cumpulsory (Marking Scheme : Correct + 4, Incorrect – 1).
- Section B contains 10 Numerical value questions out of which only 5 questions are to be attempted (Marking Scheme : Correct + 4, Incorrect 0)

Section A *Objective Type Questions*

1. When excess of D–C_6H_4–I reacts with sodium in liquid ammonia, then which of the following cannot be a product?

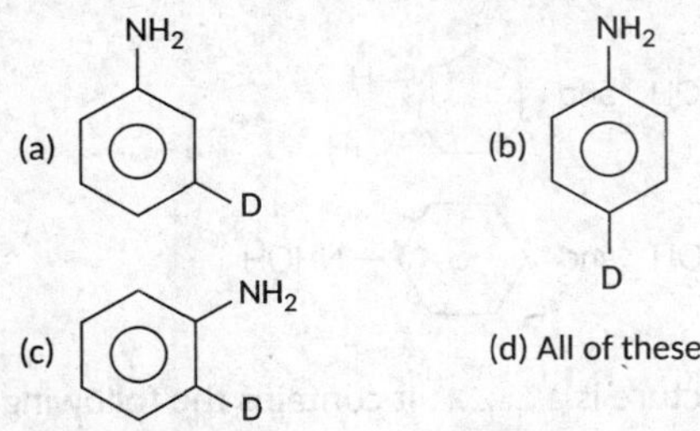

2. In which of the following options, all of the cations will form precipitate with $H_2S + HCl$?

(a) Mn^{2+}, Ni^{2+}, Fe^{2+}, Al^{3+} (b) Ca^{2+}, Ba^{2+}, Pb^{2+}, Sr^{2+}

(c) Hg^{2+}, Pb^{2+}, Cu^{2+}, Cd^{2+} (d) Hg^{2+}, Pb^{2+}, Mn^{2+}, Ba^{2+}

3. 3 g urea (molecular weight = 60) is dissolved in X g water. Vapour pressure of the system becomes 759.924 mm of Hg. What is the value of X, when vapour pressure of pure water is 760 mm of Hg?

(a) 1000 (b) 9000 (c) 7500 (d) 4500

4. $H_3CCH{=}CHCHO$ reacts with excess of HCN. Correct statement will be

(a) the final product will be $H_3CCH{=}CHCH(OH)CN$

(b) maximum 3 equivalents of HCN molecules are needed for this reaction

(c) the final product is $H_3CCH_2CH(CN)CH(OH)CN$

(d) the final product will have 2 chiral centres

5. ΔG is the available energy during the electrochemical process in a galvanic cell which can be converted into useful work. In the light of second law of thermodynamics, the change in electrode potential with temperature in the cell will be equal to

(a) $\frac{\Delta S}{nF}$ (b) $\frac{nF}{\Delta S}$

(c) $\frac{-2.303\,RT}{nF}$ (d) $-2.303\,RT \log K_{eq}$

6. Decomposition of $3A(g) \longrightarrow 2B(g) + 2C(g)$ follows first order kinetics. Initially, only A is present in the container. Pressure developed after 20 minutes and infinite time are 3.5 atm and 4 atm respectively. Which of the following is incorrect?

(a) $t_{50\%} = 20$ min

(b) $t_{87.5\%} = 60$ min

(c) $t_{99\%} = \frac{64}{3}$ min

(d) $t_{75\%} = 40$ min

7. $Ph{-}N{=}C{=}O \xrightarrow[\text{(ii) } H_2O]{\text{(i) } CH_3MgBr} P \xrightarrow[\text{(ii) } H_2O]{\text{(i) } LiAlH_4} Q$

(a) P is $Ph{-}NH{-}COCH_3$ and Q is $Ph{-}NH{-}CH_2CH_3$

(b) P is $Ph{-}NH{-}CH_3$ and Q is CO_2

(c) P is $Ph{-}N{=}C(CH_3)(OH)$ and Q is $(Ph{-}NH_2 + CH_3CH_2OH)$

(d) P is $Ph{-}NH{-}CH(OH){-}CH_3$ and Q is $Ph{-}NH{-}CH_2{-}CH_3$

8. In the given reaction,

Ph—C(CH$_3$)(Br)—C(H)(D)—Ph $\xrightarrow{\text{Alc. KOH}}$ Product(s) is (are)

(a) Both Ph(Me)C=C(Ph)(H) and Ph(Me)C=C(D)(Ph)

(b) Both Ph(Me)C=C(Ph)(D) and Ph(Me)C=C(H)(Ph)

(c) Only Ph(Me)C=C(H)(Ph)

(d) Both Ph(Me)C=C(Ph)(H) and Ph(Me)C=C(H)(Ph)

9. The ZnS structure can be obtained from the

(a) diamond by replacing two C-atoms of each ions with one Zn-atom and one S-atom respectively.

(b) graphite structure by replacing the two C-atoms of each basis with one Zn-atom and one S-atom respectively.

(c) fullerene structure by replacing two C-atoms of each basis with one Zn-atom and one S-atom.

(d) rock salt structure by replacing the Na^+ and Cl^- ion of each basis with one Zn-atom and one S-atom respectively.

10. Identify final product *R* in the following sequence of reactions.

cis-2-methylcyclohexanecarboxylic acid (CH$_3$, CO$_2$H) $\xrightarrow{SOCl_2}$ *P* $\xrightarrow{NH_3}$ *Q* $\xrightarrow[\Delta]{P_4O_{10}}$ *R*

(a) 2-methylcyclohexane with CH$_3$ and CONH$_2$

(b) 2-methylcyclohexane with CH$_3$ and CN

(c) 2-methylcyclohexane with CH$_3$ and CN (CN hashed)

(d) 2-methylcyclohexane with CH$_3$ (hashed) and CN

11. Consider the following sequence of reactions.

Cyclohexanone $\xrightarrow[OH^-]{A}$ 2-(CH—C$_6$H$_5$)cyclohexanone $\xrightarrow[\text{2. } H^+\text{, heat}]{\text{1. } LiAlH_4}$ *B*

The reactant (*A*) and the product (*B*) respectively are

(a) $C_6H_5CH_3$ and 2-(CHC$_6$H$_5$)cyclohexanol (OH)

(b) $C_6H_5CH_3$ and CHC$_6$H$_5$-substituted cyclohexene

(c) C_6H_5CHO and 2-(CHC$_6$H$_5$)cyclohexanol (OH)

(d) C_6H_5CHO and CH—C$_6$H$_5$-substituted cyclohexene

12. Cyclohexanone=O + H$_2$N—OH $\xrightarrow{\text{Heat}}$ *A* $\xrightarrow[\text{heat}]{H_2SO_4}$ *B*

The products (*A*) and (*B*) respectively are

(a) 1-(NHOH)cyclohexan-1-ol (OH, NHOH) and cyclohexylidene=N—OH

(b) cyclohexylidene=N—OH and cyclohexyl—N=O

(c) cyclohexylidene=N—OH and caprolactam (O, N—H)

(d) cyclohexylidene=N—OH and cyclohexyl—NHOH

13. The following structure is a .... It contains the following amino acids ...... , ... and ....

H$_2$N—CH(H)—CO—NH—CH(CH$_2$C$_6$H$_5$)—CO—NH—CH(CH$_2$OH)—CO—NH—CH(CH$_2$CONH$_2$)—COOH

(a) tripeptide, alanine, phenylalanine, arginine and serine

(b) tetrapeptide, alanine, phenylalanine, glutamine and serine

(c) tetrapeptide, alanine, threonine, glutamic acid cysteine and glycine

(d) tripeptide, alanine, serine, glutamine, histidine and lysine

14. Which of the following is a copolymer ?

(a) $—CH_2—\overset{CH_3}{\overset{|}{C}}=CH—CH_2—CH_2—\overset{CH_3}{\overset{|}{C}}=CH—CH_2—$

(b) $-CH_2-CH-CH_2-CH-CH_2-CH-$ (with CH_3, C_6H_5, CH_3 substituents)

(c) $-CH-CH_2-CH-CH_2-CH-CH_2-$ (with CH_3, CH_3, CH_3 substituents)

(d) $-CH_2-CH-CH_2-CH-CH_2-CH-$ (with C_6H_5 on each CH)

15. What are the constituent amines formed when the mixture of (I) and (II) undergo Hofmann bromamide degradation?

(I) $C_6H_4(D)-CONH_2$ (D at meta position) (II) $C_6H_5-\overset{15}{C}ONH_2$

(a) $C_6H_4(D)-NH_2$, $C_6H_4(D)-\overset{15}{N}H_2$, $C_6H_5-NH_2$, $C_6H_5-\overset{15}{N}H_2$

(b) $C_6H_4(D)-NH_2$, $C_6H_5-\overset{15}{N}H_2$

(c) $C_6H_5-\overset{15}{N}H_2$, $C_6H_5-\overset{15}{N}H_2$

(d) $C_6H_5-\overset{15}{N}HD$, C_6H_6

16. In the given reaction,

(bicyclic amine with N–H and ring C=C) $\xrightarrow{Br_2}$ [X]

The structure of *X* is

(a) N–H compound with Br on two ring carbons

(b) N–Br compound

(c) N–H compound with Br on two ring carbons

(d) tricyclic N compound with Br

17. What is the final product?

$$\text{Phenol} \xrightarrow[\text{AlCl}_3]{\textit{tert}\text{-butyl chloride}} \underset{(\textit{para}\text{-isomer})}{C_{10}H_{14}O} \xrightarrow[\text{(ii) } CH_3CH_2I]{\text{(i) NaOH}}$$

(a) 1-*tert*-butyl-4-ethoxybenzene
(b) 1-*tert*-butyl-4-ethylbenzene
(c) 1-*tert*-butoxy-4-ethoxybenzene
(d) *tert*-butyl ethyl ether

18. Which one of the following complexes will most likely absorb visible light ? (Atomic number Sc = 21, Ti = 22, V = 23, Zn = 30).

(a) $[Sc(H_2O)_6]^{3+}$ (b) $[Ti(NH_3)_6]^{4+}$
(c) $[V(NH_3)_6]^{3+}$ (d) $[Zn(NH_3)_6]^{2+}$

19. The reaction $A \to X$ is a first-order reaction, which takes place in a vessel with initial concentration of *A* as 10 M. The rate constant for this reaction is 4.16 h^{-1}. In the presence of a catalyst, the reaction $A \to Y$ follows second order kinetics and the rate constant is 0.2 $min^{-1}M^{-1}$. What should be the initial concentration of *A* in the presence of catalyst so that the value of $t_{1/2}$ for both the reactions is same?

(a) 30.0 M (b) 0.5 M
(c) 5.0M (d) 10.0 M

20. Hydrolysis of dimethyldichlorosilane, $(CH_3)_2SiCl_2$, followed by condensation polymerisation yields straight-chain polymer of

(a) $\sim O-Si(O)(O)-Si(O)(O)-O\sim$

(b) $\sim Si-O-O-Si\sim$

(c) $\sim O-Si(CH_3)_2-O-Si(CH_3)_2-O\sim$

(d) $\sim O-Si(CH_3)_2-Si(CH_3)_2-O\sim$

Section B *Numerical Value Questions*

21. Consider the given data for the reaction

$$H_2 + I_2 \longrightarrow 2HI$$

T (Kelvin)	$\frac{1}{T}(K^{-1})$	log *K*
769	1.3×10^{-3}	2.9
667	1.5×10^{-3}	1.1

The correct activation energy of the reaction in kcal mol^{-1} is ....

22. Among the given molecules, the number of compounds that will disproportionate in the presence of 50% NaOH solution is ....

Propanal, 2,2,2-triphenylethanal, propan-2-one, 2-phenylethanal, 4-phenylpentanal, 4-nitrobenzaldehyde, 2-hydroxybenzaldehyde, 2,2,4,4-tetramethylpentanal, 2,2,6,6-tetramethyl-cyclohexanone, 4,4-dimethylcyclohexanone

23. Among the given statements, ... statement(s) is/are correct about chemisorption.

(I) It is highly specific
(II) Heat of adsorption is low
(III) It is irreversible in nature
(IV) It depends on the surface area of the system
(V) It causes a strong chemical interaction between adsorbate and adsorbent
(VI) Low activation energy is involved in this case
(VII) Low pressure is involved in this process
(VIII) High temperature is involved in this process
(IX) It is a multilayer process
(X) Decrease of pressure does not cause desorption

24. The degree of dissociation of $Ca(NO_3)_2$ in a dilute aqueous solution containing 7g of the salt per 100 g of water at 100°C is 70 per cent. If vapour pressure of water at 100°C is 760 mm, the vapour pressure (in mm) of the solution......... .

25. Resistance of 0.2 M solution of an electrolyte is 50 Ω. The specific conductance of the solution of 0.5 m solution of same electrolyte is 1.4 Sm^{-1} and resistance of same solution of the same electrolyte is 280 Ω. The molar conductivity of 0.5 M solution of the electrolyte is $x \times 10^{-4}$ $S\,m^2\,mol^{-1}$. The value of x is ....

26. Effective atomic number of Mn and Fe in the complexes $Mn_2(CO)_{10}$ and $Co_2(CO)_8$ are x and y respectively. The value of $(x + y)$ is ....

27. (+) Sucrose has a specific rotation of +66.5°; while D-(+)-glucose and D-(–)-glucose have specific rotation of +52.5° and –92.4° respectively. After complete hydrolysis of (+)sucrose by dilute acid, the specific degree of rotation of the hydrolysis product, called invert sugar will be ....

28. Gold number of haemoglobin is 0.03. Hence, 10 mL of gold solution will require .... haemoglobin (in mg), so that gold is not coagulated by addition of 10 mL of 10% NaCl solution.

29. The molar volume of liquid benzene (density $= 0.877\ g\ mL^{-1}$) increases by a factor of 2750 as it vaporises at 20°C and that of liquid toluene (density $= 0.867\ g\ mL^{-1}$) increases by a factor of 7720 at 20°C. A solution of benzene and toluene at 20°C has a vapour pressure of 46.0 torr. The mole fraction of benzene in the vapour above the solution will be ....

30. When CH_3CHO is treated with excess of HCHO in aqueous solution of Na_2CO_3, a product, used in making explosive, is obtained finally. The number of primary alcoholic groups present in one molecule of the product will be ....

Answers

Section A

1 *(c)*	2 *(c)*	3 *(b)*	4 *(d)*	5 *(a)*
6 *(c)*	7 *(a)*	8 *(a)*	9 *(a)*	10 *(b)*
11 *(d)*	12 *(c)*	13 *(b)*	14 *(b)*	15 *(b)*
16 *(d)*	17 *(a)*	18 *(c)*	19 *(b)*	20 *(c)*

Section B

21 *(41.25)*	22 *(5)*	23 *(6)*	24 *(746.24)*	25 *(5)*
26 *(72)*	27 *(–19.95)*	28 *(0.30)*	29 *(0.45)*	30 *(4)*

See detailed solutions on page no. 279

Part Test 04

(Based on Complete Class 12 Syllabus)

JEE ADVANCED

Chemistry

SECTION 1

- This section contains **FOUR (04)** questions.
- Each question has **FOUR** options (a), (b), (c) and (d). **ONLY ONE** of these four options is the correct answer.
- For each question, choose the option corresponding to the correct answer.
- Answer to each question will be evaluated according to the following marking scheme:

Full Marks : +3 If ONLY the correct option is chosen;
Zero Marks : 0 If none of the options is chosen (i.e. the question is unanswered);
Negative Marks : −1 In all other cases.

1. List-I represents four molecules, while List-II represents their characteristic reactions; match List-I with List-II.

List-I	List-II
A. (cyclohexadiene with H and Cl)	1. Rapid elimination with almost no substitution reaction.
B. (furan with CH_2Cl)	2. Normal as well as ring substitution product.
C. (C_6H_5–CH_2–CH_2Cl) *represents ^{14}C	3. Rapid substitution with skeletal rearrangement.
D. (bicyclic bridgehead Cl)	4. Extremely sluggish substitution

Codes

	A	B	C	D
(a)	1	2	3	4
(b)	1	3	2	4
(c)	4	3	2	1
(d)	4	2	3	1

2. Cellulose upon acetylation with excess acetic anhydride/H_2SO_4 (catalytic) gives cellulose triacetate, whose structure is

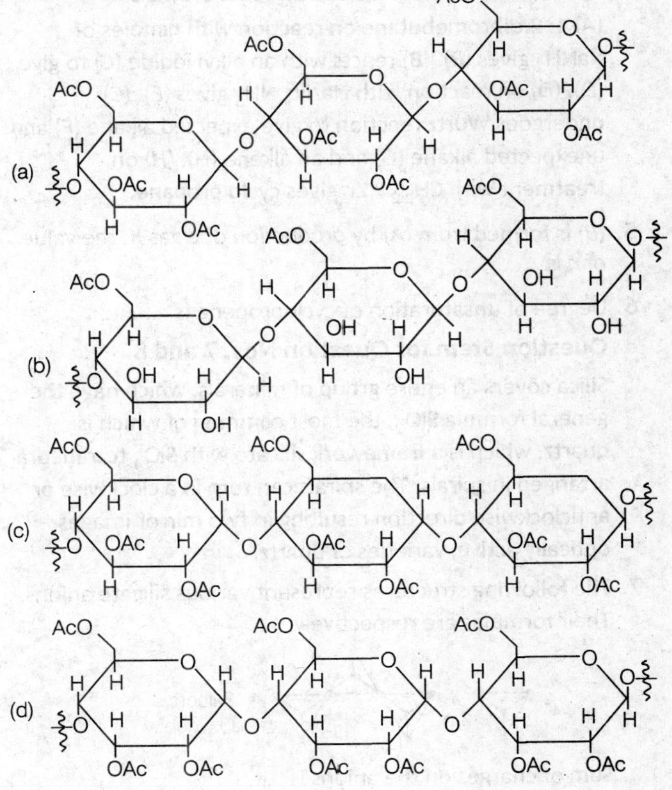

3. A nuclear explosion has taken place leading to increase in concentration of ^{14}C in nearby areas. ^{14}C concentration is C_1 in nearby areas and C_2 in areas far away.

If the age of the fossil is determined to be t_1 and t_2 at the two places respectively, then

(a) the age of the fossil will increase at the place where explosion has taken place and $t_1 - t_2 = \frac{1}{\lambda} \ln \frac{C_1}{C_2}$

(b) the age of the fossil will decrease at the place where explosion has taken place and $t_1 - t_2 = \frac{1}{\lambda} \ln \frac{C_1}{C_2}$

(c) the age of fossil will be determined to be same

(d) $\frac{t_1}{t_2} = \frac{C_1}{C_2}$

4. Which of the following facts about the complex $[Cr(NH_3)_6]Cl_3$ is incorrect?

(a) The complex is paramagnetic.

(b) The complex is an outer orbital complex.

(c) The complex gives white precipitate with silver nitrate solution.

(d) The complex involves d^2sp^3 hybridisation and is octahedral in shape.

SECTION 2

- This section contains **FOUR (04)** question stems.
- There are **TWO (02)** questions corresponding to each question stem.
- The answer to each question is a **NUMERICAL VALUE.**
- For each question, enter the correct numerical value corresponding to the answer in the designated place using the mouse and the on-screen virtual numeric keypad.
- If the numerical value has more than two decimal places, **truncate/round-off** the value to **TWO** decimal places.
- Answer to each question will be evaluated according to the following marking scheme:

Full Marks : +2 If ONLY the correct numerical value is entered at the designated place;
Zero marks : 0 In all other cases.

Question Stem for Question Nos. 5 and 6

(*A*) 1, 2-dibromobutane on reaction with *n* moles of $NaNH_2$ gives (*B*). (*B*) reacts with an alkyl iodide (*C*) to give (*D*). (*D*) on reaction with Na/liq. NH_3 gives (*E*), (*C*) undergoes Wurtz reaction to give expected alkane (*F*) and unexpected alkane (*G*) and an alkene (*H*). (*H*) on treatment with CH_2I_2 / Zn gives cyclo propane.

5. (*B*) is formed from (*A*) by production of a gas *X*, the value of *n* is ....

6. Degree of unsaturation of cyclopropene is ....

Question Stem for Question Nos. 7 and 8

Silica covers an entire group of minerals, which have the general formula SiO_2, the most common of which is quartz, which is a framework silicate with SiO_4 tetrahedra arranged in spirals. The spirals can turn in a clockwise or anticlockwise direction resulting in two mirror images, optically active, varieties of quartz.

7. The following structures represent various silicate anions. Their formulas are respectively

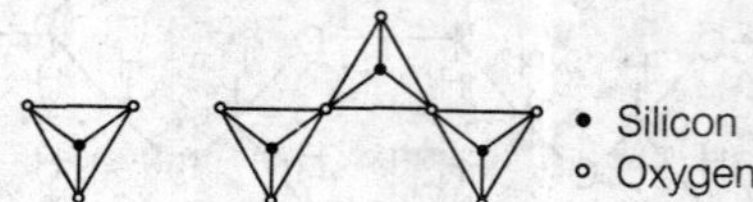

Sum of charges on the anions is ....

8. The silicate anion in the mineral kinoite is a chain of three SiO_4^{4-} tetrahedra that share corners with adjacent tetrahedra.

The mineral also contains Ca^{2+} ions, Cu^{2+} ions and water molecules in *a* : *b* : *c* ratio and the compound $Ca_2Cu_2Si_3O_{10}.2H_2O$.

Question Stem for Question Nos. 9 and 10

Knowing the standard electrode potentials of the half reactions, the standard emf of the cell can be calculated. The standard emf further helps in the calculation of free energy change, equilibrium constant of the cell reaction as well as parameters like solubility product of a sparingly soluble salt.

9. The standard electrode potential ($E°$) for Ni^{2+} / Ni and Au^{3+}/Au respectively, are −0.25 V and 1.50 V. The emf of the cell will be V

10. The standard reduction potentials for two reactions are given as follows

$AgCl(s) + e^- \longrightarrow Ag^+(s) + Cl^-(aq); E° = 0.22 \text{ V}$

$Ag^+(aq) + e^- \longrightarrow Ag(s); E° = 0.80 \text{ V}$

The solubility product of AgCl under standard conditions of temperature (298 K) is given by .... $\times 10^{-10}$ M^2.

[Antilog $(-9.81) = 1.53 \times 10^{-10}$]

Question Stem for Question Nos. 11 and 12

A solid with surface area independent of temperature adsorbs 2 mg of a gas, when in contact with the gas at a pressure of 10 kPa at 283 K. The amount of heat absorbed is 80 J, when 2 millimoles of the gas is desorbed.

11. Enthalpy of adsorption is .... kJ mol^{-1}.

12. Equilibrium pressure for the adsorption of 2 mg of the gas at 323 K is .... kPa.

log 10 = 1

Antilog (1.9142) = 82.07.

SECTION 3

- This section contains **SIX (06)** questions.
- Each question has **FOUR** options (a), (b), (c) and (d). **ONE OR MORE THAN ONE** of these four option(s) is (are) correct answer(s).
- For each question, choose the option(s) corresponding to (all) the correct answer(s).
- Answer to each question will be evaluated according to the following marking scheme:

Full Marks : +4 If only (all) the correct option(s) is(are) chosen;
Partial Marks : +3 If all the four options are correct but ONLY three options are chosen;
Partial Marks : +2 If three or more options are correct but ONLY two options are chosen, both of which are correct;
Partial Marks : +1 If two or more options are correct but ONLY one option is chosen and it is a correct option;
Zero Marks : 0 If unanswered;
Negative Marks : –2 In all other cases.

- For example, in a question, if (a), (b) and (d) are the ONLY three options corresponding to correct answers, then
choosing ONLY (a), (b) and (d) will get +4 marks;
choosing ONLY (a) and (b) will get +2 marks;
choosing ONLY (a) and (d) will get +2 marks;
choosing ONLY (b) and (d) will get +2 marks;
choosing ONLY (a) will get +1 mark;
choosing ONLY (b) will get +1 mark;
choosing ONLY (d) will get +1 mark;
choosing no option(s) (i.e. the question is unanswered) will get 0 marks and
choosing any other option(s) will get –2 marks.

13. In Dow's process of manufacture of phenol, chlorobenzene is fused with NaOH at high temperature under pressure.

$$C_6H_5Cl \xrightarrow[\text{350°C, high pressure}]{\text{NaOH}} [\text{Intermediate}] \xrightarrow{H_2O} \text{Phenol} + \underbrace{[A] + [B]}_{\text{Side products}}$$

Which of the following statements is/are correct for the above chemical reaction ?

(a) Phenol is formed *via* an intermediate which is aromatic
(b) Diphenylether is also formed as side product
(c) *para*-phenylphenol is also formed as side product
(d) Biphenylene is also formed as a side product

14. $(X) + Mg \xrightarrow[\text{ether}]{\text{Dry}} (Y) \xrightarrow[\text{(ii) } H_3O^+]{(Z)} CH_3CH_2CH_2OH$

Identify (X) and (Z) in the above sequence of reaction.

(a) (X) : CH_3CH_2Br, (Z) : HCHO
(b) (X) : CH_3Br, (Z) : $CH_2—CH_2$ (bridged by O, epoxide)
(c) (X) : CH_3Br, (Z) : CH_3CH_2CHO
(d) (X) : $CH_3—CH(Br)—CH_3$, (Z) : CH_3CHO

15. Consider the following galvanic cell.

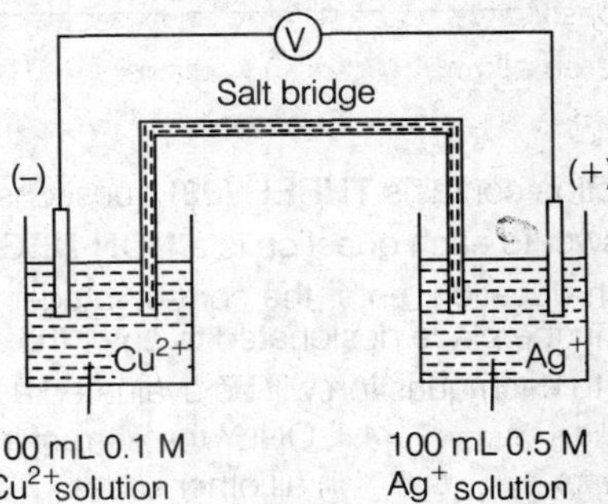

Given $E^\circ_{(Ag^+/Ag)} = 0.80$ V, $E^\circ_{(Cu^{2+}/Cu)} = 0.34$ V

Which of the following statements is/are correct ?

(a) The emf of the cell at 298 K is 0.47 V.
(b) The emf of the cell increases with increasing temperature.
(c) To reach the equilibrium the minimum mass of Cu electrode is 1.5 g.
(d) To reach the equilibrium the minimum mass of Cu electrode is 15 g.

[log 4 = 0.6020, log 10 = 1]

16. An optically active compound *A* produces two optically active products *B* and *C* in two parallel paths as shown in figure.

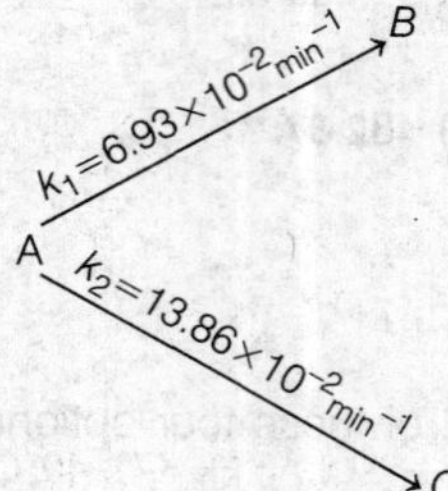

If optical activity of *A*, *B* and *C* per unit concentration are 60°, –72° and 42° respectively and initial concentration of *A* is 2 M.

Choose the right option(s) from the following:

(a) The solution will be optically active and dextrorotatory after a long time.

(b) The solution will be optically active and laevorotatory after a long time.

(c) Half-life of overall reaction is 15 min.

(d) After 75% conversion of *A* into *B* and *C*, the optical rotation of the mixture will be 36°.

17. For a reaction $A \longrightarrow P, t_{\frac{1}{2}}$ of the reaction is function of concentration of *A*, i.e. $[A_0]$ (M). The result of two experiments are given in the table.

$[A_0]$ M	0.1	0.025
$t_{\frac{1}{2}}$ (min)	100	50

Choose the correct option.

(a) Order is 2

(b) Order is $\frac{1}{2}$

(c) $t_{\frac{1}{2}} = 100\sqrt{10}$ min when $[A_0]$ is 1 M

(d) $t_{\frac{1}{2}} = 100\sqrt{2}$ min when $[A_0]$ is 0.2 M

18. Consider the following two diagrams.

make one more bubble in (I)

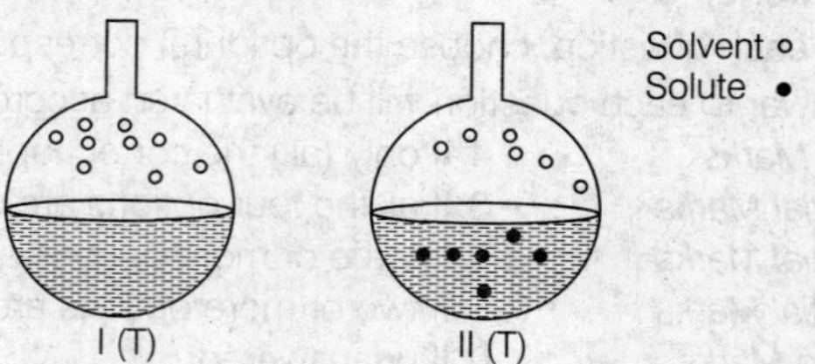

Suppose that the solute molecules on the surface of solution occupy 10% of the surface area. The correct statement(s) is(are)

(a) if the water in the left vessel *I* was transferred to a container with 10% less surface area, the vapour pressure would be lowered to same value as the vapour pressure in vessel II.

(b) mole fraction of solute in container II is $\frac{1}{3}$.

(c) boiling point of solution II is 114.44°C (K_b of water is 0.52 K kg/mol).

(d) if the cross-sectional area of surface of solution in container II is increased by 10%, the number of molecules in the vapour phase will increase by 10%.

SECTION 4

- This section contains **THREE (03)** questions.
- The answer to each question is a **NON-NEGATIVE INTEGER.**
- For each question, enter the correct integer corresponding to the answer using the mouse and the on-screen virtual numeric keypad in the place designated to enter the answer.
- Answer to each question will be evaluated according to the following marking scheme:
  Full Marks : +4 If ONLY the correct integer is entered;
  Zero Marks : 0 In all other cases.

19. A molecule A_2B (mol. wt. 166.4) occupies triclinic lattice with $a = 5$ Å, $b = 8$ Å and $c = 4$ Å. If density of AB_2 is 5.2 g cm^{-3}, calculate the number of molecules present in one unit.

20. Emf of the cell corresponding to the reaction,

$$\underset{}{Zn(s)} + 2H^+(aq) \longrightarrow \underset{(0.10\ M)}{Zn^{2+}(aq)} + \underset{(1\ atm)}{H_2(g)}$$

is 0.3175 V at 25°C. Also, at 25°C, $E^\circ_{Zn^{2+}/Zn} = -0.76$ V. The pH of solution in cathode chamber is ....

21. **Consider the pairs of ethers *a* to *f* shown below. To the right of each pair is a description of reaction conditions to be applied to each. One compound of the pair will react more rapidly than the other. The number of reactions in which first ether more rapidly cleaved than second is ....**

Ether pairs	**Conditions**
(a) O—CH(CH)$_3$)$_2$ and H_3C, H_3C, O—CH_3	(i) Treated with HBr in CH_3—CN, 40°C
(b) H_3C, H_3C, O—C(CH)$_3$)$_3$ and C_2H_5, C_2H_5, O—CH_3	(ii) Treated with H_2SO_4 in CH_3CN, 40°C
(c) O and O	(iii) Treated with H_2SO_4 in CH_3CN, 40°C
(d) CH_3O, O, OH and HO, O, OCH_3	(iv) Treated with 5% aqueous H_2SO_4, 25°C
(e) O, CH(CH)$_3$)$_2$ and O, CH(CH)$_3$)$_2$	(v) Treated with 5% aqueous H_2SO_4, 25°C
(f) —CH_2—O—C_2H_5 and —$(CH_2)_3$—O—CH_3	(vi) Treated with $H^{\oplus}$ / H_2O

SECTION 5

- This section contains **TWO (02) paragraphs.** Based on each paragraph, there are **TWO (02)** questions.
- Each question has **FOUR** options (A), (B), (C) and (D). **ONLY ONE** of these four options is the correct answer.
- For each question, choose the option corresponding to the correct answer.
- Answer to each question will be evaluated according to the following marking scheme:

Full Marks : +3 If ONLY the correct option is chosen;
Zero Marks : 0 If none of the options is chosen (i.e. question is unanswered);
Negative Marks : –1 In all other cases.

Paragraph - I

Molar conductance of NaCl varies with concentration according to the equation $\Lambda_m = \Lambda_m^o - b\sqrt{C}$ where Λ_m is molar specific conductance, Λ_m^o is molar specific conductance at infinite dilution, and C is the molar concentration. The variation is shown in the following table:

Molar concentration of NaCl	**Molar conductance is S cm^2 mol^{-1}**
4×10^{-4}	107
9×10^{-4}	97
16×10^{-4}	87

22. When a certain conductivity cell was filled with 25×10^{-4} M NaCl solution, the resistance of the cell was found to be 1000 Ω. At infinite dilution, conductance of Cl^- and SO_4^{2-} are 80 S cm^2 mol^{-1} and 160 S cm^2 mol^{-1}, respectively. What is the molar conductance of NaCl at infinite dilution?

(a) 147 S cm^2 mol^{-1}
(b) 107 S cm^2 mol^{-1}
(c) 127 S cm^2 mol^{-1}
(d) 157 S cm^2 mol^{-1}

23. What is the cell constant of the conductivity cell ?

(a) 0.385 cm^{-1} (b) 3.85 cm^{-1}
(c) 38.5 cm^{-1} (d) 0.1925 cm^{-1}

Paragraph - II

The acidity of carboxylic acid is determined by the nature of the alkyl group attached and the substituent present on it. It is affected mainly by the inductive effect of the substituent and its position with respect to the —COOH group. Electron donating substituent tend to decrease, whereas electron withdrawing substituent tend to increase the acidic strength. The acidic strength of aromatic carboxylic acid on the other hand, depends upon both the inductive and the resonance effects of the substituents.

24. Which of the following would be expected to be most highly ionised in water?

(a) $ClCH_2CH_2CH_2COOH$
(b) $CH_3CHClCH_2COOH$
(c) $CH_3CH_2CCl_2COOH$
(d) $CH_3CH_2CHClCOOH$

25. The pK_a of acetylsalicylic acid (aspirin) is 3.5. The pH of gastric juice in human stomach is about 2-3 and pH in the small intestine is about 8. Aspirin will be

(a) unionised in the small intestine and in the stomach
(b) completely ionised in the stomach and almost unionised in the small intestine
(c) ionised in the stomach and almost unionised in the small intestine
(d) ionised in the small intestine and almost unionised in the stomach

Answers

1 (a)	2 (a)	3 (a)	4 (b)	5 (3)	6 (2)	7 (– 4)	8 (3)	9 (1.75)	10 (1.53)
11 (– 40)	12 (82.10)	13 (a,b,c)	14 (a,b)	15 (a,b,c)	16 (a,d)	17 (b,c,d)	18 (b,c,d)	19 (3)	20 (8)
21 (3)	22 (c)	23 (d)	24 (c)	25 (d)					

See detailed solutions on page no. 281

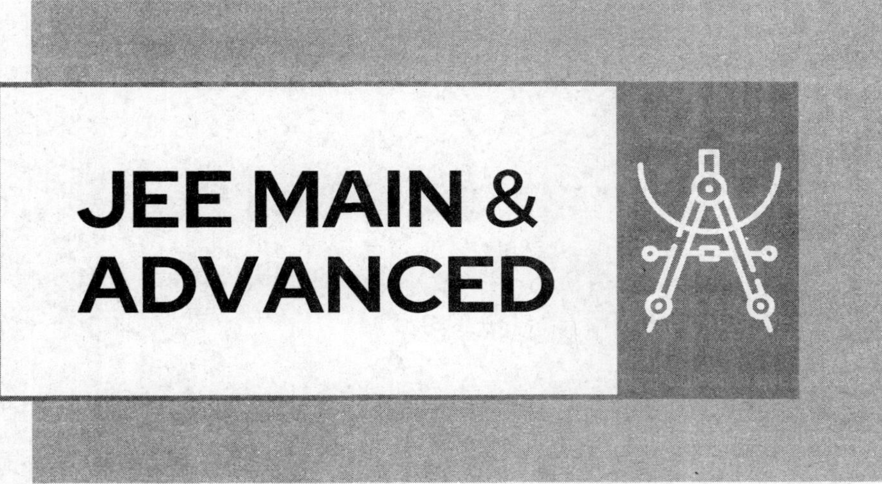

The Knockouts

10 Full Syllabus Mock Tests for JEE Main & 5 forJEE Advanced

Mock Tests given here will help you to be acquainted with Pattern & Level of JEE Main & JEE Advanced. Practicing these tests in systematic manner will ensure your good score in the Exam.

Knockout 01

JEE MAIN

Chemistry

Instructions

- This question paper contains of 30 Questions of Chemistry, divided into two sections : **Section A** Objective Type Questions and **Section B** Numerical Value Questions.
- **Section A** contains 20 Objective questions and all Questions are compulsory (Marking Scheme : Correct + 4, Incorrect – 1).
- **Section B** contains 10 Numerical value questions out of which only 5 questions are to be attempted (Marking Scheme : Correct + 4, Incorrect 0).

Section A *Objective Type Questions*

1. 1, 3-butadiene on heating with maleic anhydride would give

(a) 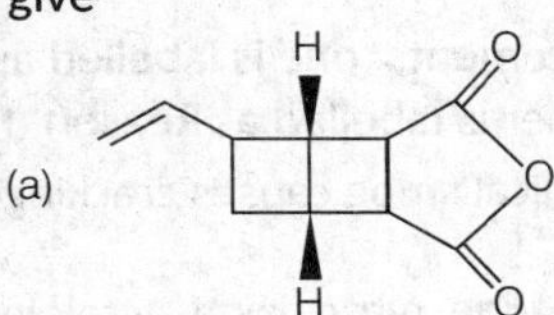

(b) 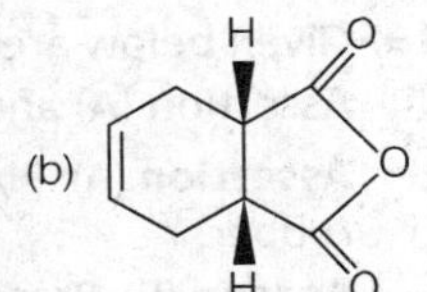

(c) 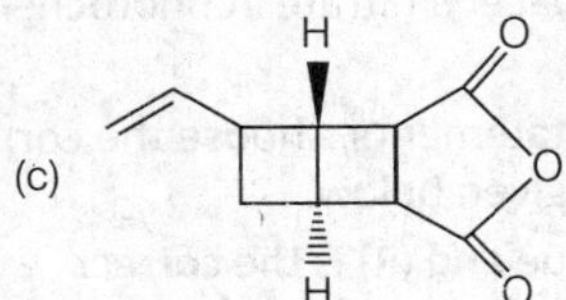

(d)

2. The rate law for a reaction between the substances A and B is given by rate $= k[A]^n [B]^m$. On doubling the concentration of A and halving the concentration of B, the ratio of the new rate to the earlier rate of the reaction will be

(a) $\frac{1}{2^{m+n}}$ (b) $2^{(m+n)}$ (c) $\frac{1}{2^{n-m}}$ (d) $2^{(n-m)}$

3. Consider the following sequence of reaction,

$X^- \xleftarrow{\Delta H_4} X \xrightarrow{\Delta H_1} X^+ \xrightarrow{\Delta H_2} X^{2+} \xrightarrow{\Delta H_3} X^{3+}$ (ΔH_5: $X^- \to X$; ΔH_6: $X^+ \to X$)

If electronic configuration of element X is $[Ne]3s^1$, then which of the following order is incorrect regarding the given enthalpies?

(a) $|\Delta H_4| = |\Delta H_5|$ (b) $|\Delta H_2| > |\Delta H_1|$
(c) $|\Delta H_2| > |\Delta H_3|$ (d) $|\Delta H_1| = |\Delta H_6|$

4. The bond angle in Cl_2O is

(a) smaller than that of F_2O
(b) greater than that of H_2O
(c) smaller than that of H_2O
(d) same as that of F_2O

5. The overall charge present on the cyclic silicate anion $[Si_6O_{18}]^{n-}$ is

(a) 6 (b) 12 (c) 18 (d) 24

6. Which of the following compounds is not yellow coloured?

(a) $K_3[Co(NO_2)_6]$ (b) $(NH_4)_3[As(Mo_3O_{10})_4]$
(c) $BaCrO_4$ (d) $Cu_2[Fe(CN)_6]$

7. Consider the following reaction,

$(H_3C)_2CH{-}CH(CH_3)_2 \xrightarrow[h\nu]{Cl_2}$ Products

Number of monochloro products (including stereoisomers) will be

(a) 2 (b) 3 (c) 4 (d) 5

8. The final product obtained from the electrolysis of 50% H_2SO_4 with high current density has

(a) S—O—O—S linkage (b) S=S linkage
(c) S—S linkage (d) S—O—S linkage

9. Compare the rate of reaction of following species with OH^-.

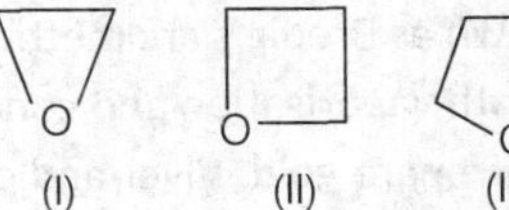

(a) I > II > III (b) I > III > II
(c) III > II > I (d) II > I > III

10. The monomer of the polymer

$$\left[-H_2C-\underset{CH_3}{\overset{CH_3}{C}}-CH_2-\underset{CH_3}{\overset{CH_3}{C}}-\right]_n$$ is

(a) $H_2C=C(CH_3)_2$ (b) $H_3C-CH=CH-CH_3$

(c) $H_3C-CH=CH_2$ (d) $H_3C-\underset{CH_3}{C}=\underset{CH_3}{C}-CH_3$

11. The correct code of matching of complex compound in Column I with their properties in Column II will be

Column I	Column II
A. $[Cr(NH_3)_6]^{3+}$	1. Tetrahedral and paramagnetic
B. $[Co(CN)_6]^{3-}$	2. Octahedral and diamagnetic
C. $[Co(CN)_4]^{2-}$	3. Octahedral and paramagnetic
D. $[Ni(Cl)_4]^{2-}$	4. Square planar and diamagnetic

Codes

	A	B	C	D
(a)	3	2	1	4
(b)	2	3	1	4
(c)	3	2	4	1
(d)	2	3	4	1

12. The number of hydrogen atoms in 0.9 g of galactose is same as

(a) 0.048 g of hydrazine (b) 0.17 g of ammonia
(c) 0.30 g of ethane (d) 0.03 g of hydrogen

13. Which of the following statements is incorrect for Lucas test, which is used to distinguish between 1°, 2° and 3° alcohols?

(a) Allyl alcohol and benzyl alcohol give immediate turbidity
(b) Alcohols which react readily with Na-metal will give turbidity at much faster rate
(c) Alcohols which give red colour during Victor-Meyer test, will give turbidity at much slower rate
(d) Lucas test involves acid-base reaction

14. Which of the following statements is incorrect for 'Electrical Disintegration' method for preparation of colloids?

(a) It is also known as Bredig's arc method.
(b) It involves both vaporisation and condensation.
(c) It is used to prepare gold, silver and platinum sols.
(d) It needs an electric arc between the electrodes of the metal immersed in the dispersed phase.

15. Which of the following antibiotics is bactericidal in nature?

(a) Erythromycin (b) Ofloxacin
(c) Tetracycline (d) Chloramphenicol

16. A metal crystallises in bcc lattice. The % of edge length which is not covered by atom is

(a) 10.4% (b) 13.4%
(c) 12.5% (d) 16%

17. The cell, $Zn|Zn^{2+}(1M)||Cu^{2+}(1M)|Cu$ of $E^\circ_{cell} = 1.10$ V, was allowed to be completely discharged at 298 K. The relative concentration of Zn^{2+} to Cu^{2+} is

(a) 9.65×10^4 (b) antilog (24.08)
(c) $10^{37.2}$ (d) 37.3

18. When benzenesulphonic acid ($C_6H_5SO_3H$), 2,6-dinitrophenol (OH with O_2N and NO_2) and benzoic acid (C_6H_5COOH) are treated with $NaHCO_3$ solution, the gases released respectively are

(a) SO_2, N_2O, CO_2 (b) SO_3, N_2O, CO_2
(c) CO_2, CO_2, CO_2 (d) CO_2, NO_2, CO_2

19. Given below are two statements, one is labelled as Assertion (A) and the other is labelled as Reason (R).

Assertion (A) Photochemical smog causes cracking of rubber.

Reason (R) Presence of ozone, nitric oxide, acrolein, formaldehyde and peroxyacetyl nitrate in photochemical smog makes it oxidising.

In the light of the above statements, choose the correct answer from the options given below.

(a) Both (A) and (R) are true and (R) is the correct explanation of (A).
(b) Both (A) and (R) are true but (R) is not the correct explanation of (A).
(c) (A) is false but (R) is true.
(d) (A) is true but (R) is false.

20. Consider the following reaction.

$$C_6H_5-CH(OH)-C(=O)-NH_2 \xrightarrow[\Delta]{Br_2/KOH} (X)$$

Here, (X) is

(a) $C_6H_5CH_2NH_2$ (b) C_6H_5CHO
(c) $C_6H_5-\underset{OH}{CH}-CH_3$ (d) $C_6H_5COOCH_3$

Section B *Numerical Value Questions*

21. In a fcc arrangement W occupies fcc arrangement, X occupies octahedral voids and Y occupies alternate tetrahedral voids, if atoms along two body diagonals are removed, then the simplest formula representing the structure is $W_aX_bY_c$. The value of $(a+b)/c$ is ....

22. The number of steps involved in the extraction of Zn from zinc blende is ....

(I) Smelting, (II) Froth-floatation, (III) Reduction, (IV) Electro-refining, (V) Electrolytic reduction, (VI) Magnetic separation

23. x and y number of electrons are present in t_{2g} set of d-orbitals of the central metal cation in $[Fe(H_2O)_5(NO)]SO_4$ (brown ring complex) respectively. The value of $(x \div y)$ is ....

24. A pentapeptide on complete hydrolysis gives glycine (G), alanine (A), leucine (L) and valine (V). On partial hydrolysis, it never gives Val-Ala. If neither $—NH_2$ nor —COOH is present at chiral centre. Number of primary structure(s) of pentapeptide possible is/are ....

25. Equal volumes of 0.2 M KI solution and 0.1 M HgI_2 solution are mixed. The van't Hoff factor of the resulting solution, assuming complete ionisation of the complex compound formed is ....

26. 1 mole of the following compound requires separately x mole of CH_3MgBr and y mole of NaOH for complete reaction of the compound. With CH_3MgBr, it liberates z L of CH_4 at STP. The value of $(x+y+z)$ is ....

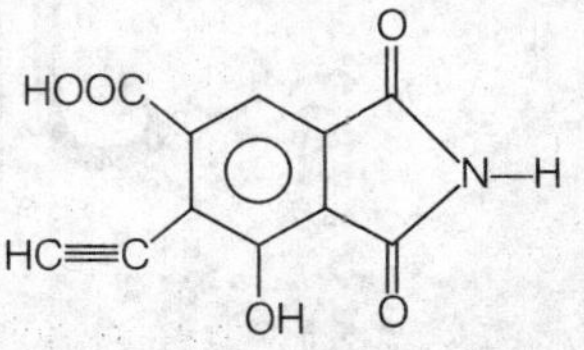

HOOC, N—H, HC≡C, OH, O, O

27. The number of chlorine atom(s) which is/are directly bonded to each beryllium in solid beryllium chloride is ....

28. $\xrightarrow[\Delta]{OH^-}$ (X)

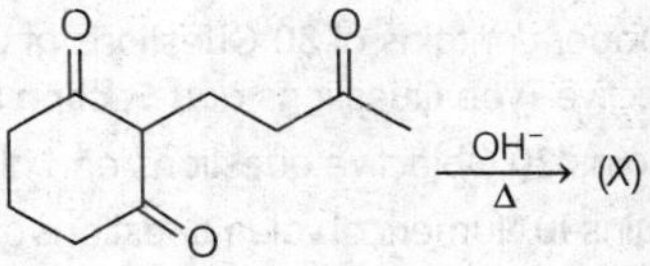

The degree of unsaturation of (X) is ......

29. K_{sp} of AgCl is 1×10^{-10}, then its solubility in 0.1 M KNO_3 is 'S' mol L^{-1}. The value of $-\log S$ is ....

30. If 'x' is the number of $lp-bp$ repulsions at 90° in I_3^- and 'y' is the number of $lp-bp$ repulsions at 90° in ICl_4^-, then the value of $\frac{x+y}{4}$ is ....

Answers

1 (b)	2 (d)	3 (c)	4 (b)	5 (b)	6 (d)	7 (b)	8 (a)	9 (a)	10 (a)
11 (c)	12 (c)	13 (b)	14 (d)	15 (b)	16 (b)	17 (c)	18 (c)	19 (a)	20 (b)
21 (3.25)	22 (4)	23 (2.50)	24 (1)	25 (3)	26 (96.6)	27 (4)	28 (5)	29 (5)	30 (3.50)

See detailed solutions on page no. 284

Knockout 02

JEE MAIN

Chemistry

Instructions

- This question paper contains of 30 Questions of Chemistry, divided into two sections : **Section A** Objective Type Questions and **Section B** Numerical Value Questions.
- **Section A** contains 20 Objective questions and all Questions are compulsory (Marking Scheme : Correct + 4, Incorrect – 1).
- **Section B** contains 10 Numerical value questions out of which only 5 questions are to be attempted (Marking Scheme : Correct + 4, Incorrect 0).

Section A *Objective Type Questions*

1. The magnetic moment of two ions M^{x+} and M^{y+} of the element M ($Z = 26$) is found to be 5.916 BM. If $x > y$, then which of the following statements is correct?

(a) M^{y+} is more stable than M^{x+}

(b) M^{y+} is less stable than M^{x+}

(c) Both are equally stable

(d) Can't be predicted

2. In which of the following cases hybridisation of underlined element is changing?

I. $\underline{Al}(OH)_3$ precipitate is dissolved in NaOH.

II. $\underline{B}_2H_6$ is dissolved in THF.

III. $\underline{Si}F_4$ vapour is passed through liquid HF.

IV. Solidification of $\underline{P}Cl_5$ vapour.

Choose the correct option.

(a) I and IV (b) I, II and IV

(c) I, III and IV (d) II, III and IV

3. Consider the following reaction,

(A) (4-nitrobenzyl chloride, CH_2Cl / NO_2) $\xrightarrow[\Delta]{KOH}$ (P)

Which of the following is not correct about the above reaction?

(a) O_2N–C_6H_4–$\overset{-}{C}H$–Cl is the intermediate

(b) 4,4′- dinitro stilbene is final product (*P*)

(c) Elimination is also taking place to get final product

(d) O_2N–C_6H_4–CH(OH)–C_6H_4–NO_2 is formed when the intermediate combines with *A*

4. The heat liberated when 1.89 g of benzoic acid is burnt in a bomb calorimeter at 25°C increases the temperature of 18.94 kg of water by 0.632°C. If the specific heat of water at 25°C is 0.998 cal/g-deg, the value of the heat of combustion of benzoic acid at constant pressure is

(a) 881.1 kcal (b) 771.2 kcal

(c) 981.1 kcal (d) 871.2 kcal

5. Which of the following is correct ?

(a) Specific conductivity of a solution decreases with dilution, whereas molar conductivity increases with dilution.

(b) Specific conductivity of a solution increases with dilution, whereas molar conductivity decreases with dilution.

(c) Both specific conductivity and molar conductivity decreases with dilution.

(d) Both specific conductivity and molar conductivity increases with dilution.

6. If the total vapour pressure of a liquid mixture *A* and *B* is given by the equation $p = 150x_A + 50$, then the ratio of the vapour pressure of pure liquid *A* and *B* is given by

(a) 3 : 2 (b) 4 : 1

(c) 3 : 1 (d) 6 : 2

7. Potential at the equivalence point in the titration of Fe^{2+} with MnO_4^- is

$$Fe^{3+} + e^- \rightleftharpoons Fe^{2+};\ E_1^\circ$$

$$MnO_4^- + 8H^+ + 5e^- \rightleftharpoons Mn^{2+} + 4H_2O;\ E_2^\circ$$

(a) $E = \dfrac{E_1^\circ + 5E_2^\circ}{6} - 0.08\ pH$ (b) $E = \dfrac{5E_1^\circ + E_2^\circ}{6} - 0.08\ pH$

(c) $E = \dfrac{E_1^\circ + E_2^\circ}{6} - 0.08\ pH$ (d) $E = E_1^\circ + E_2^\circ - 0.08\ pH$

8. If a freshly formed precipitate of SnO_2 is peptised by a small amount of NaOH. These colloidal particles may be represented as

(a) $[SnO_2]Na^+ : OH^-$ (b) $[SnO_2]Sn^{4+} : OH^-$

(c) $[SnO_2]SnO_3^{2-} : 2Na^+$ (d) $[SnO_2]SnO^{2-} : Na^+$

9. Arrange the following compounds in decreasing order of rate of electrophilic aromatic chlorination with $Cl_2 / FeCl_3$.

(A) (B)

(C) 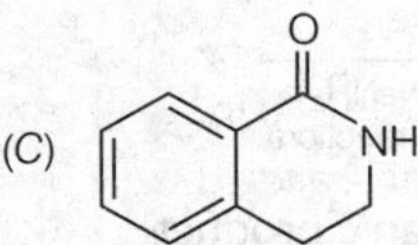 (D)

Choose the correct option.

(a) $A > B > D > C$ (b) $B > A > C > D$

(c) $B > A > D > C$ (d) $B > C > A > D$

10. Arrange the following alcohols in decreasing boiling points.

(A) H_3C ⁀⁀ OH (B) ⊥ OH

(C) (D)

Choose the correct option.

(a) $A > D > C > B$ (b) $B > D > A > C$

(c) $D > B > C > A$ (d) $A > C > D > B$

11. Which of the following statements is correct?

(a) Alkynes are more reactive than alkenes towards their reaction with HCl.

(b) Beryllium carbide on hydrolysis produces methane.

(c) Cyclohexene gives different products with HBr in the presence and absence of benzoyl peroxide.

(d) 2-fluorobutane on reaction with alcoholic KOH gives but-2-ene as a major product.

12. In a nitrosyl complex, the odd electron on nitrogen of the coordinated nitrosyl is transferred to vacant $(n-1)d$ subshell of the central metal. Hence, the spin only magnetic moment of the complex $K[Cr(CN)_4(NH_3)(NO)]$, assuming the metal ion to be in the strong field is

(a) $\sqrt{8}$ BM (b) 0 BM (c) $\sqrt{24}$ BM (d) $\sqrt{15}$ BM

13. Consider the following case of completing 1st order reaction.

$$A \xrightarrow{k_1} C, \quad A \xrightarrow{k_2} D$$

After the starting of the reaction at $t = 0$ with only A (reactant), the $[C]$ is equal to the $[D]$ at all times. The time at which all three concentrations will be equal is given by

I. $t = \dfrac{1}{k_1 + k_2} \ln 3$ II. $t = \dfrac{1}{2k_2} \ln 3$

III. $t = \dfrac{1}{2k_1} \ln 2$ IV. $t = \dfrac{1}{3k_2} \ln 2$

Choose the correct option.

(a) Only I (b) I and II

(c) I, II and III (d) None of these

14. An inorganic salt in its aqueous solution produces a white ppt. with NaOH which dissolves in excess of NaOH. Also its aqueous solution produces a light yellow ppt. with $AgNO_3$ which is sparingly soluble in NH_4OH. The probable salt is

(a) $AlBr_3$ (b) AlI_3 (c) $AlCl_3$ (d) $ZnCl_2$

15. Each NH_3 molecule has six other NH_3 molecules as nearest neighbours in solid state; ΔH of sublimation of NH_3 molecule at the m.p. is 30.8 kJ mol^{-1}, and in the absence of H-bonding estimated ΔH of sublimation is 14.4 kJ mol^{-1}. Hence, strength of H bond in solid NH_3 is

(a) 5.47 kJ mol^{-1} (b) 10.93 kJ mol^{-1}

(c) 16.40 kJ mol^{-1} (d) -16.4 kJ mol^{-1}

16. For the reaction,

OH, CH_2NH_2 $\xrightarrow{HNO_2}$ A (major product);

A is

(a) OH, CH_2OH (b) 

(c) 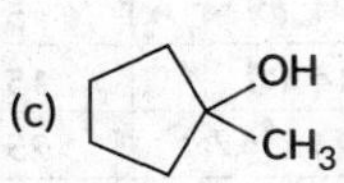 (d) 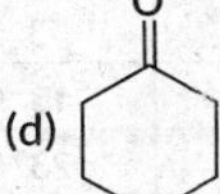

17. Match List-I with List-II.

List-I (Monomer Unit)	**List-II** (Polymer)
A. Caprolactum	1. Natural rubber
B. 2-chloro buta-1,3-diene	2. Buna-N
C. Isoprene	3. Nylon-6
D. Acrylonitrile	4. Neoprene

Choose the correct answer from the options given below.

	A	B	C	D		A	B	C	D
(a)	1	2	3	4	(b)	4	3	2	1
(c)	2	1	4	3	(d)	3	4	1	2

18. Which of the following is correct?

(a) $B < Al < Ga < In < Tl$ (Atomic size)

(b) $Li_2CO_3 < Na_2CO_3 < K_2CO_3 < Rb_2CO_3 < Cs_2CO_3$ (Solubility in water)

(c) $LiOH < NaOH > KOH > RbOH < CsOH$ (Solubility in water)

(d) $BeSO_4 < MgSO_4 < CaSO_4 < SrSO_4 < BaSO_4$ (Solubility in water)

19. End product of the following reaction is,

O= ⟨ring⟩ =O + HBr ⟶

(a) O= ⟨ring⟩ =O, Br (b) HO ⟨ring⟩ OH, Br

(c) Br ⟨ring⟩ OH, HO (d) Br ⟨ring⟩ OH, Br

20. The frequency of light emitted for the transition $n = 4$ to $n = 2$ of He^+ is equal to the transition in H-atom corresponding to which of the following?

(a) $n = 3$ to $n = 1$ (b) $n = 2$ to $n = 1$

(c) $n = 3$ to $n = 2$ (d) $n = 4$ to $n = 3$

Section B *Numerical Value Questions*

21. In the reaction with sodium hydroxide, the number of the given substances oxidised are ....

Be, B, C, Al, Si, P, S, Sn, Pb, NH_4^+, $AlCl_3$, $FeCl_3$, $SnCl_2$

22. Geometrical isomers shown by 1, 2, 3-trichlorocyclohexane are ....

23. 50 mL of 0.1 M NH_4OH is mixed with 50 mL of 0.05 M HCl. The pH of the resultant mixture is .... [$pK_b = 4.74$ NH_4OH].

24. In Duma's method for estimation of nitrogen 0.125 g of an organic compound gave 20 mL of nitrogen collected at 300 K temperature and 725 mm pressure. If the aqueous tension at 300K is 25 mm, the percentage of nitrogen in the compound is ....

25. 24×10^{23} protons are removed from 4 g of a lightest gas known, then the charge left over is 'X' Faraday. The value of X is ....

[Given : Avogadro's number $= 6 \times 10^{23}$ mol^{-1}]

26. The percentage of free volume available in 1 mole of H_2O (g) at 760 mm and 373 K is ....

[Density of H_2O (*l*) at 373 K is 0.958 g/mL].

27. A copolymer of ethene and vinyl chloride contains alternate monomers of each type. The mass percentage of vinyl chloride in this copolymer is ....

28. In the given reaction,

(butan-2-one) $\xrightarrow[\text{(ii) 'b' mole of } NaNH_2]{\text{(i) 'a' mole of } PCl_5}$ X,
(No isomerisation reaction)

where, X is molar mass of organic product.

The value of $\left(\frac{X}{a+b}\right) \div$ Mass of H in the product is ......

[Atomic mass of H = 1 amu]

29. One gram mixture of CH_3OH and CH_3CHO reacts with Benedict's reagent to give a red precipitate. The mass of the red precipitate obtained is 2.86g. The % of CH_3CHO in the mixture is ....

30. A metal complex having composition $Cr(NH_3)_4Cl_2Br$ has been isolated in two forms (A) and (B).

The form (A) reacts with $AgNO_3$ to give a white precipitate, which is readily soluble in dilute aqueous ammonia, whereas (B) gives a pale yellow precipitate soluble in concentrated ammonia. Magnetic moment of complexes A or B is .... (In Bohr Magneton).

Answers

1 *(b)*	2 *(c)*	3 *(d)*	4 *(b)*	5 *(a)*	6 *(b)*	7 *(a)*	8 *(c)*	9 *(b)*	10 *(d)*
11 *(b)*	12 *(a)*	13 *(b)*	14 *(a)*	15 *(a)*	16 *(d)*	17 *(d)*	18 *(b)*	19 *(b)*	20 *(b)*
21 *(9)*	22 *(3)*	23 *(9.26)*	24 *(16.75)*	25 *(4)*	26 *(99.94)*	27 *(69.06)*	28 *(3)*	29 *(88)*	30 *(3.87)*

See detailed solutions on page no. 287

Knockout 03

JEE MAIN

Chemistry

Instructions

- This question paper contains of 30 Questions of Chemistry, divided into two sections : **Section A** Objective Type Questions and **Section B** Numerical Value Questions.
- **Section A** contains 20 Objective questions and all Questions are compulsory (Marking Scheme : Correct + 4, Incorrect – 1).
- **Section B** contains 10 Numerical value questions out of which only 5 questions are to be attempted (Marking Scheme : Correct + 4, Incorrect 0).

Section A *Objective Type Questions*

1. List-I contains reactions and List-II contains major products.

P. 1,3-dichloro-5-nitrobenzene (NO_2, Cl, Cl) $\xrightarrow[\text{(II) } CH_3Cl]{\text{(I) NaOH, 150°C}}$ (i) Cl, OCH_3, O_2N substituted benzene

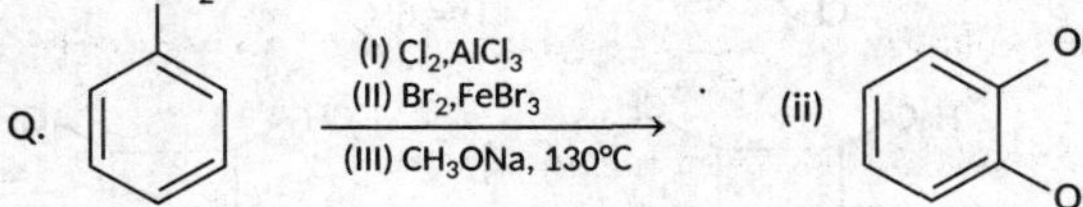

Q. Nitrobenzene (NO_2) $\xrightarrow{\text{(I) } Cl_2, AlCl_3;\ \text{(II) } Br_2, FeBr_3;\ \text{(III) } CH_3ONa, 130°C}$ (ii) benzene-1,3-diol (OH, OH)

R. Phenol (OH) $\xrightarrow{\text{(I) NaOH, } CH_3Cl;\ \text{(II) } H_2SO_4 + HNO_3;\ \text{(III) } Cl_2, AlCl_3}$ (iii) OCH_3, Cl, O_2N substituted benzene

S. 2-hydroxybenzaldehyde (OH, CHO) $\xrightarrow[\text{(II) } H^+, H_2O]{\text{(I) NaOH, } H_2O_2}$ (iv) O_2N, Cl, OCH_3 substituted benzene

Choose the correct option.

(a) P $\rightarrow$ (i); Q $\rightarrow$ (ii); R $\rightarrow$ (iii); S $\rightarrow$ (iv)
(b) P $\rightarrow$ (iii); Q $\rightarrow$ (ii); R $\rightarrow$ (i); S $\rightarrow$ (iv)
(c) P $\rightarrow$ (iv); Q $\rightarrow$ (i); R $\rightarrow$ (i); S $\rightarrow$ (ii)
(d) P $\rightarrow$ (i); Q $\rightarrow$ (ii); R $\rightarrow$ (ii); S $\rightarrow$ (iii)

2. Which of the following group of metals do not involve self reduction method during its extraction?

Fe, Cu, Sn, Pb, Al and Mg

(a) Fe, Sn, Al and Mg (b) Fe, Sn, Pb, Al and Mg
(c) Cu, Sn, Pb, Al and Mg (d) Fe, Pb, Cu and Mg

3. 7 moles of a tetra-atomic non-linear gas A at 10 atm and T K are mixed with 6 moles of another gas B at $\frac{T}{3}$ K and 5 atm in a closed vessel without energy transfer with surrounding. If final temperature of mixture was $\frac{5T}{6}$ K then, gas B is

(a) monoatomic (b) diatomic
(c) triatomic (d) tetra-atomic

4. Consider the following reactions,

(i) 1,3-butadiene + $BrCCl_3$ + Peroxide $\rightarrow A$

(ii) $RCH = CH_2 + CCl_4 \xrightarrow{\text{Peroxide}} B + C$

Identify A to C.

(a) $A \Rightarrow$ H, Br–CH(–)–CH=CH–CH$_2$–CCl_3, $B \Rightarrow R—CH_2—CHCl—CCl_3$, $C \Rightarrow R—CH(CH_2CCl_3)—CH_2—CH_2—R$

(b) $A \Rightarrow$ Br–CH$_2$–CH=CH–CH$_2$–CCl_3, $B \Rightarrow R—CHCl—CH_2—CCl_3$, $C \Rightarrow R—CH(CH_2CCl_3)—CH_2—CH(Cl)—R$

(c) $A \Rightarrow$ H, Br–CH(–)–CH=CH–CH$_2$–CCl_3, $B \Rightarrow R—CH(Cl)—CH_2—CCl_3$, $C \Rightarrow R—CH(CH_2CCl_3)—CH_2—CH_2—R$

(d) $A \Rightarrow$ Br–CH$_2$–CH=CH–CH$_2$–CCl_3, $B \Rightarrow R—CH_2—CH(Cl)—CCl_3$, $C \Rightarrow R—CH(CH_2CCl_3)—CH_2—CH(Cl)—R$

5. A 0.05 molal solution of a monobasic acid HA is 20% ionised in water. The boiling point of the resultant solution is (where, K_b for water = 0.56 K molal^{-1})

(a) 100 °C (b) 100.034 °C (c) 101 °C (d) 99.9 °C

6. What will be the correct trend of acid strength of the following aquated ions?

$[Al(H_2O)_6]^{3+}$, $[Fe(H_2O)_6]^{3+}$, $[Fe(H_2O)_6]^{2+}$, $[Hg(H_2O)]^{2+}$

(a) $[Fe(H_2O)_6]^{2+} \approx [Fe(H_2O)_6]^{3+} < [Al(H_2O)_6]^{3+} \approx [Hg(H_2O)]^{2+}$

(b) $[Fe(H_2O)_6]^{2+} \approx [Fe(H_2O)_6]^{3+} < [Al(H_2O)_6]^{3+} < [Hg(H_2O)]^{2+}$

(c) $[Fe(H_2O)_6]^{2+} < [Fe(H_2O)_6]^{3+} < [Al(H_2O)_6]^{3+} \approx [Hg(H_2O)]^{2+}$

(d) $[Fe(H_2O)_6]^{2+} < [Fe(H_2O)_6]^{3+} < [Al(H_2O)_6]^{3+} < [Hg(H_2O)]^{2+}$

7. Which of the following have *X*—O—*X* linkage? (where, *X* is the central atom of the species)

I. Pyrosilicate II. $Cr_2O_7^{2-}$

III. $S_2O_3^{2-}$ IV. Hyponitrous acid

Choose the correct option.

(a) II and III (b) I and II

(c) I, II and IV (d) All have X—O—X linkage

8. *x* g of non-electrolyte compound of molecular mass 200, when dissolved in 1 L of 0.05 M NaCl solution, the osmotic pressure of the resulting solution is found to be 4.92 atm at 27°C. Consider the complete dissociation of NaCl and ideal behaviour of solution, the value of *x* would be

(a) 10 g (b) 20.0 g

(c) 40.0 g (d) 80.0 g

9. Some oxide of *p*-block elements show colour, while some do not, among the following which pair of oxides are coloured?

(a) NO_2 and N_2O_3 (b) NO_2 and N_2O_5

(c) N_2O_4 and NO_2 (d) NO and N_2O

10. Sodium is heated in excess of air to form '*X*'. *X* absorbs CO_2 to form Na_2CO_3 and *Y*. *X* and *Y* are

(a) Na_2O_2 and O_3 (b) Na_2O_2 and O_2

(c) NaO_2 and O_2 (d) Na_2O and O_2

11. Which of the following will produce a stable non-planar carbocation?

(a) Addition of antimony pentafluoride to cycloheptatrienyl fluoride

(b) Addition of bromonium ion to propene

(c) Addition of acid to propene

(d) Addition of argentium ion to triphenylmethyl chloride

12. Consider the following compounds.

I. Cyclohexa-2,4-dien-1-one

II. Propan-2-one

III. Pentan-2,4-dione

The correct decreasing order of percentage of enolic component in the given compounds is

(a) I < II < III (b) II > III > I

(c) I > III > II (d) III > I > II

13. Reduction of 2-butyne with Na/NH_3 and Lindlar's catalyst yield product *X* and *Y* respectively. The relation between *X* and *Y* is

(a) *X* and *Y* are optical isomers.

(b) *X* and *Y* are same compound.

(c) *X* and *Y* are geometrical isomers.

(d) *X* and *Y* are positional isomers.

14. Match List-I with List-II.

	List-I (Chemical reaction)		List-II (Reagent used)
A.	$CH_3COOC_2H_5 \longrightarrow C_2H_5OH$	1.	CH_3MgBr / H_3O^+ (1.equivalent)
B.	$CH_3COOCH_3 \longrightarrow CH_3CHO$	2.	H_2SO_4 / H_2O
C.	$CH_3C{\equiv}N \longrightarrow CH_3CHO$	3.	DIBAL-H / H_2O
D.	$CH_3C{\equiv}N \longrightarrow CH_3COCH_3$	4.	$SnCl_2$, HCl / H_2O

Choose the most appropriate option given below.

	A	B	C	D
(a)	2	4	3	1
(b)	4	2	3	1
(c)	2	3	4	1
(d)	3	2	1	4

15. The major product '*X*' formed in the following reaction is

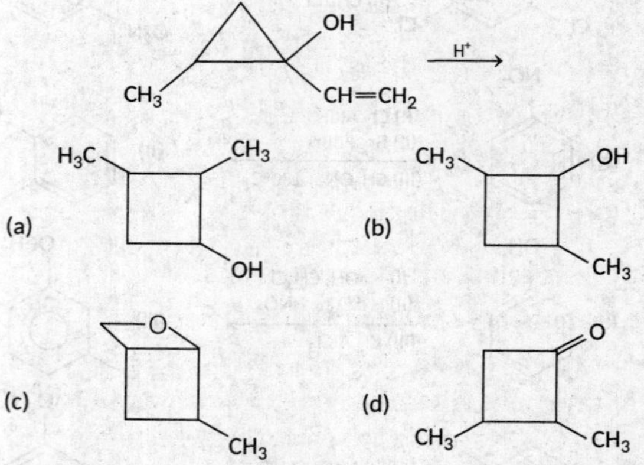

16. Choose the incorrectly matched polymer with their respective structure and name.

(a) $\left[CH_2C(Cl){=}CH{-}CH{-}CH_2 \right]_n \rightarrow$ Neoprene

(b) $\left[NH(CH_2)_6NH{-}\overset{O}{\overset{\|}{C}}{-}(CH_2)_4{-}\overset{O}{\overset{\|}{C}} \right]_n \rightarrow$ Nylon-6,6

(c) $\left[O-CH_2-CH_2-\overset{O}{\overset{\|}{C}}-C_6H_4-\overset{O}{\overset{\|}{C}}-O \right]_n \rightarrow$ Terylene

(d) $\left[CH_2-\underset{\underset{\underset{O}{\|}}{COCH_3}}{\overset{CH_3}{\overset{|}{C}}} \right]_n \rightarrow$ PMMA

17. Which of the following is correct regarding the major product (B) of the reaction?

1-amino-1-methylcyclohexane $\xrightarrow[\text{Excess}]{CH_3I} A \xrightarrow[\text{Heat}]{AgOH} B$ (Product)

(a) 1-methylcyclohexyl–$N(CH_3)_2$ which shows optical isomerism

(b) 1-methylcyclohexyl–$N(CH_3)_2OH$ which shows optical isomerism

(c) methylenecyclohexane which does not show geometrical isomerism

(d) methylenecyclohexane which shows geometrical isomerism

18. Among the following, the correct structural pairs are

NF_3, NO_3^-, BF_3, H_3O^+, HN_3

(a) [NF_3, NO_3^-] and [BF_3, H_3O^+]

(b) [NF_3, HN_3] and [NO_3^-, BF_3]

(c) [NF_3, H_3O^+] and [NO_3^-, BF_3]

(d) [NF_3, H_3O^+] and [HN_3, BF_3]

19. Given below are two statements.

Statement I On mixing equal volumes of 1 M HCl and 2 M CH_3COONa, an acidic buffer solution is formed.

Statement II Resultant mixture contains CH_3COOH and CH_3COONa which are parts of acidic buffer.

In the light of the above statements, choose the most appropriate answer from the options given below.

(a) Both Statement I and Statement II are correct.

(b) Both Statement I and Statement II are incorrect.

(c) Statement I is correct but Statement II is incorrect.

(d) Statement I is incorrect but Statement II is correct.

20. Which of the following can possibly be used as analgesic without causing addiction and modification?

(a) Morphine
(b) N-acetyl-*para*-aminophenol
(c) Diazepam
(d) Tetrahydrocatenol

Section B *Numerical Value Questions*

21. *n*-butane is produced by the mono bromination of ethane in Wurtz reaction. The volume of ethane (in L) at NTP to produce 55 g in butane, if the bromination takes place with 90% yield and the Wurtz reaction with 85% yield is ....

22. 3 g of activated charcoal was added to 50 mL of 0.06 M acetic acid solution in a flask. After an hour, 10 mL of residual CH_3COOH requires 14 mL of 0.03 M NaOH. If Freundlich adsorption isotherm is followed, i.e. $\frac{x}{m} = kC^{1/2}$ then, the value of k is $a \times 10^{-3}$. The value of a is ...... [x is the amount of adsorbate in grams adsorbed per gram of adsorbent and C is the equilibrium concentration in millimoles.]

23. Ferric hydroxide obtained during qualitative analysis of Fe^{3+} is insoluble in NaOH but when dissolved in HCl produces (B) which is when dissolved in potassium ferrocyanide produces a blue ppt. When a large excess of reagent is added, it converts into Prussian blue colour. The coordination number of Fe in complex obtained is ....

24. The cyanate content of a pesticide was determined by dissolving a 4.112 g sample in water and treating with semicarbazide hydrochloride.

$$H_2NCONHNH + CNO^- \longrightarrow H_2NCONHNHCONH_2(s)$$

The solid formed in this reaction, when filtered and dried, weighed 0.209 g.

Then percentage of KCNO in the pesticide is ....

[K = 39, O = 16, N = 14, C = 12, H = 1]

25. A sample of sugar D-ribose ($C_5H_{10}O_5$) weighing 0.727 g was placed in a calorimeter and then ignited in the presence of excess of oxygen the temperature is raised by 0.91 K.

In a separate experiment in the same calorimeter, the combustion of 0.825 g of benzoic acid, for which the internal energy of combustion is – 3251 kJ/mol, gave a temperature rise 1.94 K. The enthalpy of formation of D-ribose will be ...... $\times 10^6$ J.

[Given : $\Delta H_f^\circ CO_2 = -394$ kJ/mol, $H_2O(l) = -286$ kJ/mol]

26. The total number of chemical species among the given molecules that have $d\pi$ - $p\pi$ bonds in their structure are ....

[NO_3^-, SO_3, XeO_3, H_3PO_4, ClO_4^-, CO_3^{2-}, SO_4^{2-}, $(CN)_2$, $XeOF_2$]

27. A mixture of H_2 and I_2 in molar proportion of 2 : 3 was heated at 440°C till the reaction reach equilibrium state.

$$H_2 + I_2 \rightleftharpoons 2HI$$

The percentage of I_2 converted into HI will be ......

(K_c for the reaction is 0.02).

28. At 25°C, the inversion of sucrose proceeds with a constant half-life of 500 min at pH = 5 and 50 min at pH = 4. If the rate law for inversion of sucrose is given by $\frac{-d}{dt}[\text{sucrose}] = k\,[\text{sucrose}]^a[H^+]^b$. The value of (*b*) is ....

29. O_2 undergoes photochemical dissociation to normal oxygen atom where 1 oxygen atom is 1.969 eV more energetic than normal.

The dissociation of O_2 into 2 normal oxygen atoms is known to require 498 kJ/mol O_2.

The maximum wavelength effective (in nm) for the chemical dissociation of O_2 is ....

30. In the acid-base titration [H_3PO_4 (0.1 M) + NaOH (0.1 M)] emf of the solution is measured by coupling this electrode with suitable reference electrodes. When alkali is added, pH of the solution is in accordance with the equation,

$$E_{\text{Cell}} = E^\circ_{\text{Cell}} \times 0.059\ \text{pH}$$

For H_3PO_4, $K_1 = 10^{-3}$, $K_2 = 10^{-8}$, $K_3 = 10^{-13}$

The cell emf (in volt) at the 2nd end point of titration if E°_{cell} at this stage is 1.3805 V will be ....

Answers

1 (c)	2 (a)	3 (b)	4 (b)	5 (b)	6 (c)	7 (b)	8 (b)	9 (a)	10 (b)
11 (d)	12 (c)	13 (c)	14 (c)	15 (d)	16 (c)	17 (c)	18 (c)	19 (a)	20 (b)
21 (55.53)	22 (12.42)	23 (6)	24 (3.49)	25 (−1.27)	26 (6)	27 (5.40)	28 (1)	29 (174.17)	30 (2)

See detailed solutions on page no. 290

Knockout 04

JEE MAIN

Chemistry

Instructions

- This question paper contains of 30 Questions of Chemistry, divided into two sections : **Section A** Objective Type Questions and **Section B** Numerical Value Questions.
- **Section A** contains 20 Objective questions and all Questions are compulsory (Marking Scheme : Correct + 4, Incorrect – 1).
- **Section B** contains 10 Numerical value questions out of which only 5 questions are to be attempted (Marking Scheme : Correct + 4, Incorrect 0).

Section A *Objective Type Questions*

1. For the reaction: $2NO(g) + Cl_2(g) \rightleftharpoons 2NOCl(g)$, NO and Cl_2 are initially taken in mole ratio 2 : 1. The total pressure at equilibrium is found to be 1 atm. If mole of NOCl is one-fourth of that of Cl_2 at equilibrium, K_p for the reaction is

(a) $\frac{13}{36}$ (b) $\frac{13}{256}$

(c) $\frac{13}{512}$ (d) $\frac{13}{128}$

2. Suppose that in any Bohr atom or ion, orbits are only in even numbers like 2, 4, 6 .... . The maximum wavelength of radiation emitted in the visible region of hydrogen spectrum should be

(a) $\frac{4}{R}$ (b) $\frac{R}{4}$ (c) $\frac{36}{5R}$ (d) $\frac{16}{3R}$

3. Given below are two statements.

Statement I Concentrated HCl when kept in open air sometimes produces a cloud of white fumes.

Statement II Strong affinity of HCl gas for moisture in air result in forming of droplets of liquid solution which appear like cloudy smoke.

In the light of the above statements, choose the most appropriate answer from the options given below.

(a) Both Statement I and Statement II are correct.
(b) Both Statement I and Statement II are incorrect.
(c) Statement I is correct but Statement II is incorrect.
(d) Statement I is incorrect but Statement II is correct.

4. The number of moles of $Cr_2O_7^{2-}$ needed to oxidise 0.136 equivalent of $N_2H_5^+$ through the reaction is

$$N_2H_5^+ + Cr_2O_7^{2-} \longrightarrow N_2 + Cr^{3+} + H_2O$$

(a) 0.0226 (b) 0.087
(c) 0.136 (d) 0.488

5. Which of the following circled hydrogen is most acidic?

(a) 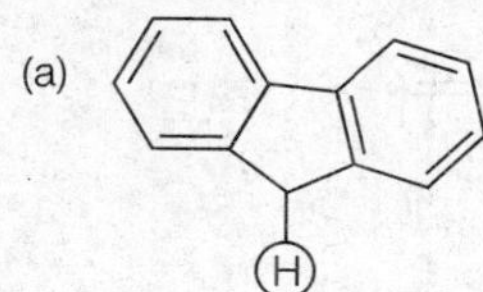

(b) 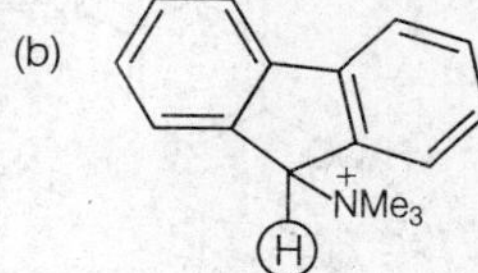

(c) 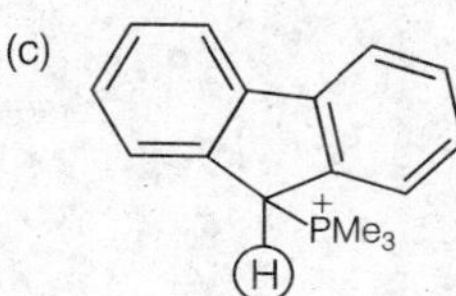

(d) 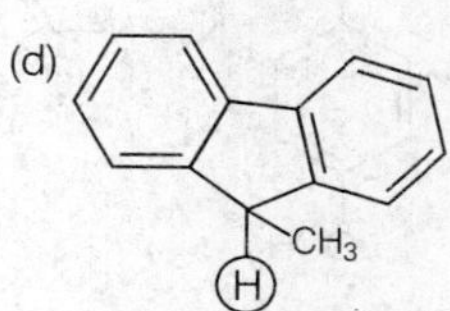

6. Choose the correct statement from the following.

(a) *p*-nitrophenol is more volatile than *o*-nitrophenol due to hydrogen bond.
(b) High boiling point of water is due to low hydrogen bonding present.
(c) Contrary to other hydrogen halides, hydrogen fluoride is present in gaseous state.
(d) Among hydrogen halides, HF has highest boiling point.

7. Which of the following is stronger acid than methanol?

(a) $CH_3—C \equiv CH$ (b) $(H_3C)_2CH—OH$

(c) $(H_3C)_3C—OH$ (d) $H_3C—\overset{+}{O}(H)—H$

8. Consider the following molecule

Find the correct order of reactivity of carbonyl groups with $LiAlH_4$

(a) $A > B > C > D$ (b) $B > C > D > A$
(c) $D > C > B > A$ (d) $B > D > C > A$

9. For the reaction,

Product of the reaction is

(a)

(b)

(c)

(d)

10. Match the following columns.

	Column I (Metal ion)		Column II (Group of Qualitative analysis)
A.	Mn^{2+}	1.	Group-III
B.	Sr^{2+}	2.	Group-II A
C.	Cu^{2+}	3.	Group-IV
D.	As^{3+}	4.	Group-II B

Codes

	A	B	C	D		A	B	C	D
(a)	1	2	3	4	(b)	1	3	2	4
(c)	3	1	2	4	(d)	2	1	3	4

11. Which of the following amino acid consists of two $—NH_2$ groups in it?

(a) Isoleucine (b) Aspartic acid
(c) Glutamic acid (d) Lysine

12. Which of the following statements regarding melamine is incorrect?

(a) It is aromatic.
(b) It contains 6 pairs of non-bonding electrons.
(c) Its molecular formula is $C_3H_8N_6$.
(d) It is a heterocyclic compound.

13. Given below are two statements, one is labelled as Assertion (A) and the other is labelled as Reason (R).

Assertion (A) Photochemical smog causes cracking of rubber.

Reason (R) Presence of ozone, nitric oxide, acrolein, formaldehyde and peroxyacetyl nitrate in photochemical smog makes it oxidising.

In the light of the above statements, choose the correct answer from the options given below.

(a) Both (A) and (R) are true but (R) is not the correct explanation of (A).
(b) Both (A) and (R) are true and (R) is the correct explanation of (A).
(c) (A) is false but (R) is true.
(d) (A) is true but (R) is false.

14. Which of the following compounds will undergo Friedel-Craft alkylation with fastest rate?

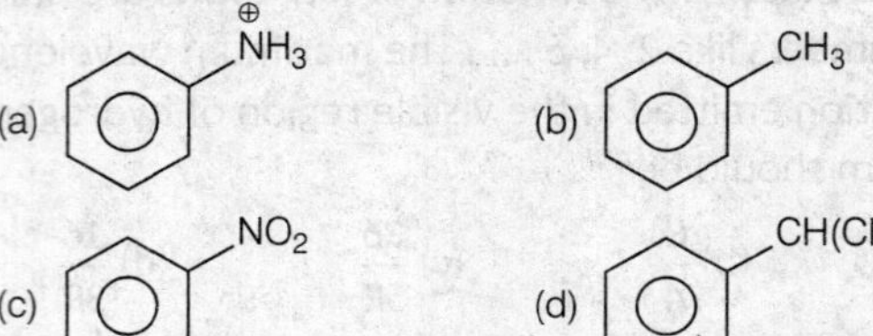

15. Consider two liquids (A) and (B) having vapour pressures p_A° and p_B° in their pure forms respectively.

The plot of $\frac{1}{x_A}$ vs $\frac{1}{y_A}$ (where x_A and y_A are the mole fractions of liquid (A) in liquid and vapour phase respectively is linear with slope and y-intercept respectively.

(a) $\frac{p_A^\circ}{p_B^\circ}, \frac{p_A^\circ - p_B^\circ}{p_B^\circ}$ (b) $\frac{p_A^\circ}{p_B^\circ}, \frac{p_B^\circ - p_A^\circ}{p_B^\circ}$

(c) $\frac{p_B^\circ}{p_A^\circ}, \frac{p_A^\circ - p_B^\circ}{p_B^\circ}$ (d) $\frac{p_B^\circ}{p_A^\circ}, \frac{p_B^\circ - p_A^\circ}{p_B^\circ}$

16. Which of the following is not obtained as a product during complete hydrolysis of XeF_4?

(a) XeO_3 (b) Xe
(c) HF (d) XeO_2F_2

17. Amphoteric oxides of Mn and Cr are

(a) MnO, CrO (b) Mn_2O_3, Cr_2O_3
(c) MnO_2, Cr_2O_3 (d) Mn_2O_7, CrO_3

18. The complex having the highest magnetic moment is

(a) $[Zn(H_2O)]^{2+}$ (b) $[Cr(H_2O)_6]^{2+}$
(c) $[Mn(H_2O)_6]^{2+}$ (d) $[Cu(H_2O)_6]^{2+}$

19. Consider the following reactions,

$$(CH_3)_3C—Cl \xrightarrow{LiAlH_4} (X)$$

$$CH_3CH{=}CHCH_2—Cl \xrightarrow{Ph_3SnH} (Y)$$

(X) and (Y) respectively are

(a) $(CH_3)_3CH$, $CH_3(CH_2)_2CH_3$
(b) $CH_2 = C(CH_3)_2$, $CH_3CH{=}CHCH_3$
(c) $CH_2 = C(CH_3)_2$, $CH_3CH_2CH_2CH_2Cl$
(d) $(CH_3)_3CH$, $CH_3CH_2CH_2CH_2Cl$

20. $C_6H_5—CH_2—O—C_6H_4—OH \xrightarrow{\text{Excess of HI}} (X) + (Y)$, which are

(a) $C_6H_5—CH_2OH$ + $I—C_6H_4—OH$
(b) $C_6H_5—CH_2I$ + $HO—C_6H_4—OH$
(c) $C_6H_5—CH_2I$ + $I—C_6H_4—OH$
(d) $C_6H_5—CH_2I$ + $HO—C_6H_4—I$

Section B Numerical Value Questions

21. The total number of compounds having at least one bridging oxo-group among the following molecules is ....

$H_4P_2O_5$, P_4O_6, N_2O_3, $H_2S_2O_3$, $H_5P_3O_{10}$

22. The number of stereoisomeric products formed in the following reaction is ....

H—C(Ph)(CHO)—D (Optical pure) + H—C(Ph)(CH₃)—MgBr $\xrightarrow[\text{(ii) } H_2O]{\text{(i) Ether}}$

23. Find out the percentage efficiency of the following cyclic process for 1 mole mono-atomic gas is ....

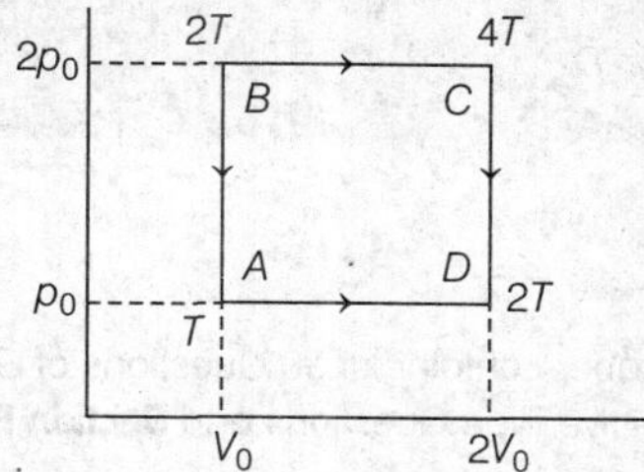

24. The spin only magnetic moment value (in Bohr magneton units) of hexacarbonylchromium is ....

25. In phosgene gas reaction at 400°C, the initial pressure are p_{CO} = 342 mm and p_{Cl_2} = 352 mm and the total pressure at equilibrium is 440 mm.

$$CO + Cl_2 \rightleftharpoons COCl_2.$$

K_p (in atm) for dissociation of phosgene at 400°C.

26. For the reaction $X(g) \rightarrow Y(g) + \frac{1}{2}Z(g)$, the pressure increases from 150 mm Hg to 170 mm Hg in 10 min. The rate of disappearance of X in mm per min is ....

27. Electrolysis of hot aqueous solution of NaCl gives $NaClO_4$. Then the number of Faraday required to deposit 500 g of $NaClO_4$ is .... (Molar mass of Na = 23 g mol^{-1}, Cl = 35.5 g mol^{-1}, O = 16 g mol^{-1})

28. The number of salt complexes which are isostructural among the given salts is ....

$FeSO_4 \cdot 7H_2O$, $MnSO_4 \cdot 4H_2O$, $ZnSO_4 \cdot 7H_2O$, $CuSO_4 \cdot 5H_2O$, $NiSO_4 \cdot 6H_2O$

29. If x is the number of exchanges possible for $3d^4$ electronic configuration, then the value of $\frac{x}{4}$ is .....

30. Consider the reaction, $XY(g) \rightleftharpoons X(g) + Y(g)$

If at a given temperature $\frac{1}{3}$rd of XY(g) is dissociated, then the ratio of equilibrium constant (K_p) and total pressure (p) at equilibrium is $x \times 10^{-2}$, then the value of x is .... .

Answers

1 *(b)*	2 *(d)*	3 *(a)*	4 *(a)*	5 *(c)*	6 *(d)*	7 *(d)*	8 *(b)*	9 *(c)*	10 *(b)*
11 *(d)*	12 *(c)*	13 *(a)*	14 *(b)*	15 *(b)*	16 *(d)*	17 *(c)*	18 *(c)*	19 *(b)*	20 *(b)*
21 *(4)*	22 *(2)*	23 *(15.38)*	24 *(0)*	25 *(0.04)*	26 *(4)*	27 *(32.65)*	28 *(2)*	29 *(1.50)*	30 *(12.50)*

See detailed solutions on page no. 293

Knockout 05

JEE MAIN

Chemistry

Instructions

- This question paper contains of 30 Questions of Chemistry, divided into two sections : **Section A** Objective Type Questions and **Section B** Numerical Value Questions.
- **Section A** contains 20 Objective questions and all Questions are compulsory (Marking Scheme : Correct + 4, Incorrect – 1).
- **Section B** contains 10 Numerical value questions out of which only 5 questions are to be attempted (Marking Scheme : Correct + 4, Incorrect 0).

Section A *Objective Type Questions*

1. A solution of a metal ion when treated with KI gives a red precipitate, which dissolves in excess of KI to give a colourless solution. The solution of the metal ion on treatment with a cobalt (II) thiocyanate produces a deep blue crystalline precipitate. The metal ion is

(a) Pb^{2+} (b) Hg^{2+}

(c) Cu^{2+} (d) Zn^{2+}

2. Ionisation energy of Al $(IE_1 + IE_2 + IE_3) = 5137$ kJ mol^{-1}

Hydration enthalpy of $Al^{3+} = -4665$ kJ mol^{-1}

Hydration enthalpy of $Cl^- = -381$ kJ mol^{-1}

From the above data regarding $AlCl_3$, select the correct statement from the following.

(a) $AlCl_3$ would remain covalent in aqueous solution

(b) Only at infinite dilution, $AlCl_3$ undergoes ionisation

(c) In aqueous solution, $AlCl_3$ becomes ionic

(d) None of the above

3. 7 moles of a tetra-atomic non-linear gas, *A* at 10 atm and *T*K is mixed with 6 moles of another gas, *B* at 5 atm and $\frac{T}{3}$K in a closed rigid vessel without energy transfer with the surrounding. If final temperature of the mixture becomes $\frac{5T}{6}$ K, then the gas *B* is ....

(Assuming all moles of energy are active)

(a) monoatomic

(b) diatomic

(c) triatomic

(d) tetra-atomic

4. Find the standard potential obtained from the cell reaction,

$$In^{2+} + Cu^{2+} \longrightarrow In^{3+} + Cu^{+}$$

Given,

$$E^\circ_{Cu^{2+}/Cu^+} = x_1 V; E^\circ_{In^{3+}/In^+} = x_2 V; E^\circ_{In^{2+}/In^+} = x_3 V$$

(a) $(x_1 + x_3 - x_2)V$ (b) $\frac{1}{3}(x_1 + x_3 - 2x_2)V$

(c) $(x_1 + x_3 - 2x_2)V$ (d) $(x_1 + 2x_2 + x_3)V$

5. There is a very little difference in acid strength in the series of phosphorus oxoacids *viz.*, H_3PO_4, H_3PO_3 and H_3PO_2 because

(a) phosphorus in three acids exist in different oxidation states.

(b) number of unprotonated oxygen atoms responsible for increase in acidity due to inductive effect remains nearly the same.

(c) phosphorus is not a highly electronegative element.

(d) phosphorus oxides are less basic.

6. The compressibility factor for a real gas at high pressure is

(a) $1 + RT/pb$ (b) 1

(c) $1 + pb/RT$ (d) $1 - pb/RT$

7. When potassium chromate is added to copper sulphate solution, there is a formation of copper (II) chromate as well as copper (II) dichromate. Formation of copper (II) dichromate is due to

(a) basic nature of $CuSO_4$ solution

(b) acidic nature of $CuSO_4$ solution

(c) oxidising nature of $K_2Cr_2O_7$ solution

(d) reducing nature of K_2CrO_4 solution

8. For the following compounds, the incorrect statement(s) with respect to nucleophilic substitution reaction is (are)

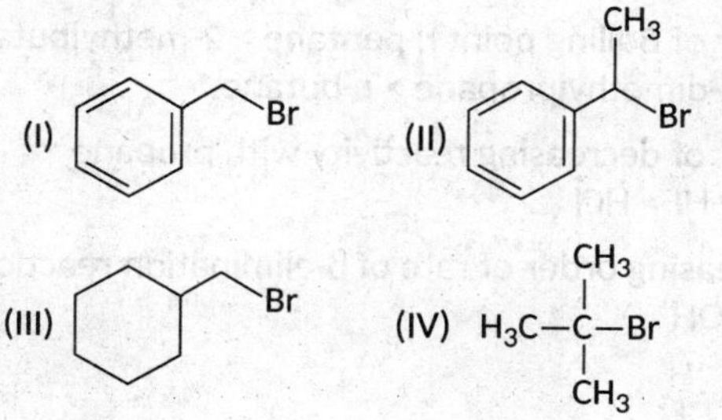

(I) (II) (III) (IV)

Choose the correct option.

(a) The compound III undergoes inversion of configuration
(b) The order of reactivity for I, II and IV is : II > I > IV
(c) I and III follow S_N2 mechanism
(d) I and IV follow S_N1 mechanism

9. Consider the following sequence of reactions,

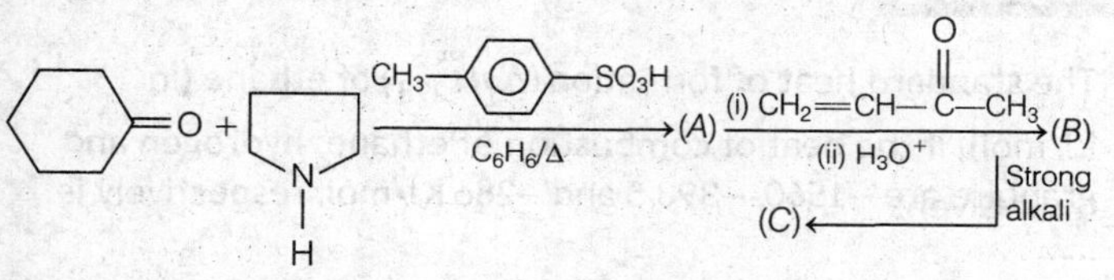

$$\text{Cyclohexanone} + \text{Pyrrolidine} \xrightarrow[C_6H_6/\Delta]{CH_3-C_6H_4-SO_3H} (A) \xrightarrow[\text{(ii) } H_3O^+]{\text{(i) } CH_2=CH-CO-CH_3} (B) \xrightarrow{\text{Strong alkali}} (C)$$

The product, (C) is

(a) 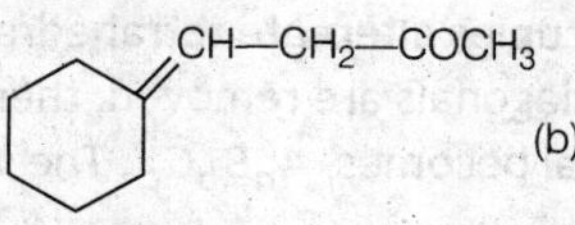 (b) 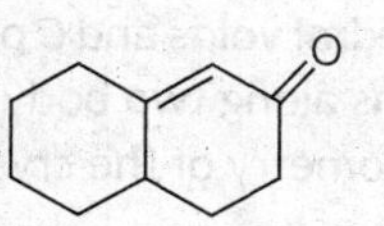 (c) 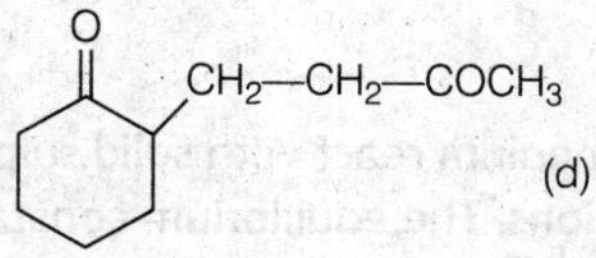 (d)

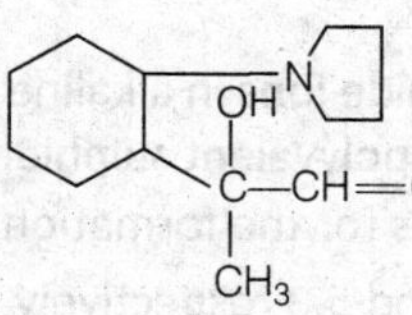

10. The major product in the reaction,

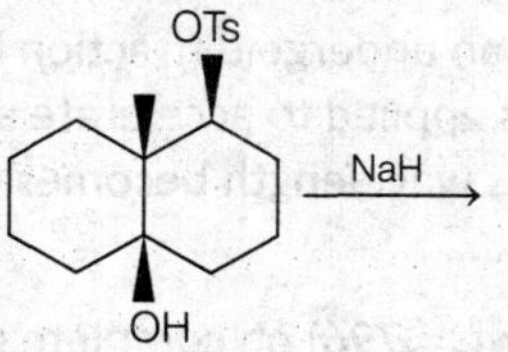

$$\xrightarrow{NaH}$$

is

(a) 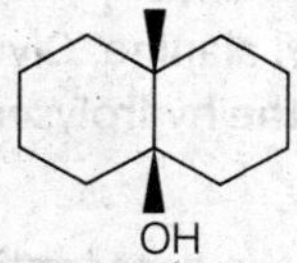 (b) 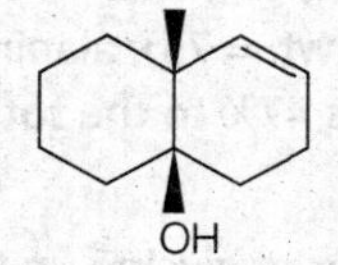 (c) 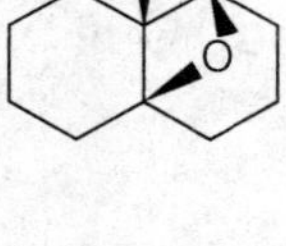 (d)

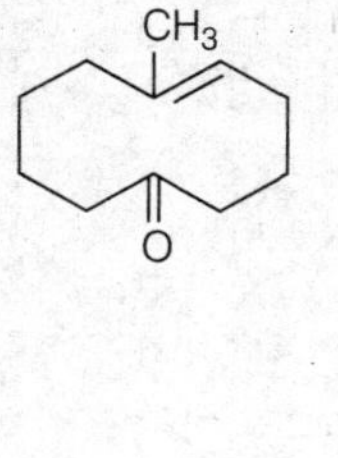

11. *A*, *B* and *C* are hydroxy compounds of the three elements *P*, *Q* and *R* respectively. *P*, *Q* and *R* belong to the same period of the periodic table.

A gives an aqueous solution of pH < 7. *B* shows reactions with both strong acids and strong bases. Aqueous solution of *C* is strongly alkaline.

Select the correct statements from the following:

I. *P*, *Q* and *R* are metals.
II. Atomic radius of *P*, *Q* and *R* decreases in the order *P* > *Q* > *R*.
III. Their order of electronegativity is, *R* < *Q* < *P*.
IV. *P*, *Q* and *R* could be P, Al and Na respectively.

Choose the correct option.

(a) I, II and IV
(b) I, III and IV
(c) III and IV
(d) All of the above

12. Standard entropy of X_2, Y_2 and XY_3 are 60, 40 and 50 J K^{-1} mol^{-1} respectively. For the reaction,

$$\frac{1}{2}X_2 + \frac{3}{2}Y_2 \longrightarrow XY_3 \quad \Delta H = -30 \text{ kJ}$$ to be at equilibrium,

the temperature will be

(a) 1250 K (b) 500 K
(c) 1000 K (d) 750 K

13. Which of the following antibiotics is bactericidal in nature?

(a) Erythromycin
(b) Tetracycline
(c) Aminoglycosides
(d) Chloramphenicol

14. The percentage of vacant space in one layer of square packing of spheres touching each other having 4 spheres is

(a) $\frac{3}{8}\pi \times 100$ (b) $100 - \frac{\pi}{6}$
(c) $\frac{3}{8}\pi$ (d) $100 - \frac{\pi}{6} \times 100$

15. In a nitrosyl complex, the odd electron on nitrogen of the coordinated nitrosyl is transferred to vacant $(n-1)d$ subshell of the central metal.

Hence, the spin only magnetic moment of the complex, $K[Cr(CN)_4(NH_3)(NO)]$ (a strong field heteroleptic complex) is

(a) $\sqrt{8}$ BM (b) Zero
(c) 4.89 BM (d) 3.87 BM

16. Consider the following reactions,

$$(CH_3)_3C—Cl \xrightarrow{LiAlH_4} X$$

$$CH_3—CH{=}CH—CH_2—Cl \xrightarrow{Ph_3SnH} Y$$

(X) and (Y) respectively are

(a) $(CH_3)_3CH, CH_3(CH_2)_2CH_3$

(b) $CH_2 = C(CH_3)_2, CH_3CH = CHCH_3$

(c) $CH_2 = C(CH_3)_2, CH_3(CH_2)_2CH_2Cl$

(d) $(CH_3)_3CH, CH_3(CH_2)_3Cl$

17. Given below are two statements, one is labelled as Assertion (A) and the other is labelled as Reason (R).

Assertion (A) Sucrose is a disaccharide and a non-reducing sugar.

Reason (R) Sucrose involves glycosidic linkage between C_1 of β-glucose and C_2 of α-fructose.

In the light of the above statements, choose the correct answer from the options given below.

(a) Both (A) and (R) are true and (R) is the correct explanation of (A).

(b) Both (A) and (R) are true but (R) is not the correct explanation of (A).

(c) (A) is true but (R) is false.

(d) (A) is false but (R) is true.

18. The following mechanism has been proposed for reaction of NO with Br_2 to form NOBr.

$$NO(g) + Br_2(g) \underset{}{\overset{\text{Fast}}{\rightleftharpoons}} NOBr_2(g)$$

$$NOBr_2(g) + NO(g) \overset{\text{Slow}}{\rightleftharpoons} 2NOBr(g)$$

If second step is rate determining step order of reaction with respect to NO is

(a) 1 (b) 2

(c) 3 (d) 0

19. Match List-I with List-II.

List-I (Name of ore/mineral)	List-I (Chemical formula)
A. Calamine	1. ZnS
B. Malachite	2. $FeCO_3$
C. Siderite	3. $ZnCO_3$
D. Sphalerite	4. $CuCO_3 \cdot Cu(OH)_2$

Choose the most appropriate answer from the options given below.

	A	B	C	D
(a)	3	4	2	1
(b)	3	4	1	2
(c)	4	3	1	2
(d)	3	2	4	1

20. Which of the following sequence of T and F is correct for hydrocarbons? Where, T represents True and F represents False statement.

(i) Order of Boiling point *n*-pentane > 2-methylbutane > 2, 2-dimethylpropane > *n*-butane.

(ii) Order of decreasing reactivity with propane HBr > HI > HCl

(iii) Decreasing order of rate of β-elimination reaction with alc. KOH

$CH_3—CH(CH_3)—CH_2Br > CH_3—CH_2—CH_2—Br > CH_3—CH_2—Br$

(a) T T T (b) F T F

(c) T F T (d) F F F

Section B *Numerical Value Questions*

21. The standard heat of formation $(\Delta_f H^\circ_{298})$ of ethane (in kJ/mol), if the heat of combustion of ethane, hydrogen and graphite are −1560, −393.5 and −286 KJ/mol, respectively is …… .

22. In a fcc lattice, *A* occupies ccp arrangement, *B* occupies octahedral voids and C occupies alternate tetrahedral voids. If atoms along two body diagonals are removed, then stoichiometry of the crystal becomes, $A_aB_bC_c$. The value of $\left(\frac{a}{bc}\right)$ is ……

23. Sulphide ions in alkaline medium react with solid sulphur to form polyvalent sulphide ions. The equilibrium constant values for the formation of S_2^{2-} and S_3^{2-} from S and S^{2-} are 1.7 and 5.3 respectively. The value of K_C for the formation of S_3^{2-} from S_2^{2-} and S is……… .

24. An electron beam can undergo diffraction by crystals. A potential of *x* volt is applied to accelerate a beam of electrons, so that its wavelength becomes equal to 1.54 Å. The value of *x* is ………. .

25. A decapeptide (M.wt. = 796) on complete hydrolysis gives glycine (M.wt. = 75), alanine and phenyl alanine. Glycine contributes 47% to the total weight of the hydrolysed products.

The number of glycine units present in the decapeptide is ………… .

26. A metal complex, $Cr(NH_3)_4Cl_2Br$ has been isolated in two forms, (*X*) and (*Y*). (*X*) reacts with $AgNO_3$ to give a white precipitate readily soluble in NH_4OH, whereas (*Y*) gives a pale yellow precipitate soluble in conc. NH_4OH. Spin only magnetic moment of complex (*X*) or (*Y*) in BM is ....

27. A copolymer of ethene and vinyl chloride contains alternate monomers of each type. The mass percentage of ethylene in the copolymer is ....

28. According to VSEPR theory, considering all types of repulsions, percentage of *lp-bp* repulsion in an ammonia molecule is found to be *a*%.

The value of *a* is ....

29. Number of sp^3 hybridised boron atoms in each of borax, diborane and boron trichloride are *x*, *y* and *z* respectively.

The value of $(yz - x)$ is ....

30. Total number of chiral centres in alitame is ....

Answers

1 (*b*)	2 (*c*)	3 (*b*)	4 (*c*)	5 (*b*)	6 (*c*)	7 (*b*)	8 (*b*)	9 (*b*)	10 (*d*)
11 (*c*)	12 (*d*)	13 (*c*)	14 (*d*)	15 (*a*)	16 (*b*)	17 (*c*)	18 (*b*)	19 (*a*)	20 (*c*)
21 (*−192.50*)	22 (*0.29*)	23 (*3.12*)	24 (*63.57*)	25 (*6*)	26 (*3.87*)	27 (*30.94*)	28 (*50*)	29 (*−2*)	30 (*4*)

See detailed solutions on page no. 296

Knockout 06

JEE MAIN

Chemistry

Instructions

- This question paper contains of 30 Questions of Chemistry, divided into two sections : **Section A** Objective Type Questions and **Section B** Numerical Value Questions.
- **Section A** contains 20 Objective questions and all Questions are compulsory (Marking Scheme : Correct + 4, Incorrect – 1).
- **Section B** contains 10 Numerical value questions out of which only 5 questions are to be attempted (Marking Scheme : Correct + 4, Incorrect 0).

Section A *Objective Type Questions*

1. At what $\frac{[Br^-]}{\sqrt{[CO_3^{2-}]}}$, does the cell have its reaction at equilibrium?

$Ag(s)\,|\,Ag_2CO_3(s)\,|\,Na_2CO_3(aq)\,||\,KBr(aq)\,|\,AgBr(s)\,|\,Ag(s)$

Given, $K_{sp}(Ag_2CO_3) = 8 \times 10^{-12}\ M^3$

$K_{sp}(AgBr) = 4 \times 10^{-13}\ M^2$

(a) $\sqrt{1} \times 10^{-7} M^{1/2}$ (b) $\sqrt{2} \times 10^{-7} M^{1/2}$
(c) $\sqrt{3} \times 10^{-7} M^{1/2}$ (d) $\sqrt{4} \times 10^{-7} M^{1/2}$

2. Find the change in pH (ΔpH) when 100 mL of 0.01 M HCl is added in a solution containing 0.1 mmoles of $NaHCO_3$ solution of negligible volume ($K_{a_1} = 10^{-7}, K_{a_2} = 10^{-11}$ for H_2CO_3).

(a) $6 + 2\log 3$
(b) $6 - \log 3$
(c) $6 + 2\log 2$
(d) $6 - 2\log 3$

3. An ideal gas is taken from the same initial pressure p_1 to the same final pressure p_2 by three different processes. If it is known that point 1 corresponds to a reversible adiabatic path and point 2 corresponds to a single stage adiabatic path, then

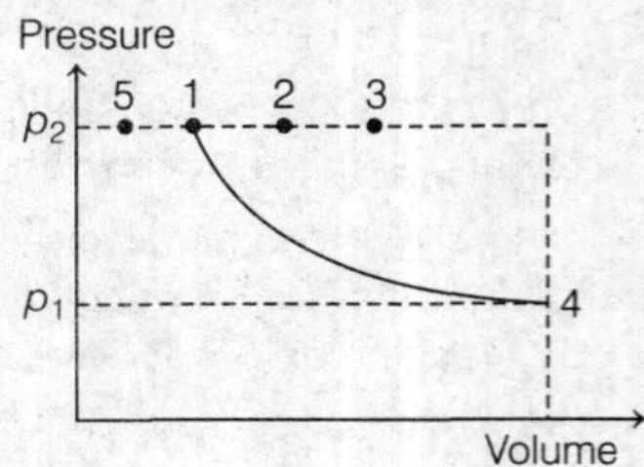

(a) point 3 may be a two stage adiabatic process
(b) the average KE of gas molecules will be maximum at point 1
(c) work done by the surrounding in reaching point 3 will be maximum
(d) if point 4 and point 5 lie along a reversible isotherm, then temperature at point 5 will be lower than that at point 1

4. Select the correct statement(s) from the following about elements of group 15.

(a) The order of stability of oxidation state for +3 is $Bi^{3+} > Sb^{3+} > As^{3+}$ and that for +5 is $As^{5+} > Sb^{5+} > Bi^{5+}$.
(b) In the case of nitrogen, all oxidation states from +1 to +4 tend to disproportionate in acidic medium.
(c) There is a considerable increase in covalent radius from N to P but from As to Bi only a small increase in covalent radius is observed.
(d) All of the above

5. Consider the following statements (S_1, S_2, S_3 and S_4) and select the correct arrangement in the order of true (T)/false (F) as given in the codes.

S_1 : For $[Pt(py)(NH_3)(NO_2)(OH)]$, number of possible geometrical isomers is six.

S_2 : The oxidation state of iron in brown ring complex, $[Fe(H_2O)NO]\,SO_4$ is +2.

S_3 : Both $[Co(ox)_3]^{3-}$ and $[CoF_6]^{3-}$ are paramagnetic.

S_4 : $CoCl_3 \cdot 3NH_3$ complex is non-conducting.

Choose the correct option.

(a) T F F T (b) T T T T
(c) T T F F (d) F T F T

6. Match the ionisation processes listed in Column I with the changes observed as listed in Column II. For this use, the codes given below.

Column I	Column II
A. $N_2 \longrightarrow N_2^+$	1. Bond order increases and magnetic property is changed.
B. $O_2^+ \longrightarrow O_2^{2+}$	2. Bond order decreases and magnetic property is not changed.
C. $B_2 \longrightarrow B_2^+$	3. Bond order increases and magnetic property is not changed.
D. $NO^- \longrightarrow NO$	4. Bond order decreases and magnetic property is changed.

[**Note** Here, change in magnetic property refers to change from diamagnetic to paramagnetic and *vice-versa*.]

Codes

	A	B	C	D		A	B	C	D
(a)	4	1	3	2	(b)	4	1	2	3
(c)	3	2	4	1	(d)	1	4	2	3

7. A compound *A* has the molecular formula C_5H_9Cl. It does not react with bromine in carbon tetrachloride. On treatment with a strong base, it produces a single compound *B*. *B* has a molecular formula C_5H_8 and reacts with bromine in carbon tetrachloride. Ozonolysis of *B* produces a compound *C* which has a molecular formula $C_5H_8O_2$. Which of the following structures is that of *A*?

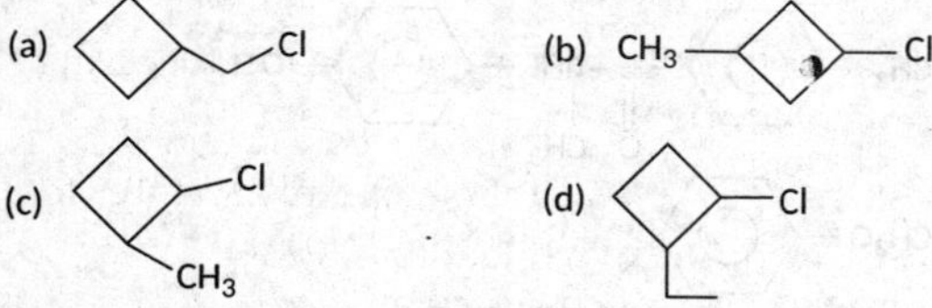

8. The major product obtained at the end of the following sequence of reaction is

(Tetrahydrofuran ring)–CH_2OH $\xrightarrow[\text{Pyridine, } \Delta]{SOCl_2}$ $\xrightarrow[(C_2H_5)_2O]{Mg}$ $\xrightarrow[H^+]{\text{epoxide}}$ Product

(a) (Tetrahydrofuran ring)–$CH_2-C(OH)(CH_3)-CH_2CH_3$

(b) (Tetrahydrofuran ring)–$CH_2-CH-C(CH_3)-CH_3$ (with O bridging CH and C)

(c) (Tetrahydrofuran ring)–$CH_2-C(CH_3)_2-CH_2OH$

(d) (Tetrahydrofuran ring)–$CH_2-CH_2-C(CH_3)_2-OH$

9. Given below are two statements.

Statement I As the electropositive character increases down the group, the stability of carbonates and hydrogen carbonates of alkali metals increases.

Statement II Lithium carbonate is not so stable to heat as lithium being very small in size polarises a larger CO_3^{2-} ion leading to the formation of more stable Li_2O and CO_2.

In the light of the above statements, choose the most appropriate answer from the options given below.

(a) Both Statement I and Statement II are correct.
(b) Both Statement I and Statement II are incorrect.
(c) Statement I is correct but Statement II is incorrect.
(d) Statement I is incorrect but Statement II is correct.

10. Match the following columns.

Column I (Separation techniques)	Column II (Mixtures)
A. Steam distillation	1. Benzoic acid + Benzaldehyde
B. Distillation	2. Ether + Toluene
C. Vacuum distillation	3. *o*-nitrophenol + *p*-nitrophenol
D. Sublimation	4. Purification of glycerol

Codes

	A	B	C	D
(a)	2	3	1	4
(b)	1	2	3	2
(c)	3	2	4	1
(d)	1	3	2	1

11. Consider the following compounds and decide as to which of the following statements is true?

(I) $CH_2=CH-CH(CH_3)-COOH$

(II) $CH_3-C(CH_3)_2-OCH_3$

(III) $CH_3O-C\equiv CH$

(IV) $CH_3-C(CH_3)(OH)-CH_2-OCH_3$

Choose the correct option.

(a) II gives no reaction with Na metal, however, 1 mole of IV on reaction with Na metal liberates 22.4 L of H_2 at STP.
(b) I will give brisk effervescence on addition of $NaHCO_3$, but will not bring any change in the colour of Br_2 water.
(c) III liberates H_2 gas, with Na metal, gives white precipitate with Tollen's reagent but does not respond towards Lucas reagent or 2, 4-DNP test.
(d) IV gives turbidity with anhydrous $ZnCl_2$.

12. At a certain temperature the following equilibrium is established

$$CO(g) + NO_2(g) \rightleftharpoons CO_2(g) + NO(g)$$

One mole of each of the four gases is mixed in one litre container and the reaction is allowed to reach equilibrium state. When excess of baryta water, $Ba(OH)_2$ is added to the equilibrium mixture, the weight of white precipitate of $BaCO_3$ obtained is 236.4 g. The equilibrium constant K_C of the reaction is (Ba = 137)

(a) 1.2 (b) 2.25
(c) 2.1 (d) 3.6

13. At a certain temperature, the first order rate constant k_1 is found to be smaller than the second order rate constant k_2. If the energy of activation E_1 of the first order reaction is greater than energy of activation E_2 of the second order reaction, then with increase in temperature

(a) k_1 will increase faster than k_2 but always will remain less than k_2
(b) k_2 will increase faster than k_1
(c) k_1 will increase faster than k_2 and becomes equal to k_2
(d) k_1 will increase faster than k_2 and becomes greater than k_2

14. The correct order of magnetic moments (spin only values in BM) among the following is

(a) $[MnCl_4]^{2-} > [CoCl_4]^{2-} > [Fe(CN)_6]^{4-}$
(b) $[MnCl_4]^{2-} > [Fe(CN)_6]^{4-} > [CoCl_4]^{2-}$
(c) $[Fe(CN)_6]^{4-} > [MnCl_4]^{2-} > [CoCl_4]^{2-}$
(d) $[Fe(CN)_6]^{4-} > [CoCl_4]^{2-} > [MnCl_4]^{2-}$

15. Find out the correct match for the following compounds regarding *cis*-and *trans*-configurations.

(I) Br, Cl (II) Br, CH_3 (III) CH_3, Br

(IV) Cl, CH_3 (V) CH_3, Br (VI) CH_3, CH_3

(a) I-*cis*, II-*trans*, VI-*cis*
(b) I-*cis*, II-*trans*, V-*cis*
(c) III-*cis*, II-*cis*, IV-*cis*
(d) II-*trans*, V-*cis*, VI-*cis*

16. A solid particle having spherical shape is assumed to react only on its surface. However, the amount of reactant contained in it is determined by its volume.

Consider the following rate law for a solid particle shrinking due to reaction :

$$-\frac{dV}{dt} = kS \quad (\because S = \text{surface area})$$

The order of the above reaction will be

(a) zero (b) 1 (c) 2/3 (d) 3/2

17. Which of the following compounds will liberate O_2 as well as N_2 gases on heating?

$NH_4NO_2(s)$ (A) $NH_4ClO_4(s)$ (B)

$NH_4IO_3(s)$ (C) $(NH_4)_2Cr_2O_7(s)$ (D)

(a) A, B and C (b) B and C
(c) B, C and D (d) A, B, C and D

18. In the reaction given below,

$CH_3O-C_6H_4-C(OH)(C_6H_4-CH_3)-CH(NH_2)-CH_3 \xrightarrow[5°C]{NaNO_2, HCl} A$ (Major product)

The product 'A' is

(a) $CH_3O-C_6H_4-C(=O)-CH(CH_3)-C_6H_4-CH_3$
(b) $CH_3-C_6H_4-C(=O)-CH(CH_3)-C_6H_4-OCH_3$
(c) $(CH_3O-C_6H_4)(CH_3-C_6H_4)CH-C(=O)-CH_3$
(d) $(CH_3O-C_6H_4)(CH_3-C_6H_4)C(CH_3)-CHO$

19. Phosphate rock (fluoroapatite) on reaction with orthophosphoric acid produces

(a) $Ca(H_2PO_4)_2 + CaF_2$ (b) $Ca_3(PO_4)_2 + CaF_2 + H_2O$
(c) $Ca(H_2PO_4)_2 + HF$ (d) $Ca_3(PO_4)_2 + HF + H_2O$

20. An evacuated glass chamber has only five H-atoms with their electrons respectively in their 1st, 2nd, 3rd, 4th and 5th excitation states. If all the electrons are grounded by de-excitation, how many total maximum number of spectral lines could be identified?

(a) 10 (b) 15 (c) 20 (d) 35

Section B *Numerical Value Questions*

21. A Tl^+/Tl couple was prepared by saturating 0.1 M KBr with TlBr and allowing the Tl^+ from the relatively insoluble bromide to equilibrate. This couple was observed to have a potential of + 0.443 V with respect to Pb^{2+}/Pb couple in which Pb^{2+} was 0.1 M. K_{sp} of TlBr is found to be $x \times 10^{-6}$ M^2. The value of x is ....

[Given, $E^\circ_{Pb^{2+}/Pb} = -0.126$ V, $E^\circ_{Tl^+/Tl} = -0.336$ V, $\frac{2.303\,RT}{F} = 0.059$, antilog $(0.5509) = 3.55$]

22. If osmotic pressure of 1 M aqueous solution of H_2SO_4 at 500 K is 90.2 atm, the value of K_{a_2} of H_2SO_4 will be ....

[Given : K_{a_1} (H_2SO_4) is infinite]

23. The percentage of the reactant molecules crossing over the energy barrier at 325 K is ....

Given, $\Delta H_{325} = 0.12$ kcal mol^{-1},

$E_a^{backward} = 0.02$ kcal mol^{-1}

$R = 2$ cal $mol^{-1}K^{-1}$, $e^{-0.215} = 0.8065$

24. A sample of $Fe_2(SO_4)_3$ and FeC_2O_4 was dissolved in dilute H_2SO_4. Complete oxidation of the reaction mixture required 40 mL of $\frac{N}{16}$ $KMnO_4$. After the oxidation, the reaction mixture was reduced by Zn and dilute H_2SO_4. On again oxidation by same $KMnO_4$ solution, 60 mL of it was required.

The ratio of millimoles of $Fe_2(SO_4)_3$ to FeC_2O_4 present in the sample will be ....

[Molar mass : $Fe_2(SO_4)_3 = 400$, $FeC_2O_4 = 144$]

25. 5.35 g of a salt, ACl (of weak base, AOH) is dissolved in 250 mL of solution. The resultant solution has a pH = 4.85. If ACl forms CsCl type crystals having density 2.2 g cm^{-3}, ionic radius of A^+ in Å is ....

[Given : $K_b(AOH) = 2 \times 10^{-5}$, $\frac{r_{A^+}}{r_{Cl^-}} = 0.731$]
[antilog $(-0.4) = 0.4$]

26. The gram-equivalent mass of XeF_4 present in water will be ....

[Xe = 131, F = 19]

27. The number of the compound(s) from the following given compounds will behave as reducing sugar in aqueous KOH solution is ....

HOH_2C, O, CH_2OH, HO, $OCOCH_3$, OH ; HOH_2C, O, CH_2OH, HO, OH ; HOH_2C, O, CH_2OH, HO, OCH_3, OH ; CH_2OH, O, CH_2OH_3, OH, HO, OH

28. 1-methyl cyclohexene on reductive ozonolysis followed by reaction with dilute NaOH gives x number of cyclic organic product(s).

On the other hand, a mixture of (HCHO + PhCHO) on treatment with conc. NaOH gives y number of organic product(s).

In another experiment, 1, 2-dimethyl cyclohexene on reaction with anhydrous *m*-CPBA gives z number of organic product(s).

The value of $\left(\frac{3y - z}{x}\right)$ will be ....

29. Liquids X and Y form ideal solution over the entire range of composition. At temperature T, equimolar binary solution of liquids X and Y has vapour pressure of 50 torr. At the same temperature, a new solution of X and Y having mole fraction x_x and x_y respectively, has a vapour pressure 25 torr. The value of x_x/x_y in the new solution is .... (Given : $p^\circ = 20$ torr).

30. First and second ionisation energies of an element M are 600 kJ mol^{-1} and 1600 kJ mol^{-1} respectively. If 1000 kJ of energy is supplied to one mole of vapours of M. It is found that x mole of $M^+(g)$ remains unoxidised. The value of x is ....

Answers

1 *(b)*	2 *(a)*	3 *(d)*	4 *(d)*	5 *(a)*	6 *(b)*	7 *(b)*	8 *(c)*	9 *(a)*	10 *(c)*
11 *(c)*	12 *(b)*	13 *(a)*	14 *(a)*	15 *(b)*	16 *(c)*	17 *(b)*	18 *(b)*	19 *(c)*	20 *(b)*
21 *(3.55)*	22 *(0.30)*	23 *(80.65)*	24 *(1.75)*	25 *(1.58)*	26 *(155.25)*	27 *(1)*	28 *(1.67)*	29 *(11.5)*	30 *(0.75)*

See detailed solutions on page no. 299

Knockout 07

JEE MAIN

Chemistry

Instructions

- This question paper contains of 30 Questions of Chemistry, divided into two sections : **Section A** Objective Type Questions and **Section B** Numerical Value Questions.
- **Section A** contains 20 Objective questions and all Questions are compulsory (Marking Scheme : Correct + 4, Incorrect – 1).
- **Section B** contains 10 Numerical value questions out of which only 5 questions are to be attempted (Marking Scheme : Correct + 4, Incorrect 0).

Section A *Objective Type Questions*

1. In a cubic packed structure of mixed oxides, the lattice is made up of oxide ions, one fifth of tetrahedral voids are occupied by divalent (X^{2+}) ions, while half of the octahedral voids are occupied by trivalent ions (Y^{3+}). The formula of the oxide is

(a) XY_2O_4 (b) X_2YO_4
(c) $X_4Y_5O_{10}$ (d) $X_5Y_4O_{10}$

2. Which of the following molecules is most suitable to disperse benzene in water?

(a) O, O^-Na^+

(b) Na^+O^-, O, O, O^-Na^+

(c) CH_3

(d) O^-Na^+

3. A compound strontium carbide when treated with water, it produces an organic compound *A*, which can also be prepared by reaction of 1, 2-dichloroethane with potassium tertiary butoxide.
Which of the following statements is correct for *A*?

I. *A* is an unsaturated compound.
II. *A* is acidic in nature.
III. *A* is a saturated compound.
IV. *A* undergoes *cis*-hydroxylation on reaction with OsO_4.

(a) I and II (b) II and III
(c) I, II and IV (d) All of these

4. Unknown salt, $X + K_2Cr_2O_7 +$ conc. $H_2SO_4 \rightarrow$ Reddish brown fumes.
Which is the correct statement regarding the above observation?

(a) It confirms presence of Cl^-.
(b) It confirms presence of Br^-.
(c) It neither confirms Cl^- nor Br^-, unless it is passed through NaOH solution.
(d) It confirms presence of both.

5. An organic compound *A* having molecular formula $C_6H_{12}O$ gives negative result to Tollen's test and iodoform test but yield phenyl hydrazone on reaction with phenyl hydrazine.
The compound may be

(a) hexanal (b) hexan-2-one
(c) hexan-3-one (d) amyl alcohol

6. Which of the following order of basic character are correct?

(a) p-$CH_3OC_6H_4NH_2$ > o-$CH_3OC_6H_4NH_2$ > m-$CH_3OC_6H_4NH_2$
(b) p-$CH_3OC_6H_4NH_2$ > m-$CH_3OC_6H_4NH_2$ > o-$CH_3OC_6H_4NH_2$
(c) o-$CH_3OC_6H_4NH_2$ > p-$CH_3OC_6H_4NH_2$ > m-$CH_3OC_6H_4NH_2$
(d) o-$CH_3OC_6H_4NH_2$ > m-$CH_3OC_6H_4NH_2$ > p-$CH_3OC_6H_4NH_2$

7. Melting point of a mixture of Na_2CO_3 and K_2CO_3 is
(a) higher than that of K_2CO_3
(b) higher than that of Na_2CO_3
(c) lower than that of K_2CO_3
(d) lower than both Na_2CO_3 and K_2CO_3

8. What will be the product when an optically active compound having IUPAC name pent-3-en-2-ol is treated with Jones reagent?
(a) Pentan-2-one (b) Pent-3-en-2-one
(c) Pentan-2-ol (d) Pent-4-en-2-one

9. Select the correct statement among the following.
(a) Co(III) is stabilised in presence of weak field ligands, while Co(II) is stabilised in presence of strong field ligands.
(b) Four coordinated complexes of Pd(II) and Pt(II) are paramagnetic and square planar.
(c) $[Ni(CN)_4]^{4-}$ ion and $[Ni(CO)_4]$ are diamagnetic, tetrahedral and square planar respectively.
(d) Ni^{2+} ion does not form inner orbital octahedral complexes.

10. When sulphur S is boiled with Na_2SO_3, a compound *A* is produced with which excess of $AgNO_3$ solution gives a compound *B*. *B* is water soluble and finally produces a black coloured sulphide *C*. Compounds *A*, *B* and *C* are respectively
(a) $Na_2S_4O_6$, Ag_2SO_4, Ag_2O (b) Na_2SO_4, Ag_2SO_4, Ag_2S
(c) $Na_2S_2O_3$, $Ag_2S_2O_3$, Ag_2S (d) $Na_2S_4O_6$, $Ag_2S_2O_3$, Ag_2O

11. Which of the following reactions will produce novolac?
I. Phenol + formaldehyde + base
II. Benzene diazonium salt + H_2O (hot) + formaldehyde + base
III. Chlorobenzene + *aq.* KOH + formaldehyde
Choose the correct option.
(a) Only I (b) I and II
(c) I, II and III (d) I and III

12. $FeCr_2O_4$ (chromite) is converted to Cr by following steps

$$\text{Chromite} \xrightarrow{\text{I}} Na_2CrO_4 \xrightarrow{\text{II}} Cr_2O_3 \xrightarrow{\text{III}} Cr$$

Reagents in I, II and III steps are

	I-Step	II-Step	III-Step
(a)	$NaHCO_3$/air, heat	Carbon, heat	Carbon, heat
(b)	NaOH/air, heat	Al, heat	Carbon, heat
(c)	NaOH/air, heat	Carbon, heat	Al, heat
(d)	Na_2CO_3/air, heat	Carbon, heat	Carbon, heat

13. Name the type of reaction for following equation,

(i) [2-chloro-3-methylbutane structure, Cl, H] $\xrightarrow{\text{NaO}-\text{Bu}^t}$ [alkene]

(ii) [Cl substrate] $\xrightarrow{\textit{Aq.}\ \text{KOH}}$ [OH product]

(iii) [alkene] $\xrightarrow{I_2}$ [diiodide, I, I]

(iv) [diene] + [ethene] $\xrightarrow{\Delta}$ [cyclohexene]

	(i)	(ii)	(iii)	(iv)
(a)	Elimination	substitution	addition	addition
(b)	Addition	elimination	addition	substitution
(c)	Elimination	addition	substitution	addition
(d)	Substitution	elimination	addition	addition

14. What will be the correct structural formula of product for the following reaction?

[1,2-dimethylcyclohexene: CH_3, CH_3] $\xrightarrow{\text{Dil. KMnO}_4} A \xrightarrow{HIO_4} B \xrightarrow{OH^-} C$

(a) [cyclohexenone with O and CH_3] (b) [cyclopentene with CHO and CH_3]
(c) [cyclohexene with CHO] (d) [cyclohexane with CHO, CHO]

15. An amino acid contains a carboxyl group and amino group, whose pK_a values are 3.30 and 9.0 respectively. The value of pH at this isoelectric point is .... and it is a ...... amino acid. Choose the correct option to fill blanks.
(a) 6.15, neutral (b) 2.34, acidic
(c) 9.60, basic (d) 6.97, basic

16. If the energy of H-atom in the ground state is $-2E$, the velocity of photoelectron emitted, when a photon having energy, E_p strikes a stationary Li^{2+} ion in ground state is given by
(a) $\sqrt{\frac{2(E_p - 9E)}{5m}}$ (b) $\sqrt{\frac{5(E_p - 9E)}{2}}$
(c) $\sqrt{\frac{2(E_p - 9E)}{7}}$ (d) $\sqrt{\frac{2(E_p - 18E)}{m}}$

17. The process which is used to purify the compounds *A* and *B* is

$C_6H_5CH_3 \xrightarrow{KMnO_4} A$; (3,4-dihydronaphthalen-2-ol, OH) $\xrightarrow{H_2SO_4} B$

(a) sublimation (b) steam distillation
(c) fractional distillation (d) decantation

18. The major product in the following reaction is

$H_2C{=}C(CH_2CH_3){-}CH{=}CH_2 \xrightarrow{\text{1 equiv.HBr}}$

(a) $H_2C{=}C(CH_2CH_3){-}CH(Br)CH_3$ (b) $H_3C{-}C(Br)(CH_2CH_3){-}CH{=}CH_2$
(c) $H_2C{=}C(CH_2CH_3){-}CH_2CH_2Br$ (d) $H_3C{-}C(CH_2CH_3){=}CH{-}CH_2Br$

19. The possible structure of the alcohol is

R—OH (alcohol) $\xrightarrow[\Delta]{\text{Conc. } H_2SO_4}$ (benzene)

(I) CH_2OH (II) OH (III) CH_2OH (IV) $=CH_2$, OH

(a) Only II (b) I, II and III
(c) I and II (d) I and III

20. In Antarctic region, slow blindness is due to
(a) damage to retina caused by IR rays
(b) inflammation of cornea due to high dose of UV-B radiation
(c) release of greenhouse gases
(d) inflammation of cornea by IR rays

Section B *Numerical Value Questions*

21. The density of a solution containing 13% by mass of sulphuric acid is 1.09 g/mL. The molarity of the solution will be ...... M.

22. 20 mL of 0.02 M $KMnO_4$ was required to completely oxidise 10 mL of oxalic acid solution. The molarity of the oxalic acid solution will be ...... M .

23. In the preparation of iron from haematite (Fe_2O_3) by the reaction with carbon as

$$2Fe_2O_3 + 3C \longrightarrow 4Fe + 3CO_2$$

The amount of 70% pure iron could be produced (m kg) from 140 kg of 80% pure Fe_2O_3 is ...... kg.

24. The equilibrium constants at 1140 K for these two reactions are

$$2CO(g) \rightleftharpoons C(s) + CO_2(g);\ K_{p_1} = 10^{-12}\ \text{atm}^{-1}$$

$$CO(g) + Cl_2(g) \rightleftharpoons COCl_2(g);\ K_{p_2} = 3 \times 10^{-3}\ \text{atm}^{-1}$$

Equilibrium constant, K_C for the following reaction at 1140 K is found to be $x \times 10^8\ M^{-1}$.

$$C(s) + CO_2(g) + 2Cl_2(g) \rightleftharpoons 2COCl_2(g)$$

The value of *x* will be ....

25. Given the following limiting molar conductivities at 250°C : HCl 425 $\Omega^{-1}\ cm^2\ mol^{-1}$; NaCl 125 $\Omega^{-1}\ cm^2\ mol^{-1}$; 82 $\Omega^{-1}\ cm^2 mol^{-1}$
If the conductivity of a 0.001 M crotonic acid solution is $3.82 \times 10^{-5}\ \Omega^{-1} cm^{-1}$. Ionisation constant of crotonic acid is found to be $x \times 10^{-5}$. The value of *x* is found to be ....

26. A triatomic linear (avoid vibration degree of freedom) gas of two moles is taken through a reversible process (ideal) starting from *P* as shown in figure.

The volume ratio $\frac{V_Q}{V_P} = 2$, if the temperature at *P* is −73°C, then work done (in kJ) by the gas in process *PQ* will be ....

(Graph: Volume (L) vs Temperature (K), points P, Q, R)

27. A bulb of constant volume is attached to a manometer tube open at other end as shown in figure.

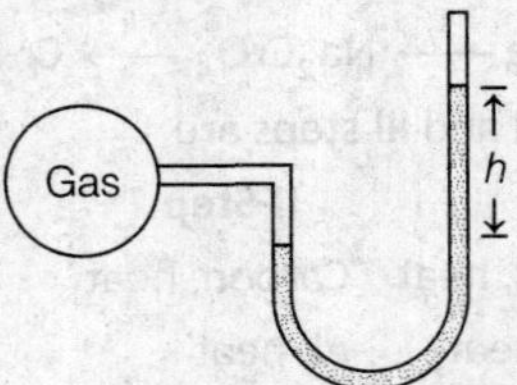

The manometer is filled with liquid of density $\left(\frac{1}{3}\right)^{rd}$ that of mercury initially *h* was 456 cm.

Through a small hole in the bulb has leaked assuming pressure decreases as $\frac{dp}{dt} = -kp$, if value of h is 228 cm after 28 min. The value of k in h^{-1} is ......

[Take, $\log \frac{57}{38} = 0.28$ and density of Hg = 136 g/mL]

28. 1.0 g of monobasic acid HA in 100 g water lowers the freezing point by 0.145 K. If 0.75 g of same acid requires 27 mL of $\frac{N}{9}$ solution for complete neutralisation, then % degree of dissociation of acid is ......

$[K_f(H_2O) = 1.86 \text{ K kg mol}^{-1}]$

29. The number of compounds, among the following which are optically inactive is ....

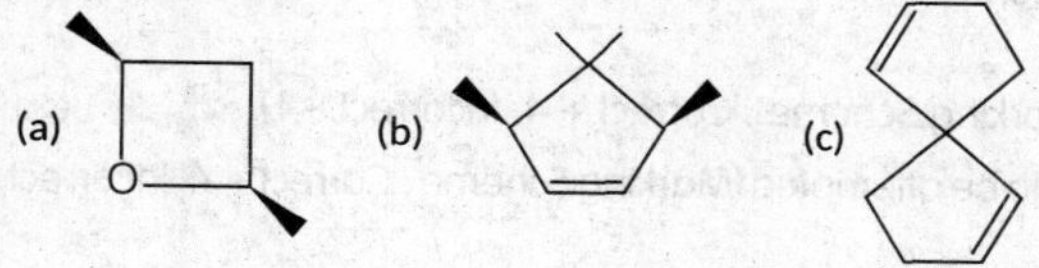

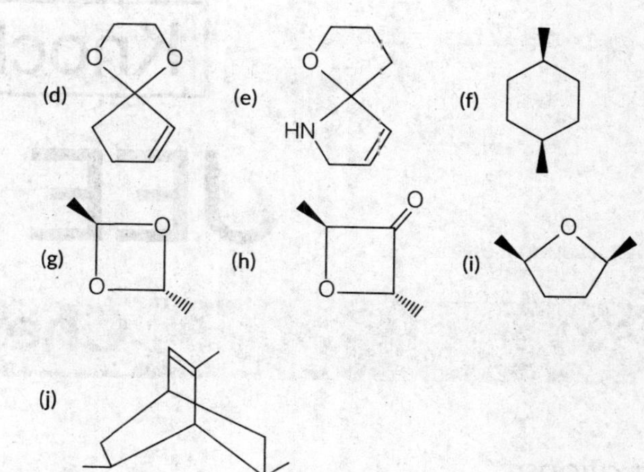

30. Excess of acidified solution of KI was added to a 25 mL H_2O_2 solution. The iodine liberated required 20 mL of 0.3 N sodium thiosulphate solution. The volume strength of H_2O_2 solution is .... g L^{-1}.

Answers

1 *(c)*	2 *(c)*	3 *(c)*	4 *(c)*	5 *(c)*	6 *(c)*	7 *(d)*	8 *(b)*	9 *(d)*	10 *(c)*
11 *(b)*	12 *(c)*	13 *(a)*	14 *(a)*	15 *(a)*	16 *(d)*	17 *(a)*	18 *(d)*	19 *(c)*	20 *(b)*
21 *(1.44)*	22 *(0.01)*	23 *(112)*	24 *(8.42)*	25 *(1.11)*	26 *(3.32)*	27 *(1.38)*	28 *(16.93)*	29 *(5)*	30 *(1.34)*

See detailed solutions on page no. 304

Knockout 08

JEE MAIN

Chemistry

Instructions

- This question paper contains of 30 Questions of Chemistry, divided into two sections :
  Section A Objective Type Questions and **Section B** Numerical Value Questions.
- **Section A** contains 20 Objective questions and all Questions are compulsory (Marking Scheme : Correct + 4, Incorrect – 1).
- **Section B** contains 10 Numerical value questions out of which only 5 questions are to be attempted (Marking Scheme : Correct + 4, Incorrect 0).

Section A *Objective Type Questions*

1. Match the compounds given in Column I with its respective uses in Column II and choose the correct option using codes.

Column I	Column II
A. Amino glycosides	1. Antifertility drug
B. Chloramphenicol	2. Bactericidal antibiotic
C. Novestrol	3. Antiseptic
D. Soframycin	4. Bacteriostatic antibiotic

Codes

	A	B	C	D		A	B	C	D
(a)	1	4	2	3	(b)	1	4	3	2
(c)	2	4	1	3	(d)	2	1	3	4

2. Which of the following statements are correct?

I. The structure given below is the disaccharide lactose,

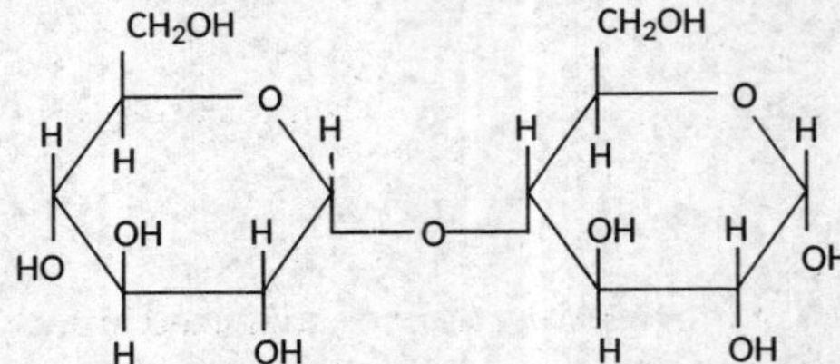

II. High content of starch is found in cereals and roots.

III. α-D glucose and β-D glucose differ in configuration at C_1.

IV. The monosaccharides allose, altrose and talose are all reducing sugars.

Choose the correct option.

(a) II, III and IV (b) I, II, III and IV
(c) II and IV (d) III and IV

3. Out of the following, statements regarding transition elements are

I. All ions are colourless.

II. When Fe^{+2} is oxidised to Fe^{+3}, equivalent weight of ion is equal to half of atomic weight.

III. Ions contain partially filled *d*-electron levels.

Choose the correct option.

(a) I and III
(b) II and III
(c) Only I
(d) I and II

4. One molecule of a substance absorbs one quantum of energy. The energy involved when 1.5 mole of the substance absorbs red light of frequency $7.5 \times 10^{14}\ s^{-1}$ will be

(a) 2.99×10^5 J (b) 3.23×10^5 J
(c) 4.49×10^5 J (d) 2.99×10^6 J

5. Out of SO_2, CO, O_3, NO and peroxyacetylnitrate (PAN), primary and secondary pollutants are

	Primary	Secondary
(a)	SO_2, O_3, NO	CO, PAN
(b)	SO_2, NO	PAN, O_3, CO
(c)	SO_2, CO, NO	PAN, O_3
(d)	PAN, O_3	SO_2, CO, NO

6. The lanthanide contraction is responsible for the fact that

(a) Zr and Y have about the same radius
(b) Zr and Nb have similar oxidation states
(c) Zr and Hf have about the same radius
(d) Zr and Ce have the same oxidation states

7. Which of the following statement is incorrect ?

(a) Mixture of CO_3^{2-} and HCO_3^- can be distinguished by phenolphthalein, which gives pink colour with HCO_3^- ions.

(b) Mixture of NO_2^- and NO_3^- can be distinguished by 'Ring test', NO_3^- ions gives brown ring, while NO_2^- ion gives a green coloured solution.

(c) To a mixture of Br^- and NO_3^- when conc. H_2SO_4 is added a reddish brown gas is evolved.

(d) Chromyl chloride test fails with Br^- and I^- ions since both chromyl bromide and chromyl iodide are non-volatile in nature.

8. Which of the following statements are correct ?

I. In octahedral complex-$d_{z^2}, d_{x^2-y^2}$ orbitals have higher energy than d_{xy}, d_{yz} and d_{zx} orbitals.

II. In tetrahedral complexes-d_{xy}, d_{yz}, d_{zx} orbitals have higher energy than d_{z^2} and $d_{x^2-y^2}$ orbitals.

III. The colour of complexes are due to transitions of electrons from one set of d-orbitals to another set of d-orbitals.

IV. $\Delta_{\text{tetrahedral}} = \frac{9}{4}\Delta_{\text{octahedral}}$

Choose the correct option.

(a) I, II and III (b) I and IV

(c) III and IV (d) II, III and IV

9. Which of the following combinations will give $C_6H_5-C(OH)(C_2H_5)-CH_3$ (2-phenyl-butan-2-ol) as the major product?

(a) $C_6H_5-\overset{O}{\overset{||}{C}}-CH_3$ and C_2H_5MgBr

(b) $C_6H_5-\overset{O}{\overset{||}{C}}-C_2H_5$ and CH_3MgBr

(c) $CH_3-\overset{O}{\overset{||}{C}}-C_2H_5$ and C_6H_5MgBr

(d) All of the above

10. [alkenol with OH] $\xrightarrow{Br_2/CCl_4}$ one of the possible products of this reaction is

(a) [structure with OH, Br, Br] (b) [tetrahydropyran structure]

(c) [structure with Br and O ring] (b) [tetrahydropyran structure]

11. For the reaction,

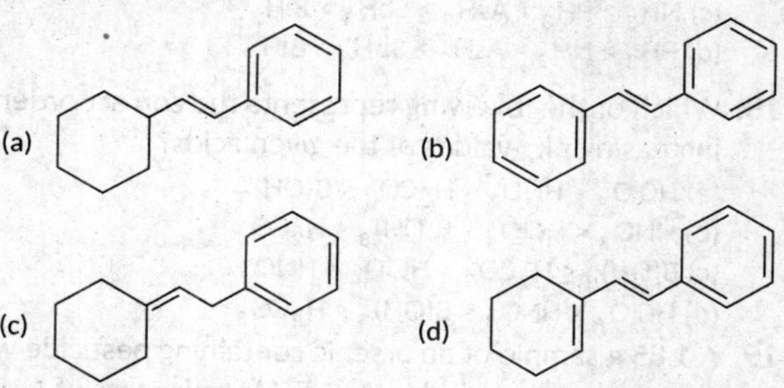

the product 'F' is

(a) [structure] (b) [structure]

(c) [structure] (d) [structure]

12. THF $\xrightarrow{\text{Excess HBr}}$, the product is

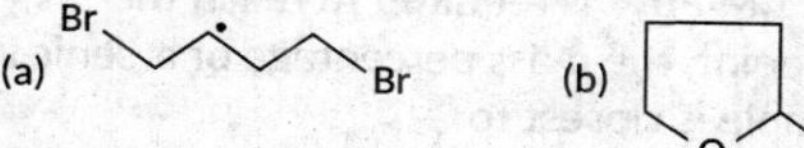

(a) [Br–(CH₂)₄–Br] (b) [2-bromotetrahydrofuran]

(c) [3-bromotetrahydrofuran] (d) HO–(CH₂)₄–Br

13. $CH_3-\underset{Ph}{\overset{OH}{C}}-CH_2-I \xrightarrow{AgNO_3}$?

The product is

(a) $CH_3-\overset{}{\underset{O}{\underset{||}{C}}}-CH_2-C_6H_5$ (b) $CH_3-CH_2-\overset{O}{\overset{||}{C}}-C_6H_5$

(c) $CH_3-\underset{Ph}{\overset{OH}{C}}-CH_3$ (d) $CH_3-\overset{Ph}{CH}-CH_2-C_6H_5$

14. Which of the following compound is used in antiknock composition to prevent deposition of oxides of lead on spark plug, combustion chamber and exhaust pipe?

(a) Glycol (b) Glycerol

(c) Toluene (d) 1, 2-dibromoethane

15. 1000 mL 0.05 M $CaOCl_2$ reacts with excess of KI and liberated I_2 is titrated with V mL of 0.1 M hypo solution, then value of V is

(a) 500 mL (b) 1000 mL (c) 2000 mL (d) 250 mL

16. Electron affinity of
(a) carbon is greater than oxygen
(b) sulphur is lesser than oxygen
(c) iodine is higher than bromine
(d) bromine is lesser than chlorine

17. Dipole moment of the hydrides of group 15 elements decreases in the order
(a) $AsH_3 > BiH_3 > SbH_3 > NH_3 > PH_3$
(b) $BiH_3 > SbH_3 > AsH_3 > PH_3 > NH_3$
(c) $NH_3 > PH_3 > AsH_3 > SbH_3 > BiH_3$
(d) $PH_3 > NH_3 > AsH_3 > SbH_3 > BiH_3$

18. Which of the following represents the correct order of increasing pK_a values of the given acids?
(a) $HClO_4 < HNO_3 < H_2CO_3 < B(OH)_3$
(b) $HNO_3 < HClO_4 < B(OH)_3 < H_2CO_3$
(c) $B(OH)_3 < H_2CO_3 < HClO_4 < HNO_3$
(d) $HClO_4 < HNO_3 < B(OH)_3 < H_2CO_3$

19. A 1.85 g sample of an arsenic containing pesticide was chemically converted to AsO_4^{3-} (Atomic mass of As = 74.9) and titrated with Pb^{2+} to form $Pb_3(AsO_4)_2$.
If 20 mL of 0.1 M Pb^{2+} is required to reach the equivalence point, the mass percentage of arsenic in the pesticide sample is closest to
(a) 8.1 (b) 2.3 (c) 5.4 (d) 3.6

20. Choose the correct one from the following alkaline earth metal sulphates, which has its hydration enthalpy greater than its lattice enthalpy.
(a) $BeSO_4$ (b) $SrSO_4$ (c) $BaSO_4$ (d) $CaSO_4$

Section B *Numerical Value Questions*

21. The number of correct statements from the following is ....
(a) Novolac is a linear polymer.
(b) Molecular forces decrease in the order.
Thermosetting > Fibres > Thermoplastic > Elastomers.
(c) 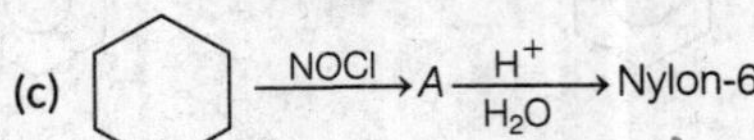

(d) Buna-S and Buna-N are addition polymers
(e) Bakelite is a copolymer

22. The number of correct statements from the following is ...
(a) Chloroxylenol gives characteristic colour with $FeCl_3$
(b) Penicillin gives positive $NaHCO_3$ test
(c) Meprobamate and chlorodiazepoxide are relatively mild tranquilizers suitable for relieving tension
(d) Brompheniramine and terfenadine are antihistamines

23. A sample was weighed using two different balances. The results were (i) 3.929 g and (ii) 4.00 g. The weight of the sample should be reported in grams as ....

24. The number of octahedral voids present in a fcc unit cell is ....

25. Considering H_2O as a weak field ligand, the number of unpaired electrons in $[Mn(H_2O)_6]^{2+}$ is ....

26. Given the cell : Cd(s) | $Cd(OH)_2(s)$ | NaOH (*aq*, 0.01 M) | $H_2(g, 1\text{ bar})$ | Pt(s) with $E_{cell} = 0.0$ V
If $E^\circ_{Cd^{2+}|Cd} = -0.39$ V, then K_{sp} of $Cd(OH)_2$ is 10^{-x}.
The value of *x* will be .... [Take $RT/F = 0.06$]

27. In an adsorption experiment, a graph between log (x/m) *versus* log *p* was found to be linear with a slope of 45°. The intercept on the log(x/m) was found to be 0.3010. The amount in grams of the gas adsorbed per gram of charcoal under a pressure of 0.5 atm is .... [log 2 = 0.3010].

28. The number of isomers [including stereoisomers] of formula $C_5H_{10}Cl_2$ are obtained from the monochlorination of S (+) 1-chloro-2-methyl butane are ....

29. Number of correct statement(s) regarding the following first-order reaction is ....
$$2N_2O_5(g) \longrightarrow 4NO_2(g) + O_2(g)$$
(a) The concentration of the reactant decreases exponentially with time.
(b) The half-life of the reaction decreases with increasing temperature.
(c) The half-life of the reaction depends on the initial concentration of the reactant.
(d) The reaction proceeds to 99.61% completion in eight half-life cycles. [log256.41 ≈ 2.41]

30. The number of the compounds from the following given compounds participate in Hofmann bromamide reaction is ....

$CH_3-\overset{O}{\overset{||}{C}}-NH_2$, $C_6H_5-\overset{Br}{\overset{|}{CH}}-\underset{O}{\underset{||}{C}}-NH_2$, $C_6H_5-\underset{O}{\underset{||}{C}}-NH_2$, $C_6H_5-NH-\overset{O}{\overset{||}{C}}-H$, $C_6H_5-\overset{O}{\overset{||}{C}}-NH-CH_3$, $C_6H_5-\overset{OH}{\overset{|}{CH}}-\overset{O}{\overset{||}{C}}-NH_2$, (phthalimide: $C_6H_4(CO)_2NH$)

Answers

1 *(c)*	2 *(a)*	3 *(c)*	4 *(c)*	5 *(c)*	6 *(c)*	7 *(b)*	8 *(a)*	9 *(d)*	10 *(c)*
11 *(a)*	12 *(a)*	13 *(a)*	14 *(d)*	15 *(b)*	16 *(d)*	17 *(c)*	18 *(a)*	19 *(c)*	20 *(a)*
21 *(4)*	22 *(4)*	23 *(4)*	24 *(4)*	25 *(5)*	26 *(15)*	27 *(1)*	28 *(7)*	29 *(3)*	30 *(5)*

See detailed solutions on page no. 308

Knockout 09

JEE MAIN

Chemistry

Instructions

- This question paper contains of 30 Questions of Chemistry, divided into two sections :
Section A Objective Type Questions and **Section B** Numerical Value Questions.
- **Section A** contains 20 Objective questions and all Questions are compulsory (Marking Scheme : Correct + 4, Incorrect − 1).
- **Section B** contains 10 Numerical value questions out of which only 5 questions are to be attempted (Marking Scheme : Correct + 4, Incorrect 0).

Section A *Objective Type Questions*

1. The heat of formation of $C_{12}H_{22}O_{11}(s)$, $CO_2(g)$ and $H_2O(l)$ are − 530, − 94.3 and −68.3 kcal/mol respectively. The amount of $C_{12}H_{22}O_{11}$ required to supply 2700 kcal of energy is

(a) 382.70 g (b) 832.74 g (c) 463.9 g (d) 684 g

2. The following alcohol after treatment with acid gives compound *A*. Ozonolysis of *A* gives octane-2, 7-dione. The compound *A* is

[Structure: cyclopentane ring bearing CH(OH)Me and Me on the same carbon] $\xrightarrow{H^+} A$

(a) [structure] (b) [structure]

(c) [structure] (d) [structure]

3. An electric current is passed through silver nitrate solution using silver electrodes. 10.79 g of silver was found to be deposited on the cathode. If the same amount of electricity is passed through copper sulphate solution using copper electrodes, the weight of copper deposited on the cathode is

(a) 1.6 g (b) 2.3 g (c) 3.2 g (d) 6.4 g

4. In the reaction,

$$CuSO_4(aq) \xrightarrow{H_2S} M \xrightarrow[KCN]{Excess} N + O$$

the final products *N* and *O* are respectively,

(a) $[Cu(CN)_4]^{2-}$, $(CN)_2$ (b) $[Cu(CN)_4]^{3-}$, $(CN)_2$

(c) CuCN, $(CN)_2$ (d) $Cu(CN)_2$, K_2S

5. $Ni + 4CO \xrightarrow{320K} Ni(CO)_4 \xrightarrow{420\ K} Ni + 4CO$

This method of purification of nickel is ....

(a) zone refining (b) froth-floatation

(c) Mond's process (d) cupellation

6. The heat liberated from the combustion of 0.5 g of carbon raised the temperature of 2000 g of water from 24°C to 26°C. The heat of combustion of carbon (per mole) is

(a) −4 kcal (b) −8 kcal (c) −62 kcal (d) −96 kcal

7. An organic compound of molecular formula C_4H_6 (*A*) precipitates with ammoniacal silver nitrate and ammoniacal cuprous chloride. *A* is an isomer of *B*, one mole of which reacts with one mole of Br_2 to form 1, 4-dibromobut-2-ene. *A* and *B* are respectively

(a) $CH_3CH_2C{\equiv}CH$ and $CH_2{=}CHCH{=}CH_2$

(b) $CH_3C{\equiv}CCH_3$ and $CH_3CH{=}C{=}CH_2$

(c) [cyclopropane ring CH_2–CH_2]$C{=}CH_2$ and cyclobutene (CH_2—CH, CH_2—CH)

(d) $CH_3C{\equiv}CCH_3$ and CH_2(CH=CH)CH_2 [bicyclic structure]

8. Given below are two statements.

Statement I Zeolites are water softener as well as catalyst.

Statement II Pores in a particular zeolite are of a fixed size and shape.

In the light of the above statements, choose the most appropriate answer from the options given below.

(a) Both Statement I and Statement II are correct.
(b) Both Statement I and Statement II are incorrect.
(c) Statement I is correct but Statement II is incorrect.
(d) Statement I is incorrect but Statement II is correct.

9. Among the given statements, which one is not true for long form of periodic table?
(a) It reflects transition in physical and chemical properties of elements.
(b) It reflects sequence of filling electrons in order or sub energy levels *s, p, d, f*
(c) It helps to predict the stable valency states of the elements.
(d) It helps to predict relative ionicity of bond between any two elements.

10. Which one of the following complexes show optical isomerism?
(a) *cis*-$[Co(en)_2Cl_2]Cl$ (b) *trans*-$[Co(en)_2Cl_2]Cl$
(c) *cis*-$[Co(NH_3)_4Cl_2]Cl$ (d) $[Co(NH_3)_3Cl_3]$

11. The major product of the following reaction is

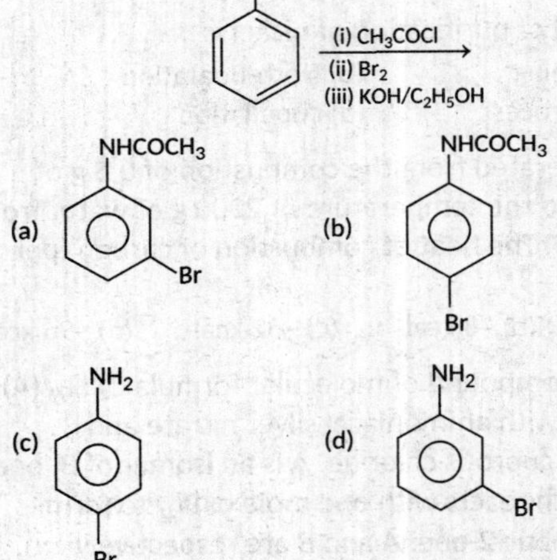

12. On treatment of 100 mL of 0.1 M solution of $CoCl_3 \cdot 6H_2O$ with excess of $AgNO_3$, 1.2×10^{22} ions are precipitated. The complex is
(a) $[Co(H_2O)_4Cl_2]Cl \cdot 2H_2O$ (b) $[Co(H_2O)_3Cl_3] \cdot 3H_2O$
(c) $[Co(H_2O)_6]Cl_3$ (d) $[Co(H_2O)_5Cl]Cl_2 \cdot H_2O$

13. Identify the set of reagents/reaction conditions, X and Y in the following set of transformations.

$$CH_3-CH_2-CH_2Br \xrightarrow{X} \text{Product} \xrightarrow{Y} CH_3-\underset{\substack{|\\Br}}{CH}-CH_3$$

(a) X = dilute aqueous NaOH, Y = HBr/ acetic acid
(b) X = concentrated alcoholic NaOH, Y = HBr/ acetic acid
(c) X = dilute aqueous NaOH, Y = $Br_2/CHCl_3$
(d) X = concentrated aqueous NaOH, Y = $Br_2/CHCl_3$

14. For one mole of a van der Waals' gas when $b = 0$ and $T = 300$ K, the *pV vs 1/V* plot is shown below. The value of the van der Waals' constant *a* (atm L^2 mol^{-2}) is

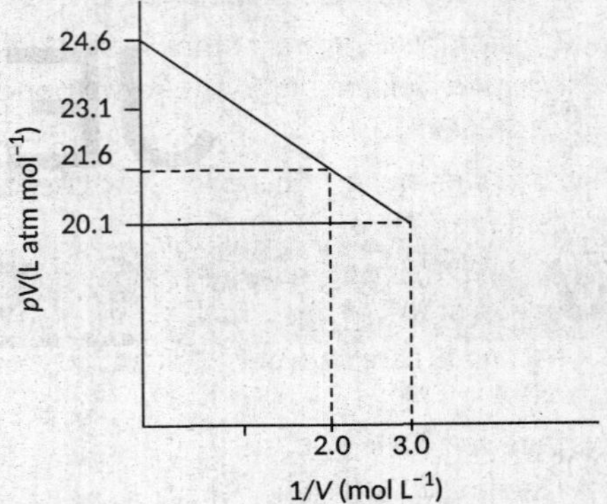

(a) 1.0 (b) 4.5 (c) 1.5 (d) 3.0

15. The molar conductivity of 0.25 mol L^{-1} formic acid is 40.1 S cm^2 mol^{-1}. Calculate its dissociation constant.
[Assuming $\Lambda^\circ_{m(H^+)} = 349.6$ S $cm^2 mol^{-1}$;
$\Lambda^\circ_{m(HCOO^-)} = 54.6$ S $cm^2 mol^{-1}$]
(a) 2.73×10^{-3} mol L^{-1} (b) 2.46×10^{-3} mol L^{-1}
(c) 4.75×10^{-3} mol L^{-1} (d) 5.27×10^{-3} mol L^{-1}

16. A hexapeptide has the composition : Ala, Gly, Phe, Val. Both the N-terminal and C-terminal units are Val. Cleavage of the hexapeptide by chemotrypsin gives two different tripeptides, both having Val as the N-terminal groups. Among the products of random hydrolysis is a Ala-Val dipeptide fragment.
What is the primary structure of the hexapeptide?
(a) Val-Gly-Phe-Val-Ala-Val (b) Val-Ala-Phe-Val-Gly-Val
(c) Val-Gly-Ala-Val-Phe-Val (d) Val-Phe-Val-Ala-Gly-Val

17. One mole of an organic compound (*A*) with the formula C_3H_8O reacts completely with two moles of HI to form X and Y. When Y is boiled with aqueous alkali, it forms Z and Z responds to the iodoform test. The compound (*A*) is
(a) propan-2-ol (b) propan-1-ol
(c) ethoxyethane (d) methoxyethane

18. Consider the following conversion

$$C_6H_{11}-\overset{\overset{O}{\|}}{C}CH_3 \xrightarrow{?} C_6H_{11}-\overset{\overset{CH_3}{|}}{\underset{\underset{OH}{|}}{C}}HCH_2CH_3$$

Which of the following sets of reagents, would successfully accomplish the conversion shown?
(a) $CH_3CH_2CH_2MgBr, H_3O^+$, PCC, CH_2Cl_2
(b) $CH_3CH_2CH_2MgBr, H_3O^+, H_2SO_4$, Heat, PCC, CH_2Cl_2
(c) $(C_6H_5)_3\overset{+}{P}-\overset{-}{\ddot{C}}HCH_2CH_3, B_2H_6, H_2O_2, HO^-$
(d) $(C_6H_5)_3\overset{+}{P}-\overset{-}{\ddot{C}}HCH_2CH_3, H_2SO_4, H_2O$

19. Given below are two statements, one is labelled as Assertion (A) and the other is labelled as Reason (R).

Assertion (A) The carbonate of lithium decomposes easily on heating to form lithium oxide and CO_2.

Reason (R) Lithium being very small in size polarises larger carbonate ion leading to the formation of more stable Li_2O and CO_2.

In the light of the above statements, choose the correct answer from the options given below.

(a) Both (A) and (R) are true and (R) is the correct explanation of (A).

(b) Both (A) and (R) are true but (R) is not the correct explanation of (A).

(c) (A) is false but (R) is true.

(d) (A) is true but (R) is false.

20. Match the species given in Column I with properties given in Column II and select the correct option using codes.

	Column I		Column II
A.	Diborane	1.	Used as a flux for soldering metals
B.	Gallium	2.	Crystalline form of silica
C.	Borax	3.	Banana bonds
D.	Alùminosilicate	4.	Low melting, high boiling substance and useful for measuring high temperature
E.	Quartz	5.	Used as catalyst in petrochemical industries

Codes

	A	B	C	D	E		A	B	C	D	E
(a)	3	4	1	5	2	(b)	4	3	1	5	2
(c)	4	3	5	2	1	(d)	1	2	5	4	3

Section B Numerical Value Questions

21. The K_{sp} of Ag_2CrO_4 is 1.1×10^{-12} at 298 K. The solubility (in mol/L) of Ag_2CrO_4 in a 0.1 M $AgNO_3$ solution is $y \times 10^{-11}$, then y is ....

22. The rate constant for the reaction,

$2N_2O_5 \longrightarrow 4NO_2 + O_2$ is $3.0 \times 10^{-5}\ s^{-1}$. If the rate is $2.40 \times 10^{-5} Ms^{-1}$, then molar concentration of N_2O_5 is .... M.

23. The entropy change (in $JK^{-1}mol^{-1}$) in surroundings when 1.00 mole of $H_2O(l)$ is formed under standard conditions is.... (given : $\Delta H_f^\circ [H_2O(l)] = -286\ kJ\ mol^{-1}$)

24. The specific conductance of $\frac{N}{10}$ KCl solution at 20°C is $0.0212\ ohm^{-1}cm^{-1}$ and the resistance of the cell containing this solution at 20°C is 5.5 ohm. The cell constant (in cm^{-1}) is ....

25. The freezing point (in K) of 1 molal NaCl (*aq*) solution having 60% dissociation ($K_f = 1.86$ K kg mol^{-1}) is ....

26. The number of incorrect statements among the following is ....

I. Clean water would have BOD value of less than 5 ppm.

II. Oxides of sulphur, N and C are the most widespread air pollutant.

III. Concentration of dissolved oxygen below 6 ppm is good for growth of fish.

IV. Photochemical smog causes infection in liver.

27. For an unknown gas at 0°C,

$$\lim_{p \to 0} \left(\frac{d}{p}\right) = 1.517\ gL^{-1}atm^{-1}$$

Molar mass of the gas is .... $g\ mol^{-1}$.

28. Number of stereogenic centre in

OH, Cl, OH, COOH, Br

is ....

29. 1 mole of ferrous oxalate is oxidised by x mol of MnO_4^- in acidic medium and also 1 mole of ferrous oxalate is oxidised by y mole of $Cr_2O_7^{2-}$ in acidic medium. The value of $A\left(\frac{x}{y}\right)$ is ....

30. The spin-only moment of $[Cu(NH_3)_4]^{2+}$ is x BM. The value of x is ....

Answers

1 *(d)*	2 *(d)*	3 *(c)*	4 *(b)*	5 *(c)*	6 *(d)*	7 *(a)*	8 *(a)*	9 *(c)*	10 *(a)*
11 *(c)*	12 *(d)*	13 *(b)*	14 *(c)*	15 *(a)*	16 *(a)*	17 *(d)*	18 *(c)*	19 *(a)*	20 *(a)*
21 *(11)*	22 *(0.80)*	23 *(959.73)*	24 *(0.12)*	25 *(270.02)*	26 *(2)*	27 *(34)*	28 *(6)*	29 *(1.20)*	30 *(1.73)*

See detailed solutions on page no. 310

Knockout 10

JEE MAIN

Chemistry

Instructions

- This question paper contains of 30 Questions of Chemistry, divided into two sections : **Section A** Objective Type Questions and **Section B** Numerical Value Questions.
- **Section A** contains 20 Objective questions and all Questions are compulsory (Marking Scheme : Correct + 4, Incorrect – 1).
- **Section B** contains 10 Numerical value questions out of which only 5 questions are to be attempted (Marking Scheme : Correct + 4, Incorrect 0).

Section A *Objective Type Questions*

1. Given, frequency of series limit of Lyman series is ν_1, frequency of first line of Lyman series is ν_2 and frequency of series limit of Balmer series is ν_3.

Find the correct relation.

(a) $\nu_3 = \frac{1}{2}(\nu_1 - \nu_3)$ (b) $\nu_1 - \nu_2 = \nu_3$

(c) $\nu_2 - \nu_1 = \nu_3$ (d) $\nu_1 + \nu_2 = \nu_3$

2. The incorrect statement about surface properties is

(a) adsorption is accompanied by decrease in enthalpy and a decrease in entropy of the system.

(b) cheese is an emulsion type of colloid in which liquid is dispersed phase and solid is dispersion medium.

(c) stability of lyophilic sols depends upon the charge and solvation of the colloidal particles.

(d) gases having higher critical temperature are easily adsorbed.

3. For the reaction, $CH_2{=}CH_2 \xrightarrow[\text{acid}]{\text{Hypochlorous}} M \xrightarrow{Q} \begin{array}{l} CH_2{-}OH \\ | \\ CH_2{-}OH \end{array}$

M and Q are

(a) CH_3CH_2OH and HCl

(b) CH_3CH_2Cl and *aq* NaOH

(c) $CH_2Cl - CH_2OH$ and *aq* $NaHCO_3$

(d) $CH_2 = CH_2$ and heat

4. For the reaction, $A + B \longrightarrow 2C + D$,

Which one is the incorrect statement?

(a) Rate of disappearance of A = rate of disappearance of B

(b) Rate of disappearance of A = rate of disappearance of D

(c) Rate of disappearance of B = 2 (rate of appearance of C)

(d) Rate of disappearance of $B = \frac{1}{2}$ (rate of appearance of C)

5. Consider the following reaction

1,4-dinitrobenzene $\xrightarrow[\Delta]{NH_4HS} A \xrightarrow[0°C-5°C]{NaNO_2 + HCl} B \xrightarrow[\Delta]{Cu_2(CN)_2 + HCN} C$

Now, excess of compound C is nitrated. The correct product will be

(a) 3, 4-dinitrocyanobenzene

(b) 2, 4-dinitrocyanobenzene

(c) 2, 4, 6-trinitrocyanobenzene

(d) mixture of (a), (b) and (c)

6. 2-butene is treated with reagent X to form *cis*-butane-2, 3-diol and separately with reagent Y to form *trans*-butane-2, 3-diol. Now reagents X and Y are respectively.

(a) $X: OsO_4 + NaHSO_3 + H_2O$ and $Y: HCO_3H$

(b) $X: HCO_3H$ and $Y: OsO_4 + NaHSO_3 + H_2O$

(c) X : Cold, dilute, alkaline $KMnO_4$ and Y : $(OsO_4 + NaHSO_3 + H_2O)$

(d) $X: C_6H_5CO_3H + H_2O$ and $Y: HCO_3H$

7. For which of the following metal extraction, all the given steps are used step by step?

Froth-floatation – roasting – bessemerisation – electrolytic refining

(a) Zn (b) Fe (c) Al (d) Cu

8. Correct order of xenon and fluorine bond length in xenon fluoride molecules is

(a) $XeF_2 > XeF_4 > XeF_6$ (b) $XeF_2 > XeF_6 > XeF_4$
(c) $XeF_6 > XeF_4 > XeF_2$ (d) $XeF_6 > XeF_2 > XeF_4$

9. Which of the following reaction does not produce an aromatic product?

(a) Cl, Cl $\xrightarrow{2SbCl_5}$ (b) Br $\xrightarrow{\text{AgNO}_3\text{ solution}}$

(c) $\xrightarrow{\text{NaOH solution}}$ (d) Br $\xrightarrow{\text{AgNO}_3\text{ solution}}$

10. The expression relating mole fraction of solute (X_2) and molarity (M) of the solutions is [d = density of the solution in gL^{-1}, M_{w_1} = Molar mass of solvent, M_{w_2} = Molar mass of solute]

(a) $\chi_2 = \dfrac{(M)(M_{w_1})}{M(M_{w_1} - M_{w_2}) + 1000d}$

(b) $\chi_2 = \dfrac{(M)(M_{w_1})}{M(M_{w_1} - M_{w_2}) - 1000d}$

(c) $\chi_2 = \dfrac{(M)(M_{w_1})}{M(M_{w_1} - M_{w_2}) - d}$

(d) $\chi_2 = \dfrac{(M)(M_{w_1})}{M(M_{w_1} - M_{w_2}) + d}$

11. $K_2Cr_2O_7$ is strongly heated with NaCl in concentrated H_2SO_4. A reddish yellow vapour is produced. That vapour is passed through NaOH solution to produce a compound X. The compound X is

(a) $K_3[CrCl_6]$ (b) CrO_5
(c) Na_2CrO_4 (d) Cr_2O_3

12. What is the percentage composition of a mixture of two enantiomers whose rotation is –10°?

[The specific rotation of pure enantiomer = – 20°]

(a) (–) form 25% and (+) form 75%
(b) (–) form 75% and (+) form 25%
(c) (–) form 35% and (+) form 65%
(d) (–) form 65% and (+) form 35%

13. Packing fraction of the element that crystallises in simple cubic arrangement is $\frac{\pi}{Q}$. The value of Q will be same as the atomic number of which of the following elements?

(a) Beryllium (b) Helium
(c) Lithium (d) Carbon

14. Which of the following polymers is correctly satisfying both the conditions addition polymerisation as well as copolymerisation?

(a) Nylon-6, 6 (b) Nylon-6
(c) Teflon (d) Buna-N-rubber

15. Which of the following will not react with sodium metal in liquid ammonia?

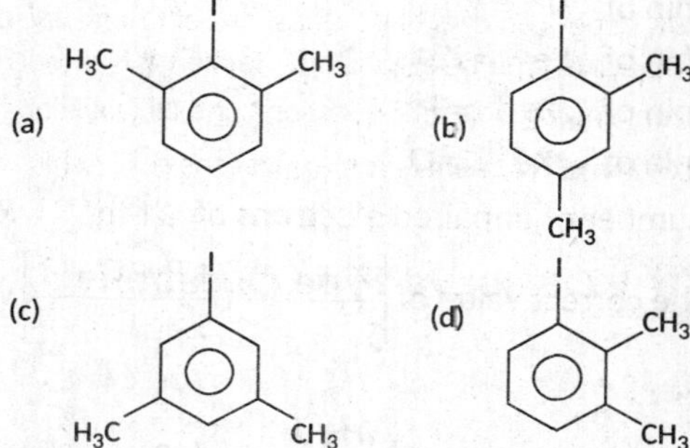

16. The pH of 0.02 M NH_4Cl (*aq*) [pK_b (NH_4OH) = 4.73] is equal to

(a) 3.48 (b) 4.48
(c) 5.48 (d) 7.48

17. The vapour density of PCl_5 is 104.25, but when heated to 230°C, its vapour density reduced to 62. The percentage dissociation of PCl_5 at this temperature will be

(a) 0.68% (b) 68%
(c) 6.8% (d) 64%

18. Excess of butan-1-ol is dehydrated with concentrated H_2SO_4. The correct product in E2 pathway will be

(a) but-1-ene only
(b) but-2-ene only
(c) but-1-ene major, but-2-ene minor
(d) but-2-ene major, but-1-ene minor

19. Proteins when heated with conc. HNO_3 give a yellow colour. This is

(a) Hoppe's test
(b) Fehling test
(c) Xanthoprotic test
(d) Benedict test

20. Ethanal is heated with $(C_6H_5)_3P{=}CH_2$ to form compound X. Compound X is treated with B_2H_6 and then H_2O_2, NaOH to form compound Y. Compound Y is treated with PCC in CH_2Cl_2 and forms compound Z. Compound Z will not take part in which of the following reactions?

(a) Aldol condensation with NaOH solution
(b) Claisen-Schmidt reaction with C_6H_5CHO + NaOEt
(c) Reaction with $H_2NCONHNH_2$
(d) Cannizzaro reaction with 50% NaOH solution

Section B *Numerical Value Questions*

21. Total spin of ${}_{30}Zn^{7+} = X$

Total spin of ${}_7N^+ = Y$

Total spin of ${}_4Be^+ = Z$

Total spin of ${}_{26}Fe^{2+} = P$

Total spin of ${}_{54}Xe^{2+} = Q$

Total number of unpaired electrons of ${}_{25}Mn^{2+} = R$

Now, the correct value of $\left[\dfrac{X+Y+Z+P+Q+R}{5}\right]$ will be ....

22. For an ideal gas, value of $\left[\dfrac{\partial^2 T}{\partial V^2}\right]_{p,n} = (13.41 - x)$. The value of x is ....

23. Bond order of $[N_2]^+ = X$

Bond order of $[O_2]^- = Y$

Bond order of $[He_2]^+ = Z$

Bond order of $[Be_2]^+ = P$

Now, the correct value of $\left[\dfrac{X+Y+Z+P}{9}\right]$ will be ....

24. Consider separate solutions of 0.500 M $C_2H_5OH(aq)$, 0.250 M KBr (aq), 0.125 M $Na_3PO_4(aq)$ and 0.1 M $Mg_3(PO_4)_2$ at 25°C.
Number of correct statement about these solutions, assuming all salts to be strong electrolytes is ....

(i) 0.125 M $Na_3PO_4(aq)$ has highest osmotic pressure.
(ii) 0.500 M $C_2H_5OH(aq)$ has highest osmotic pressure.
(iii) 0.100 M $Mg_3(PO_4)_2(aq)$ has highest osmotic pressure.
(iv) All solutions have same osmotic pressure.

25. Consider the following ions,
Sn^{4+}, Ca^{2+}, Al^{3+}, Sr^{2+}, Cr^{3+}, Co^{2+}, Mn^{2+}, Mg^{2+}, Bi^{3+}, Fe^{3+}, Ni^{2+}

Now, number of ions form precipitate with NH_4OH in presence of $NH_4Cl = X$

Number of ions form precipitate with H_2S in presence of HCl = Y

Number of ions form precipitate with H_2S in presence of $NH_4OH = Z$

The value of $[X+Y+Z]^{1/2}$ will be ....

26. Among the given statements, the number of wrong statement(s) about $H_3CCH_2CONH_2$ is ....

(a) It is stronger Lewis base than $H_3CCH_2CH_2NH_2$.
(b) It readily reacts with H_3CMgBr.
(c) It forms isocyanide after reacting with P_2O_5.
(d) It forms *n*-butanol after reacting with $NaNO_2$ + HCl at 0°C–5°C.
(e) It can form ammonia gas after boiling with NaOH.

27. Among the given statements, the correct statements about group 14 elements is/are ....

(a) Both PbI_4 and $PbBr_4$ salts do not exist.
(b) $(H_3C)_2SiCl_2$ can form both linear and cyclic silicones.
(c) CO_2 form white precipitate with $AgNO_3$ in ammoniacal solution.
(d) $PbCl_4$ is less covalent than $SnCl_4$.
(e) Al_4C_3 forms propyne after reacting with water.
(f) Dipole moment of carbon monoxide is lower than expected.

28. The number of molecules from the following will not show tautomerism is ....

$H_3CCOC(CH_3)_2COOEt$; $(H_3C)_3CNO$;

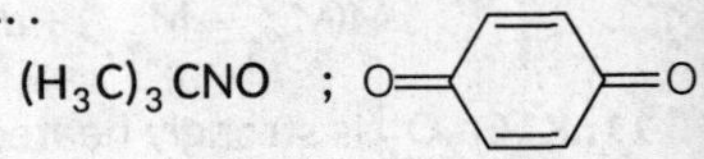

$C_6H_5CH_2CHO$; $(H_3C)_3CCHO$;

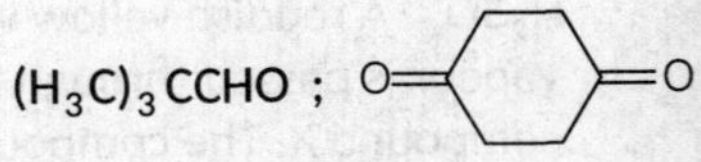

$H_3CCH_2CO_2Et$; 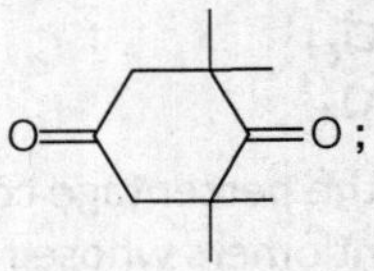 ;

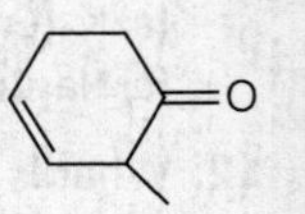

$H_3CCH{=}C(CH_3)CHO$

29. The number of molecules and ions, which will not have the effective atomic number (EAN) values equal to the atomic number of inert gases is ....

[Atomic number : Ni = 28, Fe = 26,. Mn = 25, Co = 27, Hg = 80, Pd = 46, Cr = 24, Ag = 47, Cu = 29]

$Ni(CO)_4$	$Fe(CO)_5$	$Mn_2(CO)_{10}$
$[Fe(CN)_6]^{4-}$	$[Fe(CN)_6]^{3-}$	$[Co(NH_3)_6]^{3+}$
$[Ag(NH_3)_2]^+$	$[Cr(C_2O_4)_3]^{3-}$	$[HgI_4]^{2-}$
$[Cu(NH_3)_4]^{2+}$		

30. The number of correct order is ....

I. $H_3CCH{=}CHCH_3 > (H_3C)_2C{=}CH_2 > H_3CCH = CH_2 > H_2C{=}CH_2$ [Boiling point]

II. $H_3CCH_2CH_2CH_3 > H_3CCH_2CH_3 > H_3CCH_3 > CH_4$ [Boiling point]

III. 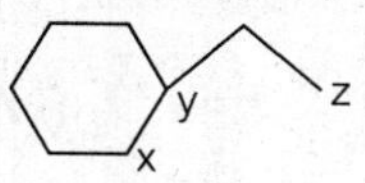 [cyclohexane ring with ethyl side chain; positions labelled x, y, z] $y > x > z$ [Reactivity order with Cl_2 in sunlight]

IV. $H_2C{=}CH{-}CH{=}CH_2 > H_2C{=}CH{-}CH_2{-}CH{=}CH_2 > H_2C{=}C{=}C{=}CH_2$ [Stability]

V. Butyne > Butene > Butane [Boiling point]

Answers

1 *(b)*	2 *(b)*	3 *(c)*	4 *(c)*	5 *(b)*	6 *(a)*	7 *(d)*	8 *(a)*	9 *(b)*	10 *(d)*
11 *(c)*	12 *(b)*	13 *(d)*	14 *(d)*	15 *(a)*	16 *(c)*	17 *(b)*	18 *(a)*	19 *(c)*	20 *(d)*
21 *(2.40)*	22 *(13.41)*	23 *(0.56)*	24 *(1)*	25 *(2.83)*	26 *(4)*	27 *(4)*	28 *(5)*	29 *(4)*	30 *(5)*

See detailed solutions on page no. 313

Knockout 11

JEE ADVANCED

Chemistry

PAPER -1

Section I

(MM : 24)

- This section contains **EIGHT** (08) questions.
- The answer to each question is a **NUMERICAL VALUE**.
- For each question, enter the correct numerical value of the answer using the mouse and the on-screen virtual numerical keypad in the place designated to enter the answer. If the numerical value has more than two decimal places, **truncate/round-off** the value to **TWO** decimal places.
- Answer to each question will be evaluated according to the following marking scheme:

Full Marks : +3 **ONLY** If the correct numerical value is entered;

Zero Marks : 0 In all other cases.

1. The fixation of photographic film involves dissolving unexposed AgBr in a hypo solution.

$$AgBr(s) + 2S_2O_3^{2-}(aq) \rightleftharpoons [Ag(S_2O_3)_2]^{3-}(aq) + Br^-(aq)$$

The molar solubility of AgBr in 0.1 M $Na_2S_2O_3$ is ....

Given :$K_{sp}(AgBr) = 5.4 \times 10^{-13}, K_f[Ag(S_2O_3)_2^{3-}] = 2.9 \times 10^{13}$

2. Two flasks of equal volume connected by a narrow tube of negligible volume are at 27°C and contain 0.6 mole of H_2 at 0.8 atm.

I (27°C) — II (117°C)

Flask-II is now immersed into a bath kept at 117°C, while the other remains at 27°C. The final pressure (in atm) of H_2 will be ....

3. The radial wave function for 1s orbital of a single-electron species is given by : $\psi_r = Ke^{-\sigma/2}$, where $\sigma = \dfrac{2Zr}{na_0}$ and K = constant [a_0 = radius of 1st Bohr orbit in H-atom = 52.9 pm, n = Principal quantum number].

The most probable distance (in pm) of 1s-electron in Be^{3+} ion is ....

4. 1.5 g of a hydrated organic compound (*A*), containing C, H and O, on mild heating rendered anhydrous and leave behind 1.07 g of solid residue (*B*). 0.675 g of *B* on complete combustion produces 0.66 g of CO_2 gas and 0.135 g of water vapour. If 1.12 g of *A* was burnt in excess of $O_2(g)$, then the weight (in g) of water molecules produced will be .... [Given : 1 mole of *B* on complete combustion produces 2 mole of CO_2]

5. The SO_2 present in air is mainly responsible for acid rain and can be estimated by MnO_4^- / H^+. A sample of air having SO_2 required 240 mL of 0.008 M $KMnO_4$. The number of millimoles of SO_2 in air will be ....

6. The work function (ϕ) of some metals is listed below. The number of metals which will show photoelectric effect when light of 300 nm wavelength falls on the metal is ....

Metal	Li	Na	K	Mg	Cu	Ag	Fe	Pt	W
ϕ (eV)	2.4	2.3	2.2	3.7	4.8	4.3	4.7	6.3	4.75

7. RNH_2 causes unsymmetrical cleavage of B_2H_6 as,

$$B_2H_6 + nRNH_2 \longrightarrow [BH_2(RNH_2)_n][BH_4]$$

The value of n is ....

8. A sample of charcoal weighing 0.6 g was brought into contact with a gas contained in a vessel of 100 mL capacity at 300 K. The pressure of the gas was found to fall from 70 torr to 40 torr. The volume (in mL) of the gas (reduced to STP) that is adsorbed per gram of the adsorbent under the condition of experiment is .... Consider the volume of charcoal as negligible.

Section II

(MM : 24)

- This section contains **SIX** (06) questions.
- Each question has **FOUR** options (a), (b), (c) and (d). **ONE OR MORE THAN ONE** of these four option(s) is/are the correct answer(s).
- For each question, choose the option(s) corresponding to (all) the correct answer(s).
- Answer to each question will be evaluated according to the following marking scheme:

Full Marks	:	+ 4 **ONLY** if (all) the correct option(s) is(are) chosen;
Partial Marks	:	+3 If all the four options are correct but **ONLY** three options are chosen;
Partial Marks	:	+2 If three or more options are correct but **ONLY** two options are chosen, both of which are correct.
Partial Marks	:	+1 If two or more options are correct but **ONLY** one option is chosen and it is a correct option.
Zero Marks	:	0 If none of the options is chosen (i.e. the question is unanswered);
Negative Marks	:	–2 In all other cases.

9. Correct reagent(s) to convert E into A is/are

$$A \xrightarrow[\text{(ii)Zn/H}_2\text{O}]{\text{(i)O}_3\text{/THF}} B \xrightarrow[\text{(ii)H}_2\text{O}]{\text{(i)Mg/Hg}} C \xrightarrow[\Delta]{\text{H}^{\oplus}} D \xrightarrow[\text{(ii)H}_2\text{O}]{\text{(i)LiAlH}_4} E$$

(a) Al_2O_3 (b) conc. H_2SO_4 (c) H_3PO_4 (d) ThO_2, Δ

10.

$$\xrightarrow{m-\text{CPBA}} A \xrightarrow{\text{H}_3\overset{18}{\text{O}}^{\oplus}} B \text{ (Major)}$$

$$A \xrightarrow[\text{H}_2\text{O}]{\overset{18}{\text{NaOH}}} C \text{ (Major)}$$

(a) A is [epoxide structure]

(b) B is [structure with CH_3, (18)OH, OH, H]

(c) B is [structure with CH_3, OH (18), OH, H]

(d) C is [structure with CH_3, OH, (18)OH]

11. Anthranilic acid can exist in the form of following structures

(I) COO^-, $\overset{+}{N}H_3$ (II) COO^-, NH_2 (III) $COOH$, $\overset{+}{N}H_3$

Which of the following statements is/are not correct regarding anthranilic acid structure?

(a) Structures I, II and III exist at pH = 7, pH < 7 and pH > 7 respectively.

(b) Structures II and III exist at pH > 7 and pH < 7 respectively.

(c) Structures I and II exist at pH > 7; structures I and III exist at pH < 7.

(d) All the structures exist in all the three mediums.

12. Which of the following statements is/are correct?

(a) The value of $C_{p,m} / C_{V,m}$ for a mixture of 1 mole of a monoatomic gas $\left(\gamma = \frac{5}{3}\right)$ and 1 mole of a diatomic gas $\left(\gamma = \frac{7}{5}\right)$ is 1.5.

(b) The work done by an ideal gas is expanding volume V_1 to volume V_2 is higher when the expansion is done isothermally as compared to that carried out adiabatically.

(c) The internal energy of an ideal gas does not change in the isothermal process.

(d) The fraction of heat utilised in increasing internal energy of a mono-atomic gas is 3/5, when the heat is supplied under constant pressure condition.

13. The first ionisation energy of magnesium is smaller as compared to that of elements X and Y, but higher than that of Z. The elements X, Y and Z, respectively are

(a) chlorine, lithium and sodium

(b) argon, lithium and sodium

(c) argon, chlorine and sodium

(d) neon, sodium and chlorine

14. 100 mL samples of two different acids X and Y are titrated with 0.1 M NaOH giving the following titration curve

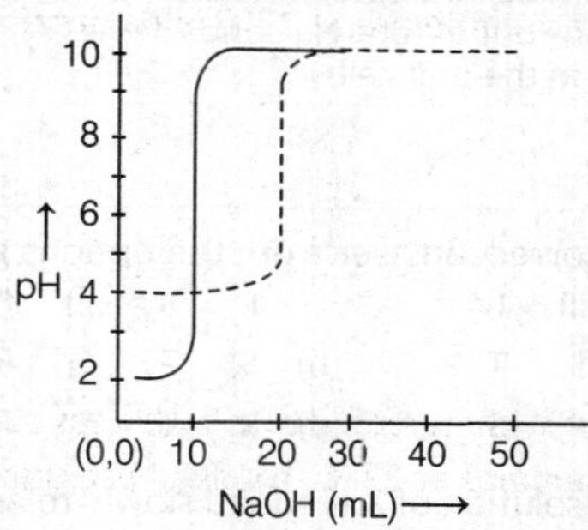

If both X and Y are monobasic acids, then the correct statement(s) is/are

(a) X has higher concentration than Y.

(b) X is a stronger acid.

(c) $[X] = 0.01$ M and $[Y] = 0.02$ M.

(d) salts of acid Y will have higher pH in aqueous solution, if their concentrations are same.

Section III (MM : 12)

- This section contains **FOUR (04)** Matching List Sets.
- Each set has **ONE** Multiple Choice Question.
- Each set has **TWO** lists: **List-I** and **List-II**.
- List-I has **FOUR** entries (I), (II), (III) and (IV) and **List-II** has **Five** entries (P), (Q), (R), (S) and (T).
- **FOUR** options are given in each Multiple Choice Question based on **List-I** and **List-II** and **ONLY ONE** of these four options satisfies the condition asked in the Multiple Choice Question.
- Answer to each question will be evaluated according to the following marking scheme

Full Marks : + 3 **ONLY** if the option corresponding to the correct combination is chosen;
Zero Marks : 0 If none of the options is chosen (i.e. the question is unanswered);
Negative Marks : –1 In all other cases.

15. Given, below is the unit of NaCl crystal

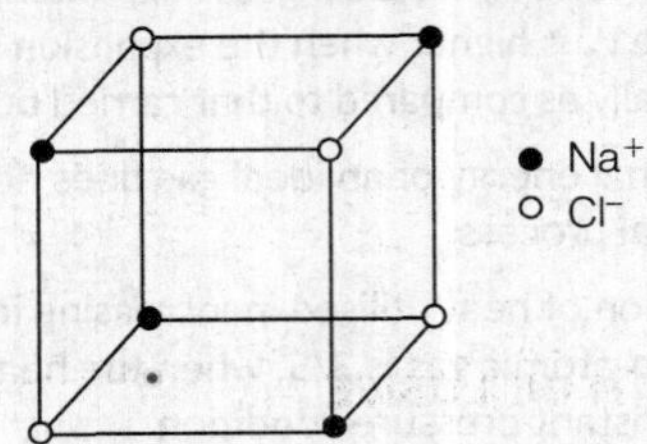

Match the question regarding the given crystal in List-I with their answer in List-II.

List-I	List-II
I. What fraction of Cl^- at each corner of the cube within the unit cell?	P. $\frac{1}{4}$
II. What fraction of a Cl^- appears in each face?	Q. $\frac{1}{2}$
III. What fraction of each Na^+ is within the unit cell?	R. $\frac{1}{8}$
IV. In the simple structure, fraction of Cl^- ions out of total Na^+ and Cl^- ions in the unit cell.	S. $\frac{2}{7}$
	T. $\frac{3}{2}$

Choose the correct answer from the options given below.

	I	II	III	IV		I	II	III	IV
(a)	P,	Q,	S,	T	(b)	S,	P,	Q,	R
(c)	R,	Q,	P,	S	(d)	R,	T,	S,	P

16. An aqueous solution of X is added slowly to an aqueous solution of Y as shown in List-I. The variation in conductivity of these reactions is given in List-II.

List-I	List-II
I. $\underset{X}{(C_2H_5)_3N} + \underset{Y}{CH_3COOH}$	P. Conductivity decreases and then increases.
II. $\underset{X}{KI(0.1 M)} + \underset{Y}{AgNO_3(0.01 M)}$	Q. Conductivity decreases and then does not change much.
III. $\underset{X}{CH_3COOH} + \underset{Y}{KOH}$	R. Conductivity remains constant.
IV. $\underset{X}{NaOH} + \underset{Y}{HI}$	S. Conductivity increases and then does not change much.
	T. Conductivity does not change much and then increases.

Match List-I with List-II and choose the correct option.

	I	II	III	IV		I	II	III	IV
(a)	S,	T,	Q,	P	(b)	S,	R,	Q,	P
(c)	Q,	T,	P,	S	(d)	P,	Q,	R,	S

17. Consider following chemical equation,

$$A_2 + B_2 \longrightarrow 2AB$$

Match the given mechanisms given in List-I with the corresponding rate laws of formation of AB given List-II and choose the correct option.

List-I	List-II
I. $A_2 \xrightarrow{k_1} 2A$ $A + B_2 \xrightarrow{k_2} AB + B$ $A + B \xrightarrow{k_3} AB$ $k_1 << k_2 \approx k_3$	P. $k\sqrt{k_1 k_2}\,[A_2]^{1/2}[B_2]^{1/2}$
II. $A_2 + B_2 \xrightarrow{k_1} A_2B_2$ $A_2B_2 \xrightarrow{k_2} 2AB$ $k_1 << k_2$	Q. $2k_1[B_2]$
III. $A_2 \rightleftharpoons 2A\ k_1$ $B_2 \rightleftharpoons 2B\ k_2$ $A + B \xrightarrow{k} AB$	R. $2k_1[A_2]$
IV. $A_2 \rightleftharpoons 2A\ k$ $B_2 \xrightarrow{k_1} 2B$ $A + B \xrightarrow{k_2} AB$ $k_1 << k_2$	S. $2k_1[A_2][B_2]$
	T. $k_1[A_2][B_2]$

Choose the correct answer from the options given below.

	I	II	III	IV		I	II	III	IV
(a)	P,	T,	S,	R	(b)	R,	S,	P,	Q
(c)	S,	T,	P,	Q	(d)	R,	S,	Q,	P

18. Match the compounds in List-I with the given properties in List-II and choose the correct option.

List-I	List-II
I. $CH\equiv C-CH_2=CH_2$	P. Compound with longest (C—H) bond
II. $CH_3-CH_2-CH_2-CH_3$	Q. Compound with shortest (C—H) bond
III. $CH_2=CH-CH=CH_2$	R. Compound which can show resonance
IV. $CH_3CH=CHCH_3$	S. Compound with allylic hydrogen
	T. Compound with longest (C—C) bond

Choose the correct answer from the options given below.

	I	II	III	IV
(a)	(Q, R),	(P),	(R, T),	(R, S)
(b)	(Q),	(P),	(R, T),	(S)
(c)	(Q, R),	(P, T),	(R),	(R, S)
(d)	(R),	(P, T),	(R),	(R, S, T)

PAPER -2

Section I

(MM : 24)

- This section contains **EIGHT** (08) questions.
- The answer to each question is a **SINGLE DIGIT INTEGER** ranging from **0 TO 9, BOTH INCLUSIVE**.
- For each question, enter the correct integer corresponding to the answer using the mouse and the on-screen virtual numeric keypad in the place designated to enter the answer.
- Answer to each question will be evaluated according to the following marking scheme:

Full Marks : + 3 If **ONLY** the correct integer is entered;
Zero Marks : 0 If the question is unanswered;
Negative Marks : −1 In all other cases.

1. The number of possible ester isomers for compound with molecular formula, $C_5H_{10}O_2$ are ....

2. Urea solution has a molarity 4 mol L^{-1} and molality 2.273 mol kg^{-1} in H_2O. Thus, density of the solution (in g mL^{-1}) is ....

3. In the redox reaction,

$$xNO_3^- + yAs_2S_3 + zH_2O \longrightarrow AsO_4^{3-} + SO_4^{2-} + H^+ + NO^+$$

What is the value of $\left(\frac{x}{2y}\right)$?

4. 1 mole of phenol reacts completely with ($x \times 68.57$) g of bromine in water to give a white precipitate. The value of x is .... [Br = 80]

5. (*Z*); but-2-ene $\xrightarrow[\text{reagent}]{\text{Baeyer's}}$ product(s)

Number of optically active product(s) obtained in the reaction is ....

6. If all carbonyl isomers of molecular mass = 86 u are separately treated with CH_3MgBr followed by acid hydrolysis, how many of them will give racemic mixture?

7. The number of step growth polymer(s) from the following given are ....

Buna-S, Protein, Cellulose, Terylene, Bakelite, Nylon-6, PVC, Polythene, Teflon, MF resin.

8. If $Br_2CH-CHBr_2$ is treated with excess of NaCN solution such that all bromides are substituted by nucleophiles. The number of different substitution products would be formed in principal which are chiral are ....

Section II (MM : 24)

- This section contains **SIX** (06) questions.
- Each question has **FOUR** options (a), (b), (c) and (d). **ONE OR MORE THAN ONE** of these four option(s) is/are the correct answer(s).
- For each question, choose the option(s) corresponding to (all) the correct answer(s).
- Answer to each question will be evaluated according to the following marking scheme:

Full Marks : + 4 **ONLY** if (all) the correct option(s) is(are) chosen;
Partial Marks : +3 If all the four options are correct but **ONLY** three options are chosen;
Partial Marks : +2 If three or more options are correct but **ONLY** two options are chosen, both of which are correct;
Partial Marks : +1 If two or more options are correct but **ONLY** one option is chosen and it is a correct option;
Zero Marks : 0 If unanswered;
Negative Marks : –2 In all other cases.

---

9. Select the incorrect statement(s)

(a) $\mu_{S+L} = \sqrt{4S(S+L) + L(L+1)}$; the orbital motion is not quenched in case of 3*d*-block elements.

(b) The magnetic moment of a divalent ion in aqueous solution is 3.87 BM, when *Z* of the element is 25.

(c) Magnetic moment, $\mu = \sqrt{n(n+2)}$ BM, where *n* is the number of unpaired electrons.

(d) The observed paramagnetism of *f*-block elements is due to both orbital motion of an electron and its spinning around its axis.

10. Select the correct statement(s) regarding the fluorides of xenon.

(a) All three fluorides are decomposed by water, XeF_2 slowly, whereas XeF_4 and XeF_6 rapidly.

(b) All three fluorides are powerful oxidising agents.

(c) XeF_4 and XeF_6 can act as fluoride ion acceptors as well as fluoride ion donors.

(d) All three fluorides are volatile and sublimable at 298 K.

11. An aqueous pink solution of Co(II) chloride changes to deep blue on addition of excess HCl. This is because

(a) $[Co(H_2O)_6]^{2+}$ is transferred into $[CoCl_6]^{4-}$

(b) $[Co(H_2O)_6]^{2+}$ is transferred into $[CoCl_4]^{2-}$

(c) tetrahedral complexes have smaller crystal field splitting than octahedral complexes

(d) tetrahedral complexes have larger crystal field splitting than octahedral complexes

12. Which of the following statements is/are incorrect regarding the compounds of group 14 elements?

(a) Maximum coordination number of carbon in commonly known compounds is 4, whereas that of silicon is 6

(b) The stability order of group 14 dihalides is $SiX_2 < GeX_2 < SnX_2 < PbX_2$.

(c) The order of boiling point of hydrides of group 14 elements is $CH_4 < SiH_4 < GeH_4 < SnH_4$.

(d) $MeSiCl_3$ on hydrolysis and subsequent condensation will produce $MeSi(OH)_3$.

13. A unit comprises of *P*, *Q* and *R* as,

(i) Atom (*P*) occupies all the corners of the lattice

(ii) Atom (*Q*) occupies all the edge centres and are also present at the alternate faces

(iii) Atoms (*R*) are present at face centres left from atoms (*Q*) and one at each body diagonal at a distance of $\frac{1}{4}^{th}$ of body diagonal from the corner.

If a 4-fold axis is passed from the given unit cell in such a way that all atoms touching the axis are removed, then the possible formula/formulae of the remaining compound will be

(a) PQ_3R_6 (b) $P_3Q_6R_7$
(c) PQR_2 (d) PQ_4R_5

14. 2 L 1 (M) solution of a complex salt, $\overset{III}{Cr}Cl_3 \cdot 6H_2O$ (molar mass = 266.5 g mol^{-1}) shows an osmotic pressure of 98.52 atm at 27°C. The solution is now treated with 1 L 6(M) $AgNO_3$. Now, which of the following statements will be correct?

(a) Mass of AgCl precipitated is 861 g.

(b) The clear solution will show an osmotic pressure = 98.5 atm.

(c) The clear solution will show an osmotic pressure = 65.6 atm.

(d) 2 moles of $[\overset{III}{Cr}(H_2O)_6](NO_3)_3$ will be present in the solution.

Section III

(MM : 12)

- This section contains **FOUR (04)** questions.
- Each question has **FOUR** options (a), (b), (c) and (d). **ONLY ONE** of these four options is the correct answer.
- For each questions, choose the option corresponding to the correct answer.
- Answer to each question will be evaluated according to the following marking scheme:

Full Marks : + 3 If **ONLY** the option is chosen;

Zero Marks : 0 If none of the options is chosen (i.e. the question is unanswered);

Negative Marks : –1 In all other cases.

15. Identify the correct product formed in the following reaction.

CH_3, CH_3, OH OH $\xrightarrow{\text{Conc. } H_2SO_4}$

(a) CH_3, O, CH_3 (b) CH_3, CH_3

(c) CH_3, CH_3, O (d) CH_3, CH_3, O

16. A red coloured metal oxide, *A* on treatment with conc. HNO_3 gives a compound *B*. *B* with HCl produces a chloride *C*, which is insoluble in cold water but soluble in hot water. *C* can also be formed by treating *A* with conc. HCl. *A*, *B* and *C* are respectively

(a) Fe_2O_3, FeO and $FeCl_3$ (b) ZnO, PbO_2 and $ZnCl_2$

(c) Mn_2O_3, MnO and $MnCl_2$ (d) Pb_3O_4, PbO_2 and $PbCl_2$

17. Select the correct statement among the following:

(a) Co(III) is stabilised in presence of weak field ligands, while Co(II) is stabilised in presence of strong field ligands.

(b) Four coordinated complexes of Pd(II) and Pt(II) are paramagnetic and square planar.

(c) $[Ni(CN)_4]^{2-}$ ion and $[Ni(CO)_4]$ are diamagnetic, tetrahedral and diamagnetic, square planar respectively.

(d) Ni^{2+} ion does not form inner-orbital octahedral complexes.

18. The major product formed in the following reaction and number of chiral centre present in the product are respectively.

CN, O $\xrightarrow[\Delta]{H_2/Pt}$

(a) NH_2, O ; 2 (b) CN, N–H ; 3

(c) N–H ; 4 (d) N–H ; 3

Answers

Paper-1

1 *(0.05)*	2 *(0.90)*	3 *(13.23)*	4 *(0.48)*	5 *(9.60)*	6 *(4.14)*	7 *(2)*	8 *(5.99)*	9 *(b,c)*	10 *(a,b,d)*
11 *(a,c,d)*	12 *(a,c)*	13 *(c)*	14 *(b,c,d)*	15 *(c)*	16 *(a)*	17 *(b)*	18 *(c)*		

Paper-2

1 *(9)*	2 *(2)*	3 *(7)*	4 *(7)*	5 *(0)*	6 *(3)*	7 *(6)*	8 *(6)*	9 *(a,b)*	10 *(a,b,c,d)*
11 *(b,c)*	12 *(d)*	13 *(a,d)*	14 *(a,c,d)*	15 *(d)*	16 *(d)*	17 *(d)*	18 *(c)*		

See detailed solutions on page no. 317

Knockout 12

JEE ADVANCED

Chemistry

PAPER-1

Section I

(MM : 24)

- This section contains **EIGHT** (08) questions.
- The answer to each question is a **NUMERICAL VALUE**.
- For each question, enter the correct numerical value of the answer using the mouse and the on-screen virtual numerical keypad in the place designated to enter the answer. If the numerical value has more than two decimal places, **truncate/round-off** the value to **TWO** decimal places.
- Answer to each question will be evaluated according to the following marking scheme:

Full Marks : +3 **ONLY** If the correct numerical value is entered;

Zero Marks : 0 In all other cases.

---

1. The pressure at the top of a tall building is 0.9659 atm compared to the earth's surface 1 atm at 298 K. If each floor has a height of 2.98 m. Then the floor number of a person living in the top floor is .... , [Assume temperature remains constant, Molar mass of air = 28.8 u, $\ln 0.9659 = -0.03469$, $g = 10\ ms^{-2}$]

2. For the reaction $A \underset{K_2\ (s^{-1})}{\overset{K_1\ (s^{-1})}{\rightleftharpoons}} B$ the graph is given, the time taken for 50% completion of equilibrium concentration of B is .... s. [Given : $K_1 = 4 \times 10^{-2}\ s^{-1}$, $\ln 2 = 0.7$]

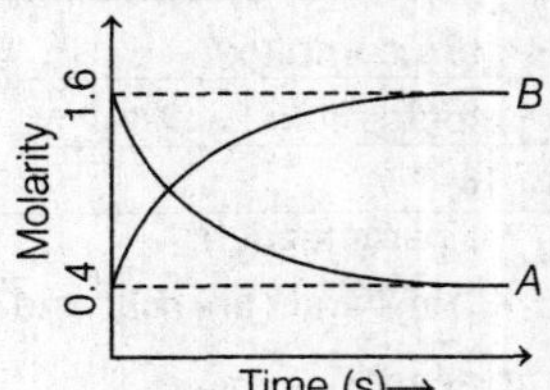

3. A 250 mL of a solution of 0.2 M Cr^{3+} is electrolysed with a current of 96.5 A. If the remaining solution contains 0.1 M Cr^{3+}, the duration of time in seconds for the process, if current efficiency is 75% will be ....

4. The molar volume of liquid benzene ($\rho = 0.877$ g/mL) increases by a factor 2794, as it vapourises at 25°C and that of liquid toluene ($\rho = 0.867$ g/mL) increases by a factor 7488 at 25°C. If a solution of benzene and toluene at 25°C has vapour pressure 46 mmHg, then the mole percentage of benzene in its vapour phase is ....

5. 2 moles of an ideal gas changed from its initial state (16 atm, 6L) to final state (4 atm, 15L) in such a way that this change can be represented by a straight line in p-V diagram. The maximum temperature attained by the gas during the above change is .... K. [Take $R = \frac{1}{12}\ L\ atm\ K^{-1} mol^{-1}$]

6. The pH of 0.05 M aqueous $NaHCO_3$ solution is .... [Given $K_1 = 4 \times 10^{-7}$, $K_2 = 5 \times 10^{-11}$, $\log 3.54 = 0.55$]

7. A sample of milk spoiled (curd) in 6 h at 27°C and the same milk needs 18 h to be spoiled in a refrigerator at 7°C. The activation energy for curdling of milk is .... kJ mol^{-1}

8. Reductive ozonolysis of a specimen of natural rubber yields 10^3 kg of ozonised organic product. From the experiment if gram-molar mass of natural rubber is $x \times 10^4$, the value of x is ....

Section II

(MM : 24)

- This section contains **SIX** (06) questions.
- Each question has **FOUR** options (a), (b), (c) and (d). **ONE OR MORE THAN ONE** of these four option(s) is/are the correct answer(s).
- For each question, choose the option(s) corresponding to (all) the correct answer(s).
- Answer to each question will be evaluated according to the following marking scheme:

Full Marks : + 4 **ONLY** if (all) the correct option(s) is(are) chosen;
Partial Marks : +3 If all the four options are correct but **ONLY** three options are chosen;
Partial Marks : +2 If three or more options are correct but **ONLY** two options are chosen, both of which are correct;
Partial Marks : +1 If two or more options are correct but **ONLY** one option is chosen and it is a correct option;
Zero Marks : 0 If none of the options is chosen (i.e. the question is unanswered);
Negative Marks : –2 In all other cases.

9. The electron of He^+ has Bohr energy, azimuthal quantum number and magnetic quantum number are 6.05 eV, 1, 0 respectively. Which of the following statement(s) is (are) correct?

(a) It may be $3p_z$ state.

(b) It's wave equation is

$$\psi = \left(\frac{\sqrt{2}}{81\sqrt{\pi}}\right)\left(\frac{2}{a_0}\right)^{3/2}(6-\sigma)\sigma\, e^{-\frac{\delta}{3}}\cos\theta$$

where, $\sigma = \frac{zr}{a_0}$.

(c) It may has *xy*-plane as nodal plane.

(d) It has one radial node at $r = 3a_0$.

10. Which of the following statement(s) is (are) incorrect regarding the defect in a solid?

(a) AgBr(*s*) crystals show both Schottky and Frenkel defects.

(b) Impurity defect by doping arsenic in silicon yields *p*-type semiconductor.

(c) Doping in crystals introduces dislocation defects.

(d) Metal deficient defect can occur with extra anion present in the interstitial voids.

11. Hydrolysis of a neutral solid (*P*) $C_{15}H_{15}ON$ gives C_7H_9N (*Q*) and $C_8H_8O_2$ (*R*). Strong oxidation of (*R*) gives a dicarboxylic acid $C_8H_6O_4$ (*S*), which can form only one monosubstituted product. The compound *S* is industrially used in manufacture of

(a) nylon-6, 6

(b) terylene

(c) glyptal

(d) dacron

12. Which of the following is(are) correct?

(a) [structure: heptane-2,6-dione chain] yields [structure: 2-methylcyclopent-1-enyl methyl ketone] as major product in aldol condensation with dil. NaOH.

(b) When (*R*) $H_3C-CH(D)-\overset{O}{\overset{||}{C}}-NH_2$ is treated with (Br_2 + KOH), the product formed is (*R*) $H_3C-CH(D)-NH_2$.

(c) [structure: 2,6-dimethylaniline, NH_2 with H_3C and CH_3] gives a foul smelling gas, when it is heated with ($CHCl_3$ + KOH).

(d) $H_3C-CH=CHCHO$ undergoes 1, 4-conjugative addition with a carbanion.

13. From the following statements choose the correct option(s).

(a) $Lu(OH)_3$ is least basic among hydroxides of lanthanoids.

(b) Zr^{4+} and Hf^{4+} possess almost same ionic radii.

(c) Ce^{4+} can act as oxidising agent.

(d) The correct increasing order of ionic radii is $Yb^{3+} < Pm^{3+} < Ce^{3+} < La^{3+}$.

14. Consider the following reactions where coordination number of Ni is 4 and choose the correct option(s).

(i) $NiCl_2$ + KCN(excess) $\longrightarrow$ *X* (cyano complex);

(ii) $NiCl_2$ + HCl $\longrightarrow$ *Y* (chloro complex)

(a) The IUPAC name of *X* is potassium tetracyanidonickelate (II)

(b) *X* is diamagnetic and *Y* is paramagnetic

(c) The hybridisation of Ni(II) in *X* and *Y* are dsp^2 and sp^3 respectively

(d) *X* and *Y* both are paramagnetic

Section III

(MM : 12)

- This section contains **FOUR (04)** Matching List Sets.
- Each set has **ONE** Multiple Choice Question.
- Each set has **TWO** lists: **List-I** and **List-II**.
- List-I has **FOUR** entries (I), (II), (III) and (IV) and **List-II** has **Five** entries (P), (Q), (R), (S) and (T).
- **FOUR** options are given in each Multiple Choice Question based on **List-I** and **List-II** and **ONLY ONE** of these four options satisfies the condition asked in the Multiple Choice Question.
- Answer to each question will be evaluated according to the following marking scheme

Full Marks : + 3 **ONLY** if the option corresponding to the correct combination is chosen;
Zero Marks : 0 If none of the options is chosen (i.e. the question is unanswered);
Negative Marks : −1 In all other cases.

15. When $\log(\Delta T_b)$ is plotted *vs* $\log(mi)$ (where, ΔT_b is elevation in boiling point, *m* the molality and *i* the van't Hoff factor) straight line cuts

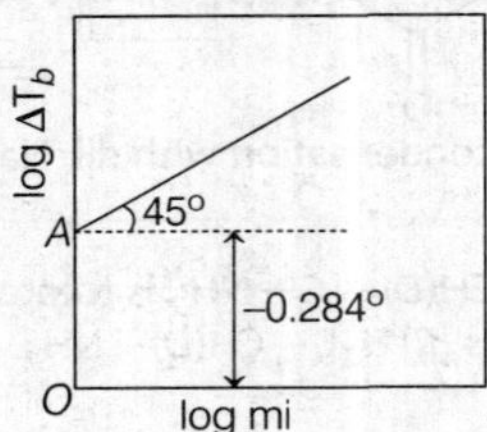

($\log \Delta T_b$) axis at – 0.284°. Match the different solutes in List-I with their corresponding values of $\log(\Delta T_b)$ in List-II and choose the correct option. (log 2 = 0.30, log 3 = 0.48, log = 0.70)

	List-I		List-II
I.	2 molal urea solution	P.	0.276
II.	2 molal NaCl solution 100% ionised	Q.	0.216
III.	2 molal K_2SO_4 solution 40% ionised	R.	0.016
IV.	2 molal $K_3Fe(CN)_6$ solution 20% ionised	S.	0.316
		T.	0.417

Choose the correct answer from the options given below.

	I	II	III	IV
(a)	P,	S,	Q,	R
(b)	Q,	T,	S,	P
(c)	R,	S,	P,	Q
(d)	R,	T,	Q,	S

16. Wavelength of the spectral line of the H-like species (atomic number Z) is given by $\frac{1}{\lambda} = \bar{R}_H Z^2 \left[\frac{1}{n_1^2} - \frac{1}{n_2^2}\right]$

	List-I		List-II
I.	Difference in wave number of the α-and β-lines in Balmer series of Be^{3+}.	P.	$\frac{2.89}{\bar{R}_H}$
II.	Maximum wave number of spectral line is Brackett series Li^{2+}.	Q.	$16\bar{R}_H$
III.	Difference in the maximum and minimum wavelength of spectral line of Paschen series in He^+.	R.	$\frac{9}{16}\bar{R}_H$
IV.	Rydberg constant in He^+.	S.	$\frac{3}{2}\bar{R}_H$
		T.	$\frac{7}{9}\bar{R}_H$

Match the given parameters in List-I with their related values in List-II and choose the correct option.

	I	II	III	IV
(a)	P,	R,	Q,	S
(b)	T,	R,	P,	Q
(c)	P,	Q,	R,	T
(d)	S,	R,	P,	Q

17. The desired compound, *X* can be prepared by reacting the major product of the reactions in List-I with one appropriate reagent in List-II, then choose the correct option.

Ph, Me, Ph, O, OH

(X)

List-I	List-II
I. $Ph(HO)C(Ph)-C(Me)(OH)Me$ + H_2SO_4	P. I_2, NaOH and acidification
II. $H_2N-C(Ph)(Ph)-CH(OH)Me$ + HNO_2	Q. $[Ag(NH_3)_2]OH$ and acidification
III. $Ph(HO)C(Me)-C(Ph)(OH)Me$ + H_2SO_4	R. HCHO, conc. NaOH and acidification
IV. $Br-C(Ph)(Ph)-CH(OH)Me$ + $AgNO_3$	S. HCN and hydrolysis
	T. H_2SO_4 and hydrolysis

Choose the correct answer from the options given below.

(a) I – P; II – Q; III – R; IV – S
(b) I – P; II – P; III – P; IV – P
(c) I – P; II – T; III – S; IV – R
(d) I – T; II – S; III – P; IV – Q

18. Match the reaction in List-I with the mechanism followed by them in List-II and choose the correct option.

List-I	List-II
I. (ditosylate, OTs OTs) + $HS^{\ominus}$ (OTs is $Cl-C_6H_4-SO_2O$)	P. S_N1
II. $C_6H_5-CH(H)-CH_2-OTs$ $\xrightarrow{t\text{-BuOK}}$	Q. Inversion
III. (diaryl tertiary alcohol with OH) $\xrightarrow{H_2SO_4}$	R. E1
IV. $C_6H_5-CH(CH_3)-CH_2I$ $\xrightarrow{Ag^+/H_2SO_4}$	S. E2
	T. Racemisation

Choose the correct answer from the options given below.

	I	II	III	IV		I	II	III	IV
(a)	P,	Q,	T,	S	(b)	Q,	S,	R,	P
(c)	S,	T,	R,	Q	(d)	Q,	P,	S,	R

PAPER-2

Section I

(MM : 24)

- This section contains **EIGHT** (08) questions.
- The answer to each question is a **SINGLE DIGIT INTEGER** ranging from **0 TO 9, BOTH INCLUSIVE**.
- For each question, enter the correct integer corresponding to the answer using the mouse and the on-screen virtual numeric keypad in the place designated to enter the answer.
- Answer to each question will be evaluated according to the following marking scheme :

Full Marks : +3 If **ONLY** the correct integer is entered;
Zero Marks : 0 If the question is unanswered;
Negative Marks : −1 In all other cases.

1. An alloy of Pb-Ag weighing 0.54 g was dissolved in dil. HNO_3 and the volume is made upto 50 mL. A silver electrode was dipped in the solution and the cell is set up as Pt(s), $H_2(g)|H^+(1M)||Ag^+(aq)|Ag(s)$. The e.m.f of the cell was 0.62 V, if $E^\circ_{cell} = 0.80$ V, the percentage of Ag in the alloy is .... [Take $\frac{2.303RT}{F} = 0.06$]

2. The number among the following amines can be prepared by Gabriel's phthalimide synthesis are ....

(i) $(CH_3)_2CHNH_2$ (ii) $H_3C-NH-CH_2CH_3$
(iii) $C_6H_5NH_2$ (iv) $C_6H_5-CH_2NH_2$
(v) cyclopentyl–NH_2 (vi) $O_2N-C_6H_3(NO_2)-NH_2$
(vii) $C_6H_5NHNH_2$

3. When cells of a skeletal vacuole of a frog were placed in a series of NaCl solutions at different concentration at 10°C, it was found that they remained unchanged in x% NaCl solution, shrank in more concentrated solution and swell in more dilute solutions. Water freezes from x% NaCl solution at −0.40°C. The osmotic pressure of the cytoplasmic cell at 10°C is .... atm. [Assume NaCl is 100% dissociated solution is very dilute, so that molarity and molality is same, $R = 0.0821$ L atm $K^{-1} mol^{-1}$ and $K_f = 1.86$ K mol^{-1} kg]

4. 10 mL of 1 mM surfactant solution forms a monolayer covering 0.24 m^2 on a polar substrate. If the polar substrate is approximately a cube, then diameter of the spherical surfactant molecule is .... Å.

5. 424 g of equimolar mixture of *o*-xylene and *p*-xylene undergoes reductive ozonolysis. The number of moles of methylglyoxal obtained is .... [Assume 100% conversion].

6. The absorption spectra of a complex shows a single band at 240 kJ/mol. If the wave length of *d-d* transition is very close to $x \times 10^{-7}$ m, then the value of x is ....

7. If the slope of Z vs p curve for a real gas is constant $\left[\text{Slope} = \frac{\pi}{492.6} \text{atm}^{-1}\right]$ at 300 K and at very high pressure, then the diameter of the gas molecule is .... Å.

8. The number of chemical species among the following that have atleast one $d\pi$-$p\pi$ bond in their structures are ....

$NO_3^-, SO_3, XeO_3, H_3PO_4, ClO_4^-, CO_3^{2-}, SO_4^{2-}, (CN)_2, XeOF_2$

Section II (MM : 24)

- This section contains **SIX** (06) questions.
- Each question has **FOUR** options (a), (b), (c) and (d). **ONE OR MORE THAN ONE** of these four option(s) is/are the correct answer(s).
- For each question, choose the option(s) corresponding to (all) the correct answer(s).
- Answer to each question will be evaluated according to the following marking scheme:

Full Marks : + 4 **ONLY** if (all) the correct option(s) is(are) chosen;
Partial Marks : +3 If all the four options are correct but **ONLY** three options are chosen;
Partial Marks : +2 If three or more options are correct but **ONLY** two options are chosen, both of which are correct;
Partial Marks : +1 If two or more options are correct but **ONLY** one option is chosen and it is a correct option;
Zero Marks : 0 If unanswered;
Negative Marks : −2 In all other cases.

---

9. Consider the complex $[Cu(NH_3)_4]^{2+}$, $[Co(NH_3)_6]^{2+}$ and $[Ni(CO)_4]$ and choose the correct statement(s).

(a) The complex $[Cu(NH_3)_4]^{2+}$ is square planar having dsp^2 mode of hybridisation with an unpaired electron in 4*p*-orbital.
(b) The complex $[Co(NH_3)_6]^{3+}$ is paramagnetic with d^2sp^3 hybridisation.
(c) The complex $[Ni(CO)_4]$ is tetrahedral and paramagnetic.
(d) Formation of volatile $Ni(CO)_4$ from impure Ni and CO(g) is a reversible reaction and at higher temperature volatile $Ni(CO)_4$ deposits pure nickel.

10. Potassium ferrocyanide is used for detection of which of the following ions?

(a) Zn^{2+} (b) Cu^{2+} (c) Fe^{3+} (d) Fe^{2+}

11. Choose the correct statement(s) from the following.

(a) All monosaccharides are reducing sugars whether it is an aldose or ketose.
(b) Hydrolysis of sucrose gives dextrorotatory glucose and laevorotatory fructose.
(c) Glucose and mannose give same osazone.
(d) Amylopectin is composed of α-D-glucose, $C_1 - C_4$ and $C_1 - C_6$ linkages.

12. The cyanide process for extraction of gold involves leaching out of gold from its ore with NaCN in presence of 'X' in water to form 'Y'. Subsequently 'Y' is treated with 'T' to obtain Au and Z. Choose the correct option(s).

(a) X is O_2 (b) T is Zn
(c) Z is $[Zn(CN)_4]^{2-}$ (d) Y is $[Au(CN)_4]^{3-}$

13. $CH_2 = CH - O - CH_2CH_3 \xrightarrow[\text{Hydrolysis}]{H_3O^+} P + Q$,

the constituents P and Q are separately isolated. Both P and Q can be identified by

(a) I_2 + NaOH (b) $NaHSO_3$
(c) Tollen's reagent (d) Brady's reagent

14. Which is(are) correct about Langmuir adsorption isotherm?

(a) It is based on kinetic theory of gases.
(b) Every adsorption site is equivalent and the ability of the particle to fit there is independent of whether or not nearby site is occupied.
(c) When the surface is fully covered, another layer starts adsorping on first layer.
(d) The rate of adsorption on a given area of surface is proportional to the pressure of the gas.

Section III

(MM : 12)

- This section contains **FOUR (04)** questions.
- Each question has **FOUR** options (a), (b), (c) and (d). **ONLY ONE** of these four options is the correct answer.
- For each questions, choose the option corresponding to the correct answer.
- Answer to each question will be evaluated according to the following marking scheme:

Full Marks : + 3 If **ONLY** the option is chosen;

Zero Marks : 0 If none of the options is chosen (i.e. the question is unanswered);

Negative Marks : –1 In all other cases.

15. At a certain temperature, 1st order rate constant k_1 is found to be smaller than 2nd order rate constant k_2. If energy of activation E_1 of 1st order reaction is greater than activation energy E_2 of 2nd order reaction, then with increase in temperature [Assume same pre-exponential factor same for both cases]

(a) k_1 will increase faster than k_2 but always remain less than k_2

(b) k_2 will increase faster than k_1

(c) k_1 will increase faster than k_2 and becomes equal to k_2

(d) k_1 will increase faster than k_2 and becomes greater than k_2

16. The height of hcp cell is h, then the height of its octahedral voids from base are

(a) $\frac{h}{2}, \frac{h}{2}$ (b) $\frac{h}{3}, \frac{2h}{3}$

(c) $\frac{h}{8}, \frac{7h}{8}$ (d) $\frac{h}{4}, \frac{3h}{4}$

17. Which one of the following is a reducing agent?

(a) $Mn(CO)_6$ (b) $Fe(CO)_5$

(c) $Mn_2(CO)_8$ (d) $Co_2(CO)_8$

18. Metal M exists in earth's crust in the form of two ores 'P' and 'Q'. Some reactions of these ores are given below. Identify P, Q, R and S

$P \xrightarrow{\text{Calcination}} R + CO_2\uparrow + H_2O$

$P \xrightarrow{KI + HCl} S + I_2 + KCl$

$Q \xrightarrow{\text{Roasting}} T + U$

$T \xrightarrow{K_2Cr_2O_7/H^+}$ Green colour

	P	Q	R	S
(a)	Malachite	Copper glance	CuO	Cu_2I_2
(b)	Magnesite	Argentite	Ag_2O	AgI
(c)	Dolomite	Copper pyrites	CuO	Cu_2I_2
(d)	Calamine	Zinc blende	ZnO	ZnI_2

Answers

Paper-1

1 (99)	2 (14)	3 (100)	4 (71.49)	5 (648)	6 (9.55)	7 (38.35)	8 (68)	9 (a,b,c,d)	10 (b,c,d)
11 (b,d)	12 (a,b,d)	13 (a,b,c,d)	14 (a,b,c)	15 (c)	16 (b)	17 (b)	18 (b)		

Paper-2

1 (1)	2 (5)	3 (5)	4 (2)	5 (6)	6 (5)	7 (5)	8 (6)	9 (a,b,d)	10 (a,b,c)
11 (a,b,c,d)	12 (a,b,c)	13 (a)	14 (a,b,d)	15 (a)	16 (d)	17 (a)	18 (a)		

See detailed solutions on page no. 322

Knockout 13

JEE ADVANCED

Chemistry

PAPER-1

Section I

(MM : 24)

- This section contains **EIGHT** (08) questions.
- The answer to each question is a **NUMERICAL VALUE**.
- For each question, enter the correct numerical value of the answer using the mouse and the on-screen virtual numerical keypad in the place designated to enter the answer. If the numerical value has more than two decimal places, **truncate/round-off** the value to **TWO** decimal places.
- Answer to each question will be evaluated according to the following marking scheme:

Full Marks : +3 **ONLY** If the correct numerical value is entered;

Zero Marks : 0 In all other cases.

1. The crystal *AB* (rock salt type) has molar mass 6.023 *Y* amu, where *Y* is an arbitary number. If the minimum distance between cation and anion is $\frac{Y^{(1/3)}}{(5)}$ nm, then theoritical density of the crystal is .... kg/m^3.

2. Salicylic acid is brominated with just sufficient bromine generated from standard bromate-bromide mixture. If white precipitate of tribromoderivative weight 33.1 g, then the mass of bromate-bromide mixture taken in gram is .... (Assume 100% conversion, Br = 80, K = 39)

3. 4.3 g of a hydrocarbon C_nH_{2n+2} is burnt completely and evolved CO_2 were absorbed in aqueous NaOH solution.
If 300 mL of 2N NaOH is needed for complete absorption, then molar mass of the hydrocarbon is .... g/mol.

4. For one mole of a van der Waals' gas when $b = 0$ and $T = 300$ K, the pV vs $\frac{1}{V}$ plot is shown below. The value of the van der Waals' constant '*a*' in atm $L^2 mol^{-2}$ is ....

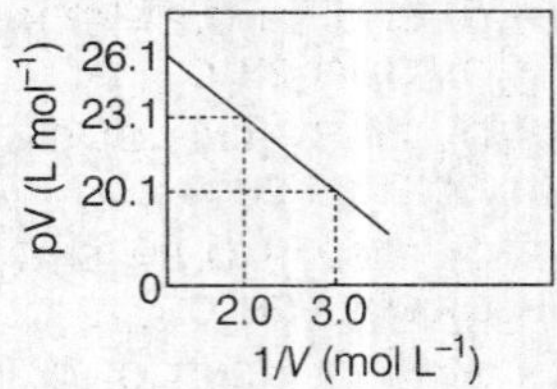

5. *x* kJ of enthalpy is required to prepare 0.01 mole of (Cl^+Cl^-) constituents of a plasma.

Given, $Cl(g) \longrightarrow Cl(g) + e^- \quad \Delta H° = 1257.5 \text{ kJ mol}^{-1}$

$Cl(g) + e^- \longrightarrow Cl^-(g), \quad \Delta H° = 359.8 \text{ kJ mol}^{-1}$

The value of *x* will be ....

6. If $K_a(HA) = K_b(BOH)$ at 298 K, and pH of 10^{-4} M BOH is 8.0, then pH of 10^{-2} M HA will be ....

7. Due to thermal pollution in air, solubility of O_2 in water is decreased and correspondingly there is rise of temperature.
Henry's law constant of $O_2(g)$ in water to 3.30×10^7 torr at 298 K and 3.52×10^7 torr at 303 K, percentage decrease due to rise in temperature by 5° at 0.20 atm will be ....

8. One of the isomers of $C_6H_4Br_2$ has zero dipole moment. This isomer on nitration with conc. HNO_3 / H_2SO_4 forms *x* type(s) of mononitro derivative with 100% yield.
Thus, *x* is ....

Section II

(MM : 24)

- This section contains **SIX** (06) questions.
- Each question has **FOUR** options (a), (b), (c) and (d). **ONE OR MORE THAN ONE** of these four option(s) is/are the correct answer(s).
- For each question, choose the option(s) corresponding to (all) the correct answer(s).
- Answer to each question will be evaluated according to the following marking scheme:

Full Marks : + 4 **ONLY** if (all) the correct option(s) is(are) chosen;
Partial Marks : +3 If all the four options are correct but **ONLY** three options are chosen;
Partial Marks : +2 If three or more options are correct but **ONLY** two options are chosen, both of which are correct.
Partial Marks : +1 If two or more options are correct but **ONLY** one option is chosen and it is a correct option.
Zero Marks : 0 If none of the options is chosen (i.e. the question is unanswered);
Negative Marks : –2 In all other cases.

9. **Consider the following process and choose the correct answer(s) from the options given below [Given, log (2.5126) = 0.40013]**

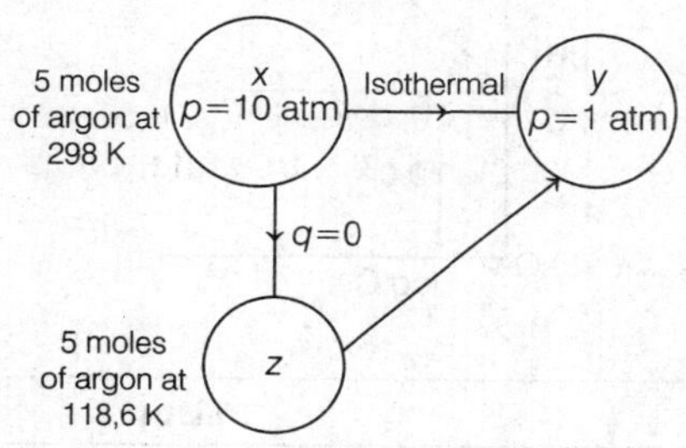

(a) $\Delta S_{x \to y} = 95.74 \text{ JK}^{-1}$

(b) $\Delta S_{x \to z} = 0$

(c) $\Delta S_{x \to y} = \Delta S_{x \to z} + \Delta S_{z \to y} = 95.76 \text{ JK}^{-1}$

(d) $\Delta S_{x \to z \to y} = 0$

10. **$NiCl_2[P(C_2H_5)_2(C_6H_5)]_2$ exhibits temperature dependent magnetic behaviour (paramagnetic/diamagnetic). The coordination geometries of Ni^{2+} in the paramagnetic and diamagnetic states respectively are**

(a) tetrahedral and tetrahedral

(b) square planar and square planar

(c) tetrahedral and square planar

(d) square planar and tetrahedral

11. **Which of the following statement(s) is (are) correct?**

(a) The degree of hydration decreases on moving down the group from Li^+ to Cs^+ in group 1.

(b) Li_2O_2 is prepared by adding hydrogen peroxide and alcohol to a concentrated solution of lithium hydroxide.

(c) Lattice energy of ionic solids having the same anion decreases with increase in the size of the cation.

(d) Lithium nitrate evolves nitrogen monoxide and oxygen on heating.

12. **In the following reaction sequence, the possible structure(s) of *B* can be**

[Reaction: 2-bromobutane $\xrightarrow[Et_2O]{Mg}$ *A*, then *A* + epoxide (with CH_3) $\xrightarrow[H_3O^+]{\text{(i) } Et_2O}$ *B*]

(a) [structure with OH, CH_3] (b) [structure with OH, CH_3] (c) [structure with O, CH_3, O] (d) [structure with OH, OH]

13. **Among the following, which reaction will give N-ethylcyclopentylamine as major product?**

(a) Cyclopentanone + $CH_3CH_2NH_2$ $\xrightarrow{H_2/Pt}$

(b) Cyclopentylamine ($-NH_2$) + CH_3CHO $\xrightarrow{H_2/Pt}$

(c) Cyclopentyl$-NH_2$ $\xrightarrow[\text{Pyridine}]{CH_3COCl}$ $\xrightarrow[\text{(ii) } H_2O]{\text{(i) } LiAlH_4\text{, diethyl ether}}$

(d) Cyclopentyl$-COCl$ $\xrightarrow[\text{Pyridine}]{CH_3CH_2NH_2}$ $\xrightarrow[\text{(ii) } H_2O]{\text{(i) } LiAlH_4\text{, diethyl ether}}$

14. ***A, B* and *C* are three complexes of chromium (III) with empirical formula $H_{12}O_6Cl_3Cr$. All the three complexes have water and chloride ion as ligands. Complex *A* does not react with concentrated H_2SO_4 whereas, complexes *B* and *C* lose 6.75% and 13.5% of their original mass respectively on treatment with concentrated H_2SO_4. The compounds *A, B* and *C* respectively are**

(a) $A = [Cr(H_2O)_5Cl]Cl_2 \cdot H_2O, B = [Cr(H_2O)_6]Cl_3,$ $C = [Cr(H_2O)_4Cl_2]Cl \cdot 2H_2O$

(b) $A = [Cr(H_2O)_6]Cl_3, B = [Cr(H_2O)_5Cl]Cl_2 \cdot H_2O,$ $C = [Cr(H_2O)_4Cl_2]Cl \cdot 2H_2O$

(c) $A = [Cr(H_2O)_5Cl]Cl_2 \cdot H_2O, B = [Cr(H_2O)_6]Cl_3,$ $C = [Cr(H_2O)_4Cl_2]Cl \cdot 2H_2O$

(d) $A = [Cr(H_2O)_6]Cl_3, B = [Cr(H_2O)_4Cl_2]Cl \cdot 2H_2O,$ $C = [Cr(H_2O)_5Cl]Cl_2 \cdot H_2O$

Section III

(MM : 12)

- This section contains **FOUR (04)** Matching List Sets.
- Each set has **ONE** Multiple Choice Question.
- Each set has **TWO** lists: **List-I** and **List-II**.
- List-I has **FOUR** entries (I), (II), (III) and (IV) and **List-II** has **Five** entries (P), (Q), (R), (S) and (T).
- **FOUR** options are given in each Multiple Choice Question based on **List-I** and **List-II** and **ONLY ONE** of these four options satisfies the condition asked in the Multiple Choice Question.
- Answer to each question will be evaluated according to the following marking scheme

Full Marks : + 3 **ONLY** if the option corresponding to the correct combination is chosen;

Zero Marks : 0 If none of the options is chosen (i.e. the question is unanswered);

Negative Marks : −1 In all other cases.

15. **Thermodynamic equilibrium constant, K is related to temperature $T(K)$ by equation**

$$\log_{10} K = -\frac{2303(K)}{T} + 4.06$$

for, $MnO_4^- + 8H^+ + 5Fe^{2+} \longrightarrow Mn^{2+} + 5Fe^{3+} + 4H_2O$

Match the thermodynamic parameters given in List-I with respective values given in List-II and choose the correct option.

List-I	List-II
I. $\Delta S°$ (in kJ mol^{-1}K^{-1})	P. 20.7
II. $\Delta H°$ (in kJ mol^{-1})	Q. 0.78
III. $\Delta G°$ (in kJ mol^{-1} at 300 K)	R. 44.1
IV. Temperature coefficient of the emf of a cell (JK^{-1})	S. 15.9
	T. 1.62×10^{-4}

	I	II	III	IV
(a)	P,	R,	Q,	T
(b)	R,	S,	Q,	P
(c)	Q,	R,	P,	T
(d)	P,	Q,	S,	R

16. For the reaction, $Br_2(g) \longrightarrow 2Br(g)$

$K_C = 38.4$ at 2400 K $\quad K_C = 84.7$ at 2600 K

Match the thermodynamic parameter in List-I with their values in List-II and choose the correct option.

List-I	List-II
I. $\Delta_r H°$ in the given temperature range (in kJ)	P. 58.0
II. K_C at 2500 K	Q. 116.0
III. $-\Delta_r G°$ at 2500 K (in kJ)	R. 205.0
IV. $-\Delta_r S°$ at 2500 K (in JK^{-1})	S. 84.4
	T. 42.8

	I	II	III	IV
(a)	P	Q	T	R
(b)	R	S	P	Q
(c)	R	P	S	Q
(d)	S	T	Q	P

17. **For a salt of weak acid (HA) and strong base (MOH) variation of pH with $\log C$ (C is molar concentration) is given**

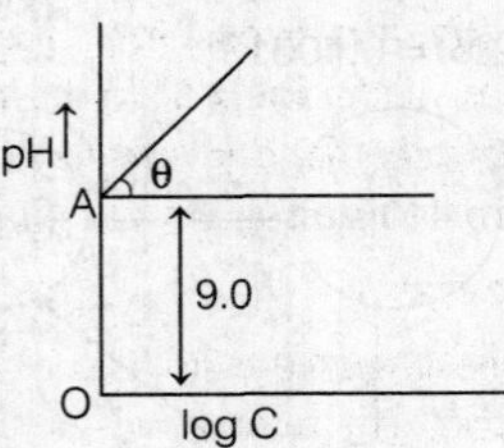

List-I	List-II
I. pK_a of the weak acid	P. 8.0
II. pH of 0.01 M salt	Q. 10.0
III. pH of 0.01 M HA	R. 4.0
IV. Percent ionisation of the 0.01 M weak acid	S. 3.0
	T. 7.0

Match the parameter in List-I with their values in List-II and choose the correct option.

	I	II	III	IV
(a)	R	Q	P	S
(b)	S	T	Q	P
(c)	R	P	S	Q
(d)	P	Q	S	T

18. **Match the following reactions given in List-I with the corresponding products in List-II and choose the correct option**

List-I	List-II
I. $[CoF_3(H_2O)_3]$	P. Diamagnetic, low spin complex
II. $[Cr(C_2O_4)_3]^{3-}$	Q. Paramagnetic, outer orbital complex
III. $[AuCl_4]^-$	R. Paramagnetic, inner orbital complex
IV. $[Fe(CN)_6]^{3-}$	S. Diamagnetic, high spin complex
	T. Paramagnetic and low spin complex

	I	II	III	IV
(a)	R	Q	P	S
(b)	P	T	R	S
(c)	P	R	Q	S
(d)	Q	R	P	T

PAPER-2

Section I

(MM : 24)

- This section contains **EIGHT** (08) questions.
- The answer to each question is a **SINGLE DIGIT INTEGER** ranging from **0 TO 9, BOTH INCLUSIVE.**
- For each question, enter the correct integer corresponding to the answer using the mouse and the on-screen virtual numeric keypad in the place designated to enter the answer.
- Answer to each question will be evaluated according to the following marking scheme:

Full Marks : + 3 If **ONLY** the correct integer is entered;
Zero Marks : 0 If the question is unanswered;
Negative Marks : −1 In all other cases.

1. The order of the following reaction,
$H_2O_2(aq) + 3I^-(aq) + 2H^+(aq) \longrightarrow I_3^-(aq) + 2H_2O(l)$ is ....

2. In a crystalline solid, atoms of A form fcc packing and atoms of B occupy all octahedral voids. When all the atoms along one body diagonal are removed, the simplest formula of the crystalline solid is found A_xB_y the sum of x and y will be ....

3. A monoelectronic species has ionisation energy 11180 kJ mol^{-1} the total number of protons present in the nucleus are ....

4. 'A' when heated forms a yellow solid 'B' which is an amphoteric oxide. B when heated in air forms a red coloured compound C. C when dissolved in concentrated HNO_3 gives a brown residue D. Oxidation state of the metal present in the compound D is ....

5. $Fe(H_2O_6)^{2+}$ appears colourless in dilute solution and it is a high spin complex. The number of unpaired electrons in $[Fe(H_2O_6)]^{2+}$ ion is ....

6. A radiation of wavelength λ illuminates a metal and ejects photoelectron of maximum kinetic energy of 1 eV. Another radiation of wavelength $\frac{\lambda}{3}$, ejects photoelectrons of maximum kinetic energy of 24 eV. The work function of metal (in eV) will be ....

7. The number of β-particles emission occurs in $(4n + 2)$ natural decay series are ....

8. $H_3C-CH_2-\underset{\displaystyle |}{\overset{CH_3}{CH}}-CH_2-CH_3 \xrightarrow[\text{(monochlorination)}]{Cl_2,\, h\nu} P$

The total number of isomeric products (P) formed is/are ....

Section II

(MM : 24)

- This section contains **SIX** (06) questions.
- Each question has **FOUR** options (a), (b), (c) and (d). **ONE OR MORE THAN ONE** of these four option(s) is/are the correct answer(s).
- For each question, choose the option(s) corresponding to (all) the correct answer(s).
- Answer to each question will be evaluated according to the following marking scheme:

Full Marks : + 4 **ONLY** if (all) the correct option(s) is(are) chosen;
Partial Marks : +3 If all the four options are correct but **ONLY** three options are chosen;
Partial Marks : +2 If three or more options are correct but **ONLY** two options are chosen, both of which are correct;
Partial Marks : +1 If two or more options are correct but **ONLY** one option is chosen and it is a correct option;
Zero Marks : 0 If unanswered;
Negative Marks : −2 In all other cases.

9. A metal salt on heating with a mixture of KCl and conc. H_2SO_4 yields an orange red vapour? The vapours on passing through an aqueous solution of KOH gives a yellow solution of compound *K*. Passing SO_2 gas through acidified solution of *K* leads to green colouration of the solution due to the formation of *M*. The compound M can be

(a) K_2CrO_4 (b) $Cr_2(SO_4)_3$ (c) $K_2Cr_2O_7$ (d) K_3CrO_8

10. Which of the following statements is (are) correct regarding the variation in the ionisation energies?

(a) In general, first ionisation energy < second ionisation energy < third ionisation energy.

(b) The noble gases He, Ne, Ar, Kr, Xe and Rn have the lowest ionisation energies in their respective periods.

(c) The group 1 metals Li, Na, K and Rb have the lowest ionisation energies in their respecitive periods.

(d) There is a general trend in increasing ionisation energy within a horizontal period.

11. Based on the compounds of group 15 elements, the correct statements is (are)

(a) $Al(CH_3)_3$ has three-centre two-electron bonds in its dimeric form.

(b) The Lewis acidity of BCl_3 is greater than that of $AlCl_3$.

(c) $AlCl_3$ has the three-centre two-electron bonds in its dimeric structure.

(d) BH_3 has the three-centre two-electron bonds in its dimeric structure.

12. In the following reaction sequence, *X* could be

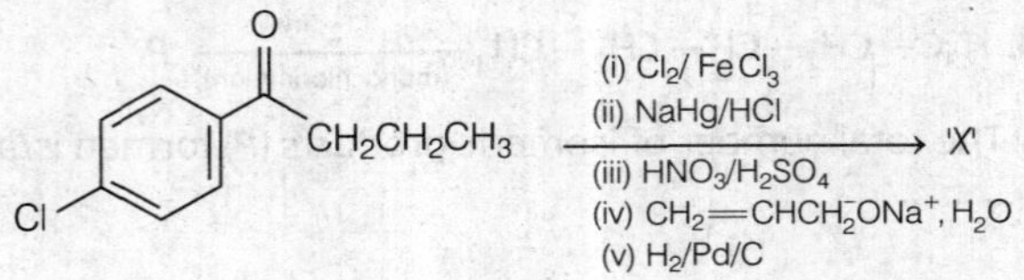

(4-chlorophenyl)–CO–$CH_2CH_2CH_3$ $\xrightarrow[\text{(iii) } HNO_3/H_2SO_4 \text{ (iv) } CH_2{=}CHCH_2ONa^+, H_2O \text{ (v) } H_2/Pd/C]{\text{(i) } Cl_2/FeCl_3 \text{ (ii) } NaHg/HCl}$ 'X'

(a) benzene ring with NO_2, butyl chain, Cl, $O(CH_2)_3CH_3$

(b) benzene ring with NO_2, butyl chain, Cl, $O(CH_2)_2CH_3$

(c) benzene ring with NO_2, butyl chain, $CH_3(CH_2)_2O$, Cl

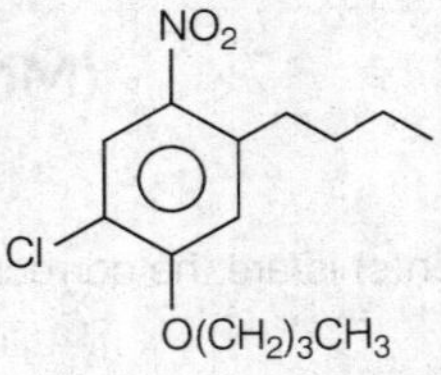

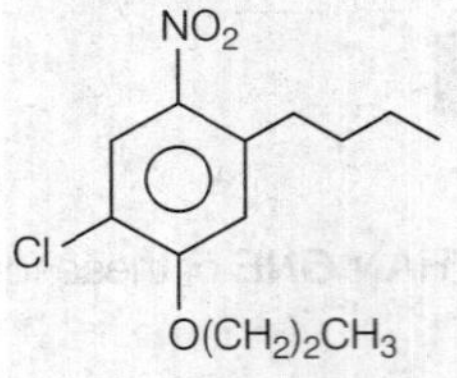

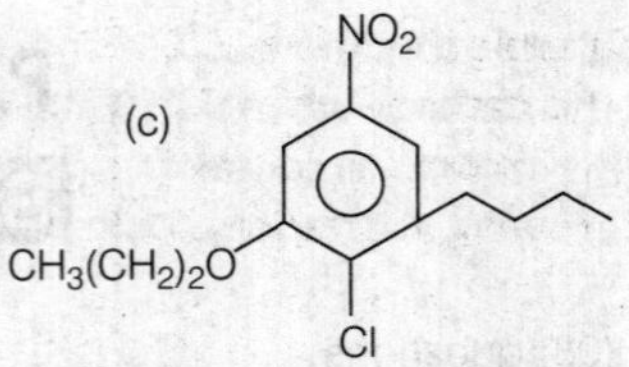

(d) benzene ring with NO_2, butyl chain, $O(CH_2)_2CH_3$, Cl

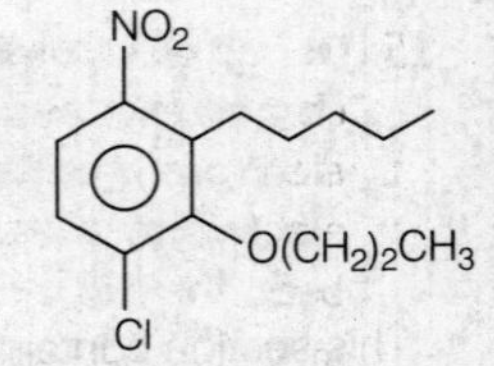

13. The reaction(s) leading to the formation of 3-hydroxypentanal is (are)

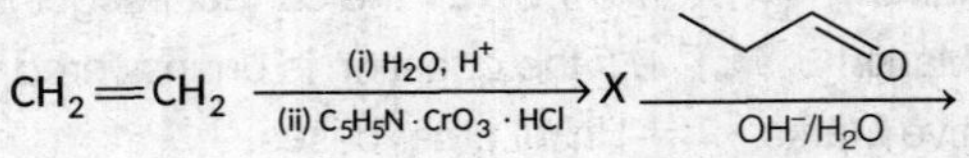

(a) $CH_2=CH_2 \xrightarrow{\text{(i) } Br_2 \text{ (ii) } KCN \text{ (iii) } H_3O^+}$

(b) $CH_2=CH_2 \xrightarrow[\text{(ii) } C_5H_5N\cdot CrO_3\cdot HCl]{\text{(i) } H_2O, H^+} X \xrightarrow[OH^-/H_2O]{\text{propanal}}$

(c) propenal + propanal $\xrightarrow{\text{(i) } OH^-/H_2O}$

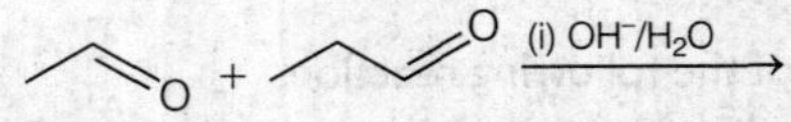

(d) (i) $CH_2=CH_2 \xrightarrow[\text{2. KOH, } N^+R_4Cl^-\text{, hexane 2,6-diol 3. } NaNH_2, NH_3]{\text{1. } Br_2, CCl_4} X$

(ii) X + propanal $\xrightarrow[\text{2. } NH_4Cl, H_2O]{\text{1. } NH_3\text{, ether}} \xrightarrow[\text{2.NaOH 3.pH7-8,} H_2O_2]{\text{1.Sia}_2\text{, BH,THF}}$

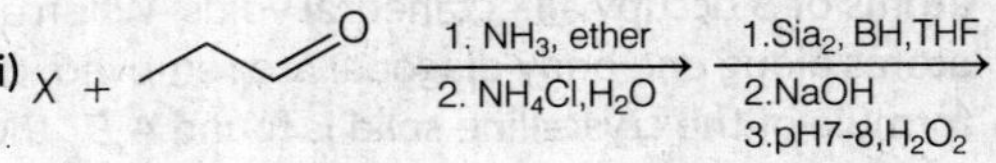

14. A mixture of $NaHCO_3$ and Na_2CO_3 required *a* mL of a HCl solution to reach the phenolphthalein end point and *b* mL of same HCl is required to reach the methyl orange point. Which of the following statements is (are) correct?

(a) Volume of HCl required for complete neutralisation of Na_2CO_3 is 2*a* mL.

(b) Volume of HCl required for complete neutralisation of $NaHCO_3$ is $(b - a)$ mL.

(c) If methyl orange is added at phenolphthalein end point, volume of HCl required to reach the end point would be $(b - a)$ mL.

(d) If the mixture is titrated against NaOH of same strength as that of HCl, $(b - 2a)$ mL of solution would be required.

Section III (MM : 12)

- This section contains **FOUR (04)** questions.
- Each question has **FOUR** options (a), (b), (c) and (d). **ONLY ONE** of these four options is the correct answer.
- For each questions, choose the option corresponding to the correct answer.
- Answer to each question will be evaluated according to the following marking scheme:

Full Marks : + 3 If **ONLY** the option is chosen;

Zero Marks : 0 If none of the options is chosen (i.e. the question is unanswered);

Negative Marks : –1 In all other cases.

15. During electrolysis under suitable conditions, 0.015 mol of chromium is deposited on the cathode when 0.090 mol of electrons is passed through a chromium containing electrolyte. Which of the following substances could have been the electrolyte?

(a) $CrCl_2$ (b) $Na_2Cr_2O_7$ (c) CrF_5 (d) $CrCl_3$

16. Platinum (IV) chloride combines with ammonia to form compounds in which the coordination number of platinum is 6. A formula unit of one of the compounds contains a cation and only two chloride ions. What is the formula of this compound?

(a) $Pt(NH_3)_6Cl_4$

(b) $Pt(NH_3)_5Cl_4$

(c) $Pt(NH_3)_4Cl_4$

(d) $Pt(NH_3)_3Cl_4$

17. Consider the following conjugated diketo compounds.

(I) (II) (III)

Which of the following is the correct decreasing order of $E°$ values ?

(a) I > II > III (b) III > II > I

(c) I > III > II (d) II > I > III

18. Consider the following reaction,

$\xrightarrow[CH_3OH]{H^+}$ Product

The most suitable product is

(a) (b)

(c) (d)

Answers

Paper-1

1 *(625)*	2 *(76.20)*	3 *(86)*	4 *(3)*	5 *(8.97)*	6 *(5)*	7 *(6.25)*	8 *(0)*	9 *(a, b, c)*	10 *(c)*
11 *(a,b,c)*	12 *(a,b)*	13 *(a,b,c)*	14 *(b)*	15 *(c)*	16 *(c)*	17 *(c)*	18 *(d)*		

Paper-2

1 *(2)*	2 *(9)*	3 *(3)*	4 *(4)*	5 *(4)*	6 *(9)*	7 *(6)*	8 *(8)*	9 *(b)*	10 *(a,c,d)*
11 *(a,b,d)*	12 *(b)*	13 *(b,c,d)*	14 *(a,c,d)*	15 *(b)*	16 *(c)*	17 *(d)*	18 *(a)*		

See detailed solutions on page no. 327

Knockout 14

JEE ADVANCED

Chemistry

PAPER-1

Section I

Instructions

- This section contains **FOUR (04)** questions.
- Each question has **FOUR** options (a), (b), (c) and (d). **ONLY ONE** of these four options is the correct answer.
- For each question, choose the option corresponding to the correct answer.
- Answer to each question will be evaluated according to the following marking scheme

Full Marks : +3 If ONLY the correct option is chosen;
Zero Marks : 0 If none of the options is chosen (i.e. the question is unanswered);
Negative Marks : −1 In all other cases.

1. The electrode potential of electrode,

$$M(s) \longrightarrow M^{n+}(aq.)$$

(2M) at 298 K is E_1. When temperature is doubled and concentration is made half, then the electrode potential become E_2. Which of the following represents the correct relationship between E_1 and E_2?

(a) $E_1 > E_2$ (b) $E_1 < E_2$
(c) $E_1 = E_2$ (d) Can't be predicted

2. A 10 mL solution of hydrogen peroxide is diluted to 250 mL with distilled water and 25 mL sample of diluted solution is titrated against $(1.023)\frac{N}{10}$ $KMnO_4$ solution required 13.32 mL. Volume strength of H_2O_2 solution is

(a) 76.16 (b) 30.464 (c) 7.616 (d) 3.046

3. Photochromic glass, used for sunglasses, darkens when exposed to bright light and become more transparent again when the light is less bright. The depth of the colour of the glass is related to the concentration of silver atoms. The following reactions are involved.

Reaction I $Ag^+ + Cl^- \rightleftharpoons Ag + Cl$

Reaction II $Cu^+ + Cl \rightleftharpoons Cu^{2+} + Cl^-$

Reaction III $Cu^{2+} + Ag \rightleftharpoons Cu^+ + Ag^+$

Which statement about these reactions is correct?

(a) Cu^+ and Cu^{2+} ions act as catalyst.
(b) Cu^+ ions act as an oxidising agent in reaction II.
(c) Reaction II is one in which light is absorbed.
(d) Ag^+ ions are oxidised in reaction I.

4. A crystalline salt *Z* was dissolved in water and then aqueous sodium hydroxide was added until present in excess. A white precipitate was formed which turned brown on exposure to the air. Which one could be *Z*?

(a) $Al_2(SO_4)_3$ (b) $FeSO_4$
(c) $MnSO_4$ (d) $NiSO_4$

Section II

- This section contains **THREE (03)** question stems.
- There are **TWO (02)** questions corresponding to each question stem.
- The answer to each question is a **NUMERICAL VALUE.**
- For each question, enter the correct numerical value corresponding to the answer in the designated place using the mouse and the on-screen virtual numeric keypad.
- If the numerical value has more than two decimal places, **truncate/round-off** the value to **TWO** decimal places.
- Answer to each question will be evaluated according to the following marking scheme
- Full Marks : +2 If ONLY the correct numerical value is entered at the designated place,
- Zero marks : 0 In all other cases.

Question Stem for Question Nos. 5 and 6

Consider the following reaction, $N_2O_4(g) \longrightarrow 2NO_2(g)$

The free energy of the reaction occurring at 298 K and 1 atm plotted against the fraction of N_2O_4 dissociated as shown in following figure.

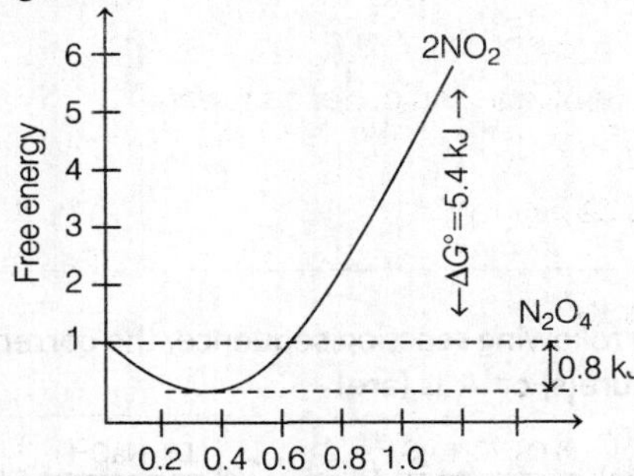

5. When two moles of NO_2 change into equilibrium mixture with N_2O_4, the $\Delta G°$ will be .... kJ.

6. When one mole of N_2O_4 changes into equilibrium mixture with NO_2, the $\Delta G°$ will be .... kJ.

Question Stem for Question Nos. 7 and 8

- Hybridisation is an analytical approach attempt to explain the observed molecular shape by constructing hybridised atomic orbitals with the appropriate inter-orbital angles. VSEPR theory suggests electron pair repulsive interaction ($lp - lp > lp - bp > bp - bp$). While from hybridisation point of view, that is deviation from normal hybridisation state because the angle between any equivalent hybrid orbital determine the fraction of s and *p*-character of the hybrid and *vice-versa*.
- This relationship can be used to determine the exact type of hybrids used by the central atom in the molecule. The subscript on *p* is called hybridisation index (*i*).

For $sp^3, i = 3$; for $sp^2, i = 2$ ... and $f_s = \frac{1}{i+1}, f_p = \frac{i}{i+1}, i = \frac{f_p}{f_s}$

When we add the f_s values for all the hybrids on a given atom the total must be equal to 1.

$$\Sigma f_s = 1.00$$

And for any hybrid generated from *s* and *p*-atomic orbitals,

$$f_s + f_p = 1.00$$

Mathematically the inter-orbital angle θ is related to hybridisation index as follows,

$$\cos\theta = \frac{-1}{i} \text{ or } i = \frac{-1}{\cos\theta}$$

7. In the NH_3 molecule, H—N—H bond angle is 107.1° ($\cos 107.1° = -0.294$). What is fraction of $s(f_s)$ present with the bonding orbital of nitrogen in NH_3?

8. Actual hybridisation of nitrogen involved with non-bonding electron pair of nitrogen in NH_3 is sp^i, where, *i* is ....

Question Stem for Question Nos. 9 and 10

For the reaction : $A \longrightarrow B + C$,

the following data were obtained at 30°C.

Experiment	[A] (mol L^{-1})	Rate (mol L^{-1} h^{-1})
I.	0.170	0.05
II.	0.340	0.10
III.	0.680	0.20

9. The rate constant for the forward reaction is .... h^{-1}.

10. In experiment I, at what time (in h) reactant 'A' will be reduced to 0.0425 M?

Section III

- This section contains **SIX (06)** questions.
- Each question has **FOUR** options (a), (b), (c) and (d). **ONE OR MORE THAN ONE** of these four option(s) is (are) correct answer(s).
- For each question, choose the option(s) corresponding to (all) the correct answer(s).
- Answer to each question will be evaluated according to the following marking scheme

  Full Marks : +4 If only (all) the correct option(s) is(are) chosen,
  Partial Marks : +3 If all the four options are correct but ONLY three options are chosen,
  Partial Marks : +2 If three or more options are correct but ONLY two options are chosen, both of which are correct,
  Partial Marks : +1 If two or more options are correct but ONLY one option is chosen and it is a correct option,
  Zero Marks : 0 If unanswered,
  Negative Marks : –2 In all other cases.
- For example, in a question, if (a), (b) and (d) are the ONLY three options corresponding to correct answers, then
  choosing ONLY (a), (b) and (d) will get +4 marks,
  choosing ONLY (a) and (b) will get +2 marks,
  choosing ONLY (a) and (d) will get +2 marks,
  choosing ONLY (b) and (d) will get +2 marks,
  choosing ONLY (a) will get +1 mark,
  choosing ONLY (b) will get +1 mark,
  choosing ONLY (d) will get +1 mark,
  choosing no option(s) (i.e. the question is unanswered) will get 0 marks and
  choosing any other option(s) will get –2 marks.

---

11. Which of the following statement(s) is (are) correct about PCl_5?

(a) Three (P—Cl) equatorial bonds lie in one plane and make an angle of 120° with each other.

(b) Two (P—Cl) axial bonds one lying above and the other lying below the equatorial plane make an angle of 90° with the plane.

(c) Axial bonds are slightly longer and slightly weaker than equatorial bonds.

(d) PCl_5 exists as $[PCl_4^+][PCl_6^-]$ in aqueous state.

12. $NiCl_2$ in the presence of dimethyl glyoxime (dmg) gives a complex which precipitates in the presence of NH_4OH, giving a bright red colour. The correct statement regarding the complex formed is(are)

(a) dmg is a strong field ligand and forces *d*-electrons of Ni(II) to pair up.

(b) The complex formed is diamagnetic.

(c) The complex is stabilised because two six membered chelate rings are formed.

(d) The complex formed is tetrahedral.

13. Which of the following reaction(s) is (are) correct about the following compounds?

(a) PCl_3 is formed when white phosphorus reacts with $SOCl_2$.

(b) NO is paramagnetic in liquid state.

(c) The percentage of *p*-character in the orbitals of phosphorus forming P—P bonds in specify white P_4 is 75%.

(d) SO_2 cannot be collected over water.

14. In the following reaction sequence, the correct structure(s) of '*A*' is (are)

$A(C_8H_{14})$ Optically active $\xrightarrow[\text{(ii) Zn/H}_2\text{O}]{\text{(i) O}_3,\ (\text{CH}_3)_2\text{S}}$ $B(C_8H_{11}O_2)$ $\xrightarrow{\text{Dil. NaOH}}$ 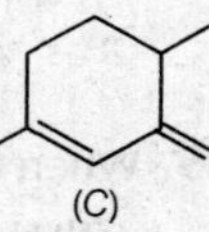 (C)

(a) 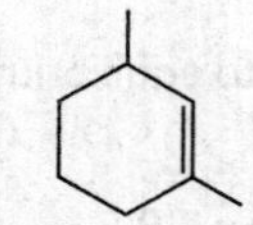 (b)

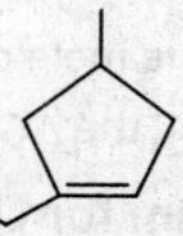

(c) 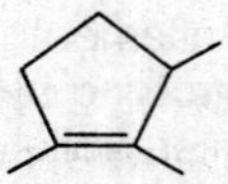 (d)

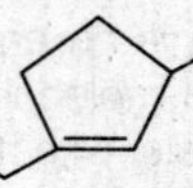

15. The reaction(s) leading to the formation of 2-methylbutan-2-ol is (are)

(a)  O $\xrightarrow[\text{(ii) NH}_4\text{Cl, H}_2\text{O}]{\text{(i) C}_2\text{H}_5\text{MgBr}}$

(b) 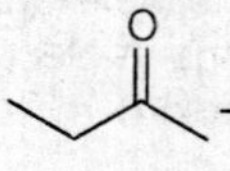 O $\xrightarrow[\text{(ii) NH}_4\text{Cl, H}_2\text{O}]{\text{(i) CH}_3\text{MgBr}}$

(c) 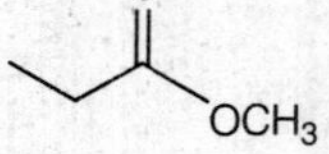 O, OCH_3 $\xrightarrow[\text{(ii) NH}_4\text{Cl, H}_2\text{O}]{\text{(i) CH}_3\text{MgBr}}$

(d) 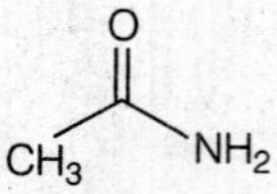 O, CH_3, $NH_2 + 2C_2H_5MgBr$ $\xrightarrow[\text{(ii) H}_3\text{O}^+]{\text{(i) THF, }\Delta}$

16. Consider two liquids A and B having pure vapour pressure p_A° and p_B° forming an ideal solution. The plot of $\frac{1}{X_A}$ *versus* $\frac{1}{Y_A}$ (where, X_A and Y_A are the mole fraction of liquid A in liquid and vapour phase respectively) is linear with slope and intercepts respectively.

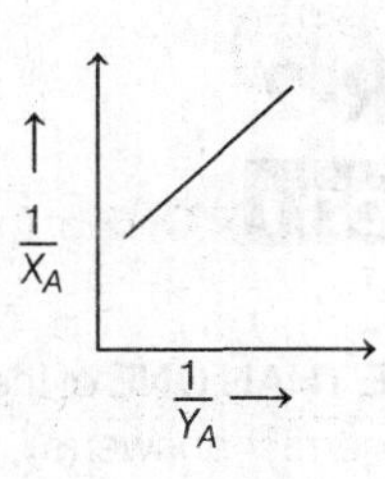

(a) $\frac{p_A^\circ}{p_B^\circ}$ and $\frac{p_A^\circ - p_B^\circ}{p_B^\circ}$

(b) $\frac{p_A^\circ}{p_B^\circ}$ and $\frac{p_B^\circ - p_A^\circ}{p_B^\circ}$

(c) $\frac{p_B^\circ}{p_A^\circ}$ and $\frac{p_A^\circ - p_B^\circ}{p_B^\circ}$

(d) $\frac{p_B^\circ}{p_A^\circ}$ and $\frac{p_B^\circ - p_A^\circ}{p_B^\circ}$

Section IV

- This section contains **THREE (03)** questions.
- The answer to each question is a **NON-NEGATIVE INTEGER.**
- For each question, enter the correct integer corresponding to the answer using the mouse and the on-screen virtual numeric keypad in the place designated to enter the answer.
- Answer to each question will be evaluated according to the following marking scheme :
  Full Marks : +4 If ONLY the correct integer is entered,
  Zero Marks : 0 In all other cases.

---

17. A counter rate meter is used to measure the activity of a radioactive sample. At a certain instant, the count rate was recorded as 475 counters per minute. Five minutes later, the count rate recorded was 270 counts per minute. The half-life period (in min) of the sample is ....

18. $CH_3-\underset{CH_3}{\overset{|}{C}}D-CH(Br)-CH_3 \xrightarrow{C_2H_5O^-/C_2H_5OH} CH_3-\overset{CH_3}{\overset{|}{C}}=CD-CH_3$

What is the order of the reaction?

19. *o*-xylene $\xrightarrow[\text{II. }(CH_3)_2S]{\text{I. }O_3}$ methyl glyoxal + glyoxal + dimethyl glyoxal

$\downarrow Br_2, Fe$

Product(s)

How many isomeric monobromo derivative(s) of the xylene can be obtained?

PAPER-2

Section I

- This section contains **SIX (06)** questions.
- Each question has **FOUR** options (a), (b), (c) and (d). **ONE OR MORE THAN ONE** of these four option(s) is (are) correct answer(s).
- For each question, choose the option(s) corresponding to (all) the correct answer(s).
- Answer to each question will be evaluated according to the following marking scheme:

Full Marks : +4 If only (all) the correct option(s) is(are) chosen,
Partial Marks : +3 If all the four options are correct but ONLY three options are chosen,
Partial Marks : +2 If three or more options are correct but ONLY two options are chosen, both of which are correct,
Partial Marks : +1 If two or more options are correct but ONLY one option is chosen and it is a correct option,
Zero Marks : 0 If unanswered,
Negative Marks : – 2 In all other cases.

- For example, in a question, if (a), (b) and (d) are the ONLY three options corresponding to correct answers, then
choosing ONLY (a), (b) and (d) will get +4 marks,
choosing ONLY (a) and (b) will get +2 marks,
choosing ONLY (a) and (d) will get +2 marks,
choosing ONLY (b) and (d) will get +2 marks,
choosing ONLY (a) will get +1 mark,
choosing ONLY (b) will get +1 mark,
choosing ONLY (d) will get +1 mark,
choosing no option(s) (i.e. the question is unanswered) will get 0 marks and
choosing any other option(s) will get –2 marks.

---

1. The correct option(s) regarding the complex $[Pt(NH_3)_2Cl_2]$ is

(a) it is diamagnetic.
(b) hybridisation of metal ion involved is dsp^2.
(c) the compound undergoes ionisation isomerism in presence of $AgNO_3$.
(d) it is tetrahedral in shape.

2. If an electron can have three values of spin quantum numbers $\left(+\frac{1}{2}, 0 \text{ and } -\frac{1}{2}\right)$. Which of the following statements would be correct?

(a) Li would have in the first period of the periodic table.
(b) The total number of elements is the second period would have been ten.
(c) There would have been 27 elements in the fourth period of periodic table.
(d) Number of periods would have been less than the number of periods present in modern periodic table.

3. $C_{10}H_{16}$ (P) on ozonisation followed by reduction with Zn – H_2O gives 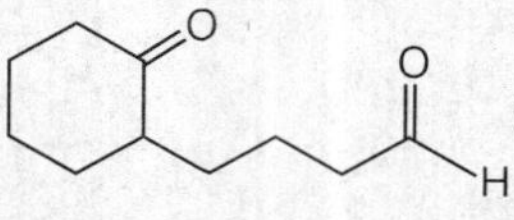 (H)

The major product(s) of the following sequence is(are)

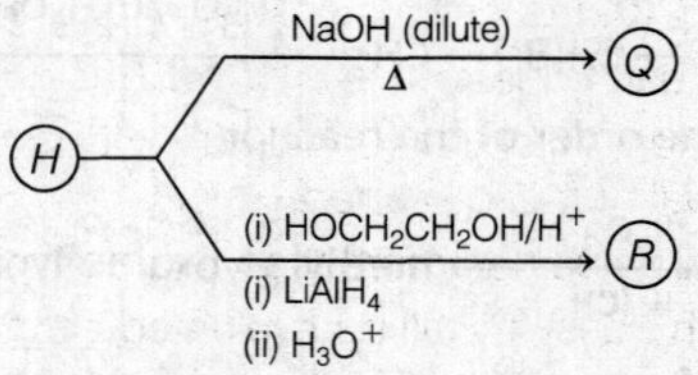

(H) — NaOH (dilute), Δ → (Q)

(H) — (i) $HOCH_2CH_2OH/H^+$; (i) $LiAlH_4$; (ii) H_3O^+ → (R)

The products Q and R are respectively.

(a) 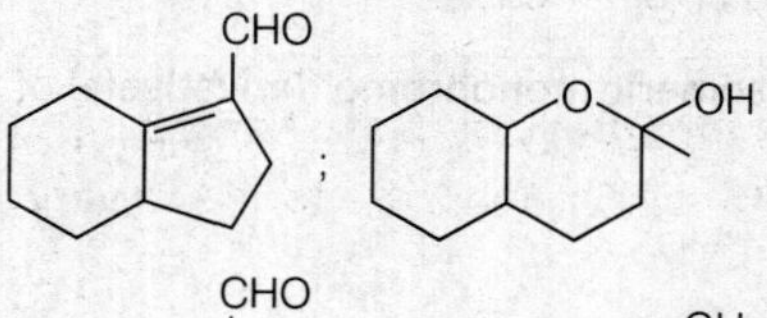 CHO ; OH
(b) 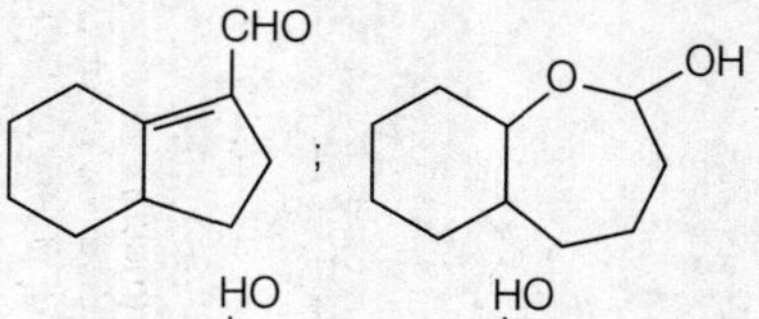 CHO ; OH
(c) 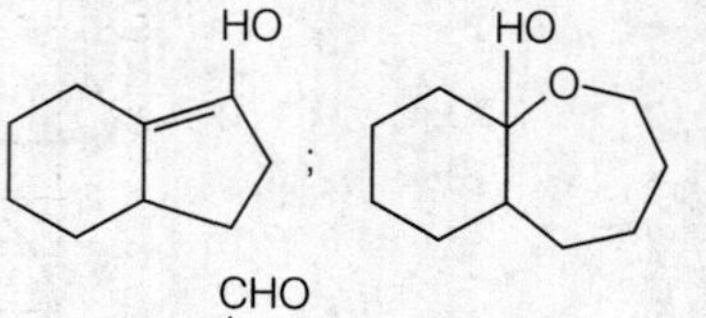 HO ; HO
(d) 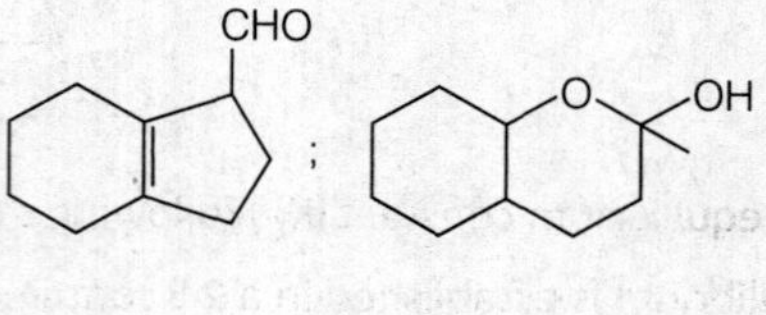 CHO ; OH

4. PhCH=CHCOOH (Q) is produced on reaction of benzaldehyde with acetic anhydride and sodium acetate followed by hydrolysis. (Q) further goes in the following sequence of reactions.

$$Q \xrightarrow[\text{MeOH}]{H_2,\ Pd/C} R \xrightarrow[\text{(ii) } AlCl_3,\ \text{heat}]{\text{(i) } SOCl_2} S$$

The major product is

(a) 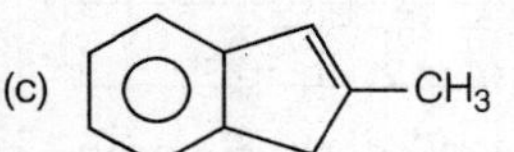

(b) 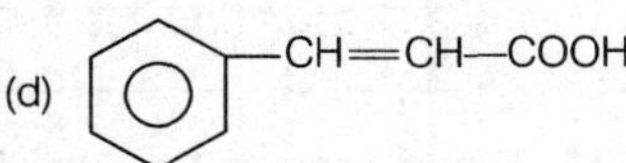

(c) $—CH_3$

(d) CH=CH—COOH

5. The lattice energy of solid NaCl is 180 kcal mol^{-1}. The dissolution of the solid in H_2O is endothermic to the extent of 1.0 kcal mol^{-1}. If the hydration energies of Na^+ and Cl^- ions are in the ratio of 6 : 5. What is the enthalpy of hydration of sodium ion?

(a) –8 kcal mol^{-1} (b) –98 kcal mol^{-1}
(c) + 82 kcal mol^{-1} (d) + 100 kcal mol^{-1}

6. A weak acid or base is titrated against a strong base or acid and the volume of titrant added, is plotted against pH as shown below.

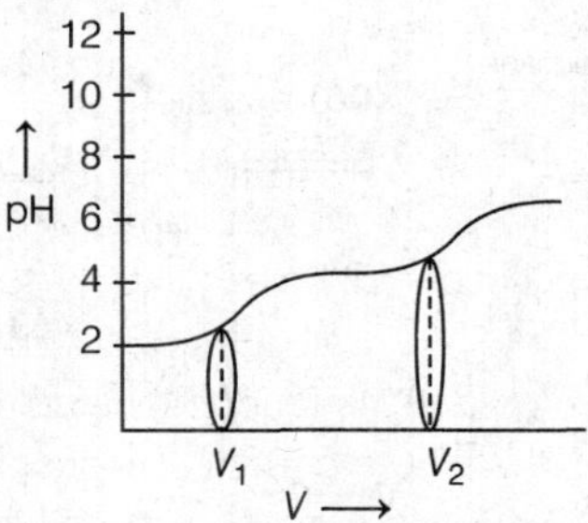

Which of the following statement(s) regarding above titration is(are) correct?

(a) The substance in a beaker is a solution of weak dibasic acid.

(b) $V_2 = 2V_1$

(c) The pH corresponding to $\left(\frac{V_1}{2}\right)$ corresponds to pK_{a_1} of the weak dibasic acid being titrated.

(d) The pH corresponding to $\left(\frac{3}{2}\right)V_1$ corresponds to pK_{a_2} of the weak dibasic acid.

Section II

- This section contains **THREE (03)** question stems.
- There are **TWO (02)** questions corresponding to each question stem.
- The answer to each question is a **NUMERICAL VALUE.**
- For each question, enter the correct numerical value corresponding to the answer in the designated place using the mouse and the on-screen virtual numeric keypad.
- If the numerical value has more than two decimal places, **truncate/round-off** the value to **TWO** decimal places.
- Answer to each question will be evaluated according to the following marking scheme:

Full Marks : +2 If ONLY the correct numerical value is entered at the designated place,
Zero Marks : 0 In all other cases.

Question Stem for Question Nos. 7 and 8

The concentration of *X*, *Y* and *Z* are found to vary with time as shown below in the graph :

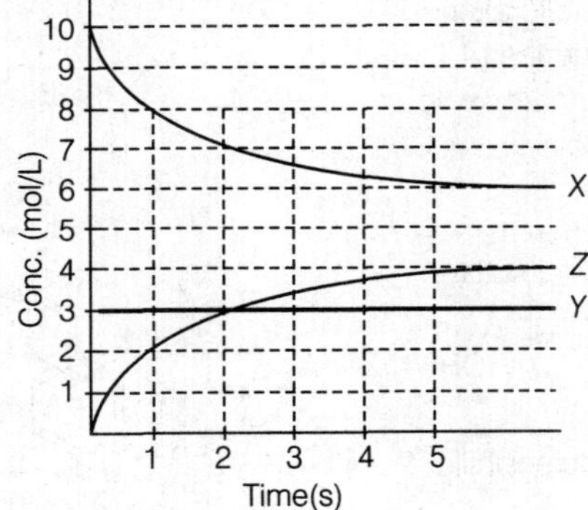

7. The value of equilibrium constant (K_C) following the graph is ....

8. If above equilibrium is established in a 2 L container by taking reactants in sufficient amount, then how many moles of component *Y* must have reacted to establish the equilibrium?

Question Stem for Question Nos. 9 and 10

The thermodynamic informations for isomerisation of alkene (C_4H_8) at 300 K are as follows

cis-2-butene ⇌(1) *trans*-2-butene

cis-2-butene: $\Delta G_f^\circ = 66$ kJ mol^{-1}, $\Delta H_f^\circ = -7$ kJ mol^{-1}

trans-2-butene: $\Delta G_f^\circ = 63$ kJ mol^{-1}, $\Delta H_f^\circ = -11.2$ kJ mol^{-1}

2-methylpropene (equilibria 2 and 3): $\Delta G_f^\circ = +58$ kJ mol^{-1}

If the temperature of the above system is increased to 400 K and equilibrium was allowed to re-establish, mole percentage of *trans*-2-butene at new equilibrium was 18.

9. Determine ΔH° (in kJ mol^{-1}) for the transformation,
***cis*-2-butene ⇌ 2-*trans*-2-butene**

10. Determine ΔS° (in JK^{-1} mol^{-1}) for the transformation,
***trans*-2-butene ⇌ *cis*-2-butene**

Question Stem for Question Nos. 11 and 12

Molar conductance of NaCl varies with concentration according to the equation $\Lambda_m = \Lambda_m^\circ - b\sqrt{c}$, where, Λ_m is molar specific conductance, Λ_m° is molar specific conductance at infinite dilution, and c is the molar concentration. The variation is shown in the following table:

Molar concentration of NaCl	Molar conductance is S cm^2 mol^{-1}
4×10^{4} M	107
9×10^{4} M	97
16×10^{-4} M	87

11. When a certain conductivity cell was filled with 25×10^{-4} M NaCl solution, the resistance of the cell was found to be 1000 Ω.

At infinite dilution, conductance of Cl^- and SO_4^{2-} are 80 S cm^2 mol^{-1} and 160 S cm^2 mol^{-1}, respectively. What is the molar conductance (in S cm^2 mol^{-1}) of NaCl at infinite dilution?

12. What is the cell constant (in cm^{-1}) of the conductivity cell?

Section III

- This section contains **TWO (02) paragraphs**. Based on each paragraph, there are **TWO (02)** questions.
- Each question has **FOUR** options (a), (b), (c) and (d). **ONLY ONE** of these four options is the correct answer.
- For each question, choose the option corresponding to the correct answer.
- Answer to each question will be evaluated according to the following marking scheme

Full Marks : +3 If ONLY the correct option is chosen,
Zero Marks : 0 If none of the options is chosen (i.e. the question is unanswered),
Negative Marks : – 1 In all other cases.

Paragraph-1

The reaction is self oxidation-reduction type and takes place in the presence of 50% aqueous or ethanolic alkali. One molecule of the aldehyde (without the presence of α-hydrogen atom) is oxidised to corresponding carboxylic acid and the other is reduced to the corresponding alcohol.

$$R_1C(R_2)(R_3)CHO \xrightarrow[\text{(ii) } H_3O^+]{\text{(i) } OH^-,\text{ Ethanol}} R_1C(R_2)(R_3)COOH + R_1C(R_2)(R_3)CH_2OH$$

The mechanism involves two distinct steps : Nucleophilic attack and hydride ion transfer.

13. Identify the product formed in the following reaction.

4-methoxybenzaldehyde $\xrightarrow[OH^-\text{(conc.)}]{CH_2O}$ Product

(a) 4-methoxybenzyl alcohol ($H_3CO-C_6H_4-CH_2OH$)
(b) 4-methoxybenzoic acid ($H_3CO-C_6H_4-COOH$)
(c) 4-hydroxybenzaldehyde ($HO-C_6H_4-CHO$)
(d) 4-hydroxybenzoic acid ($HO-C_6H_4-COOH$)

14. $\underset{(A)}{C_8H_6O_2} \xrightarrow[EtOH]{CH_2O/OH^-} \underset{(B)}{C_8H_{10}O_2} \xrightarrow{PBr_3} \underset{(C)}{C_8H_8Br_2}$

A, *B* and *C* are respectively.

(a) 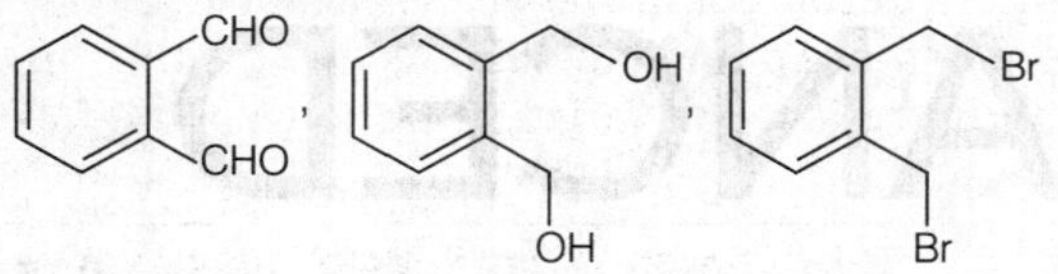 CHO, CHO ; OH, OH ; Br, Br

(b) 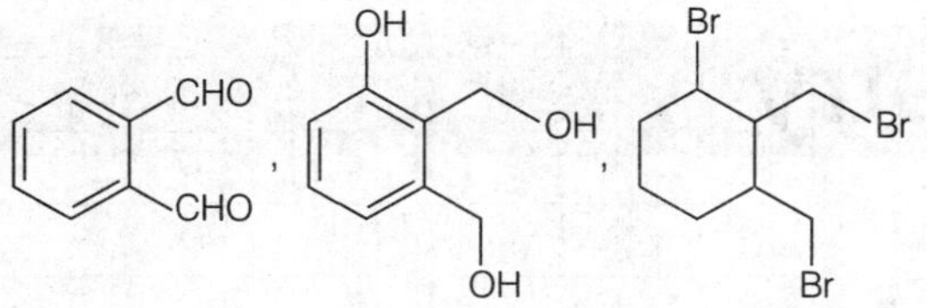 CHO, CHO ; OH, OH, OH ; Br, Br, Br

(c) 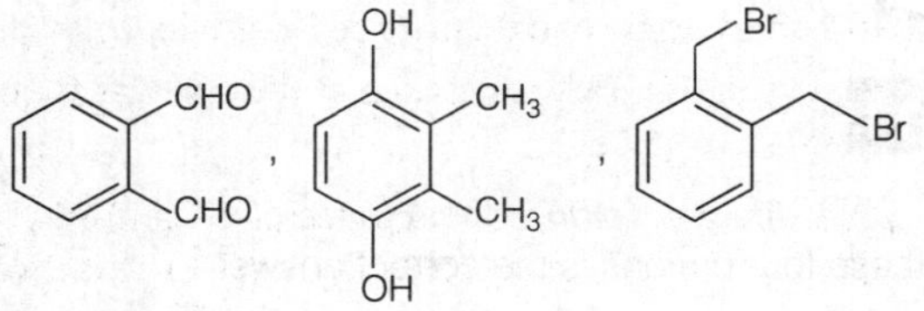 CHO, CHO ; OH, CH_3, CH_3, OH ; Br, Br

(d) All of the above

Paragraph-2

Some ligands not only donate their lone pair of electrons to the central metal atom but also accept the electron cloud from the central metal atom. This is known as synergic bonding and stability of metal carbonyls can be explained on the basis of synergic effect.

15. Select the correct order for stretching frequencies of C—O bonding.

I. *fac*-$Mo(CO)_3(PF_3)_3$ II. *fac*-$Mo(CO)_3(PCl_3)_3$

III. *fac*-$Mo(CO)_3(PMe_3)_3$

(a) I < II < III

(b) I > II > III

(c) I = II = III

(d) II > I > III

16. In which of the following complexes, the bond order is minimum?

(a) $[Mn(CO)_6]^+$ (b) $[Cr(CO)_6]$

(c) $[Ti(CO)_6]^{2-}$ (d) $[V(CO)_6]^-$

Section IV

- This section contains **THREE (03)** questions.
- The answer to each question is a **NON-NEGATIVE INTEGER.**
- For each question, enter the correct integer corresponding to the answer using the mouse and the on-screen virtual numeric keypad in the place designated to enter the answer.
- Answer to each question will be evaluated according to the following marking scheme

Full Marks : +4 If ONLY the correct integer is entered,

Zero Marks : 0 In all other cases.

17. The velocity of an electron in certain Bohr orbit of H-atom bears the ratio 1 : 275 to the velocity of light. What is the quantum number, *n* of the orbit?

18. 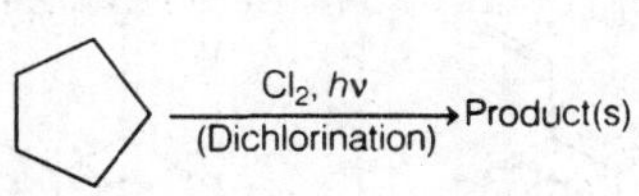 Cyclopentane $\xrightarrow[\text{(Dichlorination)}]{Cl_2,\ h\nu}$ Product(s)

Find the total number of isomeric product(s).

19. $CH_3-CHD-CH_2-\overset{O}{\overset{\|}{C}}-O-\overset{CH_3}{\underset{Ph}{C}}-CHD-CH_3 \xrightarrow{H^+,\ H_2O}$ Product(s)

If the starting ester is optically pure, how many product(s) is(are) obtained on the hydrolysis?

Answers

Paper-1

1 *(b)*	2 *(c)*	3 *(a)*	4 *(c)*	5 *(– 6.20)*	6 *(– 0.80)*	7 *(0.23)*	8 *(2.13)*	9 *(0.29)*	10 *(4.80)*
11 *(a,b,c)*	12 *(a,b)*	13 *(a,c,d)*	14 *(c)*	15 *(a,b,c)*	16 *(b)*	17 *(6)*	18 *(1)*	19 *(2)*	

Paper-2

1 *(a,b,c)*	2 *(a,c,d)*	3 *(b)*	4 *(b)*	5 *(b)*	6 *(a,b,c,d)*	7 *(0.67)*	8 *(8)*	9 *(– 4.20)*	10 *(– 4)*
11 *(127)*	12 *(0.19)*	13 *(a)*	14 *(a)*	15 *(b)*	16 *(c)*	17 *(2)*	18 *(7)*	19 *(2)*	

See detailed solutions on page no. 333

Knockout 15

JEE ADVANCED

Chemistry

PAPER-1

Section I

- This section contains **FOUR (04)** questions.
- Each question has **FOUR** options (a), (b), (c) and (d). **ONLY ONE** of these four options is the correct answer.
- For each question, choose the option corresponding to the correct answer.
- Answer to each question will be evaluated according to the following marking scheme.

Full Marks : +3 If ONLY the correct option is chosen,
Zero Marks : 0 If none of the options is chosen (i.e. the question is unanswered),
Negative Marks : −1 In all other cases.

---

1. The half-life of Tc^{99} is 6h. The total residual activity in a patient 30 h after receiving an injection containing Tc^{99} must be more than $0.01\,\mu C_i$. What is the maximum activity (in μC_i) that the sample injection can have?

(a) 0.32
(b) 0.16
(c) 0.08
(d) 0.64

2. When copper oxide is treated with sulphuric acid, it produces a compound [X] which exist as blue coloured aqueous solution and when it is heated its colour changes to white. When [X] is treated with excess of aqueous NH_3, it again produces a deep blue coloured solution of [Y]. Identify the correct statement about [X] and [Y].

(a) [X] is $Cu(SO_4)\cdot 5H_2O$ and [Y] is $[Cu(NH_3)_6]^{2+}$
(b) [X] is $[Cu(H_2O)_4]SO_4\cdot H_2O$ and [Y] is $[Cu(NH_3)_4]SO_4$
(c) [X] is $[Cu(H_2O)_4]SO_4\cdot H_2O$ and [Y] is $[Cu(NH_3)_4(H_2O)_2]^{2+}$
(d) [X] is $[Cu(H_2O)_6]SO_4$ and [Y] is $[Cu(NH_3)_4]SO_4$

3. Arrange the following polymers in increasing order of their intermolecular forces.

Nylon-6,6, Polythene, Bakelite, Buna-S
(G) (A) (U) (R)

(a) $A < R < G < U$
(b) $R < A < G < U$
(c) $U > G > A > R$
(d) $A < R < U < G$

4. Product (W) will be

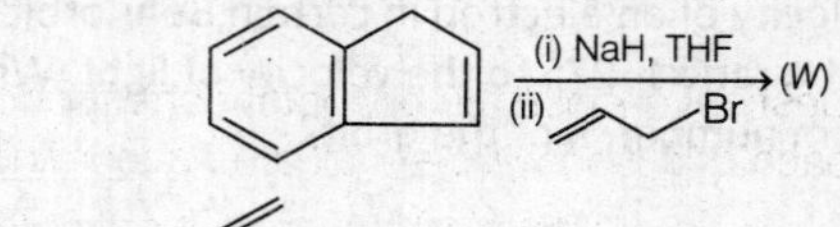

(i) NaH, THF
(ii) Br → (W)

(a) 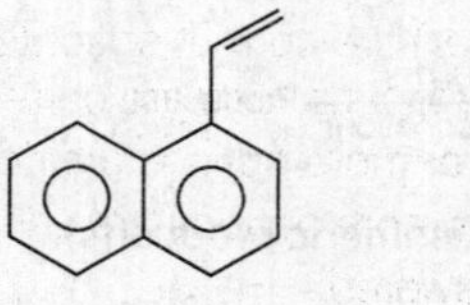
(b) 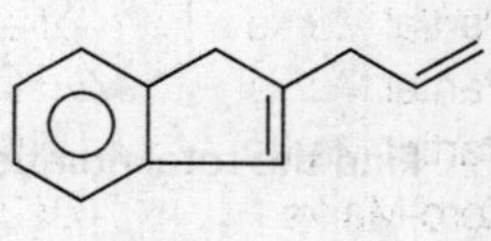
(c) 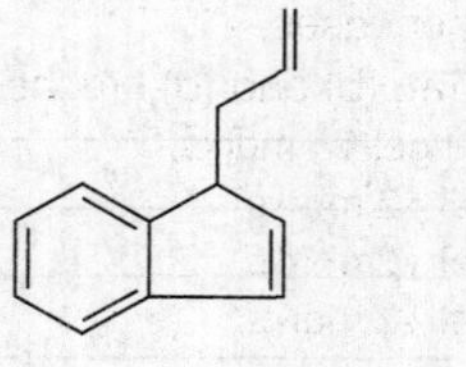
(b)

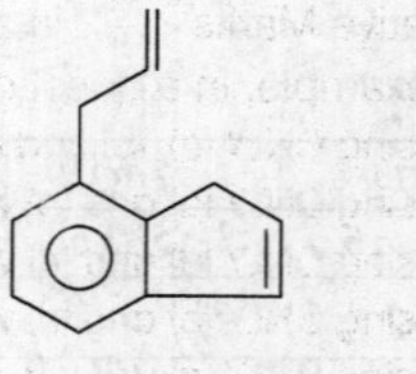

Section II

- This section contains **THREE (03)** question stems.
- There are **TWO (02)** questions corresponding to each question stem.
- The answer to each question is a **NUMERICAL VALUE.**
- For each question, enter the correct numerical value corresponding to the answer in the designated place using the mouse and the on-screen virtual numeric keypad.
- If the numerical value has more than two decimal places, **truncate/round-off** the value to **TWO** decimal places.
- Answer to each question will be evaluated according to the following marking scheme
  Full Marks : +2 If ONLY the correct numerical value is entered at the designated place,
  Zero marks : 0 In all other cases.

Question Stem for Question Nos. 5 and 6

Consider the following thermochemical changes for the formation of NaOH each involving two steps:

I. (a) $2Na(s) + 2H_2O(l) \longrightarrow 2NaOH(aq) + H_2(g)$; $\Delta H/\text{kcal} = -88$

(b) $H_2(g) + \frac{1}{2}O_2(g) \longrightarrow H_2O\ (l)$; $\Delta H/\text{kcal} = -68$

II. (a) $2Na(s) + \frac{1}{2}O_2(g) \longrightarrow Na_2O\ (s)$, $\Delta H/\text{kcal} = -100$

(b) $Na_2O(s) + H_2O(l) \longrightarrow 2NaOH(aq)$, $\Delta H/\text{kcal} = x$

5. What is the value of x in kcal?

6. What would be the value of $\Delta_f H^\circ(\text{NaOH}, aq.)$ *in kcal* mol^{-1}?

Question Stem for Questions Nos. 7 and 8

The sulphide ore of zinc (zinc sulphide) is reduced to element zinc in the following steps:

(i) $ZnS + \frac{3}{2}O_2 \longrightarrow ZnO + SO_2$ **(called roasting)**

(ii) $ZnO + CO \longrightarrow Zn + CO_2$ **(called reduction)**

On treating 5.32 kg ZnS in this way, 3.30 kg of pure zinc is formed. [Zn = 65, S = 32, O = 16]. Calculate

7. Theoretical yield of element Zn in kg.

8. Actual percentage yield of Zn which is ....

Question Stem for Question Nos. 9 and 10

Products X, Y and Z in the following chain reactions are produced as follows,

$$\underset{1.5\text{ mol}}{C_6H_5-\overset{\overset{\displaystyle O}{\|}}{C}-CH_3} \xrightarrow[CH_3COOH]{Cl_2} \underset{[x\text{ g}]}{X} \xrightarrow[\text{(ii) } H_2O]{\text{(i) NaBH}_4} Y \xrightarrow{CaO} \underset{[z\text{ g}]}{Z}$$

9. The value of X is ....

10. The value of Z is ....

Section III

- This section contains **SIX (06)** questions.
- Each question has **FOUR** options (a), (b), (c) and (d). **ONE OR MORE THAN ONE** of these four option(s) is (are) correct answer(s).
- For each question, choose the option(s) corresponding to (all) the correct answer(s).
- Answer to each question will be evaluated according to the following marking scheme
- Full Marks : +4 If only (all) the correct option(s) is(are) chosen,
- Partial Marks : +3 If all the four options are correct but ONLY three options are chosen,
- Partial Marks : +2 If three or more options are correct but ONLY two options are chosen, both of which are correct,
- Partial Marks : +1 If two or more options are correct but ONLY one option is chosen and it is a correct option,
- Zero Marks : 0 If unanswered,
- Negative Marks : – 2 In all other cases.
- For example, in a question, if (a), (b) and (d) are the ONLY three options corresponding to correct answers, then
  choosing ONLY (a), (b) and (d) will get +4 marks,
  choosing ONLY (a) and (b) will get +2 marks,
  choosing ONLY (a) and (d) will get +2 marks,
  choosing ONLY (b) and (d) will get +2 marks,
  choosing ONLY (a) will get +1 mark,
  choosing ONLY (b) will get +1 mark,
  choosing ONLY (d) will get +1 mark,
  choosing no option(s) (i.e. the question is unanswered) will get 0 marks and choosing any other option(s) will get –2 marks.

---

11. Ammonia forms the complex ion $[Cu(NH_3)_4]^{2+}$ with copper ions in the alkaline solutions but not in acidic solutions. The reason is (are)

(a) in acidic solutions, hydration protects copper ions.

(b) in acidic solutions, protons coordinate with ammonia molecules forming NH_4^+ ions and NH_3 molecules are not available.

(c) in alkaline solutions, insoluble $Cu(OH)_2$ is precipitated, which is soluble in excess of any alkali.

(d) copper hydroxide is an amphoteric substance.

12. Colourless salt (*A*), on heating with NaOH, releases a gas (*B*) that can also be obtained when Mg_3N_2 reacts with H_2O. When reaction of (*A*) with NaOH gets completed, solution obtained on reaction with $FeSO_4$ and conc. H_2SO_4 gave a brown coloured ring (*C*) between two layers. (*A*) on heating strongly forms (*D*) and (*E*). (*E*) is a neutral oxide of a dibasic acid (*F*). Which of the following statements is(are) correct?

(a) *A* is a nitrate salt.

(b) '*F*' exist as *cis*- and *trans*- isomers.

(c) The molecular formula of brown coloured ring (*C*) is $[Fe(H_2O)_5NO]SO_4$.

(d) *D* is a gas with molecular formula NH_3.

13. 3,3-dimethylbutan-1-ol reacts with $K_2Cr_2O_7, H_2SO_4$ followed by heating gives (*A*). (*A*) also undergoes the following transformations,

$$A \xrightarrow{SOCl_2} B \xrightarrow[(2\ mol)]{(CH_3)_2NH} C \xrightarrow[(ii)\ H_2O]{(i)\ LiAlH_4,\ diethyl\ ether} D$$

Identify the following compounds.

(a) (*A*) is $(CH_3)_3CCH_2COOH$

(b) (*C*) is $(CH_3)_3CCH_2-\overset{O}{\overset{||}{C}}-N(CH_3)_2$

(c) (*D*) is $(CH_3)_3CCH_2-CH_2N(CH_3)_2$

(d) (*D*) is $(CH_3)_2CHCH_2-CH_2N(CH_3)_2$

14. The product(s) may be obtained in the following reaction is(are)

(Cyclic sugar with OH, HO, HO, OH, OH groups) $\xrightarrow[H_2O]{NaBH_4}$

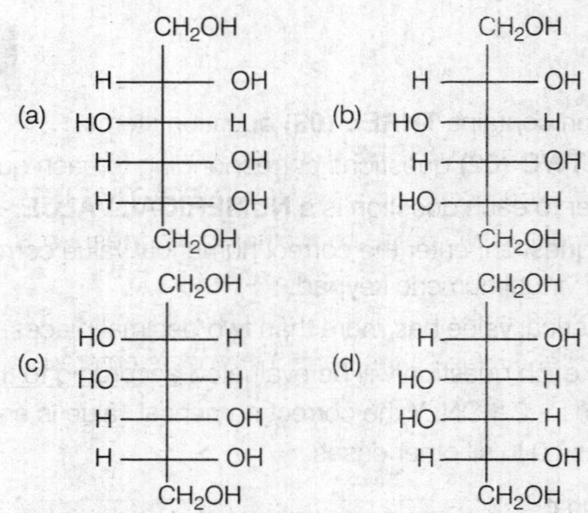

15. The two equilibrium : $AB \rightleftharpoons A^+ + B^-$ and $AB + B^- \rightleftharpoons AB_2^-$ are simultaneously maintained in a solution with equilibrium constants, K_1 and K_2 respectively. The ratio of $[A^+]$ to $[AB_2^-]$ in the solution is said to be

(a) directly proportional to the concentration of B^-.

(b) inversely proportional to the concentration of B^-.

(c) directly proportional to the square of the concentration of B^-.

(d) inversely proportional to the square of concentration of B^-.

16. Based on the isotherm given below, which of the following statements is (are) correct?

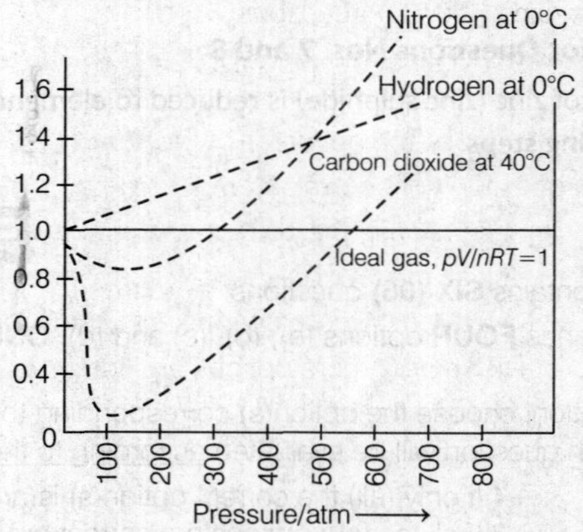

(a) For CO_2 and N_2, two effect compensate each other at a particular pressure where, $Z = 1$.

(b) For H_2 at 0°C, molecular attractive forces are weaker and size effect dominates its behaviour resulting that, $Z > 1$.

(c) For N_2 at 0°C, attractive forces are larger enough to cause negative deviation upto 300 atm, thus ($Z < 1$) after which size effect dominates, thus $Z > 1$.

(d) For CO_2, intermolecular attraction is larger even at 40°C resulting, $Z < 1$ even at high pressure.

Section IV

- This section contains **THREE (03)** questions.
- The answer to each question is a **NON-NEGATIVE INTEGER.**
- For each question, enter the correct integer corresponding to the answer using the mouse and the on-screen virtual numeric keypad in the place designated to enter the answer.
- Answer to each question will be evaluated according to the following marking scheme

Full Marks : +4 If ONLY the correct integer is entered,

Zero Marks : 0 In all other cases.

17. Addition of 0.643 g of a compound to 50 mL of benzene (density = 0.879 g/mL) lowers the freezing point from 5.51°C to 5.03°C. If K_f for benzene is 5.12 K kg mol^{-1}, the molecular weight of the compound ($i = 1$) is .... g mol^{-1}.

18. The rate constant, the activation energy and the Arrhenius parameter of a chemical reaction at 25°C are $3.0 \times 10^{-4} s^{-1}$, 104.4 kJ mol^{-1} and $6.0 \times 10^{14} s^{-1}$ respectively.

The value of the rate constant at $T \rightarrow \infty$ is .... $\times 10^{14} s^{-1}$ [Take, $10^{18.297} = 1.98 \times 10^{18}$].

19. EMF of the following cell,

Ag | $AgNO_3$ (0.1 M) || KBr (1N), AgBr(*s*) | Ag is – 0.6 V at 298 K and $10^{-11.1} = 8 \times 10^{-12}$

If $AgNO_3$ is 80% and KBr is 60% dissociated, K_{sp} of AgBr at 298 K is found to be .... $\times 10^{-12} M^2$ [Take : 0.059 = 0.06]

PAPER-2

Section I

- This section contains **SIX (06)** questions.
- Each question has **FOUR** options (a), (b), (c) and (d). **ONE OR MORE THAN ONE** of these four option(s) is (are) correct answer(s).
- For each question, choose the option(s) corresponding to (all) the correct answer(s).
- Answer to each question will be evaluated according to the following marking scheme
- Full Marks : +4 If only (all) the correct option(s) is(are) chosen,
- Partial Marks : +3 If all the four options are correct but ONLY three options are chosen,
- Partial Marks : +2 If three or more options are correct but ONLY two options are chosen, both of which are correct,
- Partial Marks : +1 If two or more options are correct but ONLY one option is chosen and it is a correct option,
- Zero Marks : 0 If unanswered,
- Negative Marks : – 2 In all other cases.
- For example, in a question, if (a), (b) and (d) are the ONLY three options corresponding to correct answers, then
choosing ONLY (a), (b) and (d) will get +4 marks,
choosing ONLY (a) and (b) will get +2 marks,
choosing ONLY (a) and (d) will get +2 marks,
choosing ONLY (b) and (d) will get +2 marks,
choosing ONLY (a) will get +1 mark,
choosing ONLY (b) will get +1 mark,
choosing ONLY (d) will get +1 mark,
choosing no option(s) (i.e. the question is unanswered) will get 0 marks and choosing any other option(s) will get –2 marks.

1. One of the most general reaction exhibited by coordination compounds is that of substitution or replacement of one ligand by another. When tetrachloridoplatinate (II) ion reacted with ammonia, yields *X* and tetraammineplatinum (II) ion reacted with chloride ion yields *Y*, here *X* and *Y* are

(a) *X* is *cis*-diamminedichloridoplatinum (II) ; *Y* is *trans*-diamminedichloridoplatinum (II)

(b) *X* is *trans*-diamminedichloridoplatinum (II) ; *Y* is *cis*-diamminedichloridoplatinum (II)

(c) *Y* is *trans*-diamminedichloridoplatinum (II) ; *X* is triamminechloridoplatinum (II)

(d) *Y* is *cis*-diamminedichloridoplatinum (III) ; *X* is triamminedichloridoplatinum (II)

2. A water soluble chloride of a poisonous element *M*, when heated with Zn/H_2SO_4 gives a colourless and extremely poisonous gaseous compound *N*, which on passing through a heated tube gives a silvery mirror of element *M*. The correct statement(s) is(are)

(a) *N* is CdH_3

(b) *M* is arsenic, silvery in colour

(c) on heating MH_3, hydrogen is evolved

(d) oxy-acids the given element (*M*) are insoluble in water

3. Benzaldehyde reacts with cyclopentanone in presence of a base to give (*A*) that on oxidation produces (*B*). (*A*) also produces *C* and *D* on reductive ozonolysis. The reaction sequence(s) are as follows

$$PhCHO + \text{(cyclopentanone)} \xrightarrow[\text{(ii) } H^{\oplus}]{\text{(i) } \overset{\ominus}{O}H} (A) \xrightarrow{KMnO_4/H^{\oplus}} (B)$$

Only one product

$(A) \downarrow$ (C) + (D)
(2 mol) (1 mol)
(Two products)

The two products (*C*) and (*D*) are

(a) *D* is (3-ethylcyclohexanone structure)

(b) *C* is CHO–CHO

(c) *D* is OHC–C(=O)–C(=O)–(ring with OHC and C=O)

(d) *C* is CHO–CH_2OH

4. Consider the following compound.

(furanose structure: HOH_2C, H / H, H, H, OH / OH, OH)

The correct structure(s) of its anomer(s) is(are)

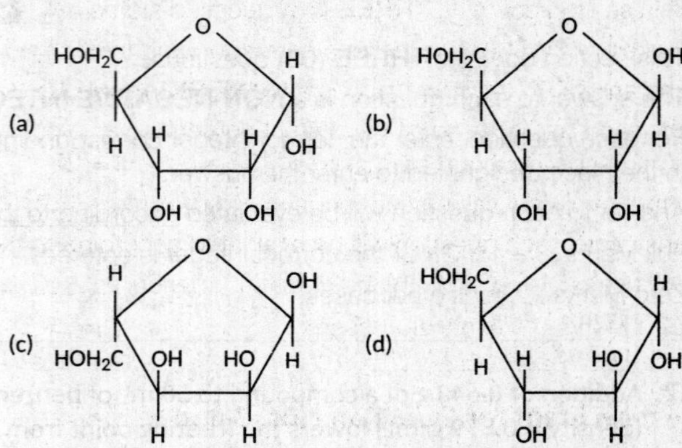

5. When the solids $Ba(OH)_2$ and NH_4SCN are taken in excess of water, a solution is produced and the temperature of the solution drops.

$$Ba(OH)_2(s) + 2NH_4SCN(s) \longrightarrow Ba(SCN)_2(aq) + 2NH_3(g) + 2H_2O(l)$$

Which statement(s) about the energy change of this reaction is(are) incorrect?

(a) The reaction is endothermic and ΔH is negative.

(b) The reaction is endothermic and ΔH is positive.

(c) The reaction is exothermic and ΔH is negative.

(d) The reaction is exothermic and ΔH is positive.

6. One mole of an ideal gas defined by the state, *A* (300 K, 2 atm) is subjected to the following change of state as,

$$A \xrightarrow[\text{heating}]{\text{Isochoric}} B\,(5.0\,\text{atm}) \xrightarrow[\text{expansion}]{\text{Adiabatic reversible}} C \xrightarrow[\text{compression}]{\text{Isothermal reversible}} A\,[C_V = 1.5\,R]$$

Which of the following *V–p* diagrams describe(s) the above mentioned cyclic process more accurately?

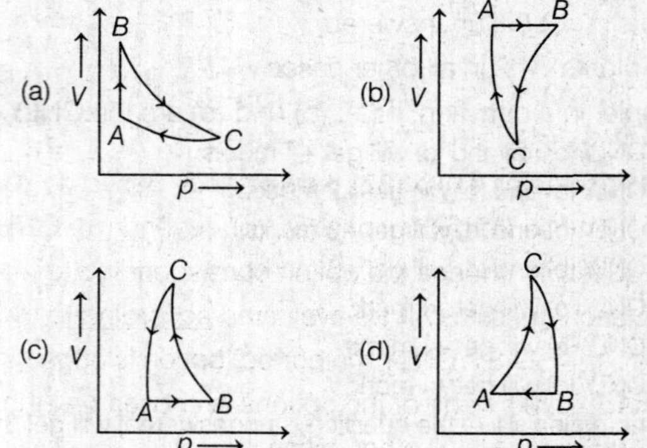

Section II

- This section contains **THREE (03)** question stems.
- There are **TWO (02)** questions corresponding to each question stem.
- The answer to each question is a **NUMERICAL VALUE.**
- For each question, enter the correct numerical value corresponding to the answer in the designated place using the mouse and the on-screen virtual numeric keypad.
- If the numerical value has more than two decimal places, **truncate/round-off** the value to **TWO** decimal places.
- Answer to each question will be evaluated according to the following marking scheme

Full Marks : +2 If ONLY the correct numerical value is entered at the designated place,

Zero Marks : 0 In all other cases.

Question Stem for Question Nos. 7 and 8

Consider the following structure of a protein,

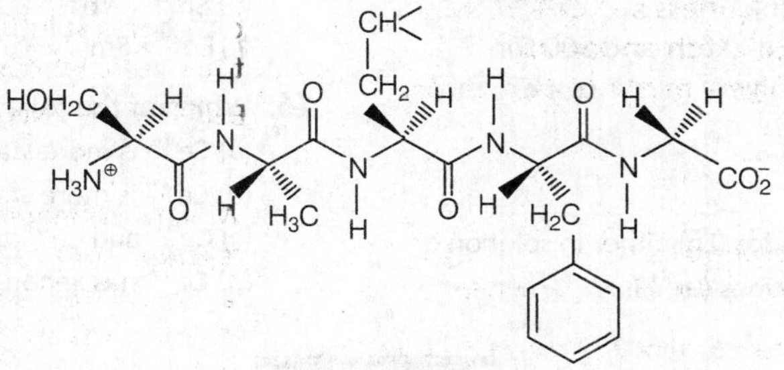

7. Number of basic group(s) [Conjugate form] present in the protein is ....

8. How many peptide linkages are present in it ?

Question Stem for Question Nos. 9 and 10

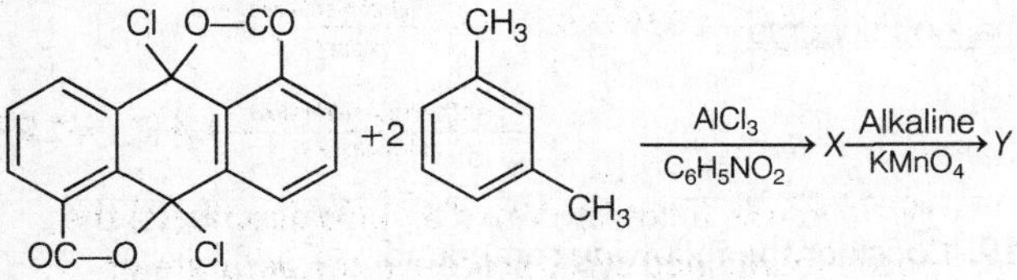

$\xrightarrow[C_6H_5NO_2]{AlCl_3} X \xrightarrow[KMnO_4]{Alkaline} Y$

9. The number of moles of sodium bicarbonate that is required to react with *Y* completely is ....

10. Degree of unsaturation in *X* is ....

Question Stem for Question Nos. 11 and 12

Consider the following radioactive disintegration of three radioelements *A*, *B* and *C* at equilibrium

$$A \xrightarrow[N_A]{t_{50} = 100 \text{ min}} B \xrightarrow[N_B]{t_{75} = 10 \text{ min}} C$$

11. At equilibrium, N_A / N_B is ....

12. The value of $\frac{\lambda_A}{\lambda_B}$ is ....

Section III

- This section contains **TWO (02) paragraphs**. Based on each paragraph, there are **TWO (02)** questions.
- Each question has **FOUR** options (a), (b), (c) and (d). **ONLY ONE** of these four options is the correct answer.
- For each question, choose the option corresponding to the correct answer.
- Answer to each question will be evaluated according to the following marking scheme
- Full Marks : +3 If ONLY the correct option is chosen,
- Zero Marks : 0 If none of the options is chosen (i.e. the question is unanswered),
- Negative Marks : – 1 In all other cases.

Paragraph-1

Given figure represents Henry's law at a given temperature for the solubility of HCl gas in cyclohexane (in terms of mole fraction) at different pressures.

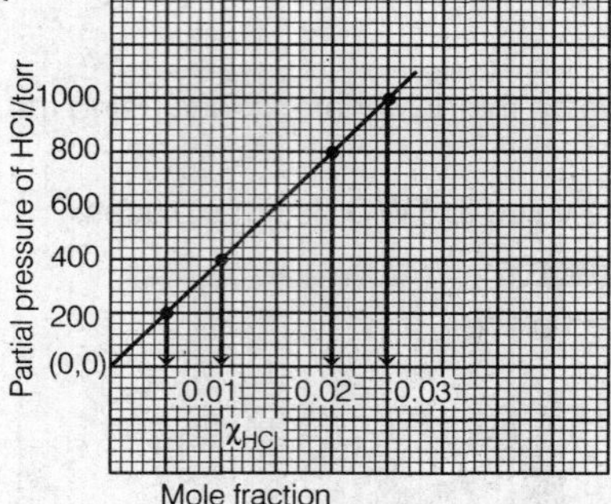

13. Henry's law constant (in torr) for HCl gas is

(a) 4×10^4 (b) 2×10^4 (c) 1×10^4 (d) 0.01×10^4

14. What is the ratio of solubility at 400 torr and 800 torr ?

(a) 2.5 (b) 0.5 (c) 25 (d) 4

Paragraph-2

The observed oxidation state of lanthanides (Ln) either in solution or insoluble compounds form tripositive cations (Ln^{3+}).

Based on the ionisation enthalpies and hydration energy factors, it is concluded that tripositive species is more stable than di or tetrapositive (Ln^{2+} or Ln^{4+}) species in aqueous solution.

In general, ions having half-filled (Tb^{4+}, Eu^{2+}, Gd^{3+}) or completely filled 4*f*-orbitals (Yb^{2+}, Lu^{3+}) or noble gas configuration (La^{3+}, Ce^{4+}) are stable. This is supported by their standard reduction potential (SRP) values. Ions with +4 oxidation state act as oxidising and ions having + 2 oxidation state act as reducing agents. Ions having same number of unpaired electrons in *f*-orbitals possess same colour.

15. Observe the following equations,

$$Sm^{3+}(aq) + e^- \longrightarrow Sm^{2+}(aq), E° = -1.55 \text{ V}$$

$$Eu^{3+}(aq) + e^- \longrightarrow Eu^{2+}(aq), E° = -0.43 \text{ V}$$

$$Yb^{3+}(aq) + e^- \longrightarrow Yb^{2+}(aq), E° = -1.55 \text{ V}$$

Based on the above equations, the correct order of reducing power is

(a) $Sm^{2+} > Yb^{2+} > Eu^{2+}$ (b) $Eu^{2+} > Yb^{2+} > Sm^{2+}$

(c) $Eu^{2+} > Sm^{2+} > Yb^{2+}$ (d) $Sm^{2+} > Eu^{2+} > Yb^{2+}$

16. Which of the following is the correct statement?

(a) Ce^{4+} is more stable than Ce^{3+} in solution.

(b) Ce^{3+} is more stable than Ce^{4+} in solution.

(c) Ce^{4+} and Ce^{3+} are equally stable.

(d) Ce^{3+} has xenon configuration.

Section IV

- This section contains **THREE (03)** questions.
- The answer to each question is a **NON-NEGATIVE INTEGER.**
- For each question, enter the correct integer corresponding to the answer using the mouse and the on-screen virtual numeric keypad in the place designated to enter the answer.
- Answer to each question will be evaluated according to the following marking scheme
- Full Marks : +4 If ONLY the correct integer is entered;
- Zero Marks : 0 In all other cases.

17. A detergent ($C_{12}H_{25}SO_4^-Na^+$) solution becomes a colloidal solution at a concentration of 10^{-4}M. On an average 10^{13} colloidal particles are present in 1 mm^3. The average number of ions contained in one colloidal particle (micelle) is .... [Given, $N_A = 6 \times 10^{23}$ mol^{-1}]

18. Apatite is a mineral that is found in tooth enamel. When fluoride tooth pastes are used, this mineral is converted to fluoroapatite, which is more resistant to acids or resistant to tooth decay. The formula of apatite is $Ca_5(PO_4)_xF$. If the compound contains 18.45% by weight of phosphorus, then the value of *x* is .... (Atomic weight of P = 31, Ca = 40, F = 19 and O = 16)

19. Consider the following compound,

Cl, C≡C—Cl, Cl, Br, Cl, I, CH_2—OSO_2CF_3

If the above compound is treated with excess of NaCN (in acetone), how many CN^- group would be incorporated by S_N2 reaction?

Answers

Paper-1

1 *(a)*	2 *(b)*	3 *(b)*	4 *(c)*	5 *(–56)*	6 *(–112)*	7 *(3.56)*	8 *(92.57)*	9 *(231.75)*	10 *(180)*
11 *(b)*	12 *(a, b, c)*	13 *(a, b, c)*	14 *(a)*	15 *(d)*	16 *(a, b, c, d)*	17 *(156)*	18 *(6)*	19 *(5)*	

Paper-2

1 *(a)*	2 *(b, c)*	3 *(b, c)*	4 *(b, c)*	5 *(a, c, d)*	6 *(c)*	7 *(1)*	8 *(4)*	9 *(6)*	10 *(18)*
11 *(20)*	12 *(0.05)*	13 *(a)*	14 *(b)*	15 *(a)*	16 *(b)*	17 *(6)*	18 *(3)*	19 *(3)*	

See detailed solutions on page no. 337

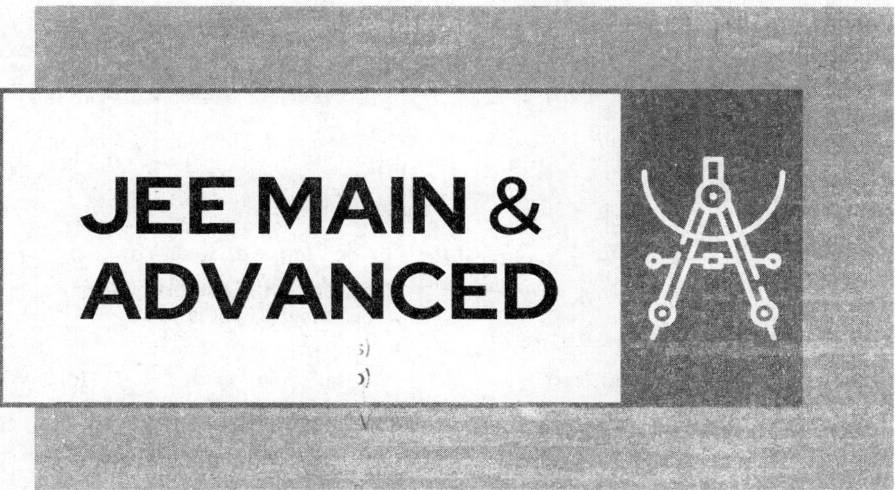

The Real Nuts

Past Year's JEE Main & Advanced Question Papers

Now you are ready for exam, so attempt these Past Exams' Papers and compare your score with the Cut Off Score of that year.

The Real Nuts

JEE MAIN 2022

(Real Nut 1-24 June 2022, Shift-I)

Chemistry

Instructions

- This question paper contains of 30 Questions of Chemistry, divided into two sections : **Section A** Objective Type Questions and **Section B** Numerical Value Questions.
- **Section A** contains 20 Objective questions and all Questions are compulsory (Marking Scheme : Correct + 4, Incorrect – 1).
- **Section B** contains 10 Numerical value questions out of which only 5 questions are to be attempted (Marking Scheme : Correct + 4, Incorrect 0).

Section A *Objective Type Questions*

1 If a rocket runs on a fuel ($C_{15}H_{30}$) and liquid oxygen, the weight of oxygen required and CO_2 released for every litre of fuel respectively are (Given, density of the fuel is 0.756 g/mL)

(a) 1188 g and 1296 g (b) 2376 g and 2592 g
(c) 2592g and 2376 g (d) 3429 g and 3142 g

2 Consider the following pairs of electrons :

(A) (a) $n = 3, l = 1, m_1 = -1, m_s = +\frac{1}{2}$
(b) $n = 3, l = 2, m_1 = 1, m_s = +\frac{1}{2}$

(B) (a) $n = 3, l = 2, m_1 = -2, m_s = -\frac{1}{2}$
(b) $n = 3, l = 2, m_1 = -1, m_s = -\frac{1}{2}$

(C) (a) $n = 4, l = 2, m_1 = 2, m_s = +\frac{1}{2}$
(b) $n = 3, l = 2, m_1 = 2, m_s = +\frac{1}{2}$

The pairs of electron present in degenerate orbitals is/are

(a) Only (A) (b) Only (B)
(c) Only (C) (d) Both (B) and (C)

3 Match List-I with List-II.

List-I	List-II
(A) $[PtCl_4]^{2-}$	(I) sp^3d
(B) BrF_5	(II) d^2sp^3
(C) PCl_5	(III) dsp^2
(D) $[Co(NH_3)_6]^{3+}$	(IV) sp^3d^2

Choose the most appropriate answer from the options given below.

(a) (A) → (II), (B) → (IV), (C) → (I), (D) → (III)
(b) (A) → (III), (B) → (IV), (C) → (I), (D) → (II)
(c) (A) → (III), (B) → (I), (C) → (IV), (D) → (II)
(d) (A) → (II), (B) → (I), (C) → (IV), (D) → (III)

4 For a reaction at equilibrium,

$$A(g) \rightleftharpoons B(g) + \frac{1}{2}C(g)$$

the relation between dissociation constant (K), degree of dissociation (α) and equilibrium pressure (p) is given by

(a) $K = \dfrac{\alpha^{1/2}p^{3/2}}{\left(1+\frac{3}{2}\alpha\right)^{1/2}(1-\alpha)}$ (b) $K = \dfrac{\alpha^{3/2}p^{1/2}}{(2+\alpha)^{1/2}(1-\alpha)}$

(c) $K = \dfrac{(\alpha p)^{3/2}}{\left(1+\frac{3}{2}\alpha\right)^{1/2}(1-\alpha)}$ (d) $K = \dfrac{(\alpha\, p)^{3/2}}{(1+\alpha)(1-\alpha)^{1/2}}$

5 Given below are two statements :

Statement I Emulsion of oil in water are unstable and sometimes they separate into two layers on standing.

Statement II For stabilisation of an emulsion, excess of electrolyte is added.

In the light of the above statements, choose the most appropriate answer from the options given below.

(a) Both Statement I and Statement II are correct.
(b) Both Statement I and Statement II are incorrect.
(c) Statement I is correct but Statement II is incorrect.
(d) Statement I is incorrect but Statement II is correct.

6 Given below are the oxides,

$$Na_2O, As_2O_3, N_2O, NO \text{ and } Cl_2O_7$$

Number of amphoteric oxides is

(a) 0 (b) 1 (c) 2 (d) 3

7 Match the List-I with List-II.

List-I	List-II
(A) Sphalerite	(I) $FeCO_3$
(B) Calamine	(II) PbS
(C) Galena	(III) $ZnCO_3$
(D) Siderite	(IV) ZnS

Choose the most appropriate answer from the options given below :

(a) (A) - (IV), (B) – (III), (C) – (II), (D) – (I)
(b) (A) - (IV), (B) – (I), (C) – (II), (D) – (III)
(c) (A) - (II), (B) – (III), (C) – (I), (D) – (IV)
(d) (A) - (III), (B) – (IV), (C) – (II), (D) – (I)

8 The highest industrial consumption of molecular hydrogen is to produce compounds of element

(a) carbon (b) nitrogen
(c) oxygen (d) chlorine

9 Which of the following statements are correct ?

(A) Both LiCl and $MgCl_2$ are soluble in ethanol.
(B) The oxides Li_2O and MgO combine with excess of oxygen to give superoxide.
(C) LiF is less soluble in water than other alkali metal fluorides.
(D) Li_2O is more soluble in water than other alkali metal oxides.

Choose the most appropriate answer from the options given below.

(a) (A) and (C) only (b) (A), (C) and (D) only
(c) (B) and (C) only (d) (A) and (D) only

10 Identify the correct statement for B_2H_6 from those given below :

(A) In B_2H_6, all B — H bonds are equivalent.
(B) In B_2H_6 there are four 3-centre-2-electron bonds.
(C) B_2H_6 is a Lewis acid.
(D) B_2H_6 can be synthesised from both BF_3 and $NaBH_4$.
(E) B_2H_6 is a planar molecule.

Choose the most appropriate answer from the options given below :

(a) (A) and (E) only (b) (B), (C) and (E) only
(c) (C) and (D) only (d) (C) and (E) only

11 The most stable trihalide of nitrogen is

(a) NF_3 (b) NCl_3 (c) NBr_3 (d) NI_3

12 Which one of the following elemental forms is not present in the enamel of the teeth?

(a) Ca^{2+} (b) P^{3+} (c) F^- (d) P^{5+}

13 In the given reaction sequence, the major product C is

$$C_8H_{10} \xrightarrow[H_2SO_4]{HNO_3} A \xrightarrow[\Delta]{Br_2} B \xrightarrow[KOH]{Alcoholic} C$$

(a) $C_6H_5-C(NO_2)=CH_2$
(b) $O_2N-C_6H_4-CH=CH_2$
(c) $O_2N-C_6H_4-C(NO_2)=CH_2$
(d) $C_6H_4(NO_2)-CH=CH_2$ (ortho)

14 Two statements are given below.

Statement I The melting point of monocarboxylic acid with even number of carbon atoms is higher than that of with odd number of carbon atoms acid immediately below and above it in the series.

Statement II The solubility of monocarboxylic acids in water decreases with increase in molar mass.

Choose the most appropriate option.

(a) Both Statement I and Statement II are correct.
(b) Both Statement I and Statement II are incorrect.
(c) Statement I is correct but Statement II is incorrect.
(d) Statement I is incorrect but Statement II is correct.

15 Which of the following is an example of conjugated diketone?

(a) $CH_3-\overset{O}{\overset{\|}{C}}-CH_2-CH_2-CH_2-\overset{O}{\overset{\|}{C}}-CH_3$
(b) $CH_3-\overset{O}{\overset{\|}{C}}-CH_2-$(cyclohexanone ring)$=O$
(c) $O=$(cyclohexa-2,5-diene ring)$=O$
(d) $C_6H_5-\overset{O}{\overset{\|}{C}}-CH_2-CH_2-\overset{O}{\overset{\|}{C}}-CH_3$

16 p-$CH_3O-C_6H_4-CH_2Br$ $\xrightarrow{\text{(i) NaCN (ii) OH}^- \text{(iii) Cyclohexanone (iv) } H_2, Ni}$ A (Major product)

The major product of the above reaction is

(a) $CH_3O-C_6H_4-CH(C_6H_{11})-CH_2-NH_2$
(b) $CH_3O-C_6H_4-C(OH)(C_6H_{10})-NH_2$
(c) $CH_3O-C_6H_4-CH(C_6H_{11})-\overset{O}{\overset{\|}{C}}-NH_2$
(d) $CH_3O-C_6H_4-CH(CH_2NH_2)-C(OH)(C_6H_{10})$ (1-hydroxycyclohexyl)

17 Which of the following is an example of polyester?

(a) Butadiene-styrene copolymer

(a) Butadiene-styrene copolymer

(b) Melamine polymer

(c) Neoprene

(d) Poly-(β)-hydroxybutyrate-co-(β)-hydroxy valerate

18 A polysaccharide 'X' on boiling with dil. H_2SO_4 at 393 K under 2-3 atm pressure yields 'Y'. 'Y' on treatment with bromine water gives gluconic acid. 'X' contains β-glycosidic linkages only. Compound 'X' is

(a) starch (b) cellulose

(c) amylose (d) amylopectin

19 Which of the following is not a broad spectrum antibiotic?

(a) Vancomycin

(b) Ampicillin

(c) Ofloxacin

(d) Penicillin-G

20 During the qualitative analysis of salt with cation Y^{2+}, addition of a reagent (X) to alkaline solution of the salt gives a bright red precipitate. The reagent (X) and the cation (Y^{2+}) present respectively are

(a) dimethylglyoxime and Ni^{2+}

(b) dimethylglyoxime and Co^{2+}

(c) Nessler's reagent and Hg^{2+}

(d) Nessler's reagent and Ni^{2+}

Section B *Numerical Value Questions*

21 Atoms of element X form hcp lattice and those of element Y occupy $\frac{2}{3}$ of its tetrahedral voids. The percentage of element X in the lattice is .... (Nearest integer)

22 At 300 K, ozone is fifty per cent dissociated. The standard free energy change at this temperature and 1 atm pressure is (–) ...... J mol^{-1} (Nearest integer) [Given, ln 1.35 = 0.3 and $R = 8.3\ JK^{-1}\ mol^{-1}$]

23 The osmotic pressure of blood is 7.47 bar at 300 K. To inject glucose to a patient intravenously, it has to be isotonic with blood. The concentration of glucose solution in gL^{-1} is .... (Molar mass of glucose = 180 g mol^{-1} $R = 0.083$ L bar K^{-1} mol^{-1}) (Nearest integer)

24 The cell potential for the following cell

$$Pt|H_2(g)|H^+(aq)||Cu^{2+}(0.01\ M)|Cu(s)$$

is 0.576 V at 298 K. The pH of the solution is .... (Nearest integer)

25 The rate constants for decomposition of acetaldehyde have been measured over the temperature range 700-1000 K. The data has been analysed by plotting ln *k* vs $\frac{10^3}{T}$ graph. The value of activation energy for the reaction is ...... kJ mol^{-1}. [Nearest integer] (Given, $R = 8.31\ J\ K^{-1}\ mol^{-1}$)

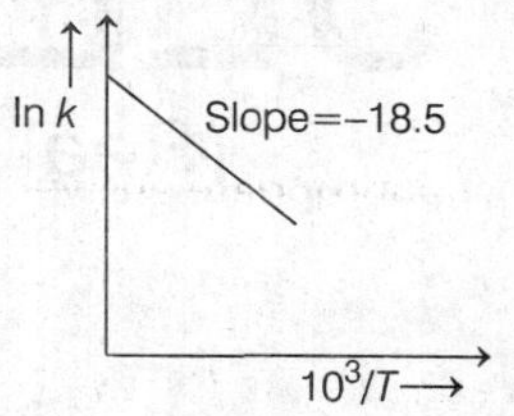

26 The difference in oxidation state of chromium in chromate and dichromate salts is ....

27 In the cobalt-carbonyl complex $[Co_2(CO)_8]$, number of Co — Co bonds is "X" and terminal CO ligands is "Y". $X + Y =$ ....

28 A 0.166 g sample of an organic compound was digested with conc. H_2SO_4 and then distilled with NaOH. The ammonia gas evolved was passed through 50.0 mL of 0.5 N H_2SO_4. The used acid required 30.0 mL of 0.25 N NaOH for complete neutralisation. The mass percentage of nitrogen in the organic compound is ....

29. Number of electrophilic centre in the given compound is ....

CH_3, O, CH_2CN

30 The major product 'A' of the following given reaction has ...... sp^2 hybridised carbon atoms.

$$\text{2, 7-dimethyl-2, 6-octadiene} \xrightarrow{H^+} \underset{\text{Major product}}{A}$$

Answers

Section A

1 *(c)*	2 *(b)*	3 *(b)*	4 *(b)*	5 *(c)*
6 *(b)*	7 *(a)*	8 *(b)*	9 *(a)*	10 *(c)*
11 *(a)*	12 *(b)*	13 *(b)*	14 *(a)*	15 *(c)*
16 *(d)*	17 *(d)*	18 *(b)*	19 *(d)*	20 *(a)*

Section B

21 *(43)*	22 *(747)*	23 *(54)*	24 *(5)*	25 *(154)*
26 *(0)*	27 *(7)*	28 *(63)*	29 *(3)*	30 *(2)*

See detailed solutions on page no. 342

The Real Nuts

JEE MAIN 2022

(Real Nut 2-26 June 2022, Shift-II)

Chemistry

Instructions

- This question paper contains of 30 Questions of Chemistry, divided into two sections : **Section A** Objective Type Questions and **Section B** Numerical Value Questions.
- **Section A** contains 20 Objective questions and all Questions are compulsory (Marking Scheme : Correct + 4, Incorrect – 1).
- **Section B** contains 10 Numerical value questions out of which only 5 questions are to be attempted (Marking Scheme : Correct + 4, Incorrect 0).

Section A *Objective Type Questions*

1 The number of radial and angular nodes in 4*d* orbital are respectively

(a) 1 and 2 (b) 3 and 2 (c) 1 and 0 (d) 2 and 1

2 Match the List I with List II.

List-I (Enzyme)	List-II (Conversion)
A. Invertase	I. Starch into maltose
B. Zymase	II. Maltose into glucose
C. Diastase	III. Glucose into ethanol
D. Maltase	IV. Cane sugar into glucose

Choose the most appropriate answer from the options given below.

	A	B	C	D		A	B	C	D
(a)	III	IV	II	I	(b)	III	II	I	IV
(c)	IV	III	I	II	(d)	IV	II	III	I

3 Which of the following elements is considered as a metalloid?

(a) Sc (b) Pb (c) Bi (d) Te

4 The role of depressants in 'froth-floatation method' is to

(a) selectively prevent one component of the ore from coming to the froth.

(b) reduce the consumption of oil for froth formation.

(c) stabilise the froth.

(d) enhance non-wettability of the mineral particles.

5 Boiling of hard water is helpful in removing the temporary hardness by converting calcium hydrogen carbonate and magnesium hydrogen carbonate to

(a) $CaCO_3$ and $Mg(OH)_2$ (b) $CaCO_3$ and $MgCO_3$

(c) $Ca(OH)_2$ and $MgCO_3$ (d) $Ca(OH)_2$ and $Mg(OH)_2$

6 *s*-block element which cannot be qualitatively confirmed by the flame test is

(a) Li (b) Na

(c) Rb (d) Be

7 The oxide which contains an odd electron at the nitrogen atom is

(a) N_2O (b) NO_2

(c) N_2O_3 (d) N_2O_5

8 Which one of the following is an example of disproportionation reaction?

(a) $3MnO_4^{2-} + 4H^+ \longrightarrow 2MnO_4^- + MnO_2 + 2H_2O$

(b) $MnO_4^- + 4H^+ + 4e^- \longrightarrow MnO_2 + 2H_2O$

(c) $10I^- + 2MnO_4^- + 16H^+ \longrightarrow 2Mn^{2+} + 8H_2O + 5I_2$

(d) $8MnO_4^- + 3S_2O_3^{2-} + H_2O \longrightarrow 8MnO_2 + 6SO_4^{2-} + 2OH^-$

9 The most common oxidation state of lanthanoid elements is +3. Which of the following is likely to deviate easily from +3 oxidation state?

(a) Ce (58)

(b) La (57)

(c) Lu (71)

(d) Gd (64)

10 The measured BOD values for four different water samples (A-D) are as $A = 3$ ppm, $B = 18$ ppm, $C = 21$ ppm, $D = 4$ ppm. The water samples which can be called as highly polluted with organic wastes, are

(a) A and B (b) A and D

(c) B and C (d) B and D

11 The correct order of nucleophilicity is

(a) $F^- > OH^-$ (b) $H_2\ddot{O} > OH^-$

(c) $R\ddot{O}H > RO^-$ (d) $NH_2^- > NH_3$

12 Oxidation of toluene to benzaldehyde can be easily carried out with which of the following reagents?

(a) CrO_3/acetic acid, H_3O^+ (b) CrO_3/acetic anhydride, H_3O^+

(c) $KMnO_4$/HCl, H_3O^+ (d) CO/HCl, anhydrous $AlCl_3$

13 The major product in the following reaction

$$\xrightarrow[\text{(ii) NaBH}_4]{\text{(i) Hg(OAc)}_2,\ \text{H}_2\text{O}} ?$$

(a) OH (b) O

(c) OH (d) OH

14 Halogenation of which one of the following will yield *m*-substituted product with respect to methyl group as a major product?

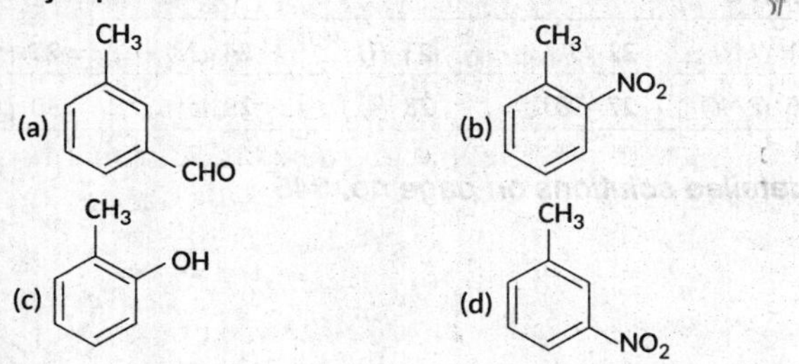

15 The reagent, from the following, which converts benzoic acid to benzaldehyde in one step is

COOH ⟶ CHO

(a) $LiAlH_4$ (b) $KMnO_4$

(c) MnO (d) $NaBH_4$

16 The final product 'A' in the following reaction sequence

$$CH_3CH_2—\overset{\overset{\large O}{\|}}{C}—CH_3 \xrightarrow{HCN} ? \xrightarrow[\text{Heat}]{95\%\ H_2SO_4} A$$

(a) $CH_3—CH{=}\underset{}{\overset{CH_3}{\overset{|}{C}}}—COOH$ (b) $CH_3—CH{=}\underset{\underset{CH_3}{|}}{C}—CN$

(c) $CH_3—CH_2—\overset{OH}{\overset{|}{\underset{\underset{CH_3}{|}}{C}}}—COOH$ (d) $CH_3—CH{=}\underset{\underset{CH_3}{|}}{C}—CONH_2$

17 Which statement is not correct for *p*-toluene sulphonyl chloride?

(a) It is known as Hinsberg's reagent.

(b) It is used to distinguish primary and secondary amines.

(c) On treatment with secondary amine, it leads to a product, that is soluble in alkali.

(d) It doesn't react with tertiary amines.

18 The final product 'C' in the following series of reactions

$$C_6H_5NO_2 \xrightarrow{\text{Sn/HCl}} A \xrightarrow[\text{HCl}]{\text{NaNO}_2} B \xrightarrow[\text{NaOH}]{\beta\text{-naphthol}} C$$

(a) N=N, OH (b) OH, N=N

(c) OH, N=N (d) N=N, OH

19 Which of the following is not an example of synthetic detergent?

(a) $CH_3—(CH_2)_{11}—C_6H_4—SO_3^-Na^+$

(b) $CH_3—(CH_2)_{16}—COO^-Na^+$

(c) $\left[CH_3—(CH_2)_{15}—\overset{\overset{CH_3}{|}}{\underset{\underset{CH_3}{|}}{N}}—CH_3\right]^+ Br^-$

(d) $CH_3(CH_2)_{16}COO(CH_2CH_2O)_nCH_2CH_2OH$

20 Which one of the following is a water soluble vitamin, that is not excreted easily?

(a) Vitamin B_2 (b) Vitamin B_1

(c) Vitamin B_6 (d) Vitamin B_{12}

Section B *Numerical Value Questions*

21 CNG is an important transportation fuel. When 100 g CNG is mixed with 208g oxygen in vehicles, it leads to the formation of CO_2 and H_2O and produced large quantity of heat during this combustion, then the amount of carbon dioxide, produced in grams is .... (Nearest integer) [Assume CNG to be methane]

22 In a solid *AB*, *A* atoms are in ccp arrangement and *B* atoms occupy all the octahedral sites. If two atoms from the opposite faces are removed, then the resultant stoichiometry of the compound is A_xB_y. The value of *x* is .... [Nearest integer]

23 Amongst SF_4, XeF_4, CF_4 and H_2O, the number of species with two lone pair of electrons is ....

24 A fish swimming in water body when taken out from the water body is covered with a film of water of weight 36 g. When it is subjected to cooking at 100°C, then the internal energy for vaporisation in kJ mol^{-1} is .... [Nearest integer] [Assume steam to be an ideal gas. Given, $\Delta_{vap}H^\circ$ for water at 373 K and 1 bar is 41.1 kJ mol^{-1}; $R = 8.31\ JK^{-1}\ mol^{-1}$]

25 The osmotic pressure exerted by a solution prepared by dissolving 2.0 g of protein of molar mass 60 kg mol^{-1} in 200 mL of water at 27°C is ...... Pa. [Integer value]
(Use, $R = 0.083$ L bar $mol^{-1} K^{-1}$)

26 40% of HI undergoes decomposition to H_2 and I_2 at 300 K. $\Delta G°$ for this decomposition reaction at one atmosphere pressure is ...... J mol^{-1}. [Nearest integer]
(Use, $R = 8.31$ JK^{-1} mol^{-1}; $\log 2 = 0.3010$, $\ln 10 = 2.3$, $\log 3 = 0.477$)

27 $Cu(s) + Sn^{2+}$ (0.001M) $\longrightarrow$ Cu^{2+}(0.01 M) + Sn(*s*)
The Gibb's free energy change for the above reaction at 298 K is $x \times 10^{-1}$ kJ mol^{-1}.
The value of *x* is .... [Nearest integer]
[Given, $E^{\ominus}_{Cu^{2+}/Cu} = 0.34$ V; $E^{\ominus}_{Sn^{2+}/Sn} = -0.14$ V; F = 96500 C mol^{-1}].

28 Catalyst *A* reduces the activation energy for a reaction by 10 kJ mol^{-1} at 300 K. The ratio of rate constants, $\frac{k', \text{catalysed}}{k, \text{uncatalysed}}$ is e^x. The value of *x* is .... [Nearest integer]
[Assume that, the pre-exponential factor is same in both the cases. Given, $R = 8.31$ JK^{-1} mol^{-1}]

29 Reaction of $[Co(H_2O)_6]^{2+}$ with excess ammonia and in the presence of oxygen results into a diamagnetic product. Number of electrons present in t_{2g}-orbitals of the product is ....

30 The moles of methane required to produce 81 g of water after complete combustion is ...... $\times 10^{-2}$ mol. [Nearest integer]

Answers

Section A

1 *(a)*	2 *(c)*	3 *(d)*	4 *(a)*	5 *(a)*
6 *(d)*	7 *(b)*	8 *(a)*	9 *(a)*	10 *(c)*
11 *(d)*	12 *(b)*	13 *(a)*	14 *(c)*	15 *(c)*
16 *(a)*	17 *(c)*	18 *(c)*	19 *(b)*	20 *(d)*

Section B

21 *(143)*	22 *(3)*	23 *(1)*	24 *(38)*	25 *(415)*
26 *(2740)*	27 *(983)*	28 *(4)*	29 *(6)*	30 *(225)*

See detailed solutions on page no. 345

The Real Nuts

JEE MAIN 2022

(Real Nut 3-29 June 2022, Shift-I)

Chemistry

Instructions

- This question paper contains of 30 Questions of Chemistry, divided into two sections : **Section A** Objective Type Questions and **Section B** Numerical Value Questions.
- **Section A** contains 20 Objective questions and all Questions are compulsory (Marking Scheme : Correct + 4, Incorrect – 1).
- **Section B** contains 10 Numerical value questions out of which only 5 questions are to be attempted (Marking Scheme : Correct + 4, Incorrect 0).

Section A *Objective Type Questions*

1 Production of iron in blast furnace follows the following equation,

$$Fe_3O_4(s) + 4CO(g) \longrightarrow 3Fe(l) + 4CO_2(g)$$

when 4.640 kg of Fe_3O_4 and 2.520 kg of CO are allowed to react then the amount of iron (in g) produced is

[Given, molar atomic mass (g mol^{-1}) Fe = 56 molar atomic mass (g mol^{-1}) O = 16 and molar atomic mass (g mol^{-1}) C = 12.]

(a) 1400 (b) 2200 (c) 3360 (d) 4200

2 Which of the following statements are correct?

(A) The electronic configuration of Cr is $[Ar]3d^5 4s^1$.

(B) The magnetic quantum number may have a negative value.

(C) In the ground state of an atom, the orbitals are filled in order of their increasing energies.

(D) The total number of nodes are given by $n-2$.

Choose the most appropriate answer from the options given below.

(a) (A), (C) and (D) only (b) (A) and (B) only

(c) (A) and (C) only (d) (A), (B) and (C) only

3 Arrange the following in the decreasing order of their covalent character :

(A) LiCl (B) NaCl (C) KCl (D) CsCl

Choose the most appropriate answer from the options given below

(a) (A) > (C) > (B) > (D) (b) (B) > (A) > (C) > (D)

(c) (A) > (B) > (C) > (D) (d) (A) > (B) > (D) > (C)

4 The solubility of AgCl will be maximum in which of the following ?

(a) 0.01 M KCl

(b) 0.01 M HCl

(c) 0.01 M $AgNO_3$

(d) Deionised water

5 Which of the following is a correct statement?

(a) Brownian motion destabilises sols.

(b) Any amount of dispersed phase can be added to emulsion without destabilising it.

(c) Mixing two oppositely charged sols in equal amount neutralises charges and stabilises colloids.

(d) Presence of equal and similar charges on colloidal particles provides stability to the colloidal solution.

6 The electronic configuration of Pt (atomic number 78) is

(a) $[Xe]\ 4f^{14}5d^9 6s^1$

(b) $[Kr]\ 4f^{14}5d^{10}$

(c) $[Xe]\ 4f^{14}5d^{10}$

(d) $[Xe]\ 4f^{14}5d^8 6s^2$

7 In isolation of which one of the following metals from their ores, the use of cyanide salt is not commonly involved ?

(a) Zinc (b) Gold

(c) Silver (d) Copper

8 Which one of the following reactions indicates the reducing ability of hydrogen peroxide in basic medium ?

(a) $HOCl + H_2O_2 \longrightarrow H_3O^+ + Cl^- + O_2$

(b) $PbS + 4H_2O_2 \longrightarrow PbSO_4 + 4H_2O$

(c) $2MnO_4^- + 3H_2O_2 \longrightarrow 2MnO_2 + 3O_2 + 2H_2O + 2OH^-$

(d) $Mn^{2+} + H_2O_2 \longrightarrow Mn^{4+} + 2OH^-$

9 Match the List-I with List-II.

List-I (Metal)	List-II (Emitted light wavelength (nm))
A. Li	I. 670.8
B. Na	II. 589.2
C. Rb	III. 780.0
D. Cs	IV. 455.5

Choose the most appropriate answer from the options given below.

	A	B	C	D		A	B	C	D
(a)	I	II	III	IV	(b)	III	II	I	IV
(c)	III	I	II	IV	(d)	IV	II	I	III

10 Match the List-I with List-II.

List-I (Metal)	List-II (Application)
A. Cs	I. High temperature thermometer
B. Ga	II. Water repellent sprays
C. B	III. Photoelectric cells
D. Si	IV. Bullet proof vest

Choose the most appropriate answer from the options given below.

	A	B	C	D		A	B	C	D
(a)	III	I	IV	II	(b)	IV	III	II	I
(c)	II	III	IV	I	(d)	I	IV	II	III

11 The oxoacid of phosphorus that is easily obtained from a reaction of alkali and white phosphorus and has two P—H bonds, is

(a) phosphonic acid (b) phosphinic acid
(c) pyrophosphorus acid (d) hypophosphoric acid

12 The acid that is believed to be mainly responsible for the damage of Taj Mahal is

(a) sulphuric acid (b) hydrofluoric acid
(c) phosphoric acid (d) hydrochloric acid

13 Two isomers '*A*' and '*B*' with molecular formula C_4H_8 give different products on oxidation with $KMnO_4/H^+$ results in effervescence of a gas and gives ketone. The compound '*A*' is

(a) but-1-ene (b) *cis*-but-2-ene
(c) *trans*-but-2-ene (d) 2-methyl propene

14 [2-bromophenol] $\xrightarrow{(CH_3)_3CLi}$ [A] $\xrightarrow[(ii)\ H_3O^+]{(i)\ CO_2}$ [2-hydroxybenzoic acid: COOH, OH]

In the given conversion the compound *A* is

(a) [benzene ring with Li and OH] (b) [benzene ring with Li and OLi]
(c) [benzene ring with Br and $OC(CH_3)_3$] (d) [benzene ring with $C(CH_3)_3$ and OH]

15 Given below are two statements.

Statement I The esterification of carboxylic acid with an alcohol is a nucleophilic acyl substitution.

Statement II Electron withdrawing groups in the carboxylic acid will increase the rate of esterification reaction.

Choose the most appropriate option.

(a) Both Statement I and Statement II are correct.
(b) Both Statement I and Statement II are incorrect.
(c) Statement I is correct but Statement II is incorrect.
(d) Statement I is incorrect but Statement II is correct.

16 [aniline, NH_2] $\xrightarrow[H_2O]{Br_2(excess)}$ *A* (Major product)

[aniline, NH_2] $\xrightarrow{(i)\ (CH_3CO)_2O,\ (ii)\ Br_2,\ CH_3COOH,\ (iii)\ HCl}$ *B* (Major product)

Consider the above reactions, the product *A* and product *B* respectively are

(a) [NH_2, Br (para)] and [NH_2, Br (para)]
(b) [NH_2, Br, Br, Br] and [NH_2, Br, Br, Br]
(c) [NH_2, Br, Br, Br] and [NH_2, Br (para)]
(d) [NH_2, Br (para)] and [NH_2, Br, Br, Br]

17 The polymer, which can be stretched and retains its original status on releasing the force is

(a) bakelite (b) nylon-6, 6
(c) buna-N (d) terylene

18 Sugar moiety in DNA and RNA molecules respectively are

(a) β-D-2-deoxyribose, β-D-deoxyribose
(b) β-D-2-deoxyribose, β-D-ribose
(c) β-D-ribose, β-D-2-deoxyribose
(d) β-D-deoxyribose, β-D-2-deoxyribose

19. Which of the following compound does not contain sulphur atom?

(a) Cimetidine (b) Ranitidine
(c) Histamine (d) Saccharin

20 Given below are two statements.

Statement I Phenols are weakly acidic.

Statement II Therefore, they are freely soluble in NaOH solution and are weaker acids than alcohols and water.

Choose the most appropriate option.

(a) Both Statement I and Statement II are correct.
(b) Both Statement I and Statement II are incorrect.
(c) Statement I is correct but Statement II is incorrect.
(d) Statement I is incorrect but Statement II is correct.

Section B *Numerical Value Questions*

21 Geraniol, a volatile organic compound, is a component of rose oil. The density of the vapour is $0.46\ gL^{-1}$ at 257°C and 100 mm Hg. The molar mass of geraniol is ...... g mol^{-1}. (Nearest integer) [Given, $R = 0.082$ L atm K^{-1} mol^{-1}]

22 17.0 g of NH_3 completely vapourises at −33.42°C and 1 bar pressure and the enthalpy change in the process is 23.4 kJ mol^{-1}. The enthalpy change for the vaporisation of 85 g of NH_3 under the same conditions is ...... kJ.

23 1.2 mL of acetic acid is dissolved in water to make 2.0 L of solution. The depression in freezing point observed for this strength of acid is 0.0198°C. The percentage of dissociation of the acid is .... (Nearest integer)

[Given, density of acetic acid is 1.02 g mL^{-1}, molar mass of acetic acid is 60 g mol^{-1} $K_f(H_2O) = 1.85$ K kg mol^{-1}]

24 A dilute solution of sulphuric acid is electrolysed using a current of 0.10 A for 2 hours to produce hydrogen and oxygen gas. The total volume of gases produced at STP is ...... cm^3. (Nearest integer) [Given, Faraday constant, $F = 96500$ C mol^{-1} at STP, molar volume of an ideal gas is 22.7 L mol^{-1}]

25 The activation energy of one of the reactions in a biochemical process is 532611 J mol^{-1}. When the temperature falls from 310 K to 300 K, the change in rate constant observed is $k_{300} = x \times 10^{-3}\, k_{310}$.

The value of x is ....

[Given, $\ln 10 = 2.3$, $R = 8.3$ J K^{-1} mol^{-1}]

26 The number of terminal oxygen atoms present in the product *B* obtained from the following reaction is ....

$$FeCr_2O_4 + Na_2CO_3 + O_2 \longrightarrow A + Fe_2O_3 + CO_2$$
$$A + H^+ \longrightarrow B + H_2O + Na^+$$

27 An acidified manganate solution undergoes disproportionation reaction. The spin-only magnetic moment value of the product having manganese in higher oxidation state is ...... BM. (Nearest integer)

28 Kjeldahl's method was used for the estimation of nitrogen in an organic compound. The ammonia evolved from 0.55 g of the compound neutralised 12.5 mL of 1 M H_2SO_4 solution. The percentage of nitrogen in the compound is .... (Nearest integer)

29 Observe structures of the following compounds.

Cl ; H_2N OH O ; NH_2 OH O ; ; OH

The total number of structures/compounds which possess asymmetric carbon atoms is ....

30 $C_6H_{12}O_6 \xrightarrow{\text{Zymase}} A \xrightarrow[\Delta]{\text{NaOI}} B + CHI_3$

The number of carbon atoms present in the product *B* is, ...

Answers

Section A

1 *(c)*	2 *(d)*	3 *(c)*	4 *(d)*	5 *(d)*
6 *(a)*	7 *(d)*	8 *(c)*	9 *(a)*	10 *(a)*
11 *(b)*	12 *(a)*	13 *(d)*	14 *(b)*	15 *(a)*
16 *(c)*	17 *(c)*	18 *(b)*	19 *(c)*	20 *(c)*

Section B

21 *(152)*	22 *(117)*	23 *(5)*	24 *(127)*	25 *(1)*
26 *(6)*	27 *(0)*	28 *(64)*	29 *(3)*	30 *(1)*

See detailed solutions on page no. 349

The Real Nuts

JEE MAIN 2022

(Real Nut 4-25 July 2022, Shift-I)

Chemistry

Instructions

- This question paper contains of 30 Questions of Chemistry, divided into two sections : **Section A** Objective Type Questions and **Section B** Numerical Value Questions.
- **Section A** contains 20 Objective questions and all Questions are compulsory (Marking Scheme : Correct + 4, Incorrect – 1).
- **Section B** contains 10 Numerical value questions out of which only 5 questions are to be attempted (Marking Scheme : Correct + 4, Incorrect 0).

Section A *Objective Type Questions*

1 SO_2Cl_2 on reaction with excess of water results into acidic mixture

$$SO_2Cl_2 + 2H_2O \longrightarrow H_2SO_4 + 2HCl$$

16 moles of NaOH is required for the complete neutralisation of the resultant acidic mixture. The number of moles of SO_2Cl_2 used is

(a) 16 (b) 8 (c) 4 (d) 2

2 Which of the following sets of quantum numbers is not allowed?

(a) $n=3, l=2, m_l=0, s=+\frac{1}{2}$

(b) $n=3, l=2, m_l=-2, s=+\frac{1}{2}$

(c) $n=3, l=3, m_l=-3, s=-\frac{1}{2}$

(d) $n=3, l=0, m_l=0, s=-\frac{1}{2}$

3 The depression in freezing point observed for a formic acid solution of concentration 0.5 mol L^{-1} is 0.0405°C. Density of formic acid is 1.05 g mol L^{-1}. The van't Hoff factor of the formic acid solution is nearly (Given, for water $K_f = 1.86$ K kg mol^{-1})

(a) 0.8 (b) 1.1 (c) 1.9 (d) 2.4

4 20 mL of 0.1 M NH_4OH is mixed with 40 mL of 0.05 M HCl. The pH of the mixture is nearest to (Given, $K_b(NH_4OH) = 1 \times 10^{-5}$, $\log 2 = 0.30$, $\log 3 = 0.48$, $\log 5 = 0.69$, $\log 7 = 0.84$, $\log 11 = 1.04$)

(a) 3.2 (b) 4.2
(c) 5.2 (d) 6.2

5. Match the List I with List II.

	List I		List II
(A)	$N_2(g) + 3H_2(g) \longrightarrow 2NH_3(g)$	(I)	Cu
(B)	$CO(g) + 3H_2(g) \longrightarrow CH_4(g) + H_2O(g)$	(II)	$Cu/ZnO-Cr_2O_3$
(C)	$CO(g) + H_2(g) \longrightarrow HCHO(g)$	(III)	$Fe_xO_y + K_2O + Al_2O_3$
(D)	$CO(g) + 2H_2(g) \longrightarrow CH_3OH(g)$	(IV)	Ni

Choose the correct answer from the options given below.

(a) (A) → (II), (B) → (IV), (C) → (I), (D) → (III)
(b) (A) → (II), (B) → (I), (C) → (IV), (D) → (III)
(c) (A) → (III), (B) → (IV), (C) → (I), (D) → (II)
(d) (A) → (III), (B) → (I), (C) → (IV), (D) → (II)

6 The IUPAC nomenclature of an element with electronic configuration [Rn] $5f^{14}6d^17s^2$ is

(a) unnilbium (b) unnilunium
(c) unnilquadium (d) unniltrium

7 The compound(s) that is(are) removed as slag during the extraction of copper is

(A) CaO (B) FeO (C) Al_2O_3
(D) ZnO (E) NiO

Choose the correct answer from the options given below.

(a) (C), (D) only (b) (A), (B), (E) only
(c) (A), (B) only (d) (B) only

8 The reaction of H_2O_2 with potassium permanganate in acidic medium leads to the formation of mainly

(a) Mn^{2+} (b) Mn^{4+}
(c) Mn^{3+} (d) Mn^{6+}

9 Choose the correct order of density of the alkali metals.

(a) Li < K < Na < Rb < Cs
(b) Li < Na < K < Rb < Cs
(c) Cs < Rb < K < Na < Li
(d) Li < Na < K < Cs < Rb

10 The geometry around boron in the product 'B' formed from the following reaction is

$$BF_3 + NaH \xrightarrow{450\ K} A + NaF$$
$$A + NMe_3 \longrightarrow B$$

(a) trigonal planar (b) tetrahedral
(c) pyramidal (d) square planar

11 The interhalogen compound formed from the reaction of bromine with excess of fluorine is a

(a) hypohalite (b) halate
(c) perhalate (d) halite

12 The photochemical smog does not generally contain

(a) NO (b) NO_2 (c) SO_2 (d) HCHO

13 A compound 'A' on reaction with 'X' and 'Y' produces the same major product but different by product 'a' and 'b'. Oxidation of 'a' gives a substance produced by ants.

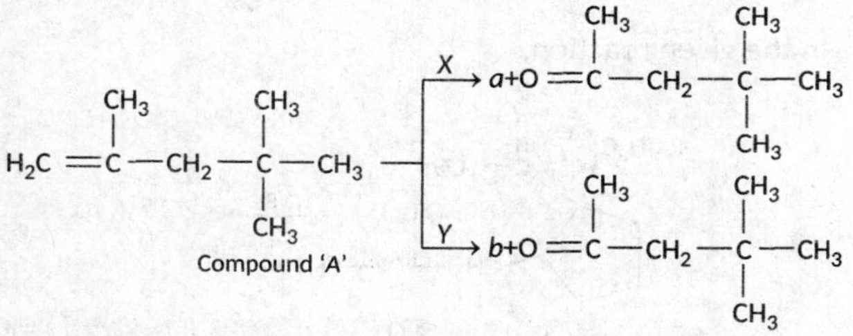

Compound 'A': $H_2C{=}C(CH_3){-}CH_2{-}C(CH_3)_2{-}CH_3$

$\xrightarrow{X}$ a + $O{=}C(CH_3){-}CH_2{-}C(CH_3)_2{-}CH_3$

$\xrightarrow{Y}$ b + $O{=}C(CH_3){-}CH_2{-}C(CH_3)_2{-}CH_3$

'X' and 'Y' respectively are

(a) $KMnO_4 / H^+$ and dil. $KMnO_4$, 273 K
(b) $KMnO_4$(dilute), 273 K and $KMnO_4 / H^+$
(c) $KMnO_4 / H^+$ and O_3, H_2O / Zn
(d) O_3, H_2O / Zn and $KMnO_4 / H^+$

14 Most stable product of the following reaction is

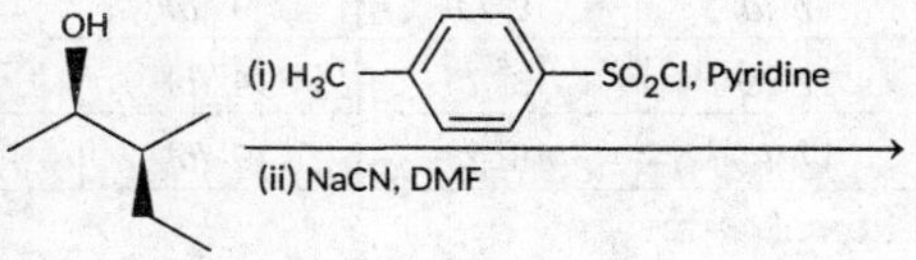

OH (i) $H_3C-C_6H_4-SO_2Cl$, Pyridine; (ii) NaCN, DMF

(a) 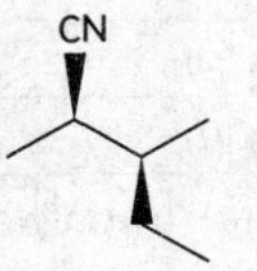 CN (b) 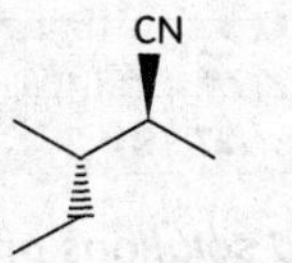 CN (c) 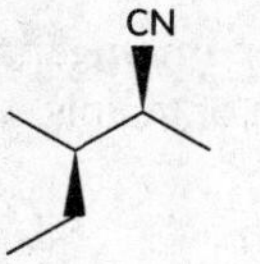 CN (d) 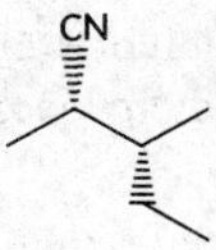 CN

15. Which one of the following reactions does not represent correct combination of substrate and product under the given conditions?

(a) 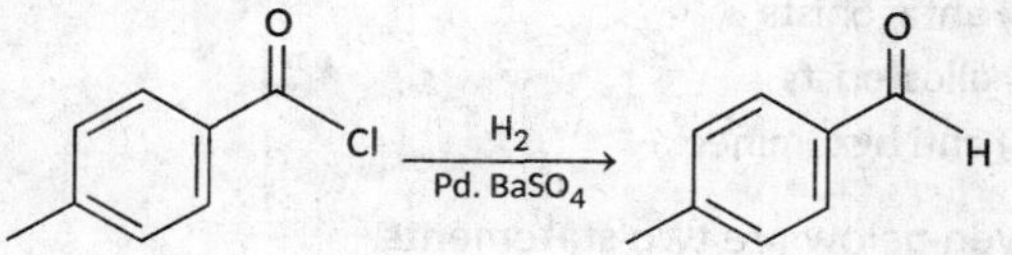 Cl, O $\xrightarrow[\text{Pd. } BaSO_4]{H_2}$ O, H

(b) 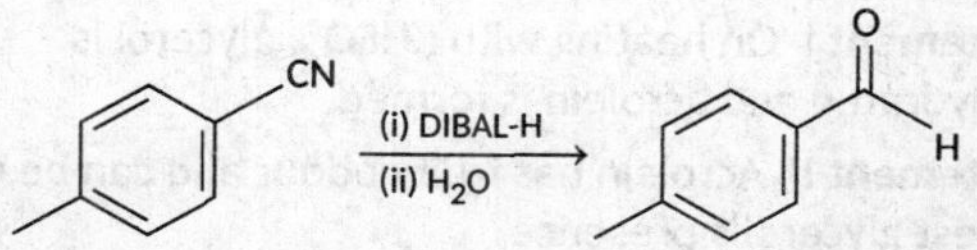 CN $\xrightarrow[\text{(ii) } H_2O]{\text{(i) DIBAL-H}}$ O, H

(c) 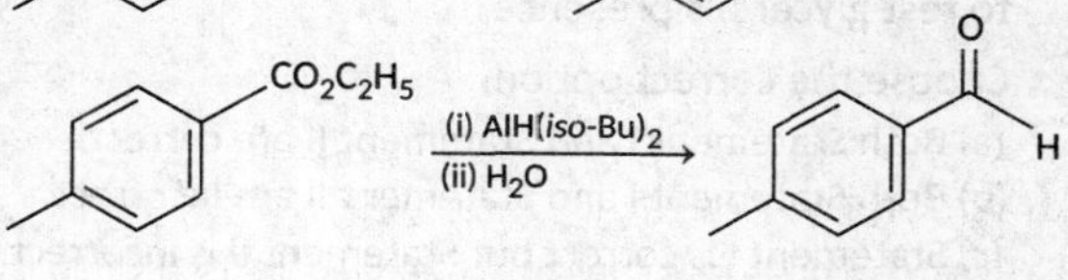 $CO_2C_2H_5$ $\xrightarrow[\text{(ii) } H_2O]{\text{(i) } AlH(iso\text{-}Bu)_2}$ O, H

(d) 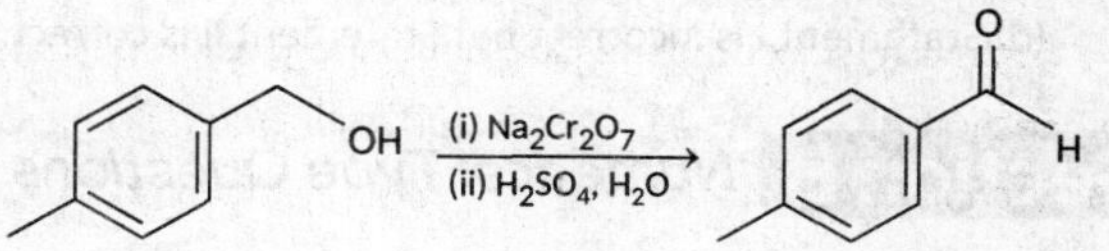 OH $\xrightarrow[\text{(ii) } H_2SO_4, H_2O]{\text{(i) } Na_2Cr_2O_7}$ O, H

16 An organic compound 'A' on reaction with NH_3 followed by heating gives compound B. Which on further strong heating gives compound C($C_8H_5NO_2$). Compound C on sequential reaction with ethanolic KOH, alkyl chloride and hydrolysis with alkali gives a primary amine. The compound A is

(a) 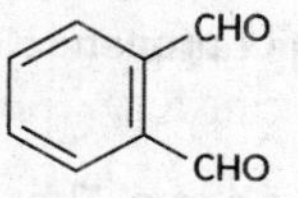 CHO, CHO (b) 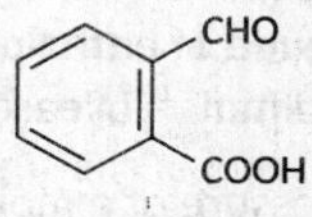 CHO, COOH
(c) 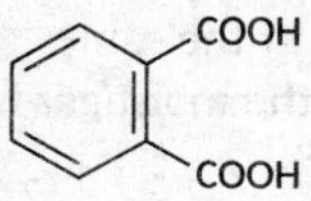 COOH, COOH (d) 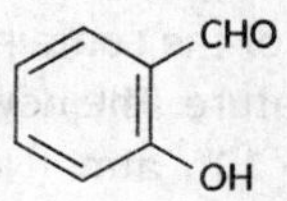 CHO, OH

17 Melamine polymer is formed by the condensation of

(a) 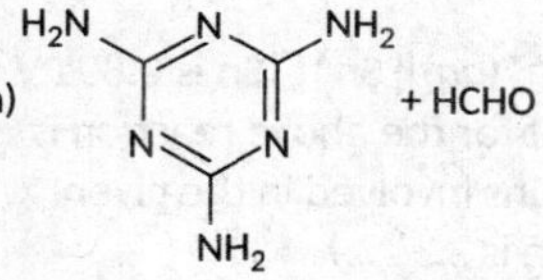 H_2N, N, NH_2, N, N, NH_2 + HCHO
(b) 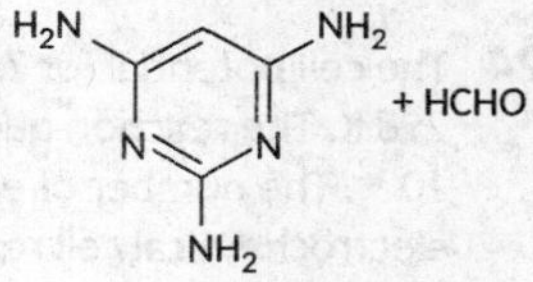 H_2N, NH_2, N, N, NH_2 + HCHO
(c) 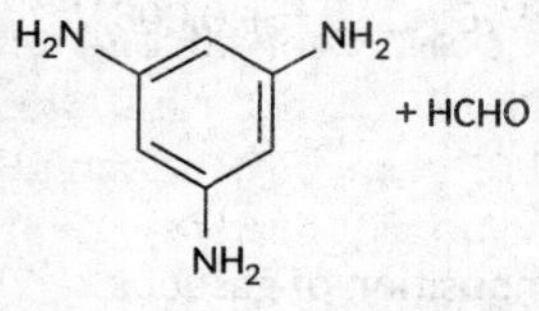 H_2N, NH_2, NH_2 + HCHO
(d) 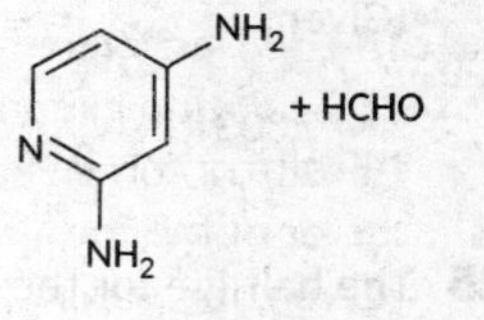 NH_2, N, NH_2 + HCHO

18 During the denaturation of proteins, which of these structures will remain intact?

(a) Primary
(b) Secondary
(c) Tertiary
(d) Quaternary

19 Drugs used to bind to receptors, inhibiting its natural function and blocking a message are called

(a) agonists
(b) antagonists
(c) allosterists
(d) anti histamines

20 Given below are two statements.

Statement I On heating with $KHSO_4$, glycerol is dehydrated and acrolein is formed.

Statement II Acrolein has fruity odour and can be used to test glycerol's presence.

Choose the correct option.

(a) Both Statement I and Statement II are correct.
(b) Both Statement I and Statement II are incorrect.
(c) Statement I is correct but Statement II is incorrect.
(d) Statement I is incorrect but Statement II is correct.

Section B *Numerical Type Questions*

21 Among the following species N_2, N_2^+, N_2^-, N_2^{2-}, O_2, O_2^+, O_2^-, O_2^{2-}, the number of species showing diamagnetism is ....

22 The enthalpy of combustion of propane, graphite and dihydrogen at 298 K are – 2220.0 kJ mol^{-1}, – 393.5 kJ mol^{-1} and –285.8 kJ mol^{-1} respectively. The magnitude of enthalpy of formation of propane (C_3H_8) is .... kJ mol^{-1}. (Nearest integer)

23 The pressure of a moist gas at 27°C is 4 atm. The volume of the container is doubled at the same temperature. The new pressure of the moist gas is .... $\times 10^{-1}$ atm. (Nearest integer)

(Given, the vapour pressure of water at 27°C is 0.4 atm.)

24 The cell potential for $Zn|Zn^{2+}(aq)||Sn^{x+}|Sn$ is 0.801 V at 298 K. The reaction quotient for the above reaction is 10^{-2}. The number of electrons involved in the given electrochemical cell reaction is ....

(Given, $E^\circ_{Zn^{2+}/Zn} = -0.763$ V, $E^\circ_{Sn^{x+}/Sn} = +0.008$ V and $\frac{2.303\,RT}{F} = 0.06$ V)

25 The half-life for the decomposition of gaseous compound A is 240 s when the gaseous pressure was 500 torr initially. When the pressure was 250 torr, the half-life was found to be 4.0 min. The order of the reaction is .... (Nearest integer)

26 Consider the following metal complexes

$[Co(NH_3)_6]^{3+}$; $[CoCl(NH_3)_5]^{2+}$

$[Co(CN)_6]^{3-}$; $[Co(NH_3)_5(H_2O)]^{3+}$

The spin-only magnetic moment value of the complex that absorbs light with shortest wavelength is .... BM. (Nearest integer)

27 Among Co^{3+}, Ti^{2+}, V^{2+} and Cr^{2+} ions, one if used as a reagent cannot liberate rH_2 from dilute mineral acid solution, its spin-only magnetic moment in gaseous state is .... BM. (Nearest integer)

28 While estimating the nitrogen present in an organic compound by Kjeldahl's method, the ammonia evolved from 0.25 g of the compound neutralised 2.5 mL of 2 M H_2SO_4. The percentage of nitrogen present in organic compound is ....

29 The number of sp^3 hybridised carbons in an acyclic neutral compound with molecular formula C_4H_5N is ....

30 In the given reaction,

(Cyclopentane ring bearing H_3C and $-C(=O)-OEt$ on one carbon, and $-CH_2-C(=O)-CH_3$ on the adjacent carbon) $\xrightarrow{\overset{\ominus}{O}Et}$ A

(where, Et is — C_2H_5)

The number of chiral carbon(s) in product A is ....

Answers

Section A

1 (c)	2 (c)	3 (c)	4 (c)	5 (c)
6 (d)	7 (d)	8 (a)	9 (a)	10 (b)
11 (b)	12 (c)	13 (d)	14 (b)	15 (d)
16 (c)	17 (a)	18 (a)	19 (b)	20 (c)

Section B

21 (2)	22 (124)	23 (22)	24 (4)	25 (1)
26 (0)	27 (5)	28 (56)	29 (1)	30 (2)

See detailed solutions on page no. 354

The Real Nuts

JEE MAIN 2022

(Real Nut 5-27 July 2022, Shift-II)

Chemistry

See Instructions Real Nut 4

Section A *Objective Type Questions*

1 The correct decreasing order of energy for the orbitals having, following set of quantum numbers

(A) $n=3, l=0, m=0$; (B) $n=4, l=0, m=0$
(C) $n=3, l=1, m=0$; (D) $n=3, l=2, m=1$

(a) (D) > (B) > (C) > (A) (b) (B) > (D) > (C) > (A)
(c) (C) > (B) > (D) > (A) (d) (B) > (C) > (D) > (A)

2 Match List I with List II.

	List-I		List-II
(A)	$\psi_{MO} = \psi_A - \psi_B$	(I)	Dipole moment
(B)	$\mu = Q \times r$	(II)	Bonding molecular orbital
(C)	$\frac{N_b - N_a}{2}$	(III)	Anti-bonding molecular orbital
(D)	$\psi_{MO} = \psi_A + \psi_B$	(IV)	Bond order

Choose the correct answer from options given below.
(a) (A)-(II), (B)-(I), (C)-(IV), (D)-(III)
(b) (A)-(III), (B)-(IV), (C)-(I), (D)-(II)
(c) (A)-(III), (B)-(I), (C)-(IV), (D)-(II)
(d) (A)-(III), (B)-(IV), (C)-(II), (D)-(I)

3 The plot of pH-metric titration of weak base NH_4OH *vs* strong acid HCl looks like

(a)
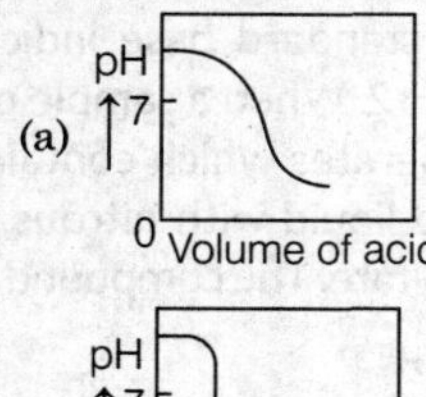

(b)
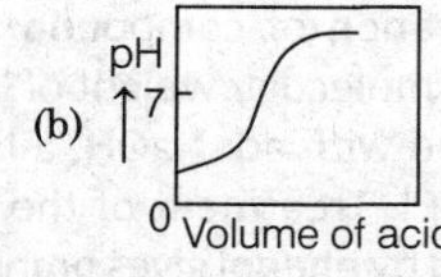

(c)
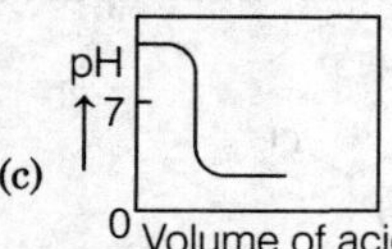

(d)
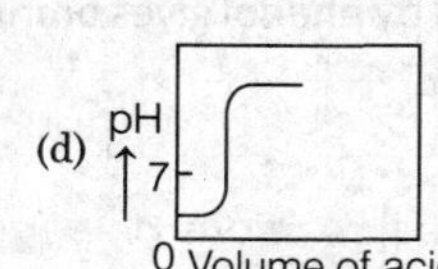

4 Given below are two statements.

Statement I For KI, molar conductivity increases steeply with dilution.

Statement II For carbonic acid, molar conductivity increases slowly with dilution.

In the light of the above statements, choose the correct answer from the options given below.
(a) Both Statement I and Statement II are correct.
(b) Both Statement I and Statement II are incorrect.
(c) Statement I is correct but Statement II is incorrect.
(d) Statement I is incorrect but Statement II is correct.

5 Given below are two statements, one is labelled as Assertion (A) and the other is labelled as Reason (R).

Assertion (A) Dissolved substances can be removed from a colloidal solution by diffusion through a parchment paper.

Reason (R) Particles in a true solution cannot pass through parchment paper but the colloidal particles can pass through the parchment paper.

In the light of the above statements, choose the correct answer from the options given below.
(a) Both (A) and (R) are correct and (R) is the correct explanation of (A).
(b) Both (A) and (R) are correct but (R) is not the correct explanation of (A).
(c) (A) is correct but (R) is not correct.
(d) (A) is not correct but (R) is correct.

6 Outermost electronic configurations of four elements A, B, C, D are given below.

(A) $3s^2$ (B) $3s^2 3p^1$ (C) $3s^2 3p^3$ (D) $3s^2 3p^4$

The correct order of fist ionisation enthalpy for them is
(a) (A) < (B) < (C) < (D) (b) (B) < (A) < (D) < (C)
(c) (B) < (D) < (A) < (C) (d) (B) < (A) < (C) < (D)

7 An element A of group 1 shows similarity to an element B belonging to group 2. If A has maximum hydration enthalpy in group 1 then B is
(a) Mg (b) Be (c) Ca (d) Sr

8 Given below are two statements, one is labelled as Assertion (A) and the other is labelled as Reason (R).

Assertion (A) Boron is unable to form BF_6^{3-}.

Reason (R) Size of B is very small.

In the light of the above statements, choose the correct answer from the options given below.

(a) Both (A) and (R) are true and (R) is the correct explanation of (A).
(b) Both (A) and (R) are true but (R) is not the correct explanation of (A).
(c) (A) is true but (R) is false.
(d) (A) is false but (R) is true.

9 In neutral or alkaline solution, MnO_4^- oxidises thiosulphate to

(a) $S_2O_7^{2-}$ (b) $S_2O_8^{2-}$ (c) SO_3^{2-} (d) SO_4^{2-}

10 Low oxidation state of metals in their complexes are common when ligands

(a) have good π-accepting character
(b) have good σ-donor character
(c) are having good π-donating ability
(d) are having poor σ-donating ability

11 Given below are two statements:

Statement I The non bio-degradable fly ash and slag from steel industry can be used by cement industry.

Statement II The fuel obtained from plastic waste is lead free.

In the light of the above statements, choose the most appropriate answer from the options given below.

(a) Both Statement I and Statement II are correct.
(b) Both Statement I and Statement II are incorrect.
(c) Statement I is correct but Statement II is incorrect.
(d) Statement I is incorrect but Statement II is correct.

12 The structure of A in the given reaction is

$$R-CO-CH_3 \xrightarrow[\text{CH}_3\text{CH}_2\text{Br}]{\text{NaOH}} \underset{\text{Major product}}{A}$$

(a) $R-C(OH)(CH_3)-CH(CH_3)Br$ (b) $R-C(OH)(CH_3)-CH_2CH_3$

(c) $R-CO-CH_2CH_2CH_3$ (d) $R-CO-CH_2CH_2CH_2CH_2-OH$

13 Major product 'B' of the following reaction sequence is

$$CH_3-\underset{CH_3}{\underset{|}{C}}=CH-CH_3 \xrightarrow[\text{CH}_3\text{OH}]{\text{Br}_2} A \xrightarrow{\text{HI}} \underset{\text{(Major product)}}{B}$$

(a) $CH_3-C(OH)(CH_3)-CH(Br)-CH_3$ (b) $CH_3-C(I)(CH_3)-CH(Br)-CH_3$

(c) $CH_3-C(Br)(CH_3)-CH(OH)-CH_3$ (d) $CH_3-C(Br)(CH_3)-CH(I)-CH_3$

14 Match List I with List II.

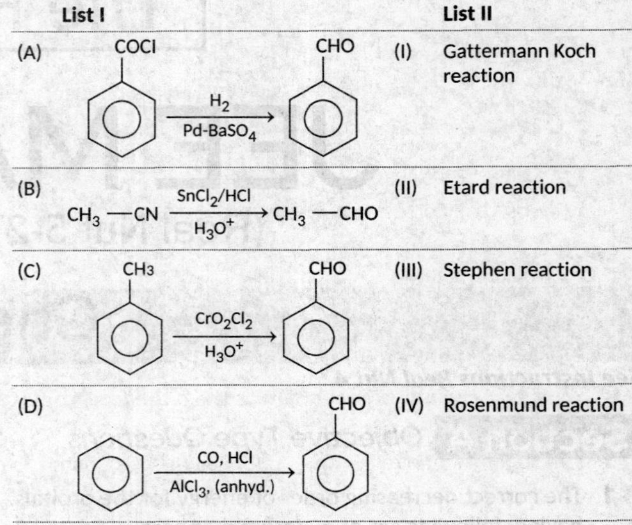

	List I		List II
(A)	$C_6H_5COCl \xrightarrow[\text{Pd-BaSO}_4]{H_2} C_6H_5CHO$	(I)	Gattermann Koch reaction
(B)	$CH_3-CN \xrightarrow[H_3O^+]{SnCl_2/HCl} CH_3-CHO$	(II)	Etard reaction
(C)	$C_6H_5CH_3 \xrightarrow[H_3O^+]{CrO_2Cl_2} C_6H_5CHO$	(III)	Stephen reaction
(D)	$C_6H_6 \xrightarrow[\text{AlCl}_3\text{ (anhyd.)}]{\text{CO, HCl}} C_6H_5CHO$	(IV)	Rosenmund reaction

Choose the correct answer from the options given below.

(a) (A) $\rightarrow$ (IV), (B) $\rightarrow$ (III), (C) $\rightarrow$ (II), (D) $\rightarrow$ (I)
(b) (A) $\rightarrow$ (I), (B) $\rightarrow$ (II), (C) $\rightarrow$ (III), (D) $\rightarrow$ (IV)
(c) (A) $\rightarrow$ (II), (B) $\rightarrow$ (III), (C) $\rightarrow$ (IV), (D) $\rightarrow$ (I)
(d) (A) $\rightarrow$ (III), (B) $\rightarrow$ (II), (C) $\rightarrow$ (I), (D) $\rightarrow$ (IV)

15 Match List I with List II.

	List I (Polymer)		List II (Monomer)
(A)	Neoprene	(I)	Acrylonitrile
(B)	Teflon	(II)	Chloroprene
(C)	Acrilan	(III)	Tetrafluoroethene
(D)	Natural rubber	(IV)	Isoprene

Choose the correct answer from the options given below.

(a) (A) $\rightarrow$ (II), (B) $\rightarrow$ (III), (C) $\rightarrow$ (I), (D) $\rightarrow$ (IV)
(b) (A) $\rightarrow$ (II), (B) $\rightarrow$ (I), (C) $\rightarrow$ (III), (D) $\rightarrow$ (IV)
(c) (A) $\rightarrow$ (II), (B) $\rightarrow$ (I), (C) $\rightarrow$ (IV), (D) $\rightarrow$ (III)
(d) (A) $\rightarrow$ (I), (B) $\rightarrow$ (II), (C) $\rightarrow$ (III), (D) $\rightarrow$ (IV)

16 An organic compound 'A' contains nitrogen and chlorine. It dissolves readily in water to give a solution that turns litmus red. Titration of compound 'A' with standard base indicates that the molecular weight of 'A' is 131 ± 2. When a sample of 'A' is treated with aq. NaOH, a liquid separates which contains N but not Cl. Treatment of the obtained liquid with nitrous acid followed by phenol gives orange precipitate. The compound A is

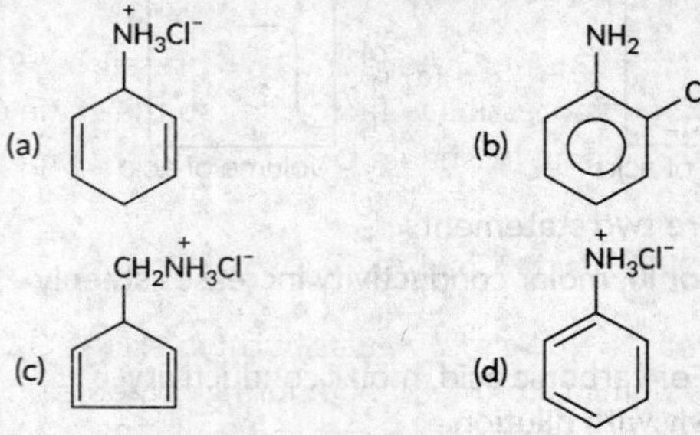

17 Match List I with List II.

List I		List II
(A) Glucose + HI	(I)	Gluconic acid
(B) Glucose + Br_2 water	(II)	Glucose pentacetate
(C) Glucose + acetic anhydride	(III)	Saccharic acid
(D) Glucose + HNO_3	(IV)	Hexane

Choose the correct answer from the options given below.

(a) (A)-(IV), (B)-(I), (C)-(II), (D)-(III)

(b) (A)-(IV), (B)-(III), (C)-(II), (D)-(I)

(c) (A)-(III), (B)-(I), (C)-(IV), (D)-(II)

(d) (A)-(I), (B)-(III), (C)-(IV), (D)-(II)

18 Which of the following enhances the lathering property of soap?

(a) Sodium stearate (b) Sodium carbonate

(c) Sodium rosinate (d) Trisodium phosphate

19 Match List I with List II.

	List I (Mixture)		List II (Purification process)
(A)	Chloroform and aniline	(I)	Steam distillation
(B)	Benzoic acid and naphthalene	(II)	Sublimation
(C)	Water and aniline	(III)	Distillation
(D)	Naphthalene and sodium chloride	(IV)	Crystallisation

Choose the correct answer from the options given below.

(a) (A) $\rightarrow$ (IV), (B) $\rightarrow$ (III), (C) $\rightarrow$ (I), (D) $\rightarrow$ (II)

(b) (A) $\rightarrow$ (III), (B) $\rightarrow$ (I), (C) $\rightarrow$ (IV), (D) $\rightarrow$ (II)

(c) (A) $\rightarrow$ (III), (B) $\rightarrow$ (IV), (C) $\rightarrow$ (II), (D) $\rightarrow$ (I)

(d) (A) $\rightarrow$ (III), (B) $\rightarrow$ (IV), (C) $\rightarrow$ (I), (D) $\rightarrow$ (II)

20 Fe^{3+} cation gives a prussian blue precipitate on addition of potassium ferrocyanide solution due to the formation of

(a) $[Fe(H_2O)_6]_2 [Fe(CN)_6]$ (b) $Fe_2[Fe(CN)_6]_2$

(c) $Fe_3[Fe(OH)_2(CN)_4]_2$ (d) $Fe_4[Fe(CN)_6]_3$

Section B *Numerical Type Questions*

21 The normality of H_2SO_4 in the solution obtained on mixing 100 mL of 0.1 M H_2SO_4 with 50 mL of 0.1 M NaOH is .... $\times 10^{-1}$N. (Nearest integer)

22 For a real gas at 25°C temperature and high pressure (99 bar) the value of compressibility factor is 2, so the value of van der Waals' constant '*b*' should be .... $\times 10^{-2}$ L mol^{-1}. (Nearest integer)

(Given, $R = 0.083$ L bar K^{-1} mol^{-1}).

23 A gas (molar mass = 280 g mol^{-1}) was burnt in excess O_2 in a constant volume calorimeter and during combustion the temperature of calorimeter increased from 298.0 K to 298.45 K. If the heat capacity of calorimeter is 2.5 kJ K^{-1} and enthalpy of combustion of gas is 9 kJ mol^{-1} then amount of gas burnt is .... g. (Nearest integer)

24 When a certain amount of solid A is dissolved in 100 g of water at 25°C to make a dilute solution, the vapour pressure of the solution is reduced to one-half of that of pure water. The vapour pressure of pure water is 23.76 mmHg. The number of moles of solute A added is .... (Nearest integer)

25 $\underset{\text{Reactant}}{[A]} \longrightarrow \underset{\text{Product}}{[B]}$

If formation of compound [*B*] follows the first order of kinetics and after 70 minutes the concentration of [*A*] was found to be half of its initial concentration. Then the rate constant of the reaction is $x \times 10^{-6} s^{-1}$. The value of *x* is .... (Nearest integer)

26 Among the following ores Bauxite, Siderite, Cuprite, Calamine, Haematite, Kaolinite, Malachite, Magnetite, Sphalerite, Limonite, Cryolite.

The number of principal ores of iron is ....

27 The oxidation state of manganese in the product obtained in a reaction of potassium permanganate and hydrogen peroxide in basic medium is ....

28 The number of molecule(s) or ion(s) from the following having non-planar structure is ....

NO_3^-, H_2O_2, BF_3, PCl_3, XeF_4, SF_4, XeO_3, PH_4^+, SO_3, $[Al(OH)_4]^-$

29 The spin only magnetic moment of the complex present in Fehling's reagent is .... BM. (Nearest integer)

30 Toluene (CH_3) $\longrightarrow$ Benzaldehyde (CHO)

5 g (92%)

In the above reaction, 5 g of toluene is converted into benzaldehyde with 92% yield. The amount of benzaldehyde produced is .... $\times 10^{-2}$ g. (Nearest integer).

Answers

Section A

1 *(a)*	2 *(c)*	3 *(a)*	4 *(b)*	5 *(c)*
6 *(b)*	7 *(a)*	8 *(b)*	9 *(d)*	10 *(a)*
11 *(a)*	12 *(c)*	13 *(b)*	14 *(a)*	15 *(a)*
16 *(d)*	17 *(a)*	18 *(c)*	19 *(d)*	20 *(d)*

Section B

21 *(1)*	22 *(25)*	23 *(35)*	24 *(6)*	25 *(165)*
26 *(4)*	27 *(4)*	28 *(6)*	29 *(2)*	30 *(530)*

See detailed solutions on page no. 358

The Real Nuts

JEE ADVANCED 2022

(Real Nut 6-Solved Paper 2022)

Chemistry

Paper 1

SECTION 1 (Maximum Marks: 24)

- This section contains **EIGHT (08)** questions.
- The answer to each question is a **NUMERICAL VALUE.**
- For each question, enter the correct numerical value of the answer using the mouse and the on-screen virtual numeric keypad in the place designated to enter the answer. If the numerical value has more than two decimal places, **truncate/round-off** the value to **TWO** decimal places.
- Answer to each question will be evaluated according to the following marking scheme:

Full Marks : +3 **ONLY** if the correct numerical value is entered;

Zero Marks : 0 In all other cases.

1. 2 moles of Hg(*g*) is combusted in a fixed volume bomb calorimeter with excess of O_2 at 298 K and 1 atm into HgO(*s*). During the reaction, temperature increases from 298.0 K to 312.8 K. If heat capacity of the bomb calorimeter and enthalpy of formation of Hg(*g*) are 20.00 kJ K^{-1} and 61.32 kJ mol^{-1} at 298 K, respectively, the calculated standard molar enthalpy of formation of HgO(*s*) at 298 K is X kJ mol^{-1}. The value of $|X|$ is ....
[Given, gas constant $R = 8.3 J K^{-1} mol^{-1}$]

2. The reduction potential ($E°$, in V) of $MnO_4^-(aq)/Mn(s)$ is
[Given, $E°_{MnO_4^-(aq)/MnO_2(s)} = 1.68$ V ;
$E°_{MnO_2(s)/Mn^{2+}(aq)} = 1.21$ V ; $E°_{Mn^{2+}(aq)/MN(s)} = -1.03$ V]

3. A solution is prepared by mixing 0.01 mole each of H_2CO_3, $NaHCO_3$, Na_2CO_3, and NaOH in 100 mL of water. pH of the resulting solution is ....
[Given, pK_{a_1} and pK_{a_2} of H_2CO_3 and 6.37 and 10.32, respectively; log 2 = 0.30]

4. The treatment of an aqueous solution of 3.74 g of $Cu(NO_3)_2$ with excess KI results in a brown solution alongwith the formation of a precipitate. Passing H_2S through this brown solution gives another precipitate X. The amount of X (in g) is ....
[Given, atomic mass of H = 1, N = 14, O = 16, S = 32, K = 39, Cu = 63, I = 127]

5. Dissolving 1.24 g of white phosphorus in boiling NaOH solution in an inert atmosphere gives a gas Q. The amount of $CuSO_4$ (in g) required to completely consume the gas Q is .... [Given, atomic mass of H = 1, O = 16, Na = 23, P = 31, S = 32, Cu = 63]

6. Consider the following reaction.

4-bromobenzyl alcohol (structure: benzene ring with CH_2OH and Br para) $\xrightarrow[Br_2]{\text{Red phosphorus}}$ *R*(major product)

On estimation of bromine in 1.00 g of *R* using Carius method, the amount of AgBr formed (in g) is ....
[Given, atomic mass of H = 1, C = 12, O = 16, P = 31, Br = 80, Ag = 108].

7. The weight percentage of hydrogen in Q, formed in the following reaction sequence, is ....

Chlorobenzene (Cl on benzene ring) $\xrightarrow[\text{2. conc. } H_2SO_4 \text{ and then conc. } HNO_3]{\text{1. NaOH, 623 K, 300 atm}}$ Q(major product)

[Given, atomic mass of H = 1 , C = 12, N = 14, O = 16, S = 32, Cl = 35

8. If the reaction sequence given below is carried out with 15 moles of acetylene, the amount of the product *D* formed (in g) is ....

$$HC\equiv CH \xrightarrow[\text{}]{\text{Iron tube (red hot)}} \underset{(80\%)}{A} \xrightarrow[AlCl_3]{H_3C\text{-}CH_2\text{-}CH_2\text{-}Cl} \underset{(50\%)}{B} \xrightarrow[-CH_3COCH_3]{1.\ O_2,\ 2.\ H_3O^+} \underset{(50\%)}{C} \xrightarrow[\text{Pyridine}]{CH_3COCl} \underset{(100\%)}{D}$$

The yields of *A*, *B*, *C* and *D* are given in parentheses. [Given, atomic mass of H = 1, C = 12, O = 16, Cl = 35]

SECTION 2 (Maximum Marks: 24)

- This section contains **SIX (06)** questions.
- Each question has **FOUR** options (a), (b), (c) and (d). **ONE OR MORE THAN ONE** of these four option(s) is (are) correct answer(s).
- For each question, choose the option(s) corresponding to (all) the correct answer(s).
- Answer to each question will be evaluated according to the following marking scheme.

Full marks	: +4	**ONLY** if (all) the correct option(s) is (are) chosen;
Partial Marks	: +3	If all the four options are correct but **ONLY** three option are chosen;
Partial Marks	: +2	If three or more options are correct but **ONLY** two options are chosen, both of which are correct;
Partial Marks	: +1	If two or more options are correct but **ONLY** one option is chosen and it is a correct option;
Zero Marks	: 0	If none of the options is chosen (i.e. the question is unanswered);
Negative marks	: −2	In all other cases.

9. For diatomic molecules, the correct statement(s) about the molecular orbitals formed by the overlap of two $2p_z$ orbitals is (are)

(a) σ orbital has a total of two nodal planes.

(b) σ^* orbital has one node in the *xz*-plane containing the molecular axis.

(c) π orbital has one node in the plane which is perpendicular to the molecular axis and goes through the center of the molecule.

(d) π^* orbital has one node in the *xy*-plane containing the molecular axis.

10. The correct option(s) related to adsorption processes is (are)

(a) chemisorption results in a unimolecular layer .

(b) the enthalpy change during physisorption is in the range of 100 to 140 $kJ\,mol^{-1}$.

(c) chemisorption is an endothermic process.

(d) lowering the temperature favors physisorption processes.

11. The electrochemical extraction of aluminium from bauxite ore involves

(a) the reaction of Al_2O_3 with coke (C) at a temperature > 2500 °C.

(b) the neutralisation of aluminate solution by passing CO_2 gas to precipitate hydrated alumina ($Al_2O_3 \cdot 3H_2O$).

(c) the dissolution of Al_2O_3 in hot aqueous NaOH.

(d) the electrolysis of Al_2O_3 mixed with Na_3AlF_6 to give Al and CO_2.

12. The treatment of galena with HNO_3 produces a gas that is

(a) paramagnetic (b) bent in geometry

(c) an acidic oxide (d) colourless

13. Considering the reaction sequence given below, the correct statement(s) is(are)

$$H_3C\text{-}CH_2\text{-}COOH \xrightarrow[2.\ H_2O]{1.\ Br_2,\ \text{red phosphorus}} P \xrightarrow[2.\ NaOH,\ 3.\ H_3O^+]{1.\ \text{potassium phthalimide } (N^{\ominus}K^{\oplus})} Q + \text{phthalic acid (benzene-1,2-dicarboxylic acid, COOH, COOH)}$$

(a) *P* can be reduced to a primary alcohol using $NaBH_4$.

(b) Treating *P* with conc. NH_4OH solution followed by acidification gives Q.

(c) Treating Q with a solution of $NaNO_2$ in aq. HCl liberates N_2.

(d) *P* is more acidic than CH_3CH_2COOH.

14. Considering the following reaction sequence,

$$\text{4-nitrotoluene } (NO_2, H_3C) \xrightarrow{P} Q \xrightarrow{R} S \xrightarrow{H_2O} T;\quad S \xrightarrow{U} \text{benzoic acid (COOH)}$$

The correct option(s) is (are)

(a) $P = H_2/Pd$, ethanol $R = NaNO_2/HCl$ U = 1. H_3PO_2 2. KMnO4 – KOH, heat

(b) P = Sn/HCl $R = HNO_2$ S = (4-methylbenzenediazonium chloride, H_3C–C_6H_4–$\overset{\oplus}{N_2}\overset{\ominus}{Cl}$)

(c) S = (4-methylbenzenediazonium chloride, H_3C–C_6H_4–$\overset{\oplus}{N_2}\overset{\ominus}{Cl}$) T = (H_3C–C_6H_4–OH) U = 1. CH_3CH_2OH 2. $KMnO_4$ – KOH, heat

(d) Q = (HOOC–C_6H_4–NO_2) $R = H_2/Pd$, ethanol T = (H_3C–C_6H_4–OH)

SECTION 3 (Maximum Marks : 12)

- This section contains **FOUR** (04) Matching List Sets.
- Each set has **ONE** Multiple Choice Question.
- Each set has **TWO** lists: **List I** and **List II**.
- **List I** has **Four** entries (I), (II), (III) and (IV) and **List II** has **Five** entries (P), (Q), (R), (S) and (T).
- **FOUR** options are given in each Multiple Choice Question based on **List I** and **List II** and **ONLY ONE** of these four options satisfies the condition asked in the Multiple Choice Question.
- Answer to each question will be evaluated according to the following marking scheme:
  Full Marks : +3 **ONLY** if the option corresponding to the correct combination is chosen;
  Zero Marks : 0 If none of the options is chosen (i.e. the question is unanswered);
  Negative Marks : –1 In all other cases.

15. **Match the rate expressions in LIST-I for the decomposition of X with the corresponding profiles provided in LIST-II. X_s and K are constants having appropriate units.**

List I	List II
(I) rate $= \dfrac{k[X]}{X_s + [X]}$ Under all possible initial concentrations of X.	(P) Half-life ($t_{1/2}$) vs Initial concentration of X
(II) rate $= \dfrac{k[X]}{X_s + [X]}$, where initial concentrations of X are much less than X_s.	(Q) Half-life ($t_{1/2}$) vs Initial concentration of X

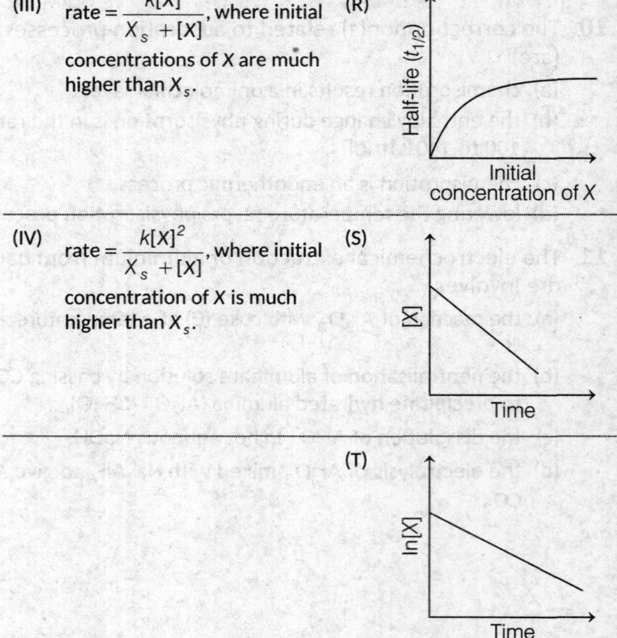

(a) I → P; II → Q; III → S; IV → T
(b) I → R; II → S; III → S; IV → T
(c) I → P; II → Q; III → Q; IV → R
(d) I → R; II → S; III → Q; IV → R

16. LIST-I contains compounds and LIST-II contains reactions.

	List I		List II
(I)	H_2O_2	(P)	$Mg(HCO_3)_2 + Ca(OH)_2 \longrightarrow$
(II)	$Mg(OH)_2$	(Q)	$BaO_2 + H_2SO_4 \longrightarrow$
(III)	$BaCl_2$	(R)	$Ca(OH)_2 + MgCl_2 \longrightarrow$
(IV)	$CaCO_3$	(S)	$BaO_2 + HCl \longrightarrow$
		(T)	$Ca(HCO_3)_2 + Ca(OH)_2 \longrightarrow$

Match each compound in LIST-I with its formation reaction(s) in LIST-II, and choose the correct option.
(a) I → Q; II → P; III → S; IV → R
(b) I → T; II → P; III → Q; IV → R
(c) I → T; II → R; III → Q; IV → P
(d) I → Q; II → R; III → S; IV → P

17. LIST-I contains metal species and LIST-II contains their properties.

	List I		List II
(I)	$[Cr(CN)_6]^{4-}$	(P)	t_{2g} orbitals contain 4 electrons
(II)	$[RuCl_6]^{2-}$	(Q)	μ (spin-only) = 4.9 BM
(III)	$[Cr(H_2O)_6]^{2+}$	(R)	Low spin complex ion
(IV)	$[Fe(H_2O)_6]^{2+}$	(S)	metal ion in + 4 oxidation state
		(T)	d^4 species

[Given, atomic number of Cr = 24, Ru = 44, Fe = 26]

Match each metal species in LIST-I with their properties in LIST-II, and choose the correct option
(a) I → R, T; II → P, S; III → Q, T; IV → P,Q
(b) I → R, S; II → P, T; III → P, Q; IV → Q, T
(c) I → P, R; II → R, S; III → R, T; IV → P, T
(d) I → Q, T; II → S, T; III → P, T; IV → Q, R

18. Match the compounds in LIST-I with the observations in LIST-II, and choose the correct option.

	List I		List II
(I)	Aniline	(P)	Sodium fusion extract of the compound on boiling with $FeSO_4$, followed by acidification with conc. H_2SO_4, gives Prussian blue colour.
(II)	*o*-cresol	(Q)	Sodium fusion extract of the compound on treatment with sodium nitroprusside gives blood red colour.
(III)	Cysteine	(R)	Addition of the compound to a saturated solution of $NaHCO_3$ results in effervescence.
(IV)	Caprolactam	(S)	The compound reacts with bromine water to give a white precipitate.
		(T)	Treating the compound with neutral $FeCl_3$ solution produces violet colour.

(a) I → P, Q; II → S; III → Q, R; IV → P
(b) I → P; II → R, S; III → R; IV → Q, S
(c) I → Q, S; II → P, T; III → P; IV → S
(d) I → P; II → T; III → Q, R; IV → P

Paper 2

Section 1 (Maximum Marks: 24)

- This section contains **EIGHT** (08) questions.
- The answer to each question is a **SINGLE DIGIT INTEGER ranging from 0 TO 9, BOTH INCLUSIVE.**
- For each question, enter the correct integer corresponding to the answer using the mouse and the onscreen virtual numeric keypad in the place designated to enter the answer.
- Answer to each question will be evaluated according to the following marking scheme:
  Full Marks : +3 If **ONLY** the correct integer is entered;
  Zero Marks : 0 If the question is unanswered;
  Negative Marks : −1 In all other cases.

1. Concentration of H_2SO_4 and Na_2SO_4 in a solution is 1 M and 1.8×10^{-2}M, respectively. Molar solubility of $PbSO_4$ in the same solution is $X \times 10^{-Y}$ M (expressed in scientific notation). The value of Y is
[Given, solubility product of $PbSO_4 (K_{sp}) = 1.6 \times 10^{-8}$, for H_2SO_4, K_{a_1} is very large and $K_{a_2} = 1.2 \times 10^{-2}$].

2. An aqueous solution is prepared by dissolving 0.1 mole of an ionic salt in 1.8 kg of water at 35 °C. The salt remains 90% dissociated in the solution. The vapour pressure of the solution is 59.724 mm of Hg. Vapour pressure of water at 35°C is 60.000 mm of Hg. The number of ions present per formula unit of the ionic salt is ....

3. Consider the strong electrolytes Z_mX_n, U_mY_p and V_mX_n. Limiting molar conductivity ($\lambda°$) of U_mY_p and V_mX_n are 250 and 440 $cm^2 \ mol^{-1}$, respectively. The value of $(m + n + p)$ is ....

Given,

Ion	Z^{n+}	U^{p+}	V^{n+}	X^{m-}	Y^{m-}
$\lambda°$ (S cm^2 mol^{-1})	50.0	25.0	100.0	80.0	100.0

$\lambda°$ is the limiting molar conductivity of ions.

The plot of molar conductivity (λ) of $Z_m X_n$ vs $C^{1/2}$ is given below.

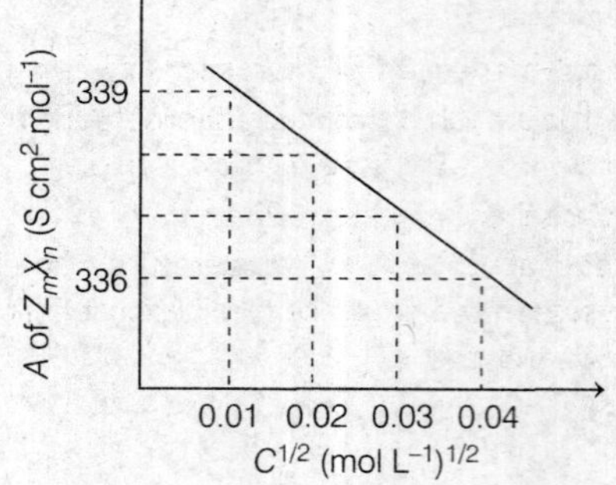

4. The reaction of Xe and O_2F_2 gives a Xe compound P. The number of moles of HF produced by the complete hydrolysis of 1 mole of P is ....

5. Thermal decomposition of $AgNO_3$ produces two paramagnetic gases. The total number of electrons present in the antibonding molecular orbitals of the gas that has the higher number of unpaired electrons is ....

6. The number of isomeric tetraenes (not containing *sp*-hybridised carbon atoms) that can be formed from the following reaction sequence is ....

1. Na, liquid NH_3
2. Br_2 (excess)
3. alc. KOH

7. The number of $-CH_2-$ (methylene) groups in the product formed from the following reaction sequence is ....

1. O_3, Zn / H_2O
2. $KMnO_4$
3. NaOH, electrolysis
4. Cr_2O_3, 770 K, 20 atm

8. The total number of chiral molecules formed from one molecule of P on complete ozonolysis (O_3, Zn / H_2O) is ....

OH OH HO HO OH

P

SECTION 2 (Maximum Marks : 24)

- This section contains **SIX (06)** questions
- Each question has **FOUR** options (a), (b), (c) and (d). **ONE OR MORE THAN ONE** of these four option(s) is (are) correct answer(s).
- For each question, choose the option(s) corresponding to (all) the correct answer(s).
- Answer to each question will be evaluated according to the following marking scheme:

Full Marks : +4 **ONLY** if (all) the correct option(s) is (are) chosen;
Partial marks : +3 If all the four options are correct but **ONLY** three options are chosen;
Partial marks : +2 If three or more options are correct but **ONLY** two options are chosen, both of which are correct;
Partial Marks : +1 If two or more options are correct but **ONLY** one options is chosen and it is a correct option;
Zero Marks : 0 if unanswered;
Negative Marks : −2 In all other cases.

9. To check the principle of multiple proportions, a series of pure binary compounds (P_mQ_n) were analysed and their composition is tabulated below. The correct option(s) is (are)

Compound	Weight % of P	Weight % of Q
1	50	50
2	44.4	55.6
3	40	60

(a) If empirical formula of compound 3 is P_3Q_4, then the empirical formula of compound 2 is P_3Q_5.
(b) If empirical formula of compound 3 is P_3Q_2 and atomic weight of element P is 20, then the atomic weight of Q is 45.
(c) If empirical formula of compound 2 is PQ, then the empirical formula of the compound 1 is P_5Q_4
(d) If atomic weight of P and Q are 70 and 35, respectively, then the empirical formula of compound 1 is P_2Q

10. The correct option(s) about entropy (S) is(are)

[R = Gas constant, F = Faraday constant, T = Temperature]

(a) For the reaction, $M(s) + 2H^+(aq) \longrightarrow H_2(g) + M^{2+}(aq)$, if $\frac{dE_{cell}}{dT} = \frac{R}{F}$, then the entropy change of the reaction is R.
(Assume that, entropy and internal energy changes are temperature, independent).
(b) The cell reaction,
$Pt(s)|H_2(g)\,1\,bar\,|H^+(aq.\,0.01M)\,||\,H^+(aq\,0.1M)\,|H_2(g), 1\,bar\,|$ $Pt(s)$, is an entropy driven process.
(c) For racemisation of an optically active compound, $\Delta S > 0$.
(d) $\Delta S > 0$, for $[Ni(H_2O)_6]^{2+} + 3en \longrightarrow [Ni(en)_3]^{2+} + 6H_2O$
(where, en = ethylenediamine).

11. The compound(s) which react(s) with NH_3 to give boron nitride (BN) is(are)

(a) B (b) B_2H_6 (c) B_2O_3 (d) HBF_4

12. The correct option(s) related to the extraction of iron from its ore in the blast furnace operating in the temperature range 900 - 1500 K is(are)

(a) Limestone is used to remove silicate impurity.
(b) Pig iron obtained from blast furnace contains about 4% carbon.
(c) Coke (C) converts CO_2 to CO.
(d) Exhaust gases consist of NO_2 and CO.

13. Considering the following reaction sequence, the correct statement(s) is(are)

Benzene + succinic anhydride $\xrightarrow{AlCl_3}$ P $\xrightarrow{Zn/Hg,\ HCl}$ Q $\xrightarrow{SOCl_2}$ R $\xrightarrow{AlCl_3}$ S $\xrightarrow{Zn/Hg,\ HCl}$ A hydrocarbon

(a) compounds P and Q are carboxylic acids.
(b) compound S decolourises bromine water.
(c) compounds P and S react with hydroxylamine to give the corresponding oximes.
(d) compound R reacts with dialkylcadmium to give the corresponding tertiary alcohol.

14. Among the following, the correct statement(s) about polymers is(are)

(a) the polymerisation of chloroprene gives natural rubber.
(b) teflon is prepared from tetrafluoroethene by heating it with persulphate catalyst at high pressures.
(c) PVC are thermoplastic polymers.
(d) ethene at 350-570 K temperature and 1000-2000 atm pressure in the presence of a peroxide initiator yields high density polythene.

SECTION 3 (Maximum Marks: 12)

- This section contains **FOUR (04)** questions.
- Each question has **FOUR** options (a), (b), (c) and (d). **ONLY ONE** of these four options is the correct answer.
- For each question, choose the option corresponding to the correct answer.
- Answer to each question will be evaluated according to the following marking scheme:
  Full Marks : +3 If **ONLY** the correct option is chosen;
  Zero Marks : 0 If none of the options is chosen (i.e. the question is unanswered);
  Negative Marks : −1 In all other cases.

15. Atom X occupies the fcc lattice sites as well as alternate tetrahedral voids of the same lattice. The packing efficiency (in %) of the resultant solid is closest to

(a) 25 (b) 35 (c) 55 (d) 75

16. The reaction of $HClO_3$ with HCl gives a paramagnetic gas, which upon reaction with O_3 produces

(a) Cl_2O (b) ClO_2 (c) Cl_2O_6 (d) Cl_2O_7

17. The reaction of $Pb(NO_3)_2$ and NaCl in water produces a precipitate that dissolves upon the addition of HCl of appropriate concentration. The dissolution of the precipitate is due to the formation of

(a) $PbCl_2$ (b) $PbCl_4$ (c) $[PbCl_4]^{2-}$ (d) $[PbCl_6]^{2-}$

18. Treatment of *D*-glucose with aqueous NaOH results in a mixture of monosaccharides, which are

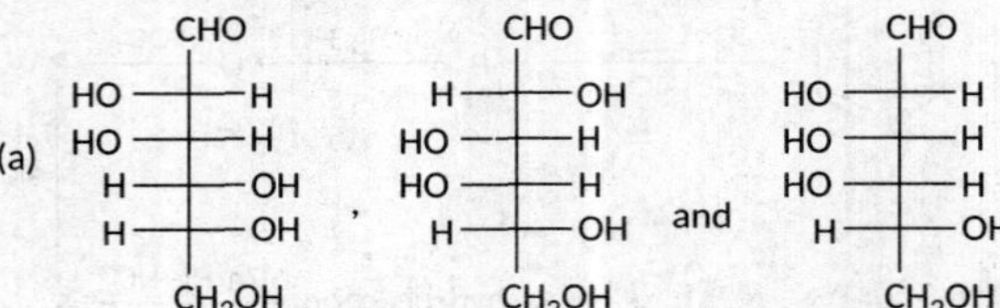

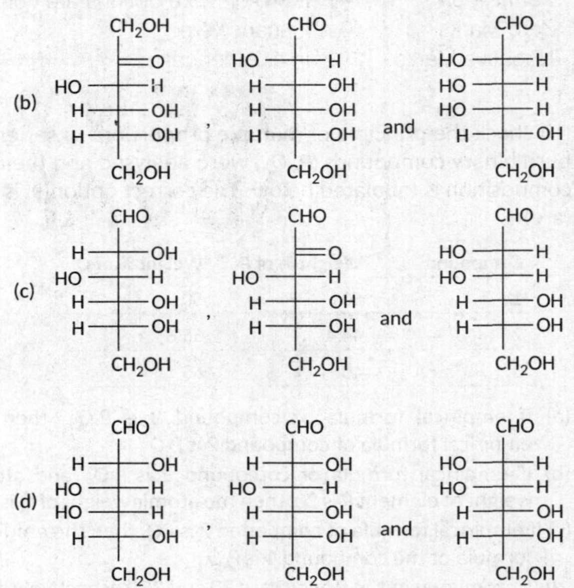

Answers

Paper ①

1	(90.39)	2	(0.77)	3	(10.02)	4	(1.58)	5	(2.38)	6	(1.50)	7	(1.31)	8	(136)	9	(a, d)	10	(a, d)
11	(b, d)	12	(a, d)	13	(c, d)	14	(a, b, c)	15	(a)	16	(d)	17	(a)	18	(d)				

Paper ②

1	(6)	2	(5)	3	(7)	4	(4)	5	(6)	6	(2)	7	(0)	8	(2)	9	(b, c)	10	(b, c, d)
11	(b, c)	12	(a, b, c)	13	(a, c)	14	(b, c)	15	(b)	16	(c)	17	(c)	18	(c)				

See detailed solutions on page no. 361

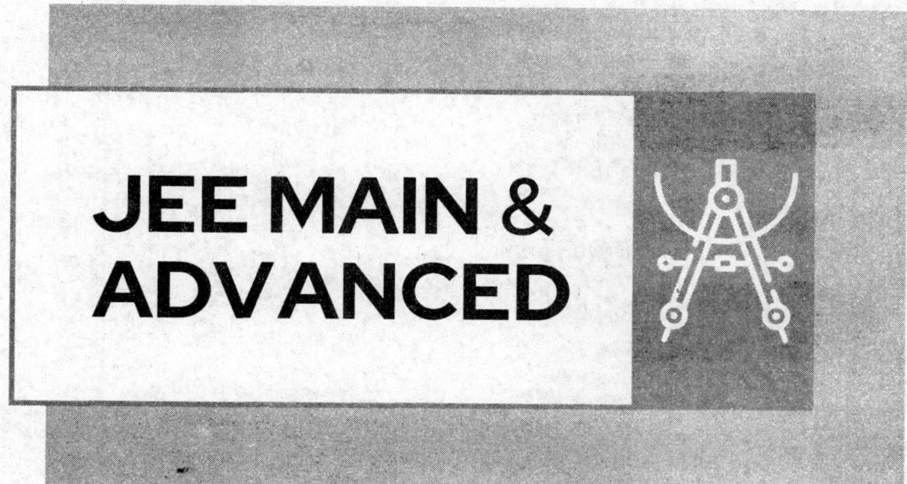

Explanations

Qualifiers, Part Tests, Knockouts, Real Nuts

THE QUALIFIERS

Qualifier 01

(Some Basic Concepts of Chemistry)

1. (a) The last three zeros in the number 134000 are not significant. Hence, the number of significant digit is 3.

2. (d) I. Law of constant or definite proportion is not valid for isotopes.

II. According to the law of multiple proportion, two elements on chemical combination can give two or more than two compounds.

$$H_2 + O_2 \longrightarrow \begin{cases} H_2O \\ H_2O_2 \end{cases}$$

III. (i) In H_2S and H_2O, for 1 g of H

$(m_S)_{H_2S} : (m_O)_{H_2O}$

$$= \frac{100 - 5.88}{5.88} : \frac{100 - 11.11}{11.11}$$

$\simeq 16 : 8$

$= 2 : 1$ ...(i)

(ii) In SO_2, $m_S : m_O = 50 : (100 - 50)$

$= 1 : 1$ ...(ii)

Ratio-(i) is the sub-multiple of ratio-(ii). So, the data illustrate the law of reciprocal proportion.

IV. For a given mass of carbon $= 12$ g, ratio of masses of hydrogen in alkane homologues : C_3H_8, C_4H_{10} and C_5H_{12} will be,

$$\frac{8}{3} : \frac{10}{4} : \frac{12}{5} = 2.67 : 2.50 : 2.40$$

It is not a simple whole number ratio.

So, it does not obey the law of multiple proportion.

3. (b) When N_A is changed from 6.022×10^{23} mol^{-1} to 6.022×10^{21} mol^{-1}, then the mass of 1 mole of C-12, i.e. mass of 6.022×10^{21} carbon-12 atoms will be

$$= \frac{12}{6.022 \times 10^{23}} \times 6.022 \times 10^{21}$$

$= 0.12$ g

4. (d) In ZnS (pure),

$$\text{Zn\%} = \frac{65.38}{(65.38 + 32.06)} \times 100 = 67.10$$

Since, the sample contains only 42.34%, Zn it is.

$$\frac{42.34}{67.10} \times 100 = 63.10\,\% \text{ pure ZnS}$$

5. (c)

$$C_xH_y + \left(x + \frac{y}{4}\right) O_2 \longrightarrow xCO_2 + \frac{y}{2} H_2O$$

1 mL $\quad \left(x + \frac{y}{4}\right)$ mL $\quad$ x mL

30 mL $\quad 30\left(x + \frac{y}{4}\right)$ mL $\quad$ 30 x mL $\quad$ [p, T : constant]

(i) $30x = 60 \Rightarrow x = 2$

(ii) $30\left(x + \frac{y}{4}\right) = 90$

$\Rightarrow \quad x + \frac{y}{4} = 3$

$\Rightarrow \quad y = 4$

$\therefore$ The hydrocarbon is C_2H_4.

6. (d) Molarity

$$= \frac{\text{Moles of solute (g)}}{\text{Volume of solution (L)}}$$

(a) $\dfrac{150}{58.5} = 2.56$ M

(b) $\dfrac{58.5 \times \dfrac{1000}{250}}{58.5} = 4$ M

(c) $\dfrac{5.85 \times 10^{-3} \times \dfrac{1000}{1}}{58.5} = 0.1$ M

(d) $\dfrac{292.5 \times \dfrac{1}{5}}{58.5} = 1$ M

7. (a) Boric acid $[B(OH)_3]$ acts as a weak monobasic acid in water.

$$H_3BO_3 + H_2O \rightleftharpoons [B(OH)_4]^{\ominus} + H^{\oplus}$$

So, molarity = normality

[$\because$ n-factor $(nf) = 1$, $N = M \times nf$]

Molar mass of $H_3BO_3 = 62$ g mol^{-1}

$$= \frac{62 \times 10^{-3}}{62} \times \frac{1000}{250} = 4 \times 10^{-3}$$

8. (c)

$$S_{final} = \frac{V_1S_1 + V_2S_2}{V_{final}}$$

$$= \frac{250 \times 5 + 500 \times 4}{2000}$$

$= 1.62$ M

[S = solution, V = volume]

9. (c) A$\rightarrow$(3), (B)$\rightarrow$(2), (C)$\rightarrow$(4), (D)$\rightarrow$(1)

A. $M = \dfrac{10 \times \%(w/w) \times d}{M_B}$

$$= \frac{10 \times 0.98 \times 1.8}{98} = 0.18 \text{ M}$$

$N = M \times n\text{-factor} = 0.18 \times 2 = 0.36$ N

B. $M = \dfrac{10 \times 9.8 \times 1.4}{98} = 1.4$ M

$N = 1.4 \times 3 = 4.2$ N [$\because \alpha\% = 100$]

C. $M = \dfrac{\dfrac{1.8 \times 10^{-3} \times N_A}{N_A}}{0.5} = 0.0036$ M

$= 0.0036$ N

($\because$ NH_4OH, n-factor $= 1$)

D. $M = \dfrac{250 \times 4 + 250 \times 2}{250 + 250} = 3$ M

($\because$ HCl, n-factor $= 1$, H_2SO_4, n-factor $= 2$)

$$N = \frac{250 \times 4 + 250 \times 4}{250 + 250} = 4 \text{ N}$$

10. (d) $w_{HNO_3} = 10 \times 1.4 = 14$ g

w_{HNO_3} in solution $= 14 \times \dfrac{70}{100} = 9.8$ g

n_{HNO_3} in solution $= \dfrac{9.8}{63} = 0.1556$ mol

Molarity of HNO_3 solution

$$= \frac{0.1556}{\dfrac{10}{1000}} = 15.56 \text{ M}$$

Volume of diluted 1 M solution

$$= \frac{10 \times 15.56}{1} = 155.6 \text{ mL}$$

Volume of water added to prepare 155.6 mL 1 M HNO_3

$= (155.6 - 10)$ mL $= 145.6$ mL

11. (b) $2Mg + O_2 \longrightarrow 2MgO$

$\Rightarrow n_{max}(Mg) = \dfrac{1.8/24.3}{2} = 0.037$ mol

$n_{max}(O_2) = \dfrac{0.8/32}{1} = 0.025$ mol

Since, $n_{max}(Mg) > n_{max}(O_2)$, the limiting reactant is O_2.

$\Rightarrow \quad n_{MgO} = 2 \times n_{max}(O_2)$

$= 2 \times 0.025 = 0.05$ mol

$\Rightarrow$ Mass of Mg consumed

$= [2 \times n_{max}(O_2)] \times 24.3$ g

$= 1.215$ g

Mass of Mg remains unreacted

$= (1.8 - 1.215)$ g $= 0.585$ g

12. (b) Number of moles of reactants taken,

$$I_2 = \frac{254}{254} = 1 \text{ mol},$$

$$Cl_2 = \frac{12.046 \times 10^{23}}{6.023 \times 10^{23}} = 2 \text{ mol}$$

$$\Rightarrow \underset{1\text{ mol}}{I_2} + \underset{2\text{ mol}}{2Cl_2} \longrightarrow \underset{1\text{ mol}}{ICl} + \underset{1\text{ mol}}{ICl_3}$$

13. (a) $\underset{1\text{ mol}}{Na_2SO_4} + \underset{1\text{ mol}}{BaCl_2} \longrightarrow \underset{1\text{ mol}}{BaSO_4}\downarrow + 2NaCl$

Given : $\frac{2}{142}$ mol $\frac{3}{208.2}$ mol

$= 0.0141$ mol $= 0.0144$ mol 0.0141 mol (Limiting quantity)

$\therefore$ Mass of $BaSO_4$ formed

$= 0.0141 \times 233.4 \text{ g} = 3.29 \text{ g}$

14. (c) $\underset{1\text{ mol}}{NaH_2PO_4} + \underset{2\text{ mol}}{2NaOH} \longrightarrow Na_3PO_4 + 2H_2O$

$$\frac{12}{120} = 0.1 \text{ mol}$$

No. of moles of NaOH required for complete reaction to occur

$= 2 \times 0.1$ mol $= 0.2$ mol.

$\because$ Molar mass of $NaH_2PO_4 = 120 \text{ g mol}^{-1}$

$$\Rightarrow \frac{V \times 1}{1000} = 0.2$$

$$\Rightarrow V = 200 \text{ mL of NaOH}$$

15. (c) Molarity $[Ba(OH)_2]$

$$= \frac{35 \times 0.1}{25} = 0.14 \text{ M}$$

We know, molality,

$$m = \frac{1000 \times M}{1000 \times d - M \times M_{solute}}$$

$$= \frac{1000 \times 0.14}{1000 \times 1.2 - 0.14 \times 171} = 0.119 \text{ m}$$

[Molar mass of $Ba(OH)_2 = 137 + 2 \times 17 = 171 \text{ g mol}^{-1}$]

16. (b) Molecular equivalent of H_2SO_4 decreased = molecular equivalent of NH_3 passed

$= (30 \times 1 - 30 \times 0.2) = 24$

$$\Rightarrow w_{NH_3} = \frac{24}{1000} \times 17 = 0.408 \text{ g}$$

$$\Rightarrow V_{NH_3} \text{ at STP} = \frac{0.408}{17} \times 22.4 \text{ L}$$

$= 0.5376$ L at STP

17. (c) No. of equivalents of,

Acid = Base

$$\Rightarrow \frac{\frac{0.4}{96}}{n} = \frac{\frac{0.5}{40}}{1} \Rightarrow n = 3$$

$\therefore$ Atomic weight of $A = 96 - 3 = 93$

18. (a) $(NH_4)_2SO_4 + 2NaOH \longrightarrow 2NH_3 + Na_2SO_4 + 2H_2O$

$\Rightarrow$ Milliequivalents of NH_3 = mmol of NH_3

$$10 \times 0.1 \times \frac{250}{25} = 10$$

$= 2 \times$ mmol of $(NH_4)_2SO_4$

$$\therefore w_{(NH_4)_2SO_4} = \frac{10}{2} \times \frac{132}{1000} = 0.66 \text{ g}$$

[$\because$ Molar mass of $(NH_4)_2SO_4 = 132 \text{ g mol}^{-1}$]

$\Rightarrow$ % $(NH_4)_2SO_4$ in the sample

$$= \frac{0.66}{0.70} \times 100 = 94.285 \simeq 94.3$$

19. (c) Phenolphthalein is used as an indicator for titration of strong base-strong acid system. When it is used in Na_2CO_3-HCl titration, it changes its pink colour to colourless, due to the formation of $NaHCO_3$ (an acidic salt) and it indicates 50% neutralisation of Na_2CO_3 by HCl.

$$\underset{\text{Pink}}{Na_2CO_3} \xrightarrow[\text{Phenolphthalein}]{HCl} \underset{\substack{\text{Colourless} \\ \text{(50\% neutralisation)}}}{NaHCO_3}$$

$$\xrightarrow{HCl} \underset{\text{(100\% neutralisation)}}{NaCl + CO_2 + H_2O}$$

So, we need a second indicator (like methyl orange or methyl red) in the same solution to indicate remaining 50% neutralisation (double titration).

20. (b) Total number of moles of C_2H_6 in the mixture $= 3 + \frac{60}{30} = 5$ mol

[$\because$ Molar mass of $C_2H_6 = 30 \text{ g mol}^{-1}$]

Number of moles of C_2H_6 left for combustion (after removal)

$$= \left(5 - \frac{2.4 \times 10^{24}}{6 \times 10^{23}}\right) = (5 - 4) = 1$$

$$\Rightarrow \underset{1\text{ mol}}{C_2H_6} + \frac{7}{2}O_2 \longrightarrow \underset{2\text{ mol}}{2CO_2} + \underset{3\text{ mol}}{3H_2O}$$

$= 2 \times 22.4$ L $\quad 3 \times 18$ g

$= 44.8$ L at STP $\quad = 54$ g

$= 54 \text{ g} \times 1 \text{ g/mL}$

$= 54$ mL

21. (3) When 0.0034 is subtracted from 1.0042, a number (1.0008) with five significant digits results.

When this number is multiplied by 1.23 (with only three significant digits), the result (1.230984) must be expressed to only three significant digits, i.e. 1.23.

22. (6) Molar mass of

$Si_2H_x = 2 \times 30 + x \times 1$

$= (60 + x) \text{ g mol}^{-1}$

$$\Rightarrow \% \text{ Si} = \frac{2 \times 30}{60 + x} \times 100 = 90.9$$

$$\Rightarrow x = 6.006 \simeq 6$$

23. (90.07)

$$w_{Al} \text{ in 13 g kaolin} = 13 \times \frac{54}{258} = 2.72 \text{ g}$$

$$w_{Al} \text{ in 87 g gibbsite} = 87 \times \frac{54}{156} = 30.11 \text{ g}$$

Total weight of Al in 100 g are $= (2.72 + 30.11) \text{g} = 32.83$ g

In kaolin, number of atoms of Al = Si. The siliceous mud takes 6 Al-atoms for 5 Si-atoms.

Hence, the precipitation of all Si-atoms from 13 g of kaolin involves the loss of

$$\frac{6}{5} \times 2.72 \text{ g} = 3.26 \text{ g of Al}$$

Fraction of Al recoverable

$$= \frac{\text{Recoverable Al}}{\text{Total Al}} = \frac{32.83 - 3.26}{32.83}$$

$= 0.9007 = 90.07\%$

24. (19)

In 100 g of compound, $Br_3C_6H_3(C_8H_8)_n$

$$\text{Br} = \frac{10.46}{80} \text{ mol} = 0.1307 \text{ mol}$$

Since, there are 3 moles of Br per mol of compound, the number of moles of

$$\text{compound} = \frac{0.1307}{3} = 0.04356 \text{ mol}$$

$\therefore$ Molecular weight of the compound

$$= \frac{100}{0.04356} = 2.29 \times 10^3 \text{ g mol}^{-1}$$

$\Rightarrow 3 \times 80 + 6 \times 12 + 3 \times 1 + n \times (8 \times 12 + 8 \times 1) = 2290$

$\Rightarrow n = 18.990 \simeq 19$

25. (3) $\underset{1\text{ mol}}{BaCl_2} \longrightarrow Ba^{2+} + \underset{2\text{ mol}}{2Cl^-}$

Volume of $BaCl_2$ solution required

$= (3 \text{ mol } Cl^-)$

$$\times \left(\frac{1 \text{ mol } BaCl_2}{2 \text{ mol } Cl^-}\right) \times \left(\frac{1 \text{ L } BaCl_2}{0.5 \text{ mol } BaCl_2}\right)$$

$= 3$ L

26. (1038.96)

On the basis of 1 m^3 of milk,

Mass of butterfat

$= (0.04 m^3) \times (865 \text{ kg}/m^3)$

$= 34.6$ kg

Mass of skimmed milk

$$=\left(\frac{1.032\text{ kg}}{1\text{L}}\times 10^3\text{ L}\right)-34.6\text{ kg}$$

$=997.4$ kg

Volume of skimmed milk

$$=(100-4)\times\frac{10}{10^3}\text{ m}^3=0.96\text{ m}^3$$

Density of skimmed milk

$$=\frac{997.4}{0.96}\text{ kg/m}^3=1038.96\text{ kg/m}^3$$

27. (0.20)

$Cu^{2+}=1\text{ L}\times 0.1\text{ M}=0.1$ mol

$$H^+=(0.1\text{ mol }Cu^{2+})\times\left(\frac{2\text{ mol }H^+}{1\text{ mol }Cu^{2+}}\right)$$

$=0.2$ mol

$$\Rightarrow [H^+]=\frac{0.2\text{ mol}}{1\text{ L}}=0.20\text{ M}$$

28. (2.43) Molar mass of the resin,

$C_8H_7SO_3Na$

$=(8\times 12+7\times 1+1\times 32+3\times 16+1\times 23)$ g/mol

$=206$ g/mol

Maximum uptake of Ca^{2+} by the resin

$$=\frac{1\text{ mol }Ca^{2+}}{(2\text{ mol resin})(206\text{ g resin / mol resin})}$$

$=2.427\times 10^{-3}\simeq 2.43\times 10^{-3}$

$=x\times 10^{-3}$ mol Ca^{+2}/g resin

$\therefore x=2.43$

29. (47.27) $2HCl+BaO\longrightarrow BaCl_2+H_2O$;

$2HCl+CaO\longrightarrow CaCl_2+H_2O$

$\Rightarrow HCl=100\times 2.5\times 10^{-3}$

$=0.25$ mol, which reacts completely with $\frac{1}{2}\times 0.25$ mol

$=0.125$ mol metal oxides

Let, moles of BaO $=n$,

moles of CaO $=(0.125-n)$

$\Rightarrow n\times 153+(0.125-n)\times 56=10$

$\Rightarrow n=0.0309$ mol BaO

$$\therefore \text{BaO}\%=\frac{0.0309\times 153}{10}\times 100$$

$=47.27=x$

30. (2.40)

HCl yields, $H^+=Cl^-=40\times 1.6$ mmol

$=64$ mmol

NaOH yields, $Na^+=OH^-$

$=60\times 2$ mmol

$=120$ mmol

$$H^++OH^-\longrightarrow H_2O$$

64 mmol of H^+ reacts with 64 mmol of OH^-, leaving $(120-64)$ mmol $=56$ mmol of OH^- in the solution.

$$\Rightarrow [Na^+]=\frac{[64\text{ (of NaCl formed)}+56\text{ (of NaOH unreacted)] mmol}}{100\text{ mL}}$$

$=1.2\text{ M}=a\text{ M}$

$$[Cl^-]=\frac{64\text{ mmol}}{100\text{ mL}}=0.64\text{ M}=b\text{ M}$$

$$[OH^-]=\frac{56\text{ mmol}}{100\text{ mL}}=0.56\text{M}=c\text{M}$$

$\Rightarrow (a+b+c)=1.2+0.64+0.56=2.40$

Qualifier 02
(States of Matter)

1. (a) Initial pressure,

$$p_1=0.94\text{ atm}\times\frac{760\text{ torr}}{1\text{ atm}}=714.4\text{ torr}$$

$\Rightarrow$ The volume of air trapped

= Length (l) times the (constant) cross-sectional area (A)

$\therefore$ At constant temperature for a given mass of the gas,

$$p_1V_1=p_2V_2=p_1l_1A=p_2l_2A$$

$$\Rightarrow\quad p_1l_1=p_2l_2$$

$\therefore p_2=p_1+$ Increase in pressure due to the weight of 8 cm Hg

$=714.4$ torr $+$ 80 mm Hg

$=(714.4+80)$ torr $=794.4$ torr

$$\Rightarrow l_2=\frac{p_1l_1}{p_2}=\frac{714.4\text{ torr}\times 10\text{ cm}}{794.4\text{ torr}}$$

$=8.99$ cm

2. (d) Gas A represents Charles' law,

$$V\propto T$$

Gas B represents Boyle's law,

$$pV=\text{constant}$$

Gas C represents Gay-Lussac's law,

$$p\propto T$$

Gas D represents non-ideal behaviour.

3. (d) $\Rightarrow$ Along $A\rightarrow B$, volume of the gas decreases, i.e. pressure increases.

$\Rightarrow$ Along $B\rightarrow C$, pressure remains constant, i.e. $V\propto T$ (Charles' law) as the straight line, extrapolated part of BC, passes through the origin.

$\Rightarrow$ Volume of the gas at A is greater than that at C. So, opposite will be their pressure values.

4. (b) From equation of state of ideal gases,

$$pV=nRT=\frac{w}{M}RT$$

$$\Rightarrow\quad p\propto\frac{1}{M}$$

[$\because V, w, T$ are constants]

$$\Rightarrow\quad \frac{p_{N_2}}{p_{O_2}}=\frac{M_{O_2}}{M_{N_2}}=\frac{32}{28}=1.14$$

$$\Rightarrow\quad p_{N_2}=1.14\times p_{O_2}$$

Thus, it can be said that pressure in the nitrogen flask is greater than that in oxygen flask.

5. (a) In 1st vessel, number of mol ratio,

$$\frac{n_P}{n_Q}=\frac{2}{3}=\frac{n_1}{n_2}$$

In 2nd vessel, number of mol ratio,

$$\frac{n_P}{n_Q}=\frac{3}{5}=\frac{n_3}{n_4}$$

$\Rightarrow$ After intermixing, Mean molar mass,

$$M_{av}=\frac{(n_1+n_3)\times M_P+(n_2+n_4)\times M_Q}{(n_1+n_2+n_3+n_4)}$$

$$=\frac{(n_1+n_3)M_P+\left(\frac{3n_1}{2}+\frac{5n_3}{3}\right)M_Q}{\left(n_1+\frac{3n_1}{2}+n_3+\frac{5n_3}{3}\right)}$$

$$=\frac{(6n_1+6n_3)M_P+(9n_1+10n_3)M_Q}{6n_1+9n_1+6n_3+10n_3}$$

$$=\frac{(6n_1+6n_3)M_P+(9n_1+10n_3)M_Q}{[(6n_1+6n_3)+(9n_1+10n_3)]}$$

If, $[(6n_1+6n_3)+(9n_1+10n_3)]=200$

then, $(6n_1+6n_3)=77$

and $(9n_1+10n_3)=123$

as $(6n_1+6n_3)<(9n_1+10n_3)$

So, M_{av} can be $\frac{77M_P+123M_Q}{200}$

6. (d) In this experiment pressure and volume of chlorine gas are kept unchanged.

So, the equation of state of an ideal gas (here, it is chlorine) is reduced to

$$pV=nRT=\frac{w}{M}RT$$

$$\Rightarrow\quad T\propto\frac{1}{w}$$

[$\because w=$ mass of Cl_2 gas)

$$\text{or}\quad \frac{T_2}{T_1}=\frac{w_1}{w_2}$$

$$\Rightarrow\frac{273+(T+30)}{273+T}=\frac{3.55}{3.20}=1.109$$

$$\Rightarrow\quad T=2.229°\text{C}\approx 2.23°\text{C}$$

7. (c) Let. n, t_1 and d_1 be the absolute viscosity, time of flow and density respectively for $CHCl_3(l)$ and n_2, t_2 and

d_2 be the corresponding values of $H_2O(l)$.

Now, $\frac{n_1}{n_2} = \frac{d_1t_1}{d_2t_2}$ = specific viscosity of water.

$= \frac{(1.49 \times 10^3) \times 15}{(1 \times 10^3) \times 39.7} = 0.5629 \simeq 0.56$

8. (c) $\frac{r_{He}}{r_{CO}} = \sqrt{\frac{M_{(CO)}}{M_{(He)}}} = \sqrt{\frac{28}{4}} = 2.645$

$\Rightarrow \quad r_{He} = 2.645 \times r_{CO}$

$\therefore \; r_{CO} = \frac{r_{He}}{2.645} = \left(\frac{6.4 \text{ mmol}}{\text{h}} \times \frac{1}{2.645}\right)$

$= 2.42$ mmol CO/h

$\Rightarrow$ Time of effusion of 10 mmol CO

$= (10 \text{ mmol CO}) \times \left(\frac{1 \text{ h}}{2.42 \text{ mmol CO}}\right) = 4.13$ h

9. (b) At constant temperature and pressure, air containing N_2 and O_2 in the volume ratio of 4 : 1 will have N_2 and O_2 in the same molar ratio, i.e. 4 : 1.

Mole fraction of N_2 in air $= \frac{4}{4+1} = \frac{4}{5}$

$\Rightarrow$ Partial pressure of N_2 in air

= mole fraction of N_2 × total pressure

$= \frac{4}{5} \times 740$ mm Hg

$= 592$ mm Hg

$= 592$ torr

10. (d) $\overline{KE} = \frac{3}{2} kT$

$[\because k$ = Boltzmann constant$]$

$\Rightarrow$ For 1 mol H_2 gas,

$N_A = \overline{KE} = \frac{3}{2} RT = 104$ kcal (given)

$\Rightarrow T = \frac{2 \times (104 \times 10^3 \text{ cal / mol})}{3 \times (1.987 \text{ cal mol}^{-1} \text{ K}^{-1})}$

$= 34893.47 \text{ K} \simeq 34900$ K

$= 3.49 \times 10^4$ K

11. (b)

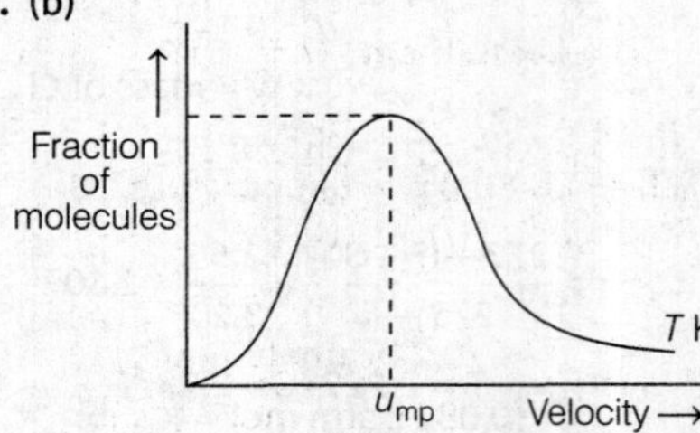

$\Rightarrow$ Fraction of molecules, i.e. distribution of molecules become maximum at most probable velocity (u_{mp}) at constant temperature. But at velocity higher and lower than u_{mp}, distribution of molecules will be lower.

where, $u_{mp} = \sqrt{\frac{2RT}{M}}$

So, (A) and (R), both are true but (R) does not explain (A).

12. (d) $p = 1 \text{ atm} = 1.013 \times 10^5 \text{ Nm}^{-2}$

$d = 1.429 \text{ g dm}^{-3} = 1.429 \text{ kg m}^{-3}$

$\Rightarrow \; c_{rms} = \sqrt{\frac{3p}{d}}$

$= \sqrt{\frac{3 \times 1.013 \times 10^5}{1.429}}$

$= 461.15 \text{ ms}^{-1}$

Another Method :

$c_{rms} = \sqrt{\frac{3RT}{M}}$

$= \sqrt{\frac{3 \times 8.31 \times 273}{(32 \times 10^{-3})}}$

$= 461.17 \text{ ms}^{-1}$

$[\because$ Molar mass of $O_2, M = 32 \text{ g mol}^{-1}$

$= 32 \times 10^{-3} \text{ kg mol}^{-1}]$

13. (a) Here, $f_1 \propto \frac{1}{r^3}, f_2 \propto \frac{1}{r^6}, f_3 \propto \frac{1}{r^6}, f_4 \propto \frac{1}{r^6}$

$\Rightarrow x = 3, y = a = b = 6$

$\Rightarrow \frac{|a+b|}{|x+y|} = \frac{6+6}{6+3} = \frac{12}{9} = 1.34$

14. (b) Compressibility factor,

$Z = \frac{pV}{nRT} = \frac{pV_m}{RT}$

$[\because V_m$ = molar volume $(n = 1)]$

$= \frac{1.5 \times 33.18}{0.082 \times (273 + 20)} = 2.071$

15. (b) $V_{ideal} = V_{real}$ − Volume correction constant (b)

$\Rightarrow V_i = V - 4 \times N_A \times \left(\frac{4}{3}\pi r^3\right) \times n$

(for n mol gas)

$\Rightarrow V_i = V - 2 \times n \times N_A \times \frac{\pi}{3} \times (2r)^3$

$\Rightarrow (2r)^3 = \frac{3(V - V_i)}{2\pi n N_A}$,

$[\because r$ = radius of He molecule (mono-atomic)$]$

$\therefore \quad 2r = \left[\frac{3(V - V_i)}{2\pi n N_A}\right]^{1/3}$

Note $b = 4 \times N_A \times \frac{4}{3}\pi r^3$ for 1 mole of a real gas.

16. (b) For 1 mole of a van der Waals' gas,

$\left(p + \frac{a}{V^2}\right)(V - b) = RT$

$\Rightarrow \left(p + \frac{a}{V^2}\right) V = RT$ (when, $b = 0$)

$\Rightarrow \quad pV = RT - a \times \frac{1}{V}$

In the plot, pV vs. $\frac{1}{V}$, slope $= -a$

$\Rightarrow$ Slope $= \frac{16.8 - 15.4}{4 - 5} = \frac{1.4}{-1} = -1.4$

$\Rightarrow \quad a = 1.4 \text{ atm L}^2 \text{ mol}^{-2}$

17. (d) (A) Pressure correction $= \frac{an^2}{V^2}$

$= \frac{3.6 \times \left(\frac{200}{40}\right)^2}{(10)^2} = 0.90$ atm (3)

(B) Free space

$= V - nb = 10 - \left(\frac{200}{40}\right) \times 0.05$

$= 9.75$ L (4)

(C) Actual volume of the gas molecules/mol gas

$= \frac{b}{4} = \frac{0.05}{4} = 0.0125$ L (2)

$\left[\because b = 4 \times N_A \times \left(\frac{4}{3}\pi r^3\right)\right]$

(D) Effective volume occupied by gas molecules

$= n \times b = \left(\frac{200}{40}\right) \times 0.05 = 0.25$ L (1)

18. (a) Reduced pressure, $\alpha = \frac{p}{p_C}$, critical pressure, $p_C = \frac{a}{27b^2}$

$\therefore \quad p = \alpha \times \frac{a}{27b^2} = \frac{a\alpha}{27b^2}$

Reduced volume, $\beta = \frac{V}{V_C}$, critical volume, $V_C = 3b$

$\therefore \quad V = \beta \times V_C = 3b\beta$

Reduced temperature, $\gamma = \frac{T}{T_C}$; critical temperature, $T_C = \frac{8a}{27Rb}$

$\therefore \quad T = \gamma \times T_C = \frac{8a\gamma}{27Rb}$

For 1 mol of a real gas,

$\left(p + \frac{a}{V^2}\right)(V - b) = RT$

$\Rightarrow \left[\frac{a\alpha}{27b^2} + \frac{a}{(3b\beta)^2}\right][3b\beta - b]$

$$= R \times \frac{8a\gamma}{27Rb}$$

$$\Rightarrow \frac{a}{9b^2}\left[\frac{\alpha}{3} + \frac{1}{\beta^2}\right] \times b[3\beta - 1] = \frac{Ra}{9Rb} \times \frac{8\gamma}{3}$$

$$\Rightarrow \left(\frac{\alpha}{3} + \frac{1}{\beta^2}\right)(3\beta - 1) = \frac{8\gamma}{3}$$

$$\Rightarrow \left(\alpha + \frac{3}{\beta^2}\right)(3\beta - 1) = 8\gamma$$

19. (d) Volume $(V) = (4\text{m})^3 = 64 \text{ m}^3$

$$= 64 \times 10^3 \text{ L}$$

Pressure (p) = Relative humidity % $\times p_{H_2O(g)}$

$$= \frac{50}{100} \times 26.8 \text{ torr}$$

$$= 13.4 \text{ torr} = \frac{13.4}{760} \text{ atm}$$

$$\Rightarrow pV = nRT = \frac{w}{M}RT$$

$$\Rightarrow w_{H_2O(g)} = M_{(H_2O)} \times pV \times \frac{1}{RT}$$

$$= 18 \times \frac{13.4}{760} \times (64 \times 10^3) \times \frac{1}{0.082 \times 300} \text{ g}$$

$$= 825.67 \text{ g} \simeq 825.7 \text{ g}$$

20. (a) By Clausius-Clapeyron equation,

$$\frac{dp}{dT} = \frac{\Delta_{vap}H^\circ}{T \times \Delta V}$$

$$\Rightarrow \frac{dp}{dT} = \frac{\Delta_{vap}H^\circ}{RT^2} \times p$$

$$\left[\because \text{For 1 mol vapour, } \Delta V = \frac{RT}{p}\right]$$

$$\Rightarrow \frac{dT}{dp} = \frac{RT^2}{\Delta_{vap}H^\circ \times p}$$

$$= \frac{(8.314 \text{ J mol}^{-1} \text{ K}^{-1}) \times (373 \text{ K})^2}{(40.6 \times 10^3 \text{ J mol}^{-1}) \times (1 \text{ atm})}$$

$$= 28.49 \text{ K atm}^{-1} \simeq 28.5 \text{ K atm}^{-1}$$

21. (4.81) From equation of the state of ideal gases,

$$pV = nRT = \frac{w}{M}RT$$

$$\Rightarrow \frac{w}{V} = \frac{pM}{RT} \quad \left[\because \begin{array}{l} p_1 = 1 \text{ atm} = 760 \text{ torr} \\ T_1 = 0°\text{C} = 273 \text{ K} \end{array}\right] \text{STP}$$

$$\Rightarrow d = \frac{pM}{RT} \quad \left[\begin{array}{l} T_2 = -100°\text{C} = 173 \text{ K} \\ \frac{d_2}{d_1} = 10^{-9} \text{ (given)} \end{array}\right]$$

So, density of a gas,

$$d \propto \frac{p}{T}$$

$$\Rightarrow \frac{d_2}{d_1} = \frac{p_2}{p_1} \times \frac{T_1}{T_2}$$

$$\Rightarrow p_2 = \frac{d_2}{d_1} \times p_1 \times \frac{T_2}{T_1}$$

$$= 10^{-9} \times 760 \times \frac{173}{273}$$

$$= 4.81 \times 10^{-7} \text{ torr}$$

$$= x \times 10^{-7} \text{ torr}$$

$$\therefore \quad x = 4.81$$

22. (37.49) No. of moles of Ar in 1 L sample,

$$n = \frac{pV}{RT}$$

$$= \frac{\left(\frac{740}{760} \text{ atm}\right) \times (1 \text{ L})}{(0.082 \text{ L atm mol}^{-1} \text{ K}^{-1}) \times (300 \text{ K})}$$

$$= 0.0395 \text{ mol}$$

$$\Rightarrow \text{Average at. wt.} = \frac{1.481 \text{ g/L}}{0.0395 \text{ mol/L}}$$

$$= 37.49 \text{ g/mol}$$

23. (76.43) As rates are inversely proportional to the times of effusion,

$$\frac{r_{O_2}}{r_{gas}} = \frac{\frac{1}{55 \text{ min}}}{\frac{1}{85 \text{ min}}} = \sqrt{\frac{M_{gas}}{M_{O_2}}}$$

$$[\because M_{O_2} = 32 \text{ g/mol}]$$

$$\Rightarrow \left(\frac{M_{gas}}{M_{O_2}}\right)^{1/2} = \frac{85}{55}$$

$$\Rightarrow M_{gas} = \frac{85^2}{55^2} \times 32 = 76.43 \text{ g/mol}$$

24. (3.14) Rate of effusion $(r) \propto$ Area of cross-section of the orifice

$$\Rightarrow \frac{r_I}{r_{II}} = \frac{[\text{Area (circular)}]_I}{[\text{Area (square)}]_{II}} = \frac{\pi r^2}{r \times r}$$

$$= \pi = 3.14$$

25. (0.75) From the reactant ratio, it is observed that the ratio of atoms $A:O = 3:4$.

Hence, empirical formula of the compound is A_3O_4.

Since, the product exerts considerable pressure, it must be a gas.

That the pressure is equal to half that of the oxygen present initially implies that the number of molecules of product is half the number of molecules of oxygen initially present.

$$\frac{3}{4}A_4(s) + 2O_2(g) \longrightarrow A_3O_4(g)$$

$\frac{3}{4} = 0.75$ mol	1 mol	1 mol
	$2 \times N_A$ molecules	$1 \times N_A$ molecules
	Pressure : p	Pressure : $\frac{p}{2}$

Hence, the number of oxygen atoms per molecule of the compound must be 4.

⇒ Molecular formula of the compound is A_3O_4 or A_xO_y

$$\therefore \quad \frac{x}{y} = \frac{3}{4} = 0.75$$

26. (1.08) $u_{rms} = \sqrt{\frac{3RT}{M}}, u_{av} = \sqrt{\frac{8RT}{\pi M}}$

$$\Rightarrow \frac{u_{rms}}{u_{av}} = \sqrt{\frac{3RT}{M} \times \frac{\pi M}{8RT}} = \sqrt{\frac{3\pi}{8}}$$

$$= \sqrt{\frac{3 \times 3.14}{8}} = 1.08$$

27. (2.75) Molecular diameter, $\sigma = 3.19 \times 10^{-8}$ cm

Number of CO molecules present in 1 cm^3 (i.e. 10^{-3} L)

$$n' = n \times N_A = \frac{pV}{RT} \times N_A$$

$$= \frac{\left(\frac{250}{760} \text{ atm}\right) \times (10^{-3} \text{ L})}{(0.082 \text{ L atm mol}^{-1} \text{ K}^{-1}) \times (300 \text{ K})} \times \frac{(6.023 \times 10^{23} \text{ mol}^{-1})}{1}$$

$$= 8.05 \times 10^{21} / \text{cm}^3$$

⇒ Mean free path,

$$l = \frac{1}{\sqrt{2}\pi\sigma^2 n'}$$

$$= \frac{1}{1.41 \times 3.14 \times (3.19 \times 10^{-8} \text{ cm})^2 \times (8.05 \times 10^{21} / \text{cm}^3)}$$

$$= 2.75 \times 10^{-8} \text{ cm}$$

$$= x \times 10^{-8} \text{ cm}$$

$$\Rightarrow x = 2.75$$

28. (111.90) Boyle temperature,

$$T_b = \frac{a}{Rb}$$

$$= \frac{(0.245 \text{ atm L}^2 \text{ mol}^{-2})}{(0.082 \text{ L atm mol}^{-1} \text{ K}^{-1}) \times (26.7 \times 10^{-3} \text{ L mol}^{-1})}$$

$$= 111.90 \text{ K}$$

29. (0.32) $Z = \frac{pV}{nRT}$

$= \frac{(40 \text{ atm}) \times (0.4 \text{ L})}{(2 \text{ mol}) \times (0.082 \text{ L atm mol}^{-1} \text{ K}^{-1}) \times 300 \text{ K})}$

$= 0.32$

30. (18.86) Surface tension of a liquid,

$$\gamma = \frac{1}{2} r \times h\,d\,g$$

Here, r = inside radius of capillary

$$= \frac{1.40}{2} = 0.70 \text{ mm}$$

$$= 0.70 \times 10^{-3} \text{ m}$$

h = height of liquid column in capillary

d = density of liquid taken = 850 kg/m^3

g = 9.80 m/s^2

γ = surface tension of the liquid

$= 0.055 \text{ N/m} = 0.055 \text{ kg/s}^2$

$$\Rightarrow \quad h = \frac{2\gamma}{r\,d\,g}$$

$$= \frac{2 \times (0.055 \text{ kg/s}^2)}{(0.70 \times 10^{-3} \text{ m}) \times (850 \text{ kg/m}^3) \times (9.80 \text{ m/s}^2)}$$

$= 0.01886 \text{ m} = 18.86 \text{ mm}$

Qualifier 03

(Atomic Structure)

1. (c) Amount of energy provided, (available) by 8 quanta of red light

$$E = 8 \times h\nu = 8 \times h \times \frac{c}{\lambda}$$

$$= 8 \times (6.63 \times 10^{-34} \text{ Js}) \times \frac{(3 \times 10^8 \text{ ms}^{-1})}{(6850 \times 10^{-10} \text{m})}$$

$$= 8 \times 2.9 \times 10^{-19} \text{ J}$$

$$= 2.32 \times 10^{-18} \text{ J } (\because \lambda = 6850 \text{ Å})$$

2.9×10^{-19} J amount of energy is required to evolve 1 molecule of O_2. Amount of energy required for average energy storage to evolve 1 molecule of O_2,

$$E' = 112 \text{ kcal/mol}$$

$$= \frac{112 \times 10^3 \times 4.184}{6.02 \times 10^{23}} \text{ J}$$

$$= 7.78 \times 10^{-19} \text{ J}$$

% efficiency of the photosynthesis process

$$= \frac{E'}{E} \times 100$$

$$= \frac{7.78 \times 10^{-19} \text{ J}}{2.32 \times 10^{-18} \text{ J}} \times 100 = 33.5\%$$

2. (a) In the expression of photoelectric effect, kinetic energy of the ejected photoelectron is

$$\text{KE} = h\nu - h\nu_0 = \frac{hc}{\lambda} - \frac{hc}{\lambda_0} \quad \text{...(i)}$$

$$\Rightarrow \quad \text{KE} = hc\left(\frac{1}{\lambda} - \frac{1}{\lambda_0}\right)$$

From de-Broglie equation,

$$\lambda' = \frac{h}{mv} = \frac{h}{\sqrt{2m \times \text{KE}}}$$

$$\left[\begin{array}{l} \because \text{KE} = \frac{1}{2} mv^2 \\ \Rightarrow mv = \sqrt{2m \times \text{KE}} \end{array}\right]$$

where, λ' = de-Broglie wavelength

$$\Rightarrow \quad \lambda' = \frac{h}{\sqrt{2m \times hc\left(\frac{1}{\lambda} - \frac{1}{\lambda_0}\right)}}$$

[from Eq. (i)]

$$= \sqrt{\frac{h^2}{2m \times hc \times \left(\frac{\lambda_0 - \lambda}{\lambda\lambda_0}\right)}}$$

$$= \sqrt{\frac{h \times \lambda\lambda_0}{2mc\,(\lambda_0 - \lambda)}}$$

or $\left[\frac{h(\lambda\lambda_0)}{2mc(\lambda_0 - \lambda)}\right]^{\frac{1}{2}}$

3. (c) Angular momentum of an electron in the nth orbit,

$$mvr = \frac{nh}{2\pi} = \frac{7h}{11} \quad \text{(given)}$$

$$\Rightarrow \quad n = \frac{7}{11} \times 2 \times \pi$$

$$= \frac{7}{11} \times 2 \times \frac{22}{7} = 4 \text{ (4}^{\text{th}} \text{ orbit)}$$

Radius of the 4th orbit of Li^{2+} ion

$$\Rightarrow \quad r_4^{Li^{2+}} = r_1^H \times \frac{n^2}{Z}$$

$$= 0.529 \times \frac{4^2}{3} \text{ Å} = 2.82 \text{ Å}$$

4. (d) When the α-particle reaches nucleus, its kinetic energy $\left(\frac{1}{2} mv^2\right)$ gets converted into potential energy $\left(\frac{Ze^2}{r}\right)$.

Now, momentum, $p = mv$ or $v = \frac{p}{m}$

$$\because \quad \frac{1}{2} mv^2 = \frac{1}{2} \frac{m}{}\left(\frac{p}{m}\right)^2 = \frac{p^2}{2m}$$

$$\Rightarrow \quad \frac{p^2}{2m}(\text{KE}) = \frac{Ze^2}{r}(\text{PE}) \quad \text{...(i)}$$

Let, at a distance r_1 from the nucleus, momentum of the α-particle $= 2p$

So, KE = PE

$$\Rightarrow \quad \frac{(2p)^2}{2m} = \frac{Ze^2}{r_1}$$

$$\Rightarrow \quad 4 \times \frac{p^2}{2m} = \frac{Ze^2}{r_1}$$

$$\Rightarrow \quad 4 \times \frac{Ze^2}{r} = \frac{Ze^2}{r_1} \quad \text{[From Eq. (i)]}$$

$$\Rightarrow \quad r_1 = \frac{r}{4}$$

5. (b) 'Hartree' is the unit (E_h or Ha) of electric potential energy which is approximately the potential energy (PE) of H-atom in its ground state.

We know,

PE = 2 × energy of an electron in an orbit

For H-atom,

$\text{PE} = 2 \times E_1^H = 2 \times (-13.6 \text{ eV atom}^{-1})$

$= -27.2 \text{ eV atom}^{-1} = 1 \text{ Ha}$

6. (a) Kinetic energy imparted by the ejected electron, $\text{KE} = \frac{1}{2} mv^2$, which is equal to IE_1 of Ne, so that ejection of an electron from the valence shell of a Ne-atom will take place.

IE_1 of Ne = 2080 kJ/mol

$$= (2080 \times 10^3 \text{ J mol}^{-1}) \times \frac{1}{(6.023 \times 10^{23} \text{ mol}^{-1})}$$

$$= 3.453 \times 10^{-18} \text{ J/atom}$$

$$\frac{1}{2} mv^2 = \text{KE} = IE_1, \text{ of Ne}$$

$$\Rightarrow \quad v = \left(\frac{2 \times IE_1}{m}\right)^{1/2}$$

$$= \left(\frac{2 \times 3.453 \times 10^{-18} (\text{J or kg m}^2 \text{ s}^{-2})}{9.1 \times 10^{-31} \text{kg}}\right)^{1/2}$$

$$= 2.754 \times 10^6 \text{ ms}^{-1}$$

$[\because m = \text{mass of electron} = 9.1 \times 10^{-31} \text{ kg}]$

7. (c) ⇒ The ideal body, which emits and absorbs radiation of all frequencies is called a black body. So, statement I is true.

⇒ The frequency distribution of black body radiation depends only on its temperature. At a given temperature, the intensity of radiation emitted increases with increase of wavelength, reaches a maximum value and then decreases with further increase in wavelength.

So, statement II is false.

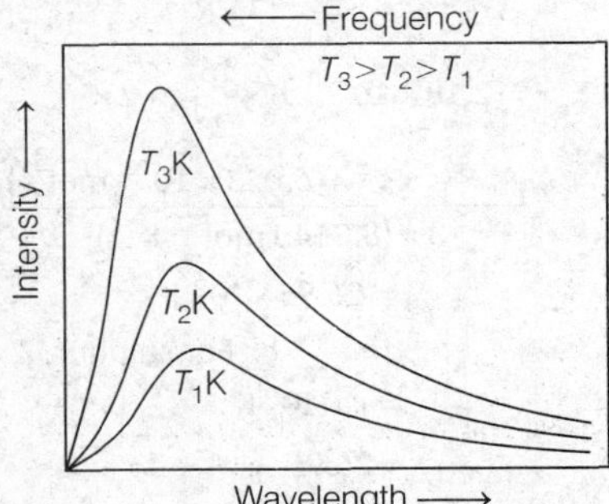

8. (b)

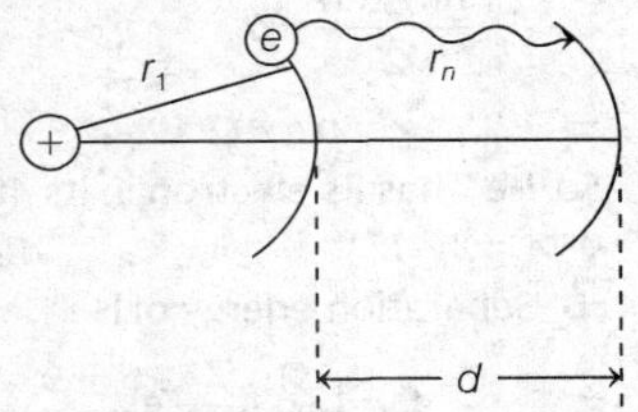

d = distance travelled by the electron of H-atom from first orbit (radius $= r_1$) to the nth orbit (ray) of radius $= r_n$

$$= r_n - r_1 = 0.7935 \text{ nm}$$

$$\Rightarrow \quad r_1 \times \frac{n^2}{Z} - r_1 = 0.7935$$

$$\left[\because r_n = r_1^H \times \frac{n^2}{Z} \text{ where, } Z = 1 \text{ for H - atom}\right]$$

$$\Rightarrow \quad r_1(n^2 - 1) = 0.7935$$

$$\Rightarrow \quad n^2 - 1 = \frac{0.7935}{0.0529} = 15$$

$$[\because r_1^H = 0.0529 \text{ nm}]$$

$$\Rightarrow \quad n = \sqrt{16} = 4$$

∴ Maximum number of spectral lines $(n_1 = 1, n_2 = 4)$

$$= \frac{(n_2 - n_1)(n_2 - n_1 + 1)}{2}$$

$$= \frac{(4-1)(4-1+1)}{2} = 6$$

9. (d) Considering particle nature (Bohr's model) and wave nature of the moving electron (de-Broglie model), we get for nth orbit circumference,

$$n\lambda_n = 2\pi r_n = 2\pi \times \left(r_1^H \times \frac{n^2}{Z}\right)$$

$$\Rightarrow \quad \lambda_n = 2\pi \times r_1^H \times \frac{n}{Z}$$

$$= 2 \times 3.14 \times 0.529 \times \frac{n}{Z} \text{ Å}$$

$$\Rightarrow \quad \lambda_n = 3.32 \times \frac{n}{Z} \text{ Å}$$

So, $\lambda_3 (\text{He}^+) = 3.32 \times \frac{3}{2} \text{ Å} = 4.98 \text{ Å}$.

10. (b) From de-Broglie equation,

$$\lambda = \frac{h}{mv}$$

For a matter wave,

$$\text{Frequency, } (\nu) = \frac{v}{\lambda} = \frac{v}{\frac{h}{mv}} \left[\because \lambda = \frac{h}{mv}\right]$$

$$\Rightarrow \nu = \frac{mv^2}{h}$$

$$\left[\because \text{KE} = \frac{1}{2} mv^2 \Rightarrow mv^2 = 2 \times \text{KE}\right]$$

$$= \frac{2 \times \text{KE}}{h}$$

11. (d) From the given diagram,

No. of waves made by the electron $= 4 =$ Orbit number (n)

Frequency of the 4th orbit of H-atom = No. of revolutions made by the electron in the 4th orbit of H-atom

$$= 6.56 \times 10^{15} \times \frac{Z^2}{n^3} \text{ s}^{-1}$$

$$= 6.65 \times 10^{15} \times \frac{1^2}{4^3} \text{ s}^{-1}$$

$$= 1.0 \times 10^{14} \text{ s}^{-1}$$

12. (a) Uncertainty in velocity,

$$\Delta v = 0.001 \text{ km/h}$$

$$= \frac{0.001 \times 10^3 \text{ m}}{3600 \text{ s}}$$

$$= 2.778 \times 10^{-4} \text{ m/s}$$

So, its uncertainty in position,

$$\Delta x = \frac{h}{4\pi m.\Delta v}$$

$$= \frac{6.626 \times 10^{-34} \text{ Js}}{4 \times 3.14 \times (500 \text{ kg}) \times (2.778 \times 10^{-4} \text{ m/s})}$$

$$= 3.798 \times 10^{-34} \text{ m}$$

So, uncertainty in momentum,

$$\Delta p = m \times \Delta v$$

$$= 500 \times (2.778 \times 10^{-4})$$

$$= 1.389 \times 10^{-1} \text{ kg m/s}$$

$$>> \Delta x = 3.798 \times 10^{-34} \text{ m}$$

⇒ Δx is wholly negligible as compared to the larger value of Δp.

13. (c) $\psi = A \sin\left(\frac{2\pi x}{\lambda}\right)$

$$\Rightarrow \quad \frac{d\psi}{dx} = \left(\frac{2\pi}{\lambda}\right) A \cos\left(\frac{2\pi x}{\lambda}\right)$$

$$\Rightarrow \quad \frac{d^2\psi}{dx^2} = -\left(\frac{2\pi}{\lambda}\right)^2 \times \left[A \sin\left(\frac{2\pi x}{\lambda}\right)\right]$$

$$= -\frac{4\pi^2}{\lambda^2} \times \psi$$

$$\Rightarrow \quad \frac{d^2\psi}{dx^2} + \frac{4\pi^2\psi}{\lambda^2} = 0$$

14. (b) When $\frac{d^2\psi}{dr^2} = 0$

The distance of the electron from the nucleus at which finding probability of the electron will be maximum.

$$\therefore \quad e^{-r/a_0} = 0$$

$$\Rightarrow \quad -\ln\left(\frac{r}{a_0}\right) = 0 = -\ln 1$$

$$\Rightarrow \quad \frac{r}{a_0} = 1$$

or $\quad r = a_0$

15. (c) Correct match is

A→(2), B→(1), C→(3)

A. Radial wave function plot, where the value of $\psi = R(r)$, which varies as +, −, +, −.

B. Radial probability density plot, where the value of $R^2 = R^2(r)$ which is always positive.

C. Radial probability function plot, where the value of ψ^2 as a function of r, is given for s-orbital.

16. (d) Writing the quadratic expression as

$$(2\gamma')^2 - 18\gamma' + 27 = 0$$

Its roots are,

$$\gamma' = \frac{18 \pm \sqrt{18^2 - 8 \times 27}}{4}$$

$$= \frac{18 \pm \sqrt{108}}{4}$$

$$= \frac{18 \pm 10.39}{4} = 1.90, 7.10$$

⇒ So, $\quad \gamma = 7.1\, a_0$

17. (c) Since, the distance from the nucleus is the same and the s-orbital is spherically symmetrical, the probability in each of the two volumes is same, i.e. 1.0×10^{-5}.

18. (d) In ground state, electronic configuration of phosphorus is,

P : $[Ne]3s^2 3p^3$
(Z=15)

or [Ne] $3s^2$ [⥮] $3p^3$ [↿|↿|↿]
$m = -1\ 0\ +1$

P has three unpaired electrons in its $3p$-subshell.

Any one of these three unpaired electrons will have,

$$n = 3, l = 1$$
$$m = 0 \text{ or } +1 \text{ or } -1$$
$$s = +\frac{1}{2} \text{ or } -\frac{1}{2}$$

So, $\left[n = 3, l = 1, m = +1, s = +\frac{1}{2}\right]$

correct combination is (option-d).

19. (d) $Cd(Z = 48) : [Kr]\,5s^2 4d^{10}$

$$Sb(Z = 51) \xrightarrow{-3e^-} Sb^{3+}$$

$[Kr]\,4p^6 5s^2 4d^{10} 5p^3$ $[Kr]\,4p^6 5s^2 4d^{10}$

Sb is a p-block element of group-15 $(5s^2 5p^3)$. So, all $5p$-electrons are lost to produce Sb^{3+}.

$$Sn\,(Z = 50) \xrightarrow{-2e^-} Sn^{2+}$$

$[Kr]\,4p^6 5s^2 4d^{10} 5p^2$ $[Kr]\,4p^6 5s^2 4d^{10}$

Sn is also a p-block element and it belongs to group-14 $(5s^2 5p^2)$.

So, all $5p$-electrons are to be removed form Sn^{2+}.

20. (d) I. When $n = 4$ (principal quantum number), total number of electrons that can be present in the 4th orbit $= 2n^2 = 2 \times 4^2 = 32$, out of which **16 electrons** will have $s = -\frac{1}{2}$ value (spin quantum number).

II. When $l = 0$ (azimuthal quantum number), it is s-orbital/subshell which can hold maximum **2 electrons** $[(2l + 1) \times 2 = (2 \times 0 + 1) \times 2 = 2]$.

III. When $l = 1$, it is a p-subshell whose capacity is **6 electrons** $[(2 \times 1 + 1) \times 2 = 6]$

IV.

$n=2$ → $l=0$ (s): one box, $m=0$; $l=1$ (p): three boxes, $m=-1\ \ 0\ \ +1$

2 electrons in each orbital
(Total = 4 electrons)

21. (8.28) $\lambda = 24\,\mu m = 24 \times 10^{-6}$ m

$$\Rightarrow \quad E = h\nu = \frac{hc}{\lambda}$$
$$= \frac{(6.626 \times 10^{-34}\text{ Js}) \times (3 \times 10^8\text{ m/s})}{(24 \times 10^{-6}\text{ m})}$$
$$= 8.28 \times 10^{-21}\text{ J}$$

22. (7.44) Stopping potential of photo-electrons,

$$V_s = \frac{h}{e}(\nu - \nu_0)$$
$$\Rightarrow \quad \nu - \nu_0 = \frac{e \times V_s}{h}$$
$$\Rightarrow \quad \nu = \frac{e \times V_s}{h} + \nu_0$$
$$= \frac{e \times V_s}{h} + \frac{c}{\lambda_0}$$
$$= \left[\frac{(1.6 \times 10^{-19}\text{ C}) \times (300\text{ V})}{(6.626 \times 10^{-34}\text{ Js})} + \frac{3 \times 10^8\text{ m/s}}{1500 \times 10^{-10}\text{ m}}\right]$$
$$= 7.44 \times 10^{16}\text{ Hz}$$

$[\because V_s = 600\text{V}, \lambda_0 = 1500\text{ Å} = 1500 \times 10^{-10}\text{ m}]$

$$= x \times 10^{16}\text{ Hz}$$
$$\therefore \quad x = 7.44$$

23. (4.52) $\Delta E = h\nu = \frac{hc}{\lambda}$

$$\Rightarrow \quad \lambda = \frac{hc}{\Delta E}$$
$$= \frac{(6.626 \times 10^{-34}\text{ Js}) \times (3 \times 10^8\text{ m/s})}{(4.4 \times 10^{-19}\text{ J})}$$
$$= 4.517 \times 10^{-7}\text{ m}$$
$$\approx 4.52 \times 10^{-7}\text{ m}$$
$$= a \times 10^{-7}\text{ m}$$
$$\therefore \quad a = 4.52$$

24. (26.95) $\bar{E} = (IE)_H \times \frac{Z^2}{n^2}$

$$= \frac{3}{2} \times k_b T$$

$\left[\because k_b = \text{Boltzmann constant} = \frac{R}{N_A}\right]$

$$\Rightarrow \quad T = \frac{(IE)_H \times \frac{Z^2}{n^2} \times 2 \times N_A}{3 \times R}$$
$$= \frac{(2.18 \times 10^{-18}\text{ J}) \times \frac{16^2}{1^2} \times 2 \times (6.023 \times 10^{23}\text{ mol}^{-1})}{3 \times (8.314\text{ J mol}^{-1}\text{ K}^{-1})}$$
$$= 26.95 \times 10^6\text{ K}$$

$[\because$ For sulphur, $Z = 16]$

$$= x \times 10^6\text{ K}$$
$$\therefore \quad x = 26.95$$

25. (4) Total number of transition,

$$\frac{n(n+1)}{2} = 6$$
$$\Rightarrow \quad n = 4$$

So, He^+ has its electron in its 4th orbit.

$\Rightarrow$ Separation energy of He^+,

$$E = 13.6 \times \frac{Z^2}{n^2}\text{ eV}$$
$$E_{He^+} = 13.6 \times \frac{(2)^2}{(4)^2}\text{ eV}$$
$$E_{He^+} = 13.6 \times \frac{4}{16} = \frac{13.6}{4}\text{ eV}$$

Ionisation energy of hydrogen

$$E_H = 13.6$$

So, $\quad E_H/E_{He^+} = 4$

26. (93.72) Transition energy, $\Delta E_{1 \to 3}$

$$= 2.18 \times 10^{-18}\left(\frac{1}{1^2} - \frac{1}{3^2}\right)\text{ J atom}^{-1}$$
$$= 1.94 \times 10^{-18}\text{ J atom}^{-1}$$

Transition energy $= \frac{3}{2} k_b T$

$$= \frac{3}{2} \times (1.38 \times 10^{-23}) \times T\text{ J atom}^{-1}$$

$(\because \; k_b = \text{Boltzmann constant} = 1.38 \times 10^{-23}\text{ J})$

$$\Rightarrow \frac{3}{2} \times 1.38 \times 10^{-23} \times T = 1.94 \times 10^{-18}$$

$$\Rightarrow T = \frac{1.94\times 10^{-18}\times 2}{3\times 1.38\times 10^{-23}}\text{ K}$$
$$= 93.719\times 10^{3}\text{ K}$$
$$\simeq 93.72\times 10^{3}\text{ K} = T'\times 10^{3}\text{ K}$$
$$\because\ T' = 93.72$$

27. (8.68) Using Davisson-Germer experiment in de-Broglie equation, we get

$$\lambda = \frac{h}{mv} = \frac{h}{\sqrt{2m\times KE}} = \frac{h}{\sqrt{2m\times e\times V}}$$

Here, $m = m_e = 9.1\times 10^{-31}$ kg

$e = 1.6\times 10^{-19}$ C

$V = 20\text{ kV} = 20\times 10^{3}$ volt

$$\Rightarrow \lambda = \frac{6.626\times 10^{-34}\text{ Js}}{[(2\times 9.1\times 10^{-31}\text{ kg})\times(1.6\times 10^{-19}\text{ C})\times(20\times 10^{3}\text{ volt})]^{1/2}}$$
$$= 8.68\times 10^{-12}\text{ m} = Y\times 10^{-12}\text{ m}$$
$$\therefore\ Y = 8.68$$

28. (3.94 or $\simeq$ 4) The maximum uncertainty in position of the electron inside the nucleus, $\Delta x = 1.34\times 10^{-15}$ m.

So, according to Heisenberg's uncertainty principle, minimum uncertainty in momentum of the electron inside the nucleus will be,

$$\Delta p = \frac{h}{4\pi\,\Delta x}$$
$$= \frac{6.626\times 10^{-34}\text{ Js}}{4\times 3.14\times(1.34\times 10^{-15}\text{ m})}$$
$$= 3.936\times 10^{-20}\text{ kg m s}^{-1}$$
$$\simeq 3.94\times 10^{-20}\text{ kg m s}^{-1}$$
$$= x\times 10^{-20}\text{ kg m s}^{-1}$$
$$\therefore\ x = 3.94$$
$$x \approx 4$$

29. (2.83) $Ti \xrightarrow{-2e^-} Ti^{2+}$

$[Ar]3d^2\,4s^2$ $[Ar]$ | 1 | 1 | | | | $3d^2$

No. of unpaired electrons, $n = 2$

Spin only magnetic moment of the compound,

$$\mu = \sqrt{n(n+2)}\text{ BM}$$
$$= \sqrt{2(2+2)}\text{ BM}$$
$$= 2.828\text{ BM} \simeq 2.83\text{ BM}$$

30. (4) Orbital angular momentum,

$$\mu_l = \sqrt{l(l+1)}\,\frac{h}{2\pi}$$
$$\Rightarrow \Sigma\mu_l = \mu_l(3s) + \mu_l(3p) + \mu_l(3d)$$
$$[l=0] \quad [l=1] \quad [l=2]$$
$$= [\sqrt{0(0+1)} + \sqrt{1(1+1)} + \sqrt{2(2+1)}]\,\frac{h}{2\pi}$$
$$= (\sqrt{2}+\sqrt{6})\times\frac{6.626\times 10^{-34}}{2\times 3.14}\text{ Js}$$
$$= 4.07\times 10^{-34}\text{ Js}$$
$$= x\times 10^{-34}\text{ Js}$$
$$\therefore\ x = 4.07 \approx 4$$

Qualifier 04
(Chemical Bonding and Molecular Structure)

1. (d)

Na (g) + Cl (g) ⟶ NaCl (s)

$-e^-$ | IE_1 $+e^-$ | EA_1

Na^+ (g) Cl^- (g) — (Lattice energy, U)

$\Rightarrow$ Net energy change for the formation of 1 mole NaCl is

$$E_{net} = IE_1 - EA_1 - U$$
$$= (495.8 - 349.4 - 776)\text{ kJ mol}^{-1}$$
$$= -629.6\text{ kJ mol}^{-1}$$

Negative sign of E_{net} indicates the process leads to release of energy of amount 629.6 kJ.

2. (b) LiCl, $BeCl_2$, BCl_3 and CCl_4 are the chlorides of Li (as Li^+), Be (as Be^{2+}), B (as B^{3+}) and C (as C^{4+}) respectively.

Here, the anion, Cl^- is common to all. So, charge and size of cation plays an important role in determining the degree of covalency in an ionic bond.

According to Fajan's rule, degree of covalency $\propto$ charge of an cation (Z_+)

$$\propto \frac{1}{\text{size of cation }(r_+)}$$

$\propto$ Polarisation power of cation

$\propto$ Ionic potential of cation $\left(\phi = \frac{Z_\oplus}{r_\oplus^2}\right)$

The order of

Size (r_+) : $C^{4+} < B^{3+} < Be^{2+} < Li^+$

Charge (Z_+) : $C^{4+} > B^{3+} > Be^{2+} > Li^+$

Polarisation power and Ionic potential of cation (ϕ) :

$$C^{4+} > B^{3+} > Be^{2+} > Li^+$$

$\Rightarrow$ Order of covalent bond nature : $CCl_4 > BCl_3 > BeCl_2 > LiCl$ (option-b)

3. (b) When, $a = 0$, the molecule is PF_5.

$a = 5$, the molecule is PCl_5.

Both of the molecules, PF_5 and PCl_5 are symmetrical and hence they have zero dipole moment, $\mu = 0$. So, PCl_5 and PF_5 are non-polar molecules [P : sp^3d; Geometry/shape : Trigonal bipyramidal]

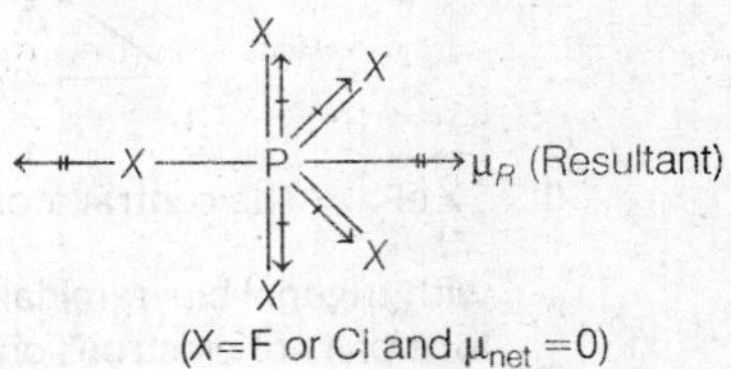

(X=F or Cl and $\mu_{net} = 0$)

$\Rightarrow$ When $a = 3$, the molecule is PCl_3F_2 in which P is sp^3d- hybridised and geometry/shape of the molecule is trigonal bipyramidal. PCl_3F_2 is structurally unsymmetrical but its net dipole moment is zero ($\mu_{net} = 0$) and it is a non-polar molecule.

In PCl_3F_2 three Cl-atoms occupy equatorial position of the trigonal plane.

So, from the plane, μ_{net} is zero. On the other hand, two F-atoms occupy axial position of the trigonal bipyramidal geometry (according to bent's rule, more electronegative atoms, here F-atoms, use axial overlapping in making of P—F covalent bonds in PCl_3F_2). So, from axial contribution to μ_{net} is also zero.

F — Cl — Cl — P — Cl — F; $\mu_{plane} = 0$; $\mu_{axis} = 0$; So, $\mu_{net} = 0$ (non-polar)

4. (d) I. $\overset{\bullet\bullet}{:}XeF_5^-$ $\Rightarrow$ The central atom (Xe) is sp^3d^3-hybridised with pentagonal bipyramidal geometry and Xe has two lone pairs of electrons on it.

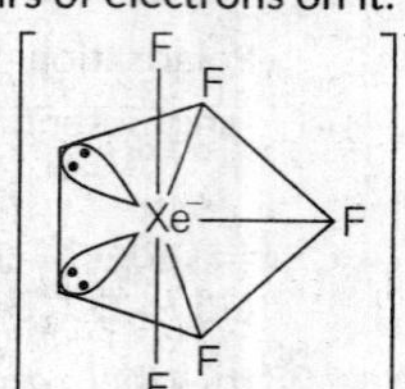

II. $\dot{:}BrF_5$ $\Rightarrow$ The central atom (Br) is sp^3d^2-hybridised with octahedral geometry and Br has one lone pair of electrons on it.

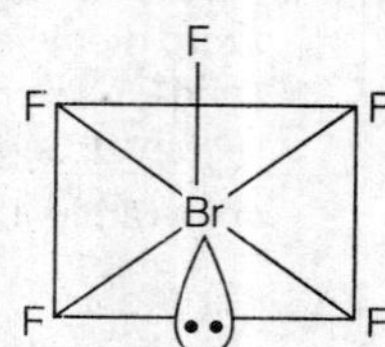

III. $\overset{\bullet\bullet}{\underset{\bullet\bullet}{:}}XeF_2$ $\Rightarrow$ The central atom (Xe) is sp^3d-hybridised with trigonal bipyramidal geometry and Xe has three lone pairs of electrons on it.

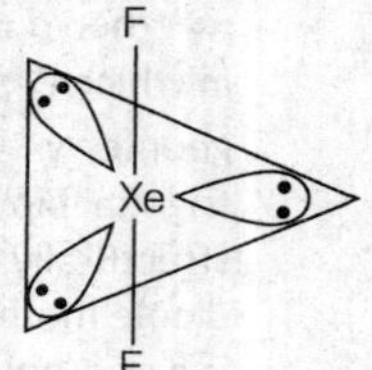

IV. $H_3\overset{+}{S}:$ $\Rightarrow$ The central atom(s) is sp^3-hybridised with tetrahedral geometry and S has one lone pair of electrons on it.

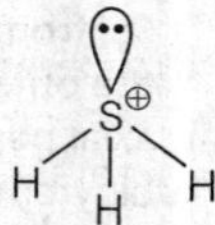

V. XeO_6^{4-} $\Rightarrow$ The central atom (Xe) is sp^3d^2-hybridised with octahedral geometry and Xe does not have lone pair of electrons on it.

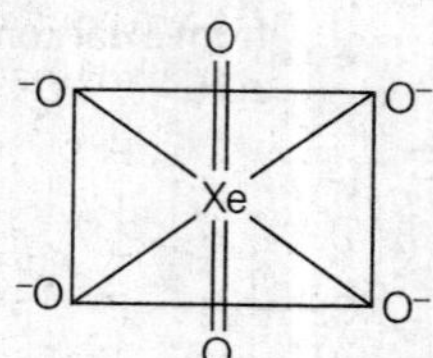

So, in II and IV, their central atoms contain same number of lone pair of electrons (1 pair).

5. (c) Presence of vacant 3*d*-orbitals in Si enables formation of $p\pi(N) - d\pi$ (Si) bond in trisilyl amine, $(SiH_3)_3N$. As a result

(i) N of $(SiH_3)_3N$ attains sp^2-hybridisation with trigonal planar geometry and shape as well.

(ii) Lone pair of N-atom looses its capability for donation to show Lewis basicity.

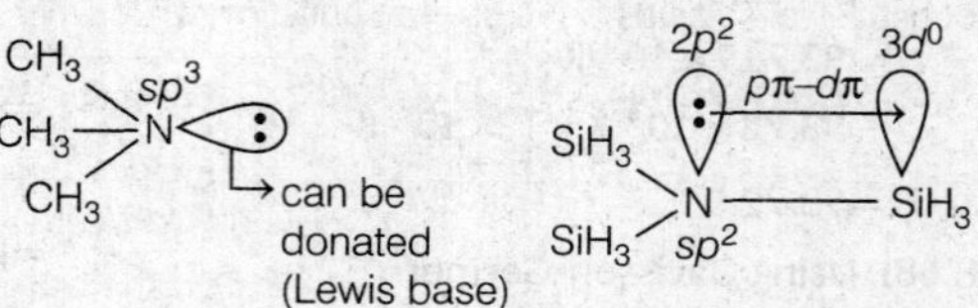

Trimethyl amine, $(CH_3)_3N$:	Trisilyl amine, $(SiH_3)_3N$
$N \rightarrow sp^3$-hybridised	$N \rightarrow sp^2$-hybridised
Geometry $\rightarrow$ tetrahedral	Geometry and shape $\rightarrow$ trigonal planar
Shape-pyramidal	
Lewis basicity $\rightarrow$ present	Lewis basicity $\rightarrow$ absent

6. (c) As in AsF_5 is sp^3d-hybridised and geometry of the molecule is trigonal bipyramidal.

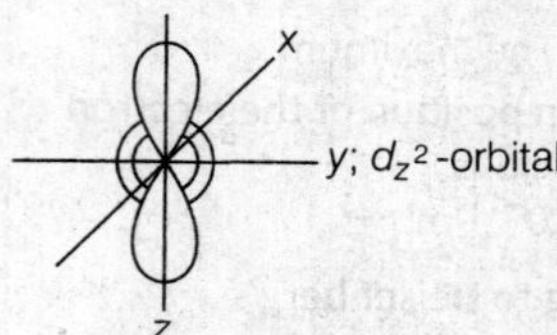

$\Rightarrow$ Here, two axial As—F bonds are formed by contribution of d_{z^2}-orbital of 4*d*-subshell of the central atom (As).

x
y; d_{z^2}-orbital
z

7. (d) $\underset{sp^3d}{\underline{Sb}F_5} + HF \longrightarrow H^{\oplus}\,[\underset{sp^3d^2}{\underline{Sb}F_6}]^{\ominus}$

sp^3d hybridisation state of Sb is changed into sp^3d^2 state.

$\Rightarrow \underset{sp^3d}{\underline{P}Cl_5} \longrightarrow \underset{sp^3}{:\underline{P}Cl_3} + Cl_2$

sp^3d hybridisation state of P is changed into sp^3 state.

$\underset{sp^2}{BCl_3} + F^- \longrightarrow \underset{sp^3}{[BFCl_3]^-}$

sp^2 hybridisation state of B is also changed into sp^3 hybridisation state.

So, option-(d) is correct.

8. (d)

Species	Hybridisation state of central atom	Geometry	Shape or structure
(*a*) CO_2	*sp*	Linear	Linear
(*b*) CH_4	sp^3	Tetrahedral	Tetrahedral
(*c*) $\dot{:}SF_4$	sp^3d	Trigonal bipyramidal	*See-saw*
(*d*) $SiCl_4$	sp^3	Tetrahedral	Tetrahedral
(*e*) $\overset{\bullet\bullet}{\underset{\bullet\bullet}{:}}XeF_2$	sp^3d	Trigonal bipyramidal	Linear
(*f*) BF_3	sp^2	Trigonal planar	Trigonal planar

$\Rightarrow$ Isostructural pairs have same structure or shape.

9. (b) Isolobal species have same hybridisation state of central atom and same geometry as well.
Isostructural species have same shape or structure.

	Species	Hybridisation of central atom	Geometry	Shape	Remarks
(a)	PH_4^+	sp^3	Tetrahedral	Tetrahedral	Isolobal but not isostructural pair
	XeO_3	sp^3	Tetrahedral	Pyramidal	
(b)	CO_2	sp	Linear	Linear	Isostructural but not isolobal pair (option-b)
	XeF_2	sp^3d	Trigonal bipyramidal	Linear	
(c)	BF_3	sp^2	Trigonal planar	Trigonal planar	In each of option-(c) and (d), each pair is neither isolobal nor isostructural
	BF_4^-	sp^3	Tetrahedral	Tetrahedral	
(d)	XeF_4	sp^3d^2	Octahedral	Square planar	
	SF_4	sp^3d	Trigonal bipyramidal	*See-saw*	

10. (a) Because of larger size of Cl-atom, it cannot participate in making of bonds with vacant *d*-orbitals of Si-atom.

Hence, $SiCl_6^{2-}$ does not exist.

Thus, both statement I and statement II are true.

11. (b) I. With increase in size and decrease in electronegativity of central atom, bond angle decreases (Drago's rule). So, for group-15 hydrides, the order of bond angle is,

$NH_3 > PH_3 > AsH_3$.

II.

(O_3) (O_3^+)

Lone pair-double bond repulsion in O_3 is greater than odd electron-double bond repulsion. Thus, $x° < y°$

III.

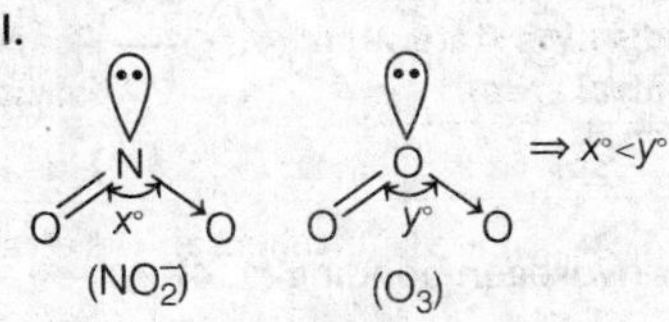

According to bent's rule, N—O bond in NO_2 has more *p*-character than that of O—O bond in O_3 and so the order of bond angle is just reversed.

IV.

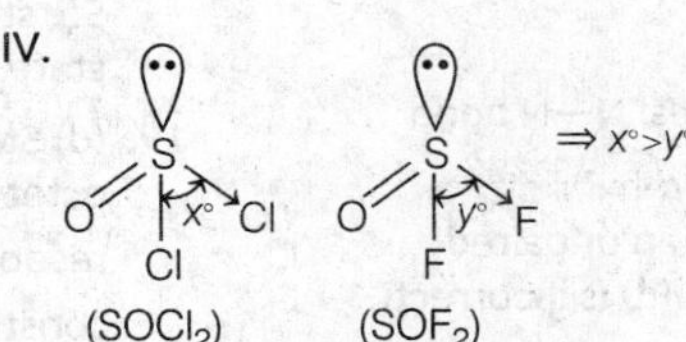

According to bent's rule, S—F bond in SOF_2 has more *p*-character than that of S—Cl bond in $SOCl_2$. Hence, opposite the order of their bond angles.

⇒ So, option (b) includes species with the lowest bond angle from each set.

12. (b) NO_2 is paramagnetic ($\mu \neq 0$) due to the presence of an unpaired electron on N-atom.

$n = 1, \mu = \sqrt{1(1+2)}$ BM $= \sqrt{3}$ BM

sp^2, 134°

$\angle ONO = 134°$ is greater than 120° (expected) which is due to more effective repulsion between two O-atoms than that created by the odd electron (not a lone pair) on N-atom.

$\Rightarrow$ $O{=}\overset{\oplus}{N}{\longrightarrow}O$ (sp) $\angle ONO = 180°$

$\Rightarrow$ (sp^2)

$\angle ONO = 115°$ is lesser than 120° (expected) which is due to repulsion between two O-atoms and O^- (more effective).

13. (c) The bond with greatest π-bond order should have the greatest double bond character and thus the shortest distance and *vice-versa*.

So, 1-2 bond is the shortest (bond order = 0.738) and 11-12 bond is the longest (bond order = 0.485)

[**Note** 1-2 bond length = 1.370 Å, 11-12 bond length = 1.436 Å]

14. (c) The resultant molecular orbitals from the options given will be as

(a)

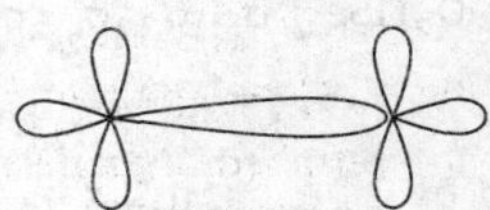

It is a σ-bond formed by head-on-head overlap of *d*-atomic orbitals.

(b)

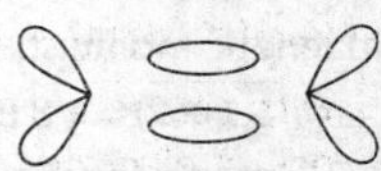

It is a π-bond formed by side-by-side overlap of *d*-atomic orbitals.

(c)

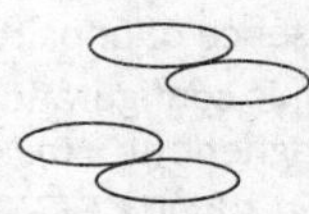

It is a δ-bond formed by angular approach (0° < θ < 90°) or overlapping of *d*-atomic orbitals.

15. (b) Atomic orbitals of same symmetry will mix up to give molecular orbitals. Let us take the molecular orbitals of B_2 and F_2 molecules,

$B_2(10e^-): \sigma_{1s^2}\, \sigma^*_{1s^2} \sigma_{2s^2} \sigma^*_{2s^2} \pi_{2p_x^1} = \pi_{2p_y^1}$

$F_2\,(18\,e^-): \sigma_{1s^2} \sigma^*_{1s^2} \sigma_{2s^2} \sigma^*_{2s^2} \sigma_{2p_z^2} \pi_{2p_x^2} = \pi_{2p_y^2}\, \pi^*_{2p_x^2} = \pi^*_{2p_y^2}$

In B_2, atomic number of boron $Z < 7$ and in F_2, atomic number of fluorine $Z > 7$.

So, after using σ_{2s} and σ^*_{2s}, π_{2p_x} and π_{2p_y} come first in B_2 but it is σ_{2p_z} comes first in case of F_2.

16. (d) $N_2(14e^-): \sigma_{1s^2}\, \sigma^*_{1s^2}\, \sigma_{2s^2}\, \sigma^*_{2s^2}\, \pi_{2p_x^2} = \pi_{2p_y^2} \sigma_{2p_z^2}$

$\Rightarrow$ Bond order $= \dfrac{10-4}{2} = 3$

$\Rightarrow$ It is diamagnetic ($\mu = 0$), as it does not have unpaired electron.

• $N_2^+(13e^-)$: $\sigma_{1s^2}\, \sigma^*_{1s^2}\, \sigma_{2s^2}\, \sigma^*_{2s^2}\, \pi_{2p_x^2} = \pi_{2p_y^2} \sigma_{2p_z^1}$

$\Rightarrow$ Bond order $= \dfrac{9-4}{2} = 2.5$

So, decrease in bond order (3 to 2.5) indicates, N—N bond weakens in N_2^+

$\Rightarrow$ It is paramagnetic due to the presence of an unpaired electron in σ_{2p_z}. So, the statement in option-(d) is incorrect.

$\Rightarrow O_2(16e^-): \sigma_{1s^2} \sigma^*_{1s^2} \sigma_{2s^2} \sigma^*_{2s^2} \sigma_{2p_z^2} \pi_{2p_x^2}$

$= \pi_{2p_y^2}\, \pi^*_{2p_x^1} = \pi^*_{2p_y^1}$

$\Rightarrow$ Bond order $= \dfrac{10-6}{2} = 2$

$\Rightarrow$ Paramagnetic moment, $\mu_1 = \sqrt{2(2+2)} = \sqrt{8}$ BM $\quad [\because n = 2]$

$\Rightarrow O_2^+(15e^-)\ \sigma_{1s^2} \sigma^*_{1s^2} \sigma_{2s^2} \sigma^*_{2s^2} \sigma_{2p_z^2} \pi_{2p_x^2}$

$= \pi_{2p_y^2}\, \pi^*_{2p_x^1} = \pi^*_{2p_y^0}$

$\Rightarrow$ Bond order $= \dfrac{10-5}{2} = 2.5$

So, during ionisation of O_2 to O_2^+ bond order increases from 2 to 2.5.

So (option-b) is correct.

Paramagnetic moment,

$\mu_2 = \sqrt{1(1+2)} = \sqrt{3}$ BM $\quad [\because n = 1]$

So, in O_2^+, paramagnetic character decreases ($\mu_2 < \mu_1$) (option-c).

So, option-(d) is the correct answer.

17. (b) Presence of unpaired electrons (n) in the molecular orbital electronic configuration will indicate the species will be paramagnetic ($\mu \neq 0$).

$\because \quad \mu = \sqrt{n(n+2)}$ BM

Li_2 $(6e^-)$: $\sigma_{1s^2}\, \sigma^*_{1s^2} \sigma_{2s^2} \Rightarrow n = 0, \mu = 0$, diamagnetic

B_2 $(10e^-)$: $\sigma_{1s^2}\, \sigma^*_{1s^2} \sigma_{2s^2} \sigma^*_{2s^2}\, \pi_{2p_x^1} = \pi_{2p_y^1}$

$n = 2, \mu \neq 0$, paramagnetic.

N_2 $(14\,e^-)$: $[Be_2]\, \pi_{2p_x^2} = \pi_{2p_y^2}\, \sigma_{2p_z^2} \Rightarrow n = 0, \mu = 0$, diamagnetic

NO $(15\,e^-)$: $[Be_2]\, \pi_{2p_x^2} = \pi_{2p_y^2}\, \sigma_{2p_z^2}\, \pi^{*1}_{2p_x}$ $n = 1, \mu \neq 0$, paramagnetic.

O_2 $(16e^-)$: $[Be_2]\, \sigma_{2p_z^2}\, \pi_{2p_x^2} = \pi_{2p_y^2}\, \pi^*_{2p_x^1}\, \pi^*_{2p_y^1}; \Rightarrow n = 2, \mu \neq 0$, paramagnetic.

F_2 $(18e^-)$: $[Be_2]\, \sigma_{2p_z^2} \pi_{2p_x^2} = \pi_{2p_y^2}\, \pi^*_{2p_x^2} = \pi^*_{2p_y^2} \Rightarrow n = 0, \mu = 0$, diamagnetic.

The set of paramagnetic molecules is, $[B_2$, NO, $O_2]$ (option-b).

18. (d) Bond order (BO) of X_2,

In ground state $[\sigma_{1s^2}\, \sigma^*_{1s^2}]$, BO $= \dfrac{2-2}{2} = 0$

In excited state $[\sigma_{1s^2}\, \sigma^*_{1s^1} \sigma_{2s^1}]$, BO $= \dfrac{3-1}{2} = 1$

We know,

stability of a species $\propto$ bond order

So, stability of X_2 in excited state is more than that in ground state.

19. (d) Structures given in options-(a), (b) and (c) are the correct octet structural formulae of N_3^- ion. These are also the resonance or canonical structures of N_3^- in which all constituent N-atom satisfy their octet as well as valency.

$\overset{-}{:N}{=}\overset{+}{N}{=}\ddot{N}{:}^- \longleftrightarrow \overset{2-}{:\ddot{N}}{—}\overset{+}{N}{\equiv}N{:} \longleftrightarrow :N{\equiv}\overset{+}{N}{—}\ddot{N}{:}^{2-}$

(1) (2) (3)

The structure in option-(d) is ruled out as a resonance form because constituent N-atoms of N_3^- are in different positions. Besides, the bond angles of 60° are less demanded by the structure require considerable strain from the normal angles of bonding.

20. (d) H-atoms, 1 and 4, are exclusively involved in association through intermolecular H-bonding. Whereas, H-atom (2) and O-atom (3) are strongly held together by intramolecular H-bonding to form a stable six-membered ring in which the O-atom (3) is sp^2-hybridised and hence more electronegative than sp^3 O-atoms of —OH groups.

6-membered ring formation (more stable)

(I) $\Rightarrow$ Intermolecular hydrogen bonding (1, 4)

(II) $\Rightarrow$ Intramolecular hydrogen bonding (2, 3)

21. (16.83) $\mu_{\text{Calculated}} = 4.8 \times 10^{-10}$ esu $\times 1.275 \times 10^{-8}$

$= 4.8 \times 1.275 \times 10^{-18}$ esu

$= (4.8 \times 1.275)$ D

Ionic character % $= \dfrac{\mu_{\text{observe}}}{\mu_{\text{calculate}}} \times 100 = \dfrac{\mu_{\text{obs}}\,(\text{in D})}{4.8 \times d\,(\text{in D})} \times 100$

$= \dfrac{1.03\text{ D}}{(4.8 \times 1.275)\text{ D}} \times 100 = 16.83$

22. (0.25) Charge (dipolar), $\delta = \dfrac{\mu_{obs}}{d}$

$$\Rightarrow \quad \delta = \frac{1.2\text{ D}}{1\times10^{-8}\text{ cm}} = \frac{1.2\times10^{-18}\text{ esu cm}}{1\times10^{-8}\text{ cm}}$$

$$= 1.2\times10^{-10}\text{ esu}$$

$$[\because 1\text{ Å} = 10^{-8}\text{ cm, 1D} = 1\times10^{-18}\text{ esu cm}]$$

The fraction of an electronic charge is

$$\frac{1.2\times10^{-10}\text{ esu}}{4.8\times10^{-10}\text{ esu}/e} = 0.25\,e$$

$$= 25\% \text{ of } e$$

23. (1.52)

0.94Å H 52.5° O 105° H

From the geometry,

$$\mu_{obs} = 2\times\mu_{O-H}\times(\cos 52.5°)$$

$$\Rightarrow \quad \mu_{O-H} = \frac{\mu_{obs}}{2\times(\cos 52.5°)}$$

$$= \frac{1.85}{2\times0.609} = 1.518\text{ D} \simeq 1.52\text{ D}$$

24. (56.97) Applying Hanney-Smith equation,

$$\%\text{ ionic character} = 16\,|\Delta\chi| + 3.5\times(\Delta\chi)^2$$

$$= 16\times1.9 + 3.5\times(1.9)^2$$

$$[\because \Delta\chi = \chi_F - \chi_H = 4.0 - 2.1 = 1.9]$$

$$= 43.03$$

$\Rightarrow$ % covalent character $= 100 - 43.03 = 56.97$

25. (4.40)

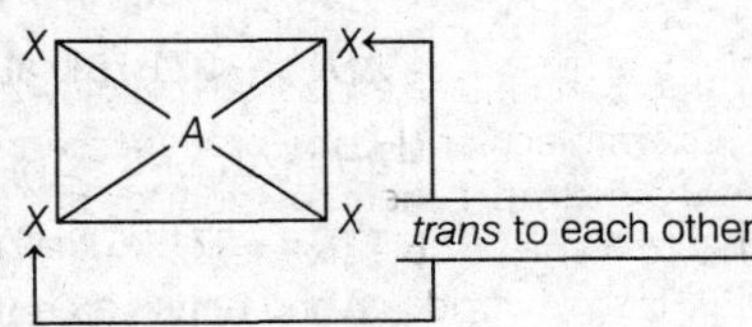

trans to each other

Distance between two *X*-atoms in *trans*-position

= bond length, $X - A - X = 2\times2.2\text{ Å} = 4.4\text{ Å}$

26. (4) All π-bonds present in compounds made by group-17 and 18 elements of periodic table are of $d\pi$-$p\pi$ type or $d\pi$ - $d\pi$ type. As, O-atom belongs to 2nd period (no *d*-orbital) of the periodic table, all π-bonds in XeO_4 are of $d\pi$(Xe)-$p\pi$(O) type.

O=Xe(=O)(=O)=O

Number of bonds, $\sigma = 4$

$$\pi = 4(d\pi\text{-}p\pi)$$

27. (4)

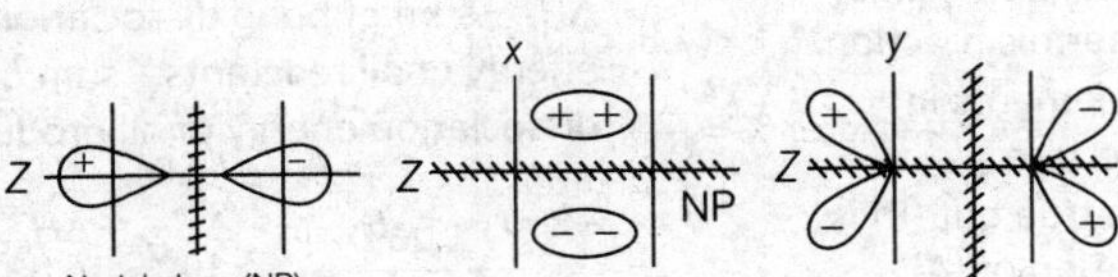

$[\overset{*}{\sigma}_{2s}]$, NP = 1 = x : $[\pi_{2px}]$: NP = 1 = y : $[\overset{*}{\pi}_{2p_y}]$, NP = 2 = z

$\Rightarrow \quad (x + y + z) = 1 + 1 + 2 = 4$

Considering, *z*-axis the molecular axis, each of bonding σ_s and bonding π_{2p_x} or π_{2p_y} MOs has one nodal plane, whereas anti-bonding MO, $\overset{*}{\pi}2_{p_x}$ or $\overset{*}{\pi}2_{p_y}$ has two nodal planes perpendicular to each other.

28. (4.75) MO electronic configuration of CO^+(13) is

$$\sigma_{1s^2}\,\overset{*}{\sigma}_{1s^2}\,\sigma_{2s^2}\,\pi_{2p_x^2} = \pi_{2p_y^2}\,\sigma_{2p_z^2}\,\overset{*}{\sigma}_{2s^1}$$

$$\text{Bond order} = \frac{10-3}{2} = 3.5 = a$$

$\Rightarrow$ In phosphate ion, PO_4^{3-}

O=P(O⁻)(O⁻)O⁻

The resonance hybrid structure is,

$[PO_4]^{3-}$

$$\text{Bond order} = \frac{\text{Number of P — O bonds in resonance}}{\text{Number of O - atoms in resonance}}$$

$$= \frac{2+1+1+1}{4}$$

$$= 1.25 = b$$

$\Rightarrow \quad (a + b) = 3.5 + 1.25 = 4.75$

29. (4)

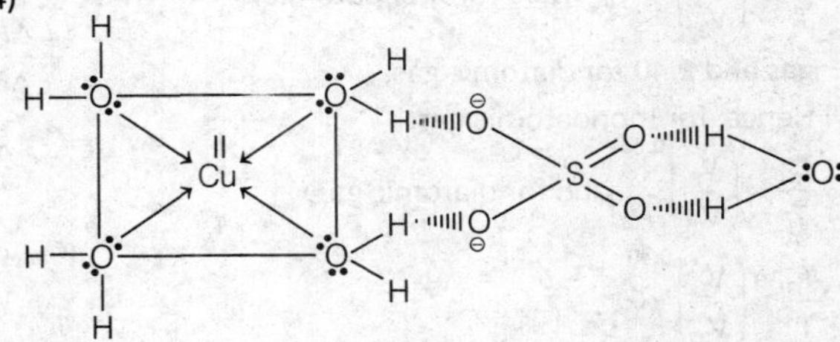

Four types of chemical bonds : Electrovalent, covalent, coordinate and hydrogen bond are present in blue vitriol $[\overset{II}{Cu}SO_4\cdot5H_2O]$ or $[\overset{II}{Cu}(H_2O)_4]^{2+}\,SO_4^{2-}\cdot H_2O$ molecule.

30. (2) In KHF_2 and 2-nitrophenol intramolecular hydrogen bonding is present.

$K^{\oplus}[F^{\ominus}\cdots H—F]^-$, (2-nitrophenol)

(KHF_2) (2-nitrophenol)

$\Rightarrow$ In 4-nitrophenol, benzoic acid(s), ice and water, intermolecular hydrogen bonding is present.

$\Rightarrow$ In $KHCl_2$, no hydrogen bonding is present.

Qualifier 05
(Chemical Theromodynamics)

1. (a) $\Delta U = q + W$

$\Rightarrow -1455 \text{ J} = 812 \text{ J} + W$

$\Rightarrow W = -2267 \text{ J}$

Negative value of workdone indicates that work is done by the system.

2. (d) Change in internal energy can be calculated using heat and work relationship.

The volume of 1 kg of water

$V_1 = \frac{1}{1000} \text{m}^3$ and of 1 kg of steam

$(V_2) = \frac{1}{0.6} \text{m}^3$

Increase in volume $(\Delta V) = V_2 - V_1$

$= \frac{1}{0.6} \text{m}^3 - \frac{1}{1000} \text{m}^3$

$= 1.7 \text{ m}^3 - 0.001 \text{ m}^3 = 1.7 \text{ m}^3$

The work done by the system is

$p\Delta V = (100 \text{ kPa})(1.7 \text{ m}^3)$

$= 1.7 \times 10^5 \text{ J}$

The heat given to convert 1 kg of water into steam $= 2.25 \times 10^6$ J

The change in internal energy is

$\Delta U = \Delta q - \Delta W$

$= 2.25 \times 10^6 - 1.7 \times 10^5$

$= 2.08 \times 10^6 \text{J}$

3. (b) For adiabatic expansion,

$\frac{T_2}{T_1} = \left(\frac{V_1}{V_2}\right)^{\gamma - 1}$, $\gamma = 1.66$ for monoatomic gas and 1.40 for diatomic gas.

Hence, for monoatomic gas,

$\frac{T_M}{T_1} = \left(\frac{V_1}{V_2}\right)^{0.66}$ and for diatomic gas,

$\frac{T_D}{T_1} = \left(\frac{V_1}{V_2}\right)^{0.40}$

$\Rightarrow$ As $\frac{V_1}{V_2} < 1$ (since, $V_2 > V_1$),

$\frac{T_M}{T_1} < 1$, i.e. $T_M < T_1$ and $\frac{T_D}{T_1} < 1$,

i.e. $T_D < T_1$

Suppose $V_2 = 10 V_1$.

Then,

$\frac{T_M}{T_D} = \left(\frac{1}{10}\right)^{0.66 - 0.40} = \left(\frac{1}{10}\right)^{0.26}$

i.e. $T_M < T_D$

Hence, $T_M < T_D < T_1$

4. (c) Work done against constant pressure $p = p_{ext}(V_1 - V_2)$

In adiabatic condition, $\Delta q = 0; W = \Delta U$.

Therefore,

$-p_{ext}(V_1 - V_2) = \frac{3}{2}R(T_1 - T_2)$ (Since, the expansion work is negative)

where, T_2 is final temperature T_1 is initial temperature

$-p_{ext}(V_1 - V_2) = \frac{3}{2}RT_1 - \frac{3}{2}RT_2$

$p_{ext} = 1$ atm; $V_2 = 3$ L; $V_1 = 1$ L

Solving, $T_2 = T_1 - \frac{2}{\left(\frac{3}{2}\right)R}$

$= T_1 - \frac{2}{1.5 \times 0.0821}$

Therefore, $T_{final} = T - \frac{2}{1.5 \times 0.082}$

5. (b) ΔH required for heating

$= m_{boiler} C_{boiler} \Delta T + m_{water} C_{water} \Delta T$

$= 900 \times 0.11 \times 90 + 400 \times 1 \times 90$

$= 44910$ kcal

Since, only 70% of heat given is used up to do so,

Thus, actual heat required

$= \frac{44910 \times 100}{70} = 64157$ kcal

6. (c) $C_p - C_V = R$

$C_p = C_V + R = \frac{5}{3}R$

$\left(\frac{\Delta H}{\Delta T}\right) = C_p$ (for 1 mole of gas)

$\Delta H = C_p \Delta T = \frac{5}{3}R(373 - 298)$

$= \frac{5}{3} \times 2 \times 75$ cal

$(R = 1.9872 \text{ cal})$

$= 250 \text{ cal mol}^{-1}$

7. (c) The enthalpy change of a reaction does not depend upon the nature of intermediate reaction steps.

This is according to Hess's law.

8. (b) In a combustion reaction, sum of enthalpies of reactants is greater than the sum of the enthalpies of products. Therefore, combustion of all organic compounds is an exothermic reaction. Also, enthalpies of all elements in their standard state are zero.

So, both (A) and (R) are true but (R) is not the correct explanation of (A).

9. (c)

Given,

$\underset{\text{(cyclopropane, } CH_2 \text{ apex)}}{H_2C—CH_2(g)} \longrightarrow CH_3CH{=}CH_2(g);$

$\Delta H = -33.0$ kJ ...(i)

$C + O_2 \longrightarrow CO_2(g); \Delta H = -393.5$ kJ ...(ii)

$H_2 + \frac{1}{2}O_2 \longrightarrow H_2O(l);$

$\Delta H = -285.8 \text{ kJ mol}^{-1}$ ...(iii)

$3C + 3H_2 \longrightarrow CH_3—CH{=}CH_2(g);$

$\Delta H = 20.42$ kJ ...(iv)

$\Rightarrow$ Eq. (iv) – Eq. (i) yields,

$3C + 3H_2 \longrightarrow$ H₂C—CH₂ (cyclopropane, CH_2 apex);

$\Delta H = 53.42$ kJ ...(v)

$\Rightarrow 3 \times$ Eq. (ii) + $3 \times$ Eq. (iii) – Eq. (v) yields

$H_2C—CH_2$ (cyclopropane, CH_2 apex) $+ \frac{9}{2}O_2 \longrightarrow 3CO_2 + 3H_2O$

$\Rightarrow \Delta_c H = [3 \times (-393.5)] + [3 \times (-285.8)] - 53.42$

$= -2091.32 \text{ kJ mol}^{-1}$

10. (d) The dissociation of $BF_3(g)$ can be written as

$BF_3(g) \longrightarrow B(g) + 3F(g);$

$\Delta H_f^\circ = -271.75$ kcal/mol

$-\Delta H = [\Delta H_B^\circ + 3 \times \Delta H_F^\circ] - [\Delta H_{BF_3}^\circ]$

$= -271.75$ kcal/mol

$\Delta H = 134.5 + 3 \times 118.86 - (-271.75)$

$= 762.83$ kcal/mol

$= 3 \times$ B—F bond energy (average)

B—F bond energy

$= \frac{762.83}{3}$ kcal/mol

$= 254.3$ kcal/mol

11. (c) Given $\Delta H_f = -200$ kJ/mol

Let the bond dissociation energy of XY, X_2 and Y_2 be x kJ/mol, x kJ/mol and $0.5x$ kJ/mol respectively.

$\frac{1}{2}X_2 + \frac{1}{2}Y_2 \longrightarrow XY$

ΔH_f = sum of bond dissociation energy of all reactants – sum of bond dissociation energy of all products

$-200 = \frac{1}{2}\Delta H_{X_2} + \frac{1}{2}\Delta H_{Y_2} - \Delta H_{XY}$

$$-200 = \frac{1}{2}(x) + \frac{1}{2}(0.5x) - x$$

$$-200 = \frac{-0.5x}{2}$$

$$x = \frac{200 \times 2}{0.5} = 800 \text{ kJ/mol}$$

12. (c) $\underset{x_1}{H_2(g)} + \underset{\frac{x_2}{2}}{\frac{1}{2}O_2(g)} \longrightarrow \underset{2x_3}{H_2O(l)}$

$$\Delta H_f = \left(E_{H-H} + \frac{1}{2}E_{O=O}\right) - 2E_{O-H}$$

$$= \left(x_1 + \frac{x_2}{2} - 2x_3\right), \text{ based on (BE)}$$

values $H_2O(g) \longrightarrow H_2O(l)$

$$\Delta H_2 = -x_4$$

$$\therefore \Delta H \text{ (net)} = \Delta H_1 + \Delta H_2$$

$$= \left(x_1 + \frac{x_2}{2} - 2x_3 - x_4\right)$$

13. (a) For adiabatic process, $\Delta U = W$

$\Rightarrow \quad W = nC_V\Delta T$

$\Rightarrow \quad \Delta T = \frac{W}{C_V}$ (for 1 mole gas)

Since, work done in reversible process is more than irreversible process. Therefore, the temperature change is more in reversible process, that is, the decrease in temperature will be more. Since, kinetic energy of ideal gases is proportional to root of temperature, so at isothermal condition, kinetic energy will not change.

From the above relations, it is clear that when an ideal gas is subjected to adiabatic expansion, its temperature decreases.

Entropy increases when an ideal gas expands isothermally because increasing the volume causes increase in randomness.

14. (a) $\Delta S = 2.303\, nR \log\left(\frac{p_1}{p_2}\right)$

$$n = \frac{\text{Given mass}}{\text{Molecular mass}}$$

$$= \frac{64}{32} = 2 \text{ mol}$$

$$\Rightarrow \Delta S = 2.303\, nR \log\left(\frac{p_1}{p_2}\right)$$

$$= 2.303 \times 2 \times 8.314 \log\left(\frac{1}{0.25}\right)$$

$$= 23.055 \text{ JK}^{-1} \simeq 23.1 \text{ JK}^{-1}$$

15. (a) Correct match is A → (2, 4), B → (2), C → (3), D → (1)

A. Entropy of vaporisation is always positive and $\Delta S = \frac{\Delta H_{vap}}{T_b}$

B. $\Delta G° = -RT \ln K$

If K is +ve, then $\Delta G° = -$ ve, i.e. spontaneous process.

C. Crystalline state is most orderly arranged state of particles, thus they have lowest entropy.

D. During adiabatic expansion of an ideal gas, $q = 0$ thus, $\Delta E = W$, i.e. work done (W) at the cost of internal energy decreases when $q = 0$, i.e. $W = -\Delta E$

16. (d) $\Delta S_{(system)} = \frac{q_{rev}}{T}$

$$\Delta S_{(system)_1} = \frac{100 \text{ J}}{298 \text{ K}} = 0.335 \text{ JK}^{-1}$$

$$\Delta S_{(system)_2} = \frac{100 \text{ J}}{298 \text{ K}} = -0.335 \text{ JK}^{-1}$$

$$\Delta S_{(system)} = \Delta S_{(system)_1} + \Delta S_{(system)_2}$$

$$= 0.335 - 0.335 = 0.00 \text{ JK}^{-1}$$

17. (a) $\Delta G°$ for the reaction,

$$CH_4(g) + 2O_2(g) \longrightarrow CO_2(g) + 2H_2O(g)$$

$$\Delta G° = \{\Delta_f G°[CO_2(g)] + 2\Delta_f G°[H_2O(g)]\} - \{\Delta_f G°[CH_4(g)] + 2\Delta_f G°[O_2(g)]\}$$

$$= \{1 \text{ mol} \times (-394.4 \text{ kJ mol}^{-1}) + 2 \text{ mol} \times (-228.6 \text{ kJ mol}^{-1})\} - (1 \text{ mol} \times (-50.79 \text{ kJ mol}^{-1}) + 2 \text{ mol} \times (0.0 \text{ kJ mol}^{-1})\}$$

$$\therefore \Delta G° = -800.8 \text{ kJ}$$

$\Rightarrow$ Maximum amount of useful work that could possibly be obtained from the combustion of 48.0 g of methane is

$$-\Delta G = W_{\text{useful work}} \text{ kJ}$$

$$= (48.0 \text{ g } CH_4)\left(\frac{1 \text{ mol } CH_4}{16.0 \text{ g } CH_4}\right)\left(\frac{800.8 \text{ kJ}}{1 \text{ mol } CH_4}\right)$$

$$= 2.40 \times 10^3 \text{ kJ}$$

18. (b) For an irreversible process to be spontaneous, $(\Delta S)_{V,E}$ (change in entropy)

$$= + \text{ ve} > 0$$

$(\Delta G)_{Tp}$ (change in Gibbs free energy)

$$= - \text{ ve} < 0$$

19. (c) $\Delta H° = [H°_{TiCl_4}(l) + H°_{O_2(g)}] - [H°_{TiO_2(s)} + H°_{Cl_2(g)}]$

$$= (-804.2 + 0) - (-944.7 + 2 \times 0)$$

$$= 140.5 \text{ kJ mol}^{-1}$$

$$\Rightarrow \Delta S° = [S°_{TiCl_4(l)} + S°_{O_2(g)}] - [S°_{TiO_2(s)} + S°_{Cl_2(g)}]$$

$$= (+252.3 + 205.1) - (+50.3 + 2 \times 233)]$$

$$= -58.9 \text{ J mol}^{-1} \text{ K}^{-1}$$

$$= -0.0589 \text{ kJ mol}^{-1} \text{ K}^{-1}$$

$$\Delta G° = \Delta H° - T\Delta S° = 140.5 - 298 \times (-0.0589)$$

$$= 158.056 \text{ kJ mol}^{-1}$$

Since, change in free energy is positive, the reaction is not spontaneous.

20. (b) **Process (i)**

$$pV^2 = K$$

$\Rightarrow \quad \frac{nRT}{V}V^2 = K$

$\Rightarrow \quad TV = \text{constant}$

$\Rightarrow \quad T \propto \frac{1}{V}$ or $T_1 \propto \frac{1}{V}$

Process (ii) $p = KV^2$

$\Rightarrow \quad \frac{nRT}{V} = KV^2$

$\Rightarrow \quad \frac{T}{V^3} = \text{constant}$

$\Rightarrow \quad T \propto V^3$

or $\quad T_2 \propto \frac{1}{V^3}$

Thus, $\quad T_2 > T_1$

21. (–8) Work done in terms of volume pressure relationship, is

$$W = -\int_{V_1}^{V_2} p\Delta V$$

Given, $\frac{p}{V} = K$, therefore $K = \frac{1}{2}$ atm L^{-1} (initial condition) where,

$$V_1 = 2\text{L and } V_2 = 6 \text{ L}$$

$$W = -\int_{V_1}^{V_2} p\Delta V = -\int_{V_1}^{V_2} KV\Delta V = -K\int_{V_1}^{V_2} \frac{V^2}{2}$$

$$= -K\left(\frac{V_2^2}{2} - \frac{V_1^2}{2}\right)$$

$$= -\frac{1}{2}\left(\frac{36}{2} - \frac{4}{2}\right)$$

$$= -8 \text{ L atm}$$

22. (60) The temperature, pressure and volume conditions at each of the points A, B, C, D can be shown as

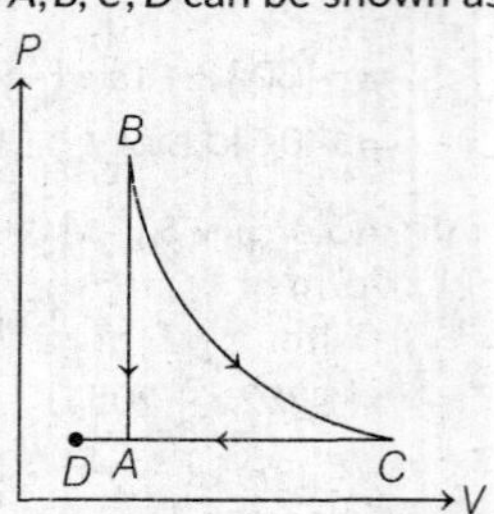

$A(p_1, V_1, T_1) : B(2p_1, V_1, 2T_1);$

$C(p_1, 2V_1, 2T_1) : D\left(2p_1, \frac{V_1}{2}, \frac{T_1}{2}\right)$

The total work done is given by

$W_{total} = W_{AB} + W_{BC} + W_{CD}$

For isochoric change (AB), $W_{AB} = 0$

For isothermal expansion (BC),

$$W_{BC} = -1 \times R \times 2T_1 \ln\left(\frac{2V}{V_1}\right)$$

$$= -2 \times 2 \times 300 \times 0.7$$

$$= -840 \text{ cal}$$

For isobaric change (CD)

$$W_{CD} = -p_1 \Delta V = -R\Delta T$$

$$= -R\left[\frac{T_1}{2} - 2T_1\right]$$

$$= \frac{3}{2}RT_1 = \frac{3}{2} \times 2 \times 300 = 900 \text{ cal}$$

Therefore, $W_{total} = -840 + 900$

$$= 60 \text{ cal}$$

23. (7992.64) To calculate the temperature of flame we have to consider adiabatic conditions where there is no loss of heat from the system. The rise in temperature can be calculated by considering the reaction to take place in the following two steps, both at constant pressure.

Step I. Reactants $(T_0, p) \rightarrow$ Product $(T_0, p) \Delta_r H_{T_0}$

Step II. Products $(T_0, p) \rightarrow$ Product $(T_1, p)\ \Delta_r H_2$

$$\Delta_r H_2 = \int_{T_0}^{T_1} C_p \text{ (products) } dT$$

Since, the overall reaction is the sum of the above two steps, that is, the net heat change is given by

$$\Delta_r H = \Delta_r H_{T_0} + \Delta_r H_2$$

Since, the reaction is considered to be adiabatic, therefore,

$$\Delta_r H = 0$$

$$\Rightarrow \quad \Delta_r H_{T_0} + \Delta_r H_2 = 0$$

$$\Rightarrow \quad \Delta_r H_2 = -\Delta_r H_{T_0}$$

$$\Rightarrow \quad -\Delta_r H_{T_0} = \int_{T_0}^{T_1} C_p dT$$

If C_p is independent of temperature, then

$$-\Delta_r HT_0 = C_p(T_f - T_o)$$

or $$T_f = \frac{\Delta_r T_0}{C_p} + T_0 \text{ ... (i)}$$

At 298 K, we have

$$\Delta_r H^\circ_{298\text{ K}} = -890.36 + 44.02 \times 2$$

$$= -802.32 \text{ kJ mol}^{-1}$$

For the reaction,

$$CH_4(g) + 2O_2(g) \longrightarrow 2H_2O(g) + CO_2(g)$$

C_p of products $= 37.11 + 2 \times 33.58$

$= 104.27 \text{ JK}^{-1} \text{ mol}^{-1}$

Substituting values of in Eq. (i) we get

$$T_f = \frac{802.32}{104.27} \times 10^3 + 298$$

$$= 7992.64 \text{ K}$$

= Temperature of the flame

24. (10.15) In reversible isothermal process

$$dW = -pdV = \frac{RT}{V_m - b} dV$$

$$\Rightarrow \quad W = -RT \int \frac{dV}{V_m - b}$$

$$= -RT \ln\left(\frac{V_2 - b}{V_1 - b}\right)$$

$$= 8.314 \times 300 \ln \frac{10 - 0.03}{0.2 - 0.03}$$

$$= 8.314 \times 300 \times \ln 58.65$$

$$= 10151.394$$

$$= 10.15 \times 10^3 \text{ J mol}^{-1}$$

$$= x \times 10^3 \text{ J mol}^{-1}$$

$$\Rightarrow \quad x = 10.15$$

25. (270) For an adiabatic process $q = 0$.

The work done is given by,

$$W = -p_{ext}(V_2 - V_1)$$

$$= -p_{ext}\left(\frac{nRT_2}{p_2} - \frac{nRT_1}{p_1}\right)$$

$\Rightarrow$ For an adiabatic process from first law,

$$\Delta U = W$$

Hence, $nC_v(T_2 - T_1) = p_{ext} nR\left(\frac{T_1}{p_1} - \frac{T_2}{p_2}\right)$ ...(i)

$\Rightarrow$ For a diatomic molecule, $C_V = \frac{5}{2}R$.

Substituting the expression of C_V in Eq. (i), we get

$$n\left(\frac{5}{2}R\right)(T_2 - T_1) = p_{ext} nR\left(\frac{T_1}{p_1} - \frac{T_2}{p_2}\right)$$

$$\Rightarrow \frac{5}{2}(T_2 - T_1) = p_{ext}\left(\frac{T_1}{p_1} - \frac{T_2}{p_2}\right)$$

$\Rightarrow$ Substituting the given values, we get

$$\frac{5}{2}(T_2 - T_1) = (0.101)\left[\frac{300}{0.507} - \frac{T_2}{0.203}\right]$$

$\Rightarrow$ Solving for T_2, we get $T_2 = 270$ K

26. (1000) Given, $\Delta Q = 3000$ J

We know, $W = p\Delta V$

$$= (2 \times 10^5 \text{N/m}^2)(10 \times 10^{-3} \text{m}^3)$$

$$= 2 \times 10^3 \text{ J}$$

$$\therefore \quad \Delta U = \Delta Q - W$$

$$= 3000 - 2000 = 1000 \text{ J}$$

27. (277.50) The reactions involved are

$$4C(s) + 5H_2 + 2S \longrightarrow$$

```
   H   H       H   H
   |   |       |   |
H—C—C—S—C—C—H
   |   |       |   |
   H   H       H   H
```

$$4C(s) + 5H_2 + 2S \longrightarrow$$

```
   H   H           H   H
   |   |           |   |
H—C—C—S—S—C—C—H
   |   |           |   |
   H   H           H   H
```

$$\Delta_f H = \Sigma n\Delta_f H \text{ (Products)} - \Sigma n\Delta_f H \text{ (Reactants)}$$

The heat of formation of $C_2H_5—S—C_2H_5$ is ΔH_f°

$(C_2H_5—S—C_2H_5) = -147.2 \text{ kJ mol}^{-1}$,

or $-147.2 = 4\Delta_a H^\circ(C) + 10\Delta_a H^\circ(H) + \Delta_a H^\circ(S) - [10\Delta H_{C-H} + 2\Delta H_{C-S} + \Delta H_{C-C}]$ ...(i)

Similarly, heat of formation of $C_2H_5—S—S—C_2H_5$ is ΔH_f°

$(C_2H_5—S—S—C_2H_5)$

$= -201.9 \text{ kJ mol}^{-1}$, or

$-201.9 = 4\Delta_a H^\circ(C) + 10\Delta_a H^\circ(H) + 2\Delta_a H^\circ(S) - [10\Delta H_{C-H} + 2\Delta H_{C-S} + 2\Delta H_{C-C} + \Delta H_{S-S}]$ ... (ii)

Subtracting Eq. (i) from Eq. (ii), we get

$$-201.9 + 147.2 = \Delta H_f^\circ - \Delta H_{S-S}$$

$$-54.7 = 222.8 - \Delta H_{S-S}$$

Solving, we get

$$\Delta H_{S-S} = 277.5 \text{ kJ mol}^{-1}$$

28. (253) The combustion reaction of naphthalene is

$$C_{10}H_8(s) + 12O_2(g) \longrightarrow 10CO_2(g) + 4H_2O(l); \Delta H^\circ = -5175 \text{ kJ}$$

$\Rightarrow \Delta H^\circ = \Sigma \Delta H_f^\circ$ (Products) $- \Sigma \Delta H_f^\circ$ (Reactants)

$\Rightarrow -5175 = -10 \times 393.5 - 4 \times 286 - \Delta H_f^\circ(C_{10}H_8)$

$\Rightarrow \Delta H_f^\circ[C_{10}H_8(s)] = 96$ kJ/mol

Also 10C (graphite) + $4H_2(g) \longrightarrow$

(Naphthalene)

$\Delta H^\circ = 10 \times 715.5 + 4 \times 436 - [6 \times 345.5 + 5 \times 617 + 8 \times 415 + 72]$

$= 349$ kJ/mol (theoretical)

Resonance energy $= 349 - 96$

$= 253$ kJ/mol

$-\Delta H_{RE}^\circ = -253$ kJ/mol

29. (613.75) At the boiling point (where liquid and vapours are in equilibrium with one another),

$\Delta G = 0 = \Delta H - T\Delta S$

or $T_{eq} = \dfrac{\Delta H}{\Delta S}$

$\Delta S^\circ = S^\circ[Hg(g)] - S^\circ[Hg(l)]$

$= (175 \times 10^{-3}\ \text{kJ mol}^{-1}\ \text{K}^{-1})$

$- (76.1 \times 10^{-3}\ \text{kJ mol}^{-1}\ \text{K}^{-1})$

$= 98.9 \times 10^{-3}\ \text{kJ mol}^{-1}\ \text{K}^{-1}$

$$T_{eq} = \frac{60.7\ \text{kJ mol}^{-1}}{98.9 \times 10^{-3}\ \text{kJ mol}^{-1}\ \text{K}^{-1}}$$

$= 613.75$ K = Boiling point of Hg (l)

30. $(-16)\ Q = (0.20\ \text{g ice})\left(\dfrac{-80\ \text{cal}}{\text{g ice}}\right)$

$= -16$ cal

Liberated heat when 1 mmol AgCl is formed $= -16$ cal/mmol

Qualifier 06
(Solutions)

1. (b) At equilibrium, let n moles of water vapour gets transferred from dilute solution (0.01 mol/100 g) to the concentrated solution (0.02 mol/100 g), i.e.

$$\frac{100}{18} - n = \frac{100}{18} + n$$

$\Rightarrow$ At equilibrium, mole fraction of two solutions will be equal.

$$\chi_{C_{12}H_{22}O_{11}} = \frac{0.01}{0.01 + \left(\dfrac{100}{18} - n\right)} = \frac{0.02}{0.02 + \left(\dfrac{100}{18} + n\right)}$$

$\Rightarrow \quad n = 1.852$

$\therefore \chi_{C_{12}H_{22}O_{11}} = 2.69 \times 10^{-3} = 0.00269$

2. (c) $m = \dfrac{\chi_B}{1 - \chi_B} \times 55.56$ for aqueous solution

$\Rightarrow \quad 5.2 = \dfrac{\chi_B}{1 - \chi_B} \times 55.56$

$\Rightarrow \quad \chi_B = \chi_{CH_3OH} = 0.0856 \simeq 0.086$

3. (d) $Ba(OH)_2 + 2HCl \longrightarrow BaCl_2 + 2H_2O$

Applying molarity equation,

$\dfrac{M_1V_1}{1} = \dfrac{M_2V_2}{2}$

$Ba(OH)_2$ HCl

$25 \times M_1 = \dfrac{0.1 \times 35}{2}$

$M_1 = \dfrac{0.1 \times 35}{2 \times 25}$

$M_1 = 0.07$ mol L^{-1}

4. (d) $V \times 4 + (1 - V) \times 10 = 1 \times 6$

$\Rightarrow \quad -6V = -4$

$\Rightarrow \quad V = \dfrac{2}{3} = 0.67$ L

[0.67 L 4 N HCl + 0.33 L 10 N HCl]

$\Rightarrow$ 1 L 6 N HCl

5. (c) Let the density of solution be 'd'

Molarity of solution given = 3.6

1 litre of solution contains 3.6 moles of H_2SO_4 or 3.6×98 grams of H_2SO_4.

Since, the solution is 29% by mass

$\dfrac{100}{d}$ mL solution contains 29 g of H_2SO_4

1000 mL solution contains 3.6×98 g of H_2SO_4.

Therefore, $3.6 \times 98 = \dfrac{29 \times d}{100} \times 1000$

$d = \dfrac{36 \times 98}{29 \times 100} = 1.22$

6. (a) When, $\chi_A = 0$, $C_2H_5OH(B)$ is pure ($\chi_B = 1$)

$\Rightarrow \quad p_B^\circ = 120 \times 0 + 138 = 138$ torr

or, $\dfrac{p_B}{x_B} = 138$ torr

When, $\chi_B = 0$, $CH_3OH(A)$ is pure ($\chi_A = 1$)

$\Rightarrow p_A^\circ = 120 \times 1 + 138 = 258$ torr

or, $\dfrac{p_A^\circ}{\chi_A} = 258$ torr

7. (c) (i) According to Raoult's law,

$p = p_p + p_H = \chi_p p_p^\circ + \chi_H p_H^\circ$

(ii) According to the combined form of Raoult's law and Dalton's law of partial pressure of gases.

$$y_p = \frac{p_p}{p} = \frac{\chi_p p_p^\circ}{p_p + p_H}$$

$$= \frac{\frac{1}{5} \times 440}{\frac{1}{5} \times 440 + \frac{4}{5} \times 120}$$

$= 0.478$

where, y_p = mole fraction of pentane in vapour phase

χ_p = mole fraction of pentane in solution phase

p_p = partial pressure of pentane

p = total vapour pressure of solution

Similarly, H$\rightarrow$ denotes for hexane.

8. (d) The value of Henry's constant can be verified from the set of experiments based on Henry's law of

$p = K_H \times \chi$

$\Rightarrow p \propto \chi$ (Temperature is constant)

$\Rightarrow$ So, plot of p vs χ will be a straight line passing through the origin with positive slope [option (a) or (d)..

$\Rightarrow$ Now, the value of K_H can be verified from the set of three experiments,

Expt-1

$K_H = \dfrac{p}{\chi} = \dfrac{82}{0.010} = 8200$ kPa

Expt-2

$K_H = \dfrac{122}{0.015} = 8133.33$ kPa

Expt-3

$K_H = \dfrac{166}{0.020} = 8300$ kPa

$K_H = 8234.5 \times$ kPa of option (d) satisfies the K_H values.

9. (d) From the plot,

I. $p_B^\circ = 135$ units, $p_A^\circ = 85$ units.

II. $A'C \Rightarrow p_A = \chi_A p_A^\circ$ (a solution of B in A)

III. $B'D \Rightarrow p_B = \chi_B p_B^\circ$ (a solution of A in B)

So, statement-I is correct.

$\Rightarrow$ Statement-II is also correct, because CD indicates, $p = p_A + p_B$

$\Rightarrow$ Statement-III is correct as,

$p_B^\circ - p_A^\circ = 135 - 85 = 50$ units

$\Rightarrow$ Statement-IV is correct as, when $\chi_B = 0.4$

$$p = 0.4 \times p_B^\circ + 0.6 \times p_A^\circ$$
$$= 0.4 \times 135 + 0.6 \times 85 = 105 \text{ units}$$

10. (c) Total vapour pressure of the solution,

(i) $p_{obs} = 200$ torr

(ii) $p_{cal} = \frac{1}{3} \times 150 + \frac{2}{3} \times 240 = 210$ torr

$\Rightarrow p_{obs} < p_{cal}$, i.e. the solution shows negative deviation from Raoult's law.

11. (d) Relative lowering of vapour pressure of a solution, is a colligative property.

$$\frac{\Delta p}{p^\circ} = \chi_B \times i$$

Since, two different solutes (urea and NaCl) are present in the same solvent (H_2O) of same strength 0.01 M.

So, vapour pressure of pure solvent, p° = constant.

Lowering of vapour pressure,

$\Delta p \propto \chi_B \times i$

$\because \chi_B$ = mole fraction of solute

i = van't Hoff factor

$i = 1$ for urea (non-dissociable/associable)

$= 2$ for NaCl

$[i = 1 + \alpha(n-1) = 1 + 1(2-1) = 2]$

assuming 100% dissociation of NaCl.

$$\Rightarrow \frac{\Delta p_{urea}}{\Delta p_{NaCl}} = \frac{0.01 \times 1}{0.01 \times 2} = \frac{1}{2}$$

[$\because$ Molarity $\propto$ Molality $\propto$ Mole fraction]

$\therefore \Delta p_{Urea} \neq \Delta p_{NaCl}$

So, Assertion is false.

$\Rightarrow$ Reason is true, because addition of a non-volatile solute in a pure solvent always decreases vapour pressure of the solution.

So, assertion is false but reason is true.

12. (d) $\Delta T_b = K_b \times m = K_b \times \frac{w_B \times 1000}{M_B \times w_A}$

$\begin{bmatrix} B = \text{solute} \\ A = \text{solvent } (H_2O) \end{bmatrix}$

(i) For dilute solution,

$$\frac{\Delta p}{p^\circ} = \chi_B = \frac{n_B}{n_A + n_B} \approx \frac{n_B}{n_A}$$
$$= 0.15 \text{ (given)}$$

$$\frac{w_B}{w_A} \times \frac{M_A}{M_B} = 0.15$$

$$\Rightarrow \frac{w_B}{M_B \times w_A} = \frac{0.15}{18}$$

$$\therefore \Delta T_b = K_b \times \left(\frac{w_B}{M_B \times w_A}\right) \times 1000$$
$$= 0.52 \times \frac{0.15}{18} \times 1000$$
$$= 4.33 \text{ K}$$

(ii) Again, $m = \frac{\chi_B}{1 - \chi_B} \times 55.56$

(for aqueous solution)

$$= \frac{0.15}{1 - 0.15} \times 55.56 = 9.80 \text{ molal}$$

So, for the solution of moderate concentration,

$\Delta T_b{}' = K_b \times m = 0.52 \times 9.80 = 5.096$ K

$\Rightarrow (\Delta T_b - \Delta T_b{}') = (4.33 - 5.096)$ K

$= -0.766$ K.

13. (d) At point A,

solvent (l) $\rightleftharpoons$ solvent (s).

So, $T_f^\circ = 279$ K

$\Rightarrow$ At B (1 m solution), $T_f = 273$ K

$\therefore \Delta T_f = 279 - 273 = 6$ K

$\therefore K_f = \frac{\Delta T_f}{m} = \frac{6}{1} = 6 \text{ K m}^{-1}$

$\Rightarrow$ At C (10% w/w solution), $T_f = 268$ K

$\therefore \Delta T_f = 279 - 268 = 11$ K

$\therefore \Delta T_f = K_f \times m$

$$= K_f \times \frac{w_B \times 10000}{M_B \times w_A}$$
$$= \frac{6 \times 10 \times 1000}{M_B \times (100 - 10)}$$
$$\therefore M_B = \frac{6 \times 10 \times 1000}{11 \times 90}$$
$$= 60.6 \text{ g mol}^{-1}$$

14. (d) $K_b = \frac{R \times (T_b^\circ)^2 \times M_A}{1000 \times \Delta_{vap} H}$

$$= \frac{(1.987 \text{ cal K}^{-1}\text{mol}^{-1}) \times [(273 + 111)\text{K}]^2 \times (92 \text{ g mol}^{-1})}{1000 \times 11217 \text{ cal mol}^{-1}}$$
$$= 2.40^\circ \text{ g mol}^{-1} \text{ K}$$

15. (c) Boiling point of CCl_4 is lower than that of $SiCl_4$. The vapour must be richer in more volatile component (CCl_4). Hence, the upper curve represents the composition of the vapour and the lower part represents the composition of the solution at their respective boiling points.

16. (c) From sucrose solution,

$$K_b = \frac{\Delta T_b}{m} = \frac{0.52}{1} = 0.52^\circ \text{ mol}^{-1} \text{ kg}$$

From AB_2 solution,

$$\Delta T_b = K_b \times m = K_b \times \frac{w_{AB_2} \times 1000}{M_{AB_2} \times w_{H_2O}}$$
$$\therefore M_{AB_2} = \frac{K_b \times w_{AB_2} \times 1000}{\Delta T_b \times w_{H_2O}}$$
$$= \frac{0.52 \times 5 \times 1000}{0.26 \times 100}$$
$$= 100$$

From A_2B solution,

$$M_{A_2B} = \frac{K_b \times w_{A_2B} \times 1000}{\Delta T_b \times w_{H_2O}}$$
$$= \frac{0.52 \times 9 \times 1000}{0.52 \times 100}$$
$$= 90$$

Now, $\left.\begin{matrix} A + 2B = 100 \\ 2A + B = 90 \end{matrix}\right] \Rightarrow \begin{matrix} A = 40 = M_A \\ B = 10 = M_B \end{matrix}$

So, the correct matching is

A – 4, B – 3, C – 2, D – 1 (option c)

17. (a) $\underset{(\alpha = 1)}{NaHSO_4} \longrightarrow \underset{0.08}{Na^+} + \underset{0.08}{HSO_4^-}$

$$\underset{0.08(1-\alpha')}{HSO_4^-} \rightleftharpoons \underset{0.08\alpha'}{H^+} + \underset{0.08\alpha'}{SO_4^{2-}}$$

$$i = \frac{0.08 + 0.08(1-\alpha') + 0.08\alpha' + 0.08\alpha'}{0.08}$$
$$= 2 + \alpha'$$

$\Rightarrow \Delta T_f = K_f \times m \times i$

$\Rightarrow 0.372 = 1.86 \times 0.08 \times (2 + \alpha')$

$\Rightarrow \alpha' = 0.5$

$$\therefore K = \frac{[H^+][SO_4^{2-}]}{[HSO_4^-]}$$
$$= \frac{[0.08\,\alpha']^2}{0.08\,[1-\alpha']}$$
$$= \frac{[0.08 \times 0.5]^2}{0.08\,[1 - 0.9]}$$
$$= 0.2$$

18. (b) When, $\pi > p_{external}$, flow of solvent molecules takes place from lower concentration (II : 0.05 M) to higher concentration (I : 0.1 M).

$\pi = CRT \times i$ or $\pi \propto C \times i$

[$\because T$ = constant]

$$\therefore \frac{\pi_1}{\pi_2} = \frac{0.1 \times 2}{0.05 \times 3}$$

$\begin{bmatrix} \because \text{When } \alpha = 1 \,(100\%) \\ i = n = 2 \text{ (NaCl)} \\ = 3 \,(BaCl_2) \end{bmatrix}$

$$= \frac{0.2}{0.15} > 1$$

19. (c) $\pi \times \frac{V}{1000} = nRT = \frac{w_B}{M_B} \times RT$

[$\because M_B$ = molar mass of insulin.
w_B = mass of insulin in g present in $V\ cm^3$ solution.]

$\Rightarrow \quad \pi = \frac{w_B}{V} \times \frac{1000\ RT}{M_B}$

$\Rightarrow \quad \pi = C \times \frac{1000RT}{M_B}$

Plot of π *vs* C results,

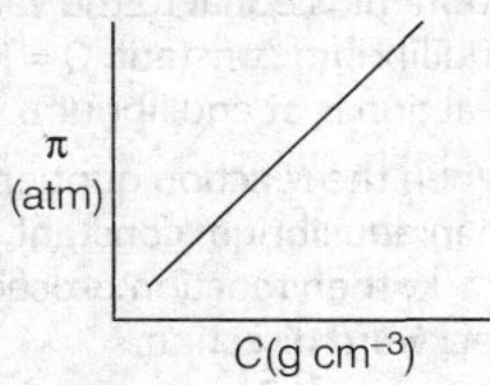

$\text{Slope} = \frac{1000RT}{M_B}$

$\Rightarrow M_B = \frac{1000RT}{\text{slope}}$

$= \frac{1000 \times 0.082 \times 300}{4.1 \times 10^{-3}}$

$= 6 \times 10^6\ g\ mol^{-1}$

20. (c) $\pi = hdg = (0.14\ m)$

$\times \left[\left(\frac{1}{1000}\ kg\right) \times 10^6\ m^{-3}\right] \times 10\ ms^{-2}$

$= 1400\ Pa = 1.4 \times 10^3\ Pa$

$= \frac{1.4 \times 10^3\ Pa}{1.013 \times 10^5\ Pa\ atm^{-1}}$

$= 0.0138\ atm$

21. (10) 109% oleum means 9 g of H_2O is present with SO_3 to give H_2SO_4.

$SO_3 + H_2O \longrightarrow H_2SO_4$
80 g 18 g
40 g 9 g

So, in 100 g sample of 109% oleum,
$SO_3 = 40\ g, H_2SO_4 = 60\ g$

$\Rightarrow \quad x = \frac{60}{98} = 0.6122, y = \frac{40}{80} = 0.5$

$\Rightarrow \quad \frac{x+y}{x-y} = \frac{0.6122 + 0.5}{0.6122 - 0.5}$

$= 9.912 \simeq 9.91$

22. (32%)

$NaHSO_4 + H_2O \rightarrow Na^+ + H_3O^+ + SO_4^{2-}$

$t = 0 \quad 1 \qquad 0$

At equil. $1-\alpha \qquad \alpha \qquad \alpha \qquad \alpha$

Total particles after dissolution of $NaHSO_4$

$1 + 1 - \alpha + \alpha + \alpha = (2 + \alpha)$

$i = \frac{(2+\alpha)}{1}$

$\Delta T_f = i \times K_f \times m$

$0.345 = (2 + \alpha) \times 1.86 \times 0.08$

$\alpha = 0.319$

$\therefore$ Percentage dissociation = 31.9%
$\approx 32\%$

23. (100) Decrease in weight of solution $\propto p$ (solution pressure)

Decrease in weight of solvent $\propto (p^\circ - p)$

$\propto \Delta p$ (lowering in VP)

$\Rightarrow \frac{\Delta p}{p} = x_2 = \frac{w_2}{w_1} \times \frac{M_1}{M_2} \begin{bmatrix} 1 \rightarrow \text{solvent} \\ 2 \rightarrow \text{solution} \end{bmatrix}$

$\Rightarrow \quad \frac{0.05}{2.5} = \frac{10 \times 18}{90 \times M_2}$

$\therefore \quad M_2 = 100$

24. (111.11)

$w_A = 100\ g, M_A = 18\ g$
$w_B = ?, M_B = 60\ g$

Reduced vapour pressure = 25%

From RLVP equation,

$\frac{p^\circ - p}{p^\circ} = x_B = \frac{\frac{w_B}{M_B}}{\frac{w_B}{M_B} + \frac{w_A}{M_A}}$

or, $\quad \frac{p^\circ - p}{p} = \frac{w_B}{w_A} \times \frac{M_A}{M_B}$

$\Rightarrow \quad \frac{100 - 75}{75} = \frac{w_B \times 18}{100 \times 60}$

$\Rightarrow \quad w_B = \frac{25 \times 100 \times 60}{75 \times 18}$

$= 111.11\ g$

25. (20.12) For immiscible solvents,

$\frac{n_1}{n_2} = \frac{p_1^\circ}{p_2^\circ} \begin{bmatrix} 1 \rightarrow \text{water} \\ 2 \rightarrow \text{nitrobenzene} \end{bmatrix}$

$\Rightarrow \frac{w_1}{w_2} \times \frac{M_2}{M_1} = \frac{p_1^\circ}{p_2^\circ}$

$\Rightarrow \frac{w_1}{w_2} = \frac{p_1^\circ}{p_2^\circ} \times \frac{M_1}{M_2} = \frac{97.7 \times 18}{3.6 \times 123} = \frac{3.97}{1.00}$

$\Rightarrow w_2\% = \frac{1}{4.97} \times 100 = 20.12\%$

26. (38.71) $\Delta T_f = K_f \times m$ [$\because$ for ethylene glycol, (B), $i = 1$]

$= K_f \times \frac{w_B \times 1000}{M_B \times w_{H_2O(l)}}$

$\Rightarrow w_{H_2O}(l) = \frac{K_f \times w_B \times 1000}{\Delta T_f \times M_B}$

$\left[\because \begin{array}{l} CH_2OH \\ | \\ CH_2OH \end{array}, M_B = 62\ g\ mol^{-1}\right]$

$= \frac{1.86 \times 50 \times 1000}{9.3 \times 62} = 161.29\ g$

$\Rightarrow$ Amount of ice separated out during cooling,

$w_{H_2O(s)} = (200 - 161.29)\ g$

$= 38.71\ g = x\ g$

27. (3.20) (i) $2AgNO_3 + K_2CrO_4 \longrightarrow Ag_2CrO_4 \downarrow + 2KNO_3$

(ii) $AgNO_3 + KCl \longrightarrow AgCl \downarrow + KNO_3$

When titration is complete, we get a ppt. of Ag_2CrO_4. At the end point,

$M_1 \times 25\ (KCl) = 1 \times 20\ (AgNO_3)$

$M_1\ (KCl) = 0.8$ molar
$= 0.8$ Molal (m)

For KCl, $i = 2$ ($\alpha = 1$, 100%)

$\Rightarrow \quad \Delta T_f = K_f \times m \times i = 2 \times 0.8 \times 2$
$= 3.20^\circ$

28. (4.57) Moles of O_2 at 1 atm (p_1) and 0°C,

$n_1 = \frac{p_1V_1}{RT} = \frac{1 \times (48.9 \times 10^{-3})}{0.082 \times 273}$

$= 2.18 \times 10^{-3}\ mol\ L^{-1}$

$= 2.18 \times 10^{-3}\ M$

According to Henry's law,

Concentration $(C) = K_H \times$ partial pressure (p)

$\therefore \quad C \propto p$

$\Rightarrow \quad \frac{C_2}{C_1} = \frac{p_2}{p_1}$

[$\because p_1 = 1\ atm, p_2 = 0.2095\ atm$]

$\therefore \quad C_2 = C_1 \times \frac{p_2}{p_1}$

$= 2.18 \times 10^{-3} \times \frac{0.2095}{1}$

$= 4.567 \times 10^{-4}\ M$

$\simeq 4.57 \times 10^{-4}\ M$

$= x \times 10^{-4}\ M$

So, $n = 4.57$

29. (7.37) Urea ($i = 1$) Cane sugar ($i = 1$)

$M_1 = 60\ g\ mol^{-1} \quad M_2 = 342\ g\ mol^{-1}$

$C_1 = \frac{\frac{3.4}{100} \times 1000}{60}\ M; \ C_2 = \frac{\frac{1.6}{100} \times 1000}{342}\ M$

$= \frac{34}{60}\ M \qquad = \frac{16}{342}\ M$

After mixing of 100 mL of each solution, the final concentration of the solution,

$C = \frac{C_1 + C_2}{2} = \frac{\frac{34}{60} + \frac{16}{342}}{2} = 0.3067\ M$

$\Rightarrow \pi = CRT$

$= 0.3067 \times 0.082 \times 293$ atm

$= 7.368$ atm $\simeq 7.37$ atm.

30. (3) For $BaCl_2$, n-factor $= 2$

$\because M = \frac{N}{2} \Rightarrow C = \frac{1}{10} N = \frac{1}{20} M$

$BaCl_2 \rightleftharpoons Ba^{2+} + 2Cl^- \ (n = 3)$

$\therefore i = 1 + \alpha(n-1) = 1 + 0.7(3-1) = 2.4$

$\pi = CRT \times i$

$= \frac{1}{20} \times 0.082 \times 300 \times 2.4$ atm

$= 2.95$ atm ≈ 3 atm

Qualifier 07
(Equilibrium)

1. (b) Gram equivalents of $Na_2CO_3 \cdot H_2O$ = moles of $Na_2CO_3 \cdot H_2O \times$ valency factor

$= \frac{0.62}{124} \times 2 = 0.01$

Gram equivalents of $(NH_4)_2SO_4$ = Volume $\times$ normality

$= \frac{100 \text{ mL}}{1000 \text{ mL}} \times 1 \text{ L} \times 0.1 \text{ N} = 0.01$

Since, gram equivalent of both $Na_2CO_3 \cdot H_2O$ and $(NH_4)_2SO_4$ are same. So, both reacts completely to form a neutral solution.

2. (c) $(\text{Rate})_f = K_f[NO]^2[O_2]$

and $(\text{Rate})_b = K_b[NO_2]^2$

At equilibrium,

$$\frac{K_f}{K_b} = \frac{[NO_2]^2}{[NO]^2[O_2]} = \frac{2.6 \times 10^3}{4.1} = K_C$$

$\therefore$ For $NO + \frac{1}{2} O_2 \rightleftharpoons NO_2$

$K'_C = \sqrt{K_C} = 25.18$

3. (a) Initially, we have

$[H_2] = [I_2] = 0.2$ M

	$[H_2]$	$[I_2]$	[HI]
Initial concentration	0.200	0.200	0
Concentration at equilibrium	0.200–x	0.200–x	+2x

Substituting the above values of equilibrium concentrations into the expression of K_C gives :

$$\Rightarrow K_C = \frac{[HI]^2}{[H_2][I_2]}$$

$$= \frac{(2x)^2}{(0.200 - x)(0.200 - x)} = 49.5$$

Take the square root of both sides of this equation, we get

$\Rightarrow \frac{2x}{0.200 - x} = 7.04$

$\Rightarrow x = 0.156$

The substances will have the following concentrations at equilibrium;

$[H_2] = [I_2] = 0.200 - 0.156 = 0.044$ M,

$[HI] = 2 \times (0.156) = 0.312$ M

4. (d) In equilibrium state,

(i) $\underset{1-x}{A(s)} \rightleftharpoons \underset{2x}{2B(g)} + \underset{3x}{3C(g)}$

$\Rightarrow K_C = [B]^2[C]^3 = (2x)^2(3x)^3$

$= 4x^2 \times 27x^3 = 108x^5$

(ii) $A(s) \rightleftharpoons \underset{2x \times y}{2B(g)} + \underset{6x}{3C(g)}$

[$\because y$ is the factor by which equilibrium concentration of B is changed]

$\Rightarrow 108x^5 = (4x^2 \times y^2) \times 216x^3$

$\Rightarrow 108 = y^2 \times 216 \times 4$

$\Rightarrow y^2 = \frac{108}{4 \times 216}$

$\Rightarrow y = \frac{1}{2\sqrt{2}}$

5. (a) The equilibrium expression for,

$2SO_3(g) \rightleftharpoons 2SO_2(g) + O_2(g)$ is,

$$K_C = \frac{[SO_2]^2[O_2]}{[SO_3]^2}$$

The equilibrium expression for the second equation,

$$SO_3(g) \rightleftharpoons SO_2(g) + \frac{1}{2}O_2(g)$$

$$K'_C = \frac{[SO_2][O_2]^{1/2}}{[SO_3]}$$

The relationship between the two equilibrium expression is,

$K'_C = \sqrt{K_C} = \sqrt{5.81 \times 10^{-7}} = 7.62 \times 10^{-4}$

6. (c) The pressure, concentration and equilibrium constants of a reaction are related by the equation,

$$K_p = K_C \times (RT)^{\Delta n_g}$$

For the given reaction, the equation becomes

$[\because \Delta n_g = (1+1) - 3 = -1]$

$\Rightarrow K_p = K_C \times (RT)^{-1}$

$\Rightarrow K_C = 1.5 \times 10^{18} \times (0.082 \times 300)^{-1}$

$= 6.10 \times 10^{16}$

	$3NO\ (g)$	$\rightleftharpoons N_2O\ (g)$	$+ NO_2(g)$
Initial conc.	0.03 mol	0	0
Final conc.	0	0.01 mole	0.01mole
Equilibrium for the reverse reaction	3x moles	0.01 - x	0.01 - x

$\Rightarrow K_C = 6.10 \times 10^{16} = \frac{(0.01 - x)^2}{(3x)^3}$

$\Rightarrow 27x^3 = \frac{1 \times 10^{-4}}{6.10 \times 10^{16}}$

[$\because K_C$ is very large $\Rightarrow 0.01 - x \simeq 0.01$]

$\Rightarrow x = 3.93 \times 10^{-8}$

$\Rightarrow$ Since, volume of vessel is 1 L,

$[NO] = 3x = 1.2 \times 10^{-7}$ M

7. (c) When the value of reaction quotient is equal to the value of the equilibrium constant, $Q = K$, the reaction is at equilibrium.

When the reaction quotient is greater than equilibrium constant, that is $Q > K$, then reaction proceed in backward direction.

When the reaction quotient is smaller than equilibrium constant, i.e. $Q < K$, then reaction proceed in forward direction.

When the equilibrium constant is much larger than i.e. $K >>> 1$ then the reaction is nearer to equilibrium.

8. (b) Given : $[N_2] = 3.0$ mol L^{-1},

$[H_2] = 2.0$ mol L^{-1}, $[NH_3] = 0.50$ mol L^{-1}

The reaction quotient for the reaction,

$N_2(g) + 3H_2(g) \rightleftharpoons 2NH_3(g)$ is

$$Q_C = \frac{[NH_3]^2}{[N_2][H_2]^3} = \frac{(0.50)^2}{3 \times (2)^3}$$

$= 0.0104$

We have $K_C = 0.061$.

Thus, at this stage of the reaction, $Q_C < K_C$.

Therefore, the reaction is not at equilibrium.

Hence, the reaction tends to move in forward direction.

9. (d) An increase in the concentration of a reactant at equilibrium, the forward reaction is favoured. Hence, adding F_2 will increase the quantity of ClF_3.

10. (b) The one with the greater number of hydrogens, i.e. HPO_4^{2-} must be Bronsted acid, and the other, PO_4^{3-} must be the Bronsted base.

Therefore, one conjugate acid-base pair is HPO_4^{2-} and PO_4^{3-}. The other two ions, HSO_4^- and SO_4^{2-} belongs to the second conjugate acid-base pair; HSO_4^- is the conjugate acid and SO_4^{2-} is the conjugate base.

11. (c) $[H^+]$ is determined by the first protic equilibrium,

$$\underset{(0.1-x)}{H_2C_6H_6O_6} \rightleftharpoons \underset{x}{H^+} + \underset{x}{HC_6H_6O_6^-}$$

$$\Rightarrow K_{a_1} = 6.8 \times 10^{-5}$$

$$= \frac{x^2}{(0.10-x)} = \frac{x^2}{0.1}$$

So, $x = [H^+] = 2.6 \times 10^{-3}$ M and

$$pH = -\log(2.6 \times 10^{-3}) = 2.58$$

The concentration of the anion $[HC_6H_6O_6^-]$, is given almost entirely by the second ionisation equilibrium.

$$HC_6H_6O_6^- \rightleftharpoons H^+ + C_6H_6O_6^{2-}$$

$$\Rightarrow K_{a_2} = \frac{[H^+][C_6H_6O_6^{2-}]}{[HC_6H_6O_6^{2-}]} = 2.7 \times 10^{-12}$$

Using the value of x from the first step,

$$2.7 \times 10^{-12} = \frac{[2.6 \times 10^{-3}][C_6H_6O_6^{2-}]}{[2.6 \times 10^{-3}]}$$

$$\Rightarrow [C_6H_6O_6^{2-}] = 2.7 \times 10^{-12} \text{ M}$$

12. (b) The reaction involved is

$$NH_4OH + CH_3COOH \rightleftharpoons CH_3COO^-NH_4^+ + H_2O$$

Before hyd.	2.5	2.5	0	0
After hyd.	0	0	2.5	2.5

In this case, pH is decided on the basis of hydrolysis of salt,

$$[CH_3COONH_4] = \frac{2.5}{100} = 2.5 \times 10^{-2} \text{ M}$$

$$\Rightarrow pH = 7 + \frac{1}{2}(pK_a - pK_b) = 7 + 0 = 7$$

$$[\because K_a = K_b = 1.8 \times 10^{-5}]$$

13. (d) The reaction is,

$$CH_3NH_2 + HCl \longrightarrow CH_3NH_3^+ + Cl^-$$

Initial conc.	0.1	0.08	0	0
Final conc.	0.02	0	0.08	0.08

The concentration of $[OH^-]$ and $[H^+]$ are

$$[OH^-] = \frac{K_b[CH_3NH_2]}{[CH_3NH_3]^+} = \frac{6 \times 10^{-4} \times 0.02}{0.08} = \frac{3}{2} \times 10^{-4} \text{ M}$$

$$[H^+] = \frac{10^{-14}}{1.5 \times 10^{-4}} = 6.7 \times 10^{-11} \text{ M}$$

14. (b) $\alpha_1 = \sqrt{K_a \cdot C_1}$

$$\Rightarrow \alpha_1 = 0.005 = \sqrt{K_a}$$

$$(\because C_1 = 1 \text{ mol L}^{-1})$$

Molarity of the diluted solution,

$$C_2 = \frac{2}{32} = \frac{1}{16} \text{ mol L}^{-1}$$

According to Ostwald dilution law,

$$\alpha_2 = \sqrt{\frac{K_a}{C_2}} = \sqrt{K_a} \times \sqrt{\frac{1}{C_2}} = 0.005\sqrt{16} = 0.02$$

$$[H_3O^+] = C_2\alpha_2 M = \frac{1 \times 0.02}{16} = 1.25 \times 10^{-3} \text{ M}$$

15. (d) At equilibrium,

$$2HI(g) \rightleftharpoons H_2(g) + I_2(g)$$

Mole: $1-\alpha$, $\frac{\alpha}{2}$, $\frac{\alpha}{2}$

$$[\because \text{Total moles} = 1 - \alpha + \frac{\alpha}{2} + \frac{\alpha}{2} = 1]$$

Partial pressure: $\frac{1-\alpha}{1} \times p_T$, $\frac{\frac{\alpha}{2}}{1} \times p_T$, $\frac{\frac{\alpha}{2}}{1} \times p_T$

$$[\because p_T = \text{total pressure}]$$

$$\Rightarrow K_p = \frac{\left(\frac{\alpha}{2} p_T\right)^2}{(1-\alpha)^2 p_T^2}$$

or $$\frac{\alpha}{1-\alpha} = 2\sqrt{K_p}$$

or $$\alpha = \frac{2\sqrt{K_p}}{1 + 2\sqrt{K_p}}$$

16. (a) Let α be the degree of dissociation of ammonia under these conditions. According to the balanced equation α moles of NH_3 decompose to produce $\frac{\alpha}{2}$ mole of N_2 and $\frac{3\alpha}{2}$ mole of H_2.

$$2NH_3 \rightleftharpoons N_2 + 3H_2$$

Initial moles	1	0	0
Moles at equilibrium	$1-\alpha$	$\frac{\alpha}{2}$	$\frac{3\alpha}{2}$

Total number of moles after decomposition $= 1 + \alpha$

Using Gay Lussac's law, $\frac{p_1}{T_1} = \frac{p_2}{T_2}$

$$\Rightarrow p_2 = p_1 \times \frac{T_2}{T_1} = 15 \times \frac{273 + 347}{273 + 27}$$

$$= 15 \times \frac{620}{300} = 31 \text{ atm}$$

$$= \frac{\text{Number of moles before decomposition}}{\text{Number of moles after decomposition}} = \frac{p_a}{p_b}$$

$$\Rightarrow \frac{1}{1+\alpha} = \frac{31 \text{ atm}}{50 \text{ atm}} = 0.62$$

$\therefore$ % decomposition of ammonia

$$= 0.62 \times 100 = 62\%$$

17. (b) HgI_2 combines with KI to form the soluble complex K_2HgI_4 and thus, the solubility of HgI_2 is expected to be less in KI due to common ion effect.

Since $I^{\ominus}$ ion is large sized and therefore it is highly polarisable.

Hence, Both (A) and (R) are true but (R) is not the correct explanation of (A).

18. (a) The reaction is,

$$NaX + H_2O \longrightarrow NaOH + HX$$

The hydrolysis constant is,

$$K_h = \frac{K_w}{K_a} = \frac{10^{-14}}{10^{-5}} = 10^{-9}$$

Now, $K_h = Ch^2 = 10^{-9}$ where, h is the degree of hydrolysis and $C = 0.1$ M

$$\Rightarrow h = \sqrt{\frac{K_h}{C}} = \sqrt{\frac{10^{-9}}{0.1}} = 10^{-4} = 10^{-2}\%$$

Therefore, % hydrolysis $= 0.01\%$

19. (a) A buffer solution containing mixture of CH_3COOH and $CH_3COO^-Na^+$ is known as acidic buffer.

When equal volume of 1 M HCl is added, the pH of the solution almost remained unchanged and acidic buffer is formed.

Hence, both A and R are true and R is the correct explanation of A.

20. (d)

Salt (type)	Solubility product	Solubility
MX (1 : 1)	$S_1^2 = 4.0 \times 10^{-8}$	$S_1 = 2 \times 10^{-4}$ M
MX_2 (1 : 2)	$4S_2^3 = 3.2 \times 10^{-14}$	$S_2 = 2 \times 10^{-5}$ M
M_3X (3 : 1)	$27S_3^4 = 2.7 \times 10^{-15}$	$S_3 = 1 \times 10^{-4}$ M

Thus, order of solubilities:

$$MX > M_3X > MX_2 \ (S_1 > S_3 > S_2)$$

21. (5.40) As shown in the balanced chemical equation, if 4.5 moles of G has been produced, then 4.5 moles of H has also been produced and 4.5 mole each of E and F have been consumed.

The quantities of reactants present at equilibrium are equal to those initially present minus what has been used up.

The quantities of products present at equilibrium are equal to those initially present plus what has been produced.

Species	Initially present	Consumed by the reaction	Produced by the reaction	Present at equilibrium
E	6.0	4.5		1.5
F	7.0	4.5		2.5
G	0.0		4.5	4.5
H	0.0		4.5	4.5

The concentrations in the two middle columns of such a table always have values related by the balanced chemical equation.

$$K = \frac{[G][H]}{[E][F]} = \frac{(4.5)\,(4.5)}{(1.5)\,(2.5)} = 5.40$$

22. (0.41) For reaction,

$$H_2(g) + S(s) \rightleftharpoons H_2S(g)$$

$$K = \frac{[H_2S]}{[H_2]} = 6.8 \times 10^{-2}$$

	Initial	Produced	Used up	Equilibrium
$[H_2]$	0.20		x	$0.20 - x \simeq 0.20$
$[H_2S]$	0.00	x		x

$$K = \frac{x}{0.20} = 6.8 \times 10^{-2}$$

$$\Rightarrow \quad x = 1.36 \times 10^{-2}\ \text{mol/L} = \frac{n}{V}$$

$$\Rightarrow p(H_2S) = \left(\frac{n}{V}\right)RT = (1.36 \times 10^{-2}\text{mol/L})$$

$$(0.0821\ \text{L}\cdot\text{atm / mol}\cdot\text{K})\ (363\ \text{K})$$

$$= 0.4053\ \text{atm} = 0.41\ \text{atm}$$

23. (–3.79) For the equilibrium,

$$6\text{HCHO} \longrightarrow C_6H_{12}O_6,$$

$$K = \frac{[C_6H_{12}O_6]}{[\text{HCHO}]^6} = \frac{1.00}{[\text{HCHO}]^6} = 6 \times 10^{22}$$

$$[\text{HCHO}]^6 = \frac{1.00}{6 \times 10^{22}} = 0.167 \times 10^{-22}$$

$$\log\,[\text{HCHO}]^6 = \log\,(0.167 \times 10^{-22})$$

$$= \log\,(0.167) - 22 = -0.777 - 22$$

$$= -22.777$$

$$\log\,[\text{HCHO}] = \frac{1}{6} \times (-22.777) = -3.79$$

24. (0.68) At equilibrium,

$$-\Delta G^\circ = 2.303\,RT \log K$$

$$\log K = \frac{-\Delta G^\circ}{2.303\,RT}$$

$$\Rightarrow \quad \log K = \frac{-460\ \text{cal mol}^{-1}}{(2.303)(1.99\ \text{cal/mol/K})(300\text{K})} = -0.334$$

$$\Rightarrow \quad K = 10^{(-0.334)} = 0.463$$

$$\Rightarrow \quad K = 0.463 = \frac{[C]\,[D]}{[A]\,[B]} = \frac{[C]^2}{[A]^2}$$

$$\Rightarrow \quad \frac{[C]}{[A]} = \sqrt{0.463} = 0.68$$

25. (0.03) $N_2H_5^+ + H_2O \rightleftharpoons N_2H_4 + H_3O^+$

Hydrolysis constant,

$$K_h = \frac{[N_2H_4][H_3O^+]}{[N_2H_5^+]} = \frac{K_w}{K_b} = \frac{1.0 \times 10^{-14}}{9.6 \times 10^{-7}}$$

$$= \frac{x^2}{0.100} = 1.04 \times 10^{-8}$$

Thus, $x = 3.22 \times 10^{-5}$

$$\%\ \text{hydrolysis} = \frac{3.22 \times 10^{-5}}{0.100} \times 100\% = 0.032\% \simeq 0.03\%$$

26. (5.04) The solution is an acidic buffer as it contains 0.01 mole of $HC_2H_3O_2$ (organic acid, a weak acid) and 0.22 mol of $NaC_2H_3O_2$

Applying Henderson's equation,

$$\text{pH} = \text{p}K_a + \log \frac{[NaC_2H_3O_2]}{[HC_2H_3O_2]}$$

$$= 4.74 + \log \frac{0.02}{0.01}$$

$$= 4.74 + \log 2 = 4.74 + 0.30 = 5.04$$

27. (50) Let x mL of 0.10 M sodium formate is added.

or $x \times 10^{-3}$ L of 0.10 M sodium formate (HCOONa) is added.

∴ Moles of HCOONa added = Molarity × Volume

$$= 0.10\ \text{M} \times x \times 10^{-3}\ \text{L}$$

$$= 0.1x \times 10^{-3}\ \text{moles}$$

Moles of HCOOH (formic acid)

$$= \text{Molarity} \times \text{Volume}$$

$$= 0.05\,\text{M} \times 50 \times 10^{-3}\ \text{L}$$

$$= 2.5 \times 10^{-3}\ \text{moles}$$

For acidic buffer, $\text{pH} = \text{p}K_a + \log \frac{[\text{Salt}]}{[\text{Acid}]}$

$$\text{pH} = \text{p}K_a + \log \frac{[\text{HCOONa}]}{[\text{HCOOH}]}$$

$$4.1 = 3.8 + \log \frac{0.1x \times 10^{-3}}{2.5 \times 10^{-3}}$$

On solving, $x = 50$ mL

Hence, volume of HCOONa used = 50 mL

28. (3.44) $CaF_2 \rightleftharpoons Ca^{2+} + 2F^-$

$$[Ca^{2+}] = \frac{1}{2}\,[F^-] = \frac{4.1 \times 10^{-4}}{2}$$

$$= 2.05 \times 10^{-4}\ \text{M}$$

$$K_{sp} = [Ca^{2+}]\,[F^-]^2$$

$$= (2.05 \times 10^{-4})(4.1 \times 10^{-4})^2$$

$$= 3.44 \times 10^{-11} = x \times 10^{-11}$$

$$\therefore \quad x = 3.44$$

29. (9.04) $Mg(OH)_2 \rightleftharpoons Mg^{2+} + 2OH^-$

$K_{sp} = [Mg^{2+}][OH^-]^2 = 1.2 \times 10^{-11}$

Any OH^- concentration higher than that contained in a saturated solution would cause precipitation. Hence, the solution must be at the point of attaining equilibrium, and the concentration of ions in solution must not be greater than those required to satisfy the solubility product constant. In this solution, $[Mg^{2+}] = 0.10$ M.

$\Rightarrow [OH^-]^2 = \frac{1.2 \times 10^{-11}}{0.10} = 1.2 \times 10^{-10}$

$\Rightarrow [OH^-] = 1.1 \times 10^{-5}$ M

$\Rightarrow$ pOH = 4.96 or pH = 9.04

30. (11) Only the ion concentrations appear in the equilibrium constant equations, because solid sulphur, S, is always in its standard state.

$S + S^{2-} \rightleftharpoons S_2^{2-}$; $K_1 = [S_2^{2-}]/[S^{2-}] = 12$

$2S + S^{2-} \rightleftharpoons S_3^{2-}$;

$K_2 = [S_3^{2-}]/[S^{2-}] = 130$

$S + S_2^{2-} \rightleftharpoons S_3^{2-}$; $K_3 = [S_3^{2-}]/[S_2^{2-}] = ?$

The desired constant, K_3, expresses the equilibrium ratio of S_3^{2-} to S_2^{2-} concentrations in a solution equilibrated with solid sulphur. Such a solution must also contain sulphide ion S^{2-}, resulting from the dissociation of S_2^{2-} by the reverse of the first equation.

Since, all four species S, S^{2-}, S_2^{2-} and S_3^{2-} are present, all the equilibria represented above must be satisfied. The three equilibrium ratios are interdependent as-

$$\frac{[S_3^{2-}]}{[S_2^{2-}]} = \frac{[S_3^{2-}]/[S^{2-}]}{[S_2^{2-}]/[S^{2-}]}$$

or $K_3 = \frac{K_2}{K_1} = \frac{130}{12} = 10.83 \approx 11$

Qualifier 08
(Redox Reactions)

1. (d) The given reaction can be balanced as

$$6I^- + ClO_3^- + 6H_2SO_4 \longrightarrow 3I_2 + Cl^- + 6HSO_4^- + 3H_2O$$

So, here, stoichiometric coefficient of HSO_4^- is 6, iodide is oxidised from I^- to I_2 and H_2O is one of the product. However, sulphur neither oxidised nor get reduced.

Hence, option (d) is incorrect.

2. (b) The chemical equation involved is :

$$2K_2\overset{+6}{Cr}O_4 + 2HNO_3 \longrightarrow K_2\overset{+6}{Cr_2}O_7 + 2KNO_3 + H_2O$$

As the oxidation state of Cr in K_2CrO_4 and $K_2Cr_2O_7$ is same, i.e. +6, so it neither gets oxidised nor gets reduced. However, potassium chromate and diluted nitric acid produce $Cr_2O_7^{2-}$ and H_2O.

Hence, option (b) is correct.

3. (c) The balanced chemical equation can be written as

$$2MnO_4^- + 5C_2O_4^{2-} + 16H^+ \longrightarrow 2Mn^{2+} + 10CO_2 + 8H_2O$$

So, $x = 2$, $y = 5$ and $z = 16$

4. (d) $Mn^{7+} + 5e^- \longrightarrow Mn^{2+}$

$Fe^{2+} \longrightarrow Fe^{3+} + e^-$

5 moles of $FeSO_4 \equiv 1$ mole of Mn^{7+}

$\therefore$ 2 moles of $FeSO_4 \equiv 2 \times \frac{1}{5} = \frac{2}{5} = a$

Also, $Fe^{2+} \longrightarrow Fe^{3+} + e^-$

$(C^{3+})_2 \longrightarrow 2C^{4+} + 2e^-$

$Mn^{7+} + 5e \longrightarrow Mn^{2+}$

5 moles of $FeC_2O_4 \equiv 3$ moles of Mn^{7+}

$\therefore$ 2 moles of $FeC_2O_4 = \frac{3}{5} \times 2 = b$

$\therefore$ Ratio of $\frac{a}{b} = \frac{1}{3}$

5. (a) The chemical equations involved are

$$K_2Cr_2O_7 + 6\overset{+2}{Fe}SO_4 + 7H_2SO_4 \longrightarrow Cr_2(SO_4)_3 + 3\overset{+3}{Fe_2}(SO_4)_3 + K_2SO_4 + 7H_2O$$

$$2KMnO_4 + 8H_2SO_4 + 10\overset{+2}{Fe}SO_4 \longrightarrow K_2SO_4 + 2MnSO_4 + 5\overset{+3}{Fe_2}(SO_4)_3 + 8H_2O$$

Consider the half reactions,

$Cr^{6+} + 3e^- \longrightarrow Cr^{3+}$

$Mn^{7+} + 5e^- \longrightarrow Mn^{2+}$

$Fe^{2+} \longrightarrow Fe^{3+} + e^-$

1 mol of $K_2Cr_2O_7$ oxidises 6 moles of Fe^{2+}, whereas 1 mole of $KMnO_4$ oxidises 5 moles of Fe^{2+}.

6. (d) As reducing agents, $C_2O_4^{2-}$ of both of the compounds get oxidised to CO_2.

$$\overset{(+3)}{C_2}\overset{(2-)}{O_4} \longrightarrow 2\overset{(+4)}{C}O_2 + 2e^-$$

n-factor $= (4-3) \times 2 = 2$

$\therefore$ Eqv. wt., $E = \frac{\text{Molar mass}}{2}$

for both of $H_2C_2O_4$ and $NaHC_2O_4$.

So, statement II is correct.

$\Rightarrow$ In acid-base neutralisation (non-redox), *n*-factor (basicity) of $H_2C_2O_4 = 2$, *n*-factor of $NaHC_2O_4 = 1$ and *n*-factor of $Ca(OH)_2 = 2$ (acidity).

So, meq. of

$H_2C_2O_4 = 100 \times (1 \times 2) = 200$

[$\because N = M \times n$-factor]

$NaHC_2O_4 = 100 \times (1 \times 1) = 100$

$Ca(OH)_2 = V \times (1 \times 2) = 2V$

In neutralisation of

$H_2C_2O_4$ - $Ca(OH)_2$: $V = \frac{200}{2} = 100$ mL

$NaHC_2O_4$ - $Ca(OH)_2$: $V = \frac{100}{2} = 50$ mL

So, statement III is incorrect.

In redox reaction, both $H_2C_2O_4$ and $NaHC_2O_4$ act as reducing agent with *n*-factor = 2 and volume of $KMnO_4$ (oxidising agent) required will be same in both of the reactions.

$$\overset{(+3)}{C_2}\overset{(2-)}{O_4} \longrightarrow \overset{(+7)}{Mn}O_4^- \xrightarrow{H^+} \overset{(+1)}{CO_2} + Mn^{2+} + H_2O$$

n-factor : 2   5

meq : $100 \times (1 \times 2)$ $V \times (1 \times 5)$

$\Rightarrow V = \frac{100 \times 2}{5} = 40$ mL in both of the cases.

So, statement IV is correct.

7. (d)

$$2\overset{(+7)}{Mn}\overset{(-2)}{O_4} \longrightarrow K_2\overset{(+6)}{Mn}O_4 + \overset{(+4)}{Mn}O_2 + \overset{0}{O_2}$$

Oxidising agent   Reducing agent

n-factor = (7 – 6) + (7–4) = 4   *n*-factor = (0 –(–2)) × 4 = 8

Total *n*-factor of $KMnO_4$ which suffers intra-molecular redox reaction is,

$= 4(\text{Mn}) + 8(\text{O}) = 12$

$\Rightarrow E_{KMnO_4} = \frac{\text{Molar mass}}{n\text{-factor}} = \frac{M}{12}$

8. (a) Fe (III) sulphate of mixture remains unoxidised by $KMnO_4$.

$$\Rightarrow Fe^{2+} + \overset{(+7)}{Mn}O_4^- \xrightarrow{H^+} Fe^{3+} + Mn^{2+} + H_2O$$

n-factor : (3 – 2) (7 – 2)

= 1   = 5

mole : 5   1

$\frac{5}{1} \times 0.2 = 1$ mol

Fe (II) sulphate

$\therefore$ Mole fraction of $FeSO_4$ in the mixture $= \frac{1}{3}$

9. (a) The net ionic equation is as follows:

$2S_2O_3^{2-} + I_3^- \longrightarrow S_4O_6^{2-} + 3I^-$

Number of moles of thiosulphate ion

$(S_2O_3^{2-}) = \frac{24.55 \times 0.102}{1000}$

$= 2.50 \times 10^{-3}$ mol

Now, 2 moles of $S_2O_3^{2-}$ ion reacts with 1 mole of I_3^- ion.

$\therefore$ No of moles of I_3^- ion

$= \frac{2.50 \times 10^{-3}}{2} = 1.25 \times 10^{-3}$ mol

So, molarity of I_3^-

$= \frac{1.25 \times 10^{-3} \text{ mol}}{10 \text{ mL}} \times 1000 = 0.125$ M

10. (b) The redox reaction are:

$Mn^{7+} + 5e^- \longrightarrow Mn^{2+}$

$(C^{3+})_2 \longrightarrow 2C^{4+} + 2e^-$

$\therefore$ *meq.* of oxalate ion = *meq.* of $KMnO_4$

$\frac{w}{E} \times 1000 = 90 \times \frac{1}{20}$ ... (i)

As $E_{C_2O_4^{2-}} = \frac{88}{2}$, the Eq. (i) becomes

$\frac{w}{44} \times 1000 = \frac{9}{2}$

$w_{C_2O_4^{2-}} = \frac{9}{2} \times \frac{44}{1000}$

So, $w_{C_2O_4^{2-}} = 0.198$ g

Now, % of oxalate ion in sample

$= \frac{0.198}{0.45} \times 100 = 44\%$

11. (4) Reaction involved.

$\overset{+2}{Mn}O_2 + 2NaOH + KNO_3 \longrightarrow Na_2\overset{+6}{Mn}O_4 + KNO_2 + H_2O$

In this reaction, oxidation number of Mn changes from +2 to +6.

So, *n*-factor = 4.

12. (0.92)

$K_2CrO_4 \Rightarrow 2K^+[\overset{+x}{Cr}O_4]^{2-}$

$x + 4(-2) = -2$

$\Rightarrow x = +6$

$CrO_5 \Rightarrow$ [structure: Cr with one =O and two peroxo O–O groups] $\rightarrow y + 4(-1) + (-2) = +6$

$K_3[CrO_8] \Rightarrow 3K^+[CrO_8]^{3-}$

[structure: $[Cr(O_2)_4]^{3-}$ with four peroxo groups] $\Rightarrow x + 8(-1) = -3$

$\Rightarrow x = +5$

CrO_2Cl_2

$b + 2(-2) + 2(-1) = 0$

$\Rightarrow b = +6$

The value of

$\frac{a+b}{x+y} = \frac{5+6}{6+6} = 0.9167 \simeq 0.92$

13. (2.07)

$a\,\overset{(+3)(-1)}{Cr\,I_3} + 6\,\overset{0}{Cl_2} + cNaOH \longrightarrow pNa_2\overset{(+6)}{CrO_4} + qNa\overset{(+7)}{I}O_4 + rNa\overset{(-1)}{Cl} + sH_2O$

Oxidising agent (OA) Reducing agent (RA)

n-factor of OA
$= (6-3)\text{Cr} + [7-(-1)] \times 3 = 27$
(Cr) (I)

n-factor of RA $= [0-(-1)] \times 2 = 2$

We know, OA : RA

n-factor > 27 : 2

mole > 2 : 27

So, $a - 2, b = 27$

By POAC method, for Cl-atom : $2b = r$

$\because r = 2 \times 27 = 54$

$\Rightarrow \frac{a+r}{b} = \frac{2+54}{27} = 2.07$

14. (1.73) *n*-factor of $BrO_3^- = (6-1) \times 1 = 5$

$\therefore$ Eqv. wt of $NaBrO_3 = E = \frac{151}{5}$

$\text{Normality} = \frac{w_{NaBrO_3}}{E_{NaBrO_3}} \times \frac{1000}{V_{mL}}$

$w_{NaBrO_3} = \frac{\text{Normality} \times E \times V_{mL}}{1000}$

$= \frac{0.672 \times \frac{151}{5} \times 85.5}{1000}$ g

$= 1.735$ g

15. (41.34)

$\overset{(0)}{P} + NaOH \longrightarrow \overset{(-3)}{P}H_3 + Na\overset{(+1)}{H_2PO_2} + H_2O$

as oxidising agent, *n*-factor $= 0-(-3) = 3$ (OA)

as reducing, agent, *n*-factor $= (1-0) = 1$ (RA)

It is a disproportionation redox reaction

$E_P = E_P^{OA} + E_P^{RA} = \frac{31}{3} + \frac{31}{1} = 41.34$

Qualifier 09
(Electrochemistry)

1. (c) For Latimer diagram,

$E_3^\circ = \frac{n_1E_1^\circ + n_2E_2^\circ}{n_3^\circ}$

Here, $\overset{(+7)}{Mn}O_4^- \longrightarrow \overset{(+4)}{Mn}O_2, n_1 = 7-4 = 3$

$\overset{(+4)}{Mn}O_2 \longrightarrow Mn^{2+}, n_2 = 4-2 = 2$

$\overset{(+7)}{Mn}O_4^- \longrightarrow Mn^{2+}, n_3 = 7-2 = 5$

$\Rightarrow 1.51 = \frac{3 \times x + 2 \times 1.23}{5}$

$\Rightarrow x = 1.69$ V

2. (b) The electrode reaction is,

$2H^+ + 2e^- \longrightarrow H_2$

$\Rightarrow E_{2H^+/H_2} = E^\circ_{2H^+/H_2} - \frac{0.0592}{2}\log\frac{p_{H_2}}{[H^+]^2}$

$\Rightarrow 0 = 0 - 0.0296 \log\frac{p_{H_2}}{(10^{-7})^2}$

[$\because E_{2H^+/H_2} = 0.00$ V, here E_{2H^+/H_2} becomes zero and at 298 K for pure water, $[H^+] = [OH^-] = 10^{-7}$ M]

$\Rightarrow \log\frac{p_{H_2}}{10^{-14}} = 0$

$\Rightarrow \log\frac{p_{H_2}}{10^{-14}} = \log 1$

$\Rightarrow p_{H_2} = 10^{-14}$ atm at which

$E_{2H^+/H_2} = 0.00$ V

3. (a) 1 g-eqv H_2 or 5.6 L of H_2 at STP is responsible for carrying 1F = 96500 C, charge = *Q*

Electrical work done by the cell of $E = 0.65$V is,

$W_{elec} = -\text{Charge} \times \text{Potential}$
$= -Q \times E_{cell}$
$= -(96500\text{ C}) \times (0.65\text{ V})$
$= -6.27 \times 10^4\text{ J}$

4. (c) The cell reaction is,

$$\underset{(0.1\text{ bar})}{H_{A_2}} + 2H_C^+ \longrightarrow 2H_A^+ + \underset{(1\text{ bar})}{H_2^C}$$

It is a concentration cell, i.e. $E^\circ_{cell} = 0$

$[OH^-]_A = \sqrt{K_b \times C}$
$= \sqrt{10^{-5} \times 0.1} = 10^{-3}\text{ M}$

$[H^+]_A = \dfrac{K_w}{[OH^-]_A} = \dfrac{10^{-14}}{10^{-3}}$
$= 10^{-11}\text{ M}$
$[\because K_w = 10^{-14}\text{ M}^2]$

$[H^+]_C = \sqrt{K_a \times C} = \sqrt{10^{-7} \times 10^{-1}}$
$= 10^{-4}\text{ M}$

$\Rightarrow E_{cell} = -\dfrac{0.0592}{2} \log Q_C$

$= -0.0296 \times \log \dfrac{[H_A^+]^2 \times p_{H_2}C}{[H_C^+]^2 \times p_{H_2}A}$

$= -0.0296 \times \log \dfrac{(10^{-11})^2 \times 1}{(10^{-4})^2 \times 0.1}$

$= -0.029 \times (-13)\text{ V}$
$= +0.3848\text{ V} \simeq +0.385\text{ V}$

5. (a) Higher the value of standard reduction potential,
$\rightarrow$ higher will be the oxidising power of the oxidised form
$\rightarrow$ lower will be the reducing power of the reduced form

$\leftarrow$ Oxidising power
$MnO_4^-, Cr_2O_7^{2-}, Cl_2, Fe^{3+}$
Reducing power $\rightarrow$

6. (b) It is true that, lower the value of standard reduction potential, higher will the reducing power of the reduced form.

Given : $\underset{(-2.71\text{V})}{E^\circ_{X^+/X}} < \underset{(+0.34\text{V})}{E^\circ_{Y^+/Y}} < \underset{(+0.08\text{V})}{E^\circ_{Z^+/Z}}$

So, the correct order of reducing power will be, $X > Y > Z$.

7. (b) At pH = 14, $[H^+] = 10^{-14}$ M and $[OH^-] = 1$ M

$K_{sp}[Cu(OH)_2] = [Cu^{2+}[OH^-]^2]$
$= 1 \times 10^{-19}\text{ M}^3$

$\therefore [Cu^{2+}] = \dfrac{1 \times 10^{-19}\text{ M}^3}{1^2\text{ M}^2} = 1 \times 10^{-19}\text{ M}$

Now, $Cu^{2+} + 2e^- \longrightarrow Cu$

$E_{Cu^{2+}/Cu} = E^\circ_{Cu^{2+}/Cu} - \dfrac{0.0592}{2} \log \dfrac{1}{[Cu^{2+}]}$

$= E^\circ_{Cu^{2+}/Cu} + \dfrac{0.0592}{2} \log [Cu^{2+}]$

$= 0.34 + 0.0296 \times \log 10^{-19}$
$= 0.34 - 0.0296 \times 19$
$= -0.22\text{V}$

8. (d) $MCl + e^- \longrightarrow M + Cl^-, E_1^\circ = 0.22\text{ V}$

$M^+ + e^- \longrightarrow M, E_2^\circ = 0.812\text{ V}$

So at equilibrium,

$MCl \rightleftharpoons M^+ + Cl^-,$

$E^\circ = E_1^\circ - E_2^\circ = (0.22 - 0.812)\text{ V}$
$= -0.592\text{ V}$

$\Rightarrow E_{cell} = E^\circ_{cell} - \dfrac{0.0592}{1} \log [M^+][Cl^-]$

$\Rightarrow \quad 0 = -0.592 - 0.0592 \log K_{sp}\ (MCl)$
$[\because \text{At equilibrium}, E_{cell} = 0]$

$\Rightarrow \log K_{sp} = -\dfrac{0.592}{0.0592} = -10$

$\therefore \quad K_{sp} = 1 \times 10^{-10}\text{ M}^2$

9. (d) In aqueous solution, ionic mobility and molar conductivity are

$K^+ \simeq NO_3^- \approx Cl^-$

During the reaction, at every moment NO_3^- of KNO_3 replaces Cl^- of KCl,

$(K^+Cl^-)(aq) + (Ag^+NO_3^-)(aq) \longrightarrow (K^+NO_3^-)(aq) + AgCl \downarrow (s)$

As if KCl solution is changed into KNO_3 solution. So, molar conductivity remains unchanged. The titration point at which all Cl^- gets precipitation at AgCl, new free cation, Ag^+ and anion, Cl^- will come in addition to K^+ and Cl^- ions. So, molar conductivity will increase beyond this point.

10. (d) 1 F ≡ 1g-eqv. of an ion
∴ 3F ≡ 3 g-eqv. of the ion

$\overset{+}{Ag} \xrightarrow{+e} Ag \quad \overset{2+}{Ge} \xrightarrow{+2e} Ge \quad \overset{3+}{Au} \xrightarrow{+3e} Au$

3F ⇒ 3 eqv. 3 eqv. 3 eqv.

Mole ratio ⇒ Ag : Ge : Au $= \dfrac{3}{1} : \dfrac{3}{2} : \dfrac{3}{3}$
$= 6 : 3 : 2$

11. (b) Volume of Ag deposited
$= 80 \times 5 \times 10^{-4}\text{ cm}^3$

Mass of Ag deposited
$= (80 \times 5 \times 10^{-4}\text{ cm}^3) \times (10.5\text{ g cm}^{-3})$
$= 0.42\text{ g}$

Number of Faraday consumed to deposit 0.42 g Ag

$= \dfrac{w_{Ag}}{E_{Ag}(l)} = \dfrac{0.42}{\frac{108}{1}} F = 3.89 \times 10^{-3}\text{ F}$

Amount of charge consumed
$= 3.89 \times 10^{-3} \times 96500\text{ C}$

For 90% current efficiency, amount of charge required
$= (3.89 \times 10^{-3} \times 96500\text{ C}) \times \dfrac{100}{90}$
$= 417.09 \simeq 417.0\text{ C}$

12. (c) Amount of Cu^{2+} consumed in electrolysis

$\dfrac{100 \times (1 - 0.4)}{1000} = 0.06\text{ mol}$
$= 0.06 \times 2\text{ eqv.}$

Amount of charge consumed,
$Q = (0.06 \times 2) \times 96500\text{ C} = i \times t$

Time taken, $t = \dfrac{Q}{i}$

$= \dfrac{0.06 \times 2 \times 96500}{0.8\text{ amp}}$
$= 14{,}475\text{ s}$
$= \dfrac{14475}{3600}\text{ h} = 4.02\text{ h}$

13. (c) Let us consider the half-cell reactions occurring in the Daniel cell.

$Zn(s) \longrightarrow Zn^{+2} + 2e^-$
$Cu^{+2} + 2e^- \longrightarrow Cu(s)$

Overall cell reaction will be

$Zn(s) + Cu^{+2}(aq) \longrightarrow Zn^{+2}(aq) + Cu(s)$

So, the no. of electrons transferred = 2

$\therefore Q = 2 \times 96500\text{ C}$
$Q = 193000\text{ C}$

14. (a)

- Oxidised: $H_2^0(g) + O_2^0(g) \longrightarrow \overset{(+1)\ (-2)}{H_2O}(l)$ + Chemical energy; Reduced

So, H_2 is used in anode (oxidation) and O_2 at cathode (reduction).

- A fuel cell is about 70% efficient compared to thermal plants (efficiency = 40%)

Hence, option, (b), (c) and (d) are incorrect.

However, fuel cell is a pollution free cell.

So, option (a) is correct.

15. (d) Leclanche cell is a primary electrochemical cell having a zinc cathode in contact with zinc chloride.

In this cell, following reaction takes place at anode:

$$Zn \longrightarrow Zn^{2+} + 2e^-$$

Ni-Cd cell are rechargeable cell using nickel oxide hydroxide and metallic cadmium as electrolyte.

Fuel cell converts combustion energy into electrical energy. The cell is

$$2H_2 + O_2 \longrightarrow 2H_2O$$

Mercury cell does not involve any ion in solution and is used for hearing aid. It is a non-rechargeable mercuric oxide battery.

16. (28.12) One mole of electrons deposits 1 eqv. of an element. So, 0.20 mole of electrons will deposit 0.20 eqv. each of Ag and Zn.

$$E_{Ag^+} = \frac{107.9}{1} = 107.9;$$

$$E_{Zn^{2+}} = \frac{65.38}{2} = 32.69$$

$$w_{Ag} = (0.20 \text{ mol } e^-) \times \left(\frac{107.9 \text{ g}}{\text{mol } e^-}\right)$$

$$= 21.58 \text{ g} = x \text{ g}$$

$$w_{Zn} = (0.20 \text{ mol } e^-) \times \left(\frac{32.69 \text{ g}}{\text{mol } e^-}\right)$$

$$= 6.538 \text{ g}$$

$$= y \text{ g}$$

$\therefore$ The value of

$$(x + y) = (21.58 + 6.538) \text{ g}$$

$$= 28.118 \text{ g} \simeq 28.12 \text{ g}$$

17. (0.23) $E^\circ_{cell} = E^\circ_{(Ag/Cl)} - E^\circ_{(calomel)}$

$$E^\circ_{(Ag/Cl)} = E^\circ_{cell} + E^\circ_{(calomel)}$$

$$= (-0.014 + 0.244) \text{ V}$$

$$= 0.23 \text{ V}$$

18. (4.8) The amount of charge on ion,

$$e = \frac{nF}{N_A} = n \times 1.6 \times 10^{-19} \text{ C}$$

$$= 3 \times 1.6 \times 10^{-19} \text{ C}$$

$$= 4.8 \times 10^{-19} \text{ C}$$

$$= x \times 10^{-19} \text{ C}$$

$$\therefore \quad x = 4.8$$

19. (132.06)

$$2Hg^{2+} + 2Cl^- + 2e \longrightarrow Hg_2Cl_2$$

$$2F \quad 1 \text{ mol} = 472 \text{ g}$$

Number of Faraday passed

$$= \frac{Q_{passed}}{96500} = \frac{i \times t \text{ C}}{96500 \text{ C}}$$

$$= \frac{5 \times (3 \times 3600)}{96500} \text{ F, which will produce}$$

$$\frac{472}{2} \times \frac{5 \times (3 \times 3600)}{96500} \times 472 \text{ g of } Hg_2Cl_2$$

$$= 132.06 \text{ g of } Hg_2Cl_2$$

20. (−0.29)

$$Mn^{2+} + 2e^- \longrightarrow Mn \quad \text{... (i)}$$

$$\Delta G^\circ = -nFE^\circ = -nF(-1.20) = 2.40 \text{ F}$$

$$Mn^{3+} + e^- \longrightarrow Mn^{2+} \quad \text{... (ii)}$$

$$\Delta G^\circ = -1 \text{ F } (1.52) = -1.52 \text{ F}$$

Now, add Eq. (i) and (ii)

$$Mn^{3+} + 3e^- \longrightarrow Mn \quad \text{... (iii)}$$

$$\therefore \Delta G^\circ = 2.40\text{F} + (-1.52)\text{F} = 0.88 \text{ F}$$

Now, use this value to calculate E° for eq. (iii).

$$\therefore \Delta G^\circ = -nFE^\circ$$

$$0.88\text{F} = -3 \times F \times E^\circ$$

$$E^\circ = -0.29 \text{ V}$$

Qualifier 10

(Chemical Kinetics)

1. (b) $4NH_3 + 5O_2 \longrightarrow 4NO + 6H_2O$

$$-\frac{1}{4}\frac{d[NH_3]}{dt} = -\frac{1}{5}\frac{d[O_2]}{dt} = +\frac{1}{4}\frac{d[NO]}{dt}$$

$$= +\frac{1}{6}\frac{d[H_2O]}{dt}$$

$$\Rightarrow \quad -\frac{6}{4}\frac{d[NH_3]}{dt} = \frac{d[H_2O]}{dt}$$

$$\Rightarrow \quad -1.5\frac{d[NH_3]}{dt} = \frac{d[H_2O]}{dt}$$

2. (c) Rate $= +\frac{1}{2}\frac{d[B]}{dt} = k_1[A]$

$\Rightarrow$ Rate of appearance of B,

$$\frac{d[B]}{dt} = 2\,k_1[A] = 2 \times (4 \times 10^{-4}\text{ s}^{-1}) \times (4\text{M})$$

$$= 3.2 \times 10^{-3} \text{ Ms}^{-1}$$

3. (d) Rate

$$= \frac{-1}{2}k_1\frac{[N_2O_5]}{\Delta t} = \frac{1}{4}\frac{\Delta[NO_2]}{\Delta t} = \frac{\Delta[O_2]}{\Delta t}$$

$$= \frac{-1}{2}k_1[N_2O_5] = \frac{1}{4}k_2[N_2O_5]$$

$$= k_3[N_2O_5]$$

$$= \frac{-1}{2}k_1 = \frac{1}{4}k_2 = k_3$$

$$= -2k_1 = k_2 = 4k_3$$

4. (a) Slow step (III), is the rate determining step,

Rate $= k_2[N_2O_2][H_2]$

But, N_2O_2 is an intermediate, whose concentrations can be expressed in terms of reactant(s) from the equilibrium step (I).

$$K_{eq} = \frac{k_1}{k_{-1}}\frac{[N_2O_2]}{[NO]^2}$$

$$\Rightarrow [N_2O_2] = \frac{k_1}{k_{-1}}[NO]^2$$

So, $\quad \text{Rate} = k_2 \times \left(\frac{k_1}{k_{-1}}[NO]^2\right) \times [H_2]$

$$= \frac{k_1k_2}{k_{-1}}[NO]^2[H_2]$$

5. (b) Statement-III is not correct, regarding order of a reaction. The correct replacement of statement-III is the statement-IV, e.g. if A and B are reactants of a chemical reaction and they are present in the slowest step of a multi-step reaction or an elementary process as

$$xA + yB \rightarrow \text{product(s)}.$$

The rate expression is, $r = k[A]^x[B]^y$

and the order of the reaction will be $n = (x + y)$.

6. (b) Statement I is incorrect but statement II is correct.

Corrected statement I Order of a reaction is the sum of powers of active masses of reactants present in the rate law expression of a reaction. Hence, the order is not related to molecularity of a reaction.

7. (d) In a first order reaction, if

a_0 = Initial concentration of reactant

a = Concentration of reactant at time 't'

$(a_0 - a) = x$ = Amount of reactant disappeared in time 't'

$$\Rightarrow \quad \ln\frac{a_0}{a} = kt$$

$$k = \frac{1}{t}\ln\frac{a_0}{a}$$

$$\Rightarrow \quad \ln\frac{a_0}{a} = kt$$

$$\Rightarrow \quad \ln\frac{a}{a_0} = -kt$$

$$\Rightarrow \quad \frac{a}{a_0} = e^{-kt}$$

$$\Rightarrow \quad \frac{a_0 - x}{a_0} = e^{-kt}$$

$$\Rightarrow \quad 1 - \frac{x}{a_0} = e^{-kt}$$

$$\Rightarrow \frac{x}{a_0} = 1 - e^{-kt} = \text{fraction of reaction}$$

disappeared in time 't', through a first order reaction.

8. (c) Since, the concentration of B is 6 M and throughout the reaction the B concentration cannot possibly fall below 5.9 m, it is useful to consider $[B]$ as constant.

So, rate $= 6\,k\,[A]$

$$\Rightarrow \quad 6k = \frac{2.303}{t}\log\frac{[A_0]}{[A]}$$

$$\Rightarrow \log\frac{[A_0]}{[A]} = \frac{6kt}{2.303}$$

$$\Rightarrow \log[A_0] - \log[A] = \frac{6kt}{2.303}$$

$[\because t = 100\text{ s}, k = 5\times10^{-3}\text{ M}^{-1}\text{s}^{-1}$ $[A_0] = 0.1\text{M}]$

$$\log[A] = \log[A_0] - \frac{6kt}{2.303}$$

$$= \log(0.1) - \frac{6\times(5\times10^{-3})\times100}{2.303}$$

$$= -1 - 1.30 = -2.30$$

$$\Rightarrow [A] = 10^{-2.30}$$

$$[A] = 5\times10^{-3}\text{M}$$

9. (c) $[B]_{\text{Max}} = [A]_0 \times \left(\frac{k_2}{k_1}\right)^x$ for the first order reaction.

$$\text{where, } x = \frac{k_2}{k_1 - k_2} = \frac{10^{-2}}{10^{-1} - 10^{-2}}$$

$$= \frac{0.01}{0.09} = \frac{1}{9}$$

$$\Rightarrow [B]_{\text{Max}} = 10\times\left(\frac{10^{-2}}{10^{-1}}\right)^{\frac{1}{9}}$$

$$= 10\times(10^{-1})^{\frac{1}{9}}$$

$$= 10\times10^{-1/9}$$

$$= 10^{1-\frac{1}{9}} = 10^{8/9}\text{ M}$$

10. (b) $(CH_3)_3COOC(CH_3)_3(g) \xrightarrow{\Delta} 2CH_3COCH_3(g) + C_2H_6(g)$

pressure at $t = 0$ p_0 0   0

$t = t$ $p_0 - x$ $2x$ x

Total $p = p_0 - x + 2x + x = p_0 + 2x$

At $t = t$

$$\Rightarrow \quad x = \frac{p - p_0}{2}$$

For the first order reaction, rate constant

$$k = \frac{1}{t}\ln\left(\frac{p_0}{p_0 - x}\right)$$

$$= \frac{1}{t}\ln\left[\frac{p_0}{p_0 - \left(\frac{p - p_0}{2}\right)}\right]$$

$$= \frac{1}{t}\ln\left[\frac{p_0}{\frac{2p_0 - p + p_0}{2}}\right]$$

$$= \frac{1}{t}\ln\left(\frac{2p_0}{3p_0 - p}\right)$$

$$= -\frac{1}{t}\ln\left(\frac{3p_0 - p}{2p_0}\right)$$

$$\Rightarrow -kt = \ln\left(\frac{3p_0 - p}{2p_0}\right)$$

11. (c) We know, half-life, $t_{50} \propto a_0^{1-n}$

So, $\quad t_{50} = k' a_0^{(1-n)}$ $(\because k = \text{constant})$

$\Rightarrow \quad \log t_{50} = \log k' + (1-n)\log a_0$

$\Rightarrow$ In the plot, $\log t_{50}$ vs $\log a_0$, slope $= (1-n) = -1$

$\Rightarrow \; n = 2$ (2nd order)

$\Rightarrow$ The rate of the reaction,

$$\frac{d[A]}{dt} = -k[A]^2$$

12. (a) For zero order reaction,

$$k = \frac{a_0 - a}{t}$$

$$\Rightarrow \quad (a_0 - a) = k\times t$$

$\Rightarrow$ In plot of $(a_0 - a)$ vs t, slope $= k =$ rate constant $= \tan 60° = \sqrt{3}$ M min^{-1}

$\Rightarrow$ Half-life, $t_{50} = \frac{a_0}{2k}$ $[\because a = a_0/2]$

$$= \frac{17.32\text{M}}{2\sqrt{3}\text{ M min}^{-1}}$$

$$= 4.99\text{ min} \simeq 5\text{ min}$$

13. (a) The expressions of the half-life are,

(i) for the 1st order reaction,

$$t_{50} = \frac{0.693}{k_1}$$

$$\Rightarrow \quad k_1 = \frac{0.693}{t_{50}} = \frac{0.693}{40}\text{s}^{-1}$$

(ii) for the zero order reaction,

$$t_{50} = \frac{a_0}{2k_0}$$

$$\Rightarrow \quad k_0 = \frac{a_0}{2\times t_{50}} = \frac{1.386\text{ mol/L}}{2\times20\text{ s}}$$

$$= \frac{1.386}{40}\text{mol/L}^{-1}\text{s}^{-1}$$

$$\therefore \quad \frac{k_1}{k_0} = \frac{\frac{0.693}{40}\text{s}^{-1}}{\frac{1.386}{40}\text{mol L}^{-1}\text{s}^{-1}}$$

$$= 0.5\text{ L/mol}$$

14. (d) For first order reaction,

$$= \frac{1}{k} = \frac{1}{\frac{0.693}{t_{50}}} = 1.44\times t_{50}$$

$[\because$ In 1st order reaction, rate constant $(k) = \frac{0.693}{t_{50}}]$

$$\Rightarrow t_{75} = \frac{2.303}{k}\log\frac{100}{25}$$

$$= 2\times\frac{2.303}{k}\log 2 = 2\times\frac{0.693}{k} = 2\times t_{50}$$

$$\Rightarrow t_{99.9} = \frac{2.303}{k}\log\frac{100}{0.1}$$

$$= \frac{2.303}{k}\log 10^3 = 3\times\frac{2.303}{k}$$

$$= (10\times0.3)\times\frac{2.303}{k}$$

$$= 10\times\left(\frac{2.303}{k}\times0.301\right) = 10\times\frac{0.693}{k}$$

$$= 10\times t_{50}$$

So, $t_{50} : t_{av} : t_{75} : t_{99.9} = 1 : 1.44 : 2 : 10$

or $t_{50} < t_{av} < t_{75} < t_{99.9}$

15. (b) Given, p_{NO}(1500 mm) >> p_{H_2} (8 mm). Hence, the rate of the reaction can be approximated as

$$\frac{dp_{(N_2O)}}{dt} = k(p_{NO})^2(p_{H_2}) = k' p_{H_2}$$

where, $k' = k(p_{NO})^2$ as change in partial pressure. NO will be negligible as compared to that of H_2 so, the reaction is assumed to follow first order kinetics.

16. (d) Correct match is

A → (3), B → (1), C → (2)

We know, $t_{50} \propto (a_0)^{1-n}$

when, $n = 0, t_{50} \propto a_0$, where $t_{50} = \frac{a_0}{2k}$

When, $n = 1, t_{50}$ becomes independent of a_0, where, $t_{50} = \frac{0.693}{k}$

$n = 2, t_{50} \propto \frac{1}{a_0}$ where,

$$t_{50} = \frac{1}{ka_0} \quad [\text{for } 2A \longrightarrow \text{product}]$$

17. (c) The increase in the rate of a reaction primarily increases due to increase in the number of molecules having threshold energy, i.e. the minimum amount of energy that to be present with reactant molecules to undergo a chemical change.

18. (c) Given, $k=\dfrac{k_1k_3}{k_2}$

$\Rightarrow \quad \ln k=\ln k_1-\ln k_2+\ln k_3$

$\Rightarrow \ln A-\dfrac{E_a}{RT}=\ln A-\dfrac{E_{a_1}}{RT}-\left(\ln A-\dfrac{E_{a_2}}{RT}\right)+\ln A-\dfrac{E_{a_3}}{RT}$

[$\because$ From Arrhenius equation, $k=A.e^{-E_a/RT}$]

or $\ln k=\ln A-\dfrac{E_a}{RT}$

$\Rightarrow \quad -\dfrac{E_a}{RT}=\dfrac{1}{RT}(E_{a_2}-E_{a_1}-E_{a_3})$

$\Rightarrow \quad E_a=E_{a_1}-E_{a_2}+E_{a_3}$

[$\because E_a=$ overall activation energy]

$=(40-30+20)=30\text{ kJ mol}^{-1}$

19. (b) According to the Arrhenius equation.

% Fraction of molecules crossing energy barrier

$=e^{-E_a/RT}\times 100=e^{\left(\frac{-3.684\times10^3}{8\times200}\right)}\times 100$

$=e^{-2.303}\times 100=\dfrac{1}{10}\times 100=10\%$

20. (c) Enthalpy of the reaction,

$\Delta_r H=(\Delta H)_{M,N}-(\Delta H)_{A,B}$

$=E_a^f-E_a^b$

$\Rightarrow -y=x-E_a^b$ [$\because$ forward change, $A+B\to M+N$ is exothermic]

$\Rightarrow E_a^b=x+y$

Where, $E_a^b=$ activation energy for the backward reaction,

$M+N\to A+B$

$E_a^f=$ activation energy for the forward reaction,

$A+B\longrightarrow M+N$

21. (1770) We know, $R=kC$

So, $R_1=kC_1$ and $R_2=kC_2$

$\therefore \dfrac{R_1}{R_2}=\dfrac{kC_1}{kC_2}$

$\dfrac{R_1}{R_2}=\dfrac{C_1}{C_2}=\dfrac{0.048}{0.03}$

$k=\dfrac{2.303}{t}\log\dfrac{C_1}{C_2}=\dfrac{2.303}{10}\log\left(\dfrac{0.048}{0.03}\right)$

$=0.047\text{ min}^{-1}$

$t_{75\%}=\dfrac{2.303}{k}\log\dfrac{100}{25}$

$=\dfrac{2.303}{0.047}\log 4=29.5\text{ min}$

$=1770$ s

22. (0.09) Since, the concentration of two reactants start equal and remain equal throughout the reaction, the reaction can be treated as a second order reaction involving two reactant.

$k=\dfrac{1}{t}\left[\dfrac{1}{[A]}-\dfrac{1}{[A_0]}\right]$

$\dfrac{1}{[A]}=kt+\dfrac{1}{[A_0]}$

$\dfrac{1}{[A]}=1\times10^{-2}\times100+\dfrac{1}{0.1}$

$=11\text{ mol/L}$

$\Rightarrow [A]=\dfrac{1}{11}\text{ mol L}^{-1}$

$=0.09$ M

23. (1.92) Since, doubling the time doubles the fractional reduction of the reactant concentration, the reaction must be of first order,

$0.12\text{ M}\xrightarrow{t=10\text{h}=t_{50}}0.06\text{M}\xrightarrow{t=20\text{ h}=2\times t_{50}}0.03\text{M}$

$\Rightarrow k=\dfrac{0.693}{10\text{h}}=\dfrac{0.693}{10\times3600\text{s}}$

$=1.92\times10^{-5}\text{ s}^{-1}$

$=x\times10^{-5}\text{ s}^{-1}$

$\therefore \quad x=1.92$

24. (3.42) Rate $=k[CH_3COOCH_3][OH^-]$

$=(0.137\text{ L mol}^{-1}\text{s}^{-1})\times(0.05\text{ mol L}^{-1})^2$

$=3.42\times10^{-4}\text{ mol L}^{-1}\text{s}^{-1}$

$=a\times10^{-4}\text{M s}^{-1}$

$\therefore a=3.42$

25. (2) We know,

$\dfrac{(t_{1/2})_1}{(t_{1/2})_2}=\left(\dfrac{a_2}{a_1}\right)^{n-1}$

$\dfrac{3.64}{1.82}=\left(\dfrac{100}{50}\right)^{n-1}$

$2=(2)^{n-1}$

or $\quad (2)^1=(2)^{n-1}$

$\Rightarrow \quad 1=n-1$

$n=2$

$\therefore$ Order of reaction $=2$

26. (0.05) Slope $=-\dfrac{0.845-0.310}{25.00-0.00}$

$=-0.0214\text{ min}^{-1}$

$\Rightarrow \quad k=-2.303\times\text{slope}$

$=-2.303\times(-0.0214\text{ min}^{-1})$

$=0.05\text{ min}^{-1}$

$\because$ The reaction follows the first order kinetics.

27. (241) Comparing,

$k=(5\times10^{11}\text{L mol}^{-1}\text{s}^{-1})\times e^{-29000\text{K}/J}$

with Arrhenius equation, $k=A.e^{-E_a/RT}$

$\Rightarrow \quad \dfrac{E_a}{RT}=\dfrac{29000\text{ K}}{T}$

$\Rightarrow \quad E_a=(29000\text{ K})\times R$

$=29000K\times8.314\text{ J mol}^{-1}\text{ K}^{-1}$

$=241106\text{ J mol}^{-1}$

$=241.10\text{ kJ mol}^{-1}$

$\approx 241\text{ kJ mol}^{-1}$

28. (3.34) $k=-\dfrac{\Delta[A]}{[A]}\times\dfrac{1}{\Delta t}$

It is seen that only fractional change in concentration $-\dfrac{\Delta[A]}{[A]}$, is needed namely $\dfrac{2}{100}=0.02$

When $\Delta t=1\text{ min}=60\text{ s}$

$\Rightarrow \quad k=\dfrac{0.02}{60\text{ s}}=3.34\times10^{-4}\text{s}^{-1}$

$=x\times10^{-4}\text{s}^{-1}$

$\therefore \quad x=3.34$

29. (71) From Arrhenius equation,

$\log k=\log A-\dfrac{E_a}{2.303RT}$

$\Rightarrow \log\dfrac{k_{T_2}}{k_{T_1}}=\dfrac{E_a}{2.303R}\times\dfrac{\Delta T}{T_1T_2}$

Hence, $k_{310}/k_{300}=Q_{10}=2.5$

$\Rightarrow \log 2.5=\dfrac{E_a}{2.303R}\times\dfrac{10}{(300\times310)}$

$\Rightarrow E_a=\dfrac{\log(2.5)\times2.303\times(8.314\times10^{-3})\times(300\times310)}{10}$

$=70.86\text{ kJ mol}^{-1}$

≈ 71.00 kJ/mol

30. (16.67) In step (i)

$\left(\dfrac{dx}{dt}\right)_I=k_1[P][Q]=3\times10^{-5}[P][Q]$

In step-(ii)

$k_3=1\times10^{10}\text{M}^{-1}\text{s}^{-1}$ (very high value), thus $X+Q\to R+S$ is faster and the rate determining step is $P\to P^{*}\to X$

$\Rightarrow \quad \left(\dfrac{dx}{dt}\right)_{II}=k_2[P]=5\times10^{-4}[P]$

When, $\quad \left(\dfrac{dx}{dt}\right)_I=\left(\dfrac{dx}{dt}\right)_{II}$

$\Rightarrow 3\times10^{-5}[P][Q]=5\times10^{-4}[P]$

$\Rightarrow \quad [Q]=\dfrac{5\times10^{-4}}{3\times10^{-5}}=16.67\text{ M}$

Qualifier 11
(Surface Chemistry)

1. (b) Physisorption is reversible because a single layer of adsorbate molecules is held together with adsorbent by weaker van der Waals' force. As activation energy of physisorption is low, it occurs at lower temperature and decreases with rise in temperature (adsorption isobar).

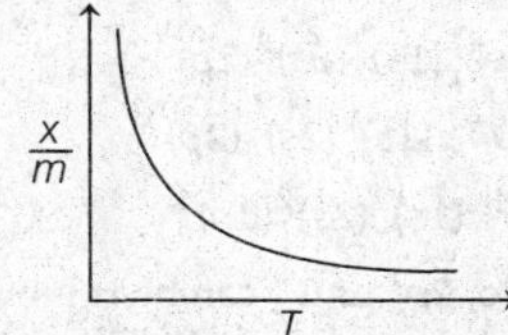

2. (c) In adsorption process, $\Delta H < 0$ (exothermic) and $\Delta S < 0$. Because during adsorption disorderness of adsorbate molecules (gas or liquid) decreases as they get adsorbed on the surface of adsorbent (solid) and there is decrease in surface energy, i.e. it is an exothermic process.

So, adsorption will be spontaneous, i.e. $\Delta G < 0$ ($\because \Delta G = \Delta H - T\Delta S$) at lower temperature.

3. (a) $\frac{x}{m} = p \times T$ is not a correct relationship regarding adsorption, because in Freundlich isotherm equation, $\frac{x}{m} = k \cdot p^{1/n}$ and in Langmuir isotherm equation, $\frac{x}{m} = \frac{ap}{1 + bp}$

where, k = Freundlich constant

a, b = Langmuir constants

4. (d) $AgNO_3(aq) + KI(aq) \longrightarrow AgI(s) + KNO_3(aq)$

$\Rightarrow$ Negatively charged colloidal sol ($AgI \cdot I^-$) will be formed when,

m mol of KI > m mol of $AgNO_3$

option (b) $100 \times 0.2 = 20$ $\quad$ $100 \times 0.1 = 10$

option (c) $100 \times 0.25 = 25$ $\quad$ $100 \times 0.15 = 15$

$\Rightarrow$ Positively charged colloidal sol ($AgI \cdot Ag^+$) will be formed when

mmol of KI < mmol of $AgNO_3$

option (a) $100 \times 0.1 = 10$ $\quad$ $100 \times 0.2 = 20$

5. (a) The reaction $SnO_2(s)$ and NaOH (*aq*) takes place as,

$SnO_2 + 2\,NaOH \longrightarrow Na_2SnO_3 \cdot + 2H_2O$

SnO_3^{2-} of Na_2SnO_3 is adsorbed by SnO_2 forming negatively charged colloidal sol, $[SnO_2]\,SnO_3^{2-} \cdot 2Na^+$.

6. (b) For chemisorption, the degree of adsorption $\left(\frac{x}{m}\right)$ increases with increase in temperature to its maximum value and then it decreases with increase in temperature at constant pressure.

7. (a) $\frac{x}{m} = k\,(p^{1/n})$

$\log\frac{x}{m} = \log k + \frac{1}{n}\log p$

From the plot, $\log\frac{x}{m}$ vs $\log p$,

Slope $= \tan 45° = \frac{1}{n} = 1$

$\Rightarrow \quad n = 1$

Intercept $= \log k = 0.6990$

$\Rightarrow \quad k = 10^{0.6990} = 5$

8. (c) For CH_3COOH, mmol

→ Initial $= 100 \times 0.5 = 50$

→ Final $= 100 \times 0.49 = 49$

mmol of CH_3COOH adsorbed $= 50 - 49 = 1$

Number of CH_3COOH molecules adsorbed $= (1 \times 10^{-3}) \times N_A$

The surface area of charcoal adsorbed by each CH_3COOH molecule,

$$= \frac{3.015 \times 10^2}{(1 \times 10^{-3}) \times (6.023 \times 10^{23})}$$

$$= 5 \times 10^{-19}\,m^2$$

$$= x \times 10^{-19}\,m^2$$

$\therefore \quad x = 5$

9. (d) As_2S_3 is negatively charged sol. So, it can be coagulated by cations.

More the charge of cations, more effective will be coagulation.

$\therefore$ Correct option is $AlCl_3$.

10. (b) Lower the coagulation or flocculation value, higher will be the flocculation power of the electrolyte.

11. (b) From the definition of gold number of a lyophilic colloid (here, it is starch)

	NaCl solution	Gold sol	Starch
Quantity $\Rightarrow$	1 mL of 10%	10 mL	0.0025 g

$= 0.0025 \times 10^{-3}$ mg

$= 2.50$ mg

12. (c) Butter is a water in oil type (*w/o*) emulsion like cold cream. Here, water is the dispersed phase and oil is the dispersion medium. Water and oil, both are liquids. So, the heterogeneous mixture of two liquids produces an emulsion.

In *o/w* type emulsions like milk and vanishing cream, oil (*o*) is the dispersed phase and water (*w*) is the dispersion medium.

13. (c) Gold number is inversely proportional to protective power, i.e.

Gol number $\propto \frac{1}{\text{Protective power}}$

As gelatin has the lowest gold number, hence, it is a better protective colloid.

14. (d) All the given statements are correct.

- Higher the mass of alkyl group (*R*) in soap (RCOONa) or detergent (RSO_3Na), lower will be the critical micelle concentration (CMC) of the associated colloid formed.
- During peptisation, the solid form (dispersed phase) of a lyophobic colloid gets converted into its colloidal sol in presence of a suitable electrolyte which provides a common ion to the lyophobic sol, e.g.

  $Fe(OH)_3(s) + FeCl_3(aq.) \longrightarrow \underset{\text{(Colloidal sol)}}{Fe(OH)_3 \cdot Fe^{3+}} \cdot + 3Cl^-(aq.)$

  Here, Fe^{3+} is the common ions which is adsorbed on the surface of $Fe(OH)_3$ particles.
- For associated colloids, micelle formation takes place above CMC and above Kraft temperature (T_k). The value of CMC decreases with increase in temperature above T_k.

15. (d) According to adsorption theory of catalysis, the reactants in their gaseous state or in their dissolved state (solution state) gets adsorbed on the surface of a suitable catalyst in its solid state. Hence, adsorption theory is given for heterogenous catalyst, adsorption of H_2 gas on nickel metal.

16. (4) $AlCl_3 \xrightarrow{H_2O} \underset{\substack{\text{Fixed layer} \\ = 1\text{ ion}}}{[Al(OH)_3] \cdot Al^{3+}} \cdot \underset{\substack{\text{Diffused layer} \\ = 3\text{ ions}}}{3OH^-}$

So, total number of ions present in the double layer $= 1 + 3 = 4$

17. (6.30) $w_{\text{oxalic acid}}$ (adsorbed)

$$= \frac{50 \times (1 - 0.5)}{1000} \times 126$$

$= 3.15$ g/0.5 g of carbon

$= 2 \times 3.15$ g/gram of carbon

$= 6.30$ g/gram of carbon or charcoal

18. (75.61) 100 mL gold sol requires 0.7561 g of X

$\therefore$ 10 mL gold sol requires 0.07561 g of X

$= 75.61$ mg of X

To check coagulation by 1 mL of 10% NaCl solution.

$\therefore$ Gold number of $X = 75.61$

19. (5.59) $\dfrac{\text{Flocculation power of } AlCl_3}{\text{Flocculation power of NaCl}}$

$$= \frac{\text{Coagulation value of NaCl}}{\text{Coagulation value of } AlCl_3}$$

$$= \frac{52 \text{ mmol/L}}{0.093 \text{ mmol/L}} = 559.13$$

$= 5.59 \times 10^2 = x \times 10^2$

$\therefore \; x = 5.59$

20. (47.5) Flocculation value of an electrolyte is expressed in milli-mol/L.

Here, mmol of KCl $= 4.75 \times 1 = 4.75$

Volume of colloidal solution $= 100$ mL $= 0.1$ L

$\Rightarrow$ Flocculation value of KCl

$$= \frac{4.75}{0.1} = 47.5$$

Qualifier 12

(Classification of Elements and Periodicity in Properties)

1. (b) Correct match is

$A \rightarrow (4), B \rightarrow (2), C \rightarrow (1), D \rightarrow (3)$

Atomic no. (Z)	Symbol	IUPAC name
105	Unp	Unnilpentium
110	Uun	Ununnilium
219	Bue	Biunennium
107	Uns	Unnilseptium

2. (d) In the 6th period, the orbitals being filled are $4f$, $5d$, $6s$ and $6p$ which follow the $(n + l)$ rule, while filling with electrons as in the order of

$$\begin{array}{lcccc} & 6s < & 4f < & 5d < & 6p \\ & 6+0 & 4+3 & 5+2 & 6+1 \\ (n+l) \Rightarrow & =6 & =7 & =7 & =7 \end{array}$$

3. (c) The relationship between radius and charge of the ions is as follows

Radius of anion $\propto$ charge on anion

$$\text{Radius of cation} \propto \frac{1}{\text{charge on cation}}$$

and it is true for an isoelectronic set of ions ($10e^-/18e^-/36e^-$ etc). So, the order will be

$$\underbrace{Br^-}_{36e^-} > \underbrace{S^{2-} > Cl^-}_{18e^-} > \underbrace{O^{2-} > Na^+ > Mg^{2+}}_{10e^-}$$

4. (b) For an element, its atomic radius is larger than its cationic radius, whereas its atomic radius is smaller than its anionic radius.

$$\Rightarrow \underset{(2.31\,\text{Å})}{r_K} > \underset{(1.34\,\text{Å})}{r_{K^+}} \text{ and } \underset{(0.64\,\text{Å})}{r_F} < \underset{(1.34\,\text{Å})}{r_{F^-}}$$

5. (a) Li^+ is the smallest alkali metal ion (M^+) in group 1. Because of its highest positive charge density and it has highest hydration enthalpy value (most negative) in group 1. In aqueous solution, size of hydrated Li^+ is largest and that of Cs^+ is smallest.

6. (a) The valence shell electronic configurations of $Cl^+ (s^2p^4)$ is more stable than that of $S^+ (s^2p^1)$. So,

IE_1 of S or IE_2 of $S^+ < IE_1$ of Cl or IE_2 of Cl^+

$[S^+ \xrightarrow{-e} S^{2+}][Cl^+ \xrightarrow{-e} Cl^{2+}]$

7. (a) Na, Mg, Al and Si belong to the third period of the periodic table. Usually, along a period IE_1, value increases from left to right. Here, we get an exception for Mg and Al. In ground state, Mg has $3s^2$ and Al has $3s^2 3p^1$ valence shell configurations. Because of $3s^2$ pairing stability, IE_1 of Mg becomes higher than Al which has $3p^1$ electron , [1| |] and it can be removed easily.

So, the IE_1 order is Na<Al<Mg<Si or Na<Mg>Al<Si.

8. (c) The sudden jump in IE values is observed from IE_4 to IE_5 (46.8 to 162.2 eV), which indicates number of valence electrons of the element is 4, i.e. it belongs to group 14.

[Group 14:C, (Si), Ge, Sn, Pb]

9. (c) The configuration $(1s)^2(2s)^2(2p)^6(3s)^2$ will maximum difference in 2nd and 3rd IE values. IE_2 implies removal of the $3s^1$ electron from the uni-positive ion and IE_3 implies removal of an electron from the stable configuration of the noble gas [Ne: [He]$(2s)^2$ $(2p)^6$] of the bi-positive ion of the same element.

10. (c) Because of the stability of $2s^2$-orbital, IE_1 (Mg) > IE_1, (Na), whereas because of stable noble gas configuration of Na^+ ($10e^-$), IE_2 (Mg) < IE_2 (Na).

11. (c) The IE_2 process implies removal of an electron from each of C^+, N^+, O^+ and F^+ species.

Their configurations are,

$C^+ : (1s)^2(2s)^2(2p)^1$

$N^+ : (1s)^2(2s)^2(2p)^2$

$O^+ : (1s)^2(2s)^2(2p)^3$

$F^+ : (1s)^2(2s)^2(2p)^4$

So, $2p^1$ of C^+ can be removed easily, whereas removal of an electron from stable $2p^3$ (half-filled) configuration of O^+ will be most difficult.

$\Rightarrow$ The order of IE_2 of X or IE_1 of X^+ is

O > F > N > C [$\because X =$ C, N, O and F]

12. (d) Neon ($Z = 10$) has stable electronic configuration. So, it is difficult to add an electron to the valence shell of any noble gas like neon. Because of the stability for noble gases,

EA = 0 and $\Delta_{eg}H > 0$

(positive electron gain enthalpy)

13. (c) Electron affinity or negative electron gain enthalpy ($-\Delta_{eg}H$) of oxygen is lowest in group 16 because of its smallest size and highest electronegativity in the group.

[$\because$ Oxygen has second highest electronegativity among all elements]

14. (b) All conversions indicate gain of an electron in the valence shell of an isolated gaseous atom in each case, i.e. first electron affinity (EA_1) process for each element. EA of an atom leads to release of energy (exothermic) while producing the gaseous anion.

Release of minimum amount of energy indicates the valence shell configuration of the atom in the LHS with which the electron is added has some additional stability. Here, it is nitrogen atom (N).

$N(g), + e^- \longrightarrow N^-(g) +$ EA (lesser amount)

$2p^3$, [1|1|1] or half-filled stability is present with nitrogen, so it is reductant to add an electron.

[$\because$ 7N:$1s^2 2s^2 2p^3$ or

$1s^2$ [1l] $2s^2$ [1l] $2p^3$ [1|1|1]

15. (c) $O^- + e^- \longrightarrow O^{2-}$, it is an endothermic process due to supply of energy (E) to overcome electrostatic repulsion between O^- ion (of high electron density) and the free electron to be added.

So, the net process becomes endothermic.

16. (a) $\overset{3}{X} \underset{|\Delta x| = 0.5}{\text{———}} \overset{3.5}{O} \underset{<|\Delta x| = 1.4}{\text{———}} \overset{2.1}{H}$

[More ionic]

$\rightleftharpoons X - \overset{\ominus}{O} + \overset{\oplus}{H}$

[Acidic solutions]

$\overset{1.72}{Y} - \overset{3.5}{O} - \overset{2.1}{H} \rightleftharpoons \overset{\oplus}{Y} + \overset{\ominus}{O}H$ $\quad O = \overset{\oplus}{\overset{*}{N}} \longrightarrow O$

[Basic solution] $\quad sp$

$|\Delta x| = 1.75 > |\Delta x| = 1.4$

[More ionic]

Higher the difference in electronegativity values (ΔX), more polar or more ionic will be the covalent bond in aqueous solution, and accordingly the nature will be (acidic or basic) of the solution.

17. (b) Electronegativity (EN) is a qualitative measure of the ability of an atom in a heteronuclear chemical bond to attract shared electrons to itself.

Electron affinity (EA) of an element is the amount of energy released when an electron is added to the valence shell of an isolated gaseous atom of an element to convert it into its gaseous uninegative ion.

18. (d) For oxides, down a group acidity decreases and along a period acidity increases with increase in non-metallic nature of the elements.

Period = 2 Gr1 Gr2 .... Gr15 Gr16

N_2O_5 Gr17

Period = 3 Na_2O MgO P_2O_5 SO_3 Cl_2O_7

19. (b) Period = 2 : Li Be B C N O F Ne

Period = 3 : Na Mg Al Si P S Cl Ar

Because of diagonal relationship of second period elements with third period elements of the periodic table, the second period elements are also called bridge elements.

20. (c) The order of electron affinity (EA) or negative electron gain enthalpy $(-\Delta_{eg} H)$ of group 17 elements (halogens) is

Cl > F > Br > I or F < Cl > Br > I

$Z = (17)\ (9)\ (35)\ (53)$

21. (1) Only group 17 consists such elements which are gases (F_2 and Cl_2), liquid (Br_2) and solids, (I_2, At_2 and Ts_2).

22. (1.25) For Al : $a = +3, |a| = 3$

Tl : $b = +1, |b| = 1$ (due to inert pair effect)

C : $c = +4$, or $-4\ |c| = 4$

F : $d = -1, |d| = 1$

$$\Rightarrow \frac{|c| + |d|}{|a| + |b|} = \frac{4 + 1}{3 + 1} = 1.25$$

23. (5) Using Slater's rule for *ns/np*-electron

$F(9e^-) \Rightarrow 1s^2\ 2s^2 2p^{(4+1)}$

$\sigma = (2 \times 0.85) + (7 - 1) \times 0.35 = 3.80$

= shielding constant

⇒ Effective nuclear charge of F($Z = 9$)

$Z^x = Z - \sigma = 9 - 3.80 = 5.20$ (for the 9th e^- of F) ≈ 5.00

24. (6) $\mu = q \cdot r$

$= (1.6023 \times 10^{-19}\ C)(1.2476 \times 10^{10} m)$

$= 1.99 \times 10^{-29}$ Cm

$1D = 3.336 \times 10^{30}$ Cm

$$\therefore \mu = \frac{1.99 \times 10^{-29}}{3.336 \times 10^{30}}$$

$= 5.99\ D \approx 6\ D$

25. (30) $I(g) + e^- \longrightarrow I^-(g)$ amount of energy released when 1 million or 10^6 atoms of I are converted into I^- is 4.9×10^{-13} J.

⇒ For 6.023×10^{23} number of I-atom, amount of energy released

$$= \frac{(4.9 \times 10^{-13}\ J)}{(10^6)} \times (6.023 \times 10^{23} mol^{-1})$$

$= 29.5127 \times 10^4\ J\ mol^{-1}$

$\approx 29.52 \times 10^4\ J\ mol^{-1}$

$= x \times 10^4\ J\ mol^{-1}$

$\therefore \quad x = 29.52$

≈ 30.00

26. (5.63) $\chi_{Mulliken} = 2.8 \times \chi_{Pauling}$

$= 2.8 \times 2.01 = 5.63$

27. (61.87) Using Haney-Smith equation,

% ionic nature $= 16|\Delta\chi| + 3.5(\Delta\chi)^2$

$= 16 \times 2.5 + 3.5 \times (2.5)^2$

$= 61.87$

28. (1.18) Using Stevenson Schomaker equation,

$d_{c-x} = r_c + r_x - 0.09|\Delta x|$

$$= \frac{d_{c-c}}{2} + \frac{dx - x}{2} - 0.09(3 - 2)$$

$$= \frac{1.54}{2} + \frac{1}{2} - 0.09 \times 1$$

$= 1.18$ Å

[∵ λ = bond length, r = covalent radius]

29. (3) In Pauling scale of electronegativity,

$\chi_C - \chi_H = 0.1018\sqrt{\Delta E}$

[∵ ΔE in kJ mol^{-1}]

Now, $\Delta E = E_{C-H} - (E_{C-C} \times E_{H-H})^{1/2}$

$= 412 - (348 \times 436)^{1/2}$

$= 22.47$ kJ mol^{-1}

$\Rightarrow \chi_C = \chi_H + 0.1018\sqrt{\Delta E}$

$= 2.1 + 0.1018 \times (22.47)^{1/2}$

$= 2.58 \approx 3.00$

30. (1.10) The Allred-Rochow scale of electronegativity is

$$\chi = 0.744 + 0.359 \times \frac{7}{r^2_{cov}\ (\text{in Å})}$$

$\Rightarrow \quad a = 0.744$ and $b = 0.359$

So, $(a + b) = 0.744 + 0.359$

$= 1.103 \simeq 1.10$

Qualifier 13

(General Principles and Processes of Isolation of Metals)

1. (b) **Carbon content (%)**

Wrought iron < steel < cast iron

Percentage of carbon

Wrought iron	Steel	Cast iron
(<0.2)	(0.2-1.5)	(2–3)
[Purest form of iron]		

2. (a) Type metal is an alloy of lead, tin and antimony. It is also called hot metal. It is used in mechanical casting for hand setting.

3. (b) Cinnabar (HgS) follows the given reactions to obtain mercury (Hg) as,

I. $\underset{\text{(Excess)}}{SnCl_2} + HgCl_2 \longrightarrow SnCl_4 + Hg \downarrow$

$[A = Sn, B = Hg]$

II. $2HgO \xrightarrow{>400^\circ C} 2Hg + O_2$

[**Note** Siderite is $FeCO_3$; malachite is $CuCO_3 . Cu(OH)_2$, horn silver is AgCl].

4. (c) In froth-floatation process during separation, NaCN is added to depress floatation of ZnS and FeS_2 to remove PbS exclusively. After complete removal of PbS, $CuSO_4$ is added to activate the floating character of ZnS. Thus, ZnS can also be removed in this way leaving behind FeS_2.

5. (b) Statement I is correct whereas all other statements are incorrect.

I. $\underset{\text{(Zinc blende)}}{2ZnS} + 3O_2 \longrightarrow 2ZnO + 2SO_2$

$ZnS + 2O_2 \longrightarrow ZnSO_4$.

So, zinc oxide and zinc sulphate are formed during roasting of ZnS.

II. Impurities gangue like As and Sb get removed as volatile As_2O_3 and Sb_2O_3.

$4M(s) + 3O_2(g) \longrightarrow 2M_2O_3(g) \uparrow$ $(M = As, Sb)$

III. Roasting is done to remove inorganic impurities like, P, As, Sb, C etc. as their volatile oxides.

IV. In roasting chemical composition of ore changes, e.g.

$\underset{\text{(Zinc blende type lattice)}}{ZnS} \longrightarrow \underset{\text{(Wurtzite type lattice)}}{ZnO}$

6. (a) As $\Delta_f H^\circ (CO_2, g) > \Delta_f H^\circ (CS_2, l)$,

smelting (carbon reduction) of metal oxide will be easier than that of metal sulphide.

7. (d) In Bessemer converter, conversion of sulphide ore of copper ($CuFeS_2$) into blister copper takes place in two steps.

Step I $CuFeS_2$ is heated in air till the part gets converted into copper oxide (Cu_2O).

Step II Copper oxide is then heated in absence of air so that Cu_2O reacts with unoxidised Cu_2S, i.e. auto-reduction takes place as,

$$2Cu_2O + Cu_2S \longrightarrow 6Cu + SO_2 \uparrow$$

8. (a) Zn and Fe can be extracted from their respective oxide ores by carbon reduction process (in blast furnace).

$$ZnO + C \xrightarrow{673\,K} Zn + CO$$

$$Fe_2O_3 + 3C \xrightarrow{1570\,K} 2Fe + 3CO$$

In McAurther- Forrest process, Ag and Au are extracted by leaching with NaCN (2-5%) in presence of air (O_2) followed by reduction with Zn.

(i) $4M(s) + 8NaCN(aq) + 2H_2O(l) + O_2(g) \longrightarrow \underset{\text{(Water soluble complex)}}{4Na[M(CN)_2](aq)} + 4NaOH(aq)$

(ii) $2Na[M(CN)_2(aq) + Zn(s) \longrightarrow 2M(s) \downarrow + Na_2[Zn(CN)_4](aq)$

where, M is Ag or Au

Anode mud is the colloidal form of Ag, Au etc., obtained around anode during electro-refining of crude (blister) copper.

Parkes process is a pyrometallurgical liquid. Liquid extraction process for removal of Ag and Au from Pb in presence of Zn.

9. (a) Near the mouth of blast furnace, which is also known as lower temperature zone (500–800 K), iron oxides get reduced to sponge iron by CO.

$Fe_2O_3 + 3CO \longrightarrow 2Fe + 3CO_2 \uparrow$

[Partially reduced]

10. (d) Liquation process is based on the principle that the metal and its impurity differ in their fusibility, where melting point of the pure metal is lower than its impurity. This method is used to purify metals like Sn, Pb, Bi, Hg etc.

11. (b) In sulphatising of zinc blende, incomplete roasting of ZnS takes place to give $ZnSO_4$.

Complete reactions are as follows

(i) $2ZnS + 3O_2 \longrightarrow 2ZnO + 2SO_2$

(ii) $ZnS + 2O_2 \longrightarrow ZnSO_4$

12. (a) $\underset{\text{(Alumina)}}{Al_2O_3} \rightleftharpoons 2Al^{3+} + 3O^{2-}$

(b) $\underset{\text{(Cryolite)}}{Na_3AlF_6}$ or $AlF_3.3NaF \rightleftharpoons 3Na^+ + Al^{3+} + 6F^-$

(c) $CaF_2 \rightleftharpoons Ca^{2+} + 2F^-$

Cathode reaction : $Al^{3+} + 3e^- \longrightarrow Al$

Anode reaction : (i) $2F^- - 2e^- \longrightarrow F_2$

(ii) $3F_2 + Al_2O_3 \longrightarrow 2AlF_3 + \frac{3}{2}O_2 \uparrow$

So, finally Al and O_2 are obtained. So, amount of Al_2O_3 decreases.

13. (b) In zone refining, the impurities of the crude metal (here, it is silicon) melt down and only the pure metal (Si) crystallises out. So, the melted form contains higher amount of impurities and lesser amount of silicon.

14. (a) Both statement I and statement II are correct.

Amalgamation process is used for extraction of gold, which occurs in native state. Finely divided auriferrous quartz is brought into contact with mercury which takes up gold forming an amalgam which on distillation yields pure gold (melting point of Au = 1065°C, Hg = −38.83°C). Due to the presence of filled $4f^{14}$ and $5d^{10}$ orbitals of poor shielding effect, there is weaker σs-s (6s–6s) type Hg-Hg- bond is present in liquid mercury.

15. (c) In Hoope's process for refining of Al (upto 99.9%) a cell is used which consists of three layers and get separated because of their difference in density. The composition of three layers is as follows :

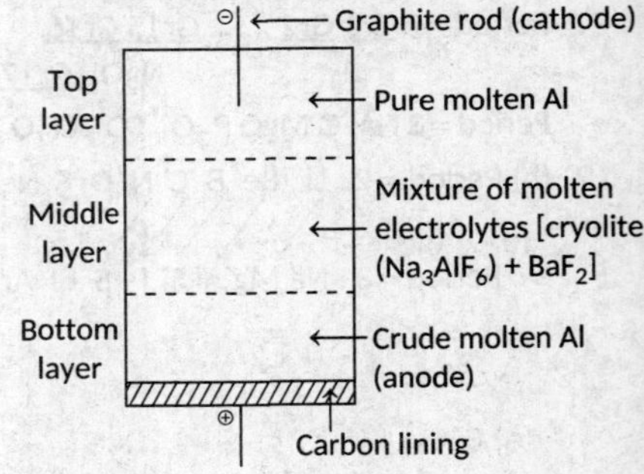

16. (b) $2M(s) + mO_2(g) \longrightarrow M_2O_m(s)$, $\Delta S < 0$

When the solid metal changes to liquid metal at its melting point, ΔS becomes more negative and so there is a sudden change in slope.

17. (d) $M(s) + O_2(g) \longrightarrow MO_2(s)$

$\Delta S<0$, so $\Delta G>0$ and ΔG *vs* temperature line curves upward

At the point P_1, melting of metals M occurs ($\Delta S > 0$)

$M(s) \longrightarrow M(l)$ and it indicates a positive slope.

At the point, P_2 boiling of liquid M takes place ($\Delta S>>0$)

$M(l) \longrightarrow M(g)$ and slope of the straight line beyond P_2 becomes more positive.

18. (d) For reduction of a metal oxide to metal, ΔG should be negative.

$$\Delta G = T\Delta S$$

(a) At $\Delta H = +ve$, $T\Delta S = +ve$

At low temp., $T\Delta S < \Delta H$

(b) At $\Delta H = +ve$, $T\Delta S = -ve$

At any temp.,

$\therefore \Delta G = \Delta H - T\Delta S = +ve$

(c) At $\Delta H = -ve$, $T\Delta S = -ve$

At high temp., $T\Delta S < \Delta H$

$\therefore \Delta G = +ve$

(d) At $\Delta H = -ve$, $T\Delta S = +ve$

At any temp.,

$\therefore \Delta G = \Delta H - T\Delta S = -ve$

Hence, the condition for the reduction of metal oxide to metal is $\Delta H = -$ ve, $T\Delta S = +$ve at any temperature.

19. (c) In Ellingham diagram, $\Delta G°$ is plotted against T and its interpretation can be done by using Gibbs equation,

$$\Delta G° = \Delta H° - T\Delta S°$$

where, the slope is $-\Delta S°$. So, negative slope of a straight line will be obtained, when $\Delta S°$ is positive.

(a) $Mg(s) + \frac{1}{2}O_2(g) \longrightarrow MgO(s)$

$$\Delta n_g = -\frac{1}{2}$$

$\Rightarrow \Delta S° < 0$

(b) $2\,Ag(s) + \frac{1}{2}O_2(g) \longrightarrow Ag_2O(s)$

$$\Delta n_g = -\frac{1}{2}$$

$\Rightarrow \Delta S° < 0$

(d) $CO(g) + \frac{1}{2}O_2(g) \longrightarrow CO_2(g)$

$$\Delta n_g = 1 - \left(1 + \frac{1}{2}\right) = -\frac{1}{2}$$

$\Rightarrow \Delta S° < 0$

But in (c) $C(s) + \frac{1}{2}O_2(g) \longrightarrow CO(g)$

$$\Delta n_g = +\frac{1}{2}$$

$\Rightarrow \Delta S° > 0$

So, for this reaction, the slope will be negative.

20. (c) $M(s) + \frac{1}{2}O_2(g) \longrightarrow MO(s)$, $\Delta n_g < 0$

$\Rightarrow \Delta S° < 0 \Rightarrow$ +ve slope

$C(s) + \frac{1}{2}O_2(g) \longrightarrow CO(g)$, $\Delta n_g > 0$

$\Rightarrow \Delta S° > 0 \Rightarrow$ −ve slope

So, the curve in option (b) is incorrect, because of the lines have +ve slope.

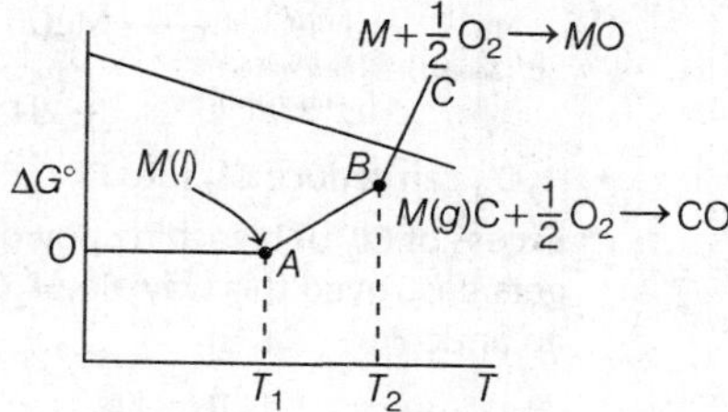

Option (c) is correct as,

T_1 = melting point of metal, M

T_2 = boiling point of metal, M

So, above temperature, T_2

M would be obtained in vapour phase

[Along, OA, M is in solid state.

AB M is in liquid state.

BC M is in vapour state].

21. (7.77) The alloy is composed of (Al + $CuAl_2$). 4.2% Cu in alloy means 100 g of alloy contains 4.2 g of Cu. So, 100 g of alloy contains,

$$(4.22Cu) \times \left(\frac{1\text{ mol Cu}}{63.5\text{g}}\right)\left(\frac{1\text{ mol }CuAl_2}{1\text{ mol Cu}}\right) \times \left(\frac{117.5\text{ g }CuAl_2}{1\text{mol }CuAl_2}\right) = 7.77\text{ g }CuAl_2$$

$\therefore$ % $CuAl_2 = 7.77$

22. (18) Beryl is $Be_3Al_2Si_6O_{18}$, a mineral of beryllium aluminium cyclosilicate.

$\therefore$ $m = 3, n = 6$

$\Rightarrow$ $mn = 3 \times 6 = 18$

23. (2) All these substances contain metal in their combined form. Pig iron and blister copper contain iron and copper in their elemental form respectively.

Copper matte $= Cu_2O + FeS$

Argentite $= Ag_2S$

Alumina $= Al_2O_3$

24. (1.10) In Portland cement,

$$\frac{\%CaO}{\%SiO_2 + \%Al_2O_3 + \%Al_2O_3} = 1.9 - 2.1$$

$\Rightarrow$ $a = 1.9, b = 2.1$

$\Rightarrow$ $\frac{b}{a} = \frac{2.1}{1.9} = 1.10$

25. (4) ZnO, PbO, SnO_2 and Fe_2O_3 can be reduced by carbon in carbon reduction method.

26. (+2) Complete ionic equation is as follows

$$\underset{\text{Galena}}{PbS} + \frac{3}{2}O_2 \longrightarrow \underset{\text{Lead oxide}}{PbO} + \underset{\text{Sulphur dioxide}}{SO_2}$$

Oxidation of S in PbS = −2

Oxidation of S in SO_2 = +4

So, the difference is +2.

27. (5.6) All group I metal carbonates are stable to heat except Li_2CO_3 which resembles group 2 metal carbonates in various properties.

Here, Li_2CO_3 only on heating liberates CO_2 gas.

$$Li_2CO_3(s) \xrightarrow{\Delta} Li_2O(s) + CO_2(s)$$

1 mol   1 mol

0.25 mol   0.25 mol

$\Rightarrow V_{CO_2} = 0.25\text{ mol} \times 22.4\text{ L/mol at STP}$

$= 5.6$ L at STP

$\therefore$ $x = 5.6$

28. (3) Among the given metals,

Zr, Ti can be refined by van-Arkel method

Ni is purified by Mond process

Both of the above two methods are vapour phase refining.

29. (6) (i) It is the Mond process,

$$Ni + 4CO \xrightarrow{330\text{ K}} Ni(CO)_4 \xrightarrow{470\text{K}} Ni + 4CO$$

$\therefore$ $x = 4$

(ii) It is the van Arkel method,

$$Zr + 2I_2 \xrightarrow{523\text{ K}} ZrI_4 \xrightarrow{1700\text{ K}} Zr + 2I_2$$

$\therefore$ $y = 2$

$\Rightarrow$ $(x + y) = 4 + 2 = 6$

30. (−1.60) The overall reaction of the Hall-Heroult process is,

$$2Al_2O_3 + 3C \longrightarrow 4Al + 3CO_2\uparrow$$

$$\Delta_r G° = 3\Delta_f G°(CO_2) - 2\Delta_f G°(Al_2O_3)$$

$[\because \Delta_f G°(\text{element}) = 0]$

$= 3 \times (-394) - 2 \times (-1520)$

$= 1858\text{ kJ} = 1858 \times 10^3\text{ J}$

No. of electrons involved in the reaction, $n = 12$

Now, $\Delta G° = -nFE°$

$$\Rightarrow \quad E° = -\frac{\Delta G°}{nF} = -\frac{1858 \times 1000}{12 \times 96500}$$

$= -1.60$ V

Qualifier 14
(Hydrogen)

1. (a) I. Boiling point values,
$P_2 = 20.89\text{ K} < D_2 = 23.67\text{ K} < T_2 = 25\text{ K}$

II. Bond dissociation enthalpy values,
$D_2 = 443.35\text{ kJ mol}^{-1} > P_2 = 435.88\text{ kJ mol}^{-1}$

III. Bond length values, $D_2 = P_2 = 74.14$ pm

IV. Because of the order (II), reactivity order of P_2 and D_2 with Cl_2 will be, $P_2 > D_2$, i.e.

$H_2 + Cl_2 \xrightarrow{\text{Rate}=r_1} 2HCl$ [$\because H_2$ is P_2]

$D_2 + Cl_2 \xrightarrow{\text{Rate}=r_2} 2DCl$

Here, $r_1 > r_2$

2. (d)

- Electrolysis of warm aqueous solution of $Ba(OH)_2$ by nickel electrodes gives product of very pure H_2 gas (purity > 99.95%) at the cathode.
- In water-gas shift reaction, water gas or *syn* gas ($CO + H_2$) reacts with steam.
- In presence of iron chromate ($FeCrO_4$) catalyst to give a satisfactory yield of H_2 gas.

$$CO + H_2 + H_2O(g) \xrightarrow[673\text{ K}]{FeCrO_4}$$

$$CO_2(g) + 2H_2(g) \xrightarrow[-CO_2]{NaAsO_3\text{ solution}} \underset{\text{(Pure)}}{H_2}$$

Sodium arsenite ($NaAsO_3$) removes CO_2 gas.

- In Bosch reaction, elemental carbon (graphite) is formed by reaction between CO_2 and H_2.

$$CO_2(g) + 2H_2(g) \xrightarrow[800\text{ K}]{Fe} C(s) + H_2O(g).$$

It is based on two-step mechanism whose rate determining step (slow) is just reverse to the water gas shift reaction.

(i) $CO_2 + 2H_2 \xrightarrow{\text{Slow}} CO + H_2O$

(ii) $CO + H_2 \xrightarrow{\text{Fast}} C + H_2O$

3. (a) *Ortho* and *para* hydrogen are the allotropes of hydrogen and they vary with their nuclear spin as,

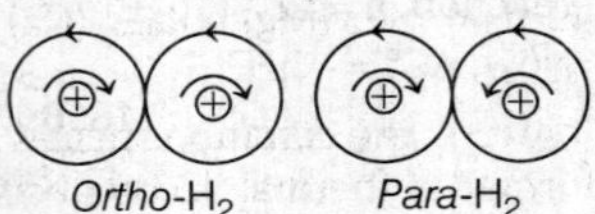

At 298 K; *ortho* $-H_2$: *para* $-H_2$ $= 75:25$

With increase in temperature, *ortho* % can be 80% (max). With decrease in temperature, *para* % increases upto almost 100% at 20 K.

4. (c) Correct match is A → (3), B → (1), C → (2), D → (4).

- Permutit (zeolite) can soften a permanent hard or temporary hard water into soft water.

$$\underset{[Z:\text{Zeolite}]}{Na_2Z} + \underset{\substack{[\text{Hard water}]\\[\text{permanent}]}}{MgCl_2} \longrightarrow Mg(Z)\downarrow + 2NaCl$$

- H_2O_2 can reduce Cl_2 into Cl^-. Excess of Cl_2 of bleaching powder gets destroyed this way. So, H_2O_2 is an antichlor.

$$\overset{(-1)}{H_2O_2} + \overset{(0)}{Cl_2} \longrightarrow 2H\overset{(-1)}{Cl} + \overset{(0)}{O_2}$$

Tritium (^3_1H) is radioactive $\left(\frac{n}{p} = \frac{2}{1} = 2\right)$ and it is β^--emitter.

$$^3_1H \longrightarrow {}^3_2He + {}^{\ 0}_{-1}e(\beta^-)$$

- H_2O is an amphoteric solvent, as it can act as an acid and a base as well.

$$\underset{[\text{Acid}]}{H_2O} + \underset{[\text{Base}]}{NH_3} \rightleftharpoons OH^- + NH_4^+$$

$$\underset{[\text{Base}]}{H_2O} + \underset{[\text{Acid}]}{H_2S} \rightleftharpoons H_3O^+ + HS^-$$

5. (b) Pure hydrogen (99.9%) can be prepared by electrolysis of water using platinum electrodes in the presence of small amount of acid or alkali.

$$2H_2O(l) \longrightarrow 2H_2(g) + O_2(g)$$

Hydrogen obtained through this process is used as an efficient fuel source.

6. (b) In ice cold condition, dichromate ($Cr_2O_7^{2-}$) and H_2O_2 react to form an unstable blue coloured compound, CrO_5, chromium peroxide which easily migrates in either medium to attain stability.

$$Cr_2O_7^{2-} + 2H^+ + 4H_2O_2 \longrightarrow \underset{\text{(Blue)}}{2CrO_5} + 5H_2O$$

7. (c) H_2O_2 acts as reducing agent in those reactions where it releases electrons.

So, in reactions II and IV, H_2O_2 releases two electrons. Hence, reactions II and IV are known as reduction reactions and H_2O_2 is a reducing agent in these reactions.

While, in reactions I and III, two electrons are being added, so I and III represents oxidation reactions.

8. (d) H_2O_2 can act both as an oxidant and reductant.

$$\overset{(-1)}{H_2O_2} + \overset{(-1)}{H_2O_2} \longrightarrow \overset{(-2)}{H_2O} + \overset{(0)}{O_2}$$
(I: $H_2O_2 \to H_2O$; II: $H_2O_2 \to O_2$)

In conversion-I, H_2O_2 acts as an oxidising agent, as itself is reduced into H_2O [decrease in oxidation number (ON) of O-atom ; −1 to −2].

In conversion-II, H_2O_2 is reduced into OH [as oxidation number (ON) decreases from −1 to −2]

In conversion III, H_2O is reduced into H_2O [as oxidation number (ON) decreases from −1 to −2].

Only in the reaction (given in option-d), one of the products in RHS is O_2. So, in this reaction H_2O_2 acts as a reducing agent.

9. (a) H_2O_2 is thermally unstable and readily gets disproportionated into H_2O and O_2.

$$2H_2\overset{(-1)}{O_2} \longrightarrow 2H_2\overset{(-2)}{O} + \overset{(0)}{O_2}$$

While producing H_2O [itself reduced, $O(-1) \to O(-2)$], H_2O_2 acts as an oxidising agent and O_2 is produced because of reducing nature of H_2O_2 [itself oxidises, $O(-1) \to O(0)$].

So, both of the statements, I and II are correct.

10. (d) Heavy water when reacts with $(CH_3)_3CMgCl$, it produces $(CH_3)_3CD$ and $Mg(OD)Cl$.

$$D_2O + (CH_3)_3CMgCl \longrightarrow (CH_3)_3CD + Mg(OD)Cl$$

11. (0.16) We know, x vol.

$$H_2O_2 = \frac{x}{5.6} N\ H_2O_2$$

$$\Rightarrow 0.9 \text{ vol. } H_2O_2 = \frac{0.9}{5.6} N\ H_2O_2 = 0.16\ N\ H_2O_2$$

12. (4) All the given statements are correct.

(a) $[Fe(CN)_6]^{4-} + 1/2\ H_2O_2 + H^+ \longrightarrow [Fe(CN)_6]^{3-} + H_2O$

(b) $\underset{\substack{\text{Sodium}\\\text{metaborate}}}{2NaBO_2} + 2H_2O_2 + 6H_2O \longrightarrow \underset{\text{Sodium peroxoborate}}{Na_2[B_2(O_2)_2(OH)_4]\cdot 6H_2O}$

(c) OH, C_2H_5

OH

2-ethyl anthraquinol

↓ Air (O_2)

O, C_2H_5 $+ H_2O_2$ Hydrogen peroxide

O

2-ethyl anthraquinone

(d) On decomposition of H_2O_2, and oxygen are formed.

$$H_2O_2 \longrightarrow H_2O + \frac{1}{2}O_2$$

13. (1.20) Here, the soluble complexes are $[Be(OH)_4]^{2-}$ and $[Al(OH)_4]^-$.

$\therefore x = a = 4,\ y = 2, b = 1$

$\Rightarrow \quad \dfrac{x+y}{a+b} = \dfrac{4+2}{4+1} = 1.20$

14. (10) Degree of hardness of water,

$$Q = \frac{w_{salt}\ (9/10^6\ \text{g of water})}{E_{salt}} \times 50\ \text{ppm}$$

$$= \frac{\frac{12\times10^{-3}\ \text{g}}{10^3\ \text{g}}\times10^6}{\frac{120}{2}} \times 50 = 10\ \text{ppm}$$

$[\because 1\text{L}\ H_2O = 1\ \text{kg}\ H_2O = 10^3\ \text{g}\ H_2O$

$E_{MgSO_4} = \dfrac{24+96}{2} = \dfrac{120}{2} = 60]$

15. (0.75) Sodium aluminosilicate is $Na_2[Al_2Si_2O_8 \cdot xH_2O]$ or $Na_2[Al_2Si_2O_8 \cdot x'H_2O]$.

$\Rightarrow \quad x = y = z = 2, x' = 8$

$\therefore \quad \dfrac{x+y+z}{x'} = \dfrac{2+2+2}{8} = 0.75$

Qualifier 15

s-Block Elements (Alkali and Alkaline Earth metals)

1. (d) Ionic hydrides $\Rightarrow CaH_2$ (hydrolith)

Covalent hydrides-electron-deficient $\Rightarrow BeH_2$, LiH and B_2H_6

—electron-precise $\Rightarrow CH_4$

—electron - rich $\Rightarrow \ddot{N}H_3$

Metallic or non-stoichiometric or Interstitial hydride $\Rightarrow LaH_{2.87}$

NOTE (i) Be and Li are *s*-block metals, but BeH_2 and LiH are covalent hydrides ($\bar{e}$-deficient) because of higher degree of covalency by Be^{2+} and Li^+ ions.

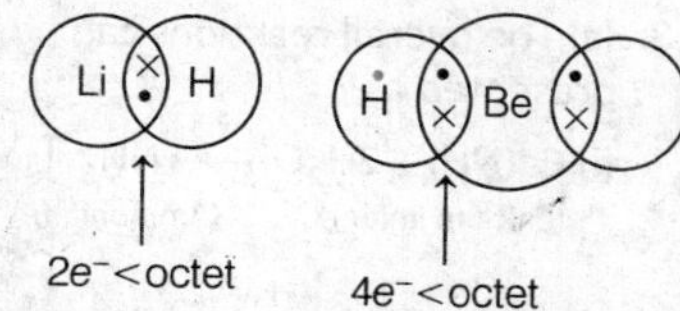

(ii) In B_2H_6, B is sp^3-hybridised but still electron-deficient due to the presence of two 3C—2*e* (bridge bonds) bonds.

H H H B B H H H

3C—2e⁻ bond

2. (a) The thermal stability of alkali metal (group 1) hydrides depends on *M*—H bond strength. H-atom is smaller in size. The size of the alkali metals increases down the group, i.e. from Li to Cs. Hence, LiH bond is most stable, while CsH is least stable. So, the order of their thermal stability is, LiH > NaH > KH > RbH > CsH.

3. (c)
- The strength of alkali metal hydroxides increases down the group with increase in their metallic character.
- With decrease in size of hydrated alkali metal ions in water, their electrical conductivity increases down the group.
- As size of halide increases from F to I, lattice energy decreases. Hence, melting points follow the order : *M*F > *M*Cl > *M*Br > *M*I.
- Lithium halides have lower melting points as compared to the corresponding halides of sodium.

4. (d) Highest positive values of sublimation enthalpy ($\Delta_{sub}H°$) and ionisation enthalpy ($\Delta_i H°$) of Li get compensated by highest negative value of enthalpy of hydration ($\Delta_{hyd}H°$) of Li^+ ion because of its highest charge density in group 1.

$Li(s) \longrightarrow Li\ (g),\ \Delta_{sub}H° = x_1$ (say)

$Li(g) \xrightarrow{-e^-(g)} Li^+(g),\ \Delta_i H° = x_2$ (say)

$Li^+(g) + e^-(g) \xrightarrow{H_2O(l)} Li^+(aq),$
$+ e^-(aq),\ \Delta_{hyd}H° = -x_3$ (say)

$Li(s) \xrightarrow{H_2O(l)} Li^+(aq) + \bar{e}\ (aq.), \Delta H$

where,

$\Delta H = (x_1 + x_2 - x_3) < 0$ or – ve value

$[\because |(x_1 + x_2)| < |x_3|]$.

5. (a) During the preparation of washing soda ($Na_2CO_3 \cdot 10H_2O$) from brine solution (NaCl), Sodium bicarbonate ($NaHCO_3$) is collected as residue which (crystalline form) on heating gives Na_2CO_3.

(i) $NaCl(aq) + NH_3(g) + CO_2(g) + H_2O(l) \downarrow \longrightarrow NaHCO_3(s) + NH_4Cl$

(ii) $2NaHCO_3(s) \xrightarrow{\Delta} Na_2CO_3(s) + CO_2 \uparrow (g) + H_2O \uparrow (g)$

So, preparation of Na_2CO_3 is possible because of lower solubility of $NaHCO_3$ in water which is 96 gL^{-1} at 293 K. Whereas, $KHCO_3$ is fairly soluble in water (solubility = 224 gL^{-1} at 293 K), so $KHCO_3$ cannot be collected as residue so that it cannot be heated to give K_2CO_3.

6. (b) Both Zn and Al on reaction with NaOH solution (separately) form soluble salts, sodium zincate (Na_2ZnO_2) and sodium aluminate ($NaAlO_2$) respectively with evolution of H_2 gas in both of the reactions.

$Zn(s) + 2NaOH(aq) \longrightarrow Na_2ZnO_2(aq) + H_2 \uparrow (g)$

$2Al(s) + 2NaOH(aq) + 2H_2O(l) \longrightarrow 2NaAlO_2(aq) + 3H_2(g)$

So, the statement I is true but the statement II is false.

7. (c) Calgon is sodium hexameta phosphate, $(NaPO_3)_6$ or $Na_2[Na_4(PO_3)_6]$, from which $4Na^+$ ions of the coordination sphere (cage) get replaced by $2Mg^{2+}$ ions to give the precipitate.

$Na_2[Na_4(PO_3)_6] + \underset{\text{(Permanent hard water)}}{2MgCl_2} \longrightarrow \underset{\text{(Precipitate)}}{Na_2[Mg_2(PO_3)_6] \downarrow} + 4NaCl$

8. (a) Statement I is correct. It is true that alkaline earth metals (group 2) are harder and denser than alkali metals (group 1), but alkali metals are more electropositive than alkaline earth metals. The correct order of IE (Na) and IE (Mg) is as follows IE_1 (Na) < IE_1 (Mg) but IE_2 (Na) > IE_2 (Mg)

9. (d) Here, the common species (*X*) formed in thermal decomposition reactions in oxygen (O_2), which is a colourless paramagnetic gas (due to the presence of one unpaired electron in each of $\pi^*_{2p_x}$ and $\pi^*_{2p_y}$ MOs).

$$4\,LiNO_3(s) \xrightarrow{\Delta} 2Li_2O(s) + 4NO_2(g) + O_2(g)(X)$$

$$2NaNO_3(s) \xrightarrow{\Delta} 2NaNO_2(s) + O_2(g)(X)$$

$$2Mg(NO_3)_2(s) \xrightarrow{\Delta} 2MgO(s) + 2NO_2(g) + 3O_2(g)(X)$$

10. (b) These are group 2 metal hydrides made of the common anion H^- and alkaline earth metal ions M^{2+}.

The order of size of M^{2+} type ions is, $Ba^{2+} > Ca^{2+} > Mg^2 > Be^{2+}$.

So, according to Fajans' rule, degree of covaleny is maximum in BeH_2 and degree of ionic nature (which increases down the group) is maximum in BaH_2.

11. (d) Due to the increase in ionic character down the group, lattice energy (U) of group 2 metal sulphates ($\overset{(II)}{M}SO_4$) also increases down the group. An ionic compound will be water soluble only when, enthalpy of solution, $|\Delta_{sol}H°| > |\Delta°_u H|$.

$|\Delta_{sol}H°|$ of Be^{2+} is maximum because of its highest value of $|\Delta_{hyd}H°|$ (hydration enthalpy). As a result, their order of solubility in water becomes

$BeSO_4 > MgSO_4 > CaSO_4 > SrSO_4 > BaSO_4$.

12. (a) Charge/Radius ratio of Be^{2+} is nearly same as that of Al^{3+}.

Hence, Be resembles Al in some cases and they maintain diagonal relationship in the periodic table.

In excess of alkali, $Be(OH)_2$ and $Al(OH)_3$ become soluble due to formation of $[Be(OH)_4]^{2-}$ and $[Al(OH)_4]^-$ respectively.

$$Be(OH)_2(s) + 2OH^-(aq) \longrightarrow [Be(OH)_4]^{2-}(aq)$$

$$Al(OH)_3(s) + OH^-(aq) \longrightarrow [Al(OH)_4]^-(aq)$$

In vapour phase, $BeCl_2$ and $AlCl_3$ forms dimers

$(BeCl_2)_2 \Rightarrow$ Cl—Be(μ-Cl)₂Be—Cl

$(AlCl_3)_2 \Rightarrow$ $Cl_2Al(\mu\text{-}Cl)_2AlCl_2$

Be^{2+} and Al^{3+} can form complexes with excess of F^-.

$$Be^{2+} + 4F^- \longrightarrow [BeF_4]^{2-}$$

$$Al^{3+} + 6F^- \longrightarrow [AlF_6]^{3-}$$

13. (c) The overall reactions can be presented as,

(i) $\underset{\text{(Calcium imide)}}{Ca(NH)} + 2H_2O \longrightarrow \underset{\text{(Ammonia)(P)}}{NH_3}\uparrow + Ca(OH)_2$

(ii) $\underset{(P)}{2NH_3} + \underset{\text{(Bleaching powder)}}{3CaOCl_2} \xrightarrow{[O]} \underset{(Q)}{N_2}\uparrow + 3CaCl_2 + 3H_2O$

(iii) $\underset{(Q)}{N_2} + 3Mg \xrightarrow{\Delta} \underset{\text{(White Solid) (R)}}{Mg_3N_2}$

(iv) $\underset{(R)}{Mg_3N_2} + 6H_2O \xrightarrow{\Delta} \underset{(P)}{2NH_3} + 3Mg(OH)_2$

14. (10) In liquid ammonia solution, coordination number of alkali and alkaline metal ions in ammoniated form are 4 and 6 respectively.

$\therefore \quad x = 4, a = 6$

$\Rightarrow \quad (x + a) = 4 + 6 = 10$

15. (4) Li of group 1 and Sr of group 2 give crimson red colour to the flame.

$\Rightarrow \quad x = 2$

Be and Mg of group 2 do not impart colour to the flame in the flame test because of their higher IE values.

$\Rightarrow \quad y = 2$

$\therefore \quad (xy) = 2 \times 2 = 4$

16. (0.75)

$$CaSO_4 \cdot 2H_2O \xrightarrow{120°C} CaSO_4 \cdot \frac{1}{2}H_2O + 1\frac{1}{2}H_2O$$

(Hemihydrate of $CaSO_4$) [Plaster of Paris] ($\because x = 1.5$)

$$CaSO_4 \cdot 2H_2O \xrightarrow{>120°C} CaSO_4 + 2H_2O$$

(Dead burnt plaster) ($\therefore y = 2$)

$$\Rightarrow \quad (x \div y) = \frac{1.5}{2} = 0.75$$

17. (4.71) A typical 70 kg adult person contains, 90 g of Na, 170 g of K, 25 g of Mg and 1200 g of Ca.

So, $x = 90, y = 170, a = 25, b = 1200$

$$\Rightarrow \quad \frac{a+b}{x+y} = \frac{25+1200}{90+170} = 4.71$$

Qualifier 16

(p-block Elements)

1. (c) Atomic size of Ga should be larger than Al but the order is reverse, which is due to poor shielding of $3d^{10}$ electrons of Ga-atom. As a result, effective nuclear charge of the nucleus can reach to the valence $4s^2 4p^1$ electrons of Ga-atom easily.

Hence, due to addition of a new shell in comparison to Al-atom, atomic radius of Ga (135 pm) is slightly smaller than that of Al (143 pm).

2. (c) The given reactions can be shown as,

(i) $2Al + N_2 \xrightarrow{\Delta} \underset{(P)}{2AlN}$,

$\underset{(P)}{AlN} + 3H_2O \xrightarrow{\Delta} \underset{(Q)}{Al(OH)_3} + \underset{(R)}{NH_3}$

(ii) $2Al + \underset{(R)}{2NH_3} \xrightarrow{\Delta} \underset{(P)}{2AlN} + \underset{(S)}{3H_2}$

So, P : Aluminium nitride, AlN;

Q : Aluminium hydroxide, $Al(OH)_3$;

R : Ammonia, NH_3;

S : Hydrogen, H_2

3. (c)
- B and N_2 are chemically less active and they react only at very high temperature (900°-1000°C) to give boron nitride, BN.
- Al, Ga and In are stable in their +3 oxidation states. So, they can form tri-iodine (MI_3).
- Due to inert pair effect, Tl shows only +1 oxidation state. TlI_3 in aqueous solution dissociates into Tl^+ and I_3^- (a polyhalide ion).
- During formation of M_2O_3 type of oxides by a group 13 elements, only Ga is superficially oxidised by O_2 to give Ga_2O_3.

4. (b) Al_2Cl_6 undergoes stronger dipole-dipole interactions with solvent H_2O molecules.

Hence, solubility of Al_2Cl_6 in water is developed which is further favoured due to higher hydration enthalpy of Al^{3+}.

Complete reaction is as follows

$$Al_2Cl_6(g) + 12H_2O(l) \longrightarrow 2[Al(H_2O)_6]^{3+}(aq) + 6Cl^-(aq)$$

5. (b)
- There are two types of bonds in diborane
  (i) $3C—2e^-$ bond
  (ii) $2C—2e^-$ bond

  As in $3C—2e^-$ bond, $2e^-$s are shared by 2H and 1B atom.

Thus, this B—H bond is larger than B—H bond (2C—2*e*). The two bond lengths are 119 pm (terminal bond) and 134 pm (bridge bond).

(diagram: B_2H_6 structure — H–B–H terminal angle 120°, bridge angle 97°, bridge bond 134 pm, terminal bond 119 pm)

Hence, statement I is false.

- H—B—H (terminal) bond angle is 120°.
- H—B—H (bridge) bond angle is 97°.

Thus, statement II is true.

6. (a) In the reaction condition, $(CH_3)_3SiCl$ will be hydrolysed to give $(CH_3)_3Si$—OH and its —OH group will now combine with the propagating part of the silicon, i.e. —Si—O—H unit. It can be shown as,

$$(CH_3)_3Si—Cl \xrightarrow[-HCl]{H_2O} (CH_3)_3Si—O—H$$

H—O—Si—O—Si—O— (Active silicon) $\xrightarrow{-H_2O}$ $CH_3—Si(CH_3)_2—O—Si—O—Si—O—$

This terminal of the silicon get blocked

7. (a) Pb is a heavy metal, whereas F is a smaller sized atom. So, thermodynamic stability of PbF_4 is lower, $\Delta_f H°(PbF_4) = 113\ \text{kJ mol}^{-1}$ (positive value). Under suitable conditions, PbF_4 can supply F_2.

The *d*-orbitals in Pb have poor shielding thus, *s*-orbital electrons are strongly attracted toward nucleus. Hence, Pb^{2+} is more stable than Pb^{4+}. So, PbF_2 is more stable than PbF_4.

8. (b) In $(CH_3)_3SiOH$, there is a tendency to form $d\pi(Si) \leftarrow p\pi(O)$ back bond and for which the O-atom becomes more electronegative as it acquires a +ve charge. So, the —OH group of $(CH_3)_3SiOH$ can release $H^{\oplus}$ easily and showing its acidic property.

$$(CH_3)_3Si—\ddot{O}—H \longrightarrow (CH_3)_3\overset{\ominus}{Si} \leftarrow \overset{\oplus}{O}—H \rightleftharpoons (CH_3)_3\overset{\ominus}{Si}=O + H^{\oplus}$$

($3d^0$, $2p^2$)

As carbon atom does not have vacant *d*-orbital, it cannot form $d\pi$-$p\pi$ bond.

So, tertiary butyl alcohol is less active.

9. (d) With increase in size of the central atom of the hydride, its molecular size also increases.

So, larger BiH_3 and SbH_3 molecules are associated by van der Waals' force of attraction in liquid state, whereas ammonia molecules are associated by intermolecular hydrogen bonding in that state.

So, the order of their boiling points is

$$\underbrace{BiH_3 > SbH_3}_{\text{van der Waals' force}} > \underbrace{NH_3}_{\text{Weaker H-bonding}} > AsH_3 > PH_3$$

10. (d) Co-existence of +1 and +3 oxidation states of Ga is observed in solid $GaCl_3$ or Ga_2Cl_4 as, $\overset{[I]}{[Ga]}^+ \overset{[III]}{[GaCl_4]}^-$

Ionic compositions of crystalline PCl_5 and ICl_3 are

$$2PCl_5(s) \equiv P_2Cl_{10}(s) \longrightarrow [PCl_4]^+[PCl_6]^-$$

$$2\,ICl_3(s) \equiv I_2Cl_6(s) \longrightarrow [ICl_2]^+[ICl_4]^-$$

11. (a)
- Pure HNO_3 is a deep yellow or yellowish brown liquid as it contains dissolved NO_2.
- $[H_2SO_4(98.3\%) + H_2O(1.7\%)]$ is a higher boiling (338°C) azeotrope (positive deviation from Raoult's law).
- $\underset{\substack{\text{(Conc. } H_2SO_4)\\ \text{Bronsted acid}}}{H^+} + \underset{\substack{\text{(Conc. } HNO_3)\\ \text{Bronsted base}}}{H\ddot{O}—NO_2} \longrightarrow H_2O^{\oplus}—NO_2 \xrightarrow{-H_2O} \underset{\text{(Nitronium ion)}}{\overset{\oplus}{NO_2}}$
- Covalents nitrates are less stable to heat and on heating, it decomposes completely into metal, NO_2 and O_2. e.g.

$$2AgNO_3 \xrightarrow{\Delta} 2Ag + 2NO_2 + O_2$$

Whereas, ionic nitrates are more stable to heat and decomposes to metal nitrite and O_2 only. e.g.

$$2KNO_3 \xrightarrow{\Delta} 2KNO_2 + O_2$$

12. (d)
- The reaction of white phosphorus (P_4) and thionyl chloride ($SOCl_2$) produce phosphorus trichloride (PCl_3), SO_2 and dimer of sulphur monochloride, $(SCl)_2$ or S_2Cl_2.

$$P_4 + 8SOCl_2 \longrightarrow 4PCl_3 + 4SO_2 + 2S_2Cl_2$$

- White P_4 on reaction with sulphuryl chloride (SO_2Cl_2) yields phosphorus pentachloride (PCl_5) and SO_2 gas only.

$$P_4 + 10SO_2Cl_2 \longrightarrow 4PCl_5 + 10SO_2$$

13. (d) S—S linkages are present in dithionous acid ($H_2S_2O_4$), dithionic acid ($H_2S_2O_6$) and polythionic acid ($H_2S_nO_6$), but it is absent in pyrosulphuric acid ($H_2S_2O_7$). Their structures are as follows

HO—S(=O)—S(=O)—OH ($H_2S_2O_4$)

HO—S(=O)₂—S(=O)₂—OH ($H_2S_2O_6$)

HO—S(=O)₂—[S—S]$_{n-2}$—S(=O)₂—OH ($H_2S_nO_6$)

HO—S(=O)₂—O—S(=O)₂—OH ($H_2S_2O_7$)

14. (b) (I) $\underset{[A]}{SO_3^{2-}}(aq.) + 2H^+(aq) \longrightarrow \underset{[B]}{SO_2}(g) + H_2O(l)$

(II) $\underset{[B]}{\overset{(+4)}{3SO_2}}(g) + \underset{\text{(Orange coloured)}}{K_2\overset{(+6)}{Cr_2}O_7}(s) + \underset{(+6)}{H_2SO_4}(aq.) \longrightarrow K_2SO_4(aq.) + \underset{\text{[C] (Green solution)}}{\overset{(+3)}{Cr_2}(SO_4)_3}(aq.) + H_2O(l)$

A : Sulphite salt (SO_3^{2-})

B : Sulphur dioxide gas (SO_2), which reduces dichromate solution

C : Chromium sulphate, $Cr_2(SO_4)_3$

15. (c) • In group 17, oxidising power of halogens and acid strength of hydrogen halides (HX) decrease down the group. So, the order given in options (a) and (d) are correct.

• Among oxoacids of chlorine, HOCl or Cl(OH) is thermally least stable, i.e. strongest oxidising agent.

$$\underset{\text{(Hypochlorous acid)}}{HOCl} \xrightarrow{298K} HCl + [O]$$

Hence, the order of their oxidising power is :

$$HOCl > HClO_2 > HClO_3 > HClO_4$$
or or or or
$$Cl(OH) > OCl(OH) > O_2Cl(OH) > O_3Cl(OH)$$

• But, the correct order of bond energy or bond dissociation enthalpy ($\Delta_{diss}H°$) of halogens is

$$Cl_2 > Br_2 > F_2 > I_2$$

$\Delta_{diss}H°$ (kJ/mol) 242.6 192.8 158.8 151.1

→ Steric repulsion between larger I-atoms make the I—I weakest.

→ Electrostatic repulsion between two F-atoms of high electron density weakens the F—F bond.

16. (a) In halogen family (group 17), the order of

(i) oxidising power : $F_2 > Cl_2 > Br_2 > I_2$

(ii) reducing power : $Cl_2 < Br_2 < I_2$ [$\because F_2$ does not show reducing property]

So, in reaction (a) I_2 cannot oxidise Cl^- to Cl_2. Hence, the reaction is non-spontaneous, $\Delta G° > 0$.

$$2K\overset{(-1)}{Cl} + \overset{(0)}{I_2} \longrightarrow 2K\overset{(-1)}{I} + \overset{(0)}{Cl_2}$$

But in reaction (b), Br_2 can oxidise I^- to I_2 and it becomes feasible, i.e. $\Delta G° < 0$.

$$2Na\overset{(-1)}{I} + \overset{(0)}{Br_2} \longrightarrow 2Na\overset{(-1)}{Br} + \overset{(0)}{I_2}$$

Among halogen, I_2 is the strongest reducing agent and reaction (c) is also spontaneous, i.e. $\Delta G° < 0$.

$$2K\overset{(+5)}{ClO_3} + \overset{(0)}{I_2} \longrightarrow 2K\overset{(+5)}{IO_3} + \overset{(0)}{Cl_2}$$

17. (c) The reactions can be computed as,

(i) $2F_2 + \underset{\text{(Cold, dilute)}}{2NaOH} \longrightarrow \underset{(A)}{2NaF} + \underset{(B)}{OF_2} + H_2O$

(ii) $2Cl_2 + \underset{\text{(Dry slaked lime)}}{2Ca(OH)_2} \longrightarrow \underset{(C)}{Ca(OCl)_2} + \underset{(D)}{CaCl_2} + 2H_2O$

18. (a)

$$\underset{\text{Lewis base}}{[Ph_4As]^{\oplus}:\ddot{Cl}:^{\ominus}} + \underset{\text{Lewis acid}}{\overset{3d^0}{:\ddot{Cl}}—Cl} \longrightarrow [Ph_4As]^{\oplus}[Cl—\ddot{Cl}—Cl]^{\ominus}$$

Vacant 3d-orbital

or $[Ph_4As]^{\oplus}[Cl_3]^-$

In this reaction, Cl_2 acts as a Lewis acid, because it accepts lone pair of electrons from $Cl^{\ominus}$ of $[Ph_4As][Cl]$ and forms a trichloride ion, Cl_3^-.

19. (c) Any π-bond present in any compound made by group 17 elements or Xe of group 18, is always of *dπ-pπ* type. While making a π-bond, unpairing of *np*-electrons and finally that of ns^2 electrons takes place into the next available vacant *d*-orbitals.

So, in excited state, all unpaired electrons present in *p*- and *s*-orbitals will make σ and *pπ-pπ* bonds but unpaired electrons of *d*-orbitals will make *dπ-pπ* bonds only.

As halogens and Xe have np^5 and np^6 configurations, unpairing of *p*-electrons will lead to form *dπ-pπ* only.

20. (b) • $IE_1(Xe \rightarrow Xe^+ + e^-) = 1170 \text{ kJ mol}^{-1}$

$IE_1(O_2 \rightarrow O_2^+ + e^-) = 1175 \text{ kJ mol}^{-1}$

So, IE values of Xe and O_2 are nearly equal.

• $XeOF_2$ is a T-shaped molecule.

⟶ Xe (sp^3d)
⟶ Geometry : Trigonal bipyramidal

• XeF_2 is a linear molecule.

⟶ Xe (sp^3d)
⟶ Geometry : Trigonal bipyramidal
⟶ Shape : Linear
Equatorial position

• XeF_4 is a square planar or pseudo octahedral molecule.

⟶ Xe (sp^3d^2)
⟶ Geometry : Octahedral
⟶ Shape : Square planar or pseudo octahedral

21. (5) The bases weaker than TlOH are, $Tl(OH)_3$, $Ga(OH)_3$, $In(OH)_3$, $B(OH)_3$ and NH_4OH.

22. (256) Borax ($Na_2B_4O_7.10H_2O$) is structurally represented as $Na_2[B_4O_5(OH)_4].8H_2O$ or

⇒ No. of BO_4 and BO_3 units $= 2 = x = y$

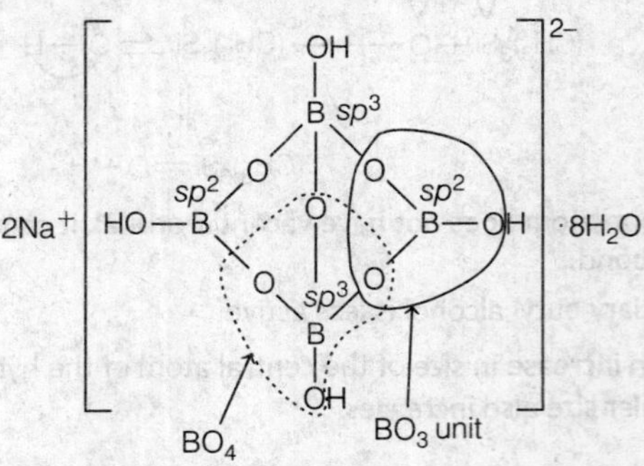

sp^3 boron $= sp^2$ boron $= 2 = a = b$

$\Rightarrow (ab)^{xy} = (2 \times 2)^{2\times 2} = 4^4 = 256$

23. (4) Disubstituted borazine is $B_3N_3H_4X_2$.

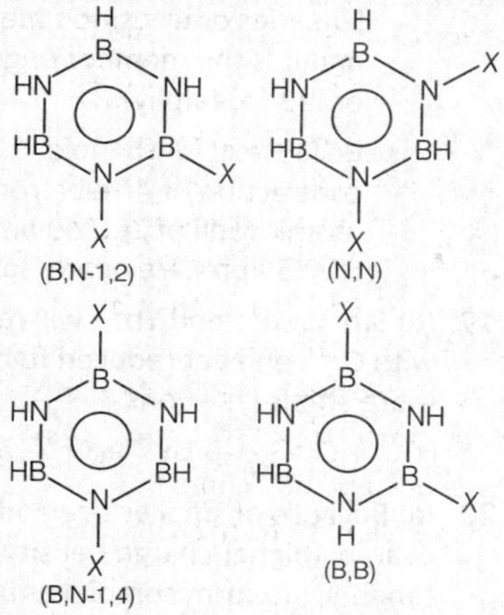

(B,N-1,2) (N,N) (B,N-1,4) (B,B)

24. (62) Boric acid (H_3BO_3) is a weak monobasic acid in water.

$$H_3BO_3 + H_2O \rightleftharpoons [B(OH)_4]^{\ominus} + H^{\oplus}$$

(basicity or *n*-factor = 1)

$$E_{B(OH)_3} = \frac{\text{Molar mass}}{n\text{-factor}} = \frac{3\times1 + 11 + 3\times16}{1} = 62$$

25. (0.60) C_{60} contains 12 pentagons and 20 hexagons.

$$\Rightarrow \quad p = 12, h = 20 \Rightarrow \frac{p}{h} = \frac{12}{20} = 0.6$$

26. (1.50)

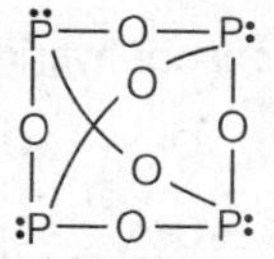

$[P_4O_6]$

P—O—P bonds = 6 = *x*

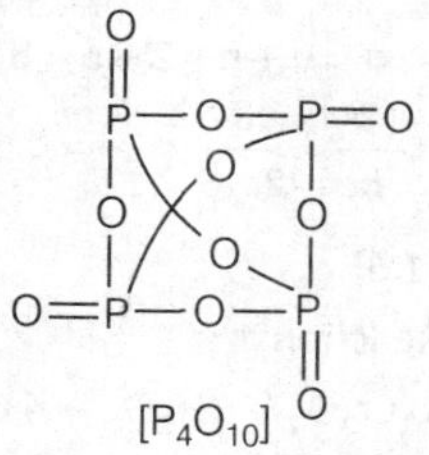

$[P_4O_{10}]$

P—O—P bonds = 6 = *y*

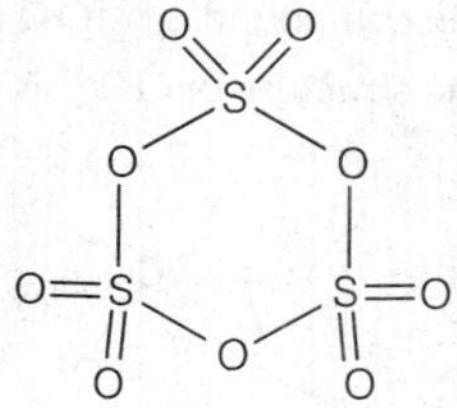

$[S_3O_9]$

S—O—S bonds = 3 = *z*

$$\Rightarrow \quad \frac{y+z}{x} = \frac{6+3}{6} = 1.5$$

27. (6) Except O_2 and CO_2, all others react with PCl_5 to give $POCl_3$.

$$PCl_5 + H_2O \longrightarrow POCl_3 + 2HCl$$
$$PCl_5 + SO_2 \longrightarrow POCl_3 + SOCl_2$$
$$2PCl_5 + H_2SO_4 \longrightarrow 2POCl_3 + SO_2Cl_2 + 2HCl$$
$$6PCl_5 + P_4O_{10} \longrightarrow 10POCl_3$$
$$PCl_5 + C_2H_5OH \longrightarrow POCl_3 + C_2H_5Cl + HCl$$
$$PCl_5 + CH_3COOH \longrightarrow POCl_3 + CH_3COCl + HCl$$

28. (16) H_2SO_4 crystallises at −190°C is $H_2SO_4.2H_2O$ (white). Chlorine water crystallises at 0°C is $Cl_2.8H_2O$ (greenish-yellow)

So, $n = 2, m = 8 \Rightarrow mn = 8\times2 = 16$

29. (16) Interhalogens are known with the formulae as *AB*, AB_3, AB_5 and AB_7.

Thus, values of *n* can be 1, 3, 5 and 7.

∴ The sum of possible *n* values

$$= 1 + 3 + 5 + 7 = 16$$

30. (25.50)

(i) $\underset{(1:0.5)}{Xe + F_2} \xrightarrow[1\text{ bar}]{Ni/400°C} XeF_2(s)$

$\Rightarrow x = 0.5$

(ii) $\underset{(1:5)}{Xe + 2F_2} \xrightarrow[7\text{ bar}]{Ni/600°C} XeF_4(s)$

$\Rightarrow y = 5$

(iii) $\underset{(1:20)}{Xe + 3F_2} \xrightarrow[60\text{-}70\text{ bar}]{Ni/300°C} XeF_6(s)$

$\Rightarrow z = 20$

$\Rightarrow (x + y + z) = (0.5 + 5 + 20) = 25.5$

Qualifier 17

(*d*-and *f*-Block Elements)

1. (b) The colour shown by a substance is complementary to the colour absorbed by the substance. Complementary colours of red and blue/green are blue/green and red respectively.
2. (d) • Complexation of Cu^+ ion with H_2O molecules is not favourable as it does not have vacant *d*-orbitals (it has $3d^{10}$ configuration) to accommodate lone pair of electrons of H_2O.
   • Cu^+ ion disproportionates in aqueous medium as,
   $2Cu^+ \longrightarrow Cu^{2+} + Cu$,
   $E° = 0.18$ V
   Positive $E°$ value of the reaction supports spontaneity of the reaction ($\Delta G° < 0$).
3. (d) • Because of the smaller energy gap between $(n-1)d$ and *ns* sub-shells, transition metals can show variable oxidation states with a minimum value of (+2) except few metals like Ag, Au etc., which also show (+1) oxidation state.
   • V^{2+} and Mn^{2+} are very weak reducing agents because of their more negative $E°_{M^{2+}/M}$ values.
   $E°_{V^{2+}/V} = E°_{Mn^{2+}/Mn} = -1.18$ V
   • Atomic radii (in pm) of 3*d*-series metals show the trend as,
   $\underset{(164)}{Sc} > \underset{(147)}{Ti} > \underset{(135)}{V} > \underset{(129)}{Cr} < \underset{(137)}{Mn} > \underset{(126)}{Fe} \simeq \underset{(125)}{Co} = \underset{(125)}{Ni} < \underset{(128)}{Cu} < \underset{(137)}{Zn}$
4. (d) • $_{44}Ru$ (Ruthenium) and $_{76}Os$ of d^6-family (group 8) can show +8 oxidation state, which is the maximum value of oxidation state that can be achieved, e.g. OsO_4.
   • In the first row (3*d*) transition series, manganese, $_{25}Mn$ can show +7 (maximum in 3*d*-series) oxidation state because of its $3d^5 4s^2$ configuration.
   • Tungsten ($_{74}W$) has the highest melting point (MP 3400°C) among transition metals.
   • Promethium ($_{59}Pm$) is the only radioactive lanthanoid.
   So, the correct matching is
   [A→(3), B→(1), C→(4), D→(5)], i.e. option (d).
5. (b) There is a space around the Os atom for four bonded oxygen atoms but not for eight F or Cl atoms.
   Eight F or Cl atoms around Os have steric hindrance which contributes to the unstability of the complex.
6. (d) Group-3 or IIIB (d^1-family) transition metals do not show variable oxidation states. They show +3 oxidation state only. These elements are $_{21}Sc(3d^1)$, $_{39}Y(4d^1)$, $_{57}La(5d^1)$ and $_{89}Ac(6d^1)$.
   The stable oxidation state of lanthanides is +3. So, if the oxidation state of ion is < +3 then, it gets oxidised to +3. And if oxidation state of ion is > +3 then, it gets inducted to +3.

7. (b) In $K_2Cr_2O_7$, Cr (metal, *M*) is present in its highest oxidation state +6 and Cr(+6) becomes able to accept the π^*-electron pair or charge from the ligand (*L*), i.e. O-atom. It takes place ($L \rightarrow M$) in visible region.

Hence, $K_2Cr_2O_7$ is intense orange coloured even in the absence of *d*-electron(s) ($Cr^{+6}: 3d^0 4s^0$).

8. (c) $\underset{\substack{\text{(Yellow)}\\ \text{[Potassium}\\ \text{chromate]}}}{\overset{(+6)}{2K_2CrO_4}} + H_2SO_4 \longrightarrow \underset{\substack{\text{(Orange)}\\ \text{[Potassium}\\ \text{dichromate]}}}{\overset{(+6)}{K_2Cr_2O_7}} + K_2SO_4 + H_2O$

So, statement I is correct, but statement II is incorrect, because the colour change in the reaction is not due to change in oxidation state of Cr, as it remains unchanged (+6).

9. (a) A paramagnetic substance is attracted towards the magnetic field. To put the beam back, more weight to be added on the balancing beam.

Hence, the apparent mass becomes greater than the actual mass. So, the value of the given ratio will be >1.

10. (b)
- As the inner orbitals get filled from Sc to Cu, effective nuclear charge on outer $e^{\ominus}$s increases. So, molar volume decreases. As density is inversely proportional to volume, hence, density increases.
- The enthalpy of atomisation drops at manganese because of half-filled stable electronic configuration. Thus, this statement is incorrect.
- On moving down a group, the the valence shell increases by 1. Hence, electrons have less effective nuclear charge and are loosely bound. Thus, higher oxidation states increases as $e^{\ominus}$s are easy to loose.
- Melting point first increases and then decreases. This is because from Sc to Cr, no. of unpaired $e^{\ominus}$s are increasing but from Fe to Zn, no. of unpaired $e^{\ominus}$s are decreasing.

11. (c) It is a condensation reaction because this reaction leads to the removal of H_2O.

$$2CrO_4^{2-} + 2H^+ \rightleftharpoons Cr_2O_7^{2-} + H_2O$$

12. (b) **Alkaline medium**

$$\overset{(+7)}{2MnO_4^-} + 2OH^- \longrightarrow \underset{\text{(Manganate ion)}}{\overset{(+6)}{2MnO_4^{2-}}} + H_2O + [O]$$

Acidic medium

$$\overset{(+7)}{MnO_4^-} + 8H^+ + 5e^- \longrightarrow Mn^{2+} + 4H_2O$$

13. (d) When MnO_2 (pyrolusite) is fused with KOH in presence of air (O_2), it is oxidised to give a dark green coloured compound, potassium manganate (K_2MnO_4).

$$\overset{(+4)}{2MnO_2} + 4KOH + O_2 \longrightarrow \overset{(+6)}{2K_2MnO_4} + 2H_2O$$

This reaction is the first step of two step reactions for the preparation of $KMnO_4$ from MnO_2.

14. (c) Amongst lanthanoids, $_{63}$Eu has abnormally higher atomic radius (199 pm). This may be attributed to $4f^7 5d^0 6s^2$ electronic configuration where 4*f*-subshell is half-filled and 6*s*-subshell/orbital is fully-filled.

15. (b) With decrease in ionic size of Ln^{3+}, effective nuclear charge increases. Tendency to donate electron(s) decreases and hence, basicity decreases.

16. (c) $\begin{bmatrix} Ce^{3+} \rightarrow 4f^1, Eu^{3+} \rightarrow 4f^6 \\ n = 1, 14 - n = 13 \neq 6 \end{bmatrix}$,

$\begin{bmatrix} Pr^{3+} \rightarrow 4f^2, Gd^{3+} \rightarrow 4f^7 \\ n = 2, 14 - n = 12 \neq 7 \end{bmatrix}$

$\begin{bmatrix} Sm^{3+} \rightarrow 4f^5, Dy^{3+} \rightarrow 4f^9 \\ n = 3, 14 - n = 9\,(4f^9) \end{bmatrix}$,

$\begin{bmatrix} Lu^{3+} \rightarrow 4f^{14}, Tm^{3+} \rightarrow 14f^{12} \\ n = 12, 14 - n = 2 \neq 14 \end{bmatrix}$

The ions having $(4f)^n$ and $(4f)^{14-n}$ electrons have the same colour. Hence, $Sm^{3+}(4f^5)$ and $Dy^{3+}(4f^9)$ have same colour.

17. (d) Lanthanoid hydroxides, $Ln(OH)_3$ are more basic than transition metal hydroxides like $Fe(OH)_3$ and *p*-block metal hydroxides like $Al(OH)_3$ but less basic than *s*-block metal hydroxides like $Sr(OH)_2$, $Ca(OH)_2$ and NaOH.

18. (a)
- With decrease in ionic nature of the metal hydroxides, their basicity also decreases from $La(OH)_3$ to $Ce(OH)_3$ and least basicity is observed with $Lu(OH)_3$.
- Lanthanum ($_{57}$La) belongs to 5*d*-series of transition metals and it is the member of group 3 or IIIB (d^1 family).
- Because of lanthanoid contraction of 4*f*-electrons atomic radii of Zr (160 pm) and Hf (159 pm) are nearly same.

19. (d) Sm^{3+}, Eu^{3+} and Yb^{3+} will react with Cr^{2+} and get reduced to their more stable Ln^{2+} ions.

$$Ln^{3+} + Cr^{2+} \longrightarrow Ln^{2+} + Cr^{3+}, \Delta G^\circ < 0$$

20. (a) Because of smaller size and higher charge, (higher charge density) the tendency to form complexes by actinoid metal ions is greater than that of lanthanoids.

21. (31.60)

$$\overset{+7}{KMnO_4} \xrightarrow{H^{\oplus}} Mn^{2+} + K^+ + H_2O$$

n-factor $= (7 - 2) = 5$

$$\Rightarrow E_{KMnO_4} = \frac{39 + 55 + 4 \times 16}{5} = 31.6$$

22. (0.67)

$Cr_2O_7^{2-} \Rightarrow$ [structure: O–Cr(=O)(=O)–O–Cr(=O)(=O)–O with resonance arrows]

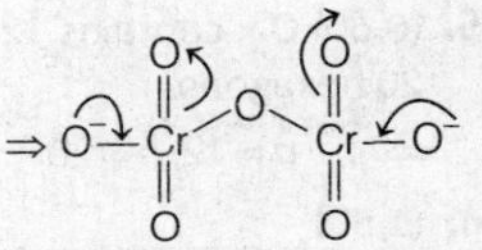

its resonance hybrid structure is,

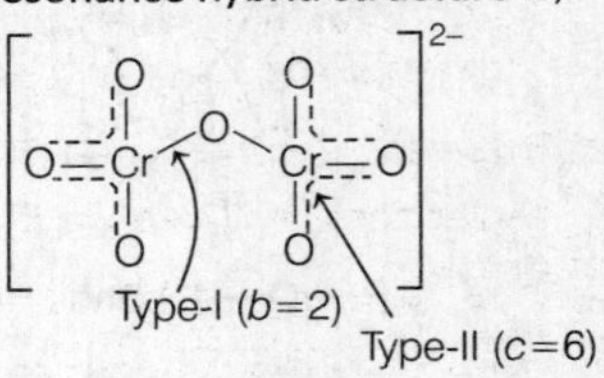

[structure: $[O_3Cr\text{–}O\text{–}CrO_3]^{2-}$ with Type-I (b=2) and Type-II (c=6) bonds marked]

Type-I (b=2)

Type-II (c=6)

$$\Rightarrow a = b + c = 2 + 6 = 8$$

$$\Rightarrow \frac{a}{bc} = \frac{8}{2 \times 6} = \frac{8}{12} = 0.67$$

23. (1.6)

Reaction is ;

$$K_2Cr_2O_7 + 7H_2O_2 + 4KOH \longrightarrow 2K_3CrO_8 + 9H_2O$$

The compound is $K_3[CrO_8]$.

The structure of CrO_8^{3-} is

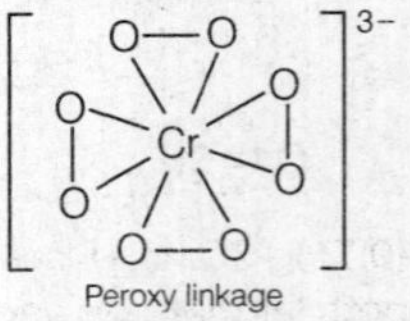

[structure: $[Cr(O_2)_4]^{3-}$]

Peroxy linkage

$$\Rightarrow a = 8 \text{ and } b + 8(-1) = -3$$

$$\Rightarrow b = +5$$

So, the value of $\frac{a}{b} = \frac{8}{5} = 1.6$

24. (7) $HNO_3, FeCl_3, O_3, Cl_2, H_2O_2, CuSO_4$, acidified $K_2Cr_2O_7$ can oxidise aqueous iodide to iodine. Alkaline $KMnO_4$ oxidise *aq.* iodide to $IO_3^{\ominus}$.

$Na_2S_2O_3$ is a strong reducing agent which on reaction with I_2, produces I^-.

$$2Na_2S_2O_3 + I_2 \longrightarrow 2NaI + Na_2S_4O_6$$

$\therefore$ No reaction takes place between $Na_2S_2O_3$ and of NaI.

25. (14.7) The reaction is

$$4\overset{(+6)(-2)}{K_2Cr_2O_7} \longrightarrow 4K_2\overset{(+6)}{Cr}O_4 + 2\overset{(+3)}{Cr_2}O_3 + 3\overset{(0)}{O_2}\uparrow$$

- *n*-factor of O-atom (reducing agent) $= [(0-(-2)\times 7)] = 14 = (nf)_O$
- (*n*-factor of Cr-atom (oxidising agent) $= [(6-3)\times 2] = 6 = (nf)_{Cr}$

$$E_{K_2Cr_2O_7} = \frac{\text{(Molar mass) } K_2Cr_2O_7}{(nf)_{Cr} + (nf)_O}$$

$$= \frac{2\times 39 + 2\times 52 + 7\times 16}{6+14} = \frac{294}{20} = 14.7$$

26. (6) All of the given pairs (six) have nearly same radii.

For the pairs : Reasons for same radii (approx.) are:

[(Zr, Hf) (Zr^{4+}, Hf^{4+}) (Nb, Ta) (Nb^{3+}, Ta^{3+})]

$\Rightarrow$ Lanthanoid contraction

[(Cr, Mn) (Mn, Fe)] $\Rightarrow$ Influence of $3d^5$ electrons in determining Z_{eff} of nucleus.

27. (8.94) ${}_{64}Gd^{2+} \Rightarrow [Xe]4f^7 5d^1$ which has 8 unpaired electrons, $n = 7+1 = 8$

$$\Rightarrow \mu = \sqrt{n(n+2)} \text{ BM} = \sqrt{8(8+2)} \text{ BM} = 8.94 \text{ BM}$$

28. (1.25) $x = 5$ $(Cr^{2+}, Sm^{2+}, Eu^{2+}, Tm^{2+}$ and Yb^{2+}, which get oxidised to their +3 state)

$y = 4$ $(Ce^{4+}, Pr^{4+}, Tb^{4+}$ and Dy^{4+} which get reduced to their +3 state)

The value of $\frac{x}{y} = \frac{5}{4} = 1.25$

29. (78.57) All actinoids (5*f*-family) are radioactive, so, $y = 14$. In actinoid family, ${}_{93}Np$ to ${}_{103}Lr$ are transuranic $(Z > 92)$ elements.

$\therefore \quad x = 11$

$\Rightarrow \quad \frac{x}{y} = \frac{11}{14} = 78.57\times 10^{-2} = a\times 10^{-2}$

$\therefore \quad a = 78.57$

30. (0.75) +3 and +4 are the common oxidation states of both lanthanoids and actinoids, where +3 oxidation state is more frequent to both.

$\therefore x = 3, y = 4$ and $\frac{x}{y} = \frac{3}{4} = 0.75$

Qualifier 18

(Coordination Compounds)

1. (c) A bidentate ligand can substitute two monodentate ligands which are *cis* to each other. Since, the complex is not responding to $AgNO_3$, the Br^- ions is in coordination sphere.

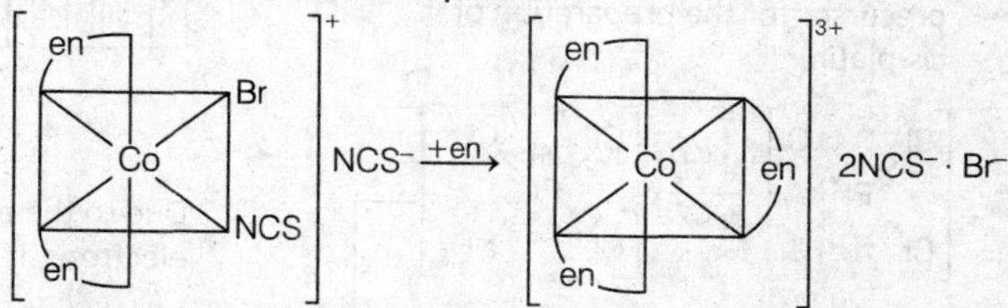

2. (d) Glycinate ion is not ambidentate ligand. It is a bidentate ligand. So, cannot exhibit linkage isomerism.

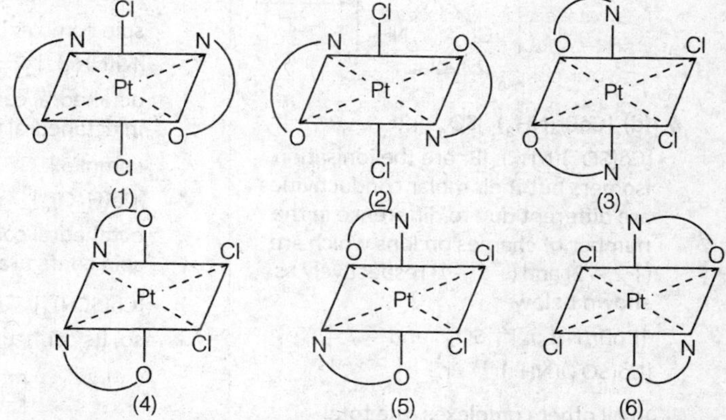

Structures (1), (2), (3), (4) and (5) are geometrical isomers, whereas (5) and (6) are optical isomers.

3. (a) The IUPAC name of $K_2[Cr(CN)_2O_2(O)_2(NH_3)]$ is potassium amminedicyanidodioxoperoxo chromate (VI).

4. (c) The geometrical isomers are

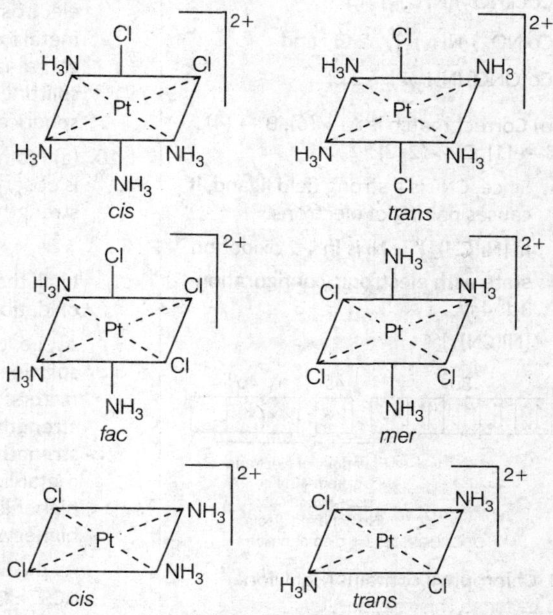

5. (a) *cis*-platin is used as an anti-tumor agent. Its formula is *cis*-$Pt(NH_3)_2Cl_2$.

It is prepared from tetrachloroplatinate(II). Chloride ligand has greater *trans* effect than ammonia ligand.

That's why $PtCl_4^{2-}$ is used as the precursor for the preparation of *cis*-platin.

$[PtCl_4]^{2-} \xrightarrow[-Cl^-]{NH_3} [PtCl_3(NH_3)]^- \xrightarrow[-Cl^-]{NH_3} [PtCl_2(NH_3)_2]$

cis-platin

6. (d) $[CoBr(NH_3)_5]SO_4$ and $[Co(SO_4)(NH_3)_5]Br$ are the ionisation isomers but their molar conductivities are different due to difference in the number of charges on ions which are $(+2, -2)$ and $(+1, -1)$ respectively as shown below

$[CoBr(NH_3)_5]^{2+} SO_4^{2-}$ and

$[Co(SO_4)(NH_3)_5]^+ Br^-$

In all other complexes, the total charges are same for both complexes.

$[PtCl_2(NH_3)_4]^{2+} 2Br^-$ and

$[PtBr_2(NH_3)_4]^{2+} 2Cl^-$

$[CoCl_2(NH_3)_4]^+ NO_2^-$ and

$[CoCl(NO_2)(NH_3)_4]^+ Cl^-$

$[Co(NO_2)(NH_3)_5]^{2+} 2Cl^-$ and

$[Co(ONO)(NH_3)_5]^{2+} 2Cl^-$

7. (a) Correct match is A → (6), B → (4), C → (1), D → (2, 3)

A. Since, CN^- is a strong field ligand, it causes pairing of electrons.

In $[Ni(CN)_4]^{2-}$, Ni is in +2 oxidation state with electronic configuration $3d^8 4s^0$.

$[Ni(CN)_4]^{2-} =$

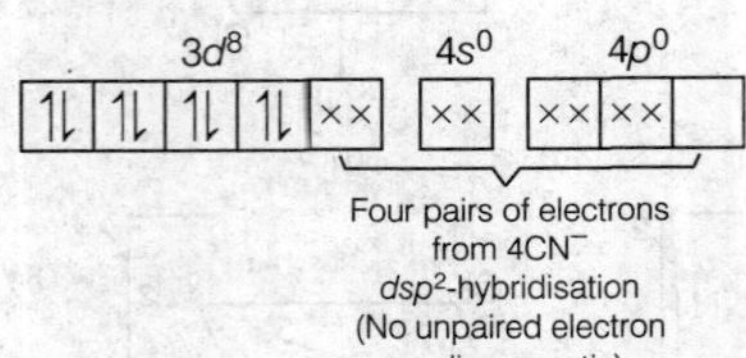

B. Chlorophyll contains Mg^{2+} ion.

C. Ziegler-Natta catalyst is $Ti^{4+} + (C_2H_5)_3Al$.

D. $[NiCl_4]^{2-}$

In this case, Cl^- is a weak field ligand, so it does not cause pairing.

$[Ni(Cl)_4]^{2-} =$

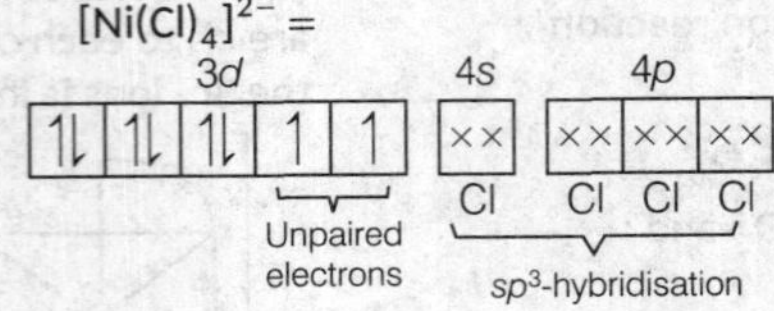

Due to the presence of unpaired electrons, it is paramagnetic.

8. (d) $[NiCl_4]^{2-} \Rightarrow Ni^{2+}(3d^8)$; it is a tetrahedral complex and gets splitted in tetrahedral field as $e_{2g}^4 t_{2g}^4$ (high spin complex).

$[Ni(NH_3)_6]^{2+} \Rightarrow Ni^{2+}(3d^8)$; it is an octahedral complex and gets splitted in octahedral field as $t_{2g}^6 e_g^2$ (high spin complex).

$[Co(H_2O)_6]^{3+} \Rightarrow Co^{3+}(3d^6)$; it is an octahedral complex and it has low spin configuration $t_{2g}^4 e_g^2$.

$[Co(SCN)_4]^{2-}$ is tetrahedral complex, so, its configuration is $e_g^4 t_{2g}^3$.

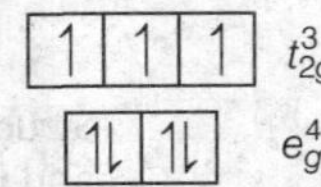

9. (a) Statement (a) is incorrect, whereas all other statements are correct.

Crystal field theory is based mainly on electrostatic interaction between metal ion and ligands. In six and four coordinate complexes, *d*-orbital splitting takes place due to the loss of spherically symmetric field.

10. (a) From the spectrochemical series, it is observed that the ligand field strength of the given ligands runs as

$$NCS^- > Cl^- > Br^-$$

In all the complexes, Co shows +2 oxidation state.

Δ_t, i.e. tetrahedral ligand-field splitting parameter depends on many factors. One of them is the ligand field strength. Greater is the ligand-field strength, more will be the metal-ligand interaction causing higher ligand field splitting and hence, higher Δ_t.

As the ligand field strength runs : $NCS^- > Cl^- > Br^-$, Δ_t will follow the following order : III > I > II.

11. (a) The spin-only magnetic moment is given by $\mu = \sqrt{[n(n+2)]}$ BM, where, *n* is the number of unpaired electron(s).

According to the question, the magnetic moment of octahedral Co(+2) complex is 4.0 BM.

Hence, $\sqrt{[n(n+2)]} = 4 \Rightarrow n = 3$

Hence, in octahedral Co(+2) complex has only three unpaired electrons. This condition is satisfied by the electronic configurations denoted by options-(a), (c) and (d).

But, in case of an octahedral complex after the half-filling of t_{2g} and e_g-orbitals, electrons will fill up fully first the lower energy t_{2g}-orbital. This rule is maintained by only option (a).

Hence, the electronic configuration of the complex is : $t_{2g}^5 e_g^2$.

12. (b) When a weak ligand (H_2O) is substituted by a strong ligand (NH_3), Δ_o increases. So, radiation having a shorter wavelength will be absorbed. But the splitting is not very much large. Thus, it will absorb at 580 nm.

13. (c) $[Co(H_2O)_6]^{2+}$ and $[CoCl_4]^{2-}$ are symmetrically octahedral and tetrahedral complexes respectively. Both are d^7 systems.

The electronic configuration of Co^{2+} in the complexes are $t_{2g}^5 e_g^2$ and $e_g^4 t_{2g}^3$. Hence, *d-d* transition is Laporte forbidden.

But, due to vibronic coupling, Laporte selection rule become partly relaxed. Hence *d-d* transition may become partly allowed and hence, the complex become intense colour. But, vibronic coupling does not occur in symmetrical octahedral complex due to the presence of centre of symmetry. That's why it will appear as light pink colour.

But, due to the absence of centre of inversion in the tetrahedral complex, here vibronic coupling will occur which will make the *d-d* transition partly allowed. Hence, the tetrahedral complex will appear as intense blue colour.

14. (a) All of the given complexes are octahedral complexes. Greater is the energy gap between t_{2g} and

e_g levels, smaller will be the absorption (λ_{max}). The energy gap depends on extent of interaction between the metal and ligand. Greater is the interaction, higher will be the energy gap and hence, lower will be the absorption.

Greater is field strength of a ligand, more close it can go to the metal causing greater interaction. Hence, the energy gap will be increased and the λ_{max} will be decreased.

The order of ligand field strength of the given ligands :

$CN^- > en > H_2O > F^-$.

Hence, order of the energy gap of given complexes will be :

$[Cr(CN)_6]^{3+} > [Cr(en)_3]^{3+} > [Cr(H_2O)_6]^{3+} > [CrF_6]^{3-}$

Hence, the order of the absorption (λ_{max}) will be

$[CrF_6]^{3+} > [Cr(H_2O)_6]^{3+} > [Cr(en)_3]^{3+} > [Cr(CN)_6]^{3-}$.

15. (a) In haemoglobin, Fe is present in + 2 oxidation state. When it is bound with oxygen, oxy-haemoglobin is formed.

Hence, the colour changes from blue to red. The oxidation state also changes from + 2 to + 3. Fe^{3+} has d^5 electronic configuration. Due to higher positive charge on metal, pairing of electrons will occur causing the formation of low spin complex. Hence, electron can be transferred from t_{2g}-orbital to e_g-orbital. As a result of *d-d* transition, the complex will become red in colour.

16. (c) **Statement I** The oxidation state of nickel is +2 in both complexes, $[NiCl_4]^{2-}$ and $[Ni(CN)_4]^{2-}$. Thus, the primary valencies of these complexes are same.

Statement II CN^- is a strong field ligand whereas Cl^- is a weak field ligand. Thus, crystal field splitting for $[Ni(CN)_4]^{2-}$ is higher/more than $[NiCl_4]^{2-}$. Hence, $[Ni(CN)_4]^{2-}$ absorbs more energy or lower wavelength than $[NiCl_4]^{2-}$. So, statement II is also incorrect.

17. (b) Strong Jahn-Teller distortion in an octahedral field is observed due to the unsymmetrical occupancy of electrons in the e_g level.

Weak Jahn-Teller distortion in an octahedral field is observed due to the unsymmetrical occupancy of electrons in the t_{2g} level.

The *d*-electronic configuration of high spin d^2, d^4, d^5 systems and low spin d^6 system are as follows

High spin $d^2 : t_{2g}^2\, e_g^0$; high spin $d^4 : t_{2g}^3 e_g^1$, high spin $d^5 : t_{2g}^3\, e_g^2$; low spin $d^6 : t_{2g}^6 e_g^0$

The high spin d^4 system has unsymmetrically filled e_g-orbital. Hence, in case of octahedral high spin d^4 system, strong Jahn-Teller distortion will be observed.

18. (d) In all the complexes, the number of lone pairs available for back bonding in Cr-atom is 3. CH_3NH_2 ligand is not a π-acceptor ligand. So, as the number of CH_3NH_2 increases the number of lone pairs available for each CO molecule from metal atom increases and hence the *M*—C bond strength increases.

19. (d) Statement (d) is incorrect, whereas all other statements are correct. $[Cd(CN)_4]^{2-}$ is less stable than $[Cu(CN)_4]^{3-}$ and these properties get reflected in qualitative analysis to distinguish between Cu^+ and Cd^{2+}.

20. (a) In $[Ni(H_2O)_6]^{2+}$, NH_3 can attack at six coordination sites, but as the number of H_2O molecules substituted increases the probability of the coordination sites for the attack decreases. So, K_f values decreases.

21. (6) Since, the effective atomic number of molybdenum must be 54 and its atomic number is 42, 12 electrons (54 – 42) must be donated by the CO molecules. Hence, each six CO molecules must donate a pair of electrons, resulting in the formula $Mo(CO)_6$.

22. (16) The complex *bis*(dimethyl glyoximato) nickel (II) is

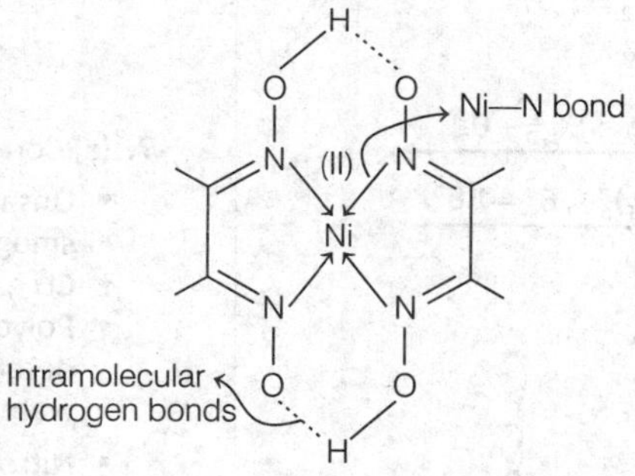

No. of Ni—N bonds, $x = 4$

No. of Ni—O bonds, $y = 0$

No. of intramolecular hydrogen bonds, $z = 2$

$\therefore \quad (z - y)^x = (2 - 0)^4 = 2^4 = 16$

23. (8120) In $[Ti(H_2O)_6]^{3+}$ complex, Ti is present in + 3 oxidation state. Hence, the Ti is a one electron system. In case of an octahedral complex with d^1 electronic configuration the electron occupy the t_{2g}-orbital. Hence, the crystal field stabilisation energy

$= 0.4\, \Delta_o = 0.4 \times 20300 = 8120\ cm^{-1}$.

24. (1260) For a d^4 ion in low-spin state has configuration, $t_{2g}^4 e_g^0$ ($n = 4$).

The net crystal field stabilisation energy is

$CFSE = -1.6\, \Delta_o + P$

$= -1.6(13{,}900\ cm^{-1}) + 23500\ cm^{-1}$

$= +\,1260\ cm^{-1}$

25. (1.46) The enthalpy of hydration of Cr^{2+} is $0.6\, \Delta_o$ higher for this d^4 weak field ion than it would be in the absence of CFSE. Thus,

$-0.6\, \Delta_o = (-\,460\ kcal/mol)$
$-(-\,435\ kcal/mol) = -25\ kcal/mol$

$$\Delta_o = \left(\frac{-\,25\ kcal/mol}{-\,0.6}\right)\left(\frac{350\ cm^{-1}}{1\ kcal/mol}\right)$$

$= 14{,}583.3\ cm^{-1}$

$= \underline{1.46} \times 10^4\ cm^{-1}$

$= \underline{x} \times 10^4\ cm^{-1}$

So, the value of x is 1.46.

26. (21000)

$Cr = 3d^5 4s^1, Cr^{2+} = 3d^4$ (i.e. $t_{2g}^3\, e_g^1$)

$CFSE = (-\,0.4 \times 3 + 0.6)\, \Delta_o$

$= -\,0.6\, \Delta_o$

$-\,0.6\, \Delta_o = (-\,460) - (-\,424)$

$= -\,36\ kcal\ mol^{-1}$

$$\Delta_o = \frac{36}{0.6} = 60\ kcal\ mol^{-1}$$

$= 60 \times 350\ cm^{-1}$

$= 21000\ cm^{-1}$

27. (–2) Crystal field splitting energy,

$\Delta E = h\nu$

$$\Delta E = \frac{hc}{\lambda}$$

$$= \frac{6.62 \times 10^{-34} \times 3 \times 10^8}{544 \times 10^{-9}}$$

$\Delta E = 3.65 \times 10^{-19}$ J per ion

$$\Delta E = 3.65 \times 10^{-19} \times 6.022 \times 10^{+23} \text{ J mol}^{-1}$$
$$\Delta E = 219.79 \text{ kJ mol}^{-1}$$
$$\Delta E = 21979 \times 10^{-2} \text{ kJ mol}^{-1}$$

So, x is -2.

28. (7.72) $Cu^{2+} + 4NH_3 \rightleftharpoons [Cu(NH_3)_4]^{2+}$;

$$K_s = \frac{[Cu(NH_3)_4^{2+}]}{[Cu^{2+}][NH_3]^4} = 1 \times 10^{12}$$

The reaction between Cu^{2+} and NH_3 goes almost for completion, as is suggested by the large magnitude of the formation constant. Thus, the equilibrium concentration of the tetraamine complex is approximately 0.10 M.

- If x mol/L Cu^{2+} ion still remains uncoordinated, the concentration of the complex will be $0.10 - x$.
- With the formation of 0.10 M $Cu(NH_3)_4^{2+}$, which requires 4 mol NH_3 per mol complex, the ammonia concentration becomes $1.00 - 4(0.10) = 0.60$ M. (Dissociation of the complex provides $4x$ mol NH_3 per x mol Cu^{2+}). In summary

Species	Initial concentration	Used up	Produced	Equilibrium concentration
$[Cu^{2+}]$	0.10	$0.10 - x$		x
$[NH_3]$	1.00	$4(0.10 - x)$		$0.60 + 4x \cong 0.60$
$[Cu(NH_3)_4^{2+}]$	0.00		$0.10 - x$	$0.10 - x \cong 0.10$

$$\Rightarrow \quad K_s = \frac{0.10}{x(0.60)^4} = 1 \times 10^{12} \Rightarrow x = 7.72 \times 10^{-13} \text{ M}$$

29. (0.39) K_f (formation constant) $= \dfrac{[Fe(H_2O)_5NCS]^{2+}}{[Fe(H_2O)_6]^{3+}[SCN^-]}$

$$= \frac{7.3 \times 10^{-5}}{(0.2)(10^{-3} - 7.3 \times 10^{-5})} = 0.39$$

30. (35) The overall formation constant of $[Co(NH_3)_6]^{2+}$ ion in aqueous solution is 10^5 and the standard potentials for the reaction of Co^{3+} *(aq.)* and $[Co(NH_3)_6]^{3+}$ *(aq.)* are as follows

$$Co^{3+}(aq.) + e^- \rightleftharpoons Co^{2+}(aq.);\ E^\circ = -1.9 \text{ V}$$
$$[Co(NH_3)_6]^{3+}(aq.) + e^- \rightleftharpoons [Co(NH_3)_6]^{2+}(aq.);\ E^\circ = +0.1 \text{ V}$$

Calculation of the overall formation constant of the $[Co(NH_3)_6]^{2+}$.

$$Co^{2+} + 6NH_3 \rightleftharpoons [Co(NH_3)_6]^{2+};\ k_1 = 10^5$$
$$Co^{+3} + 6NH_3 \rightleftharpoons [Co(NH_3)_6]^{+3};\ k_2 = ?$$
$$Co^{+3} + e^- \longrightarrow Co^{+2};\ E^\circ = 1.9 \text{ V}$$
$$Co(NH_3)_6^{2+} \longrightarrow Co(NH_3)_6^{+3} + e^-;\ E^\circ = -0.1$$
$$Co^{3+} + Co(NH_3)_6^{2+} \rightleftharpoons Co^{+2} + Co(NH_3)_6^{+3};\ E^\circ = 1.8 \text{ V}$$

$$E^\circ = \frac{0.059}{1} \log \frac{k_2}{k_1} = 1.8$$
$$= 0.059 \log \frac{k_2}{10^5} = 1.8$$
$$\Rightarrow \quad k_2 = 10^{35} = 10^x$$

Qualifier 19
(Environmental Chemistry)

1. (d) Carbon monoxide is highly toxic to living beings, because it has an ability to form more stable carboxyhaemoglobin complex with haemoglobin due to which the transport of oxygen to the organs and tissues is blocked.

2. (d) Statement (d) is incorrect, whereas all other statements are correct.
PSCs (Polar Stratospheric Clouds) of type II provide an active site for the conversion of chlorine nitrate ($ClONO_2$) and HCl into HOCl and Cl_2.

$$ClONO_2 + H_2O \xrightarrow{PSCs} HOCl + HNO_3$$
$$ClONO_2 + HCl \longrightarrow Cl_2 + HNO_3$$

3. (a) In Antarctica, ozone depletion is due to the formation of chlorine nitrate.
The steps involved are

(i) $\dot{Cl}O + NO_2 \longrightarrow \underset{\text{Chlorine nitrate}}{ClONO_2}$

(ii) $ClONO_2 + H_2O \longrightarrow HOCl + HNO_3$

(iii) $HOCl \xrightarrow{h\nu} \dot{O}H + \dot{Cl}$

The HOCl so formed can get converted into chlorine radicals. Thus, supporting ozone depletion.

4. (d) The statement (d) is correct, whereas all other statements are incorrect.
During the formation of photochemical smog, the level of ozone in the atmosphere goes down.

$$NO + O_3 \xrightarrow{h\nu} NO_2 + O_2$$

In the atmosphere, the organic compounds rapidly react with O_3, NO_2 to form other noxious photochemical products known as peroxyacetyl nitrate (PAN) and acrolein.

5. (b) Photochemical smog has high concentration of oxidising agents and it can be checked by controlling the release of NO_2, hydrocarbons, ozone (O_3) etc. Plantation of some plants like pinus helps in controlling photochemical smog.

6. (a) Freons (CF_2Cl_2) and chlorofluorocarbons ($CFCl_3$) are less reactive halogenated hydrocarbons. Thus, they find their way to stratosphere without being destroyed in troposphere.
But they liberate free radical ($Cl^\bullet$) by action of UV-light. Hence, both statements are correct.

$$CF_2Cl_2 \xrightarrow{h\nu} CF_2Cl^\bullet + Cl^\bullet$$
$$CF_2Cl_3 \xrightarrow{h\nu} {}^\bullet CFCl_2 + Cl^\bullet$$

7. (a) Correct match is A→ (4), B→ (3), C→ (1), D→ (2).

- Unsaturated hydrocarbons result in photochemical smog.
- CH_4, CO_2, CFCs etc., cause global warming.
- Polychlorinated biphenyls (PCBs) of synthetic detergents increases BOD level of water (polluted water).
- Nitrogen oxides are also responsible for acid rain.

8. (a) Methyl isocyanate reacts with α-naphthol to give sevin.

$$\underset{(\alpha\text{-naphthol})}{\text{C}_{10}\text{H}_7\text{OH}} + \underset{\text{(Methyl isocyanate)}}{CH_3-N=C=O} \longrightarrow \underset{\text{Sevin}}{\text{C}_{10}\text{H}_7-O-\overset{O}{\overset{\|}{C}}-NHCH_3}$$

9. (d) Using plastic cans for storing substances will not come under green chemistry. Water in lakes and rivers have been polluted by the use of plastic materials, as plastic materials are non-biodegradable.

10. (b) The gas $CF_2Cl_2(X)$ which gets broken down by powerful UV radiations in stratosphere as shown in the following reaction.

$$CF_2Cl_2(g) \xrightarrow{UV} \dot{C}l(g) + \dot{C}F_2Cl(g)$$

11. (4) CO_2, CH_4, O_3 and CFCs cause global warming.

12. (4) $N_2 + O_2 \longrightarrow NO \xrightarrow{O_2} NO_2 \xrightarrow{O_3} NO_3 + O_2$

$NO_3 + NO_2 \longrightarrow N_2O_5 \xrightarrow{H_2O} 2HNO_3 (pH < 7)$

So, four nitrogenous oxides, (NO, NO_2, NO_3, N_2O_5) are formed during formation of HNO_3 in thunderstorm.

13. (0.35) Ozone concentration in Jakarta, Indonesia $= 0.015 \text{ mg m}^{-3} = 0.015 \text{ mg L}^{-1}$

Ozone concentration in Tokyo, Japan is 20 ppmV (i.e. by volume). This means that there are 20 μmol of ozone for every 1.0 mol of the components of air.

$\therefore$ 22.4 L (1 mol) mixture of gases contains = 20 μmol of ozone.

1 L mixture of gases will contain $= \frac{20 \times 10^{-6}}{22.4}$ mol of O_3

$= 0.893 \times 10^{-6} \text{ mol} = 0.893 \times 10^{-6} \times 48 \text{ g } O_3$

$= 42.86 \times 10^{-3} \text{ mg } O_3 = 0.043 \text{ mg L}^{-1} O_3$

Hence, $\frac{\text{concentration of ozone in Jakarta}}{\text{concentration of ozone in Tokyo}} = \frac{0.015}{0.043}$

$= 0.348 \simeq 0.35$

14. (3.20) $\text{COD} = \frac{\text{Number of mg of } O_2 \text{ require}}{\text{Volume of water (in litre)}}$

One gram equivalent of any oxidant can give, one equivalent weight of oxygen (8 g)

$49 \text{ g} K_2Cr_2O_7 \longrightarrow 8 \text{ g } O_2$

$1.96 \times 10^{-3} \text{ g} K_2Cr_2O_7 \longrightarrow \frac{8 \times 1.96 \times 10^{-3}}{49} \text{ g } O_2 = 3.2 \times 10^{-4} \text{ g } O_2$

$= 0.32 \text{mg } O_2$

Chemical oxygen demand of the given 100 mL or 0.1 L sample of water $= \frac{0.32}{0.1} = 3.2$ ppm

15. (0.12) COD value is 40 ppm. It means 10^6 g of water sample requires 40 g of oxygen to oxidise the organic matter in it.

$10^6 \text{ g water} \longrightarrow 40 \text{ g } O_2$

$500 \text{ g water} \longrightarrow \frac{40 \times 500}{10^6} = 2 \times 10^{-2} \text{ g of } O_2$

500 mL water sample requires 2×10^{-2} g of O_2, to oxidise the organic matter present in it.

$8 \text{ g } O_2 \longrightarrow 49 \text{ g } K_2Cr_2O_7$

$2 \times 10^{-2} \text{ g } O_2 \longrightarrow \frac{49 \times 2 \times 10^{-2}}{8} \text{ g of } K_2Cr_2O_7 = 0.12 \text{ g } K_2Cr_2O_7$

Amount of $K_2Cr_2O_7$ required to oxidise the organic matter present in the water sample is 0.12 g.

Qualifier 20

(Purification and Characterisation of Organic Compounds)

1. (b) Sugar can be separated from water by recrystallisation. A mixture of aniline and water can be separated by steam distillation. Water having lower boiling point (100°C) vapourises leaving behind aniline (boiling point 184°C). Mixture of water and toluene can be separated by differential extraction as they are immiscible in nature and less dense toluene stand above the water layer (more dense). Hence, A→ 4, B→ 2, C→ 3.

2. (d) The solid with lesser solubility crystallises out first followed by the other. Hence, they can be separated by fractional crystallisation.

3. (a) Both statements I and II are correct. Simple distillation can be used to separate a mixture of two liquids which do not react and have boiling point difference of more than 20°C. Hence, a mixture of propan-1-ol and propanone can be separated by simple distillation.

4. (a) In a mixture of two liquids, the liquid having lower boiling point vapourises first and can be distillated in other flask of condensing it. Liquid remaining in the flask has higher boiling point than the liquid that is distillated. The compositions of both liquids also depend upon the length of fractionating column.

5. (d) Essential oils are insoluble in water and have high vapour-pressure at 373 K but are miscible with water-vapour in vapour phase, it means these are steam volatile. Hence, steam distillation technique is used for the extraction of essential oils.

6. (d) In chromatography technique, the purification of a compound is independent of physical state of the pure compound.

7. (c) The general principle of chromatography is that mobile phase move over the stationary phase. The mixture of substances to be tested which may be in solid or liquid state acts as the stationary phase, while the pure solvent liquid or gas which is allowed to pass over the stationary phase is called mobile phase.

8. (c) In Beilstein test, a (clean) copper wire is heated in the non-luminous flame of the Bunsen burner until it ceases to impart any green or bluish green colour to the flame. The heated end of the wire is dipped into the organic compound and is again introduced into the Bunsen flame. The appearance of a bluish green or green flame is due to the formation of volatile cupric halides which shows the presence of halogens in the given organic compound.

9. (d) In Kjeldahl's method, organic compound containing nitrogen is heated with concentrated sulphuric acid in presence of a catalyst $CuSO_4$, which converts the nitrogen in the compound to ammonium sulphate.

10. (c) The presence of both nitrogen and sulphur in the Lassaigne's test in an organic compound shows a blood red colouration with $FeCl_3$ solution. This is due to the formation of NaCNS in the sodium fusion extract.

$$Na + C + N + S \longrightarrow NaSCN \xrightarrow{FeCl_3} \underset{(Red)}{[Fe(SCN)_3]} + NaCl$$

11. (c) For Lassaigne's test of N, compound must contain C in addition to nitrogen, so that NaCN can be formed in the sodium extract. Here, hydrazine hydrochloride ($NH_2NH_2 \cdot HCl$) will not respond.

12. (c) Sodium fusion extract is heated with dilute HNO_3 to decompose NaCN or Na_2S (if present) to HCN and H_2S gases, respectively.

$$NaCN(aq.) + HNO_3(aq.) \longrightarrow NaNO_3(aq.) + HCN(g)\uparrow$$
$$Na_2S(aq.) + 2HNO_3(aq.) \longrightarrow 2NaNO_3(aq.) + H_2S(g)\uparrow$$

13. (d) Weight of substance taken $= 295 \times 10^{-3}$ g

Volume of acid taken = 20 mL of 0.1 N HCl

Now, 15 mL of 0.1 N NaOH = 15 mL of 0.1 N HCl

[$\because$ For HCl and NaOH, 1M = 1N]

Volume of acid used = 20 − 15 = 5 mL of 0.1 N HCl

$$\%\text{Nitrogen} = \frac{14 \times \text{Volume} \times \text{Normality}}{\text{Weight of substance taken}} \times 100$$
$$= \frac{14 \times 5 \times 10^{-3}\ L \times 1\ gL^{-1}}{295 \times 10^{-3}\ g} \times 100 = 23.73\%$$

14. (d) Percentage of Br

$$= \frac{\text{Atomic mass of Br} \times \text{Weight of AgBr}}{\text{Molecular mass of AgBr} \times \text{Weight of organic substance}} \times 100$$
$$= \frac{80 \times 141 \times 100}{188 \times 250} = 24\%$$

15. (c) % of nitrogen

$$= \frac{1.4 \times \text{m.eq. of } H_2SO_4 \text{ used to neutralise } NH_3}{\text{Mass of the compound}}$$

[$\because$ For H_2SO_4, 1M = 2N and for NaOH, 1M = 1N]

$$= \frac{1.4 \times \left(60 \times \frac{1}{10} \times 2 - 20 \times \frac{1}{10}\right)}{1.4} = 10\%$$

16. (c) Let V mL of 0.1 M H_2SO_4 be left unused. Then using molarity equation,

$$V_1 \times M_1 \times n_1(H_2SO_4) = V_2 \times M_2 \times n_2(NaOH)$$
$$V_1 \times 0.1 \times 2 = 20 \times 0.5 \times 1$$
$$\Rightarrow \quad V_1 = 50 mL$$

Volume of acid used = (100 − 50) mL = 50 mL of 0.1 M H_2SO_4

$$\text{Percentage of nitrogen present} = \frac{1.4 \times 50 \times 0.1 \times 2}{0.30} = 46.6\%$$

$$\text{Nitrogen present in urea } (NH_2CONH_2) = \frac{28}{60} \times 100 = 46.6\%$$

(as 14 is the atomic mass of N and 60 is the molecular mass of urea). This is equal to the percentage of nitrogen obtained above. Thus, the compound present is urea.

17. (a) Pressure of dry nitrogen = (732.7 − 12.7) mm = 720 mm

$$\text{Volume of nitrogen at NTP} = \frac{720 \times 22.4}{280} \times \frac{273}{760}\ cm^3$$

$$\%\text{ of N} = \frac{28}{22400} \times \frac{720 \times 22.4}{280} \times \frac{273}{760} \times \left(\frac{1}{\frac{5}{19}}\right) \times 100 = 9.828\%$$

18. (c) From the given data, we have

Element	Percentage composition	Relative number of moles	Simple molar ratio
C	20.00	20/12 = 1.66	1.66/1.66 = 1
H	6.67	6.67/1 = 6.67	6.67/1.66 = 4
N	46.67	46.67/14 = 3.33	3.33/1.66 = 2
O	100 − 20.00 − 6.67 − 46.67 = 26.66	26.66/16 = 1.66	1.66/1.66 = 1

The solid residue has empirical/molecular formula, CH_4N_2O or $(NH_2)_2CO$ which gives violet colour with alkaline $CuSO_4$. So, it is urea.

19. (d) For minimum weight, insulin must have atleast one sulphur atom.

Minimum mass of sulphur in one insulin molecule = 32 g

As 100 g of insulin contains 3.4 g sulphur.

$$\text{So, 32 g of sulphur is present in } \frac{100 \times 32}{3.4} = 940\text{ g}$$

20. (c) $\%\text{ of Ag} = \frac{\text{Weight of silver}}{\text{Weight of silver salt}} \times 100 = 60$

$$\frac{\text{Weight of silver salt}}{\text{Weight of silver}} = \frac{100}{60}$$

$$\text{Equivalent weight of salt} = \frac{\text{Weight of silver salt}}{\text{Weight of silver}} \times \text{Equivalent mass of silver}$$
$$= \frac{100}{60} \times 108 = 180\text{ g}$$

Equivalent weight of acid = Equivalent weight of salt − Equivalent weight of Ag + Basicity

Equivalent weight of acid = 180 − 108 + 1 = 73 g

Molecular weight of acid = Basicity × Equivalent mass = 1 × 73 = 73 g

21. (50) Let the volume of 1N H_2SO_4 taken = V mL

Now, 60 mL of N/2 NaOH = 30 mL of 1N NaOH = 30 mL of 1N H_2SO_4

Thus, volume of acid left unused = 30 mL of 1N H_2SO_4

$\therefore$ Volume of 1N H_2SO_4 used = (V − 30) mL

$$\text{Now, \% of N} = \frac{1.4 \times N_1 \times V}{w}$$

or $\quad 56 = \frac{1.4 \times 1 \times (V - 30)}{0.50}$ or V = 50 mL

22. (73.29) The percentage of C and H can be determined as :

$$\%\ C = \frac{12 \times \text{mass of } CO_2 \times 100}{44 \times \text{mass of organic compound}}$$
$$\%\ C = \frac{12}{44} \times \frac{0.147}{0.2} \times 100 = 20.045$$
$$\%\ H = \frac{2 \times \text{mass of } H_2O \times 100}{18 \times \text{mass of organic compound}}$$

$$\% H = \frac{2}{18} \times \frac{0.12}{0.2} \times 100 = 6.666$$

$\therefore \quad \% O = (100 - 20.045 - 6.666) = 73.289 \simeq 73.29$

23. (15.55) % N (By Duma's method)

$$= \frac{28 \times \text{volume of } N_2 \text{ at NTP} \times 100}{22400 \times \text{weight of compound}} = \frac{28 \times 31.1 \times 100}{22400 \times 0.25}$$

$= 15.55\%$

24. (5.33) Calculation of empirical formula

Element	Percentage	Atomic mass	Relative number of atoms	Simplest ratio of atoms
Carbon	34.62	12	$\frac{34.62}{12} = 2.88$	$\frac{2.88}{2.88} = 1 \times 3 = 3$
Hydrogen	3.84	1	$\frac{3.84}{1} = 3.84$	$\frac{3.84}{2.88} = 1.33 \times 3 = 4$
Oxygen	61.54 (by difference)	16	$\frac{61.54}{16} = 3.84$	$\frac{3.84}{2.88} = 1.33 \times 3 = 4$

Empirical formula of the acid $= C_3H_4O_4$; Empirical formula mass $= (3 \times 12) + (4 \times 1) + (4 \times 16) = 104$

Calculation of molecular mass : 20 mL 0.1 N NaOH $= 0.1075 \text{ g mol}^{-1}$

So, 1000 mL 1 N NaOH $= \frac{0.1075}{20 \times 0.1} \times 1000$ g acid $= 53.75$ g acid

Equivalent mass of the acid $= 53.75 \text{ g mol}^{-1}$

Molecular mass of the acid = Equivalent mass × basicity $= 53.75 \times 2 = 107.50$

$$n = \frac{\text{Molecular mass}}{\text{Empirical mass}} = \frac{107.50}{104.0} \simeq 1$$

$\therefore$ Molecular formula $= C_3H_4O_4 = C_aH_bO_c$

$\Rightarrow \quad a = 3, b = c = 4$

$\therefore \quad \frac{bc}{a} = \frac{4 \times 4}{3} = 5.33$

25. (14.59) Volume of $\frac{N}{10}$ HCl taken = 50 mL

Volume of $\frac{N}{10}$ NaOH used for neutralisation of unused acid $= 23.2$ mL

Now, $N_1V_1(\text{NaOH}) = N_2V_2(\text{HCl})$

23.2 mL of $\frac{N}{10}$ NaOH = 23.2 mL of $\frac{N}{10}$ HCl

$\therefore$ Volume of $\frac{N}{10}$ HCl unused = 23.2 mL

$\therefore$ Volume of $\frac{N}{10}$ HCl required for neutralisation of NH_3

$= 50 - 23.2 = 26.8$ mL

26.8 mL of $\frac{N}{10}$ HCl = 26.8 mL of $\frac{N}{10}$ NH_3

1000 mL of 1 N NH_3 solution contains nitrogen = 14 g

26.8 mL of NH_3 solution contains nitrogen $= \frac{14 \times 26.8}{10 \times 1000}$ g

Percentage of nitrogen $= \frac{14 \times 26.8 \times 100}{10 \times 1000 \times 0.257} = 14.59\%$

26. (20.24) Mass of $BaSO_4 = 0.582$ g

We know $\underset{233}{BaSO_4} \equiv \underset{32}{S}$

$\Rightarrow$ 233 g of $BaSO_4$ contains sulphur = 32 g

0.582 g of $BaSO_4$ contains sulphur $= \frac{32}{233} \times 0.582$ g

$\Rightarrow$ Percentage of sulphur $= \frac{\text{Wt. of sulphur}}{\text{Wt. of compound}} \times 100$

$= \frac{32 \times 0.582}{233 \times 0.395} \times 100 = 20.24\%$

27. (9.75) Weight of compound = 0.198 g

Weight of $CO_2 = 0.524$ g

Weight of water = 0.132 g

$$\% C = \frac{12}{44} \times \frac{\text{wt. of } CO_2}{\text{wt. of compound}} \times 100 = \frac{12 \times 0.524}{44} \times \frac{100}{0.198}$$

$= 72.18$ %

So, $x = 72.18$

$$\% H = \frac{2}{18} \times \frac{\text{wt. of } H_2O}{\text{wt. of substance}} \times 100 = \frac{2 \times 0.132}{18} \times \frac{100}{0.198} = 7.4\ \%$$

So, $y = 7.4$

Thus, $\frac{x}{y} = \frac{72.18}{7.4} = 9.75$

28. (298.67) Molecular mass of the compound

$$= \frac{\text{Wt. of organic substance taken}}{\text{Air displaced at STP}} \times 22400$$

$$= \frac{0.2}{15} \times 22400 = 298.67$$

29. (4) Volume after explosion and cooling, i.e. vol. of CO_2 formed + evolved $O_2 = 95$ mL

Volume after introducing KOH solution, i.e. volume of CO_2 formed = 20 mL

Volume absorbed by alkaline pyrogallol, i.e. volume of unused $O_2 = 95 - 20 = 75$ mL

$\therefore$ Volume of O_2 used $= 100 - 75 = 25$ mL

Applying the combustion equation,

$$\underset{10\,\text{mL}}{C_xH_y} + \underset{10\left(x+\frac{y}{4}\right)\text{mL}}{\left(x + \frac{y}{4}\right)O_2} \longrightarrow \underset{10x\,\text{mL}}{xCO_2} + \underset{\text{Negligible volume}}{\frac{y}{2}H_2O}$$

$\Rightarrow \quad 10x = 20$ and $10\left(x + \frac{y}{4}\right) = 25$

$\therefore \quad x = 2$ and $10\left(2 + \frac{y}{4}\right) = 25$

$\Rightarrow \quad y = 2$

$\Rightarrow$ The hydrocarbon is C_2H_2.

$\Rightarrow \quad (x + y) = 4$

30. (73.34)

$$\% C = \frac{\text{Mass of carbon}}{\text{Molecular mass of } CO_2} \times \frac{\text{Mass of } CO_2}{\text{Mass of substance}} \times 100$$

$$C\% = \frac{12}{44} \times \frac{0.22}{0.24} \times 100 = 25$$

%H = 1.66 (given)

%O = (100 − %C − %H)

$\therefore \quad O\% = (100 - 25 - 1.66) = 73.34$

Qualifier 21

(Some Basic Principles of Organic Chemistry)

1. (b) In case of compounds I and III, carbon atoms are sp^3-hybridised. Hence, the expected H—C—H bond angle in both molecules is 109°28′.

But in case of I, due to the lesser internal C—C—C bond angle (60°) [angle strain], the external H—C—H bond angle become more than 109°28′ but it should be less than 120°.

⇒ In case of II, as the C-atom is sp^2-hybridised then, H—C—H bond angle will be around 120°.

2. (c) A simplest ketone of molecular formula $C_5H_{10}O$ (general formula $C_nH_{2n}O$) can show all types of structural isomerism which are

(i) Chain isomerism

Pentan-2-one , 3-methylbutan-2-one

(ii) Position isomerism as well as metamerism

Pentan-2-one , Pentan-3-one

(iii) Functional isomerism

Pentan-2-one , Pent-3-en-2-ol

(iv) Tautomerism

Pentan-2-one (Keto-form) ⇌ Pent-2-en-2-ol (Enol-form)

3. (c) Tautomerism is shown by carbonyl compound having α-H atoms.

(a) Me_3C—CO, Me_3COC—C—H, Me_3COC ⇌ $(Me_3COC)_2C$=C(OH)CMe_3 ;

(b) cyclohexene-dione ⇌ phenol (OH) with C=O ;

(d) cyclohexane-1,2-dione ⇌ 2-hydroxycyclohex-2-enone (OH)

But, compound (c) will not show tautomerism as there is no α-H to any >C=O.

4. (c)

I. COOH / H—C—NH_2 / Me $\xrightarrow[\text{rotation}]{180° \text{ in plane}}$ Me / H_2N—C—H / COOH ⋮ Me / H—C—NH_2 / COOH

Mirror-image relationship : Enantiomers

II. Et / H—C—Br / Br—C—H / Me $\xrightarrow[\text{rotation}]{180° \text{ in plane}}$ Me / H—C—Br / Br—C—H / Et ≡ Me / H—C—Br / Br—C—H / Et

Superimposable relationship : Identical

III. Ph / HO—C—H / H_2N—C—H / Me $\xrightarrow[\text{rotation}]{180° \text{ in plane}}$ Me / H—C—NH_2 / H—C—OH / Ph ≢ Me / H—C—NH_2 / HO—C—H / Ph

No mirror-image relationship : Diastereomers

IV. Et / H—C—Cl / H—C—Br / Me $\xrightarrow[\text{rotation}]{180° \text{ in plane}}$ Me / Br—C—H / Cl—C—H / Et ; Me / Cl—C—H / Br—C—H / Et

Structural isomers

Hence, the compounds in I to IV are enantiomers, identical, diastereomers and structural isomers respectively.

5. (d) Let us analyse the given molecule by converting the flying-wedge projection to Fisher projection.

HO, H, H_3C, Br, H, O, OH ≡ COOH / H—C—Br / H—C—OH / CH_3

COOH (2) ; H (4) — Br (1) ; (3)

1 ⟶ 2 ⟶ 3 ⇒ Anti-clockwise ⇒ 2S
⇓
But, 4th group is at horizontal plane (2R)

H (4′) — OH (1′) ; 2′ ; CH_3 (3′)

1 ⟶ 2′ ⟶ 3′ ⇒ Anti-clockwise ⇒ 2S
⇓
But, 4th group is at horizontal plane (3R)

6. (c) The structure of *sec*-butyl phenyl vinyl methane:

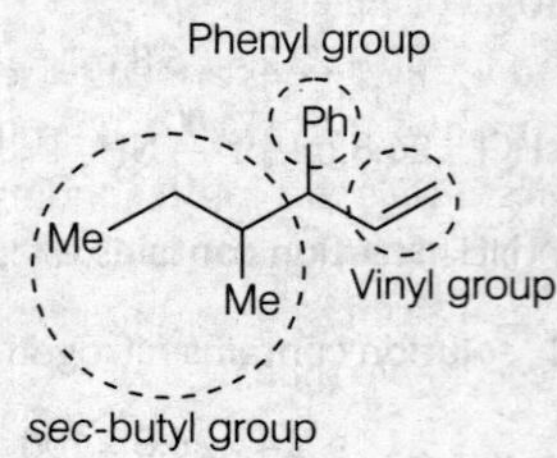

7. (d) Structure is as follows

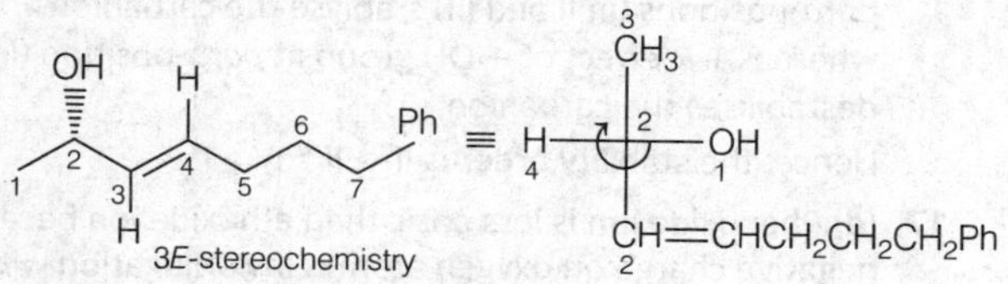

3E-stereochemistry

$1 \rightarrow 2 \rightarrow 3 \Rightarrow$ Clockwise rotation : *R*

But 4th group is at horizontal plane : 2*S*

As the longest chain contains seven carbons, its name will be hept. The principal functional group is —OH situated at C-2 position. Hence, it will be 2-ol. It contains one double bond at C-3 position. So, it will be 3-ene.

Its *R/S* stereochemistry is: 2*S* and *E/Z* stereochemistry is; 3*E*. Thus, its name will be (2*S*, 3*E*)-7-phenylhept-3-en-2-ol.

8. (a)

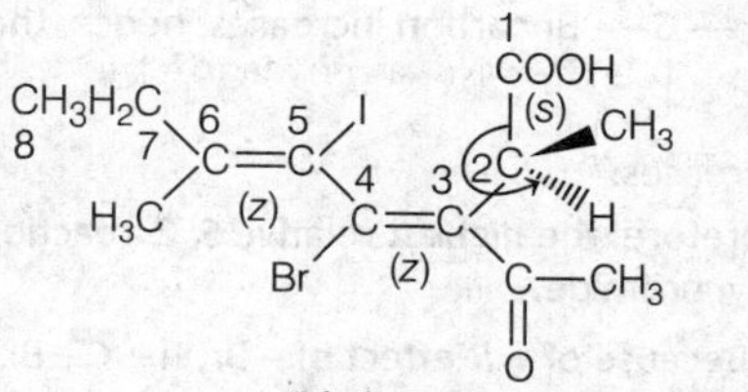

(Methoxycarbonyl) (ester)

(2*S*, 3*Z*, 5*Z*) -4-bromo-5-iodo-2, 6-dimethyl-3-methoxycarbonyloctanoic acid.

9. (d) The C_a— C_b carbons in compounds (a), (b), (c) and (d) are 1°, 1°, 2° and 3° respectively. Homolytic breaking of a bond leads to the formation of radicals. Greater is the stability of radicals, higher will be the chance of breaking the bond.

(a) $H_3C_a—C_bH_3 \longrightarrow \dot{C}_aH_3 + \dot{C}_bH_3$

(b) $CH_3C_aH_2C_bH_2CH_3 \longrightarrow CH_3\dot{C}_aH_2 + CH_3\dot{C}_bH_2$

(c) $Me_2C_aHC_bHMe_2 \longrightarrow Me_2\dot{C}_aH + Me_2\dot{C}_bH$

(d) $Me_3C_aC_bMe_3 \longrightarrow Me_3\dot{C}_a + Me_3\dot{C}_b$

The radicals generated after cleavage of compounds in options (a), (b), (c) and (d) are 1°(methyl), 1°(ethyl), 2° and 3° respectively. The stability order of various radicals is as follows 3° > 2° > 1° (ethyl) > 1° (methyl).

Hence, homolytic cleavage is easiest in $Me_3C_a—C_b—Me_3$.

10. (b) The ease of leaving groups depend on the stability of leaving groups. Greater is the stability of a leaving group, higher will be its leaving group ability.

In case of *C* and *D*, the anions are stabilised by three resonating structures. But, as —CF_3, group has very strong −*I* effect, it will stabilise the corresponding anion more than the anion *C*, while methyl group in *C* will increase electron density on oxygen atom by its +*I*-effect making it unstable. Hence, *D* is more stable than *C*.

In case of *A*, two canonicals can be drawn which are degenerate in nature. Hence, *A* is moderately stable. But, in case of *B*, —Me group by its electron donating effect (+*I*-effect) will increase the electron density on oxygen atom and making it unstable. Hence, it is least stable.

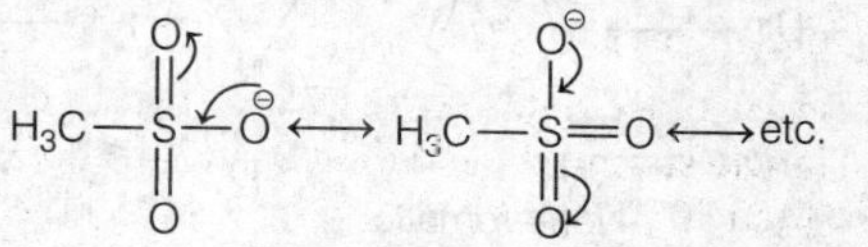

Resonance occurs in *C*

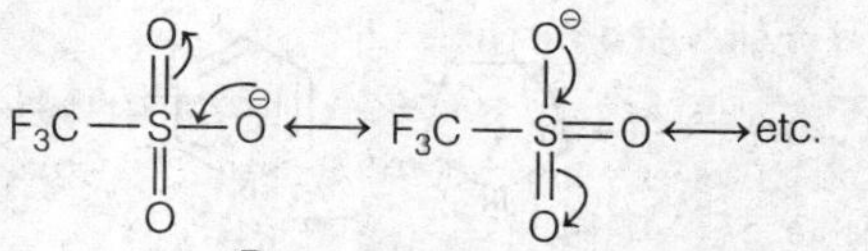

Resonance occurs in *D*

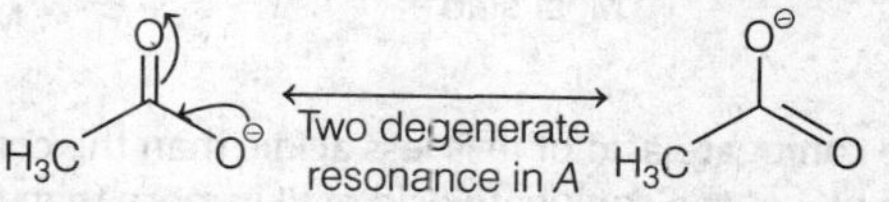

Two degenerate resonance in *A*

Thus, the order of ease of the following leaving groups would be : *D* > *C* > *A* > *B*.

11. (d) In water, hydration enthalpy is most negative and least negative for F^- and I^- respectively. So, size of hydrated ions is largest for F^- and smallest for I^-. As powerful nucleophile should have smaller size, hence, I^- is the most powerful nucleophile in water among the halides.

12. (c) In case of alkene, greater is the number of hyperconjugated structures, higher will be its stability. The greater stability of the $Me_2C═CH_2$ is due to hyperconjugation by methyl groups. Here, six hyperconjugable α-H atoms are present and hence, six hyperconjugated structures can be drawn. But, in case of $MeCH_2CH═CH_2$ only two hyperconjugable α-H atoms are present.

13. (c) Carbocation is an electron deficient species. Oxygen sulphur, nitrogen and fluorine atoms contain one lone pair of electrons. Hence, all of these will undergo resonance (+*R*) with the carbocations. The order of electronegativity of atoms: F > O > N > S.

Out of F, O and N, nitrogen will donate its electron pair to the carbocation more generously than both of oxygen and fluorine. Sulphur being less electronegative will also donate its electron pair to the sp^2-carbon. But, sulphur being larger in size resonance will occur between two orbitals of different size making the overlap less effective. Hence, resonance will occur most efficiently in (c).

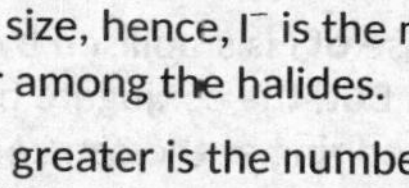

+*R*

(c)

14. (c) All of the given compounds are basic in nature. Hence, the conjugate acids of these compounds will be positively charged species. Lesser is the stability of the conjugate acid, more easily it will get deprotonated and hence, higher will be its acidity and hence, lower will be its pK_a.

The conjugate acid of I is very unstable. The conjugate acid will readily give up the proton to attain stability due to aromaticity. Hence, the conjugate acid of I is highly acidic and its pK_a will be very low.

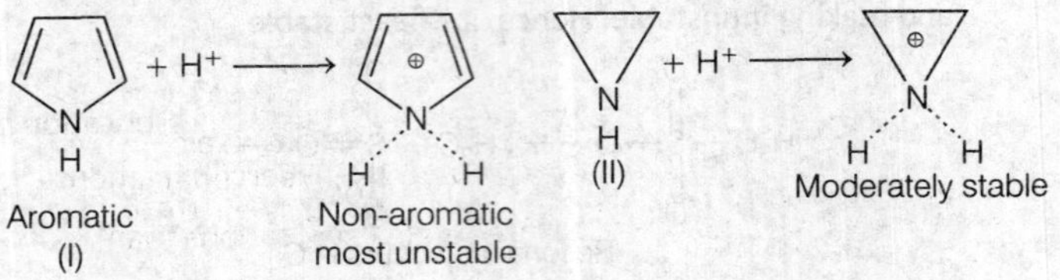

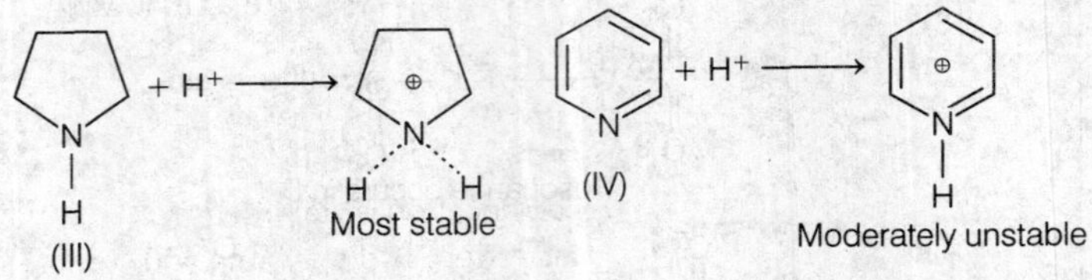

Aromatic (I) + H^+ ⟶ Non-aromatic most unstable

(II) + H^+ ⟶ Moderately stable

(III) + H^+ ⟶ Most stable

(IV) + H^+ ⟶ Moderately unstable

The conjugate acid of III is less acidic than the conjugate acid of II. The pK_a of the conjugate acid of III is more than the pK_a of the conjugate acid of II.

Therefore, the correct order of pK_a is III > II > IV > I.

15. (c) Acidity of a compound depends on the stability of the conjugate base. Greater is the stability of the conjugate base, higher will be the acidity of acid.

The conjugate base of I is stabilised by the resonance involving two phenyl rings. But, the conjugate bases of II and III contains one five membered ring at the centre of the system. The conjugate base obtained from the compounds II and III are stabilised by the resonance involves two and three phenyl rings respectively. Hence, the conjugate base of III is more stable than the conjugate base of II.

Therefore, the correct order of acidity of the compounds is III > II > I.

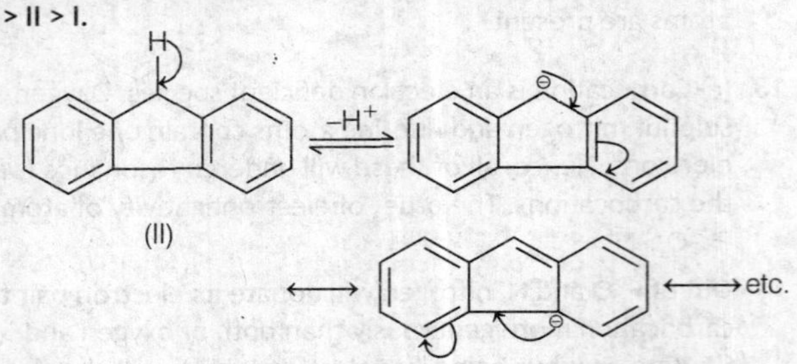

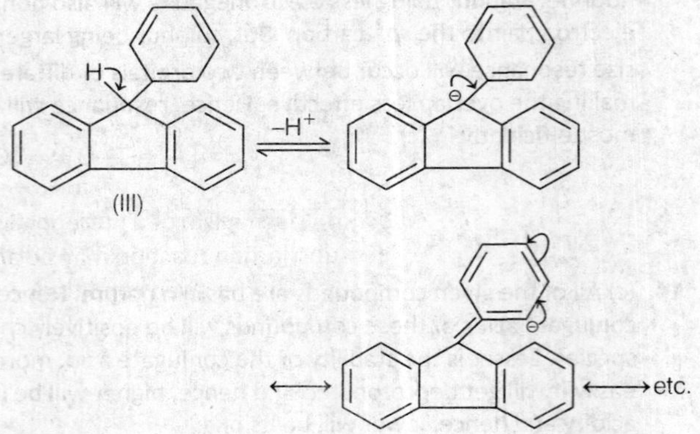

(II) $\xrightleftharpoons{-H^+}$ ⟷ ⟷ etc.

(III) $\xrightleftharpoons{-H^+}$ ⟷ ⟷ etc.

16. (c) –*R*-effects of —NO_2 group(s) at *ortho* and *para*-positions (in II and III) stabilise the carbanions, whereas + *R*-effect of —OH group at *para*-position (in I) destabilises the carbanion,

Hence, the stability order is III > II > IV > I.

17. (d) Phenoxide ion is less basic than ethoxide ion because negative charge on oxygen atom is in conjugation with π-bonds of phenyl ring. Therefore, statement II is correct. Hence, phenoxide ion gains proton less likely than ethoxide. So, K_1 is less than K_2. Thus, statement I is incorrect.

18. (a) Greater is the steric hindrance around the electrophilic centre, higher will be the activation energy of the transition state and hence lower will be the reaction rate. On moving from ethyl to propyl to 2-methylpropyl to 2, 3-dimethylpropyl bromide, the steric crowding around the —C—Br carbon increases, hence, the reaction rate decreases.

Therefore, the highest relative S_N2 reaction rate will be of ethyl bromide.

19. (a) Because of + *R*-effect of – Br, the C—Br bond of bromobenzene achieves a double bond nature, i.e. C—Br bond energy increases which causes lesser reactivity in nucleophilic substitution reaction .

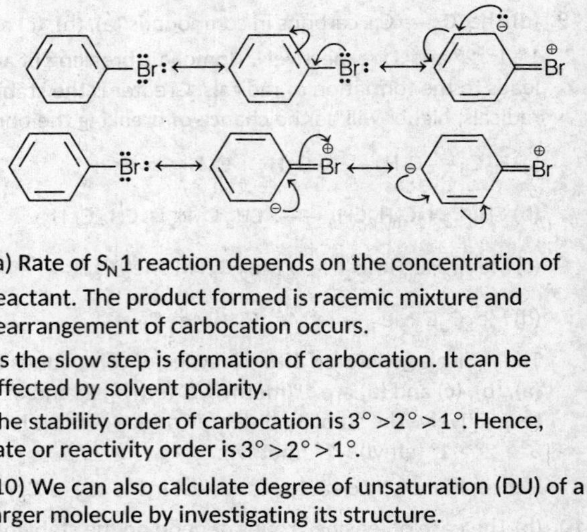

20. (a) Rate of S_N1 reaction depends on the concentration of reactant. The product formed is racemic mixture and rearrangement of carbocation occurs.

As the slow step is formation of carbocation. It can be affected by solvent polarity.

The stability order of carbocation is 3° > 2° > 1°. Hence, rate or reactivity order is 3° > 2° > 1°.

21. (10) We can also calculate degree of unsaturation (DU) of a larger molecule by investigating its structure.

Each value of DU corresponds to the number of π-bond or ring present in the molecule. In the given molecule,

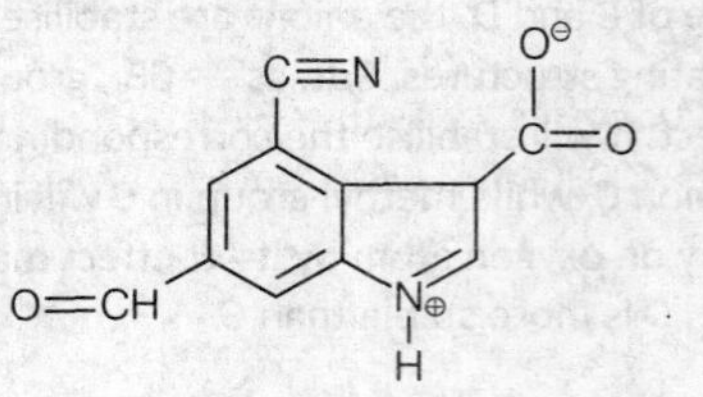

Substituent	DU
C=C	3
H–C=O (aldehyde, —C(H)=O)	1
O^-–C=O (—C(O⁻)=O)	1
—C≡N	2
—C(H)=$N^{\oplus}$(H)—	1
Six membered ring	1
Five membered ring	1
Total = 10	

22. (19) 60% *R*-enantiomer exhibit + 90° optical rotation
Then, 100% *R*-enantiomer will exhibit

$$\frac{100}{60}\times(+90°) = +150° \text{ optical rotation}$$

Hence, 100% *S*-enantiomer will exhibit − 150° optical rotation.

If − 150° optical rotation corresponds to 100% *S*-enantiomer.

So, − 135° optical rotation corresponds to

$$\frac{100}{(-150°)}\times(-135°) = 90\%$$

S-enantiomer
Hence, the rest 10% is an equal mixture of *R* and *S* enantiomeric forms.
Total *S*-enantiomeric form $= (90\% + 5\%) = 95\%$ and total *R*-enantiomeric form $= 5\%$

⇒ The ratio of *S* and *R*-enantiomers $= 95 : 5 = 19 : 1$

23. (80) For 90% optically pure 2-arylpropanoic acid $[\alpha]_D = +135°$
For 100% optically pure 2-arylpropanoic acid,

$$[\alpha]_D = 135° \times \frac{100}{90} = +150°$$

+ 150° corresponds to 100% pure sample.

∴ + 120° corresponds to $\{(120\times100)/(150)\} = 80\%$ pure sample

24. (0.20) Number of moles become half on halving its volume.
Hence, rotation also becomes half, i.e. $\theta = 0.20°$.

25. (4) Number of stereocentres(*) = 4

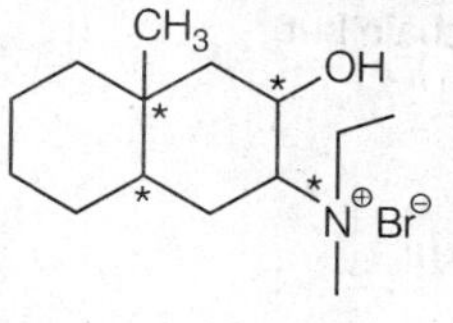

(Structure: decalin ring system bearing CH_3 at ring-fusion carbon (*), OH (*), and $\overset{\oplus}{N}$ $Br^{\ominus}$ (*) substituents; stereocentres marked *)

26. (2)

$$H_3C-\overset{*}{C}H(OH)-\overset{*}{C}H(OH)-\overset{*}{C}H(OH)-CH_3$$

Number of chiral carbons (*), $n = 3$
Number of *meso*-form

$$= 2^{\left(\frac{n-1}{2}\right)} = 2^{\left(\frac{3-1}{2}\right)} = 2$$

27. (8)

Primary amines

I. $CH_3-CH_2-CH_2-CH_2-NH_2$

II. $CH_3-CH_2-CH(NH_2)-CH_3$

III. $CH_3-CH(CH_3)-CH_2-NH_2$

IV. $CH_3-C(CH_3)(NH_2)-CH_3$

Secondary amines

I. $CH_3-CH_2-CH_2-N(H)-CH_3$

II. $CH_3-CH_2-N(H)-CH_2-CH_3$

III. $CH_3-CH(CH_3)-N(H)-CH_3$

Tertiary amine

$CH_3-CH_2-N(CH_3)-CH_3$

28. (5) H_2O, HF, CH_3CH_2-OH, CH_3-CH_2-SH and (cyclopentadiene) are more acidic than $HC\equiv CH$.

29. (4) In $CH_3-\overset{\oplus}{C}H-CH_3$, carbocation is stabilised by 6-hyperconjugations.
More stable carbocations than $CH_3-\overset{\oplus}{C}H-CH_3$ are as follows:

II. In $C_6H_5-\overset{\oplus}{C}H-CH_3$, carbocation is stabilised by +*R*-effect of phenyl ring and 3-hyperconugations.

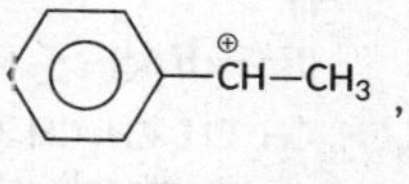

III. In $(CH_3)_3C^{\oplus}$, carbocation is stabilised by 9-hyperconjugations.

VI. In $H_2C=CH-\overset{\oplus}{C}H-CH_3$, carbocation is stabilised by resonance and 3-hyperconjugations.

VIII. $CH_3-\overset{\oplus}{C}H-OCH_3$, the lone pair of $e^{\ominus}$s of oxygen atom stabilises the carbocation and hyperconjugations also stabilise carbocation.

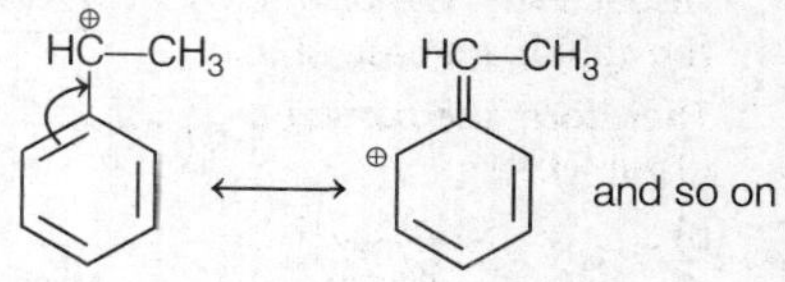

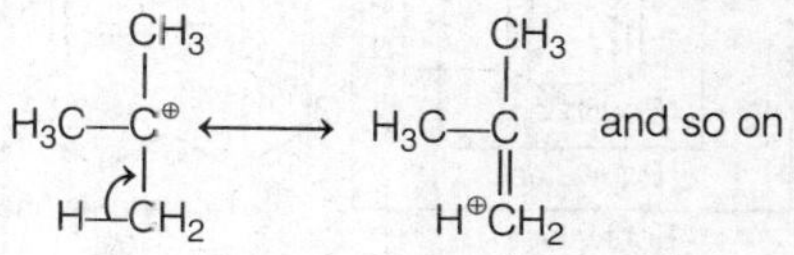

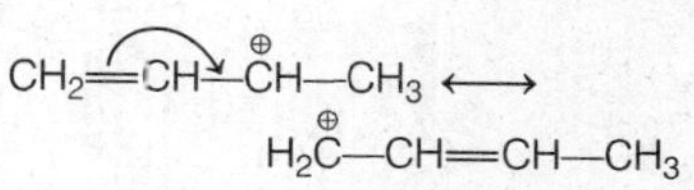

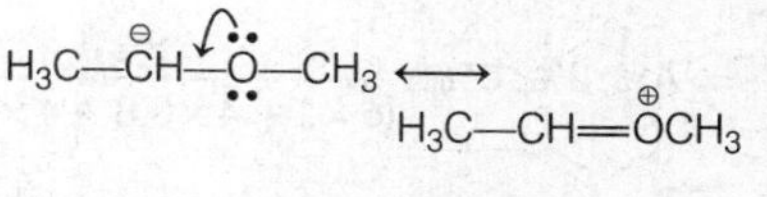

$C_6H_5-\overset{\oplus}{C}H-CH_3 \longleftrightarrow$ (ring-delocalised form, $HC-CH_3$ exocyclic double bond, ⊕ on ring) and so on

$H_3C-\overset{\oplus}{C}(CH_3)-CH_2-H \longleftrightarrow H_3C-C(CH_3)=CH_2\ H^{\oplus}$ and so on

$CH_2=CH-\overset{\oplus}{C}H-CH_3 \longleftrightarrow \overset{\oplus}{H_2C}-CH=CH-CH_3$

$H_3C-\overset{\oplus}{C}H-\ddot{O}-CH_3 \longleftrightarrow H_3C-CH=\overset{\oplus}{O}CH_3$

30. (4) Mechanism of a nucleophilic substitution reaction may be affected by all of the given conditions – I, II, III and IV.

Qualifier 22
(Hydrocarbons)

1. (b) Higher is the intermolecular force of attraction, higher will be the boiling point of the compound.

For alkanes, the intermolecular force of attraction is of van der Waals' type which increases with length of carbon chain but decreases with branching of the carbon chain.

(a) $CH_3-C(CH_3)_2-CH_2-CH(CH_3)-CH_3$ [Branching is present]
(*Iso*-octane)

(b) $CH_3CH_2CH_2CH_2CH_2CH_2CH_2CH_3$ [Straight chain]
(*n*-octane)

(c) $CH_3-C(CH_3)_2-C(CH_3)_2-CH_3$ [More branching is present]
(2,2,3,3-tetramethylbutane)

(a), (b) and (c) have same molecular formula. i.e. C_8H_{18}.

(d) $CH_3-CH_2-CH_2-CH_3$ [Straight chain]
(*n*-butane)

⇒ Taking the options, the order of their boiling point will be, (b) > (a) > (c) > (d).

2. (b) (a) Kolbe's electrolysis of sodium ethanoate yields ethane at anode along with CO_2.

$$CH_3CO\overset{-}{O}\overset{+}{Na}(aq.) \xrightarrow[\text{(Electrolysis)}]{\text{Pt-electrodes}} \underbrace{CH_3-CH_3}_{\text{(Ethane)}} + CO_2 \text{ (At anode)} + \underbrace{H_2}_{\text{At cathode}} + \underbrace{NaOH}_{\text{In solution}}$$

(b)
1° 2° 2° 2° 2° 1°
$CH_3\ CH_2\ CH_2\ CH_2\ CH_2\ CH_3$ (*n*-hexane) $\xrightarrow[Cl_2/UV]{\text{Monochlorination}}$ 1-chlorohexane (*A*) + 2-chlorohexane (*B*) + 3-chlorohexane (*C*)

Equivalent; Equivalent; Equivalent

$$\Rightarrow A\%:B\%:C\% :: \frac{6\times1}{(6\times1+4\times3.8+4\times3.8)}\times100 : \frac{4\times3.8}{36.4}\times100 : \frac{4\times3.8}{36.4}\times100$$

$$:: 16.48 : 41.76 : 41.46$$

[Abstractable 1°-H to give A = 6
Abstractable 2°-H to give B or C = 4]

(c) The C—H bonds of cyclopropane involves more *s*-character than those of an alkane, as cyclopropane is the only planar cycloalkane.

(d) The chair conformation of cyclohexane is more stable than its boat conformation.

3. (b) Twist boat conformation of cyclohexane is optically active because of its molecular disymmetry.

(Twist boat conformation of cyclohexane)

4. (b)

Newman projection: front carbon CH_3, H, H; rear carbon $C(CH_3)_3$, H, H
(I)

It is the *Gauche* conformation (Newman projection) of the second structure given, i.e.

(2, 2-dimethylpentane)
(II)

whose C_3-C_4 bond is considered for conformation. So, (I) and (II) are same molecule.

5. (c) The acidity can be determined by the relative stability of conjugate bases.

I. Cyclopentadiene—H ⟶ cyclopentadienyl anion (*A*) + $H^{\oplus}$

II. Cyclopropene—H ⟶ cyclopropenyl anion (*B*) + $H^{\oplus}$

III. $H-C\equiv C-H \longrightarrow HC\equiv C^{\ominus} + H^{\oplus}$ (*C*)

IV. $CH_3-C\equiv CH \longrightarrow CH_3-C\equiv C^{\ominus} + H^{\oplus}$ (*D*)

Compound *A* is aromatic so, it is most stable. Hence, (I) is most acidic. Compound *B* is anti-aromatic so, it is least stable. Hence, (II) is least acidic.

Out of *C* and *D*, due to +*I*-effect of methyl group in *D*, the negative charge is less stable. Hence, *D* is less stable than *C*. So, (IV) is less acidic than (III). Therefore, the order of acidity is

I > III > IV > II

6. (a) Addition of bromine to 1-butene in presence of CCl_4 gives 1,2-dibromobutane as the final product.

$$\underset{\text{1-butene}}{CH_3-CH_2-CH=CH_2} + Br_2 \xrightarrow{CCl_4} \underset{\text{1,2-dibromobutane}}{CH_3-CH_2-\overset{*}{C}H(Br)-CH_2-Br}$$

The product has only one chiral or asymmetric carbon.

$\therefore$ No. of optical isomers $= 2^n = 2^1 = 2$

Hence, both the statements are correct.

7. (d) Lower the value of heat of hydrogenation, more stable will be the alkene. Further more, stability of an alkene is the direct measure of its number of hyperconjugative (HP) structures.

Number of α-H atom to sp^2-carbon = number of hyperconjugative structures.

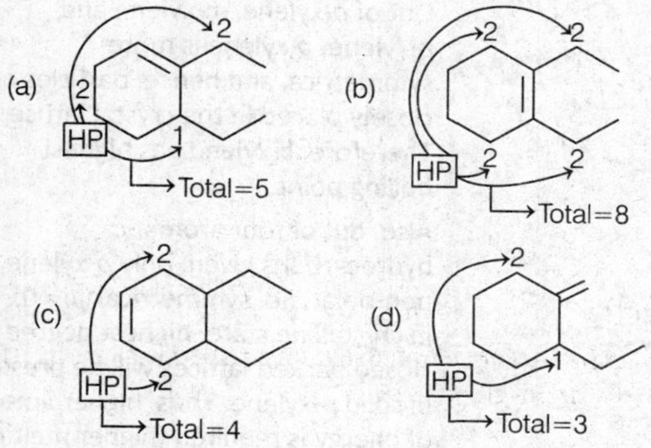

(a) Total=5 (b) Total=8

(c) Total=4 (d) Total=3

$\Rightarrow$ (d) (c) (a) (b)

$\rightarrow$ Increasing order of number of hyperconjugations.

$\rightarrow$ Increasing order of stability.

$\rightarrow$ Decreasing order of heat of hydrogenation value.

So, (d) 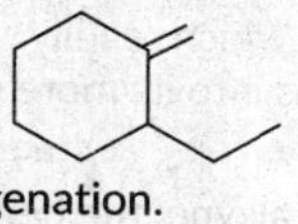 has maximum value of heat of hydrogenation.

8. (d) Potassium tertiary butoxide, $t\text{-BuO}^{\ominus}\text{K}^{\oplus}$ or $CH_3-C(CH_3)_2-O^{\ominus}K^{\oplus}$ is a larger base which prefers to abstract a less hindered β-hydrogen atom through E2 mechanism (β-elimination) to give less substituted alkene as the major product (Hofmann elimination).

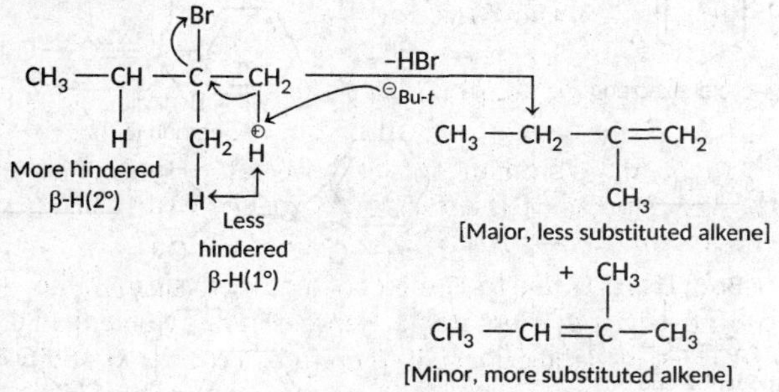

$CH_3-CH(H)-CBr(CH_3)-CH_2-H \xrightarrow[\ominus Bu\text{-}t]{-HBr} CH_3-CH_2-C(CH_3)=CH_2$ [Major, less substituted alkene] $+ CH_3-CH=C(CH_3)-CH_3$ [Minor, more substituted alkene]

More hindered β-H(2°); Less hindered β-H(1°)

9. (c) Br_2 undergoes electrophilic addition by its counter electrophile Br^+ with an alkene to give a bromonium ion complex (I). The complex (I) is then suffers anti-addition of the nucleophile, Br^- to give an anti-1,2-dibromo compound (option-c).

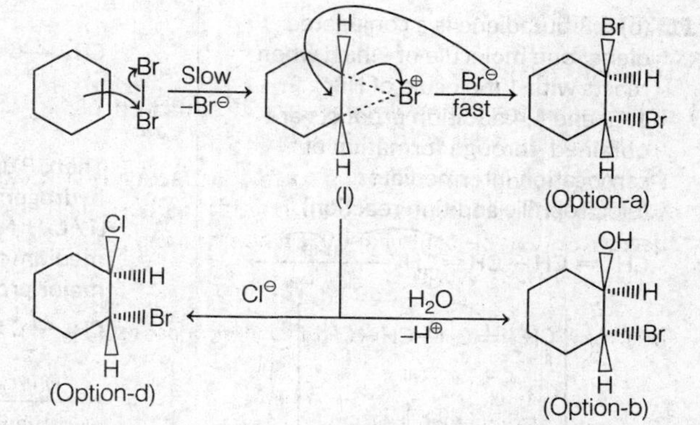

Cyclohexene $+ Br_2 \xrightarrow[-Br^{\ominus}]{\text{Slow}}$ bromonium ion (I) $\xrightarrow[\text{fast}]{Br^{\ominus}}$ (Option-a)

(I) $\xrightarrow{Cl^{\ominus}}$ (Option-d); (I) $\xrightarrow[-H^{\oplus}]{H_2O}$ (Option-b)

Other two nucleophiles, H_2O and Cl^- come from brine solution (saturated aqueous solution of NaCl) present along with Br_2 in the mixture. The product mentioned in option (c) will not be obtained as one Br-atom is present with the intermediate (I) of the reaction.

10. (c) The given alkene undergoes electrophilic addition of H^+ available in dilute acid (H_2SO_4, H_2O) to give alcohols.

In electrophilic addition reaction, carbocation intermediate formed may be rearranged into its more stable form to give the major product.

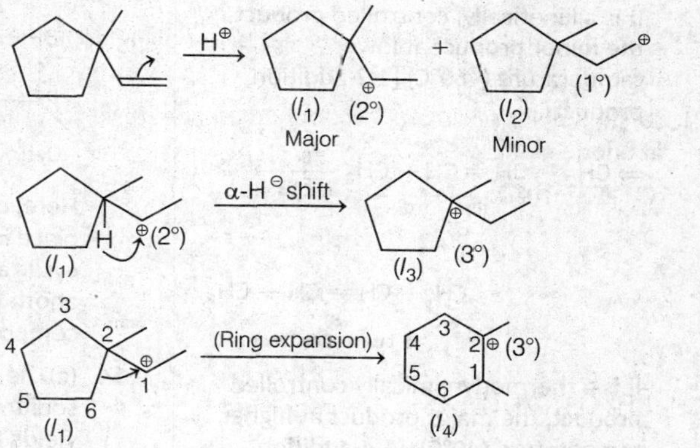

$\xrightarrow{H^{\oplus}}$ (I_1) (2°) Major $+$ (I_2) (1°) Minor

(I_1) (2°) $\xrightarrow{\alpha\text{-H}^{\ominus}\text{ shift}}$ (I_3) (3°)

(I_1) $\xrightarrow{\text{(Ring expansion)}}$ (I_4) (3°)

$\Rightarrow$ Stability of carbocation intermediates obtained,

$$I_4 > I_3 > I_1 > I_2$$
(3°) (3°) (2°) (1°)

I_4 is more stable than I_3 because of its thermodynamic stability.

$\Rightarrow$ So, yield % of the products (alcohols) will also follow the order as obtained from the respective carbocation.

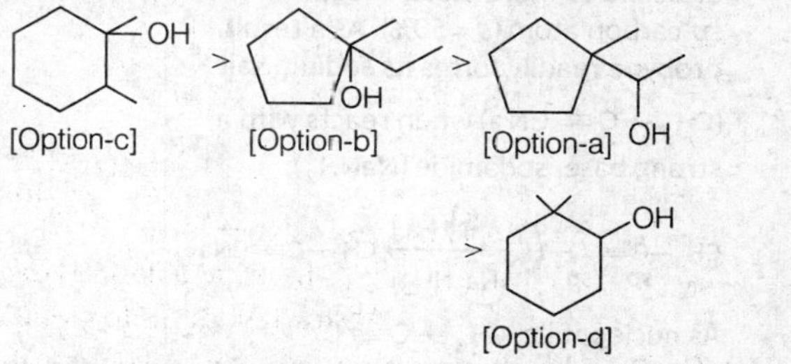

[Option-c] > [Option-b] > [Option-a] > [Option-d]

11. (b) 1,3-butadiene is a conjugated diene, one molecule of which when reacts with 1 molecule of HBr, 1, 2- and 1,4-addition products are obtained through formation of carbocation intermediates (electrophilic addition reaction).

$\Rightarrow$

$$\underset{4}{CH_2}=\underset{3}{CH}-\underset{2}{CH}=\underset{1}{CH_2}\xrightarrow[\text{Slow, }-Br^-]{H-Br}$$

$$\left[\underset{4}{CH_2}=\underset{3}{CH}-\overset{\oplus}{\underset{2}{CH}}-\underset{1}{CH_3}\ (I)\ \underset{40°C}{\overset{-60°C}{\rightleftharpoons}}\ \overset{\oplus}{\underset{4}{CH_2}}-\underset{3}{CH}=\underset{2}{CH}-\underset{1}{CH_3}\ (II)\right]$$

$$\Rightarrow \underset{4}{CH_2}=\underset{3}{CH}-\overset{\oplus}{\underset{2}{CH}}-\underset{1}{CH_3}\ (I)\xrightarrow[\text{Fast}]{Br^-}CH_2=CH-\overset{Br}{\overset{|}{CH}}-CH_3$$

(*A*) (3-bromobutene)

It is a kinetically, controlled product, the minor product at lower temperature (−60°C) [1,2-addition product].

$$\Rightarrow \overset{\oplus}{\underset{4}{CH_2}}-\underset{3}{CH}=\underset{2}{CH}-\underset{1}{CH_3}\ (II)\xrightarrow[\text{Fast}]{Br^-}\overset{Br}{\overset{|}{CH_2}}-CH=CH-CH_3$$

(*B*) (1-bromo-2-butene)

It is a thermodynamically controlled product, the major product at higher temperature (40°C). [1,4-addition product]

So, $CH_2=CH-CH=CH_2\xrightarrow[40°C]{HBr}\underset{(Minor)}{A}+\underset{(Major)}{B}$ [Option (b)]

12. (b) Propyne has one acidic H-atom attached to more electronegative *sp*-carbon atom ($s=50\%$). As a result, propyne readily forms its sodium salt ($CH_3-C\equiv\overset{-}{C}\overset{+}{N}a$) when reacts with a strong base, sodamide ($NaNH_2$).

$$CH_3-\underset{sp}{C}\equiv\underset{sp}{\overset{\delta-}{C}}-\overset{\delta+}{H}\ \ \overset{+}{Na}\overset{-}{:NH_2}\xrightarrow{-NH_3}CH_3-C\equiv\overset{-}{C}\overset{+}{N}a$$

As nucleophile, $CH_3-C\equiv C^{\ominus}$ attacks ethyl bromide (CH_3CH_2Br, 1°-bromide) in S_N2 pathway to produce the higher homologue of propyne, i.e pent-2-yne ($CH_3-C\equiv C-CH_2-CH_3$) or (*P*).

$$CH_3-C\equiv\overset{-}{C}\overset{\oplus}{N}a\xrightarrow[S_N2,\ -NaBr]{CH_3-CH_2-Br}\underset{(P)}{CH_3-C\equiv C-CH_2CH_3}$$

Then, *P* undergoes, anti-addition of hydrogen atoms selectively by use of $Li/C_2H_5NH_2$ at −78°C in neutral medium to give (*E*)-pent-2-ene as the major product(*Q*).

$$\underset{(P)}{CH_3-C\equiv C-CH_2CH_3}\xrightarrow[\text{(ii) }NH_4Cl]{\text{(i) }Li/C_2H_5NH_2/-78°C}$$

$(CH_3)(H)C=C(H)(CH_2CH_3)$ *Trans* or Major (*Q*) + $(CH_3)(H)C=C(CH_2CH_3)(H)$ *cis* or (*Z*) (Minor)

13. (d)

(Cyclic alkene) $\xrightarrow[\text{(ii) }Zn/H_2O]{\text{(i) }O_3/THF}$ cyclic 1,4-dione

Here, cleavage $C_1=C_4$ bond takes place in reductive ozonolysis of a cyclic alkene. As a result, we get another cyclic 1,4-dicarboxyl compound.

14. (c)The reduction of benzene with sodium in presence of liquid ammonia yields 1, 4-cyclohexadiene.

Benzene $\xrightarrow[NH_3(l)]{Na}$ 1,4-cyclohexadiene

15. (b)

$$\underset{\text{2-pentyne}}{CH_3CH_2-C\equiv C-CH_3}\xrightarrow{HBr}\underset{\text{3-bromopent-2-ene (A)}}{CH_3CH_2-\overset{Br}{\overset{|}{C}}=\overset{H}{\overset{|}{C}}-CH_3}$$

$$\underset{\text{2-pentyne}}{CH_3CH_2-C\equiv C-CH_3}\xrightarrow{HBr}\underset{\text{2-bromopent-2-ene (B)}}{CH_3CH_2-\overset{H}{\overset{|}{C}}=\overset{Br}{\overset{|}{C}}-CH_3}$$

We get, isomeric bromo compounds *A* and *B* of molecular formula, C_5H_9Br.

$\Rightarrow$ *A* and *B* are positional isomers (structural).

$\Rightarrow$ Each of *A* and *B* shows geometrical isomerism (*cis* + *trans*).

$\therefore$ Total number of stereoisomers (geometrical) $=2\times2=4$

16. (d) With increase in molecular mass, boiling point increases. So, toluene has least boiling point.

Out of *o*-xylene, *m*-xylene and *p*-xylene, *p*-xylene is more symmetrical and hence, particles are closely placed in the crystal lattice. Therefore, *p*-xylene has highest boiling point.

Also, out of four aromatic hydrocarbons given, only *p*-xylene is non-polar, i.e. symmetrical ($\mu=0$). So, in crystalline state, highest degree of closed packed lattices will be present in solid *p*-xylene. Thus, higher amount of energy is required (higher melting point) to break down its lattices.

17. (a) An alkyne undergoes nucleophilic addition of H_2O (hydration) in presence of $Hg^{2+}/H^+/H_2O$ to produce an enol first which readily tautomerises into its more stable keto-form.

In the given alkyne, the benzyl-carbon has more partial positive charge (δ^+) which favours attack of the nucleophile (H_2O) to this carbon easily.

$C_6H_5-C\equiv C-C_2H_5 \xrightarrow{Hg^{2+}}$ Hg^{2+}-complex (Benzylic carbon (δ^+)) $\xrightarrow{H_2\ddot{O}:}$ $C_6H_5(HO)C=C(Hg^+)C_2H_5$ (Enol) $\rightarrow$ $C_6H_5-\overset{O}{\overset{\|}{C}}-CH(Hg^+)C_2H_5$ (keto) $\xrightarrow{-Hg^{2+}}$ $C_6H_5-\overset{OH}{\overset{|}{C}}=CH-C_2H_5$ (Enol) $\rightleftharpoons$ $C_6H_5-\overset{O}{\overset{\|}{C}}-CH_2-C_2H_5$

(Keto) $\Rightarrow$ more stable (major, *A*)

So, *A* is formed as the major product.

18. (b) In (a), (c) and (d), the group attached to phenyl ring deactivates the ring as they are electron-withdrawing groups. But methyl is a electron-donating group. So, it activates the ring for further substitution. Hence, polysubstitution may takes place in case of toluene only.

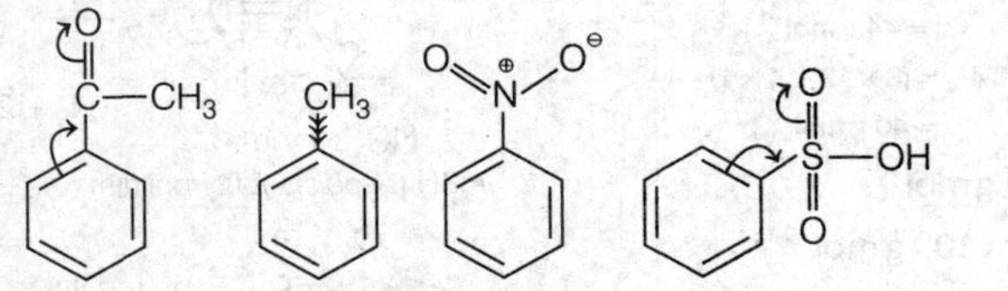

(a) (b) (c) (d)

19. (d)

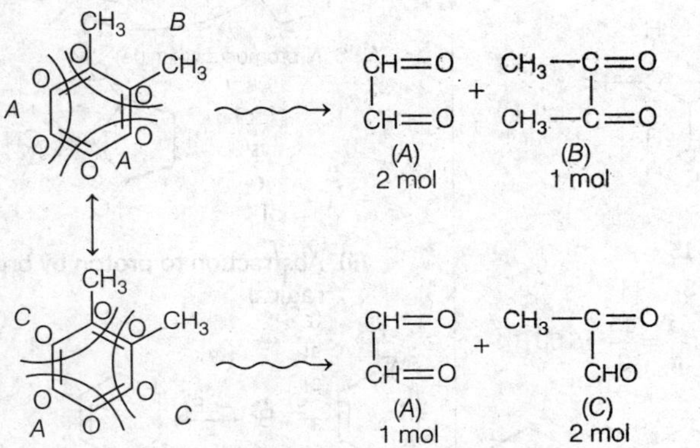

$CH=O$ + $CH_3-C=O$ / $CH=O$ $CH_3-C=O$ — (*A*) 2 mol, (*B*) 1 mol

$CH=O$ + $CH_3-C=O$ / $CH=O$ CHO — (*A*) 1 mol, (*C*) 2 mol

So, *o*-xylene on complete ozonolysis (reductive) produces 3 moles of glyoxal (*A*), 1 mole of dimethyl glyoxal (*B*) and 2 moles of methyl glyoxal (*C*).

$\Rightarrow A:B:C = 3:1:2$

20. (b)

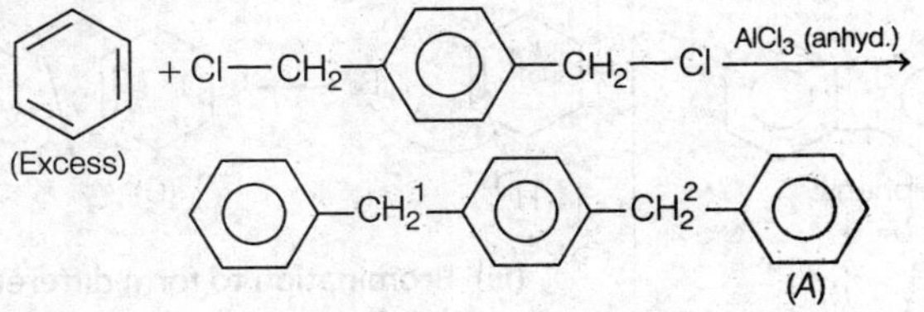

(Excess) + $Cl-CH_2-C_6H_4-CH_2-Cl \xrightarrow{AlCl_3 \text{ (anhyd.)}}$ $C_6H_5-CH_2^1-C_6H_4-CH_2^2-C_6H_5$ (*A*)

NBS is used for bromination at the benzyl position.

In (*A*) there are two benzyl positions marked as 1 and 2.

Thus, bromination occurs at 1 and 2 to give product *B*.

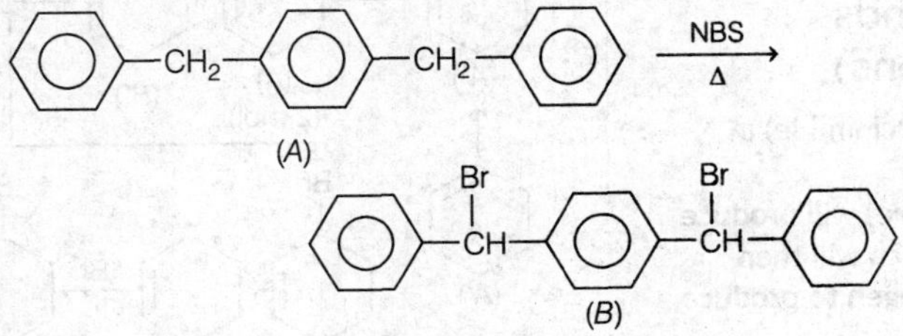

$C_6H_5-CH_2-C_6H_4-CH_2-C_6H_5$ (*A*) $\xrightarrow[\Delta]{NBS}$ $C_6H_5-CH(Br)-C_6H_4-CH(Br)-C_6H_5$ (*B*)

21. (256) Monochlorinated products for cyclopentane are

$\xrightarrow{Cl_2}$ (chlorocyclopentane)

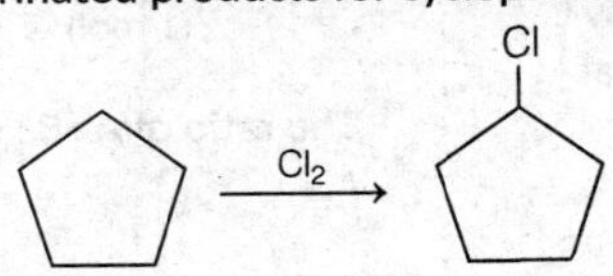

So, $x = 1$

Dichlorinated products for cyclopentane are

$\xrightarrow{Cl_2}$ (1,1-dichloro) + (1,2-dichloro) + (1,3-dichloro)

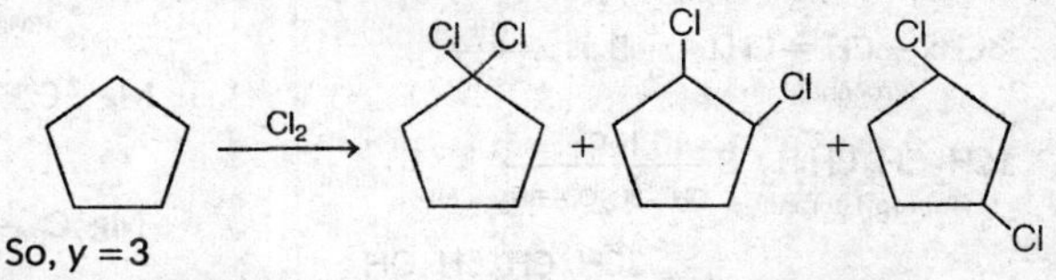

So, $y = 3$

Trichlorinated products for cyclopentane are

$\xrightarrow{Cl_2}$ (trichloro isomers) + … + … + …

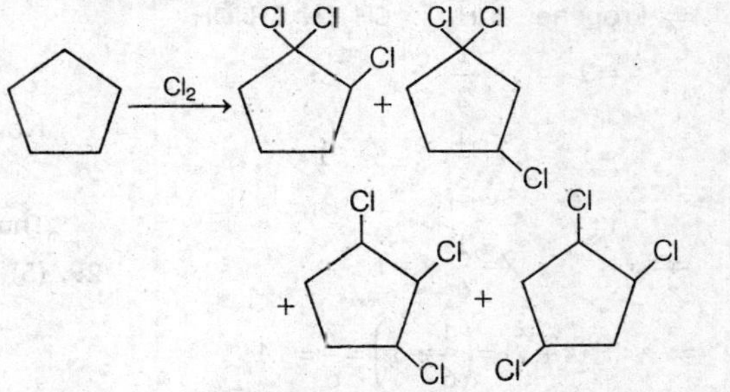

So, $z = 1$. Thus, $(x+y)^z = (1+3)^4 = (4)^4 = 256$

22. (3) The given molecule has three types of hydrogens, i.e. 1°, 2° and 3°. So, total three mono brominated products are formed.

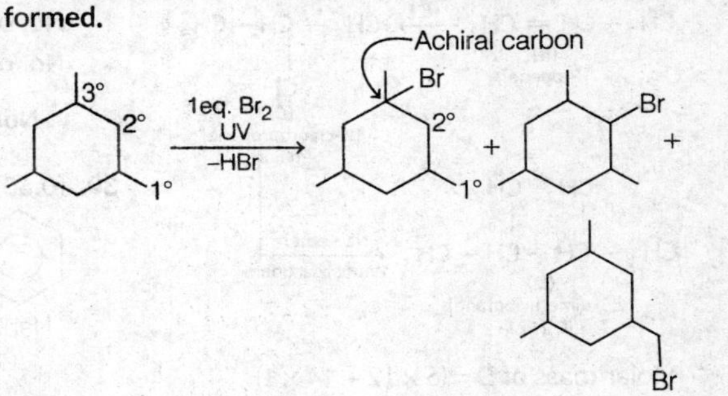

$\xrightarrow[\text{UV}, -HBr]{\text{1eq. } Br_2}$ (Achiral carbon) + … + …

23. (12.50) $CH_3-CH(CH_3)-CH_2-CH_3$ (1°, 1°, 1°)

Iso-pentane (C_5H_{12})

$\Rightarrow$ Total number of 1°-H atoms $= 3 \times 3 = 9$

$\therefore$ Mass % of 1°-H atoms $= \dfrac{9 \times 1}{(5 \times 12 + 12 \times 1)} \times 100 = 12.50\% = x\%$

So, $x = 12.50$

24. (27.77) Selectivity in chlorination is,

1°-H : 2°-H : 3°-H = 1 : 3.8 : 5

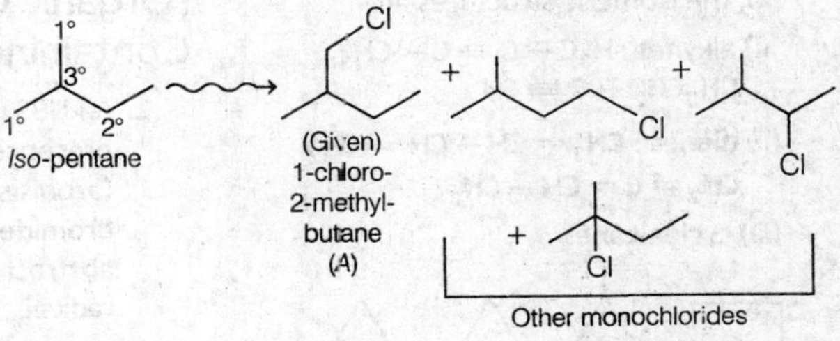

$\Rightarrow$ *Iso*-pentane (1°, 3°, 1°, 2°) ⟶ (Given) 1-chloro-2-methyl-butane (*A*) + … + … + … (Other monochlorides)

$\Rightarrow a\% = \dfrac{6 \times 1}{(6 \times 1 + 3 \times 1 + 2 \times 3.8 + 1 \times 5)} \times 100$

$= \dfrac{6}{21.6} \times 100 = 27.77\% = a\%$

25. (1.16)

$$3CH_3-CH=CH_2+\frac{1}{2}B_2H_6 \xrightarrow{THF}$$
(Propene)

$$(CH_3CH_2CH_2)_3B \xrightarrow[OH^-,\,3H_2O,\,-BH_3]{H_2O_2} 3CH_3CH_2CH_2OH$$
(Tripropyl borane) (Propan-1-ol)

$\Rightarrow$ Propene : B_2H_6 : $CH_3CH_2CH_2OH$

$= 3 : \frac{1}{2} : 3$

$= 1 : \frac{1}{6} : 1$
(x) (y)

$\Rightarrow$ $x=\frac{1}{6}, y=1$

$\Rightarrow$ $(x+y)=\left(\frac{1}{6}+1\right)=\frac{7}{6}=1.16$

26. (40) $CH_3-C\equiv CH \xrightarrow[H_2]{\text{Lindlar's catalyst}}$
(A) [Propyne]

$CH_3-CH=CH_2 \xrightarrow{HCl} CH_3-CH(Cl)-CH_3$
(B) [Propene] (C) [2-chloropropane] (major)

$CH_3-CH(CH_3)-CH(CH_3)-CH_3 \xleftarrow[\text{Wurtz reaction}]{\text{Na / ether}}$
(D) [2,3-dimethylbutane] (C_6H_{14})

Molar mass of $D=(6\times12+14\times1)$
$=86\text{ g mol}^{-1}$

$\Rightarrow$ Molar mass of
$A(C_3H_4)=(3\times12+4\times1)$
$=40\text{ g mol}^{-1}$

27. (8) Degree of unsaturation of C_4H_6 is,

$$DU=\frac{2n_C-n_H+2}{2}$$
$$=\frac{2\times4-6+2}{2}=2$$

So, the isomeric structures are

(i) alkynes : $H_3C-C\equiv C-CH_3$, $CH_3CH_2-C\equiv CH$

(ii) dienes : $CH_2=CH-CH=CH_2$, $CH_2=C=CH-CH_3$

(iii) cycloalkanes :

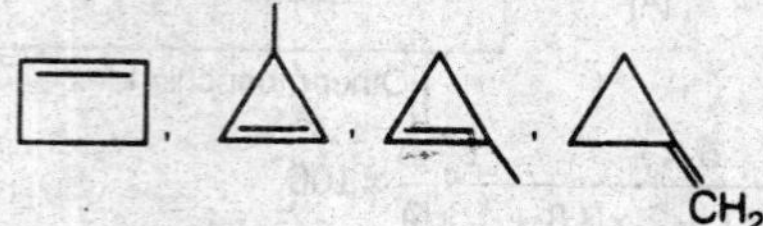

Total $=2+2+4=8=x$

28. (1.76) Mg_2C_3 (Magnesium carbide) or

$$Mg^{2+}C_3^{4-} \xrightarrow[-Mg(OD)_2]{D_2O} C_3D_4 \;(A)$$

$$Mg_2C_3 \xrightarrow[-Mg(OH)_2]{H_2O} C_3H_4 \;(B)$$

[Molar mass of A, $C_3D_4=(3\times12+4\times2)$
$=44\text{ g mol}^{-1}$]

[Molar mass of B, $C_3H_4=(3\times12+4\times1)$
$=40\text{ g mol}^{-1}$]

Now, $44\times40=1760\text{ g mol}^{-1}$
$=1.76\times10^3\text{ g mol}^{-1}$

Thus, the value of x is 1.76.

29. (5)

No. of σ-bonds, $\sigma=15$

No. of π-bonds, $\pi=3$

$\therefore$ Number of bonds, $\frac{\sigma}{\pi}=\frac{15}{3}=5.00$

30. (0.60)

Naphthalene $x=2$ Anthracene $y=3$

Phenanthrene $a=3$ Biphenyl $b=0$

$$\Rightarrow \frac{a+b}{x+y}=\frac{3+0}{2+3}=\frac{3}{5}=0.60$$

Qualifier 23
(Organic Compounds Containing Halogens)

1. (c) NBS (N-bromosuccinimide) in presence of AIBN (azo*bis*isobutyronitrile) will produce bromide radical, which will then abstract allylic hydrogen to produce radical.

It will undergo resonance followed by the combination with bromide radical to give different products with different extents.

The reaction scheme with possible mechanism is shown below

(i) Reaction of NBS with AIBN to produce bromine radical

AIBN (Azo*bis*isobutyronitrile) $\xrightarrow{\Delta}$ $N_2 + 2$ (CN) radical

NBS (N-bromosuccinimide) + radical ⟶ N–C(CN) succinimide + Br•

(ii) Abstraction to proton by bromine radical

+ Br• $\xrightarrow{-HBr}$ (A′)

Resonance ⟶ (B′) / (B′)

OR

+ Br• ⟶ (C) / (C′)

(iii) Bromination to form different products

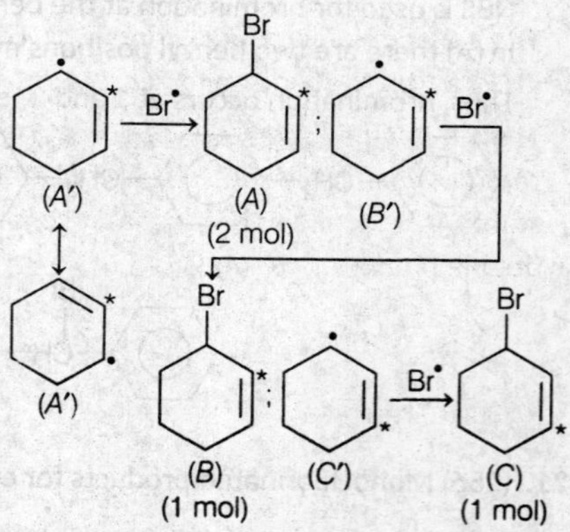

The ratio of A : B : C is 2 : 1 : 1.

2. (d) The reaction scheme with possible mechanism are shown below

CH_3 CH_3 ≡ ≡ H_3C CH_3 CH_3 CH_3 Br — Br CH_3

⟶ H_3C CH_3 Br Br

(*d*)

Angle strain in cyclopropane is very high, so it readily undergoes electrophilic addition with Br_2 as it responds similarly with propane.

3. (c) Assertion is correct and Reason is incorrect.

Br $\xrightarrow{Br_2/Fe}$ Br Br + Br Br

Bromobenzene 1, 4-dibromobenzene (Major) 1, 2-dibromobenzene (Minor)

Bromine orientation is controlled by its mesomeric effect (+ *M*) and it also gives stabilisation to the arenium ion.

Br $Br^{\oplus}$ ⟶ (+*M*) :Br: Br H Arenium ion

4. (d) In case of butadiene system, bromination leads to the formation of two products; 1, 2-addition product and 1, 4-addition product.

The 1,2-addition product is kinetically controlled product (KCP) as it is formed at a faster rate.

The 1,4-addition product, i.e. 1, 4-dibromobut-2-ene is thermodynamically controlled product (TCP) which is more stable. It is the major product as it contains more substituted double bond.

(Buta-1, 3-diene) Br — Br ⟶ Br

⟷ $\overset{\ominus}{Br}$ Br ⟶ Br Br

(1, 4-dibromobut-2-ene)
$(BrCH_2CH{=}CHCH_2Br)$

5. (a) The following is the mechanism involved in the given reaction,

$\xrightarrow[-Cl^-]{HCl}$ $H^{\oplus}$ $\overset{\ominus}{Cl}$ ⟶ Cl

3° carbocation

6. (a) The given reaction involves the formation of cyclic bromonium ion intermediate. Hence, the first bromine addition occurs as Br^+ ion and this ion will act as the electron acceptor, while ethylene will act as the electron donor species. From the M.O. diagram of Br_2, it can be shown that the LUMO of Br_2 is σ^* orbital. Hence, molecular orbital interactions involved in the first step of the following reaction is

$$\pi_{C=C} \longrightarrow \sigma^*_{Br—Br}$$

7. (a) Iodide > bromide > chloride > fluoride

With increase in size as well as number of halogen atoms in the benzene ring, density of halobenzene increases.

The size of halogen decreases in the order as iodine > bromine > chlorine > fluorine.

Thus, considering above facts the increasing order density given compounds is (i) < (ii) < (iii) < (iv).

8. (b) —CH_3 group is a weak activator and —Cl group is a deactivator. So, to compare the dipole moment of the chloroderivatives, we have to consider the formula

$$\mu = \sqrt{\mu_1^2 + \mu_2^2 + 2\mu_1\mu_2 \cos\theta},$$

greater the value of θ, smaller is the dipole moment.

9. (c) At first methoxide will pick up one acidic α-proton to produce anion which will displace the bromide ion to generate cyclopropanone moiety which undergo nucleophilic attack by methoxide ion and followed by rearrangement which will lead to the generation of compound in option - (c). This is known as Favorskii rearrangement.

H $\overset{\ominus}{O}Me$ Br Br O ⟶ Br Br O

$\xrightarrow{-Br^-}$ Br O $^{\ominus}OMe$ ⟶ Br O OMe $\xrightarrow{-Br^-}$ COOMe

10. (b) The given compound contains active keto-methyl ($—COCH_3$) group. Hence, in presence of NaOH and Br_2, it undergoes bromoform reaction to give $CHBr_3$ and chiral acid salt, which on acidification, produces chiral acid. The final acid is chiral in nature as it contains one chiral centre (*). The reaction scheme is shown below.

O O H O $\xrightarrow[2.\ H^{\oplus}]{1.\ NaOH/Br_2}$ O O * H OH O + $CHBr_3$

11. (c) Bromide is a good leaving group. Hence, in presence of strong base $MeO^-/MeOH$, the compound will undergo elimination *via* E2 pathway.

The stereo-electronic requirement for an E2 reaction is that the eliminating groups must have *anti*-periplanar geometry. Here, the given substrate has E-geometry, the two ethyl groups are present on the same side of the double bond. Hence, MeO^- will abstract a proton from ethyl group and force to remove bromide group and leading to the formation of 2, 3-hexadiene.

$$\xrightarrow[-HBr]{E2} \overset{4}{C}H(\overset{5}{C}H_2\overset{6}{C}H_3)=\overset{3}{C}=\overset{2}{C}H-\overset{1}{Me}$$

(2, 3-hexadiene)

$MeO^{\ominus}$

[(E)-3- bromo-3-hexene]

12. (a) With AgCN, due to greater covalency of Ag—C bond, N is the donor atom. In KCN, CN^- exists as free ion, better carbon donor and forms the bond.

$$R—X \xrightarrow[-KX]{\overset{\oplus}{K}\ddot{C}N} R—CN\text{(major)}$$

$$R—X \xrightarrow[-AgCN]{Ag—C\equiv N:} R—\ddot{N}\equiv C:\text{(major)}$$

[∵ CN^- is an ambident nucleophile]

13. (c) In E2-elimination, α -Br and β-H remain *anti-* or *trans-* to each other.

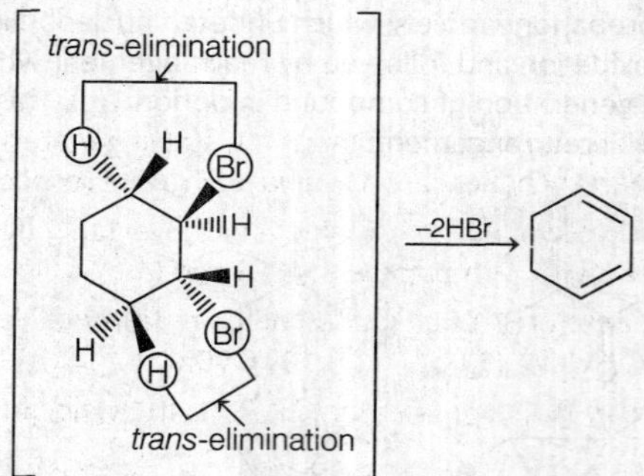

14. (a) Stability of the transition state (TS) indicates, that activation energy will be lower, i.e. rate of formation of the product will be faster.
More the conjugation, more stable is the transition state. II gives the aromatic product, (benzene) whereas I and III produce (1,3-cyclohexadiene) and (cyclohexene) respectively.

15. (a) Correct match is A-(3), B-(1), C-(2), D-(4).

A. In S_N1 reaction, the carbocation intermediate gets attacked by the nucleophile in the faster step to give a product whose inversion and retention in configuration occur, i.e. racemisation takes place.

B. **In bromination**, an alkene produces α, β-dibromoalkane, i.e. a *vicinal* (*vic*-) dibromide is formed.

$$>C=C< \xrightarrow{Br_2/CCl_4} >C(Br)—C(Br)<$$

Alkene (*vic*-dibromide)

C. **Alkylidene dihalide** is an α, α-dihalide or *geminal* (*gem*-) dihalide.

$$—C—CX_2—$$

(*gem*-dihalide)

D. **Dehydrohalogenation** (—HX) of an alkyl halide in elimination reaction forms an alkene and it follows Saytzeff rule to give more substituted alkene as the major product.

$$CH_2(H)—CH(X)—CH(H)—CH_3 \xrightarrow[\text{Base}]{-HX} CH_2—CH=CH—CH_3$$

[More substituted alkene] (Major Product)

$$+ CH_2=CH—CH_2—CH_3$$

[Least substituted alkene] (Minor product)

16. (b) It does not react with isopropyl magnesium bromide due to steric hindrance caused by two bulkier group.

17. (c) With Grignard reagent (RMgX); HCHO, R—CHO, $R—\overset{O}{\overset{\|}{C}}—R$ and $R—C\equiv CH$ will give RCH_2OH (1°), R_2CHOH (2°), $R_3C—OH$ (3°) and RH(hydrocarbon) respectively.

18. (a) An alkyl halide containing an alcoholic —OH group can be converted to Grignard reagent. First protecting the —OH group to a *tert*-butyldimethylsilyl ether which is inert to Grignard reagent. The protecting group is finally liberated by treatment with fluoride ion.

19. (d) The reaction mechanism for the reaction is as follows

$$\text{Morpholine} \xrightarrow[-KHCO_3]{DMSO,\ K_2CO_3} \text{Morpholine anion} \xrightarrow{F—C_6H_4—SO_2—CH_3} \text{intermediate} \xrightarrow{-F^-} MeO_2S—C_6H_4—N(\text{morpholine})$$

From the mechanism, it is evident that the reaction is an aromatic nucleophilic substitution (ArS_N2) and as the substitution reaction occurs at the carbon at which fluorine is attached, it is also an example of aromatic *ipso* substitution reaction.

20. (d) Presence of electron withdrawing group (EWG) at *ortho/para* makes the reaction more feasible.

So, here the rate of reactivity is (d) > (c) > (a) > (b).

21. (6)

⇒ X is benzyne, [structure] or [structure]

in which 6π-electrons are involved in aromaticity and it remains perpendicular to the σ-plane.

22. (2.97) Let, in the mixture of 10 g of *n*-butane and 2-butene, *x* g of 2-butane is present. The molecular weight of 2-butene is 56. One mole of 2-butene will react with one equivalent of bromine. Hence, the amount of bromine required is 160 g. In the mixture of two, only but-2-ene will undergo bromination.

$$\underset{\substack{\text{(2-butene)}\\56\text{ g}}}{H_3C—CH=CH—CH_3} + \underset{160\text{ g}}{Br_2} \longrightarrow CH_3—CH(Br)—CH(Br)—CH_3$$

As 56 g of 2-butene consumed 160 g of bromine.

Hence, x g of 2-butene consumed $= \frac{160x}{56} = \frac{20x}{7}$ g

According to the question, $\frac{20x}{7} = 8$ or, $x = \frac{56}{20} = 2.8 \text{ g} = a$ g

$a = 2.8$

The total molecular weight of *n*-butane and 2-butene $= (56 + 58) = 114$. When hydrogenation is carried out, only 2-butene will be hydrogenated. Hence, the gain in molecular weight of the mixture = 2.

$$\underset{\text{(But-2-ene) } M = 56\text{ g}}{H_3C—CH=CH—CH_3} + H_2 \longrightarrow \underset{(n\text{-butane) } M = 58\text{ g}}{CH_3CH_2CH_2CH_3}$$

So, 114 g of mixture of hydrogenation cause the gain of 2 g of weight.

Hence, 10 g of mixture on hydrogenation cause the gain of

$$= \frac{2 \times 10}{114} = 0.17 \text{ g of weight.}$$

$\Rightarrow \quad b = 0.17$

$\Rightarrow \quad (a + b) = 2.8 + 0.17 = 2.97$

23. (29.55)

$$\underset{\text{(Acetophenone)}}{C_6H_5COCH_3} + 3I_2 \xrightarrow{Aq.\ NaOH} C_6H_5CO\overset{-}{O}\overset{+}{Na} + \underset{\substack{\text{(Iodoform)}\\[A]}}{CHI_3(s)\downarrow}$$

	Acetophenone	$3I_2$	CHI_3
	1×120 g	3×254 g	1×394 g
Amount :	12 g	76.2 g	39.4 g

Hence, from the reaction scheme, it is evident that one mole of acetophenone reacts with three moles of iodine.

Hence, 120 g of acetophenone will react with 762 g of iodine to give 394 g of CHI_3.

So, 12 g of acetophenone will react with $\frac{3 \times 254}{120} \times 12 \text{ g} = 76.2$ g of iodine to give 39.4 g of CHI_3.

According to the question, the yield of solid *A* is 75%.

Hence, the amount of *A* obtained $= (39.4 \times 0.75) = 29.55$ g

24. (6) The following six compounds will undergo rearrangement in S_N1 reaction with their carbocation intermediate.

[structures: Br, I, Cl/Br, Cl, Cl, Cl substituted compounds]

25. (6) The following six halides will respond to both S_N1 and S_N2 pathways.

$C_6H_5—CH_2—Br$, $(CH_3)_2CHBr$, $H_3C—O—CH_2Cl$, [OTs structure], [Br cyclohexane], [cyclopentyl–CH_2Cl]

26. (60) The molecular weight of the starting material and the isomeric products are 199 and 118 g/mol respectively.

Hence, 199 g of the bromide *A* will give 118 g (for 100% reaction) of isomeric products *B* and *C*.

But, here only 1.062 g of *B* and *C* are formed. Hence, the % of overall yield: $(1.062/1.18)\ 100 = 90\%$.

Now, as the ratio of *B* and *C* is 2 : 1, the yields for their formation, $A = 90 \times \frac{2}{3}\% = 60\%$.

27. (3)

$$Cl—\overset{O}{\overset{\|}{C}}—OC_2H_5 \xrightarrow[-MgBrCl]{\overset{\ominus\oplus}{R}MgBr} R—\overset{O}{\overset{\|}{C}}—OC_2H_5 \xrightarrow[-Mg(OEt)Br]{\overset{\ominus\oplus}{R}MgBr}$$

$$R—\overset{O}{\overset{\|}{C}}—R \xrightarrow[\substack{\text{(ii) } H_3O^+\\-Mg(OH)Br}]{\text{(i) }\overset{\ominus\oplus}{R}MgBr} R—\overset{OH}{\underset{R}{C}}—R \text{ (3° alcohol)}$$

Number of moles of Grignard reagent used $x = 3$

28. (6)

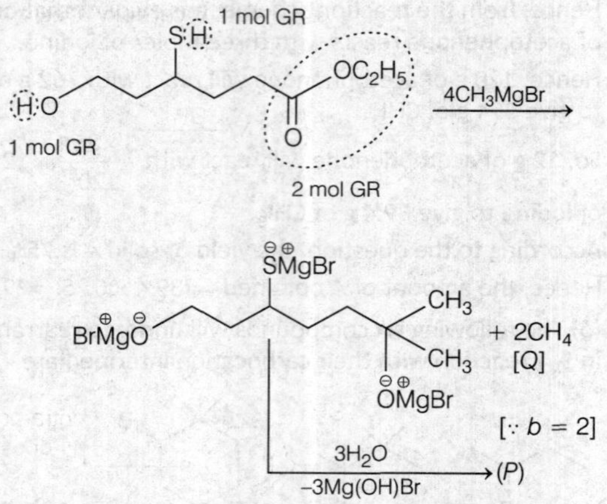

1 mol GR, 1 mol GR, 2 mol GR; $\xrightarrow{4CH_3MgBr}$

$\overset{\ominus\oplus}{SMgBr}$, $\overset{\oplus}{Br}\overset{\ominus}{Mg}O$ ... + $2CH_4$ [Q], $\overset{\ominus\oplus}{OMgBr}$ [∵ b = 2]

$\xrightarrow[-3Mg(OH)Br]{3H_2O}$ (P)

⇒ $a = 4$ [∵ GR = Grignard Reagent (CH_3MgBr)]

⇒ $a + b = 4 + 2 = 6$

29. (33.6)

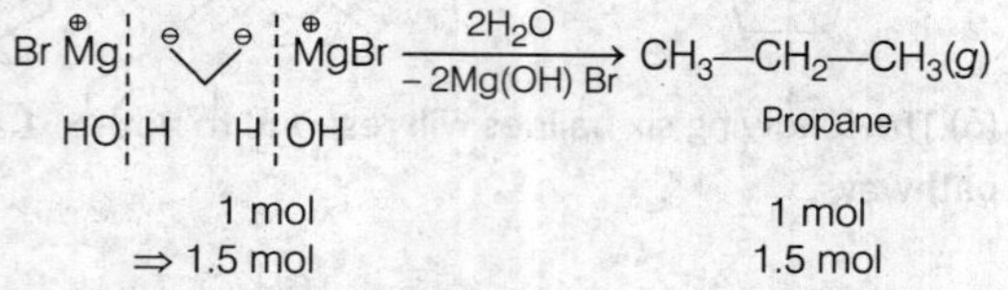

$\overset{\oplus}{Br}\ \overset{\ominus}{Mg}$ ... $\overset{\oplus}{MgBr}$ $\xrightarrow[-2Mg(OH)Br]{2H_2O}$ $CH_3—CH_2—CH_3(g)$ Propane

HO H   H OH

1 mol ⇒ 1.5 mol   1 mol 1.5 mol

⇒ $V_{C_3H_8(g)} = 1.5 \times 22.4$ L

$= 33.6$ L $= x$ L at STP

$x = 33.6$

30. (6) The final step follows Hofmann elimination to give,

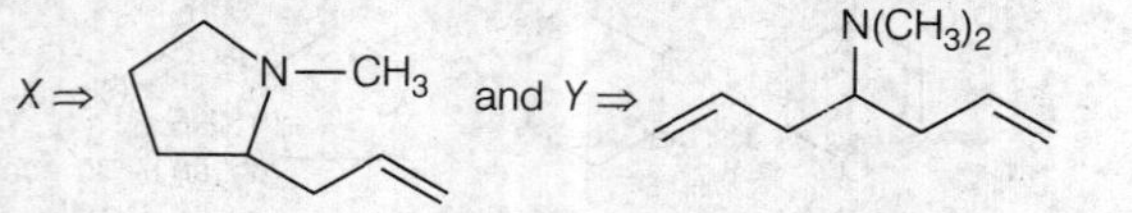

X ⇒ (N—CH_3 pyrrolidine with allyl group) and Y ⇒ ($N(CH_3)_2$ diene)

⇒ Total number of $\pi - e^-$s = number of π-bonds $\times 2 = 3 \times 2 = 6$

Qualifier 24
(Organic Compounds Containing Oxygen)

1. (a) The reagent having greater value of nucleophilic character undergo faster nucleophilic substitution reaction. Steric hindrance plays an important role. According to which greater the steric hindrance in the nucleophile, lower will be its reactivity towards S_N2.

So, the order of reactivity towards S_N2 reaction is as follows

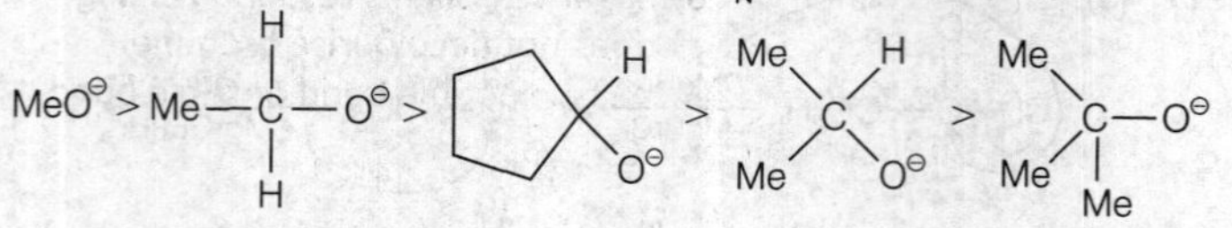

$MeO^{\ominus} > Me—CH_2—O^{\ominus} >$ (cyclopentyl-$O^{\ominus}$) $>$ $Me_2CH—O^{\ominus}$ $>$ $Me_3C—O^{\ominus}$

i.e. II > III > V > IV > I

2. (c) The conversion of an α, β-diol to α-hydroxy ketone on reaction with protic acid is known as pinacol-pinacolone rearrangement and this reaction is believed to proceed as,

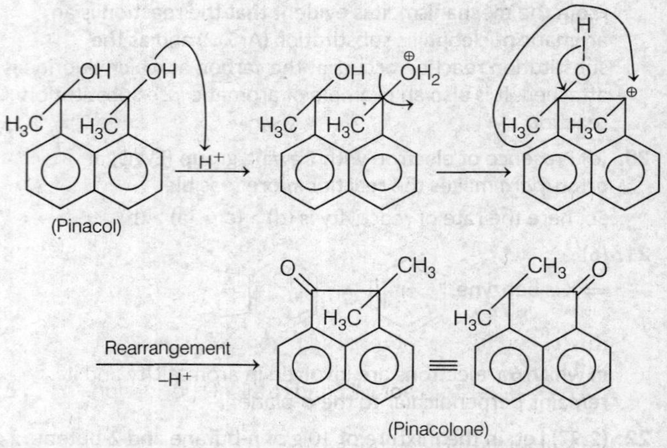

(Pinacol) $\xrightarrow{H^+}$ → $\xrightarrow[-H^+]{\text{Rearrangement}}$ (Pinacolone)

3. (b) As aldehyde group is an electron withdrawing group, it will deactivate the ring and it is *meta* orienting group. However, hydroxyl group is an electron donating group, it will activate the ring and it is *ortho* and *para* orienting group.

Also, an aldehyde group is bulkier than a hydroxyl group. Hence, the bromo group will occupy the *ortho* position with respect to hydroxyl group.

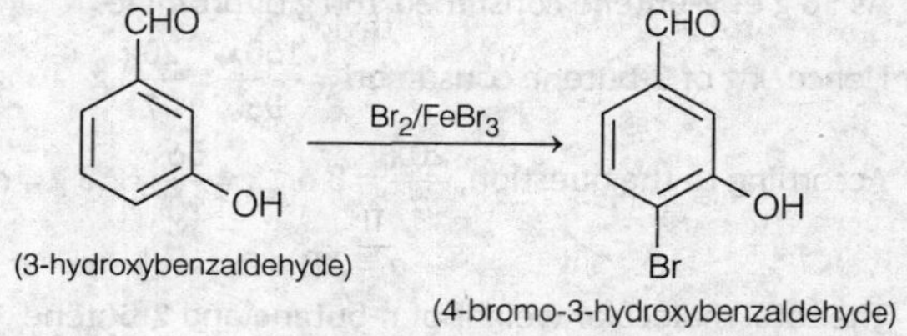

(3-hydroxybenzaldehyde) $\xrightarrow{Br_2/FeBr_3}$ (4-bromo-3-hydroxybenzaldehyde)

4. (d) When phenol is treated with NaOH and CO_2, sodium salicylate is formed *via* the formation of six membered chelated ring which on acidic hydrolysis will produce salicylic acid (*E*).

As phenolic hydroxyl oxygen is more nucleophilic than the carboxyl oxygen, so when salicylic acid is treated with acetic anhydride, acetylation will occur at phenolic hydroxyl oxygen causing the formation of aspirin.

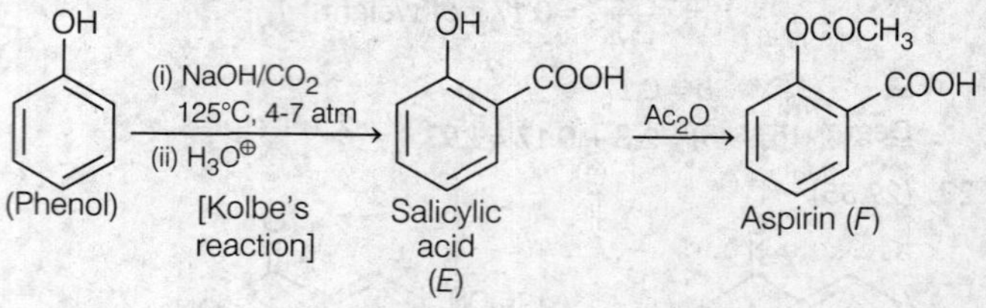

(Phenol) $\xrightarrow[\text{(ii) } H_3O^{\oplus}]{\text{(i) NaOH/}CO_2\text{, 125°C, 4-7 atm}}$ Salicylic acid (*E*) [Kolbe's reaction] $\xrightarrow{Ac_2O}$ Aspirin (*F*) ($OCOCH_3$, COOH)

5. (a) Molecular formula ($C_9H_{12}O$) shows that four isomers are of alcohols, $C_6H_5—C_nH_{2n}—OH$ (1°, 2° or 3°) as they liberate H_2 gas on treatment with Na.

Hence, 4 isomers are

(a) Ph–CH₂–CH(OH)–CH₃ (b) Ph–C(CH₃)₂–OH (c) Ph–CH(OH)–CH₂–CH₃ (d) Ph–CH₂–CH₂–CH₂–OH

(b), (c) and (d) do not respond to iodoform test.

(b) $\xrightarrow[H^+]{KMnO_4}$ Does not respond to $KMnO_4$ oxidation.

(a) Fulfills all the conditions.

6. (b) Deuteroboration reaction involves the *cis*-addition of $-D$ and $-BD_2$ units of $BD_3\left(\text{or } \frac{1}{2}B_2D_6\right)$ to the more substituted positions of the double bond. So, methyl and $-BD_2$ units are *trans* to each other.

Hence, oxidation by using hydrogen peroxide and sodium hydroxide will lead hydration in anti-Markownikoff's manner to form *trans* 2-deutero-2-methylcyclopentan-1-ol (*A*). The reaction scheme is shown below

1-methylcyclopentene $\xrightarrow{B_2D_6/THF}$ (Me, D, BD_2, H) $\xrightarrow{H_2O_2/NaOH}$ (Me, D, OH, H) (*A*)

7. (b) Molecular structure of compound having molecular formula $C_{14}H_{10}O_2$ is determined by calculating degree of unsaturation (*U*),

$$U=(C+1)-\frac{H}{2}-\frac{X}{2}+\frac{N}{2}=(14+1)-\frac{10}{2}=15-5=10$$

Degree of unsaturation is 10 in which 2 units are already used as diketo group $\left(\text{—}\overset{O}{\overset{\|}{C}}\text{—}\overset{O}{\overset{\|}{C}}\text{—}\right)$

Rest 8 unit of unsaturation is satisfied by two phenyl ring each having, $U=4$.

Hence, correct structure is

C_6H_5–CO–CO–C_6H_5 (Benzil)

Conversion of benzil to benzylic acid in the presence of base is known as benzylic acid rearrangement.

In general, benzylic acid is α-hydroxycarboxylic acid. The reaction is believed to occur as,

C_6H_5–CO–CO–C_6H_5 $\xrightarrow{OH^-}$ C_6H_5–C(O⁻)(OH)–CO–C_6H_5 ⟶ HO–CO–C(O⁻)(C_6H_5)–C_6H_5 —(Intramolecular H-abstraction)⟶ ⁻O–CO–C(OH)(C_6H_5)–C_6H_5 $\xrightarrow{H^+}$ HO–CO–C(OH)(C_6H_5)–C_6H_5

Benzylic acid

8. (c) MnO_2 causes oxidation of allylic alcohol. Allylic alcohol is an alcohol where hydroxy group is attached to a saturated carbon atom adjacent to a double bond.

(a) Hex-3-en-1-ol (not an allylic alcohol)

(b) Cyclohex-3-en-1-ol (not an allylic alcohol)

(c) Hex-2-en-1-ol $\xrightarrow{MnO_2}$ Hex-2-en-1-one

This is an allylic alcohol (1°). Hence, it will undergo oxidation reaction with MnO_2.

9. (c) The compound contains carbonyl group gives positive 2, 4-DNP test.

Those compounds which give iodoform test contain a keto methyl group (not aldehydic) $\text{—}\overset{O}{\overset{\|}{C}}\text{—}CH_3$. The presence of this group is also confirmed by negative Tollen's test and Fehling test. The compound which does not decolourise bromine water means it does not have free double bond or triple bond.

Given, molecular formula $= C_9H_{10}O$

$$U=(9+1)-\frac{10}{2}=5$$

Degree of unsaturation is 5. Thus, there must be a benzene ring ($U=4$) and one C=O group ($U=1$).

Ph–CH₂–CO–CH₃ $\xrightarrow[\text{[O]}]{\text{Drastic oxidatior}}$ PhCOOH (Benzoic acid) ($C_7H_6O_2$) + CH_3COOH (Acetic acid)

So, compound *A* is C_6H_5–CH_2–$\overset{O}{\overset{\|}{C}}$–$CH_3$

10. (a) When an alkene is treatment with dil. $KMnO_4$, it produces *vicinal cis*-diol.

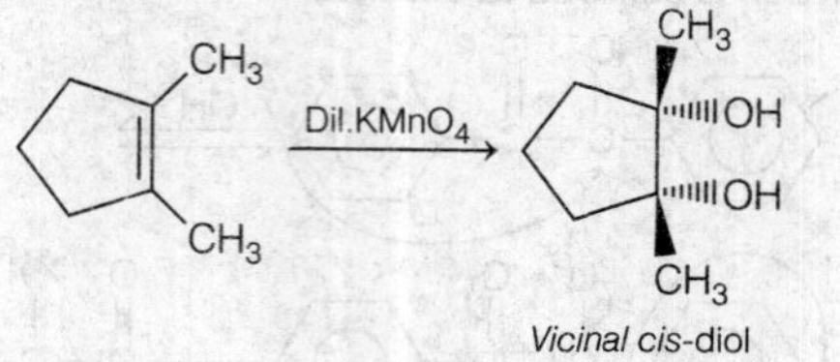

Dil.$KMnO_4$ → *Vicinal cis*-diol (*A*)

Now, *cis* diol undergoes Malaprade oxidation in presence of HIO_4 to form (*B*). It is believed to proceed as,

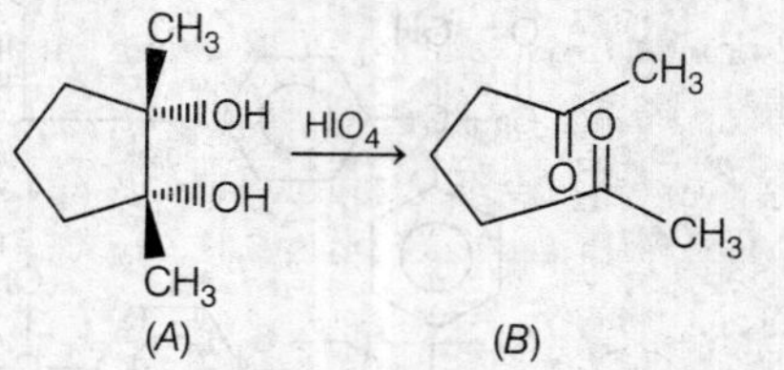

(*A*) —HIO_4→ (*B*)

This diketone undergoes intramolecular aldol reaction to produce the cyclic α, β-unsaturated ketone (*C*) as follows,

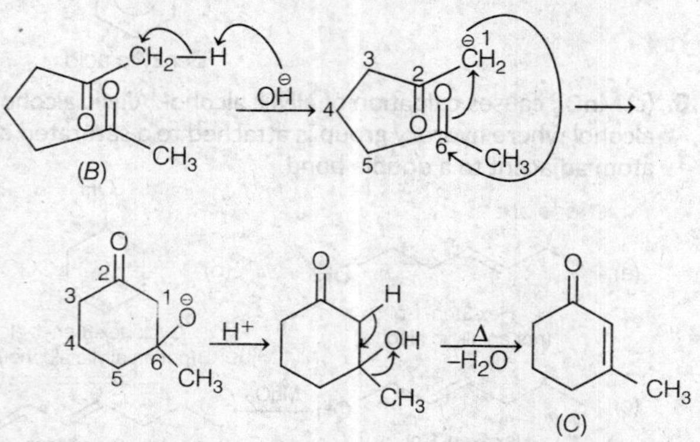

(*B*) —$\overset{\ominus}{OH}$→ ...

—H^+→ ... —Δ, $-H_2O$→ (*C*)

11. (d) When the given compound (*A*) is cleaved by ozonolysis reaction, a di-carbonyl compound (*B*) will be formed. This compound (*B*) in presence of *aq*. NaOH will undergo aldol-condensation reaction to produce α, β-unsaturated carbonyl compound which is (*R*).

The reaction scheme with possible mechanism is shown below

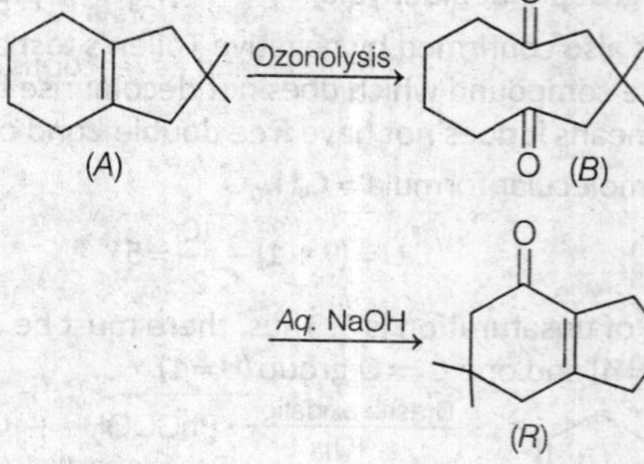

(*A*) —Ozonolysis→ (*B*)

—*Aq*. NaOH→ (*R*)

Mechanism showing conversion of diketone (*B*) to final product R:

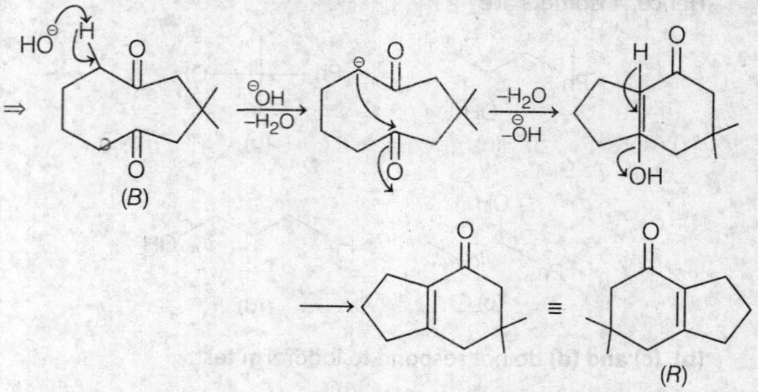

(*B*) —$\overset{\ominus}{OH}$, $-H_2O$→ ... —$-H_2O$, $-\overset{\ominus}{OH}$→ ... → ... ≡ (*R*)

12. (d) The conversion of cyclopentyl methylketone to 1-cyclopentyl-1-methylethene by use of Wittig reagent, i.e. phosphorus ylide (*B*) is known as Wittig reaction.

$\Rightarrow \quad [B] : PPh_3 = CH_2$ or $Ph_3\overset{\oplus}{P}—\overset{\ominus}{C}H_2$

The reaction occurs as follows

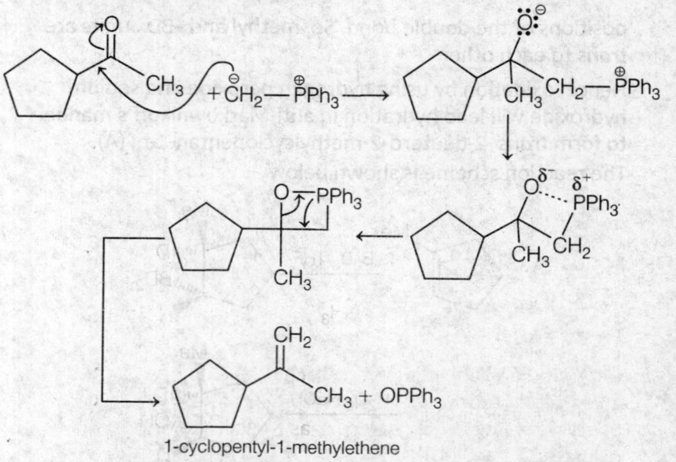

$+ \overset{\ominus}{C}H_2—\overset{\oplus}{P}Ph_3$ → ... → ... → $CH_3 + OPPh_3$

1-cyclopentyl-1-methylethene

When carbonyl compound is treated with amalgamated zinc in presence of concentrated HCl, it converts $>C{=}O$ to $>CH_2$. This reaction is known as Clemmensen reduction.

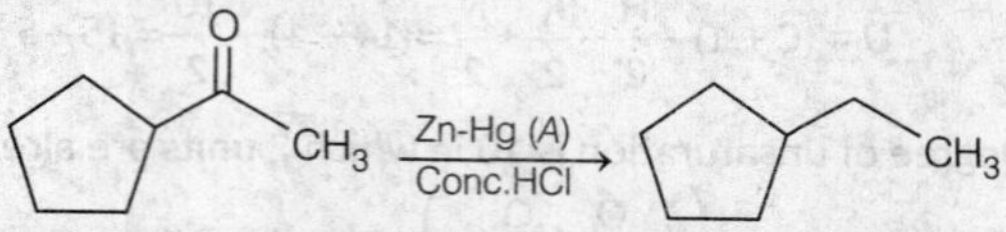

—Zn-Hg (*A*), Conc.HCl→

This is a direct method for the conversion of ketone to hydrocarbon.

13. (a) The reaction involves the following steps:

***Step* 1.** Attack of nucleophile (OH^-) on electrophilic site, i.e. carbonyl carbon-atom.

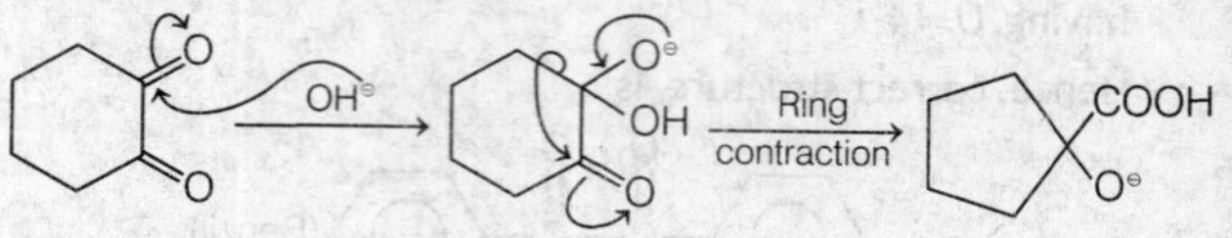

—$OH^{\ominus}$→ ... —Ring contraction→ (COOH, $O^{\ominus}$)

***Step* 2.** Acid workup to form the final product.

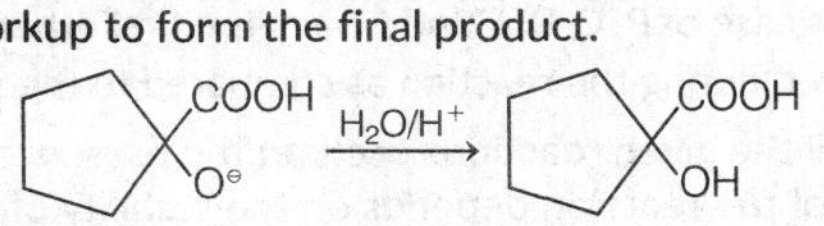

$$\text{(cyclopentane with COOH and } O^{\ominus}) \xrightarrow{H_2O/H^+} \text{(cyclopentane with COOH and OH)}$$

14. (c) Protection of carbonyl group takes place by formation of acetal.

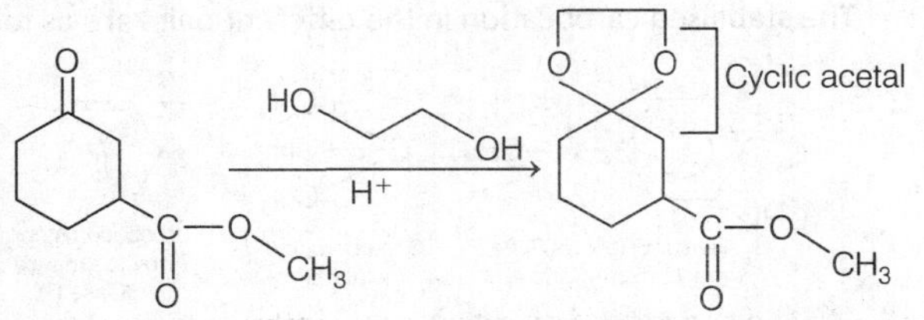

$$\xrightarrow[H^+]{HO\text{—}CH_2CH_2\text{—}OH}$$

Cyclic acetal

(Keto group is protected)

Addition of Grignard reagent to an ester group leads to formation of ketone and then a 3°-alcohol after hydrolysis.

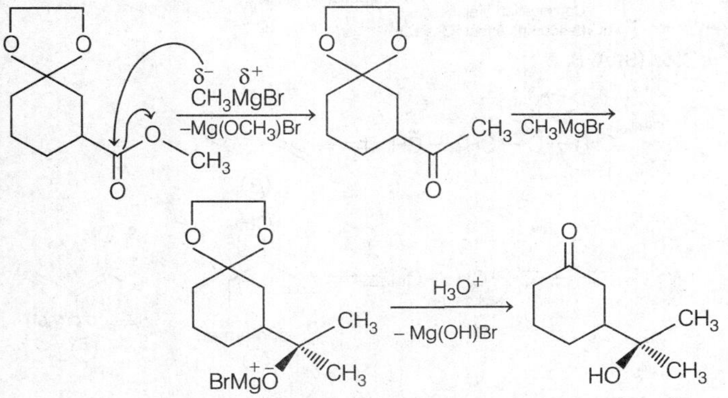

$\overset{\delta-}{CH_3}\overset{\delta+}{MgBr}$, $-Mg(OCH_3)Br$ → CH_3MgBr → $\xrightarrow[-Mg(OH)Br]{H_3O^+}$

15. (a) Amino alcohol adjacent to each other undergo cleavage to give fragment product in a same way as in diol. The oxidation occurs in this reaction is known as Malaprade or periodate oxidation.

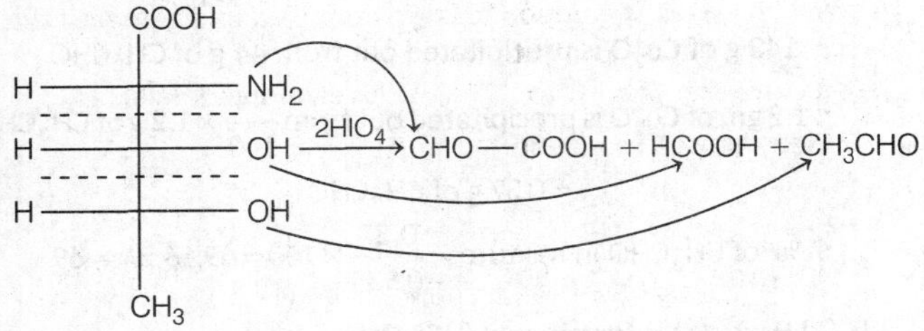

$$HOOC\text{—}CH(NH_2)\text{—}CH(OH)\text{—}CH(OH)\text{—}CH_3 \xrightarrow{2HIO_4} CHO\text{—}COOH + HCOOH + CH_3CHO$$

16. (c)

$$\underset{(\beta\text{-keto acid})}{Ph\text{—}CO\text{—}CH_2\text{—}COOH} \xrightarrow[(-CO_2)]{\text{Heat, Decarboxylation}} \underset{\substack{(E)\\ \text{(Acetophenone)}}}{Ph\text{—}CO\text{—}\overset{*}{C}H_3}$$

$$\xrightarrow[\text{Iodoform reaction}]{I_2,\ NaOH} \underset{\substack{(F)\\ \text{(Benzoate salt)}}}{Ph\text{—}CO\text{—}\overset{\ominus}{O}\overset{\oplus}{Na}} + \underset{\substack{(G)\\ \text{(Iodoform)}}}{\overset{*}{C}HI_3}$$

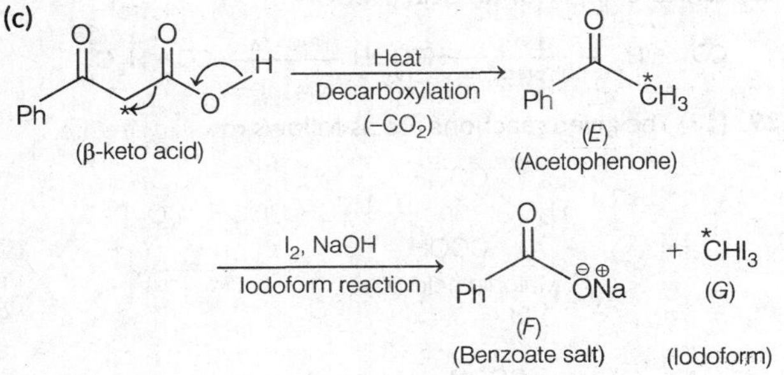

17. (c) (i) Mass of benzene (solute) $w = 0.816$ g,

Mass of the compound A, $W = 7.5$ g,

$$\Delta T_f = 5.51 - 1.59 = 3.92$$

Molecular weight of (A), $M = \dfrac{1000\, K_f \times w}{\Delta T_f \times W}$

$$\Rightarrow \quad M = \frac{1000 \times 4.9 \times 0.816}{3.92 \times 7.5} = 136$$

(ii) For (A)

Element	%	Relative number of atoms	Simplest ratio
C	70.58	5.88	4
H	5.88	5.88	4
O	23.54	1.47	1

∴ Empirical formula of (A) = C_4H_4O and empirical formula weight = 68

$$\Rightarrow \quad n = \frac{\text{Molecular formula weight}}{\text{Equivalent formula weight}} = \frac{136}{68} = 2$$

∴ Molecular formula of (A) is $(C_4H_4O)_2 = C_8H_8O_2$

(iii) Also given, $\underset{(A)}{C_8H_8O_2} \xrightarrow[-CO_2]{\text{Sodalime, }\Delta} \underset{(B)}{C_7H_8} \xrightarrow[H^+]{[O]} \underset{(C)}{C_6H_5\text{—}COOH} \xrightarrow[\Delta]{\text{Sodalime}} \underset{(D)}{\text{Benzene}}$

(Equivalent wt. = 122)

Thus, (A) should be

$C_6H_4(CH_3)(COOH)$ (*o, m, p*-toluic acid) or $C_6H_5CH_2COOH$ (Phenyl acetic acid)

∴ Reactions are as follows :

$$\underset{(A)}{C_6H_4(CH_3)(COOH)} \xrightarrow[-Na_2CO_3]{\text{Sodalime (NaOH+CaO)}} \underset{\substack{(B)\\ \text{(Toluene)}}}{C_6H_4(CH_3)(H)} \xrightarrow{[O]} \underset{\substack{(C)\\ \text{(Benzoic acid)}}}{C_6H_5COOH} \xrightarrow{\text{Sodalime}} \underset{(D)}{C_6H_6}$$

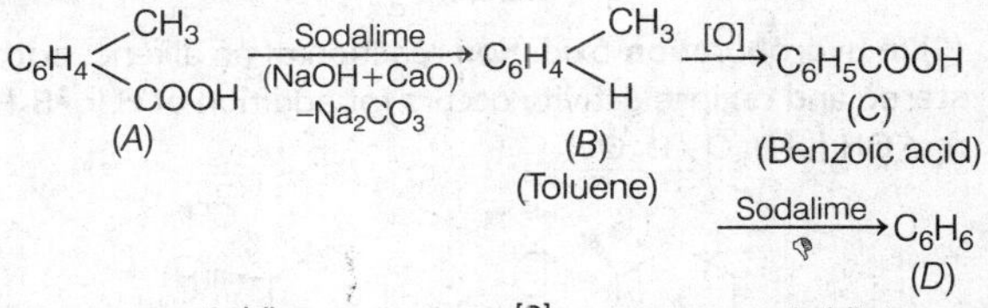

$$\underset{(A)}{C_6H_5CH_2COOH} \xrightarrow{\text{Sodalime}} \underset{(B)}{C_6H_5CH_3} \xrightarrow{[O]} \underset{(C)}{C_6H_5COOH} \xrightarrow[\Delta]{\text{Sodalime}} \underset{(D)}{C_6H_6}$$

18. (c) In 2, 4, 6-trinitrobenzoic acid, the decarboxylation takes place most easily, because of stronger −*I*-effect of three nitro groups, whereas in the dicarboxylic acid with one carbon atom having two carboxylic groups, it is also easier to remove CO_2. Also, decarboxylation is easier in case of unsaturated benzoic acid as compared to saturated benzoic acid.

Hence, the order of ease of decarboxylation is IV > III > II > I.

19. (a) An ester (A) will be $C_6H_5COOC_2H_5$ and its reactions are as follows

$$\underset{(A)}{C_6H_5COOC_2H_5} \xrightarrow{CH_3MgBr} C_6H_5\text{—}\underset{CH_3}{\overset{\overset{-\ +}{OMgBr}}{C}}\text{—}OC_2H_5 \xrightarrow{-(C_2H_5O)MgBr} C_6H_5\text{—}\overset{O}{\overset{\|}{C}}\text{—}CH_3$$

$$\xrightarrow{CH_3MgBr} C_6H_5\text{—}\underset{CH_3}{\overset{\overset{-\ +}{OMgBr}}{C}}\text{—}CH_3 \xrightarrow{H_2O} C_6H_5\text{—}\underset{CH_3}{\overset{OH}{C}}\text{—}CH_3 \xrightarrow{\text{Conc. } H_2SO_4} \underset{(B)}{C_6H_5\text{—}\underset{CH_3}{C}{=}CH_2}$$

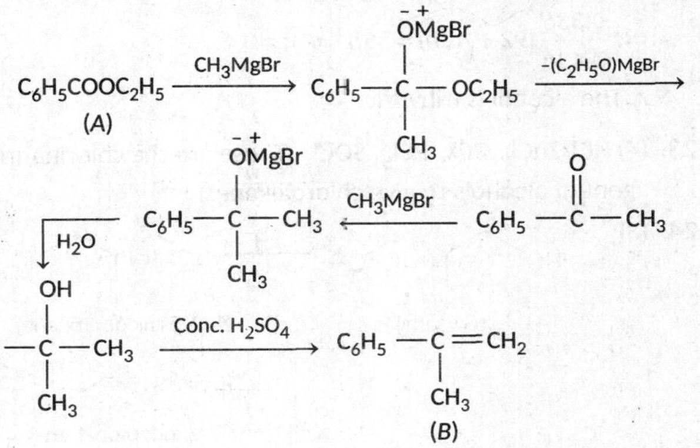

$$C_6H_5-\underset{\underset{CH_3}{|}}{C}=CH_2 \xrightarrow[\text{(ii) Zn/}H_2O \;-CH_2O]{\text{(i) }O_3} C_6H_5-\underset{\underset{O}{\|}}{C}-CH_3 \xrightarrow[\text{NaOH}]{I_2} CHI_3\downarrow + C_6H_5\overset{-\,+}{COONa}$$

(B) (C_8H_8O) (Iodoform)

20. (a) In acyl S_N2 reaction, the rate of reaction of acid derivatives follows the order

Acid chloride > Acid anhydride > Ester > Acid amide.

e.g. Hydrolysis of acid chloride (ROCl) and ester (*RCOOR*).

$$CH_3-\overset{\overset{O}{\|}}{C}-Cl \longleftrightarrow CH_3-\overset{\overset{O^{\ominus}}{|}}{\underset{\oplus}{C}}-Cl$$

Chloro group is highly electronegative. In this compound, only inductive effect operates which makes the compound less stable.

$$CH_3-\overset{\overset{O}{\|}}{C}-O-C_2H_5 \longleftrightarrow CH_3-\overset{\overset{O^{\ominus}}{|}}{\underset{\oplus}{C}}-\ddot{O}-C_2H_5 \longleftrightarrow CH_3-\overset{\overset{O^{\ominus}}{|}}{C}=\overset{\oplus}{O}-C_2H_5$$

Electronegativity of oxygen is less than Cl. In this compound, resonance dominates over inductive effect which increases its stability.

Hence, both Assertion and Reason are true and Reason is the correct explanation of Assertion.

21. (2) In hydroboration-oxidation reaction of an alkene, both stereo and regioselectivity occurs for addition of H (of B_2H_6) and OH (of H_2O / H_2O_2)

[Structures: 2-methylcyclopentanol stereoisomers with CH$_3$, H, OH, H] and [enantiomer]

22. (3) We know, $\frac{w}{W}(M + 42n) = 56n$;

Given: $w = 0.336$ g, $W = 0.436$ g, $M = 92$

w = weight of KOH for hydrolysis

W = weight of acetyl derivative of polyhydric alcohol

M = molecular mass of acetyl derivative of polyhydric alcohol

n = number of hydroxyl groups

$$\Rightarrow \frac{0.336}{0.436}(92 + 42n) = 56n \Rightarrow n = 3$$

∴ The alcohol is trihydric.

23. (4) $HCl/ZnCl_2$, PCl_3, PCl_5, $SOCl_2$: These are the chlorinating agent of alcohols to give chloroalkanes.

24. (3)

HO–CH$_2$–CH(OH)–CH$_2$–OH (Glycerol) $\xrightarrow[-3H_2O]{3HI}$ I–CH$_2$–CH(I)–CH$_2$–I (1, 2, 3-triiodopropane) $\xrightarrow{-I_2}$ CH$_2$=CH–CH$_2$–I (3-iodoprop-1-ene)

25. (5) In case of *B*, *C*, *D*, *E* and *F* pairs the first ether is more rapidly cleaved during the reaction as compared to the second one.

As, all the given reactions occur in the presence of acid, so the rate of the reaction depends on the stability of carbocation which is higher for 3° or carbocation that is stabilised by resonance or mesomeric effect.

The stabilised carbocation in the different pairs are as follows:

- 3,5-dimethylphenyl–$\overset{+}{O}$(H)–CH_3 — Reaction follows S_N2 mechanism (Case *A*)
- $^+C(CH_3)_3$ — 3° carbocation (Case *B*)
- Allylic cation — Carbocation stabilised by resonance (Case *C*)
- Cyclohexyl cation with OH — Carbocation stabilised by mesomeric effect (Case *D*)
- Allylic cation — Resonance stabilised carbocation (Case *E*)
- $C_6H_5\overset{+}{C}H_2$ — Resonance stabilised carbocation (Case F)

26. (3) *A*, *B*, *F*

$CH_2(H)-\overset{\overset{O}{\|}}{C}-CH_2-CH_3 \rightleftharpoons$ $CH_2=C(OH)-CH_2CH_3$ (B)

$CH_3-\overset{\overset{O}{\|}}{C}-\underset{\underset{H}{|}}{CH}-CH_3 \rightleftharpoons$ $CH_3C(OH)=CHCH_3$ (*E*-conformer) (A) + $CH_3C(OH)=CHCH_3$ (*Z*-conformer) (F)

27. (69) Let the mass of acetaldehyde is *x* g, then mass of ethanol is (0.535 – *x*) g. When acetaldehyde is heated with Fehling's solution, it gives 1.2 g of red precipitate.

$$CH_3CHO + 2Cu^{2+} + 5OH^- \longrightarrow CH_3COO^{\ominus} + \underset{\text{Red ppt.}}{Cu_2O} + 3H_2O$$

∵ 143 g of Cu_2O is precipitated out from 44 g of CH_3CHO

∴ 1.2 gm of Cu_2O is precipitated out from $\frac{44}{143} \times 1.2$ g of CH_3CHO

$= 0.37$ g of CH_3CHO

∴ % of CH_3CHO in mixture $= \frac{0.37}{0.535} \times 100 = 69.16\ \% \simeq 69$

28. (2) Here, (X) is formic acid (HCOOH).

$$CO_2 + H_2 \xleftarrow[\text{High pressure}]{160°} \underset{(X)}{HCOOH} \xrightarrow{P_2O_5/\Delta} CO + H_2O$$

29. (13) The given reactions are as follows :

$$H_2C\begin{matrix}COOH\\COOH\end{matrix} \xrightarrow{\Delta} CH_3COOH + CO_2\uparrow;$$

Malonic acid (X)
$[n_C = 3 = x]$

$$\begin{matrix}CH_2-COOH\\|\\CH_2-COOH\end{matrix} \xrightarrow{\Delta} \begin{matrix}CH_2-CO\\|\\CH_2-CO\end{matrix}\!\!>O + H_2O$$

Succinic acid (Y) $[n_C = 4 = y]$ (Succinic anhydride)

$$\begin{matrix} CH_2CH_2—COOH \\ | \\ CH_2CH_2—COOH \end{matrix} \xrightarrow{\Delta} \begin{matrix} CH_2—CH_2 \\ | \\ CH_2—CH_2 \end{matrix}\!\!>\!C=O + H_2O + CO_2\uparrow$$

Adipic acid (Z) $[n_c = 6 = z]$ (Cyclopentanone)

$\Rightarrow x + y + z = 3 + 4 + 6 = 13$

30. (5) According to the given statement,

$$R\!\!-\!\!(NH\!\!-\!\!H)_n + Cl\!\!-\!\!\overset{O}{\overset{\|}{C}}\!\!-\!\!CH_3 \xrightarrow{-nHCl} R\!\!-\!\!(NH\!\!-\!\!\overset{O}{\overset{\|}{C}}\!\!-\!\!CH_3)_n$$

Molar mass $= M_1$ n mol; Mass of CH_3CO unit $=43$; Molar mass $= M_2$

Number of $—NH_2$ group

$$= \frac{\text{Mol. weight of product } (M_2) - \text{Mol. weight of reactant } (M_1)}{42}$$

$$= \frac{390 - 180}{42} = 5$$

Qualifier 25

(Organic Compounds Containing Nitrogen)

1. (c) In the given resonating structures, structure II is not an acceptable canonical structure because the nitrogen has ten valence electrons which is not possible.

2. (b) Hofmann bromamide reaction ($KOH + Br_2 \longrightarrow KOBr$) of succinimide produces the conjugate base of 3-amino-propanoic acid (B).

Succinic acid $\xrightarrow[\Delta]{\text{Urea}}$ (A) (Succinimide) $\xrightarrow{\text{KOBr}}$ (NBS) $\longrightarrow$ ... $\longrightarrow$ (Isocyanate) $\xrightarrow[-CO_2]{H_2O/\overset{\ominus}{O}H} \longrightarrow$ $\overset{\ominus}{O}OC—CH_2CH_2—NH_2$ (B)

3. (c) When an 1° amine ($R—NH_2$) reacts with an aldehyde ($R—CHO$), an aldimine is formed, which on catalytic hydrogenation produces a secondary amine.

$$R—NH_2 + O=CH—R \xrightarrow{-H_2O} R—\ddot{N}=CH—R \text{ (Aldimine)}$$

$$\xrightarrow{Pt/H_2,\Delta} R—\ddot{N}H—CH_2R \text{ (2° amine)}$$

4. (d) Electron releasing groups increase the basic strength of amines, whereas electron withdrawing groups decrease the basic strength of N-bases.

Therefore, the order of basic strength will be III > II > IV > I. Since, in I, —NH group is placed between two electrons withdrawing groups, it is less basic among the given compounds.

5. (b) In Hinsberg test, a primary amine (RNH_2) forms a white precipitate (A) with benzene sulphonyl chloride ($C_6H_5SO_2Cl$) known as Hinsberg reagent. The precipitate (A) gets dissolved in *aq.* KOH.

$$C_6H_5SO_2Cl + RNH_2 \xrightarrow{-HCl} \underset{\text{N-alkyl benzene sulphonamide (A)}}{RNHSO_2C_6H_5} \xrightarrow{Aq.\ KOH} [R—\overset{\ominus}{N}SO_2C_6H_5]K^+(aq) + H_2O$$

6. (b) The overall reactions can be represented as,

(i) Toluene on sulphonation gives *ortho* and *para*-toluene sulphonic acid.

Toluene $\xrightarrow[\Delta]{\text{Conc. } H_2SO_4}$ *o*-toluene sulphonic acid + *p*-toluene sulphonic acid

(ii) *ortho*-toluene sulphonic acid undergoes series of reaction to give final product saccharin (A)

o-toluene sulphonic acid $\xrightarrow{PCl_5}$ (o-$CH_3C_6H_4SO_2Cl$) $\xrightarrow{NH_3}$ (o-$CH_3C_6H_4SO_2NH_2$) $\xrightarrow[35°C]{Aq.\ KMnO_4}$ (o-$HOOC—C_6H_4—SO_2NH_2$) $\xrightarrow[-H_2O]{\Delta}$ Saccharin (A)

7. (c) In strong acidic condition of mixed acid, ($HNO_3 + H_2SO_4$), aniline ($Ph—NH_2$) gets protonated into anilinium ion ($Ph—\overset{\oplus}{N}H_3$) where, $—\overset{\oplus}{N}H_3$ is a *meta*-directing group for electrophile ($NO_2^{\oplus}$).

So, *m*-nitroaniline is the second major product (47%).

Aniline $\xrightarrow[H_2SO_4\ (MA)]{HNO_3}$ *p*-nitroaniline 51% (*p*-) + *m*-nitroaniline 47% (*m*-) + *o*-nitroaniline 2% (*o*-)

Nitroanilines

8. (c) There is no direct method for nitration of aniline, since aniline undergoes oxidation on nitration. Therefore, by protecting —NH_2 group in aniline by acetylation method, we can obtain nitro derivatives. Hence, Assertion is correct.

However, acetylation decreases the electron-density in benzene ring thereby preventing oxidation. Hence, Reason is incorrect.

9. (a) NMe_2 group is an electron donating group.

Under the highly acidic condition —NMe_2 group will get protonated and will get converted into —$\overset{+}{N}HMe_2$, which is a very strong electron withdrawing group. Hence, it will deactivate the ring through −*I* and −*R*-effect and it will behave as *meta*-orienting group. Therefore, N, N-dimethyl aniline on nitration with conc. H_2SO_4 and HNO_3 mixture will give *m*-nitro-N, N-dimethyl aniline as the major product. The reaction scheme is as follows

(N, N-dimethyl aniline) $\xrightarrow{H^+}$ $\xrightarrow{NO_2^+}$ (*m*-nitro-N, N-dimethylaniline)

10. (a) Nitration in naphthalene produce 1-nitronaphthalene (*A*) and 2-nitronaphthalene (*B*) depending upon the reaction temperature. At room temperature, kinetically controlled product (KCP) is formed, while at high temperature, thermodynamically controlled product (TCP) is formed. The σ-complex corresponding to C-1 attack is more stable than the σ-complex corresponding to C-2 attack, thus, *A* will form at a faster rate than *B*.

Hence, at room temperature *A* will be the product.

(Naphthalene) $\xrightarrow[\text{(Room temperature)}]{HNO_3/H_2SO_4}$ (Major) [*A*] + (Minor) [*B*]

11. (c) The most convenient method to obtain *m*-dibromobenzene is as follows

(Nitrobenzene) $\xrightarrow[H_2SO_4, \Delta]{\text{Fuming } HNO_3}$ (*m*-dinitrobenzene) $\xrightarrow[C_2H_5OH, \Delta]{Fe/HCl}$ (1, 3-diaminobenzene) $\xrightarrow[\text{Diazotisation}]{HONO}$ $\xrightarrow[\text{Sandmeyer reaction}]{CuBr}$ (*m*-dibromobenzene)

12. (b) The reaction takes place as,

(*m*-dinitrobenzene) $\xrightarrow[\text{(ii) Partial reduction}]{\text{(i) } (NH_4)_2S}$ $\xrightarrow[\text{[Diazotisation followed by Sandmeyer reaction]}]{\text{(i) } NaNO_2/HCl \text{ (ii) } CuCl/HCl}$ (*m*-nitrochlorobenzene) (*P*)

13. (a) It is a Balz-Schiemann reaction. It is a chemical reaction in which primary aromatic benzene is converted into aryl fluoride *via* diazonium tetrafluoroborate intermediate.

$\xrightarrow[HNO_2]{HBF_4}$ [$\overset{\oplus}{N}{\equiv}N\overset{\ominus}{B}F_4$] $\xrightarrow{\Delta}$

Benzene diazonium tetrafluoroborate into fluorobenzene

14. (d) When the given amine compound is treated with $NaNO_2$ and HCl at 0°C-5°C, unstable diazonium chloride will form, which will readily breaks down into unstable 1° carbocation.

Hence, readily bond migration (ring expansion) will occur to generate more stable 2° carbocation which will be readily attacked by the nucleophile, water to form (d) as the major product.

The reaction scheme with possible mechanism is shown below

(Aliphatic 1°-amine) $\xrightarrow[\text{(Diazotisation)}]{NaNO_2, HCl}$ $\xrightarrow{-N_2}$ $\longrightarrow$ $\xrightarrow{H_2\ddot{O}}$ $\xrightarrow{-H^+}$ (d)

15. (c) The overall reaction takes place as,

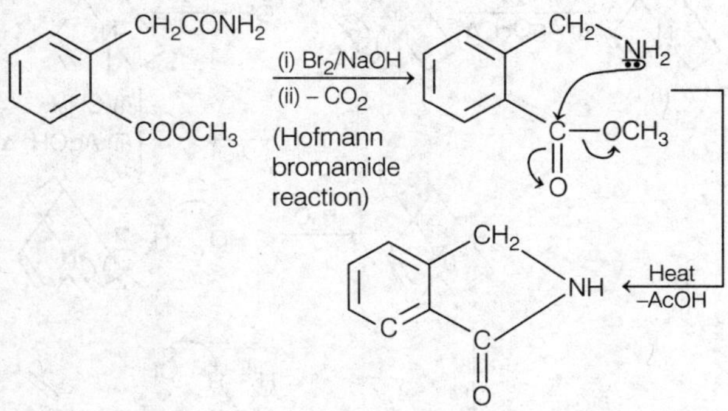

CH_2CONH_2 / $COOCH_3$ —(i) Br_2/NaOH (ii) – CO_2 (Hofmann bromamide reaction)→ CH_2 / NH_2 / C—OCH_3 / O —Heat –AcOH→ CH_2 / NH / C / C / O

16. (a) This is known as Hofmann degradation reaction. This is used to prepare one carbon less primary amine from the corresponding amide. The reaction scheme with possible mechanism are as follows

(i) Br_2 + NaOH ⟶ NaOBr

(ii)

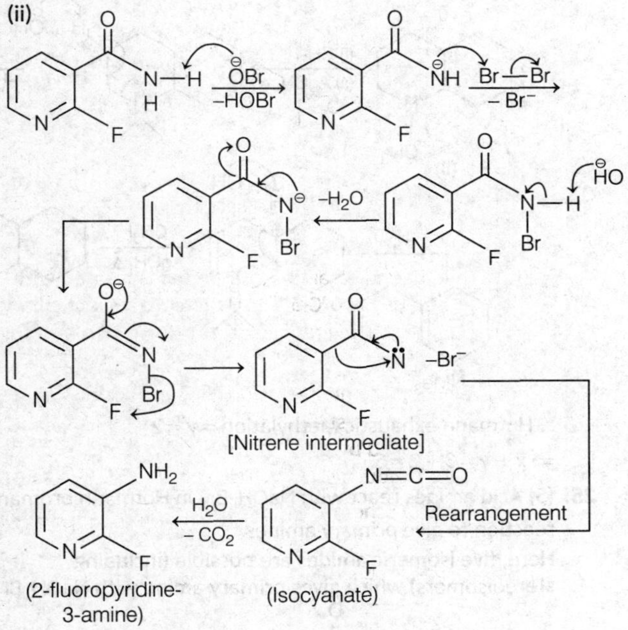

O / N—H / H / N / F —$\overset{\ominus}{O}Br$, –HOBr→ O / $\overset{\ominus}{N}H$ / N / F —Br—Br, – Br^-→ O / N—H / Br / N / F —$\overset{\ominus}{HO}$, –H_2O→ O / $N^{\ominus}$ / Br / N / F → $O^{\ominus}$ / N / Br / N / F ⟶ O / $\ddot{N}$ –Br^- / N / F [Nitrene intermediate] —Rearrangement→ N=C=O / N / F (Isocyanate) —H_2O, – CO_2→ NH_2 / N / F (2-fluoropyridine-3-amine)

17. (b) Aniline on reaction with acetic acid derivatives will produce acetanilide (*A*). Compounds of options – (a), (c) and (d) are the acetic acid derivatives.

Hence, these on reaction with aniline will produce acetanilide. But, compound of option – (b) is an aldehyde compound, which is not derivative of acetic acid. Thus, on reaction with aniline, it will produce imine compound (*B*) which is commonly known as Schiff's base. Hence, it will not form acetanilide with aniline.

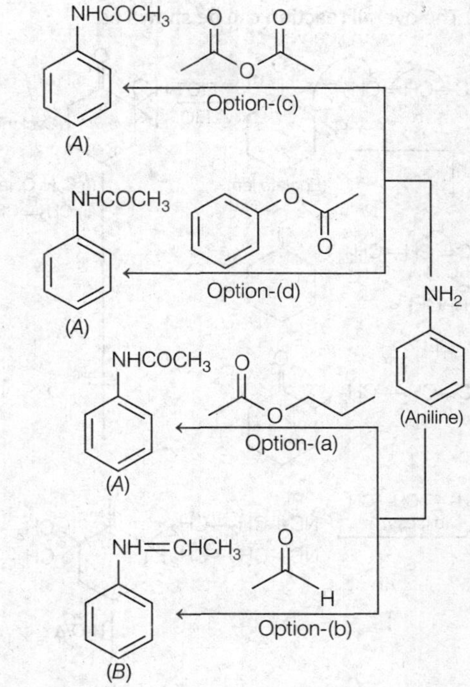

NH_2 (Aniline) —Option-(c), O O O→ $NHCOCH_3$ (*A*)

NH_2 (Aniline) —Option-(d), O O→ $NHCOCH_3$ (*A*)

NH_2 (Aniline) —Option-(a), O O→ $NHCOCH_3$ (*A*)

NH_2 (Aniline) —Option-(b), O H→ NH=$CHCH_3$ (*B*)

18. (b) When anthranilic acid is treated with $NaNO_2$ in presence of HCl, corresponding diazonium salt (*X*) will be formed which on treatment with mild base (*B*) will generate benzyne as the reactive intermediate *P*. This intermediate benzyne will undergo Diels-Alder 1, 4-addition reaction with 2-methyl-1, 3-butadiene (*Y*) to give corresponding cyclohexene ring containing compound *Q*.

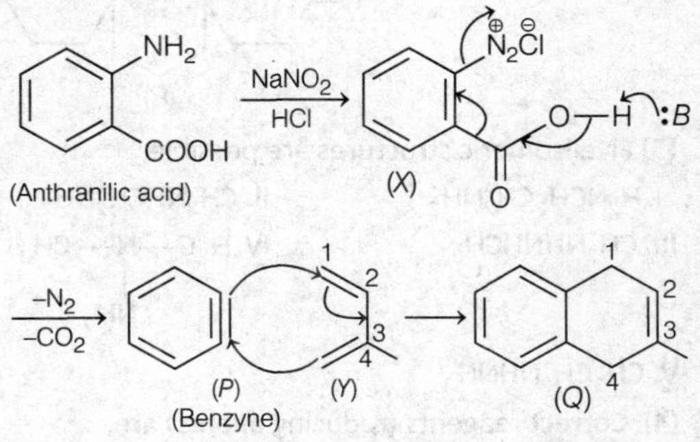

NH_2 / COOH (Anthranilic acid) —$NaNO_2$, HCl→ $\overset{\oplus}{N}_2\overset{\ominus}{Cl}$ / O—H :*B* / O (*X*) —$-N_2$, $-CO_2$→ (*P*) (Benzyne) + 1 2 3 4 (*Y*) ⟶ 1 2 3 4 (*Q*)

19. (d) (*R'R*) and (*R'S*) are diastereomers and have different physical (and chemical) properties like water solubility, boiling point, melting point etc.

Mixture of diastereomers is optically active, hence the product mixture in step 1 is optically active.

⇒ (*R'R*) and (*R'S*) have identical structural formula but they are enantiomers, i.e. they produce non-superimposable mirror images (optically active).

20. (c) The overall reaction can be shown as,

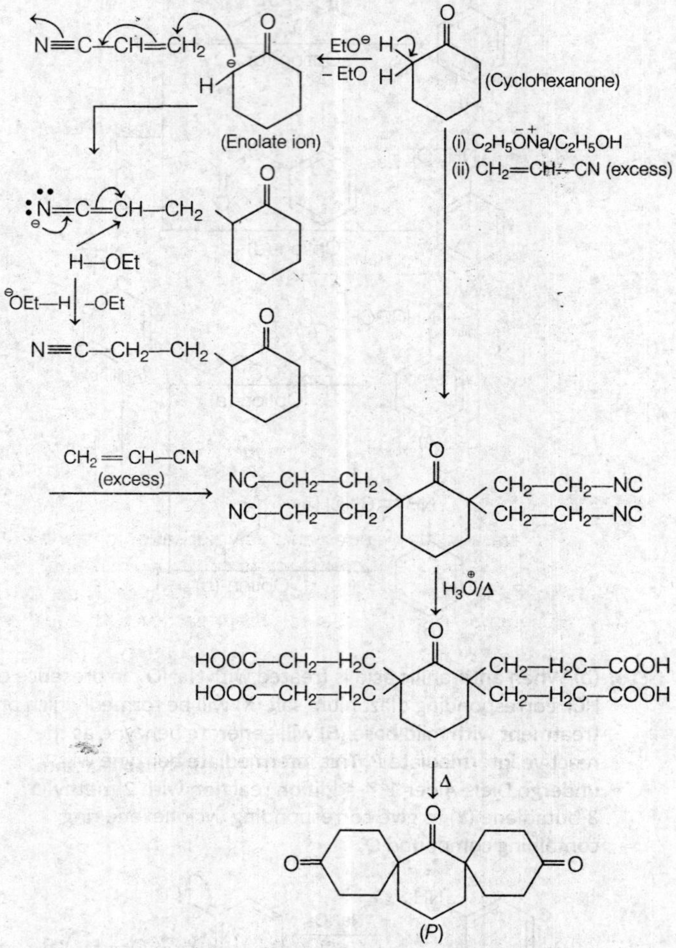

(Cyclohexanone) → (i) $C_2H_5\overset{-}{O}\overset{+}{Na}/C_2H_5OH$ (ii) $CH_2{=}CH{-}CN$ (excess)

$EtO^{\ominus}$, – EtO → (Enolate ion)

$N{\equiv}C{-}CH{=}CH_2$

H—OEt

$\overset{\ominus}{O}Et{-}H$ | –OEt

$N{\equiv}C{-}CH_2{-}CH_2$

$CH_2{=}CH{-}CN$ (excess) → $NC{-}CH_2{-}CH_2$, $NC{-}CH_2{-}CH_2$ ... $CH_2{-}CH_2{-}NC$, $CH_2{-}CH_2{-}NC$

$H_3\overset{\oplus}{O}/\Delta$

$HOOC{-}CH_2{-}H_2C$, $HOOC{-}CH_2{-}H_2C$ ... $CH_2{-}H_2C{-}COOH$, $CH_2{-}H_2C{-}COOH$

Δ

(P)

21. (5) Five isomeric structures are possible,

I. $H_2NCH_2CH_2NH_2$ II. $CH_3NHCH_2NH_2$

III. $CH_3NHNHCH_3$ IV. $H_3C{-}N(NH_2){-}CH_3$

V. $CH_3CH_2NHNH_2$

22. (4) Correct reagents (reducing agents) are,

I. $H_2/Ni/\Delta$

II. metal/acid

III. $LiAlH_4$

IV. Na/EtOH (Mendius reaction)

23. (5) $LiAlH_4$ can reduce nitroalkanes/arenes (a), iminol (b), alkyl/arylnitrile (c), acid amide (d) and alkylazide (f) into respective 1°-amines.

24. (5)

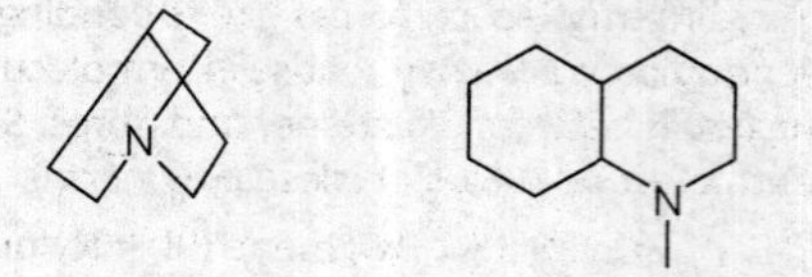

(I) (II)

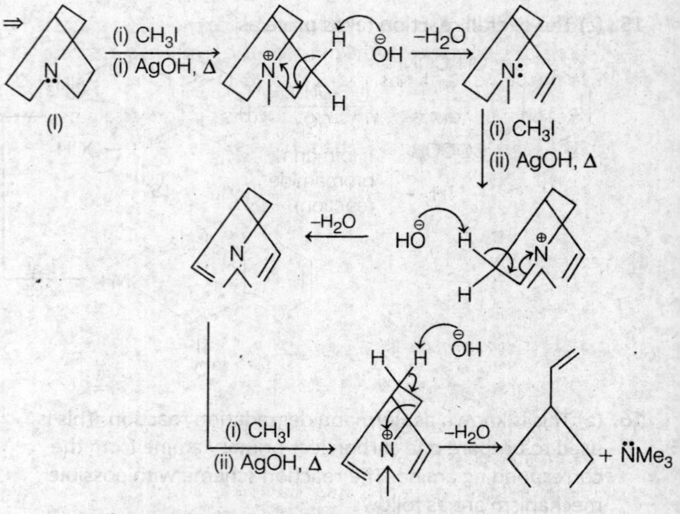

⇒ (I) (i) CH_3I (i) AgOH, Δ → $\overset{\ominus}{O}H$, $-H_2O$ → (i) CH_3I (ii) AgOH, Δ → $H\overset{\ominus}{O}$, $-H_2O$ → (i) CH_3I (ii) AgOH, Δ → $\overset{\ominus}{O}H$, $-H_2O$ → + $\ddot{N}Me_3$

∴ Hofmann Exhaustive Methylation = $x=3$

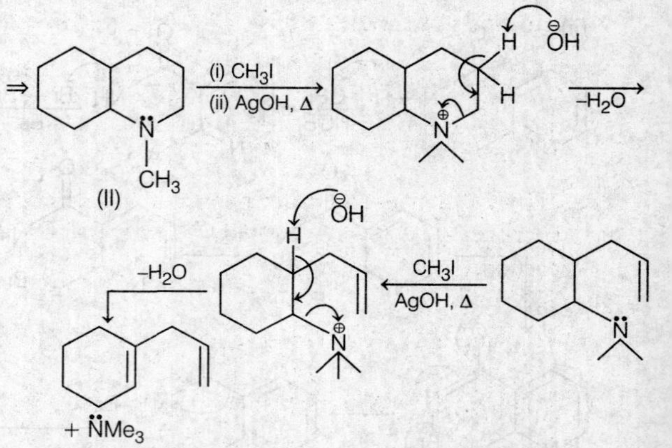

⇒ (II) CH_3 (i) CH_3I (ii) AgOH, Δ → $\overset{\ominus}{O}H$, $-H_2O$ → CH_3I AgOH, Δ → $\overset{\ominus}{O}H$, $-H_2O$ → + $\ddot{N}Me_3$

∴ Hofmann exhaustic methylation = $y=2$

$\Rightarrow x+y=3+2=5.$

25. (5) Acid amides react with NaOH, Br_2 in Hofmann bromamide reaction to give primary amines.

Here, five isomeric amides are possible (including stereoisomers) which gives primary amine with NaOH, Br_2.

$CH_3CH_2CH_2{-}\overset{O}{\overset{\|}{C}}{-}NH_2$; $CH_3CH_2{-}\underset{CH_3}{\overset{\bullet}{C}H}{-}\underset{O}{\underset{\|}{C}}{-}NH_2(\pm)$

$(CH_3)_2CH{-}CH_2{-}\overset{O}{\overset{\|}{C}}{-}NH_2$; $CH_3{-}\underset{CH_3}{\overset{CH_3}{C}}{-}\overset{O}{\overset{\|}{C}}{-}NH_2$

26. (4)

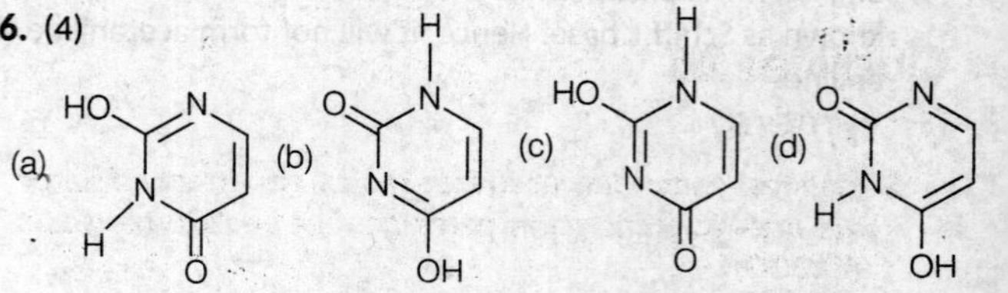

(a) (b) (c) (d)

These four molecules are tautomers of the given forms. They are not resonance forms because the hydrogen atoms are not in the same positions.

(Resonance forms must have all atoms in identical positions with same number of unpaired electrons.)

27. (2.45) $Ph-\ddot{N}H_2 + CHCl_3 \xrightarrow{KOH} Ph-\ddot{N}=\ddot{C}$ (I)

or $Ph-\overset{+}{N}\equiv \overset{-}{C}:$ (II)
(Phenyl isocyanide)

In chloroform ($CHCl_3$),

Hybridisation state of $C = sp^3$ $[\because x=3] = sp^x$

Oxidation state of $C = +2$ $[\because |a| = 2]$

In phenyl isocyanide (Ph—NC) [Here, C-atom of the NC groups is originated from $CHCl_3$],

Hybridisation state of $C = sp^2 \text{(in II)} = sp^y$

$= sp \text{ (in I)} = sp^z$ $[\because y=2, z=1]$

Oxidation state of $C = +2$ $[\because |b| = 2]$

$\Rightarrow [(x+y+z)+(a-b)]^{1/2}$

$= [(3+2+1)-(2-2)]^{1/2}$

$= (6)^{1/2} = 2.449 \approx 2.45$

28. (3) Only 1° amines (aliphatic or aromatic) give carbylamine reaction, i.e. (1), (3) and (5) will respond to carbylamine reaction.

29. (48)

Aniline (NH_2 on benzene) $+ 3Br_2 \xrightarrow[-3HBr]{Br_2/H_2O}$ 2,4,6-tribromoaniline

1 mol → 3 mol
0.1 mol → 0.3 mol

[White precipitate of 2, 4, 6-tribromoaniline]

$\Rightarrow w_{Br_2} = 0.3 \times 160 \text{ g} = 48 \text{ g} = x \text{ g (I)}$

$\therefore$ $x = 48$

30. (4) Only 1° amine give Hofmann's mustard oil reaction, which are

ethylamine ($CH_3CH_2NH_2$); 2-amino compound (NH_2 on secondary carbon); $Ph-C(C_2H_5)(CH_3)-NH_2$; $C_6H_5-CH_2-NH_2$

Qualifier 26
(Polymers)

1. (a) Most commonly used free radical generator/initiator are organic or inorganic peroxides like benzoyl peroxide $(PhCOO)_2$.

2. (c) Melamine formaldehyde resin, a cross-linked polymer, will be formed by

Melamine (2,4,6-triamino-1,3,5-triazine) + HCHO ⟶ H_2N, $NHCH_2OH$, NH_2 substituted triazine

Melamine formaldehyde resin

$\xrightarrow{\text{Polymerisation}}$ $[-HN-(\text{triazine})-NH-CH_2-]_n$ (cross-linked through NH)

3. (b) The correct match of nylon-6, 6 is

$$\left[-\overset{O}{\overset{\|}{C}}-(CH_2)_4-\overset{O}{\overset{\|}{C}}-\underset{H}{\underset{|}{N}}-(CH_2)_6-\overset{H}{\overset{|}{N}}-\right]_n$$

4. (c) In radical, cationic or anionic polymerisation of styrene ($C_6H_5-CH=CH_2$), benzyl free radical, cation or anion formed are stable species because of resonance. Thus, styrene can undergo all these polymerisation reaction with equal ease.

5. (a) Correct match is A ⟶ (3), B ⟶ (1), C ⟶ (2), D ⟶ (4)

Nylon-6 ⇒ $\left[-\overset{O}{\overset{\|}{C}}-(CH_2)_5-NH-\right]_n$ Polycaprolactam

PVC ⇒ $\left[-CH_2-\overset{Cl}{\overset{|}{CH}}-\right]_n$ Polyvinyl chloride

Acrilan ⇒ $\left[-CH_2-\overset{CN}{\overset{|}{CH}}-\right]_n$ Polyacrylonitrile

Natural rubber ⇒

$$\left[\begin{matrix}H_3C & & H \\ & C=C & \\ H_2C & & CH_2\end{matrix}\right] \quad CH_2 - C(CH_3)=C - CH_2 \quad \textit{cis}\text{-polyisoprene}$$

6. (d) Buna-S is an elastomer, it has weakest intermolecular forces (van der Waals' force). Nylon-6,6 is a fibre, thus has strong intermolecular forces like H-bonding. Polythene is a thermoplastic polymer, whose intermolecular forces are present in between elastomer and fibres. So, the order of intermolecular forces of these polymers is

Buna-S (II) < Polythene (III) < Nylon-6,6 (I)

7 (b) Complete sequence of reaction is as follows

(Cyclohexanoxime) $\xrightarrow[\text{Beckmann rearrangement}]{H_2SO_4}$ (Caprolactam) [X] $\xrightarrow{540\text{ K}}$ $\left[-NH-(CH_2)_5-\overset{O}{\overset{\|}{C}}-\right]_n$ (Nylon-6)

Nylon-6 is the condensation homopolymer of caprolactam.

8. (a) Polymer *B* obtained is dextron, which is a condensation polymer of glycine and caprolactam. It contains ($-\overset{O}{\overset{\|}{C}}-NH-$) bond. So, it is a polyamide polymer and it is biodegradable.

$$\text{Caprolactam} \xrightarrow{H_2O} \underset{A}{H_2N-(CH_2)_5-\overset{O}{\overset{\|}{C}}-OH} + \underset{\text{Glycine}}{H_2N-CH_2-\overset{O}{\overset{\|}{C}}-OH}$$

$$\xrightarrow{-H_2O} \left(-HN-(CH_2)_5-\overset{O}{\overset{\|}{C}}-HN-CH_2-\overset{O}{\overset{\|}{C}}-\right)_n$$

Amide bond

(*B*)

9. (a) 3-hydroxybutanoic acid and 3-hydroxypentanoic acid react to form biodegradable polymer, PHBV. Glycine and amino caproic acid also react to form biodegradable polymer, nylon-2-nylon-6.

10. (c) PHBV is a biodegradable polymer. Its structure is

$$\left(-O-\underset{CH_3}{\underset{|}{CH}}-CH_2-\overset{}{\underset{O}{\underset{\|}{C}}}-O-\underset{CH_2CH_3}{\underset{|}{CH}}-CH_2-\underset{O}{\underset{\|}{C}}-\right)_n$$

Complete reaction is as follows

$$n\underset{\text{3-hydroxybutanoic acid}}{CH_3-\overset{OH}{\overset{|}{CH}}-CH_2-COOH} + n\underset{\text{3-hydroxpentanoic acid}}{CH_3CH_2-\overset{OH}{\overset{|}{CH}}-CH_2-COOH}$$

$\xrightarrow[-H_2O]{\text{Polymerisation}}$ PHBV or Poly-β-hydroxybutyrate-co-β-hydroxy valerate

11. (5) PVC, PAN, neoprene, PMMA and polystyrene are the chain growth addition polymers.

12. (2) *Gutta-percha* and natural rubber contain isoprene units. The *cis*-polyisoprene is called natural rubber and *trans*-isoprene is called *gutta-percha*.

13. (30.94) The structure of the copolymer is

$$nCH_2=CH_2 + nCH_2=CHCl \longrightarrow (CH_2CH_2CH_2CHCl)_n$$

Mol. wt. of ethylene = 28 u

Mol. wt. of vinyl chloride = 62.5 u

Empirical formula wt. of copolymer = 28 + 62.5 = 90.5

Weight percent of ethylene in the copolymer

$$= \frac{28}{90.5} \times 100 = 30.94$$

14. (1.33) Polydispersity index,

$$PDI = \frac{\overline{M_W}}{\overline{M_N}} = \frac{40000}{30000} = 1.33$$

15. (729) Monomers for melamine polymer are melamine and formaldehyde. Thus, *X* is melamine.

No. of carbon atoms, $x = 3$

No. of nitrogen atoms, $y = 6$

Melamine (*X*) + $H-\overset{O}{\overset{\|}{C}}-H$ (Formaldehyde) $\longrightarrow$ (*Y*)

No. of double bonds in *X* and *Y* are 3 each. So, total no. of double bonds, $z = 3 + 3 = 6$

Thus, $(z-x)^y = (6-3)^6$

$$= 3^6 = 729$$

Qualifier 27
(Biomolecules)

1. (b) D-(+)-sucrose (invert sugar) is an equimolar mixture of D-(+)-glucose and D-(−)-fructose. It is called invert sugar due to the fact that on hydrolysis, there is a change in the sign of rotation from positive to negative.

2. (a) Cellulose is a straight chain polysaccharide composed of D-glucose units, which are joined by β-glycosidic linkages between C-1 of one glucose and C-4 of the next glucose. In each unit, only three hydroxy groups are free to form acetate, that's why it is called cellulose triacetate whose structure is shown in option (a).

3. (c) The structure of *A* matches with structure (c), as

CHO–C(HO)(H)–$(CHOH)_2$–CH_2OH ($C_5H_{10}O_5$) (*A*) $\xrightarrow[-4\,AcOH]{4\,Ac_2O}$ CHO–C(H_3COCO)(H)–$(CHOCOCH_3)_2$–$CHOCOCH_3$ (It is a tetraacetate)

(*A*) $\xrightarrow{[H]\ HI}$ $H_3C–CH(CH_3)–CH_2–CH_3$ (*Iso*-pentane)

(*A*) $\xrightarrow{[O]\ Br_2/H_2O}$ COOH–C(HO)(H)–$(CHOH)_2$–CH_2OH (Carboxylic acid, $C_5H_{10}O_6$)

4. (d) Assertion is false but Reason is true. In maltose, two α-D-glucose units are joined by $C_1 - C_4$ glycosidic linkage.

α-D-glucose — O — α-D-glucose

(Maltose)

5. (d) In case of sugar molecule, two compounds are said to be epimer, if they involve change in conformation in any asymmetric carbon atom when more than one asymmetric carbon is present. In case of *P* and *Q*, this condition is satisfied. Hence, *P* and *Q* are epimers (C_3-epimers). Similarly, *Q* and *R*, also satisfied the given condition. Hence, *Q* and *R* are also epimers (C_4-epimers).

6. (b) Complete reaction is as follows

⇒ When the D-aldopentose is treated with a series of reagents – (i) KCN, HCN ; (ii) H_2, Pd/$BaSO_4$; (iii) H^+ / H_2O, a mixture (*B*) of epimeric hexoses is formed which are D-glucose and D-mannose. This reaction is known as Fisher-Kiliani reaction.

D-ribose (*A*) $\xrightarrow[(iii)\ H^+/H_2O]{(i)\ KCN,\ HCN;\ (ii)\ H_2, Pd/BaSO_4}$ D-glucose + D-mannose (*B*)

⇒ On the other hand, when the D-aldo-pentose is treated with a series of reagents- (i) Br_2 / H_2O, (ii) $Ca(OH)_2$, (iii) $H_2O_2 / Fe_2(SO_4)_3$, a tetrose (*A*) is formed. This reaction is known as Ruff's reaction.

D-ribose $\xrightarrow[(iii)\ H_2O_2,\ Fe_2(SO_4)_3]{(i)\ Br_2/H_2O;\ (ii)\ Ca(OH)_2}$ D-erythrose (*A*) + CO_2

7. (d) That compound will give positive Benedict's test which contains free hemi-acetal unit. In case of carbohydrates, osazone formation will occur if it contains the following unit

^{1}CHO–^{2}CHOH– or, $^1CH_2OH$–^{2}CO–

In case of sucrose, neither hemi-acetal unit is present nor the following above mentioned residue is present in the molecule.

Hence, it will not give Benedict's test and will not form osazone.

α-D-glucose — O — β-D-fructose

Structure of sucrose

8. (c) In presence of methylating agent, dimethyl sulphate $[(CH_3)_2SO_4]$ and strong base NaOH, all the hydroxyl group will get converted to the corresponding methyl ether. Then on acidic hydrolysis anomeric (C-1) methoxy group will undergo hydrolysis to give back hydroxyl group at the anomeric carbon.

The mechanism involves the displacement of leaving group by the internal nucleophilic attack by the pyranose ring oxygen. The reaction scheme with mechanism is shown below

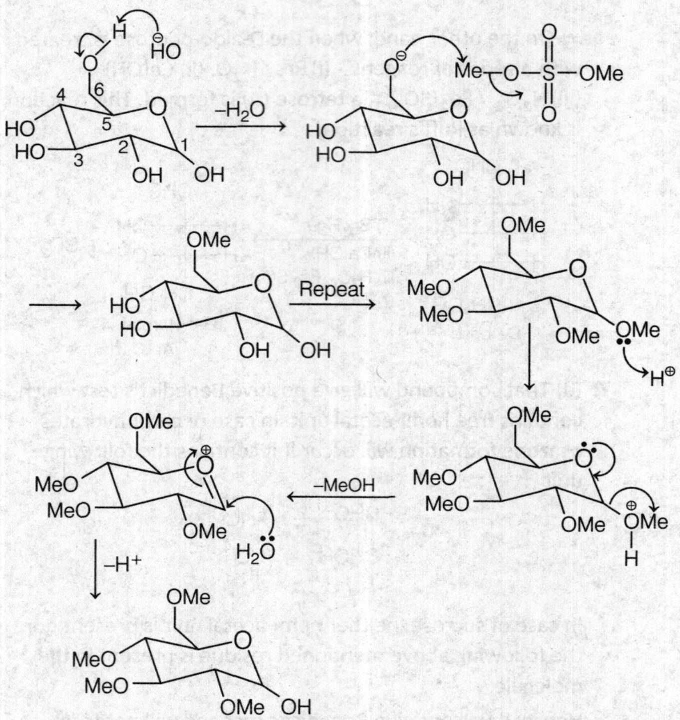

$$\xrightarrow{-H_2O} \quad \xrightarrow{\text{Repeat}} \quad \xrightarrow{-MeOH} \quad \xrightarrow{-H^+}$$

Labels in the scheme: $Me{-}O{-}S(=O)_2{-}OMe$, OMe, MeO, $H^{\oplus}$, $H_2\ddot{O}$

9. **(b) Formation of violet colour takes place, when glucose reacts with conc. HCl.**

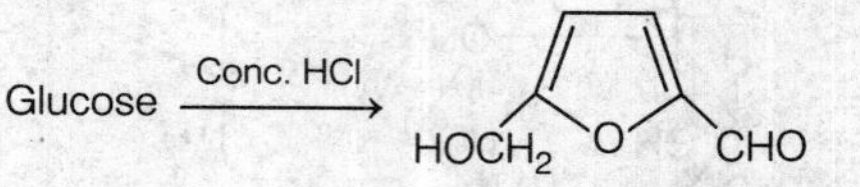

$$\text{Glucose} \xrightarrow{\text{Conc. HCl}} \text{HOCH}_2\text{-furan-CHO}$$

(Violet in colour)
(5-hydroxymethyl furfural)

10. **(b) Complete reaction is as follows**

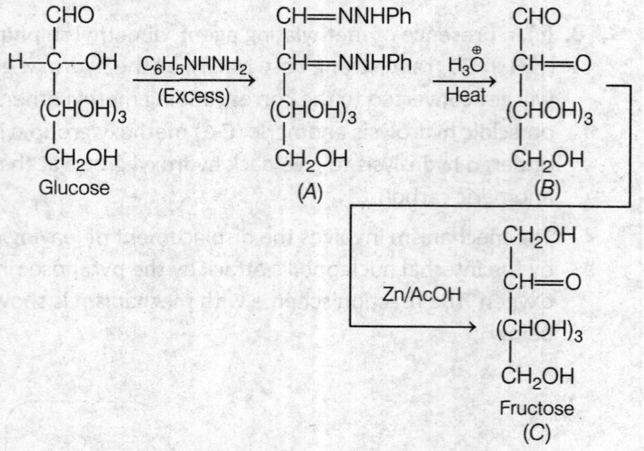

$$\underset{\text{Glucose}}{CHO{-}CH(OH){-}(CHOH)_3{-}CH_2OH} \xrightarrow[\text{(Excess)}]{C_6H_5NHNH_2} \underset{(A)}{CH{=}NNHPh{-}C({=}NNHPh){-}(CHOH)_3{-}CH_2OH} \xrightarrow[\text{Heat}]{H_3\overset{\oplus}{O}} \underset{(B)}{CHO{-}C{=}O{-}(CHOH)_3{-}CH_2OH}$$

$$\xrightarrow{\text{Zn/AcOH}} \underset{\text{Fructose } (C)}{CH_2OH{-}C{=}O{-}(CHOH)_3{-}CH_2OH}$$

11. **(b) Lactose (milk sugar) is composed of β-D-galactose and β-D-glucose through C_1 (of β-D-galactose) and C_4 (of β-D-glucose) glycosidic linkage.**

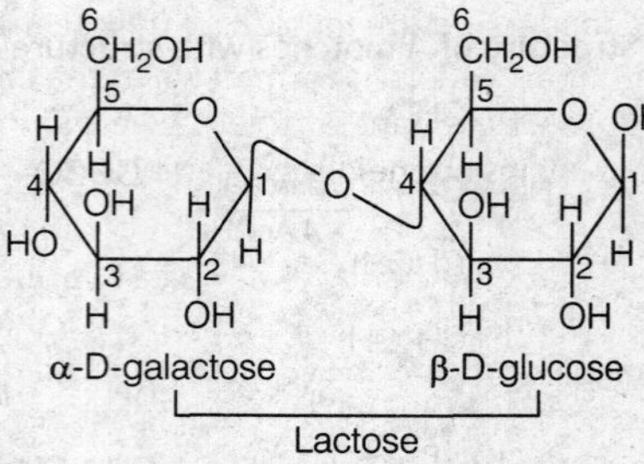

α-D-galactose — β-D-glucose
Lactose

12. **(a) The backbone of nucleic acid molecule consists of an alternating sugar and phosphate groups one linked by phosphate ester bond which can be shown as,**

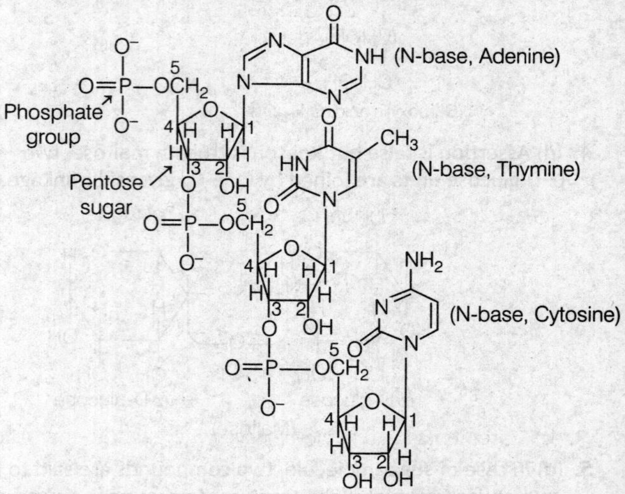

Labels in the structure: Phosphate group; Pentose sugar; NH (N-base, Adenine); (N-base, Thymine); (N-base, Cytosine)

13. **(d) There are two types of nucleobase : Purine and pyrimidine. Purine nucleobase contains adenine and guanine, while pyrimidine nucleobase contains uracil, thymine and cytosine bases respectively.**

Glycine in its Zwitter ion form bears no chiral centres and can superimposed on its mirror image. Thus, it is achiral is while due to presence of four different groups attached in proline is chiral.

⇒ DNA is composed of N-bases, pentose sugar and phosphoric acid. Phosphoric acid units get attached with sugar through glycosidic bonds.

14. **(c) One strand of DNA : A T C G T A T G**

Complementary strand : T A G C A T A C

15. **(a) γ-carboxyglutamic acid (X) is present in the protein, prothrombin which readily gets decarboxylated ($-CO_2$) to another amino acid, i.e. glutamic acid (A).**

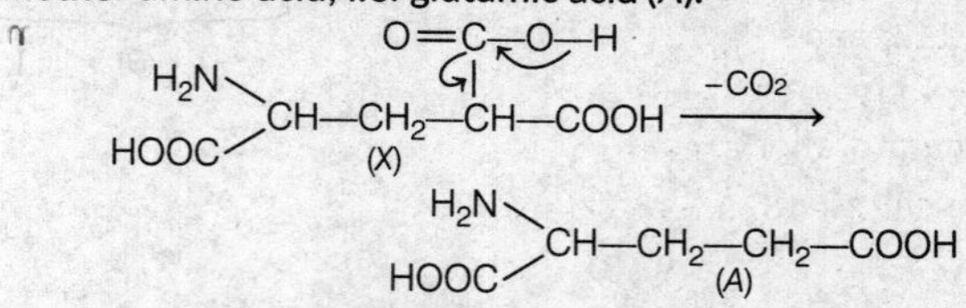

$$\underset{(X)}{(H_2N)(HOOC)CH{-}CH_2{-}CH(COOH){-}COOH} \xrightarrow{-CO_2} \underset{(A)}{(H_2N)(HOOC)CH{-}CH_2{-}CH_2{-}COOH}$$

So, presence of X cannot be detected in prothrombin.

16. (a) Secondary structure involves α-helical and β-pleated sheet like structures. α-helix is formed when the chain of α-amino acid coils as a right handed screw, whereas in β-pleated sheet the chains are held together by a large number of H-bonds.

17. (b) The triplet of nucleotides having a specific sequence of bases is known as codon. More than one codon can specify same amino acid. Specificity of a codon is determined by first two bases, the third base of codon is not very important.

18. (c) The overall reaction can be shown as,

$$C_6H_5-CH(COOC_2H_5)_2 \xrightarrow[-HBr]{Br_2/CCl_4} \underset{(A)}{C_6H_5-C(Br)(COOC_2H_5)_2}$$

$$\xrightarrow[-KBr]{\text{Phthalimide-NK}} C_6H_4(CO)_2N-C(C_6H_5)(COOC_2H_5)_2$$

[Gabriel phthalimide reaction]

$$\xrightarrow{H_3\overset{\oplus}{O}} H_2N-C(C_6H_5)(COOH)_2 \xrightarrow{-CO_2} \underset{\text{(An amino acid)}}{H_2N-CH(C_6H_5)-COOH}$$

19. (c) Statements I and IV are correct, whereas statements II and III are incorrect.

⇒ All naturally occurring α-amino acids are optically active except glycine (H_2N-CH_2-COOH).

Most naturally occurring amino acids have L-configuration.

⇒ In proteins, α-amino acid units are connected by peptide (amide linkage) linkages.

20. (a) Neutral amino acids have isoelectric point at neutral region, i.e. 7. Acidic amino acids have isoelectric point at acidic region, i.e. less than 7, while basic amino acids have isoelectric point at basic region, i.e. more than 7. *A*, *B* and *C* are glycine, glutamic acid and lysine respectively. These are neutral, acidic and basic amino acids respectively.

Hence, *A*, *B* and *C* will have isoelectric point around 7, less than 7 and more than 7. Hence, the isoelectric points at 9.5, 6.0 and 3.1 corresponds to *C*, *A* and *B*.

21. (1.74) Let the % of α-D-glucose (I) present is x and that of β-D-glucose (II) is $(100 - x)$.

α-D-glucose and β-D-glucose shows the specific rotations of +112° and +18.7° respectively. According to the problem,

$[x \times 112 + (100 - x) \times 18.7] = 52.7 \times 100 = 5270$ (during mutarotation)

$$\Rightarrow 112x + 1870 - 18.7x = 5270$$

$$\Rightarrow \quad 93.3x = 3400$$

$$\Rightarrow \quad x = 36.44$$

Hence, at the equilibrium α-D-glucose and β-D-glucose present are 36.44 and 63.56 respectively. So, at equilibrium, the ratio of (II) and (I) is: 63.56/36.44 = 1.74

22. (7)

(i) D-glucose: ^1CHO, H–[2]–OH, HO–[3]–H, H–[4]–OH, H–[5]–OH, $_6CH_2OH$

$$\xrightarrow{5HIO_4} \underset{\substack{5\text{ mol}\\(C_1-C_5)\\{[a=5]}}}{HCOOH} + \underset{\substack{1\text{ mol}\\(C_6)\\{[b=1]}}}{HCHO}$$

(ii) D-fructose: $^1CH_2OH$, [2] C=O, HO–[3]–H, H–[4]–OH, H–[5]–OH, $_6CH_2OH$

$$\xrightarrow{5\,HIO_4} \underset{\substack{4\text{ mol}\\(C_1-C_5)\\{[c=4]}}}{HCOOH} + \underset{\substack{2\text{ mol}\\(C-1,\ C_6)\\{[d=2]}}}{HCHO}$$

$$\Rightarrow \left(\frac{a}{b} + \frac{c}{d}\right) = \frac{5}{1} + \frac{4}{2} = 7$$

23. (3)

$$\underset{\text{Glucose}}{CHO-(CHOH)_4-CH_2OH} + \underset{\text{(Phenylhydrazine)}}{3C_6H_5NHNH_2} \longrightarrow$$

$$\underset{\text{Glucosazone}}{HC{=}NNHC_6H_5-C{=}NNHC_6H_5-(HO-C-H)-(H-C-OH)-(H-C-OH)-CH_2OH} + NH_3 + 2H_2O + PhNH_2$$

24. (27.99) Let α % = x

So, $x \times (150.7) + (100 - x) \times (52.8) = 80.2 \times 100$

$$\Rightarrow \quad 150.7x - 52.8x = 8020 - 5280 \Rightarrow x = 27.99$$

25. (4.88) Difference in mass of compound = 390 − 180 = 210

weight of $CH_3CO—$ group is 43 g.

∴ Therefore, no. of $—NH_2$ group $= \frac{210}{43} = 4.88$

26. (1)

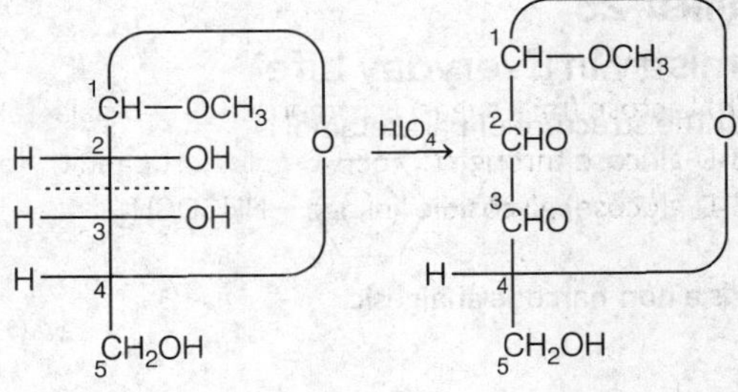

As C_1 and C_4 of the substrate are present in the optimum oxidised state, $C_1 - C_2$, $C_3 - C_4$ and $C_4 - C_5$ bond will not be cleaved by HIO_4, only $C_2 - C_3$ will be cleaved by one mole of HIO_4.

27. (3.25) The ionisation of the various protons of Glutamic acid are as follows

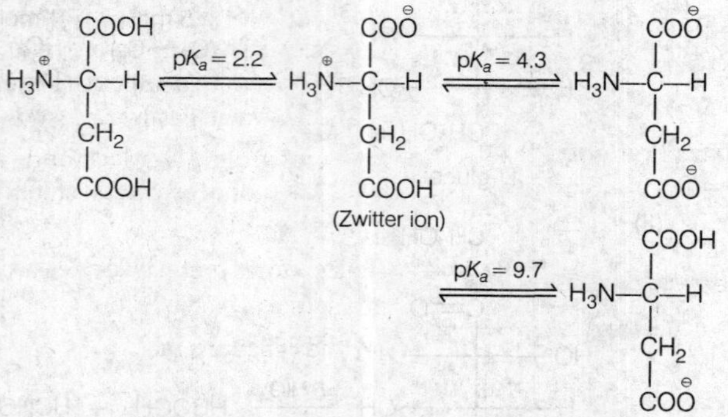

$$\underset{\text{COOH}}{\overset{\text{COOH}}{H_3\overset{\oplus}{N}-C-H}} \xrightleftharpoons{pK_a = 2.2} \underset{\text{COOH (Zwitter ion)}}{\overset{COO^{\ominus}}{H_3\overset{\oplus}{N}-C-H}} \xrightleftharpoons{pK_a = 4.3} \underset{COO^{\ominus}}{\overset{COO^{\ominus}}{H_3N-C-H}} \xrightleftharpoons{pK_a = 9.7} \underset{COO^{\ominus}}{\overset{\text{COOH}}{H_3N-C-H}}$$

(each with CH_2 side chain)

Hence, from the above ionisation process, the isoelectric point of glutamic acid can be calculated as

$pH_i = (pK_a$ of α-COOH + pK_a of side chain COOH)/2

$= (2.2 + 4.3) / 2 = 3.25$

28. (81.00) The number of polypeptides $= (n)^m$

where, n = value of polypeptide,
i.e. for dipeptide $n = 2$
for tripeptide $n = 3$ etc.

$\Rightarrow m$ = number of different amino acids

$\Rightarrow (n)^m = (3)^4 = 3 \times 3 \times 3 \times 3 = 81$ = number of tetrapeptides

29. (5.00) Let, the number of glycine units present in the decapeptide unit $= n$

$$\Rightarrow \frac{n \times M_{Glycine}}{M_{Decapeptide}} \times 100 = 47$$

$$\Rightarrow \frac{n \times 75}{796} \times 100 = 47$$

$$\Rightarrow n = 4.98 = 5$$

30. (−2.00) pH = 14, indicates a strongly basic medium at which only basic groups of the amino acid will be stabilised.

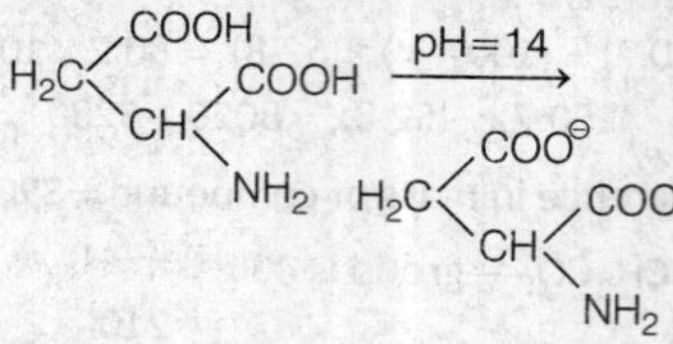

$$H_2C(COOH)-CH(COOH)-NH_2 \xrightarrow{pH=14} H_2C(COO^{\ominus})-CH(COO^{\ominus})-NH_2$$

Net charge $= 2 \times (-1) = -2$

Qualifier 28

(Chemistry in Everyday Life)

1. (d) The structure of paracetamol is

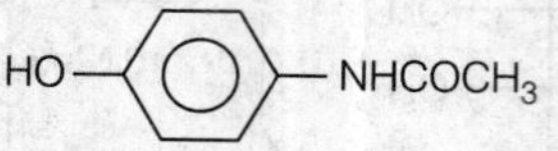

HO–C_6H_4–$NHCOCH_3$

It is a non-narcotic analgesic.

2. (d) Reserpine is a tranquilizer. Its structure is as given,

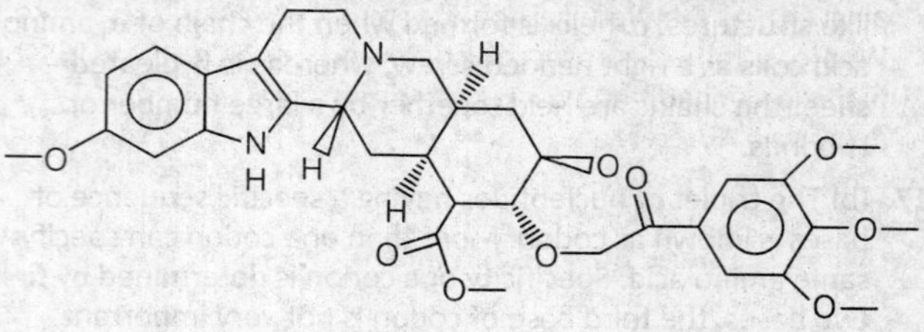

[Structure of reserpine]

3. (b) (I) and (II) are the examples of antidepressant drugs.

I → Iproniazid

II → Phenelzine (Brand name-Nardil)

These two drugs inhibit the enzymes which catalyse the degradation of noradrenaline, which is one of the neurotransmitters that plays a role in mood changes.

4. (a) Narrow spectrum antibiotics are effective against gram-positive or gram-negative bacteria.

Whereas broad spectrum antibiotics kill or inhibit a wide range of gram-positive and gram-negative bacteria.

Limited spectrum antibiotics are effective against a single organism or disease.

5. (c) Antacids are those which are used when over production of acid in the stomach causes irritation and pain.

It is used in the treatment of hyperacidity. Cimetidine and ranitidine are used as antacids, while phenelzine and equanil are not. Phenelzine is used as an antidepressant and equanil is a mild tranquilizer for relieving hypertension.

6. (b) Correct match is A→(4), B→(3), C→(1), D→(2).

- Pathogen is an infectious agent or a germ that cause disease.
- Bacteriostatic is an antimicrobial agent that stops bacteria from reproducing, i.e. it show static or inhibitory effect on microbes.
- Bactericidal is an antimicrobial agent that kill bacteria.
- Disinfectant is a chemical substance that inhibit or destroy microorganisms on inert surfaces.

7. (a) Both statements I and II are correct.

Boric acid (H_3BO_3) in dilute aqueous solution is weak antiseptic.

$$H_3BO_3 + H_2O \rightleftharpoons [B(OH)_4]^- + H^+$$

Boric acid acts as a weak monobasic acid in water.

8. (a) Cationic detergents are quaternary ammonium salts of amines

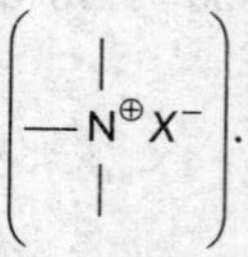

$$\left(-\overset{|}{\underset{|}{N^{\oplus}}} X^- \right)$$

where, X = Cl, Br, $OCOCH_3$

These detergents have germicidal properties.

9. (c) Detergents with straight chain alkyl groups are biodegradable. Whereas, if the hydrocarbon chain is highly branched, then bacteria cannot degrade the detergent in environment easily. It may cause pollution with effluents in ponds, rivers etc. Hence, both (a) and (b) are biodegradable detergents.

10. (c) The boiling point of glycerol is 290°C at 1 atm pressure. It decomposes before it distils at this temperature. Hence, the distillation is carried out under reduced pressure by applying vacuum which helps to decrease the boiling point of glycerol and thus, its decomposition is prevented.

11. (3) Statements II, III and IV are correct, while statement I is incorrect. The drugs that bind the receptor site and inhibit its natural function are called antagonists. Agonists are those drugs that mimic the natural messenger by switching on the receptor. They are useful where there is lack of natural chemical messenger.

12. (5) Salvarsan, prontosil, sulphanilamide, azodye and chloramphenicol are the antibiotic drugs. Chlordiazepoxide is a tranquilizer, while terfenadine is an antihistamine.

13. (6)

$$\begin{array}{l} CH_2-O-\overset{O}{\overset{\|}{C}}-C_{17}H_{35} \\ | \\ CH-O-\overset{O}{\overset{\|}{C}}-C_{17}H_{35} \\ | \\ CH_2-O-\underset{O}{\underset{\|}{C}}-C_{17}H_{35} \end{array} + \underset{\text{Sodium hydroxide}}{3NaOH}$$

Glyceryl ester of stearic acid

$$\longrightarrow \underset{\text{Sodium stearate}}{3\,C_{17}H_{35}COONa} + \underset{\text{Glycerol}}{\begin{array}{l} CH_2-OH \\ | \\ CH-OH \\ | \\ CH_2-OH \end{array}}$$

From this reaction the value of,

$x + y = 3 + 3 = 6$

14. (1.53) When sweetness of sucrose $= 1$, that of alitame $= 2000$, saccharin $= 550$, sucralose $= 600$

$\Rightarrow$ When sweetness of sucrose $= x = 1$ then, that of alitame, $xy = 1 \times 2000$

Saccharin, $xz = 1 \times 550$

Sucralose, $xw = 1 \times 600$

$$\Rightarrow \quad y = \frac{2000}{x} = 2000$$

$$z = \frac{550}{x} = 550$$

$$\Rightarrow \quad w = \frac{600}{x} = 600$$

$$\Rightarrow \quad w(y + z) = 600\,(2000 + 550)$$

$$= 1.53 \times 10^6 = p \times 10^6$$

$$\therefore \quad p = 1.53$$

15. (25) Formula of sodium laurylsulphate is $CH_3(CH_2)_{10}CH_2O\overset{-}{S}O_3\overset{+}{N}a$.

Here, $a = 10$

Formula of cetyltrimethyl ammonium bromide is $CH_3(CH_2)_{15}-\overset{+}{N}(CH_3)_3\overset{-}{Br}$.

Here, $b = 15$

$\therefore a + b = 10 + 15 = 25$

Qualifier 29

(Principles Related to Practical Chemistry

1. (b) Detection of the chlorine is not possible in $CHCl_3$.

In (a), (C—Cl) bond is weakened by strong (EWG) $-NO_2$ groups at *ortho* and *para*-position.

In (b), but C—Cl bond is purely covalent in $CHCl_3$.

In (c), $C_6H_5-\overset{\oplus}{C}H_2$ benzyl carbocation is stabilised by resonance and thus Cl^- ions become free.

In (d) $CH_2{=}CH\overset{\oplus}{C}H_2$ allyl carbocation is stabilised by resonance and thus, behaves as an ionic chloride.

2. (b) Phenolic —OH gives violet colour with neutral $FeCl_3$ solution.

The given compound is *m*-cresol which on nitration gives three nitro-derivatives.

$$\text{m-cresol (OH, }CH_3\text{)} \xrightarrow[(ArS_E2)]{NO_2^+} \text{(OH, }NO_2\text{, }CH_3\text{)} + \text{(OH, }CH_3\text{, }NO_2\text{)} + O_2N\text{–(OH, }CH_3\text{)}$$

3. (b)

$$\underset{\text{(Aniline)}}{Ph-NH_2} + \underset{\text{(Acetic anhydride)}}{CH_3-\overset{O}{\overset{\|}{C}}-O-\overset{O}{\overset{\|}{C}}-CH_3} \xrightarrow[CH_3COOH]{\text{Glacial}} \underset{\text{(Acetanilide)}}{Ph-NHCOCH_3} + CH_3COOH$$

Small amount of Zn-dust is added to the reaction mixture to prevent oxidation and to decolourise the coloured impurities by reduction.

4. (a) K_{sp} of group I metal chloride is $\le 10^{-4}$, K_{sp} of other metal chloride is more than 10^{-4}.

Hence, other metal chlorides are not precipitated by dil. HCl.

5. (a) The reactions are,

(i) $AgBr + \underset{(A)}{2Na_2S_2O_3} \longrightarrow \underset{(B)}{Na_3[Ag(S_2O_3)_2](aq)} + NaBr$

(ii) $2AgNO_3 + \underset{(A)}{Na_2S_2O_3} \longrightarrow$

$\underset{\substack{\text{(White)} \\ (C)}}{Ag_2S_2O_3} + H_2O \longrightarrow \underset{\substack{\text{Black ppt.} \\ (D)}}{Ag_2S\downarrow} + H_2SO_4$

6. (b) The preferential systematic analysis of the given basic radicals can be shown as

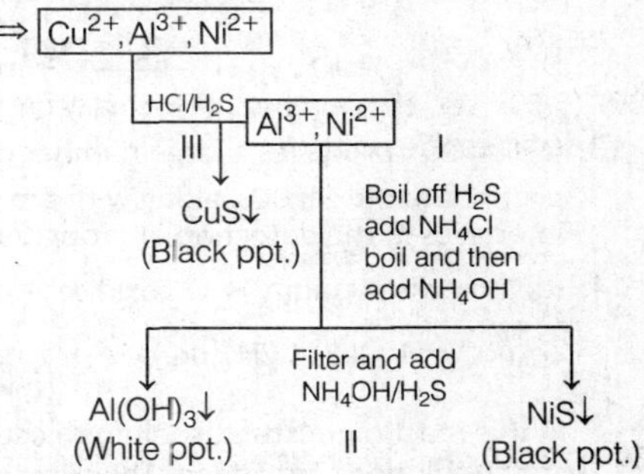

7. (c) $Al(OH)_3$ reacts with NaOH to form $NaAlO_2$ which is soluble in NaOH. $Cr(OH)_3$ reacts with NaOH to form Na_2CrO_4 which is also soluble in NaOH and $Fe(OH)_3$ is basic, it does not react with NaOH.

8. (c) $CoS \xrightarrow{\text{Aqua-regia}} CoCl_2 \xrightarrow{NaHCO_3}$

$Na_4[Co(CO_3)_3] \xrightarrow[H_2O]{Br_2}$

$\underset{\text{Green solution}}{Na_3[Co(CO_3)_3]}$

(i) ZnS and MnS are soluble in dil. HCl.

(ii) $NiCl_2$ reacts with $NaHCO_3$ to form $NiCO_3$ which converts into NiO_3 (black) by bromine water.

9. (d) Reactions with $CoCl_2$ are as follows

- $CoCl_2 \xrightarrow{NaHCO_3} CoCO_3 \xrightarrow{Na_2CO_3} Na_4[Co(CO_3)_3]$

$$\xrightarrow[NaHCO_3]{Br_2} \underset{\text{Green solution}}{2Na_3[Co(CO_3)_3]}$$

- $CoCl_2 + 4NH_4SCN \longrightarrow \underset{\text{Blue colour}}{(NH_4)_2[Co(CNS)_4]}$
- $CoCl_2 \xrightarrow[CH_3COOH]{KNO_2} \underset{\text{Yellow ppt.}}{K_3[Co(NO_2)_6]}$

10. (b) Only ZnS and MnS are soluble in dil. HCl. The given test is given by MnS.

$$MnS \xrightarrow{HCl} MnCl_2 \xrightarrow{NH_4OH} Mn(OH)_2 \xrightarrow{HNO_3} Mn(NO_3)_2$$

$$\xrightarrow[[O]]{PbO_2/HNO_3} \underset{\text{Pink colour}}{HMnO_4}$$

11. (c) Formation of the compounds are as follows

$$3Fe^{2+} + 2\underset{\text{(Ferricyanide)}}{[Fe^{III}(CN)_6]^{3-}} \longrightarrow \underset{\text{Turnbull's blue}}{Fe_3^{II}[Fe^{III}(CN)_6]_2} \text{ (Ferro-ferricyanide)}$$

$$4Fe^{3+} + 3\underset{\text{(Ferrocyanide)}}{[Fe^{II}(CN)_6]^{4-}} \longrightarrow \underset{\text{Prussian's blue}}{Fe_4^{III}[Fe^{II}(CN)_6]_3} \text{ (Ferri-ferrocyanide)}$$

12. (b) Correct match is A→ (4), B→ (3), C→ (1), D→ (2)

A. $4Fe^{3+} + 3[Fe(CN)_6]^{4-} \longrightarrow \underset{\text{Prussian blue (4)}}{Fe_4[Fe(CN)_6]_3}$

B. $Fe^{3+} + 3CNS^- \longrightarrow \underset{\text{Blood red (3)}}{[Fe(CNS)_3]}$

C. $Ni^{2+} + 2DMG \longrightarrow \underset{\text{Cherry red (1)}}{[Ni(DMG)_2]}$

D. $2Mn^{2+} + 5PbO_2 + 4H^+ \xrightarrow{H^+} \underset{\text{Pink (2)}}{2MnO_4^-} + 5Pb^{+2} + 2H_2O$

13. (c) Na_2CO_3 produces a large number of CO_3^{2-} ions which can precipitate out $MgCO_3$ along with group V cations. Hence, it interferes in the detection of group V cations.

14. (d) In acidic medium, H_2O_2 oxidises I^- to I_2.

$$2I^-(aq.) + H_2O_2(l) + 2H^+(aq.) \longrightarrow \underset{\text{(Violet)}}{I_2(g)} + 2H_2O\,(l)$$

In this reaction mixture, sodium thiosulphate ($Na_2S_2O_3$) and starch solutions are added. The excess of I_2, thus produced (concentration of KI or $H_2O_2 > Na_2S_2O_3$) reacts with starch giving the blue colour.

$$I_2(g) + 2S_2O_3^{2-}(aq) \longrightarrow 2I^-(aq) + S_4O_6^{2-}(aq)$$

$$I_2 + \text{Starch} \longrightarrow \text{Starch-iodide complex (blue)}$$

15. (c) Complete reaction is as follows

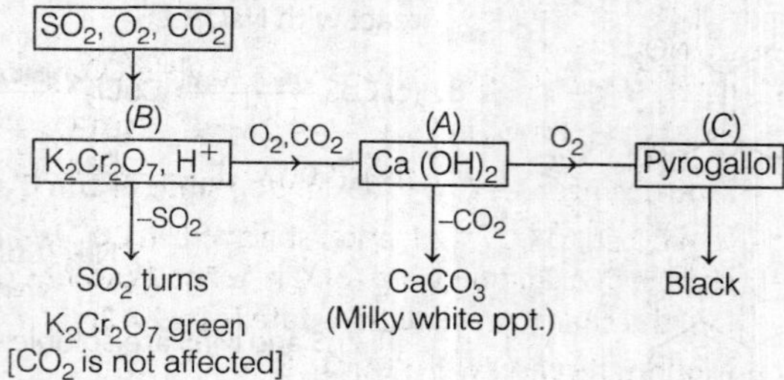

⇒ Thus, order is *B*, *A*, *C*.

16. (a) The white waxy solid (*A*) is white phosphorus. When white phosphorus is heated in an inert atmosphere at 573 K, it changes to red phosphorus. (*B*) is red phosphorus.

(*A*) on heating with KOH liberates phosphine gas (*C*) which is poisonous gas with rotten fish smell.

$$P_4 + 3KOH + 3H_2O \longrightarrow \underset{\substack{\text{Phosphine} \\ (C)}}{PH_3} + 3KH_2PO_2$$

White phosphorus (P_4) burns with excess of Cl_2 to form phosphorus pentachloride (*D*).

$$P_4 + 10Cl_2 \xrightarrow{\text{Heat}} \underset{(D)}{4PCl_5}$$

Hydrolysis of (*D*) gives phosphoric acid (*E*).

$$PCl_5 + 4H_2O \longrightarrow \underset{(E)}{H_3PO_4} + 5HCl$$

17. (a)

(i) Gas (*X*) is absorbed in acidified $K_2Cr_2O_7$ and the solution turns green, so (*X*) is SO_2.

$$\underset{(X)}{3SO_2} + K_2Cr_2O_7 + H_2SO_4 \longrightarrow K_2SO_4 + \underset{\text{Green}}{Cr_2(SO_4)_3} + H_2O$$

(ii) Gas (*Y*) is absorbed in lime water turning it white, so *Y* is CO_2.

$$Ca(OH)_2 + \underset{(Y)}{CO_2} \longrightarrow \underset{\text{White}}{CaCO_3} \downarrow + H_2O$$

(iii) Gas (*Z*) is absorbed in pyrogallol, so (*Z*) is O_2.

$$\underset{(Z)}{O_2} + \text{Pyrogallol} \longrightarrow \text{Absorbed (black)}$$

18. (d) Assertion is incorrect and Reason is correct.

Ring test is given by NO_3^- ion where NO_2^- is the interfering radicals, while NO_2^- ion gives thiourea test and sulphanilic acid test.

19. (c) Amount of heat evolved during dissolution of hydrated copper sulphate $= m \times s \times t$

$$= (w + 200) \times 4.2 \times (t_2 - t_1)\text{ J}$$

[∵ Specific heat of the solution = specific heat of water $= 4.2\text{ J g}^{-1}{}^\circ\text{C}^{-1}$]

$\Rightarrow$ Heat evolved by $\frac{w}{249.5}$ mol $CuSO_4 \cdot 5H_2O$

$$= (w + 200) \times 4.2 \times (t_2 - t_1)\text{ J}$$

$\Rightarrow$ Heat or enthalpy of dissolution of $CuSO_4 \cdot 5H_2O$ is,

$$\frac{(w + 200) \times 4.2 \times (t_2 - t_1)}{w} \times 249.5\text{ J/mol}$$

20. (c) Experiments mentioned in options (a) and (b) will result in formation of lyophilic or hydrophilic sols which are 'starch sol' and 'sol of egg albumin' respectively.

Experiment mentioned in option (c) leads to the formation of a brown coloured lyophobic sol of $Fe(OH)_3$ which is a positive colloid as well as it adsorbs Fe^{3+} ions from the solution.

$$2FeCl_3(aq) + 3H_2O(l) \xrightarrow{\Delta} \underset{\text{[Sol particles]}}{Fe(OH)_3 \cdot Fe^{3+}} + 3HCl(aq) + 3Cl^-(aq)$$

21. (6)

(i) $CH_3CH_2-\underset{\underset{CH_3}{|}}{CH}-CH_2OH \xrightarrow[-H_2O]{\text{Conc. } H_2SO_4, \Delta}$ $CH_3-CH_2-\underset{\underset{CH_3}{|}}{CH}=CH_2$ $+ CH_3-CH=C(CH_3)_2$ (Major)

(ii) $CH_3-CH_2-\underset{\underset{CH_3}{|}}{C}=CH_2 \xrightarrow[\text{(ii) } H_2O_2/OH^-]{\text{(i) } BH_3/THF}$ $CH_3-\underset{\underset{OH}{|}}{CH}-CH(CH_3)_2$ (A, as 2°alcohol)

⇒ *A* is a 2° alcohol and it will react with the given reagents as,

$CH_3-\underset{\underset{OH}{|}}{CH}-CH(CH_3)_2$ (A as 2°alcohol)

- $\xrightarrow{NaOH + I_2}$ $CHI_3 + (CH_3)_2CH-\overset{-+}{COONa}$ (Haloform reaction)
- $\xrightarrow{\text{Conc. HCl}/ZnCl_2}$ 2-chloro-3-methylbutane (Lucas test)
- $\xrightarrow{Cr_2O_7^{2-}/H^+}$ 3-methylbutan-2-one $+ Cr^{3+}$(Green)
- $\xrightarrow{MnO_4^-/H^+}$ 3-methylbutan-2-one $+ Mn^{2+}$(Colourless)
- $\xrightarrow{CAN}$ 3-methylbutan-2-one [CAN is cerium (IV) ammonium nitrate, $(NH_4)_2Ce(NO_3)_6$]
- $\xrightarrow{Cu, 300°C}$ 3-methylbutan-2-one

22. (4) Aldehydes reduce Tollen's reagent to metallic silver (mirror).

The isomeric aldehydes are,

pentanal, 2-methylbutanal, 3-methylbutanal and 2,2-dimethylpropanal

23. (1) Acids stronger than H_2CO_3 can liberate CO_2 from $NaHCO_3$. Here, it is picric acid (III).

24. (2)

$\overset{\oplus}{:N}\equiv N-Ph$ + (Alkaline β-naphthol) $\xrightarrow{\text{[Coupling]}}$ intermediate ($:N=\ddot{N}-Ph$) $\xrightarrow{-H^+}$ 1-(phenylazo)-2-naphthol ($N=N-Ph$, OH)

[Azo dye]
(Reddish orange ppt.)

So, two π-bonds are involved in conjugation with each other, which are one $C=C$ π-bond of β-naphthol and one $N\equiv N$ π-bond of benzene diazonium chloride ($Ph-N_2^+$).

25. (4) $AgNO_3$ reacts with Cl^- to give white ppt. of AgCl.

$C_6H_5CH_2Cl$ and $CH_3-CH=CH-CH_2-Cl$ gives $Cl^{\ominus}$ ion as the cation formed is resonance stabilised.

$C_6H_5CH_2-Cl \longrightarrow C_6H_5\overset{\oplus}{C}H_2 + Cl^{\ominus}$

$CH_3-CH=CH-CH_2-Cl \longrightarrow CH_3-CH=CH + Cl^{\ominus}$ (with $\overset{\oplus}{C}H_2$)

7-chlorocycloheptatriene and 3-chlorocyclopropene gives $Cl^{\ominus}$ ion as the cation formed is aromatic.

$C_7H_7Cl \longrightarrow C_7H_7^{\oplus} + Cl^{\ominus}$

$C_3H_3Cl \longrightarrow C_3H_3^{\oplus} + Cl^{\ominus}$

26. (3) Oxalic acid reacts with $KMnO_4$ to yield CO_2 gas.

$$5C_2O_4^{2-} + 2MnO_4^- + 16H^+ \longrightarrow 2Mn^{2+} + 10CO_2 + 8H_2O$$

reducing agent is $C_2O_4^{2-}$. Oxidation state of C in $C_2O_4^{2-}$ is +3 . It is oxidised to CO_2. Oxidation state of C in CO_2 is + 4. Thus, the change in oxidation state for C is 1. For 2 carbons of oxalate ion, the change in oxidation state is $1 \times 2 = 2$.

Mohr' salt reacts with $KMnO_4$ is

$$5Fe^{2+} + MnO_4^- + 8H^+ \longrightarrow Mn^{2+} + 5Fe^{3+} + 4H_2O$$

Fe^{2+} is reducing agent. Its oxidation state is changing from +2 to +3. Therefore, the change is 1.

Hence, the total change in the oxidation state of the reducing agents/species is $2 + 1 = 3$.

27. (5) PbS, CuS, HgS, CoS and Bi_2S_3 are black in colour. MnS can be red, green or brown coloured powder. SnS_3 is a golden-yellow powder.

28. (8) Coordination no. of Fe in given complex ion is 6 so, $P = 6$.

$$S - 1 + 5 \times 0 = +2$$
$$S = +3$$

Oxidation number, S of Fe is +3

$$Fe^{3+} = d^5$$

As both CNS^- and H_2O are weak field ligands so, no pairing of electrons occur.

1	1	1	1	1

Thus, no. of unpaired electrons, $Q = 5$

No. of paired electrons in d-orbital, $R = 0$

Hence, $(P + Q) + R^2 - S = (6 + 5) + (0)^2 - 3 = 11 - 3 = 8$

29. (3) In brown ring, $[Fe(H_2O)_5NO]SO_4$, Fe is present in +1 oxidation state where H_2O, is a weak field ligand. NO is strong field ligand, so pairing of electrons occur.

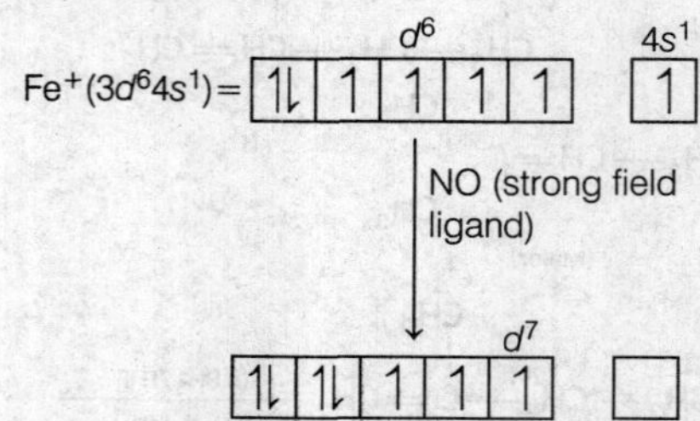

$\Rightarrow$ Number of unpaired electrons in Fe = 3

30. (2) NaOH can dissolve $Cr(OH)_3$ [a green ppt.] and $Al(OH)_3$ [a white ppt.] into soluble Na_2CrO_4 and $NaAlO_2$ respectively.

PART TESTS

Part Test 01

1. (b) As we move from left to right across a period, ionisation enthalpy increases with increasing atomic number.

But $N(1s^2 2s^2 2p^3)$ has a stable half filled electronic configuration. So, its ionisation enthalpy is greater than oxygen.

Hence, the correct order of increasing first ionisation enthalpy is B < C < O < N.

2. (b) The hydration energy is maximum in case of Li^+. Therefore, its hydration sphere is most bulky and its mobility is least as compared to other alkali metal ions. Therefore, its conductance is also least.

3. (a) $4PH_3(g) \longrightarrow P_4(g) + 6H_2(g)$

$t = 0$: 100 mL, 0, 0

$t = t$: 0, $\frac{100}{4}$ mL, $\frac{6 \times 100}{4}$ mL

$\Rightarrow$ New volume $= 25 + 150 = 175$ mL

$\therefore$ Change in volume $= 175 - 100 = 75$ mL

4. (b) $\Delta G = \Delta H - T\Delta S$

At 1000 K,

$$\Delta G = -283 \text{ kJ} - 1000 \text{ K} \times \left(\frac{-97}{1000} \text{kJ}\right) = -186 \text{ kJ}$$

At 1500 K,

$$\Delta G = -283 \text{ kJ} - 1500 \text{ K} \times \left(\frac{-97}{1000} \text{kJ}\right) = -137.5 \text{ kJ}$$

At 3000 K,

$$\Delta G = -283 \text{ kJ} - 3000 \text{ K} \times \left(\frac{-97}{1000} \text{kJ}\right) = +8.0 \text{ kJ}$$

At 3500 K,

$$\Delta G = -283 \text{ kJ} - 3500 \text{ K} \times \left(\frac{-97}{1000} \text{kJ}\right) = +56.5 \text{ kJ}$$

Thus, at 1000 K and at 1500 K, the reaction will be spontaneous ($\Delta G < 0$).

5. (a) Number of spherical nodal planes $= (n - l - 1)$

for, $4s \Rightarrow (4 - 0 - 1) = 3$

$4p \Rightarrow (4 - 1 - 1) = 2$

$4d \Rightarrow (4 - 2 - 1) = 1$

6. (c) Number of milligram of Ca^{2+} ion $= 3.75 \times 40 = 150$

$\therefore$ 200 g sample hard water contains 150 mg of Ca^{2+}.

$\therefore$ 10^6 g sample hard water contains

$$\frac{150}{200} \times 10^6 \times 10^3 = 750 \times 10^6 = 750 \text{ ppm}$$

7. (b) A chiral molecule has non-superimposable mirror images.

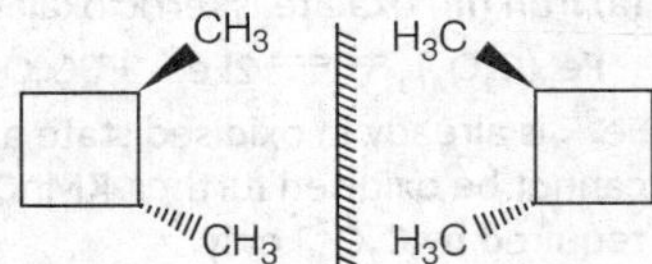

8. (b) Lattice energy $\propto q_1 q_2 \propto \frac{1}{r}$

Hence, it is maximum of A_2B_3 $(2A^{3+} . 3B^{2-})$ and minimum for $A_2B(2A^+ . B^{2-})$.

Charge (q) on A (A^{3+}) of A_2B_3 is higher than $A(A^+)$ of A_2B.

So, correct order of lattice energy is $A_2B_3 > AB > A_2B$.

9. (c) The atomic orbital overlap is the key feature that explains the bond formation.

Bonding orbitals are formed by in-phase overlap of atomic orbitals, while antibonding orbitals are formed by out-of-phase overlap between atomic orbitals.

10. (a) We know that

$$p(V - nb) = nRT$$

$\Rightarrow p(V_m - b) = RT$ (where, $V_m = V/n$)

The compressibility factor is given by

$$Z = \frac{pV_m}{RT} = 1 + \frac{pb}{RT}$$

Suppose pressure and temperature are p' and T' when its molar volume is $10b$, then $p'(V_m - b) = RT'$

$$\Rightarrow \frac{p'}{RT'} = \frac{1}{10b - b} = \frac{1}{9b}$$

$$\Rightarrow Z = 1 + \frac{p'b}{RT'} = 1 + \frac{1}{9} = \frac{10}{9}$$

11. (d) $\underset{1-x}{A(s)} \rightleftharpoons \underset{2x}{2B(g)} + \underset{3x}{3C(g)}$

$$K_c = 4x^2 \times 27x^3 = 108x^5$$

$\Rightarrow A(s) \rightleftharpoons \underset{2x \times C}{2B(g)} + \underset{6x}{3C(g)}$

$\Rightarrow 108x^5 = 4x^2 \times C^2 \times 216x^3$

$\Rightarrow 108 = C^2 \times 216 \times 4$

$\Rightarrow C^2 = \frac{108}{4 \times 216} \Rightarrow C = \frac{1}{2\sqrt{2}}$

12. (c) The reaction can be expressed as

$$PCl_5(g) \rightleftharpoons PCl_3(g) + Cl_2(g)$$

$0.1 - 0.052$, $0 + 0.52$, $0 + 0.52$

0.048, 0.052, 0.052

Total number of moles $= 0.048 + 0.052 + 0.052 = 0.152$ mol

If p is pressure of PCl_5, PCl_3 and Cl_2, then

$$K_p = \frac{p_{PCl_3} \times p_{Cl_2}}{p_{PCl_5}}$$

$$1.78 = \frac{\left(\frac{0.052}{0.152}\right) \times p \times \left(\frac{0.052}{0.152}\right) \times p}{\left(\frac{0.048}{0.152}\right) \times p}$$

$$1.78 = \frac{0.342 \times p \times 0.342 \times p}{0.3158\, p}$$

$1.78 = 0.3703\, p$

$4.8 = p$

So, $p = 4.8$ (due to PCl_5, PCl_3 and Cl_2).

$p_{\text{solvent}} = 5.5 - 4.8 = 0.7$

Since $p \propto$ number of moles, we have

$$\frac{p_{(Cl_2, PCl_3 \text{ and } PCl_5)}}{p_{\text{solvent}}} = \frac{\text{Total moles of } Cl_2, PCl_3 \text{ and } PCl_5}{n_{\text{solvent}}}$$

$$\Rightarrow \frac{4.8}{0.7} = \frac{0.152}{n_{\text{solvent}}}$$

$n_{\text{solvent}} = 0.022$ mol

$= 0.022 \times 154$

$= 3.388$ g

13. (a) Balanced chemical equation is

$$2K_2Cr_2O_7 + 3Sn + 28HCl \longrightarrow 3SnCl_4 + 4KCl + 4CrCl_3 + 14H_2O$$

$2(2 \times 39 + 2 \times 52 + 7 \times 16) = 2 \times 294 = 588$ g; $3 \times 118.7 = 356.1$ g

Now, 356.1 g Sn react with $K_2Cr_2O_7 = 588$ g

1 g Sn will react with

$$K_2Cr_2O_7 = \frac{588}{356.1} = 1.651 \text{ g}$$

$\Rightarrow$ Equivalent weight of $K_2Cr_2O_7$

$$= \frac{\text{Molecular weight}}{6} = \frac{294}{6} = 49$$

Decinormal $K_2Cr_2O_7$ solution means 1000 mL solution contains 4.9 g

$K_2Cr_2O_7$, that is 4.9 g $K_2Cr_2O_7$ is present in 1000 mL solution.

Thus, 1.651 g $K_2Cr_2O_7$ will be present in

$$= \frac{1000}{4.9} \times 1.651 = 336.9 \text{ mL}$$

14. (c) The rate of dissolution of NaCl in water is more than that of D_2O (heavy water) due to isotopic effect.

Molecule	H_2O	D_2O
Solubility of NaCl	359 g L^{-1}	305 g L^{-1}

15. (a) The alkali metals dissolve in liquid ammonia giving deep blue solutions, which are conducting in nature.

$$M + (x+y)NH_3 \longrightarrow [M(NH_3)_x]^+ + [e(NH_3)_y]^-$$

The blue colour is due to the ammoniated electron which absorbs energy in the visible region of light and thus, imparts blue colour to the solution.

16. (c) Silica is unreactive but its product when it reacts with H_2SO_4 and CaF_2 followed by hydrolysis is,

(i) $H_2SO_4 + CaF_2 \longrightarrow HF + CaSO_4$

(ii) $4HF + SiO_2 \longrightarrow SiF_4 + 2H_2O$

(iii) $SiF_4 + 4H_2O \longrightarrow 4HF + Si(OH)_4$ or $SiO_2.2H_2O$ (Silicic acid)

$\Rightarrow$ SiF_4 comes in contact with a drop of H_2O and hydrolysed to silicic acid. This can be seen as white solid (opaque) forming on the surface of drop of water.

17. (a) Peroxyacetyl nitrate is a constituent of photochemical smog.

$\Rightarrow$ Polycyclic aromatic compounds are carcinogenic in nature.

$\Rightarrow$ Dioxins are produced during waste incineration.

$\Rightarrow$ IR active molecules absorbs IR rays and are responsible for global warming.

18. (b) According to Markownikoff's rule, deuterium (D) will get attached to the carbon with fewer alkyl substituents and the chloride (Cl) will get attached to the carbon with more alkyl substituents.

2-cyclohexyl-4-methylpent-2-ene $\xrightarrow{DCl}$ (product with Cl, D, H)

19. (c) Major stable carbocation shown below leads to major product.

(Biphenyl)–CH=CH–Ph $\xrightarrow{H^+}$ (Biphenyl)–$\overset{+}{C}H$–CH_2–Ph

It has more resonance structures than other possible carbocations.

20. (a) Iron (III) oxalate is ferric oxalate.

$$Fe_2(C_2O_4)_3 \rightleftharpoons 2Fe^{3+} + 3C_2O_4^{2-}$$

Fe^{3+} is already in oxidised state and cannot be oxidised further. $KMnO_4$ is required by $C_2O_4^{2-}$ only.

$$2MnO_4^- + 5C_2O_4^{2-} \longrightarrow 2Mn^{2+} + 10CO_2$$

2 moles of MnO_4^- oxidise $= 5$ moles of $C_2O_4^{2-}$

1 mole of MnO_4^- oxidise $= 2.5$ moles of $C_2O_4^{2-}$

$= \frac{2.5}{3}$ moles of $Fe_2(C_2O_4)_3 = 0.83$ mol

Thus, (A) $\rightarrow$ (3)

$\Rightarrow$ Iron (II) sulphate (IV) is ferrous sulphite $FeSO_3$.

$$\overset{+2}{Fe}\overset{+4}{S}O_3 \rightleftharpoons Fe^{2+} + SO_3^{2-}$$

Both ions are oxidised by $KMnO_4$ in acidic medium.

$$5Fe^{2+} + MnO_4^- \longrightarrow Mn^{2+} + 5Fe^{3+}$$

$$5SO_3^{2-} + 2MnO_4^- \longrightarrow 2Mn^{2+} + SO_4^{2-}$$

$$5FeSO_3 \equiv 3MnO_4^-$$

1 mole of $MnO_4^- \equiv \frac{5}{3}$ moles of $FeSO_3 = 1.67$ mol

Thus, (B) $\rightarrow$ (4)

$\Rightarrow$ Iron (II) oxalate is ferrous oxalate FeC_2O_4.

$$FeC_2O_4 \rightleftharpoons Fe^{2+} + C_2O_4^{2-}$$

Both ions are oxidised by MnO_4^- in acidic medium.

$$2MnO_4^- + 5C_2O_4^{2-} \longrightarrow CO_2 + H_2O + Mn^{2+}$$

$$MnO_4^- + 5Fe^{2+} \longrightarrow Mn^{2+} + Fe^{3+} + H_2O$$

$$3MnO_4^- \equiv 5FeC_2O_4$$

$$1MnO_4^- \equiv \frac{5}{3}FeC_2O_4 = 1.67 \text{ mol}$$

Thus, (C) $\rightarrow$ (4)

$\Rightarrow$ Iron (III) sulphate (VI) is ferric sulphate.

$$Fe_2(SO_4)_3 \rightleftharpoons 2Fe^{3+} + 3SO_4^{2-}$$

Both ions are in oxidised state and no further reaction with MnO_4^- is possible.

Hence, $KMnO_4$ is not used.

Thus, (D) $\rightarrow$ (2)

$\Rightarrow$ Iron (III) sulphate (IV) is ferric sulphite $Fe_2(SO_3)_3$.

$$Fe_2(SO_3)_3 \rightleftharpoons 2Fe^{3+} + 3SO_3^{2-}$$

Only SO_3^{2-} is oxidised.

$$5SO_3^{2-} + 2MnO_4^- \longrightarrow 2Mn^{2+} + 5SO_4^{2-}$$

$2MnO_4^-$ oxidise $= 5$ moles of $SO_3^{2-} = \frac{5}{3}$ moles of $Fe_2(SO_3)_3$

$1MnO_4^-$ oxidises $= \frac{5}{6}$ moles of $Fe_2(SO_3)_3 = 0.83$ mol

Thus, (E) $\rightarrow$ (3)

21. (40)

$$N_2O(g) \rightleftharpoons N_2(g) + \frac{1}{2}O_2(g)$$

$$p^\circ(1-\alpha) \qquad p^\circ(\alpha) \qquad p^\circ\left(\frac{\alpha}{2}\right)$$

$\Rightarrow$ When temperature of N_2O is doubled, its pressure also become doubled.

$\therefore$ Pressure of N_2O at 900 K $(p^\circ) = 2$ atm

$\Rightarrow$ Total pressure at equilibrium $= 2.4$ atm

$$\Rightarrow p^\circ(1-\alpha) + p^\circ(\alpha) + p^\circ\left(\frac{\alpha}{2}\right) = 2.4$$

$$\Rightarrow p^\circ\left(1 + \frac{\alpha}{2}\right) = 2.4 \qquad [p^\circ = 2]$$

$$\Rightarrow \alpha = 0.4$$

$\therefore$ Degree of dissociation of $N_2O(g) = 40\%$

22. (7)

In case of (ii), (iii), (iv). (v), (vii). (viii) and (ix) first intermediate is more stable than the second one.

The second intermediate is more stable than the first, which is due to-

$\Rightarrow +I$ effect of CH_3 in (i).

$\Rightarrow$ allylic (2°) conjugation in (vi).

$\Rightarrow$ higher LFCF bond angle in (x)

23. (0.33)

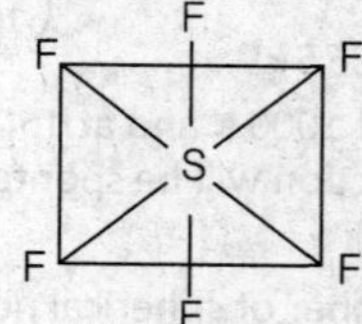

$\angle FSF = 90°$, bonds $= 12(a)$

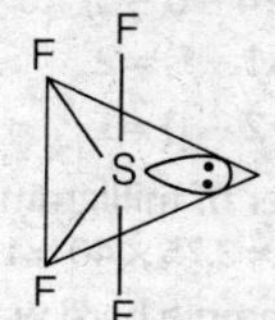

$\angle FSF = 90°$, bonds $= 0 (b)$ (due to presence of one lone pair)

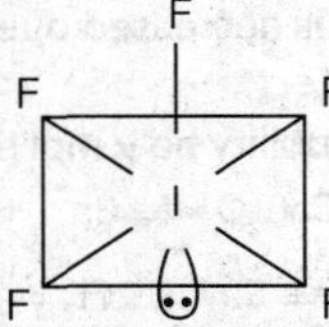

$\angle FIF = 90°$, bonds $= 0$ (c) (due to presence of one lone pair)

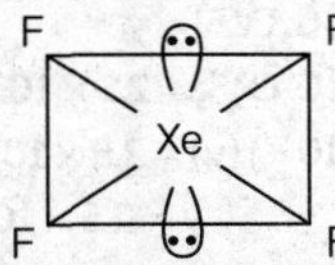

$\angle FXeF = 90°$, bonds $= 4$ (*d*) (two lone pairs are present in opposite direction)

$$\Rightarrow \frac{b+c+d}{a} = \frac{0+0+4}{12} = 0.33$$

24. (195.46)

The amount of Fe_2O_3 that would be required to react completely with the given amount of Al moles.

$$Fe_2O_3 = (4.20 \text{ moles of Al}) \times \left(\frac{1 \text{ mole of } Fe_2O_3}{2 \text{ moles of Al}}\right)$$

$$= 2.10 \text{ moles } Fe_2O_3$$

⇒ Since, only 1.75 mole of Fe_2O_3 are supplied, it is the limiting reactant. This can be confirmed by calculating the amount of Al that would be required to react completely with all of the available Fe_2O_3.

$$\text{Moles of Al} = (1.75 \text{ mole of } Fe_2O_3)\left(\frac{2 \text{ moles of Al}}{1 \text{ mole of } Fe_2O_3}\right)$$

$$= 3.50 \text{ moles of Al}$$

Since, an excess (4.20 mol − 3.50 mol = 0.70 mol) of Al is present, Fe_2O_3 must be the limiting reactant, as determined above.

⇒ Amount of Fe(*g*) formed from this mixture of reactants $= (1.75 \text{ mol of } Fe_2O_3)$

$$\left(\frac{2 \text{ moles of Fe}}{1 \text{ mole of } Fe_2O_3}\right)\left(\frac{55.847 \text{ g Fe}}{1 \text{ mole of Fe}}\right)$$

$$= 195.46 \text{ g Fe}$$

25. (6)

$$\Rightarrow \frac{1}{\lambda} = 109.678 \text{ cm}^{-1} \times \left(\frac{1}{n_2^2} - \frac{1}{n_1^2}\right)$$

$$= \left(\frac{1}{410.3 \text{ nm}}\right)\left(\frac{1 \text{ nm}}{1 \times 10^{-9} \text{ m}}\right)\left(\frac{1 \text{ m}}{100 \text{ cm}}\right)$$

$$\Rightarrow \left(\frac{1}{4.103 \times 10^{-5} \text{ cm}}\right) = 109{,}678 \text{ cm}^{-1} \times \left(\frac{1}{2^2} - \frac{1}{n_1^2}\right)$$

$$\Rightarrow \frac{2.437 \times 10^4 \text{ cm}^{-1}}{109{,}678 \text{ cm}^{-1}} = \frac{1}{4} - \frac{1}{n_1^2}$$

$$\Rightarrow \frac{1}{n_1^2} = \frac{1}{4} - 0.222$$

$$\Rightarrow n_1 = 6$$

26. (−2870.80)

The given values can be represented in the chemical reactions as

$$Ca(s) + Cl_2(g) \xrightarrow{-795 \text{ kJ mol}^{-1}} CaCl_2(s)$$

121 kJ mol^{-1} [Ca(s) → Ca(g)]; 242.8 kJ mol^{-1} [$Cl_2(g)$ → 2Cl(g)]

$$Ca(g) \quad 2Cl(g) \xrightarrow{-355 + 2 \text{ kJ mol}^{-1}}$$

2422 kJ mol^{-1} → $2Cl^-(g) + 2Ca^{2+}(g)$ → ΔH → $CaCl_2(s)$

Applying Hess's law of constant heat summation, we get

$$-795 = 121 + 242.8 + 2422 + (-355 \times 2) + \Delta H$$

$$\Rightarrow \Delta H = -2870.8 \text{ kJ mol}^{-1}$$

27. (2.11) $\Delta G^\circ_{500} = -RT \ln K_p$

$$= -(8.314 \text{ JK}^{-1}\text{mol}^{-1})(500 \text{ K}) \ln (6.25 \times 10^{-3})$$

$$= 2.11 \times 10^4 \text{ J}$$

28. (1.10) The reaction involved is

$$\underset{s}{Ag_2CrO_4} \rightleftharpoons \underset{\substack{0.1 + 2S = 0.1 \\ = 0.1}}{2Ag^+} + \underset{s}{CrO_4^{2-}}$$

The solubility product is

$$K_{sp} = [Ag^+]^2 [CrO_4^{2-}]$$

$$\Rightarrow 1.1 \times 10^{-12} = (0.1)^2 \times S$$

$$\text{Therefore, } S = [CrO_4^{2-}] = \frac{1.1 \times 10^{-12}}{(0.1)^2}$$

$$= 1.10 \times 10^{-10} \text{ mol L}^{-1}$$

29. (8) There are 8 chiral carbon atoms are present.

(Structure: H_3C, CH_3, CH_3, CH_3, CH_3, HO)

30. (5) The structures of five possible alkenes are as follows

(Structures: $H_3C—CH_2—CH_2$, H, $C=C$, CH_3; $H_3C—CH_2—CH_2$, CH_3, $C=C$, H; $H_3C—CH_2$, $CH_2—CH_3$, $C=C$, H; H, $CH_2—CH_3$, $C=C$, $CH_3—CH_2$; $H_3C—CH_2—CH_2—C—CH_2—CH_3$)

Part Test 02

1. (a) The correct match is A-(ii), B-(i), C-(iv), D-(iii).

⇒ Singlet carbene is sp^2-hybridised with one empty *p*-orbital,

⇒ Options (A) and (C) are conceptual.

⇒ Option (B) is a *see-saw* structure, as lone-pair lies In equatorial position, hence there is more reduction in *equatorial* bond angle than in *axial* bonds.

$[\angle F_{ax}—S—F_{ax} = 173°, \angle F_{eq}—S—F_{eq}]$

2. (b) Complete reaction as follows :

$$H_3C—C \equiv C—H \xrightarrow{\overset{\ominus}{N}H_2} H_3C—C \equiv \overset{\ominus}{C} Na^+$$

(OTs-cyclohexane) → $H_3C—C \equiv C—$(cyclohexyl) $\xrightarrow{\text{Na / liq.} NH_3}$ H_3C, H, $C=C$, H, cyclohexyl (*B*) $\xrightarrow{m\text{CPBA}}$ H, O, CH_3, H (*C*)

3. (c) Option (a) refers to a polluted air condition because particulate matter of size greater than 1 μ can get into the lungs and act as site for adsorption of carcinogenic material.

$\Rightarrow$ Option (b) refers to a polluted air condition because the rain with pH of about 5 is called acid rain and contains nitric and sulphuric acids. It is formed by the presence of oxides of sulphur and nitrogen in the air that exceed the permitted values.

$\Rightarrow$ Option (c) refers to a non-polluted environment because hydrogen-containing chlorofluorocarbons are destroyed in the troposphere itself, and not taken to stratosphere, where they can cause destruction of ozone.

$\Rightarrow$ Option (d) refers to a polluted air condition because levels of SO_2 at even 5 ppm can cause irritation of respiratory tract and eyes. SO_3 is harmful even at the concentration of 1 ppm which causes discomfort particularly to the elders.

4. (c) The reaction is,

$$\underset{0.1-a}{HCOOH} \rightleftharpoons \underset{a+b}{H^+} + \underset{a}{HCOO^-}$$

and

$$\underset{0.1-b}{HOCN} \rightleftharpoons \underset{b+a}{H^+} + \underset{b}{OCN^-}$$

$$\Rightarrow \quad K_{a(HCOOH)} = \frac{(a+b)a}{0.1-a} \quad \text{...(i)}$$

$$K_{a(HOCN)} = \frac{(a+b)b}{0.1-b} \quad \text{...(ii)}$$

$\because \quad (0.1-a) = (0.1-b) \cong 0.1$

Dividing Eq. (i) by Eq. (ii), we get

$$\frac{a}{b} = \frac{1.8}{3.3}$$

$\Rightarrow \quad b = 1.83\,a$

Now substracting Eq. (i) from Eq. (ii)

$$\frac{(a+b)b-(a+b)a}{0.1} = 3.3\times10^{-4} - 1.8\times10^{-4}$$

$$b^2 - a^2 = 1.5\times10^{-4} \quad \text{...(iii)}$$

$\because$ We know, $b = 1.83a$

Put the value in equation (iii)

On putting and solving,

we get,

$a = 7.99\times10^{-3}$ M

$b = 1.83\times a$

$b = 1.83\times7.99\times10^{-3}$

$b = 14.6\times10^{-3}$ M

Therefore, $[H^+] = (a+b)$

$= 22.59\times10^{-3}$

5. (4.06) Mole fraction of $CH_3OH = 0.1$

Mole fraction of $CH_3CH_2OH = 0.3$

Mole fraction of $H_2O = 0.6$

Sum of mole fraction = 1.0

Thus, moles of $CH_3OH = 1 (= 32\text{ g})$

$\Rightarrow$ Moles of $CH_3CH_2OH = 3 (= 138\text{ g})$

Moles of $H_2O = 6\ (= 108\text{ g})$

$\Rightarrow$ Molality of CH_3OH

$$= \frac{\text{Moles of } CH_3OH}{\text{kg of solvent } (H_2O + CH_3OH)}$$

$$= \frac{1}{246/1000} = 4.065 \text{ molal} = 4.06 \text{ molal}$$

6. (49.64)

Mass percentage of CH_3CH_2OH

$$= \frac{\text{Mass of solute}}{\text{Mass of solution}}$$

$$= \frac{138}{278}\times100 = 49.64\%$$

7. (4.56) $n = \dfrac{pV}{RT}$

$$= \frac{1 \text{ bar}\times(4/3)\pi\,(3)^3\text{m}^3}{0.0831\times10^{-3}\text{ bar m}^3\text{ mol}^{-1}\text{ K}^{-1}\times298\text{ K}}$$

$= 4.565\times10^3$ mol $= 4.56$ K mol

8. (128.90)

$w = 4.565\times2$ kg $= 9.130$ kg

Density $= 1.22$ kg m^{-3}

$\therefore$ Mass = Volume × Density

$$= \frac{4}{3}\pi(27)\times1.22 = 138.03 \text{ kg}$$

$\Rightarrow$ Mass that the balloon can lift (pay load) = mass of air − mass of H_2

$= 138.03$ kg $- 9.130$ kg

$= 128.90$ kg

9. (2.50)

$\Rightarrow C_2O_4^{2-}$ is oxidised to CO_2 by MnO_4^- in acidic medium.

$$C_2O_4^{2-} \longrightarrow 2CO_2 + 2e^-$$

$$MnO_4^- + 8H^+ + 5e^- \longrightarrow Mn^{2+} + 4H_2O$$

$\Rightarrow$ Thus, 1×10^{-4} M $MnO_4^- = 5\times10^{-4}$ N MnO_4^-

and $\quad xMC_2O_4^{2-} = 2xNC_2O_4^{2-}$

$\Rightarrow \quad N_1V_1 = N_2V_2$

$(N_1V_1)_{C_2O_4^{2-}} = (N_2V_2)_{MnO_4^-}$

$\Rightarrow \quad N_1[C_2O_4^{2-}]\times1000 = 5\times10^{-4}\times200$

$\Rightarrow \quad N_1[C_2O_4^{2-}] = 1\times10^{-4}$ N

$\Rightarrow \quad M_1[C_2O_4^{2-}] = 0.5\times10^{-4}$ M

$= [Ca^{2+}]$

$K_{sp} = [Ca^{2+}]\,[C_2O_4^{2-}]$

$= 2.5\times10^{-9}$ M^2

10. (10)

In presence of 1×10^{-3}M $CaCl_2$, solubility is decreased due to common ion.

$\Rightarrow$ Let solubility be y mol L^{-1}

$$CaC_2O_4 \rightleftharpoons \underset{y}{Ca^{2+}} + C_2O_4^{2-}$$

$\Rightarrow \quad CaCl_2 \rightleftharpoons Ca^{2+} + 2Cl^- = 1.0\times10^{-3}$ M

$\therefore \quad [Ca^{2+}] = (1\times10^{-3} + y)$ M

$\approx 1\times10^{-3}$ M, $y << \sqrt{K_{sp}}$

$\Rightarrow \quad [C_2O_4^{2-}] = y$

$\Rightarrow [Ca^{2+}]\,[C_2O_4^{2-}] = 2.5\times10^{-9}$

$\Rightarrow \quad (1\times10^{-3})(y) = 2.5\times10^{-9}$

$\therefore \quad y = 2.5\times10^{-6}$ M

Thus, $\quad \underset{CaC_2O_4}{(2M_1)V_1} = \underset{MnO_4^-}{(5M_2)V_2}$

$\Rightarrow 2\times2.5\times10^{-6}\times1000$

$= 5\times1\times10^{-4}\times V_2$

$\therefore \quad V_2 = 10$ mL

11. (33.18)

I. $\frac{1}{2}N_2(g) + \frac{1}{2}O_2(g) \longrightarrow NO$, $\quad \Delta H = +90.25$ kJ

II. $NO(g) + \frac{1}{2}O_2(g) \longrightarrow NO_2$, $\quad \Delta H = -57.07$ kJ

III. $\frac{1}{2}N_2(g) + O_2(g) \longrightarrow NO_2$, $\quad \Delta H = +33.18$ kJ

$(I + II \equiv III)$

NO_2 is formed in (III) from its elements.

Thus, $\Delta_f H^\circ(NO_2) = +\ 33.18$ kJ mol^{-1}

12. (− 57.07)

NO is oxidised to NO_2 in II.

Thus, $\Delta_c H^\circ(NO) = -57.07$ kJ mol^{-1}

13. (a), (b), (c)

B_2H_6 contains two $3C-2e$ as well as four $2C-2e$ bonds.

$$\Rightarrow \underset{(X)}{3B_2H_6} + 6NH_3 \xrightarrow{450\text{ K}} \underset{\substack{\text{Borazine} \\ \text{(Inorganic benzene)} \\ (Y)}}{2B_3N_3H_6} + 12H_2$$

$$\Rightarrow \underset{(X)}{B_2H_6} + NH_3 \xrightarrow[\text{High temperature}]{\text{Excess of } NH_3} \underset{\substack{\text{(Boron nitride)} \\ (Z)}}{(BN)_x}$$

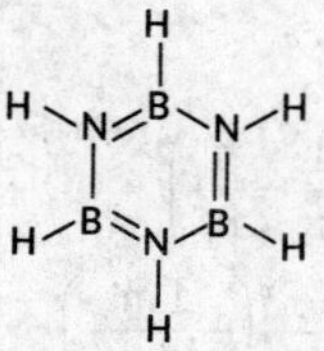

Borazine

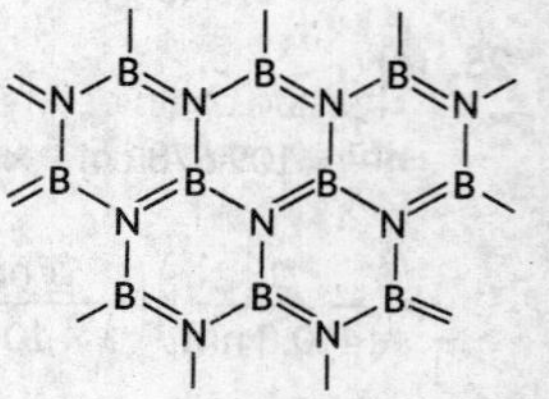

Boron nitride structure

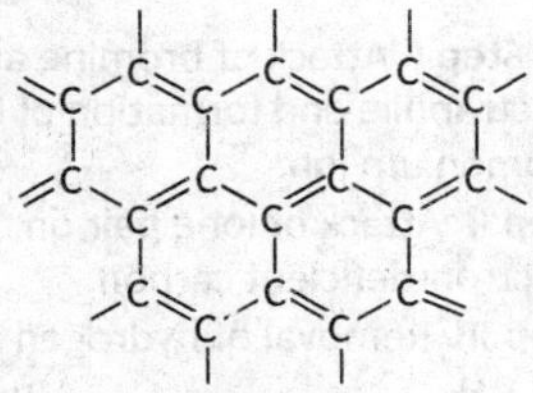

Graphite structure

14. (b), (d) The reactions involved are

$Na_2Z + CaSO_4(\text{or } CaCl_2) \longrightarrow CaZ + Na_2SO_4(\text{or } 2NaCl)$

$Na_2Z + MgCl_2(\text{or } MgSO_4) \longrightarrow MgZ + 2NaCl \text{ (or } Na_2SO_4)$

$Na_2Z + Ca(HCO_3)_2 \text{ (or } Mg(HCO_3)_2) \longrightarrow CaZ(\text{or } MgZ) + 2NaHCO_3$

15. (b), (c), (d)

⇒ In the reduction reaction, $H_2C_2O_4$ and $NaHC_2O_4$ are converted to CO_2, so

$(C^{3+})_2 \longrightarrow 2C^{4+} + 2e^-$

Therefore, equivalent weight = molecular weight/2.

⇒ On titration with 1 M $KMnO_4$:

$Mn^{7+} + 5e^- \longrightarrow Mn^{2+}$

Therefore,

$\Rightarrow \quad M_{equiv} H_2C_2O_4 = M_{equiv} KMnO_4$

$100 \text{ mL} \times 1 \text{ M} \times 2 = V \text{ mL} \times 1 \text{ M} \times 5$

$\Rightarrow \quad M_{equiv} NaHC_2O_4 = M_{equiv} KMnO_4$

$100 \text{ mL} \times 1 \text{ M} \times 2 = V \text{ mL} \times 1 \text{ M} \times 5$

⇒ So, 100 mL of 1 M solution of each is neutralised by equal volumes of 1 M $KMnO_4$.

16. (a), (b), (c), (d)

⇒ In option (a) : Ionisation enthalpy ∝ 1/(shielding effect)

⇒ In option (b) : Be and Mg have valence shell electron completely filled (ns^2). So, more IE is required as compared to B and Al (ns^2np^1).

⇒ In option (c) : Due to lanthanide contraction, the atomic and ionic radii of niobium and tantalum are almost the same.

⇒ In option (d) : The metallic radii of K is higher (10-15%) than the single covalent radii of potassium.

17. (a), (b)

The side chain of any type of benzene ring is oxidised to benzoic acid.

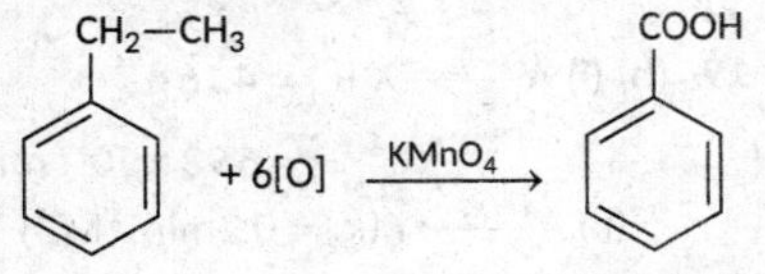

$C_6H_5CH_2-CH_3 + 6[O] \xrightarrow{KMnO_4} C_6H_5COOH + CO_2 + 2H_2O$

$C_6H_5CH_2-OH + 2[O] \xrightarrow{KMnO_4} C_6H_5COOH + 2H_2O$

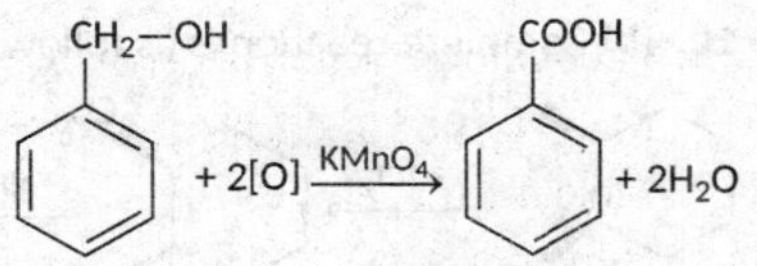

18. (a), (b), (c), (d)

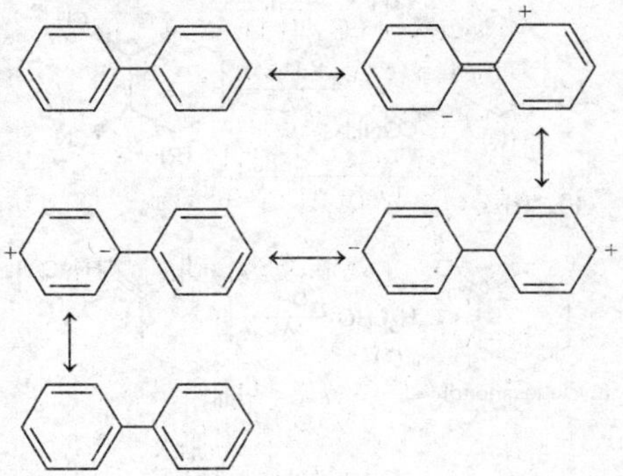

19. (9) $\Rightarrow \left(\dfrac{\partial p}{\partial V_m}\right) = 0$ means the gas is at critical state.

$\Rightarrow \dfrac{p_C V_C}{RT_C} = \dfrac{x}{24}$ but for van der Waals' gas

$\Rightarrow \dfrac{p_C V_C}{RT_C} = \dfrac{3}{8} \Rightarrow x = 9$

20. (46) $\Delta G^\circ = \Delta H^\circ - T\Delta S^\circ$

$= -2.303\, RT \log_{10} K$

$\text{Slope} = -\dfrac{\Delta H^\circ}{2.303\, R} = -\tan 45^\circ = -1$

$\Rightarrow \quad \Delta H^\circ = 2.303 \times 2 = 4.606 \text{ cal/mol}$

$= Q \text{ cal/mol}$

$\Rightarrow \quad 10Q = 10 \times 4.606 = 46$

21. (35) Let amount of Fe_3O_4 and Fe_2O_3 in the sample be x and y moles respectively, then the mixture contains x mole of FeO and $(x + y)$ moles of Fe_2O_3.

$Fe_2O_3 + 2KI + 3H_2SO_4 \longrightarrow 2FeSO_4 + I_2 + K_2SO_4 + 3H_2O$

$I_2 + 2Na_2S_2O_3 \longrightarrow Na_2S_4O_6 + 2NaI$

⇒ m equivalence of $Fe_2O_3 = m$ equivalence of $I_2 = m$ equivalence of $Na_2S_2O_3$

$\Rightarrow (x + y) \times 2 \times 1000 = 5 \times 11 \times 0.5 \quad \text{...(i)}$

⇒ After 1st titration all Fe is in Fe^{2+} state in the acidified solution.

$\underset{x \text{ mol}}{Fe_3O_4} \longrightarrow \underset{x \text{ mol}}{FeO} + \underset{x \text{ mol}}{Fe_2O_3} \xrightarrow{KI} \underset{2x \text{ mol}}{2Fe^{2+}}$

$\underset{y \text{ mol}}{Fe_2O_3} \longrightarrow \underset{2y \text{ mol}}{2\,FeO}$

⇒ From 2nd titration $(3x + 2y) \times 1000$

$= 2 \times 12.8 \times 0.25 \times 5 \quad \text{... (ii)}$

⇒ Solving Eqs. (i) and (ii)

$x = 0.0045 \text{ mol}$

$= 0.0045 \times 232 + 1.044 \text{ g}$

$\Rightarrow \quad \% Fe_3O_4 = \dfrac{1.044 \times 100}{3}$

$= 34.8 = 35$

22. (b) For Q, there is a large gap between IE_1 and IE_2. Hence, element Q is an alkali metal, which can form QX type of compound.

23. (a) For R or S, there is a large gap between IE_2 and IE_3. Hence, both are alkaline earth elements.

Since, IE_1 of $(S) > IE_1$ or (R), $r_{S^{2+}} < r_{R^{2+}}$ and $r_{S^{2+}(aq)} > r_{R^{2+}(aq)}$,

where, r is radius. Hence, ionic mobility order is $R^{2+}_{(aq)} > S^{2+}_{(aq)}$.

24. (a) In general, the ease of reduction decreases in the order mono-substituted > 1,1-disubstituted, 1,2-*cis*-disubstituted, 1, 2-*trans*-disubstituted > trisubstituted > tetra-substituted.

Therefore, II > III > IV > I.

25. (b)

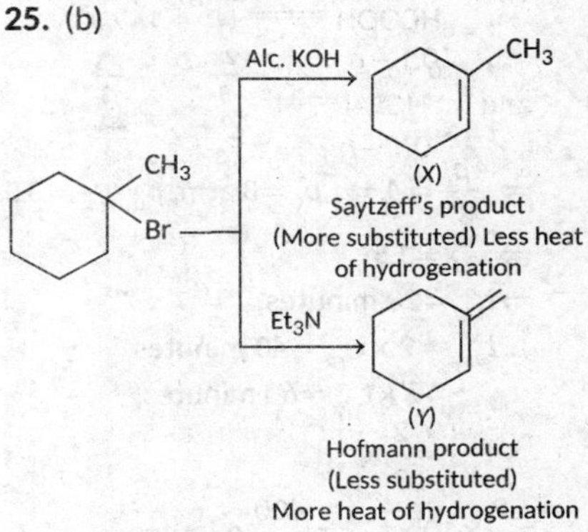

1-bromo-1-methylcyclohexane —Alc. KOH→ (X) Saytzeff's product (More substituted) Less heat of hydrogenation

—Et_3N→ (Y) Hofmann product (Less substituted) More heat of hydrogenation

Part Test 03

1. (c) The correct structure of the intermediate formed when excess of D–C_6H_4–I reacts with Na in liq. NH_3 is given below.

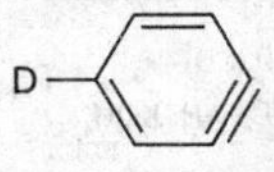

⇒ Hence, *para* and *meta*-isomers are formed, while *ortho* products cannot be a product.

2. (c) In group-II, we get sulphide precipitates of metal ions which are, HgS, PbS, CuS and CdS.

3. (b) $\dfrac{p^\circ - p}{p^\circ} = \dfrac{w_{urea}}{M_{urea}} \times \dfrac{M_{water}}{X}$

$\Rightarrow \dfrac{760 - 759.924}{760} = \dfrac{3}{60} \times \dfrac{18}{X}$

So, $X = 9000$ g

4. (d) **Step 1**

$CH_3CH{=}CHCHO + HCN \longrightarrow H_3CCH(CN)CH{=}CHOH$

Step 2

$H_3CCH(CN)CH{=}CHOH \xrightleftharpoons{\text{Tautomerism}} H_3CCH(CN)CH_2CHO$

Step 3 $H_3CCH(CN)CH_2CHO + HCN \longrightarrow H_3C\overset{*}{C}H(CN)CH_2\overset{*}{C}H(OH)CN$

The final product has two chiral centres.

5. (a) According to the second law of thermodynamics,

$$\frac{d(\Delta G)}{dT} = -\Delta S$$

$$\therefore \quad \frac{d(-nFE_{cell})}{dT} = -\Delta S$$

$$\Rightarrow \quad \frac{dE_{cell}}{dT} = \frac{\Delta S}{nF}$$

6. (c) $3A(g) \longrightarrow 2B(g) + 2C(g)$

	$3A(g)$	$2B(g)$	$2C(g)$
$t = 0$	p_0	0	0
$t = 20$	$p_0 - x$	$\frac{2x}{3}$	$\frac{2x}{3}$
$t = \infty$		$\frac{2p_0}{3}$	$\frac{2p_0}{3}$

$\Rightarrow \dfrac{4p_0}{3} = 4 \Rightarrow p_0 = 3$ atm, $p_0 + \dfrac{x}{3} = 3.5$

$\Rightarrow x = 1.5$

$\Rightarrow t_{1/2} = 20$ minutes,

$t_{75\%} = 2 \times t_{1/2} = 40$ minutes,

$t_{87.5\%} = 3 \times t_{1/2} = 60$ minutes,

$t_{99\%} = \dfrac{2}{3} \times t_{99.9\%}$

$= \dfrac{2}{3} \times 10 \times t_{50\%} = \dfrac{400}{3}$ minutes

7. (a) $Ph{-}N{=}C{=}O \xrightarrow[\text{(ii) } H_2O]{\text{(i) } CH_3MgBr} PhNH{-}\underset{\underset{O}{\|}}{C}{-}CH_3 \xrightarrow[\text{(ii) } H_2O]{\text{(i) } LiAlH_4} Ph{-}NH{-}CH_2{-}CH_3$

(Amide) (P) (2° amine) (Q)

8. (a) Complete reaction is as follows

Ph(CH₃)C(Br)–C(H)(D)Ph $\xrightarrow{\text{Alc. KOH}}$ (Ph)(Me)C=C(Ph)(H) and (Ph)(Me)C=C(D)(Ph)

9. (a) In ZnS (zinc blende), S^{2-} ions form ccp lattice [corners + face centres] and Zn^{2+} ions occupy alternate tetrahedral voids.

10. (b) Complete reaction is as follows

2-methylcyclohexanecarboxylic acid (CO_2H, CH_3) $\xrightarrow{SOCl_2}$ (P) (COCl) $\xrightarrow[\Delta]{NH_3}$ (Q) ($CONH_2$) $\xrightarrow[\Delta]{P_4O_{10}}$ (R) (CN)

11. (d)

(Cyclohexanone) $+ C_6H_5CHO \xrightarrow[\Delta]{OH^-}$ (A) 2-benzylidenecyclohexanone ($=CH{-}C_6H_5$) $\xrightarrow{LiAlH_4}$ 2-benzylidenecyclohexanol (OH, $=CH{-}C_6H_5$) $\xrightarrow[\Delta]{H^+}$ (B) ($=CHC_6H_5$)

12. (c)

Cyclohexanone $=O + H_2N{-}OH \xrightarrow[\text{Nucleophilic addition}]{\Delta}$ (A) oxime ($=N{-}OH$) $\xrightarrow[\text{Beckmann Rearrangement}]{H_2SO_4, \Delta}$ (Caprolactam) (B)

13. (b) The given structure is a tetrapeptide. It contains the following amino acids, alanine, serine, phenylalanine and glutamine.

14. (b) Homopolymers are formed by polymerisation of the same type of monomers. Copolymers are formed when a mixture of more than one monomeric species is allowed to polymerise. e.g. Buna-N is a copolymer of acrylonitrile and 1,3-butadiene. From the given options, (b) represents a copolymer.

15. (b) Amine produced after Hofmann bromamide degradation is one carbon less than the starting compound.

D-substituted benzamide ($C(=O){-}NH_2$) $\xrightarrow{Br_2/KOH}$ D-substituted aniline (NH_2)

D-substituted benzamide ($C(=O){-}^{15}NH_2$) $\xrightarrow{Br_2/KOH}$ aniline ($^{15}NH_2$)

16. (d) **Step I** Attack of bromine atom as electrophile and formation of cyclic bromonium ion.

Step II Attack of lone pair on electron-deficient carbon.

Step III Removal of hydrogen as H^+.

(Reaction scheme: $Br{-}Br$ → cyclic bromonium ion → N^+ bicyclic intermediate; Br^- removes H → bicyclic amine with Br)

17. (a) Complete reaction is as follows

Phenol $+$ tert-butyl chloride (Cl) $\xrightarrow{AlCl_3}$ (*para*-isomer $C_{10}H_{14}O$) $\xrightarrow[\text{(ii) } CH_3CH_2I]{\text{(i) NaOH}}$ 1-*tert*-butyl-4-ethoxybenzene

18. (c) Complex compound with unpaired electron in its *d*-orbital may undergo *d*-*d* transition and absorbs light of visible region.

$\Rightarrow [V(NH_3)_6]^{3+}$

The electronic configuration of

$V = 3d^3 4s^2$

The electronic configuration of

$V^{3+} = 3d^2 4s^0$

$\Rightarrow$ Here, *d*-*d* transition is possible and thus electrons may absorb light of the visible region.

(d^2 splits into t_{2g}^2 and e_g^0, separated by Δ_o)

19. (b) (i) $A \xrightarrow{k_1} X$ ($k_1 = 4.16\,h^{-1}$

$= 6.93 \times 10^{-2}\,min^{-1}$)

(ii) $A \xrightarrow{k_2} Y$ ($k_2 = 0.2\,min^{-1}\,M^{-1}$)

For (i), $t_{1/2}=\frac{0.693}{6.93\times10^{-2}}=10$ min

(for first-order reaction)

It is independent of initial concentration.

⇒ Also, for (ii)

$t_{1/2}=\frac{1}{k_2 a}$ (for a second-order reaction)

or, $a=\frac{1}{(0.2\,\text{min}^{-1}\text{M}^{-1}\times10\,\text{min})}=0.5$ M

20. (c) Complete reaction is as follows

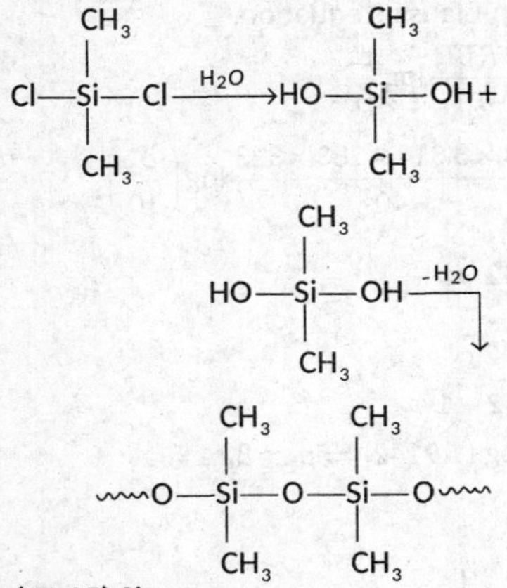

$Cl-Si(CH_3)_2-Cl \xrightarrow{H_2O} HO-Si(CH_3)_2-OH +$

$HO-Si(CH_3)_2-OH \xrightarrow{-H_2O}$

$\sim\sim O-Si(CH_3)_2-O-Si(CH_3)_2-O\sim\sim$

21. (41.25) Slope

$=\frac{(2.9-1.1)}{(1.3-1.5)\times10^{-3}}=-9\times10^3$

$\therefore\quad E_a=-2.303\,R$ (slope)

$\therefore\quad E_a=(-2.303).(1.99).(-9\times10^3)$

$=41.25$ kcal mol^{-1}

22. (5) Molecules that do not possess α-hydrogen atom readily undergoes disproportionation reaction. This reaction is called Cannizzaro reaction.

These molecules are
2, 2, 2-triphenylethanal,
4-nitrobenzaldehyde,
2-hydroxybenzaldehyde,
2,2,4,4-tetramethylpentanal,
2,2,6,6-tetramethylcyclohexanone.

23. (6) The correct statements are

I. It is highly specific.
III. It is irreversible in nature.
IV. It depends on the surface area of the system.
V. It causes a strong chemical interaction between adsorbate and adsorbent.
VIII. High temperature is involved in this process.
X. Decrease of pressure does not cause desorption.

24. (746.24)

$\underset{1-x}{Ca(NO_3)_2} \longrightarrow \underset{x}{Ca^{2+}} + \underset{2x}{2NO_3^-}$

$\therefore\quad i=\frac{1-x+x+2x}{1}=1+2x=2.4$

$\Rightarrow\quad \frac{p_A^\circ-p_S}{p_S}=i\frac{n_B}{n_A}$

$\Rightarrow\quad \frac{760-p_S}{p_S}=2.4\times\frac{\frac{7}{164}}{\frac{100}{18}}$

$\Rightarrow\quad \frac{760-p_S}{p_S}=\frac{2.4\times7\times18}{164\times100}=\frac{378}{20500}$

$\Rightarrow 20878\times p_S=20500\times760$

$\Rightarrow\quad p_S=746.24$ mm

25. (5) For the first solution,

$\kappa=1.4$ S m^{-1}, $R=50\,\Omega$, $M=0.2$ M

$\therefore 1.4=\frac{1}{50}\times\frac{l}{A}$

$\Rightarrow \frac{l}{A}=50\times1.4\,\text{m}^{-1}$

For second solution,

$R=280\,\Omega,\ \frac{l}{A}=50\times1.4\,\text{m}^{-1}$

$\kappa=\frac{1}{280}\times50\times1.4$

Now, molar conductivity

$\Lambda_m=\frac{\kappa}{1000\,M}=\frac{\frac{1}{280}\times1.4\times50}{1000\times0.5}$

$=\frac{1}{4\times500}$

$=5\times10^{-4}$ S m^2 mol^{-1}

$=x\times10^{-4}$ S m^2 mol^{-1}

$\therefore\ x=5$

26. (72)

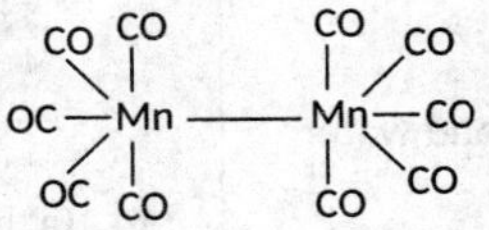

$(OC)_5Mn-Mn(CO)_5$

EAN $=25+10+1=36=x$

$(OC)_4Co-Co(CO)_4$

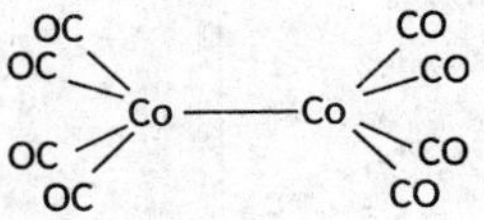

EAN $=27+8+1=36=y$

$\therefore\ x+y=72$

27. (−19.95) Net specific rotation

$=\frac{52.5^\circ-92.4^\circ}{2}=\frac{-39.9^\circ}{2}=-19.95^\circ$

28. (0.30) $0.03=\frac{\text{Mass of haemoglobin}\times10}{100}$

$\therefore$ Mass of haemoglobin $=0.30$ mg

29. (0.45) In the vapour phase,

1 mole of (or 78 g) benzene has volume at 20°C

$=\frac{78\times1}{0.877}\times2750$ mL

1 mole of (or 92 g) benzene has volume at 20°C

$=\frac{92\times1}{0.867}\times7720$ mL

⇒ The vapour pressure of pure benzene and toluene are,

$\frac{p_B^\circ}{760}\times\frac{78\times2750}{0.877\times1000}=1\times0.0821\times293$

$p_B^\circ=74.74$ mm Hg

$\frac{p_T^\circ}{760}\times\frac{92\times7720}{0.877\times1000}=1\times0.0821\times293$

$p_T^\circ=22.32$ mm Hg

⇒ Given that, $p_{mix}=46$ mm Hg

$\Rightarrow\quad p_{mix}=p_B^\circ x_B+p_T^\circ x_T$

$\Rightarrow\quad 46=74.74\,x_B+22.32\,(1-x_B)$

On solving, we get $x_B=0.45$

30. (4) $CH_3CHO+HCHO \xrightarrow[\text{Excess}]{Na_2CO_3}$

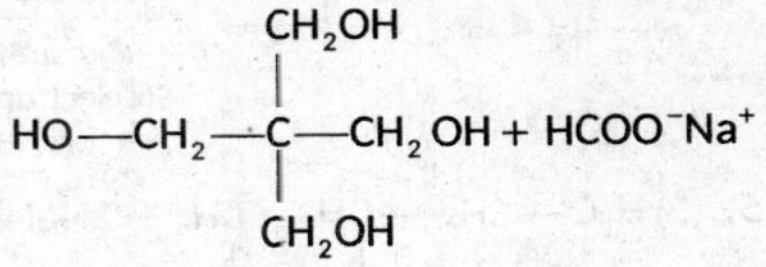

$HO-CH_2-C(CH_2OH)_2-CH_2OH+HCOO^-Na^+$

Part Test 04

1. (a) The correct match is

A → 1, B → 2, C → 3, D → 4

A → 1 to gain aromaticity

B → 2 giving (furan with CH_2X) and (furan with X and CH_2X)

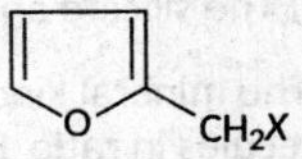

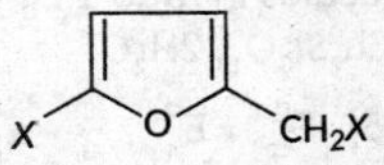

[X is a nucleophile]

C → 3 giving $C_6H_5-\overset{*}{C}H_2-CH_2X$ and $C_6H_5-CH_2-\overset{*}{C}H_2X$ *via* (Phenoium ion)

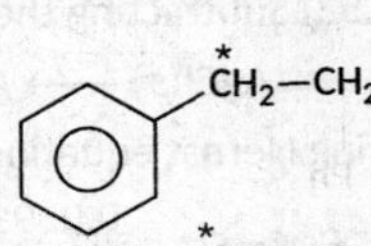

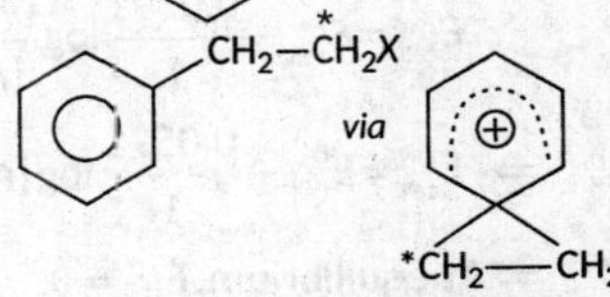

D→4 due to steric crowding at bridge head (neither S_N1 nor S_N2)

2. (a) The correct structure of cellulose triacetate is shown below.

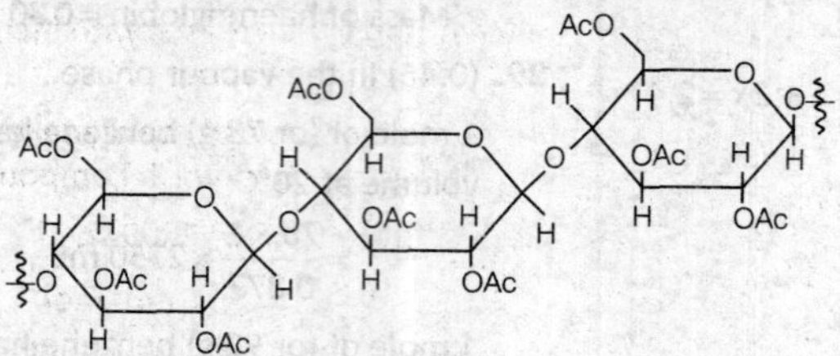

It contains β-1, 4-glycosidic linkage.

3. (a) The fossil has certain activity, say λN. It is the same at the two sites. The concentration at the two sites (which is proportional to the initial activity) differs due to which the age of the fossil calculated at the two locations will vary.

Since, $N = N_0 e^{-\lambda t}$ ⇒ Therefore, we get $t_1 - t_2 = \frac{1}{\lambda} \ln \frac{C_1}{C_2}$

i.e. the age of the fossil will increase where the explosion has taken place.

4. (b) In $[Cr(NH_3)_6]Cl_3$, the electronic configuration of Cr^{3+} is $3d^3$ and the hybridisation is d^2sp^3, thus forming an inner orbital octahedral complex. The compound is paramagnetic as there are three unpaired electrons. This compound gives white precipitate on reaction with $AgNO_3$ due to the reaction with Cl^- ions.

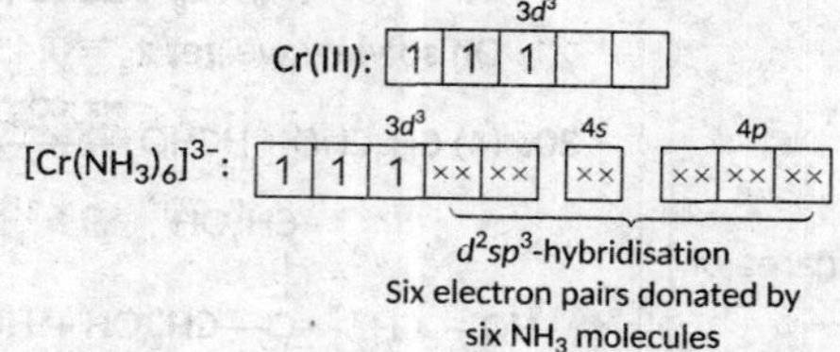

5. (3) $H_3C—CH_2—\underset{Br}{CH}—\underset{Br}{CH_2} + 2NaNH_2 \longrightarrow \underset{(A)}{CH_3—CH_2—C \equiv CH}$

$\xrightarrow{NaNH_2} \underset{(B)}{CH_3—CH_2—C \equiv C^-Na^+} + \underset{(X)}{NH_3}$

6. (2) Cyclopropene

Degree of unsaturation = One ring + One π-bond = 2

7. (−4) The silicate anions are SiO_3^{2-} and $Si_3O_7^{2-}$.

8. (3) The mineral kinoite contains Ca^{2+} ions, Cu^{2+} ions and water molecules in ratio 1 : 1 : 1 and the compound is $Ca_2Cu_2Si_3O_{10}.2H_2O$.

9. (1.75) $E^\circ_{cell} = E^\circ_{Au^{3+}/Au} - E^\circ_{Ni^{2+}/Ni} = 1.50 - (-0.25) = 1.75\ V$

10. (1.53) Subtracting the given equations

$AgCl(s) \longrightarrow Ag^+(aq) + Cl^-(aq)\ ; E^\circ = -0.58\ V$

Using Nernst equation, we get

$$E_{cell} = E^\circ_{cell} - \frac{0.0591}{1} \log \frac{[Ag^+][Cl^-]}{[AgCl(s)]}$$

$$\Rightarrow E_{cell} = E^\circ_{cell} - \frac{0.0591}{1} \log [Ag^+][Cl^-] \qquad [\text{as } [AgCl(s)] = 1]$$

⇒ At equilibrium, $E_{cell} = 0$.

Also, $K_{sp} = [Ag^+][Cl^-]$

So, $E^\circ_{cell} = -0.0591 \times \log K_{sp}$

$\Rightarrow -0.58 = 0.0591 \times \log K_{sp}$

$\Rightarrow \quad K_{sp} = \text{antilog}(-0.58/0.0591) = 1.53 \times 10^{-10}\ M^2$

11. (−40)

⇒ Heat absorbed in desorption = 80 J

For 2 millimoles of adsorbate

Thus, heat evolved in adsorption

$= -80\ J/2\ \text{millimol} = -40\ J/\text{millimol}$

$= -40 \times 1000\ J/mol = -40\ kJ\ mol^{-1}$

12. (82.10) By Clapeyron-Clausius equation,

$$\Delta H = \frac{2.303\, RT_1T_2}{(T_1 - T_2)} \log \frac{p_2}{p_1},$$

$$\Rightarrow -40 \times 10^3 = \frac{2.303 \times 8.314 \times 283 \times 323}{-40} \log\left(\frac{p_2}{10}\right)$$

$$\Rightarrow \quad \log\left(\frac{p_2}{10}\right) = 0.9142$$

$\log p_2 - \log 10 = 0.9142$

$\log p_2 = 0.9142 + 1$

$p_2 = \text{Antilog}\ (1.9142) \Rightarrow p_2 = 82.1\ kPa$

13. (a,b,c)

Cl, H, $\xrightarrow{OH^\ominus}$ Benzyne(aromatic)

(Mechanism: benzyne + phenoxide ⟷ resonance structures → biphenyl-O⁻ → biphenyl–OH)

14. (a, b)

(a) $\underset{(X)}{CH_3—CH_2—Br} + Mg \xrightarrow{\text{Dry ether}} CH_3—CH_2MgBr \xrightarrow[\text{(ii) } H_3O^+]{\text{(i) HCHO}} CH_3—CH_2—CH_2—OH$

(b) $\underset{(X)}{CH_3Br} + Mg \xrightarrow{\text{Dry ether}} CH_3MgBr \xrightarrow[H_3O^+]{CH_2—CH_2 \text{ (epoxide, O)}} CH_3CH_2CH_2OH$

15. (a,b,c)

(a) $E^\circ_{cell} = 0.80 - 0.34 = 0.46$

$2Ag^+ + Cu \rightleftharpoons Cu^{2+} + 2Ag$

$$\Rightarrow E = 0.46 - \frac{0.0591}{2}\log\frac{[Cu^{2+}]}{[Ag^+]^2}$$
$$= 0.46 - \frac{0.0591}{2}\log\frac{0.1}{0.25}$$
$$0.46 - \frac{0.0591}{2}\times(-0.397)$$
$$= 0.46 + 0.0117$$
$$= 0.47\ V$$

(b) When the Q is less than unity, increasing temperature will make ΔG more negative and will make ther eaction more spontaneous by increasing cell voltage, $Q = 0.2421$.

(c) At equilibrium,
$$\log K = \frac{nE^\circ}{0.0591}$$
$$= \frac{2\times 0.46}{0.0591} = 15.56 \simeq 15.6$$
$$K = 4\times 10^{15}$$
i.e. essentially no Ag^+ will remain.

$\Rightarrow$ Initial millimole of $Ag^+ = 100\times 0.5 = 50$

We must take 25 m moles of Cu^{2+} ion stoichiometrically.

Mass of Cu(s) $= 0.025\times 63.5 = 1.5$ g

16. (a, d) After a long time $[C_A] \approx 0$,
$$[C_B] = \frac{1}{3}\times 2 = \frac{2}{3}\ M$$
$$\Rightarrow \quad [C_C] = \frac{2}{3}\times 2 = \frac{4}{3}\ M,$$

Rotation of final solution
$$= 60\times 0 + (-72)\times\frac{2}{3} + 42\times\frac{4}{3} = +8^\circ$$
[so dextrorotatory]

$\Rightarrow$ Options (b) and (c) are incorrect as overall.
$$K = K_1 + K_2 = (6.93 + 13.86)\times 10^{-2}$$
$$= 20.79\times 10^{-2}\ min^{-1}$$
$$\text{Overall } t_{\frac{1}{2}} = \frac{0.693}{20.79\times 10^{-2}}\ min$$
$$= \frac{10}{3}\ min$$

Options (a) and (d) are correct as after 75% completion $[C_A] = 0.5$ M, $[C_B] = 0.5$ M, $[C_C] = 1$ M

Final rotation of the mixture
$$= 60\times\frac{1}{2} + (-72)\times\frac{1}{2} + 42\times 1 = +36^\circ$$

17. (b, c, d) $\Rightarrow \dfrac{(t_{1/2})_1}{(t_{1/2})_2} = \left\{\dfrac{[A_2]}{[A_1]}\right\}^{n-1}$
$$\Rightarrow \frac{100}{50} = \left(\frac{0.025}{0.1}\right)^{n-1} = \left(\frac{1}{4}\right)^{n-1}$$
$\Rightarrow 2 = 2^{2-2n}$ and on solving $n = \dfrac{1}{2}$

i.e. order of the reaction is $\dfrac{1}{2}$.
$$\Rightarrow \text{For option (c)}: \frac{100}{t_{\frac{1}{2}}} = \left(\frac{1}{0.1}\right)^{\frac{1}{2}} = \frac{1}{\sqrt{10}}$$
$$\Rightarrow t_{\frac{1}{2}} = 100\sqrt{10}$$
$$\Rightarrow \text{For option (d)}: \frac{100}{t_{\frac{1}{2}}} = \left(\frac{0.2}{0.1}\right)^{-\frac{1}{2}} = \frac{1}{\sqrt{2}}$$

18. (b, c, d)

Vapour pressure of a pure solvent does not depend on its surface area.

Also, $p = p_o x_1$
$$\Rightarrow 6 = 9x \text{ and } x_1 = \frac{2}{3}, x_2 = \frac{1}{3}$$
$$\Rightarrow \text{Also, } \frac{n_2}{n_1} = \frac{x_2}{x_1} = \frac{1}{2}$$
$$\text{Molality } \frac{n_2}{n_1}\times\frac{1000}{18} = \frac{1000}{36}$$
$$\Rightarrow \Delta T_b = \frac{0.52\times 1000}{36} = 14.44$$

Also, increasing cross-sectional area of liquid increases the number of molecules in vapour phase in same proportion.

19. (3) $\Rightarrow$ Volume of unit cell $= a\times b\times c$
$$= 5\times 10^{-8}\times 8\times 10^{-8}\times 4\times 10^{-8}$$
$$= 1.6\times 10^{-22}\ cm^3$$
$\Rightarrow$ Mass of unit cell
$$= 1.6\times 10^{-22}\times 5.2 = 8.32\times 10^{-22}\ g$$
$\Rightarrow$ Number of molecules in one unit cell
$$= \frac{8.32\times 10^{-22}\times 6\times 10^{23}}{166.4} = 3.01 \approx 3$$

20. (8) $E = 0.3175 = 0.76 - \dfrac{0.06}{2}\log\dfrac{[Zn^{2+}]}{[H^+]^2}$
$$\Rightarrow \log\frac{(0.1)}{[H^+]^2} = \frac{0.76 - 0.3175}{0.03} = 14.75$$
$$\Rightarrow \log(0.1) + 2\log\frac{1}{[H^+]} = 14.75$$
$$\Rightarrow \quad pH = \frac{14.75 + 1}{2} = 7.88 \approx 8$$

21. (3) In (b), (c) and (f) first ether more rapidly cleaved than second one. In ethers.

- order of bond breaking is $1^\circ > 2^\circ > 3^\circ$.
- stability increases with increase in number of rings.
- bond cleavage rapidly takes place in simple ether w.r.t. compound ether.

22. (c) Given that $R = 1000\ \Omega$,
$$\Lambda^\circ_{m(Cl^-)} = 80\ S\ cm^2\ mol^{-1}$$
$$\text{and } \Lambda^\circ_{m(SO_4^{2-})} = 160\ S\ cm^2\ mol^{-1}$$
$\Rightarrow$ Now applying equations,
$$\Lambda^\circ_{m(NaCl)} = 107 + b\sqrt{c} \quad \text{... (i)}$$
$$\Lambda^\circ_{m(NaCl)} = 97 + b\sqrt{c} \quad \text{... (ii)}$$
$\Rightarrow$ Subtracting Eq. (ii) from Eq. (i), we get
$$0 = 10 + b(2\times 10^{-2}) - b(3\times 10^{-2})$$
$$10 = b(3\times 10^{-2} - 2\times 10^{-2})$$
$$10 = 10^{-2}b \text{ or } b = 10^3$$
Therefore,
$$\Lambda^\circ_{m(NaCl)} = \Lambda_{NaCl} + b\sqrt{c}$$
$$= 107 + 10^3\sqrt{4\times 10^{-4}}$$
$$= 107 + 10^3(2\times 10^{-2})$$
$$= 107 + 20 = 127\ S\ cm^2\ mol^{-1}$$

23. (d) $\Lambda^\circ_m = \Lambda_m - b\sqrt{C}$
$$= 127 - 10^3\sqrt{25\times 10^{-4}}$$
$$= 127 - 10^3\times 5\times 10^{-2} = 77$$
$$\Rightarrow \quad \Lambda^\circ_m = \kappa\times C$$
$$\Rightarrow \quad 77 = \kappa\times\frac{1000}{25\times 10^{-4}}$$
Hence, $\kappa = 77\times 25\times 10^{-7} = 1925\times 10^{-7}$
$$\Rightarrow \text{Now, } \kappa = \frac{1}{R}\times\frac{l}{A}$$
$$\Rightarrow \quad \frac{l}{A} = 1925\times 10^{-7}\times 1000$$
$$= 0.1925\ cm^{-1}$$

24. (c) Greater the $-I$ effect, greater will be its acidic strength.
$$CH_3CH_2CCl_2COOH + H_2O \rightleftharpoons CH_3CH_2CCl_2COO^- + H_3O^+$$

25. (d) The reaction is

Unionised form $\xleftarrow[\text{Stomach}]{H^+}$ (benzene ring with $COCH_3$ and $COOH$)

$\xrightarrow[\text{Intestine}]{H^+}$ (benzene ring with $COCH_3$ and COO^-) Ionised form

THE KNOCKOUTS

Knockout 01

1. (b) It is an example of pericyclic reaction [$(4n+2)$ cyclo addition], i.e. Diels - Alder reaction.
In this reaction, a conjugated diene (buta-1, 3-diene) undergoes 1, 4-addition with (dienophile) maleic anhydride.

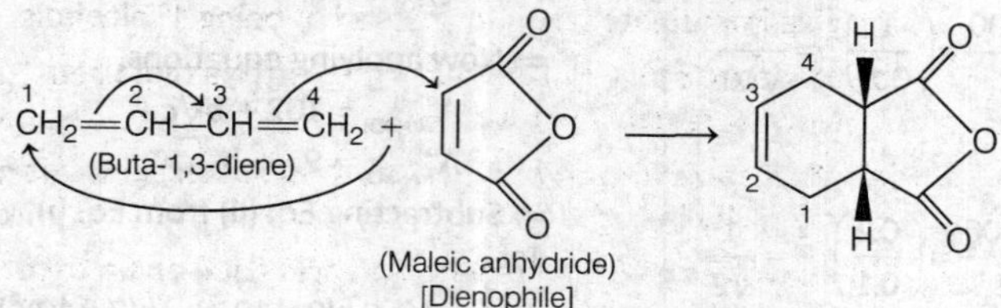

2. (d) Rate $(r)=k[A]^n[B]^m \Rightarrow$ Initial rate, $r_1=k[A]^n[B]^m$

Final rate, $r_2=k[2A]^n\left[\frac{B}{2}\right]^m=2^{n-m}k[A]^n[B]^m$

$\Rightarrow \frac{r_2}{r_1}=\frac{2^{n-m}\times k[A]^n[B]^m}{k[A]^n[B]^m}=2^{n-m}$

3. (c) ΔH_1, ΔH_2 and ΔH_3 indicate ΔIE_1, ΔIE_2 and ΔIE_3 of X. So, $IE_1 < IE_2 < IE_3$ is $\Delta H_1 < \Delta H_2 < \Delta H_3$.
Here, ΔH_4 is the EA of X and ΔH_5 is the IE of X^-. Whereas, ΔH_1 is the IE_1 of X and ΔH_6 is the EA_1 of X^+.
$\Rightarrow$ When a reaction is reversed, magnitude of enthalpy change remains same.

4. (b) Because of larger size of Cl-atoms, $\angle ClOCl$ in Cl_2O is greater than $\angle HOH$ in H_2O. Whereas, because of higher electron density of F-atoms, it has strong electrostatic repulsion between F and O atoms in F_2O. The order of their bond angles is $Cl_2O > H_2O > F_2O$

$\Rightarrow$ Cl 110° Cl H 108° H F 103° F

5. (b) General formula of cyclic silicates is $[(SiO_3)n]^{2n-}$, where three or more tetrahedral SiO_4^{4-} units are linked cyclically.
$[Si_6O_{18}]^{n-}$ can be written as $[(SiO_3)_6]^{n-}$ or $[(SiO_3)_6]^{12-}$, where $n=12$

6. (d) $2Cu^{2+}(aq)+[Fe(CN)_6]^{4-}(aq) \longrightarrow Cu_2[Fe(CN)_6]\downarrow(s)$
[Blue] [Ferrocyanide] (Chocolate brown ppt.)

7. (b)

(2, 3-dimethylbutane) $\xrightarrow[-HCl]{Cl_2/h\nu \text{ Monochlorination}}$ (P) 1-chloro-2,3-dimethyl butane + (Q) 2-chloro-2,3-dimethyl butane

Total products = 3

i.e. (P) Two stereoisomers (R) and (S) or (±) + (Q) Only one product

8. (a) In the manufacturing of H_2O_2, 50% H_2SO_4 is electrolysed by Pt-electrodes to produce peroxodisulphuric acid or Marshall's acid ($H_2S_2O_8$) at the anode. $H_2S_2O_8$ gets hydrolysed to give H_2O_2 and H_2SO_4 (raw material). $H_2S_2O_8$ has S—O—O—S linkage as

$H_2S_2O_8 \xrightarrow{2H_2O} H_2O_2 + 2H_2SO_4$

9. (a) Epoxide undergoes ring opening with bases. Greater the ring strain, greater is the reactivity towards base. Angle strain is maximum in (I) and it is minimum in (III).

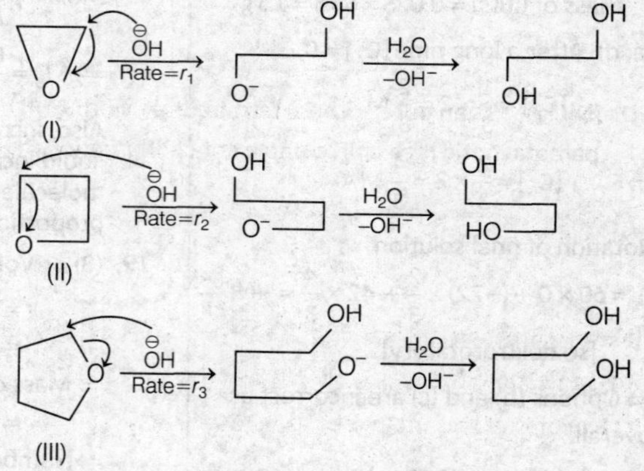

$\Rightarrow$ Rate of reaction is : $r_1 > r_2 > r_3$ or I > II > III

10. (a) Cationic addition polymerisation occurs as,

$H_2C=C(CH_3)_2 \xrightarrow{H^+} (CH_3)_3C^{\oplus}$, which adds to $H_2C=C(CH_3)_2$ to give $H_3C—C(CH_3)_2—CH_2—C^{\oplus}(CH_3)_2 \longrightarrow$ and so on

11. (c)

A. $[\overset{III}{Cr}(NH_3)_6]^{3+}$ is an octahedral complex of $Cr^{3+}(3d^3)$ with NH_3 molecules (ligands). It is an inner-orbital complex $[Cr(III): d^2sp^3]$ paramagnetic, high-spin complex of configuration, $t_{2g}^3 e_g^0$.

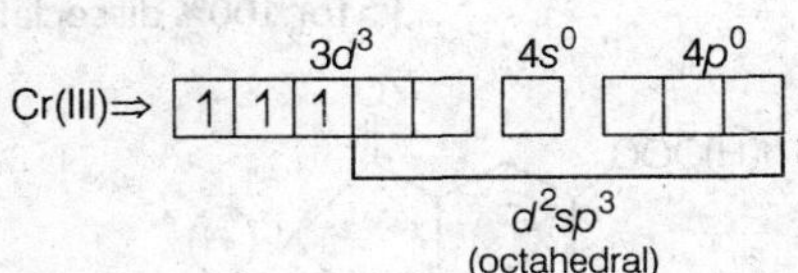

Number of unpaired electron(s) = 3 and $\mu \neq 0$

B. $[\overset{III}{Co}(CN)_6]^{3-}$ is an inner-orbital octahedral complex $[Co(III): d^2sp^3]$ diamagnetic, low-spin complex of configuration, $t_{2g}^6 e_g^0$.

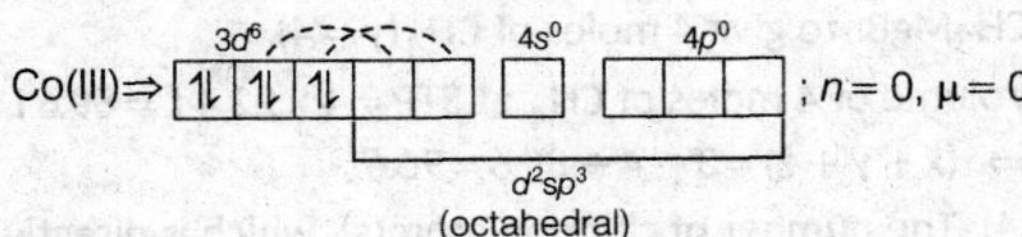

C. $[\overset{II}{Co}(CN)_4]^{2-}$ is an inner-orbital complex $[Co(II): dsp^2]$ dimagnetic, low-spin complex of configuration, $t_{2g}^6 e_g^1$.

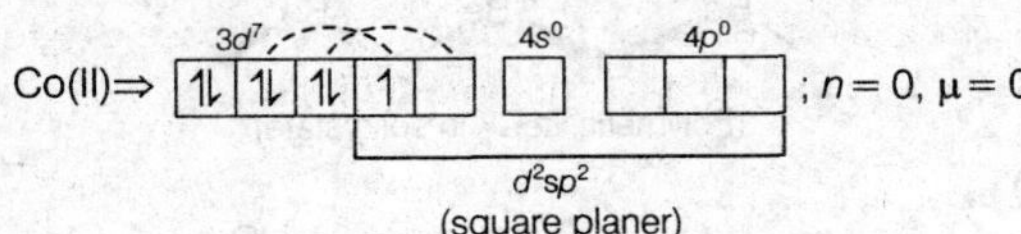

D. $[\overset{II}{Ni}Cl_4]^{2-}$ is an outer-orbital tetrahedral $[Ni(II): sp^3]$ paramagnetic high-spin complex of configuration $t_{2g}^6 e_g^2$.

3d⁸ 4s⁰ 4p⁰

Ni(II)⇒ [1L 1L 1L 1 1] [ ] [ ] ; n=2, μ≠0

sp^3

[**Note** (i) Strength of ligands : $CN^- > NH_3 > Cl^-$; (ii) Spin only magnetic moment, $\mu = \sqrt{n(n+2)}$ BM]

12. (c) No. of H-atoms in 0.9 g of galactose, $C_6H_{12}O_6$

$(M = 180\ g/mol) = \frac{0.9}{180} \times 12 \times N_A = 0.06\ N_A$

($\because N_A$ = Avogadro number)

$\Rightarrow$ No. of H-atoms in 0.048 g of hydrazine, N_2H_4 ($M = 32$ g/mol)

$= \frac{0.048}{32} \times 4 \times N_A = 0.006\ N_A$

$\Rightarrow$ No. of H-atoms in 0.17 g ammonia, NH_3 ($M = 17$ g/mol)

$= \frac{0.17}{17} \times 3 \times N_A = 0.03\ N_A$

$\Rightarrow$ No. of H-atoms in 0.30 g ethane, C_2H_6 ($M = 30$ g/mol)

$= \frac{0.30}{30} \times 6 \times N_A = 0.06\ N_A$

$\Rightarrow$ No. of H-atoms in 0.03 g hydrogen, H_2 ($M = 2$ g/mol)

$= \frac{0.03}{2} \times 2 \times N_A = 0.03\ N_A$

Thus, the number of hydrogen atoms in 0.9 g of galactose is same as 0.30 g of ethane.

13. (b) Statement (b) is incorrect, whereas all other statements are correct.

(a) $CH_2{=}CH{-}\overset{+}{C}H_2$ of allyl alcohol ($CH_2{=}CH{-}CH_2OH$) and $C_6H_5{-}\overset{+}{C}H_2$ of benzyl alcohol ($Ph{-}CH_2OH$) are resonance stabilised carbocations, so these alcohols will give immediate turbidity instead of being 1° alcohols.

(b) 1° alcohols give fastest reactivity with Na metal, but slowest reactivity in Lucas test.

(c) 1° alcohols (red colour in Victor-Meyer test) gives slowest reactivity in Lucas test.

(d) It involves reaction between an acid (HCl) and a base ($R{-}OH$).

14. (d) Statement (d) is incorrect, whereas all other statements are correct.

The corrected form is the electric arc is struck between the electrodes of metals immersed in the dispersion medium (concentrated alkali).

15. (b) Ofloxacin have bactericidal or killing effect, whereas the other three are bacterostatic (inhibitory) in nature.

16. (b) For bcc, $r = \frac{\sqrt{3}}{4}a$ where, r = radius of sphere (atom); a = edge length of unit cell

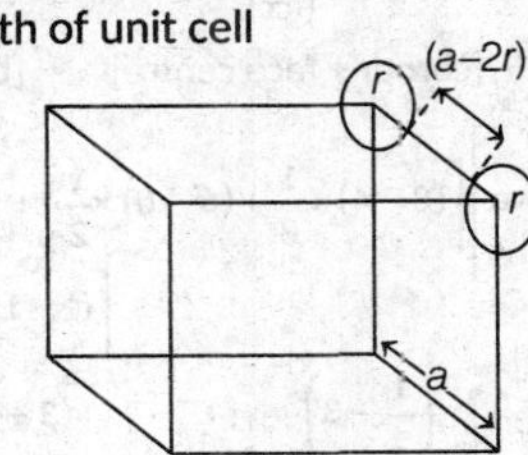

Edge length not covered by atom $= a - 2r$

$$a - 2\left(\frac{\sqrt{3}}{4}\right)a = a\left(\frac{2-\sqrt{3}}{2}\right)$$

$\Rightarrow$ % of edge length not covered

$$= \frac{a\left(\frac{2-\sqrt{3}}{2}\right)}{a} \times 100 = 0.134 \times 100 = 13.4\%$$

17. (c) $Zn + Cu^{2+} \longrightarrow Zn^{2+} + Cu$, $Q = \frac{[Zn^{2+}]}{[Cu^{2+}]}$

$\Rightarrow \quad E = E° - \frac{0.0591}{2}\log Q \quad [\because n = 2]$

For complete discharge, $E = 0$

$\Rightarrow \quad E° = \frac{0.0591}{2}\log Q$

$\Rightarrow \quad Q = 10^{2\times E°/0.0591} = 10^{2\times 1.10/0.0591}$

$= 10^{37.2} = \frac{[Zn^{2+}]}{[Cu^{2+}]}$

18. (c) Acids which are stronger than carbonic acid (H_2CO_3) give effervescence of CO_2 gas from aqueous $NaHCO_3$ or Na_2CO_3.

$$\underset{\text{[Stronger than } H_2CO_3]}{H^{\oplus}} + HCO_3^- \longrightarrow H_2O + CO_2$$

⇒ Here, $PhSO_3H$ (benzene sulphonic acid), 2, 4-dinitrophenol and PhCOOH (benzoic acid) are stronger than H_2CO_3.

⇒ So, CO_2 is evolved in all the cases, as it comes from $NaHCO_3$.

19. (a) Both Assertion and Reason are true and Reason is the correct explanation of Assertion. Excessive cracking of rubber indicates the presence of atmospheric photochemical oxidants of photochemical smog are ozone, nitric oxide, acrolein, formaldehyde and PAN.

20. (b)

$$\text{PhCH(OH)CONH}_2 \xrightarrow[\text{(Hofmann degradation)} \; -K_2CO_3]{Br_2/KOH,\ \Delta} \text{PhCH(OH)NH}_2$$

$$\text{PhCH(OH)NH}_2 \xrightarrow[-NH_3,\ -H_2O]{\overset{\ominus}{O}H} \underset{\text{(X) (Benzaldehyde)}}{\text{PhCH=O}}$$

21. (3.25) Let us find the empirical/molecular formula of the crystal as,

	W	:	X	:	Y
	(fcc) [corner + face centre]		(OV) [bc + ec]		[TV] [alternate]
[After removal of all atoms from two body diagonals]	$\left[(8-4)\times\frac{1}{8}+(6-0)\times\frac{1}{2}\right]$	:	$\left[(1-1)+(12-0)\times\frac{1}{4}\right]$	:	[4–2]
⇒	$\left(\frac{1}{2}+3\right)$	:	(3 + 0)	:	2
⇒	7	:	6	:	4

∴ The formula becomes, $W_7X_6Y_4 \equiv W_aX_bY_c$

⇒ $a=7, b=6, c=4$

⇒ $\frac{a+b}{c}=\frac{7+6}{4}=3.25$

22. (4) As zinc blende (ZnS) is a sulphide ore, extraction of Zn will follow the following sequence of metallurgical steps.

(II) → (I) → (III) → (IV)

23. (2.50) In the brown ring complex, iron is present in + 1 oxidation state [Fe(I) : $3d^6 4s^1$] and it forms an outer orbital complex, octahedral [Fe(I) : sp^3d^2], high-spin paramagnetic complex of configuration ($t_{2g}^5 e_g^2$).

$Fe^+ \Rightarrow 3d^6 4s^1 \Rightarrow$ [⥮ | 1 | 1 | 1 | 1] $3d^6$ [1] $4s^1$ [| |] $4p^0$ [| | | |] $4d^0$ (sp^3d^2)

$Fe(3d^7)$ in $[Fe(H_2O)_5NO]^{2+}$

e_g: [1 | 1] ($d_{x^2-y^2}$, d_{z^2})

Δ_0

t_{2g}: [⥮ | ⥮ | 1] (d_{xy}, d_{yz}, d_{zx})

⇒ $x=5, y=2$

∴ $\frac{x}{y}=\frac{5}{2}=2.50$

24. (1) Only one primary pentapeptide is possible of structure G-A-L-V-G.

25. (3) $\underset{2\text{ mmol}}{2KI} + \underset{1\text{ mmol}}{HgI_2} \rightarrow K_2[HgI_4] \rightleftharpoons 2K^{\oplus} + [HgI_4]^{2-}$

[No. of ions formed, $n=3$]

⇒ van't Hoff factor, $i=1+\alpha(n-1)=1+1\times(3-1)=3$

[∵ for 100% dissociation, $\alpha=1$]

26. (96.6)

(Structure: benzene ring fused to a five-membered imide ring (C=O, N–H⁴, C=O), bearing a ^{1}(H)OOC– group, a ^{2}(H)C≡C– group and an –O(H)$_3$ group.)

⇒ Three acidic H-atoms (1, 3 and 4) will react with 3 moles of NaOH ($x=3$).

⇒ Four acidic H-atoms (1, 2, 3 and 4) will react with 4 moles of CH_3MgBr to give 4 moles of CH_4 ($y=4$).

Volume of 4 moles of CH_4 at STP $=4\times22.4$ L $=89.6$ L $=z$L

⇒ $(x+y+z)=3+4+89.6=96.6$

27. (4) The number of chlorine atom(s), which is directly bonded to each beryllium in solid beryllium chloride is 4.

(Polymeric $BeCl_2$ in solid state)

28. (5)

(Reaction scheme: 2-(3-oxobutyl)cyclohexane-1,3-dione $\xrightarrow{\overset{\ominus}{O}H,\ -H_2O}$ enolate ($\ddot{C}H_2$) → intramolecular addition giving bicyclic alkoxide (O^-) $\xrightarrow{-OH^-,\ H_2O}$ bicyclic hydroxy diketone $\xrightarrow[-H_2O]{\Delta}$ (X), bicyclic enone diketone)

In (X), degree of unsaturation = (No. of π-bonds + No. of rings)
$=3+2=5$

29. (5) KNO_3 does not affect the solubility of AgCl as (K^+, NO_3^-) are not common ion to (Ag^+, Cl^-).

⇒ $AgCl \rightleftharpoons \underset{S}{Ag^+} + \underset{S}{Cl^-}$

⇒ $K_{sp}=S^2$

and $S=\sqrt{10^{-10}}=10^{-5}$ mol/L

⇒ $-\log S=5$

30. (3.50)

$x = 3 \times 2 = 6$ $y = 2 \times 4 = 8$

$\therefore \frac{x+y}{4} = \frac{8+6}{4} = 3.50$

Knockout 02

1. (b) Considering ionisation of M ($Z = 26$) as,

$M [3d^6 4s^2] \xrightarrow{-e^-} M^+ [3d^6 4s^1], n=5, \mu = 5.916$ BM $\xrightarrow{-2e^-} M^{3+} [3d^5], n=5, \mu = 5.916$ BM

[$\because$ Spin only magnetic moment, $\mu = \sqrt{n(n+2)}$ BM, n = no. of unpaired electrons]

So, $x = 3, y = 1$ and because of half-filled $3d^5$ configuration, M^{3+} is more stable than M^+.

2. (c) In I, III and IV hybridisation of underlined element is changing.

I. Formation of $Na[Al(OH)_4]$,

$\underline{Al}(OH)_3 + NaOH \longrightarrow Na[\underline{Al}(OH)_4]$

$\Rightarrow [Al: sp^2 \longrightarrow sp^3]$

II. $\underline{B}_2H_6 +$ O(THF) $\rightarrow$ [$H_3\underline{B} \leftarrow$ O(THF)]

$\Rightarrow [B: sp^3 \longrightarrow sp^3$, no change]

III. $[\underline{Si}F_4 + HF \longrightarrow H_2\underline{Si}F_6 \Rightarrow [Si: sp^3 \longrightarrow sp^3d^2]$ (sp^3d^2)

IV. $\underline{P}Cl_5 \longrightarrow [\underline{P}Cl_4]^+[\underline{P}Cl_6]^- \Rightarrow [P: sp^3d \rightarrow sp^3$ and $sp^3d^2]$

So, in I, III and IV change in hybridisation state of the central underlined atoms take place.

3. (d) Let us study the mechanism of the reaction in which the steps involved are

(i) abstraction of acidic benzylic H-atom

(ii) S_N2 reaction and

(iii) elimination

EWG (O_2N) (A) (*p*-nitrobenzyl chloride) $\xrightarrow[(i)]{\overset{\ominus}{OH}, -H_2O}$ (Intermediate carbanion) $\xrightarrow[(ii)]{S_N2, -Cl^-}$ ... $\xrightarrow[(iii)]{\overset{\ominus}{OH}/\Delta \text{ (Elimination)}, -HCl}$ O_2N–C₆H₄–CH=CH–C₆H₄–NO_2

(4,4′-dinitro-stilbene) (*P*)

4. (b)

$\Rightarrow$ Heat capacity, $C_V = 18.94 \times 0.998 \times 10^3$

$= 18.902 \times 10^3$ cal/deg

Moles of benzoic acid $= \frac{1.89}{122}$

$\Rightarrow C_p = C_V + R = 18.902 \times 10^3 + 2$

$= 18.904 \times 10^3$ cal/deg

Heat of combustion $= \frac{C_p \times \Delta t}{\text{Moles}} = \frac{18.904 \times 10^3 \times 0.632 \times 122}{1.89}$

$= 771.2 \times 10^3$ cal $= 771.2$ kcal

5. (a) Statement (a) is correct, whereas all other statements are incorrect.

Specific conductivity of solution decreases with dilution due to decrease in concentration of electrolyte present in unit volume of the solution enclosed by two electrodes in the conductivity cell.

Molar conductance increases due to increase in degree of dissociation of the electrolyte.

6. (b) Total vapour pressure of the solution, $p = 150x_A + 50$

(i) For pure liquid, $A \Rightarrow x_A = 1$

$p_A^\circ = 150 \times 1 + 50 = 200$ unit

(ii) For pure liquid, $B \Rightarrow x_A = 0$

$p_B^\circ = 150 \times 0 + 50 = 50$ unit

$\therefore \frac{p_A^\circ}{p_B^\circ} = 200:50 = 4:1$

7. (a) $E = E_1^\circ - \frac{0.0591}{5}\log\frac{[Fe^{2+}]}{[Fe^{3+}]}$

$E_2 = E_2^\circ - \frac{0.0591}{5}\log\frac{[Mn^{2+}]}{[MnO_4^-][H^+]^8}$

$\Rightarrow E_1 = E_2 = E_{equiv}$ at equivalence point

$\Rightarrow 6E_{equiv} = (E_1^\circ + 5E_2^\circ) - 0.0591\log\frac{[Fe^{2+}][Mn^{2+}]}{[MnO_4^-][Fe^{3+}][H^+]^8}$

Since, $\frac{[Fe^{2+}][Mn^{2+}]}{[MnO_4^-][Fe^{3+}]} = 1$ at equivalence point

$\therefore E_{equiv} = \left(\frac{E_1^\circ + 5E_2^\circ}{6}\right) - 0.08$ pH

8. (c) $SnO_2 + NaOH \longrightarrow Na_2SnO_3$
$[SnO_2]SnO_3^{2-}$; $2Na^+$, it is a negatively charged colloidal sol.

9. (b) In both (*A*) and (*B*), lone pair of N undergo resonance (+*R*) with the benzene ring, but in (*A*) lone pair of N is also delocalised with $\rangle$=O group (–*R*) which decreases the rate of aromatic electrophilic substitution, ArS_E2 (chlorination).
In (*C*) and (*D*) –*R* effect of $\rangle$=O, group is operative with the ring (more in *D*) which decreases rate of ArS_E2 reaction. So, correct order is *B* > *A* > *C* > *D*.

10. (d) Molar mass is same for all.
As branching increases in (*C*) to (*D*) to (*B*), surface area decreases which causes a decrease in van der waals' force and boiling point decreases.
⇒ (*A*) is a dihydric alcohol which is strongly associated with other molecules through intermolecular hydrogen bonding. So, the correct order is *A* > *C* > *D* > *B*.

11. (b) Statement (b) is correct, whereas other statements are incorrect.
Alkenes are more reactive than alkynes in electrophilic addition reaction, e.g. reaction with HCl.

$$Be_2C + 4H_2O \longrightarrow 2Be(OH)_2 + \underset{\text{(Methane)}}{CH_4}$$

Cyclohexene (Symmetrical alkene) $\xrightarrow[\text{HBr/Peroxide}]{\text{HBr or}}$ Bromocyclohexane

(Only one product from cyclohexene)

$$CH_3CH_2-\underset{H}{CH}-CH_2F \xrightarrow[-HF]{\text{Alc. KOH, }\Delta} \underset{\text{(Major)}}{\text{But-1-ene}}$$

Hofmann elimination is observed as —F is a poor leaving group.

12. (a) During the formation of the inner-orbital octahedral complex of Cr (III) $[d^2sp^3]$, reduction of Cr (III) into Cr (II) takes place as,

$$\underset{3d^3}{Cr^{+3}} + \overset{+}{N}O \longrightarrow \underset{3d^4}{Cr^{2+}} + NO^+$$

In strong field ligand,

d^4: e_g^0 ⇒ No. of unpaired electrons (*n*) = 2
t_{2g}^4 (⇅ ↑ ↑) ⇒ $\mu = \sqrt{2(2+2)} = \sqrt{8}$ BM

13. (b) When, $k_1 = k_2$
$\frac{2}{3}$rd *A* reacted for $[A] = [C] = [D]$

$$(k_1 + k_2) = \frac{1}{t}\ln\frac{[A_0]}{[A_0]/3}$$

$$\Rightarrow t = \frac{1}{(k_1 + k_2)}\ln 3$$

$$t = \frac{1}{2k_1}\ln 3 = \frac{1}{2k_2}\ln 3$$

14. (a) Inorganic salt like aluminium bromide reacts with sodium hydroxide to give $Al(OH)_3$.

$$AlBr_3 + 3NaOH \longrightarrow \underset{\text{(White gelatinous ppt.)}}{Al(OH)_3} + 3NaBr$$

$$H_2O + \underset{\text{(Soluble)}}{NaAlO_2} \xleftarrow[\text{(excess)}]{\text{NaOH}} Al(OH)_3$$

The white precipitate of $Al(OH)_3$ gets dissolved in excess of NaOH to give a water soluble salt, sodium aluminate, $NaAlO_2$.

$$3AgNO_3 + AlBr_3 \longrightarrow \underset{\text{(Light yellow ppt.)}}{3\,AgBr} + Al(NO_3)_3$$

Thus, the probable salt is $AlBr_3$.

15. (a) Total strength of all H-bonds
$= 30.8 - 14.4 = 16.4$ kJ mol^{-1}
There are six nearest neighbours, but each hydrogen bond involves 2 molecules.
Hence, effective neighbours = 3
Hence, strength of H-bond

$$= \frac{16.4}{3} = 5.47 \text{ kJ mol}^{-1}$$

16. (d)
1-(aminomethyl)cyclopentanol ($-OH$, $-CH_2NH_2$) $\xrightarrow[-H_2O]{HNO_2}$ ($-OH$, $-CH_2\overset{\oplus}{N_2}$) $\xrightarrow{-N_2}$ ($-OH$, $-\overset{+}{C}H_2$) 1° carbocation $\xrightarrow[\text{(ring expansion)}]{\text{1,2-alkyl shift}}$ cyclohexyl cation (OH) $\xrightarrow{+H_2O}$ Enol $\xrightleftharpoons{\text{Tautomerises}}$ cyclohexanone

17. (d) Caprolactam is the monomeric unit of nylon-6. 2-chlorobuta-1, 3-diene is the monomeric unit of neoprene.
2-methylbuta-1, 3-diene (isoprene) is the monomeric unit of natural rubber.
Acrylonitrile is the monomeric unit of buna-N.

18. (b) Correct order is present in only option (b).
For group 13 elements, atomic size varies as : B < Ga < Al < In < Tl
Water solubility of group-1 metal hydroxides follow the order
LiOH < NaOH < KOH < RbOH < CsOH
Water solubility of group-2 metal sulphates decreases down the group.
$BeSO_4 > MgSO_4 > CaSO_4 > SrSO_4 > BaSO_4$

19. (b)
p-Benzoquinone → (resonance, $O^{\ominus}$, ⊕) $\xrightarrow{\overset{\oplus\ \ominus}{HBr}}$ 2-bromo-4-hydroxy-cyclohexadienone (OH, Br, O) $\xrightleftharpoons{\text{Tautomerises}}$ 2-bromohydroquinone (OH, Br, OH)

20. (b) ⇒ $\nu = \frac{\Delta E}{h}$ and

$$\Delta E = 2.18 \times 10^{-18} Z^2\left[\frac{1}{n_1^2} - \frac{1}{n_2^2}\right] \text{J}$$

$$\therefore \nu = \frac{2.18 \times 10^{-18}}{h} Z^2\left[\frac{1}{n_1^2} - \frac{1}{n_2^2}\right]$$

$$\Rightarrow \nu(He^+) = \frac{2.18 \times 10^{-18}}{h}(Z^2)\left[\frac{1}{2^2} - \frac{1}{4^2}\right]$$

$$= \frac{2.18 \times 10^{-18}}{h}(4)\left[\frac{3}{16}\right]$$

$$= \frac{2.18 \times 10^{-18}}{h} \times \frac{3}{4}$$

In case of $n_1 = 1$ and $n_2 = 2$

$$= \frac{2.18 \times 10^{-18}}{h}\left[\frac{1}{1^2} - \frac{1}{2^2}\right] = \nu(H)$$

$$= \frac{2.18 \times 10^{-18}}{h} \times \left(\frac{3}{4}\right)$$

Thus, $n_1 = 1$ and $n_2 = 2$

21. (9) The reactions of the elements with NaOH can be computed as,

$$\underset{\substack{+H_2}}{\overset{+2}{Na_2BeO_2}} \leftarrow Be^0 \quad \underset{+H_2}{\overset{+3}{Na_3BO_3}} \leftarrow B^0 \quad \underset{\substack{+Na\\+H_2}}{\overset{+4}{Na_2CO_3}} \leftarrow C^0 \quad \underset{+H_2}{\overset{+3}{NaAlO_2}} \leftarrow Al^0$$

$$Si^0 \rightarrow \underset{+H_2}{\overset{+4}{Na_2SiO_3}} \quad P^0 \rightarrow \underset{+PH_3}{\overset{+1}{NaH_2PO_2}} \quad S^0 \rightarrow \underset{+Na_2S}{\overset{+2}{Na_2S_2O_3}}$$

$$Sn^0 \rightarrow \underset{+H_2}{\overset{+4}{Na_2SnO_3}} \quad Pb^0 \rightarrow \underset{+H_2}{\overset{+4}{Na_2PbO_3}}$$

$$\overset{+3}{AlCl_3} + 3NaOH \longrightarrow \underset{\text{White gelatineous}}{\overset{+3}{Al(OH)_3}} + 3NaCl$$

$$\overset{+3}{FeCl_3} + 3NaOH \longrightarrow \underset{\text{Reddish brown}}{\overset{+3}{Fe(OH)_3}} + 3NaCl$$

$$\overset{+2}{SnCl_2} + 2NaOH \longrightarrow \underset{\text{White}}{\overset{+2}{Sn(OH)_2}} + 2NaCl$$

22. (3)

[Three structures of 1,2,3-trichlorocyclohexane with Cl substituents shown with wedge/dash bonds]

So, three geometrical isomers are possible for 1, 2, 3-trichlorocyclohexane.

23. (9.26) Meq. of NH_4OH

$= 50 \times 0.1 = 5$ meq

Meq. of $HCl = 50 \times 0.05 = 2.5$ meq

	NH_4OH +	$HCl \longrightarrow$	NH_4Cl +	H_2O
$t = 0$	5 meq	2.5 meq	0	
$t = t$	(5 – 2.5) = 2.5 meq.	0	2.5 meq (salt)	

After reaction 2.5 meq salt is formed which is a salt of strong acid (HCl) and weak base (NH_4OH).

In the solution 2.5 meq weak base and 2.5 meq salt of same base is present, which is a basic buffer solution.

Now, on applying Henderson's equation,

$$pOH = pK_b + \log\frac{[\text{Salt}]}{[\text{Base}]}$$

$$= 4.74 + \log\frac{2.5}{2.5} = 4.74$$

$\therefore$ pH $= 14 - 4.74 = 9.26$

24. (16.75) Vol. of $N_2 = 20$ mL.

Pressure of dry $N_2 = 725 - 25 = 700$ mm

$$= \frac{700}{760} \text{ atm}$$

$T = 300\,K$

$$\Rightarrow \quad pV = \frac{w_{N_2}}{M_{N_2}} RT$$

$$\Rightarrow \quad \frac{700}{760} \times \frac{20}{1000} = \frac{w_{N_2}}{28} \times 0.0821 \times 300$$

$[\because M_{N_2} = 28 \text{ g/mol}]$

$$w_{N_2} = \frac{7 \times 2 \times 28}{760 \times 0.0821 \times 300}$$

$= 0.02094$ g

$$\therefore \% \text{ of } N_2 = \frac{0.02094}{0.125} \times 100 = 16.75$$

25. (4) The lightest known gas is $H_2 (M = 2\text{g/mol})$

$\Rightarrow 4 \times 6 \times 10^{23}$ atoms $= 24 \times 10^{23}$ atoms = Number of H-atoms

After removal of 24×10^{23} atoms of hydrogen $= 24 \times 10^{23}$ protons

$= 24 \times 10^{23}$ electrons are left

$\because$ Amount of charge left

$$= \frac{24 \times 10^{23}}{6 \times 10^{23}} = 4 \text{ Faraday } (X)$$

26. (99.94) Vol. occupied by 1 mole of H_2O (g) at 373 K $= nRT/p$

$$= \frac{1 \times 0.0821 \times 373}{1} = 30.62 \text{ L}$$

Vol. of 1 mole of H_2O (*l*)

$$= \frac{M}{p} = \frac{18}{0.958} = 18.789 \text{ mL}$$

$= 18.789 \times 10^{-3}$ L

% of vol. occupied by liquid water

$$= \frac{18.89 \times 10^{-3}}{30.62} \times 100$$

$= 0.0613\%$

% of free volume

$= (100 - 0.0613) = 99.9386\% \simeq 99.94\%$

27. (69.06)

$$nH_2C{=}CH_2 + n(CH_2{=}CHCl) \longrightarrow \left[CH_2{-}CH_2{-}CH_2{-}CHCl \right]_n$$

Molar mass of $C_2H_4 = 28$ g/mol and that of C_2H_3Cl = 62.5 g / mol

$\therefore$ Empirical formula mass of copolymer

$= 28 + 62.5 = 90.5$

% of vinyl chloride

$$= \frac{62.5}{90.5} \times 100 = 69.06\%$$

28. (3)

$$\underset{\text{Butanone}}{CH_3{-}CH_2{-}\overset{\overset{O}{\|}}{C}{-}CH_3} + \underset{(a=1)}{PCl_5} \xrightarrow{-POCl_3} \underset{\text{2,2-dichlorobutane}}{CH_3CH_2CCl_2CH_3} \xrightarrow[-HCl]{NaNH_2}$$

$$\underset{\text{2-chloro but-2-ene}}{CH_3CH{=}CClCH_3} \xrightarrow[-HCl\ (b=2)]{NaNH_2} \underset{\text{But-2-yne}}{H_3C{-}C{\equiv}C{-}CH_3} \text{ or } H{-}\overset{H}{\underset{H}{C}}{-}C{\equiv}C{-}\overset{H}{\underset{H}{C}}{-}H$$

Molar mass of but-2-yne (X)

$= (12 \times 4) + (1 \times 6) = 54$ amu $= X$

$$\Rightarrow \frac{X}{a+b} \div w_H = \left(\frac{54}{1+2}\right) \div 6 = \frac{18}{6} = 3.00$$

29. (88) 1 mol CH_3CHO produces 1 mol Cu_2O

Molar mass of $CH_3CHO = 44$ g/mol and that of $Cu_2O = 143$ g / mol

$$\therefore \text{Produced } Cu_2O = \frac{2.86}{143} = \frac{2}{100}$$

$= 0.02$ mole

$=$ mole of CH_3CHO

Mass of CH_3CHO in mixture

$= 0.02 \times 44 = 0.88$ g

$\therefore$ % of CH_3CHO in mixture

$$= \frac{0.88}{1} \times 100 = 88\%$$

30. (3.87) $\underset{(B)}{[Cr(NH_3)_4Cl_2]Br} \xrightarrow{AgNO_3}$

$[Cr(NH_3)_4Cl_2]^+ + NO_3^-$

\+ AgBr

Yellow precipitate Partially soluble in concentrated NH_3, i.e. $[Ag(NH_3)_2]Br$

$$\underset{(A)}{[Cr(NH_3)_4BrCl]Cl} \xrightarrow{AgNO_3} [Cr(NH_3)_4ClBr]^+$$

$+ NO_3^- +$ AgCl

White ppt. soluble in concentrated NH_3, i.e. $[Ag(NH_3)_2]Cl$

Hybridisation of Cr(III) in *A* or *B* $\longrightarrow d^2sp^3$ having 3 unpaired electrons (*n*)

$\Rightarrow \mu = \sqrt{3(3+2)}$

$= \sqrt{15} = 3.8729 = 3.87$BM

Knockout 03

1. (c) The reactions associated with P, Q, R and S are as follows

(P) 3,5-dichloronitrobenzene $\xrightarrow[150°C]{NaOH}$ 3-chloro-5-nitrophenoxide (O^-) $\xrightarrow{CH_3Cl}$ 1-chloro-3-methoxy-5-nitrobenzene (NO_2, Cl, OCH_3) (iv)

(Q) Nitrobenzene $\xrightarrow{Cl_2, AlCl_3}$ m-chloronitrobenzene $\xrightarrow[FeBr_3]{Br_2}$ (Br, Cl, NO_2 substituted benzene) $\xrightarrow[130°C]{CH_3\bar{O}Na^+}$ (NO_2, Cl, OCH_3 substituted benzene) (i)

(R) Phenol (OH) $\xrightarrow[CH_3Cl]{NaOH}$ Anisole (OCH_3) $\xrightarrow[HNO_3]{H_2SO_4}$ p-nitroanisole (OCH_3, NO_2) $\xrightarrow[AlCl_3]{Cl_2}$ (OCH_3, Cl, NO_2) (i)

(S) Salicylaldehyde (OH, CHO) $\xrightarrow[\text{-HOCOONa}]{\text{(ii) NaOH, } H_2O_2 \text{ (Dakin's reaction)}}$ Catechol (OH, OH) (ii)

2. (a) Out of the given elements, only Cu and Pb undergo self reduction. The sulphide of Pb, Cu are heated in air to either convert the complete ore or part of ore into oxide or sulphate, which react with remaining sulphide ore to give metal and SO_2 (self reduction). So, option which contains any of these two metals is not correct and can not be extracted by involving self reduction method.

3. (b) C_V (gas A) $= \frac{3}{2}R + \frac{3}{2}R + 6R = 9R$

Let C_V for gas B be a.

Heat lost by the gas

$$A = 7 \times 9R \times \left(T - \frac{5T}{6}\right)$$

and heat gain by the gas

$$B = 6a\left(\frac{5T}{6} - \frac{T}{3}\right)$$

$$\Rightarrow \quad 63R\left(\frac{T}{6}\right) = 6a\left(\frac{T}{2}\right)$$

$$\Rightarrow \quad a = \frac{7}{2}R$$

So, C_V (of gas B) $= \frac{7R}{2}$ and it is a diatomic gas.

4. (b) (i) This is a free radical addition reaction which gives mainly 1,4-addition.

buta-1,3-diene $+ \dot{Br}\dot{C}Cl_3 \longrightarrow$ $Br-CH_2-CH=CH-CH_2-CCl_3$ (A)

(ii) $R-CH=CH_2 + \dot{C}Cl_3\ \dot{Cl} \longrightarrow R-CH(Cl)-CH_2-CCl_3$ Major (B) (Less steric hindrance)

$+ R-CH(CCl_3)-CH_2Cl$ Minor

Product C can be obtained by the combination of two intermediate free radicals.

$$R\dot{C}HCH_2CCl_3 + RCH(Cl)\dot{C}H_2 \longrightarrow R-CH(CH_2CCl_3)-CH_2-CH(Cl)-R \ (C)$$

5. (b) Weak acid is 20% ionised so, $\alpha = \frac{20}{100} = 0.2$

For a monobasic acid,

$\alpha = \frac{i-1}{n-1}$, where i = van't Hoff factor and n is the number of ionised species or ions.

$$\alpha = \frac{i-1}{2-1}$$

$$\Rightarrow \quad \alpha = i - 1$$

$$i = 1 + \alpha$$

$$= 1 + 0.2 = 1.2$$

$$\Delta T_b = iK_b m$$

$$T_b - T_b^\circ = 1.2 \times 0.56 \times 0.05$$

$$= 0.034$$

T_b° (boiling point of water) $= 100\,°C$

$\therefore \quad T_b = 100 + 0.034 = 100.034\,°C$

6. (c) The weakest acid is the Fe^{2+} complex on account of its relatively large ionic radius and low charge. The increase of charge to + 3 increase the acidic strength.

The greater acidity of Al^{3+} can be explained by its smaller radius.

The anomalous ion in the series is the Hg^{2+} complex. This complex reflects the failure of an ionic model, because in the complex there is a large transfer of positive charge to oxygen as a result of covalent bonding.

7. (b)

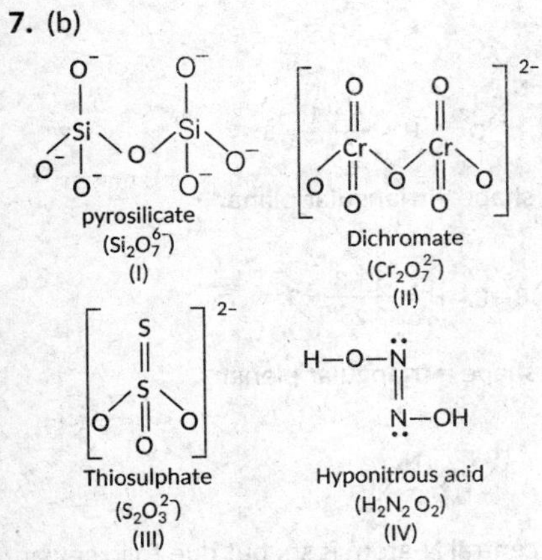

(I) have Si—O—Si linkage
(II) Cr—O—Cr linkage but no such linkage is present in (III) and (IV).

8. (b) Osmotic pressure, $\pi = iCRT$

$$4.92 = \left\{\frac{x}{200} + 2 \times 0.05\right\} 0.0821 \times 300$$

atm $\qquad [\because$ for NaCl, $\alpha = 1 \Rightarrow i = 2]$

$$\Rightarrow \quad \frac{x}{200} + 0.1 = \frac{4.92}{0.0821 \times 300}$$

$$\therefore \quad \frac{x}{200} + 0.1 = 0.2$$

$$\Rightarrow \quad x = 0.1 \times 200 = 20 \text{ g}$$

9. (a) NO_2 is a brown coloured gas, because molecular orbital electronic configuration of NO_2 confirms the presence of unpaired electrons, which can easily undergo transition from ground state energy level to excited state level by absorbing light of suitable wavelength.

N_2O_3 is a blue coloured liquid because low or difference between occupied and unoccupied energy levels of electrons among molecules of N_2O_3, it absorbs a part of visible light spectrum which cause colour in N_2O_3.

10. (b) The reactions involved are

$$\underset{\text{Sodium}}{2Na} + \underset{\text{(Air) excess}}{O_2} \longrightarrow \underset{X}{Na_2O_2}$$

$$\underset{X}{2Na_2O_2} + 2CO_2 \longrightarrow 2Na_2CO_3 + \underset{Y}{O_2}$$

11. (d)

(a) Cycloheptatrienyl fluoride $\xrightarrow{SbF_5}$ (Aromatic) (Tropylium carbocation) $[SbF_6]^{\ominus}$

(Cycloheptatrienyl fluoride) (Aromatic) (Tropylium carbocation)

(b) (Propene) $+ Br^+ \rightleftharpoons$ bromonium ion (Br^+, CH—CH_2)

(c) (Propene) $+ H^+ \longrightarrow$ carbocation

(d) Triphenylmethyl chloride $+ Ag^+ \longrightarrow$ triphenylmethyl carbocation $+ AgCl$

45°tilted to each other
(Non-planar)

Option (d) gives a non-planar carbocation. This non-planar structure is due to steric hindrance of three phenyl rings which remain to plane by 45° like wings of a fan.

12. (c) Structure of given compounds are

(Non-aromatic) Cyclohexa-2, 4-dien-1-one ⇌ OH (Aromatic) I

Propan-2-one ⇌ OH (enol) II

Pentan-2,4-dione ⇌ (intramolecular H-bonded enol) III

⇒ In (I) aromaticity as well as conjugation stabilises the enolic form of structure (I).

Hence, (I) has maximum stability. (III) has more % enolic component due to intramolecular H-bonding which stabilises the structure.

⇒ Greater the stability of enolic form, greater will be the percentage of enolic component.

Hence, the order of % enolic component is

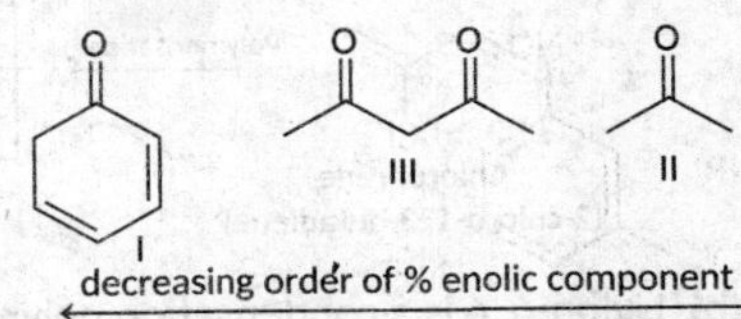

13. (c) 2-Butyne is reduced by Na/NH_3 to give trans-2-butene.

$$CH_3-C\equiv C-CH_3 \xrightarrow{Na/NH_3}$$

X (*trans*-2-butene)

Lindlar's catalyst (H_2, Pd-$CaCO_3$, quinoline) reduces 2-butyne to *cis*-2-butene.

$$CH_3-C\equiv C-CH_3 \xrightarrow[\text{catalyst}]{\text{Lindlar's}}$$

Y (*cis*-but-2-ene)

As products X and Y are *trans* and *cis* isomers respectively of 2-butene. Hence, they are geometrical isomers.

14. (c) $\underset{\text{Ester}}{CH_3COOC_2H_5} \xrightarrow[H_2O]{H_2SO_4} \underset{\text{Alcohol}}{C_2H_5OH}$

$\underset{\text{Ester}}{CH_3COOCH_3} \xrightarrow[H_2O]{\text{DIBAL-H}} \underset{\text{Aldehyde}}{CH_3CHO}$

$\underset{\text{Nitrile}}{CH_3C\equiv N} \xrightarrow[HCl/H_2O]{SnCl_2} \underset{\text{Aldehyde}}{CH_3CHO}$

$\underset{\text{Nitrile}}{CH_3-C\equiv N} \xrightarrow[H_3O^+]{CH_3MgBr}$ [1 | 1 |]

15. (d)

$\xrightarrow{H^+}$ ... Ring Expansion ... $\xrightarrow{-H^{\oplus}}$

16. (c) (a) Neoprene is an addition homopolymer of chloroprene.]

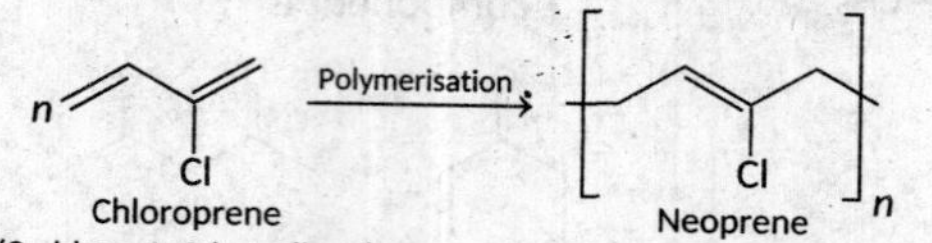

n Chloroprene (2-chloro-1, 3-butadiene) $\xrightarrow{\text{Polymerisation}}$ Neoprene

(b) Nylon-6, 6 is a condensation polymer of adipic acid and hexamethylene diamine.

$$nH_2N—(CH_2)_6—NH_2 + nHOOC—(CH_2)_4—COOH$$

Hexamethylene diamine, Adipic acid

$$\xrightarrow[\text{High Pressure}]{553\text{ K}} \left[NH—(CH_2)_6—NH—\overset{O}{\overset{\|}{C}}—(CH_2)_4—\overset{O}{\overset{\|}{C}}\right]_n$$

Nylon-6, 6

(c) Terylene is a condensation polymer of terephthalic acid or benzene-1, 4-dicarboxylic acid and ethylene glycol.

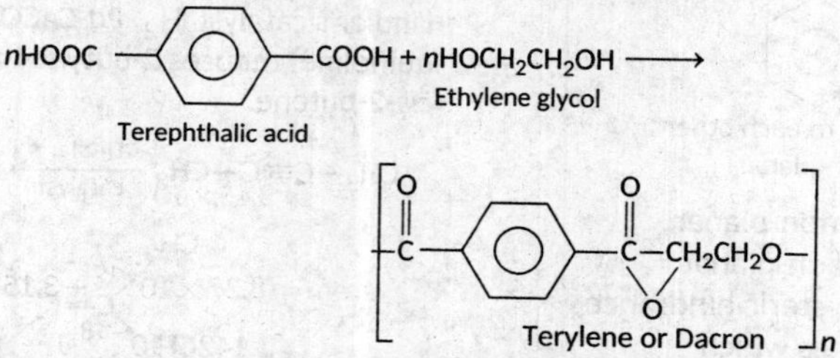

$$nHOOC—C_6H_4—COOH + nHOCH_2CH_2OH \longrightarrow$$

Terephthalic acid, Ethylene glycol

$$\left[\overset{O}{\overset{\|}{C}}—C_6H_4—\overset{O}{\overset{\|}{C}}—CH_2CH_2O—\right]_n$$

Terylene or Dacron

(d) PMMA (polymethyl methacrylate) is an addition polymer of methyl methacrylate.

$$nCH_2{=}C(COOCH_3)(CH_3) \xrightarrow{\text{Polymerisation}} \left[CH_2—\underset{CH_3}{\overset{COOCH_3}{C}}—\right]_n$$

Methyl methacrylate, PMMA

17. (c) **Hofmann elimination** The reaction of an amine with excess of CH_3I produces a quaternary ammonium salt which on further treatment with AgOH followed by heating undergoes Hofmann elimination to produce less substituted product in major amount.

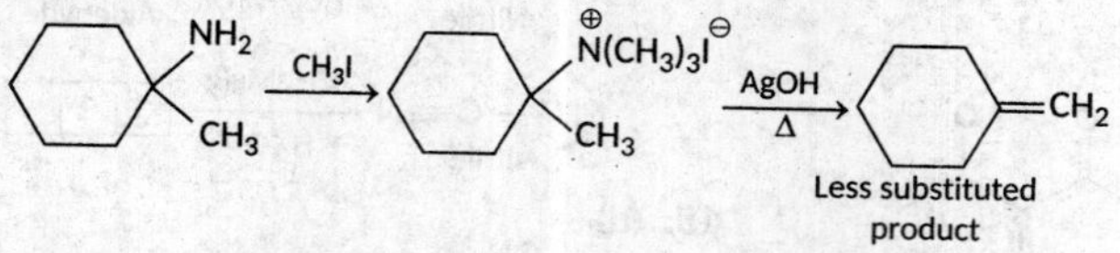

1-methylcyclohexylamine (NH_2, CH_3) $\xrightarrow{CH_3I}$ $\overset{\oplus}{N}(CH_3)_3\overset{\ominus}{I}$ (CH_3) $\xrightarrow[\Delta]{AgOH}$ methylenecyclohexane ($=CH_2$)

Less substituted product

The product does not show geometrical isomerism.

18. (c) **Structure of NF_3**

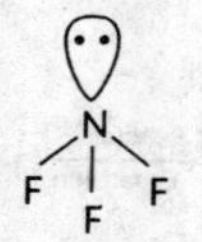

$$H = \frac{5+3}{2} = 4$$

Hybridisation $= sp^3$, according to VSEPR shape is pyramidal

Structure of H_3O^+

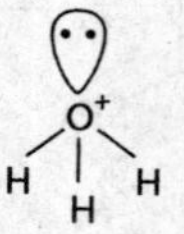

$$H = \frac{6+3-1}{2} = 4$$

Hybridisation $= sp^3$, shape = pyramidal

Structure of NO_3^-

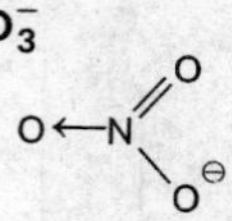

$$H = \frac{5+1}{2} = 3$$

Hybridisation $= sp^2$, shape = triangular planar

Structure of BF_3

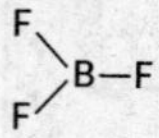

$$H = \frac{3+3}{2} = 3$$

Hybridisation $= sp^2$, shape = triangular planar

Structure of HN_3

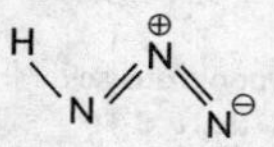

$$H—N{=}\overset{\oplus}{N}{=}\overset{\ominus}{N}$$

The hybridisation of central N-atom is sp, but due to irregular distribution of electron cloud, its structure is slightly bent. Hence, option (c) is correct regarding isostructural pairs.

19. (a) A buffer solution containing mixture of CH_3COOH and CH_3COONa is known as acidic buffer. When an equal volume of 1 M HCl is added, the pH of the solution almost remains unchanged and acidic buffer is formed.

The acetate ion reacts with H^+ ion to form acetic acid thus, the solution contains CH_3COOH and CH_3COONa in equal amounts.

20. (b) N-acetyl *para*-aminophenol can be used as an analgesic without causing addiction and modification.

21. (55.53) Given, reactions are

(i) $2C_2H_6 + 2Br_2 \longrightarrow 2C_2H_5Br + 2HBr$

(ii) $2C_2H_5Br + 2Na \longrightarrow C_4H_{10} + 2NaBr$

Mole ratio of reactions (i) and (ii)

$$C_2H_6 : C_2H_5Br : C_4H_{10} :: 2:2:1$$

Now, mole of butane formed $= \frac{55}{58}$ mol

[∵ Molar mass $(C_4H_{10}) = 58$ g/mol]

Mole of C_2H_5Br actually required

$$= \frac{2\times55}{58}\times\frac{100}{85} \quad (\because \text{Reaction efficiency is } 85\%)$$

Now, similarly mole of C_2H_6 actually required

$$= \frac{2\times55}{58}\times\frac{100}{85}\times\frac{100}{90} = 2.479 \text{ mol}$$

Therefore, volume of C_2H_6 at NTP actually required

$$22.4\times2.479 \text{ L} = 55.53 \text{ L}$$

22. (12.42) Given, initial conc. of $CH_3COOH = 0.06$ M

∴ Residual CH_3COOH is unadsorbed CH_3COOH.

10 mL of M' (unadsorbed) $CH_3COOH = 14$ mL of 0.03 M NaOH

$$\therefore \quad M' = \frac{14\times0.03}{10} = 0.042 \text{ M}$$

Initial millimoles of $CH_3COOH = 50\times0.06 = 3$

Unadsorbed millimoles of $CH_3COOH = 50\times0.042 = 2.1$

Thus, equilibrium concentration of $CH_3COOH = 2.1$

CH_3COOH adsorbed $= 3.0 - 2.1 = 0.9$ millimol

$$= \frac{0.9}{1000}\times60 \text{ g} = 0.054 \text{ g} = x$$

m = adsorbent = 3 g

$\Rightarrow \frac{x}{m} = kC^{1/2} \Rightarrow \frac{0.054}{3} = k \times (2.1)^{1/2}$

$\Rightarrow \quad k = 12.42 \times 10^{-3} = a \times 10^{-3}$

$\therefore \quad a = 12.42$

23. (6) $Fe(OH)_3 + HCl \longrightarrow FeCl_3$

$\xrightarrow{K_4[Fe(CN)_6]}$ Blue ppt. $\xrightarrow{\text{Excess } K_4[Fe(CN)]_6} \overset{III}{Fe_4}[\overset{II}{Fe}(CN)_6]_3$ (Prussian blue)

Coordination number of Fe(II) in complex is 6.

24. (3.49) Moles of precipitate

$= \frac{0.209}{118} = 1.77 \times 10^{-3}$ mol= mol of KCNO

Mass of KCNO $= 1.77 \times 10^{-3} \times 81 = 0.1434$ g

$KCNO\% = \frac{0.1434}{4.112} \times 100 = 3.487\% \simeq 3.49\%$

25. (– 1.27)

From the combustion of benzoic acid, the heat capacity of calorimeter and its constant C can be determined as

$\frac{3251}{122} \times 10^3 \times 0.825\ J = 1.94 \times C$

$\therefore \quad C = 11332.07\ JK^{-1}$

Heat produced in combustion of 0.727 g D-ribose

$= 0.910 \times 11332.07 = 10312.18 J$

Internal energy of combustion of D-ribose $= -\frac{10312.18}{0.727} \times 150$

$= -2.13 \times 10^6\ J\ mol^{-1}$

[∵ Molar mass of D-ribose = 150 g/mol] 0.727

The combustion reaction is

$C_5H_{10}O_5(s) + 5O_2(g) \longrightarrow 5CO_2(g) + 5H_2O(l)$

$\because \Delta n_g = 0,\ \Delta H = \Delta E$

$\Rightarrow -2.13 \times 10^6 = -5(394 + 286) \times 1000 - \Delta H_f^\circ$ (D-ribose)

ΔH_f° (D-ribose) $= -1.27 \times 10^6$ J

26. (6) SO_3, XeO_3, H_3PO_4, ClO_4^-, SO_4^{2-}, $XeOF_2$ have $d\pi$ - $p\pi$ bonding. This type of bonding is important in the compounds containing third (or higher) period elements (Si, P, S,Cl, etc.) These elements have vacant d-orbitals.

These vacant d-orbital form $(d-p)\ \pi$ bonding with N, O, F which have lone pair electrons in their p-orbitals.

27. (5.40) $H_2 + I_2 \rightleftharpoons 2HI$

Initially 2 3 0

At equilibrium $2-x$ $3-x$ $2x$

$K_C = \frac{[HI]^2}{[H_2][I_2]} = \frac{(2x)^2}{(2-x)(3-x)}$

$\Rightarrow \quad 0.02 = \frac{4x^2}{x^2 - 5x + 6}$

$\Rightarrow \quad 0.02x^2 - 0.1x + 0.12 = 4x^2$

$3.98x^2 + 0.1x - 0.12 = 0$

By solving for x, we get $x = 0.162$

So, % I_2 converted $= \frac{x}{[I_2]_0} \times 100 = \frac{0.162}{3} \times 100$

% I_2 converted = 5.40

28. (1) Since, the inversion of sucrose proceeds with constant $t_{1/2}$. The order w.r.t. sucrose is 1.

$\frac{-d\,(\text{sucrose})}{dt} = k\,(H^+)^b\,(\text{sucrose})^1$

Let $k(H^+)^b = k$

$\Rightarrow \quad \frac{-d\,(\text{sucrose})}{dt} = k\,(\text{sucrose})^1$

Hence, $k = \frac{0.693}{t_{1/2}} = k\,(H^+)^b$

$\frac{0.6932}{k} = t_{1/2}(H^+)^b = \text{constant}$

$\Rightarrow \quad 500 \times (10^{-5})^b = 50(10^{-4})^b$

$\Rightarrow \quad 10^{1-5b} = 10^{-4b}$

$\Rightarrow \quad b = 1$

29. (174.17) For normal O-atoms

$\Rightarrow \left(\frac{498 \times 10^3\ J}{mol\ O_2}\right)\left(\frac{1\ mol\ O_2}{6.02 \times 10^{23}\ molecules\ O_2}\right) = 8.27 \times 10^{-19}\ J$

Extra energy for excited 'O'-atom

$1.967\ eV \times \left(\frac{1.60 \times 10^{-19}}{1\ eV}\right) = 3.15 \times 10^{-19}\ J$

Total energy for excited 'O'-atom $= (8.27 \times 10^{-19} + 3.15 \times 10^{-19})$ J

$= 1.142 \times 10^{-18}$ J

$\Rightarrow \lambda = \frac{hc}{E}$

$= \frac{(6.63 \times 10^{-34}\ J.s)\ (3 \times 10^8\ m/s)}{1.142 \times 10^{-18}\ J}$

$= 1.74167 \times 10^{-7}\ m = 174.17$ nm

30. (2) pH at the 2nd end point of titration is given as

$pH = \frac{pK_2 + pK_3}{2} = \frac{8 + 13}{2} = 10.5$

$\Rightarrow \quad E_{cell} = E^\circ_{cell} + 0.059$ pH

$\therefore \quad E_{cell} = 1.3805 + 0.059 \times 10.5 = 2$ V

Knockout 04

1. (b) Pressure $(p) \propto$ number of moles (n) at constant volume and temperature.

$2NO(g) + Cl_2(g) \rightleftharpoons 2NOCl(g)$

$t = 0$ $2p$ p 0

$t = t_{eq}$ $2p - 2x$ $p - x$ $2x$

Total pressure $p_T = 2p - 2x + p - x + 2x$

$3p - x = 1$ and $2x = \frac{p - x}{4}$ (∵ Mole of NOCl $= \frac{1}{4} \times$ mole of Cl_2)

Solving, $x = \frac{1}{26}$ and $p = \frac{9}{26}$

$K_p = \frac{(2x)^2}{(2p - 2x)^2 (p - x)} = \frac{4 \times x^2}{(16x)^2 \times 8x}$

$= \frac{4x^2}{2048 \times x^3} = \frac{1}{512x} = \frac{1}{512 \times \frac{1}{26}} = \frac{13}{256}$

2. (d) Maximum wavelength radiation means minimum energy radiation which is emitted when transition occurs from $4 \rightarrow 2$ (visible or Balmer region).

$$\Rightarrow \frac{1}{\lambda} = R\left(\frac{1}{4} - \frac{1}{16}\right) \Rightarrow \frac{1}{\lambda} = R \times \frac{12}{4 \times 16} = \frac{3R}{16} \text{ or } \lambda = \frac{16}{3R}$$

3. (a) Oxygen in air reacts with emitted HCl gas to form a cloud of chlorine gas which appear as white fumes.

$$\underset{\text{Air}}{4HCl + O_2} \longrightarrow \underset{\text{Cloud of white fumes}}{2Cl_2} + 2H_2O$$

4. (a) Equivalents of $Cr_2O_7^{2-} = 0.136 =$ Equivalents of $N_2H_5^+$

$\Rightarrow$ Number of moles of $Cr_2O_7^{2-} = \frac{0.136}{n\text{-factor of } Cr_2O_7^{2-}}$

$= \frac{0.136}{6} = 0.0226$

$[\because Cr_2O_7^{2-} \rightarrow 2Cr^{3+}, n\text{-factor } (6-3) \times 2 = 6]$

5. (c)

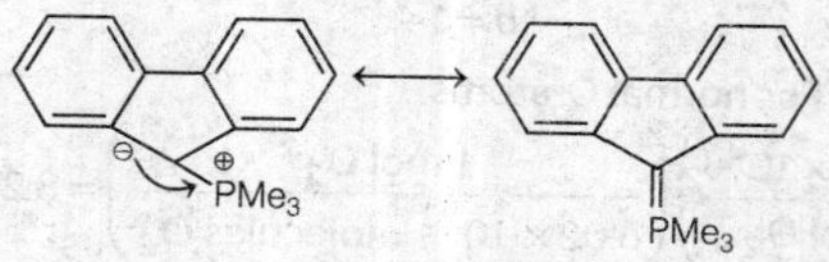

[Resonance structures: fluorenyl anion with $\overset{\oplus}{P}Me_3$ ⟷ fluorenylidene $=PMe_3$]

Negative charge can be delocalised in vacant 3*d*-orbitals of phosphorus and also in addition to phenyl rings. So, the anion is more stabilised by resonance. N and C do not have vacant *d*-orbitals.

6. (d) Statements (a), (b), (c) are incorrect, while statement(d) is correct as HF has highest boiling point due to H-bonding.

7. (d) Protonated methanol is a stronger acid than methanol, because + ve charge on O-atom is unstable.

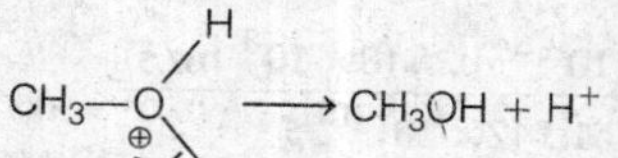

$$CH_3-\overset{\oplus}{O}H_2 \longrightarrow CH_3OH + H^+$$

8. (b) Reactivity of carbonyl groups (their polarity too) follow the order

Acid chlorides > Aldehydes > Ketones > Esters
(*B*) (*C*) (*D*) (*A*)

H^- of $LiAlH_4$ shows nucleophilic addition reaction with $\rangle C=O$ group where, rate of the reaction is directly proportional to the polarity of $\rangle C=O$ group.

9. (c) —OH converts phenol to phenoxide ion which is strongly activating than $-OCH_3$ group, so attack occurs (coupling) at *ortho*-position w.r.t hydroxyl group as the *para*-position is blocked by $-OCH_3$ group.

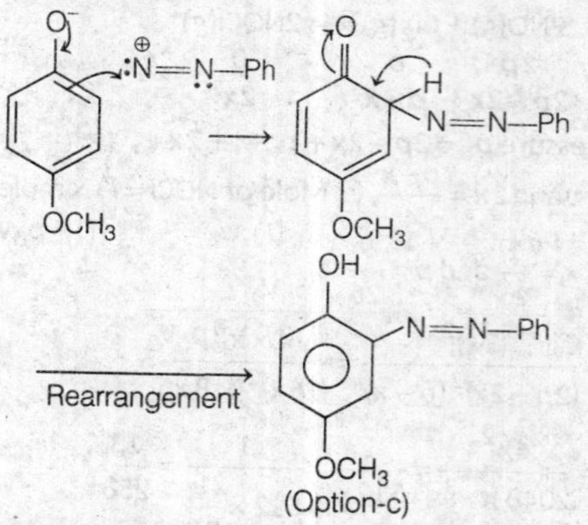

[Scheme: p-methoxyphenoxide + $\overset{\oplus}{N}{=}N{-}Ph$ ⟶ intermediate (C=O, H, N=N—Ph, OCH_3) —Rearrangement⟶ 2-hydroxy-5-methoxyazobenzene: OH, N=N—Ph, OCH_3 (Option-c)]

This reaction is called coupling reaction (ArS_E2).

10. (b) Correct match is $A \rightarrow (1), B \rightarrow (3), C \rightarrow (2), A \rightarrow (4)$.

A. Mn^{2+} ions are precipitated as hydroxide by ammonia solution in the presence of ammonium chloride. Hence, Mn^{2+} belongs to group III.

B. Sr^{2+} ions belong to group IV because its carbonates precipitate in a mixture of ammonium carbonate, ammonium chloride or ammonium solution.

C. Cu^{2+} ions belong to group IIA because its basic sulphide is insoluble in yellow ammonium sulphides.

D. As^{3+} ions are grouped in sub group II B as its acidic sulphides are soluble in yellow ammonium sulphide due to formation of complex.

11. (d) Lysine consists of two $-NH_2$ groups. Its structure is as follows

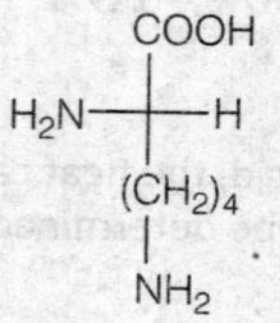

[Structure: COOH / H_2N—C—H / $(CH_2)_4$ / NH_2] (Lysine, a basic amino acid)

12. (c)

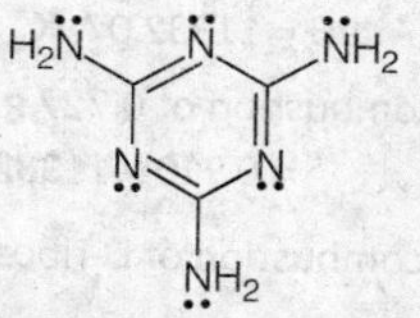

[Structure: melamine — triazine ring with three NH_2 groups]

Molecular formula of melamine is $C_3H_6N_6$.

13. (a) Both (A) and (R) are true but (R) is not the correct explanation of (A). It is because, cracking of rubber is caused by the atmospheric ozone formed in the photochemical smog formation process.

14. (b)

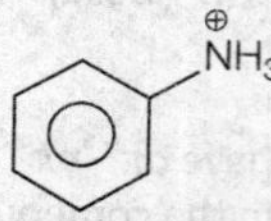

- [$C_6H_5\overset{\oplus}{N}H_3$] do not undergo Friedel-Crafts reaction due to strong deactivating effect of $-\overset{\oplus}{N}H_3$. 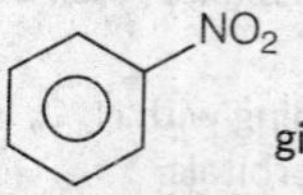
- [$C_6H_5NO_2$] gives poor yield in Friedel-Crafts since $-NO_2$ is a powerful deactivator. 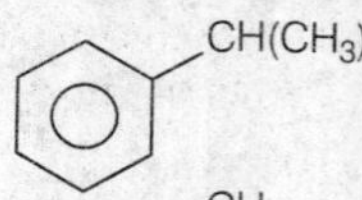
- [$C_6H_5CH(CH_3)_2$] $\Rightarrow \alpha$-H = 1 and +*I* slower rate. 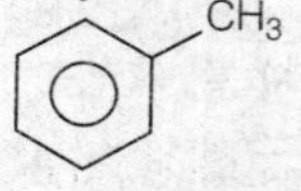
- [$C_6H_5CH_3$] $\Rightarrow \alpha$-H = 3 and +*I* fastest rate.

$\Rightarrow$ Three α-H atoms (benzylic) give hyperconjugative stability to the σ-complex (X) of Friedel-Craft reaction.

$\Rightarrow$ (X) : [σ-complex with CH_3, H, + and H, R] where R^+ is the electrophile.

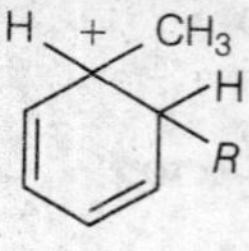

15. (b) From Raoult-Dalton's combined phase law,

$$y_A = \frac{p_A}{p_{total}}$$

$$\Rightarrow \quad y_A = \frac{p_A^\circ x_A}{p_A^\circ x_A + p_B^\circ x_B}$$

$$\Rightarrow \quad \frac{1}{y_A} = 1 + \left(\frac{p_B^\circ}{p_A^\circ}\right) \cdot \frac{x_B}{x_A}$$

$$\Rightarrow \quad \frac{1}{y_A} = 1 + \left(\frac{p_B^\circ}{p_A^\circ}\right) \times \frac{(1-x_A)}{x_A} = \left(\frac{p_B^\circ}{p_A^\circ}\right) \times \frac{1}{x_A} + \left(1 - \frac{p_B^\circ}{p_A^\circ}\right)$$

$$\Rightarrow \quad \frac{1}{y_A} = \left(\frac{p_B^\circ}{p_A^\circ}\right) \cdot \frac{1}{x_A} + \left(\frac{p_A^\circ - p_B^\circ}{p_A^\circ}\right)$$

$$\frac{1}{x_A} \times \left(\frac{p_B^\circ}{p_A^\circ}\right) = \frac{1}{y_A} - \left(\frac{p_A^\circ - p_B^\circ}{p_A^\circ}\right)$$

$$\Rightarrow \quad \frac{1}{x_A} = \left(\frac{p_A^\circ}{p_B^\circ}\right) \times \frac{1}{y_A} - \left(\frac{p_A^\circ - p_B^\circ}{p_A^\circ}\right) \times \frac{p_A^\circ}{p_B^\circ}$$

$$\Rightarrow \quad \frac{1}{x_A} = \left(\frac{p_A^\circ}{p_B^\circ}\right) \cdot \frac{1}{y_A} + \left(\frac{p_B^\circ - p_A^\circ}{p_B^\circ}\right)$$

$$y = mx + C$$

$$\text{Slope } (m) = \frac{p_A^\circ}{p_B^\circ}$$

$$\text{and } y = \text{intercept} = \left(\frac{p_B^\circ - p_A^\circ}{p_B^\circ}\right)$$

16. (d) The complete hydrolysis equation of XeF_4 is

$$6XeF_4 + 12H_2O \longrightarrow 4Xe + 2XeO_3 + 24HF + 3O_2$$

So, complete hydrolysis of XeF_4 does not produce XeO_2F_2.

17. (c) All the possible oxides of Mn and Cr are

MnO_2, Cr_2O_3 } Amphoteric

{ $MnO \Rightarrow$ Basic
$Mn_2O_3 \Rightarrow$ Weakly basic
$Mn_2O_7 \Rightarrow$ Strongly acidic

{ $CrO \Rightarrow$ Basic
$CrO_3 \Rightarrow$ Acidic

For transition metals, lower oxidation number of the metals in its oxides make the oxides basic, e.g. + 2 state of Mn in MnO and that of Cr in CrO.

Whereas highest oxidation number enhances their acidic nature, e.g. $\overset{+7}{Mn}_2O_7$ and $\overset{+6}{Cr}O_3$.

So, intermediate oxidation states + 4 of Mn in MnO_2 and + 3 of Cr in Cr_2O_3 make them amphoteric.

18. (c) H_2O is a weak field ligand, so cannot force pairing of electron(s).

$[Zn(H_2O)_6]^{2+} \Rightarrow (d^{10}) t_{2g}^6 e_g^4 \Rightarrow n = 0$

$[Cr(H_2O)_6]^{2+} \Rightarrow (d^4) t_{2g}^3 e_g^1 \Rightarrow n = 4$

$[Mn(H_2O)_6]^{2+} \Rightarrow (d^5) t_{2g}^3 e_g^2 \Rightarrow n = 5$

$[Cu(H_2O)_6]^{2+} \Rightarrow (d^9) t_{2g}^6 e_g^3 \Rightarrow n = 1$

Spin only magnetic moments, $\mu = \sqrt{n(n+2)}$ BM

So, $\mu \propto n$ where n is the number of unpaired electrons.

19. (b) $LiAlH_4$ causes elimination in 3° alkyl halides using its base, H^- and form $CH_2{=}C(CH_3)_2$

Ph_3SnH reduces all three type of alkyl halides.

Complete reaction is as follows

$$(CH_3)_3C{-}Cl \xrightarrow{LiAlH_4} \underset{(X)}{CH_2{=}C(CH_3)_2}$$

$$CH_3CH{=}CHCH_2{-}Cl \xrightarrow{Ph_3SnH} \underset{(Y)}{CH_3CH{=}CHCH_3}$$

20. (b) Complete reaction is as follows

$$C_6H_5{-}CH_2{-}\ddot{O}{-}C_6H_4{-}OH \xrightarrow{H{-}I} Ph{-}CH_2{-}\overset{H}{\overset{|}{O^{\oplus}}}{-}C_6H_4{-}OH$$

[Cannot be broken due to partial double bond character]

$$\xrightarrow{I^\ominus} PhCH_2I + HO{-}C_6H_4{-}OH$$

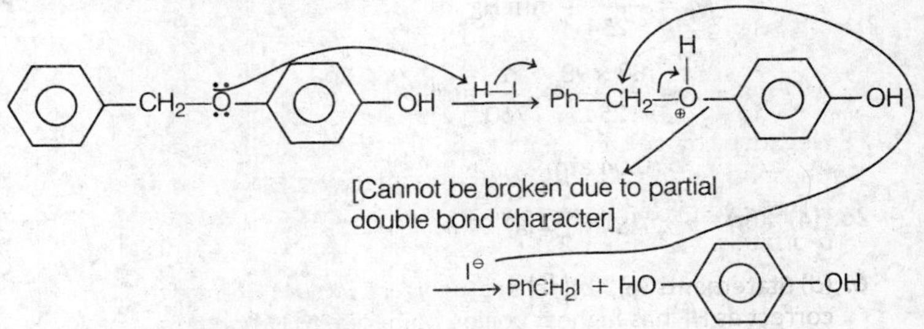

21. (4) $H_4P_2O_5$ contains 1 bridging oxo group.

P_4O_6 contains 6 bridging oxo-groups.

N_2O_3 contains 1 bridging oxo-group.

$H_2S_2O_3$ does not contain any bridging oxo-group.

$H_5P_3O_{10}$ contains 2 bridging oxo groups.

22. (2) In the reaction, two stereoisomeric products will be formed.

Total three chiral carbon atoms are present. The configuration at two chiral carbon atoms is same in the two isomers.

However, the configuration at one chiral carbon atom is different in the two isomers.

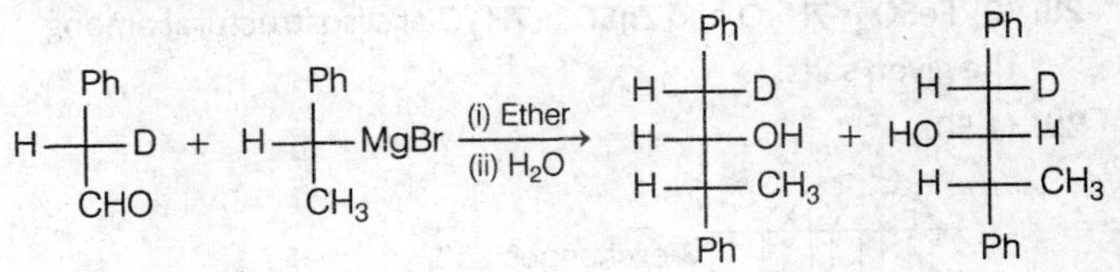

$$\text{H}{-}\overset{\text{Ph}}{\underset{\text{CHO}}{C}}{-}\text{D} + \text{H}{-}\overset{\text{Ph}}{\underset{\text{CH}_3}{C}}{-}\text{MgBr} \xrightarrow[\text{(ii) } H_2O]{\text{(i) Ether}}$$

Product 1 (top to bottom, Ph at top and bottom): H–C–D; H–C–OH; H–C–CH₃ + Product 2 (Ph at top and bottom): H–C–D; HO–C–H; H–C–CH₃

23. (15.38)

$A \to B$; $w_1 = 0$, $\Delta U_1 = 1 \times C_V(T)$, $q_1 = C_V(T)$

$B \to C$; $w_2 = -2p_0V_0$, $\Delta U_2 = 1 \times C_V(2T)$, $q_2 = C_V(2T) + 2p_0V_0$

$C \to D$; $w_3 = 0$, $\Delta U_3 = 1 \times C_V(-2T)$, $q_3 = -C_V(2T)$

$D \to A$; $w_4 = p_0V_0$, $\Delta U_4 = -1 \times C_V(T)$, $q_4 = -C_V(T) - p_0V_0$

$$\text{Efficiency} = \frac{|w|}{q_{absorbed}} = \frac{p_0V_0}{C_VT + C_V2T + 2p_0V_0}$$

$$= \frac{RT}{3 \times C_V \times T + 2RT} = \frac{RT}{3 \times \frac{3R}{2} \times T + 2RT}$$

$$= \frac{2}{13} = 0.1538 = 15.38\%$$

Note (i) For one mole mono-atomic gas, $C_V = \frac{3R}{2}$.

(ii) Heat is absorbed in $A \rightarrow B$ and $B \rightarrow C$ processes.

24. (0) In hexacarbonylchromium, $Cr(CO)_6$ there is no unpaired electrons due to $3d^6$ configuration.

25. (0.04) $CO + Cl_2 \rightleftharpoons COCl_2$

342 mm 352 mm 0

(342 – p) mm (352 – p)mm p mm

$\Rightarrow p_{total} = 342 - p + 352 - p + p = 440$

$\Rightarrow p = 254$ mm

$$K_p = \frac{p_{COCl_2}}{p_{CO} \times p_{Cl_2}} = \frac{254}{88 \times 98}$$

For $COCl_2 \rightleftharpoons CO + Cl_2$

$$K_p' = \frac{88 \times 98}{254} \text{ mm Hg}$$

$$= \frac{88 \times 98}{254} \times \frac{1}{760} \text{ atm}$$

$$= 0.04 \text{ atm}$$

26. (4) $X(g) \longrightarrow Y(g) + \frac{1}{2} Z(g)$

(150 – p) (p) $\left(\frac{p}{2}\right)$

$$150 - p + p + \frac{p}{2} = 170 = \text{Total pressure}$$

$\Rightarrow p = 40$ mm

So, pressure of $X(g)$ decreases by 40 mm in 10 min.

Rate of disappearance $= \frac{40}{10} = 4$ mm/min

27. (32.65) $\underset{-1}{Cl^-} \longrightarrow \underset{+7}{ClO_4^-}$ (n-factor = 8)

Number of Faraday = Number of equivalent of $NaClO_4$ formed

$$= \frac{500}{122.5} \times 8 = \frac{4000}{122.5} = 32.65$$

28. (2) $FeSO_4 \cdot 7H_2O$ and $ZnSO_4 \cdot 7H_2O$ are isostructural among the given salts.

29. (1.50)

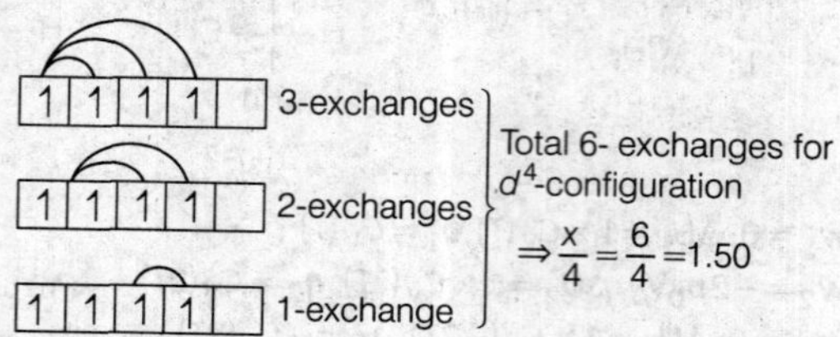

30 (12.50)

$$XY(g) \rightleftharpoons X(g) + Y(g)$$

	$XY(g)$	$X(g)$	$Y(g)$
$t = 0$	1	0	0
$t = t_{eq}$	$1-\alpha$	α	α

Total no. of moles at equilibrium $= 1 - \alpha + 2\alpha$

$= 1 + \alpha$

Partial pressure at $t = t_{eq}$

$$\left(\frac{1-\alpha}{1+\alpha}\right)p \quad \left(\frac{\alpha}{1+\alpha}\right)p \quad \left(\frac{\alpha}{1+\alpha}\right)p$$

$$K_p = \frac{\left(\frac{\alpha}{1+\alpha}\right)p \cdot \left(\frac{\alpha}{1+\alpha}\right)p}{\left(\frac{1-\alpha}{1+\alpha}\right)p} = \frac{\alpha^2}{1-\alpha^2} \times p$$

$$\Rightarrow \frac{K_p}{p} = \frac{\left(\frac{1}{3}\right)^2}{1 - \left(\frac{1}{3}\right)^2} = \frac{1}{9} \times \frac{9}{8} = \frac{1}{8} \qquad \left[\because \alpha = \frac{1}{3}\right]$$

$$\Rightarrow \frac{K_p}{p} = \frac{100}{8} \times 10^{-2} = 12.50 \times 10^{-2}$$

Knockout 05

1. (b) (i) $Hg^{2+}(aq) + 2I^-(aq) \longrightarrow HgI_2(s)$ (Red ppt.)

$HgI_2(s) + 2KI(aq) \longrightarrow K_2[HgI_4](aq)$ (Colourless)

(ii) $Hg^{2+}(aq) + 2Co(SCN)_2(aq) \longrightarrow Co[Hg(SCN)_4] \downarrow (s) + Co^{2+}$ (Deep blue ppt.)

2. (c) $\Delta_{hyd}H(AlCl_3) = -4665 + 3 \times (-381)$

$= -5808$ kJ mol^{-1}

Now, $|\Delta_{hyd}H| > \Sigma$ IE (5137 kJ mol^{-1})

So, $AlCl_3$ would remain ionic in aqueous solution.

$AlCl_3(g) + 6H_2O(l) \longrightarrow [Al(H_2O)_3]^{3+}(aq) + 3Cl^-(aq)$

3. (b) For gas A,

$$C_V^A = \frac{3R}{2} + \frac{3R}{2} + 6R = 9R$$

$\Rightarrow$ Heat lost by gas $A = nC_V\, dT$

$$= 7 \times 9R \times \left(T - \frac{5T}{6}\right)$$

$$= \frac{63R}{6} \times T = Q_1$$

Heat gained by gas

$$B = 6 \times C_V^B \times \left(\frac{5T}{6} - \frac{T}{3}\right)$$

$$= 3 \times C_V^B \times T = Q_2$$

Now, $Q_1 = Q_2$

$$\therefore \frac{63R}{6} \times T = 3 \times C_V^B \times T$$

$$\Rightarrow C_V^B = C_V \text{ of gas } B = \frac{7R}{2}$$

Hence, the gas B is diatomic.

4. (c) (i) $Cu^{2+} + e^- \longrightarrow Cu^+$;

$\Delta G_1^\circ = -1 \times F \times E_1^\circ = -Fx_1$

(ii) $In^{3+} + 2e^- \longrightarrow In^+$; $\Delta G_2^\circ = -2 \times F \times E_2^\circ = -2\,Fx_2$

(iii) $In^{2+} + e^- \longrightarrow In^+; \Delta G_3^\circ = -1 \times F \times E_3^\circ = -Fx_3$

For the reaction,

$In^{2+} + Cu^{2+} \longrightarrow In^{3+} + Cu^+ \ (n=1)$

$$\Delta G^\circ = \Delta G_1^\circ + \Delta G_3^\circ - \Delta G_2^\circ$$

$$\Rightarrow -1 \times F \times E_3^\circ = -Fx_1 - Fx_3 - (-2Fx_2)$$

$$\Rightarrow E_3^\circ = (x_1 + x_3 - 2x_2)V$$

5. (b) The acidic strength of an oxoacid depends on the inductive effect $(-I)$ of unprotonated oxygen atoms [O=P<].

If the number of unprotonated oxygen atoms increases, $-I$ effect also increases and hence the acidic strength will increase

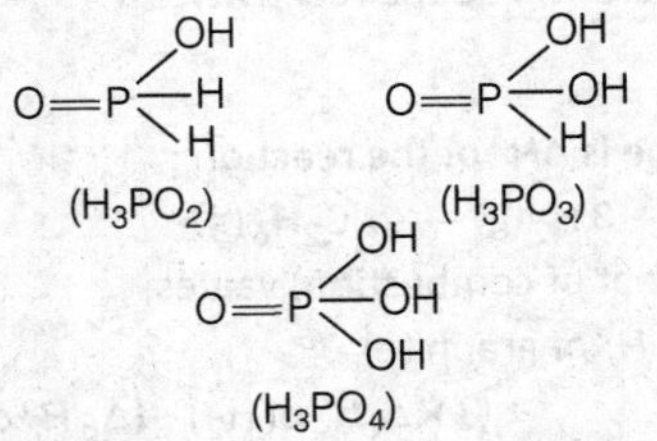

(H_3PO_2) (H_3PO_3) (H_3PO_4)

Since, all the three acids have the same number of unprotonated oxygen atoms, their acidic strength is also nearly same.

6. (c) $\left(p + \frac{a}{V^2}\right)(V - b) = RT$

At high pressure, pressure correction is neglected

$$\therefore \quad p(V-b) = RT$$

$$pV - pb = RT$$

$$\Rightarrow \frac{pV}{RT} - \frac{pb}{RT} = 1$$

$$\Rightarrow Z = 1 + \frac{pb}{RT}$$

7. (b) Aqueous solution of $CuSO_4$ is acidic.

$CuSO_4 + 2H_2O \rightleftharpoons Cu(OH)_2 + H_2SO_4$ In acidic medium, chromate salt changes into dichromate salt.

CrO_4^{2-} (Chromate) $\xrightarrow[(H_2SO_4)]{H^+}$ $Cr_2O_7^{2-}$ (Dichromate)

$CrO_4^{2-} \xrightarrow{Cu^{2+}} CuCrO_4$ Copper (II) chromate

$Cr_2O_7^{2-} \xrightarrow{Cu^{2+}} CuCr_2O_7$ Copper (II) dichromate

8. (b)

(a) The compound (III) undergoes inversion of configuration due to presence of chiral carbon atom.

(b) The order of reactivity for I, II and IV is II > IV > I according to stability of carbocation.

(c) I and III will follow S_N2 mechanism because both of the compounds contains primary carbon.

(d) I and IV follow S_N2 mechanism because they will form most stable carbocation.

9. (b)

(i) Cyclohexanone + H–N(pyrrolidine) → ; Δ, $-H_2O$; $-H^\oplus$ → (A)

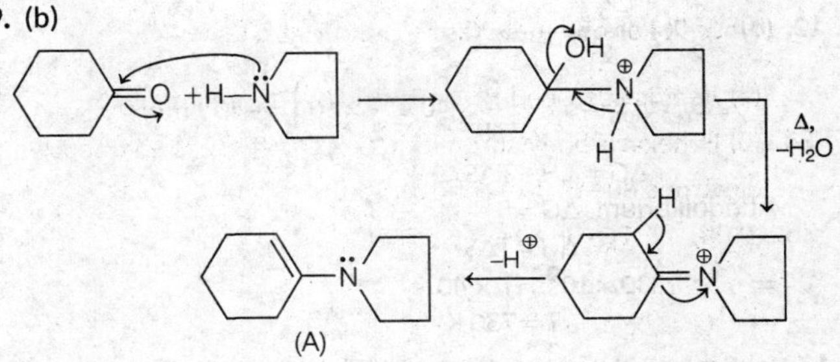

(ii) (D) + $CH_2{=}CH{-}\overset{O}{\overset{||}{C}}{-}CH_3$ —Michael reaction→ ; $\xleftarrow{H_3O^+}$ $CH_2{-}CH_2{-}\overset{}{C}{-}CH_3$ (numbered 4, 3, 2, 1; ring carbons 5, 6) ; $CH_2{-}CH{=}C(O^-){-}CH_3$

$\xrightarrow[\text{(Robinson annulation)}]{OH^- \text{ Intramolecular (1,6) aldol reaction}}$ (C)

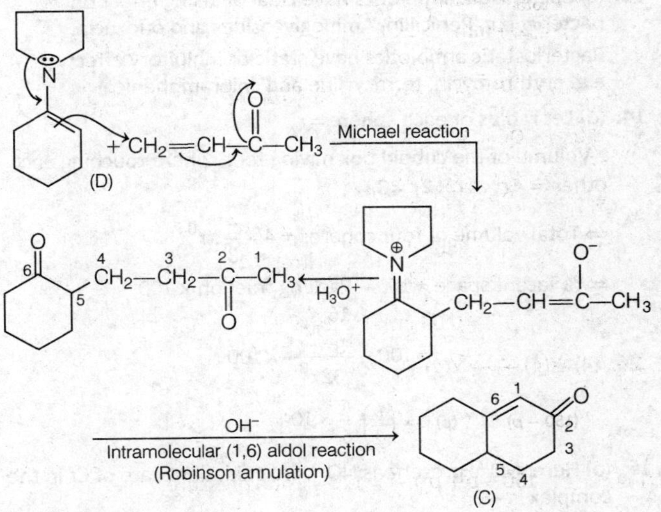

10. (d)

OTs ; $\xrightarrow[-H_2]{NaH}$ OTs (good leaving group) ; $O^\ominus Na^\oplus$; (Acidic H -atom) ; – TsONa ; CH_3 ; (Option -d)

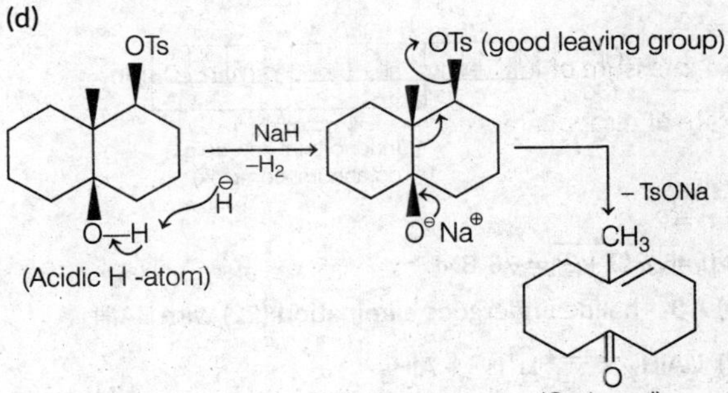

11. (c) Na (*R*), Al(*Q*) and P(*P*) belong to the third period and the decreasing order of radius and electronegativity as,

Radius : Na > Al > P

Electronegativity : P > Al > Na

Na and Al are metals and P is non-metal

Hydroxy compounds of,

P(P) is H_3PO_4 : acidic, pH < 7
(*A*)

Q(Al) is $Al(OH)_3$: amphoteric
(*B*)

R(Na) in NaOH : basic, pH > 7
(*C*)

12. (d) $\frac{1}{2}X_2 + \frac{3}{2}Y_2 \longrightarrow XY_3$

$$\Delta S_{reaction} = 50 - \left(\frac{3}{2}\times 40 + \frac{1}{2}\times 60\right) = -40 \text{ J mol}^{-1}$$

$$\Delta G = \Delta H - T\Delta S$$

At equilibrium, $\Delta G = 0$

$$\Delta H = T\Delta S$$

$\Rightarrow$ $30 \times 10^3 = T \times 40$

$\Rightarrow$ $T = 750$ K

13. (c) Bactericidal antibiotics have cidal or killing effect on bacteria, e.g. Penicillin, Aminoglycosides and ofloxacin.

Bacteriostatic antibiotics have static or inhibitory effect, e.g. erythromycin, tetracycline and chloramphenicol.

14. (d) Let radius of each sphere $= r$

$\therefore$ Volume of the cuboid box having four sphere touching each other $= 4r \times 4r \times 2r = 32r^3$

$\Rightarrow$ Total volume of four spheres $= 4 \times \frac{4}{3}\pi r^3$

$\Rightarrow$ % vacant space $= 100 -$ Packing fraction $\times 100$

$$= 100 - \frac{\frac{16}{3}\pi r^3}{32r^3} \times 100$$

$$= 100 - \frac{\pi}{6} \times 100$$

15. (a) Here, NO is present as NO^+. So, oxidation state of Cr in the complex is + 2.

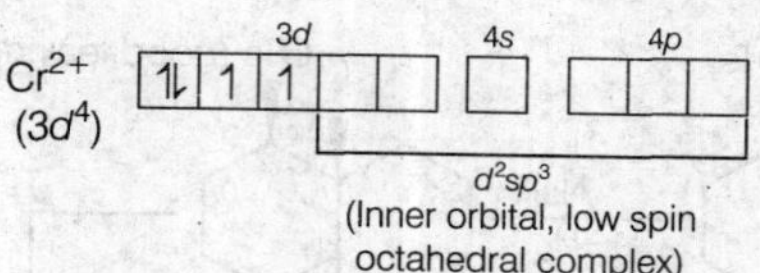

$\therefore$ $n = 2$

$\Rightarrow \mu = \sqrt{2(2+2)} = \sqrt{8}$ BM

16. (b) A 3°- halide undergoes elimination (E2) with $LiAlH_4$.

(i) $LiAlH_4 \rightleftharpoons Li^+H^- + AlH_3$

(ii) $(CH_3)_2\overset{3°}{C}-Cl$ (*tert*-butyl chloride) with $CH_2-H^- Li^+$ $\xrightarrow{-H_2, Cl^-}$ $(CH_3)_2C{=}CH_2$ (Isobutylene) (*X*)

Ph_3SnH, i.e. TPH selectively reduces alkyl halide (1°/2°/3°) but does not reduce $C{=}C$ and $C{\equiv}C$.

$$\underset{\text{(1-chloro-but-2-ene)}}{CH_3-CH{=}CH-CH_2Cl} \xrightarrow{Ph_3SnH} \underset{\text{(But-2-ene) (Y)}}{CH_3-CH{=}CH-CH_3\,(Y)}$$

17. (c) Assertion is true but Reason is false. Sucrose is formed by linkage of C_1 of α – D-glucose and C_2 of β – D-fructose.

18. (b) Given the rate determining step

$$\text{Rate} = k[NOBr_2][NO] \quad \text{... (i)}$$

$$K_{eq} = \frac{[NOBr_2]}{[NO][Br_2]}$$

$\therefore$ $[NOBr_2] = K_{eq}[NO][Br_2]$

Substitute value in Eq. (i)

$\Rightarrow$ Rate $\propto [NO]^2[Br]^1$

$\therefore$ Order is 2.

19. (a) The correct match of the ores and their chemical formula is :

A $\rightarrow$ 3, B $\rightarrow$ 4, C $\rightarrow$ 2, D $\rightarrow$ 1

20. (c) (i) The given order is true because boiling point of alkanes increases with increase in molecular mass and decreases with branching.

(ii) The correct order is HI > HBr > HCl. As the size of halogen increases, the strength of H—*X* bond decreases and hence, the reactivity increases.

(iii) The given order is true because it is based on the fact that more the number of β-substituents (alkyl groups), more stable alkene will be formed on β-elimination and hence, more will be the reactivity.

21. (–192.50)

$\Delta_f H°$ of ethane is $\Delta H°$ of the reaction :

$2C(\text{graphite}) + 3H_2(g) \longrightarrow C_2H_6(g)$

From $\Delta_c H°$ (heat of combustion) values,

$\Delta_f H° = (2 \times \Delta_c H°$ of graphite)

$+ (3 \times \Delta_c H°$ of $H_2) - (\Delta_c H°$ of $C_2H_6)$

$= (-2 \times 286) + (-393.5 \times 3) - (-1560)$ kJ mol^{-1}

$= -192.50$ kJ mol^{-1}

22. (0.29)

	A (ccp)	:	*B* (octahedral = ec + bc) void	:	*C* (50% TV)
After removal from two body diagonals	$[(8-4)\times\frac{1}{8} + (6-0)\times\frac{1}{2}]$	:	$[(12-0)\times\frac{1}{4} + (1-1)]$	:	$[\frac{1}{2}\times 8 - 2]$
$\Rightarrow$	$\frac{7}{2}$	:	3	:	2
$\Rightarrow$	7	:	6	:	4

$\Rightarrow$ $a = 7, b = 6, c = 4$

$\therefore$ $\frac{a}{bc} = \frac{7}{6\times 4} = 0.29$

23. (3.12) (i) $S + S^{2-} \rightleftharpoons S_2^{2-}$; $K_{C_1} = 1.7$

(ii) $2S + S^{2-} \rightleftharpoons S_3^{2-}$; $K_{C_2} = 5.3$

So, for the equilibrium, $S_2^{2-} + S \rightleftharpoons S_3^{2-}$

$$K_C = \frac{K_{C_2}}{K_{C_1}} = \frac{5.3}{1.7} = 3.117 \simeq 3.12$$

24. (63.57) $\lambda = \frac{h}{mv} = \frac{h}{\sqrt{2m \times KE}} = \frac{h}{\sqrt{2m \times e \times V}}$

$$V = \frac{h^2}{\lambda^2} \times \frac{1}{2 \times m \times e}$$

$$= \frac{(6.626\times 10^{-34})^2}{(1.54\times 10^{-10})^2 \times 2 \times (9.1\times 10^{-31}) \times (1.6\times 10^{-19})} \text{ volt}$$

$= 63.57$ Volt $= x$ Volt

$\therefore$ $x = 63.57$

25. (6) Total number of bonds of the decapeptide to be hydrolysed $= 10 - 1 = 9$ per molecule

$\therefore$ Total weight of H_2O added $= 9 \times 18 = 162$ g

Total weight of hydrolysed product $= 796 + 162 = 958$ g

$\therefore$ Total weight of glycine obtained $= 958 \times \frac{47}{100} = 450.26$ g

$\Rightarrow$ Number of glycine molecule in the protein $= \frac{450.26}{75} = 6$

26. (3.87)

$Cr(NH_3)_4Cl_2Br$ —
- $[Cr(NH_3)_4(Br)Cl]Cl \xrightarrow{AgNO_3} AgCl$ (White ppt.) (X)
- $[Cr(NH_3)_4Cl_2]Br \xrightarrow{AgNO_3} AgBr$ (Pale yellow ppt.) (Y)

In (X) or (Y), Cr(III) is d^2sp^3-hybridised having 3 unpaired electrons (n).

$Cr^{3+}(3d^3) \Rightarrow$ [3d: 1 1 1 _ _][4s: _][4p: _ _ _] ($3d^3$, $4s^0$, $4p^0$; d^2sp^3)

$\mu = \sqrt{n(n+2)}$

$= \sqrt{3(3+2)}$ BM

$= 3.87$ BM

27. (30.94) $n(CH_2{=}CH_2) + n(CH_2{=}CHCl) \longrightarrow$

Ethene (Chloroethene)

$-\!\!\left[CH_2 - CH_2 - CH_2 - \underset{Cl}{\underset{|}{CH}}\right]\!\!-_n$

Mol. wt. of $C_2H_4 = 28$, $C_2H_3Cl = 62.5$

$\Rightarrow$ Empirical formula mass of the copolymer

$= (28 + 62.5) = 90.5$

% vinyl chloride (C_2H_3Cl) $= \frac{28}{90.5} \times 100 = 30.94$

28. (50)

NH_3 (N with lone pair, bonded to three H)

Total no. of repulsions,

$bp - bp = 3$

$lp - bp = 3$

$lp - lp = 0$

$\Rightarrow \%\ lp - bp$ repulsion $= \frac{3}{6} \times 100 = 50 = a$

$\therefore \quad a = 50$

29. (−2) In borax ($Na_2B_4O_7 \cdot 10H_2O$), $2sp^3$ boron atoms are present.

$\therefore \quad x = 2$

In diborane (B_2H_6), $2sp^3$ boron atoms are present.

$\therefore \quad y = 2$

In BCl_3, no sp^3 boron atoms are present.

$\therefore \quad z = 0$

$(yz - x) = 2 \times 0 - 2 = -2$

30. (4)

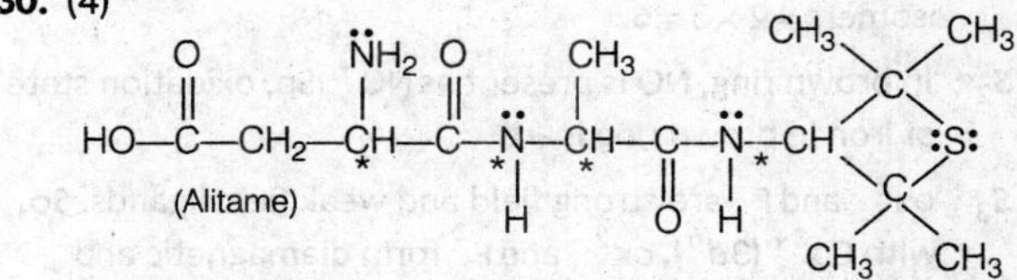

Total no. of chiral centres,

Carbon (C^*) $= 2$

Nitrogen (N^*) $= 2$ Total $= 4$

Knockout 06

1. (b) Anode : $Ag(s) \longrightarrow Ag^+(aq) + e^-$

Cathode : $Ag^+(aq) + e^- \longrightarrow Ag$

Net reaction : $Ag^+(AgBr) \longrightarrow Ag^+(Ag_2CO_3)$

It is an electrolyte concentration cell ($E° = 0$).

At equilibrium ($E = 0$).

$$0 = 0 + \frac{0.059}{1} \log \frac{(K_{sp}(AgBr)/[Br^-])}{[K_{sp}(Ag_2CO_3)/[CO_3^{2-}]]^{1/2}}$$

$$\Rightarrow \frac{K_{sp}(AgBr)}{[Br^-]} = \left(\frac{K_{sp}(Ag_2CO_3)}{[CO_3^{2-}]}\right)^{\frac{1}{2}}$$

$$\Rightarrow \frac{[Br^-]}{([CO_3^{2-}])^{1/2}} = \frac{K_{sp}(AgBr)}{(K_{sp}(Ag_2CO_3))^{1/2}}$$

$$= \frac{4 \times 10^{-13}\ M^2}{(8 \times 10^{-12}\ M^3)^{1/2}}$$

$$= \sqrt{2} \times 10^{-7}\ M^{1/2},$$

2. (a) pH of $NaHCO_3 = \frac{pK_{a_1} + pK_{a_2}}{2} = \frac{7 + 11}{2} = 9$ (initial)

Now, $H^+ + HCO_3^- \longrightarrow H_2CO_3$

$\therefore$ Number of mmoles of HCl left

$= (100 \times 0.01) - 0.1 = 0.9$

$pH = -\log(9 \times 10^{-3}) = 3 - 2\log 3$ (final)

$\Rightarrow \quad \Delta pH = 9 - (3 - 2\log 3) = 6 + 2\log 3$

3. (d) Since, work done on the system is maximum in single stage compression, all other adiabatic points will fall between 1 and 2.

4. (d) (a) It is due to inert pair effect of heavier *p*-block elements.

(b) Example : $3H\overset{+3}{N}O_2 \longrightarrow H\overset{+5}{N}O_3 + 2\overset{+2}{N}O + H_2O$

(c) It is due to the presence of completely filled *d*-and/or *f*-orbitals in heavier elements.

r_{cov} (pm) : N = 70, P = 110, As = 120, Sb = 140, Bi = 150

5. (a) $S_1 \rightarrow T, S_2 \rightarrow F, S_3 \rightarrow F, S_4 \rightarrow T$

S_1 : A square planar complex of molecular formula M_{abcd} can give three geometrical isomers. Here, NO_2 and ONO show linkage isomerism. So, number of geometrical isomers $= 2 \times 3 = 6$.

S_2 : In brown ring, NO is present as NO^+. So, oxidation state of iron in brown ring is +1.

S_3 : ox^{2-} and F^- are strong field and weak field ligands. So, with Co^{3+} $(3d^6)$, ox^{2-} and F^- form diamagnetic and paramagnetic octahedral complexes respectively.

S_4 : Co(III) forms octahedral complex, $[Co(NH_3)_3Cl_3]$ which is a neutral complex and so it is non-conducting.

6. (b) (A) $BO(N_2) = \frac{10-4}{2} = 3$; $BO(N_2^+) = \frac{9-4}{2} = 2.5$

$\Rightarrow n = 0, \mu = 0$ $\Rightarrow n = 1, \mu \neq 0$

(B) $BO(O_2^+) = \frac{10-5}{2} = 2.5$; $BO(O_2^{2+}) = \frac{10-4}{2} = 3$

$\Rightarrow n = 1,\ \mu \neq 0$ $\Rightarrow n = 0,\ \mu = 0$

(C) $BO(B_2) = \frac{6-4}{2} = 1$; $BO(B_2^+) = \frac{5-4}{2} = 0.5$

$\Rightarrow n = 2, \mu_1 \neq 0$ $\Rightarrow n = 1, \mu_2 \neq 0\ (\mu_1 > \mu_2)$

(D) $BO(NO^-) = \frac{10-6}{2} = 2$; $BO(NO) = \frac{10-5}{2} = 2.5$

$\Rightarrow n = 2, \mu_1 \neq 0$ $n = 1, \mu_2 \neq 0\ (\mu_1 > \mu_2)$

7. (b) Out of four structures of *A* as given, only the structures of option-(a) and option-(b) will give a single alkene (*B*) on separate treatment with strong base (E2-elimination).

(i) A(C_5H_9Cl) $\xrightarrow[\text{(-HCl)}]{\text{Strong base (E2)}}$ cyclobutylidene $=CH_2$ (*B*) $[C_5H_8]$

(ii) CH_3–cyclobutyl–Cl $\xrightarrow[\text{(-HCl)}]{\text{Strong base (E2)}}$ CH_3–cyclobutene (*B*) $[C_5H_8]$

Between two structures of (*B*) [both decolourise red colour of Br_2/CCl_4], only the second one (obtained from option-b) will give ozonolysis product, *C* in which the number of carbon atoms remains unchanged, i.e. $C_5H_8O_2$ (*C*).

CH_3–cyclobutene $\xrightarrow[\text{(ii) Zn/H}_2\text{O}]{\text{(i) O}_3\text{/THF}}$ CH_3–CH(CHO)–CH_2–CHO ($C_5H_8O_2$)

but methylenecyclobutane $\xrightarrow[\text{(ii) Zn/H}_2\text{O}]{\text{(i) O}_3\text{/THF}}$ cyclobutanone (C_4H_6O) + $CH_2{=}O$

So, option-(b) is the correct structure of *A*.

8. (c)

(Tetrahydrofuran-2-yl)CH_2OH $\xrightarrow[\text{Py, }\Delta]{SOCl_2}$ (Tetrahydrofuran-2-yl)CH_2Cl $\xrightarrow[\text{ether}]{Mg}$ (Tetrahydrofuran-2-yl)$\overset{-}{C}H_2\overset{+}{Mg}Cl$

2,2-dimethyloxirane $\xrightarrow{H^\oplus}$ protonated epoxide (1°, 3°) $\xrightarrow{S_N1 \text{ solvolysis}}$ $CH_2(OH)$–$\overset{\oplus}{C}(CH_3)$–$CH_3$ [More stable (3°) carbocation]

(Tetrahydrofuran-2-yl)$\overset{\ominus}{C}H_2\overset{\oplus}{Mg}Cl$ [Grignard reagent (Nucleophile)] attacks the carbocation →

(Tetrahydrofuran-2-yl)CH_2–$C(CH_3)_2$–CH_2OH (Option-c)

9. (a) **Statement I** is true, because with increase in size of alkali metal ions down the group, electropositive or ionic nature of carbonate and bicarbonate salts also increase. Hence, their stability also increase down the group.

Statement II is also true, because degree of polarisation of smaller sized Li^+ is very high and hence, it can polarise larger CO_3^{2-} easily to give Li_2O and CO_2.

$Li_2CO_3 \longrightarrow Li_2O^{2-} + O{=}C{=}O$ or $Li_2O + CO_2$

10. (c) The correct match is $A \rightarrow 3, B \rightarrow 2, C \rightarrow 4, D \rightarrow 1$.

A. *o*-nitrophenol and *p*-nitrophenol can be separated by steam distillation as *p*-nitrophenol is not steam volatile due to presence of intermolecular hydrogen bonding, while *o*-nitrophenol is steam volatile due to presence of intramolecular hydrogen bonds.

B. Distillation is used to separate ether from toluene because they have large difference in boiling point, i.e. 75°C.

C. The purification of glycerol is carried out through vacuum distillation in an inert atmosphere.

D. As benzoic acid is sublimable volatile compound, it can be separated from benzaldehyde by sublimation.

11. (c) CH_3–CH(COOH)–$CH{=}CH_2$ (I)

$\Rightarrow$ liberates $\frac{1}{2}$ mole H_2, i.e. 11.2 L of $H_2(g)$ at STP.

$\Rightarrow$ effervescence of $CO_2(g)$ with $NaHCO_3(aq)$

$\Rightarrow$ decolouration of red colour of Br_2/H_2O

$$CH_3-\overset{CH_3}{\underset{CH_3}{\overset{|}{\underset{|}{C}}}}-OCH_3$$ ⇒ it does not have acidic H-atom and so does not react with metallic Na
(II)

$CH_3O-C\equiv C-H$ ⇒ acidity of H-atom of an 1-yne can be tested as,
(III)

$$\xrightarrow{Na} CH_3O-C\equiv \overset{-\,+}{CNa} + \frac{1}{2}H_2\uparrow$$

$$\xrightarrow[\text{reagent}]{\text{Tollen's}} CH_3O-C\equiv CAg\downarrow \text{ (white ppt.)}$$

–ve test with Lucas reagent (no —OH group)

–ve test with 2,4-DNP (no $>C=O$ group)

$$CH_3-\overset{CH_3}{\underset{OH}{\overset{|}{\underset{|}{C}}}}-CH_2-OCH_3$$ ⇒ can give white turbidity with anhyd. $ZnCl_2$ and conc. HCl
(IV)

12. (b)

	$CO(g)$ +	$NO_2(g)$ ⇌	$CO_2(g)$ +	$NO(g)$
$t=0$	1	1	1	1
$t=t_{eq}$	$1-x$	$1-x$	$1+x$	$1+x$

$$\Rightarrow \underset{1\text{ mol}}{CO_2} + Ba(OH)_2 \longrightarrow \underset{1\text{ mol}}{BaCO_3\downarrow} + H_2O$$

$$\frac{236.4}{197} = 1.2 \text{ mol}$$

(At equilibrium)

$$\Rightarrow 1+x=1.2 \Rightarrow x=0.2$$

$$\Rightarrow K_C = \frac{(1+x)^2}{(1-x)^2} = \frac{1.2^2}{0.8^2} = 2.25$$

13. (a) (i) Rate constant

$$\frac{\text{1st order reaction}}{k_1} < \frac{\text{2nd order reaction}}{k_2}$$

where, $k_1 < k_2$ at a given temperature.

(ii) E_1 = Activation energy for first order

E_2 = Activation energy for second order

where, $E_1 > E_2$

So, according to van't Hoff isotherm equation,

$$\frac{d(\ln k)}{dT} = \frac{E_a}{RT^2}$$

→ E_a does not change with temperature.

→ k increases with temperature whereas, k_1 will increase faster than k_2 as,

$k \propto$ temperature and $E_a \propto \frac{1}{k}$ and according to steady-state-approximation, k_1 will always remain lower than k_2.

14. (a) Number of unpaired electrons in the compound $[MnCl_4]^{2-}$, $[CoCl_4]^{2-}$ and $[Fe(CN)_6]^{4-}$ are 5, 3 and 0 respectively.

As number of unpaired electrons increases, the magnetic moment values also increases.

15. (b) For di-substituted chair conformations of cyclohexane, its geometrical isomers (configurational) are given as,

	(1, 2) or (1, 4)	(1, 3)
trans :	*aa* and *ee*	*ae*
cis :	*ae*	*aa* and *ce*
	II : *ee* → *trans*	I : *ee* → *cis*
	III : *ae* → *cis*	V : *ee* → *cis*
	IV : *ee* → *trans*	VI : *ae* → *trans*

[*a* : axial substituent, *e* : equatorial substituent]

16. (c) $-\frac{dV}{dt} = kS = k(4\pi r^2) = k'r^2$ $[\because k' = 4\pi k]$

$$= k'\left(\frac{3V}{4\pi}\right)^{2/3} \qquad \left[\because V = \frac{4}{3}\pi r^3\right]$$

$$\Rightarrow -\frac{dV}{dt} = k''(V)^{2/3} \qquad \left[\because k'' = k' \times \left(\frac{3}{4\pi}\right)^{2/3}\right]$$

∴ Order of the reaction is 2/3.

17. (b) (A) $NH_4NO_2(s) \xrightarrow{\Delta} N_2\uparrow(g) + 2H_2O(g)$

(B) $2NH_4ClO_4(s) \xrightarrow{\Delta} N_2\uparrow(g) + 2O_2(g) + Cl_2(g) + 4H_2O(g)$

(C) $2NH_4IO_3(s) \xrightarrow{\Delta} N_2\uparrow(g) - O_2(g) + I_2(g) + 4H_2O$

(D) $(NH_4)_2Cr_2O_7(s) \xrightarrow{\Delta} Cr_2O_3(s) + N_2\uparrow(g) + 4H_2O(g)$

18. (b)

$CH_3O-C_6H_4-C(OH)(C_6H_4-CH_3)-CH(NH_2)-CH_3$

$\downarrow$ $NaNO_2/HCl/5°C$ [Diazotisation of 1°-amine]

$CH_3O-C_6H_4-C(OH)(C_6H_4-CH_3)-CH(\overset{\oplus}{N_2}\overset{\ominus}{Cl})-CH_3$

$\downarrow -N_2$

CH_3

$\overset{+R}{CH_3O}$ — C$_6$H$_4$ — $\overset{+}{C}$—CH_2—CH_3 (OH)

Rearrangement

CH_3—C$_6$H$_4$—$\overset{\oplus}{C}$(:$\ddot{O}$—H)—CH—CH_3 (C$_6$H$_4$—OCH_3)

$\downarrow -H^+$

CH_3—C$_6$H$_4$—C(=O)—CH(CH_3)—C$_6$H$_4$—OCH_3

(Option-b)

19. (c) $\underset{\text{(Fluoroapatite)}}{3Ca_3(PO_4)_2 \cdot CaF_2} + \underset{\text{Orthophosphoric acid}}{14H_3PO_4} \longrightarrow 10\,Ca(H_2PO_4)_2 + 2HF$

20. (b) $n_1 = 1$ (ground state)

$n_2 = 5$ th excited state $= 5 + 1 = 6$ (max.)

Total number of spectral lines

$$= \frac{(n_2 - n_1)(n_2 - n_1 + 1)}{2}$$

$$= \frac{(6-1)(6-1+1)}{2} = \frac{5 \times 6}{2} = 15$$

21. (3.55) $Pb^{2+} + 2e^- \longrightarrow Pb$

$$E = E° - \frac{0.059}{2} \log \frac{1}{[Pb^{2+}]} = -0.126 - \frac{0.059}{2} \log \frac{1}{0.1}$$

$$= -0.1555\text{ V}$$

$$E_{cell} = E_{Pb^{2+}/Pb} - E_{Tl^+/Tl}$$

$$E_{Tl^+/Tl} = E_{Pb^{2+}/Pb} - E_{cell}$$

$$= -0.1555 - 0.443 = -0.5985\text{ V}$$

$Tl^+ + e^- \longrightarrow Tl$

$$E = E° - \frac{0.059}{1} \log \frac{1}{[Tl^+]}$$

$$= E° + 0.059 \log [Tl^+]$$

$$\log [Tl^+] = \frac{E - E°}{0.059}$$

$$= \frac{-0.5985 + 0.336}{0.059} = -4.449$$

$$[Tl^+] = 3.55 \times 10^{-5}\text{ M}$$

$$K_{sp}\,(TlBr) = [Tl^+]\,[Br]^-$$

$$= (3.55 \times 10^{-5}) \times 0.1\text{ M}^2$$

$$= 3.55 \times 10^{-6}\text{ M}^2$$

$$= x \times 10^{-6}\text{ M}^2$$

$\therefore \quad x = 3.55$

22. (0.30)

$$\underset{\underset{-}{1\,M}}{H_2SO_4} \xrightarrow{K_{a_1} \to \alpha} \underset{\underset{1\,M}{0}}{H^+} + \underset{\underset{1\,M}{0}}{HSO_4^-}$$

$$\underset{\underset{1-x}{1\,M}}{HSO_4^-} \xrightarrow{K_{a_2}} \underset{\underset{1+x}{1\,M}}{H^+} + \underset{\underset{x}{0}}{SO_4^{2-}}$$

$\Rightarrow$ Total moles $= 1 - x + 1 + x + x = 2 + x$

$$\pi = CRT$$

$\Rightarrow 90.2 = (2 + x) \times 0.082 \times 500$

$\Rightarrow \quad x = 0.2$

$$K_{a_1} = \frac{[H^+]\,[SO_4^{2-}]}{[HSO_4^-]} = \frac{(1 + 0.2) \times 0.2}{(1 - 0.2)}$$

$$= 0.30$$

23. (80.65)

$\Rightarrow \quad \Delta H = E_a^f - E_a^b$

$\therefore \quad E_a^f = \Delta H + E_a^b$

$$= (0.12 + 0.02) = 0.14\text{ kcal mol}^{-1}$$

Percentage of reactant molecules crossing over the energy barrier

$$= 100 \times e^{-E_a^f/RT}$$

$$= 100 \times e^{-\frac{0.14 \times 10^3}{2 \times 325}}$$

$$= 100 \times 0.8065 = 80.65\%$$

24. (1.75) Let, number of millimoles of $Fe_2(SO_4)_3 = a$, $FeC_2O_4 = b$

As, $Fe_2(SO_4)_3$ is not oxidisable,

$\Rightarrow b \times 3 = 40 \times \frac{1}{16}$ $\left[\because \overset{+2}{Fe}\overset{+3}{C_2}O_4 \xrightarrow{[O]} Fe^{3+} + \overset{+4}{C}O_2 \quad \text{n-factor} = 1 + 2 = 3\right]$

$\therefore \quad b = \frac{40}{48}$

After reduction, $(2a + b)$ millimoles of Fe^{2+} get oxidised by 60 mL $\frac{N}{16}$ $KMnO_4$

$(2a + b) \times 1 = 60 \times \frac{1}{16}$ $\quad [\because Fe^{2+} \to Fe^{3+}]$

$$n_f = 1$$

$\therefore \quad a = \left(\frac{60}{16} - \frac{40}{48}\right) \times \frac{1}{2} = \frac{70}{48}$

$\Rightarrow \quad a : b = \frac{70}{48} : \frac{40}{48} \Rightarrow \frac{7}{4} \Rightarrow 1.75$

25. (1.58) $\text{pH} = 7 - \frac{1}{2}(pK_b + \log c)$

[$\because$ ACl is a salt of weak base (AOH) and strong acid (HCl)]

$\Rightarrow 4.85 = 7 - \frac{1}{2}(4.7 + \log c)$

$\Rightarrow \log c = -0.4$

$\Rightarrow \quad c = 0.4\,M$

Molar mass of ACl = M' (say)

$\Rightarrow \quad 0.4 = \dfrac{5.35}{M'} \times \dfrac{1000}{250}$

$\Rightarrow \quad M' = 53.5\,g\,mol^{-1}$

Now, $\quad d = \dfrac{Z \times M'}{a^3 \times N_A}$

$\Rightarrow \quad a = \left(\dfrac{Z \times M'}{d \times N_A}\right)^{1/3} \qquad [\because Z \text{ of CsCl structure} = 2]$

$= \left(\dfrac{2 \times 53.5}{2.2 \times 6.023 \times 10^{23}}\right)^{1/3}$ cm

$= 4.32 \times 10^{-8}$ cm

$= 4.32$ Å

For CsCl type of lattice,

$2(r_{A^+} + r_{Cl^-}) = \sqrt{3} \times a \qquad \left[\because r_{Cl} = \dfrac{r_{A^+}}{0.731}\right]$

$\Rightarrow \left\{2\left(r_{A^+} + \dfrac{r_{A^+}}{0.731}\right)\right\} = \sqrt{3} \times 4.32$

$\Rightarrow \quad 2 \times \dfrac{1.731}{0.731} \times r_{A^+} = \sqrt{3} \times 4.32$

$\Rightarrow \quad r_{A^+} = 1.579\,Å \simeq 1.58\,Å$

26. (155.25) $6\overset{+4}{Xe}F_4 + 12H_2O \longrightarrow 4\overset{0}{Xe} + 2\overset{+6}{Xe}O_3 + 24HF + 3O_2$

It is a disproportionation redox reaction.

$E_{XeF_4} = E^{\text{ox. agent}}_{XeF_4} + E^{\text{red. agent}}_{XeF_4}$

$= \dfrac{M}{(4-0)} + \dfrac{M}{6-4} = \dfrac{M}{4} + \dfrac{M}{2} = \dfrac{3M}{4}$

$= \dfrac{3 \times 207}{4} = 155.25 \quad [\text{Molar mass}, M = (131 + 4 \times 19 = 207)]$

NOTE XeF_4 reacts with water in a very fast manner to give Xe, XeO_3, HF and O_2. So, like most of the solutes, it is not a simple mixture of XeF_4 and water.

27. (1) Ester in presence of aqueous KOH solution gives following reaction.

Furanose (HOH_2C, CH_2OH, OH, OH, $O-\overset{O}{\overset{\|}{C}}-Me$) $\xrightarrow{Aq.\ KOH}$ Hemiketal ($HOCH_2$, CH_2OH, OH, OH, $O^{\ominus}$) + $Me-\overset{O}{\overset{\|}{C}}-O^{\ominus}$

Hemiketal → open chain ($HOCH_2$, $O^{\ominus}$, CH_2OH, C=O, OH, OH) $\xrightarrow{\text{Tollen's reagent}}$ Positive silver mirror test

28. (1.67)

1-methyl cyclohexene $\xrightarrow[2.\ Zn/H_2O]{1.\ O_3/THF}$ $\overset{7}{CH_3}-\overset{O}{\overset{\|}{\underset{6}{C}}}-\overset{5}{CH_2}-\overset{4}{CH_2}-\overset{3}{CH_2}-\overset{2}{CH_2}-\overset{1}{CH}=O$

$\xrightarrow{\text{Dil. }OH^-\ \text{(Aldol condensation)}}$ three products: (1,7), (1,5), (2,6)

$\Rightarrow x = 3$

$\underset{\text{(Methanal)}}{HCHO} + \underset{\text{(Benzaldehyde)}}{PhCHO}$ (No α-H atom) $\xrightarrow[\text{(Cannizzaro reaction)}]{\text{Conc. }OH^-}$ $HCOO^- + PhCH_2OH\ [y = 2]$

1,2-dimethyl cyclohexene $\xrightarrow{m\text{-CPBA}}$ epoxide (Me, Me) $\Rightarrow z = 1$

$\Rightarrow \quad \dfrac{3y - z}{x} = \dfrac{3 \times 2 - 1}{3} = 1.67$

29. (11.5) According to Raoult's law,

$p_t = p^\circ_X x_X + p^\circ_Y x_Y$

In case of equimolar binary solution of X and Y,

$50 = p^\circ_X \times \dfrac{1}{2} + p^\circ_Y \times \dfrac{1}{2}$

$\Rightarrow \quad p^\circ_X + p^\circ_Y = 100$

$\Rightarrow \quad p^\circ_Y = 100 - p^\circ_X$

$\Rightarrow \quad p^\circ_Y = 100 - 20$

$= 80$ torr

Now, a new solution has total vapour pressure of 25 torr.

$25 = 20 \times x_X + 80 \times x_Y$

As $\quad x_X + x_Y = 1$

$\Rightarrow \quad x_Y = 1 - x_X$

$\Rightarrow \quad 25 = 20 \times x_X + 80(1 - x_X)$

$\Rightarrow \quad x_X = 0.92$

$\Rightarrow \quad x_Y = 0.08$

So, $\quad \dfrac{x_X}{x_Y} = \dfrac{0.92}{0.08} = 11.5$

30. (0.75)

(i) $\underset{1\text{ mol}}{M(g)} \underset{+\ 600\text{ kJ mol}^{-1}}{\xrightarrow{IE_1/-e}} \underset{1\text{ mol}}{M^+(g)}$

So, from 1000 kJ amount of heat, 600 kJ of heat is used up for complete conversion of 1 mole of $M(g)$ into 1 mole of $M^+(g)$.

(ii) $M^+(g) \xrightarrow{IE_2/-e} M^{2+}(g)$

For this conversion, only $\dfrac{(1000-600)\text{ kJ}}{1600\text{ kJ mol}^{-1}\ (IE_2)}$

i.e. $\dfrac{400}{1600} = 0.25$ mole of $M^+(g)$ will be converted into 0.25 mole of M^{2+} and $(1-0.25)$ mole $= 0.75$ mole of M^+ will remain unoxidised.

Knockout 07

1. (c) In ccp, anions occupy primitives of the cube, while cations occupy voids. In ccp, there are two tetrahedral voids and one octahedral hole.

For one oxygen atom, there are two tetrahedral holes and one octahedral hole.

Since, one fifth of the tetrahedral voids are occupied by divalent cations (X^{2+}), number of divalent cations in tetrahedral voids $= 2 \times 1/5$

Since, half of the octahedral voids are occupied by trivalent cations (Y^{3+}), number of trivalent cations $= 1 \times 1/2$.

So, the formula of the compound is $X_{2/5}Y_{1/2}O$ or $X_4Y_5O_{10}$.

2. (c) Benzene is non-polar in nature. As we know that a non-polar molecule dissolves more in non-polar substances.

Therefore, metamethyl nonylbenzene being non-polar from both sides will disperse more to benzene. All other substances (a, b and d) have either one polar end or both sides polar end.

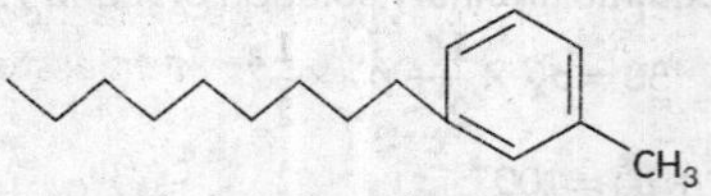

Non-polar end (Non-polar end) (Metamethyl nonylbenzene)

$\equiv H_{19}C_9-C_6H_4-CH_3$

3. (c) When strontium carbide (SrC_2) is treated with water, it produces alkyne.

$$SrC_2 \xrightarrow{H_2O} H-C\equiv C-H\ (A)$$

When 1, 2-dichloroethane is treated with $\overset{+\,-}{KO}$ but, it produces the alkyne, A.

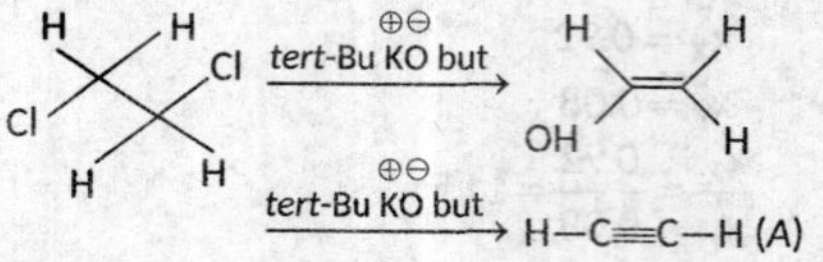

$$ClCH_2-CH_2Cl \xrightarrow{tert\text{-Bu}\overset{\oplus\ominus}{KO}\text{ but}} CH_2=CHCl \xrightarrow{tert\text{-Bu}\overset{\oplus\ominus}{KO}\text{ but}} H-C\equiv C-H\ (A)$$

Properties of alkyne (A)

(i) Since the alkyne prepared is ethyne. Hence, it is acidic due to attachment of hydrogen to *sp* hybridised carbon atom.

(ii) On reaction with OsO_4, it undergoes *cis*-hydroxylation as follows

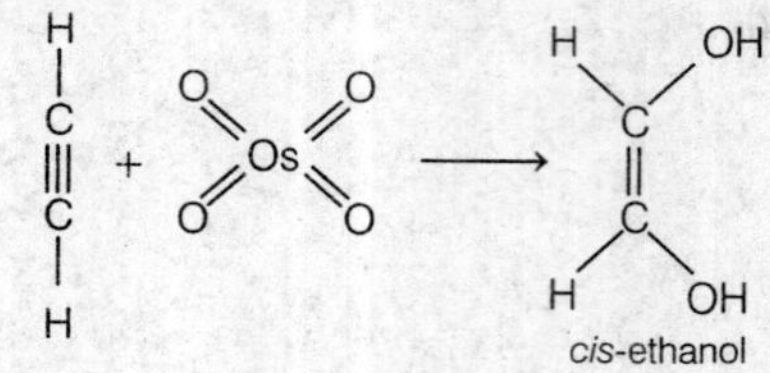

$$H-C\equiv C-H + OsO_4 \longrightarrow H(OH)C=C(OH)H$$

cis-ethanol

4. (c) When a chloride salt is heated with $K_2Cr_2O_7$ and conc. H_2SO_4, red vapours of CrO_2Cl_2 is obtained.

$$4Cl^- + Cr_2O_7^{2-} + 6H^+ \longrightarrow \underset{\text{Reddish brown}}{2CrO_2Cl_2} \uparrow + 3H_2O$$

$$CrO_2Cl_2 + OH^- \longrightarrow \underset{\text{Yellow solution}}{CrO_4^{2-}} + 2Cl^- + 2H_2O$$

While heating of a bromide salt with $K_2Cr_2O_7$ and H_2SO_4 instead of forming CrO_2Br_2, we get reddish brown fumes of Br_2.

$$6Br^- + Cr_2O_7^{2-} + H^+ \longrightarrow \underset{\text{Reddish brown}}{3Br_2} \uparrow + Cr^{3+} + 7H_2O$$

$$2NaOH + Br_2 \longrightarrow \underset{\text{Colourless}}{NaBr} + NaOBr + H_2O$$

5. (c) **Iodoform test** is given by the compound having at least $CH_3CH(OH)$ group or $CH_3-\underset{H}{C}=O$.

Since, the compound gives negative test, there must be absence of terminal methyl ketone or 2-ol group.

Reagent used in iodoform test $= \overset{\ominus}{O}X(X_2 + \overset{\ominus}{O}H)$

$$R-\overset{O}{\overset{\|}{C}}-CH_3 \xrightarrow{\overset{\ominus}{O}X} \text{+ve iodoform test}$$

$$R-\overset{O}{\overset{\|}{C}}-CH_2-CH_3 \xrightarrow{\overset{\ominus}{O}X} \text{–ve iodoform test}$$

Tollen's test is given by aldehyde not by ketone. Since compound gives negative Tollen's test, this confirms that there is absence of aldehyde group in the compound.

Aldehyde as well as ketone both gives the formation of phenyl hydrazone, when treated with phenyl hydrazine.

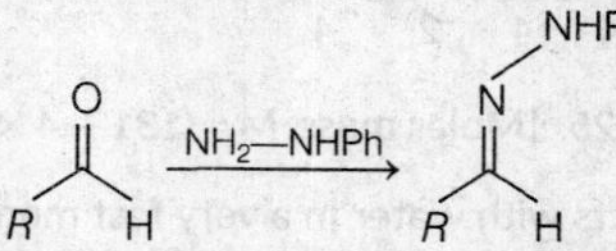

$$R(H)C=O \xrightarrow{NH_2-NHPh} R(H)C=N-NHPh$$

Based on the above observations, the molecule is a non-terminal carbonyl compound, i.e. a ketone.

The correct structure of the compound (A, $C_6H_{12}O$) is

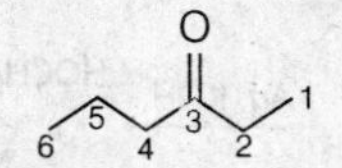

(hexan-3-one; carbons numbered 1 to 6)

6. (c) The structures of given compounds are as follows

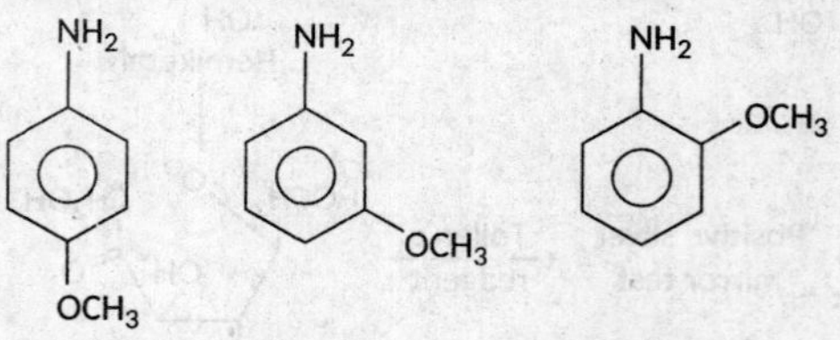

NH_2 / OCH_3 *para*-isomer, *meta*-isomer, *ortho*-isomer

According to the principle of *ortho*-effect, the basic strength of *ortho*-substituted aniline is more basic than other isomers due to the steric and electronic factors.

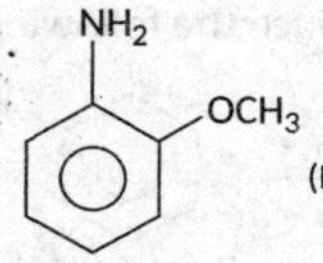

NH_2, OCH_3 (ortho-anisidine) (Maximum basic strength)

This occurrence in comparison to others is due to loss of planarity in *o*-substituted aniline. The correct order is,

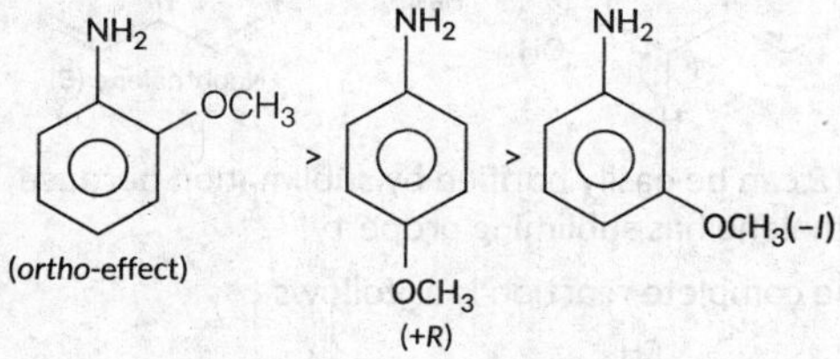

o-anisidine (*ortho*-effect) > p-anisidine (OCH_3 (+R)) > m-anisidine ($OCH_3(-I)$)

$-OCH_3$ group shows $+R$ effect at *p*-position, while at *m*-position it shows $-I$ effect. $+R$ effect (EDG) increases basicity but $-I$ effect decreases basicity.

7. (d) On mixing Na_2CO_3 and K_2CO_3 both will treat each other as impurity. Hence, causes decrease in melting point of mixture.

8. (b) Structure of pent-3-en-2-ol is,

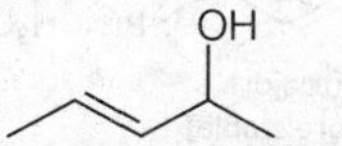

Jones reagent on treatment with allylic alcohol produces alkylic ketone. Jones reagent does not oxidise C=C double bond only oxidises the alcoholic group.

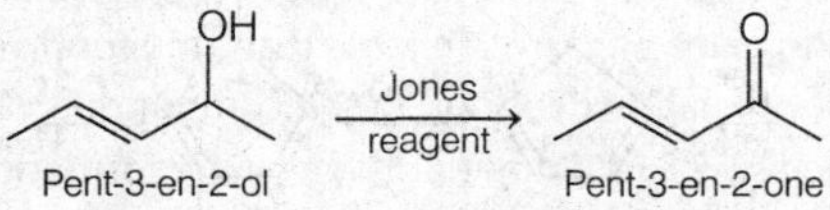

Pent-3-en-2-ol $\xrightarrow{\text{Jones reagent}}$ Pent-3-en-2-one

Jones reagent H_2CrO_4 is an aqueous solution of acetone.

9. (d) Statement (d) is correct, whereas statements (a), (b) and (c) are incorrect.

(a) Both Co^{2+} and Co^{3+} are stabilised in presence of strong field ligands due to higher CFSE values.

(b) Due to higher Z_{eff} values on the valence shell Pd^{2+} and Pt^{2+} cations always form inner orbital complex but are diamagnetic in nature.

(c) $[Ni(CO)_4]$; sp^3, tetrahedral and diamagnetic.

$[Ni(CN)_4]^{4-}$; dsp^2, square planar and diamagnetic.

(d) For Ni^{2+};

⥮	⥮	⥮	↿	↿

In octahedral field, electronic distribution remains unaffected and it always forms outer-orbital octahedral $[Ni(II) : sp^3d^2]$ paramagnetic complex.

10. (c) Complete reactions are as follows

I. $Na_2SO_3 + S \xrightarrow{\Delta} \underset{(A)}{Na_2S_2O_3}$

II. $\underset{(A)}{Na_2S_2O_3} + 2AgNO_3 \longrightarrow 2NaNO_3 + \underset{(B)}{Ag_2S_2O_3}$

III. $\underset{(B)}{Ag_2S_2O_3} + H_2O \longrightarrow \underset{(C)}{Ag_2S} + H_2SO_4$

11. (b) Reactions I and II produce novolac. Complete reactions are as follows

I. (Phenol) + HCHO (Formaldehyde) $\xrightarrow{\overset{\ominus}{O}H}$ n o-hydroxybenzyl alcohol (CH_2OH) → $[-C_6H_3(OH)-CH_2-C_6H_3(OH)-CH_2-]_n$

Linear polymer (Novolac)

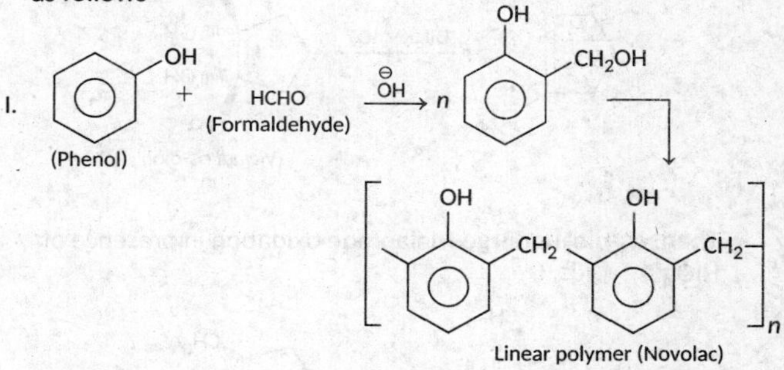

II. Benzene diazonium salt + hot H_2O + HCHO + base

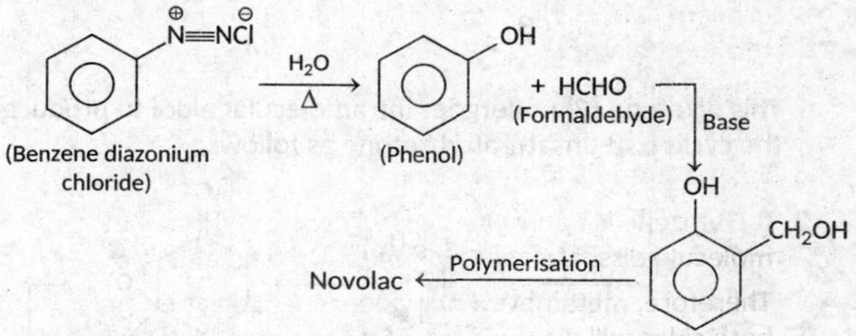

(Benzene diazonium chloride) $\xrightarrow[\Delta]{H_2O}$ (Phenol) + HCHO (Formaldehyde) $\xrightarrow{\text{Base}}$ o-hydroxybenzyl alcohol $\xrightarrow{\text{Polymerisation}}$ Novolac

Novolac is a linear polymer of formaldehyde and phenol.

12. (c) The given conversion is based on extraction of chromium from chromite ore using various sequential steps. These are as follows

Chromite $\xrightarrow[\text{Heat(fusion)}]{\text{NaOH/Air (I)}}$ Na_2CrO_4 $\xrightarrow[\text{Carbon reduction}]{C/\Delta\text{(II)}}$

$Cr_2O_3 \xrightarrow[\text{Aluminium reduction}]{Al/\Delta\text{(III)}} Cr$

13. (a) (i) **Elimination reaction**

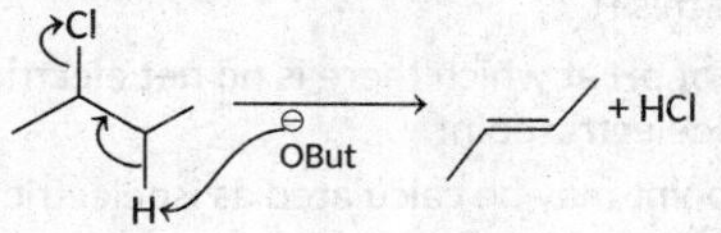

Alkyl chloride $\xrightarrow{\overset{\ominus}{O}But}$ alkene + HCl

(ii) **Substitution reaction**

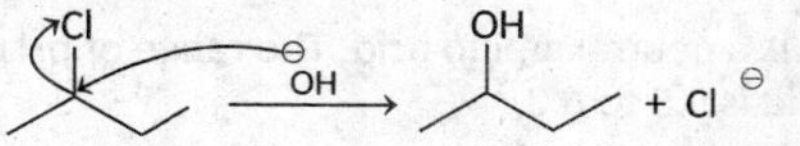

Alkyl chloride $\xrightarrow{\overset{\ominus}{O}H}$ alcohol + $Cl^{\ominus}$

(iii) **Addition reaction**

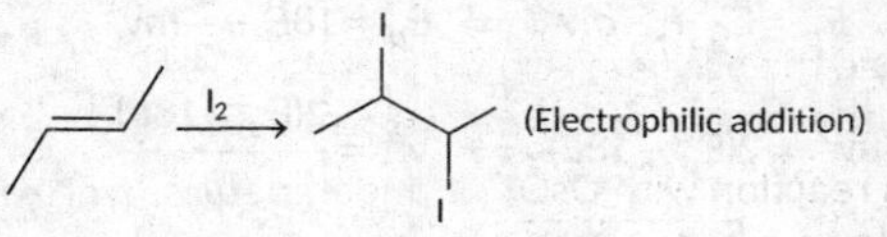

Alkene $\xrightarrow{I_2}$ diiodide (Electrophilic addition)

(iv) **Addition reaction**

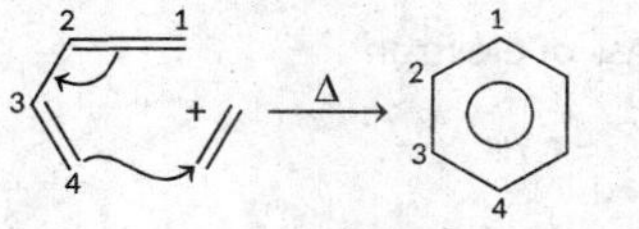

Butadiene + ethylene $\xrightarrow{\Delta}$ cyclohexene

(Diels-Alder 1, 4-addition)

14. (a) The alkene on treatment with cold and dilute alkaline $KMnO_4$ (Baeyer's reagent) produces *vicinal cis*-diol. This reaction is known as hydroxylation reaction.

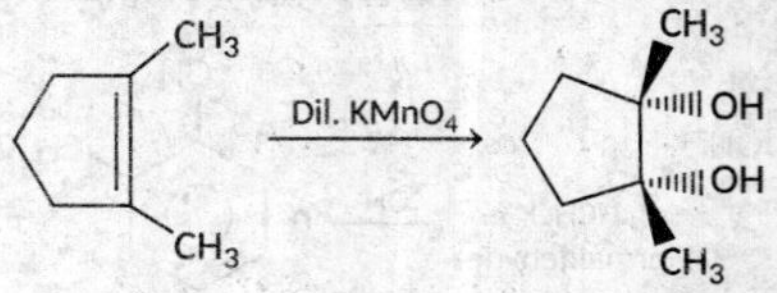

(*Vicinal cis*-diol) (*A*)

Then, *cis*-diol undergo Malaprade oxidation in presence of HIO_4.

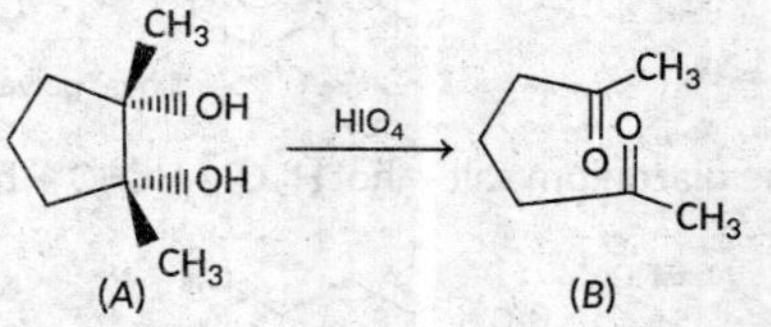

This diketone (*B*) undergoes intramolecular aldol to produce the cyclic α, β-unsaturated ketone as follows

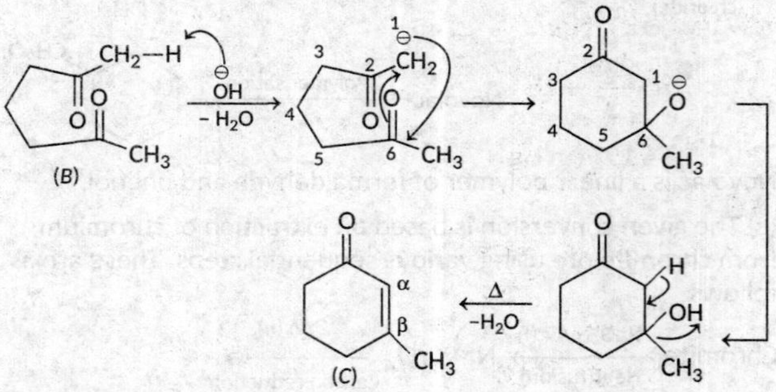

15. (a) Amino acid has two functional groups, i.e. carboxylic (COOH) and amino (NH_2), which means it has an acidic and a basic group. The acidic group looses its hydrogen and basic group gains this H^+.

The nature of pH at which there is no net electrical charge is known as isoelectric point.

Isoelectric point may be calculated as isoelectric pH

$$=\frac{pK_{a_1}+pK_{a_2}}{2}=\frac{9.00+3.30}{2}=6.15$$

Hence, it is a neutral amino acid. The range of pH of neutral amino acid is 5.5 to 6.3.

16. (d) Work function of $Li^{2+}=(-2E)\times 3^2=18E=E_0$

$$\Rightarrow \quad E_p=E_0+\frac{1}{2}mv^2 \Rightarrow E_p=18E+\frac{1}{2}mv^2$$

$$\Rightarrow \quad mv^2=2(E_p-18E) \Rightarrow v^2=\frac{2(E_p-18E)}{m}$$

$$\Rightarrow \quad v=\sqrt{\frac{2(E_p-18E)}{m}}$$

where, $m=$ mass of electron

17. (a) The given reactions will produce the following products

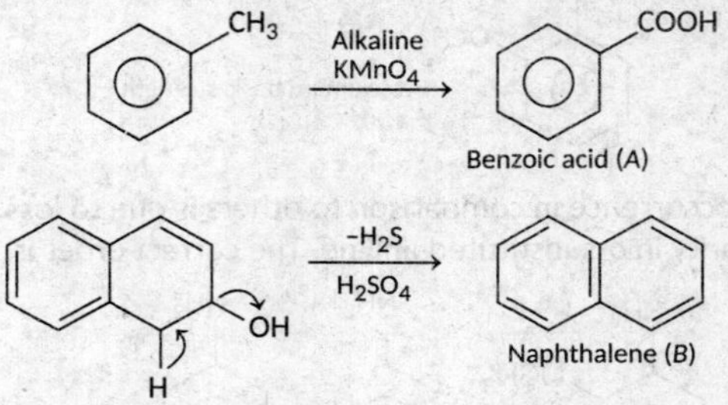

Benzoic acid (*A*)

Naphthalene (*B*)

A and *B* can be easily purified by sublimation because naphthalene has subliming property.

18. (d) The complete reaction is as follows

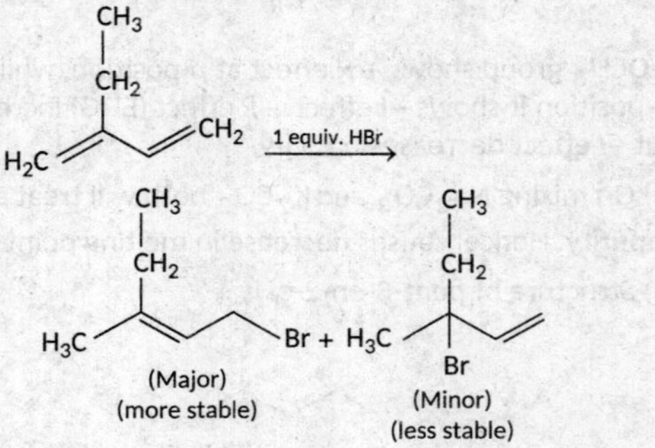

(Major) (more stable) + (Minor) (less stable)

19. (c)

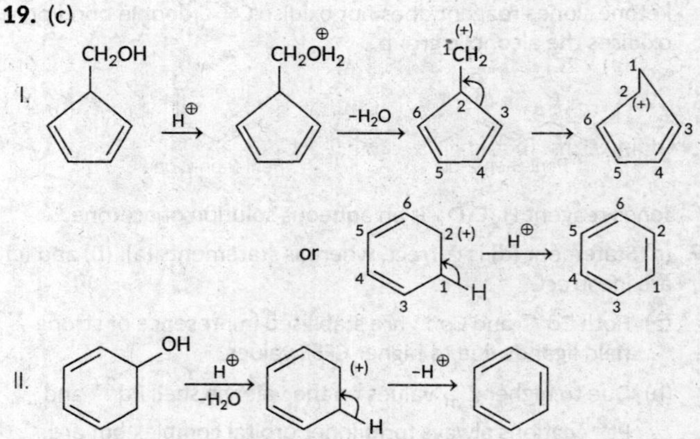

20. (b) In human eye, cornea absorbs UV-B radiation, which causes inflammation of cornea and such exposure may permanently damage cornea.

21. (1.44) Volume of 100 g of the solution $=\frac{100}{d}$ mL $=\frac{100}{1.09}$ mL

$$=\frac{100}{1.09\times 1000}\text{ L}=\frac{1}{1.09\times 10}\text{ L}$$

$\Rightarrow$ Number of moles of H_2SO_4 in 100 g of the solution $=\frac{13}{98}$ mol

$$\Rightarrow \text{Molarity}=\frac{\text{No. of moles of } H_2SO_4}{\text{Volume of solution in litre}}$$

$$=\frac{13}{98}\times\frac{1.09\times 10}{1}=1.445\text{ M}$$

22. (0.01M) The concerned reaction is,

$$2KMnO_4 + 3H_2SO_4 + 5(COOH)_2 \longrightarrow K_2SO_4 + 2MnSO_4 + 10CO_2 + 8H_2O$$

[For $KMnO_4$] $V_1 = 20$ mL, $M_1 = 0.02$ M, $n_1 = 2$

[For oxalic acid] $V_2 = 10$ mL, $M_2 = ?$, $n_2 = 5$

$$\frac{M_1V_1}{n_1} = \frac{M_2V_2}{n_2} \Rightarrow \frac{0.02 \times 20}{2} = \frac{M_2 \times 10}{5}$$

$$\Rightarrow M_2 = \frac{0.02 \times 20 \times 5}{10 \times 2} = 0.1 \text{ M}$$

23. (112) The reaction is,

$$2Fe_2O_3 + 3C \longrightarrow 4Fe + 3CO_2$$

Number of moles of $Fe_2O_3 = \left(\frac{140 \times 1000}{2 \times 56 + 48}\right) \times \frac{80}{100}$

$$= \frac{140 \times 1000 \times 0.8}{160} \text{ mol}$$

Mass of 80% pure iron produced

$$= \frac{140 \times 1000 \times 0.8}{160} \times \frac{2 \times 56}{0.7} = 112000 \text{ g}$$

$$= 112 \text{ kg}$$

24. (8.42) $C(s) + CO_2(g) \rightleftharpoons 2CO(g)$ ...(i)

$K'_{p_1} = 10^{12}$ atm^{-1}, where $K'_{p_1} = \frac{1}{K_{p_1}} = \frac{1}{10^{-12}}$

$2\,CO(g) + 2Cl_2(g) \rightleftharpoons 2COCl_2(g)$ ...(ii)

$K'_{p_2} = (3 \times 10^{-3})^2$ atm^{-1} $\quad [\because K'_{p_2} = (K_{p_2})^2]$

Adding Eqns. (i) and (ii), we get

$\Rightarrow \quad C(s) + CO_2(g) + 2Cl_2(g) \rightleftharpoons 2COCl_2(g)$

$\Rightarrow \quad K_p = K'_{p_1} \times K'_{p_2}$

$\Rightarrow \quad K_p = (10^{12}) \times (9 \times 10^{-6}) = 9 \times 10^6$ atm^{-1}

$\Rightarrow \quad \Delta n_g = 2 - (1 + 2) = -1,$

$\Rightarrow \quad K_p = K_c\,(RT)^{-1}$

$\Rightarrow \quad K_C = K_p(RT)$

$= 9 \times 10^6 \times 0.0821 \times 1140$

$= 8.42 \times 10^8$ M^{-1} $= x \times 10^8$ M^{-1}

Hence, $x = 8.42$

25. (1.11) Limiting molar conductivity of the dissociated crotonic acid (HC).

$$\overset{\circ}{\Lambda}_{m(HC)} = \overset{\circ}{\Lambda}_{(HCl)} + \overset{\circ}{\Lambda}_{m(NaCl)} - \overset{\circ}{\Lambda}_{m(NaCl)}$$

$= (425 + 82 - 125)\ \Omega^{-1}$ cm^2 mol^{-1}

$= 382\ \Omega^{-1}$ cm^2 mol^{-1}

Molar conductivity of HC,

$$\Lambda_{m(HC)} = \frac{K}{C} = \frac{3.82 \times 10^{-5}}{0.001} \times 1000$$

$= 38.2\ \Omega^{-1}$ cm^2 mol^{-1}

The degree of dissociation, $\alpha = \frac{\Lambda_{m(HCl)}}{\overset{\circ}{\Lambda}_{m(HCl)}}$

$$= \frac{38.2\Omega^{-1}\text{cm}^2\text{mol}^{-1}}{382\Omega^{-1}\text{cm}^{-2}\text{mol}^{-1}} = 0.1$$

$\Rightarrow \quad K_a = \frac{C\alpha^2}{1-\alpha} = \frac{(0.001) \times (0.1)^2}{1 - 0.1}$

$= 1.11 \times 10^{-5} = x \times 10^{-5}$

$\therefore \quad x = 1.11$

26. (3.32) $W = -p\Delta V = -nR\Delta T = -2 \times 8.314 \times \Delta T$

Temperature at $P = -73 + 273 = 200$ K $= T_p$

$$\frac{V_Q}{V_p} = \frac{T_Q}{T_p} \Rightarrow 2 = \frac{T_Q}{200} \Rightarrow T_Q = 400 \text{ K}$$

$W = -p\Delta V = -nR\Delta T$

$= -2 \times 8.314 \times (400 - 200)$

$= 3325.6$ J $= 3.32$ kJ

27. (1.38) Given, $\frac{dp}{dt} = -kp$

$\Rightarrow \quad p = p_o e^{kt}$

$\Rightarrow \quad p_o = \frac{456}{3} + 76 = 228$ cm Hg

Now, At $t = 28$ min,

$p = \frac{228}{3} + 76$

$= 152$ cm Hg

$228\, e^{-kt} = 152$

$k = \frac{2.303}{t} \log \frac{228}{152}$

$= \frac{2.303}{28} \log \frac{57}{38}$

$= \frac{2.303}{28} \times 0.28 \times 60$ h^{-1}

$= 1.38$ h^{-1}

28. (16.93) Depression in freezing point of the solution,

$$\Delta T_f = K_f \times \frac{w_{acid}}{M_{acid} \times w_{H_2O}} \times 1000$$

$$0.145 = 1.86 \times \frac{1 \times 1000}{M_{acid}\ 100}$$

$$M_{acid} = \frac{18.6}{0.145} = 128.28 \text{ g mol}^{-1}$$

M_{acid}(observed) $= 128.28$

M_{acid} (normal)

$$\left\{ \begin{array}{l} \frac{0.75}{M_{acid}} \times 1000 = 27 \times \frac{1}{9} \\ M_{acid}(\text{normal}) = 150 \end{array} \right.$$

$$i = \frac{150}{128.28} = 1.1693$$

$\Rightarrow \quad i = 1 + \alpha$

$\Rightarrow \quad 1 + \alpha = 1.1693$

$\Rightarrow \quad \alpha = 0.1693, \Rightarrow \quad \%\alpha = 16.93$

29. (5) (a), (b), (f), (g) and (i) contains plane of symmetry and thus, they are optically inactive.

30. (1.34) The reaction involved in the liberation of I_2 is

$$2KI + H_2O_2 \longrightarrow I_2 + 2KOH$$

Now, let normality of 25 mL H_2O_2 be 'x' N.

Use, $\underset{(H_2O_2)}{N_1V_1} = \underset{(Na_2S_2O_3 \text{ or } I_2)}{N_2V_2}$

$\Rightarrow x \times 25 = 0.3 \times 20$

$\Rightarrow x = 0.24$

∴ We know, volume strength $= \text{Normality} \times \text{Weq.}$

Equiv. weight of H_2O_2 in terms of $O_2 = 5.6$ L

$\Rightarrow$ Volume strength $= 0.24 \times 5.6 = 1.34 \text{ g L}^{-1}$

Knockout 08

1. (c) Correct match is A→(2), B→(4), C→(1), D→(3).

A. Amino glycosides-Bactericidal (2), it has cidal or killing effect on microbes.
B. Chloroamphenicol-Bacteriostatic antibiotic (4), it shows static or inhibitory action on microbes.
C. Novestrol-Antifertility drug(1), it is a progesterone derivative.
D. Soframycin-Antiseptic (3), which can be applied on the living tissues such as wounds, ulcers and diseased skin surfaces.

2. (a) Statements II, III and IV are correct, whereas statement I is incorrect.

I. The given structures represent the disaccharide, maltose.
II. Starch content in cereals and roots is very high.
III. α-D glucose and β-D glucose are anomers as they vary in configurations at C-1
IV. Allose, altrose and talose are reducing sugars. These are monosaccharides.

3. (c) Ions of transition elements are colourless.

$$Fe^{2+} \longrightarrow Fe^{3+} + e^-$$

$$\text{Equivalent weight} = \frac{\text{Atomic weight}}{\text{No. of electron lost}} = \frac{\text{At. wt.}}{1}$$

4. (c) Energy of one molecule, $E = h\nu$

$\Rightarrow$ 1.5 mole molecule $= 1.5 \times N_A$ molecules

$\Rightarrow$ Energy of 1.5 mole molecule,

$$E' = 1.5 \times 6.023 \times 10^{23} \times h\nu$$

$$= 1.5 \times 6.023 \times 10^{23} \times 6.626 \times 10^{-34} \times 7.5 \times 10^{+14} = 4.49 \times 10^5 \text{ J}$$

5. (c) • Primary pollutants are SO_2, SO_3, CO, NO, NO_2 etc.
• Secondary pollutants are O_3, HCHO, PAN etc.

6. (c) Due to poor shielding of $(n-2)f$-electrons, the size of Zr and Hf are almost same. It is due to lanthanide contraction.

7. (b) Statement (b) is incorrect, whereas all other statements are correct.

Nitrite ion (NO_2^-) interferes the ring test of nitrate ion (NO_3^-). Here, NO_2^- inhibits the oxidation of NO to NO^+ which acts as a positively charged ligand in the brown ring complex.

$[Fe(H_2O)_5(NO^+)]SO_4$

8. (a) Statements (I), (II) and (III) are correct, whereas statement (IV) is incorrect.

Crystal field stabilisation energy, CFSE (Δ) of tetrahedral complex is lower than that of octahedral complex

$$\Delta_t = \frac{4}{9}\Delta_o$$

9. (d) All the given options will produce 2-phenylbutan-2-ol as the major product.

(a) Acetophenone + ethyl magnesium bromide

Ph–CO–CH$_3$ + Et-MgBr $\xrightarrow{H_2O}$ 2-phenylbutan-2-ol + Mg(OH)Br

(2- phenyl- butan-2-ol)

(b) 1-phenylpropan-1-one + methyl magnesium bromide

Ph–CO–Et + CH_3—MgBr $\xrightarrow{H_2O}$ 2-phenylbutan-2-ol + Mg(OH)Br

(2- phenylbutan-2-ol)

(c) Butan-2-one + phenyl magnesium bromide

CH_3—C(=O)—Et + PhMgBr $\longrightarrow$ 2-phenylbutan-2-ol + Mg (OH)Br

(2- phenylbutan-2-ol)

10. (c)

6-methylhept-5-en-2-ol $\xrightarrow[\text{(Electrophilic addition)}]{Br_2/CCl_4}$ (Bromonium ion)

(1,6-attack) → (Major) six-membered cyclic ether with Br at C-5

(1,5-attack) → (Minor) [Option-c] five-membered cyclic ether with Br on side chain

11. (a) The overall reaction can be shown as,

Cyclohexanone $\xrightarrow[\text{(ii) } H_2O^+]{\text{(i) } LiAlH_4}$ Cyclohexanol (*A*) $\xrightarrow{Br_2+P}$ 1-bromo cyclohexane (*B*) $\xrightarrow{Mg/Et_2O}$ Cyclohexyl magnesium bromide $\xrightarrow[\text{(iii) } NH_4Cl(aq)]{\text{(ii) HCHO}}$ Cyclohexyl methanol (*C*) $\xrightarrow{PCC}$ Cyclohexane carbaldehyde (*D*) $\xrightarrow[\text{(ii) } H_2O]{\text{(i) } Ph-CH_2MgX}$ (Secondary alcohol) (*E*) $\xrightarrow{Al_2O_3}$ (Alkene) (*F*) Ph (option-a)

12. (a) Tetrahydrofuran (THF) $\xrightarrow[-Br]{H-Br}$ $\xrightarrow{Br^-}$ $HO\text{-}CH_2CH_2CH_2CH_2\text{-}Br$ 4-bromo-1-butanol $\xrightarrow[-H_2O]{HBr}$ $Br\text{-}CH_2CH_2CH_2CH_2\text{-}Br$ 1,4-dibromobutane

It is solvolysis (S_N2) of a cyclic ether (THF here).

13. (a) Complete reaction is as follows

$$CH_3-\underset{Ph}{\overset{OH}{C}}-CH_2-I \xrightarrow[-AgI]{AgNO_3} CH_3-\underset{Ph}{\overset{OH}{C}}-\overset{\oplus}{C}H_2 \xrightarrow{+R,\ -H^+} CH_3-\overset{O}{\overset{\|}{C}}-CH_2-Ph \text{ (1-phenylpropan-2-one)}$$

14. (d) $Pb(C_2H_5)_4 \xrightarrow{\text{Heat}} Pb + 4CH_3\dot{C}H_2$ (Ethylradical)

$$\underset{Br}{CH_2}-\underset{Br}{CH_2} + Pb \longrightarrow CH_2=CH_2 + PbBr_2$$

As leaded gasoline burns, lead metal gets deposited in engine, which is removed by adding ethylene dibromide. The lead bromide is volatile and is carried off with exhaust gases from engine.

15. (b) $[Ca\overset{(0)}{O}\overset{(+2)}{Cl_2} + Na_2\overset{(+2.5)}{S_2}O_3 \longrightarrow Na_2S_4O_6 + Na\overset{(-1)}{Cl}$

$\Rightarrow n_f$ of $CaOCl_2 = 2\ n_f$ of $Na_2S_2O_3 = 1]$

Number equivalent of hypo = Number equivalent of $CaOCl_2$

$$N_1V_1 = N_2V_2$$
$$0.05 \times 2 \times 1000 = 0.1 \times V_2$$
$$\therefore \quad V_2 = 1000 \text{ mL}$$

16. (d) The order of electron affinity is Cl > Br > I > S > O > C. On moving from chlorine to bromine to iodine, the electron affinity decreases. This is because the increase in atomic size decreases the effective nuclear charge. Hence, the additional electron feels less attraction by the large atom.

17. (c) Dipole moment of $M\ddot{H}_3$ type of hydrides of group 15 elements decreases down the group as the electronegativity of the central atom *M* decreases.

18. (a) Greater the $pK_a(-\log K_a)$ value, weaker will be the acid. Perchloric acid ($HClO_4$) is the strongest acid ($pK_a = -8$) followed by nitric acid (HNO_3).

19. (c) $3Pb^{2+} + 2AsO_4^{3-} \longrightarrow Pb_3(AsO_4)_2$

3 moles of Pb^{2+} reacts with 2 moles of AsO_4^{3-}

$\therefore$ 1 mole of Pb^{2+} will react with $= \frac{2}{3}$ moles of AsO_4^{3-}

Normality = Molarity × Volume

$$N_{Pb^{2+}} = 0.1 \times \frac{20}{1000} = 2 \times 10^{-3}$$
$$N_{AsO_4^{3-}} = \frac{2}{3} \times 2 \times 10^{-3} = 0.00133$$
$$N_{As} = N_{AsO_4^{3-}} = 0.00133$$
$$W_{As} = N_{As} \times M_{As}$$
$$= 0.00133 \times 74.9 = 0.0996 \text{ g}$$
$$\% \text{ of As} = \frac{0.0996}{1.85} \times 100 \approx 5.38 \approx 5.4\%$$

20. (a) The solubility of sulphates of group 2 metals in water decreases down the group. Also, hydration energy decreases down the group, while lattice energy remains almost constant.
Hence, hydration energy of $BeSO_4$ is more in magnitude than its lattice energy.

21. (4) Statements (a), (b), (d) and (e) are correct, whereas statement (c) is incorrect.

Correct reaction is

Cyclohexane $\xrightarrow{\text{Oxidation}}$ Cyclohexanone $\xrightarrow{NH_2OH}$ Cyclohexanone oxime (N–OH) $\xrightarrow{\text{Conc. } H_2SO_4}$ Caprolactam $\xrightarrow{H_2O,\ 533\text{-}543\text{ K}}$ $H_3\overset{+}{N}-(CH_2)_5-CO\overset{-}{O}K$ $\xrightarrow[\text{Polymerisation}]{\text{Heat}}$ $\left(\overset{H}{N}-(CH_2)_5-\overset{O}{\overset{\|}{C}}\right)_n$ Nylon-6

22. (4) All are the correct statements.

23. (4) $\frac{3.929 + 4.0}{2} = 3.9645 = 4$

(rounded off to the measurement with lowest number of decimal point)

24. (4) Octahedral voids are present at edge centres $\left(Z = 12 \times \frac{1}{4} = 3\right)$ and at the body centre ($Z = 1$) of a fcc unit cell.

25. (5) Mn^{2+} ($3d^5$) (i.e.) 5 unpaired electrons because H_2O is weak field ligand and does not force to pairing.

26. (15) $E_{cell} = E^\circ_{cell} - \frac{0.06}{2} \log \frac{[Cd^{2+}]}{[H^+]^2}$

$\therefore \quad 0 = 0.39 - 0.03 \log \frac{[Cd^{2+}][OH^-]^2}{K_w^2}$

$\Rightarrow \log \frac{K_{sp}}{K_w^2} = \frac{0.39}{0.03} = 13$

$\therefore \quad K_{sp} = 10^{13} \times (10^{-14})^2 = 10^{-15}$

27. (1) According to the Freundlich equation,

$$\frac{x}{m} = kp^{1/n}$$

or, $\log \frac{x}{m} = \log k + \frac{1}{n} \log p$

$\therefore$ Plot of $\log \frac{x}{m}$ *versus* $\log p$ is linear with slope of 45°.

Thus, slope $= \frac{1}{n} = \tan \theta = \tan 45° = 1$ or $n = 1$

[$\because x$ = amount of gas in gram, m = amount of charcoal in gram]

Intercept $= \log k = 0.3010$ or $k = 2$

At $p = 0.5$ atm

$$\frac{x}{m} = kp^{1/n} = 2 \times (0.5)^1 = 1.00$$

28. (7)

$Cl-CH_2-CH(CH_3)-CH_2-CH_3 \xrightarrow{\text{Monochlorination}} P + Q + R + S + T$

[S(+) 1-chloro-2-methylbutane]

(P) $Cl-CH(Cl)-\overset{*}{C}H(CH_3)-CH_2-CH_3 = 1$ [no change in chiral centre (*)]

(Q) $Cl-CH_2-\overset{*}{C}H(CH_2-Cl)-CH_2-CH_3 = 1$

(R) $Cl-CH_2-\overset{*}{C}(CH_3)(Cl)-CH_2-CH_3 (\pm) = 2$

(S) $Cl-CH_2-\overset{*}{C}H(CH_3)-CH_2-\overset{**}{C}H(Cl)-CH_3 = 2(**)$

[no change in chiral centre (*)]

(T) $Cl-CH_2-\overset{*}{C}H(CH_3)-CH_2-CH_2-Cl = 1$

[no change in chiral centre (*)]

29. (3) According to first order reaction, $-d[N_2O_5]/dt = k[N_2O_5]$.

Then half-life period for first-order reaction is

$t_{1/2} = \frac{\ln 2}{k} = \frac{0.693}{k}$ so, $t_{1/2}$ is independent of initial concentration of the reactant.

With increase in temperature, k increases (according to Arrhenius equation), so $t_{1/2}$ decreases.

If the reaction completes to 99.61% completion, then,

$$t = \left(\frac{2.303}{k}\right) \log \frac{a}{a-x}$$

where, $a = 100$ and $(a - x) = (100 - 99.61) = 0.39$

$$t_{99.61} = \left(\frac{2.303}{k}\right) \log \frac{100}{0.39}$$

$$= \left(\frac{2.303}{k}\right) 2.41$$

$$= 8 \times \frac{0.693}{k} = 8 \times t_{1/2}$$

$\therefore$ Statements (a), (b) and (d) are correct.

30. (5) The following amides respond to Hofmann bromamide reaction.

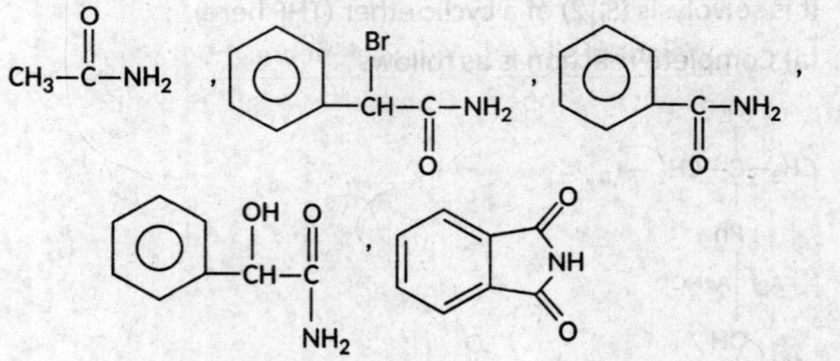

$CH_3-C(=O)-NH_2$, $C_6H_5-CH(Br)-C(=O)-NH_2$, $C_6H_5-C(=O)-NH_2$,

$C_6H_5-CH(OH)-C(=O)-NH_2$, phthalimide (NH)

Knockout 09

1. (d) $C_{12}H_{22}O_{11}(s) + 12O_2(g) \longrightarrow 12CO_2(g) + 11H_2O(l)$

$\Delta H^\circ_C = [12\Delta_f H^\circ_{(CO_2)} + 11\Delta_f H^\circ_{(H_2O)}] - [\Delta_f H^\circ_{(C_{12}H_{22}O_{11})}]$

$= [12(-94.3) + 11(-68.3)] - [-530]$

$= -1352.9 \text{ kcal mol}^{-1}$

Thus, number of moles of $C_{12}H_{22}O_{11}$ required for 2700 kcal of energy

$= \frac{2700}{1352.9} \approx 2$ mol

$= 2 \times 342 = 684$

[$\because$ Molar mass of $C_{12}H_{22}O_{11} = 342$ g/mol]

2. (d) The alcohol on treatment with acid gives an alkene (A) which on ozonolysis will give octane-2, 7-dione. The reaction can be shown as

CH(OH)Me, Me $\xrightarrow{H^+}$ (A) $\xrightarrow{O_3}$ Octane-2,7-dione

The mechanism of formation of A is

$\xrightarrow{H^+, -H_2O}$ Ring expansion $\xrightarrow{H^+}$ (A)

3. (c) Number of equivalents of silver formed = number of equivalents of copper formed

In $AgNO_3$, Ag is in + 1 oxidation state and in $CuSO_4$, Cu is in + 2 oxidation state.

$\therefore$ Equivalent weight of Ag $= \frac{108}{1} = 108$

Equivalent weight of Cu $= \frac{63.5}{2} = 31.75$

$$\frac{\text{Weight of silver}}{\text{Weight of copper}} = \frac{\text{Equivalent weight of silver}}{\text{Equivalent weight of copper}}$$

$$\frac{10.79}{w_{Cu}} = \frac{108}{31.75}$$

$$w_{Cu} = \frac{10.79 \times 31.75}{108} = 3.17\ g \simeq 3.2\ g$$

4. (b) $\underset{(M)}{CuSO_4 + H_2S \longrightarrow CuS} + H_2SO_4$

$CuS + \underset{(excess)}{KCN} \longrightarrow \underset{(N)}{[Cu(CN)_4]^{3-}} + \underset{(O)}{(CN)_2}$

5. (c) Mond's process for refining of nickel is based on principle that nickel is heated in presence of carbon monoxide to form nickel tetracarbonyl, which is a volatile complex.

6. (d) Amount of heat liberated by 0.5 g of carbon

$= mc\Delta T = 2000 \times 1 (26 - 24) = 4000$ cal

$= 4$ kcal

Calorific value $= \frac{4\ \text{kcal} \times 1}{0.5}$

$= 8$ kcal per g

$\therefore$ Heat of combustion $= -8 \times 12$

$= -96$ kcal per mol

7. (a) The organic compound (A) forms white precipitate with $AgNO_3/NH_4OH$ and red precipitate with Cu_2Cl_2 / NH_4OH, it must be a terminal alkyne or 1-yne.

$\underset{(A)}{\underset{\text{(But-1-yne)}}{CH_3-CH_2-C{\equiv}CH}}$

$\xrightarrow{AgNO_3/NH_4OH}$ $\underset{\text{(White ppt.)}}{CH_3-CH_2-C{\equiv}\overset{\ominus\oplus}{CAg}\downarrow}$

$\xrightarrow{Cu_2Cl_2/NH_4OH}$ $\underset{\text{(Red ppt.)}}{CH_3-CH_2-C{\equiv}\overset{\ominus\oplus}{CCu}\downarrow}$

$\underset{(B)}{\underset{\text{(Buta-1,3-diene)}}{\overset{1}{C}H_2{=}\overset{2}{C}H-\overset{3}{C}H{=}\overset{4}{C}H_2}} \xrightarrow[\text{(1,4-addition)}]{Br_2(1\ mol)}$ Br—Br

$\xrightarrow{-Br^{\ominus}}$ $\overset{\oplus}{C}H_2-CH{=}CH-CH_2Br$ (1, 2, 3, 4) $\xrightarrow{Br^{\ominus}}$ $\underset{\text{(1,4-dibromobut-2-ene)}}{BrCH_2-CH{=}CH-CH_2Br}$

8. (a) Zeolites are water softener and also behave as catalyst in which pores of fixed shape and size are present.

9. (c) It does not help to predict the stable valency state of elements.

10. (a) Optical isomerism arises in those compounds where the mirror images are non-superimposable. Complexes like $[M(AA)_2X_2]$ (only *cis*-form) and $[M(AA)_3]$ exhibit optical isomerism.

cis-$[Co(en)_2Cl_2]Cl$ (optically active)

trans-$[Co(en)_2Cl_2]Cl$ (optically inactive due to plane of symmetry)

$[Co(NH_3)_4Cl_2]Cl$ can exist in both *cis* and *trans*-forms, which are given below.

trans- $[Co(NH_3)_4Cl_2]Cl$ (optically inactive)

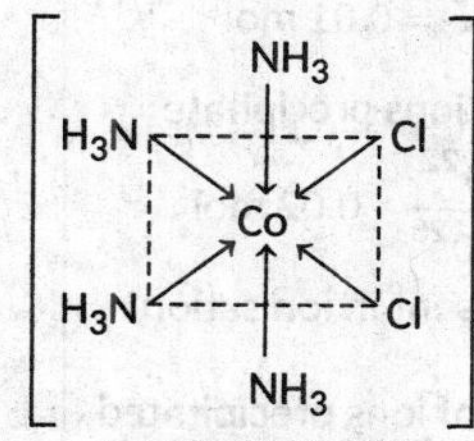

cis- $[Co(NH_3)_4Cl_2]Cl$ (optically inactive)

$[Co(NH_3)_3Cl_3]$ exists in *fac*- and *mer*-isomeric forms and both are optically inactive.

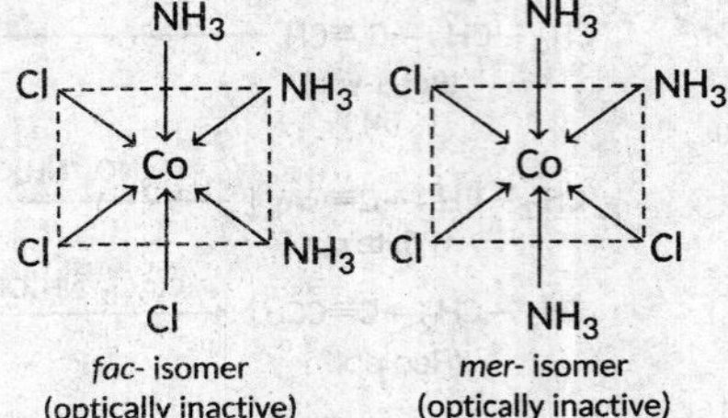

fac- isomer (optically inactive) *mer*- isomer (optically inactive)

11. (c) Complete reaction is as follows

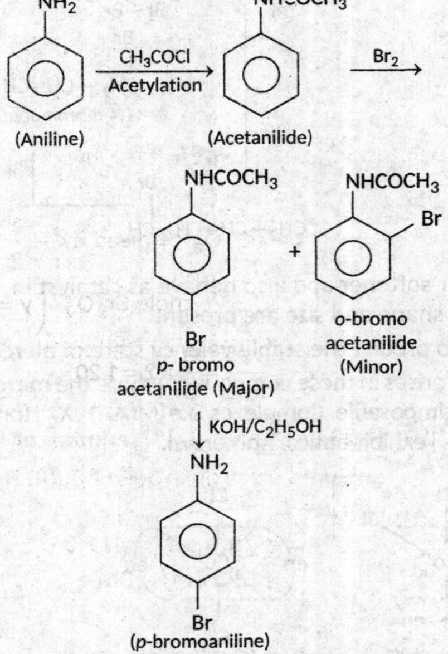

$-NH_2$ group is highly activating group, hence reaction can take place at all the *ortho/para* positions. However, if the ring is deactivated by acetylation, then monohaloaniline derivative (*para*) is obtained as a major product.

12. (d) Molarity (*M*)

$$= \frac{\text{Number of moles of solute}}{\text{Volume of solution (in L)}}$$

Number of moles of complex

$$= \frac{\text{Molarity} \times \text{Volume (in mL)}}{1000}$$

$$= \frac{0.1 \times 100}{1000} = 0.01 \text{ mol}$$

Number of moles of ions precipitate

$$= \frac{1.2 \times 10^{22}}{6.02 \times 10^{23}} = 0.02 \text{ mol}$$

$\therefore$ Number of Cl^- present in ionisation sphere

$$= \frac{\text{Number of moles of ions precipitated}}{\text{Number of moles of complex}}$$

$$= \frac{0.02}{0.01} = 2$$

$\therefore$ 2 Cl^- are present outside the square brackets, i.e. in ionisation sphere. Thus, the formula of complex is $[Co(H_2O)_5Cl]Cl_2 \cdot H_2O$.

13. (b)

$$\underset{\text{1-bromopropane}}{CH_3-CH_2-CH_2Br} \xrightarrow[\substack{80^\circ C \\ -HBr}]{\text{Alc. NaOH }(X)} \underset{\text{Propene}}{CH_3-CH{=}CH_2} \xrightarrow[\text{Acetic acid}]{\text{HBr }(Y)} \underset{\text{2-bromopropane}}{CH_3-\underset{\underset{Br}{|}}{C}H-CH_3 \text{ (major)}}$$

(*X*) Step 1 Haloalkanes on reaction with alcoholic NaOH undergoes elimination reaction to give alkenes.

(*Y*) Step 2 The formed alkene then reacts with HBr to give monobrominated product. This product is in accordance with Markownikov's addition rule.

14. (c) The van der Waals' equation of state is

$$\left(p + \frac{n^2a}{V^2}\right)(V - nb) = nRT$$

For one mole and when $b = 0$, the above equation condenses to

$$\left(p + \frac{a}{V^2}\right)V = RT$$

$$pV = RT - \frac{a}{V} \quad \text{...(i)}$$

Eq. (i) is a straight line equation between pV and $\frac{1}{V}$ whose slope is $-a$.

Equating with slope of the straight line given in the graph,

$$-a = \frac{20.1 - 21.6}{3 - 2} = -1.5$$

$$a = 1.5 \text{ atm L}^2 \text{ mol}^{-1}$$

15. (a) $\Lambda_m^c = 40.1 \text{ S cm}^2\text{mol}^{-1}$

$$\Lambda_m^\circ = \Lambda_{m(HCOO^-)}^\circ + \Lambda_{m(H^+)}^\circ$$

$$= (54.6 + 349.6) \text{ S cm}^2\text{mol}^{-1}$$

$$= 404.2 \text{ S cm}^2\text{mol}^{-1}$$

$$\alpha = \frac{\Lambda_m^c}{\Lambda_m^\circ} = \frac{40.1}{404.2} = 0.0992$$

Now, $HCOOH \overset{H_2O}{\rightleftharpoons} HCOO^-(aq) + H^+(aq)$

Initial conc.	C	0	0
Equili conc.	C(1 − α)	Cα	Cα

$$K_a = \frac{C\alpha^2}{1-\alpha} = \frac{0.25 \times (0.0992)^2}{(1 - 0.0992)}$$

$$= 2.73 \times 10^{-3} \text{ mol L}^{-1}$$

16. (a) Val-Gly-Phe-Val-Ala-Val on random hydrolysis gives Ala-Val dipeptide fragment which indicates the connected presence of Ala and Val.

17. (d) Molecular formula C_3H_8O $(C_nH_{2n+2}O)$ suggests that the organic compound is either alcohol or ether. Since, the compound on reaction with HI gives two different compounds, it must be an unsymmetrical ether and its formula must be $CH_3OC_2H_5$ (methoxyethane). The reactions are as follows

(i) $\underset{\substack{\text{Methoxyethane} \\ (A)}}{CH_3OC_2H_5} + 2HI \longrightarrow \underset{\substack{\text{Methyl iodide} \\ (X)}}{CH_3I} + \underset{\substack{\text{Ethyl iodide} \\ (Y)}}{C_2H_5I} + H_2O$

(ii) $\underset{(Y)}{C_2H_5I} + \underset{\text{Aqueous}}{NaOH} \longrightarrow \underset{\substack{\text{Ethanol} \\ (Z)}}{C_2H_5OH} + NaI$

(iii) $\underset{(Z)}{C_2H_5OH} + \underset{\text{Aqueous}}{6NaOH} + 4I_2 \longrightarrow \underset{\text{Iodoform}}{CHI_3} + HCO\overset{-}{O}\overset{+}{N}a + 5H_2O + 5NaI$

18. (c) Complete reaction is as follows

$$\text{C}_6\text{H}_{11}-\underset{\underset{CH_3}{|}}{C}{=}O \xrightarrow[-Ph_3PO]{(C_6H_5)_3\overset{\oplus}{P}\overset{\ominus}{C}HCH_2CH_3} \underset{(A)}{\text{C}_6\text{H}_{11}-\underset{\underset{CH_3}{|}}{C}{=}CHCH_2CH_3} \xrightarrow[2.\ H_2O_2/OH^-]{1.\ B_2H_6} \underset{(B)}{\text{C}_6\text{H}_{11}-\underset{\underset{CH_3}{|}}{C}H-\underset{\underset{OH}{|}}{C}HCH_2CH_3}$$

Carbonyl compounds reacts with $(C_6H_5)_3\overset{+}{P}-\overset{-}{\ddot{C}}HCH_2CH_3$ to form phosphonium ylide (Wittig reaction) which then gives the alkene (*A*). The formed alkene (*A*) then reacts with B_2H_6 to give addition product (*B*) which is in accordance to anti-Markownikov's rule.

19. (a) Assertion and Reason both are correct and Reason is the correct explanation of the Assertion.

The thermal stability of carbonates increases down the group. Hence, Li_2CO_3 is least stable.

$$Li_2CO_3 \xrightarrow{\Delta} Li_2O + CO_2 \uparrow$$

Due to small size of Li^+, strong polarising power distorts the electron cloud of CO_3^{2-} ion. High lattice energy of Li_2O than Li_2CO_3 also favours the decomposition of Li_2CO_3.

20. (a) Correct match is A $\rightarrow$ (3), B $\rightarrow$ (4), C $\rightarrow$ (1), D $\rightarrow$ (5), E $\rightarrow$ (2).

A. BH_3 is unstable and readily forms diborance B_2H_6 by $(3C-2e^-)$ electron bond [banana bond] (3).

B. Gallium with low melting point and high boiling point makes it useful to measure high temperatures (4).

C. Borax is used as a flux for soldering metals for heat, scratch resistance cooking in earthenwares (1)

D. Aluminosilicate is used as catalyst in petrochemical industries (5).

E. Quartz is a crystalline form of silica (2).

21. (11) Solubility of Ag_2CrO_4 in 0.1 M $(AgNO_3) = x$ M

$$\underset{}{Ag_2CrO_4} \rightleftharpoons \underset{2x}{2Ag^+} + \underset{x}{CrO_4^{2-}},$$

$$AgNO_3 \rightleftharpoons \underset{0.1}{Ag^+} + \underset{0.1}{NO_3^-}$$

Total $[Ag^+] = (2x + 0.1) \simeq 0.1$ M,

$[CrO_4^{2-}] = x$ M

$$[Ag^+]^2[CrO_4^{2-}] = K_{sp}(Ag_2CrO_4)$$

$$(0.1)^2(x) = 1.1 \times 10^{-12}$$

$$x = 1.1 \times 10^{-10} \text{ M}$$

$$= 11 \times 10^{-11} \text{ M}$$

$$= y \times 10^{-11} \text{ M}$$

$\therefore \quad y = 11$

22. (0.80) For the given reaction,

$$2N_2O_5 \longrightarrow 4NO_2 + O_2$$

$$\text{Rate} = k[N_2O_5]$$

$$[N_2O_5] = \frac{\text{Rate}}{k} = \frac{2.40 \times 10^{-5}}{3 \times 10^{-5}} = 0.8 \text{ M}$$

23. (959.73) Complete reaction is as follows:

$$H_2(g) + \frac{1}{2}O_2(g) \longrightarrow H_2O(l),$$

$$\Delta H_f^\circ = -286 \text{ kJ/mol}$$

Energy released by the reaction is absorbed by its surroundings as,

$$\Delta S = \frac{\Delta q}{T} = \frac{+286 \times 10^3 \text{ Jmol}^{-1}}{298 \text{ K}}$$

$$= 959.73 \text{ JK}^{-1}\text{mol}^{-1}$$

24. (0.12) $\qquad \kappa = C \times \frac{l}{a}$

$$\left(\frac{l}{a}\right)_{\text{cell constant}} = \kappa \times \frac{1}{C}$$

$\Rightarrow \kappa \times R =$ Specific conductance $\times$ Resistance

$$= 0.0212 \text{ ohm}^{-1} \text{ cm}^{-1} \times 5.5 \text{ ohm}$$

$$= 0.1166 \text{ cm}^{-1} \simeq 0.12 \text{ cm}^{-1}$$

25. (270.02) $NaCl \longrightarrow Na^+ + Cl^-$

$$i = 1 + \alpha(n-1) = 1 + \frac{60}{100}(2-1) = 1.6$$

Molality = 1m

$$\Delta T_f = K_f \times m \times i$$

$$\Rightarrow 0 - T_f = 1.86 \times 1 \times 1.6 = 2.976$$

$\therefore$ Freezing point, $T_f = -2.976°C$

$$= 270.02 \text{ K}$$

26. (2) Statement (III) and statement (IV) are incorrect, while statement (I) and (II) are correct.

27. (34) Given, $\lim_{p \to 0}\left(\frac{d}{p}\right) = 1.517$

From equation of state of an ideal gas.

$$pV = nRT = \frac{w}{M}RT$$

$$p = \frac{w}{V}\frac{RT}{M} = d \times \frac{RT}{M}$$

$$M = \left(\frac{d}{p}\right) \times RT$$

$$= 1.517 \times 0.0821 \times 273$$

$$= 34.00 \text{ g mol}^{-1}$$

28. (6)

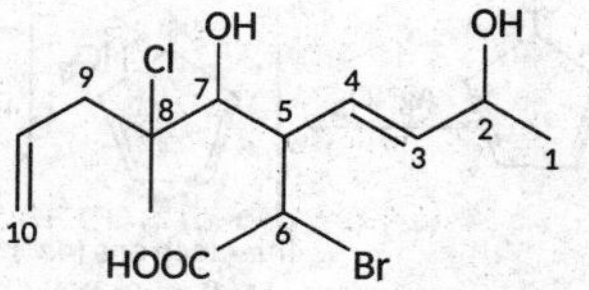

Number of stereogenic centres
= Number of chiral carbon atom
+ Number of asymmetric $-C{=}C-$
$= 5(C_2, C_5, C_6, C_7 \text{ and } C_8) + 1(C_3 - C_4$ double bond)
$= 6$

29. (1.20) 5 moles of FeC_2O_4 oxidised by 3 moles of $MnO_4^\ominus$.

Complete reaction is as follows:

$$[\overset{+2}{Fe}\,\overset{(+3)}{C_2}O_4 + \overset{(+7)}{Mn}O_4^- \xrightarrow{H^+} Fe^{3+} + 2\overset{(+4)}{C}O_2 + Mn^{2+} + 4H_2O]$$

n-f : 3   5
mol : 5   3

1 mole of FeC_2O_4 oxidised by $\rightarrow \frac{3}{5}$ moles $MnO_4^\ominus$

$\therefore \quad \left(x = \frac{3}{5}\right)$

2 moles of FeC_2O_4 oxidised by $\rightarrow$ 1 mole $Cr_2O_7^{2-}$

$$[\overset{(+2)}{Fe}\,\overset{(+3)}{C_2}O_4 + Cr_2O_7^{2-} \xrightarrow{H^+} Fe^{3+} + \overset{(+4)}{C}O_2 + Cr^{3+}]$$

n-f : 3   6
mol : 6   3
       2   1

1 mole of FeC_2O_4 oxidised by $\rightarrow \frac{1}{2}$ mole $Cr_2O_7^{2-}$ $\left(y = \frac{1}{2}\right)$

$$\therefore \quad \frac{x}{y} = \frac{3/5}{1/2} = \frac{3}{5} \times 2 = 1.20$$

30. (1.73) In $[Cu(NH_3)_4]^{2+}$, number of unpaired electron in $3d^9$ of Cu(II) is one $(n = 1)$

$$\mu_m = \sqrt{n(n+2)} = \sqrt{1 \times 3}$$

$$= 1.73 \text{ BM} = x\text{BM}$$

$\therefore \quad x = 1.73$

Knockout 10

1. (b) $\nu_1 = RcZ^2\left(\frac{1}{n_1^2} - \frac{1}{n_2^2}\right)$

$$\nu_1 = RcZ^2\left(\frac{1}{1^2} - \frac{1}{\infty^2}\right) = RcZ^2$$

$$\nu_2 = RcZ^2\left(\frac{1}{1^2} - \frac{1}{2^2}\right) = \frac{3RcZ^2}{4}$$

$$\nu_3 = RcZ^2\left(\frac{1}{2^2} - \frac{1}{\infty^2}\right) = \frac{RcZ^2}{4}$$

$\therefore \nu_1 - \nu_2 = \nu_3$

2. (b) The incorrect option is (b).

Cheese is a gel type of colloid in which liquid is dispersed phase and solid is dispersion medium.

3. (c) $CH_2{=}CH_2 \xrightarrow{HOCl} \underset{(M)}{CH_2(Cl)-CH_2(OH)} \xrightarrow[(Q)\ Aq.\ NaHCO_3]{} CH_2(OH)-CH_2(OH)$

4. (c) Statement (c) is incorrect, whereas statements (a), (b) and (d) are correct.

$$A + B \longrightarrow 2C + D$$

$$-\frac{d[A]}{dt} = -\frac{d[B]}{dt} = \frac{1}{2}\frac{d[C]}{dt} = \frac{d[D]}{dt}$$

So, rate of disappearance of *B*, i.e. $\left[-\frac{d[B]}{dt}\right] = \frac{1}{2} \times$ rate of appearance of *C*, i.e. $\left[+\frac{d[C]}{dt}\right]$

5. (b) Complete reaction is as follows

1,4-dinitrobenzene $\xrightarrow[\Delta]{NH_4HS}$ 4-nitroaniline (A) $\xrightarrow[0°C\text{-}5°C]{NaNO_2/HCl}$ (B) $p\text{-}O_2N\text{-}C_6H_4\text{-}\overset{\oplus}{N_2}\overset{\ominus}{Cl}$ $\xrightarrow[\Delta]{Cu_2(CN)_2^+,\ HCN}$ (C) $p\text{-}O_2N\text{-}C_6H_4\text{-}CN$

Now, both $-NO_2$ and $-CN$ are strongly meta orienting groups in ArS_E2 reaction and $-NO_2$ is stronger *metal* orienting group than $-CN$ group. So, the product after nitration of (*C*) will be,

(2,4- dinitrocyanobenzene)

6. (a) The given reaction can be written as follows

$>C=C< \longrightarrow$ (Osmate ester intermediate) $\xrightarrow[(ii)\ H_2O]{(i)\ NaHSO_3}$ $>\underset{OH}{C}-\underset{OH}{C}<$ (*cis*-diol)

[α, β-hydroxylation of but-2-ene takes place to give *cis*-butane-2, 3-diol]

$>C=C<$ (Alkene) $\xrightarrow{HCO_3H}$ epoxide $\xrightarrow{H_2O}$ $>C(OH)-C(OH)<$ (*trans*-diol)

[α, β -anti-hydroxylation of but-2-ene takes place to give *trans*-butane-2, 3-diol]

7. (d) Froth-floatation method is used for sulphide ores (here, it could be Zn from ZnS and Cu from Cu_2S).

Among the given metals Zn and Cu need this in the first step.

But only Cu needs bessemerisation followed by electrolytic refining.

8. (a) Correct order of ionic character is

$$XeF_2 < XeF_4 < XeF_6.$$

Xe—F bonds in XeF_2 show partial covalent and partial ionic character.

$$F-\overset{+}{Xe}......F^- \longleftrightarrow F^-......\overset{+}{Xe}-F$$

As number of F-atoms around Xe increases, the effective nuclear charge on Xe increases which results strong attraction between Xe and F-atoms.

∴ Bond length order ⇒ $XeF_2 > XeF_4 > XeF_6$

9. (b)

(a) 7,8-dichlorocyclooctatriene $\xrightarrow{2SbCl_5}$ cyclooctatetraene dication (2+) $+ 2[SbCl_6]^-$
(4*n* +2) π-electrons (6e⁻) [Aromatic]

(b) bromocyclopentadiene $\xrightarrow{AgNO_3}$ $\left[\text{cyclopentadienyl cation } \overset{\oplus}{}\overset{\ominus}{NO_3}\right]$ + AgBr↓
4*n*π-electrons (4e⁻) [Anti-aromatic]

(c) cyclopentadiene $\xrightarrow{NaOH}$ $\left[\text{cyclopentadienide } \overset{\ominus}{}\overset{\oplus}{Na}\right] + H_2O$
(4*n* + 2) π-electrons (6e⁻) [Aromatic]

(d) bromocycloheptatriene $\xrightarrow{AgNO_3}$ $\left[\text{tropylium } \overset{\oplus}{}\overset{\ominus}{NO_3}\right]$ + AgBr↓
(4*n* + 2) 6π-electrons [Aromatic]

So, compounds of options (a), (c) and (d) produce aromatic compounds and the reactions are highly spontaneous. But the compound of option (b) produces an anti-aromatic compound and the reaction are non-spontaneous.

10. (d) Let volume of solution be 1 L

∴Weight of solution $= (1 \times d) = d$ g

⇒ Number of moles of solute n_2 in 1L solution $= M = \frac{w_2}{M_{w_2}}$

$\therefore \quad w_2 = (M)\,M_{w_2}$

w_1 = weight of solvent

$= (w_{\text{Solution}} - w_{\text{Solute}}) = [d - (M \cdot M_{w_2})]$

Number of moles of solvent

$$(n_1) = \frac{w_1}{M_{w_1}} = \frac{[d-(MM_{w_2})]}{M_{w_1}}$$

∴

$$\chi_2 = \frac{n_2}{n_1 + n_2} = \frac{M}{\left[\frac{d-(MM_{w_2})}{M_{w_1}}\right] + M} = \frac{(M)(M_{w_1})}{M(M_{w_1} - M_{w_2}) + d}$$

11. (c) It is chromyl chloride test (dry test) of ionic chloride salts (it is NaCl here). The reddish yellow vapour is chromyl chloride (CrO_2Cl_2) which gives a yellow precipitate of sodium chromate (Na_2CrO_4) when passed through NaOH solution.

(i) $K_2Cr_2O_7 + 6H_2SO_4 + 4NaCl \xrightarrow{\Delta} 2KHSO_4 + 4NaHSO_4 + 2CrO_2Cl_2 \uparrow + 3H_2O$

(ii) $CrO_2Cl_2 + 4NaOH \longrightarrow \underset{\text{Compound (X)}}{Na_2CrO_4} + 2NaCl + 2H_2O$

12. (b) % of excess (–) enantiomer $= \frac{[\alpha]_{obs}}{[\alpha]_D}$

$$= \frac{(-10°) \times (100)}{(-20°)} = 50\%$$

[∵ $[\alpha]_D$ = Specific rotation of pure enantiomer = −20°]

So, 50% of the mixture contains (–) enantiomer and 50% is the racemate [i.e. 25% (+) form and 25% (–) form].

Total percentage of (–) form = (50% + 25%) = 75% and total percentage of (+) form = 25%

13. (d) In simple unit cell, $a = 2r$ and $Z = 1$

$$\text{Packing fraction} = \frac{\text{Occupied volume}}{\text{Total volume}}$$

$$= \frac{1 \times \frac{4}{3}\pi r^3}{a^3} = \frac{\frac{4}{3}\pi r^3}{(2r)^3} = \frac{\pi}{6}$$

$$\left[\begin{array}{l} \because r = \text{radius of sphere} \\ a = \text{edge length of the unit cell} \\ Z = \text{rank of the simple cube} \\ = 8 \times \frac{1}{8} = 1 \end{array}\right]$$

$\therefore \quad Q = 6$

It is the atomic number of carbon ($^{12}_{6}C$).

14. (d) (a) Nylon-6, 6 is the polymer of $H_2N-(CH_2)_6-NH_2$ (hexamethylene diamine) and $(CH_2)_4(COOH)_2$ (adipic acid). It is an example of condensation polymerisation as well as copolymerisation.

(b) Nylon-6 is the polymer of (cyclic lactam: C=O, NH) (Caprolactam). It is an example of condensation and homopolymerisation.

(c) Teflon is the polymer of $F_2C=CF_2$ (Tetrafluoroethylene). It is an example of homopolymerisation as well as addition polymerisation.

(d) Buna-N-Rubber is the polymer $H_2C=CH-CH=CH_2$ (buta-1, 3-diene) + $H_2C=CH(CN)$ (acrylonitrile). It is an example of both addition polymerisation as well as co-polymerisation.

15. (a) Those aromatic iodides will react with sodium in liquid ammonia, where at least one hydrogen must be present on the carbon which is at β-position (or *ortho*) with respect to that iodide group.

(Structure: benzene ring with I at top, H_3C and CH_3 at α-adjacent positions, β positions marked) will not take part in this reaction, as both β-positions are blocked by $-CH_3$ groups.

16. (c) NH_4Cl is a salt of strong acid (HCl) and weak base (NH_4OH). The expression of pH of the solution obtained by hydrolysis of NH_4Cl.

[$\because$ C = Molar concentration of $NH_4Cl = 0.02$ M]

$$pH = \frac{1}{2}[pK_w - pK_b - \log C]$$

$$= \frac{1}{2}[14 - 4.73 - (\log 0.02)]$$

$$= \frac{1}{2}[14 - 4.73 + 1.698]$$

$$pH = 5.48$$

17. (b) The reaction is

$$PCl_5(g) \rightleftharpoons PCl_3(g) + Cl_2(g)$$

Now, $\alpha = \dfrac{D-d}{(n-1)d}$

$\because n$ = Number of gaseous molecules in RHS for 1 mole of $PCl_5 = 2$

D = Initial vapour density = 104.25

d = Final vapour density = 62

$$\therefore \quad \alpha = \frac{(104.25-62)}{(2-1)62} = 0.68$$

$\therefore$ Percentage of dissociation of $PCl_5(g)$ at 230°C = 68%

18. (a) As butan-1-ol is an 1°-alcohol, it will undergo E2-elimination with conc. H_2SO_4 to give only but-1-ene. It can be shown as

(i) $H_2SO_4 \rightleftharpoons H^{\oplus} + HSO_4^-$ (Conc.)

(ii) $CH_3CH_2CH(H)-CH_2\ddot{O}H$ (Butan-1-ol) $\xrightleftharpoons{H^{\oplus}}$ $CH_3CH_2-CH(H)-CH_2-\overset{\oplus}{O}H_2$ (β; $HSO_4^{\ominus}$) $\xrightarrow[-H_2SO_4]{\beta\text{-elimination}, -H_2O}$ $CH_3CH_2-CH=CH_2$ (But-1-ene)

In E2 mechanism, carbocation formation does not take place.

19. (c) Protein + Conc. $HNO_3 \longrightarrow$ Yellow colour

Protein which consist α-amino acids containing benzene ring such as tyrosine, yellow colour is due to nitration of benzene ring.

20. (d)

$$\underset{\text{(Ethanal)}}{CH_3CHO} \xrightarrow[\Delta \text{ [Wittig reaction]}]{(C_6H_5)_3P=CH_2} \underset{\text{(X) (Propene)}}{H_3C-CH=CH_2}$$

$$\xrightarrow[\text{(i) } H_2O_2,\ NaOH \text{ [Hydroboration-Oxidation]}]{\text{(i) } B_2H_6} \underset{\text{(Y) (Propan-1-ol)}}{CH_3-CH_2-CH_2OH}$$

$$\xrightarrow[{[O]}]{PCC,\ CH_2Cl_2} \underset{\text{(Z) (Propanal)}}{CH_3CH_2CHO}$$

Now, compound Z (propanal) contains α-hydrogen atoms. So, it will take part in aldol condensation reaction and Claisen-Schmidt reaction. It will also react with semicarbazide, $H_2NCONHNH_2$, but it will not take part in Cannizzaro reaction with 50% NaOH solution, as propanal has two α-H atoms.

21. (2.40) $Zn^{7+} \rightarrow 1s^2 2s^2 2p^6 3s^2 3p^6 3d^5$

[1|1|1|1|1]

Total spin $= 5 \times \frac{1}{2} = 2.5 = X$

$\Rightarrow N^+ \rightarrow 1s^2, 2s^2\ (2p^2)$ [1|1|]

Total spin $= 2 \times \frac{1}{2} = 1 = Y$

$\Rightarrow Be^{\oplus} \rightarrow 1s^2 2s^1$

[1]

Total spin $= 1 \times \frac{1}{2} = 0.5 = Z$

$\Rightarrow Fe^{2+} \rightarrow 1s^2 2s^2 2p^6 3s^2 3p^6 3d^6$

[1↓|1|1|1|1]

Total spin $= 4 \times \frac{1}{2} = 2 = P$

$\Rightarrow Xe^{2\oplus} \rightarrow$ [1↓|1|1] $(5p^4)$

Total spin $= 2 \times \frac{1}{2} = 1 = Q$

$\Rightarrow Mn^{2+} \rightarrow 1s^2 2s^2 2p^6 3s^2 3p^6 3d^5$

[1|1|1|1|1]

Unpaired electrons = 5 = R

$$\therefore \frac{[X+Y+Z+P+Q+R]}{5}$$

$$= \frac{2.5+1+0.5+2+1+5}{5}$$

$$= \frac{7+5}{5} = 2.40$$

22. (13.41) For an ideal gas the correct relationship between T and ∂V will be

$$T = KV$$

[when p and n are constant]

$$\therefore \quad \left[\frac{\partial T}{\partial V}\right] = K$$

$$\therefore \quad \left[\frac{\partial^2 T}{\partial V^2}\right]_{p,n} = 0 = (13.41 - x)$$

$$\Rightarrow \quad x = 13.41$$

23. (0.56) BO of N_2^+ will be $\dfrac{10-5}{2} = 2.5 = X$

BO of O_2^- will be $\dfrac{10-7}{2} = 1.5 = Y$

BO of He_2^+ will be $\dfrac{4-3}{2} = 0.5 = Z$

BO of Be_2^+ will be $\dfrac{8-7}{2} = 0.5 = P$

$$\therefore \left[\frac{X+Y+Z+P}{9}\right] = \frac{2.5+1.5+0.5+0.5}{9}$$

$$= \frac{5}{9} = 0.56$$

24. (1) For C_2H_5OH, $\pi = 1 \times 0.5 \times RT = 0.5RT$

For KBr, $\pi = 2 \times 0.25 \times RT = 0.5RT$

For $Mg_3(PO_4)_2$, $\pi = 5 \times 0.1\, RT = 0.5RT$

For Na_3PO_4, $\pi = 4 \times 0.125 \times RT = 0.5RT$

So, all are isotonic solution. Therefore, only (iv) statement is correct.

25. (2.83)

Precipitation as hydroxide with NH_4OH in presence of NH_4Cl	Precipitation as sulphide with H_2S in presence of HCl	Precipitation as sulphide with H_2S in presence of NH_4OH
Fe^{3+}	Bi^{3+}	Mn^{2+}
Cr^{3+}	Sn^{4+}	Ni^{2+}
Al^{3+}	$Y = 2$	Co^{2+}
$X = 3$		$Z = 3$

$$\therefore [X+Y+Z]^{1/2} = (3+2+3)^{1/2}$$

$$= 8^{1/2} = 2.8284 \approx 2.83$$

26. (4)

$$CH_3CH_2-\overset{\overset{O}{\|}}{C}-\ddot{N}H_2 \longleftrightarrow CH_3CH_2-\underset{\underset{O^{\ominus}}{|}}{C}=\overset{\oplus}{N}H_2$$

For this resonance, this compound (amide) is a weaker Lewis base than $CH_3CH_2CH_2NH_2$ and does not react with CH_3MgBr.

$$CH_3CH_2-CONH_2 \xrightarrow[\Delta]{P_2O_5} \underset{\text{(Alkyl cyanide)}}{CH_3CH_2-C\equiv N} + H_2O$$

$$CH_3CH_2-CONH_2 \xrightarrow[0°C\text{-}5°C]{NaNO_2 + HCl} \underset{\text{(Carboxylic acid)}}{CH_3CH_2-\overset{\overset{O}{\|}}{C}-OH} + N_2\uparrow + H_2O$$

$$CH_3CH_2-CONH_2 \xrightarrow[\Delta]{NaOH} CH_3CH_2COO^-Na^+ + NH_3\uparrow$$

So, wrong statements are *a*, *b*, *c* and *d*.

27. (4) Pb^{4+} is a strongly oxidising agent due to inert pair effect, itself gets reduced to Pb^{2+} by Br^-/I^-. I^- and Br^- are strongly reducing agents and get oxidised by Pb^{4+} to I_2 and Br_2 respectively.

$$\overset{+4\ -1}{PbX_4} \longrightarrow \overset{+2}{PbX_2} + \overset{0}{X_2}$$
$[X = Br, I]$

So, PbI_4 and $PbBr_4$ do not exist.

$$(CH_3)_2SiCl_2 \xrightarrow[-2HCl]{2H_2O} (CH_3)_2Si(OH)_2 \xrightarrow{\text{Polymerisation}} \text{Linear/Cyclic silicones}$$

$CO_2 + AgNO_3 + H_2O \longrightarrow$ No reaction

Radius : $Pb^{4+} > Sn^{4+}$

Smaller the size of cation, covalency becomes higher and so, covalency order : $SnCl_4 > PbCl_4$

$$Al_4C_3 + 12H_2O \longrightarrow 4Al(OH)_3 + 3CH_4\uparrow$$

Dipole moment of CO molecule is lower than expected due to $p\pi$-$p\pi$ back bonding.

$\therefore$Correct statements will be : (a), (b), (d) and (f).

28. (5) Tautomerism will not be shown by those compounds which

(1) do not have α-hydrogen atom(s)

(2) forms very unstable enol-structures

It will be shown by

(cyclohexane-1,4-dione with α-H) ; $C_6H_5CH_2CHO$ (α-H), (2-methylcyclohexanone with α-H), (5,5-dimethylcyclohexane-1,3-dione with α-H) , $H_3CCOC(CH_3)_2COOEt$

29. (4) EAN values are shown as follows

Complex	EAN value
$[Ni(CO)_4] \rightarrow (28-0) + 4\times 2$	= 36 (Kr configuration)
$[Fe(CO)_5] \rightarrow (26-0) + 5\times 2$	= 36 (Kr configuration)
$[Mn_2(CO)_{10}] \rightarrow (25-0) + 5\times 2 + 2\times\frac{1}{2}$	= 36 (Kr configuration) on Mn—Mn bond is present
$[Fe(CN)_6]^{4-} \rightarrow (26-2) + 6\times 2$	= 36 (Kr configuration)
$[Fe(CN)_6]^{3-} \rightarrow (26-3) + 6\times 2$	= 35 (No inert gas configuration)
$[Co(NH_3)_6]^{3+} \rightarrow (27-3) + 6\times 2$	= 36 (Kr configuration)
$[Ag(NH_3)_2]^+ \rightarrow (47-1) + 2\times 2$	= 50 (No inert gas configuration)
$[Cr(C_2O_4)_3]^{2-} \rightarrow (24-3) + 6\times 2$	= 33 (No inert gas configuration)
$[HgI_4]^{2-} \rightarrow (80-2) + 4\times 2$	= 86 (Rn configuration)
$[Cu(NH_3)_4]^{2+} \rightarrow (29-2) + 4\times 2$	= 35 (No inert gas configuration)
$[Ni(CO)_4]$, $[Fe(CO)_5]$, $Mn_2(CO)_{10}$, $[Fe(CN)_6]^{4-}$, $[Co(NH_3)_6]^{3+}$ $[HgI_4]^{2-}$	have EAN value equal to atomic number of inert gases.

30. (5) Boiling point of a compound depends on the following two factors:

(a) **Surface area** Higher the surface area, higher is the boiling point due to higher van der Waals' force of attraction.

So, (I) and (II) are correct orders.

(b) **Dipole moment in the compound** Higher the dipole moment, higher is the intermolecular force of attraction.

Now, due to *s*-character, dipole moment order is alkyne > alkene > alkane (when number of carbon atoms is constant)

So, (V) is correct order.

Reactivity with Cl_2 in sunlight order is :

$$\underset{(y)}{3^\circ \text{ carbon}} > \underset{(x)}{2^\circ \text{ carbon}} > \underset{(z)}{1^\circ \text{ carbon}}$$

Hence, (III) is the correct order.

Now, more the number of resonating structures, higher will be the stability.

∴ (IV) is the correct order.

Knockout 11

Paper 1

1. (0.05) $AgBr(s) \rightleftharpoons Ag^+(aq) + Br^-(aq); K_1 = K_{sp}$

$Ag^+(aq) + 2S_2O_3^{2-}(aq) \rightleftharpoons Ag(S_2O_3)_2^{3-}(aq); K_2 = K_f$

$AgBr(s) + 2S_2O_3^{2-}(aq) \rightleftharpoons Ag(S_2O_3)_2^{3-}(aq) + Br^-(aq);$

$K = K_{sp} \times K_f$

0.1 M	0	0
(0.1 − 2x)M	x	x

$\Rightarrow \quad K = K_{sp} \times K_f = 5.4 \times 10^{-13} \times 2.9 \times 10^{13}$

$= 15.66$

$\Rightarrow \quad K = \dfrac{x^2}{(0.1-2x)^2} = 15.66 \Rightarrow x = 0.05$ M

2. (0.90) Given : $T_1 = 300$ K, $p_1 = 0.8$ atm, $V_I = V_{II} = V, n = 0.6$ mol (i.e. 0.3 mol in each bulb)

On heating flask-II at 117°C, *n* moles of H_2 gas will be diffused from flask-II to flask-I, therefore Flask-I contains (0.3 + *n*) mol and flask-II contains (0.3 − *n*) mol of H_2.

$\Rightarrow p_2 \times V = (0.3+n) \times R \times 300$... in I... (i)

$p_2 \times V = (0.3-n) \times R \times 390$ ...in II...(ii)

$\Rightarrow \quad n = 0.04$ mol

$\Rightarrow$ Initially : $0.8 \times 2V = 0.6 \times 0.0821 \times 300 = 9.236$ L

$\Rightarrow$ From Eq. (ii)

$$p_2 = \frac{(0.3-0.04) \times 0.0821 \times 390}{9.236} \text{ atm} = 0.90 \text{ atm}$$

3. (13.23)

$\Rightarrow f(r) = 4\pi r^2 \psi_r^2 = Kr^2 e^{-2Zr/na_0}$

For 1*s*-orbital, $n = 1$ and $f(r) = Kr^2 e^{-2Zr/a_0}$

For maximum probability, $\dfrac{df(r)}{dr} = 0$

$\Rightarrow \quad 2r \times e^{-2Zr/a_0} + r^2 \times \left(\dfrac{-2Z}{a_0}\right) \times e^{-2Zr/a_0} = 0$

$\Rightarrow \quad r \times e^{-2Zr/a_0}\left[2 - \dfrac{2rZ}{a_0}\right] = 0$

$\therefore \quad 2 - \dfrac{2rZ}{a_0} = 0 \Rightarrow r = \dfrac{a_0}{Z} = \dfrac{52.9}{4} = 13.23$ pm

4. (0.48) Empirical formula (EF) of anhydrous *A*,

$C\% = \dfrac{12}{44} \times \dfrac{0.66}{0.675} \times 100 = 26.67 \rightarrow \dfrac{26.67}{12} = 2.22 \rightarrow 1$

$H\% = \dfrac{2}{18} \times \dfrac{0.135}{0.675} \times 100 = 2.23 \rightarrow \dfrac{2.23}{1} = 2.23 \rightarrow 1$ $\quad CHO_2$

$O\% = 100 - (26.67 + 2.23) = 71.10 \rightarrow \dfrac{71.10}{16} = 4.44 \rightarrow 2$

Mass of H_2O in $A = 1.50 - 1.07 = 0.43$ g

EF mass of $CHO_2 = 45$ g

Simple ratio of $CHO_2 : H_2O = \dfrac{1.07}{45} : \dfrac{0.43}{18} = 1:1$

Molecular formula of *A* is $(CHO_2 \cdot H_2O)_n$.

As, one mole of *B* on complete combustion produces 2 mole of $CO_2, n = 2$

Molecular formula of $B = C_2H_2O_4$ and $A = C_2H_2O_4 \cdot 2H_2O$

$$\Rightarrow \underset{\substack{(A)\\126\text{ g}\\1.12\text{ g}}}{C_2H_2O_4 \cdot 2H_2O} \xrightarrow[\Delta]{O_2} 2CO_2 + \underset{\substack{3 \times 18\text{ g}}}{3H_2O}$$

$\dfrac{3 \times 18}{126} \times 1.12 = 0.48$ g

5. (9.60)

$$\overset{+4}{SO_2} + \overset{+7}{MnO_4^-} \xrightarrow{H^+} \overset{+6}{SO_4^{2-}} + Mn^{2+}$$

$n-f = 6-4 = 2$ $\quad n-f = 7-2 = 5$

mol = 5 $\quad$ mol = 2

$\Rightarrow MnO_4^-$ required = 240×0.008 mmol

SO_2 required = $240 \times 0.008 \times 5$ mmol

= 9.60 mmol

6. (4.14) $\Rightarrow \dfrac{1}{2}mv^2 = KE = E - \phi$

To show photoelectricity, energy of light (*E*) > work function (ϕ) of the metal

$\Rightarrow E = \dfrac{hc}{\lambda} = \dfrac{(6.62 \times 10^{-34} \text{ Js}) \times (3 \times 10^8 \text{ ms}^{-1})}{(300 \times 10^{-9} \text{ m})}$

$= 6.62 \times 10^{-19}$ J

$= \dfrac{6.62 \times 10^{-19} \text{ J}}{1.6 \times 10^{-19} \text{ J/eV}} = 4.14$ eV

So, only 4 metals (Li, Na, K, Mg) will show photoelectric effect.

7. (2)

$B_2H_6 + 2RNH_2 \longrightarrow [BH_2(RNH_2)_2]^\oplus [BH_4]^\ominus$

8. (5.99)

$\Rightarrow V_2 = \dfrac{p_1V_1}{p_2} = \dfrac{70 \times 100}{40} = 175\,\text{mL}$

$\Rightarrow$ Volume of the gas adsorbed

$= 175 - 100 = 75$ mL

$\Rightarrow$ Volume of the gas adsorbed per gram of charcoal

$= \dfrac{75}{0.6} = 125\,\text{mL/g}$

$\Rightarrow$ At STP condition,

$V_S = \dfrac{pV}{T} \times \dfrac{T_S}{p_S}$

$= \dfrac{40 \times 125}{300} \times \dfrac{273}{760} = 5.99$ mL

9. (b,c)

$\Rightarrow$ (A) $\xrightarrow[\text{(ii)}Zn/H_2O]{\text{(i)}O_3/THF}$ (B) $\xrightarrow[\text{(ii)}H_2O]{\text{(i)}Mg/Hg}$ HO–(C)–OH $\xrightarrow[\Delta]{H^+}$ HO–(carbocation) $\xrightarrow{\text{Rearrangement}}$; $-H^{\oplus}$; (D) $\xrightarrow[\text{(ii) } H_2O]{\text{(i) } LiAlH_4}$ (E) $\xrightarrow[-H_2O]{\text{(E1) conc. } H_2SO_4 \text{ or } H_3PO_4}$ $\xrightarrow{\text{Ring expansion}}$ $\xrightarrow{-H^{\oplus}}$ (A)

$\Rightarrow Al_2O_3$ or ThO_2 shows dehydration of an alcohol into alkene *via*. E2 elimination.

10. (a,b, d)

$\xrightarrow{m\text{-CPBA}}$ (A) $\xrightarrow{H_3O^{\oplus}}$ (3°, $\oplus$, OH) $\xrightarrow[-H^{\oplus}]{H_2\overset{18}{O}(18)}$ (B) (CH_3, $\overset{18}{OH}$, OH, H)

(A) $\xrightarrow{\ominus\overset{18}{O}H}$ (CH_3, $O^{\ominus}$, (18) OH) $\xrightarrow[-OH^-]{H_2O}$ (C) (CH_3, OH, (18) OH)

11. (a,c,d)

(III) COOH, $\overset{+}{N}H_3$ $\xleftarrow{pH<7}$ (I) COO^-, $\overset{+}{N}H_3$ $\xrightarrow{pH>7}$ (II) COO^-, NH_2

(III) All are acidic groups; (I) Zwitter ion (pH = p_IH = 7); (II) All are basic groups.

12. (a, c) $\Rightarrow C_{p,m}^{\text{mix}} = \dfrac{1}{2}(C_p^1 + C_p^2) = \dfrac{1}{2}\left(\dfrac{5R}{2} + \dfrac{7R}{2}\right) = 3R$

$C_{V,m}^{\text{mix}} = \dfrac{1}{2}(C_V^1 + C_V^2)$

$= \dfrac{1}{2}\left(\dfrac{3R}{2} + \dfrac{5R}{2}\right) = 2R$

$\gamma_{\text{mix}} = \dfrac{C_{p,m}^{\text{mix}}}{C_{V,m}^{\text{mix}}} = \dfrac{3R}{2R} = 1.5$

$\Rightarrow W_{\Delta Q=0} < W_{\Delta T=0}$, because from the given plot, it is clear that : $(\text{area})_{\text{isothermal}} > (\text{area})_{\text{adiabatic}}$

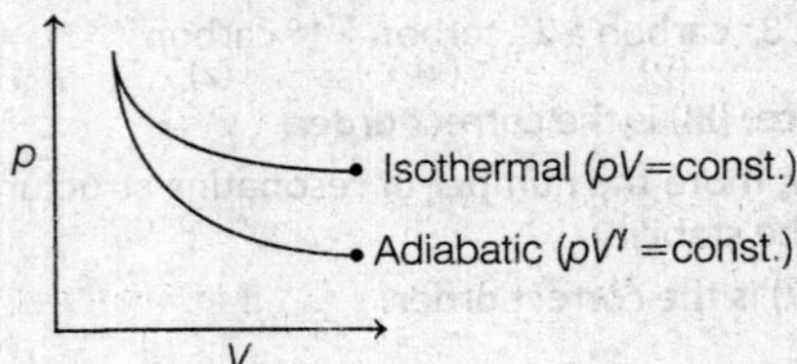

$\Rightarrow$ Internal energy of an ideal gas depends only on temperature.

$\Rightarrow$ Fraction of heat used in increasing internal energy

$= \dfrac{dU}{dq_p} = \dfrac{dU}{dH} = \dfrac{nC_V\,dT}{nC_p\,dT}\ (p = \text{constant})$

$= \dfrac{C_{V,m}}{C_{p,m}} = \dfrac{5R/2}{3R/2} = \dfrac{5}{3}$ [mono-atomic gas]

13. (c) The order of first ionisation energy of 3rd period is as follows

Na < Al < Mg < Si < S < P < Cl < Ar

On moving along a period from left to right, nuclear charge increases that outweighs the shielding effect. As a result, outermost electrons are held more tightly.

Hence, ionisation enthalpy increases. Ionisation enthalpy of group 2 is greater than group 13 and that of group 15 is greater than group 16. This is due to fully filled and half-filled orbitals.

$\therefore$ X, Y and Z are argon, chlorine and sodium respectively.

14. (b,c,d) Statements (b,c,d) are correct, whereas statement (a) is incorrect.

(a) X reaches end point earlier than Y, hence X is present in lower concentration.

(b) Greater change in pH of X at end point indicates that X is stronger acid than Y.

(c) Volume of NaOH required to neutralise Y is twice to that required for X, so $[X] = \dfrac{1}{100} = 0.01$ M

and $[Y] = \dfrac{2}{100} = 0.02$ M.

(d) Weaker acid (Y) produces a stronger conjugate base (salt).

15. (c) (i) An atom at the corner contributes 1/8 of its volume to each of 8 adjacent cubes.

Thus, (I) - (R)

(ii) An atom on the face of the unit cell contributes 1/2 of its volume of the cell.

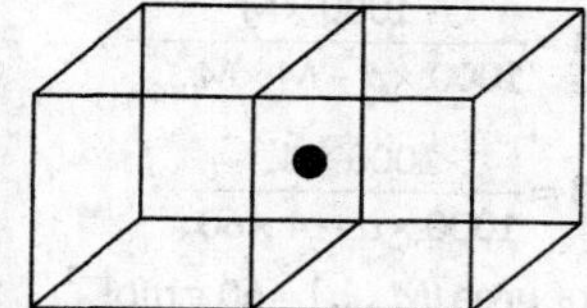

Thus, (II) - (Q)

(iii) Atoms on the edge of the unit cell contribute 1/4 of their volume to the unit cell.

Thus, (III)-(P)

(iv) Total Cl^- contributing to the cell

$= 8$ at corners $+ 6$ at the faces $= 14\ Cl^-$

Total Cl^- at the unit cell

$= \left(8 \times \frac{1}{8}\right)$ at the corner $+ \left(6 + \frac{1}{2}\right)$ at the faces $= 4\ Cl^-$

Thus, fraction $= 4/14 = 2/7$

Thus, (IV) - (S)

16. (a) (I) X and Y both are weak electrolytes, hence have minimum conductance. When $X[(C_2H_5)_3N]$ is added to $Y(CH_3COOH)$ ions are formed, hence conductance increases.

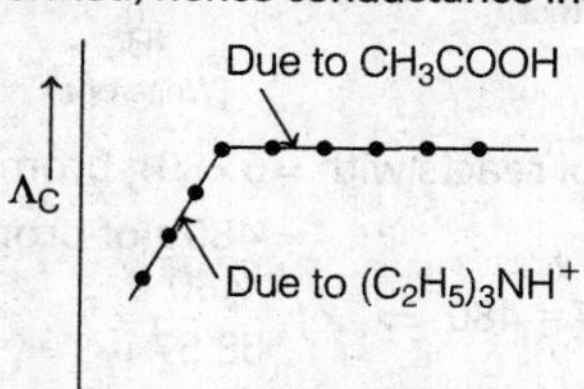

$$\underset{(Y)}{CH_3COOH} + \underset{(X)}{(C_2H_5)_3N} \longrightarrow CH_3COO^- + (C_2H_5)_3NH^+$$

After complete reaction further addition of Y, makes no change in conductance.

Thus, (I) $\rightarrow$ (S)

(II) Net reaction is

$$\underset{(X)}{I^-} + \underset{(Y)}{Ag^+} \longrightarrow \underset{\text{Insoluble}}{AgI(s)}$$

Where, $X(I^-)$ is added to $Y(Ag^+)$ insoluble AgI is formed. Hence, there is no change in conductance.

After complete reaction of Ag^+, further addition of I^- cause increase in conductance.

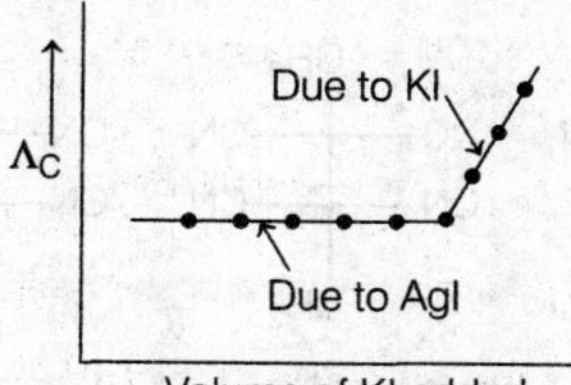

Thus, (II) $\rightarrow$ (T)

(III) KOH is a strong electrolyte. As $CH_3COOH(X)$ is added, OH^- is neutralised by CH_3COOH.

$$\underset{(Y)}{OH^-} + \underset{(X)}{CH_3COOH} \longrightarrow CH_3COO^- + H_2O$$

$$CH_3COO^- + H_2O \longrightarrow CH_3COOH + OH^-$$

But being in small extent, conductance decreases. After complete reaction of KOH, on further addition of CH_3COOH, (weak) there is no change in conductance.

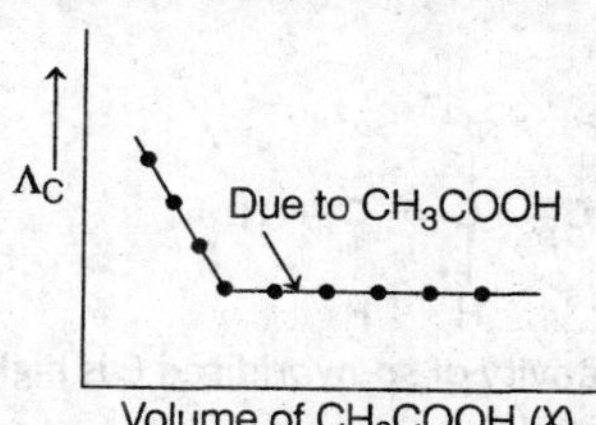

Thus, (III) $\rightarrow$ (Q)

(IV) NaOH(X) and HI(Y), H_2O is formed hence, conductance decreases. After complete reaction of OH^-, further addition of NaOH(X), causes increase in conductance.

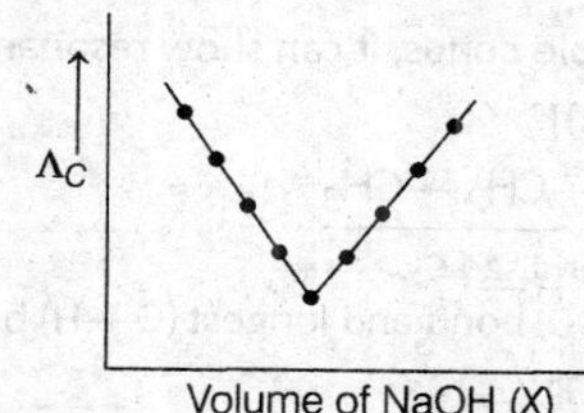

Thus, (IV) $\rightarrow$ (P)

17. (b) As, $k_1 << k_2 \approx k_3$ in mechanism (I) based on relative values, it is clear that rate determining step is $A_2 \xrightarrow{k_1} 2A$

$$\therefore \quad -\frac{d[A_2]}{dt} = \frac{1}{2}\frac{d[AB]}{dt} = k_1[A_2]$$

$$\therefore \quad \frac{d[AB]}{dt} = 2k_1[A_2]$$

Thus, (I) - (R)

$\Rightarrow$ In mechanism (II)

$$k_1 << k_2$$

Thus, rate determining step is

$$A_2 + B_2 \longrightarrow A_2B_2$$

$$= \frac{d[A_2]}{dt} = \frac{1}{2}\frac{d[AB]}{dt}$$

$$\frac{d[AB]}{dt} = -2\frac{d[A_2]}{dt} = -2[-k_1[A_2][B_2]]$$

$$= 2k_1[A_2][B_2]$$

Thus, (II) - (S)

$\Rightarrow$ In mechanism (III)

$$k_1 = \frac{[A]^2}{[A_2]} \text{ and } [A] = \sqrt{k_1[A_2]}$$

Similarly, $[B] = \sqrt{k_2[B_2]}$

$$\frac{d[A]}{dt} = k[A][B] = k\sqrt{k_1k_2}\,[A_2]^{1/2}[B_2]^{1/2}$$

Thus, (III) - (P)

$\Rightarrow$ For mechanism (IV)

$$k_1 << k_2$$

Thus rate determining step is $B_2 \rightarrow 2B$

$$k = \frac{[A]^2}{[A_2]}$$

$$\therefore \quad [A] = \sqrt{k(A_2)}$$

$$\frac{d[AB]}{dt} = -2\frac{d[B_2]}{dt} = -2 - [-k_1[B_2]] = 2k_1[B_2]$$

Thus, (IV) - (Q)

18. (c) I. $\underset{}{H—\overset{sp}{C}\equiv\overset{sp}{C}—\underset{H}{\overset{sp^2}{C}}=\underset{H}{\overset{sp^2}{C}}—H}$

Electronegativity of *sp*-hybridised C is higher, than that of sp^2-hybridised C.

(C—H) bond is shortest attached to *sp*-hybridised C.

(C—H) bond is shortest attached to *sp*-hybridised C.

Due to multiple bonds, it can show resonance to *sp*-hybridised C.

Due to multiple bonds, it can show resonance.

Thus [(I)-(Q,R)]

(II) $\underbrace{CH_3—CH_2—CH_2—CH_3}_{sp^3\text{–hybridised C}}$

Longest (C—C) bond and longest (C—H) bond.

Thus (II) - (P, T)

(III) $CH_2=CH—CH=CH_2$

Due to multiple bonds, resonance is possible

$$CH_2=CH—CH=CH_2 \longleftrightarrow \overset{\oplus}{C}H_2—CH=CH—\overset{\ominus}{C}H_2$$

Thus, (III) - (R)

(IV) $CH_3CH=CHCH_3$ (Allylic, Allylic)

Thus, (IV)-(R, S)

Paper 2

1. (9)

[Structures of isomeric esters $C_5H_{10}O_2$: $HCOOCH_2CH_2CH_2CH_3$, $HCOOCH(CH_3)CH_2CH_3$, $HCOOCH_2CH(CH_3)_2$, $HCOOC(CH_3)_3$, $CH_3COOCH_2CH_2CH_3$, $CH_3COOCH(CH_3)_2$, $CH_3CH_2COOCH_2CH_3$, $CH_3CH_2CH_2COOCH_3$, $(CH_3)_2CHCOOCH_3$]

2. (2) ⇒ Molality of urea solution $(m) = 2.273$

Molarity of urea solution = 4 mol L^{-1}

$$m = \frac{1000 \times M}{1000 \times d - M \times M_{urea}}$$

$$\Rightarrow \quad 2.273 = \frac{1000 \times 4}{1000 \times d - 4 \times 60}$$

$\because$ Molar mass of urea $(M_{urea}) = 60 \text{ g mol}^{-1}$

$$\Rightarrow \quad d = 1.99 \text{ g mL}^{-1} \simeq 2 \text{ g mL}^{-1}$$

3. (7) $\overset{+5}{NO_3^-} + \overset{+3}{As_2}\overset{-2}{S_3} + H_2O \longrightarrow \overset{+5}{AsO_4^{3-}} + \overset{+6}{SO_4^{2-}} + H^+ + \overset{+3}{NO^+}$

$n-f : (5-3) \quad As : (5-3) \times 2 = 4$

$= 2 \qquad S : [+6-(-2)] \times 3 = 24$

Total = 28

Mole : 28(x) $\qquad$ 2(y)

$$\Rightarrow \text{So, } \frac{x}{2y} = \frac{28}{2 \times 2} = 7$$

4. (7)

Phenol (1 mol) + $3Br_2$ (3 mol) $\xrightarrow{H_2O}$ 2,4,6-tribromophenol [White ppt.] + 3HBr

1 mol of phenol reacts with $= 6 \times 80$ g bromine

$= 480$ g of bromine

Given, $x \times 68.57 = 480 \Rightarrow x = \dfrac{480}{68.57} = 7$

5. (0)

(*Z*) or (*cis*)- but-2-ene $\xrightarrow[\text{(Baeyer's reagent) [syn-addition]}]{\text{Cold, dilute } KMnO_4/OH^-}$ *meso*-butane-2,3 diol [optically inactive]

6. (3) The isomeric carbonyl compounds of molecular formula, $C_5H_{10}O$ (86 u) are

(4), (6) and (7) ⟶ give racemic mixture of alcohols) = (5) ⟶ is a pure enantiomer and will give diastereomers = (1), (2), (3) ⟶ give achiral alcohols.

7. (6) Protein, Cellulose, Nylon-6, Terylene, Bakelite, MF resin.

8. (6)

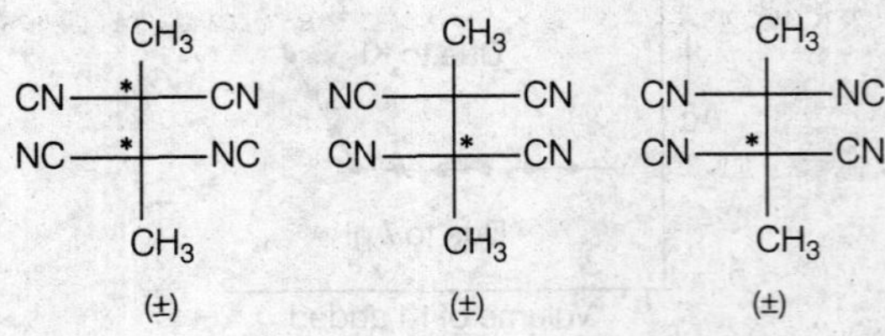

9. (a,b) For the compounds of first series (3*d*) of transition metals, the contribution of orbital angular momentum (*L*) is effectively quenched and hence no significance of μ_{S+L}.

$\Rightarrow$ M^{2+} of $Z = 25$ has $3d^5$ configuration, i.e. $n = 5$

$\therefore \quad \mu = \sqrt{5(5+2)} = 5.916$ BM

10. (a,b,c,d)

$\Rightarrow H_2O$

$\xrightarrow{XeF_2} Xe + HF + O_2$

$\xrightarrow{XeF_4} Xe + HF + O_2 + XeO_3$

$\xrightarrow{XeF_6} HF + XeO_3$

$\Rightarrow \quad XeF_4 + NaF \longrightarrow Na^{\oplus}\,[XeF_5]^{\ominus}$ $\quad [F^{\ominus}$ acceptor$]$

$XeF_4 + SbF_5 \longrightarrow [XeF_3]^{\oplus}\,[SbF_6]^{\ominus}$ $\quad [F^{\ominus}$ donor$]$

$\Rightarrow$ The above are also true for XeF_6.

11. (b, c) Pink colour of aqueous solution of Co(II) chloride is due to electronic transition of electrons from t_{2g} to e_g energy level of $[Co(H_2O)_6]^{2+}$ complex.

$\Rightarrow$ When excess of HCl is added to this solution, $[Co(H_2O)_6]^{2+}$ gets converted into $[CoCl_4]^{2-}$.

$\Rightarrow$ Tetrahedral complexes have smaller crystal field splitting than octahedral complexes, because, $\Delta_t = \frac{4}{9}\Delta_o$.

12. (d) $MeSiCl_3$ on hydrolysis produces $MeSi(OH)_3$, which on subsequent condensation forms a cross-linked polymeric silicon.

$$CH_3 - \underset{\underset{\left[\,\right]_n}{|}}{\overset{\overset{\left[\,\right]_n}{|}}{Si}} - \left[O\right]_n$$

13. (a,d) $\quad P \quad : \quad Q \quad : \quad R$

(Corners) (Edge centres and alternate face centres) (remaining face centres and alternate, Td, void positions)

$$= 8 \times \frac{1}{8} : \left(12 \times \frac{1}{4} + 2 \times \frac{1}{2}\right) : \left(4 \times \frac{1}{2} + 4\right) = 1 : 4 : 6$$

$\therefore$ Formula of the compound is PQ_4R_6.

Now, as per the conditions given, there are two possibilities :

(i) *Q* are removed from 4-fold axis and the remaining number of *Q* becomes $= 4 - 2 \times \frac{1}{2} = 3$ and the formula becomes PQ_3R_6.

(ii) *R* is removed from 4-fold axes and the remaining numbers of *R* becomes $= 6 - 2 \times \frac{1}{2} = 5$ and the formula becomes PQ_4R_5.

14. (a,c,d) $\Rightarrow \quad \pi = CRT \times i$

$\Rightarrow \quad 98.52 = 1 \times 0.082 \times 300 \times n$

$\Rightarrow \quad n = 4$

$\because$ When, $\quad \alpha = 1$

$\Rightarrow \quad i = 1 + \alpha(n-1) = n$

$\therefore$ The complex can be written as, $\overset{III}{[Cr(H_2O)_6]Cl_3}$

$\Rightarrow [Cr(H_2O)_6]Cl_3(aq) + 3AgNO_3(aq) \longrightarrow$

1 mol, 2×1 mol (given) ; 3 mol, 6 mol (also given)

$3AgCl\downarrow(s) + [Cr(H_2O)_6](NO_3)_3(aq)$

3 mol, 6 mol, $= 6 \times 143.6$ g, $= 861$ g ; 1 mol, 2 mol $\Downarrow$ Molarity $= \frac{2}{2+1}$ M $= \frac{2}{3}$ M

$\Rightarrow$ For the clear solution,

$\pi = CRT \times i = \frac{2}{3} \times 0.082 \times 300 \times 4 \qquad [\because i = n = 4]$

$= 65.6$ atm

15. (d) In the given reaction, pinacol-pinacolone rearrangement takes place.

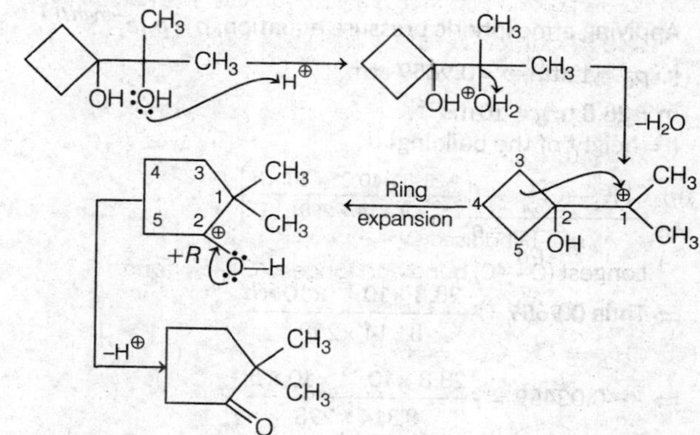

16. (d) (i) Pb_3O_4 on treatment with conc. HNO_3 gives PbO_2 (*B*).

$$\underset{(A)}{Pb_3O_4} \xrightarrow{\text{Conc.}HNO_3} \underset{(B)}{PbO_2} + Pb(NO_3)_2 + H_2O$$

[Red coloured mixed oxide : $PbO_2 \cdot 2PbO$]

(ii) PbO_2 with HCl produces lead chloride, $PbCl_2$ (*C*).

$$\underset{(B)}{PbO_2} \xrightarrow{HCl} \underset{(C)}{PbCl_2} + Cl_2 + H_2O$$

Insoluble in cold water but soluble in hot water

(iii) Pb_3O_4 on treating with HCl, gives $PbCl_2$ (*C*) alongwith chlorine gas and water.

$$\underset{(A)}{Pb_3O_4} \xrightarrow{HCl} \underset{(C)}{PbCl_2} + Cl_2 + H_2O$$

17. (d) Statement (d) is correct, whereas other statements are incorrect.

$\Rightarrow$ Both Co(III) and Co(II) are stabilised by strong field ligands due to higher CFSE values.

$\Rightarrow$ Due to higher Z_{eff} values, Pd(II) and Pt(II) always form inner-orbital low-spin diamagnetic square planar complexes.

$\Rightarrow [Ni(CN)_4]^{2-}$: Diamagnetic, square planar

$[Ni(CO)_4]$: Diamagnetic, tetrahedral.

18. (c)

$\xrightarrow[\Delta]{H_2/Pt}$ $\xrightarrow{-H_2O}$

The product formed has 4 chiral centres.

Knockout 12

Paper 1

1. (99)

Applying atmospheric pressure equation, $p = p_0 e^{-mgh/RT}$

[$\because p_0 = 1$ atm, $p = 0.9659$ atm,
$m = 28.8$ u, $g = 10\,ms^{-2}$,
h = height of the building]

$$\Rightarrow \frac{p}{p_0} = e^{\left(\frac{-28.8\times10^{-3}\times10\times h}{8.314\times298}\right)}$$

$$\Rightarrow \ln 0.9659 = \frac{-28.8\times10^{-3}\times10\times h}{8.314\times298}$$

$$\Rightarrow -0.03469 = -\frac{28.8\times10^{-3}\times10\times h}{8.314\times298}$$

On solving, $h = 298.4$ m

Number of floors in the building

$$= \frac{298.4}{2.98} = 100$$

Top floor must be 99th floor.

2. (14)

Equilibrium constant, $K = \frac{[B]_{eq}}{[A]_{eq}} = \frac{1.6}{0.4} = 4$

$$\Rightarrow 4 = \frac{K_1}{K_2} = \frac{4\times10^{-2}}{K_2}$$

$$\Rightarrow K_2 = 10^{-2}\,s^{-1}$$

For 50% completion of equilibrium concentration (X_e), time taken, $t_{eq} = \frac{1}{K_1+K_2}\ln\frac{X_e}{50\% \text{ of } X_e}$

$$= \frac{1}{4\times10^{-2}+10^{-2}}\ln\frac{X_e}{0.5X_e}$$

$$= \frac{1}{5\times10^{-2}}\ln 2 = 14\text{ s.}$$

3. (100)

Gram equivalence deposited $= \frac{250\times0.1\times3}{1000}$

$$\Rightarrow \text{Time} = \frac{250\times0.1\times3}{1000}\times\frac{96500}{96.5}\times\frac{100}{75} = 100\text{ s}$$

4. (71.49)

$$V_B \text{ at } 298\text{ K} = \frac{78\times2794}{0.877\times1000}\text{ L},$$

$$V_T \text{ at } 298\text{ K} = \frac{92\times7488}{0.867\times1000}\text{ L}$$

[$\because V_B$ = volume of benzene, V_T = volume of toluene]

$$\Rightarrow \frac{p_B^\circ}{760}\times\frac{78\times2794}{0.877\times1000} = 1\times0.082\times298 \quad \text{...(i)}$$

$$\frac{p_T^\circ}{760}\times\frac{92\times7488}{0.867\times1000} = 1\times0.082\times298 \quad [\because pV = nRT] \text{...(ii)}$$

Solving Eqs. (i) and (ii)

$p_B^\circ = 74.74$ mm; $p_T^\circ = 23.37$ mm

$$\Rightarrow 46 = p_B^\circ X_B + p_T^\circ(1 - X_B)$$

[Applying Raoult's law]

Putting p_B° and p_T° solving $X_B = 0.44$ (in liquid phase)

$\Rightarrow$ In vapour phase

$$74.74\times0.44 = 46\,(X'_B)_g$$

$$\Rightarrow (X'_B)_g = 0.7149$$

$$\Rightarrow (X'_B)_g\,\% = 71.49$$

5. (648) Slope $= -\frac{4}{3}$, $\left[\because m = \frac{4-16}{15-6}\right]$

$$\Rightarrow p = -\frac{4}{3}V + C$$

$$\Rightarrow 16 = -\frac{4}{3}\times6 + C$$

$$\Rightarrow C = 24;\ p = -\frac{4}{3}V + 24 \quad \text{...(i)}$$

$$\therefore p = -\frac{4}{3}\times\frac{2RT}{p} + 24$$

[$\because$ 2 moles of gas has taken, i.e. $V = \frac{2RT}{p}$]

$$\Rightarrow 3p^2 - 72p + 8RT = 0 \quad \text{...(ii)}$$

Differentiating we get,

$$6p - 72 + 8R\frac{\partial T}{\partial p} = 0 \text{ [For maxima]}$$

or, $\frac{\partial T}{\partial p} = \frac{72-6p}{8R} = 0$ or, $p = 12$ atm

Putting the value of p in Eq. (ii) and solving $T_{max} = 648$ K

6. (9.55)

Since, $NaHCO_3$ is amphiprotic compound, it will ionise as well as hydrolyse

$$HCO_3^- \rightleftharpoons H^+ + CO_3^{2-}$$

$$\text{... } K_2 = 5\times10^{-11} \quad \text{...(i)}$$

$$HCO_3^- + H_2O \rightleftharpoons H_2CO_3 + \overset{\ominus}{O}H,$$

$$K_h = \frac{K_w}{K_1} = 2.5\times10^{-8} \quad \text{...(ii)}$$

Since, hydrolysis equilibrium is ~1000 times greater, it will predominate

$\Rightarrow \quad OH^{\ominus} = \sqrt{K_h \cdot C}$

$= \sqrt{2.5 \times 10^{-8} \times 5 \times 10^{-2}}$

$\Rightarrow \quad [OH^-] = 3.54 \times 10^{-5}$ M,

$\Rightarrow \quad pOH = 5 - 0.55 = 4.45$

$\Rightarrow \quad pH = 14 - 4.45 = 9.55$

7. (38.35) Rate constant of reaction (k) and time vary as,

$$k \propto \frac{1}{\text{time}}$$

$$\Rightarrow \frac{k_{27^\circ}}{k_{7^\circ}} = \frac{18}{6} = 3$$

$$\Rightarrow \log \frac{k_{27}}{k_7} = \frac{E_a}{2.303R}\left[\frac{T_2 - T_1}{T_1 T_2}\right]$$

$$\Rightarrow \log 3 = \frac{E_a \times 20}{2.303 \times 8.31 \times 300 \times 280}$$

On solving $E_a = 38.35$ kJ mol^{-1}

8. (68) $n\,CH_2{=}C(CH_3){-}CH{=}CH_2 \xrightarrow{\text{Polymerise}} \left[-CH_2-C(CH_3){=}CH-CH_2-\right]_n$

$\xrightarrow{\text{Reductive ozonolysis}} n\,O{=}CH{-}CH_2{-}CH_2{-}C({=}O){-}CH_3$ (Molar mass = 100 g/mol)

$\Rightarrow \quad n \times 100 = 10^3 \times 10^3$

$n = 10^4$ unit

Gram molar mass of natural rubber

$= 68 \times 10^4$

9. (a, b, c, d)

$$\Rightarrow \quad E_n = -13.6\frac{Z^2}{n^2}$$

$$\Rightarrow \quad -6.05 = -13.6\frac{2^2}{n^2}$$

solving, $n = 3$ and as magnetic quantum number (m) is 0, it is $3p_z$ orbital.

Hence, option (a) is correct.

$\Rightarrow$ (b) is correct as the wave function will be ψ_{310}.

$\Rightarrow$ (c) is correct, since ψ involves only $\cos\theta$.

$\Rightarrow$ (d) is correct, for radial node : $6 - \sigma = 0$

$$\Rightarrow \quad \sigma = 6 \Rightarrow \frac{2r}{a_0} = 6$$

$$\Rightarrow \quad r = 3a_0$$

10. (b, c, d)

Statements (b), (c) and (d) are incorrect, whereas statement (a) is correct.

Option (b) is incorrect since doping of As in silicon produces 'n'-type semiconductor.

Option (c) is incorrect as doping in crystals does not create dislocation defects.

Option (d) is incorrect since anion cannot occupy interstitial voids as it is bigger in size.

11. (b, d)

Compound (S) is terephthalic acid, $HO_2C-C_6H_4-CO_2H$

obtained from oxidation of (R) which is 4-methylbenzoic acid,

$H_3C-C_6H_4-CO_2H$ is one of the hydrolysis products of compound (P) which has structure

$H_3C-C_6H_4-C({=}O)-NH-C_6H_4-CH_3$, ($S$) is terephthalic acid and is confirmed as it can form only one monosubstituted product (by E^+, electrophile) as

$H_3C-C_6H_4-C({=}O)-NH-C_6H_3(E)-CH_3$ in ArS_E2 reaction.

$S + $ (n-mol) $CH_2OH{-}CH_2OH$ (n-mol) (Ethylene glycol) $\xrightarrow[-H_2O]{\text{Condensation}} \left[-O-C({=}O)-C_6H_4-C({=}O)-O-CH_2CH_2-\right]_n$ (Terylene or Dacron)

12. (a, b, d)

Option (a) is correct as the mode of reaction is intramolecular aldol where methylene carbon forms carbanion (enolate ion).

Option (b) is correct as in Hofmann degradation stereochemistry (R-configuration) of the migrating group remains same.

Option (c) is incorrect as approach of reagent is hindered due to steric effect of two methyl groups in *ortho* positions of aniline in carbylamine reaction.

Option (d) is correct, it is Michael's addition.

13. (a, b, c, d)

Option (a) is correct as with increase in atomic number ($_{58}Ce \rightarrow {}_{71}Lu$), basicity of $Ln(OH)_3$ decreases, where Ln = lanthanoids.

Option (b) is correct because of lanthanide contraction, size of Zr^{4+} and Hf^{4+} is nearly same.

Option (c) is correct as +3 is the most stable oxidation state of Ln^{3+} ions. So, Ce^{4+} easily gets reduced to Ce^{3+}. Hence, it acts as oxidising agent.

Option (d) is correct as ionic radii values are La^{3+}(103), Ce^{3+}(102), Pm^{3+}(97), Yb^{3+}(86.8) in picometer. Hence, size of Ln^{3+} decreases from La^{3+} to Ce^{3+} to Lu^{3+}.

14. (a, b, c)

$X: K_2[Ni(CN)_4]$; $Y: H_2[NiCl_4]$

Option (b) and (c) are correct as $\overset{\ominus}{CN}$ is a strong field ligand having paired up d^8 configuration and Ni(II) undergoes

dsp^2-hybridisation with no unpaired electrons in X while $Cl^{\ominus}$ being a weak field ligand, it cannot pair up d^8 configuration and Ni(II) undergoes sp^3-hybridisation in Y having two unpaired electrons.

15. (c) $\Delta T_b = K_b mi$

$\log \Delta T_b = \log K_b + \log(mi)$

$y = c + mi$

$(m' = \text{slope}) = \tan\theta = \tan 45° = 1$

$c = \text{intercept on } \log(\Delta T_b) \text{ axis} = -0.284°$

Thus, when $mi = 1$, $\log mi = 0$

$\therefore \log K_b = \log \Delta T_b = -0.284°$

(I) For 2 molal urea solution, $m = 2, i = 1$ (non-electrolyte)

$\log \Delta T_b = -0.284 + \log 2$

$= -0.284 + 0.300 = 0.016°$

Thus, (I)-(R)

(II) For NaCl $(y = 2)$

$i = 1 + (y-1)x = 1 + x$

$= 1 + 1 = 2$

$\therefore \log(mi) = \log 4 = \log 2^2$

$= 2\log 2 = 0.60$

$\log \Delta T_b = -0.284 + 0.60 = 0.316$

Thus, (II)-(S)

(III) For K_2SO_4, $(y = 3)$

$\therefore \quad i = [1 + (y-1)x]$

$= (1 + 2x) = 1 + 2 \times 0.4 = 1.8$

$\therefore \quad \log(mi) = \log 3.6$

$= \log 36 - \log 10 = \log(2^2 \times 3^2) - \log 10$

$= 2\log 2 + 2\log 3 - \log 10$

$= 2 \times 0.3 + 2 \times 0.48 - 1$

$= 0.6 + 0.96 - 1 = 0.56$

$\therefore \quad \log \Delta T_b = -0.284 + 0.56 = 0.276$

Thus, (III)-(P)

(IV) For $K_3[Fe(CN)_6]$, $(y = 4)$

$\therefore \quad i = 1 + (y-1)x = 1 + 3x$

$= 1 + 3 \times 0.2 = 1.6$

$\therefore \quad \log(mi) = \log 3.2$

$= \log 32 - \log 10$

$= 5\log 2 - \log 10$

$= 1.5 - 1.0 = 0.5$

$\therefore \quad \log \Delta T_b = -0.284 + 0.500 = 0.216$

Thus, (IV)-(Q)

16. (b) For α-line in Balmer series, $n_1 = 2$ and $n_2 = 3$

For β-line $n_1 = 2, n_2 = 4$

(I) $\therefore \quad \bar{v} = \frac{1}{\lambda} = \bar{R}_H Z^2 \left[\frac{1}{n_1^2} - \frac{1}{n_2^2}\right]$

$$\bar{v}_\alpha = \bar{R}_H (4)^2 \left[\frac{1}{2^2} - \frac{1}{3^2}\right] = \bar{R}_H (16)\left[\frac{5}{36}\right] = \frac{20\bar{R}_H}{9}$$

$$\bar{v}_\beta = \bar{R}_H (4)^2 \left[\frac{1}{2^2} - \frac{1}{4^2}\right] = \bar{R}_H (16)\left[\frac{12}{64}\right] = 3\bar{R}_H$$

$$\text{Difference} = 3\bar{R}_H - \frac{20}{9}\bar{R}_H = \frac{7}{9}\bar{R}_H$$

Thus, [(I)-(T)]

(II) For maximum wave number

$n_2 \to \infty$

$$\therefore \quad \bar{v}_{max} = \frac{\bar{R}_H Z^2}{n_1^2}$$

For Brackett series in Li^{2+}

$n_1 = 4$

$$\therefore \quad \bar{v}_{max} = \frac{9}{16}\bar{R}_H$$

Thus, [(II)-(R)]

(III) If v is maximum, λ is minimum

$$\frac{1}{\lambda_{min}} = \bar{R}_H Z^2 \left[\frac{1}{n_1^2}\right] = \bar{R}_H (2)^2 \left[\frac{1}{3^2}\right]$$

$\therefore \frac{1}{\lambda_{min}} = \frac{4}{9}\bar{R}_H$ in Paschen series of He^+.

If $\bar{v}$ is minimum, λ is minimum, λ is maximum and is at $n_2 = (n_1 + 1)$

$$\because \quad \frac{1}{\lambda_{max}} = 4\bar{R}_H \left[\frac{1}{3^2} - \frac{1}{4^2}\right]$$

$$= 4\bar{R}_H \left[\frac{7}{144}\right] = \frac{7}{16}\bar{R}_H$$

$$\therefore \lambda_{max} - \lambda_{min} = \left[\frac{36}{7} - \frac{9}{4}\right]\frac{1}{R_H} = \frac{2.89}{R_H}$$

$\therefore$ [(III)-(P)]

$\Rightarrow$ Rydberg constant of $He^+ = \bar{R}_H (Z^2) = 16\bar{R}_H$

Thus, [(IV)-(Q)]

17. (b) Major product in (I), (II), (III) and (IV) is common which is

Ph(Me)C(Ph)–C(=O)–CH_3 $\xrightarrow[\text{(ii) } H_3O^+]{\text{(i) Iodoform reaction}}$ X + $CHI_3\downarrow$

[Using reagent (P) of List-II]

In all the reactions, (I) is finally obtained by Pinacol-Pinacolone rearrangement in which the migratory aptitude follows the order:

H > aryl (Ph) > alkyl (Me)

Here, X is Me–C(Ph)(Ph)–COOH (2, 2-diphenylpropan-1-oic acid)

18. (b)

(I) OTs ... OTs ← Good leaving group + $HS^{\ominus}$ ⟶ S_N2 with inversion (Chiral)

Thus, [(I)-(Q)]

(II) t-BuOK

BuO^- is sterically hindered base causing elimination by E2 mechanism.

Thus, [(II)-(S)]

(III) H^+, E1, H_2SO_4

3° alcohol changes to $(—OH_2^+)$ — a good leaving group. Thus a carbocation is formed.

Thus, [(III)-(R)]

(IV) $C_6H_5—CH(CH_3)—CH_2I + Ag^+ \longrightarrow C_6H_5—CH(CH_3)—\overset{\oplus}{C}H_2 + AgI\downarrow$ (A)

a better leaving; a good electrophile

$\xrightarrow{H_2O}$ $C_6H_5—CH(CH_3)CH_2OH$ (A)

(A) $\xrightarrow{\text{1, 2-hydride shift}}$ $C_6H_5—\overset{\oplus}{C}(CH_3)—CH_3 \xrightarrow{H_2O} C_6H_5—C(OH)(CH_3)—CH_3$

Thus, S_N1

Thus, [(IV)-(P)]

Paper 2

1. (1) The cell reaction is

$$H_2 + 2Ag^+ \longrightarrow 2H^+ + 2Ag$$

$$\Rightarrow \quad E = E° - \frac{0.06}{2}\log\frac{[H^+]^2}{[Ag^+]^2}$$

$$\Rightarrow \quad 0.62 = 0.80 + 0.06\log[Ag^+] \quad [\because [H^+] = 1\,M]$$

$\therefore$ $\log[Ag^+] = -3, [Ag^+] = 10^{-3}$ M

$\Rightarrow$ Mass of Ag^+ in 50 mL solution

$$= 54 \times 10^{-4}\text{ g}$$

$$\% = \frac{54 \times 10^{-4} \times 100}{0.54} = 1\%$$

2. (5) Only 1°-aliphatic amines can be prepared from Gabriel's phthalimide synthesis, where a halogen is replaced by NH_2 group. In chlorobenzene, Cl is attached to sp^2-hybridised carbon, hence aniline can not be prepared while halogen atom in 2, 4-dinitrochlorobenzene is replaceable, hence compound (vi) can be prepared.

So, (i), (iv), (v), (vi) and (vii) can be prepared.

3. (5) x% NaCl solution is isotonic with cytoplasmic cell, on applying depression of freezing point equation,

$$\Delta T_f = i \times K_f \times C_m$$

$$\Rightarrow \quad 0.40 = 2 \times 1.86 \times C_m$$

$$\Rightarrow \quad C_m = \frac{0.40}{3.72}\text{ M}$$

$$\Rightarrow \quad \pi = i \times C_m \times RT$$

$$\pi = 2 \times \frac{0.40}{3.72} \times 0.0821 \times 283 = 4.99\text{atm} \simeq 5\text{ atm}$$

4. (2) 10 mL of 1 mM solution contains 10^{-5} mole

$\therefore$ Number of molecules in one face $= \frac{6 \times 10^{23} \times 10^{-5}}{6} = 10^{18}$

Number of molecules in one edge $= \sqrt{10^{18}} = 10^9$

$\Rightarrow$ Area of 1 face $= \frac{0.24}{6} = 0.04\text{ m}^2$

edge length $= \sqrt{0.04}$ m $= 0.2$ m

10^9 molecules are covering 0.2 m length [monoatomic layer]

$\therefore$ 1 molecule is covering 2×10^{-10} m length, i.e. 2 Å.

5. (6) Molar mass of xylene (C_8H_{10}) is 106.

$\therefore$ 424 g is 4 mole each of which is 2 mol.

o-xylene (1 mol) $\xrightarrow{\text{Ozonolysis}}$ $2CH_3—\underset{O}{\underset{\|}{C}}—CHO + H—\underset{O}{\underset{\|}{C}}—\underset{O}{\underset{\|}{C}}—H$ (2 mol)

$\updownarrow$

o-xylene (1 mol) $\xrightarrow{\text{Ozonolysis}}$ $CH_3—\underset{O}{\underset{\|}{C}}—\underset{O}{\underset{\|}{C}}—CH_3 + 2H—\underset{O}{\underset{\|}{C}}—\underset{O}{\underset{\|}{C}}—H$

2 moles of o-xylene produces 2 moles of methylglyoxal

p-xylene, 2 mol (symmetrical) $\xrightarrow{\text{Ozonolysis}}$ $2CH_3—\underset{O}{\underset{\|}{C}}—CHO + H—\underset{O}{\underset{\|}{C}}—\underset{O}{\underset{\|}{C}}—H$ (4 mol)

Total moles of methylglyoxal $= (2 + 4) = 6$ mol

6. (5) Energy of the monochromatic radiation,

$$E = \frac{240\text{ kJ}}{6 \times 10^{23}}\text{ per molecule} = \frac{240 \times 10^3}{6 \times 10^{23}}\text{ J/molecule}$$

$$= 40 \times 10^{-20}\text{ J/molecule}$$

$$\Rightarrow \quad E = \frac{hc}{\lambda}$$

$$\Rightarrow \quad \lambda = \frac{6.63 \times 10^{-34} \times 3 \times 10^8}{40 \times 10^{-20}}$$

$$= 0.4925 \times 10^{-6}\text{ m} \approx 5 \times 10^{-7}\text{ m}$$

7. (5) For 1 mole of a van der Waals' real gas,

$$\left(p+\frac{a}{V^2}\right)(V-b)=RT$$

$\Rightarrow$ At very high pressure $Z=1+\frac{pb}{RT}$ $\left[\text{Slope}=\frac{b}{RT}\right]$

$$\Rightarrow \quad \frac{\pi}{492.6}=\frac{b}{RT}$$

$$\Rightarrow \quad b=\frac{\pi RT}{492.6}=\frac{\pi\times 0.0821\times 300}{492.6}\text{ L mol}^{-1}$$

$$\Rightarrow \quad \text{Again } b=4\times\frac{4}{3}\pi r^3\times N_A$$

$$=\frac{\pi\times 0.0821\times 10^3\times 300}{492.6}\text{ cm}^3$$

$$\Rightarrow \quad r^3=\frac{0.0821\times 10^3\times 300\times 3}{492.6\times 16\times 6\times 10^{23}}\text{ and on solving}$$

$$r^3=\frac{10^{-21}}{4\times 4\times 4}\text{ cm}^3 \qquad [\because N_A=6\times 10^{23}\text{mol}^{-1}]$$

$$\Rightarrow \quad r=\frac{1}{4}\times 10^{-7}\text{ cm}$$

$$=\frac{10}{4}\times 10^{-8}\text{ cm}=2.5\text{ Å}$$

$$\Rightarrow \quad d=2r=5\text{ Å}.$$

8. (6) Only $p\pi$-$p\pi$: $NO_3^-, CO_3^{2-}, (CN)_2$

$\Rightarrow$ Only $d\pi$-$p\pi$:

$XeO_3, ClO_4^-, XeOF_2, H_3PO_4$

$\Rightarrow$ One $p\pi$-$p\pi$, rest $d\pi$-$p\pi$: SO_3, SO_4^{2-}

9. (a, b, d) Statements (a), (b) and (d) are correct whereas (c) is incorrect.

(a) $[Cu(NH_3)_4]^{2+} : 3d^9\ (Cu^{2+})$

$\Rightarrow$

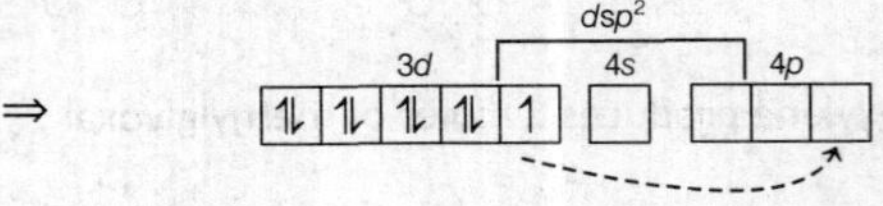

It is an inner orbital square planar [Cu(II) : dsp^2] paramagnetic complex.

(b) $[Co(NH_3)_6]^{3+} : 3d^6\ (Co^{3+})$

$\Rightarrow$

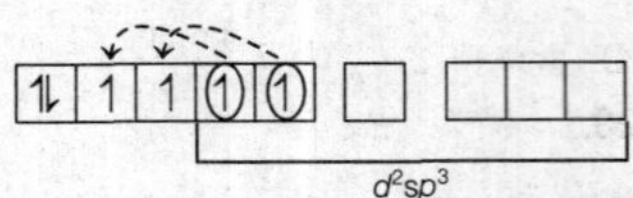

It is an inner orbital octahedral [Co(III) : d^2sp^3] diamagnetic complex.

(c) $[Ni(CO)_4] : 3d^8 4s^2\ (Ni^0)$

$\Rightarrow$

sp^3

It is a tetrahedral [Ni(0) : sp^3] diamagnetic complex.

So, option — (c) is not correct.

(d) Mond process :

$$\text{Crude Ni} \underset{}{\overset{4\text{ CO, 350 K}}{\rightleftharpoons}} \underset{\text{(Volatile compound)}}{[Ni(CO)_4]} \xrightarrow{470\text{ K}} \underset{\text{(Pure)}}{Ni} + 4CO$$

10. (a, b, c) The identification test reactions of the given ions are,

$$2ZnSO_4 + K_4[Fe(CN)_6] \longrightarrow \underset{\text{Bluish white ppt.}}{\overset{II\quad II}{Zn_2[Fe(CN)_6]}}\downarrow + 2K_2SO_4$$

$$2CuSO_4 + K_4[Fe(CN)_6] \longrightarrow \underset{\text{Reddish-brown}}{\overset{II\quad II}{Cu_2[Fe(CN)_6]}}\downarrow + 2K_2SO_4$$

$$FeCl_3 + K_4[Fe(CN)_6] \longrightarrow \underset{\text{Prussian blue}}{\overset{III\quad II}{Fe_4[Fe(CN)_6]_3}}\downarrow + 3KCl$$

11. (a, b, c, d)

(a) All monosaccharides are reducing sugars.

(b) Hydrolysis of sucrose gives D-glucose and L-fructose.

$$\underset{\text{(Sucrose)}}{C_{12}H_{22}O_{11}} + H_2O \longrightarrow \underset{\text{D-glucose}}{C_6H_{12}O_6} + \underset{\text{L-fructose}}{C_6H_{12}O_6}$$

(c) Glucose and mannose cannot be distinguished by osazone formation as they are epimers.

(d) In amylopectin of starch, α-D-glucose units are held together by C_1-C_4 and C_1-C_6 (cross) linkages.

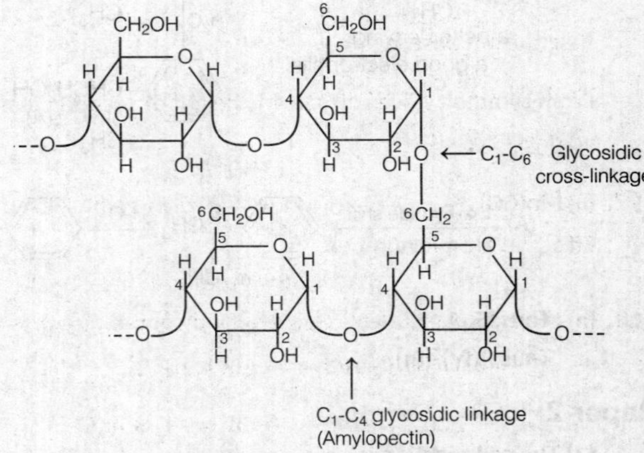

12. (a, b, c) The reactions involved are as follows

(i) $4Au + 8NaCN + 2H_2O + \underset{(A)}{O_2} \longrightarrow \underset{(Y)}{4Na[Au(CN)_2]} + 4NaOH$

(ii) $\underset{(Y)}{2Na[Au(CN)_2]} + \underset{(T)}{Zn} \longrightarrow \underset{(Y)}{Na_2[Zn(CN)_4]} + 2Au$

13. (a) $CH_2=CH-O-C_2H_5 \xrightarrow{\text{Hydrolysis}}$ (H, OH)

$$CH_2=CH(\text{enol}) + C_2H_5OH \rightleftharpoons$$ (O—H)

$$\underset{'P'}{CH_3CHO} + \underset{'Q'}{C_2H_5OH}$$

$\Rightarrow$ Both P and Q can be separately identified by iodoform test.

(i) $CH_3-CH=O \xrightarrow{NaOH, I_2}$

$HCOONa + CHI_3\downarrow$ (yellow ppt.)

(ii) $C_2H_5OH \xrightarrow[\text{(NaOI)}\ [O]]{NaOH, I_2} CH_3CHO \xrightarrow[NaOH]{I_2}$

14. (a, b, d)

As Langmuir is based on mono-atomic layer over the surface, hence option (c) is incorrect.

$\Rightarrow$ Langmuir isotherm, $\theta = \frac{ap}{1 + bp}$

where, θ is the fraction of surface covered by adsorbate.

p is the pressure of the gas; a and b are Langmuir constants.

15. (a) Applying Arrhenius equation for both the reactions,

$$k_1 = Ae^{-\frac{E_1}{RT}};\ k_2 = Ae^{-\frac{E_2}{RT}}$$

$$\Rightarrow \frac{k_2}{k_1} = e^{\frac{E_1 - E_2}{RT}}$$

As $k_2 > k_1$ and $E_1 > E_2$, i.e. $E_1 - E_2 = (+)\text{ve}$

Thus, on increasing temperature, $\frac{k_2}{k_1}$ decreases and when $\frac{E_1 - E_2}{RT} = 1$

$k_2 = 2.72\,k_1$ and thus, k_1 remain always less than k_2.

16. (d) Height of crystal lattice is h so, effective height of one layer is $\frac{h}{2}$. Octahedral void is exactly in between two layers. Then

height from base is $\frac{\frac{h}{2}}{2} = \frac{h}{4}$.

From symmetry, we can say any height of second octahedral void will be $\frac{h}{4} + \frac{h}{2} = \frac{3h}{4}$

17. (a) $Mn(CO)_6 - e^- \longrightarrow [Mn(CO)_6]^{\oplus}$ most stable because

Effective atomic number

$= (25 - 1) + 6 \times 2 = 36 =$ Atomic number of Kr

18. (a) Malachite is $CuCO_3 \cdot Cu(OH)_2$ and copper glance is Cu_2S

$$\Rightarrow \underset{(P)}{\text{Malachite}} + HCl \longrightarrow CuCl_2,$$

$$2CuCl_2 + 4KI \longrightarrow \underset{(S)}{Cu_2I_2} + I_2 + 4KCl$$

$$\Rightarrow \underset{(Q)}{Cu_2S} \xrightarrow{\text{Roasting}} \underset{(U)}{Cu_2O} + \underset{(T)}{SO_2},$$

$$\underset{(T)}{SO_2} + K_2Cr_2O_7 + H^+ \longrightarrow \underset{\text{Green}}{Cr^{3+}} + SO_4^{2-}$$

Knockout 13

Paper 1

1. (625)

$$a = \frac{2Y^{\frac{1}{3}}}{5} \times 10^{-9}\,\text{m} = \text{edge length of the unit cell.}$$

$\Rightarrow$ Density of the crystal,

$$\rho = \frac{4 \times 6.023 \times Y \times 10^{-3}}{6.023 \times 10^{23} \times \left\{\frac{(2Y)^{\frac{1}{3}}}{5}\right\}^3 \times 10^{-27}} = 625\,\text{kg/m}^3$$

[$\because$ Rank of rock salt type crystal (AB), $z = 4$]

2. (76.20)

Bromate-bromide mixture is a mixture of ($5\,KBr + KBrO_3$) which generates bromine (Br_2) as,

$$\underset{5\text{ mole}}{5KBr} + \underset{1\text{ mole}}{KBrO_3} + H_2SO_4 \longrightarrow \underset{3\text{ mole}}{3Br_2} + \underset{3\text{ mole}}{3K_2SO_4} + 3H_2O$$

[Salicylic acid] + $3Br_2$ (0.3 mole) $\longrightarrow$ 2,4,6-tribromophenol $\downarrow$ (33.1 g *i.e.* $\frac{1}{10}$ mole)

$\Rightarrow$ Mole of KBr = 0.5 mole of

$KBrO_3 = 0.1$ [$\equiv 0.3$ mole Br_2]

$\Rightarrow$ Total mass $= (119 \times 0.5 + 167 \times 0.1)$

$= 76.2$ g

3. (86) Moles of hydrocarbon taken $= \frac{4.3}{14n + 2}$ mol

and mole of CO_2 formed $= \frac{300 \times 1}{1000} = 0.3$ [n-factor of $CO_2 = 2$]

$\Rightarrow$ 1 mole of hydrocarbon produces n mole CO_2

$$\Rightarrow \frac{4.3 \times n}{14n + 2} = 0.3$$

$$\Rightarrow n = 6$$

$\therefore$ Molar mass of hydrocarbon

$= 14 \times 6 + 2 = 86$ g/mol

4. (3) $\Rightarrow$ van der Waals' equation for one mole of gas is

$$\left(p + \frac{a}{V^2}\right)(V - b) = RT$$

At 300 K, $b = 0$

$$\therefore \quad pV + \frac{a}{V} = RT$$

$$\Rightarrow \quad pV = \left(RT - \frac{a}{V}\right)$$

$\Rightarrow$ At $\frac{1}{V} = 2.0$, $pV = 23.1$ and at $\frac{1}{V} = 3.0$, $pV = 20.1$

$$\therefore \quad 20.1 = RT - 3a$$

$$23.1 = RT - 2a$$

$$\Rightarrow \quad a = 3$$

5. (8.97)

	ΔH°
$Cl(g) \longrightarrow Cl^+(s) + e^-$	1257.5 kJ
$Cl(g) + e^- \longrightarrow Cl^-(g)$	−359.8 kJ
$2Cl(g) \longrightarrow Cl^+Cl^-$	897.7 kJ mol^{-1}

Thus, for 0.01 mole (Cl^+Cl^-),

$\Delta H = 8.977\text{ kJ} \approx 8.97\text{ kJ} = x\text{kJ}$

$\Rightarrow \quad x = 8.97$

6. (5) For a weak base

$$[OH^-] = \sqrt{K_b C}$$

$$\therefore \quad pOH = \frac{1}{2}[pK_b - \log C]$$

If $pH(BOH) = 8.0$, then $pOH = 6.0$

$$6 = \frac{1}{2}[pK_b - \log 10^{-4}]$$

$$\Rightarrow \quad 12 = [pK_b + 4]$$

$$\Rightarrow \quad pK_b = 8 = pK_a$$

$\Rightarrow$ For a weak acid,

$$pH = \frac{1}{2}[pK_a - \log C] = \frac{1}{2}[8 - \log 0.01]$$

$$= \frac{1}{2}[8 + 2] = 5$$

7. (6.25) At 298 K,

$$p_{O_2} = K_H \chi_{O_2}$$

$$\therefore \chi_{O_2} \text{ (at 298)} = \frac{0.20 \times 760}{3.30 \times 10^7}$$

$$= 4.606 \times 10^{-6}$$

and at 303 K,

$$\therefore \chi_{O_2} \text{(at 303)} = \frac{0.20 \times 760}{3.52 \times 10^7} = 4.318 \times 10^{-6}$$

$$\text{Decrease} = (4.606 - 4.318) \times 10^{-6}$$

$$= 0.288 \times 10^{-6}$$

$$\% \text{ decrease} = \frac{0.288 \times 10^{-6}}{4.606 \times 10^{-6}} \times 100$$

$$= 6.252 \simeq 6.25$$

8. (0)

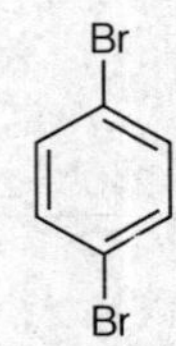

Dipole moment = Zero

Br-atom is *o*, *p*-directing and deactivating.

Thus, nitration is not possible.

Br

$\leftarrow$ *o*-to I, but *m*-to II

$\leftarrow$ *o*-to II, but *m*-to I

Br

(II)

9. (a, b, c)

(a) $\Delta S(x \to y)$ taking place at constant temperature, i.e. isothermal.

$$\therefore \Delta S = 2.303\, nR \log \frac{V_2}{V_1} = 2.303\, nR \log \frac{p_1}{p_2}$$

$$= 2.303 \times 5 \times 8.314 \log \left(\frac{10}{1}\right) = 95.74 \text{ JK}^{-1}$$

Thus, (a) is the correct option.

(b) $\because q = 0$ (adiabatic)

$$\Rightarrow \quad \Delta S(x \to z) \frac{q}{T} = 0$$

Thus, (*B*) is the correct option.

(c) $x \to z$ takes place adiabatically, hence temperature falls to 118.6 K.

$$\Delta S_{x \to z} = 0,\ C_p = \frac{5}{2}R \text{ for monoatomic gas.}$$

$$\Delta S_{z \to y} = 2.303\, nC_p \log \frac{T_2}{T_1}$$

$$= 2.303 \times 5 \times 2.5 \times 8.314 \log \frac{298}{118.6} = 95.76 \text{ JK}^{-1}$$

$$\text{Thus, } \Delta S_{x \to y} = \Delta S_{x \to z} + \Delta S_{z \to y}$$

$$= (0 + 95.76) \text{ JK}^{-1} = 95.76 \text{ JK}^{-1}$$

$\therefore$ (c) is the correct option.

(d) $\Delta S_{x \to z \to y} \neq 0$

Thus, (d) is the incorrect option.

10. (c) In the given complex, $NiCl_2[P(C_2H_5)_2(C_6H_5)]_2$, nickel is in +2 oxidation state and the electronic configuration of Ni^{2+} ion can be explained as,

Ni^{2+}: $3d^8$ [⥮ ⥮ ⥮ 1 1] [×× ×× ×× ××] $\Delta \Rightarrow$ Tetrahedral and paramagnetic

sp^3-hybridised

Ni^{2+}: $3d^8$ [⥮ ⥮ ⥮ ⥮ ⥮] [×× ×× ×× ××] Δ_1

dsp^2-hybridised

The above electronic arrangement gives dsp^2-hybridisation of Ni(II) and therefore, have square planar geometry and diamagnetic behaviour.

11. (a, b, c) Statements (a), (b) and (c) are correct, whereas statement (d) is incorrect.

Li^+ ion being the smallest in size and has the highest charge/size ratio amongst the alkali metal ions, get much more hydrated (i.e. holds more water molecules in its hydration sphere) than Na^+ ion and later gets more hydrated than K^+ ion and so on.

On heating, lithium nitrate evolves lithium oxide, nitrogen dioxide and oxygen as shown in following reaction.

$$4LiNO_3 \xrightarrow{\Delta} 2Li_2O + 4NO_2 + O_2$$

12. (a, b) $(CH_3CH_2\overset{-}{C}HCH_3)\overset{+}{M}gBr$ attack to less substituted carbon of epoxide ring from the side opposite to $-CH_3$ group to give *A* as the major product and *B* will be the minor product.

Here *A* is, $\ominus$ $\oplus$ MgBr a (Grignard reagent), where acts as a nucleophile (bulkier)

2°, 3°, (in Et_2O) [S_N2], CH_3, $\overset{-+}{OMgBr}$, H_2O, OH

A (As major product)

whereas [structure: OH, CH_3] is *B* as minor product.

13. (a, b, c) Reactions (a, b and c) all give N-ethylcyclopentylamine as major product.

Cyclopentanone $=O$ + $CH_3CH_2NH_2$ $\xrightarrow{-H_2O}$ cyclopentylidene$=N—CH_2CH_3$ (Schiff's base) $\xrightarrow{H_2/Pt}$ cyclopentyl$-NH-C_2H_5$

Cyclopentylidene$=NH_2$ + CH_3CHO $\xrightarrow{-H_2O}$ cyclopentyl$-N=CH—CH_3$ $\xrightarrow{H_2/Pt}$ cyclopentyl$-NH-C_2H_5$

Cyclopentyl$-NH_2$ $\xrightarrow[\text{Pyridine}]{CH_3\overset{O}{\overset{\|}{C}}Cl}$ cyclopentyl$-NH\overset{O}{\overset{\|}{C}}CH_3$ $\xrightarrow[\text{(ii) } H_2O]{\text{(i) } LiAlH_4, \text{ diethyl ether}}$ cyclopentyl$-NHC_2H_5$

14. (b) Molar mass of the coordination compound,

$H_{12}O_6Cl_3Cr = 12\times 1 + 6 \times 16 + 3\times 35.5 + 52$

$= 266.5$

A, *B* and *C* are isomeric octahedral complexes of Cr(III).

As *A* does not react with conc. H_2SO_4, all six H_2O molecules must be present in the coordination sphere.

So, *A* is $[Cr(H_2O)]_6Cl_3$

B is $[Cr(H_2O)_5Cl]Cl_2\cdot H_2O$, because one molecule of H_2O present outside the coordination sphere will be absorbed by conc. H_2SO_4 and will lose a mass by, $\frac{1\times 18}{266.5}\times 100 = 6.75\%$

Then, *C* is $[Cr(H_2O)_4Cl_2]Cl\cdot 2H_2O$, as here decrease in mass with conc. H_2SO_4 is double to the compound, *B*, i.e. $2\times 6.75\% = 13.5\%$

15. (c)

$\Rightarrow$ For $MnO_4^- + 8H^+ + 5Fe^{2+} \longrightarrow Mn^{2+} + 5Fe^{3+} + 4H_2O$

Electrons exchange = 5

$$\log_{10} K = -\frac{2303(K)}{T} + 4.06$$

Thermodynamic equation is

$$\log_{10} K = -\frac{\Delta H^\circ}{2.303RT} + \frac{\Delta S^\circ}{2.303R}$$

(I) On comparison : $\frac{\Delta S^\circ}{2.303R} = 4.06$

$\therefore \Delta S^\circ = 2.303\times 4.06\times R$

$= 2.303\times 4.06\times 8.314\times 10^{-3}$ kJ mol^{-1} K^{-1}

$= 0.078$ kJ mol^{-1}K^{-1}

Thus, [(I)-(Q)]

(II) $\frac{\Delta H^\circ}{2.303R} = 2303$

$\therefore \Delta H^\circ = 2.303\times 2303\times R$

$= 2.303\times 2303\times 8.314\times 10^{-3}$ kJ mol^{-1}

$= 44.1$ kJ mol^{-1}

Thus, [(II)-(R)]

(III) $\Delta G^\circ = \Delta H^\circ - T\Delta S$

$= 44.1 - 300\times 0.078$

$= 20.7$ kJ mol^{-1}

Thus, [(III)-(P)]

(IV) Temperature coefficient of the cell reaction

$$\left(\frac{dE_{cell}}{dT}\right) = \frac{\Delta S^\circ}{nF}\text{ (in J)} = \frac{0.078\times 1000}{5\times 96500} = 1.62\times 10^{-4}\text{ JK}^{-1}$$

$\therefore$ [(IV)-(T)]

16. (c) (I) $\Delta_r H^\circ = \frac{2.303RT_1T_2}{T_2 - T_1}\log\frac{K_{T_2}}{K_{T_1}}$

$$= \frac{2.303\times 8.314\times 10^{-3}\times 2400\times 2600}{200}\log\frac{84.7}{38.4} = 205\text{ kJ}$$

Thus, [(I)-(R)]

(II) $\Delta H^\circ = \frac{2.303RT_1T_2}{(T_2 - T_1)}\log\frac{K_{T_2}}{K_{T_1}} = \frac{2.303RT_1T_3}{(T_3 - T_1)}\log\frac{K_{T_3}}{K_{T_1}}$

$$\frac{2600}{200}\log\frac{84.7}{38.4} = \frac{2500}{10.0}\log\frac{K_{T_3}}{38.4}$$

$\therefore \quad \log\frac{K_{T_3}}{38.4} = 0.1784$

$\Rightarrow \quad \frac{K_{T_3}}{38.4} = 1.51$

$K_{T_3} = 57.98 \approx 58.0 = K_C$

Thus, [(II)-(P)]

(III) $\Delta G^\circ = -2.303\,RT\log K_{T_3}$

$= -2.303\times 8.314\times 10^{-3}\times 2500\log 58.0 = -84.4$ kJ

$\therefore -\Delta G^\circ = 84.4$ kJ

Thus, [(III)-(S)]

(IV) $\Delta G° = \Delta H° - T\Delta S°$

$\therefore T\Delta S° = \Delta H° - T\Delta S°$

$$\Delta S° = \frac{\Delta H° - \Delta G°}{T}$$

$$= \frac{250 - (-84.4)}{2500}$$

$$= 0.11576 \text{ kJ K}^{-1} = 115.76 \text{ J K}^{-1}$$

$$\approx 116 \text{ JK}^{-1}$$

Thus, [(IV)-(Q)]

17. (c) Salt of weak acid (HA) and strong base (MOH) is alkaline due to hydrolysis

$$A^- + H_2O \rightleftharpoons HA + OH^-$$

Thus, $pH = \left(7 + \frac{pK_a}{2}\right) + \frac{\log C}{2}$

$y = (\text{constant}) + mx$

Hence, constant = intercept $= \left(7 + \frac{pK_a}{2}\right)$

$= OA = 9$

$m = \text{slope} = \frac{1}{2}$

thus, $7 + \frac{pK_a}{2} = 9$

$\therefore$ $pK_a = 4$

Thus, [(I)-(R)]

$\Rightarrow$ When $C = 0.01$

$$pH = 9 + \frac{\log 0.01}{2} = 9 - \frac{2}{2} = 8$$

Thus [(II)-(P)]

$\Rightarrow$ pH of weak acid

$$pH = \frac{1}{2}(pK_a - \log C) = \frac{1}{2}[4 - \log 0.01] = 3$$

Thus, [(III)-(S)]

By Ostwald's dilution law,

$$\alpha = \sqrt{\frac{K_a}{C}} = \sqrt{\frac{10^{-4}}{0.01}} = \sqrt{10^{-2}} = 0.1$$

Thus, percentage ionisation $= 0.1 \times 100 = 10\%$

Thus, [(IV)-(Q)]

18. (d)

(I) $[CoF_3(H_2O)_3]$ is a coordination compound of Co (III) and weak field ligands (F^- and H_2O).

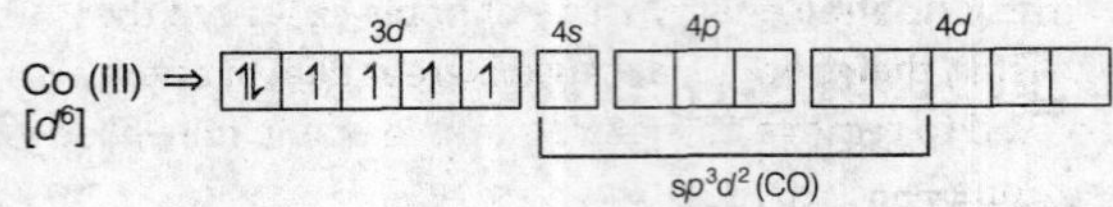

$\Rightarrow$ Paramagnetic $[n = 4, \mu = n(n+2)\text{BM} \neq 0]$, Outer orbital and High spin complex

So, [(I)-(Q)]

(II) $[Cr(C_2O_4)_3]^{3-}$ is a complexed ion of Cr(III) and strong field ligand $(C_2O_4^{2-})$.

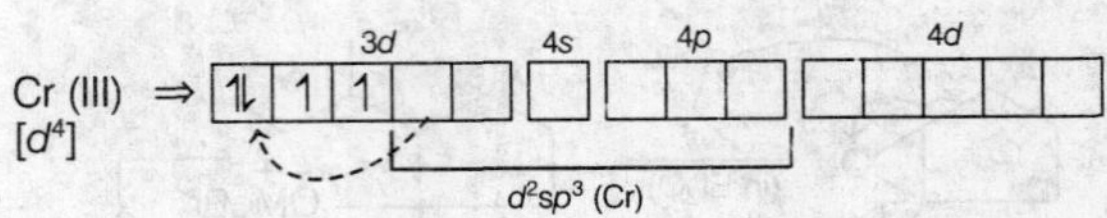

$\Rightarrow$ Paramagnetic $(n = 2, \mu \neq 0)$, Inner orbital and Low spin complex

So, [(II)-(R)]

(III) $[AuCl_4]^-$ is a complexed ion of Au(III) and strong field ligand (Cl^-)

Au (II) ⇒ [d8] 5d 6s 6p — dsp² (Au)

Diamagnetic $(n = 0, \mu = 0)$ Inner Orbital Low spin complex

So, [(III)-(P)]

(IV) $[Fe(CN)_6]^{3-}$ is a complexed ion of Fe(III) and strong field ligand (CN^-)

Fe (III) ⇒ [d5] — d²sp³

$\Rightarrow$ Paramagentic $(n = 1, \mu \neq 0)$, Inner Orbital and Low spin complex.

So, [(IV)-(T)]

Paper-2

1. (2) Comparing the observations in the series of experiments,

$$\frac{r_2}{r_1} = \left(\frac{[H_2O_2]_2}{[H_2O_2]_1}\right)^x \times \left(\frac{[I^-]_2}{[I^-]_1}\right)^y$$

[Let order of the reaction is $-x$ w.r.t H_2O_2 and y w.r.t I^-].

$$\Rightarrow \frac{2.3 \times 10^{-4}}{1.15 \times 10^{-4}} = \left(\frac{0.1}{0.1}\right)^x \times \left(\frac{0.2}{0.1}\right)^y = 2^y$$

$$\Rightarrow 2 = 2^y \Rightarrow y = 1$$

Similarly, $\frac{r_3}{r_1} = \left(\frac{[H_2O_2]_3}{[H_2O_2]_1}\right)^x \times \left(\frac{[I^-]_3}{[I^-]_1}\right)^y$

$$\Rightarrow \frac{2.3 \times 10^{-4}}{1.15 \times 10^{-4}} = \left(\frac{0.2}{0.1}\right)^x \times \left(\frac{0.1}{0.1}\right)^y = 2^x$$

$$\Rightarrow 2 = 2^x \Rightarrow x = 1$$

$\therefore$ The rate law for the formation of I_3^-,

rate $= k[H_2O_2]^x[I^-]^y = k[H_2O_2][I^-]$ and

order of the reaction $(n) = x + y = 1 + 1 = 2$

2. (9) Number of atoms of A in fcc = 4 [Corners + Face centres]

Number of atoms of B at octahedral voids

= 4 [Edge centres + Body centre]

$\Rightarrow$ Number of effective atoms of A after removal

$= 4 - 2 \times \frac{1}{8} = \frac{15}{4}$ (two corners of the body diagonal are removed)

$\Rightarrow$ Number of effective atoms of B after removal $= 4 - 1 = 3$ (body centre of the body diagonal is removed)

$\Rightarrow A : B = \frac{15}{4} : 3 = 5 : 4$

So, simplest formula $= A_5B_4$ and $x + y = 9$

3. (3) Ionisation energy.

$$IE = \frac{Z^2}{n^2} \times 21.69 \times 10^{-19} \text{ J atom}^{-1}$$

$$\Rightarrow \quad \frac{11180 \times 10^3}{6.023 \times 10^{23}} = \frac{Z^2}{1^2} \times 21.69 \times 10^{-19}$$

$$\Rightarrow \quad Z^2 = 8.56 \simeq 9$$

$\Rightarrow Z = 3 =$ Total number of protons in the nucleus of the species.

4. (4)

In compound, *D*, i.e. PbO_2 $\overset{-2}{O}=\overset{+4}{Pb}=\overset{-2}{O}$ oxidation state of Pb = + 4.

5. (4)

$\Rightarrow H_2O$ is a weak field ligand and $[Fe(H_2O)_6]^{2+}$ is a high spin complex.

$\Rightarrow Fe^{2+} : 3d^6 \Rightarrow t_{2g}^4 e_g^2$

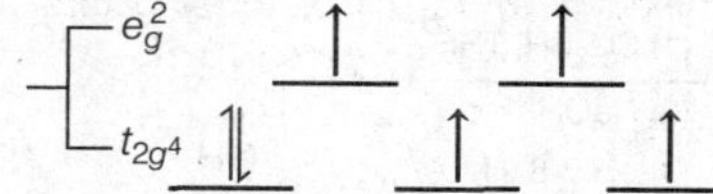

$\Rightarrow$ Number of unpaired electrons = 4

6. (9) When an incident light of energy, *E* falls on a metal of work function $E°$, the expression of kinetic energy (KE) of the ejected photoelectron will be,

$$\Rightarrow \quad E = E° + KE$$

Case I : $\frac{hc}{\lambda} = E° + 2\text{eV}$ ...(i)

Case II : $\frac{3hc}{\lambda} = E° + 24\text{ eV}$ ...(ii)

$$\Rightarrow \quad 3(E° + 2\text{eV}) = E° + 24\text{ eV}$$

$$3E° + 6\text{eV} = E° + 24\text{ eV}$$

$$\Rightarrow \quad E° = \frac{24 - 6}{2}\text{ eV} = 9\text{ eV}$$

7. (6) In $(4n + 2)$ decay series, U^{238} gets ended into Pb^{206},

$${}^{238}_{92}U \xrightarrow[(8\alpha,\ 6\beta)]{} {}^{206}_{82}Pb$$

Number of α-particles emitted

$$= \frac{\Delta A}{4} = \frac{238 - 206}{4} = 8$$

Number of β-particles emitted

$$= 2N_\alpha - \Delta Z = 2 \times 8 - (92 - 82) = 6$$

8. (8) Total number of isomeric monochlorides $= 2 + 4 + 1 + 1 = 8$

The products (*P*) can be shown as,

$ClCH_2-CH_2-\overset{*}{C}H(CH_3)-CH_2-CH_3$
(2) [1 × (±)]

$CH_3-\overset{*}{C}H(Cl)-\overset{*}{C}H(CH_3)-CH_2-CH_3$
(4) [2 × (±)]

$CH_3-CH_2-CCl(CH_3)-CH_2-CH_3$
(1)

$CH_3-CH_2-CH(CH_2Cl)-CH_2-CH_3$
(1)

9. (b) (i) $\underset{(A)}{K_2Cr_2O_7} + 6H_2SO_4 + 4KCl \longrightarrow 6KHSO_4 + 3H_2O + \underset{\substack{(J)\\ \text{Chromyl chloride}}}{2CrO_2Cl_2}$

When a mixture of a metal chloride (ionic chloride) and potassium dichromate is heated with conc. H_2SO_4, an orange red vapour of chromyl chloride is evolved.

(ii) $4KOH + \underset{(J)}{CrO_2Cl_2} \longrightarrow \underset{\substack{\text{(Yellow solution)}\\ (K)}}{K_2CrO_4} + 2KCl + 2H_2O$

(iii) $\underset{(K)}{2CrO_4^{2-}} + H^+ \longrightarrow Cr_2O_7^{2-} + H_2O$

$Cr_2O_7^{2-} + H_2SO_4 + 3SO_2 \longrightarrow SO_4^{2-} + \underset{\substack{(M)\\ \text{(Green coloured)}}}{Cr_2(SO_4)_3} + H_2O$

M is Cr(III) sulphate.

10. (a, c, d) In general, the ionisation energy decreases on descending a group and increase on crossing a period because removal of successive electrons become more difficult and first ionisation energy < second ionisation energy < third ionisation energy.

$\Rightarrow$ The ionisation energy value of noble gases are the highest in their periods because a great deal of energy is required to remove an electron from a stable fully-filled shell of electrons.

11. (a, b, d)

(a) ⇒

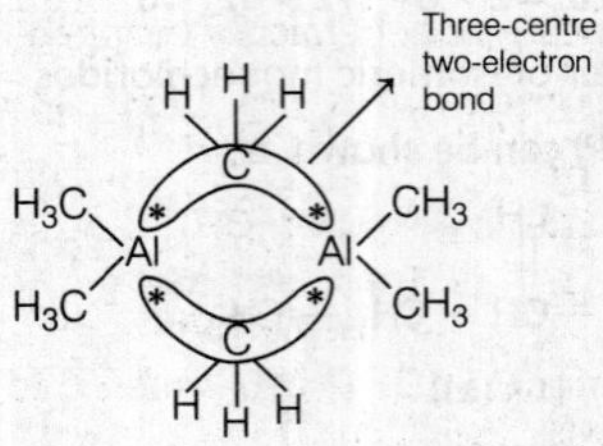

Three-centre two-electron bond

H_3C, CH_3 / Al–CH_3–Al bridges

It is the dimeric form of $Al(CH_3)_3$, i.e. $Al_2(CH_3)_6$.

(b) ⇒ BCl_3 is stronger Lewis acid than $AlCl_3$ due to greater extent of $p\pi$-$p\pi$ back bonding in $AlCl_3$.

(c) ⇒

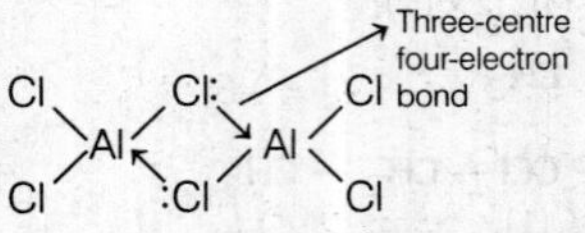

Three-centre four-electron bond

(Al_2Cl_6, the dimer of $AlCl_3$)

(d) ⇒

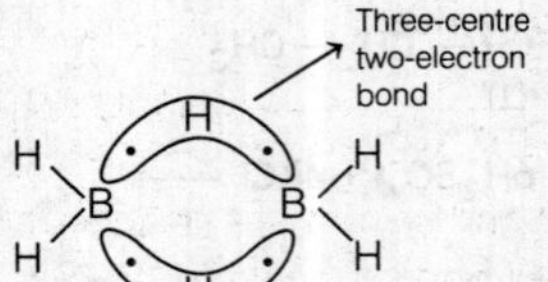

Three-centre two-electron bond

B_2H_6 (diborane, the dimer of BH_3)

12. (b) The overall reaction sequence can be represented as,

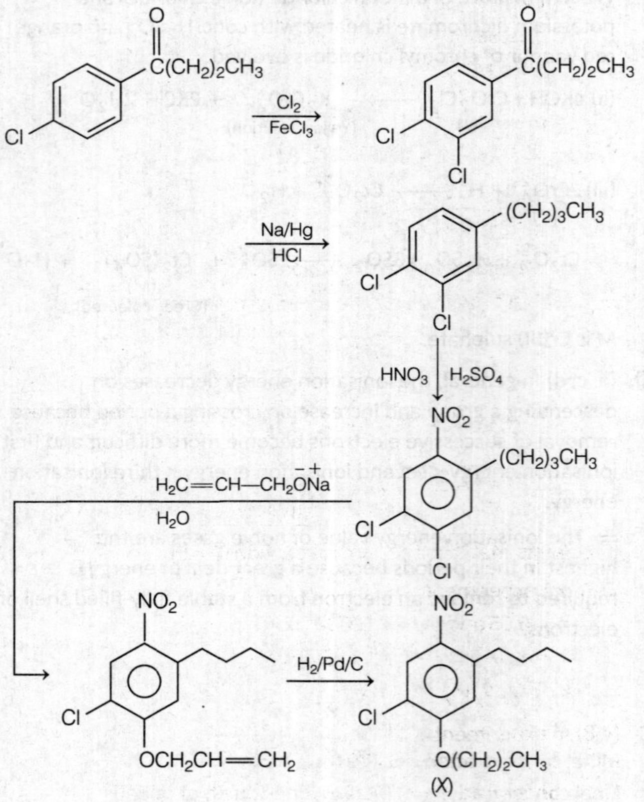

4-chlorophenyl–$C(=O)(CH_2)_2CH_3$ $\xrightarrow[FeCl_3]{Cl_2}$ 3,4-dichlorophenyl–$C(=O)(CH_2)_2CH_3$ $\xrightarrow[HCl]{Na/Hg}$ 3,4-dichlorophenyl–$(CH_2)_3CH_3$ $\xrightarrow{HNO_3,\ H_2SO_4}$ nitro compound (with NO_2, $(CH_2)_3CH_3$, Cl, Cl) $\xrightarrow[H_2O]{H_2C{=}CH{-}CH_2\overset{-}{O}\overset{+}{Na}}$ compound with NO_2, butyl, Cl and $OCH_2CH{=}CH_2$ $\xrightarrow{H_2/Pd/C}$ compound with NO_2, butyl, Cl and $O(CH_2)_2CH_3$ (X)

13. (b, c, d)

(b) ⇒ (I) $CH_2{=}CH_2$ (Ethene) $\xrightarrow[H^+]{H_2O}$ [Ethanol] $\xrightarrow[(PCC)]{(i)\ C_5H_5NCrO_3.HCl}$ [Acetaldehye]

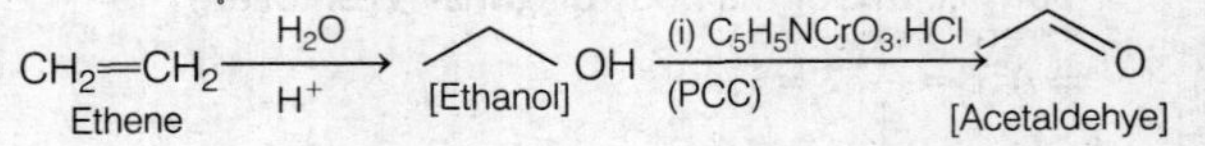

(II) acetaldehyde + propanal $\xrightarrow{NaOH/H_2O\ (Aldol\ condensation)}$ [3-hydroxy-2-methylbutanal] + [3-hydroxy pentanal] + [3-hydroxy-butanal] + [3-hydroxy-2-methyl pentanal]

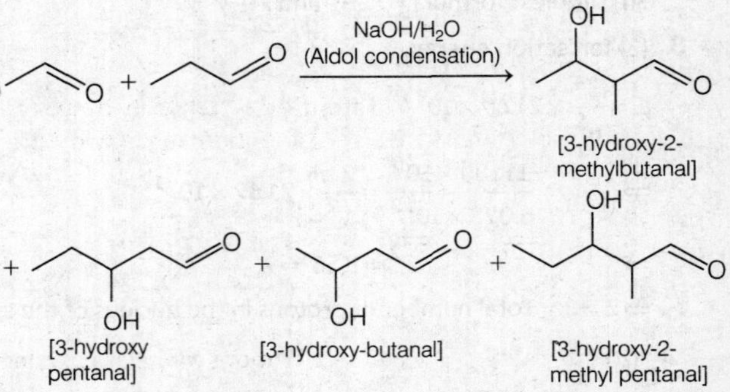

(c) ⇒ Reactions are similar to the last step reactions of (b) (II).

(d) ⇒ $CH_2{=}CH_2$ $\xrightarrow[CCl_4]{Br_2}$ [1, 2-dibromoethane] $\xrightarrow{KOH\ \overset{+}{N}H_4\overset{-}{Cl}}$ $HC{\equiv}CH$ [Ethyne]

$CH{\equiv}CH$ [Ethyne] $\xrightarrow[(1\ eqv)\ in\ liq.\ NH_3]{NaNH_2}$ $\equiv{-}Na^+$ [Ethynyl sodium] (X) + [Propanal] $\xrightarrow[(ii)\ NH_4Cl,\ H_2O]{(i) NH_3,\ ether}$ [Pent-1-yn-3-ol]

[Pent-1-yn-3-ol] $\xrightarrow{(1)\ Sia_2BH,\ THF;\ (2)\ NaOH;\ (3)\ pH\ 7\text{-}8,\ H_2O_2}$ [3- hydroxypentanal]

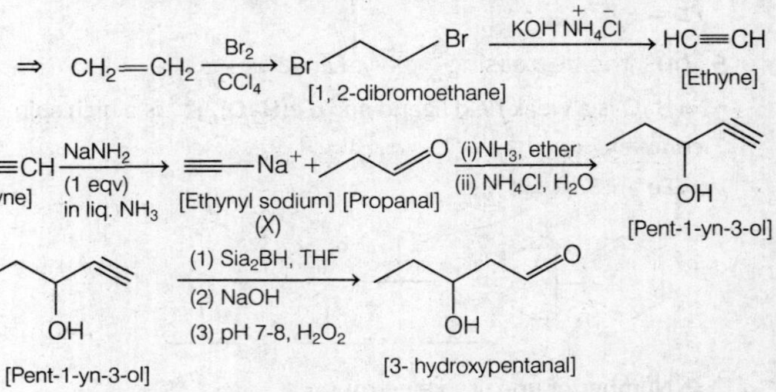

14. (a, c, d) Let the mixture contains x and y moles of $NaHCO_3$ and Na_2CO_3 respectively.

$\Rightarrow x = a$ and $x + 2y = b$

Thus, for complete neutralisation of Na_2CO_3, $2y$ mol HCl (i.e. $2a$ volume) would be required.

$\therefore$ Volume of HCl required for complete neutralisation of $NaHCO_3 = x = (b - 2a)$ mL

If methyl orange is added at phenolphthalein end point, then $(x + y)$ mol HCl $= (b - a)$ mL HCl would be required.

If the mixture is titrated against NaOH, only $NaHCO_3$ will react and x mol NaOH, i.e. $(b - 2a)$ mL NaOH would be required.

15. (b) $Cr^{n+} + ne^- \longrightarrow Cr$

To deposit 0.015 mol of Cr, 0.015 n mol of electrons are required.

$\therefore \quad 0.015n = 0.090$

$n = 6$

Hence, the compound is $Na_2Cr_2O_7$.

16. (c) In Pt(IV) complex, coordination number of Pt(IV) will be six. Now, on the basis of Werner's theory, the given compounds can be represented as (assuming 100% dissociation in water),

(A) $Pt(NH_3)_6Cl_4$ as $[\overset{IV}{Pt}(NH_3)_6]^{4+}.4Cl^-$ ⇒ 5 ions

(B) $Pt(NH_3)_5Cl_4$ as $[\overset{IV}{Pt}(NH_3)_5Cl]^{3+}.3Cl^-$ ⇒ 4 ions

(C) $Pt(NH_3)_4Cl_4$ as $[\overset{IV}{Pt}(NH_3)_4Cl_2]^{2+}\cdot 2Cl^-$ ⇒ 3 ions

(D) $Pt(NH_3)_3Cl_4$ as $[\overset{IV}{Pt}(NH_3)_3Cl_3]^{3+}\cdot Cl^-$ ⇒ 2 ions

17. (d) Greater the stability of the product (hydroxyl or enol form) higher the tendency to be reduced and greater the reduction potential value.

(I) 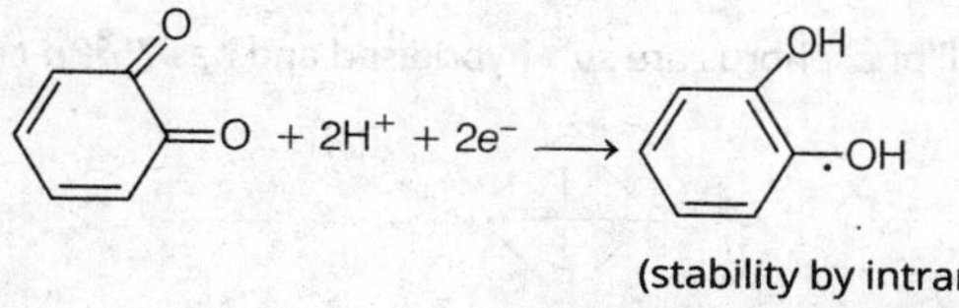 cyclohexadienedione $=O + 2H^+ + 2e^- \longrightarrow$ catechol (OH, OH)

(stability by intramolecular H-bonding of two *ortho* groups)

(II) 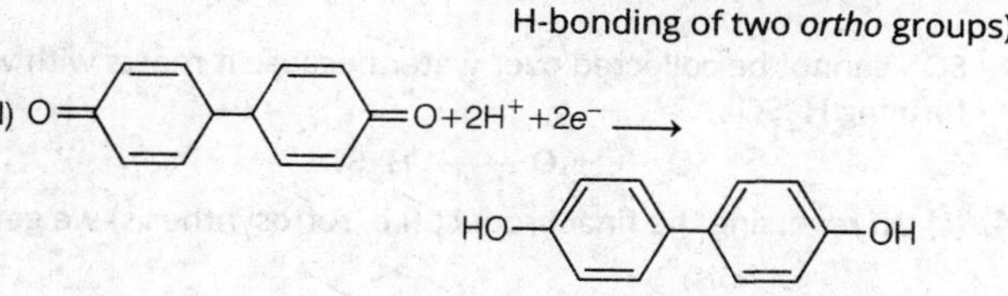 $O=\!\!$ diphenoquinone $=\!O + 2H^+ + 2e^- \longrightarrow$ HO–C$_6$H$_4$–C$_6$H$_4$–OH

(more conjugated system)

(III) 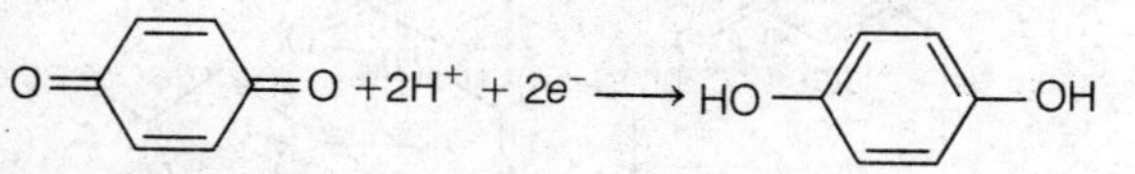 $O=$ C$_6$H$_4$ $=O + 2H^+ + 2e^- \longrightarrow$ HO–C$_6$H$_4$–OH

Thus, the decreasing order of $E°$ values is II > I > III.

18. (a) Let us study the reaction mechanism to understand the feasibility of formation the product,

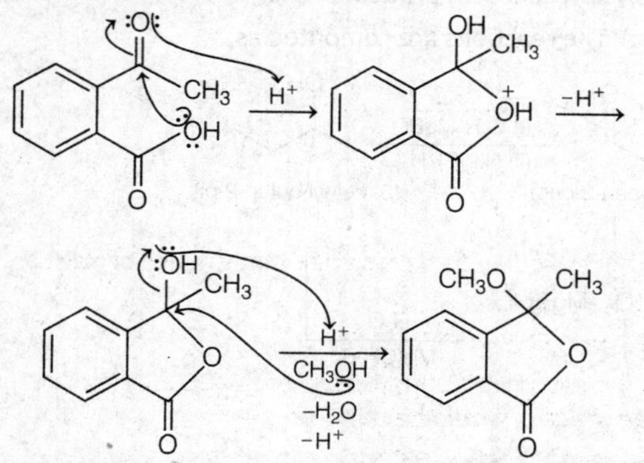

[Mechanism: keto acid with CH_3, H^+ $\longrightarrow$ cyclic intermediate (OH, CH_3, $\overset{+}{O}H$) $\xrightarrow{-H^+}$ hydroxy lactone; then $\xrightarrow{H^+,\ CH_3OH,\ -H_2O,\ -H^+}$ lactone with CH_3O and CH_3 (Option-a)]

Knockout 14

Paper 1

1. (b) **Case I** $E_1 = E° - \frac{2.303RT}{nF} \log \frac{[M^{n+}]}{[M]}$ at 298 K.

$\Rightarrow \quad E_1 = E° - \frac{0.059}{n} \log 2 \ [\because [M^{n+}] = 2\ M]$

Case II When temperature is doubled and the concentration is halved.

$\Rightarrow \quad E_2 = E° - \frac{2.303R \times 2T}{nF} \log 1 \left[\because [M^{n+}] = \frac{1}{2} \times 2\ M = 1\ M\right]$

$\Rightarrow \quad E_2 = E° - 0 = E°$

Thus, $E_2 > E_1$

2. (c) Milli-equivalent of H_2O_2

$= \text{milli-equivalent of } KMnO_4 = 13.32 \times 1.023 \times \frac{1}{10} = 1.36$

$\Rightarrow$ Normality of H_2O_2 solution = 1.36 N

$\Rightarrow$ Volume strength of H_2O_2 solution = 1.36 × 5.6 vol

= 7.616 vol $\quad [\because 1\ N\ H_2O_2 = 5.6 \text{ Volume } H_2O_2]$.

3. (a) Since, Cu^+ ions are used up in reaction II but reappeared in reaction III and Cu^{2+} is produced in reaction II but used up in reaction III, they are not chemically changed in the reaction.

4. (c) Mn(II) salt (Z) gives a white precipitate, Mn(II) hydroxide in excess of *aq* NaOH.

$$Mn^{2+} + 2OH^- \longrightarrow Mn(OH)_2 \downarrow$$

[White ppt. insoluble in excess OH^-]

On aerial oxidation, $Mn(OH)_2$ gets oxidised to brown coloured manganese dioxide (MnO_2)

$$2Mn(OH)_2 + O_2 \longrightarrow 2H_2O + 2MnO_2$$

Brown solid

5. (–6.20) For 2 mol NO_2,

$$2NO_2 \rightleftharpoons N_2O_4$$

$\Delta G° = G_2 - G_1$

$\Delta G° = (-0.8) + (-5.4) = -6.2$ kJ

6. (–0.80) For 1 mol NO_2,

$$N_2O_4 \rightleftharpoons 2NO_2$$

$\Delta G° = -0.8$ kJ

7. (0.23) Hybridisation index,

$$i = \frac{-1}{\cos\theta} = \frac{-1}{\cos 107.1°} = \frac{-1}{-0.294} = 3.40$$

The three N—H bonds which are arranged at bond angle of 107.1° use $sp^{3.4}$ hybridisation state.

$$\Rightarrow f_s = \frac{1}{i+1} = \frac{1}{3.4+1} = 0.227 \simeq 0.23$$

8. (2.13) Total

$f_s = f_{s\,(\text{Bonding})} + f_{s\,(\text{Non-bonding})}$

$\Rightarrow \ 1 = 3 \times 0.227 + f_{s\,(\text{Non-bonding})}$

$\Rightarrow f_{s\,(\text{Non-bonding})} = 1 - 0.681 = 0.319$

Now, $f_p = 1 - f_s = 1 - 0.319 = 0.681$

$$\Rightarrow \quad i = \frac{f_p}{f_s} = \frac{0.681}{0.319} = 2.13$$

9. (0.29) Rate of the forward reaction.

$\Rightarrow r_f = k_f [A]^n$, where *n* is the order of reaction.

	[A]	Rate
	0.170	0.05
twice	0.340	0.10 (twice)
twice	0.680	0.20 (twice)

It suggests that it is a 1st order reaction ($n = 1$)

$\Rightarrow$ From experiment I,

$r_f = 0.05$ and $[A] = 0.170$ M

$r_f = k_f [A] \Rightarrow 0.05 = k_f \times 0.170$

$\Rightarrow k_f = 0.29\ h^{-1}$

10. (4.8) In experiment I,

Initial concentration = 0.170 M

Final concentration = 0.0425 M (one-fourth of initial)

order of reaction = 1

$\Rightarrow$ Half-life time,

$$t_{1/2} = \frac{0.693}{k} = \frac{0.693}{0.294} = 2.4\,h$$

One-fourth will take

$$= 2 \times t_{1/2} = 2.4\,h \times 2 = 4.8\,h$$

11. (a, b, c) Statements (a), (b) and (c) are correct, whereas statement (d) is incorrect.

P-atom in PCl_5 is sp^3d-hybridised and PCl_5 has trigonal bipyramidal geometry.

$\Rightarrow$ Axial P—Cl bonds (P — Cl_a) are longer and weaker whereas equatorial P—Cl bonds (P — Cl_e) are shorter and stronger.

$\Rightarrow \angle Cl_aPCl_e = 90°, \angle Cl_ePCl_e = 120°$

$\Rightarrow$ In solid state, PCl_5 exists as $[PCl_4^+][PCl_6^-]$

Cl_a, Cl_e, Cl_e, P, Cl_e, Cl_a

12. (a, b) $NiCl_2$ in presence of dimethyl glyoxime (dmg) gives a complex $[Ni(dmg)_2]$

$$2\ \begin{matrix} CH_3—C{=}N—OH \\ | \\ CH_3—C{=}N—OH \end{matrix} + Ni^{2+} \longrightarrow [Ni(dmg)_2] + 2\overset{\oplus}{H}$$

(Bright red)

The red coloured complex precipitated by Ni^{2+} and dmg from slightly ammoniacal solution has square planar geometry.

The formation of this complex is used both for the detection and quantitative estimation of Ni(II) ion.

The dmg loses a proton and forms a stable complex molecule.

The complex is stabilised because two five-membered chelate rings are formed and also by intramolecular hydrogen bonding.

13. (a, c, d) White phosphorus on reaction with thionyl chloride ($SOCl_2$) produces phosphorus trichloride.

$$P_4(s) + 8SOCl_2(l) \longrightarrow 4PCl_3(l) + 4SO_2(g) + 2S_2Cl_2(g)$$

NO is paramagnetic in gaseous state because in gaseous state, it has one unpaired electron.

But in liquid state it is diamagnetic.

$$2\,\dot{N}{=}\ddot{O}:\ (g) \longrightarrow \begin{bmatrix} N{=}O \\ \vdots\ \ \vdots \\ O{=}N \end{bmatrix} \text{(Liquid)}$$

In P_4, all phosphorus are sp^3-hybridised and has 75% *p*-character.

(P_4 tetrahedron, each P: sp^3)

SO_2 cannot be collected over water because it reacts with water forming H_2SO_3.

$$SO_2 + H_2O \longrightarrow H_2SO_3$$

14. (c) On reversing the final product (i.e. retrosynthesis) we get,

(C) $\longrightarrow$ (D) $\longrightarrow$ (B) $\longrightarrow$ (A)

$\Rightarrow$ Here, (*C*) is the condensation product of (*D*) and (*B*) is the ozonolysis (reductive) product of (*A*).

15. (a, b, c) The reactions are computed as,

(a) (Propan-2-one) $\xrightarrow[\text{(ii) } NH_4Cl/H_2O]{\text{(i) } \overset{\ominus}{C_2H_5}\overset{\oplus}{Mg}Br}$ (2-methyl butan-2-ol)

via $\overset{\delta-}{O}—\overset{\delta+}{Mg}Br$ intermediate $\xrightarrow[-Mg(OH)Br]{H_2O}$

(c) (Methyl propanoate) $\xrightarrow[-Mg(OCH_3)Br]{\overset{\ominus}{CH_3}\overset{\oplus}{Mg}Br}$ (*b*) $\xrightarrow[\text{(ii) } H_2O]{\text{(i) } CH_3MgBr}$ (2-methylbutan-2-ol)

(d) CH_3CONH_2 (Ethanamide) does not undergo acyl S_N2 reaction with Grignard reagent, because for nature of $—CONH_2$ group where $—NH_2$ is in resonance with $>C{=}O$

$$Me—C(=O)—\ddot{N}H_2 \longleftrightarrow Me—C(—O^-)=\overset{+}{N}H_2$$

16. (b) Mole fraction of liquid A in vapour phase, i.e.

$$Y_A = \frac{X_A p_A^\circ}{X_A(p_A^\circ - p_B^\circ) + p_B^\circ} \quad \text{...(i)}$$

On reversing Eq. (i), we have

$$\frac{1}{Y_A} = \left(\frac{p_A^\circ - p_B^\circ}{p_A^\circ}\right) + \frac{p_B^\circ}{p_A^\circ}\left(\frac{1}{X_A}\right)$$

or

$$\frac{1}{X_A} = \left(\frac{p_B^\circ - p_A^\circ}{p_B^\circ}\right) + \frac{p_A^\circ}{p_B^\circ}\left(\frac{1}{Y_A}\right) \quad \text{...(ii)}$$

On comparing Eq. (ii) with $y = mx + c$, we get

$$\text{slope} = \frac{p_A^\circ}{p_B^\circ}; \text{Intercept} = \frac{p_B^\circ - p_A^\circ}{p_B^\circ}$$

17. (6) $\Rightarrow \frac{\lambda N_0}{\lambda N} = \frac{475}{270}$ or $\frac{N_0}{N} = 1.759$

$\Rightarrow$ After 5 min,

$$\lambda = \frac{2.303}{t}\log\frac{N_0}{N} = \frac{2.303}{5}\log 1.759 = 0.1129\ \text{min}^{-1}$$

$$\Rightarrow \text{Half-life period} = \frac{0.693}{\lambda} = \frac{0.693}{0.1129} = 6.138\ \text{min} \simeq 6\ \text{min}$$

18. (1)

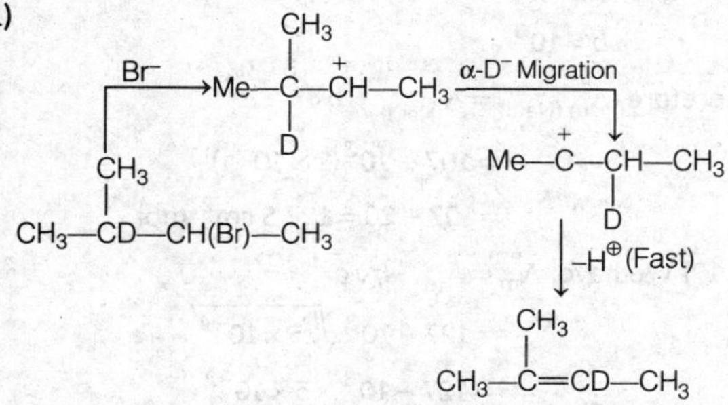

$CH_3-CD(CH_3)-CH(Br)-CH_3$ → (Br^-) $Me-C(CH_3)(D)-\overset{+}{C}H-CH_3$ → α-D^- Migration → $Me-\overset{+}{C}(CH_3)-CH(D)-CH_3$ → $-H^{\oplus}$ (Fast) → $CH_3-C(CH_3)=CD-CH_3$

The reaction involves E1 mechanism (order = 1) as migration of D^- takes place to form more stable 3° carbocation, As C—H bond is weaker than C—D bond, in faster step, H^+ gets eliminated.

19. (2)

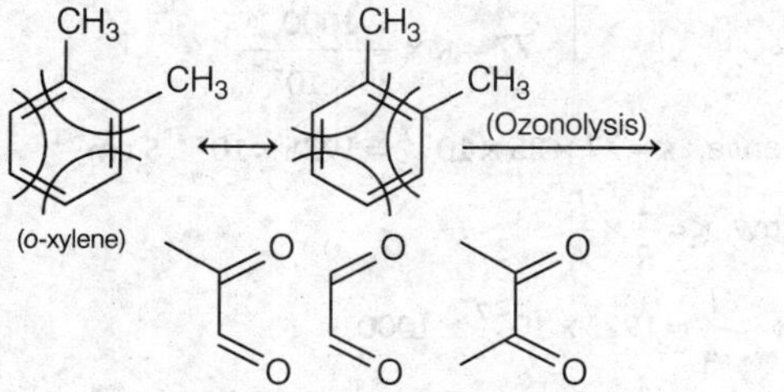

(o-xylene) ⟷ (resonance structure) → (Ozonolysis) → Methylglyoxal (2 mol) + Glyoxal (3 mol) + Dimethylglyoxal (1 mol)

ortho-xylene or 1,2-dimethylbenzene on mono-bromination will give 2 products.

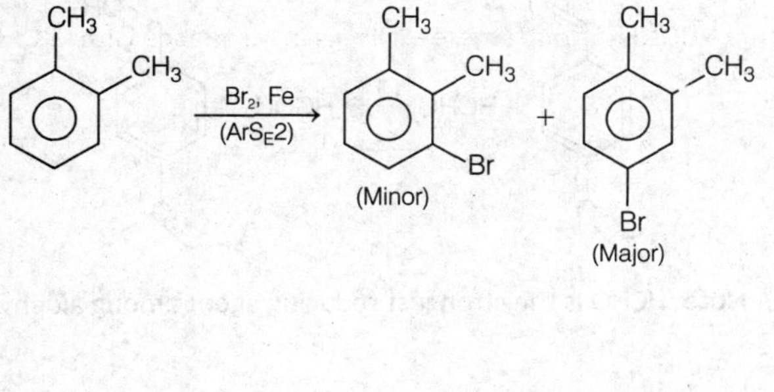

o-xylene → Br_2, Fe (ArS_E2) → 3-bromo-1,2-dimethylbenzene (Minor) + 4-bromo-1,2-dimethylbenzene (Major)

Paper 2

1. (a, b, c) In $[Pt(NH_3)_2Cl_2]$, platinum is in +2 oxidation state. d^2 configuration. It has dsp^2 configuration with square planar geometry. Number of unpaired electron is zero. So, it is diamagnetic in nature.

The complex $[Pt(NH_3)_2Cl_2]$ undergoes ionisation isomerism in presence of $AgNO_3$.

2. (a, c, d) Statements (a), (c), (d) are correct, whereas statement (b) is incorrect.

In the given situation, first period would have 3 elements H, He and Li.

$\Rightarrow$ Number of elements in the 2nd period will be,

$2s + 2p = 3 + 9 = 12$

$\Rightarrow$ Number of elements in the 4th period will be, $18 + 9 = 27$

$\Rightarrow$ Number of periods will be less than 7.

3. (b) Compound (*H*) undergoes aldol condensation reaction followed by dehydration of aldol that gives α, β- unsaturated carbonyl compound (*B*), not the β, γ-unsaturated carbonyl as major product.

As a result, *Q* is (bicyclic α,β-unsaturated aldehyde with CHO; β, α labelled)

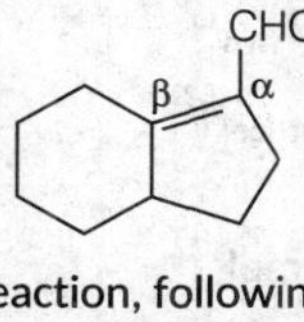

In the second reaction, following steps take place.

(i) In first step, the more reactive aldehyde group is acetylated and then ketonic group is reduced with $LiAlH_4$.

(ii) In the final step, hemiacetal formation occur at aldehyde group and led to the formation of

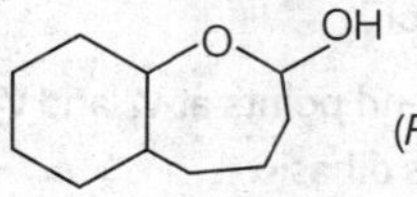

(*R*) (cyclic hemiacetal with OH)

4. (b)

$CH_3\overset{O}{\overset{\|}{C}}O\overset{O}{\overset{\|}{C}}CH_3$ (+ $CH_3CO\bar{O}\overset{+}{N}a$)

(Benzaldehyde) C_6H_5CHO + $\overset{\ominus}{C}H_2-\overset{O}{\overset{\|}{C}}-O-\overset{O}{\overset{\|}{C}}-CH_3$

Perkin reaction → $C_6H_5-CH(O^-)-CH_2\overset{O}{\overset{\|}{C}}O\overset{O}{\overset{\|}{C}}CH_3$

↓ $H^{\oplus}$(– AcOH)

$C_6H_5-CH(OH)-CH_2\overset{O}{\overset{\|}{C}}OH$

↓ $-H_2O$

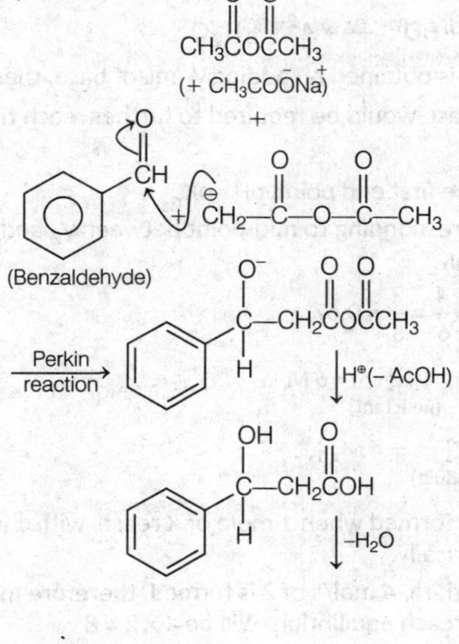

(Q) CH=CHCOOH
↓ MeOH | H_2, Pd/C
(R) CH=CHCH$_2$OH
↓ (i) $SOCl_2$
CH=CHCH$_2$Cl
↓ Δ | (ii) $AlCl_3$
CH=CH—$\overset{+}{C}H_2$$AlCl_4^-$
↓ (ArS_E2)
(S)
(Option-b)

5. (b) Using the formula,
enthalpy of solution = lattice energy + hydration enthalpy

Or $\Delta_{sol}H^\circ = \Delta_{lattice}H^\circ + \Delta_{hyd}H^\circ$

$\therefore \quad \Delta_{hyd}H^\circ = \Delta_{sol}H^\circ - \Delta_{lattice}H^\circ$

$= 1.0 - 180$

$= -179.0 \text{ kcal mol}^{-1}$

$\Rightarrow$ The ratio of hydration energies of Na^+ and Cl^- is 6 : 5.

$\therefore$ Hydration energy of Na^+

$= \frac{6}{11} \times (-179.0) = -97.63$

$\simeq -98.0 \text{ kcal mol}^{-1}$

6. (a, b, c, d) The two end points at V_1 and V_2 indicate that weak acid being titrated is dibasic.

$$H_2A + OH^- \longrightarrow H_2O + HA^-$$

$$HA^- + HO^- \longrightarrow A^{2-} + H_2O$$

If first end point is obtained on adding V_1 mL of base, then V_2 mL of same base would be required to further reach the 2nd end point.

At half-way of the first end point, $pH = pK_{a_1}$.

Similarly, pH corresponding to mid-point between V_2 and V_1 corresponds to pK_{a_2}.

7. (0.67) $K_C = \frac{[Z]}{[X]} = \frac{4}{6} = \frac{2}{3} = 0.67$

[$\because$ At equilibrium, $\underset{\text{(Reactant)}}{[X]} = 6\text{ M}$,

$\underset{\text{(Product)}}{[Z]} = 4\text{ M}_X$]

8. (8) 1 mole of *Z* is formed when 1 mole of *X* reacts with 1 mole of *Y* stoichiometrically.

To attain equilibrium, 4 mol/L of *Z* is formed, therefore moles of *Y* required to reach equilibrium will be $4 \times 2 = 8$

9. (−4.20) At 300 K,

ΔG° (*cis*-2-butene $\longrightarrow$ *trans*-2-butene)

$= (63 - 66) \text{ kJ mol}^{-1} = -3 \text{ kJ mol}^{-1}$

$\Rightarrow \Delta H^\circ$ (*cis*-2-butene $\rightarrow$ *trans*-2-butene)

$= [-11.2 - (-7)] \text{ kJ mol}^{-1} = -4.2 \text{ kJ mol}^{-1}$

10. (−4)

ΔS° (*cis*-2-butene $\rightarrow$ *trans*-2-butene)

$$= \frac{\Delta H^\circ - \Delta G^\circ}{T} = \frac{-4.2 + 3}{300} \times 1000 = -4 \text{ JK}^{-1} \text{ mol}^{-1}$$

11. (127)

Given that, $R = 1000\ \Omega$, $\Lambda^\circ_{m(Cl^-)} = 80 \text{ S cm}^2\text{mol}^{-1}$,

$\Lambda^\circ_{m(SO_4^{2-})} = 160 \text{ S cm}^2 \text{ mol}^{-1}$

$\Rightarrow$ Now applying the equation,

$$\Lambda^\circ_{m\,(NaCl)} = 107 + b\sqrt{c} \quad \text{...(i)}$$

$$\Lambda^\circ_{m\,(NaCl)} = 97 + b\sqrt{c} \quad \text{...(ii)}$$

Subtracting Eq. (ii) from Eq. (i), we get

$0 = 10 + b(2 \times 10^{-2}) - b(3 \times 10^{-2})$

$\Rightarrow \quad b = 10^3$

Therefore, $\Lambda^\circ_{m\,(NaCl)} = \Lambda_{(NaCl)} + b\sqrt{c}$

$= 107 + 10^3(2 \times 10^{-2})$

$= 107 + 20 = 127 \text{ S cm}^2 \text{ mol}^{-1}$

12. (0.19) We have, $\Lambda^\circ_m = \Lambda_m - b\sqrt{c}$

$= 127 - 10^3\sqrt{25 \times 10^{-4}}$

$= 127 - 10^3 \times 5 \times 10^{-2}$

$= 77 \text{ S cm}^2\text{mol}^{-1}$

$$\Lambda^\circ_m = \frac{\kappa(\text{S cm}^{-1}) \times 1000(\text{cm}^3/\text{L})}{\text{Molarity (mol/L)}}$$

$\Rightarrow \quad 77 = \kappa \times \frac{1000}{25 \times 10^{-4}}$

Hence, $\kappa = 77 \times 25 \times 10^{-7} = 1925 \times 10^{-7} \text{ S cm}^{-1}$

Now, $\kappa = \frac{1}{R} \times \frac{l}{A}$

$\Rightarrow \quad \frac{l}{A} = 1925 \times 10^{-7} \times 1000$

$= 0.19255 \text{ cm}^{-1} \simeq 0.19 \text{ cm}^{-1}$

13. (a) It is cross Cannizzaro reaction in which HCHO is oxidised and other aldehyde gets reduced.

(4-methoxybenzaldehyde) + HCHO $\xrightarrow{OH^-}$ $HCOO^-$ + (4-methoxybenzyl alcohol)

Note HCHO is the strongest reducing agent among aldehydes.

14. (a)

$$\text{C}_6\text{H}_4(\text{CHO})_2 \; [C_8H_6O_2] \; (A) + HCHO \xrightarrow{OH^-} \text{C}_6\text{H}_4(\text{CH}_2\text{OH})_2 \; [C_8H_{10}O_2] \; (B) + HCOO^-$$

$$\text{C}_6\text{H}_4(\text{CH}_2\text{OH})_2 \; (B) \xrightarrow{PBr_3} \text{C}_6\text{H}_4(\text{CH}_2\text{Br})_2 \; [C_8H_8Br_2] \; (C)$$

15. (b) In metal carbonyls, when CO groups are replaced with groups that have low or no ability to back accept electron density in their low-lying antibonding orbitals, the remaining CO groups must accept more electrons from the metal.

Thus, the CO stretching frequency decreases. In the given three compounds, PF_3 has better π-acceptor capabilities than PCl_3, so C—O stretching frequency is maximum in *fac*-$Mo(CO)_3(PF_3)_3$.

PMe_3 is a weak π-donor ligand, so it does not take any electron density from the metal and the C—O stretching frequency is the minimum.

16. (c) When π-back bonding takes place between metal and carbonyl group, the electron density of the metal is accommodated in the empty π^* obitals of CO group and the bond order decreases.

The extent of π-back bonding follows the order :

$[Ti(CO)_6]^{2-} > [V(CO)_6]^- > [Cr(CO)_6] > [Mn(CO)_6]^+$.

It is maximum in $[Ti(CO)_6]^{2-}$ because, in addition to metal electron density, carbonyl groups also accommodate the negative charge on the metal, hence the bond order is minimum.

17. (2) $\quad \dfrac{v}{c} = \dfrac{1}{125}$

or $\quad v = \dfrac{3 \times 10^{10}}{275} \text{ cm s}^{-1}$

On comparing with

$$v = \frac{nh}{2\pi mr},$$

where, $r = 0.529 \times 10^{-8} n^2$ cm

($Z = 1$ for H-atom)

$$\Rightarrow \quad v = \frac{nh}{2\pi m \times (0.529 \times 10^{-8} n^2 \text{ cm})}$$

$$\Rightarrow \quad n = \frac{h}{2\pi mv \times (0.529 \times 10^{-8} \text{ cm})}$$

$$= \frac{6.626 \times 10^{-27} \text{ erg. s}}{2 \times 3.14 \times (9.1 \times 10^{-28} \text{ g}) \times \left(\dfrac{3 \times 10^{10}}{275} \text{ cm s}^{-1}\right) \times (0.529 \times 10^{-8} \text{ cm})} = 2.031 \approx 2$$

18. (7) The isomeric dichloro products are,

[Structures: 1,1-dichlorocyclopentane; cis- and trans-1,2-dichlorocyclopentane; cis- and trans-1,3-dichlorocyclopentane (enantiomers)]

Total number of products = 7

19. (2)

$$CH_3\overset{*}{C}HD-CH_2-\overset{O}{\overset{\|}{C}}-O-\underset{Ph}{\overset{CH_3}{C^*}}-\overset{*}{C}HD-CH_3 \xrightarrow[\text{Alkyl cleavage}]{H^+, H_2O}$$

$$\underset{\text{(2 products)}}{CH_3\overset{*}{C}HD-CH_2-\overset{O}{\overset{\|}{C}}-OH} + HO-\underset{Ph}{\overset{CH_3}{C^*}}-\overset{*}{C}HD-CH_3$$

The cleavage of C—O—C bond does not change optical purity of the carboxylic acid and alcohol components.

Knockout 15

Paper 1

1. (a) Applying the concept of half-life time of radioactive decay,

$N_0 = N \times 2^n$

$\Rightarrow$ n = Number of half lives $= T / t_{1/2}$ or $T = n \times t_{1/2}$

$\Rightarrow N_0$ = Initial activity

N = Activity observed = 0.01 μC_i

$\Rightarrow$ Total time taken $(T) = nt_{1/2}$

$\Rightarrow \quad = 30 \text{ h} = n6$

$\Rightarrow n = 5$ h

$\Rightarrow$ Initial activity $= 0.01 \times 2^5 = 0.32 \, \mu C_i$

2. (b) When copper (II) oxide is treated with sulphuric acid, it produces copper sulphate $[X]$.

$$CuO + H_2SO_4 \longrightarrow \underset{[X]}{CuSO_4} + H_2O$$

In aqueous solution, it exists as pentahydrate copper sulphate which is blue in colour.

$[Cu(H_2O)_4]SO_4 \cdot H_2O \longrightarrow$ Blue colour

$\Rightarrow$ When copper sulphate is treated with excess of aqueous solution of ammonia, it produces $[Cu(NH_3)_4]^{2+}$ which has deep blue colour.

$$\underset{}{[Cu(H_2O)_4]SO_4 \cdot H_2O} + NH_3 \longrightarrow \underset{[Y]}{[Cu(NH_3)_4]SO_4}$$

Deep blue colour (needle like crystals)

$\Rightarrow [X] = [Cu(H_2O)_4]SO_4 \cdot H_2O$; $[Y] = [Cu(NH_3)_4]SO_4$

3. (b) Order of strength of intermolecular forces in polymers is :

Elastomer < Thermoplastic < Fibre < Thermosetting

So, buna-S < polythene < nylon-6, 6 < bakelite, i.e. $R < A < G < U$.

4. (c) The reaction is computed as,

Indene $\xrightarrow[-H_2\uparrow]{\overset{\oplus\ \ominus}{NaH}}$ indenyl anion (Stable) [Both rings become aromatic] $\xrightarrow{\text{allyl bromide } (S_N2')}$ 3-(but-3-enyl)indene $+ Br^{\ominus}$ (when, $S_N2' > S_N2$)

5. (–56) Applying Hess's law of constant heat summation,

$\Rightarrow$ add I (a) and I (b) :

$$2Na\,(s) + \frac{1}{2}O_2(g) + H_2O(l) \longrightarrow 2NaOH(aq);$$

$$\Delta H_1^\circ = -88 - 68 = -156 \text{ kcal} \quad \text{...(III)}$$

$\Rightarrow$ add II (a) and II (b) :

$$2Na\,(s) + \frac{1}{2}O_2(g) + H_2O(l) \longrightarrow 2NaOH(aq.);$$

$$\Delta H_2^\circ = (-100 + x)\text{kcal} \quad \text{...(IV)}$$

$\Rightarrow$ Both (III and IV) represent same chemical change, hence

$$\Delta H_1^\circ = \Delta H_2^\circ$$

$$\Rightarrow \quad -156 \text{ kcal} = -100 + x$$

$$\therefore \quad x = -56 \text{ kcal}$$

6. (–112) The expression of $\Delta_f H^\circ(NaOH, aq)$ is,

$Na + \frac{1}{2}O_2 + \frac{1}{2}H_2 \longrightarrow NaOH$, where

$$\Delta_f H^\circ = \frac{1}{2}[\Delta H(IIa) + \Delta H\,(IIb) + \Delta H\,(Ib)]$$

$$= \frac{1}{2}(-100 - 56 - 68) \text{ kcal mol}^{-1}$$

$$= -112 \text{ kcal mol}^{-1}$$

7. (3.56) $\underset{97\,g}{ZnS} \longrightarrow \underset{65\,g}{Zn}$

5.32×10^3 g ZnS gives

$$\frac{65}{97} \times 5.32 \times 10^3 \text{ g Zn} = 3565 \text{ g} = 3.565 \text{ kg}.$$

Theoretical yield of Zn = 3.56 kg

8. (92.57)

Actual yield of Zn = 3.30 kg

$$\text{Thus, \% yield} = \frac{\text{Actual yield}}{\text{Theoretical yield}} \times 100$$

$$= \frac{3.30}{3.565} \times 100 = 92.57\%$$

9. (231.75) $\underset{(X)}{C_6H_5—\overset{O}{\overset{||}{C}}—CH_2Cl}$;

$\underset{(Y)}{C_6H_5—\overset{OH}{\overset{|}{CH}}—CH_2Cl}$;

$\underset{(Z)}{C_6H_5—CH—CH_2}$ (epoxide, O bridging CH and CH_2)

In the reactions,

(X) is $C_6H_5—\overset{O}{\overset{||}{C}}—CH_2Cl\ (C_8H_7OCl)$

Molar mass $= 8 \times 12 + 7 \times 1 + 1 \times 16 + 1 \times 35.5 = 154.5 \text{ g mol}^{-1}$

$$W_X = 1.5 \text{ mol} \times M_x = 1.5 \times 154.5 \text{ g} = 231.75 \text{ g} = x \text{ g}$$

10. (180)

(Z) is $C_6H_5—CH—CH_2\ (C_8H_8O)$ (epoxide)

Molar mass $= 8 \times 12 + 8 \times 1 + 1 \times 16 = 120 \text{ g mol}^{-1}$

$W_Z = 1.5 \text{ mol} \times M_Z = 1.5 \times 120 \text{ g} = 180 \text{ g} = z \text{ g}$

11. (b) Ammonia forms the complex ion $[Cu(NH_3)_4]^{2+}$ with copper ions in the alkaline solutions but not in acidic solutions. The reason is that in acidic solutions, protons coordinate with ammonia molecules forming NH_4^+ ions and NH_3 molecules are not available as ligands to coordinate with Cu(II).

12. (a, b, c) According to the question,

$$(A) \xrightarrow{NaOH, \Delta} (B) \xleftarrow{H_2O} Mg_3N_2$$

A has NH_4^+ ion and (B) is NH_3.

(i) $Mg_3N_2 + 6H_2O \longrightarrow 3Mg(OH)_2 + \underset{(B)}{2NH_3}$

(ii) $\underset{(\text{of } A)}{NH_4^+} + NaOH \xrightarrow{\Delta} Na^+ + \underset{(B)}{NH_3} + H_2O$

Resultant solution after NH_3 has escaped completely contains Na^+ and anion of (A), which also gives ring test of NO_3^-. Thus, (A) is NH_4NO_3.

(i) $\underset{(A)}{NH_4NO_3} + NaOH \xrightarrow{\Delta} \underset{(B)}{NH_3}\uparrow + NaNO_3 + H_2O$

(ii) **Ring – Test**

$$NaNO_3 + H_2SO_4 \longrightarrow NaHSO_4 + HNO_3$$

$$3H_2SO_4 + 6FeSO_4 + 2HNO_3 \longrightarrow 3Fe_2(SO_4)_3 + 2NO + 4H_2O$$

$$[Fe(H_2O)_6]SO_4 + NO \longrightarrow \underset{\text{Brown coloured ring }(C)}{[Fe(H_2O)_5NO]SO_4} + H_2O$$

$\Rightarrow \quad \underset{(A)}{NH_4NO_3} \xrightarrow{\Delta} \underset{(D)}{N_2O} + \underset{(E)}{2H_2O}$

$N_2O + H_2O \longrightarrow \underset{\text{(Hypo nitrous acid)}}{H_2N_2O_2(F)}$

It exists in following two geometrical isomeric forms,

trans   cis

13. (a, b, c) The reaction sequence can be shown as,

$CH_3-C(CH_3)_2-CH_2CH_2OH$ or $(CH_3)_3C-CH_2CH_2OH$ (1°alcohol) (3,3-dimethylbutan-1-ol) $\xrightarrow[H_2SO_4,\ H_2O,\ \Delta]{[O]\ K_2Cr_2O_7}$ $\underset{\text{(Carboxylic acid)}}{\underset{(A)}{(CH_3)_3CCH_2COOH}} \xrightarrow[-SO_2,\ -HCl]{SOCl_2} \underset{\text{(Acid chloride)}}{\underset{(B)}{(CH_3)_3CCH_2COCl}}$

$\xrightarrow[-HCl]{(CH_3)_2NH} \underset{\text{(N,N-dimethyl amide)}}{\underset{(C)}{(CH_3)_3CCH_2-\overset{O}{\overset{\|}{C}}-N(CH_3)_2}} \xrightarrow[\text{(ii)}H_2O]{\text{(i) LiAlH}_4\text{, ether}} \underset{\text{(3°amine)}}{\underset{(D)}{(CH_3)_3CCH_2-CH_2N(CH_3)_2}}$

14. (a) Reactant is β-D glucopyranosyl (β-D-glucose), so the product formed will also be D-glucose (*s*-orbital). In this reaction, $NaBH_4$ reduces —CHO(C-1) group into —CH_2OH.

15. (d) $AB \rightleftharpoons A^+ + B^-, K_1$ ...(i)

$AB + B^- \rightleftharpoons AB_2^-, K_2$ ...(ii)

$2AB \rightleftharpoons A^+ + AB_2^- \Rightarrow K = K_1 \times K_2$

$\Rightarrow$ Also, subtracting Eqs. (ii) from (i), we have,

$AB_2^- \rightleftharpoons A^+ + 2B^-;\ K = \frac{K_1}{K_2}$

$$\Rightarrow \quad \frac{K_1}{K_2} = \frac{[A^+][B^-]}{[AB]} \times \frac{[AB][B^-]}{[AB_2^-]} = \frac{[A^+][B^-]^2}{[AB_2^-]}$$

$$\Rightarrow \quad \frac{[A^+]}{[AB_2^-]} = \frac{K_1}{K_2} \times \frac{1}{[B^-]^2}$$

$$\Rightarrow \quad \frac{[A^+]}{[AB_2^-]} \propto \frac{1}{[B^-]^2}$$

16. (a, b , c, d)

(a) At a particular pressure (separately for O_2 and N_2) ideal behaviour is reached.
Thus, $Z = 1$

(b) For H_2, attractive force is zero.
Hence, $p(V - b) = RT$ or $pV = RT + Pb$

$$\Rightarrow \quad Z = \frac{pV}{RT} = \left(1 + \frac{pb}{RT}\right) \quad \therefore Z > 1$$

(c) For N_2 (in low pressure range) p is low, V is high

Thus, $(V - b) = V$ or $\left(p + \frac{a}{V^2}\right)V = RT$

$$\Rightarrow \quad pV = RT - \frac{a}{V}$$

$$\Rightarrow \quad Z = \frac{pV}{RT} = \left(1 - \frac{a}{RTV}\right) \quad \therefore Z < 1$$

(d) This statement is also correct [same as in (c)].

17. (156)

Given : $K_f = 5.12$ K kg mol^{-1}, $w_{solute} = 0.643$ g,

$\Delta T_f = T_0 - T_i = 5.51 - 5.03 = 0.48$

$w_{solvent} = 50$ mL $\times 0.879$ g/mL $= 43.95$ g and $i = 1$

$$\Rightarrow \quad \Delta T_f = K_f \times m \times i = K_f \times \frac{w_{solute} \times 1000}{M_{solute} \times w_{solvent}} \times 1$$

$$\Rightarrow M_{solute} = \frac{K_f \times w_{solute} \times 1000}{\Delta T_f \times w_{solvent}}$$

$$= \frac{5.12 \times 0.643 \times 1000}{0.48 \times 43.95} = 156.06 \text{ g mol}^{-1}$$

$$\simeq 156 \text{ g mol}^{-1}$$

18. (6) Given, $T_1 = 25°C = 298$ K, $T_2 = T$ (say),

$E_a = 104.4$ kJ mol^{-1} = 104.4×10^3 J mol^{-1}

$k_1 = 3 \times 10^{-4}$ s^{-1} and $k_2 = ?$

$\Rightarrow$ Applying Arrhenius equation,

$$\log \frac{k_2}{k_1} = \frac{E_a}{2.303\,R}\left[\frac{1}{T_1} - \frac{1}{T_2}\right]$$

$$\Rightarrow \log \frac{k_2}{3 \times 10^{-4}} = \frac{104.4 \times 10^3}{2.303 \times 8.314} \times \left[\frac{1}{298} - \frac{1}{T}\right]$$

$$\Rightarrow \log \frac{k_2}{3 \times 10^{-4}} = \frac{104.4 \times 10^3}{2.303 \times 8.314} \times \frac{1}{298} \quad \left[\text{as } T \to \infty, \frac{1}{T} \to 0\right]$$

$$\Rightarrow \log \frac{k_2}{3 \times 10^{-4}} = 18.297$$

$$\Rightarrow \quad \frac{k_2}{3 \times 10^{-4}} = 10^{18.297} \Rightarrow \quad \frac{k_2}{3 \times 10^{-4}} = 1.98 \times 10^{18}$$

$$\Rightarrow \quad k_2 = 1.98 \times 10^{18} \times 3 \times 10^{-4}$$

$$= 5.94 \times 10^{14} \text{ s}^{-1} \simeq 6 \times 10^{14} \text{ s}^{-1}$$

19. (5) The above cell is a concentration cell, i.e. $E^\circ_{cell} = 0$

$\Rightarrow$ The half-cell reactions are

Anode reaction

$Ag \text{ (anode)} \rightleftharpoons Ag^{\oplus} \text{ (0.1 M)} + e^-$

Cathode reaction

$Ag^{\oplus}\text{(cathode)} + e^- \rightleftharpoons Ag(s)$

Cell reaction

$Ag^{\oplus}\text{(cathode)} + e^- \rightleftharpoons Ag^{\oplus}\text{(0.1 M) (anode)}$

Since, $AgNO_3$ is 80% ionised,

$$[Ag^{\oplus}]_a = 0.1 \times \frac{80}{100} = 0.08 \text{ M}$$

$$\Rightarrow \quad E_{cell} = E^\circ_{cell} - \frac{0.06}{1}\log\frac{[Ag^{\oplus}]_a}{[Ag^{\oplus}]_c}$$

$$\Rightarrow -0.6\ V = 0 - 0.06\log\frac{0.08}{[Ag^{\oplus}]_c}$$

$$\Rightarrow \quad \log\frac{0.08}{[Ag^{\oplus}]_c} = \frac{0.6}{0.06} = 10$$

$$\Rightarrow \quad \log[Ag^+]_c = \log 0.08 - 10$$

$$= (\log 2^3 - \log 100) - 10$$

$$= 0.9 - 2 - 10 = -11.1$$

$$\therefore \quad [Ag^+]_c = 10^{-11.1} = 8\times10^{-12}\ M$$

$[\because$ for KBr, $1\ N = 1M]$

Since, KBr is 60% dissociated,

$$[Br^{\ominus}] = 1\times\frac{60}{100} = 0.6\ M$$

$$\Rightarrow K_{sp}(AgBr) = [Ag^{\oplus}][Br^{\ominus}]$$

$$= 8\times10^{-12}\times0.6 = 4.8\times10^{-12}M^2$$

$$\simeq 5\times10^{-12}M^2$$

Paper 2

1. (a) The *trans* effect causes the introduction of the ligand *trans* to chloride rather than *trans* to ammonia in both the cases,

$$\Rightarrow \left[\begin{matrix} & Cl & \\ Cl- & Pt & -Cl \\ & Cl & \end{matrix}\right]^{2-} \xrightarrow[-Cl^-]{+NH_3}$$

(Tetrachloridoplatinate (II) ion)

$$\left[\begin{matrix} & Cl & \\ Cl- & Pt & -NH_3 \\ & Cl & \end{matrix}\right]^{-} \xrightarrow[-Cl^-]{+NH_3} \left[\begin{matrix} & Cl & \\ Cl- & Pt & -NH_3 \\ & NH_3 & \end{matrix}\right] \; (X)$$

$$\Rightarrow \left[\begin{matrix} & NH_3 & \\ H_3N- & Pt & -NH_3 \\ & NH_3 & \end{matrix}\right]^{2+} \xrightarrow[-NH_3]{+Cl^-}$$

(Tetraammineplatinum(II) ion)

$$\left[\begin{matrix} & NH_3 & \\ H_3N- & Pt & -Cl \\ & NH_3 & \end{matrix}\right]^{+} \xrightarrow[-NH_3]{+Cl^-} \left[\begin{matrix} & NH_3 & \\ Cl- & Pt & -Cl \\ & NH_3 & \end{matrix}\right] \; (Y)$$

2. (b, c) The poisonous element M may be As (Arsenic).

On the basis of the given informations,

$$\Rightarrow AsCl_3 + 6[H] \xrightarrow[H_2SO_4]{Zn} \underset{(N)}{AsH_3} + 3HCl;$$

$$2AsH_3 \xrightarrow{\Delta} \underset{(M)}{2As} + 3H_2\uparrow$$

$\Rightarrow$ Oxy acids of As (H_3AsO_3, H_3AsO_4) are water soluble.

3. (b, c)

PhCHO + cyclopentanone (H at α-carbon) $\xrightarrow[-H_2O]{\overset{\ominus}{O}H}$ Ph—CH(OH)—(2-oxocyclopentyl) $\xrightarrow[-H_2O]{H^{\oplus}}$ [Ph—$\overset{\oplus}{C}$H—(2-oxocyclopentyl)] $\xrightarrow{\text{Ring expansion}}$ [Ph—$\overset{\oplus}{\text{cyclohexanone}}$] $\xrightarrow{-H^+}$ 3-phenylcyclohex-2-en-1-one (A) $\xrightarrow[KMnO_4/H^+]{[O]}$ HOOC–(keto acid with Ph) (B)

(A) $\xrightarrow[(ii)Zn/H_2O]{(i)O_3/THF}$ 2 CHO–CHO (C) (Glyoxal) + OHC–C(=O)–C(=O)–CH₂–CH₂–CH₂–C(=O)–CHO (D)

(C) (Glyoxal); (D) (2,3,7-trioxooctan-1,8- dial)

4. (b, c)

Furanose structure: HOH_2C at C-5, ring O, C-1 (H, OH), C-2 (H, OH), C-3 (H, OH), C-4.

It is an aldofuranose. Anomers differ in configuration of anomeric carbon, i.e. at (C–1) position.

5. (a, c, d) When temperature of a system drops during a chemical reaction, then that process is called endothermic process, in which heat is consumed by the reaction ($\Delta H > 0$).

$\Rightarrow \Delta H$ = [heat of system before the reaction (larger value) – heat of system after reaction (smaller value)] > 0.

6. (c) $A \xrightarrow[300\ K,\ 2\ atm]{\Delta V = 0} B \xrightarrow[5\ atm,\ 750\ K]{\text{Adiabatic reversible expansion}} C$

$\xrightarrow[300\ K]{\text{Isothermal reversible compression}} A\ (300\ K,\ 2\ atm)$

$$\Rightarrow C_V = 1.5R,\ C_p = 2.5R$$

$$\Rightarrow \quad \gamma = \frac{5}{3} \text{ and } 1-\gamma = \frac{-2}{3} \Rightarrow \quad \frac{\gamma}{1-\gamma} = \frac{-5}{2}$$

$$\Rightarrow \text{Between } B \text{ and } C: p\times(T)^{\frac{\gamma}{(1-\gamma)}} = \text{constant}$$

$$\Rightarrow 5(750)^{-5/2} = p\times(300)^{-5/2}$$

$[\because B\ (p = 5\ atm, T = 750\ K);\ C\ (p = ?, T = 300\ K)]$

$$\Rightarrow p = 5\left(\frac{750}{300}\right)^{-5/2} = 5\times0.10 = 0.5\ atm$$

Therefore, $p(C) < p(A)$ and hence, graph (C) behaves most appropriately.

7. (1) Here, $-COO^-$ (one) is the conjugate basic group present in *C*-terminal position.

8. (4) Between five molecules of amino acids, only four amide (peptide) linkages are possible.

9. (6) Since, 1 mole of $NaHCO_3$ reacts with 1 mole of $-COOH$. Here, (in product *Y*) 6—COOH groups are present, so 6 moles of $NaHCO_3$ are required.

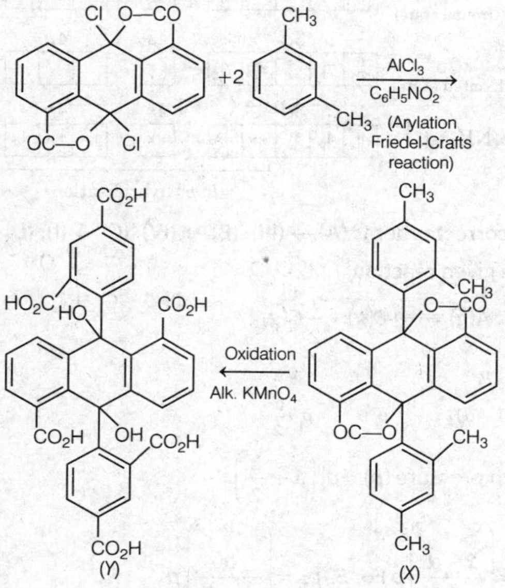

$\xrightarrow[\text{(Arylation Friedel-Crafts reaction)}]{AlCl_3,\ C_6H_5NO_2}$ (X) $\xrightarrow[\text{Alk. } KMnO_4]{\text{Oxidation}}$ (Y)

10. (18)

Each degree of unsaturation = One π-bond or one ring

$\Rightarrow$ Degree of unsaturation in *X*

= Number of π-bonds + Number of rings

$$= [\underset{\text{[in 4 rings]}}{4 \times 3} + \underset{\text{[in 2 C=O groups]}}{2 \times 1}] + 4 = 18$$

11. (20) For radioactive disintegration at equilibrium,

$$N_A \lambda_A = N_B \lambda_B$$

$$\Rightarrow \quad N_A \frac{0.693}{(t_{50})_A} = N_B \frac{0.693}{(t_{50})_B}$$

$$\Rightarrow \quad \frac{N_A}{N_B} = \frac{(t_{50})_A}{(t_{50})_B}$$

$$\Rightarrow \quad (t_{50})_A = 100 \text{ min}$$

and $(t_{50})_B = \dfrac{(t_{75})_B}{2} = \dfrac{10}{2} = 5 \text{ min}$

$$\therefore \quad \frac{N_A}{N_B} = \frac{100}{5} = 20$$

12. (0.05) From above answer,

$$\frac{\lambda_A}{\lambda_B} = \frac{N_B}{N_A} = \frac{1}{20} = 0.05$$

13. (a) Based on given figure, pressure of HCl $\propto \chi_{HCl}$

$$\Rightarrow \quad p_{HCl} = K_H \chi_{HCl}$$

$$\therefore \quad K_H = \frac{p_{HCl}}{\chi_{HCl}}$$

$\Rightarrow$ When $\chi_{HCl} = 0.01$, $p_{HCl} = 400$ torr

$$\therefore \quad K_H = \frac{400}{0.01} = 4 \times 10^4 \text{ torr}$$

14. (b) At $p_{HCl} = 400$ torr, $\chi_{HCl} = 0.01$ and $p_{HCl} = 800$ torr, $\chi_{HCl} = 0.02$

$$\therefore \quad \frac{\chi_{HCl}(400 \text{ torr})}{\chi_{HCl}(800 \text{ torr})} = \frac{0.01}{0.02} = 0.5$$

15. (a) More negative the standard reduction potential value, stronger is the reducing agent.

16. (b) Ce^{4+} is $[Xe]4f^0$, it readily gets converted into more stable oxidation state of +3 by gain of an electron. So, in aqueous solution, Ce^{4+} is a good oxidising agent.

17. (6) Number of sodium lauryl sulphate $[C_{12}H_{25}SO_4^-Na^+]$ molecules in colloidal solution $= 10^{-4} \times 6 \times 10^{23} = 6 \times 10^{19}$

$\Rightarrow$ Number of sodium lauryl sulphate per $mm^3 = (6 \times 10^{19}) \times 10^{-6}$

$$= 6 \times 10^{13}$$

$\Rightarrow$ Number of colloidal particles per $mm^3 = 10^{13}$

So, number of molecules per colloidal particle $= \dfrac{6 \times 10^{13}}{10^{13}} = 6$

18. (3) In apatite, % P $= \dfrac{x \times 31}{5 \times 40 + 31x + 64x + 19} \times 100$

$$\Rightarrow \quad 18.45 = \frac{3100x}{219 + 95x}$$

$$\Rightarrow 18.45 \times 219 + 18.45 \times 95x = 3100x$$

$$\Rightarrow \quad 1347.25x = 4040.5$$

$$\therefore \quad x = 2.999 \simeq 3$$

19. (3) Only the circled groups (leaving groups) will be substituted by CN^- (nucleophile) in S_N2 reaction.

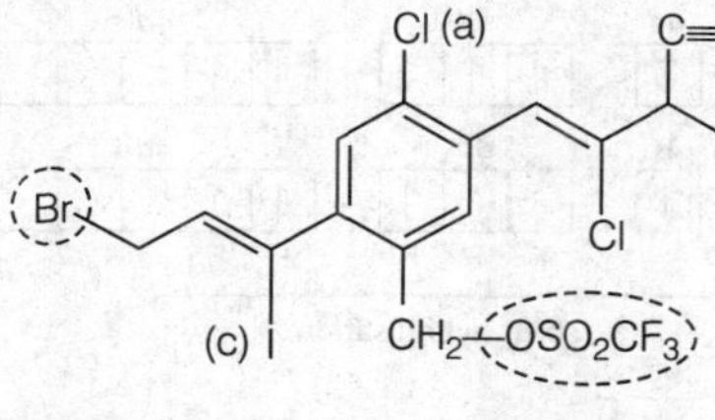

Cl (a), C≡C—Cl (b), Cl, Br, Cl, (c) I, CH_2—OSO_2CF_3

Cl(a) (aryl), Cl(b) and I(c) (vinyl) are attached to sp^2, *sp* and sp^2-carbons respectively and they will not be substituted here.

$\therefore$ Number of circled groups = 3

THE REAL NUTS

24 JUNE 2022, SHIFT-I

1. (c) The chemical reaction involved is as follows

$$C_{15}H_{30} + \frac{45}{2}O_2 \longrightarrow 15CO_2 + 15H_2O$$

Mass of the fuel $(C_{15}H_{30}) = 0.756 \times 1000 = 756$ g

Number of moles of fuel $= \frac{756}{210} = 3.6$ mol

Now, weight of oxygen required $= 3.6 \times \frac{45}{2} \times 32 = 2592$ g

and weight of CO_2 released $= 3.6 \times 15 \times 44 = 2376$ g

2. (b) Electrons pair of the same shells and the same subshell have same energy and these electrons pairs are found in degenerated orbitals. So, only pairs of electron of (B) are present in degenerate orbitals.

3. (b) The hybridisation of the given complexes are described as follows

(A) $[PtCl_4]^{2-}$

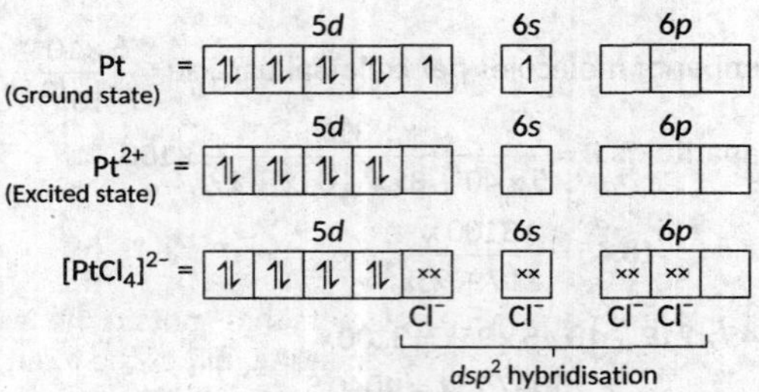

(B) BrF_5

	4s	4p	4d
Br (Ground state) =	⇅	⇅ ⇅ 1	
Br (Excited state) =	⇅	1 1 1	1 1
BrF_5 =	⇅	1 1 1 (F F F)	1 1 (F F)

sp^3d^2 hybridisation

(C) PCl_5

	3s	3p	3d
P (Ground state) =	⇅	1 1 1	
P (Excited state) =	1	1 1 1	1
PCl_5 =	1 (Cl)	1 1 1 (Cl Cl Cl)	1 (Cl)

sp^3d hybridisation

(D) $[Co(NH_3)_6]^{3+}$

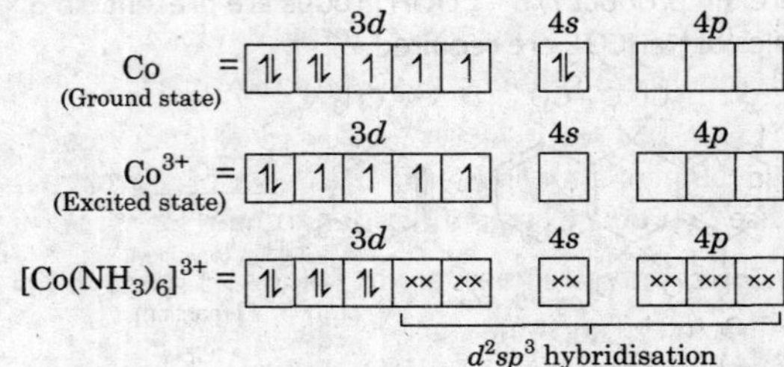

Thus, the correct order is (A) $\rightarrow$ (III), (B) $\rightarrow$ (IV), (C) $\rightarrow$ (I), (D) $\rightarrow$ (II)

4. (b) For the given reaction,

$$A(g) \rightleftharpoons B(g) + \frac{1}{2}C(g)$$

Initial :	p_i	0	0
At equili :	$p_i(1-\alpha)$	$p_i\,\alpha$	$p_i \cdot \frac{\alpha}{2}$

Equilibrium pressure $(p) = p_i\left(1 + \frac{\alpha}{2}\right)$

For A, $p_A = \left(\frac{1-\alpha}{1+\frac{\alpha}{2}}\right)p$ For B, $p_B = \left(\frac{\alpha}{1+\frac{\alpha}{2}}\right)p$

For C, $p_C = \left(\frac{\frac{\alpha}{2}}{1+\frac{\alpha}{2}}\right)p$

Now, dissociation constant $(K) = \frac{p_C^{1/2} \cdot p_B}{p_A}$

$$K = \frac{\left(\frac{\frac{\alpha}{2}}{1+\frac{\alpha}{2}}\right)^{1/2} p^{1/2} \cdot \left(\frac{1-\alpha}{1+\frac{\alpha}{2}}\right)p}{\left(\frac{1-\alpha}{1+\frac{\alpha}{2}}\right)p} = \frac{\alpha^{3/2}\, p^{1/2}}{(2+\alpha)^{1/2}(1-\alpha)}$$

5. (c) Statement I is correct but statement II is incorrect.

Corrected statement II For stabilisation of an emulsion, an additional component is used known as an emulsifying agent. This emulsifying agent can be proteins, gums, natural and synthetic soaps, etc.

6. (b) Na_2O is a basic oxide as it contains oxide ion which has a strong tendency to combine with hydrogen ions, hence, it is a strong base.

As_2O_3 is an amphoteric oxide because it dissolves in both dilute acid and warm with formation of salts.

N_2O is a neutral oxide as it does not form salt when it is reacted with either base or acid.

NO is a neutral oxide because it does not react with water to form oxyacids.

Cl_2O_7 is an acidic oxide because it forms acid on reaction with water.

Hence, the number of amphoteric oxides is 1.

7. (a) A→ IV, B→ III, C→ II, D→ I

(A) Sphalerite is an ore of zinc. Its formula is ZnS.

(B) Calamine is an ore of zinc. Its formula is $ZnCO_3$.

(C) Galena is an ore of lead. Its formula is PbS.

(D) Siderite is an ore of iron. Its formula is $FeCO_3$.

8. (b) Molecular hydrogen is widely used by industries for the production of ammonia. More than 50% of hydrogen is only utilise to produce compounds of nitrogen.

9. (a) Corrected statements are as follows:

(A) Both LiCl and $MgCl_2$ are soluble in ethanol.

(B) The oxides Li_2O and MgO do not form superoxides.

(C) Due to small size of Li^+ and F^- ions, the lattice enthalpy of LiF is very high. Hence, it is less soluble in water than other alkali metal oxides.

(D) Li_2O is less soluble in water than other alkali metal oxides because lithium oxide has high lattice enthalpy than hydration enthalpy.

10. (c) The structure of B_2H_6 is given below

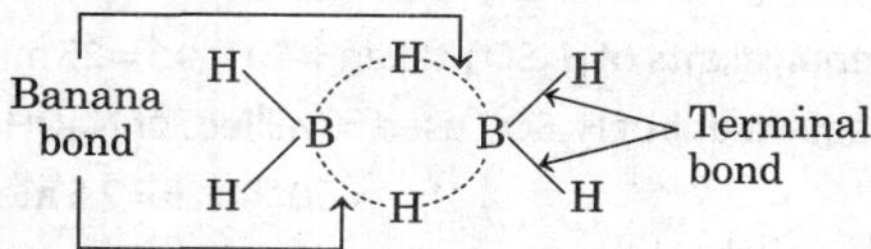

(A) In B_2H_6, not all B—H bonds are equivalent.

(B) There are two types of bonds present in B_2H_6, four normal covalent bonds and two 3-centre-2-electrons bonds.

(C) Compounds that are electron deficient and able to accept a pair of electron. So, B_2H_6 is an electron deficient compound and acts as Lewis acid.

(D) B_2H_6 can be synthesised from both BF_3 and $NaBH_4$ as follows:

$$BF_3 + LiAlH_4 \longrightarrow 2B_2H_6 + 3LiF + 3AlF_3$$

$$NaBH_4 + I_2 \longrightarrow B_2H_6 + 2NaI + H_2$$

(E) B_2H_6 is a non-planar molecule.

11. (a) NF_3 is the most stable trihalide of nitrogen because both nitrogen and fluorine have comparable sizes and electronegativity. The order of stability is

$$NF_3 > NCl_3 > NBr_3 > NI_3.$$

12. (b) Tooth enamel is made up of calcium phosphate and fluoride ions team up with calcium and phosphate in enamel to create the most powerful defence system to prevent cavity.

13. (b) Degree of unsaturation in C_8H_{10} = 4.

Ethylbenzene $\xrightarrow[H_2SO_4]{HNO_3}$ 4-nitroethylbenzene (A) $\xrightarrow[\Delta]{Br_2}$ 1-bromo-1-(4-nitrophenyl)ethane (B) $\xrightarrow{\text{Alc. KOH}}$ 4-nitrostyrene (C)

14. (a) Both Statement I and Statement II are correct.

I. The melting point of monocarboxylic acid with even number of carbon atoms is higher than that of with odd number of carbon atoms acids of carbon atom because of close packing in crystal lattice with even number of carbon atom acids.

II. With increase in molar mass, the size of hydrophobic part increases and hence, solubility decreases.

15. (c) Conjugated diketone has two ketone group directly attached to carbon atom containing double bond.

Hence, O=⟨cyclohexa-2,5-diene⟩=O is a conjugated diketone.

16. (d) The complete reaction is as follows

4-methoxybenzyl bromide $\xrightarrow{NaCN}$ 4-methoxybenzyl cyanide $\xrightarrow{OH^-}$ carbanion ($^-$CH–CN), which adds to cyclohexanone → alkoxide (O$^\ominus$) $\xrightarrow{H_2, Ni}$ (A) (HO–cyclohexyl with CH(Ar)CH$_2$NH$_2$)

(A)
Major product

17. (d) Polyester are those polymers that contain the 'ester' functional group in every repeating unit of the main chain.

$$\text{e.g.} \left[O-\underset{CH_3}{\underset{|}{CH}}-CH_2-\overset{O}{\overset{\|}{C}}-O-\overset{CH_3}{\overset{|}{CH}}-CH_2-\underset{O}{\underset{\|}{C}} \right]_n$$

Poly-β-hydroxybutyrate-co-β-hydroxy valerate.

18. (b) As cellulose contains β-glycosidic linkages. So, compound 'X' is cellulose. On treatment with bromine water, gives

$$\underset{\text{(X)}}{\underset{\text{Cellulose}}{(C_6H_{10}O_5)_n}} \xrightarrow[\text{393 K, 2-3 atm}]{\text{Dil. } H_2SO_4} \underset{\text{(Y)}}{\underset{\text{Glucose}}{n(C_6H_{12}O_6)}} \xrightarrow[Br_2/\text{water}]{[O]} \underset{\text{Gluconic acid}}{(C_6H_{12}O_7)_n}$$

19. (d) Among the given drugs, penicillin-G is a narrow spectrum antibiotic and others are broad spectrum antibiotics.

20. (a) The reagent dimethylglyoxime (*X*) is added to the alkaline solution of nickel salt and a bright red precipitate is formed.

$$Ni^{2+} + \underset{(X)}{DMG^-} \longrightarrow \underset{\text{Bright red precipitate}}{[Ni(DMG)_2]\downarrow}$$

So, here the cation (Y^{2+}) is Ni^{2+} and *X* is dimethylglyoxime.

21. (43) Element X form hcp lattice. So, the atoms at corners are shared by 6 unit cells, atoms shared at face centered are 2 unit cell and one atom is shared in middle layer.

Hence, effective number of atoms of X in unit cell

$$=\frac{1}{6}\times 12+\frac{1}{2}\times 2+1\times 3=6$$

Now, number of tetrahedral voids $=2\times 6=12$

So, the number of atoms of $Y=\frac{2}{3}\times 12=8$

So, the percentage of element X in the lattice $=\frac{6}{14}\times 100$

$$=42.8\%\simeq 43\%$$

22. (747) The given chemical equation is

$$2O_3(g) \rightleftharpoons 3O_2(g)$$

At 300 K, $\frac{2}{5}$ $\frac{3}{5}$

Now, equilibrium constant $(K_p)=\frac{(p_{O_2})^3}{(p_{O_3})^2}=\frac{0.216}{0.16}=1.35$

To calculate standard free energy change, formula to be used is

$$\Delta G^\circ=-RT\ln K_p$$
$$=-8.3\times 300\times \ln(1.35)$$
$$=-8.3\times 300\times 0.3=-747 \text{ J/mol}$$

23. (54) At 300 K, the osmotic pressure of blood $(\pi)=7.47$ bar

Molar mass of glucose $=180 \text{ g mol}^{-1}$.

We know, $\pi=CRT$

$$7.47=C\times 0.083\times 300$$

$$\Rightarrow \quad C=\frac{7.47}{0.083\times 300}=0.3 \text{ M}$$

Concentration of glucose solution $=0.3$ M

Now, concentration in $\text{gL}^{-1}=0.3\times 180=54 \text{ gL}^{-1}$

24. (5) The cell potential of the given cell $(E_{cell})=0.576$ V

Reaction at anode $\quad H_2 \longrightarrow 2H^+ + 2e^-$

Reaction at cathode $\quad Cu^{2+} + 2e^- \longrightarrow Cu$

Overall reaction $\quad Cu^{2+} + H_2 \longrightarrow 2H^+ + Cu$

According to Nernst equation, $E_{cell}=E^\circ_{cell}-\frac{0.059}{2}\log\frac{[H^+]^2}{[Cu^{2+}]}$

$$0.576=0.34-0.0295\log\frac{[H^+]^2}{(0.01)}$$
$$0.236=-0.0295\ [2\log[H^+]-\log(0.01)]$$
$$0.236=-0.059\ \log[H^+]-0.059$$
$$0.295=-0.059\log[H^+]$$
$$5=-\log[H^+]=\text{pH}$$

$\therefore$ pH of solution $=5$.

25. (154) According to given Arrhenius plot,

$$\ln k=\ln A-\frac{E_a}{10^3RT}\times 10^3$$

$$\ln k=\ln A+\frac{10^3}{T}\left[\frac{-E_a}{10^3R}\right]$$

where, $\frac{-E_a}{10^3R}$ represent slope.

$\therefore \quad \text{Slope}=\frac{-E_a}{10^3R}=-18.5$

$\therefore \quad E_a=18.5\times 10^3\times 8.31=153.735\simeq 154$ kJ/mol

26. (0) Oxidation state of chromium in chromate $(CrO_4^{2-})=+6$

Oxidation state of chromium in dichromate $(Cr_2O_7^{2-})=+6$

So, the difference of both oxidation states of chromium $=0$

27. (7) The structure of $[Co_2(CO)_8]$ is

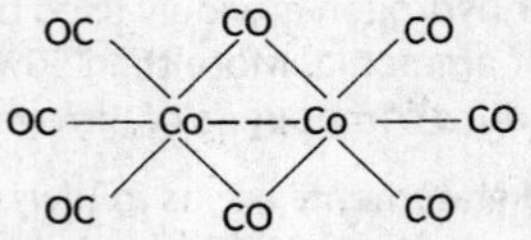

OC, CO, CO (top); OC—Co—Co—CO; OC, CO, CO (bottom)

Number of Co—Co bond $(X)=1$

Number of terminal CO ligands $(Y)=6$

$\therefore \quad X+Y=1+6=7$

28. (63) Mass of organic compound $=0.166$ g

Reactions involved are

$$\text{Organic compound} + \text{Conc.}H_2SO_4 \longrightarrow (NH_4)_2SO_4 \xrightarrow{NaOH} NH_3 \xrightarrow{H_2SO_4} (NH_4)_2SO_4$$

Milliequivalents of H_2SO_4 taken $=50\times 0.5=25$ meq.

Milliequivalent of H_2SO_4 used $=$ Millieq. of NaOH

$$=30\times 0.25=7.5 \text{ meq.}$$

Milliequivalent of $NH_3=$ Millieq. of H_2SO_4 used $=7.5$ m eq.

Using the Kjeldahl's method formula,

$$\%N=\frac{1.4\times \text{millieq. of } NH_3}{\text{Weight of organic compound}}$$
$$=\frac{1.4\times 7.5}{0.166}=63.25\approx 63$$

29. (3) The given compound have 3 electrophilic centres.

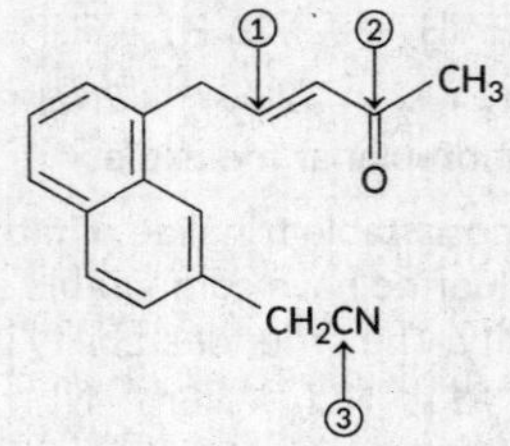

(structure with electrophilic centres marked ①, ② near the CH_3 ketone side chain and ③ at CH_2CN)

30. (2)

2, 7-dimethyl-2, 6-octadiene $\xrightarrow{H^+}$ carbocation $\xrightarrow{\text{Intramolecular attack}}$ cyclic carbocation $\xrightarrow{-H^+}$ (A) (sp^2, sp^2 marked)

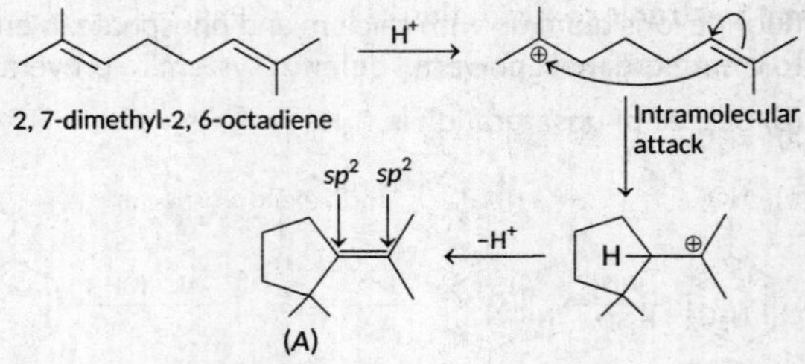

In major product (A), there are 2 carbon atoms which are sp^2 hybridised.

26 JUNE 2022, SHIFT-II

1. (a) For $4d$, principal quantum number $(n) = 4$

Azimuthal quantum number $(l) = 2$

$\therefore$ Number of angular nodes = value of $l = 2$

Number of radial nodes $= (n - l - 1) = (4 - 2 - 1) = 1$

2. (c) A. Cane sugar $\xrightarrow{\text{Invertase}}$ Glucose + Fructose

B. Glucose $\xrightarrow{\text{Zymase}}$ Ethanol + CO_2

C. Starch $\xrightarrow{\text{Diastase}}$ Maltose

D. Maltose $\xrightarrow{\text{Maltase}}$ Glucose

Correct matching is A $\rightarrow$ IV, B $\rightarrow$ III, C $\rightarrow$ I, D $\rightarrow$ II.

3. (d) Sc, Pb and Bi are metals while Te is a metalloid.

Elements on the left side of periodic table are classified as metals, on the right side as non-metals and elements between them as metalloids. Elements B, Si, Ge As, Sb and Te are considered as metalloids.

4. (a) Depressants prevent one component of the ore from coming to the froth making separation easy. For example in galena ore, the depressant (NaCN) prevents impurity (ZnS) from coming to the froth.

5. (a) $Mg(HCO_3)_2 \xrightarrow{\text{Boil}} Mg(OH)_2 \downarrow + 2CO_2 \uparrow$

$Ca(HCO_3)_2 \xrightarrow{\text{Boil}} CaCO_3 \downarrow + H_2O + CO_2 \uparrow$

Soluble $Mg(HCO_3)_2$ and $Ca(HCO_3)_2$ on boiling form precipitates $Mg(OH)_2$ and $CaCO_3$, respectively which can be filtered off easily.

6. (d)

s-block element	Flame colour
Li $1s^2\,2s^1$	Crimson red
Na $[Ne]\,3s^1$	Yellow
Rb $[Kr]\,5s^1$	Red violet
Be $1s^2\,2s^2$	No colour

Be due to its small size and stable electronic configuration (completely filled orbitals), has high ionisation energy. Energy of flame is not sufficient to excite electrons to higher energy levels. Hence, Be does not give flame test.

7. (b) Electronic configuration of $N = 1s^2\,2s^2\,2p^3$.

$\therefore$ N has 5 valence electrons.

(a) N_2O $\ddot{N}{\equiv}N \rightarrow O$

(b) NO_2 $O{=}\dot{N}{\rightarrow}O$ (odd electron species)

(c) N_2O_3 $O{=}\ddot{N}{-}N(=O){\rightarrow}O$

(d) N_2O_5 $O{=}N(\rightarrow O){-}O{-}N(\rightarrow O){=}O$

8. (a)

Reduction (gain of electrons)

$$\overset{+6}{3MnO_4^{2-}} + 4H^+ \longrightarrow \overset{+7}{2MnO_4^-} + \overset{+4}{MnO_2} + 2H_2O$$

Oxidation (loss of electrons)

A chemical reaction in which when the same species undergoes both reduction and oxidation is called disproportionation reaction.

9. (a) Ce will show +3 oxidation state but it is likely to deviate easily to +4 oxidation state to attain a noble gas configuration.

$Ce = [Xe]\,4f^1\,5d^1\,6s^2$

$Ce^{3+} = [Xe]\,4f^1\,5d^0$

$Ce^{4+} = [Xe]\,4f^0$ (Noble gas configuration)

10. (c) Higher the BOD (Biochemical Oxygen Demand) level, higher is the organic waste in water. Clean water has BOD < 5 ppm, while highly polluted water has BOD > 17 ppm.

$\therefore$ Water samples *B* and *C* with BOD 18 ppm and 21 ppm respectively are highly polluted.

11. (d) (a) F^- is less nucleophilic than OH^- as

$$\text{Nucleophilicity} \propto \frac{1}{\text{Electronegativity of atom}}$$

and electronegativity of F > O.

Hence, nucleophilicity of $F^- < OH^-$.

(b) H_2O is less nucleophilic than OH^- due to less electron density on donor atom oxygen in H_2O. Hence, nucleophilicity of $H_2O < OH^-$.

(c) RO^- is more nucleophilic than ROH due to more electron density on donor atom oxygen in RO^-. Hence, nucleophilicity of $ROH < RO^-$.

(d) NH_2^- is more nucleophilic than NH_3 due to more electron density of nitrogen atom. Hence, the nucleophilicity of $NH_2^- > NH_3$.

12. (b) Benzaldehyde is formed by oxidation of toluene with chromic oxide in the presence of acetic anhydride, followed by acidic hydrolysis.

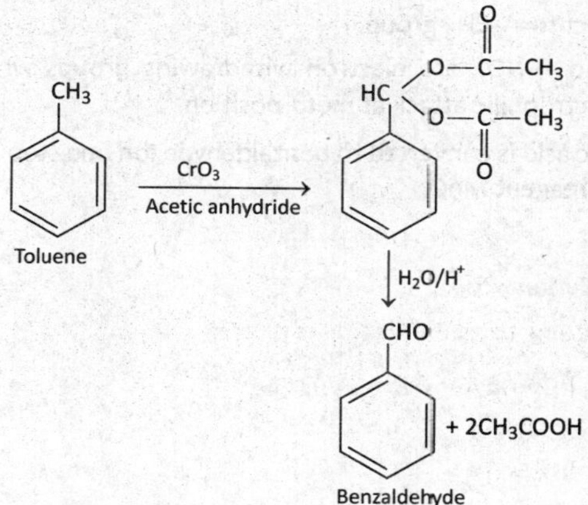

13. (a) This is oxymercuration-demercuration reaction.

Step 1 Alkene reacts with mercury (II) acetate and forms cyclic mercurinium ion.

(i) $Hg(OAc)_2$ → + $\overset{\ominus}{O}Ac$

Step 2 Attack of nucleophile occurs and this mechanism follows Markownikoff's rule of regioselectivity.

$\oplus$Hg + $\ddot{O}H_2$ → $\overset{\oplus}{O}H_2$ $Hg(OAc)_2$

Step 3 Deprotonation takes place in presence of base acetate ion which gives alcohol.

$H-\ddot{O}-H$ $\overset{\oplus}{O}H$ $Hg(OAc)_2$ $\xrightarrow{-H^+}$ OH $Hg(OAc)_2$

Step 4 Addition of $NaBH_4$ reduces the acetyl mercury by a hydrogen atom. $NaBH_4$ acts as a reducing agent.

OH $Hg(OAc)_2$ $\xrightarrow{(ii)\ NaBH_4}$ OH

14. (c) Since, —OH is better electron releasing group than —CH_3. So, electrophile will attack at *ortho* and *para*-position with respect to —OH group.

CH_3 OH

para-position with respect to —OH group is the *meta*-position with respect to —CH_3 group.

—CHO and —NO_2 are electron withdrawing groups which lead to electrophilic attack at *meta*-position.

15. (c) Benzoic acid is converted to benzaldehyde ion one step by the use of reagent MnO.

$$C_6H_5-\overset{O}{\overset{\|}{C}}-OH + HO-\overset{O}{\overset{\|}{C}}-H \xrightarrow[\Delta]{MnO} C_6H_5-\overset{O}{\overset{\|}{C}}-H + CO_2 + H_2O$$

16. (a)

$$CH_3-CH_2-\overset{O}{\overset{\|}{C}}-CH_3 \xrightarrow{H^+CN^\ominus} CH_3-CH_2-\overset{OH}{\overset{|}{C}}(CN)-CH_3 \xrightarrow[\text{Heat}]{95\%\ H_2SO_4} CH_3-CH=\overset{CH_3}{\overset{|}{C}}-COOH$$

Mechanism

$$CH_3CH_2-\overset{\ddot{O}H}{\overset{|}{C}}(CN)-CH_3 \xrightarrow[\text{Protonation}]{H_2SO_4,\ \oplus H,\ \Delta} CH_3-CH(H)-\overset{\overset{\oplus}{O}H_2}{\overset{|}{C}}(CN)-CH_3 \quad \overset{\ominus}{O}SO_3H$$

Elimination

$$CH_3-CH=C(CN)-CH_3 \xrightarrow[\text{Acid-catalysed hydrolysis of nitrile}]{H_2SO_4} CH_3-CH=C(CONH_2)-CH_3 \text{ (Amide)} \xrightarrow{H^+} CH_3-CH=C(COOH)-CH_3$$

17. (c) Hinsberg reagent is *p*-toluene sulphonyl chloride.

CH_3 — benzene ring — SO_2Cl

Hinsberg reagent can distinguish primary and secondary amines. It reacts with primary amine to give product which is soluble in alkali while reacts with secondary amine to give product insoluble in alkali. Hinsberg reagent doesn't react with tertiary amines.

18. (c) Nitrobenzene is first treated with Sn/HCl to give aniline (*A*) as a product. Aniline undergoes diazotisation reaction to give *B* (diazonium salt). This '*B*' undergoes coupling reaction with β-naphthol to form azo dye.

Nitrobenzene $\xrightarrow[\text{Reduction}]{Sn/HCl}$ Aniline (*A*) $\xrightarrow[HCl]{NaNO_2}$ Benzene diazonium chloride (*B*) $\xrightarrow{\beta\text{-naphthol, NaOH}}$ Azo dye (*C*)

Mechanism

β-naphthol + $C_6H_5N^{\oplus}{\equiv}N$ $\xrightarrow[\text{NaOH}]{\alpha\text{-attack}}$ [resonance-stabilised intermediates] ⟶ Azo dye (*C*)

19. (b) Synthetic detergents are cleansing agents and can be classified as anionic, cationic and non-ionic detergents.

$CH_3-(CH_2)_{11}-C_6H_4-SO_3^{\ominus}Na^+$ is an example of anionic detergent.

$[CH_3(CH_2)_{15}-N(CH_3)_2-CH_3]^+Br^-$ is an example of cationic detergent.

$CH_3(CH_2)_{16}COO(CH_2CH_2O)_nCH_2CH_2OH$ is an example of non-ionic detergent.

$CH_3-(CH_2)_{16}COO^-Na^+$, sodium stearate is not a synthetic detergent but a soap made from glycerol ester of stearic acid (fat) and base through saponification.

20. (d) Vitamin B_{12} is the water soluble vitamin that is not excreted in urine easily as excess of it is stored in liver.

21. (143) Given, mass of CNG $[CH_4]$ = 100 g

Mass of O_2 = 208 g

$$CH_4 + 2O_2 \longrightarrow CO_2 + 2H_2O$$

	CH_4	O_2
Moles	$\frac{100}{16} = 6.25$	$\frac{208}{32} = 6.5$
Moles / stoichiometric coefficient	$\frac{6.25}{1} = 6.25$	$\frac{6.5}{2} = 3.25$

So, O_2 is limiting reagent.

Mole-Mole Analysis

$$\frac{n_{O_2}}{2} = \frac{n_{CO_2}}{1}$$

$$\frac{6.5}{2} = n_{CO_2}$$

$$n_{CO_2} = 3.25$$

∴ Mass of $CO_2 = 3.25 \times 44 = 143$ g.

22. (3) A atoms are in ccp arrangement.

∴ Number of atoms A = 4

If 2 atoms of opposite faces are removed then number of atoms,

$$A = 4 - \left(2 \times \frac{1}{2}\right) = 3$$

In ccp arrangement, octahedral voids occur at 12 edges and at body centre.

B atoms occupy octahedral sites $= 12 \times \frac{1}{4} + 1 \times 1 = 4$

So, compound is A_3B_4 and value of *x* is 3.

23. (1) In SF_4, Total lone pairs = 13

In XeF_4, Total lone pairs = 14

In CF_4, Total lone pairs = 12

In H_2O, Total lone pairs = 2

24. (38) $H_2O(l) \longrightarrow H_2O(g)$

Given, weight of water = 36 g

Moles of $H_2O = \frac{36\text{ g}}{18\text{ g}} = 2$ moles

Internal energy, $\Delta U = \Delta H - \Delta n_g RT \quad (\Delta n_g = 1 - 0 = 1)$

$$= 41.1 - \frac{1 \times 8.314 \times 373\text{ kJ/mol}}{1000}$$

$$= 38\text{ kJ/mol}$$

25. (415) Osmotic pressure, $\pi = iCRT$

where, C = concentration of solution, R = gas constant,

T = temperature = 27° C = 300 K, i = van't Hoff factor

Given, mass of protein = 2 g

Molar mass of protein = 60 kg mol^{-1} = 60,000 g mol^{-1}

Volume of water = 200 mL = 0.2 L

Concentration, $C = \frac{\text{Given mass}}{\text{Molar mass}} \times \frac{1}{\text{Volume solution}}$

$$\pi = 1 \times \frac{2 \times 0.083 \times 300}{60000\text{ g/mol} \times 0.2\text{ L}}$$

$$\pi = 0.00415\text{ bar} \qquad (1\text{ bar} = 10^5\text{ Pascal})$$

So, $\pi = 0.00415 \times 10^5$ Pa

$$\pi = 415\text{ Pa}$$

26. (2740) 40% of HI undergoes decomposition to H_2 and I_2 at 300 K.

$$HI \rightleftharpoons \frac{1}{2}H_2 + \frac{1}{2}I_2$$

	HI	$\frac{1}{2}H_2$	$\frac{1}{2}I_2$
t = initial	1	0	0
t = equilibrium	(1 − 0.4)	$\frac{0.4}{2} = 0.2$	$\frac{0.4}{2} = 0.2$

$$K_p = \frac{[H_2]^{1/2}[I_2]^{1/2}}{[HI]}$$

$$= \frac{[0.2]^{1/2}[0.2]^{1/2}}{1 - 0.4} = \frac{0.2}{0.6} = \frac{1}{3}$$

$$\Delta G = \Delta G^\circ + RT\ln K \qquad (\text{at equilibrium } \Delta G = 0)$$

$$0 = \Delta G^\circ + RT\ln K$$

$$\Delta G^\circ = -RT\ln K = -8.314 \times 300 \times \ln\left(\frac{1}{3}\right)$$

$$= -8.314 \times 300 \times 2.303\log\left(\frac{1}{3}\right)$$

$$= -8.314 \times 300 \times 2.303(\log 1 - \log 3)$$

$$= +2740\text{ J/mol}$$

27. (983) The given reaction is as follows

$Cu(s) + Sn^{2+}(0.001\text{ M}) \longrightarrow Cu^{2+}(0.01\text{ M}) + Sn(s)$

$$E^\circ_{cell} = E^\circ_{cathode} - E^\circ_{anode}$$

$$= (-0.14) - (0.34) = -0.48\text{ V}$$

$$E_{cell} = E^\circ_{cell} - \frac{0.059}{2}\log\frac{[Cu^{2+}]}{[Sn^{2+}]}$$

$$= -0.48 - 0.0295\log\frac{0.01}{0.001}$$

$$= -0.5095\text{ V}$$

$$\Delta G = -nFE_{cell}$$

$$= -2 \times 96500 \times (-0.5095)$$

$$= 98333.5\text{ J/mol}$$

$$= 98.3335\text{ kJ/mol or } 983.335 \times 10^{-1}\text{ kJ/mol}$$

$$\Delta G \approx 983 \times 10^{-1}\text{ kJ mol}^{-1}$$

28. (4) According to Arrhenius equation,

$$k = Ae^{-E_a/RT}$$

For catalyst A, $k_{catalysed} = Ae^{-E'_a/RT}$

For uncatalysed, $k_{uncatalysed} = Ae^{-E_a/RT}$

We are given that, $\frac{k_{catalysed}}{k_{uncatalysed}} = e^x$

$$\frac{k_{catalysed}}{k_{uncatalysed}} = e^{(E_a - E'_a)/RT} = e^{10000\text{ J/mol}/(8.314 \times 300)}$$

$$= e^{4.009} = e^x$$

$\therefore \quad x = 4$

29. (6) $[Co(H_2O)_6]^{2+} + NH_3(\text{excess}) \xrightarrow{O_2} [CO(NH_3)_6]^{3+} + 6H_2O$

Diamagnetic (means no unpaired electrons)

$[Co(NH_3)_6]^{3+}$ is low spin complex and diamagnetic in nature.

So, configuration of Co^{3+} = [Ar] $3d^6\,4s^0$

$$= [Ar](t_{2g}^6 e_g^0)\,4s^0$$

$\therefore$ Total number of electrons in t_{2g} orbital of $[Co(NH_3)_6]^{3+}$ is 6.

30. (225) $CH_4 + 2O_2 \longrightarrow CO_2 + 2H_2O$

Mole-mole analysis

$$\frac{n_{CH_4}}{1} = \frac{n_{H_2O}}{2}$$

$$\frac{\text{Mass of } CH_4}{\text{Molar mass of } CH_4} = \frac{1}{2} \times \frac{\text{Mass of } H_2O}{\text{Molar mass of } H_2O}$$

Mass of water to be produced = 81 g

Mass of $CH_4 = \frac{1}{2} \times \frac{81}{18} \times 16 = 36$ g

So, moles of $CH_4 = \frac{36\text{ g}}{16\text{ g}} = 2.25$ mol or 225×10^{-2} mol

29 JUNE 2022, SHIFT-I

1. (c) The chemical reaction for production of iron in blast furnace is $Fe_3O_4(s) + 4CO(g) \longrightarrow 3Fe(l) + 4CO_2(g)$

Amount of Fe_3O_4 reacting = 4.640 kg, i.e. 4640 g

$$\therefore \text{Moles of } Fe_3O_4 \text{ reacting} = \frac{\text{Amount of } Fe_3O_4 \text{ reacting}}{\text{Molar mass of } Fe_3O_4}$$

Molar mass of $Fe_3O_4 = (56 \times 3 + 16 \times 4)$ g/mol
$= (168 + 64)$ g/mol
$= 232$ g/mol

So, moles of Fe_3O_4 reacting $= \frac{4640}{232} = 20$ moles

Similarly, amount of CO reacting = 2.520 kg, i.e. 2520 g

Molar mass of CO = (12 + 16) g/mol = 28 g/mol

$\therefore$ Moles of CO reacting $= \frac{2520}{28} = 90$ moles

In the given reaction,

for 1 mole of $Fe_3O_4 \longrightarrow$ 4 moles of CO are required.

for 20 moles of $Fe_3O_4 \longrightarrow 4 \times 20 = 80$ moles of CO are required.

As number of moles of Fe_3O_4 reacting is less than number of moles of CO, it is the limiting reagent and product formed will depend on number of moles of Fe_3O_4.

$\therefore$ Moles of iron formed $= 3 \times$ moles of Fe_3O_4
$= 3 \times 20 = 60$ moles

Weight of iron produced $= 60 \times 56$ (in g) $= 3360$ g

2. (d) (A) Cr has atomic number 24.
Its electronic configuration is $[Ar]\,3d^5 4s^1$ and not $[Ar]\,3d^4 4s^2$ as half-filled orbitals are more stable.

(B) Magnetic quantum number can have values from $-l$ to $+l$ including 0. (where, l is azimuthal quantum number). Thus, the magnetic quantum number may have a negative value.

(C) According to the Aufbau's principle, electrons fill lower-energy atomic orbitals before filling the higher-energy atomic orbitals.
Hence, in the ground state of an atom, the orbitals are filled in order of their increasing energies.

(D) Total number of nodes present in atomic orbital is given by the formula $n - 1$, where n is principal quantum number.
So, the formula "$n - 2$" is incorrect.
(A), (B) and (C) are correct statements.

3. (c)

	Alkali metal	Halide
Size increases, polarising power decreases ↓	Li^+	Cl^-
	Na^+	Cl^-
	K^+	Cl^-
	Cs^+	Cl^-

As the halide is same (Cl^-) in all given compounds, the polarisability due to halide is same.

According to Fajan's rule, as the size of cations of same charge increases, the charge density on cations decreases, so their polarising power decreases and hence, their covalent character also decreases. (Covalent character $\propto$ polarising power.)

$\therefore$ The decreasing order of their covalent character is

LiCl > NaCl > KCl > CsCl

i.e. (A) > (B) > (C) > (D)

4. (d) According to common-ion effect, addition of a solute with a common ion to a solution, decreases the solubility of the solute added and can lead to its precipitation as the reaction shifts towards the left of the equilibrium. The solubility of AgCl will be maximum in deionised water as rest all the solutions (0.01 M KCl, 0.01 M HCl and 0.01 M $AgNO_3$) have a common ion with the solute being added (AgCl). Thus, AgCl will be most soluble in deionised water.

5. (d) (a) Brownian motion stabilises sols as the random movement of sol particles does not get the dispersed phase particles to settle and thus prevents coagulation.

(b) Any amount of dispersed phase cannot be added to emulsion as it destabilises the emulsion.

(c) When two oppositely charged sols are mixed in equal amounts, their charges get neutralised and they get partially or completely precipitated. This condition is called as mutual coagulation. Coagulation leads to instability in colloids.

(d) Presence of equal and similar charges on colloidal particles provides stability to the colloidal solution as the same charged particles repel each other and hence, prevent coagulation to occur.
Hence, statement (d) is correct.

6. (a) The atomic number of Pt is 78. Its exceptional electronic configuration can be written as $[Xe]\,4f^{14}5d^9 6s^1$.

According to Aufbau's principle of filling electrons, the electronic configuration of Pt should be $[Xe]\,4f^{14}\,5d^8 6s^2$. But as the number of electrons increases, interelectronic repulsion also increases. In higher atomic number elements energy difference between shells becomes less. Hence, $6s$ and $5d$ come closer due to which electronic transition from $6s$ to $5d$ is easily done. Therefore, we have the electronic configuration as $[Xe]\,4f^{14}5d^9 6s^1$.

7. (d) In isolation of copper from its ore, use of cyanide is not commonly involved. It is extracted from chalcopyrite by heating it strongly with silica (SiO_2), calcium carbonate ($CaCO_3$) (as flux) and excess of air. The reaction can be written as

$$2CuFeS_2 + 2SiO_2 + 4O_2 \longrightarrow Cu_2S + 2FeSiO_3 + 3SO_2$$

$$Cu_2S + O_2 \longrightarrow 2Cu + SO_2$$

For ZnS, KCN is used as depressant.

Cyanide process is used in extracting gold and silver from the ores by dissolving them in cyanide salt solution

8. (c) Reducing ability of any species is its ability to reduce the other species in the reaction and itself getting oxidised. In the following reaction,

$$2\overset{+7}{Mn}O_4^- + 3H_2O_2 \longrightarrow 2\overset{+4}{Mn}O_2 + 3O_2 + 2H_2O + 2OH^-$$

Oxidation state of Mn changes from +7 to +4, i.e. it is accepting electrons and is getting reduced. Thus, H_2O_2 is acting as reducing agent in the given reaction.

Reduction

(a) $\overset{+1}{HOCl} + H_2O_2 \longrightarrow H_3O^+ + Cl^- + O_2$

Here, H_2O_2 is acting as a reducing agent but the medium is acidic.

Oxidation

(b) $\overset{+2\ -2}{PbS} + 4\overset{+1\ -1}{H_2O_2} \longrightarrow \overset{+2\ +6\ -2}{PbSO_4} + 4\overset{+1\ -2}{H_2O}$

Reduction

Oxidation

(d) $\overset{+2}{Mn} + H_2O \longrightarrow \overset{+4\ -1}{Mn + HO}$

In reactions (b) and (d), H_2O_2 is acting as an oxidising agent.

9. (a) Alkali metals impart a characteristic colour to an oxidising flame on heating. When they are heated, the outermost orbital electron excites to a higher energy level and while coming back to the ground state, emission of radiation occurs. The emitted radiation is invisible region of electromagnetic spectrum and has a characteristic wavelength as mentioned below

Metal	Colour of flame	Wavelength (nm)
Li	Crimson red	670.8
Na	Yellow	589.2
Rb	Red violet	780.0
Cs	Blue	455.5

The correct match is (A)-(I), (B)-(II), (C)-(III), (D)-(IV).

10. (a) Cs has low ionisation energy. On exposure to sunlight Cs can easily emit electrons. Hence, Cs is used in making photoelectric cells.

Ga has high boiling point, low vapour pressure and is less toxic (than mercury). Therefore, Ga is used in making high temperature thermometer.

B is a network solid and hence is used in making bullet proof vests.

Silicon is an inorganic synthetic polymer consisting atoms of Si and O. Silicones being surrounded by non-polar alkyl groups are water repelling in nature.

Thus, the correct match is (A)-(III), (B)-(I), (C)-(IV), (D)-(II).

11. (b) White phosphorus reacts with alkali in presence of CO_2 (inert atmosphere) as

$$\underset{\text{White phosphorus}}{P_4} + NaOH \xrightarrow[CO_2]{\text{Inert atmosphere}} PH_3 + NaH_2PO_2 \xrightarrow{H^+} H_3PO_2)$$

The structure of H_3PO_2 is

H–P(=O)(–OH)–H ⟵ Hypophosphorus or phosphinic acid

Two P—H bonds

12. (a) Acid rain (rain or any form of precipitation) is caused by emissions of SO_x and NO_x which react with water molecules in the atmosphere to form acids. The acids mainly responsible for the damage of Taj Mahal are sulphuric acid (H_2SO_4) and nitric acid (HNO_3) which react with the marble (Limestone) of the Taj Mahal to form calcium sulphate and calcium nitrate, respectively, that corrodes the marble.

$$H_2SO_4 + \underset{\text{Limestone}}{CaCO_3} \longrightarrow \underset{\substack{\text{(Calcium sulphate)}\\ \text{Dissolve in water}}}{CaSO_4} + H_2O + CO_2$$

13. (d) $=\overset{H}{\overset{|}{C}}—R$ gets oxidised to $RCOOH$ (acid) whereas $=\overset{R'}{\overset{|}{C}}—R$ gets oxidised to $R—\overset{R'}{\overset{|}{C}}=O$ (ketone).

$$\underset{\text{2-methyl propene}}{(H)_2\overset{1}{C}=\overset{2}{C}(CH_3)\overset{3}{C}H_3} + [O] \xrightarrow{KMnO_4/H^+} \underset{\text{Acetone}}{O=C(CH_3)_2} + \underset{\substack{\text{Carbon dioxide}\\ \text{(Cause of effervescence)}}}{CO_2\uparrow} + \underset{\text{Water}}{H_2O}$$

But-1-ene will give :

$$\underset{\text{But-1-ene}}{(H)_2\overset{1}{C}=\overset{2}{C}H—\overset{3}{C}H_2—\overset{4}{C}H_3} + [O] \xrightarrow{KMnO_4/H^+} \underset{\text{Propanaldehyde}}{O=C(H)—CH_2—CH_3} + \underset{\text{Carbon dioxide}}{CO_2} + \underset{\text{Water}}{H_2O}$$

$$\underset{\text{Propanaldehyde}}{O=C(H)—CH_2—CH_3} + [O] \xrightarrow[\substack{\text{Further}\\ \text{oxidises}}]{KMnO_4/H^+} \underset{\text{Propanoic acid}}{CH_3—CH_2—COOH}$$

But-2-ene, on oxidation forms :

$$CH_3—\overset{H}{\overset{|}{C}}=\overset{H}{\overset{|}{C}}—CH_3 \xrightarrow{KMnO_4/H^+} 2CH_3COOH$$

Thus, the isomer 'A' is 2-methyl propene.

14. (b) 2-Bromophenol (Br, OH) $\xrightarrow{(CH_3)_3\,CLi}$ A (Li, OLi) + $(CH_3)_3C—Br$

A + O=C=O ⟶ (C(=O)O⁻ Li⁺, OLi) $\xrightarrow{H_3O^+}$ Salicylic acid (COOH, OH)

15. (a) The esterification of carboxylic acid with an alcohol is a nucleophilic acyl substitution reaction

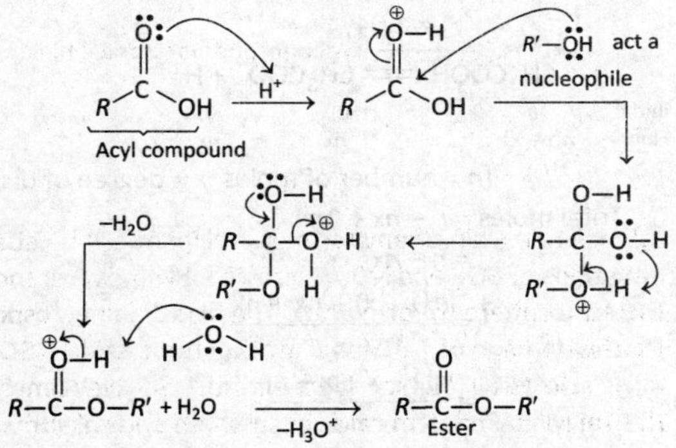

Acyl compound

$R'-\ddot{O}H$ act a nucleophile

$\xrightarrow{H^+}$ ... $\xrightarrow{-H_2O}$

$R-\overset{O}{\overset{\|}{C}}-O-R' + H_2O \xrightarrow{-H_3O^+} R-\overset{O}{\overset{\|}{C}}-O-R'$ Ester

Electron withdrawing groups in the carboxylic acid will increase the rate of esterification reaction by making carbonyl carbon of acyl group more electron deficient, thereby increasing the rate of nucleophilic attack by alcohol.

Hence, both the statements are correct.

16. (c)

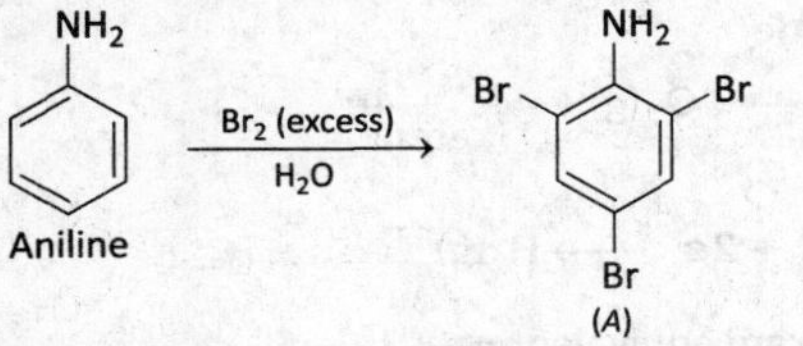

Aniline $\xrightarrow[H_2O]{Br_2 \text{ (excess)}}$ 2,4,6-tribromoaniline (*A*)

$—NH_2$ being a ring activating and *o*, *p*-directing group will direct the incoming $—Br^+$ (formed by reaction of Br_2 (excess) + $H_2O \longrightarrow \overset{\delta-}{HO}—\overset{\delta+}{Br}$) at *ortho* and *para*-position.

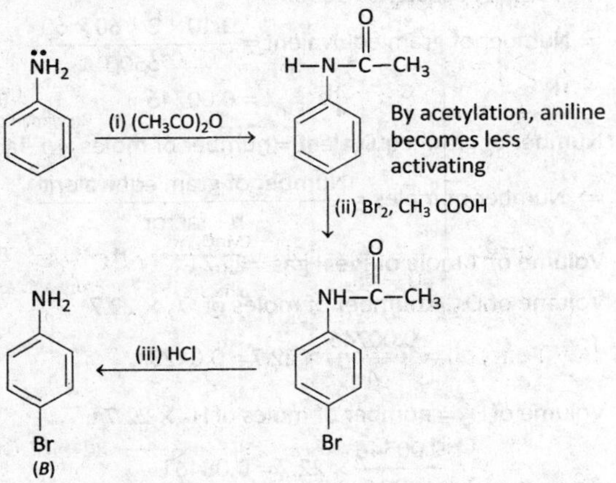

Aniline $\xrightarrow{\text{(i) } (CH_3CO)_2O}$ acetanilide ($H-N-\overset{O}{\overset{\|}{C}}-CH_3$)

By acetylation, aniline becomes less activating

$\xrightarrow{\text{(ii) } Br_2, CH_3COOH}$ p-bromoacetanilide $\xrightarrow{\text{(iii) HCl}}$ p-bromoaniline (*B*)

17. (c) Buna-N being a synthetic rubber (elastomer) can be stretched. It retains its original status when the force is released/removed.

Nylon-6, 6 is a fibre.

Bakelite is a thermosetting polymer.

Terylene is also a polyester fibre.

18. (b)

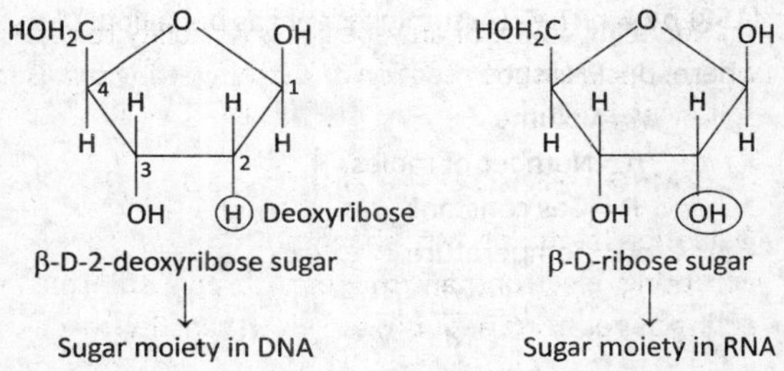

β-D-2-deoxyribose sugar (Deoxyribose) → Sugar moiety in DNA

β-D-ribose sugar → Sugar moiety in RNA

19. (c) Histamine does not contain sulphur atom. Rest all cimetidine, ranitidine and saccharin contain sulphur.

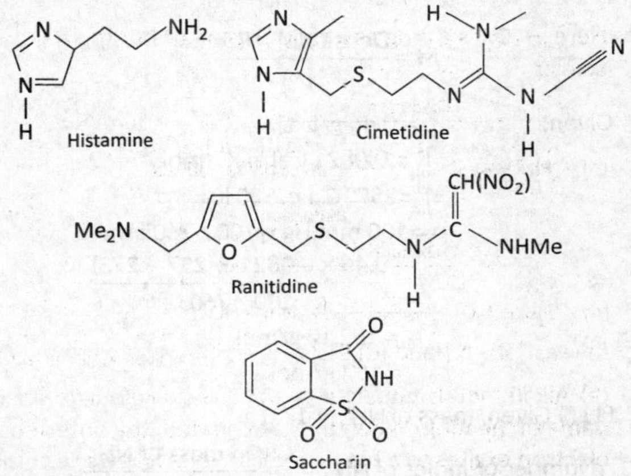

Histamine

Cimetidine

Ranitidine

Saccharin

20. (c) (I) Phenol is weakly acidic. Alcohols and phenols are weak acids. This is due to the polarisation of the O — H bond making H partially positively charged. It is a weaker acid as compared to carboxylic acid.

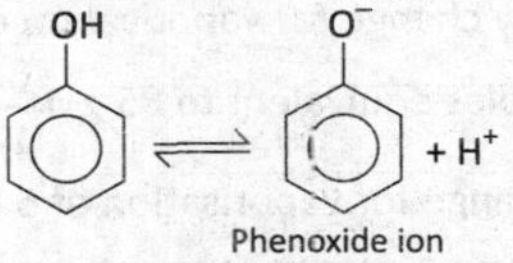

Phenol $\rightleftharpoons$ Phenoxide ion $+ H^+$

The conjugate base formed by carboxylic acid is more stable as compared to phenoxide ion.

(II) Phenols are freely soluble in NaOH solution and are stronger acids than alcohols and water. This is due to more stability of phenoxide ion (conjugate base formed) as negative charge on the oxygen atom is delocalised on the ring (resonance) as compared to stability of alkoxide (conjugate base of alcohol) and hydroxide ion (conjugate base of water)

$$R—O—H \rightleftharpoons R—O^- + H^+$$

Alkoxide (Destabilised due to + *I*-effect of alkyl group)

Stability order: Phenoxide $> \bar{O}H > R—O^{\ominus}$

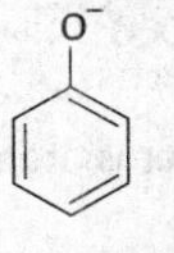

Hence, Statement I is correct but Statement II is incorrect.

21. (152) $pV = nRT \leftarrow$ (Assuming ideal gas behaviour)

where, p = Pressure

V = Volume

n = Number of moles

R = Gas constant

T = Temperature

$$p = \frac{wt}{M} \times \frac{RT}{V}$$

On rearranging,

$$p = \text{density} \times \frac{RT}{M}$$

$$M = \frac{\text{Density}(\rho) \times RT}{p}$$

Given, $\rho = 0.46$ g/L

$R = 0.0821$ L atm $K^{-1}mol^{-1}$

$T = 257°$ C, i.e. 530 K

$p = 100$ mm Hg $= 100/760$ atm

$$\Rightarrow M = \frac{0.46 \times 0.0821 \times (257 + 273)}{100/760}$$

$= 152.12$ g/mol

≈ 152 g/mol

22. (117) Given, mass of $NH_3 = 17.0$ g

$$\therefore \text{Number of moles of } NH_3 = \frac{\text{Given mass of } NH_3}{\text{Molar mass of } NH_3}$$

$$= \frac{17}{17} = 1$$

Enthalpy change for vaporising 1 mole $NH_3 = 23.4$ kJ/mol

Now, enthalpy change for vaporisation of 85 g NH_3 will be :

number of moles equivalent to 85 g $= \frac{85}{17} = 5$

$\therefore$ Enthalpy change for vaporisation of 5 moles of NH_3

$= 5 \times 23.4$ kJ/mol

$= 117$ kJ

23. (5) Number of moles of acetic acid $= \frac{V \times \rho}{\text{Molar mass}}$

V = Volume of acetic acid = 1.2 mL

ρ = Density of acetic acid = 1.02 gm L^{-1}

Molar mass of acetic acid = 60 g mol^{-1}

$$= \frac{(1.2)\text{mL} \times (1.02)\text{g/m}}{(60)\text{g/mol}} = 0.0204 \text{ mol}$$

$$\text{Molality } (m) = \frac{\text{Moles of solute}}{\text{Mass of solvent (g)}} \times 1000$$

$$= \frac{0.0204}{2000} \times 1000$$

(As 2 L solution in water is prepared so mass of solvent becomes 2000 g).

$= 0.0102$

$\Delta T_f = i \times K_f \times m$

ΔT_f = Depression in freezing point $= 0.0198°$ C

$$i = \frac{\Delta T_f}{K_f \times m} = \frac{0.0198}{1.85 \times 0.0102}$$

$= 1.049$

$$CH_3COOH \rightleftharpoons CH_3COO^- + H^+$$

	CH_3COOH	CH_3COO^-	H^+
Initial	n	0	0
Final	$n(1-x)$	nx	nx

[n = number of moles, x = degree of dissociation]

Total moles $= n - nx + 2nx$

$= n - nx$

$$i = \frac{n(1-x) + nx + nx}{n}$$

$$= \frac{n[1 - x + x + x]}{n}$$

$\Rightarrow$ $i = 1 + x$

$\therefore$ $1.049 = 1 + x$

x (degree of dissociation) $= 1.049 - 1$

$= 0.049$

≈ 0.05

% degree of dissociation $= 0.05 \times 100 = 5\%$

24. (127) **At anode**

$$2H_2O \longrightarrow O_2(g) + 4H^+ + 4e^-$$

At cathode

$$2H^+ + 2e^- \longrightarrow H_2(g)$$

Number of gram equivalent $= \frac{i \times t}{F}$

i = current passed = 0.10 A

t = time = 2 hours $= 2 \times 60 \times 60$ seconds

F = Faraday constant = 96500

$$\Rightarrow \text{Number of gram equivalent} = \frac{0.10 \times 2 \times 60 \times 60}{96500}$$

$= 0.00746$

Number of gram equivalent = number of moles $\times n$-factor

$$\Rightarrow \text{Number of moles} = \frac{\text{Number of gram equivalent}}{n\text{ - factor}}$$

Volume of 1 mole of ideal gas = 22.7 L

Volume of O_2 = number of moles of $O_2 \times 22.7$

$$= \frac{0.00746}{4} \times 22.7 = 0.0423 \text{ L}$$

Volume of H_2 = number of moles of $H_2 \times 22.7$ L

$$= \frac{0.00746}{2} \times 22.7 = 0.0846 \text{ L}$$

Total volume = (0.0423 + 0.0846) L = 0.1269 L

≈ 127 mL or 127 cm^3

25. (1) Given,

$E_a = 532611$ J/mol, $T_1 = 310$K, $T_2 = 300$ K

$$k_{300} = x \times 10^{-3} k_{310}$$

$$\therefore \quad x = \frac{k_{300}}{k_{310} \times 10^{-3}}$$

$$\log\left(\frac{k_2}{k_1}\right)=\frac{E_a}{2.303\,R}\times\left[\frac{1}{T_1}-\frac{1}{T_2}\right]$$

$$=\frac{532611}{2.303\times 8.3}\times\left[\frac{1}{310}-\frac{1}{300}\right]$$

$$\log\frac{k_2}{k_1}=-2.9960$$

Taking antilog,

$$\frac{k_2}{k_1}=\text{antilog}\,(-2.9960)=1.009\times10^{-3}$$

$$x=\frac{k_2}{k_1}\times\frac{1}{10^{-3}}$$

$$=\frac{1.009\times10^{-3}}{10^{-3}}=1.009\approx 1$$

26. (6) The balanced equation will be

$$4FeCr_2O_4+7O_2+8Na_2CO_3\longrightarrow \underset{(A)}{8Na_2CrO_4}+2Fe_2O_3+8CO_2$$

$$2Na_2CrO_4+H^+\longrightarrow \underset{(B)}{Na_2Cr_2O_7}+2Na^++H_2O$$

$Na_2Cr_2O_7$ Na^+ $\bar{O}-Cr(=O)_2-O-Cr(=O)_2-\bar{O}$ Na^+

Number of terminal oxygen atoms is 6.

27. (0) Disproportionation reaction of acidified manganate solution is

$$3MnO_4^{2-}+4H^+\longrightarrow 2\overset{+7}{Mn}O_4^-+\overset{+4}{Mn}O_2+2H_2O$$

Higher oxidation state of manganese is +7 (in MnO_4^-).

Electronic configuration of Mn in +7 oxidation state will be

Mn (25) : [Ar] $4s^2 3d^5$

$Mn^{(+7)}$: [Ar]

i.e. It does not have any unpaired electron magnetic moment (μ)

$$=\sqrt{n(n+2)}$$

where, n is number of unpaired electrons.

$\therefore$ Magnetic moment (μ) = 0 as $n=0$.

28. (64) Mass of organic compound = 0.55 g

Volume of 1M H_2SO_4 solution required for neutralisation = 12.5 mL

In Kjeldahl's method, the ammonia produced is twice the amount of H_2SO_4.

$\therefore$ 12.5 mL of 1 M H_2SO_4 = 25 mL of 1 M NH_3

As 1000 mL of 1 M NH_3 contains 14 g N.

$\therefore$ 25 mL of 1 M NH_3 contains $\left(\frac{14}{1000}\times25\right)$ g of N.

$\therefore$ % of N in 25 mL 1M NH_3 will be

$$=\frac{14}{1000}\times25\times\frac{100}{0.55}$$

$$=63.63\%\cong64\%$$

29. (3) An asymmetric carbon atom is a carbon atom attached to four different atoms or group of atoms. There are three compounds which possess asymmetric carbon atoms.

Cl — Symmetric carbon

H_2N, H H, OH, O — No aymmetric carbon

NH_2, OH, O — Symmetric carbon

No asymmetric carbon

OH — has asymmetric carbons

30. (1) $C_6H_{12}O_6\xrightarrow[-2CO_2]{\text{Zymase}}\underset{\substack{\text{Ethanol}\\(A)}}{2C_2H_5OH}\xrightarrow{\text{NaOI},\,\Delta}\underset{\substack{\text{Sodium formate}\\(B)}}{HCOO^-Na^+}+CHI_3$

Number of carbon atoms present in the product B is 1.

$$\underset{\text{Ethanol}}{C_2H_5OH}\xrightarrow[\Delta,\,\text{Oxidation}]{I_2/\text{NaOH}}\underset{\text{Acetaldehyde}}{CH_3-\overset{O}{\overset{\|}{C}}-H}\xrightarrow[I_2]{\text{NaOH}}HCOO^-+CHI_3$$

25 JULY 2022, SHIFT-I

1. (c) The given balanced chemical equation is

$$SO_2Cl_2 + 2H_2O \longrightarrow H_2SO_4 + 2HCl$$

Number of moles of NaOH required for complete neutralisation $= 16$

Now, as given chemical equation is balanced, so stoichiometric coefficients are equal to their moles respectively.

Number of moles of $H^+ = 2$ moles [from H_2SO_4] + 2 moles [HCl]

$= 4$ moles

Now, 1 mole of SO_2Cl_2 gives 4 moles of H^+ and 16 moles of NaOH are used in neutralisation of these 4 moles.

So, moles of SO_2Cl_2 used

$$= \frac{\text{Moles of NaOH used in neutralisation}}{\text{Moles of acid } [H^+]}$$

$$= \frac{16}{4} = 4$$

2. (c) Given, principal quantum number $= 3$

Now, for azimuthal quantum number (l) has possible values

$l = 0$ to $n-1$

$= 0, 1, 2$

l cannot be equal to the value of n.

So, option (c) $n = 3; l = 3; m_l = -3; s = -\frac{1}{2}$ is not allowed.

3. (c) Given, concentration of formic acid (HCOOH) $= 0.5 \text{ mol L}^{-1}$

Density of formic acid $= 1.05 \text{ g mL}^{-1}$.

$$K_f = 1.86 \text{K kg mol}^{-1}$$

$$\Delta T_f = 0.0405°\text{C}$$

Now, $p = \frac{M}{V} \Rightarrow M = p \cdot V = 1.05 \times 0.5 = 0.525 \text{ g}$

According to formula,

$$\Delta T_f = iK_f m \quad (m = \text{molarity})$$

Let us take, mass of solution $= 1 \text{ kg} = 1000 \text{ g}$

Mass of solvent $= 1000 - 0.525 = 999.475 \text{ g}$ (formic acid)

So $\quad m = \frac{0.525 \times 1000}{46 \times 999.475} = 0.0114$

$$\Delta T_f = iK_f (0.0114)$$

$\Rightarrow \quad i = \frac{0.0405}{1.86 \times 0.0114} = 1.92$

4. (c) $NH_4OH + HCl \longrightarrow NH_4Cl + H_2O$ [weak base + strong acid]

Salt formed

	NH_4OH	HCl	NH_4Cl	H_2O
Volume	20 mL	40 mL		
Conc.	0.1 M	0.05 M		
Millimoles (V × C)				
Time, t = 0	2	2	–	–
After complete neutralisation	–	–	2	

2 mmoles of NH_4Cl remain as a solution.

Total volume of NH_4Cl solution = 60 mL

Concentration of $NH_4Cl = \frac{2}{60} = \frac{1}{30}$

Now, $\quad pH = \frac{1}{2}[pK_w - pK_b - \log C]$

$$= \frac{1}{2}[14 - 5 - (-1.48)] = 5.24$$

Option (c) is correct.

5. (c) (A) $N_2(g) + 3H_2(g) \longrightarrow 2NH_3 \rightarrow$ It is Haber process in which oxide of iron is used as catalyst whereas K_2O and Al_2O_3 are used as promoter.

(B) $CO(g) + 3H_2(g) \longrightarrow CH_4(g) + H_2O \rightarrow$ Ni is used as a catalyst here.

(C) $CO(g) + H_2(g) \longrightarrow HCHO(g) \rightarrow$ In this reaction, Cu is used as a catalyst.

(D) $CO(g) + 2H_2(g) \longrightarrow CH_3OH(g) \rightarrow$ This reaction is completed in presence of Cu / ZnO—Cr_2O_3.

Hence, correct match is

(A) → (III), (B) → (IV), (C) → (I), (D) → (II).

6. (d) Electronic configuration $= [Rn] 5f^{14} 6d^1 7s^2$

Atomic number of Rn = 86

Atomic number of given element will be 86 + 14 + 1 + 2 = 103

IUPAC nomenclature is

1 0 3
↓ ↓ ↓
unn nil tri +ium
= Unniltrium

7. (d) During copper extraction, iron containing slag is attained that is heated with SiO_2 in reverberatory furnace.

The reaction involved is

$$FeS \xrightarrow{O_2} FeO + SiO_2 \longrightarrow \underset{\text{(Slag)}}{FeSiO_3}$$

8. (a) The balanced chemical equation for the given reaction is

$$2KMnO_4 + 5H_2O_2 + 3H_2SO_4 \longrightarrow K_2SO_4 + 2MnSO_4 + 8H_2O + 5O_2$$

Now, $MnSO_4$ is formed as product in which is Mn is in its + 2 state, i.e. Mn^{2+}.

9. (a) Density $= \frac{\text{Mass}}{\text{Volume}}$ and volume ∝ size of the atom.

On moving down the group, size increases which implies volume also increases.

Also on moving down the group, atomic mass increases.

But increase in atomic mass compensate the bigger atomic size.

∴ On moving down the group, density of alkali metals increases whereas potassium being an exception due to an unusual increase in atomic size.

So, density order is Li < K < Na < Rb < Cs.

10. (b) Complete and balanced reaction is

$$2BF_3 + 6NaH \xrightarrow{450\,K} \underset{\substack{\text{(Diborane)}\\(A)}}{B_2H_6} + 6NaF$$

$$B_2H_6 + 2\overset{\ominus}{N}Me_3 \longrightarrow \underset{(B)}{2BH_3 \cdot NMe_3}$$

BH_3 is electron deficient, so NMe_3 forms a coordinate bond with it.

Structure = (B with NMe$_3$ coordinated and three H, tetrahedral)

Shape/geometry = tetrahedral

11. (b) Balanced reaction is

$$Br_2 + 5F_2 \longrightarrow 2BrF_5 \xrightarrow{H_2O} \underset{\text{Bromate}}{HBrO_3}$$

(a) Hypohalite = salt | ester of hypohalous acid (HOX) = OX type e.g. : OCl

(b) Halate = XO_3 type species e.g. : ClO_3

(c) Perhalate = XO_4 type species e.g. : ClO_4

(d) Halide = XO_2 type species e.g. : ClO_2

Hydrolysis of BrF_5

$$BrF_5 + 3H_2O \longrightarrow \underset{\text{(Halate)}}{HBrO_3} + 5HF$$

12. (c) Photochemical smog is mixture of pollutants that are formed when nitrogen oxides and volatile organic compounds (VOCs) reacts in sunlight.

It also contains ozone, nitric oxide, formaldehyde except SO_2.

13. (d) $\underset{(A)}{H_2C=C(CH_3)-CH_2-C(CH_3)_2-CH_3} \xrightarrow{X} a + CH_3-C(=O)-CH_2-C(CH_3)_2-CH_3$

This is an ozonolysis reaction.

$H_2C=C(CH_3)-CH_2-C(CH_3)_2-CH_3$ (ozonide) $\xrightarrow{X} \underset{\boxed{a}}{H-C(=O)-H} + CH_3-C(=O)-CH_2-C(CH_3)_2-CH_3$

X = O_3, H_2O/Zn

$\boxed{a} \xrightarrow{[O]} H-C(=O)-OH$

Formic acid (Produced by ants)

$\underset{(A)}{H_2C=C(CH_3)-CH_2-C(CH_3)_2-CH_3} \xrightarrow{Y} \underset{\boxed{b}}{H-C(=O)-OH} + O=C(CH_3)-CH_2-C(CH_3)_2-CH_3$

Y = $H^+/KMnO_4$

14. (b)

Alcohol (OH) $\xrightarrow{\text{Pyridine (Act as base)}}$ alkoxide ($O^{\ominus}$) $\xrightarrow[\text{Protection of OH group}]{H_3C-C_6H_4-SO_2Cl}$ $R-O-SO_2-C_6H_4-CH_3$ $\xrightarrow[(S_N2\text{ reaction})]{NaCN,\ DMF}$ R–CN + $\overset{\oplus\ominus}{NaO}-S(=O)_2-C_6H_4-CH_3$

By product

(Inversion of stereochemistry takes place)

15. (d) $Na_2Cr_2O_7$, H^+/H_2O being strongest oxidising agent convert primary alcohols to carboxylic acids.

$$\text{Ar}-CH_2CH_2OH \xrightarrow[\text{(ii) } H^+/H_2O]{\text{(i) } Na_2Cr_2O_7} \text{Ar}-CH_2COOH$$

Carboxylic acid

16. (c) $A + NH_3 \xrightarrow{\Delta} B \xrightarrow{\Delta} C(C_8H_5NO_2) \xrightarrow[RCl,\ NaOH/H_2O]{\text{Alc. KOH}} \underset{(1°)}{\text{Amine}}$

Now, degree of unsaturation in C is

$$\text{Degree of unsaturation} = nC - \frac{nH}{2} + \frac{nN}{2} - \frac{nX}{2} + 1$$

$$= 8 - \frac{5}{2} + \frac{1}{2} + 1 = 8 - 25 + 0.5 + 1 = 7$$

which suggest a benzene ring with two doubly bonded oxygen.

$\underset{\boxed{A}}{\text{Phthalic acid}} \xrightarrow[\Delta]{NH_3} \underset{\boxed{B}}{C_6H_4(CONH_2)(COOH)} \xrightarrow[\Delta]{\text{Strong}}$ Phthalimide (N–H)

$\xrightarrow[\text{KOH}]{\text{Ethanolic}}$ Potassium phthalimide ($\overset{\ominus}{N}\ \overset{\oplus}{K}$) $\xrightarrow{R-Cl}$ N-alkylphthalimide (N–R) $\xrightarrow{OH^{\ominus}/H_2O}$ RNH_2 + $C_6H_4(COO^{\ominus})_2$

17. (a) Melamine and formaldehyde condensate to form melamine polymer.

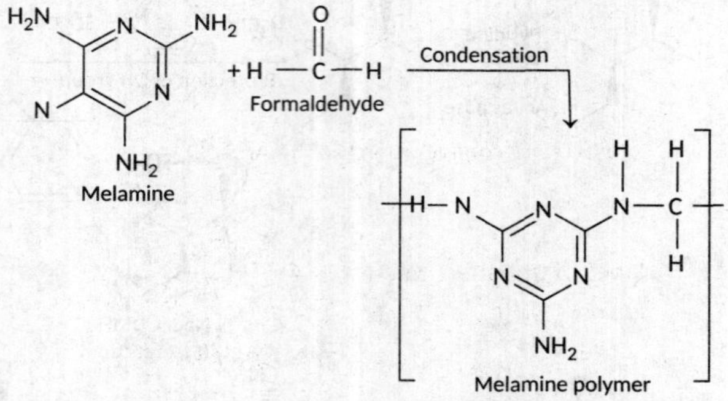

Melamine $+ H-\overset{O}{\overset{||}{C}}-H$ (Formaldehyde) $\xrightarrow{\text{Condensation}}$ Melamine polymer

18. (a) Primary structure is the sequence of amino acids linked together to form polypeptide chain.

Secondary structure is protein backbone stabilised by inter and intra-molecular hydrogen bonding of amide groups.

Tertiary structure is overall 3D arrangement of its polypeptide chain.

After denaturation, hydrogen bonds are broken hence, secondary and tertiary structures are destroyed.

19. (b) Antagonists are the drugs that bind to the receptor sites and inhibit its natural function.

20. (c) When glycerol is heated with $KHSO_4$, it get dehydrated and from acrolein.

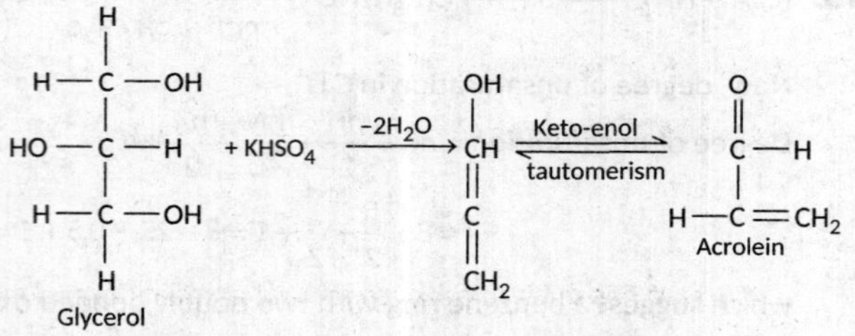

Glycerol $+ KHSO_4 \xrightarrow{-2H_2O}$ $CH(OH)=C=CH_2$ $\underset{\text{tautomerism}}{\xrightarrow{\text{Keto-enol}}}$ $O=CH-CH=CH_2$ (Acrolein)

Acrolein formed has unpleasant smell.

Hence, statement I is correct but statement II is incorrect.

21. (2) To decide magnetic nature of molecule, we need to find the number of unpaired electrons present in it.

Molecule	Electronic configuration	Unpaired electron	Nature
E.C. of N_2	$\sigma1s^2\sigma1s^{*2}\sigma2s^2\sigma2s^{*2}$ $\pi2p_x^2=\pi2p_y^2\sigma2p_z^2$	Unpaired electron = 0	Diamagnetic in nature
E.C. of N_2^+	$\sigma1s^2\sigma1s^{*2}\sigma2s^2\sigma^*2s^{*2}$ $\pi2p_x^2=\pi2p_y^2\,\sigma2p_z^1$	Unpaired electron = 1	Paramagnetic in nature
E.C. of N_2^-	$\sigma1s^2\sigma1s^{*2}\sigma2s^2\sigma2s^{*2}$ $\pi2p_x^2=\pi2p_y^2\sigma2p_z^2$ $\pi2p_x^{*1}$	Unpaired electron=1	Paramagnetic in nature
E.C. of N_2^{2-}	$\sigma1s^2\sigma1s^{*2}\sigma2s^2\sigma2s^{*2}$ $\pi2p_x^2=\pi2p_y^2\,\sigma2p_z^2$ $\pi2p_x^{*1}=\pi2p_y^{*1}$	Unpaired electron=2	Paramagnetic in nature
E.C. of O_2^-	$\sigma1s^2\sigma1s^{*2}\sigma2s^2\sigma2s^{*2}$ $\sigma2p_z^2$ $\pi2p_x^2=\pi2p_y^2\pi2p_x^{*2}$ $\pi2p_y^{*1}$	Unpaired electron=1	Paramagnetic in nature
E.C. of O_2	$\sigma1s^2\sigma1s^{*2}\sigma2s^2\sigma2s^{*2}$ $\sigma2p_z^2\pi2p_x^2=\pi2p_y^2$ $\pi2p_x^{*1}=\pi2p_y^{*1}$	Unpaired electron=2	Paramagnetic in nature
E.C. of O_2^+	$\sigma1s^2\sigma1s^{*2}\sigma2s^2\sigma2s^{*2}$ $\sigma2p_z^2\pi2p_x^2=\pi2p_y^2$ $\pi2p_x^{*1}$	Unpaired electron=1	Paramagnetic in nature
E.C. of O_2^{2-}	$\sigma1s^2\sigma1s^{*2}\sigma2s^2\sigma2s^{*2}$ $\sigma2p_z^2\pi2p_x^2=\pi2p_y^2$ $\pi2p_x^{*2}=\pi2p_y^{*2}$	Unpaired electron=0	Diamagnetic in nature

So, only N_2 and O_2^{2-} are diamagnetic in nature.

22. (124) Combustion reaction for propane, graphite and dihydrogen are

(i) $C_3H_8(g)+5O_2(g)\longrightarrow 3CO_2(g)+4H_2O(l)$

$$\Delta H_{(i)}=-2220\text{ kJ mol}^{-1}$$

(ii) $C(\text{graphite})+O_2(g)\longrightarrow CO_2(g)\,\Delta H_{(ii)}=-393.5\text{ kJ mol}^{-1}$

(iii) $H_2(g)+\frac{1}{2}O_2(g)\longrightarrow H_2O(l)\quad \Delta H_{(iii)}=-285.8\text{ kJ mol}^{-1}$

Reaction for formation of propane is

$3\,C(\text{graphite})+4H_2(g)\longrightarrow C_3H_8(g)$

$$\Delta H_{\text{reaction}}=3\Delta H_{(ii)}+4\Delta H_{(iii)}-\Delta H_{(i)}$$
$$=3(-393.5)+4(-285.8)-(-2200)$$
$$=-123.7\text{ kJ mol}^{-1}$$

23. (22) Initial pressure of gas = 4 atm (moist)

Initial volume of container = V

Final volume of container = $2V$

Pressure of gas = ?

The vapour pressure of water is 0.4 atm.

So, initial pressure of gas = moist gas – vapour pressure of water

$$=4-0.4=3.6\text{ atm}$$

Using ideal gas equation,

$$p_1V_1=nRT \text{ and } p_2V_2=nRT$$

So, $p_1V_1=p_2V_2\Rightarrow p_2=\dfrac{3.6\times V}{2V}$

$$p_2=1.8\text{ atm}$$

Final pressure of gas which is moist $=1.8+0.4$

$$=2.2\text{ atm}$$
$$=22\times10^{-1}\text{ atm}$$

24. (4) Given, $E^\circ_{Zn^{2+}/Zn}=-0.763$ V

$E^\circ_{Sn^{x+}/Sn}=0.008$ V

$E_{cell}=0.801$ V

$$\frac{2.303RT}{F} = 0.06\text{ V}$$

Q = potential quotient $= 10^{-2}$

Reactions of half-cell are

A : $Zn \longrightarrow Zn^{2+} + 2e^-; E^\circ_{cell} = E^\circ_{Sn^{x+}/Sn} - E_{Zn/Zn^{2+}}$

$= 0.008 - (-0.763)$

C : $Sn^{x+} + xe^- \longrightarrow Sn$

$Zn + Sn^{x+} + xe^- \longrightarrow Sn + Zn^{2+} + 2e^-; E^\circ_{cell} = 0.771\text{ V}$

Applying Nernst equation,

$$E_{cell} = E^\circ_{cell} - \frac{2.303\,RT}{nF}\log Q$$

$$0.801 = 0.771 - \frac{0.06}{n}\log 10^{-2}$$

$$0.801 - 0.771 = \frac{-0.06}{n}(-2\log 10)$$

$$0.03 = \frac{0.12}{n}$$

$\therefore$ $n = 4$

25. (1) Given, $(t_{1/2})_{p_1} = 240$ s; $p_1 = 500$ torr

$(t_{1/2})_{p_2} = 4$ min; $p_2 = 250$ torr

$= 4 \times 60$

$= 240$ s

Given information proves that, $t_{1/2}$ is independent of pressure of gas.

So, order of the reaction is 1.

26. (0) Oxidation state of Co in all the given complexes $= +3$.

The inner orbital and outer orbital nature of complex depends on the chemical nature of ligands and also crystal field splitting depends on strength of ligands.

Ligand strength order is $\overset{\ominus}{C}N > NH_3 > H_2O > Cl^-$.

Crystal field splitting energy $(\Delta_0) = \dfrac{hc}{\lambda}$

$\boxed{\Delta_0 \propto \dfrac{1}{\lambda}}$ $\Rightarrow$ complex having shortest wavelength is that which have highest Δ_0.

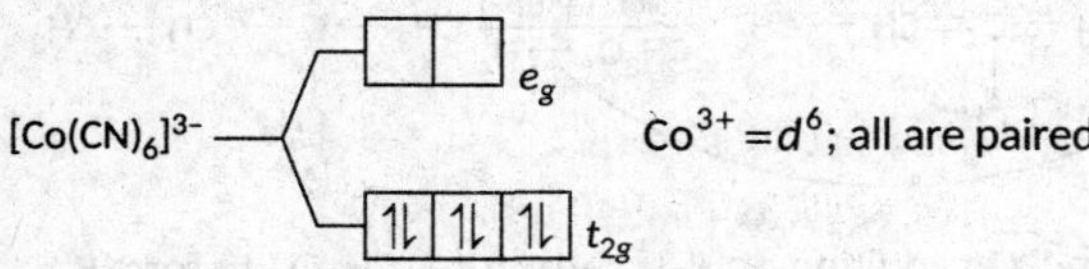

Hence, number of unpaired electrons $(n) = 0$

So, spin only magnetic moment $= \sqrt{n(n+2)}$

$\mu_{spin} = 0$

27. (5) Electronic configuration of $Co^{3+} = d^6$

Electronic configuration of $Ti^{2+} = 3d^0 4s^2$

or $V^{2+} = 3d^1 4s^2$

Electronic configuration of $Cr^{2+} = 3d^4$.

$E^\circ_{Co^{3+}/Co^{2+}} = 1.97 \rightarrow$ it would not be able to liberate hydrogen from dil. acid.

$Co^{3+} + e^- \longrightarrow Co^{2+}$; $E^\circ = 1.97$

So, electronic configuration $[Co^{3+}] = [Ar]3d^6$ (with e_g: ↑ ↑ and t_{2g}: ↑↓ ↑ ↑)

Number of unpaired electron = 4

$\mu_{spin} = \sqrt{n(n+2)}$

$\Rightarrow$ $\mu_{spin} = \sqrt{4(4+2)} = 4.92 \approx 5$

$\Rightarrow$ $\mu_{spin} = 5$

28. (56) Given, volume of $H_2SO_4 = 2.5$ mL

Molarity of $H_2SO_4 = 2$

Millimole of $H_2SO_4 = 2 \times 2.5 = 5$ m moles

Millimoles of NH_3 neutralised $= 2 \times 5 = 10$ millimoles (2 = n-factor of H_2SO_4)

Moles of NH_3 neutralised $= 10 \times 10^{-3}$ moles

Weight of N present in compound will be $= 10 \times 10^{-3} \times 14$

$= 0.14$ g

Mass of compound $= 0.25$ g

% of N in compound $= \dfrac{0.14}{0.25} \times 100 = 56\%$

29. (1) Molecular formula $= C_4H_5N$

Degree of unsaturation $= nC - \dfrac{nH}{2} + \dfrac{nN}{2} - \dfrac{nX}{2} + 1$

$= 4 - \dfrac{5}{2} + \dfrac{1}{2} + 1 = 3$

Compound has one nitrogen, so it must contain CN and it is acyclic.

(structures with C≡N) or (structure with C≡N) are two possibilities.

Number of sp^3 hybridised carbon = 1

30. (2)

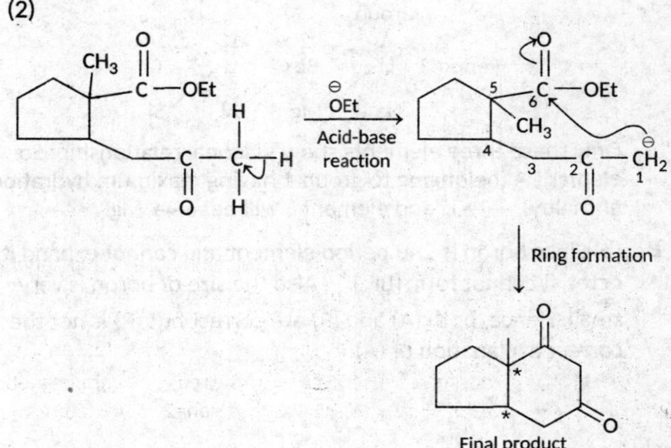

Final product (A)

There are two chiral centres in A.

27 JULY 2022, SHIFT-II

1. (a) The energy of orbitals depends on their $(n+l)$ value. Greater the $(n+l)$ value higher is the energy.

(A) $n+l=3+0=3$ (B) $n+l=4+0=4$

(C) $n+l=3+1=4$ (D) $n+l=3+2=5$

Hence, correct order of energy is D > B > C > A.

2. (c) (A) $\psi_{MO}=\psi_A-\psi_B$, made by destructive interference of atomic orbital, i.e. antibonding molecular orbital.

(B) $\mu=Q\times r$, it is the formula for dipole moment.

(C) $\frac{N_b-N_a}{2}$, it gives bond order of molecule.

(D) $\psi_{MO}=\psi_A+\psi_B$, made by constructive interference of atomic orbital, i.e. bonding molecular orbital.

So, the correct match is

(A) $\rightarrow$ (III), B $\rightarrow$ (I), (C) $\rightarrow$ (IV), D $\rightarrow$ (II).

3. (a) Since, NH_4OH is a weak base and HCl is a strong acid, thus initial pH will be higher than 7 due to presence of NH_4OH. As we add HCl the pH of solution starts to drop till equivalence point and will drop till acidic pH of HCl.

4. (b) Molar conductance of strong electrolyte increases on dilution but slowly, while molar conductance of weak electrolyte increases on dilution but steeply.

$$KI \longrightarrow \text{Strong electrolyte}$$

$$H_2CO_3 \text{ (carbonic acid)} \longrightarrow \text{Weak electrolyte}$$

5. (c) Since parchment paper is semipermeable, thus it allows particles of solution to pass through it but will not let pass the particles of colloids. Thus (A) is correct but (R) is not correct.

6. (b) As we move from left to right in a period ionisation enthalpy increases gradually, but ionisation enthalpy of fully and half-filled orbitals are higher than normal values due to higher stability.

Hence, the correct order will be B < A < D < C.

7. (a) This relation is called diagonal relationship, i.e. 2nd period elements show similar behaviour like diagonal element of next group. e.g.

Group	1	2	13	14
Period 2	Li	Be	B	C
	Na	Mg	Al	Si

(Li ↘ Mg, Be ↘ Al, B ↘ Si)

Only these three elements show diagonal relationship. So element A (belonging to group 1 having maximum hydration enthalpy) $\longrightarrow$ Li and element B will be $\longrightarrow$ Mg.

8. (b) Since boron is 2nd period element and cannot expand its octet, it cannot form $[BF_6]^{3-}$. Also the size of boron is very small. Hence, both (A) and (R) are correct but (R) is not the correct explanation of (A).

9. (d) In alkaline medium, $\overset{+7}{Mn}O_4^-$ gets reduced to $\overset{+4}{Mn}O_2$ and in this reaction, it oxidises as

$$\underset{\text{Thiosulphate ion}}{S_2O_3^{2-}} \longrightarrow \underset{\text{Sulphate ion}}{SO_4^{2-}}$$

Balanced reaction

$$8MnO_4^- + 3S_2O_3^{2-} + H_2O \longrightarrow 8MnO_2 + 6SO_4^{2-} + 2OH^-$$

10. (a) Ligands like CO forms σ-coordinate bond with central metal and also accepts π-electron of metals by back bonding, such ligands are called π-acceptor ligands.

More the electron density on central metal having π-acceptor ligands, less is its oxidation state and greater is the strength of π-bond.

11. (a) Both statement I and statement II are correct.

Cement industry requires silicates and fly in large amount as raw material which they obtain from steel industry.

Fuels obtained from plastic waste has very high octane rating and contains no lead.

12. (c) NaOH is a base, it attack on acidic H and forms a carbanion.

$$R-\overset{O}{\overset{\|}{C}}-CH_3 \xrightarrow[-H_2O]{NaOH} R-\overset{O}{\overset{\|}{C}}-\overset{\ominus}{C}H_2$$

Ethyl bromide attacks on carbanion as electrophile to give the final product.

$$R-\overset{O}{\overset{\|}{C}}-\overset{\ominus}{C}H_2 + CH_3CH_2Br \longrightarrow R-\overset{O}{\overset{\|}{C}}-CH_2CH_2CH_3$$

13. (b) **Step I** Addition of CH_3O^- and Br^- on unsaturated part of alkene.

$$CH_3-\underset{CH_3}{\underset{|}{C}}=CH-CH_3 \xrightarrow[CH_3O-H]{Br-Br} \underset{(A)}{CH_3-\underset{CH_3}{\underset{|}{\overset{OCH_3}{\overset{|}{C}}}}-\overset{Br}{\overset{|}{CH}}-CH_3}$$

Step II On addition of HI, I^- substitutes CH_3O^- to form B.

$$\underset{(B)}{CH_3-\underset{CH_3}{\underset{|}{\overset{I}{\overset{|}{C}}}}-\overset{Br}{\overset{|}{CH}}-CH_3}$$

14. (a) The correct match is A - (IV), B-(III), C-(II), D-(I).
These are all named reactions

A. $C_6H_5COCl \xrightarrow[\text{Pd-BaSO}_4]{H_2} C_6H_5CHO$ ⟶ Rosenmund reaction

B. $CH_3-CN \xrightarrow[H_3O^+]{SnCl_2/HCl} CH_3CHO$ ⟶ Stephen reduction

C. $C_6H_5CH_3 \xrightarrow[H_3O^+]{CrO_2Cl_2} C_6H_5CHO$ ⟶ Etard reaction

D. $C_6H_6 \xrightarrow[\text{AlCl}_3\text{(anhy.)}]{\text{CO, HCl}} C_6H_5CHO$ ⟶ Gattermann-Koch reaction

15. (a) The correct match is as follows

	List I (Polymer)		List II (Monomer)
(A)	Neoprene	(II)	Chloroprene
(B)	Teflon	(III)	Tetrafluoroethene
(C)	Acrilan	(I)	Acrylonitrile
(D)	Natural rubber	(IV)	Isoprene

16. (d) *A*. turns litmus solution red means it is acidic.
$A + NaOH \longrightarrow B$ (contains only N, not Cl and liquid ⟶ (suggests aniline)
$B + HNO_2 \longrightarrow C$ {It suggest diazotisation reaction}
C + Phenol ⟶ Orange precipitate {It suggest coupling followed by diazotisation}

So, reactions involved are as follows :

$C_6H_5\overset{+}{N}H_3Cl^-$ (A) $+ NaOH \longrightarrow C_6H_5NH_2$ (B) $+ NaCl + H_2O$

$C_6H_5NH_2 + HNO_2 \xrightarrow{(0\text{-}5°C)} C_6H_5\overset{+}{N_2}Cl^-$

$C_6H_5\overset{+}{N_2}Cl^- + HO-C_6H_5 \longrightarrow C_6H_5-N{=}N-C_6H_4-OH$

Orange coloured dye

17. (a) The correct match is as follows
(A) Glucose + HI/Red P ⟶ (IV) *n*-hexane
(B) Glucose + Br_2 water ⟶ (I) Gluconic acid
(C) Glucose + Acetic acid ⟶ (II) Glucose pentaacetate
(D) Glucose + HNO_3 ⟶ (III) Saccharic acid

18. (c) Rosin, a gum is added in soap to enhance its lather forming ability as well as enhances the quality of soap.
Thus, sodium rosinate is the correct option.

19. (d) (A) Chloroform and aniline ⟶ (III) can be separated by simple distillation as difference in their boiling points is more than 25° C.
(B) Benzoic acid and naphthalene ⟶ (IV) they can be separated more. conveniently by crystallisation.
(C) Water and aniline ⟶ (I) steam distillation
(D) Naphthalene and NaCl ⟶ (II) sublimation (as naphthalene is sublime and NaCl is non-sublime).

20. (d) $2Fe^{3+} + 3K_4[Fe(CN)_6] \longrightarrow \overset{III}{Fe_4}[\overset{II}{Fe}(CN)_6]_3$
Ferriferrocyanide
Prussian blue ppt.

It is a 3 – 2 complex, where counter Fe is in +3 oxidation state and central metal Fe is in +2 oxidation state.

21. (1) Reaction involved

	H_2SO_4	+ $2NaOH$ ⟶	Na_2SO_4	+ H_2O
Initial millimoles	10	5	–	–
Final millimoles	7.5	0	2.5	–

So, millimoles of H_2SO_4 left = 7.5
Volume of solution = 100 + 50 = 150 mL

Thus molarity of $H_2SO_4 = \dfrac{\text{millimoles of } H_2SO_4}{\text{volume of solution}} = \dfrac{7.5}{150} = \dfrac{1}{20}$ M

n-factor of H_2SO_4 is 2.
Thus, normality, *N* = molarity × *n*-factor

$$= \frac{1}{20} \times 2 = \frac{1}{10} = 1 \times 10^{-1}\ N$$

22. (25) van der Waals' equation,

$$\left(p + \frac{an^2}{V^2}\right)(V - nb) = nRT$$

Considering 1 mole of gas ($n = 1$) and high pressure

i.e $\left(p + \dfrac{an^2}{V^2}\right) \approx (p)$

Modified equation will be

$$p(V - b) = RT$$
$$pV - pb = RT$$

Dividing by *RT* throughout,

$$\frac{pV}{RT} - \frac{pb}{RT} = 1 \Rightarrow Z = 1 + \frac{pb}{RT}$$

Now, given $Z = 2, p = 99, R = 0.083, T = 298$ K

$$b = \frac{(Z-1)}{p} \times RT = \frac{(2-1)}{99} \times 0.083 \times 298$$
$$= 25 \times 10^{-2}\ \text{L mol}^{-1}$$

23. (35) Given, molar mass of gas = 280

Increase in temperature of calorimeter = 298.45 K − 298.0 K

$$\Delta T = 0.45\ \text{K}$$

Heat of calorimeter, $C_{\text{Calorimeter}} = 2.5\ \text{kJ K}^{-1}$

Enthalpy of calorimeter $\Delta H_{\text{Comb}} = 9\ \text{kJ mol}^{-1}$

$$q = C\,\Delta T = 2.5 \times 0.45 = 1.125\ \text{kJ}$$

Considering $q = \Delta H$ (enthalpy change)

So, total enthalpy change = q = 1.125 kJ

Enthalpy change for 1 mole of gas, $\Delta H = 9\ \text{kJ mol}^{-1}$

Thus, $n_{\text{gas}} = \dfrac{q}{\Delta H} = \dfrac{1.125\ \text{kJ}}{9\ \text{kJ mol}^{-1}}$

and mass of gas taken = $n_{\text{gas}} \times$ molar mass

$$= \frac{1.125}{9} \times 280 \simeq 35\ \text{g}$$

24. (6) Vapour pressure of pure water, $p^\circ_{H_2O} = 23.76$ mmHg

Vapour pressure of solution, $p_s = \dfrac{p^\circ_{H_2O}}{2} = 11.88$ mmHg

According to the expression of relative lower vapour pressure.

$$\frac{p^\circ_{H_2O} - p_s}{p^\circ_{H_2O}} = \chi_A \quad \{\chi_A = \text{mole fraction of solid } A\}$$

$$\frac{23.76 - 11.88}{23.76} = \frac{n_A}{n_A + n_{H_2O}} \quad \left[n_{H_2O} = \frac{100}{18} = 5.55\right]$$

$$\frac{1}{2} = \frac{n_A}{n_A + 5.55}$$

or $\quad n_A \simeq 6$

25. (165) Since, after 70 minutes, the concentration of reactant [A] is halved.

So, $t_{1/2} = 70$ min

Half-life of first order reaction is given as

$$t_{1/2} = \frac{0.6932}{k} \quad [k = \text{rate constant for 1st order reaction}]$$

$$k = \frac{0.6932}{t_{1/2}} = \frac{0.6932}{70} = 0.0099\ \text{min}^{-1}$$

$$= \frac{0.0099}{60}\ \text{s}^{-1} = 165 \times 10^{-6}\ \text{s}^{-1}$$

26. (4) The principal ores of iron are siderite ($FeCO_3$), haematite (Fe_2O_3), magnetite (Fe_3O_4), limonite ($2Fe_2O_3 \cdot 3H_2O$).

27. (4) Reaction involved

$$2MnO_4^- + 3H_2O_2 \longrightarrow 2MnO_2 + 3O_2 + 2H_2O + 2OH^-$$

Oxidation state of product → +4

Oxidation state of Mn in $MnO_2 = x \times 2(-2) = 0 \Rightarrow x = +4$

28. (6) General planar structures linear, bent, T-shaped, trigonal planar and square pyramidal

NO_3^- → Trigonal planar (✗)

H_2O_2 → Open book like (3D) (non-planar) (✓)

BF_3 → Trigonal planar (✗)

PCl_3 → Pyramidal (✓)

XeF_4 → Square planar (✗)

SF_4 → *See-saw* (✓)

XeO_3 → Pyramidal (✓)

PH_4^+ → Tetrahedral (✓)

SO_3 → Trigonal planar (✗)

$[Al(OH)_4]^-$ → Tetrahedral (✓)

29. (2) Fehling solution contains $Cu^{2+} \rightarrow d^9$ configuration

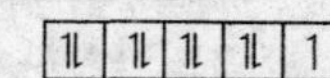

∴ Number of upaired $e^-(n) = 1$

So, spin magnetic moment (μ).

$$= \sqrt{n(n+2)}\ \text{BM} = \sqrt{1(3)} = 1.73\ \text{BM} \simeq 2\ \text{BM}$$

30. (530) The given reaction is

$$C_6H_5CH_3 \xrightarrow{92\%} C_6H_5CHO$$

Number of moles of toluene

$$= \frac{\text{Mass of toluene}}{\text{Molecular mass of toluene}} = \frac{5}{92}$$

Thus, for 100% yield moles of benzaldehyde formed $= \dfrac{5}{92} \times 1$

For 92% yield moles of benzaldehyde formed

$$= \frac{5}{92} \times 0.92 = 0.05\ \text{mol}$$

= yield of benzaldehyde × molecular mass of benzaldehyde

So, mass of benzaldehyde formed = 0.05 × 106

$$= 5.3\ \text{g} = 530 \times 10^{-2}\ \text{g}$$

JEE ADVANCED

Paper 1

1. (90.39) The combustion reaction is

$$2Hg(g) + O_2(g) \longrightarrow 2HgO(s)$$

Given, heat capacity of calorimeter, $C = 20 \text{ kJ K}^{-1}$

Initial temperature, $T_i = 298 \text{ K}$

Final temperature, $T_f = 312.8 \text{ K}$

Change in temperature, $\Delta T_f = 312.8 - 298 = 14.8 \text{ K}$

Heat evolved in reaction, $q = C\Delta T = 20 \times 14.8 = 296 \text{ kJ}$

Since, the reaction is taking place under constant volume

$$\Delta U_r = -296 \text{kJ}$$

Enthalpy of reaction, $\Delta H_r^\circ = \Delta U^\circ + \Delta n_g RT$

$$\Delta H_r^\circ = -296 \text{ kJ} - 3 \text{ mol}^{-1} \times 8.3 \times 10^{-3} \text{kJ K}^{-1} \text{ mol}^{-1} \times 298 \text{ K}$$

$$\Delta H_r^\circ = -296 \text{ kJ} - 7.42 \text{ kJ} = -303.42 \text{ kJ}$$

Also, $\Delta H_r^\circ = 2\Delta H_f^\circ(\text{HgO}(s)) - 2\Delta H_f^\circ(\text{Hg}(g)) - \Delta H_f^\circ(\text{O}_2(g))$

$$-303.42 = 2\Delta H_f^\circ(\text{HgO}(s)) - 2 \times 61.32 \text{ kJ mol}^{-1} - 0$$

$$\Delta H_f^\circ[\text{HgO}(s)] = -303.42 + 122.64 = -180.78 \text{ kJ}$$

$$\Delta H_f^\circ[\text{HgO}(s)] = \frac{-180.78}{2} = -90.39 \text{ kJ mol}^{-1}$$

So, the value of $(X) = 90.39 \text{kJ mol}^{-1}$

2. (0.77) Latimer diagram

$$\overset{+7}{MnO_4^-} \xrightarrow[n_1=3]{E_1^\circ = 1.68 \text{ V}} \overset{+4}{MnO_2} \xrightarrow[n_2=2]{E_2^\circ = 1.21 \text{ V}} \overset{+2}{Mn^{2+}} \xrightarrow[n_3=2]{E_3^\circ = -1.03 \text{ V}} \overset{0}{Mn}$$

$$E_4^\circ = ?\ n_4 = 7$$

So, $\quad n_4E_4^\circ = n_1E_1^\circ + n_2E_2^\circ + n_3E_3^\circ$

$$7E_4^\circ = 3 \times 1.68 + 2 \times 1.21 + 2 \times (-1.03)$$

$$\Rightarrow \quad E_4^\circ = \frac{5.04 + 2.42 - 2.06}{7} = \frac{5.4}{7} = 0.77 \text{ V}$$

$$E^\circ_{MnO_4^-(aq)/Mn(s)} = +0.77 \text{ V}$$

3. (10.02)

Moles of NaOH, $n_{NaOH} = 0.01$ mol

Moles of H_2CO_3, $n_{H_2CO_3} = 0.01$ mol

Moles of $NaHCO_3$, $n_{NaHCO_3} = 0.01$ mol

Moles of Na_2CO_3, $n_{Na_2CO_3} = 0.01$ mol

Acid-base reaction can be written as

	H_2CO_3	+ NaOH	$\longrightarrow NaHCO_3$	$+ H_2O$
$t = 0$	0.01 mol	0.01 mol	0.01 mol	-
Complete reaction	0	0	0.02 mol	-

Final moles of Na_2CO_3 and $NaHCO_3$ are 0.01 mole and 0.02 mole respectively.

This is a buffer solution,

By Henderson – Hasselbalch equation

$$pH = pK_{a_2} + \log\frac{[\text{Salt}]}{[\text{Acid}]}$$

$$pH = pK_{a_2} + \log\frac{[NaHCO_3]}{[H_2CO_3]}$$

$$= 10.32 + \log\frac{0.02}{0.01}$$

$$= 10.32 - \log 2$$

$$= 10.32 - 0.30 = 10.02$$

4. (1.58) Given, mass of $Cu(NO_3)_2 = 3.74$g

Molar mass of $Cu(NO_3)_2 = 63 + 2 \times 14 + 6 \times 16$

$$= 63 + 28 + 96 = 187 \text{ g mol}^{-1}$$

Moles of $Cu(NO_3)_2 = \frac{3.74}{187} = 0.02$ mol

Reaction involved,

$$2Cu(NO_3)_2 + 4KI \longrightarrow 2\,CuI(s) + I_2 + 4KNO_3$$

2 moles of $Cu(NO_3)_2$ forms 2 moles of CuI.

So, 0.02 mole of $Cu(NO_3)_2$ will form 0.02 mole of CuI.

Reaction involved on passing H_2S gas,

$$2\,CuI + H_2S \longrightarrow Cu_2S + 2HI$$

2 moles of CuI form 1 mole of Cu_2S and 0.02 mole of CuI will form 0.01 mole Cu_2S.

Molar mass of $Cu_2S = 2 \times 63 + 32$

$$= 126 + 32 = 158 \text{ g mol}^{-1}$$

Mass of Cu_2S formed $= 0.01 \times 158 = 1.58$ g.

5. (2.38) Mass of white phosphorus, $P_4 = 1.24$ g

Molar mass of $P_4 = 4 \times 31 = 124 \text{ g mol}^{-1}$

Moles of $P_4 = \frac{1.24}{124} = 0.01$ mol

Reaction involved,

$$P_4(s) + 3NaOH(aq) + 3H_2O(l) \longrightarrow PH_3(g) + 3NaH_2PO_2(aq)$$

NaOH is present in excess, so P_4 is limiting reagent. Thus, amount of PH_3 formed is 0.01 mole.

Reaction of PH_3 with $CuSO_4$, can written as

$$2PH_3 + 3CuSO_4 \longrightarrow Cu_3P_2 + 3H_2SO_4$$

2 moles PH_3 reacts with 3 moles $CuSO_4$ by double displacement reaction.

0.01 mole PH_3 reacts with $\frac{3\times 0.01}{2} = 0.015$ mole $CuSO_4$.

Molar mass of $CuSO_4 = 63 + 32 + 4\times 16$

$= 63 + 32 + 64 = 159\ g\ mol^{-1}$

Mass of $CuSO_4 = 0.015 \times 159$

$= 2.38\ g$

6. (1.50) By Carius method,

$$2P + 3Br_2 \longrightarrow 2PBr_3$$
(Red P)

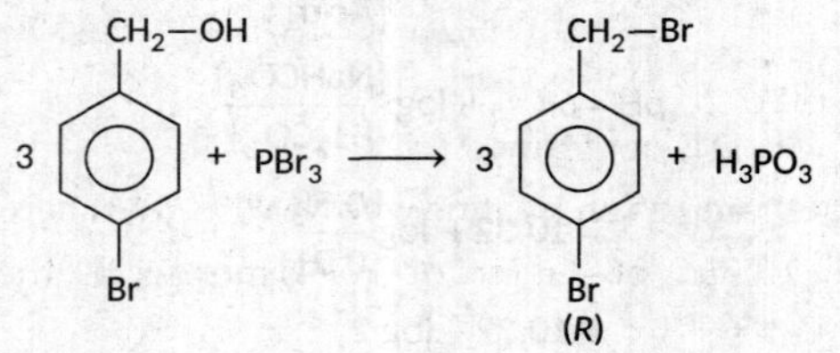

3 (4-bromobenzyl alcohol, $CH_2—OH$ / Br) + PBr_3 ⟶ 3 (4-bromobenzyl bromide, $CH_2—Br$ / Br) *(R)* + H_3PO_3

Given, mass of *R* (major product) = 1 g

Molar mass of $R = 2\times 80 + 7\times 12 + 6\times 1$

$= 250\ g\ mol^{-1}$

Moles of $R = \frac{1}{250}$ mol

1 mole of *R* contain 2 moles of Br, so can give 2 moles AgBr.

So, $\frac{1}{250}$ moles of *R* will give $\frac{2}{250}$ moles AgBr.

Molar mass of AgBr = 108 + 80 = 188 g mol^{-1}

Mass of AgBr $= \frac{2\times 188}{250}$

$= \frac{188}{125} = 1.50\ g$

7. (1.31)

Complete reaction is

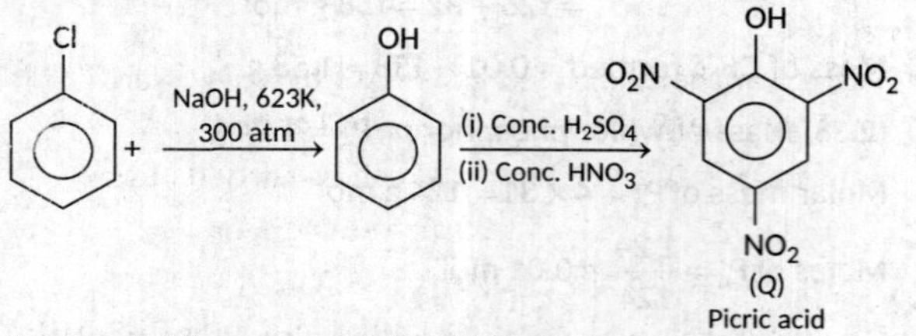

Chlorobenzene (Cl) $\xrightarrow{\text{NaOH, 623K, 300 atm}}$ Phenol (OH) $\xrightarrow[\text{(ii) Conc. } HNO_3]{\text{(i) Conc. } H_2SO_4}$ 2,4,6-trinitrophenol (OH, O_2N, NO_2, NO_2) *(Q)* Picric acid

Molecular formula of *Q* is $C_6H_3N_3O_7$.

Moles of hydrogen in *Q* = 3 moles

Mass of hydrogen in 1 mole *Q* = 3 g

Molar mass of $Q = 6\times 12 + 3\times 1 + 3\times 14 + 7\times 16$

$= 72 + 3 + 42 + 112$

$= 229\ g$

% weight of H $= \frac{\text{Mass of H} \times 100}{\text{Mass of Q}}$

$= \frac{3}{229}\times 100$

$= \frac{300}{229} = 1.31\%$

8. (136)

Given, reaction sequence is as follows.

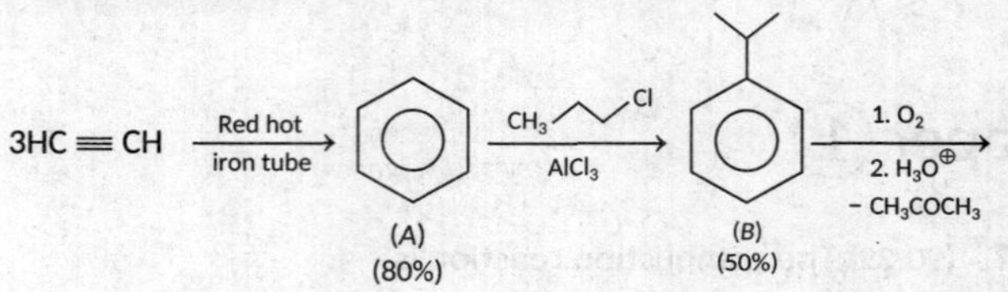

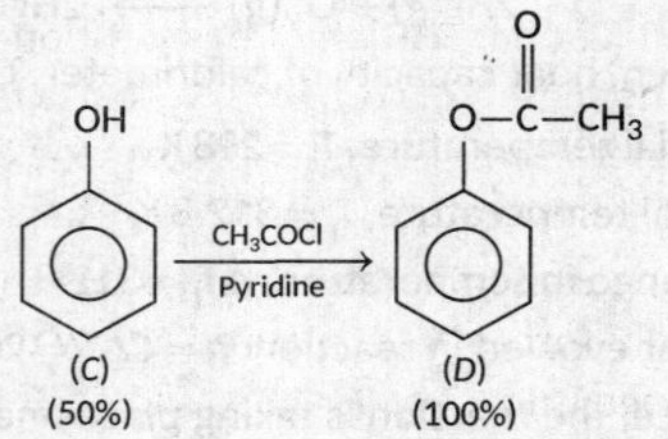

$3HC \equiv CH \xrightarrow[\text{iron tube}]{\text{Red hot}}$ Benzene *(A)* (80%) $\xrightarrow[AlCl_3]{CH_3CH_2CH_2Cl}$ Cumene *(B)* (50%) $\xrightarrow[2.\ H_3O^{\oplus}]{1.\ O_2}$ $-\ CH_3COCH_3$

Phenol (OH) *(C)* (50%) $\xrightarrow[\text{Pyridine}]{CH_3COCl}$ Phenyl acetate ($O—\overset{O}{\overset{\|}{C}}—CH_3$) *(D)* (100%)

3 mol $HC \equiv CH$ = 1 mol $A \times \frac{80}{100} = 0.8$ mol of *A*

15 mol $HC \equiv CH = 0.8\times 15 = 4$ mol of *A*

1 mol *A* forms = 1 mol $B \times \frac{50}{100} = 0.5$ mol *B*

4 mol *A* forms = 0.5 × 4 = 2 mol *B*

1 mol *B* forms = 1 mol $C \times \frac{50}{100} = 0.5$ mol *C*

2 mol *B* forms = 2 × 0.5 = 1 mol *C*

1 mol *C* forms = 1 mol *D*

Molecular formula of $D = C_8H_8O_2$

Molar mass of $D = 12\times 8 + 1\times 8 + 2\times 16$

$= 96 + 8 + 32 = 136\ g\ mol^{-1}$

So, mass of *D* = 1 mol × 136 g / mol = 136 g.

9. (a, d)

(a) 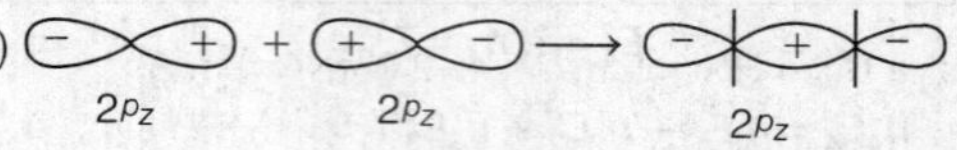 $2p_z$ + $2p_z$ ⟶ $2p_z$ ($\sigma 2p_z$ has total two nodal planes)

So, statement (a) is correct.

(b) 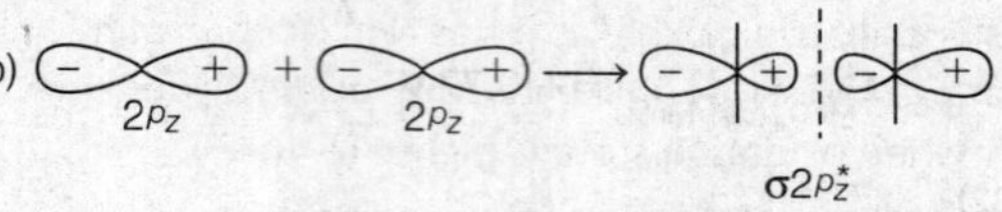 $2p_z$ + $2p_z$ ⟶ $\sigma 2p_z^*$

(Total 3 nodal planes. The nodal plane between two orbitals is *xy* not *xz*.) Since, the orbitals are along *z*-axis.

So, statement (b) is incorrect.

(c) 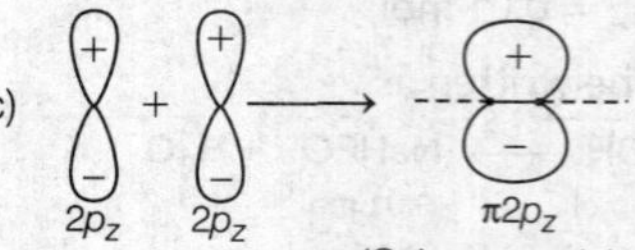 $2p_z$ + $2p_z$ ⟶ $\pi 2p_z$

(Only one nodal plane passing through the internuclear axis and is parallel to molecular axis and not perpendicular.)

So, statement (c) is also incorrect.

(d) $2p_z$ + $2p_z$ ⟶ π^*2p_z
(Two nodal planes are present, one is present in the *xy*-plane.)

So, statement (d) is correct.

10. (a, d) **Chemisorption** Chemisorption is due to the formation of chemical bond. Chemisorption is favoured at high temperatures. The enthalpy change in chemisorption is very high i.e. 80 to 240 kJ mol^{-1}. It results in a unimolecular layer.
Physisorption Physisorption is due to the formation of van der Waals' forces. It is favoured at low temperature. The enthalpy change is low i.e. 20–40 kJ mol^{-1}. It results in multimolecular layer. Hence, statements (a) and (d) are correct related to adsorption processes.

11. (b, d)

(a) Al_2O_3 reacts with coke at temperature higher than 2500°C to form carbides. Thus, reduction of Al_2O_3 with coke (C) at a temperature greater than 2500°C is not carried out. Hence, option (a) is incorrect.

(b) Aluminate solution on passing CO_2 gas gives neutralisation reaction and forms precipitates of hydrated alumina ($Al_2O_3 \cdot 3H_2O$). So, it is a correct option.

(c) Dissolution of Al_2O_3 in hot aqueous NaOH takes place at 473 K - 523 K and 35–36 bar pressure. As no conditions are mentioned. So, option (c) is not completely correct.

(d) Electrolysis of Al_2O_3 is done by mixing it with Na_3AlF_6 to produce Al and CO_2. So, it is a correct statement.

12. (a, d) Galena is an ore of PbS. It reacts with HNO_3 to produce NO gas.

$$3\,PbS(s) + \text{Dil. } 8\,HNO_3(aq) \longrightarrow 3\,Pb(NO_3)_2(aq) + 3S(s) + 2NO(g) + 4H_2O(l)$$

NO contains $7 + 8 = 15$ electrons. So, it is paramagnetic in nature as electrons are unpaired. NO is a colourless, neutral oxide of nitrogen. Also it is linear as it contains only 2 atoms.
NO is not an acidic oxide as it has N in ionic form having lower oxidation state (+2) unlike its other acidic oxides such as NO_2, N_2O_5 when oxidation state is higher (+4, +5).
Hence, statements (a) and (d) are correct.

13. (c, d) The correct reaction sequence is

H_3C-CH_2-COOH $\xrightarrow[\text{2. } H_2O]{\text{1. } Br_2/\text{Red P}}$ $CH_3CH(Br)COOH$ (*P*) $\xrightarrow{\text{1. potassium phthalimide}}$ N-phthalimido propanoic acid $\xrightarrow[\text{3. } H_3O^{\oplus}]{\text{2. NaOH}}$ phthalic acid + $CH_3CH(NH_2)COOH$ (*Q*)

(a) $NaBH_4$ is a weak reducing agent, so it can't reduce carboxylic acids to alcohol.

$CH_3CH(Br)COOH$ (*P*) $\xrightarrow{NaBH_4}$ *X*

(b) *P* on treatment with NH_4OH and followed by acidification gives α-alcohol acid derivative.

$CH_3CH(Br)COOH$ (*P*) $\xrightarrow{NH_4OH}$ $CH_3CH(OH)COOH$

So, Q is not formed.

(c) 1° amines on treating with $NaNO_2$ / HCl liberates N_2 gas.

(d) Because of –*I*-effect of Br, P is more acidic than Q.

$CH_3CH(Br)COOH$ > CH_3CH_2COOH

14. (a, b, c)
The reaction products involved are

p-nitrotoluene $\xrightarrow{P}$ p-toluidine (*Q*) $\xrightarrow{R}$ p-$CH_3C_6H_4N_2Cl$ (*S*) $\xrightarrow{H_2O}$ p-cresol (*T*)
(*S*) $\xrightarrow{(U)}$ benzoic acid

$-NO_2$ can be converted to $-NH_2$ by using reducing agents such as H_2 / Pd-ethanol or Sn/HCl. Thus, *P* is H_2 / Pd ethanol or Sn/HCl.
$-NH_2$ can be converted to $-N_2Cl$ by using $NaNO_2$ / HCl or HNO_2. Hence, *R* is either $NaNO_2$ / HCl or HNO_2.
Conversion of *S* to benzoic acid can be carried out by
1. H_3PO_2 2. $KMnO_4$ – KOH, Δ or
1. CH_3-CH_2-OH 2. $KMnO_4$ –KOH, Δ
Diazonium salt on treatment with water forms phenol. Thus, option (a), (b) and (c) are correct.

15. (a) (I) $\text{Rate} = \dfrac{k[X]}{X_s + [X]}$

Case I $[X] >>>> X_s$; So, $X_s + [X] \approx [X]$

∴ $\text{Rate} = \dfrac{k[X]}{[X]} = K$

Zero order reaction,
So, I ⟶ P, S

Case II $[X] << X_s$; $[X] + X_s \approx X_s$

∴ $\text{Rate} = \dfrac{k[X]}{X_s} = K'[X]$

Ist order reaction,

So, I $\longrightarrow$ Q, T

Case III $[X] \approx X_s; [X] + X_s = 2[X]$

$\therefore$ Rate $= \dfrac{k[X]}{2[X]} = \dfrac{k}{2}$

I $\longrightarrow$ P, Q, R, S, T

The graph of half-life should start from origin.

(II) Rate $= \dfrac{k[X]}{X_s + [X]}$

$\because \quad [X] <<< X_s$

$\therefore \quad [X] + X_s \approx X_s$

$\therefore \quad$ Rate $= \dfrac{k[X]}{X_s} = k'[X]$

First order reaction,

$\therefore \quad$ II $\longrightarrow$ Q, T

(III) $\quad$ Rate $= \dfrac{k[X]}{X_s + [X]}$

$\because \quad [X] >>> X_s$

$\therefore \quad [X] + X_s \approx [X]$

$\Rightarrow \quad$ Rate $= \dfrac{k[X]}{[X]} = k$

Zero order reaction.

$\therefore \quad$ III $\longrightarrow$ P, S

(IV) Rate $= \dfrac{k[X]^2}{X_s + [X]}$

$\because \quad [X] >>> X_s$

$\therefore \quad [X] + X_s \approx [X]$

Rate $= \dfrac{k[X]^2}{[X]} = k[X]$

First order reaction.

$\therefore \quad$ IV $\longrightarrow$ Q, T

Hence, the correct match is

I $\rightarrow$ P, II $\rightarrow$ Q, III $\rightarrow$ S, IV $\rightarrow$ T.

16. (d) Formation reactions given in List-II are

(P) $Mg(HCO_3)_2 + 2Ca(OH)_2 \longrightarrow \underset{(IV)}{2CaCO_3} + \underset{(II)}{Mg(OH)_2} + 2H_2O$

(Q) $BaO_2 + H_2SO_4 \longrightarrow BaSO_4 + \underset{(I)}{H_2O_2}$

(R) $Ca(OH)_2 + MgCl_2 \longrightarrow \underset{(II)}{Mg(OH)_2} + CaCl_2$

(S) $BaO_2 + 2HCl \longrightarrow \underset{(III)}{BaCl_2} + \underset{(I)}{H_2O_2}$

(T) $Ca(HCO_3)_2 + Ca(OH)_2 \longrightarrow \underset{(IV)}{2CaCO_3} + 2H_2O$

Thus, the correct matches are

(I) $\rightarrow$ Q, S $\qquad$ (II) $\rightarrow$ R, P

(III) $\rightarrow$ S $\qquad$ (IV) $\rightarrow$ P, T

So, as per given options

I-Q, II-R, III-S, IV-P

Hence, option (d) is correct.

17. (a) (I) $[Cr(CN)_6]^{4-}$

Oxidation number of Cr = +2 ; $[Ar](3d^4 4s^0)$

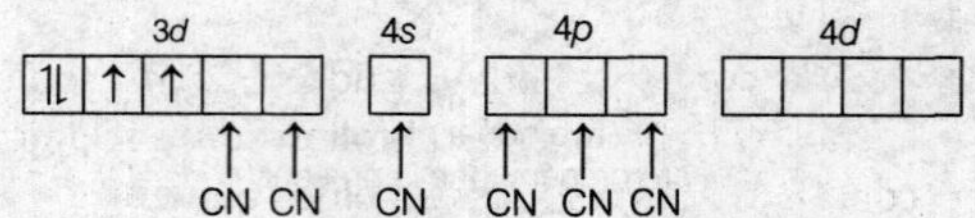

Hybridisation $= d^2sp^3$ (inner sphere complex)as CN^- is strong ligand.

Low spin complex ion $\rightarrow$ [ ][ ] e_g

[⥮][↑][↑] t_{2g}

d^4 species $\rightarrow t_{2g}$ contains 4 electrons

$\mu = 2.8$ BM (2 unpaired electrons)

(I) $\rightarrow$ R,P,T

(II) $[RuCl_6]^{2-}$

Oxidation number of Ru = +4; [Kr] $(3d^4 4s^0)$

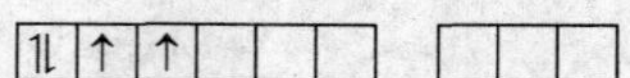

d^2sp^3 hybridisation.

Low spin complex [ ][ ] e_g

 t_{2g}

d^4 species $\rightarrow t_{2g}$ contains 4 electrons

$\mu = 2.8$ BM (2 unpaired electrons)

(II) $\rightarrow$ P, R, S and T

(III) $[Cr(H_2O)_6]^{2+}$ $H_2O \longrightarrow$ Weak field ligand.

Oxidation number of Cr = +2 ; [Ar] $(3d^4 4s^0)$

3d [↑][↑][↑][↑][ ] 4s [ ] 4p [ ][ ][ ] 4d [ ][ ][ ][ ][ ]

sp^3d^2 hybridisation (outer sphere complex)

high spin complex [1][ ] e_g

[1][↑][↑] t_{2g}

d^4 species $\rightarrow t_{2g}$ contains 3 electrons

$\mu = 4.9$ BM (4 unpaired electrons)

(III) $\rightarrow$ Q and T

(IV) $[Fe(H_2O)_6]^{2+}$

Oxidation number of Fe = +2 ; $[Ar](3d^6 4s^0)$

3d [⥮][↑][↑][↑][↑] 4s [ ] 4p [ ][ ][ ] 4d [ ][ ][ ][ ][ ]

sp^3d^2 hybridisation. (outer sphere complex) high spin complex

d^6 species $\rightarrow t_{2g}$ contains 4 electrons $\qquad e_g$ 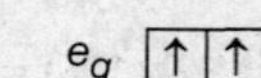

$\mu = 4.9$ BM (4 unpaired electrons) $\qquad t_{2g}$ 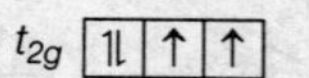

(IV) $\rightarrow$ P and Q

Hence, the correct matches are

(I) $\rightarrow$ R, T $\qquad$ (II) $\rightarrow$ P, S

(III) $\rightarrow$ Q, T $\qquad$ (IV) $\rightarrow$ P, Q

18. (d) (I) Aniline →

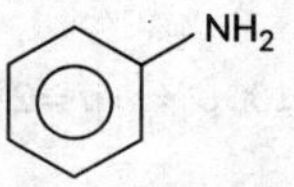

Aniline contains both C and N, so its sodium fusion extract with boiling $FeSO_4$ followed by acidification with conc. H_2SO_4 gives Prussian blue colour.

$$\underset{\text{Sodium extract}}{Fe^{2+} + 6CN^-} \longrightarrow [Fe(CN)_6]^{4-}$$

$$3[Fe(CN)_6]^{4-} + 4Fe^{3+} \longrightarrow \underset{\text{Prussian blue}}{Fe_4[Fe(CN)_6]_3 \cdot xH_2O}$$

Aniline reacts with bromine water to form white precipitates of tribromide.

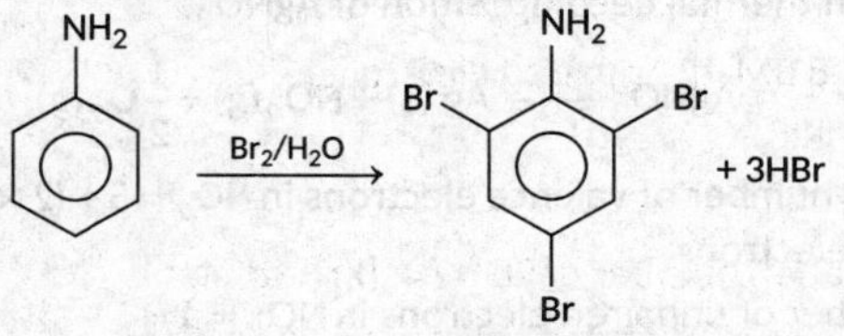

$$\text{Aniline} \xrightarrow{Br_2/H_2O} \underset{\text{(White ppt.)}}{\text{2,4,6-tribromoaniline}} + 3HBr$$

I → P, S

(II) *o*-cresol contains phenolic —OH group which gives violet coloured complex with $FeCl_3$ solution.

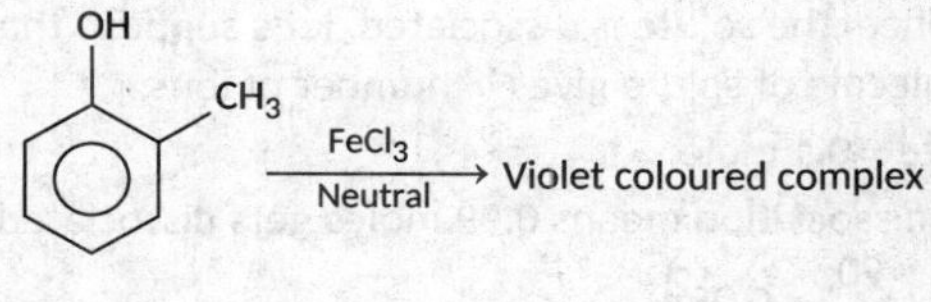

$$\text{o-cresol} \xrightarrow[\text{Neutral}]{FeCl_3} \text{Violet coloured complex}$$

(II) → T

(III) Cysteine → $HS-CH_2-CH(NH_2)-COOH$

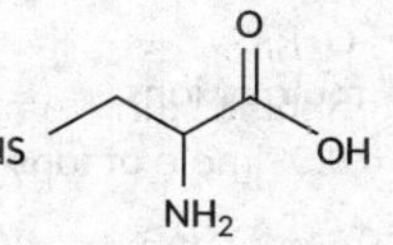

It contains both S and N.

So, its sodium fusion extract will give blood red colour with Fe^{3+}. As it contains carboxylic acid group, so it gives brisk effervescences with $NaHCO_3$.

(III) → Q, R

(IV) Caprolactam

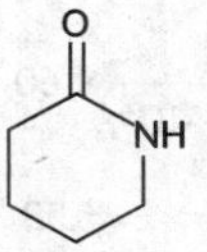

It contains C and N so, its sodium fusion extract will give Prussian blue colour on boiling with $FeSO_4$ followed by acidification with concentrated H_2SO_4.

IV → P

Paper (2)

1. (6) H_2SO_4 being a strong acid ionises completely.

	$H_2SO_4 \xrightarrow{K_{a_1}}$	H^+	$+ HSO_4^-$
t = 0	1M	0	0
t = t	0	1M	1M

Na_2SO_4 is a salt of strong acid and strong base, so it also ionises completely.

	$Na_2SO_4 \longrightarrow$	$2Na^+$	$+ SO_4^-$
t = 0	1.8×10^{-2}M	0	0
t = t	0	$2\times(1.8\times 10^{-2})$M	1.8×10^{-2}M

HSO_4^- is a weak acid as its $K_{a_2} = 1.2\times 10^{-2}$

	$HSO_4^- \rightleftharpoons$	H^+	$+ SO_4^-$
t = 0	1M	1M	1.8×10^{-2}M
t = t	$1-x$	$1+x$	$1.8\times 10^{-2}+x$

$$K_{a_2} = \frac{[H^+][SO_4^-]}{[HSO_4^-]}$$

$$1.2\times 10^{-2} = \frac{(1+x)(1.8\times 10^{-2}+x)}{(1-x)}$$

$$1.2\times 10^{-2}(1-x) = (1+x)(1.8\times 10^{-2}+x)$$

$$x^2 + 1.03x + 0.06 = 0$$

Solving the quadratic equation, $x = -0.006$

This means that some of the sulphate ions will associate with H^+ to form HSO_4^-, thereby reducing the concentration of SO_4^- in solution.

$$[SO_4^-] = (1.8\times 10^{-2} + x)\text{M}$$
$$= (1.8\times 10^{-2} - 0.6\times 10^{-2})\text{M}$$
$$= 1.2\times 10^{-2}\text{M}$$

$PbSO_4$ is weak electrolyte as evident by its K_{sp} (1.6×10^{-8}).

Let the molar solubility of $PbSO_4$ = S mol/L

$$PbSO_4 \rightleftharpoons \underset{S}{Pb^{2+}} + \underset{S+1.2\times 10^{-2}}{SO_4^{2-}}$$

$$K_{sp} = [Pb^{2+}][SO_4^{2-}]$$

$$1.6\times 10^{-8} = (S)(S + 1.2\times 10^{-2})$$

Since $K_{sp} <<< 1.2\times 10^{-2}$; therefore S is neglected in $(S + 1.2\times 10^{-2})$

$$1.6\times 10^{-8} = S\times 1.2\times 10^{-2}$$

$$\Rightarrow \quad S = \frac{1.6\times 10^{-8}}{1.2\times 10^{-2}} = 1.3\times 10^{-6}$$

$$S = X\times 10^{-Y} = 1.3\times 10^{-6} \Rightarrow X = 1.3$$

$$Y = 6$$

2. (5) Since, the solute is dissociated, let's suppose that 1 molecule of solute gives 'i' number of ions.

Solute = 0.1 mole

90% dissociation means 0.09 moles gets dissociated

$$\left(0.1 \times \frac{90}{100} = 0.09\right)$$

1 mole of solute = 'i' mole of ions

0.09 mole of solute = 0.09 mole of ions

$$p_{solution} = X_{solvent} \times p_{solvent}$$

$$= \frac{n_{solvent}}{n_{solute} + n_{solvent}} \times p_{solvent}$$

$$\Rightarrow \quad n_{solvent} = \frac{1.8 \times 10^3 \text{ g}}{18 \text{ g}} = 10^2$$

$$59.7 = \frac{10^2}{(i \times 0.09) + 10^2} \times 60$$

$$0.09i + 10^2 = \frac{100 \times 60}{59.7} \Rightarrow i = 5.58$$

$$i = 5$$

3. (7) All electrolytes are strong electrolyte

$$U_mY_p = m\lambda^\circ{}_U^{p+} + p\lambda^\circ{}_Y^{m-}$$

$$250 = m \times 25 + p \times 100 \qquad \text{...(i)}$$

$$V_mX_n = m\lambda^\circ{}_V^{n+} + n\lambda^\circ{}_X^{m-}$$

$$440 = m \times 100 + n \times 80 \qquad \text{...(ii)}$$

$$Z_mX_n = m\lambda^\circ{}_Z^{n+} + n\lambda^\circ{}_X^{m-}$$

Following the relation, $\lambda_m^C = \lambda_m^\circ - K\sqrt{C}$ for strong electrolytes,

$$\text{Slope} = -K$$

Intercept on Y-axis = λ_m°

$$-K = \frac{\Delta Y}{\Delta X} = \frac{339 - 336}{0.01 - 0.04} = -100$$

$$\lambda_m^C = \lambda_m^\circ - K\sqrt{C}$$

$$\Rightarrow \quad \lambda_m^\circ = \lambda_m^C + K\sqrt{C}$$

$$\lambda_m^\circ = 339 + 100 \times 0.01 = 340$$

$$\Rightarrow \quad \lambda^\circ(Z_mX_n) = 340$$

$$\lambda^\circ(Z_mX_n) = m\lambda^\circ{}_Z^{n+} + n\lambda^\circ{}_X^{m-}$$

$$340 = m \times 50 + n \times 80 \qquad \text{...(iii)}$$

Writing Eq. (i), Eq. (ii) and Eq. (iii),

$$250 = 25m + 100p \qquad \text{...(i)}$$

$$440 = 100m + 80n \qquad \text{...(ii)}$$

$$340 = 50m + 80n \qquad \text{...(iii)}$$

From Eq. (ii) and Eq. (iii),

$$440 - 340 = 100m - 50m$$

$$m = 2$$

From Eq. (i),

$$250 = 25 \times 2 + 100p \Rightarrow p = 2$$

From Eq. (ii),

$$440 = 100 \times 2 + 80n \Rightarrow n = 3$$

So, $m + n + p = 2 + 3 + 2 = 7$.

4. (4) The reaction of Xe with O_2F_2 gives XeF_4 as follows

$$Xe + 2\,O_2F_2 \longrightarrow XeF_4 + 2\,O_2$$

Hydrolysis of XeF_4

$$6XeF_4 + 12\,H_2O \longrightarrow 4\,Xe + 24HF + 2XeO_3 + 3O_2$$

6 moles of XeF_4 will give 24 moles of HF.

5. (6) On thermal decomposition of $AgNO_3$.

$$AgNO_3 \longrightarrow Ag\,(s) + NO_2(g) + \frac{1}{2}O_2(g)$$

Total number of valence electrons in $NO_2 = 5 + (2 \times 6)$ = 17 electrons

Number of unpaired electrons in NO_2 = 1

Writing electronic configuration of O_2

$O_2 = \sigma 1s^2, \sigma 1s^{*2}, \sigma 2s^2, \sigma 2s^{*2}, \sigma 2p_z^2, \pi 2p_x^2 = \pi 2p_y^2,$
$\pi^* 2p_x^1 = \pi^* 2p_y^1$

So oxygen gas has 2 unpaired electrons. The total number of electrons present in anti-bonding molecular orbitals of the gas is 6.

6. (2) The given reaction sequence can be written as

1. Na, liq. NH_3 → *trans*-alkene

2. Br_2(excess) (Addition of Br_2 molecule)

Br Br Br Br

3. alc. KOH dehydrohalogenation

a b c d (A) + a b c d (B)

'a' and 'b' have fixed *cis* configuration 'd' does not show *cis-trans* isomerism but 'c' can show *cis-trans* isomerism. A and B are two isomers around 'c' bond.

7. (0)

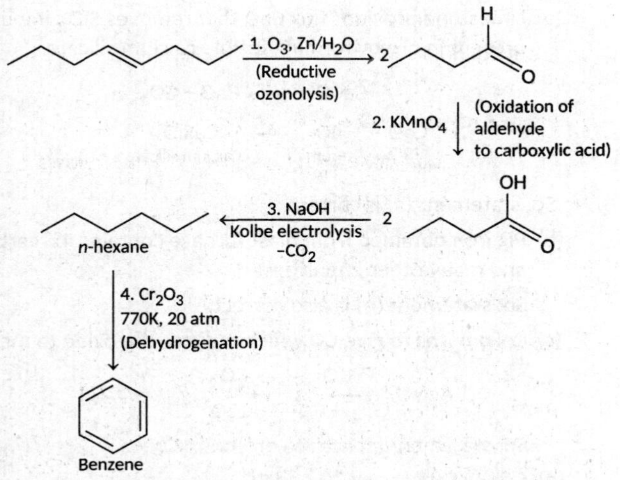

1. O_3, Zn/H_2O (Reductive ozonolysis) → 2 (butanal)
2. $KMnO_4$ (Oxidation of aldehyde to carboxylic acid)
3. NaOH, Kolbe electrolysis, $-CO_2$ → *n*-hexane
4. Cr_2O_3, 770K, 20 atm (Dehydrogenation) → Benzene

So, the number of methylene, i.e. $-CH_2-$ group in benzene is zero.

8. (2)

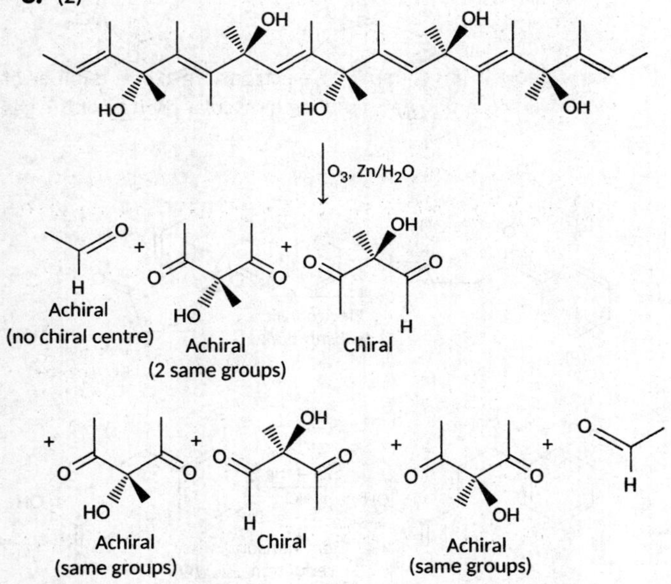

O_3, Zn/H_2O

Achiral (no chiral centre) + Achiral (2 same groups) + Chiral + Achiral (same groups) + Chiral + Achiral (same groups) + Achiral

So there are 2 chiral molecules produced on ozonolysis.

9. (b, c) (a) If empirical formula of compound 3 is P_3Q_4.

We know that,

$$\frac{3\times M_P}{4\times M_Q}=\frac{\%\text{ of }P}{\%\text{ of }Q}$$

where, M_P = molar mass of P

M_Q = molar mass of Q

$$\frac{3M_P}{4M_Q}=\frac{40}{60}=\frac{2}{3}$$

$$\frac{M_P}{M_Q}=\frac{8}{9}$$

If empirical formula of compound 2 is P_3Q_5.

$$\frac{3M_P}{5M_Q}=\frac{44}{55}$$

$$\frac{M_P}{M_Q}=\frac{20}{15}=\frac{4}{3}$$

Since molecular weight ratio does not come out equal in two compounds, '2' and '3'. So, statement (a) is not correct.

(b) If empirical formula of '3' is P_3Q_2

$$\frac{3M_P}{2M_Q}=\frac{40}{60}=\frac{2}{3}$$

$$\frac{M_P}{M_Q}=\frac{4}{9}$$

If atomic weight of $P=20$ and that of $Q=45$

$$\frac{M_P}{M_Q}=\frac{20}{45}=\frac{4}{9}$$

So, statement (b) is correct.

(c) If empirical formula of 2 is PQ

$$\frac{M_P}{M_Q}=\frac{44}{55}=\frac{4}{5}$$

and compound '1' is P_5Q_4

$$\frac{5M_P}{4M_Q}=\frac{50}{50}=\frac{1}{1}$$

Putting value of $\frac{M_P}{M_Q}=\frac{4}{5}$, we get $\frac{5}{4}\times\frac{4}{5}=1$

So, statement (c) is correct.

(d) $M_P=70, M_Q=35$

If empirical formula of compound '1' is P_2Q.

$$\frac{2M_P}{M_Q}=\frac{50}{50}=1$$

$$2M_P=M_Q$$

$$M_P=\frac{M_Q}{2} \qquad (M_P \text{ is half of } M_Q)$$

But, M_P is shown as double to M_Q.

So, this statement is not correct.

So, only statements (b) and (c) are correct.

10. (b, c, d)

(a) The Gibb's function is related to entropy though its temperature dependence.

$$\left(\frac{d\Delta G}{dT}\right)_p=-\Delta S \qquad \text{...(i)}$$

For reaction,

$$M(s)+2H^+\longrightarrow H_2(g)+M^{2+}(aq)$$

$$M\longrightarrow M^{2+}+2e^{\ominus}$$

$$2H^++2e^{\ominus}\longrightarrow H_2$$

So, $n=2$

From Eq. (i),

$$-nF\left(\frac{dE}{dT}\right)_p=-\Delta S$$

$$nF\frac{dE}{dT}=\Delta S$$

Given, $$\frac{dE}{dT}=\frac{R}{F}$$

$$nF\times\frac{R}{F}=\Delta S$$

$$2\times F\times\frac{R}{F}=\Delta S$$

$$2R=\Delta S$$

So, statement (a) is not correct.

(b) $$\underset{(0.1\,M)}{H_2+2H^+(aq)}\longrightarrow\underset{(0.01\,M)}{2H^+(aq)}+H_2$$

$$\Delta G=\Delta H-T\Delta S$$

$\Delta H=0$ for concentration cell reaction (as the reactant and product are same)

$$\Delta G=-T\Delta S$$

Since, the concentration cell is not having equal concentration of H^+ ion in half cells. So, is in working condition.

So, $$\Delta G=-\text{ve}$$
$$-\text{ve}=-T\Delta S$$
$$\Delta S=+\text{ve}$$
$$\Delta S>0$$

So, statement (b) is correct as the entropy is increasing as the cell works.

(c) The optically active compound reacts in the formation of mixture of enantiomers on racemisation. This causes increase in entropy $\Delta S>0$.

Therefore, statement (c) is correct.

(d) $[Ni(H_2O)_6]^{2+}+3\,en\longrightarrow[Ni(en)_3]^{2+}+6H_2O$

Number of particles on product side is more than that on reactant side. So, entropy is increasing $\Delta S>0$.

Statements (b), (c) and (d) are correct.

11. (b,c)

(a) Boron metal reacts with NH_3 to form various compounds but not BN.

$$B+NH_3\longrightarrow BNH_2/B_2NH/B_3N$$

(b) Hydrides of boron react with hydride of N to give boron nitrides and hydrogen gas is released.

$$B_2H_6+\underset{(Excess)}{2NH_3}\longrightarrow 2BN+6H_2$$

(c) Oxides of boron react with hydride of nitrogen to form boron nitride and eliminate water.

$$B_2O_3+2NH_3\longrightarrow 2BN+3H_2O$$

(d) HBF_4 is fluoroboric acid. It reacts with basic ammonia to form salt ammonium fluoroborate.

$$HBF_4+NH_3\longrightarrow\underset{\text{Ammonium fluoroborate}}{NH_4BF_4}$$

So, options (b) and (c) are correct.

12. (a, b, c)

(a) Limestone provides flux CaO that removes SiO_2 impurity present in ore by forming fusible calcium silicate.

$$CaCO_3\xrightarrow{\Delta}CaO+CO_2$$

$$\underset{\text{From limestone}}{CaO}+\underset{\text{From ore}}{SiO_2}\longrightarrow\underset{\text{Calcium silicate}}{CaSiO_3}$$

So, statement (a) is correct.

(b) Pig iron obtained from blast furnace contains 4% carbon and many other impurities.

So, statement (b) is also correct.

(c) Coke burns to give CO which reduces the oxide to metal.

$$C+O_2\longrightarrow CO_2$$
$$CO_2+C\longrightarrow 2CO$$

So, statement (c) is also correct.

(d) Exhaust gases are CO and CO_2.

So, statement (d) is incorrect.

13. (a, c)

+ $AlCl_3$ →

$\overset{\ominus}{AlCl_3}$

Electrophilic substitution

(P)

Zn — Hg / HCl

Clemmenson reduction (aldehyde is reduced to $-CH_2-$)

(Q)

$SOCl_2$

(R)

$AlCl_3$ (Electrophilic substitution)

$\overset{\ominus}{AlCl_4}$

(S)

Zn/Hg/HCl (Clemmenson reduction)

Hydrocarbon

(a) Compounds P and Q are carboxylic acid. So, (a) is correct.

(b) Compound S is ketone and it does not decolourise Br_2/water. So, (b) is incorrect.

(c) Compound P and S are ketones and react with hydroxylamine to form oxime.

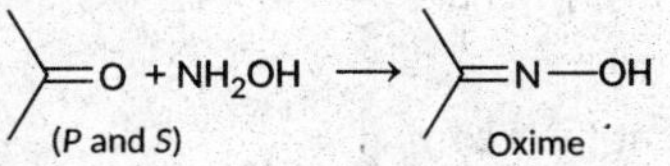

$$>C=O + NH_2OH \longrightarrow >C=N-OH$$

(P and S) Oxime

So, (c) is correct.

(d) Compound R reacts with organo metallic, dialkylcadmium to give ketone.

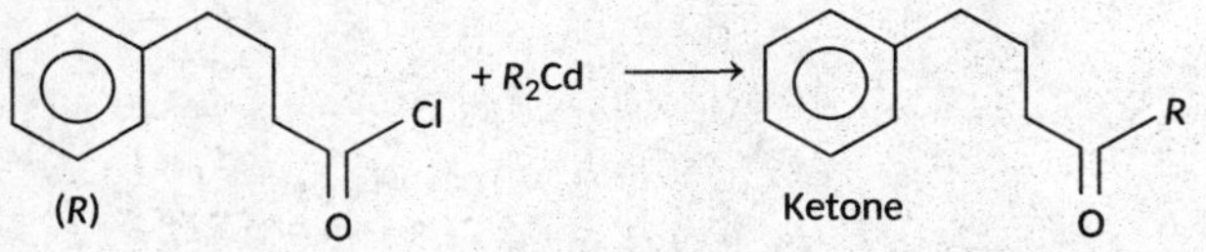

$$(R)\ C_6H_5CH_2CH_2COCl + R_2Cd \longrightarrow C_6H_5CH_2CH_2COR\ \text{(Ketone)}$$

No alcohol is formed. So, (d) is incorrect.

∴ So, statements (a) and (c) are correct.

14. (b, c)

(a) The polymerisation of chloroprene gives synthetic rubber, not natural rubber.

(b) Teflon is obtained from tetrafluoroethylene

$$nCF_2{=}CF_2 \xrightarrow[\text{catalyst}\ \Delta,\ \text{high pressure}]{\text{Persulphate}} [-CF_2-CF_2-]_n$$

(c) PVC are thermoplastic polymers and not thermosetting as it becomes soft on heating and can be reshaped.

(d) Ethene yields low density polythene when at 350 – 370 K and 1000 – 2000 atm pressure in the presence of peroxide.

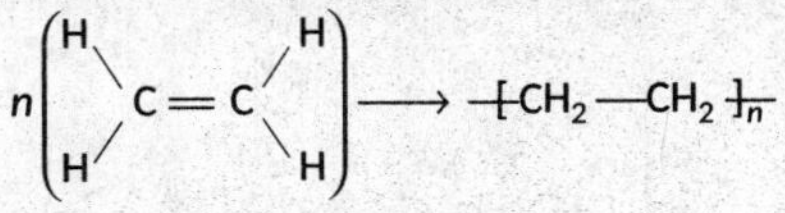

$$n\,(H_2C{=}CH_2) \longrightarrow -[CH_2-CH_2]_n-$$

So, statements (b) and (c) are correct.

15. (b) For fcc lattice,

$$\frac{\sqrt{3}}{4}a = 2R$$

So, $a = \frac{8R}{\sqrt{3}}$

where, 'a' is edge length and R is radius.

There are 8 tetrahedral voids in fcc but only 4 are occupied.

Number of atoms on lattice sites in fcc $= 8 \times \frac{1}{8} + 6 \times \frac{1}{2} = 4$

Total number of atoms in fcc $= 4 + 4 = 8$

$$\%\ \text{packing efficiency} = \frac{\text{Volume of 8 atoms}}{\text{Volume of cell}} \times 100$$

$$\%\ \text{packing} = \frac{8 \times \frac{4}{3}\pi R^3}{a^3} \times 100$$

$$= \frac{8 \times \frac{4}{3}\pi R^3}{\left(\frac{8R}{\sqrt{3}}\right)^3} \times 100$$

$= 33.3\%$

$\cong 35\%$

So, option (b) is correct.

16. (c) $2HClO_3 + 2HCl \longrightarrow \underset{\text{(Gas)}}{2ClO_2} + \underset{\text{(Gas)}}{Cl_2} + 2H_2O$

Chlorine is diamagnetic as it has 14 valence electrons which is even number.

ClO_2 is paramagnetic as it has $7 + 6 + 6 = 19$ valence electrons (odd number).

ClO_2 reacts with O_3 to give ClO_3 and O_2,

$$ClO_2 + O_3 \longrightarrow ClO_3 + O_2$$

ClO_3, forms dimer to give Cl_2O_6. So, option (c) is correct.

17. (c) $Pb(NO_3)_2 + 2NaCl \longrightarrow \underset{\text{(ppt.)}}{PbCl_2} + 2NaNO_3$

Nitrates are soluble.

$$\underset{\text{(Solid)}}{PbCl_2} + \underset{\text{(From HCl)}}{2Cl^-} \longrightarrow [PbCl_4]^{2-}$$

Solid $PbCl_2$ reacts with chloride ion to form ion $[PbCl_4]^{2-}$ which is soluble. So, option (c) is correct.

18. (c)

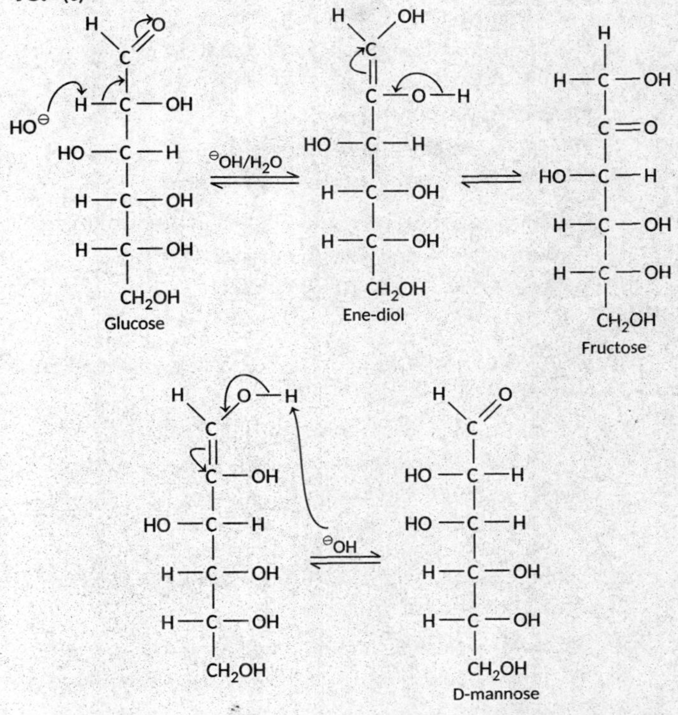

Glucose $\underset{}{\overset{^{\ominus}OH/H_2O}{\rightleftharpoons}}$ Ene-diol $\rightleftharpoons$ Fructose

Glucose: CHO, H–C–OH, HO–C–H, H–C–OH, H–C–OH, CH_2OH (attack by $HO^{\ominus}$ on H of C-2)

Ene-diol: H–C–OH, $\Vert$ C–OH, HO–C–H, H–C–OH, H–C–OH, CH_2OH

Fructose: H–C(H)–OH, C=O, HO–C–H, H–C–OH, H–C–OH, CH_2OH

Ene-diol $\overset{^{\ominus}OH}{\rightleftharpoons}$ D-mannose

D-mannose: CHO, HO–C–H, HO–C–H, H–C–OH, H–C–OH, CH_2OH

D-mannose and D-glucose are anomers and D-fructose is ketose isomer of glucose.

So, option (c) is correct.